# A-Level
# Biology
## The Complete Course for OCR A

Enzymes, biotechnology, epistasis… and that's just for starters. A-Level Biology is packed full of tricky concepts that you'll need to get your head around.

That's why you'll love this brilliant CGP book. It's the perfect companion to the OCR A course — brimming with crystal clear explanations, exam practice, advice on practical investigations and maths skills… everything you need!

It even includes a free Online Edition to read on your PC, Mac or tablet.

### How to get your free Online Edition
Go to **cgpbooks.co.uk/extras** and enter this code...

4129 6155 7770 8996

This code will only work once. If someone has used this book before you, they may have already claimed the Online Edition.

# Contents

## Introduction
How to use this book ... i

## How Science Works
The Scientific Process ... 1

## Module 1

### Development of Practical Skills
1. Planning an Experiment ... 5
2. Carrying Out an Experiment ... 9
3. Processing Data ... 11
4. Presenting Data ... 17
5. Drawing Conclusions and Evaluating ... 23
Exam-style Questions ... 29

## Practical Skills

### Practical Skills for the Practical Endorsement
1. General Practical Skills ... 30
2. Working Safely ... 32
3. Keeping Scientific Records ... 34
4. Practical Activity Groups ... 36

## Module 2

### Section 1: Cell Structure
1. Cells and Organelles ... 38
2. Organelles Working Together ... 44
3. Prokaryotic Cells ... 46
4. How Microscopes Work ... 47
5. Using Microscopes ... 52
Exam-style Questions ... 57

### Section 2: Biological Molecules
1. Water ... 59
2. Macromolecules and Polymers ... 62
3. Carbohydrates ... 63
4. Lipids ... 66
5. Proteins ... 69
6. Inorganic Ions ... 74
7. Biochemical Tests for Molecules ... 76
8. Separating Molecules ... 82
Exam-style Questions ... 86

### Section 3: Nucleotides and Nucleic Acids
1. Nucleotides ... 88
2. Polynucleotides and DNA ... 91
3. DNA replication ... 94
4. Genes and Protein Synthesis ... 96
5. Transcription and Translation ... 99
Exam-style Questions ... 103

### Section 4: Enzymes
1. Action of Enzymes ... 105
2. Factors Affecting Enzyme Activity ... 109
3. Enzyme-Controlled Reactions ... 112
4. Cofactors and Enzyme Inhibition ... 116
Exam-style Questions ... 122

## Section 5: Biological Membranes

| | |
|---|---|
| 1. Cell Membranes — The Basics | 124 |
| 2. Cell Membranes and Signalling | 130 |
| 3. Diffusion and Osmosis | 132 |
| 4. Facilitated Diffusion and Active Transport | 139 |
| **Exam-style Questions** | **145** |

## Section 6: Cell Division and Cellular Organisation

| | |
|---|---|
| 1. The Cell Cycle and Mitosis | 147 |
| 2. Sexual Reproduction and Meiosis | 151 |
| 3. Stem Cells and Differentiation | 155 |
| 4. Tissues, Organs and Systems | 160 |
| **Exam-style Questions** | **164** |

# Module 3

## Section 1: Exchange and Transport

| | |
|---|---|
| 1. Specialised Exchange Systems | 166 |
| 2. Gas Exchange in Mammals | 171 |
| 3. Ventilation in Mammals | 174 |
| 4. Gas Exchange in Fish and Insects | 177 |
| 5. Dissecting Gas Exchange Systems | 180 |
| **Exam-style Questions** | **183** |

## Section 2: Transport in Animals

| | |
|---|---|
| 1. Circulatory Systems | 185 |
| 2. Blood Vessels | 188 |
| 3. Heart Basics | 191 |
| 4. Electrical Activity of The Heart | 195 |
| 5. Haemoglobin | 199 |
| **Exam-style Questions** | **204** |

## Section 3: Transport in Plants

| | |
|---|---|
| 1. Xylem and Phloem | 206 |
| 2. Water Transport | 211 |
| 3. Transpiration | 214 |
| 4. Translocation | 218 |
| **Exam-style Questions** | **222** |

# Module 4

## Section 1: Disease and the Immune System

| | |
|---|---|
| 1. Pathogens and Communicable Diseases | 224 |
| 2. Defence Against Pathogens | 227 |
| 3. The Immune System | 230 |
| 4. Antibodies | 234 |
| 5. Primary and Secondary Immune Responses | 236 |
| 6. Immunity and Vaccinations | 238 |
| 7. Antibiotics and Other Medicines | 242 |
| **Exam-style Questions** | **246** |

## Section 2: Biodiversity

| | |
|---|---|
| 1. Investigating Biodiversity | 248 |
| 2. Genetic Diversity | 254 |
| 3. Factors Affecting Biodiversity | 256 |
| 4. Biodiversity and Conservation | 259 |
| **Exam-style Questions** | **266** |

## Section 3: Classification and Evolution

| | |
|---|---|
| 1. Classification Basics | 268 |
| 2. The Evolution of Classification Systems | 272 |
| 3. Variation | 275 |
| 4. Investigating Variation | 278 |
| 5. Adaptations | 284 |
| 6. The Theory of Evolution | 287 |
| 7. More on Evolution | 290 |
| **Exam-style Questions** | **293** |

# Module 5

## Section 1: Communication and Homeostasis

| | |
|---|---|
| 1. Communication Basics | 295 |
| 2. The Nervous System | 296 |
| 3. The Nervous Impulse | 300 |
| 4. Synapses | 305 |
| **Exam-style Questions** | **309** |
| 5. The Hormonal System and Glands | 311 |
| 6. Homeostasis Basics | 315 |
| 7. Control of Body Temperature | 318 |
| 8. Control of Blood Glucose Concentration | 322 |
| **Exam-style Questions** | **330** |

## Section 2: Excretion

| | |
|---|---|
| 1. The Liver and Excretion | 332 |
| 2. The Kidneys and Excretion | 337 |
| 3. The Kidneys and Water Potential | 342 |
| 4. Kidney Failure | 345 |
| 5. Detecting Chemicals | 348 |
| **Exam-style Questions** | **351** |

## Section 3: Animal Responses

| | |
|---|---|
| 1. The Nervous System | 353 |
| 2. 'Fight or Flight' Response and Heart Rate | 357 |
| 3. Muscle Contraction | 363 |
| 4. Nerve Impulses and Muscle Contraction | 371 |
| **Exam-style Questions** | **375** |

## Section 4: Plant Responses and Hormones

| | |
|---|---|
| 1. Plant Responses | 377 |
| 2. The Effects of Plant Hormones | 383 |
| **Exam-style Questions** | **389** |

## Section 5: Photosynthesis

| | |
|---|---|
| 1. Storing and Releasing Energy | 391 |
| 2. Photosynthesis and the Light-dependent Reaction | 394 |
| 3. Light-independent Reaction | 399 |
| 4. Limiting Factors in Photosynthesis | 402 |
| 5. Photosynthesis Experiments | 407 |
| **Exam-style Questions** | **411** |

## Section 6: Respiration

| | |
|---|---|
| 1. Aerobic Respiration | 413 |
| 2. Anaerobic Respiration | 420 |
| 3. Respiratory Substrates | 422 |
| 4. Respiration Experiments | 424 |
| **Exam-style Questions** | **429** |

# Module 6

## Section 1: Cellular Control

| | |
|---|---|
| 1. Regulating Gene Expression | 431 |
| 2. Body Plans | 435 |
| 3. Gene Mutations | 438 |
| **Exam-style Questions** | **442** |

## Section 2: Patterns of Inheritance

| | |
|---|---|
| 1. Types and Causes of Variation | 443 |
| 2. Genetic Terms | 446 |
| 3. Genetic Diagrams — Monogenic Crosses | 448 |
| 4. Genetic Diagrams — Multiple Allele and Dihybrid Crosses | 452 |
| 5. Linkage | 455 |
| 6. Epistasis | 460 |
| 7. The Chi-Squared Test | 463 |
| **Exam-style Questions** | **469** |

## Section 3: Evolution

| | |
|---|---|
| 1. Evolution by Natural Selection and Genetic Drift | 471 |
| 2. The Hardy-Weinberg Principle | 476 |
| 3. Artificial Selection | 479 |
| 4. Speciation | 481 |
| **Exam-style Questions** | **485** |

## Section 4: Manipulating Genomes

| | |
|---|---|
| 1. Common Techniques | 487 |
| 2. DNA Profiling | 492 |
| 3. Genetic Engineering | 493 |
| 4. Genetically Modified Organisms | 495 |
| 5. Gene Therapy | 499 |
| 6. Sequencing Genes and Genomes | 501 |
| **Exam-style Questions** | **509** |

## Section 5: Cloning and Biotechnology

| | |
|---|---|
| 1. Plant Cloning | 511 |
| 2. Animal Cloning | 515 |
| 3. Biotechnology — The Use of Microorganisms | 519 |
| 4. Biotechnology — Culturing Microorganisms | 523 |
| 5. Immobilised Enzymes | 530 |
| **Exam-style Questions** | **534** |

## Section 6: Ecosystems

| | |
|---|---|
| 1. Ecosystems and Energy Flow | 536 |
| 2. Recycling in Ecosystems | 543 |
| 3. Succession | 546 |
| 4. Investigating Ecosystems | 550 |
| **Exam-style Questions** | **555** |

## Section 7: Populations and Sustainability

| | |
|---|---|
| 1. Variation in Population Size | 557 |
| 2. Conservation of Ecosystems | 561 |
| 3. Human Impact on Ecosystems | 565 |
| **Exam-style Questions** | **569** |

## Exam Help

| | |
|---|---|
| 1. The Exams | 571 |
| 2. Command Words | 573 |
| 3. Time Management | 573 |

## Reference

| | |
|---|---|
| Answers | 574 |
| Glossary | 643 |
| Acknowledgements | 659 |
| Index | 663 |

# How to use this book

## Learning Objectives
- These tell you exactly what you need to learn, or be able to do, for the exam.
- There's a specification reference at the bottom that links to the OCR A specification.

## Exam Tips
There are tips throughout the book to help with all sorts of things to do with answering exam questions.

## Examples
These are here to help you understand the theory.

## Tips
These are here to help you understand the theory.

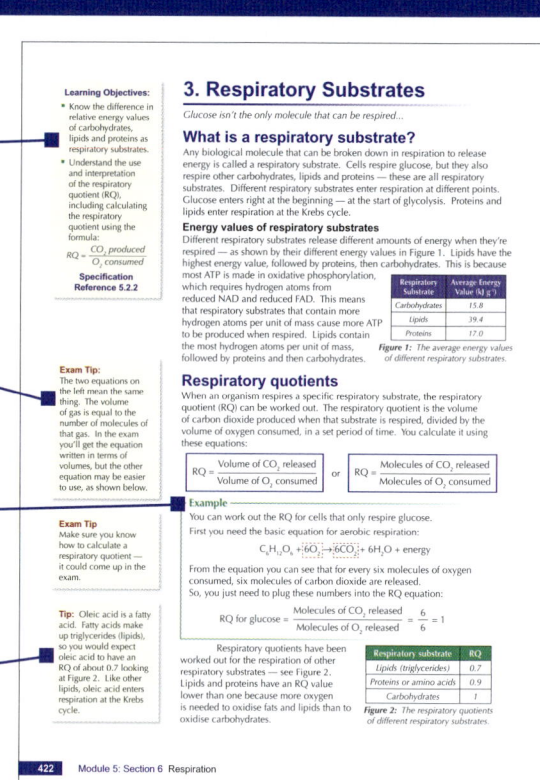

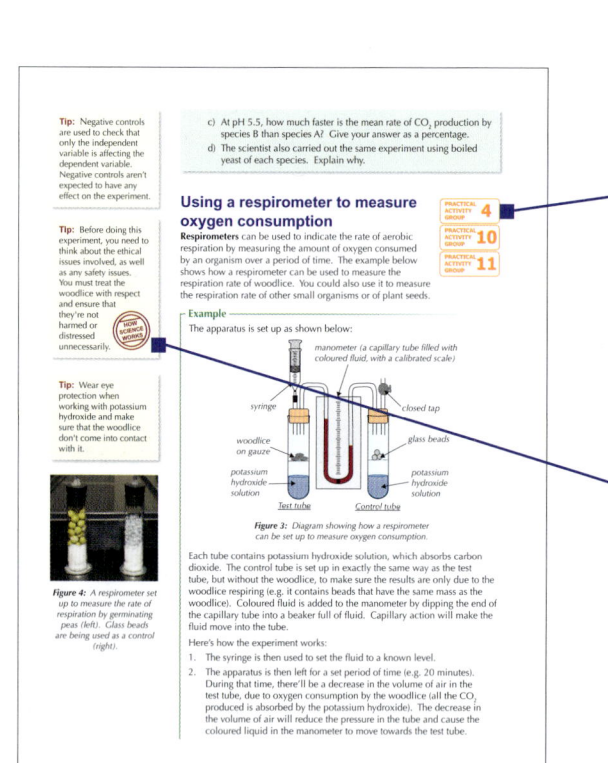

## Practical Activity Groups
You need to show you've mastered some key practical skills in your Practical Endorsement. Information on the skills you need and opportunities to apply them are marked up throughout the book.

## How Science Works
- You need to know about How Science Works. There's a section on it at the front of the book.
- How Science Works is also covered throughout the book wherever you see this symbol.

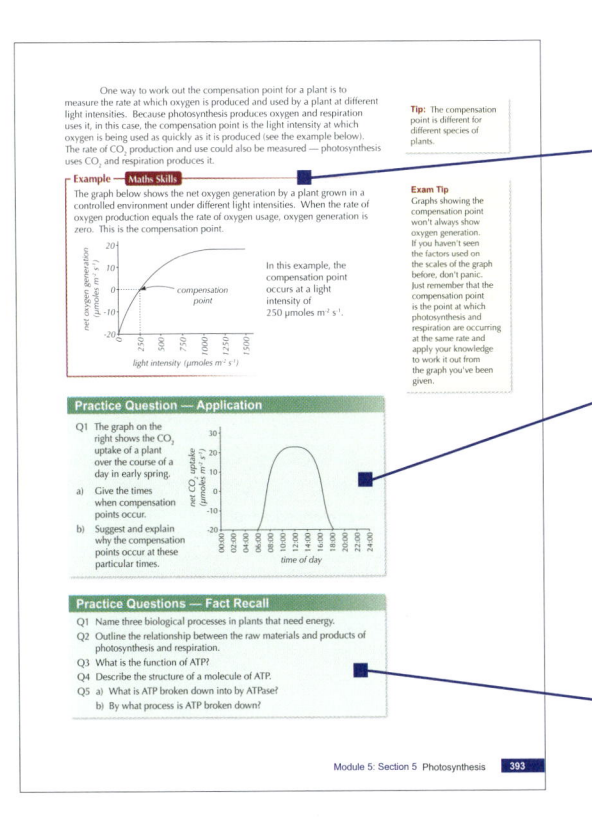

## Maths Skills

There's a range of maths skills you could be expected to apply in your exams. Examples that show these maths skills in action are marked up like this.

## Practice Questions — Application

- Annoyingly, the examiners expect you to be able to apply your knowledge to new situations — these questions are here to give you plenty of practice at doing this.
- All the answers are in the back of the book (including any calculation workings).

## Practice Questions — Fact Recall

- There are a lot of facts you need to learn — these questions are here to test that you know them.
- All the answers are in the back of the book.

## Exam-style Questions

- Practising exam-style questions is really important — you'll find some at the end of each section.
- They're the same style as the ones you'll get in the real exams — some will test your knowledge and understanding and some will test that you can apply your knowledge.
- All the answers are in the back of the book, along with a mark scheme to show you how you get the marks.

## Exam Help

There's a section at the back of the book stuffed full of things to help with your exams.

## Glossary

There's a glossary at the back of the book full of useful words — perfect for looking up key words and their meanings.

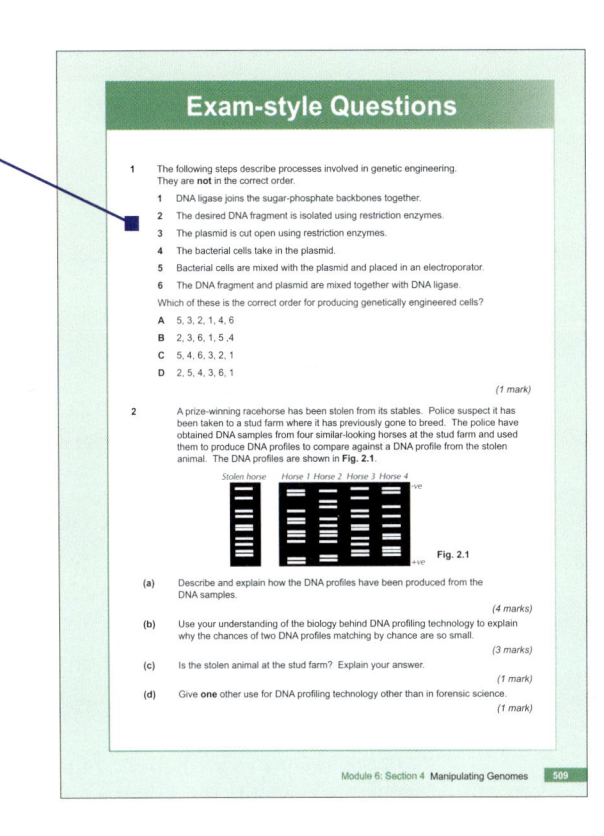

Published by CGP

Editors:
Keith Blackhall, Ellen Burton, Emily Forsberg and George Wright.

Contributors:
Sophie Anderson, Gloria Barnett, James Foster, Paddy Gannon, Barbara Green,
Derek Harvey and Adrian Schmit.

ISBN: 978 1 78908 667 6

With thanks to Hayley Thompson for the proofreading.
With thanks to Jan Greenway for the copyright research.

Printed and bound by Bell and Bain Ltd, Glasgow.
Clipart from Corel®

Illustrations by: Sandy Gardner Artist, email sandy@sandygardner.co.uk

Text, design, layout and original illustrations © Coordination Group Publications Ltd. (CGP) 2020
All rights reserved.

Photocopying more than 5% of this book is not permitted, even if you have a CLA licence.
Extra copies are available from CGP with next day delivery • 0800 1712 712 • www.cgpbooks.co.uk

# How Science Works

## The Scientific Process

*Science tries to explain how and why things happen. It's all about seeking and gaining knowledge about the world around us. Scientists do this by asking questions and suggesting answers and then testing them, to see if they're correct — this is the scientific process.*

### Developing theories

A **theory** is a possible explanation for something. Theories usually come about when scientists observe something and wonder why or how it happens. Scientists also sometimes form a **model** too — a simplified picture of what's physically going on.

**Tip:** A theory is only scientific if it can be tested.

#### Examples

- Darwin came up with his theory of evolution by natural selection after observing wildlife (e.g. finches) and fossils during a trip around South America and the Galapagos Islands.
- The theory that smoking causes lung cancer was developed after it was observed that many people who contracted lung cancer also smoked.
- John Snow came up with the theory that cholera is transmitted in water, rather than air, after observing lots of cases of cholera clustered around a water pump.
- Edward Jenner came up with the idea that being infected with cowpox protected you from getting smallpox after observing that milkmaids didn't get smallpox.

*Figure 1:* Drawings of finches that Darwin made in the Galapagos Islands.

### Testing theories

The next step is to make a **prediction** or **hypothesis** — a specific testable statement, based on the theory, about what will happen in a test situation. Then an experiment or study is carried out to provide evidence that will support the prediction (or help to disprove it). If it's disproved it's back to the drawing board — the theory is modified or a completely new one is developed.

**Tip:** The results of one experiment can't prove that a theory is true — they can only suggest that it's true. They can however disprove a theory — show that it's wrong.

#### Examples

- Louis Pasteur designed an experiment to test his idea that 'germs' in the air caused disease and decomposition. He boiled two flasks of broth, both of which were left open to the air. One of the flasks had a curved neck (see Figure 2) to trap any airborne bacteria so they couldn't get into the broth. The broth in the flask with the curved neck stayed fresh, whereas the other broth went off. This provided evidence to support his theory. (After more evidence like this modern microbiology was born.)
- Edward Jenner tested his idea that getting cowpox protected people from getting smallpox by infecting a boy with cowpox, then exposing him to smallpox. The boy didn't get smallpox, which provided evidence to support his theory. (Eventually this led to the development of a smallpox vaccine.)

*Figure 2:* Pasteur's experiment — the flask with the curved neck stayed fresh.

How Science Works

**Tip:** Some well known biological journals are Nature, The Lancet and the British Medical Journal.

**Tip:** Scientific findings are also communicated at conferences around the world.

**Tip:** Even negative results are communicated — knowing that something is wrong improves scientific knowledge.

**Tip:** Once an experimental method is found that gives good evidence it becomes a protocol — an accepted method to test that particular thing that all scientists can use.

**Tip:** Sometimes data from one experiment can be the starting point for developing a new theory.

# Communicating results

The results are then published — scientists need to let others know about their work. Scientists publish their results in **scientific journals**. These are just like normal magazines, only they contain scientific reports (called papers) instead of the latest celebrity gossip.

Scientific reports are similar to the lab write-ups you do in school. And just as a lab write-up is reviewed (marked) by your teacher, reports in scientific journals undergo **peer review** before they're published. The report is sent out to peers — other scientists who are experts in the same area. They examine the data and results, and if they think that the conclusion is reasonable it's published. This makes sure that work published in scientific journals is of a good standard.

But peer review can't guarantee the science is correct — other scientists still need to reproduce it. Sometimes mistakes are made and flawed work is published. Peer review isn't perfect but it's probably the best way for scientists to self-regulate their work and to publish quality reports.

# Validating theories

Other scientists read the published theories and results, and try to test the theory themselves in order to validate it (back it up). This involves:
- Repeating the exact same experiments.
- Using the theory to make new predictions and then testing them with new experiments.

**Examples**
- In 1998 a study was published that linked the MMR vaccine to autism (a developmental disorder). Other scientists then conducted different studies to try to find the same link, but their results didn't back up (validate) the theory.
- In the 1940s a study was published linking smoking and lung cancer. After this many more studies were conducted all over the world that validated the conclusion of the first study.

# How do theories evolve?

If multiple experiments show a theory to be incorrect then scientists either have to modify the theory or develop a new one, and start the testing again. If all the experiments in all the world provide good evidence to back a theory up, the theory is thought of as scientific 'fact' (for now) — see Figure 3. But it will never become totally indisputable fact. Scientific breakthroughs or advances could provide new ways to question and test the theory, which could lead to new evidence that conflicts with the current evidence. Then the testing starts all over again... And this, my friend, is the tentative nature of scientific knowledge — it's always changing and evolving.

Develop a theory → Test the theory → Communicate the results → Validate the theory → Evidence supports it → Theory accepted

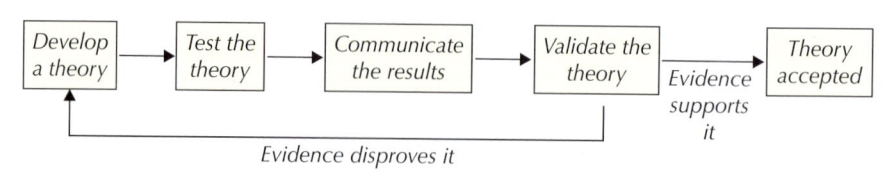

Evidence disproves it (loops back to Develop a theory)

**Figure 3:** Flow diagram summarising the scientific process.

### Example

For many years, many people (including scientists) believed in spontaneous generation — the theory that life can arise from non-living organic matter. This theory was supported by observations such as maggots arising from rotting meat, and sterilised broth becoming cloudy with bacteria.
Over time, the theory was disproved by scientists such as Francesco Redi, whose experiments showed that maggots only arose from meat if flies laid their eggs on it (see Figure 4), and Louis Pasteur, whose experiment with a curved-neck flask (see page 1) showed that there were bacteria in the air that could cause decomposition.

*Figure 4:* Redi's experiment — the meat in the sealed flask (that flies couldn't enter) didn't produce maggots.

## Collecting evidence

### 1. Evidence from lab experiments

Results from controlled experiments in laboratories are great. A lab is the easiest place to control **variables** (quantities that have the potential to change) so that they're all kept constant (except for the one you're investigating). This means you can draw meaningful conclusions.

**Tip:** Module 1 (p. 5-29) is all about designing and carrying out experiments.

### Example

If you're investigating how pH affects enzyme activity, you need to keep everything but the pH of the solution constant. This means controlling things like the temperature of the solution, the concentration of the substrate, etc. Otherwise there's no way of knowing if it's the change in pH that's affecting the rate, or some other changing variable.

### 2. Designing studies

There are things you can't investigate in a lab — you have to do a study instead. You still need to try and make the study as controlled as possible to make it valid. But in reality it's very hard to control all the variables that might be having an effect. You can do things to help, but you can't easily rule out every possibility.

**Tip:** There's more about variables and drawing conclusions from lab experiments on pages 5 and 23.

### Examples

- You can't investigate whether stress causes heart attacks in the lab, so you have to do a study. You could compare the number of heart attacks suffered by a group of people with a high amount of stress to the number suffered by a group with a low amount of stress. But there are always differences between groups of people. The best you can do is to have a well-designed study using matched groups — choose two equally-sized groups of people (those who have quite stressful jobs and those who don't) who are as similar as possible (same mix of ages, same mix of diets etc.) apart from the amount of stress they suffer. But you still can't rule out every possibility.
- It's also tricky to investigate whether adding fertiliser to farmland causes an increase in algal growth in nearby rivers, in the lab. You'd have to do a study on a river that's next to a fertilised field. However, there are variables other than the amount of fertiliser which may have an effect on the amount of algae, such as water temperature and amount of sunlight. You can't easily rule out every possibility. In this case, using a **negative control** too, e.g. a river next to an unfertilised field, can be a useful method for accounting for the effects of variables beyond your control — the results for the negative control could be used as a comparison, so any difference in the results could be attributed to the fertiliser.

**Tip:** In fieldwork, the effect of variables beyond your control can be reduced by methods such as random sampling (see p. 249).

**Tip:** There's more about negative controls on page 6.

How Science Works

## Science and decision making

Scientific knowledge is used by society (that's you, me and everyone else) to make decisions — about the way we live, what we eat, what we drive, etc. All sections of society use scientific evidence to make decisions, e.g. politicians use it to devise policies and individuals use science to make decisions about their own lives.

**Tip:** Don't get mixed up — it's not the scientists who make the decisions, it's society. Scientists just produce evidence to help society make the decisions.

### Examples
- The maximum amount of salt people are advised to eat per day was reduced in government guidelines in 2004, due to the results of a study which showed that reducing salt intake could significantly reduce heart disease.
- Leaded petrol in cars was phased out in many countries after it was found to cause air pollution that damaged the brain.

## Factors affecting decision making

Other factors can influence decisions about science or the way science is used:

### Economic factors
Society has to consider the cost of implementing changes based on scientific conclusions. Sometimes it decides the cost outweighs the benefits.

**Tip:** Economic factors just mean anything to do with money, and social factors just mean anything to do with people.

#### Example
The NHS can't afford the most expensive drugs without sacrificing something else. Sometimes they decide to use a less effective, but less expensive drug, despite evidence showing there's a more effective one.

### Social factors
Decisions affect people's lives — sometimes people don't want to follow advice, or are strongly against some recommendations.

#### Examples
- Scientists may suggest banning smoking and alcohol to prevent health problems, but shouldn't we be able to choose whether we want to smoke and drink or not?
- Scientists may be able to cure many diseases using stem cells, but some people are strongly against the idea of embryonic stem cell research.

**Tip:** The people making the decisions can be affected by lots of other things too, e.g. public opinion, the media and whether they might benefit from a particular decision.

### Environmental factors
Some scientific research and breakthroughs might affect the environment. Not everyone thinks the benefits are worth the possible environmental damage.

#### Examples
- Scientists believe unexplored regions like remote parts of rainforests might contain untapped drug resources. But some people think we shouldn't exploit these regions because any interesting finds may lead to deforestation and reduced biodiversity in these areas.
- Scientists have developed genetically modified (GM) crops (e.g. with frost resistance, or high nutrient content), but some people think the possible environmental harm they could do outweighs their benefits.

*Figure 5:* Man protesting against the production of genetically modified organisms (GMOs).

# Module 1 | Development of Practical Skills

## 1. Planning an Experiment

*You have to do practical work in class as part of your course. You'll be asked about it in exams too, so you need to know how to plan the perfect experiment.*

### Testing a theory
Before you start planning an experiment, you need to be clear about what you're trying to find out. You should start off by making a **prediction** or **hypothesis** — see page 1. You then need to plan a good experiment that will provide evidence to support the prediction — or help disprove it.

### Getting good results
A good experiment is one that will give results that are:
- **Precise** — precise results don't vary much from the mean. Precision is reduced by **random error**.
- **Repeatable and reproducible** — repeatable means that if the same person repeats the experiment using the same methods and equipment, they will get the same results. Reproducible means that if someone different does the experiment, using a slightly different method or piece of equipment, the results will still be the same.
- **Valid** — valid results answer the original question. To get valid results you need to control all the variables (see below) to make sure you're only testing the thing you want to.
- **Accurate** — accurate results are really close to the true answer.

Here are some things you need to consider when designing a good experiment:

#### 1. Variables
**Variables** are quantities that have the potential to change, e.g. temperature, pH. In an experiment you usually change one variable and measure its effect on another variable.
- The variable that you change is called the **independent variable**.
- The variable that you measure is called the **dependent variable**.

All the other variables should be controlled — when you're investigating a variable you need to keep everything else that could affect it constant. This means you can be sure that only your independent variable is affecting the thing you're measuring (the dependent variable).

> **Example**
> For an investigation into how temperature affects an enzyme's activity:
> - Temperature is the independent variable.
> - Enzyme activity is the dependent variable.
> - pH, volume, substrate concentration and enzyme concentration should all stay the same (and the quantities should be recorded to allow someone else to reproduce the experiment).

---

**Learning Objectives:**
- Know how to design experiments, including how to solve problems set in a practical context.
- Be able to evaluate whether an experimental method is appropriate to meet the expected outcomes.
- Be able to identify variables that must be controlled, where appropriate.
- Be able to select suitable apparatus, equipment and techniques for carrying out an experiment.

**Specification Reference 1.1.1**

**Tip:** If you're studying a sample of a population (p. 249), a larger sample size will increase the accuracy of your results.

**Exam Tip**
Examiners love getting you to suggest improvements to methods — e.g. how a method could be improved to make the results more precise, so make sure you know how to design a good experiment.

**Tip:** There's more on how enzymes work on pages 105-111.

## 2. Controls

**Negative controls** are used to check that only the independent variable is affecting the dependent variable. Negative controls aren't expected to have any effect on the experiment.

> **Example**
> When investigating how temperature affects an enzyme's activity, you should measure a negative control at each temperature you're investigating. The controls should contain everything used except the enzyme. No enzyme activity should be seen with these controls.

**Positive controls** can also be used. They should show what a positive result of the experiment should look like, to check that it is possible.

> **Example**
> If the product of an enzyme-catalysed reaction changes the colour of an indicator solution, a positive control for an experiment using this reaction would be a solution of the product and indicator, showing the colour change.

In studies, **control groups** are used. The subjects in the study are split into two groups — the experimental group and the control group. The control group is treated in exactly the same way as the experimental group, except for the factor you're investigating.

> **Example**
> If you were investigating the effect of margarine containing omega-3 fish oils on heart disease, you'd have two groups — an experimental group that would be given margarine containing omega-3 fish oils, and a control group that would be given margarine without fish oils. This is done so that you can tell any reduction in heart disease is due to the fish oil, not some other substance in the margarine.

When testing new drugs to see if they work, control groups should always be used. The control group is treated in exactly the same way as the experimental group, except they're given a **placebo** instead of the drug.

## 3. Repeats

Taking several repeat measurements and calculating the mean can reduce the effect of random error on your experiment, making your results more precise. Doing repeats and getting similar results each time also shows that your data is repeatable. This makes it more likely that the same results could be reproduced by another scientist in an independent experiment.

> **Example**
> For an investigation into how temperature affects enzyme activity, the experiment should be repeated at least three times at each temperature used. A mean result should be calculated for each temperature (see page 11).

Repeating measurements also reduces the likelihood that the results are due to chance — see below.

## 4. Sample Size

Sample size is the number of samples in the investigation, e.g. the number of people in a drug trial. As with carrying out repeats, having a large sample size reduces the likelihood that the results are due to chance (e.g. if you get the same result twice it might be because of chance, but if you get it 100 times it's much more likely that it's not due to chance).

---

**Exam Tip**
If you get an exam question asking why a control is important in a particular experiment, make sure your answer is specific to that experiment (not just generally about why controls are good).

**Tip:** In a study with human participants, you should try to keep the variables of all the participants the same, e.g. they should all be the same age, sex, etc.

**Tip:** A placebo is a dummy pill or injection that looks exactly like the real drug, but doesn't contain the drug. It's used to make sure that people don't improve just because they think they're being treated.

**Tip:** Precise results are sometimes referred to as reliable results.

**Tip:** Scientists can use statistical tests to figure out if a result is likely to be due to chance or not. See page 16 for more.

Module 1: Development of Practical Skills

## Taking accurate measurements

When you're planning an experiment you need to decide what it is you're going to measure and how often you're going to take measurements.

> **Example**
> If you're investigating the rate of respiration, you could either measure the volume of oxygen used over time or the volume of carbon dioxide produced over time. You could take measurements at 30 second or 60 second intervals, for example.

Then you need to choose the most appropriate apparatus, equipment and techniques for the experiment.

The measuring apparatus you use has to be sensitive enough to measure the changes you're looking for. For example, if you need to measure changes of 1 cm$^3$ you need to use a measuring cylinder that can measure in 1 cm$^3$ increments. It'd be no good trying with one that only measures 10 cm$^3$ increments — it wouldn't be sensitive enough. And if you need to measure small changes in pH, a pH meter (which can measure pH to several decimal places) would be more sensitive than indicator paper.

The equipment and apparatus you choose has to be appropriate for the function it needs to perform.

*Figure 1: pH meters can be used to measure small changes in pH.*

> **Example**
> If you are studying the nuclei of cells under the microscope you need to stain them with a dye that stains nuclei, e.g. methylene blue. It would be no good staining them with eosin, as this doesn't stain the nuclei.

The technique you use has to be the most appropriate one for your experiment. E.g. if you want to make a series of solutions for a calibration curve, you'd usually use a serial dilution technique (see p. 79).

**Tip:** There's more about choosing the correct technique on page 9.

## Risk assessments

In order to work safely, you need to carry out a risk assessment for your experiment. To do this, you need to identify:

- All the dangers in the experiment, for example any hazardous chemicals, microorganisms or naked flames.
- Who is at risk from these dangers — this could be you and your lab partner, but it could also be anyone who is in the same room or building.
- What can be done to reduce the risk. You should wear a lab coat and goggles as a standard precaution, but you may need to take other safety precautions, such as carrying out your experiment in a fume cupboard.

## Ethical issues

You also need to consider any ethical issues in your experiment.

*Figure 2: Chemicals marked with hazard warning signs.*

> **Example**
> If you're using living animals (e.g. insects) you must treat them with respect. This means handling them carefully and keeping them away from harmful chemicals, extreme heat sources and other things that might cause them physical discomfort.

Module 1: Development of Practical Skills  7

**Tip:** A potometer is a piece of apparatus used to estimate transpiration rate by measuring a plant's water uptake. There's loads more about transpiration rate on pages 214-215.

## Practice Questions — Application

Q1 A student wants to investigate the effect of light intensity on transpiration rate. She sets up a potometer as shown below.

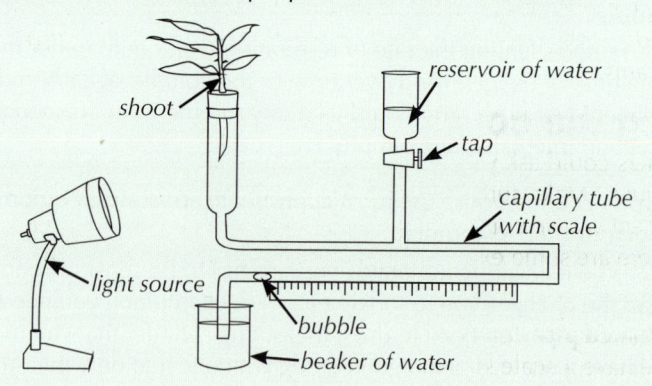

[Diagram of potometer setup with labels: shoot, reservoir of water, tap, capillary tube with scale, light source, bubble, beaker of water]

The student first measures the distance the bubble moves along the tube in ten minutes when the light source is 0 cm away from the shoot (i.e. right next to it). She then repeats the experiment with the light source 30 cm away from the shoot, then again with the light source 60 cm away.

a) Name the independent variable in this investigation.
b) Name two variables in this investigation that the student should keep the same.
c) Give one thing the student could do to make to her results more precise.

Q2 Emezie wants to investigate the effect of substrate concentration on the activity of the enzyme catalase, which catalyses the breakdown of hydrogen peroxide into oxygen and water. Her experiment involves mixing catalase and hydrogen peroxide in a sealed boiling tube with a delivery tube attached.

a) Suggest an appropriate piece of equipment for measuring how much gas has been given off by the reaction.
b) Suggest a negative control for this experiment.

**Tip:** You can read all about how to measure the rate of an enzyme-controlled reaction on pages 112-113.

## Practice Questions — Fact Recall

Q1 What does it mean if your results are repeatable?
Q2 What are valid results?
Q3 What is a dependent variable?
Q4 What does a negative control show?
Q5 What does a positive control show?
Q6 What three things should you consider when carrying out a risk assessment?

# 2. Carrying Out an Experiment

As part of your A-level in Biology, you're expected to carry out Practical Activity Groups (PAGs) and be familiar with the techniques and apparatus involved in each one. You could be asked about the skills you've learnt in your exams.

## Using the correct apparatus and techniques

Examiners could ask you about a whole range of different apparatus and techniques. Make sure you know how to use all the instruments and equipment you've come across in class and can carry out all the techniques too. Here are some examples of equipment you should be able to use:

--- Examples ---
**Graduated pipettes**
These have a scale so you can measure specific volumes. Make sure you read the volume from the bottom of the meniscus (the curved upper surface of the liquid) when it's at eye level — see Figure 1.

**Water baths**
Make sure you allow time for water baths to heat up before starting your experiment. Don't forget that your solutions will need time to get to the same temperature as the water before you start the experiment too.

**Data loggers**
Decide what you are measuring and what type of data logger you will need, e.g. temperature, pH. Connect an external sensor to the data logger if you need to. Decide how often you want the data logger to take readings depending on the length of the process that you are measuring.

Make sure you perform all techniques carefully and that any apparatus is set up correctly — this will help to minimise errors which would affect your results.

## Using appropriate units

Make sure you're measuring things using appropriate units — to choose the correct units to use, you might have to think about how you're going to analyse them later.

--- Example ---
If you're measuring time, it might be better to use seconds rather than minutes — when you come to processing your results, it'll be easier to work with a result of 73 seconds than a result of 1.217 minutes.

Also, make sure you record your units properly, e.g. if you're measuring the length of something and accidently write cm instead of mm, any calculations you do will be affected and your conclusions may be wrong.

## Recording data

As you get your results, you need to record them. It's a good idea to draw a **table** to record the results of your experiment in. When you draw a table, make sure you include enough rows and columns to record all of the data you need to. You might also need to include a column for processing your data (e.g. working out the mean — see page 11). Make sure each column has a heading so you know what's going to be recorded where. The units should be in the column heading, not the table itself — see Figure 2 on the next page.

---

**Learning Objectives:**
- Know how to use a wide range of practical apparatus and techniques correctly.
- Be able to select appropriate units for measurements.
- Be able to present observations and data in an appropriate format.
- Be able to identify anomalies in experimental measurements.

**Specification References 1.1.2, 1.1.4**

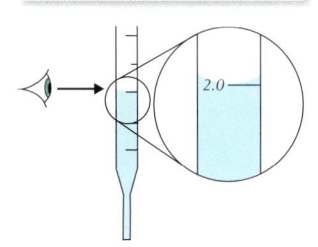

**Figure 1:** Measuring volume using the bottom of the meniscus.

**Tip:** A data logger (or data recorder) is an electronic device that can record data over time using a sensor. They can sometimes be connected to a computer.

Module 1: Development of Practical Skills

**Tip:** If you're recording your data as decimals, make sure you do it to a consistent number of decimal places, because when you're analysing your results, it makes sense to compare values that have been rounded to the same level of accuracy.

**Tip:** Frequency is just the number of times that something occurs.

**Figure 2:** Table showing the number of different species and the length of hedgerows found on three farms.

| Farm | Length of hedgerows (km) | Number of species |
|---|---|---|
| 1 | 49 | 21 |
| 2 | 90 | 28 |
| 3 | 155 | 30 |

(data, heading, units, column labels; row indicated)

### Using frequency tables

A **frequency table** is just a table that shows how many of each value there are. They usually have three columns. The first column just gives the values or names of the different pieces of data. The second column shows a mark for each piece of data — this is the **tally**. The third column is the **frequency**, which you get by adding up the tally marks.

You can draw a frequency table for data you've already collected, or to record the data straight into.

#### Example — Maths Skills

To record the number of individuals of different species of bird observed in a garden:

1. Draw a table with three columns. Give the columns the headings 'species', 'tally' and 'frequency'.
2. Record the data by drawing a tally mark in the right row to represent each piece of data.
3. Add up the tally marks in each row when you've finished recording your data. This is the frequency.

| species | tally | frequency |
|---|---|---|
| sparrow | ||||| || | 7 |
| blue tit | |||| | 4 |
| goldfinch | || | 2 |
| blackbird | ||||| ||||| | 10 |

**Tip:** To record 5 results you write ||||, not |||||. This makes it easier to keep track of the numbers.

## Anomalous results

When you look at all the data in your table, you may notice that you have a result that doesn't seem to fit in with the rest at all. These results are called **anomalous results**.

You should investigate anomalous results — if you can work out what happened (e.g. you measured something totally wrong) you can ignore them when processing your results. However, you can't just exclude a value just because you don't like the look of it.

**Tip:** Doing repeats makes it easier to spot anomalous results.

### Practice Questions — Fact Recall

Q1 The diagram on the right shows a pipette with graduations to mark every 0.1 cm³. What volume of water is shown to be in the pipette?

Q2 If your experiment uses a water bath, why should you wait a while after switching it on before carrying out the experiment?

Q3 What is a frequency table?

Q4 What is an anomalous result?

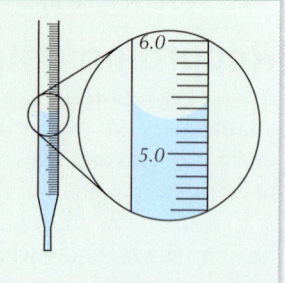

# 3. Processing Data

*Processing data means taking raw data and doing some calculations with it, to make it more useful. This is where your maths skills really come in.*

## Summarising your data

Once you've collected all your data, it's useful to summarise it using a few handy-to-use figures — like the mean and the range.

### Mean and range

When you've done repeats of an experiment you should always calculate a **mean** (a type of average). To do this add together all the data values and divide by the total number of values in the sample.

You might also need to calculate the **range** (how spread out the data is). To do this find the largest data value and subtract the smallest data value from it. You shouldn't include anomalous results when calculating the mean or the range.

--- **Example** — **Maths Skills** ---

**Compare the mean result and range for test tubes A and B in the table on the right.**

| Test tube | Repeat (g) |      |      |
|-----------|------------|------|------|
|           | 1          | 2    | 3    |
| A         | 27.8       | 37.0 | 32.2 |
| B         | 47.5       | 50.2 | 45.3 |

To calculate the means:
- Add up the three data values for A, then divide by three.
  A: (27.8 + 37.0 + 32.2) ÷ 3 = 97.0 ÷ 3 = **32.3 g**
- Do the same for B.
  B: (47.5 + 50.2 + 45.3) ÷ 3 = 143.0 ÷ 3 = **47.7 g**

  **B has the higher mean.**

To find the range of results for each test tube, subtract the smallest result from the largest result.
A: 37.0 − 27.8 = **9.2 g**    B: 50.2 − 45.3 = **4.9 g**    **B has the smaller range.**

You might be asked to work out the mean rate from a table in your exam. To do this, just divide the amount of change by the difference in time.

--- **Example** — **Maths Skills** ---

**The table on the right shows the number of cases of disease X for four different years.**

**Calculate the average increase in number of cases per year between 1992 and 2004.**

| Year | Number of cases |
|------|-----------------|
| 1992 | 127             |
| 1998 | 212             |
| 2004 | 247             |

- Work out the increase in the number of cases between 1992 and 2004.
  247 − 127 = 120
- Work out the difference in the number of years.
  2004 − 1992 = 12
- Divide the increase in number of cases by the difference in years.
  120 ÷ 12 = 10

  So the average increase in number of cases per year is **10**.

**Learning Objectives:**
- Be able to process, analyse and interpret qualitative and quantitative experimental results, including reaching valid conclusions where appropriate.
- Be able to use appropriate mathematical skills for analysis of quantitative data.
- Understand the appropriate use of significant figures.

**Specification Reference 1.1.3**

**Exam Tip**
At least 10% of marks in the exams will come from assessment of maths skills.

**Tip:** Averages and range values have the same units as the data used in the calculation.

**Tip:** When people talk about an <u>average</u>, they are usually referring to the <u>mean value</u>.

Module 1: Development of Practical Skills

## Standard deviation

**Standard deviation** can be more useful than the range because it tells you how values are spread about the mean rather than just the total spread of data. A small standard deviation means the repeated results are all similar and close to the mean, i.e. they are precise. There's more on standard deviation on p. 279.

## Median and mode

Like the mean, the **median** and **mode** are both types of average.

To calculate the median, put all your data in numerical order. The median is the middle value in this list. If you have an even number of values, the median is halfway between the middle two values.

To calculate the mode, count how many times each value comes up. The mode is the number that appears most often. A set of data might not have a mode — or it might have more than one.

**Tip:** If all the values in your data are different, there won't be a mode at all.

### Example — Maths Skills

The number of days survived without watering was recorded for a species of drought-resistant plant. The results were as follows:

26  24  29  24  22  26  25  27  24  21  22  27

Calculate the median and mode of these results.

1. Put the data in numerical order:

    21  22  22  24  24  24  25  26  26  27  27  29

2. Find the middle value (the median):

    *There are 12 values, so the median is between the 6th and 7th numbers. The 6th number is 24 and the 7th number is 25, so the median is **24.5**.*

3. Count how many times each value comes up to find the mode:

    *24 comes up three times. None of the other numbers come up more than twice. So the mode is **24**.*

**Tip:** To find the value halfway between two numbers, add the two numbers together and then divide by two. E.g. 24 + 25 = 49, 49 ÷ 2 = 24.5.

### Practice Questions — Application

**Q1** The maximum volume of air breathed out was measured for ten people using a spirometer. The results are listed below.

3.9 dm$^3$   3.5 dm$^3$   3.1 dm$^3$   3.9 dm$^3$   3.4 dm$^3$
3.5 dm$^3$   3.7 dm$^3$   3.9 dm$^3$   4.2 dm$^3$   3.2 dm$^3$

a) What is the range of these results?

b) Calculate the median and mode of these results.

**Q2** The Benedict's test was used on three different glucose solutions and the absorbance of each solution was measured using a colorimeter. The results are shown in the table on the right. Calculate the mean absorbance for each solution.

| Solution | Absorbance (arbitrary units) | | |
|---|---|---|---|
| | 1 | 2 | 3 |
| A | 0.81 | 0.84 | 0.82 |
| B | 0.54 | 0.55 | 0.11 |
| C | 0.12 | 0.12 | 0.15 |

**Tip:** When analysing results, you need to watch out for any that are anomalous (see page 10).

**Tip:** There's more about the Benedict's test and using colorimetry to measure the absorbance of the solution on pages 79-80.

**Q3** The number of individuals of a species in a forest was recorded in three different years. The results are shown in the table on the right. What was the mean decrease in number of individuals per year between 1995 and 2015?

| Year | Number |
|---|---|
| 1995 | 292 |
| 2005 | 169 |
| 2015 | 105 |

# Calculating percentages

Calculating **percentages** helps you to compare amounts from samples of different sizes. To give the amount X as a percentage of sample Y, you need to divide X by Y, then multiply by 100.

### Example — Maths Skills

A tissue sample containing 50 cells is viewed under the microscope. 22 are undergoing mitosis. What percentage of cells are undergoing mitosis?
1. Divide 22 by 50: $22 \div 50 = 0.44$
2. Multiply by 100: $0.44 \times 100 =$ **44%**

## Calculating percentage change

Calculating **percentage change** helps to quantify how much something has changed, e.g. the percentage of plants that were killed with a herbicide in a particular year compared to the previous year.
To calculate it you use this equation:

$$\text{Percentage change} = \frac{\text{final value} - \text{original value}}{\text{original value}} \times 100$$

A positive value indicates an increase and a negative value indicates a decrease.

### Example — Maths Skills

Three sets of potato chips were weighed, then each set was placed in a solution containing a different concentration of sucrose. After 24 hours the chips were removed from the solution, patted dry and weighed again. **Calculate the percentage change in mass for the chips in each solution.**

| Concentration of sucrose (M) | 0.0 | 0.2 | 0.4 |
|---|---|---|---|
| Mass before (g) | 7.7 | 9.8 | 8.6 |
| Mass after (g) | 9.4 | 10.2 | 7.1 |

Potato chips in 0.0 M sucrose solution:
$$\text{Percentage change} = \frac{(9.4 - 7.7)}{7.7} \times 100 = \frac{1.7}{7.7} \times 100 = \mathbf{22\%}$$

Potato chips in 0.2 M sucrose solution:
$$\text{Percentage change} = \frac{(10.2 - 9.8)}{9.8} \times 100 = \frac{0.4}{9.8} \times 100 = \mathbf{4.1\%}$$

Potato chips in 0.4 M sucrose solution:
$$\text{Percentage change} = \frac{(7.1 - 8.6)}{8.6} \times 100 = \frac{-1.5}{8.6} \times 100 = \mathbf{-17\%}$$

# Using ratios

**Ratios** can be used to compare lots of different types of quantities. For example, an organism with a surface area to volume ratio of 2 : 1 would theoretically have a surface area twice as large as its volume.

Ratios are usually most useful in their simplest (smallest) form. To simplify a ratio, divide each side by the same number. It's in its simplest form when there's nothing left you can divide by. To get a ratio of X : Y in the form X : 1, divide both sides by Y.

**Exam Tip**
Rather that having to calculate a percentage, sometimes you might just have to give your answer as a fraction i.e. X/Y. To simplify a fraction, divide the top and bottom of the fraction by the same number. To get the fraction as simple as possible, you might have to do this more than once.

**Exam Tip**
The examiners just love getting you to calculate percentage changes, including percentage increases and decreases, so make sure you learn this formula.

**Tip:** Percentage change can be either positive or negative, depending on whether the value has gone up or down. However, percentage increase and percentage decrease are both written as positive numbers because the direction of the change has already been taken into account.

**Tip:** If you're not sure what number to divide by to simplify a ratio, start by trying to divide both sides by a small number, e.g. 2 or 3, then check to see if you can simplify your answer further. E.g. you could simplify 28 : 36 by dividing each side by 2 to get 14 : 18. But you could simplify it further by dividing by 2 again to get 7 : 9. You can't simplify the ratio any further, so it's in its simplest form.

**Tip:** There's more about genetic polymorphism on page 254.

**Tip:** For ratio questions like Q2b here, remember to give your answer in its simplest form.

---

### Examples — Maths Skills

- To simplify the ratio 28 : 36, divide both sides by 4. You get **7 : 9**.
- To write the ratio 28 : 36 in the form of X : 1, just divide both sides by 36:
  $28 \div 36 = 0.78 \qquad 36 \div 36 = 1$
  So the ratio is **0.78 : 1**.
- The method still works when one or both sides are less than one — so to write the ratio 2.7 : 0.45 in the form of X : 1, just divide both sides by 0.45:
  $2.7 \div 0.45 = 6 \qquad 0.45 \div 0.45 = 1$
  The ratio is **6 : 1**.

### Practice Questions — Application

**Q1** In a sample of 65 genes in a population, 36 genes were found to be polymorphic. What percentage of the genes in the sample were polymorphic?

**Q2** A study investigated the number of people admitted for a chest infection in three different hospitals between 2004 and 2008. The table on the right shows some of the results of the study.

| Hospital | Number of cases per 1000 patients |||
|---|---|---|---|
| | 2004 | 2006 | 2008 |
| A | 22 | 24 | 29 |
| B | 14 | 16 | 19 |
| C | 25 | 28 | 31 |

a) Which hospital had the largest percentage increase in the number of people admitted for chest infections between 2004 and 2008?

b) Use the values in the table to calculate the ratio of cases in Hospital A : Hospital B in 2006.

---

**Tip:** You may also want to round measurements to a certain number of significant figures when you're recording your data, e.g. if you're using a data logger that records data to several decimal places.

**Tip:** When rounding a number, if the next digit after the last significant figure you're using is <u>less than 5</u> you should round it <u>down</u>, and if it's <u>5 or more</u> you should round it up.

## Rounding to significant figures

The first **significant figure** of a number is the first digit that isn't a zero. The second, third and fourth significant figures follow on immediately after the first (even if they're zeros). When you're processing your data you may well want to round any really long numbers to a certain number of significant figures.

### Example

0.6874976 rounds to **0.69** to **2 s.f.** and to **0.687** to **3 s.f.**

When you're doing calculations using measurements given to a certain number of significant figures, you should give your answer to the lowest number of significant figures that was used in the calculation.

### Example — Maths Skills

For the calculation: 1.2 ÷ 1.85 = 0.648648648...

1.2 is given to 2 significant figures. 1.85 is given to 3 significant figures. So the answer should be given to 2 significant figures.

Round the final significant figure (0.6<u>4</u>8...) up to 5: *1.2 ÷ 1.85 =* **0.65**

The lowest number of significant figures in the calculation is used because the fewer digits a measurement has, the less accurate it is. Your answer can only be as accurate as the least accurate measurement in the calculation.

Module 1: Development of Practical Skills

# Writing numbers in standard form

When you're processing data you might also want to change very big or very small numbers that have lots of zeros into something more manageable — this is called standard form.

**Examples**

1 000 000 can be written $1 \times 10^6$. 0.017 can be written $1.7 \times 10^{-2}$.

To do this you just need to move the decimal point left or right. The number of places the decimal point moves is then represented by a power of 10 — this is positive for big numbers, and negative for numbers smaller than one.

**Example — Maths Skills**

**To write 16 500 in standard form:**

1. Move the decimal point to give the smallest number you can between 1 and 10.

    $16\ 500 \longrightarrow 1.6500$

2. Count the number of places the decimal point has moved.

    *The decimal point has moved four places to the left.*

3. Write that number as the power of ten. If the decimal point has moved to the left, the power is positive. If the decimal point has moved to the right, the power is negative.

    $16\ 500 = \mathbf{1.65 \times 10^4}$

**Tip:** When you're writing a measurement in standard form, make sure you keep the same number of significant figures. E.g. $0.00400\ cm^3 = 4.00 \times 10^{-3}\ cm^3$. This'll make sure that you don't lose any accuracy.

**Tip:** Double check you've got it right by doing the multiplication — you should end up with the number you started with. So for this example, you'd check $1.65 \times 10^4 = 16\ 500$.

# Converting between units

When processing your data, you need to have all the data in the correct units. Make sure you can convert between common units of time, length and volume.

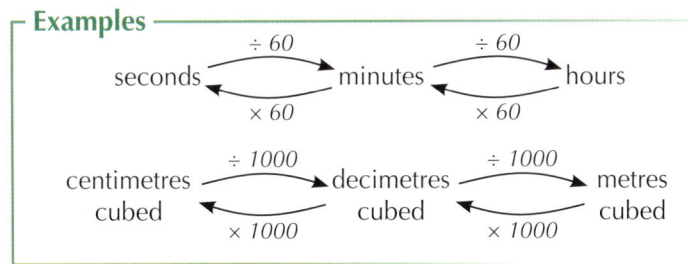

**Examples**

seconds $\xrightarrow{\div 60}$ minutes $\xrightarrow{\div 60}$ hours
seconds $\xleftarrow{\times 60}$ minutes $\xleftarrow{\times 60}$ hours

centimetres cubed $\xrightarrow{\div 1000}$ decimetres cubed $\xrightarrow{\div 1000}$ metres cubed
centimetres cubed $\xleftarrow{\times 1000}$ decimetres cubed $\xleftarrow{\times 1000}$ metres cubed

**Tip:** One decimetre cubed ($1\ dm^3$) is the same as one litre (1 L).

**Examples — Maths Skills**

1. **The total lung capacity of a patient is 5430 $cm^3$. What is the patient's lung capacity in $dm^3$?**

    There are 1000 $cm^3$ in one $dm^3$, so you need to divide by 1000:
    $5430\ cm^3 \div 1000 = \mathbf{5.430\ dm^3}$

2. **The volume of oxygen produced over time was measured for an enzyme-controlled reaction. The initial rate of reaction was found to be 8.4 $cm^3\,min^{-1}$. What is this rate in $cm^3\,s^{-1}$?**

    $8.4\ cm^3\,min^{-1}$ means $8.4\ cm^3$ oxygen was produced per minute. You want to find out the volume produced per second. There are 60 seconds in one minute, so you need to divide the volume by 60:
    $8.4\ cm^3\,min^{-1} \div 60 = \mathbf{0.14\ cm^3\,s^{-1}}$

**Tip:** Make sure your answer makes sense — if you're converting from a small unit (e.g. $cm^3$) to a larger unit (e.g. $dm^3$) you need to <u>divide</u> the value, so your answer should be <u>smaller</u> than the number you started with.

Module 1: Development of Practical Skills   15

**Tip:** Qualitative data is <u>descriptive</u> — there's more about it on the next page.

**Tip:** Quantitative results can be <u>discrete</u> or <u>continuous</u> data (see pages 17-19).

**Tip:** < means 'less than', << means 'much less than', > means 'greater than', >> means 'much greater than', ≤ means 'less than or equal to' and ≥ means 'greater than or equal to'.

**Tip:** If the result of your statistical test is greater than the critical value at a P value of less than 2% (< 0.02), or even 1%, you can be even more confident that the difference is significant.

**Exam Tip**
When you're talking about the results of a statistical test and using the 95% confidence limit, make sure you refer to the probability as less than 0.05 or 5%, <u>not</u> 0.05%.

**Exam Tip**
In the exams, you could be asked to calculate the result of a statistical test and interpret it.

# Statistical tests

Statistical tests are used to analyse data mathematically. They can be used to analyse quantitative (numerical) or qualitative (non-numerical) results. You can be more confident in your **conclusions** (see page 26) if they're based on results that have been analysed using a statistical test.
If you're planning on analysing your data using a statistical test, you first need to come up with a **null hypothesis** — this is a special type of hypothesis that states there is no significant difference (or correlation) between the things you're investigating. You then collect data to try to disprove the null hypothesis before analysing it statistically. There's more on null hypotheses on page 282.

### Student's t-test
You can use the Student's t-test when you have two sets of data that you want to compare, e.g. whether males and females performed well in the same test. It tests whether there is a significant difference in the means of the two data sets.

The value obtained is compared to a critical value, which helps you decide how likely it is that the results or 'differences in the means' were due to chance. If the value obtained from the t-test is greater than the critical value at a probability (or **P value**) of 5% or less (≤ 0.05), then you can be 95% confident that the difference is significant and not due to chance. This is called a **95% confidence limit** — which is good enough for most biologists to reject the null hypothesis. For more on the Student's t-test, see pages 360-362.

### Chi-squared test
You can use the Chi-squared test when you have categorical (grouped) data and you want to know whether your observed results are statistically different from your expected results. You compare your result to a critical value — if it's larger than the critical value at P = 0.05, you can be 95% certain it's significant. See pages 463-465 for more on the chi-squared test.

### Spearman's rank correlation coefficient
Spearman's rank correlation coefficient allows you to work out the degree to which two sets of data are correlated (see page 23 for more on correlation). It is given as a value between 1 and –1. A value of 1 indicates a strong positive correlation, 0 means there is no correlation and –1 is a strong negative correlation. You can then compare your result to a critical value to find out whether or not the correlation is significant. See pages 281-283 for more on how to use the Spearman's rank correlation coefficient.

## Practice Questions — Application

Q1 Write 0.0045 in standard form.

Q2 Give the answers to the following calculations to the correct number of significant figures:
   a) 4.53 × 3.142        b) 0.315 ÷ 0.025

Q3 A student was investigating the effect of light intensity on plant growth. He measured the heights of seedlings grown under a lamp and the heights of seedlings grown in a cupboard, then used the Student's t-test to compare the heights of the two groups. The value obtained was greater than the critical value at P = 0.05. What does this tell you about the student's results?

Module 1: Development of Practical Skills

# 4. Presenting Data

*Presenting your data can make it easier for you to understand your results and spot any trends. There are several different ways to do it though, and you need to be able to choose the best way for the data you've got.*

## Qualitative and discrete data

**Qualitative** data is non-numerical data, e.g. blood group, hair colour.
**Discrete** data is numerical data that can only take certain values in a range, e.g. shoe size, number of patients. You can use **bar charts** or **pie charts** to present these types of data.

### Example — Maths Skills

The table shows the results of a survey into people's blood groups.

| Blood group | Number of people |
|---|---|
| A | 9 |
| B | 8 |
| AB | 2 |
| O | 17 |

To draw a bar chart from it:

1. **Space out each category evenly on the x-axis.**
   The blood groups are the categories so they go on the x-axis. Space each category out evenly. The bars for different categories shouldn't touch each other.

2. **Choose a sensible scale for your y-axis.**
   The number of people (the thing that was measured in this survey) goes on the y-axis. The highest number of people is 17, so an axis running from 0 to 20 would work nicely.

3. **Draw a bar for each category.**

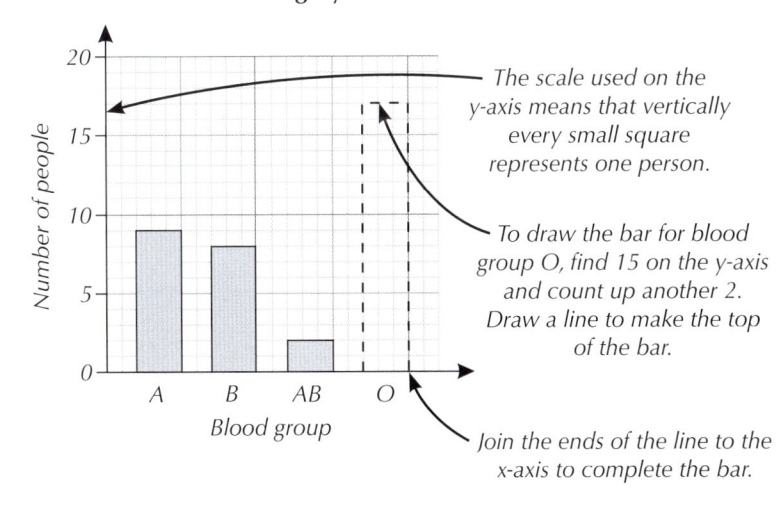

   - The scale used on the y-axis means that vertically every small square represents one person.
   - To draw the bar for blood group O, find 15 on the y-axis and count up another 2. Draw a line to make the top of the bar.
   - Join the ends of the line to the x-axis to complete the bar.

**Learning Objectives:**
- Be able to plot suitable graphs from experimental results, including selecting and labelling axes with appropriate scales, quantities and units.
- Understand how to interpret graphs of experimental results.
- Be able to measure gradients and intercepts of graphs.

**Specification Reference 1.1.3**

**Tip:** Qualitative data can also be called categorical data — all the data can be sorted into categories and values between categories don't exist.

**Exam Tip**
If you are asked to draw a graph or chart in your exam, don't forget to label the axes (including the quantity and units), choose a sensible scale and make sure that it covers at least half the graph paper.

**Tip:** Graph paper tends to be divided vertically and horizontally into groups of 10 squares. So axes that go up in 1s, 2s, 5s or 10s make data a lot easier to plot.

**Tip:** You can choose the width of the bars — just make sure they're all the same.

**Tip:** This bar chart shows that most people in the survey had blood group O.

Module 1: Development of Practical Skills

## Continuous data

**Continuous** data is data that can take any value in a range, e.g. height or weight. You can use **line graphs** or **histograms** to present this type of data.

### Line graphs

Line graphs often show how a variable changes over time. The data on both axes is continuous.

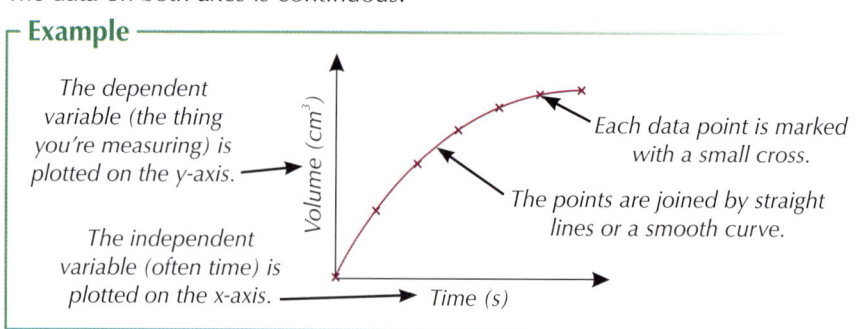

**Tip:** The graph on the right is a line graph. Line graphs look a bit like scattergrams (see next page), but the points on line graphs are joined together.

--- Example ---

The dependent variable (the thing you're measuring) is plotted on the y-axis.

The independent variable (often time) is plotted on the x-axis.

Each data point is marked with a small cross.

The points are joined by straight lines or a smooth curve.

(y-axis: Volume (cm$^3$); x-axis: Time (s))

**Tip:** The line graph on the right shows that the volume increases over time but the rate of increase is slowing down. There's more about rate on page 20.

### Histograms

Histograms are a useful way of displaying frequency data when the independent variable is continuous. They may look like bar charts, but it's the area of the bars that represents the frequency (rather than the height). The height of each bar is called the **frequency density**.

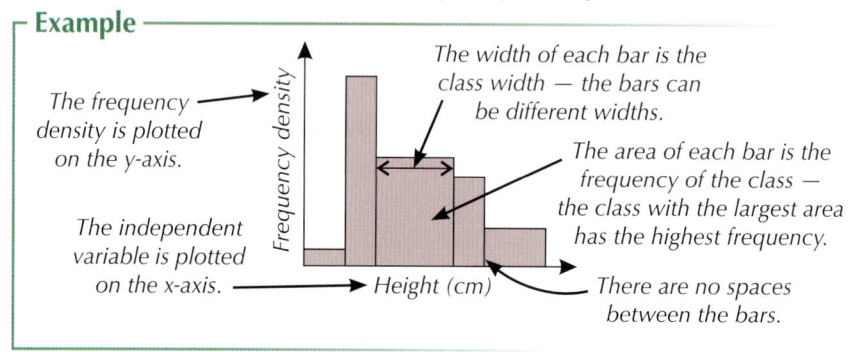

**Tip:** Don't be fooled by the height of the bars in a histogram — the tallest bar doesn't always belong to the class with the greatest frequency.

--- Example ---

The frequency density is plotted on the y-axis.

The independent variable is plotted on the x-axis.

The width of each bar is the class width — the bars can be different widths.

The area of each bar is the frequency of the class — the class with the largest area has the highest frequency.

There are no spaces between the bars.

(y-axis: Frequency density; x-axis: Height (cm))

**Tip:** If all the class widths are the same, you can just plot the frequency on the y-axis.

You calculate the frequency density using this formula:

$$\text{frequency density} = \text{frequency} \div \text{class width}$$

--- Example — Maths Skills ---

The table on the right shows the results of a study into variation in pea plant height. The heights of the plants were grouped into four classes.

| Height of pea plant (cm) | Frequency |
|---|---|
| $0 \leq x < 5$ | 5 |
| $5 \leq x < 10$ | 14 |
| $10 \leq x < 15$ | 11 |
| $15 \leq x < 30$ | 3 |

**Tip:** The continuous data here has been split into classes. $0 \leq x < 5$ means the data in the class is more than or equal to 0 and less than 5.

1. To draw a histogram of the data, you first need to work out the width of each class. Write the class width in a new column.

| Class width |
|---|
| 5 − 0 = **5** |
| 10 − 5 = **5** |
| 15 − 10 = **5** |
| 30 − 15 = **15** |

Module 1: Development of Practical Skills

2. Use the formula on the previous page to calculate the frequency density for each class and write it in another new column.

| Frequency density |
|---|
| 5 ÷ 5 = **1** |
| 14 ÷ 5 = **2.8** |
| 11 ÷ 5 = **2.2** |
| 3 ÷ 15 = **0.2** |

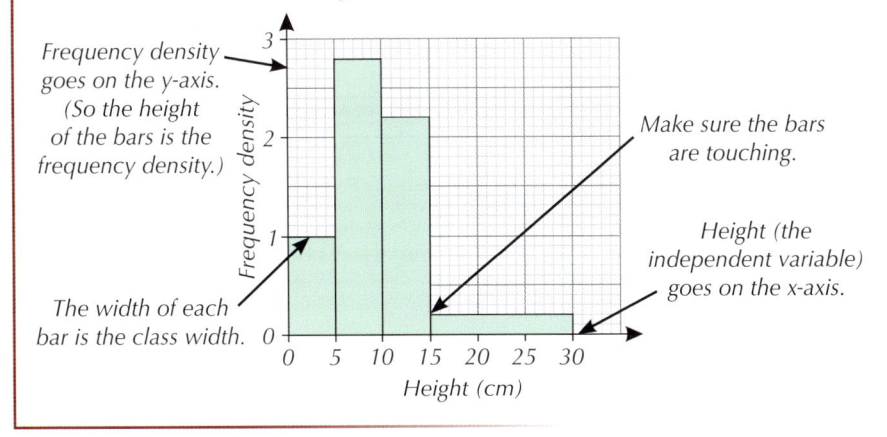

**Tip:** You might have to round the frequency density — if so, choose a sensible number of decimal places that will be possible to plot using your graph's scale.

3. Work out a suitable scale for each axis, then plot the histogram. It should look something like this:

*Frequency density goes on the y-axis. (So the height of the bars is the frequency density.)*

*Make sure the bars are touching.*

*Height (the independent variable) goes on the x-axis.*

*The width of each bar is the class width.*

**Tip:** You can calculate the frequency of a class from a histogram by rearranging the formula: frequency = frequency density × class width.

**Tip:** The width of the whole histogram shows the range of results (how spread out they are).

## Scattergrams

When you want to show how two variables are related (or correlated, see page 23) you can use a **scattergram**. Both variables must be numbers.

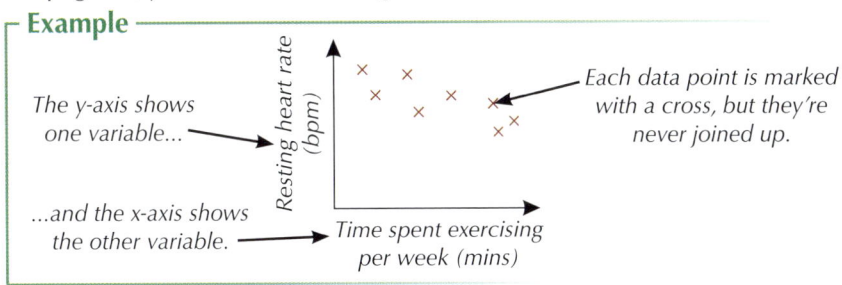

**Tip:** Scattergrams can also be called scatter graphs, or scatter diagrams.

― Example ―

*The y-axis shows one variable...*

*Each data point is marked with a cross, but they're never joined up.*

*...and the x-axis shows the other variable.*

**Tip:** Data that's made up of numbers is called quantitative data.

**Tip:** You should never join the points together on a scattergram.

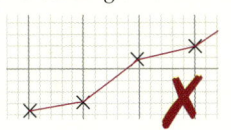

You can draw a **line** (or curve) **of best fit** on a scattergram to help show the trend in your results. To do so, draw the line through or as near to as many points as possible, ignoring any anomalous results.

A line of best fit shows a trend rather than changes between data points.

― Example ―

The number of organisms of one species on a rocky beach was recorded at different distances from the shore. The graph below shows the results, including a line of best fit.

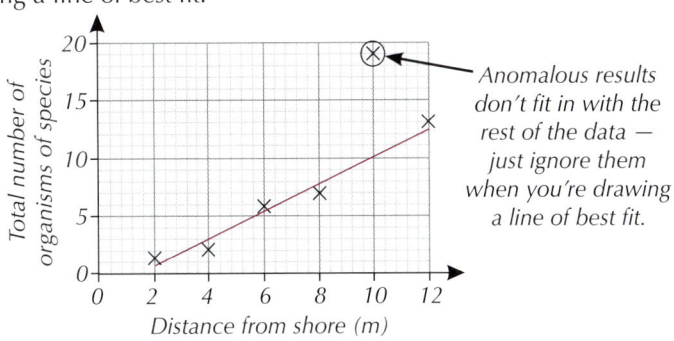

*Anomalous results don't fit in with the rest of the data — just ignore them when you're drawing a line of best fit.*

**Tip:** A trend shown by a scattergram is called a correlation. The graph on the left shows a positive correlation — as the distance from the shore increases, the total number of organisms of one species increases. There's more about correlation and what it means on page 23.

Module 1: Development of Practical Skills

## Finding the rate from a graph

Rate is a measure of how much something is changing over time. Calculating a rate can be useful when analysing your data, e.g. you might want to the find the rate of a reaction. You can find the rate from a graph that shows a variable changing over time by finding the **gradient** (how steep it is):

**Tip:** Linear graphs are graphs with a straight line.

### Linear graphs

For a linear graph you can calculate the rate by finding the gradient of the line, using the equation:

**Tip:** When using this equation to find a rate, x should always be the time.

$$\text{Gradient} = \frac{\text{Change in } y}{\text{Change in } x}$$

**Change in y** is the change in value on the y-axis and **change in x** is the change in value on the x-axis.

The equation of a straight line can always be written in the form $y = mx + c$, where $m$ is the gradient and $c$ is the y-intercept (this is the value of y when the line crosses the y-axis).

--- Example --- Maths Skills ---

**Tip:** The graph on the right is a straight line graph in which one variable increases in proportion with the other. The symbol for 'proportional to' is '∝'. Here, you can say that volume of oxygen released ∝ time.

To find the rate at which oxygen is produced in the graph on the right:

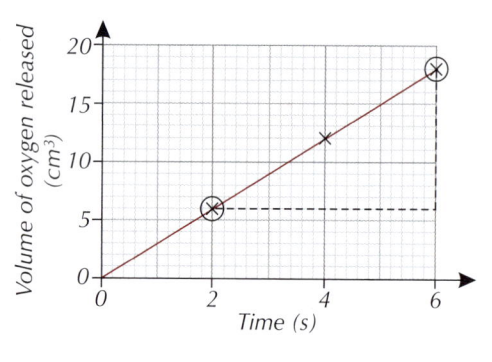

1. Pick two points on the line that are easy to read and a good distance apart.

2. Draw a vertical line down from one point and a horizontal line across from the other to make a triangle.

**Tip:** When drawing a triangle to calculate a gradient like this, the hypotenuse of the triangle should be at least half as long as the line of the graph itself.

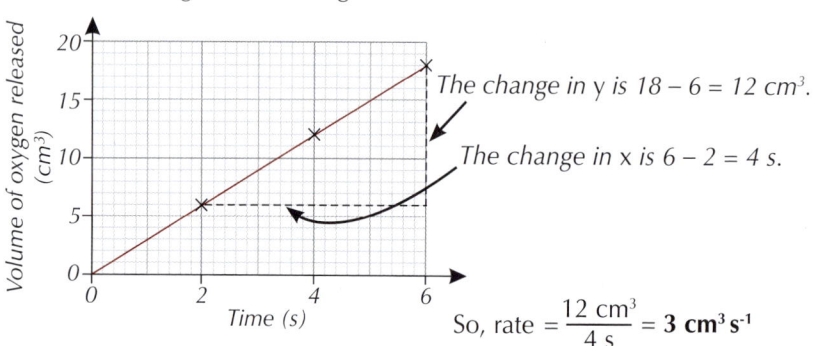

3. Use the scales on the axes to work out the length of each line. The vertical side of the triangle is the change in y and the horizontal side of the triangle is the change in x.

The change in y is 18 − 6 = 12 cm³.

The change in x is 6 − 2 = 4 s.

**Tip:** The units for the gradient are the units for y divided by the units for x. Remember, cm³ s⁻¹ means the same as cm³/s (centimetres cubed per second).

So, rate = $\frac{12 \text{ cm}^3}{4 \text{ s}}$ = **3 cm³ s⁻¹**

To find the equation of the line you need the gradient (which is the same as the rate) and the y-intercept (where the line crosses the y-axis).

*The gradient is 3 and the line crosses the y-axis where y is 0.*

So the equation for the line is $y = 3x + 0$.

Since $c = 0$, the equation can be written as just **y = 3x**.

Knowing the equation of the line allows you to estimate results not plotted on the graph:

### Example — Maths Skills

**For the reaction shown in the graph on the right, estimate the volume of oxygen released after 20 seconds.**

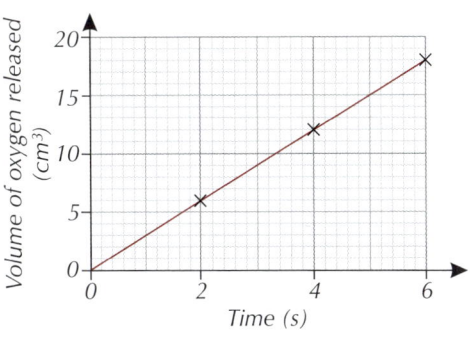

The equation for the line is $y = 3x$ (see previous page), where $y$ is the volume of oxygen released (in cm³) and $x$ is the time (in seconds).
To find the value of $y$ when $x$ is 20 s, just replace $x$ with 20 in the equation.
$$y = 3 \times 20 = \mathbf{60 \text{ cm}^3}$$

**Tip:** This is an estimate because you are assuming that the relationship between the two variables doesn't change after six seconds (so as time increases, the volume of oxygen released keeps increasing at the same rate).

## Curved graphs

For a curved (non-linear) graph you can find the rate by drawing a **tangent**. A tangent is a straight line that touches a single point on the curve.

### Example — Maths Skills

To find the rate of reaction when time = 30 seconds on the graph below:

1. Position a ruler on the graph at the point on the curve where you want to know the rate (so on this graph, find the point on the curve where $x = 30$).

2. Angle the ruler so there is equal space between the ruler and the curve on either side of the point.

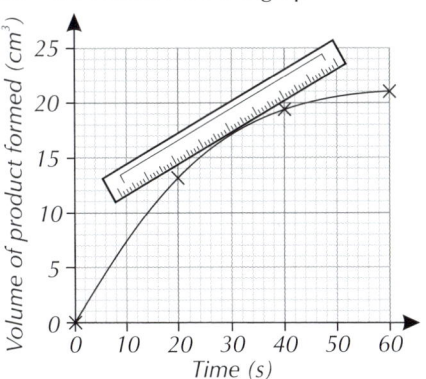

**Tip:** Look at the gaps on either side of the point — keep wiggling the ruler about until the two gaps look about the same size.

3. Draw a line along the ruler to make the tangent. Extend the line right across the graph — it'll help to make your gradient calculation easier as you'll have more points to choose from.

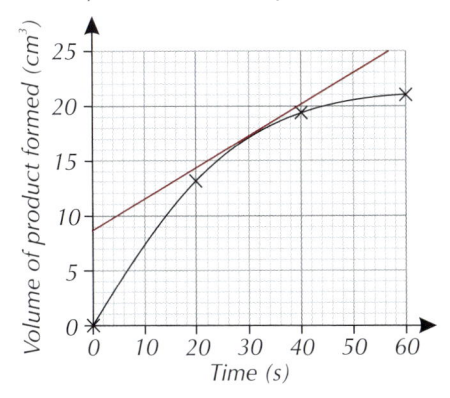

**Tip:** Always use a sharp pencil when drawing a tangent to draw a neat line — you'll need to read points off the line in the next step, so make sure the line's nice and clear.

Module 1: Development of Practical Skills    21

4. To find the rate, calculate the gradient of the tangent in the same way you would calculate the gradient of a straight line graph (see p. 20).

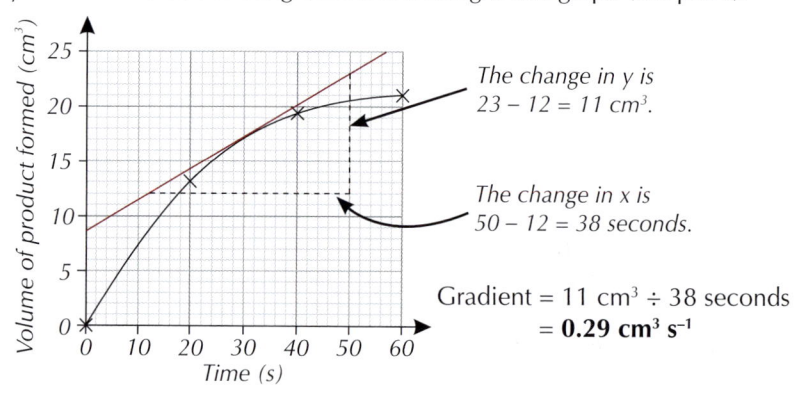

**Tip:** Remember, gradient = change in y ÷ change in x.

**Tip:** Remember, the gradient of a tangent only tells you the rate at that particular point on the graph.

The change in y is 23 − 12 = 11 cm³.

The change in x is 50 − 12 = 38 seconds.

Gradient = 11 cm³ ÷ 38 seconds = **0.29 cm³ s⁻¹**

## Practice Questions — Application

**Q1** A scientist is investigating the variation in wingspan in a species of bird. The results are shown in the table on the right. What type of graph should the scientist use to display this data? Explain your answer.

| Wingspan (cm) | Frequency |
|---|---|
| 14 ≤ x < 16 | 2 |
| 16 ≤ x < 18 | 5 |
| 18 ≤ x < 20 | 9 |
| 20 ≤ x < 22 | 4 |

**Q2** A group of students was investigating the effect of temperature on the respiration rate of locusts. Their results are shown in the graph below.

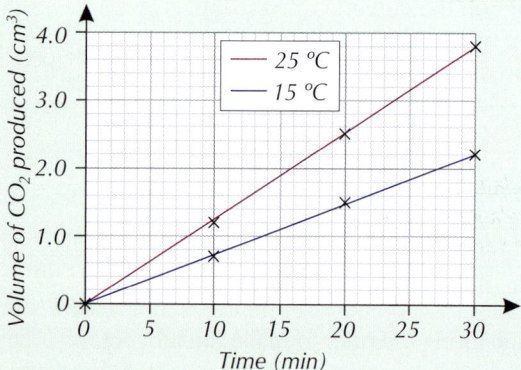

**Tip:** Respiration rate can be investigated by measuring volume of $O_2$ used or the volume of $CO_2$ produced.

a) What is the rate of $CO_2$ production at 25 °C?

b) Assuming that the respiration rate remains constant, how much $CO_2$ will have been produced during the experiment at 15 °C after 50 minutes?

**Q3** The concentration of product produced during an enzyme-controlled reaction was measured over time. The table below shows the results. Plot a suitable graph for the data in the table.

| Time (s) | 0 | 10 | 20 | 30 | 40 | 50 | 60 |
|---|---|---|---|---|---|---|---|
| Product concentration (µmol/dm³) | 0 | 6.1 | 10.3 | 12.5 | 13.6 | 14.1 | 14.2 |

# 5. Drawing Conclusions and Evaluating

*You need to be able to draw conclusions from your results and evaluate them. You also need to be able to draw conclusions from other people's data and evaluate them — which is what you're likely to be asked to do in your exams.*

## Drawing conclusions from data

Conclusions need to be **valid**. A conclusion can only be considered as valid if it answers the original question.

### Correlations and causal relationships

You can often draw conclusions by looking at the relationship (**correlation**) between two variables:

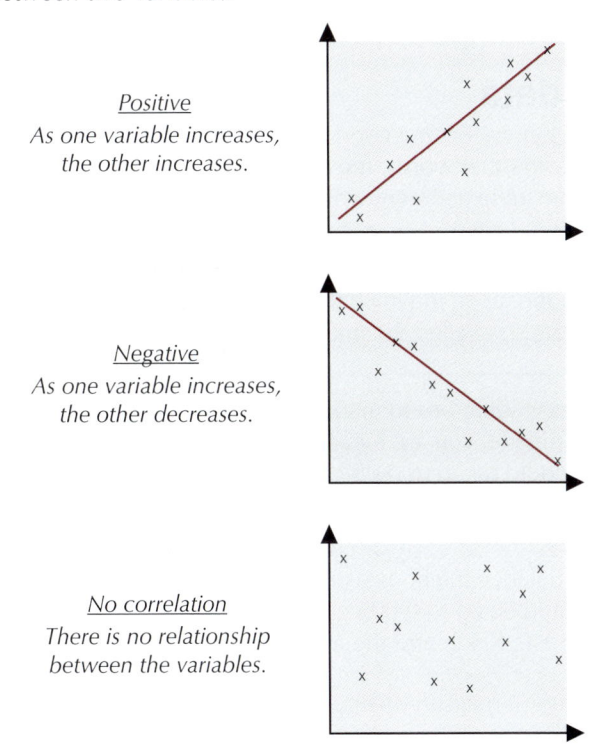

*Positive*
As one variable increases, the other increases.

*Negative*
As one variable increases, the other decreases.

*No correlation*
There is no relationship between the variables.

You have to be very careful when drawing conclusions from data like this because a correlation between two variables doesn't always mean that a change in one variable causes a change in the other (the correlation could be due to chance or there could be a third variable having an effect).

If there's a relationship between two variables and a change in one variable does cause a change in the other it's called a **causal relationship**. It can be concluded that a correlation is a causal relationship if every other variable that could possibly affect the result is controlled.

### Drawing specific conclusions

When you're making a conclusion you can't make broad generalisations from data — you have to be very specific. You can only conclude what the results show and no more.

**Learning Objectives:**
- Understand how to evaluate results and draw conclusions.
- Understand precision and accuracy of measurements and data, including margins of error, percentage errors and uncertainties in apparatus.
- Be able to identify the limitations in experimental procedures.
- Be able to refine experimental design by suggesting improvements to the procedures and apparatus.

**Specification Reference 1.1.4**

**Tip:** The closer the points are to the line of best fit, the stronger the correlation. You can calculate a correlation coefficient (see p. 16) to get a numerical value for how strong the correlation is.

**Tip:** In reality, concluding that a correlation is a causal relationship is very hard to do — correlations are generally accepted to be causal relationships if lots of studies have found the same thing, and scientists have figured out exactly how one factor causes the other.

Module 1: Development of Practical Skills 23

### Example — Maths Skills

**Figure 1** shows the results from a study into the effect of penicillin dosage on the duration of fever in men.

**What you can conclude from these results:**
The only conclusion you can draw is that there's a negative correlation between penicillin dosage and duration of fever in men (as the dosage of penicillin increases, the duration of fever in men decreases).

**What you can't conclude from these results:**
You can't conclude that this is true for any other antibiotic, any other symptom or even for female patients — the results could be completely different. Without more information and the results from more studies, you can't conclude that the increasing penicillin dosage has caused the reduction in duration of fever either.

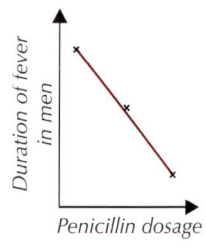

**Figure 1:** The relationship between penicillin dosage and the duration of fever in men.

**Exam Tip**
Being able to recognise correlations and causal relationships comes up a lot in Biology. It's really important that you learn how to do this and understand the difference between the two.

## Uncertainty in data

When you draw a conclusion, it's often a good idea to talk about the uncertainty in your data — in other words, the amount of error there might be. The results you get from an experiment won't be completely perfect — there'll always be a degree of uncertainty in your readings or measurements due to limits in the sensitivity of the apparatus you're using.

A ± sign tells you the range in which the true value lies (to within a certain probability). The range is called the **margin of error**.

**Tip:** A reading is when you make a judgement about one value, e.g. when you read a value off a mass balance. A measurement is when you judge two values and find the difference, e.g. when you measure length with a ruler.

### Examples

- A 10 $cm^3$ pipette has graduations to mark every 0.1 $cm^3$. If you measure a volume using the pipette, you are measuring to the nearest 0.1 $cm^3$ — the real volume could be up to 0.05 $cm^3$ less or 0.05 $cm^3$ more. The uncertainty value of the pipette is ± 0.05 $cm^3$, and so its margin of error is 0.1 $cm^3$ (see Figure 2).

- An electronic mass balance might measure to the nearest 0.01 g, but the real mass could be up to 0.005 g smaller or larger. It has an uncertainty value of ± 0.005 g, and the margin of error is 0.01 g.

If you're combining readings or measurements, you'll need to combine their uncertainties:

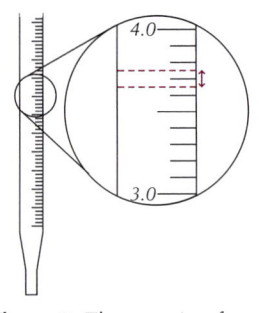

**Figure 2:** The margin of error for a reading of 3.7 $cm^3$ using a 10 $cm^3$ pipette.

### Example — Maths Skills

In a serial dilution, 5 $cm^3$ of glucose solution is transferred using a pipette that measures to the nearest 0.5 $cm^3$. It is added to 10 $cm^3$ water that was measured in a graduated cylinder with graduations to mark every 1 $cm^3$.
The uncertainty in the pipette is ± 0.25 $cm^3$.
The uncertainty in the graduated cylinder is ± 0.5 $cm^3$.
So the total uncertainty will be 0.25 $cm^3$ + 0.5 $cm^3$ = **± 0.75 $cm^3$**.

**Tip:** If the total uncertainty of combined errors is ± 0.75 $cm^3$, the margin of error will be 2 × 0.75 = 1.5 $cm^3$. This is the same as adding the two separate margins of error together.

### Calculating percentage error

If you know the uncertainty value of your measurements, you can calculate the percentage error using this formula:

$$\text{percentage error} = \frac{\text{uncertainty}}{\text{reading}} \times 100$$

## Example — Maths Skills

50 cm$^3$ of HCl is measured with an uncertainty value of ± 0.05 cm$^3$. What is the percentage error?

$$\frac{0.05}{50} \times 100 = \mathbf{0.1\%}$$

**Tip:** The percentage error is the error as a <u>percentage</u> of the measured value, so you can use it to compare the uncertainty of two readings or measurements (see below).

## Minimising errors in data

One obvious way to reduce errors in your measurements is to buy the most sensitive equipment available. In real life there's not much you can do about this one — you're stuck with whatever your school or college has got. But there are other ways to lower the uncertainty in experiments.

### Example — Measuring a greater amount of something

So using a 500 cm$^3$ cylinder to measure 100 cm$^3$ of liquid will give you a percentage error of:  $\frac{2.5}{100} \times 100 = \mathbf{2.5\%}$

But if you measure 200 cm$^3$ in the same cylinder, the percentage error is:  $\frac{2.5}{200} \times 100 = \mathbf{1.25\%}$

Hey presto — you've just halved the uncertainty.

**Tip:** You can also minimise errors by using a <u>larger sample size</u>, as this reduces the chance of getting a freak result — see page 6.

## Evaluating results

When you evaluate your results, you need to think about whether they were repeatable and reproducible and whether they were valid.

### Repeatability
- Did you take enough repeat readings or measurements?
- Would you do more repeats if you were to do the experiment again?
- Do you get similar data each time you carried out a repeat measurement?

If you didn't do any repeats, or enough repeats, you can't be sure your data is repeatable. Your repeated results need to be similar too. If you repeated a measurement three times and got a completely different result each time, your results aren't repeatable (or precise).

### Reproducibility
Have you compared your results with other people's results and if so, were they similar? If not, you can't be sure your data is reproducible.

### Validity
- Does your data answer the question you set out to investigate?
- Were all the variables controlled?

If you didn't control all the variables, you haven't answered the original question and your data isn't valid.

### Example
You could only conclude from your results that the rate of activity of an enzyme is fastest at a particular temperature (see page 109) if you controlled all the other variables that could have affected enzyme activity in your experiment, e.g. pH, enzyme concentration, etc.

**Exam Tip**
If you're given data or a method to evaluate in the exam, you should be asking similar questions, e.g. were all the variables controlled? And if not, how should they have been controlled?

**Tip:** Think about whether other scientists could gain data showing the same relationships that are shown in your data.

**Tip:** If you don't control all other variables in your experiment, you can't tell if any trend in your results is linked to just the independent variable.

Module 1: Development of Practical Skills

**Tip:** This is where you take the uncertainty of your measurements (see page 24) into account. Think about the size of the margin of error, and whether you could have reduced the uncertainty.

## Evaluating methods

When you evaluate your method, you need to think about how you could improve your experiment if you did it again. Here are some things to consider:

- Is there anything you could have done to make your results more precise or accurate?
- Were there any limitations in your method, e.g. should you have taken measurements more frequently?
- Was your sample size large enough?
- Were there any sources of error in your experiment?
- Could you have used more sensitive apparatus or equipment?

## Having confidence in your conclusion

Once you've evaluated your results and method, you can decide how much confidence you have in your conclusion. For example, if your results are repeatable, reproducible and valid and they back up your conclusion then you can have a high degree of confidence in your conclusion.

You can also consider these points if you're asked to evaluate a conclusion in the exam.

**Exam Tip**
Data questions are fairly common in the exams. You might be given a conclusion for the data and asked to evaluate it — this just means you have to give reasons why it is (or isn't) a valid conclusion. You could also be asked how far data supports a conclusion — it requires a similar type of answer.

---Example---

A study examined the effect of farm hedgerow length on the number of species in a given area. The number of species present during a single week on 12 farms was counted by placing ground-level traps. All the farms were a similar area. The traps were left out every day, at 6 am for two hours and once again at 6 pm for two hours. The results are shown in Figure 3:

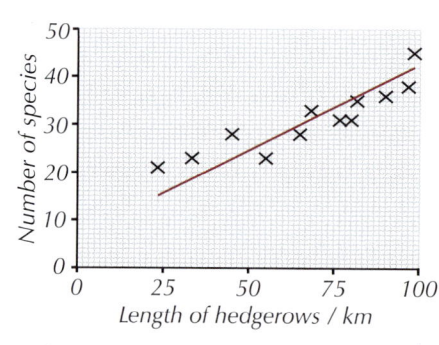

**Figure 3:** Scattergram to show relationship between number of species and length of hedgerows.

**A journalist who read this study concluded that longer hedgerows cause the number of species in a given area to increase. Does the data support this conclusion? Explain your answer.**

**Yes** — The data in the graph supports the conclusion as it shows that as the length of hedgerows increases, the number of species increases — the length of the hedgerows has a positive correlation with the number of species in that area.

**No** — You can't conclude that the increasing length of the hedgerows caused the increase in the number of species. Other factors may have been involved, for example, the number of predators in an area may have decreased or the farmers may have used less pesticide there.

Also, the study is quite small — they only used 12 farms. The trend shown by the data may not appear if 50 or 100 farms were studied, or if the farms were studied for a longer period of time.

The results are also limited by the method of trapping. Traps were placed on the ground, so species like birds weren't included, and they weren't left overnight, so nocturnal animals wouldn't get counted, etc. This could have affected the results.

Importantly, you're not told if all the other variables were controlled, e.g. you don't know if all the farms had a similar type of land, similar weather, the same crops growing, etc. This means you don't know how valid the study is — you can't be sure that the factor being investigated (hedgerows) is the only one affecting the thing being measured (number of species).

**Overall** — The limits of the study mean that the journalist's conclusion isn't well supported.

**Tip:** The method used to collect the data can bias the results. Bias is when someone intentionally or unintentionally favours a particular result — in the example on the left, the method of trapping gives results that are biased towards ground-dwelling species.

## Practice Questions — Application

Q1 a) What is the uncertainty of a pipette that has graduations every 0.5 cm³?

b) What is the percentage error of a measurement of 6.0 cm³ water made with the pipette in part a)?

Q2 A scientist was investigating the effect of temperature on the activity of enzyme X. She timed how long it took for 5 cm³ of product to be produced by enzyme X at 10 °C, keeping all variables other than temperature constant. The scientist repeated the experiment at 20 °C, 30 °C, 40 °C, 50 °C and 60 °C, then used the results to calculate a rate of reaction for each temperature. The results of the investigation are shown in Figure 4.

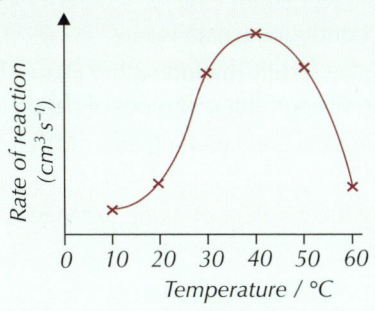

**Figure 4:** *Graph to show the effect of temperature on the rate of an enzyme-controlled reaction.*

a) A science magazine came to the following conclusion from this data:

**"Enzyme X works best at 40 °C."**

Does the data support this conclusion? Explain your answer.

b) Give one way in which the method for this experiment could be improved to provide more precise results.

c) The scientist is also interested in the effect of temperature on the activity of enzyme Z. Could she use the results of the experiment above to predict the effect of temperature on enzyme Z? Explain your answer.

Module 1: Development of Practical Skills

# Section Summary

Make sure you know...

- The definitions of the terms precise, repeatable, reproducible, valid and accurate, when referring to experimental results.
- How to plan a good experiment and evaluate whether a method is appropriate to meet an expected outcome, including the consideration of variables (the independent variable, the dependent variable, and variables that need to be controlled), controls (positive controls, negative controls and control groups), repeats and sample size.
- How to select equipment that is of the right size, scale and sensitivity for an experiment.
- How to select the most appropriate technique(s) to use for an experiment.
- How to carry out a risk assessment for an experiment and identify any ethical issues.
- How to use lots of different techniques and equipment.
- How to choose the most appropriate units for your measurements.
- How to record results into a table of data, including frequency tables.
- How to identify anomalous results in data.
- How to process, analyse and interpret results, including:
    - How to calculate a mean, median, mode and range from a data set.
    - What standard deviation is.
    - How to calculate a percentage and percentage change.
    - How to write two values as a ratio, in the form X : Y or X : 1.
    - How to correctly use significant figures and standard form when processing data.
    - How to convert between units.
    - What the Student's t-test, chi-squared test and Spearman's rank correlation coefficient are used for and what the results of these tests can tell you about data.
- What qualitative and quantitative (discrete and continuous) data is.
- The different types of graphs you can use to display results (including bar charts, histograms, line graphs and scattergrams), and which type to use for different types of data.
- How to plot a graph, including selecting suitable axes and labelling them with appropriate scales, quantities and units.
- How to find the rate from a graph by calculating the gradient of a line or tangent.
- How to find the equation of a straight line graph.
- That two variables may have a positive, a negative or no correlation.
- That correlation between variables doesn't always mean that they have a causal relationship (where a change in one causes a change in the other).
- How to draw conclusions that are supported by data.
- What uncertainty in an experiment is and how to calculate the margin of error and percentage error of a measurement.
- How to minimise errors in experiments.
- How to evaluate results (including being able to identify repeatable, reproducible and precise results), identify the limitations in an experiment and suggest ways in which an experiment could be improved.
- How to evaluate how well a conclusion is supported by a set of results.

# Exam-style Questions

**Q1** Which of the following has the largest percentage error?

A  50 g measured to the nearest 1 g.

B  5.0 g measured to the nearest 0.1 g.

C  10 g measured to the nearest 0.2 g.

D  15 g measured to the nearest 0.5 g.

*(1 mark)*

**Q2** The effect of temperature on diffusion rate in cells was investigated, using agar jelly as a model of cell cytoplasm. Pink agar jelly, prepared with phenolphthalein and dilute sodium hydroxide, was cut into four equal-sized cubes. Each cube was placed into a test tube of hydrochloric acid at a different temperature and the time taken for the cube to become colourless was recorded. The experiment was repeated three times at each temperature. **Table 2.1** shows the results.

| Temperature (°C) | Time taken for cube to become colourless (s) ||||
| --- | --- | --- | --- | --- |
|  | Repeat 1 | Repeat 2 | Repeat 3 | Mean |
| 10 | 728 | 414 | 425 | 420 |
| 20 | 343 | 330 | 351 | 341 |
| 30 | 240 | 231 | 228 | 233 |
| 40 | 187 | 166 | 172 | 175 |

**Table 2.1**

(a) (i) Give two benefits of repeating the experiment at each temperature.

*(2 marks)*

(ii) Draw a graph of these results, including a line of best fit.

*(3 marks)*

(b) Describe any correlation shown by the graph.

*(1 mark)*

(c) Write a conclusion for this investigation, based on the results shown by the graph.

*(2 marks)*

(d) Hydrochloric acid is an irritant and can cause damage if it comes into contact with skin or eyes. Suggest two ways that the risk from hydrochloric acid could be reduced in this investigation.

*(2 marks)*

(e) A student wants to repeat this experiment. Suggest two pieces of additional information that could be added to the method above, so that these results are more likely to be reproducible.

*(2 marks)*

# Practical Skills for the Practical Endorsement

## What is the Practical Endorsement?

The Practical Endorsement is assessed slightly differently to the rest of your course. Unlike the exams, you don't get a mark for the Practical Endorsement — you just have to get a pass grade. The Practical Endorsement is split into twelve categories, called Practical Activity Groups (PAGs). Each PAG covers a variety of practical techniques, for example, using a light microscope or separating biological compounds. All the PAGs you need to do are listed on page 36 and the practical techniques are listed on pages 36-37. In order to pass the Practical Endorsement, you'll have to carry out at least one experiment for each PAG, and demonstrate that you can carry out each of the required techniques. You'll do the experiments in class, and your teacher will assess you as you're doing them.

You'll need to keep a record of all of the assessed practical activities that you carry out throughout the A-Level course.

**Tip:** Throughout this book, experiments and skills that you could use for your Practical Endorsement are marked with a big PAG stamp, like this one:

**PRACTICAL ACTIVITY GROUP 7**

## 1. General Practical Skills

*The way you do an experiment is important. You should follow all the steps in a method, whether you were given it or planned it yourself. Doing this ensures that you work safely and makes your results more likely to be precise.*

### Solving problems in a practical context

Practical experiments are used to solve problems or test whether a theoretical model works in a practical setting. If you're given a method to follow for an experiment, you should carry out each step, as described, in the correct order.

It's possible you'll be given a problem and asked to solve it using your own knowledge. In Module 1, there's loads of information about how to plan and carry out experiments correctly (see pages 5-10). Here's a quick round-up of some of the things you'll need to think about when you plan an experiment:

- Identify the aim of your experiment.
- Work out how to achieve the aim — you'll often need to identify the independent and dependent variables for the investigation.
- Identify all the control variables (and how to control them).
- Think about how to make your data as precise and accurate as possible.

**Tip:** Experiments are often used to test scientific theories to see if they are true in a practical context.

**Tip:** Variables include things like temperature, time, mass, volume and colour.

**Tip:** Precise results are results that don't vary much from the mean. Accurate results are close to the true value.

### Recording and analysing data

After planning, you can carry out your experiment, working carefully to make sure your results are precise. The relevant techniques will be covered throughout this book — they should be carried out safely (see pages 32-33) and correctly.

**Recording data**

As you carry out your experiment, you should record your results in a well laid-out table, leaving space for any data analysis you might want to do later. Your table should have a heading for each column, including any units. See pages 9-10 for more on recording data in tables.

**Tip:** Any recorded results that don't fit in with the rest of the data are called anomalous results. If you can work out that they were due to a mistake when carrying out your experiment, you can leave them out of your data analysis.

## Processing data

When you've got results from several repeats of an experiment, you should calculate the **mean**. Module 1 details other measures you can use to summarise your data, including the **mode**, **median**, **range** and **standard deviation** (see pages 11-12). **Percentages** and **ratios** are useful for comparing quantities (see pages 13-14).

You can use statistical tests to analyse your data mathematically. You can be more confident in your conclusions if they're based on data that's been analysed in this way. The statistical tests you should be able to use are:

- **Spearman's rank correlation coefficient** (see pages 281-283) — This allows you to work out the degree to which two sets of data are correlated.
- **Student's t-test** (see pages 360-362) — This tests whether there is a significant difference in the means of two data sets.
- **Chi-squared test** (see pages 463-465) — This is used when your data is categorical (grouped) and tests whether your observed results are statistically different from your expected results.

**Tip:** Processing data is useful because you're summarising your results — it's a lot quicker and easier to understand figures like the mean and range than a lot of raw data.

**Tip:** Qualitative data can also be called categorical data — all the data can be sorted into categories and values between categories don't exist.

## Presenting data

Presenting your data can make it easier for you to understand your results and spot any trends. There are several different ways to do it though, and you need to be able to choose the best way for the data you've got.

Pages 17-19 in Module 1 show different ways to present data, including:

- Drawing **bar charts** or **pie charts** for **qualitative** or **discrete** data.
- Drawing **line graphs** or **histograms** for **continuous** data.
- Drawing **scattergrams** to show how two variables are related. You can draw a **line** (or curve) **of best fit** on the scattergram to help show the trend in your results. The trend is called the **correlation**.

**Tip:** You need to be able to find the rate of reaction from a graph. This includes using a tangent if the graph line is a curve.

**Tip:** A correlation between two variables can be positive (as one variable increases, the other increases), negative (as one variable increases, the other decreases), or there may be no correlation present.

## Conclusions and evaluations

When you've collected and analysed your data, it's time to wrap up your experiment with some conclusions and an evaluation. Conclusions explain what your results showed. They need to be supported by the data you collected, and shouldn't make sweeping generalisations. If you've found a correlation between two variables, you should be cautious about claiming that the change in one has caused the change in the other — there may be another factor that is causing both variables to change.

An evaluation is a chance for you to look at what you did and think about how you could have improved your method to improve the validity, accuracy and precision of your results. You should consider how well your results address the original aim of your experiment, how you could reduce errors in your results, and whether you need to repeat your experiment further to show your results can be reproduced.

**Tip:** When evaluating your experiment, you could comment on the uncertainty of your measurements and work out the margin of error or percentage error. The smaller these values are, the more precise your results will be. Look back at pages 24-25 for how to work them out.

**Tip:** A hazard is anything that has the potential to cause harm or damage. The risk associated with that hazard is the probability of someone (or something) being harmed if they are exposed to the hazard.

**Tip:** The CLEAPSS® website has a database with details of the potential harm lots of the hazardous chemicals you're likely to come across could cause. It also has student safety sheets, and your school or college may have CLEAPSS® Hazcards® you can use. These are all good sources of information if you're writing a risk assessment.

**Tip:** This isn't a comprehensive list of all the types of chemical hazards you may encounter — just some of the more common ones.

**Figure 1:** The hazard symbols for flammable (left), and corrosive (right).

**Tip:** Hazard symbols like the ones above are gradually replacing the older orange symbols. 'Harmful' and 'irritant' are being replaced by 'moderate hazard'. Its symbol looks like this: →

# 2. Working Safely

*When you do an experiment, you need to carry out a risk assessment and work safely at all times. This reduces the risk of anyone being hurt.*

## Risks and hazards

Many biology experiments have risks associated with them. These can include risks associated with the equipment you're using, as well as risks associated with chemicals or biological material. When you're planning an experiment, you need to identify all the hazards and what the risk is from each hazard — this is a risk assessment. A risk assessment includes working out how likely it is that something could go wrong, and how serious it would be if it did go wrong. You then need to think of ways to reduce these risks.

### Chemicals

Any hazardous chemicals you use should come with a list of dangers associated with them — this can be found on the bottle they come in, or looked up on something called a Material Safety Data Sheet. The table below shows some common hazard words that you may come across:

| Hazard word | Potential harm | Example chemicals | Examples of how to reduce the risk |
|---|---|---|---|
| Corrosive | May cause chemical burns to tissues such as skin and eyes. | Potassium hydroxide | Use as little of the substance as possible. If the chemical is a solution, use it in low concentrations. Wear a lab coat, goggles and gloves when handling the chemical. |
| Irritant | May cause inflammation and discomfort. | Hydrochloric acid (2-6.5 M), hydrogen peroxide (1.5-2.3 M), Biuret reagent | Use as little of the substance as possible. If the chemical is a solution, use it in low concentrations. Wear a lab coat, goggles and gloves when handling the chemical. |
| Flammable | May catch fire. | Ethanol, propanone, some chromatography solvents, ninhydrin spray | Keep the chemical away from any naked flames. If you have to heat it, use an electric water bath instead of a Bunsen burner. |
| Harmful | May cause damage to health when breathed in, swallowed or absorbed via the skin. | Enzymes (as powders), ninhydrin spray | Use as little of the substance as possible. If the chemical is a solution, use it in low concentrations. Wear a lab coat, goggles and gloves when handling the chemical. |

You may come across some volatile chemicals during your course (e.g. ninhydrin spray, some chromatography solvents). Volatile chemicals easily evaporate at room temperature and the vapours they produce may be hazardous — for example, they may be flammable or harmful if inhaled. Because of this, volatile substances should be used in a fume cupboard and you should take additional precautions based on the hazards associated with the vapour. Hazardous powders that may be inhaled (e.g. enzyme powders) should also be used in a fume cupboard.

Practical Skills for the Practical Endorsement

### Heating substances

Some of the experiments that you are expected to do during your course may involve heating a solution. You should only heat a solution in a boiling tube directly over a Bunsen burner if it is not flammable. Solutions heated over a Bunsen burner can boil, so there is a risk of hot liquid splashing out of the tube. There is also a risk of burns from a hot boiling tube. You can reduce these risks by using a test tube holder to hold the boiling tube, with the open end pointing away from you and others, not filling more than one tenth of the tube with liquid and by wearing safety goggles to protect your eyes.

A water bath (Figure 2) is a more controlled way to heat substances, as it can be heated to a specific temperature and there is less risk of a flammable substance catching fire. Test tubes placed in the water bath are warmed to the same temperature as the water. You should move test tubes in and out of the water bath using a test tube holder to reduce the risk of scalding. You should also leave test tubes to cool down after being removed from the water, as the glassware can become hot (depending on the temperature of the water bath).

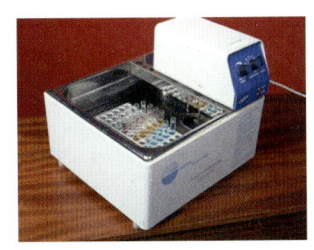

*Figure 2: A water bath.*

**Tip:** If the mixture you're heating contains hazardous chemicals (e.g. hydrochloric acid), it makes sense to use a water bath so there is less chance of the mixture splashing on to your skin.

### Using dissection tools

The tools used for dissection include scalpels, dissecting scissors, tweezers and pins. You need to take precautions to reduce the risk of injuring yourself or others with these tools, e.g. by cutting in a direction away from yourself and carrying the tools in a tray when moving through the classroom, so that any blades or sharp points are not exposed. Blunt tools are more likely to slip while you are cutting, so you should make sure that your equipment is sharp before you start the dissection. You should also make sure all the tools you are using are free from rust, to reduce the likelihood of them breaking.

**Tip:** When dissecting, you should take care to position your fingers away from where you're cutting.

### Biohazards

Some of the experiments that you are expected to do during your course may include possible biohazards (biological material that presents a risk to human health). You need to take appropriate precautions to reduce the risk of pathogenic (disease-causing) microorganisms spreading between objects or people, e.g. wash your hands after dissecting animal tissue, change and disinfect a spirometer mouthpiece between users. If you're culturing microorganisms, the microorganisms that you will be expected to work with should not be pathogenic. However, you need to take care that your cultures do not become contaminated with pathogenic bacteria. When you are culturing microorganisms, it is important to use aseptic techniques — see page 527 for more.

In experiments using insects, you need to be careful — some people are allergic to insects and/or their droppings, so gloves should be worn when handling live insects if you're in doubt as to whether a reaction could occur.

**Tip:** Although any microorganisms you use in the lab should be safe, you should always treat them as though they are pathogenic in case the samples have become contaminated.

**Tip:** Enzyme powders may also cause allergic reactions. If you're using them, make sure you're wearing safety goggles and gloves.

### Glassware

Many pieces of equipment that you may use during your course are made of glass (e.g. test tubes, potometers, microscope slides). Broken glass can cause serious injury, so you should take care to transport glass items safely and check them for cracks and flaws before you use them. Any broken pieces of glass should be moved away from the work area immediately and disposed of in an appropriate container (not the normal waste bin).

**Tip:** Don't try to pick up broken glass with your hands — it's a lot safer to use a dustpan and brush.

## Appropriate clothing

When working in the lab, you should make sure that you are wearing sensible clothing to reduce the risk of injury, e.g. open shoes or sandals won't protect your feet against spillages. You should also wear a lab coat to protect your skin and clothing. It's all about using your common sense really.

**Tip:** If you have long hair, it should be tied back if you're working near an open flame.

# 3. Keeping Scientific Records

*When you carry out experiments, it's important to keep records of everything you do. The records should be detailed and clear enough that a complete stranger would be able to read them and understand what you did.*

## Records of scientific experiments

Throughout your A-Level Biology course, you should keep a record of all the experiments you carry out, the results you obtain and the solutions to any data analysis you do. This could be done in a physical lab book, or kept in folders on a computer. However you choose to keep your records, the information for each experiment should include:

- The aim of the experiment.
- A detailed method for how you carried out the experiment, including the quantities of all the chemicals and any safety precautions you had to take.
- The results of your experiment, clearly set out in a table. The results may be hand-written, or a print-out of data collected by a data logger.
- Any other important observations you made whilst carrying out your experiment, for example, anything that went wrong or anything you did slightly differently from how it was described in the method.
- The solutions to any analysis you did on your results, or any graphs drawn using your results. These should be clearly labelled to show what analysis has been done or what graph has been drawn.
- Citations of any references you used.

**Tip:** Try to keep all your lab reports in the same place — write them in the same book, or keep them in the same folder on your computer. That way you'll know where everything is.

**Tip:** A clear and detailed method is important, as it could be used by another scientist who is trying to reproduce your results.

**Tip:** There's loads more detail about making observations, recording data and analysing your results in Module 1.

## Sources of information

It's possible you'll have to do some research to find out information before you get started with an experiment. Useful sources of information include:

**PRACTICAL ACTIVITY GROUP 12**

### Websites

Using the Internet for research is really convenient, but you have to be slightly wary as not all the information you find will be true. It's hard to know where information comes from on forums, blogs and websites that can be edited by the general public, so you should avoid using these. Websites of organisations such as the Nuffield Foundation and the National Health Service (NHS) provide lots of information that comes from reliable scientific sources.
To decide whether a website gives reliable information, think about the following things:

- Who has written the information — was it a scientist, a teacher, or just a member of the public?
- Whether or not anyone will have checked the source — articles on websites for scientific organisations will have people reading through the information and checking all the facts. Information on forums or blogs is likely to have been written by an individual, and won't necessarily have been thoroughly checked.
- What the purpose of the website is — if it's a website all about Biology, then it's likely whoever has written it will know quite a lot. If it's a website where you can also find out how to make a plant pot from an old teacup and some PVA glue, then the depth and quality of the information may not be enough.

**Tip:** If you're unsure whether the information on a website is true or not, try and find the same piece of information in a different place. The more sources you can find for the information, the more likely it is to be correct.

Practical Skills for the Practical Endorsement

## Textbooks
Your school or public library is likely to have textbooks covering specific areas of Biology in a lot of detail.

## Scientific papers
You can find papers in online catalogues, such as SciFinder or PubMed, as well as in journals that are often available in public libraries.

**Tip:** Scientific papers are checked by other scientists who are experts in the subject of the paper. This is called peer review (see page 2).

The source you do your research from needs to give the right level of information. It's no good trawling through a scientific paper if you're just looking for the boiling point of a compound — the information will be far too detailed, and you'll probably end up wading through lots of complicated information that you don't need to understand. Equally, if you're researching the theory behind an experiment, you want a source that gives enough detail. A GCSE textbook will probably be too simplistic — you're better off finding a book that deals specifically with the subject in a library instead.

# Using references and making citations

It sounds obvious, but when you're using the information that you've found during your research, you can't just copy it down word for word. Any data you're looking up should be copied accurately, but you should rewrite everything else in your own words.

PRACTICAL ACTIVITY GROUP 12

When you've used information from a source, you need to cite the reference properly. Citations allow someone else to go back and find the source of your information. This means they can check your information and see you're not making things up out of thin air. Citations also mean you've properly credited other people's data that you've used in your work.

Citations are included in the main text of a report and are usually written in brackets after the relevant piece of information. They can either include the entire reference or link the information to a list of references at the end of the report (e.g. using a number — see Figure 1). References for each piece of information may include the title of the book, paper or website where you found the information, the author and/or the publisher of the document and the date the document was published.

**Tip:** There are lots of slightly different ways of referencing sources, but the important thing is that it's clear where you found the information.

**Tip:** You should include page numbers with your citation if you quote directly from the text or copy a diagram.

**Referencing a website:** include the URL and the date accessed.

**Referencing a book:** include the author, book title and publication year.

**Referencing a paper:** include the authors, publication year, title of the paper, the journal it was published in, the volume number and page numbers.

*Report*

90% of people with diabetes have Type II diabetes (2, p. 434)...

*References*

1. http://www.diabetes.co.uk/diabetes_care/blood-sugar-level-ranges.html [Accessed 06 June 2015]

2. McConnell T.H.; The Nature of Disease: Pathology for the Health Professions; 2007

3. King H., Aubert R.E., Herman W.H.; 1998. Global burden of diabetes, 1995-2025: prevalence, numerical estimates, and projections. Diabetes Care. 21: 1414-1431

**Figure 1:** *Example of a citation in the main text of a report and the corresponding references document.*

# 4. Practical Activity Groups

*This section tells you all the Practical Activity Groups you'll be expected to have carried out for A-Level Biology, as well as the techniques included in them. These will be covered in more detail as they crop up throughout the book.*

## PAGs

There are 12 Practical Activity Groups (PAGs) that you should have covered by the end of your A-Level course. These are shown in the table below, along with an example of the type of activity you could carry out for each one.

| | PAG | Example activity |
|---|---|---|
| 1 | Microscopy | Examining cells in a pondwater sample (see pages 53-54). |
| 2 | Dissection | Dissection of a kidney (see p. 340). |
| 3 | Sampling techniques | Investigating biodiversity in a habitat (see pages 249-251). |
| 4 | Rates of enzyme controlled reactions | Investigating effect of temperature on the rate of an enzyme-controlled reaction (see p. 112). |
| 5 | Colorimeter / Potometer | Determining the concentration of glucose in a solution (see page 80). / Estimating transpiration rate (see page 215). |
| 6 | Chromatography / Electrophoresis | Separating the pigments from leaves (see pages 407-408). |
| 7 | Microbiological techniques | Investigating the effect of temperature on the growth of a microorganism (see p. 528). |
| 8 | Transport in and out of cells | Investigating the effect of temperature on the rate of diffusion using model cells (see p.133). |
| 9 | Qualitative testing | The iodine test for starch (see page 77). |
| 10 | Investigation using a data logger / Computer modelling | Recording data from a spirometer using a data logger (see pages 175-176). |
| 11 | Investigation into the measurement of plant or animal responses | Investigating how exercise affects heart rate (see pages 359-360). |
| 12 | Research skills | Researching online for further information on a topic (see page 34). |

**Tip:** Research skills include being able to cite sources of information. There's more about citations on p. 35.

## Practical techniques

As part of each PAG you'll be expected to show that you can carry out certain techniques, such as:

- using appropriate apparatus and instrumentation (e.g. a potometer) to record quantitative measurements
- using lab glassware for different techniques, such as making serial dilutions
- using a light microscope and a graticule
- making scientific drawings of observations with labels
- identifying biological molecules using qualitative reagents

**Tip:** Quantitative measurements include measurements of mass, time, volume, temperature, length and pH.

Practical Skills for the Practical Endorsement

- separating biological compounds, using thin layer or paper chromatography or electrophoresis
- using organisms safely and ethically to measure plant or animal responses, or physiological functions
- using microbiological aseptic techniques, including using nutrient broth and agar plates
- using instruments safely in dissections
- using sampling techniques when carrying out fieldwork
- using ICT to collect data (e.g. via a data logger) or software to process data

All of these techniques should be covered across all of the PAGs.

**Tip:** Each individual PAG won't cover every single one of these techniques, but you should have covered all the techniques you need to know by the end of your course.

## Ethical issues

One of the practical techniques is knowing how to use any organisms involved in your experiments safely and ethically. This means that when you're planning an experiment involving animals or humans, you need to take any ethical issues into account.

Animals need to be treated humanely — they should be handled carefully and any wild animals captured for studying (e.g. during a biodiversity investigation) should be returned to their original habitat. Any animals (e.g. insects) being raised for dissection should be cared for in a humane way, e.g. they should not be kept in overcrowded conditions, and they should be killed humanely to minimise suffering.

If you are carrying out an experiment involving other students (e.g. investigating the effect of exercise on heart rate), the participants should not be forced to undergo testing against their will, or feel pressured to participate.

**Tip:** Animals kept in the lab should be kept in a safe environment (away from any chemicals or other hazards), have a clean enclosure, access to food and water, and they should not be subjected to extreme temperatures.

**Tip:** Many PAGs involve the use of organisms, e.g. PAG2, PAG3 and PAG11.

# Module 2 Section 1: Cell Structure

## 1. Cells and Organelles

**Learning Objectives:**
- Be able to understand the ultrastructure of eukaryotic cells and the functions of the different cellular components.
- Be able to describe the functions of the following cellular components:
  - plasma membrane
  - cell wall
  - nucleus
  - nuclear envelope
  - nucleolus
  - lysosomes
  - ribosomes
  - rough and smooth endoplasmic reticulum (ER)
  - Golgi apparatus
  - mitochondria
  - chloroplasts
  - centrioles
  - cilia
  - flagella.

**Specification Reference 2.1.1**

*No doubt you learnt about cell structure at GCSE, but there's a lot more to it at A-level — as you're about to find out...*

### Prokaryotes and eukaryotes

There are two main types of organism — eukaryotes and prokaryotes. Prokaryotic organisms are **prokaryotic cells** (i.e. they're single-celled organisms) and eukaryotic organisms are made up of **eukaryotic cells**. Both types of cells contain **organelles** (see below). Eukaryotic cells are complex and include all animal and plant cells. Prokaryotic cells are smaller and simpler, e.g. bacteria. There's more on prokaryotic cells on page 46.

### Organelles

Organelles are parts of cells. Each one has a specific function.
If you examine a cell through an electron microscope (see page 49) you can see its organelles and the internal structure of most of them — this is known as the **cell ultrastructure**. Everything you need to know about eukaryotic cell organelles is covered over the next few pages.

### Animal and plant cells

Animal and plant cells are both eukaryotic. Eukaryotic cells are generally a bit more complicated than prokaryotic cells and have more organelles. You've probably been looking at animal and plant cell diagrams for years, so hopefully you'll be familiar with some of the bits and pieces...

#### Animal cells

Figure 1 shows the organelles found in a typical animal cell. You can compare these to the ones found in a typical plant cell on the next page.

**Tip:** The term 'cells' was first coined by Robert Hooke in the 17th century. Understanding what goes on inside cells is a key concept in biology because all living organisms are made up of them. Improvements in light microscopy and the development of electron microscopes (see p. 49) have been key to the advancement of our knowledge of the structure and function of cells.

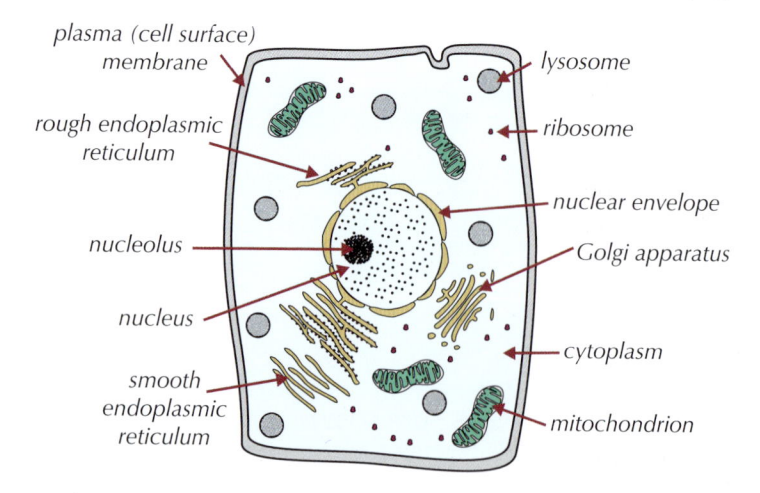

*Figure 1: The structure and ultrastructure of a typical animal cell.*

## Plant cells

Plant cells have all the same organelles as animal cells, but with a few added extras:

- a cell wall with plasmodesmata ('channels' for exchanging substances between adjacent cells),
- a vacuole (compartment that contains cell sap),
- and of course good old chloroplasts (the organelles involved in photosynthesis).

These organelles are all shown in Figure 2.

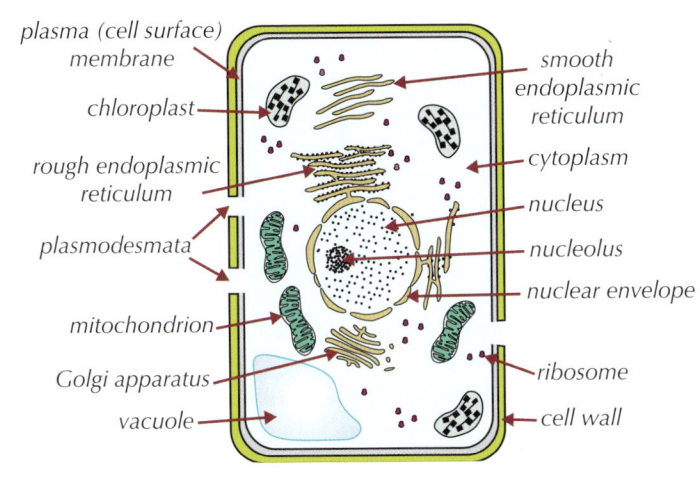

**Figure 2:** The structure and ultrastructure of a typical plant cell.

# Functions of organelles

This table contains a big list of organelles — you need to know the structure and function of them all. Sorry. Most organelles are surrounded by membranes, which sometimes causes confusion — don't make the mistake of thinking that a diagram of an organelle is a diagram of a whole cell. They're not cells — they're parts of cells.

---

### Plasma membrane (Also called the cell surface membrane)

**Description**
The membrane found on the surface of animal cells and just inside the cell wall of plant cells and prokaryotic cells.
It's made mainly of lipids and protein.

**Function**
Regulates the movement of substances into and out of the cell. It also has receptor molecules on it, which allow it to respond to chemicals like hormones.

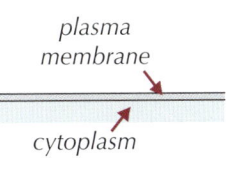

### Cell wall

**Description**
A rigid structure that surrounds plant cells. It's made mainly of the carbohydrate cellulose.

**Function**
Supports plant cells.

---

**Exam Tip**
As well as being able to interpret diagrams of cells like Figure 1 and Figure 2, you're also expected to be able to interpret photos of cells and their organelles, taken through different types of microscopes. (These are called micrographs or photomicrographs.)

**Tip:** There are lots of different types of plant and animal cells and they won't all look exactly like the ones shown here or contain exactly the same organelles (e.g. not all plant cells contain chloroplasts). Make sure you know all the distinguishing features for each cell type.

**Tip:** There's more on the structure and function of the plasma membrane on pages 124-126.

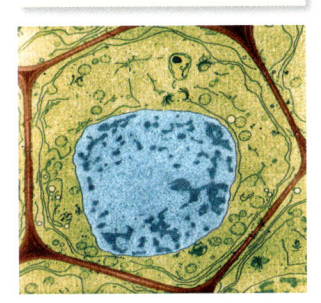

**Figure 3:** An electron micrograph of a plant cell. The cell walls appear red/brown.

**Tip:** In addition to plants, other organisms (e.g. fungi and bacteria) can have cell walls too but they aren't made of cellulose — see p. 46.

Module 2: Section 1 Cell Structure

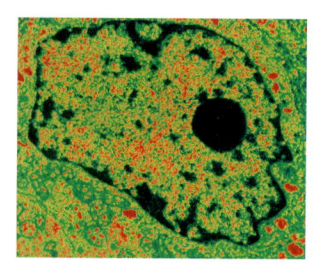

*Figure 4: An electron micrograph of a nucleus, showing the nucleolus, nuclear envelope and nuclear pores.*

**Tip:** There's more on DNA and RNA on pages 88-89.

**Tip:** Organelles in electron micrographs won't always look exactly the same as the ones shown here, e.g. they may vary in size and shape and they can be viewed from different angles, which can affect their appearance.

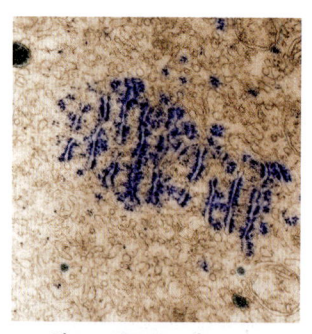

*Figure 5: An electron micrograph showing SER (red-brown) and RER (blue).*

## Nucleus
### Description
A large organelle surrounded by a nuclear envelope (double membrane), which contains many pores. The nucleus contains chromatin (which is made from DNA and proteins) and often a structure called the nucleolus.

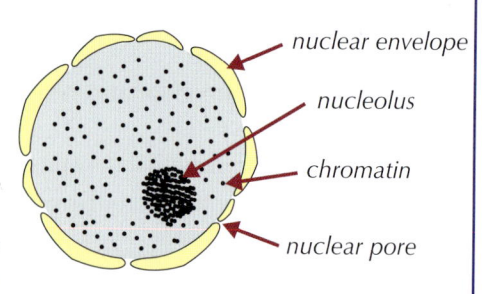

### Function
The nucleus controls the cell's activities (by controlling the transcription of DNA — see p. 99). DNA contains instructions to make proteins — see page 96. The pores allow substances (e.g. RNA) to move between the nucleus and the cytoplasm. The nucleolus makes ribosomes (see below).

*Labels: nuclear envelope, nucleolus, chromatin, nuclear pore*

## Lysosome
### Description
A round organelle surrounded by a membrane, with no clear internal structure.

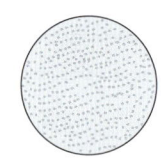

### Function
Contains digestive enzymes. These are kept separate from the cytoplasm by the surrounding membrane, and can be used to digest invading cells or to break down worn out components of the cell.

## Ribosome
### Description
A very small organelle that either floats free in the cytoplasm or is attached to the rough endoplasmic reticulum. It's made up of proteins and RNA (see page 89). It's not surrounded by a membrane.

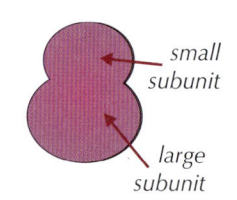

### Function
The site where proteins are made.

*Labels: small subunit, large subunit*

## Rough endoplasmic reticulum (RER)
### Description
A system of membranes enclosing a fluid-filled space. The surface is covered with ribosomes.

### Function
Folds and processes proteins that have been made at the ribosomes.

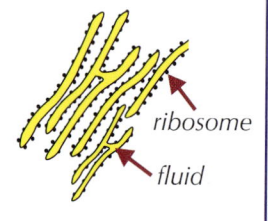

*Labels: ribosome, fluid*

## Smooth endoplasmic reticulum (SER)
### Description
Similar to rough endoplasmic reticulum, but with no ribosomes.

### Function
Synthesises and processes lipids.

Module 2: Section 1 Cell Structure

## Vesicle

**Description**
A small fluid-filled sac in the cytoplasm, surrounded by a membrane.

**Function**
Transports substances in and out of the cell (via the plasma membrane) and between organelles. Some are formed by the Golgi apparatus or the endoplasmic reticulum, while others are formed at the cell surface.

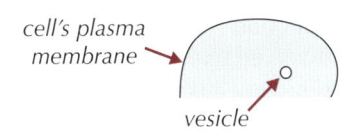

## Golgi apparatus

**Description**
A group of fluid-filled, membrane-bound, flattened sacs. Vesicles are often seen at the edges of the sacs.

**Function**
It processes and packages new lipids and proteins. It also makes lysosomes.

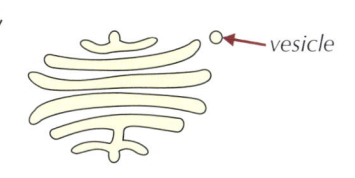

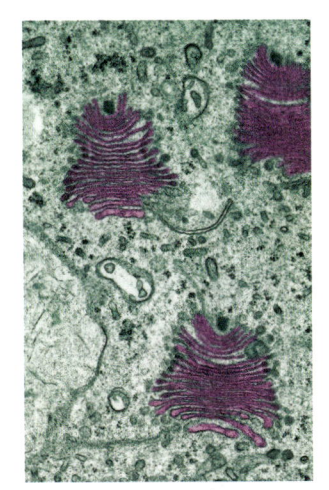

*Figure 6: An electron micrograph of Golgi apparatus.*

**Exam Tip**
Never say mitochondria produce energy in the exam — they produce ATP or release energy (energy can't be made).

## Mitochondrion

**Description**
It's usually oval-shaped. It has a double membrane — the inner one is folded to form structures called cristae. Inside is the matrix, which contains enzymes involved in respiration.

**Function**
The site of aerobic respiration, where ATP is produced. Mitochondria are found in large numbers in cells that are very active and require a lot of energy.

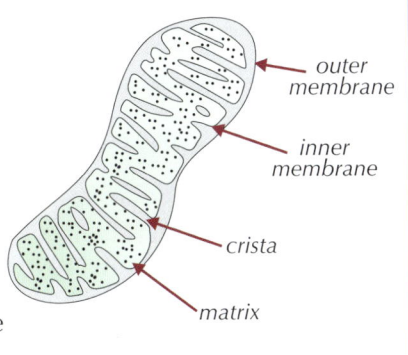

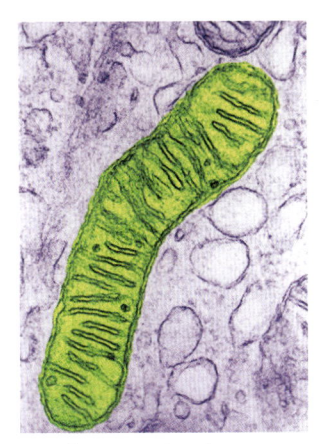

*Figure 7: An electron micrograph of a mitochondrion.*

## Chloroplast

**Description**
A small, flattened structure found in plant cells.
It's surrounded by a double membrane, and also has membranes inside called thylakoid membranes.
These membranes are stacked up in some parts of the chloroplast to form grana. Grana are linked together by lamellae — thin, flat pieces of thylakoid membrane.

**Function**
The site where photosynthesis takes place. Some parts of photosynthesis happen in the grana, and other parts happen in the stroma (a thick fluid found in chloroplasts).

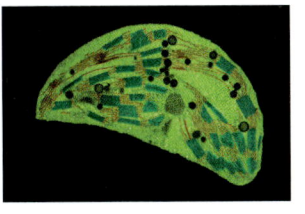

*Figure 8: An electron micrograph of a chloroplast.*

Module 2: Section 1 Cell Structure

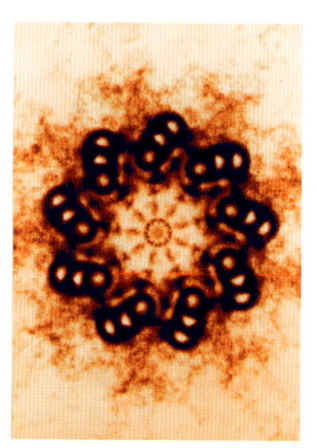

*Figure 9: An electron micrograph of centrioles in a tumour cell.*

**Tip:** Cilia in the trachea (windpipe) are used to sweep dust and dirt out of the lungs — see page 171.

**Tip:** The only example of a flagellum found in humans is the 'tail' of a sperm cell.

**Tip:** The formation of microtubules inside flagella and cilia is known as the '9 + 2' formation because there are nine pairs of microtubules surrounding two central microtubules.

**Tip:** 'Cilium' and 'flagellum' are singular. The plural versions are 'cilia' and 'flagella'.

**Tip:** You can find out more about electron micrographs on pages 49-50.

## Centriole
**Description**
Small, hollow cylinders, made of microtubules (tiny protein cylinders). Found in animal cells, but only some plant cells.

**Function**
Involved with the separation of chromosomes during cell division (see page 148).

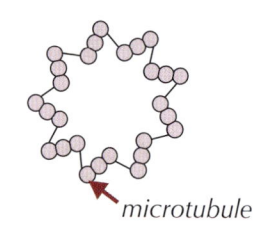

*microtubule*

## Cilia
**Description**
Small, hair-like structures found on the surface membrane of some animal cells. In cross-section, they have an outer membrane and a ring of nine pairs of protein microtubules inside, with a single pair of microtubules in the middle.

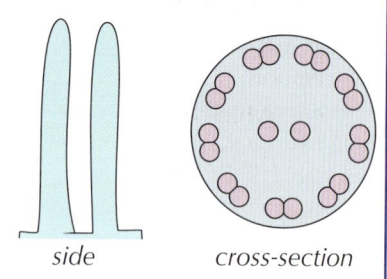

*side    cross-section*

**Function**
The microtubules allow the cilia to move. This movement is used by the cell to move substances along the cell surface.

## Flagellum
**Description**
Flagella on eukaryotic cells are like cilia but longer. They stick out from the cell surface and are surrounded by the plasma membrane. Inside they're like cilia too — two microtubules in the centre and nine pairs around the edge.

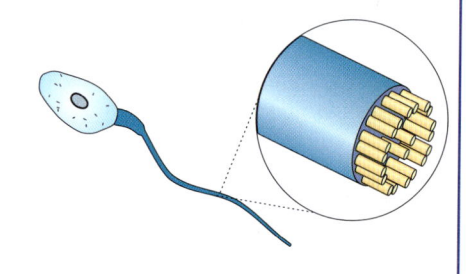

**Function**
The microtubules contract to make the flagellum move. Flagella are used like outboard motors to propel cells forward (e.g. when a sperm cell swims).

### Practice Questions — Application
Q1 Identify the organelle(s) labelled 'A' in the following electron micrographs. Give the function of each organelle.
a)    b)

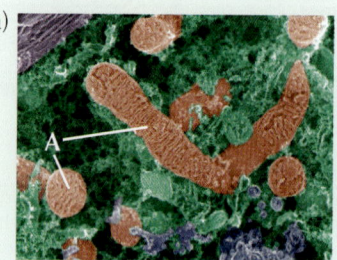

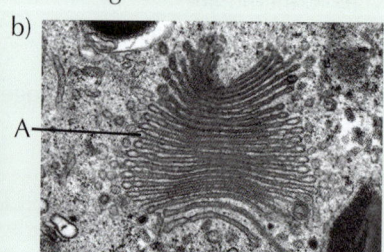

Module 2: Section 1  Cell Structure

**Exam Tip**
Electron micrographs in the exam are often in black and white (see p. 50), so don't be thrown seeing them like this.

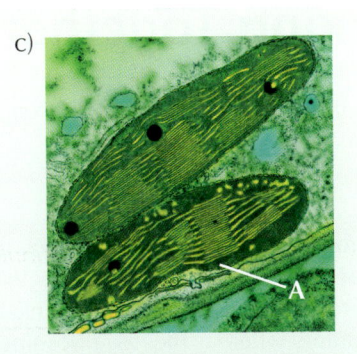

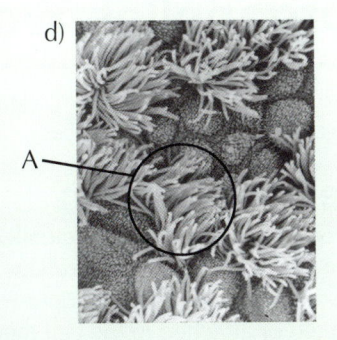

Q2 The images below each show a different type of cell.
  a) Name organelle X in Image A.
  b) Name organelle Y in Image B.
  c) Which of the images is a plant cell? Explain your answer.

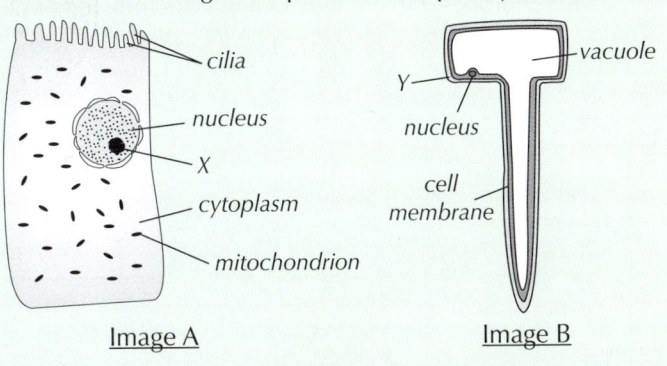

Image A

Image B

## Practice Questions — Fact Recall

Q1 Name the organelles labelled A-H on the plant cell below.
Q2 Name three organelles that can be found in plant cells, but not in animal cells. 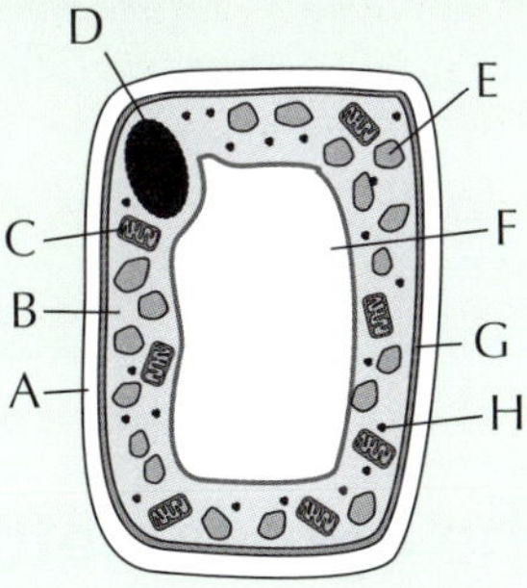
Q3 Describe the functions of the nucleus.
Q4 Give one function of a lysosome.
Q5 Describe how the structure of the rough endoplasmic reticulum is different from the smooth endoplasmic reticulum.
Q6 What is the function of the smooth endoplasmic reticulum?
Q7 Which organelle is responsible for making lysosomes?
Q8 Name the organelle responsible for the separation of chromosomes during cell division.
Q9 Draw a labelled cross-section of a cilium.

**Exam Tip**
Remember you could be asked about the structure and function of any of the organelles in the table on pages 39-42, so make sure you learn them all.

Module 2: Section 1 Cell Structure

**Learning Objectives:**
- Be able to describe the interrelationship between the organelles involved in the production and secretion of proteins.
- Be able to explain the importance of the cytoskeleton in providing mechanical strength to cells, aiding transport within cells and enabling cell movement, and how the dynamic nature of the cytoskeleton facilitates these actions.

**Specification Reference 2.1.1**

**Tip:** Protein production in prokaryotes is slightly different as they don't have the same organelles as eukaryotes.

**Tip:** Proteins may be stored at the rough endoplasmic reticulum until they are needed by the Golgi apparatus.

# 2. Organelles Working Together

*There are loads of organelles, each with an important role. But it's when they work together that they start to become really impressive.*

## Protein production

Figure 1 shows the variety of organelles involved in protein production. Each one has a different role. Proteins are made at the ribosomes — the ribosomes on the rough endoplasmic reticulum (RER) make proteins that are excreted or attached to the cell membrane, whereas the free ribosomes in the cytoplasm make proteins that stay in the cytoplasm.

New proteins produced at the RER are folded and processed (e.g. sugar chains are added) in the RER. Then they're transported from the RER to the Golgi apparatus in vesicles. At the Golgi apparatus, the proteins may undergo further processing (e.g. sugar chains are trimmed or more are added). The proteins enter more vesicles to be transported around the cell. E.g. glycoproteins (found in mucus) move to the cell surface and are secreted.

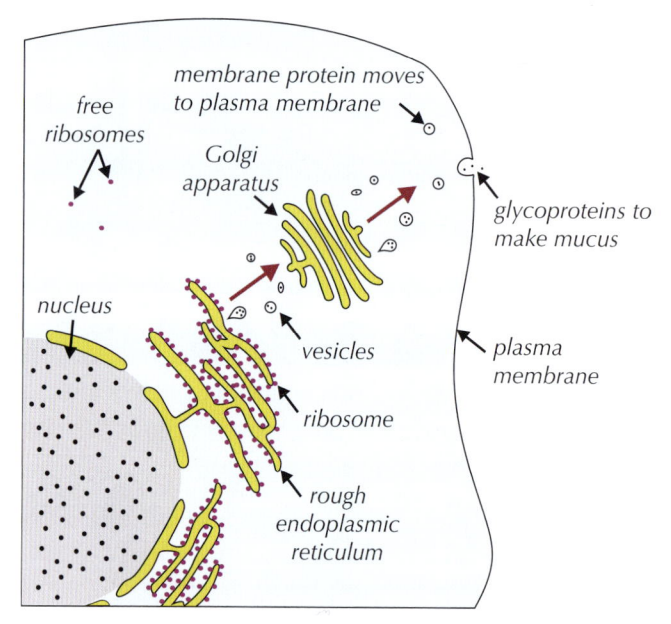

*Figure 1: Protein production in a eukaryotic cell.*

## The cytoskeleton

The organelles in cells are surrounded by the cytoplasm. The cytoplasm is more than just a solution of chemicals though — it's got a network of protein threads running through it. These protein threads are called the cytoskeleton. In eukaryotic cells the protein threads are arranged as **microfilaments** (very thin protein strands) and **microtubules** (tiny protein cylinders). These are shown in Figure 2 and Figure 4 (on the next page).

The cytoskeleton has four main functions:

1. The microtubules and microfilaments support the cell's organelles, keeping them in position.
2. They also help to strengthen the cell and maintain its shape.
3. As well as this, they're responsible for the transport of organelles and materials within the cell.

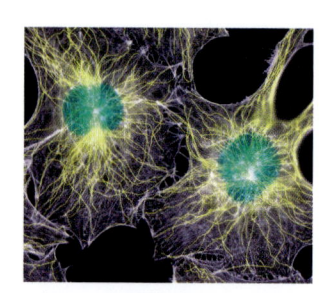

*Figure 2: A fluorescent light micrograph of two cells and their cytoskeleton. The microfilaments appear purple, microtubules are shown in yellow and the nuclei are green.*

44    Module 2: Section 1   Cell Structure

**Examples**
- The movement of chromosomes when they separate during cell division depends on contraction of microtubules in the spindle (see page 148 for more on cell division).
- The movement of vesicles around the cell relies on cytoskeletal proteins.

**Tip:** A cytoskeleton is found in prokaryotes as well as eukaryotes, but the prokaryotic cytoskeleton contains different proteins.

4. The proteins of the cytoskeleton can also cause the cell to move.

**Example**
The movement of cilia and flagella is caused by the cytoskeletal protein filaments that run through them. So in the case of single cells that have a flagellum (e.g. sperm cells), the cytoskeleton propels the whole cell.

*Figure 3:* Sperm cells are propelled by their cytoskeleton.

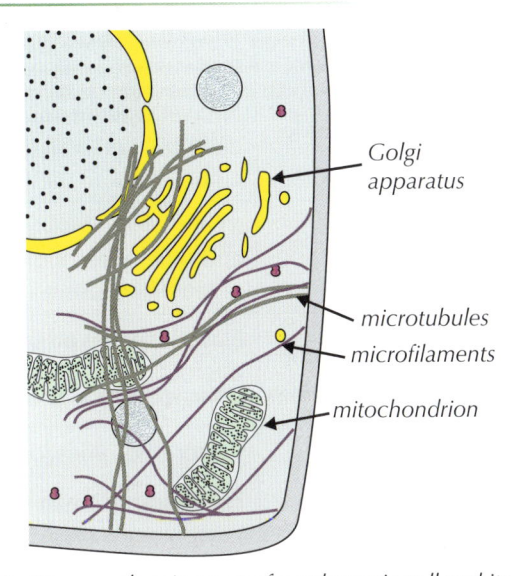

*Figure 4:* Diagram showing part of a eukaryotic cell and its cytoplasm.

**Tip:** The assembly of microtubules and microfilaments, and the movement of materials along them, requires energy from respiration. So microtubules and microfilaments can be prevented from functioning using respiratory inhibitors.

The cytoskeleton is dynamic (constantly changing), which allows it to respond to changes in the cell and carry out its functions.

### Practice Questions — Application
Recent research has shown abnormalities in the Golgi apparatus in some brain cells in Alzheimer's sufferers. The Golgi apparatus in some cells were visualised as small, round, disconnected elements.

Q1 How would the appearance of normal Golgi apparatus differ to the abnormal ones described above?

Q2 Suggest what effect these altered Golgi apparatus might have on protein production.

Q3 Structural abnormalities have also been seen in the cytoskeleton of brain cells in some Alzheimer's sufferers. Suggest how abnormalities in the cytoskeleton may affect protein production.

### Practice Questions — Fact Recall
Q1 Describe the role of the ribosomes and RER in protein production.
Q2 Describe the main functions of the cytoskeleton.

**Learning Objective:**
- Be able to describe the similarities and differences in the structure and ultrastructure of prokaryotic and eukaryotic cells.

**Specification Reference 2.1.1**

**Tip:** A micrometre (μm) is one millionth of a metre, or 0.001 mm.

**Tip:** When DNA is linear it has two distinct ends (imagine a long strand of DNA). Circular DNA on the other hand loops round and connects to itself to form a complete ring.

**Tip:** Prokaryotes are always single-celled organisms, but eukaryotes can be single-celled or multicellular.

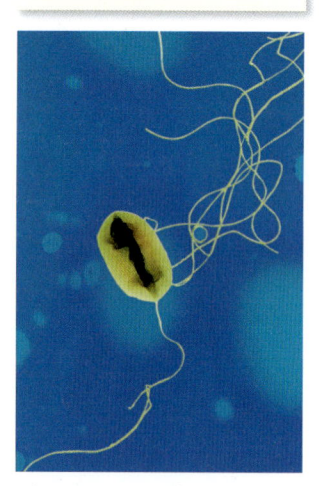

*Figure 1:* A prokaryotic cell. The long strands extending from the cell are flagella.

**Tip:** Flagella and plasmids aren't always present in prokaryotic cells.

# 3. Prokaryotic Cells

*Prokaryotic cells are different from eukaryotic cells.*

## Prokaryotes vs eukaryotes

The table below summaries the differences between prokaryotic and eukaryotic cells:

| Prokaryotic cells | Eukaryotic cells |
|---|---|
| Extremely small cells (less than 2 μm diameter) | Larger cells (about 10-100 μm diameter) |
| DNA is circular | DNA is linear |
| No nucleus — DNA free in cytoplasm | Nucleus present — DNA is inside nucleus |
| Cell wall made of a polysaccharide, but not cellulose or chitin | No cell wall (in animals), cellulose cell wall (in plants) or chitin cell wall (in fungi) |
| Few organelles and no membrane-bound organelles, e.g. no mitochondria | Many organelles — mitochondria and other membrane-bound organelles present |
| Flagella (when present) made of the protein flagellin, arranged in a helix | Flagella (when present) made of microtubules arranged in a '9 + 2' formation |
| Small ribosomes (20 nm or less) | Larger ribosomes (over 20 nm) |
| **Examples:** *E. coli* bacterium, *Salmonella* bacterium | **Examples:** Human liver cell, yeast, amoeba |

## Bacterial cells

Prokaryotes like bacteria are roughly a tenth the size of eukaryotic cells. This means that normal microscopes aren't really powerful enough to look at their internal structure. Figure 2 below shows a bacterial cell as seen under an electron microscope (see page 49).

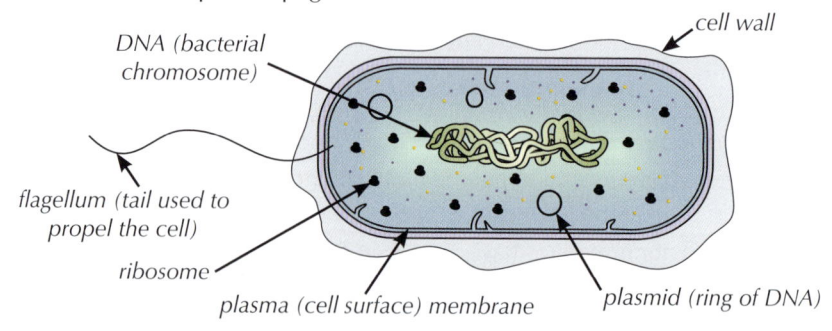

*Figure 2:* A bacterial cell — an example of a prokaryote.

Labels: DNA (bacterial chromosome); cell wall; flagellum (tail used to propel the cell); ribosome; plasma (cell surface) membrane; plasmid (ring of DNA)

### Practice Questions — Fact Recall
Q1 Give three differences between prokaryotes and eukaryotes.
Q2 Give one similarity between prokaryotic and eukaryotic cells.

# 4. How Microscopes Work

*Investigating cells involves donning a lab coat and digging out your microscope.*

## Magnification and resolution of microscopes

We all know that microscopes produce a magnified image of a sample, but resolution is just as important...

### Magnification

Magnification is how much bigger the image is than the specimen (the sample you're looking at). It's calculated using the formula shown on the right.

$$\text{magnification} = \frac{\text{image size}}{\text{object size}}$$

In the exam, you might be told the actual and magnified size of an object and then be asked to calculate the magnification. You can do this by using the formula above. You might also have to rearrange the formula to work out the image size or the object size.

--- **Examples** — Maths Skills ---

**Calculating magnification**

If you have a magnified image that's 5 mm wide and your specimen is 0.05 mm wide the magnification is:

$$\text{magnification} = \frac{\text{image size}}{\text{object size}} = \frac{5}{0.05} = \times\,100$$

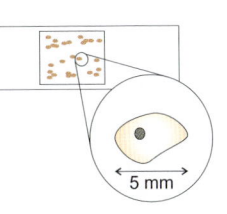

**Calculating image size**

If your specimen is 0.1 mm wide and the magnification of the microscope is × 20, then the image size is:

$$\text{image size} = \text{magnification} \times \text{object size} = 20 \times 0.1 = \textbf{2 mm}$$

**Calculating object size**

If you have a magnified image that's 5 mm wide and the magnification is × 50, then the object size is:

$$\text{object size} = \frac{\text{image size}}{\text{magnification}} = \frac{5}{50} = \textbf{0.1 mm}$$

When you're calculating magnification you need to make sure that all lengths are in the same unit, e.g. all in millimetres. When dealing with microscopes these units can get pretty tiny. The table below shows common units:

| Unit | How many millimetres it is: |
|---|---|
| Millimetre (mm) | 1 mm |
| Micrometre (μm) | 0.001 mm |
| Nanometre (nm) | 0.000001 mm |

To convert × 1000, × 1000 (smaller to bigger columns); To convert ÷ 1000, ÷ 1000.

The table shows that millimetres are three orders of magnitude ($10^3$ or 1000 times) bigger than micrometres, which are three orders of magnitude bigger than nanometres.

--- **Example** — Maths Skills ---

To convert from a smaller unit to a bigger unit you divide by 1000. So to convert 6 micrometres to millimetres you divide 6 by 1000 = 0.006 mm. To go from a bigger unit to a smaller unit you times by 1000.

---

**Learning Objectives:**

- Be able to use and manipulate the magnification formula.

$$\text{magnification} = \frac{\text{image size}}{\text{object size}}$$

- Understand the difference between magnification and resolution, including the differences in resolution and magnification that can be achieved by a light microscope and both transmission and scanning electron microscopes.
- Understand the use of microscopy to observe and investigate different types of cell and cell structure in a range of eukaryotic organisms.
- Appreciate the images produced by light microscopes, electron microscopes and laser scanning confocal microscopes.
- Be able to interpret photomicrographs of cellular components in a range of eukaryotic cells.

**Specification Reference 2.1.1**

**Exam Tip**

If you find rearranging formulas hard you can use a formula triangle to help:

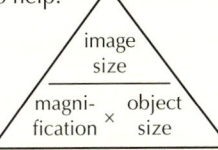

image size / (magnification × object size)

Just put your finger over the one you want and read off the formula. E.g. the formula to work out object size is image size ÷ magnification.

Module 2: Section 1 Cell Structure

**Tip:** A microscope can't distinguish between objects that are smaller than its maximum resolution.

**Tip:** The maximum resolution you can achieve through a light microscope is 0.2 µm (see next page). That means that any separate objects less than 0.2 µm apart from each other will be seen as one single object.

**Exam Tip**
Don't forget that when you're doing calculations the units need to be the same, e.g. all in millimetres (mm), or all in micrometres (µm).

**Exam Tip**
You're allowed a calculator in your exam — make sure you use one in calculation questions like these.

## Resolution

Resolution is how detailed the image is. More specifically, it's how well a microscope distinguishes between two points that are close together. If a microscope lens can't separate two objects, then increasing the magnification won't help.

### Example
When you look at a car in the dark that's a long way away you see the two headlights as one light. This is because your eyes can't distinguish between the two points at that distance — your eyes produce a low resolution image. When the car gets a bit closer you can see both headlights — a higher resolution image.

## Practice Questions — Application

Q1  Image A shows a cartilage cell under a × 3150 microscope.
   a) What is the diameter of the nucleus (labelled A) in millimetres?
   b) What is the diameter of the cell (labelled B) in millimetres?

Q2  A researcher is examining some ribosomes under a microscope. Ribosomes are around 0.00002 mm long. Calculate the size of the image when viewed through a × 40 microscope. Give your answer in millimetres.

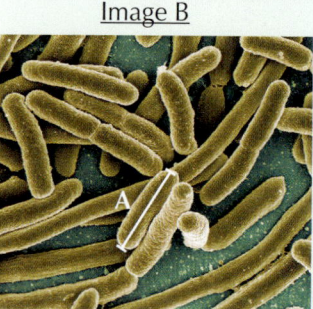

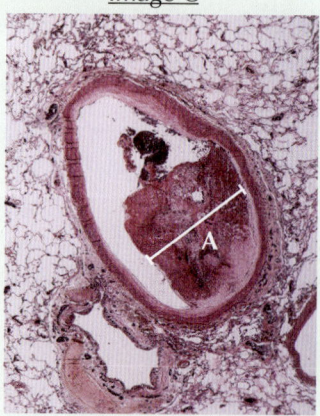

Q3  Rhinovirus particles are around 0.023 µm in diameter. They appear 0.035 mm under a microscope. What is the magnification of the microscope?

Q4  Image B shows some bacteria. It was taken using a × 7000 microscope. How long is the bacterium labelled A, in micrometres?

Q5  Image C shows a blood clot (labelled A) in an artery. The clot is 2 mm in diameter.
   a) What is the magnification of the microscope?
   b) The diameter of the artery is 3 mm. If the same specimen was examined under a × 50 microscope, what would the diameter of the artery in the image be?

Q6  A mitochondrion is 10 µm long. In a microscope image it is 10 mm. What is the magnification of the microscope?

Module 2: Section 1 Cell Structure

# Types of microscope

## Light microscopes
They use light (no surprises there). They have a lower resolution than electron microscopes. They have a maximum resolution of about 0.2 micrometres (μm). So they're usually used to look at whole cells or tissues. The maximum useful magnification of a light microscope is about × 1500.

## Laser scanning confocal microscopes
These are a special type of light microscope that use laser beams (intense beams of light) to scan a specimen that's usually tagged with fluorescent dyes.

A laser beam is focused through a lens which is aimed at a beam splitter. This splits the beam and some of the light is directed to the specimen. When the laser hits the dyes it causes them to give off fluorescent light. This light is then focused through a pinhole onto a detector. The detector is hooked up to a computer, which generates an image. The pinhole means that any out-of-focus light is blocked, so these microscopes produce a much clearer image than a normal light microscope.

These microscopes can be used to look at objects at different depths in thick specimens. Multiple images produced by the microscope can be combined by the computer to generate 3D images of a specimen.

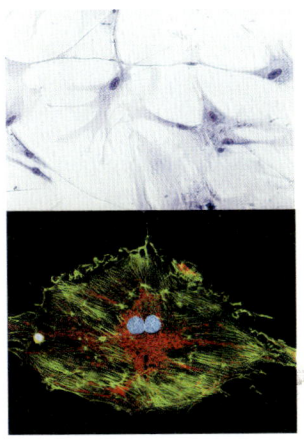

*Figure 1:* Lung cells seen under a light microscope (top) and a laser scanning confocal microscope (bottom).

*Figure 2:* The internal workings of a laser scanning confocal microscope. The image shows the laser beam (red) being focused onto the beam splitter.

## Electron microscopes
Electron microscopes use electrons instead of light to form an image. They have a higher resolution than light microscopes so give more detailed images.

# Types of electron microscope
There are two types of electron microscope:

## Transmission electron microscope (TEM)
TEMs use electromagnets to focus a beam of electrons, which is then transmitted through the specimen to produce 2D images. Denser parts of the specimen absorb more electrons, which makes them look darker on the image you end up with.

TEMs are good because they provide high resolution images, so they can be used to look at very small organelles, e.g. ribosomes. They can also be used to look at the internal structures of organelles in detail. But specimens viewed on TEMs need to be quite thinly sliced. The angle at which specimens are cut can affect how they appear (see Figure 3).

## Scanning electron microscope (SEM)
SEMs scan a beam of electrons across the specimen. This knocks off electrons from the specimen, which are gathered in a cathode ray tube to form an image. The images produced show the surface of the specimen and can be 3D but they give lower resolution images than TEMs.

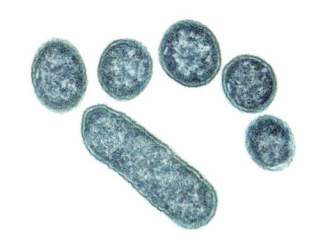

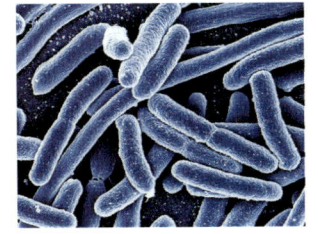

*Figure 3:* A TEM image (top), and SEM image (bottom) of E. coli bacteria. The E. coli in the TEM have been cut at different angles.

## Interpretation of electron micrographs

You need to be able to interpret the micrographs that are produced by both transmission and scanning electron microscopes. The micrographs produced from transmission and scanning electron microscopes are different — this is due to how they are produced (see previous page).

**Tip:** For more about the structure and function of mitochondria take a look back at page 41.

### Examples

A transmission electron micrograph shows a cross section through a sample. The micrograph in Figure 4 shows internal structures of a mitochondrion — it's like you've taken a slice through the mitochondrion.

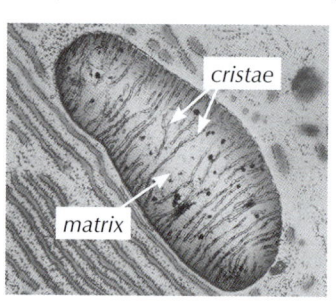

**Figure 4:** A transmission electron micrograph of a mitochondrion.

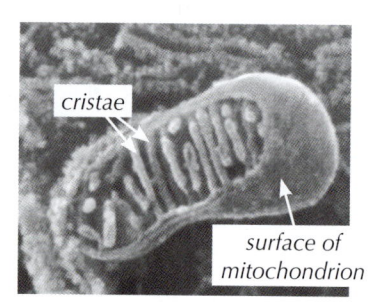

**Figure 5:** A scanning electron micrograph of a mitochondrion.

A scanning electron micrograph shows the surface of a sample. In Figure 5 the outer surface of a mitochondrion can be seen. This micrograph also shows the outer surfaces of the structures inside the mitochondrion (cristae) because in this particular sample the outer membrane of the organelle has been cut open exposing the internal structures.

**Tip:** Figures 4 and 5 show the difference in resolution between TEM and SEM micrographs. Figure 4 has been produced by a TEM and has a much higher resolution (it's much clearer and you can see more fine detail) than the SEM micrograph in Figure 5.

**Tip:** Have a look at the electron micrographs in this section. Try and work out if they've been produced using a TEM or a SEM.

### Producing electron micrographs

To prepare samples for use with electron microscopes they are treated with a solution of heavy metals (like lead) — this process is the equivalent of staining samples that are to be viewed with a light microscope (see page 52 for more about this). The metal ions act to scatter the electrons that are fired at the sample and give contrast between different structures.

The images produced by electron microscopy are always black and white, although colour can be added to images after they've been made to make them easier to interpret.

**Tip:** Adding colour to electron micrographs can make it easier to distinguish between different structures (e.g. you could make red blood cells appear red). There are examples of coloured micrographs on pages 39-43).

## Comparing types of microscope

You need to know about the magnification and resolution of light microscopes and both types of electron microscope. All the important numbers are shown in Figure 6.

|  | light microscope | TEM | SEM |
| --- | --- | --- | --- |
| maximum resolution | 0.2 µm | 0.0002 µm | 0.002 µm |
| maximum magnification | x 1500 | can be more than x 1 000 000 | usually less than x 500 000 |

**Figure 6:** Comparison table of light and electron microscope features.

**Tip:** TEMs have the highest resolution because they can distinguish between the smallest objects (or objects that are only 0.0002 µm apart).

Module 2: Section 1 Cell Structure

## Practice Questions — Application

Q1 Read the information in the table below.

| object | diameter / μm |
|---|---|
| *E. coli* bacterium | 2.0 |
| nuclear pore | 0.05 |
| human egg cell | 100 |
| DNA helix | 0.002 |
| mitochondrion | 0.7 |
| influenza virus | 0.1 |

For each object, state the type of microscope(s) it could be resolved by.

Q2 Two teams of scientists are studying the human immunodeficiency virus (HIV). HIV has a diameter of 0.12 μm. Team One are focusing on HIV surface proteins and how they bind to immune system cells. The second team is studying the internal structure of the virus. Suggest what specific type of microscope each team might use during their studies. Explain your answer.

Q3 A team of researchers are investigating the function of a particular set of proteins within a tissue. In a thick sample of tissue they have tagged the different types of protein with fluorescent dyes so that they can identify them.
Suggest the type of microscope that the team could use to gain an understanding of what is happening at different depths of the sample. Explain why your suggestion is suitable.

**Exam Tip**
If you understand the differences between the types of microscopes, you'll then be able to decide which microscope is the most useful in any given situation.

## Practice Questions — Fact Recall

Q1 State the formula for calculating the magnification of a microscope.
Q2 Explain the difference between magnification and resolution.
Q3 In laser scanning confocal microscopy what type of dyes are used?
Q4 How do transmission electron microscopes work?
Q5 How do scanning electron microscopes work?
Q6 Which type of electron microscope can produce an image of the 3D surface of a sample?
Q7 What is the maximum resolution for:
  a) a light microscope,
  b) a transmission electron microscope,
  c) a scanning electron microscope?
Q8 Which has a higher maximum magnification, a TEM or SEM?
Q9 What type of microscope would you use to study an object that is 0.001 μm long?

**Exam Tip**
Make sure you understand the difference between resolution and magnification — you could be asked to explain it in the exam.

## Learning Objectives:

- Be able to explain the use of staining in light microscopy, including the use of differential staining to identify different cellular components and cell types.
- Understand representations of cell structure as seen under the light microscope using drawings and annotated diagrams of whole cells or cells in sections of tissue.
- Be able to prepare and examine microscope slides for use in light microscopy, including the use of an eyepiece graticule and stage micrometer (PAG1).

**Specification Reference 2.1.1**

# 5. Using Microscopes

*Now you know how they work you need to grasp how to actually use them.*

## Microscopes — what you need to know

You need to know a few things about using microscopes. These are:

**PRACTICAL ACTIVITY GROUP 1**

- How to prepare a slide for use with a light microscope — this includes the use of stains.
- How to use a light microscope — this includes using an eyepiece graticule and stage micrometer to work out the size of specimens you're looking at.
- How to produce and interpret drawings and annotated diagrams of cells viewed under a light microscope.

## Staining samples

In light microscopes the beam of light passes through the object being viewed. An image is produced because some parts of the object absorb more light than others. Sometimes the object being viewed is completely transparent. This makes the whole thing look white because the light rays just pass straight through. To get round this, the object can be stained.

For the light microscope, this means using some kind of dye. These dyes are called stains. Common stains include methylene blue and eosin (see below). The stain is taken up by some parts of the object more than others, which means that some parts become more heavily stained than others. The contrast between heavily stained and more lightly stained parts means that the different parts of cells can be seen.

Different stains can be used to make particular parts of cells show up.

### Examples

Methylene blue can be used to stain DNA (see Figure 1) and Giemsa stain is commonly used to differentiate between different types of blood cells (Figure 2).

**Tip:** An important thing to remember here is that an image is produced after staining because it makes some parts of the specimen appear darker (or a different colour) to other parts.

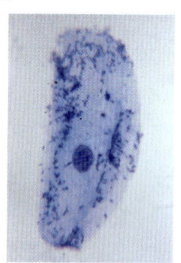

**Figure 1:** A cheek cell stained with methylene blue. The nucleus is visible as the roughly oval structure in the cell.

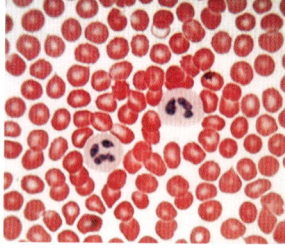

**Figure 2:** A human blood sample treated with Giemsa stain. Red blood cells are stained red and the nuclei present in the two white blood cells are stained purple.

It's possible to use more than one stain at once.

### Example

The stains haematoxylin and eosin are often used together (called H&E staining) to highlight different parts of cells (see Figure 3). Eosin dyes the cytoplasm pink. Haematoxylin stains the RNA and DNA present in cells a purple/blue colour — this highlights cell structures where these molecules are found (e.g. the nucleus and ribosomes).

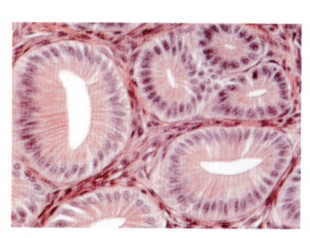

**Figure 3:** A light micrograph showing cells from the large intestine epithelium. Stained nuclei (purple) and cytoplasms (pink) are visible.

Module 2: Section 1 Cell Structure

## How to prepare a microscope slide

If you want to look at a specimen under a light microscope, you need to stick it on a slide first. A slide is a strip of clear glass or plastic. Slides are usually flat, but some of them have a small dip or well in the centre (useful if your specimen's particularly big or a liquid).

There are two main ways of preparing a microscope slide:

### Dry Mount

This is the simplest way of preparing a slide for examination under a microscope. This technique is particularly useful for observing specimens such as hairs, parts of insects, pollen, parts of flowers, etc.

Here's how to dry mount a specimen:

- Firstly, your specimen needs to let light through it for you to be able to see it clearly under the microscope. So if you've got quite a thick specimen, you'll need to take a thin slice to use on your slide.
- Use tweezers to pick up your specimen and put it in the middle of a clean slide.
- Pop a cover slip (a square of thin, transparent plastic or glass) on top. Your slide is now ready to use.

**Tip:** Take care when preparing slides — glass slides and cover slips can expose sharp edges if they break. Also, make sure you do a risk assessment before doing any practical work like this to identify any other hazards, e.g. some stains are harmful chemicals.

**Tip:** In a dry mount there's just a (relatively) dry specimen under the cover slip.

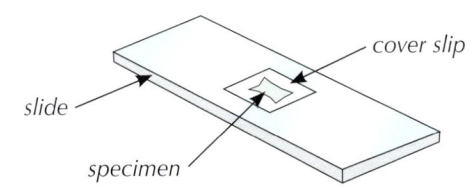

*Figure 4: A dry mount slide.*

### Wet Mount

Wet mounts involve your specimen being in a liquid (usually water). They are more difficult to carry out than dry mounting but can produce slides that give a really clear view of a specimen. This technique can be used with a variety of specimens including living samples (e.g. tiny aquatic organisms).

Here's how to wet mount a specimen:

- Start by pipetting a small drop of water onto the slide. Then use tweezers to place your specimen on top of the water drop.
- To put the cover slip on, stand the slip upright on the slide, next to the water droplet. Then carefully tilt and lower it so it covers the specimen. Try not to get any air bubbles under there — they'll obstruct your view of the specimen.
- Once the cover slip is in position, you can add a stain. Put a drop of stain next to one edge of the cover slip. Then put a bit of paper towel next to the opposite edge. The stain will get drawn under the slip, across the specimen.

**Tip:** Wet mounts are also used for liquid specimens (e.g. a sample of pond water). For these you won't need to add any water as your sample itself will provide the liquid. This is an example of when you might use a slide that has a well.

**Tip:** A smear slide is a special type of wet mount. These are often used for blood samples. It involves spreading the liquid thinly over the central area of the slide. A cover slip can then be applied and any excess liquid wiped off the slide.

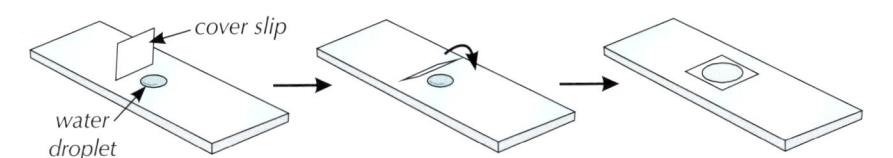

*Figure 5: A wet mount slide.*

Module 2: Section 1 Cell Structure

# How to use a light microscope

You're expected to be able to use a light microscope to view a specimen (e.g. a sample of plant tissue or a sample of human skin cells).

**Tip:** The appearance of light microscopes can vary (e.g. they might have two eyepieces rather than one) but they should have the same basic features shown in Figure 7.

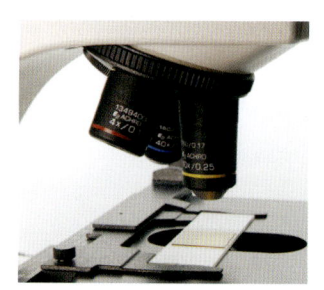

## How to use a light microscope to view a specimen

1. Start by clipping the slide containing the specimen onto the stage.
2. Select the lowest-powered objective lens (i.e. the one that produces the lowest magnification).
3. Use the coarse adjustment knob to bring the stage up to just below the objective lens.
4. Look down the eyepiece (which contains the ocular lens). Use the coarse adjustment knob to move the stage downwards, away from the objective lens, until the image is roughly in focus.
5. Adjust the focus with the fine adjustment knob, until you get a clear image of what's on the slide.
6. If you need to see the slide with greater magnification, swap to a higher-powered objective lens and refocus.

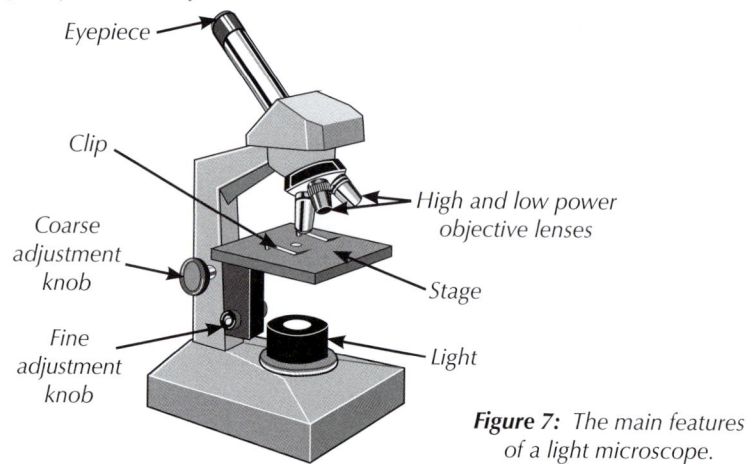

*Figure 6: Some microscopes have a slide holder rather than clips. This grips the sides of a slide and allows fine movement of the slide on the stage.*

*Figure 7: The main features of a light microscope.*

If you're asked to draw what you can see when using a microscope to look at a specimen, make sure the relative sizes of objects in your drawing are accurate and that you write down the magnification the specimen was viewed under. You'll also need to label your drawing and give it a title.

**Tip:** Your drawing should be done using a sharp pencil (not pen) and take up at least half the space available. Don't colour in or shade your drawing and make sure outlines are drawn neatly, not sketched. Also the pencil lines of your labels need to be straight, should not cross each other and should touch the part you are labelling.

## How to use an eyepiece graticule and stage micrometer

Sometimes, you might want to know the size of your specimen. And that's where the eyepiece graticule and stage micrometer come in — they're a bit like rulers.

- An **eyepiece graticule** is fitted onto the eyepiece. It's like a transparent ruler with numbers, but no units. So when you look through the eyepiece you'll see a scale (see Figure 8 on the next page).
- The **stage micrometer** is placed on the stage — it is a microscope slide with an accurate scale (it has units) and it's used to work out the value of the divisions on the eyepiece graticule at a particular magnification.

**Tip:** An eyepiece graticule (often simply referred to as a graticule) is just a transparent disc with a scale on it. They can be slotted inside the eyepiece (you take the eyepiece apart to put it inside) or some eyepieces have them already built-in.

This means that when you take the stage micrometer away and replace it with the slide containing your specimen, you'll be able to measure the size of the specimen. This works because you'll have worked out what lengths the divisions on your eyepiece graticule actually represent.

The example on the next page demonstrates how to use an eyepiece graticule and stage micrometer.

54    Module 2: Section 1   Cell Structure

### Example — Maths Skills

1. Line up the eyepiece graticule and the stage micrometer.
2. Each division on the stage micrometer is 0.1 mm long (see Figure 8).
3. At this magnification, 1 division on the stage micrometer is the same as 4.5 divisions on the eyepiece graticule.
4. To work out the size of 1 division on the eyepiece graticule, you need to divide 0.1 by 4.5:

    1 division on eyepiece graticule = 0.1 ÷ 4.5 = 0.02... mm

5. So if you look at an object under the microscope at this magnification and it's 20 eyepiece divisions long, you know it measures:

    20 × 0.02... = **0.4 mm** (1 s.f.)

    If you look at a different object under the microscope and it's 37 eyepiece divisions long, you know it measures:

    37 × 0.02... = **0.8 mm** (1 s.f.)

    But don't forget, if you change to a different magnification you'll need to re-do the calibration.

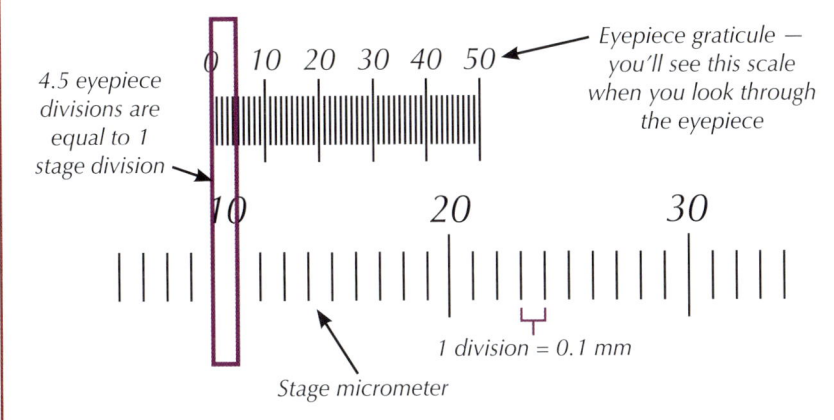

**Tip:** Remember: at a different magnification, 1 division on the stage micrometer will be equal to a different number of divisions on the eyepiece graticule — so the eyepiece graticule will need to be re-calibrated.

**Tip:** Each division on an eyepiece graticule can be called an eyepiece unit (epu).

*Figure 8: Calibrating an eyepiece graticule to a stage micrometer.*

### Practice Question — Application

**Q1** An eyepiece graticule and a stage micrometer are being calibrated. Each division on the stage micrometer is 2 μm long. At this magnification, 5 divisions on the stage micrometer is the same as 8 divisions on the eyepiece graticule.

   a) Calculate the size of one division on the eyepiece graticule.
   b) Calculate the width of the animal cell labelled X shown in the diagram below.

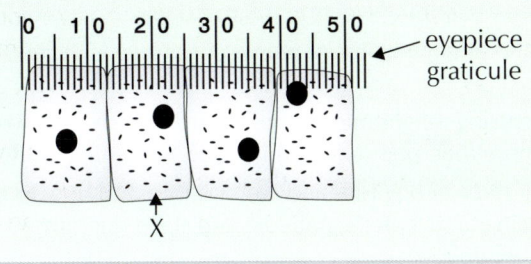

Module 2: Section 1 Cell Structure

### Practice Questions — Fact Recall

Q1  Explain why some samples need to be stained before they can be viewed under a light microscope.
Q2  Explain why a variety of different stains are used for staining samples.
Q3  Name two stains that can be used with samples in light microscopy.
Q4  Name two ways of preparing a microscope slide.
Q5  What is placed over a sample once it is placed onto a slide?
Q6  Name the part of a light microscope that you look through.
Q7  Describe what a stage micrometer is.

## Section Summary

Make sure you know:
- What prokaryotes and eukaryotes are.
- The ultrastructure of eukaryotic cells, such as animal and plant cells, and the cellular components that they contain, e.g. the different organelles that are present in different eukaryotic cells.
- The structure and function of the following cellular components: the plasma membrane, cell wall, nucleus, nuclear envelope, nucleolus, lysosomes, ribosomes, rough and smooth endoplasmic reticulum, vesicles, Golgi apparatus, mitochondria, chloroplasts, centrioles, cilia and flagella.
- That organelles work together to make proteins. Proteins are made at the ribosomes, then folded and processed in the rough endoplasmic reticulum. They are then transported to the Golgi apparatus in vesicles, processed further, and are transported around the cell before being secreted.
- That in eukaryotes the cytoplasm contains protein threads known as the cytoskeleton — arranged as microfilaments and microtubules. The cytoskeleton supports organelles, provides strength to the cell and maintains its shape, transports organelles and material within the cell and enables cell movement, and the cytoskeleton's dynamic nature is important in allowing these actions to happen.
- The similarities and differences between the ultrastructure of prokaryotes and eukaryotes.
- How to use the magnification formula: magnification = image size ÷ object size. You also need to know how to manipulate this formula, e.g. how to rearrange it to calculate object size or image size.
- The difference between magnification (how much bigger the image is than the sample) and resolution (how detailed the image is).
- How microscopy allows the study of cells and cell structure.
- That a laser scanning confocal microscope uses laser beams to scan a specimen which is tagged with fluorescent dyes. The images produced result from fluorescent light emitted by specimens.
- That a transmission electron microscope (TEM) transmits a beam of electrons through a specimen and produces micrographs that show 2D images of the specimen.
- That a scanning electron microscope (SEM) scans a beam of electrons across a specimen and produces micrographs that show 3D images of the surface of the specimen.
- How to interpret photomicrographs of cellular components, including photos from TEMs and SEMs.
- The different magnification and resolution that can be achieved from a light microscope, a transmission electron microscope and a scanning electron microscope.
- How to understand drawings and annotated diagrams of whole cells or cells in sections of tissue as seen under the light microscope.
- That staining is often required before using a light microscope in order to see the different cellular structures and organelles, and that more than one stain can be used to highlight different parts.
- How to prepare slides for use in light microscopy (dry and wet mounts) and how to examine specimens and work out their size using an eyepiece graticule and stage micrometer.

# Exam-style Questions

**1** Abnormal mitochondria have been found in diseased heart tissue, suggesting a link between mitochondria and heart disease. To investigate this further, a group of scientists produced a strain of mice with abnormal mitochondria.

ABnormal mice developed symptoms of heart disease after just one year. Normal mice showed similar symptoms after two years.

**(a) (i)** Describe the main function of mitochondria.

*(1 mark)*

**(ii)** Suggest why abnormal mitochondria might be problematic in heart tissue.

*(2 marks)*

**(b)** **Fig. 1.1** shows mitochondria in the normal mice and the abnormal mice.

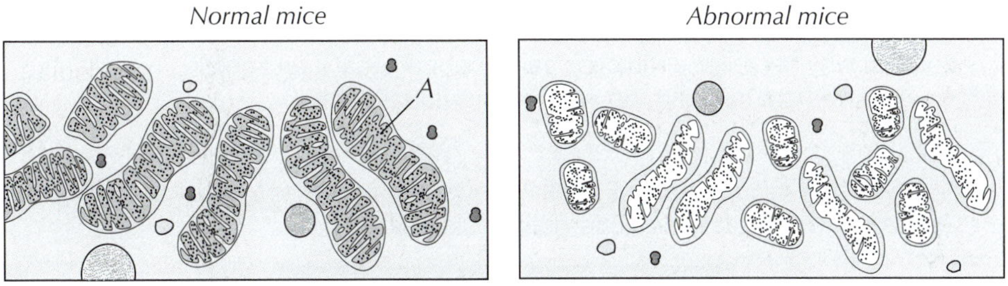

*Normal mice*            *Abnormal mice*

**Fig. 1.1**

**(i)** Describe **two** differences between the mitochondria found in the abnormal and normal mice.

*(2 marks)*

**(ii)** The mitochondrion labelled **A** in the normal mouse is about 1.5 µm in length. Calculate the magnification of the image.

*(2 marks)*

**2** A scientist is studying secretory epithelial cells from the stomach under a light microscope.

The microscope has a magnification of × 100 and a resolution of 0.2 µm.

**(a) (i)** The ribosomes in the epithelial cells are 25 nm in diameter. Will the scientist be able to see them using the light microscope? Explain your answer.

*(2 marks)*

**(ii)** Explain the difference that you would expect to see if the ribosomes in the stomach cells were compared to those in bacterial cells.

*(2 marks)*

**(iii)** State **two** differences the scientist would observe if he compared the stomach cell to a plant cell.

*(2 marks)*

Module 2: Section 1 Cell Structure

(iv) Before looking at the epithelial cells under the microscope the scientist applies two stains to the specimen.

Suggest why the scientist has done this.

*(1 mark)*

(b) The scientist sees an image of an epithelial cell that is 4 mm in diameter. Calculate the actual diameter of the cell. Give your answer in millimetres.

*(2 marks)*

(c)* One of the main functions of secretory epithelial cells in the stomach is to produce and secrete digestive enzymes.

Describe the role of each organelle involved in the production and secretion of these proteins.

*(6 marks)*

**3** Penicillins are a group of antibiotics that are only effective against prokaryotic cells. They work by inhibiting cell wall synthesis, leading to cell lysis (bursting).

(a) Explain why penicillin antibiotics can clear bacterial infections in humans without harming the infected individual's cells.

*(2 marks)*

(b) The electron micrograph in **Fig. 3.1** shows an intact *Staphylococcus aureus* bacterium (right) and one undergoing lysis (left).

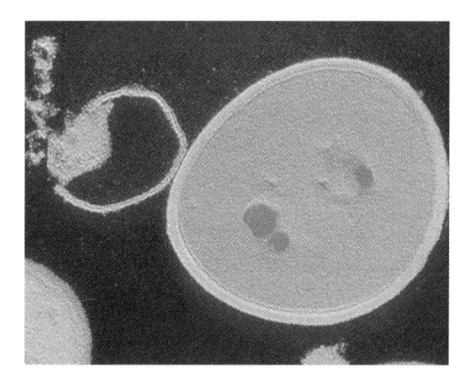

**Fig. 3.1**

(i) Suggest **one** reason why an electron microscope was used to view these cells rather than a light microscope.

*(2 marks)*

(ii) Name the type of electron microscope that was used to produce the micrograph seen in **Fig 3.1**. Give a reason for your answer.

*(2 marks)*

(c) Give **two** ways in which you could distinguish between a prokaryotic cell and a eukaryotic cell in an electron micrograph.

*(2 marks)*

\* The quality of your response will be assessed in this question.

# Module 2  Section 2: Biological Molecules

# 1. Water

*Water is essential for life. The next few pages will show you what it is about water that makes it so important.*

## Functions of water

Water is vital to living organisms. It makes up about 80% of a cell's contents and has loads of important functions, inside and outside cells, such as:

- Water is a reactant in loads of important chemical reactions, including hydrolysis reactions (see page 62).
- Water is a solvent, which means some substances dissolve in it. Most biological reactions take place in solution (e.g. in the cytoplasm of eukaryotic and prokaryotic cells) so water's pretty essential.
- Water transports substances. The fact that it's a liquid and a solvent means it can easily transport all sorts of materials, like glucose and oxygen, around plants and animals.
- Water helps with temperature control because it has a high specific heat capacity and a high latent heat of evaporation (see next page).
- Water is a habitat. The fact that it helps with temperature control, is a solvent and becomes less dense when it freezes (see next page) means many organisms can survive and reproduce in it.

### Learning Objectives:
- Be able to describe how hydrogen bonding occurs between water molecules.
- Be able to relate the properties of water to the roles of water for living organisms, including as a solvent, transport medium, coolant and a habitat.
- Be able to illustrate these roles using examples of prokaryotes and eukaryotes.

**Specification Reference 2.1.2**

## Structure of water

To understand the structure of water, you need to know a bit about the chemistry involved in holding water molecules together.

### Polarity of water

A molecule of water ($H_2O$) is one atom of oxygen (O) joined to two atoms of hydrogen ($H_2$) by shared electrons — see Figure 1.

Because the shared negative hydrogen electrons are pulled towards the oxygen atom, the other side of each hydrogen atom is left with a slight positive charge. The unshared negative electrons on the oxygen atom give it a slight negative charge. This makes water a polar molecule — it has a partial negative charge ($\delta-$) on one side and a partial positive charge ($\delta+$) on the other (see Figure 2).

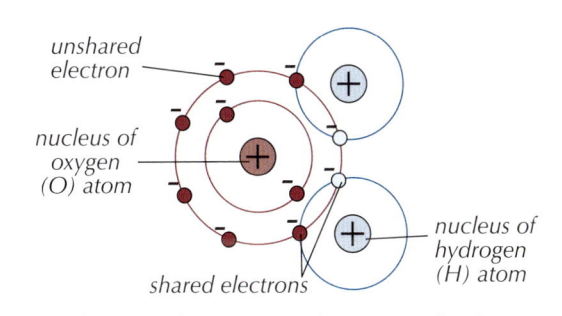

**Figure 1:** *The structure of a water molecule.*

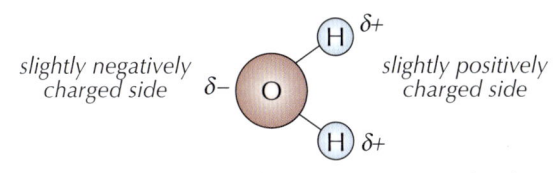

**Figure 2:** *The slight charges on a water molecule.*

**Exam Tip**
Examiners like asking you to relate structure to properties and function, so make sure you're clear on the structure of water.

**Tip:** '$\delta$' is the Latin letter 'delta'. So you read $\delta+$ as 'delta positive' and $\delta-$ as 'delta negative'.

**Exam Tip**
Be careful not to write that a water molecule has a positive and a negative side — you must make it clear that one side has a partial positive charge and the other side has a partial negative charge.

Module 2: Section 2  Biological Molecules

### Hydrogen bonding

The slightly negatively-charged oxygen atoms attract the slightly positively-charged hydrogen atoms of other water molecules. This attraction is called **hydrogen bonding** and it gives water some of its useful properties.

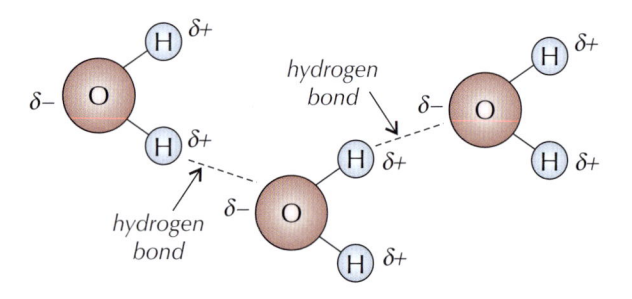

**Figure 3:** *Diagram showing how hydrogen bonds hold water molecules together.*

> **Exam Tip**
> If you're asked to draw water molecules in the exam, make sure you draw the hydrogen bonds as dashed lines and include the partial charges (δ+ or δ−) on all the atoms.

## Properties of water

The structure of a water molecule gives it some useful properties, and these help to explain many of its functions:

### High specific heat capacity

Hydrogen bonds give water a high **specific heat capacity** — this is the energy needed to raise the temperature of 1 gram of a substance by 1 °C. The hydrogen bonds between water molecules can absorb a lot of energy. So water has a high specific heat capacity — it takes a lot of energy to heat it up. This means water doesn't experience rapid temperature changes, which is one of the properties that makes it a good habitat — the temperature under water is likely to be more stable than it is on land.

### High latent heat of evaporation

It takes a lot of energy (heat) to break the hydrogen bonds between water molecules. So water has a high latent heat of evaporation — a lot of energy is used up when water evaporates (changes from a liquid to a gas). This is useful for living organisms because it means water's great for cooling things. This is why some mammals, like us, sweat when they're too hot. When sweat evaporates, it cools the surface of the skin.

### Very cohesive

Cohesion is the attraction between molecules of the same type (e.g. two water molecules). Water molecules are very cohesive (they tend to stick together) because they're polar. This helps water to flow, making it great for transporting substances. It also helps water to be transported up plant stems in the transpiration stream (see page 213).

> **Tip:** Latent heat is the heat energy that's needed to change a substance from one state to another, e.g. from a liquid to a gas.

### Lower density when solid

At low temperatures water freezes — it turns from a liquid to a solid. Water molecules are held further apart in ice than they are in liquid water because each water molecule forms four hydrogen bonds to other water molecules, making a lattice shape. This makes ice less dense than liquid water — which is why ice floats. This is useful for living organisms because, in cold temperatures, ice forms an insulating layer on top of water — the water below doesn't freeze. So organisms that live in water, like fish, don't freeze and can still move around.

## Good solvent

A lot of important substances in biological reactions are ionic (like salt, for example). This means they're made from one positively-charged atom or molecule and one negatively-charged atom or molecule (e.g. salt is made from a positive sodium ion and a negative chloride ion). Because water is polar, the slightly positive end of a water molecule will be attracted to the negative ion, and the slightly negative end of a water molecule will be attracted to the positive ion. This means the ions will get totally surrounded by water molecules — in other words, they'll dissolve (see Figure 4).

**Tip:** Most biological reactions take place in solution, so water's pretty essential.

**Tip:** Remember — a molecule is polar if it has a slightly negatively-charged side and a slightly positively-charged side.

**Tip:** Polar molecules, such as glucose, dissolve in water because hydrogen bonds form between them and the water molecules.

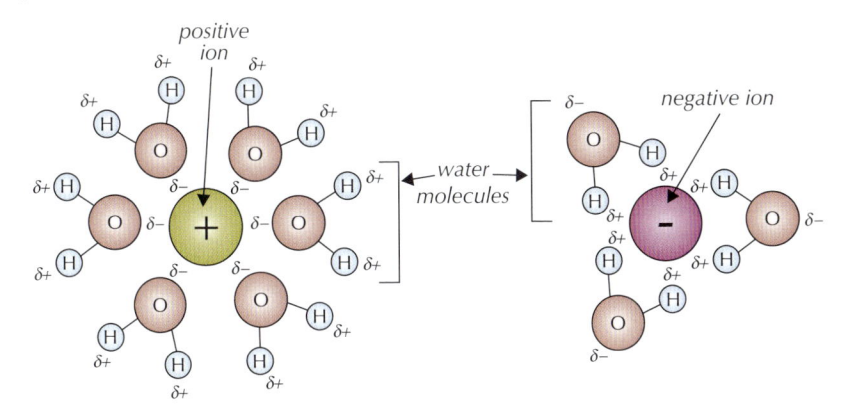

*Figure 4: A positive ion (left) and a negative ion (right) dissolved in water.*

Water's polarity makes it useful as a solvent in living organisms. E.g. in humans, important ions (see pages 74-75) can dissolve in the water in blood and then be transported around the body.

### Practice Questions — Fact Recall

Q1  Give three functions of water that are important to living organisms.
Q2  Why is water classed as a polar molecule?
Q3  Label this diagram of a water molecule showing the name and charge on each atom.
Q4  What is a hydrogen bond?
Q5  Draw a diagram showing four water molecules hydrogen bonded together.
Q6  Explain why water has a high specific heat capacity.
Q7  Explain why water is good for cooling things.
Q8  Give two reasons why the polarity of water makes it good for transporting substances.
Q9  The diagrams on the right show molecular models of liquid water and ice.
   a) Which diagram, A or B, is a molecular model of ice? Give a reason for your answer.
   b) Explain how the formation of ice can be beneficial for organisms.
Q10 Describe how an $Mg^{2+}$ ion dissolves in water.

**Exam Tip**
If you're asked in the exam about how a particular ion dissolves in water, don't get put off by the ion itself — just figure out if it's positively charged or negatively charged. E.g. in Q10 here $Mg^{2+}$ is a positively charged magnesium ion.

Module 2: Section 2 Biological Molecules

**Learning Objectives:**
- Understand the concept of monomers and polymers.
- Understand the importance of condensation and hydrolysis reactions in a range of biological molecules.

**Specification Reference 2.1.2**

**Tip:** Nucleic acids are also polymers. Their monomers are called nucleotides. There's more about nucleic acids on pages 91-92.

**Tip:** Lipids aren't classed as polymers because they do not consist of repeating units (monomers).

**Exam Tip**
If you're asked to show a condensation reaction, don't forget to put the water molecule in as a product.

**Tip:** A condensation reaction <u>removes</u> one molecule of water, but a hydrolysis reaction <u>adds</u> one molecule of water.

**Tip:** It's easy to remember what a hydrolysis reaction does as 'hydro' means water and 'lysis' means breaking down.

# 2. Macromolecules and Polymers

*The cells of all living organisms are made up of loads of different types of biological molecules. Some of these are macromolecules and some are polymers as well...*

## What are macromolecules?
**Macromolecules** are complex molecules with a relatively large molecular mass. Examples of biological macromolecules include proteins, some carbohydrates and lipids. Polymers are a group of macromolecules.

## What are polymers?
Most carbohydrates and all proteins are **polymers**. Polymers are large, complex molecules composed of long chains of **monomers** joined together.
Monomers are small, basic molecular units. Examples of monomers include monosaccharides (see next page) and amino acids (see p. 69).

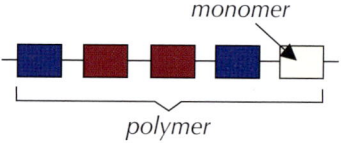

**Figure 1:** A polymer.

## Making polymers
Most biological polymers are formed from their monomers by **condensation** reactions. A condensation reaction forms a chemical bond between monomers, releasing a molecule of water — see Figure 2.

**Figure 2:** Example of the formation of a polymer.

## Breaking down polymers
Biological polymers can be broken down into monomers by **hydrolysis** reactions. A hydrolysis reaction breaks the chemical bond between monomers using a water molecule. It's basically the opposite of a condensation reaction.

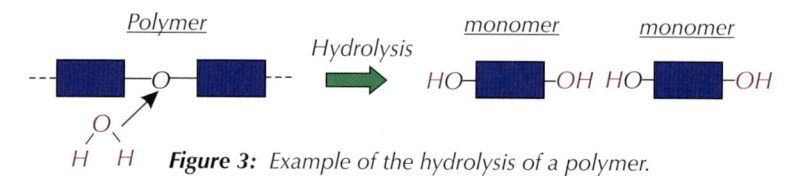

**Figure 3:** Example of the hydrolysis of a polymer.

### Practice Questions — Fact Recall
Q1 What is a polymer?
Q2 What is a monomer?
Q3 Give two examples of monomers.
Q4 Explain what happens in a condensation reaction between two monomers.
Q5 What type of reaction involves the breakage of a chemical bond between two monomers using water?

Module 2: Section 2  Biological Molecules

# 3. Carbohydrates

*Carbohydrates are needed by living organisms for things like energy storage and support — their function is related to their structure.*

## What are carbohydrates made from?

Most carbohydrates are polymers. All carbohydrates are made up of the same three chemical elements — carbon (C), hydrogen (H) and oxygen (O). For every carbon atom in the carbohydrate there are usually two hydrogen atoms and one oxygen atom.

The monomers that make up carbohydrates are called **monosaccharides**. You need to know the structures of two different monosaccharides — glucose and ribose.

### Glucose

Glucose is a monosaccharide with six carbon atoms. This means it's a hexose monosaccharide. There are two forms of glucose — alpha (α) and beta (β). They both have a ring structure — see Figure 1.

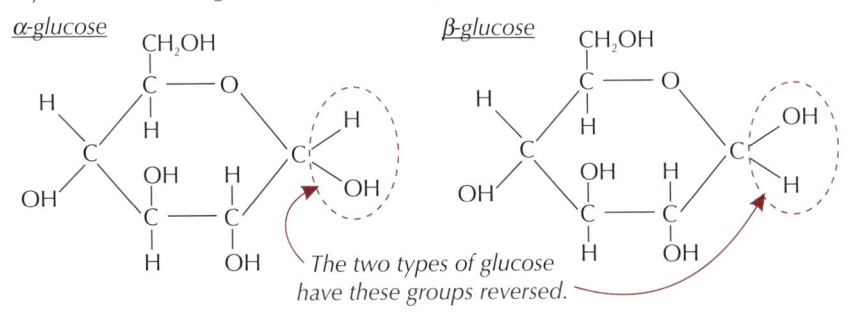

*Figure 1: The structures of α-glucose and β-glucose.*

Glucose's structure is related to its function as the main energy source in animals and plants. Its structure makes it soluble, so it can be easily transported. Its chemical bonds contain lots of energy.

### Ribose

Ribose is a monosaccharide with five carbon atoms — this means it's a pentose monosaccharide. You need to know its structure (see Figure 2).

*Figure 2: The structure of ribose.*

Ribose is the sugar component of RNA nucleotides (see p. 89).

## Polysaccharide formation

Monosaccharides are joined together by **glycosidic bonds**. During synthesis, a hydrogen atom on one monosaccharide bonds to a hydroxyl (OH) group on the other, releasing a molecule of water — this is a **condensation** reaction (see previous page). The reverse of this synthesis reaction is **hydrolysis** — a molecule of water reacts with the glycosidic bond, breaking it apart.

---

**Learning Objectives:**
- Know the chemical elements that make up carbohydrates (C, H and O).
- Understand the difference between a hexose and a pentose monosaccharide.
- Recall the ring structure and properties of glucose (a hexose monosaccharide) and the structure of ribose (a pentose monosaccharide).
- Understand the structural difference between α-glucose and β-glucose.
- Recall the synthesis and breakdown of disaccharides (including sucrose, lactose and maltose) and polysaccharides by the formation and breakage of glycosidic bonds.
- Recall the structure of starch (amylose and amylopectin), glycogen and cellulose molecules.
- Know how the structures and properties of glucose, starch, glycogen and cellulose molecules relate to their functions in living organisms.

**Specification Reference 2.1.2**

**Tip:** Although most carbohydrates are polymers, single monosaccharides are also called carbohydrates.

Module 2: Section 2 Biological Molecules

**Tip:** Structures aren't always drawn with everything on them, e.g. when you get a line with nothing on the end, like this ↘ it just means there's a carbon there, with other elements (like hydrogen) attached to it.

A **disaccharide** is formed when two monosaccharides join together:

--- Example ---
Two α-glucose molecules are joined together by a glycosidic bond to form maltose.

H₂O is removed → glycosidic bond

synthesis ⇌ hydrolysis    + H₂O

Other disaccharides are formed in a similar way. Sucrose is a disaccharide formed when α-glucose and fructose join together. Lactose is a disaccharide formed by the joining together of galactose with either α-glucose or β-glucose.

A **polysaccharide** is formed when more than two monosaccharides join together:

--- Example ---
Lots of α-glucose molecules are joined together by glycosidic bonds to form amylose.

glycosidic bonds

## Functions of carbohydrates

You need to know about the relationship between the structure and function of three polysaccharides — starch, glycogen and cellulose.

### Starch

**Tip:** You can test for the presence of starch using the iodine test (see page 77).

Starch is the main energy storage material in plants. Cells get energy from glucose and plants store excess glucose as starch (when a plant needs more glucose for energy it breaks down starch to release the glucose). Starch is insoluble in water so it doesn't cause water to enter cells by osmosis (see p. 134), which would make them swell. This makes it good for storage. Starch is a mixture of two polysaccharides of alpha-glucose — amylose and amylopectin:

**Tip:** Hydrogen bonds between α-glucose molecules help to hold amylose in its helical structure.

- **Amylose** is a long, unbranched chain of α-glucose. The angles of the glycosidic bonds give it a coiled structure, almost like a cylinder. This makes it compact, so it's really good for storage because you can fit more in to a small space.

**Exam Tip**
Always specify whether you're talking about α-glucose or β-glucose — you won't get a mark for only saying glucose.

- **Amylopectin** is a long, branched chain of α-glucose. Its side branches allow the enzymes that break down the molecule to get at the glycosidic bonds easily. This means that the glucose can be released quickly.

one α-glucose molecule

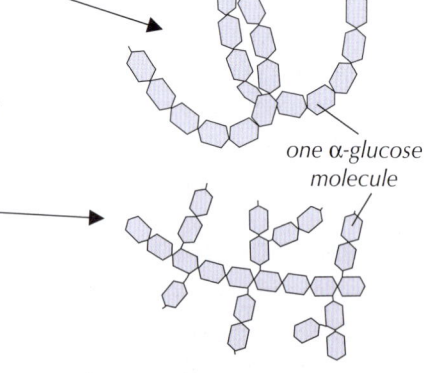

**Figure 3:** The structures of amylose (top) and amylopectin (bottom).

## Glycogen

Glycogen is the main energy storage material in animals. Animal cells get energy from glucose too, but animals store excess glucose as glycogen — another polysaccharide of alpha-glucose. Its structure is very similar to amylopectin, except that it has loads more side branches coming off it — see Figure 4. Loads of branches means that stored glucose can be released quickly, which is important for energy release in animals. It's also a very compact molecule, so it's good for storage.

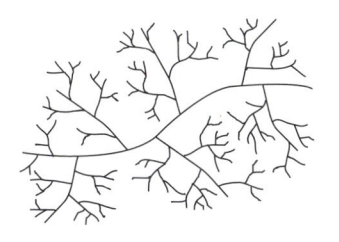

*Figure 4:* The structure of glycogen.

**Exam Tip**
If you're asked about the function of glycogen in the exam, make sure you say it acts as an energy store or reserve — you won't get marks just for saying it 'contains energy'.

## Cellulose

Cellulose is the major component of cell walls in plants. It's made of long, unbranched chains of beta-glucose. When beta-glucose molecules bond, they form straight cellulose chains. The cellulose chains are linked together by **hydrogen bonds** to form strong fibres called **microfibrils** — see Figure 5. The strong fibres mean cellulose provides structural support for cells (e.g. in plant cell walls).

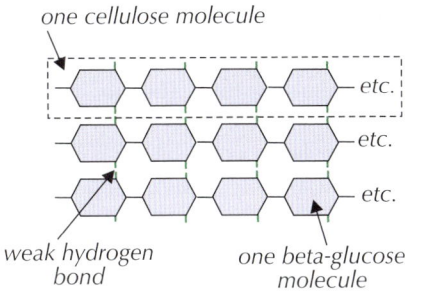

*Figure 5:* The structure of a cellulose microfibril.

*Figure 6:* Coloured scanning electron micrograph (SEM) of cellulose microfibrils in a plant cell wall.

**Tip:** A hydrogen bond is a relatively weak bond formed between hydrogen atoms and other atoms, e.g. nitrogen or oxygen.

### Practice Question — Application

**Q1** Look at the following monosaccharides.

α-glucose      galactose 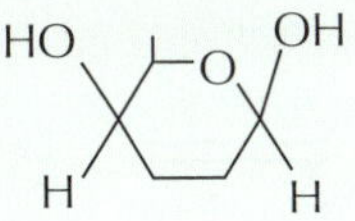      fructose

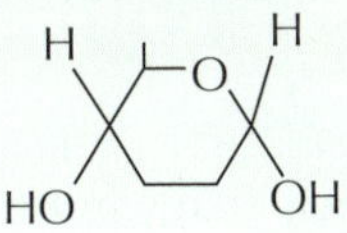

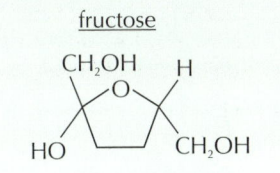

Draw the disaccharide that would be formed from a condensation reaction between:

a) α-glucose and galactose     b) α-glucose and fructose

### Practice Questions — Fact Recall

**Q1** What three chemical elements are found in carbohydrates?

**Q2** What is the difference between a hexose monosaccharide and a pentose monosaccharide?

**Q3** Draw the structure of:
   a) an α-glucose molecule,    b) a ribose molecule.

**Q4** Name the bond that forms between two monosaccharides to make a disaccharide.

**Q5** What two monosaccharides make up a sucrose molecule?

**Q6** Describe the structure of glycogen and explain how its structure makes it suited to its function.

**Q7** Sketch and label a diagram of a microfibril.

**Exam Tip**
Don't panic if you're asked to draw a diagram in the exam — you don't have to be the best artist in the world, but make sure you add labels to point out all the important bits.

Module 2: Section 2 Biological Molecules

### Learning Objectives:

- Know the chemical elements that make up lipids (C, H and O).
- Recall the structure of a triglyceride as an example of a macromolecule.
- Be able to describe the synthesis and breakdown of triglycerides by the formation (esterification) and breakage of ester bonds between fatty acids and glycerol.
- Be able to outline the structure of a saturated and an unsaturated fatty acid.
- Recall the structure of a phospholipid as an example of a macromolecule.
- Be able to explain how the properties of triglyceride, phospholipid and cholesterol molecules relate to their functions in living organisms, including hydrophobic and hydrophilic regions and energy content, illustrated using examples of prokaryotes and eukaryotes.

**Specification Reference 2.1.2**

# 4. Lipids

*Lipids are commonly known as fats or oils. They're found in plants and animals, and have a variety of different functions.*

## What are lipids?

Lipids are macromolecules — see page 62. They all contain the chemical elements carbon, hydrogen and oxygen. There are three types of lipid you need to know about — triglycerides, phospholipids and cholesterol.

## Triglycerides

Triglycerides have one molecule of glycerol with three fatty acids attached to it. They're synthesised by the formation of an **ester bond** between each fatty acid and the glycerol molecule.

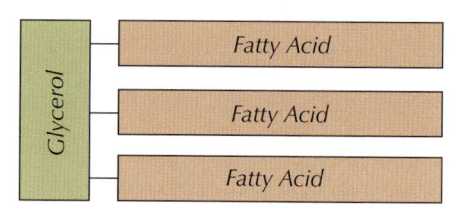

**Figure 1:** Structure of a triglyceride.

### Ester bonds

One triglyceride molecule has three ester bonds. Each ester bond is formed by a condensation reaction (in which a water molecule is released). The process in which triglycerides are synthesised is called **esterification**. Triglycerides break down when the ester bonds are broken. Each ester bond is broken in a hydrolysis reaction (in which a water molecule is used up).

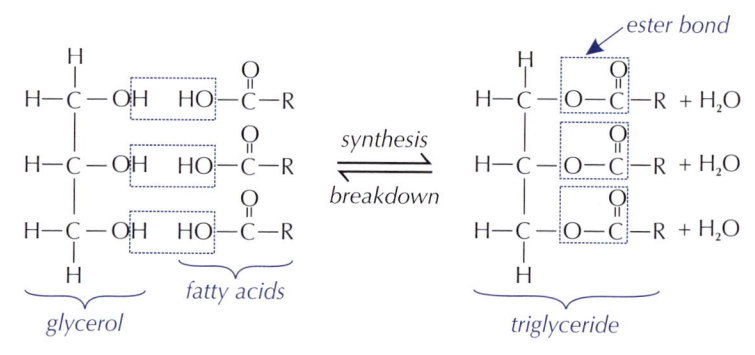

**Figure 2:** The esterification and breakdown of a triglyceride.

### Fatty acids

Fatty acid molecules have long 'tails' made of hydrocarbons (compounds that contain only carbon and hydrogen atoms). The tails are 'hydrophobic' (they repel water molecules). These tails make lipids insoluble in water. All fatty acids have the same basic structure, but the hydrocarbon tail varies — see Figure 3.

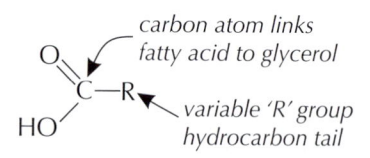

**Figure 3:** Structure of a fatty acid.

There are two kinds of fatty acids — saturated and unsaturated. The difference is in their hydrocarbon tails (see next page).

**Tip:** The variable R group can be any hydrocarbon.

Module 2: Section 2 Biological Molecules

- **Saturated fatty acids** don't have any double bonds between their carbon atoms in their hydrocarbon tails. The fatty acid is 'saturated' with hydrogen.

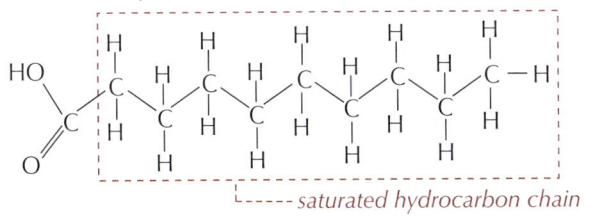

*Figure 4: Saturated fatty acid.*

*Tip: Most animal fats are saturated — the fatty acids in these lipids are saturated so they have no double bonds.*

*Tip: The general formula for a saturated fatty acid is $C_nH_{(2n+1)}COOH$.*

- **Unsaturated fatty acids** have at least one double bond between carbon atoms, which causes the chain to kink.

*Figure 5: Unsaturated fatty acid.*

*Tip: Most plant fats are unsaturated — some of the fatty acids in these lipids are unsaturated meaning they have double bonds.*

## Phospholipids

Phospholipids are pretty similar to triglycerides, except one of the fatty acid molecules is replaced by a phosphate group. The phosphate group is hydrophilic (it attracts water molecules) and the fatty acid tails are hydrophobic.

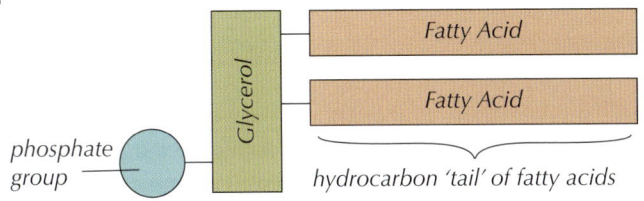

*Figure 6: Structure of a phospholipid.*

*Tip: Remember, a phospholipid has a phosphate group.*

## Cholesterol

Cholesterol is another type of lipid — it has a hydrocarbon ring structure attached to a hydrocarbon tail. The ring structure has a polar hydroxyl (OH) group attached to it.

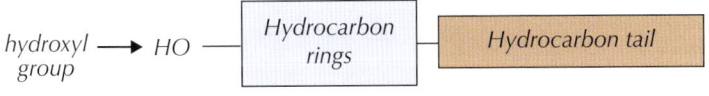

*Figure 7: Structure of cholesterol.*

*Tip: In a hydrocarbon ring structure, the carbon atoms are literally arranged in a ring-like shape instead of a long chain.*

## Functions of lipids

You need to know how the properties of triglycerides, phospholipids and cholesterol are related to their functions:

### Triglycerides

In animals and plants, triglycerides are mainly used as energy storage molecules. Some bacteria (e.g. *Mycobacterium tuberculosis*) use triglycerides to store both energy and carbon. Triglycerides are good for storage because the long hydrocarbon tails of the fatty acids contain lots of chemical energy — a load of energy is released when they're broken down. Because of these tails, lipids contain about twice as much energy per gram as carbohydrates.

Module 2: Section 2 Biological Molecules

**Tip:** Storage molecules also need to be insoluble because otherwise they'd just dissolve (and release whatever they were storing) whenever they came into contact with water.

Triglycerides are also insoluble, so they don't cause water to enter the cells by osmosis (see p. 134) which would make them swell. The triglycerides bundle together as insoluble droplets in cells because the fatty acid tails are hydrophobic (water-repelling) — the tails face inwards, shielding themselves from water with their glycerol heads — see Figure 8.

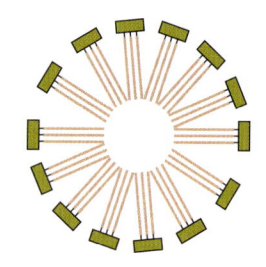

*Figure 8: Diagram showing an insoluble triglyceride droplet.*

### Phospholipids

Phospholipids are found in the cell membranes of all eukaryotes and prokaryotes. They make up what's known as the phospholipid bilayer (see p. 125). Cell membranes control what enters and leaves a cell. Phospholipid heads are hydrophilic and their tails are hydrophobic, so they form a double layer with their heads facing out towards the water on either side. The centre of the bilayer is hydrophobic, so water-soluble substances can't easily pass through it — the membrane acts as a barrier to those substances.

**Tip:** There's more about the role of phospholipids and cholesterol in cell membranes on pages 125-126.

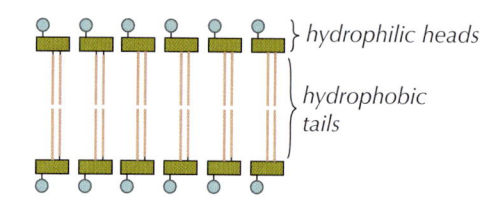

*Figure 9: A phospholipid bilayer.*

### Cholesterol

In eukaryotic cells, cholesterol molecules help to regulate the fluidity of the cell membrane by interacting with the phospholipid bilayer. Cholesterol has a small size and flattened shape — this allows cholesterol to fit in between the phospholipid molecules in the membrane. At higher temperatures, they bind to the hydrophobic tails of the phospholipids, causing them to pack more closely together. This helps to make the membrane less fluid and more rigid. At lower temperatures, cholesterol prevents phospholipids from packing too close together, and so increases membrane fluidity.

**Tip:** 'Polar' means it has a slightly negatively-charged bit and a slightly positively-charged bit — see p. 59.

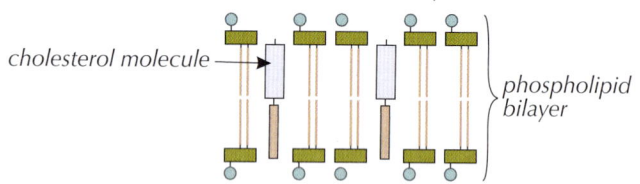

*Figure 10: Cholesterol molecules within a cell membrane.*

> ### Practice Questions — Fact Recall
> Q1 What are the main three chemical elements that make up lipids?
> Q2 What are the components of a triglyceride?
> Q3 What type of bond links glycerol to a fatty acid in a triglyceride?
> Q4 Explain the difference between a saturated fatty acid and an unsaturated fatty acid.
> Q5 Give two reasons why triglycerides are used as energy storage molecules.
> Q6 Explain how the structure of phospholipids make them suited to their function.
> Q7 Describe the role cholesterol molecules have in cell membranes.

Module 2: Section 2 Biological Molecules

# 5. Proteins

*Proteins have lots of useful functions in organisms. Their function is related to their structure, which is determined by the basic units they're made from and the bonds between them.*

## What are proteins made from?

Proteins are polymers. The monomers of proteins are amino acids. A **dipeptide** is formed when two amino acids join together. A **polypeptide** is formed when more than two amino acids join together. Proteins are made up of one or more polypeptides.

*Monomer* — one amino acid

*Dipeptide* — two amino acids

*Polypeptide* — more than two amino acids

*Proteins* — one or more polypeptides

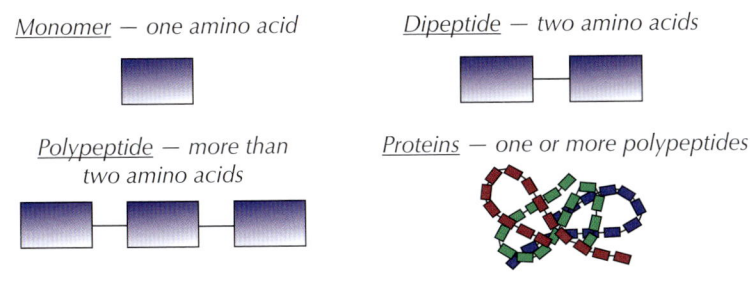

**Figure 1:** *Amino acids join together to form peptides and proteins.*

## Amino acid structure

All amino acids have the same general structure — a carboxyl group (-COOH) and an amino group (-NH$_2$) attached to a carbon atom. The difference between different amino acids is the variable group they contain (shown as R in Figure 2).

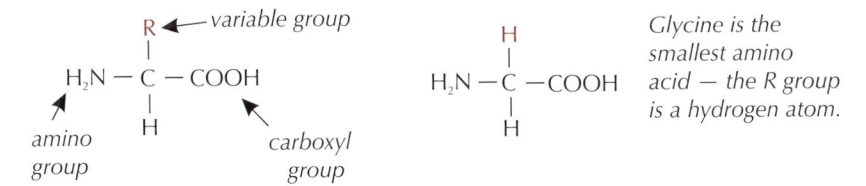

*Glycine is the smallest amino acid — the R group is a hydrogen atom.*

**Figure 2:** *The general structure of an amino acid (left) and the structure of glycine (right).*

All amino acids contain the chemical elements carbon, oxygen, hydrogen and nitrogen. Some also contain sulfur.

## Dipeptide and polypeptide formation

Amino acids are linked together by **peptide bonds** to form dipeptides and polypeptides. A molecule of water is released during the reaction — it's a **condensation reaction**. The reverse of this reaction adds a molecule of water to break the peptide bond — it's a **hydrolysis** reaction.

*a molecule of water is formed during condensation.*

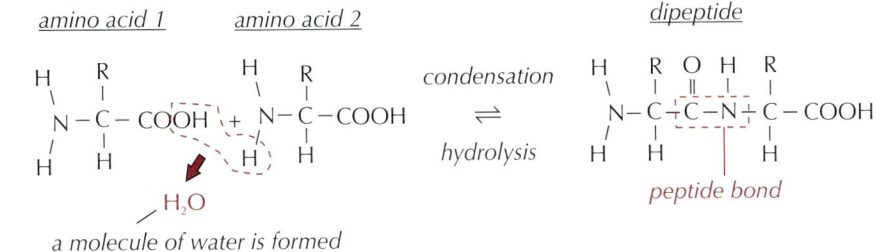

**Figure 3:** *Dipeptide formation.*

---

**Learning Objectives:**
- Know the general structure of an amino acid (C, H, O, N and S).
- Know the chemical elements that make up proteins.
- Understand the synthesis and breakdown of dipeptides and polypeptides by the formation and breakage of peptide bonds.
- Recall the levels of protein structure, including primary, secondary, tertiary and quaternary structure.
- Understand the role of hydrogen bonds, ionic bonds, hydrophobic and hydrophilic interactions and disulfide bonds in the structure of proteins.
- Recall the structure and function of globular proteins, including a conjugated protein, using examples of haemoglobin (as a conjugated protein), a named enzyme and insulin.
- Recall the properties and functions of fibrous proteins, including collagen, keratin and elastin.

**Specification Reference 2.1.2**

**Tip:** Remember, condensation reactions <u>form</u> a water molecule, hydrolysis reactions <u>use</u> a water molecule.

Module 2: Section 2 Biological Molecules

**Tip:** If you compare these amino acids to the basic amino acid structure on the previous page you can spot the R groups, e.g. for alanine it's -CH₃.

### Practice Questions — Application

Q1  Look at the following amino acid structures.

Glycine

$$H_2N - \underset{\underset{H}{|}}{\overset{\overset{H}{|}}{C}} - COOH$$

Alanine

$$H_2N - \underset{\underset{H}{|}}{\overset{\overset{CH_3}{|}}{C}} - COOH$$

Valine

$$H_2N - \underset{\underset{H}{|}}{\overset{\overset{CH(CH_3)_2}{|}}{C}} - COOH$$

Draw the dipeptides and polypeptide that would be formed from a condensation reaction between:
a) glycine and valine.
b) alanine and glycine.
c) glycine, alanine and valine.

Q2  Draw the amino acids produced from the hydrolysis of the dipeptide below.

$$H_2N - \underset{\underset{H}{|}}{\overset{\overset{H}{|}}{C}} - \overset{\overset{O}{\|}}{C} - \underset{\underset{}{|}}{\overset{\overset{H}{|}}{N}} - \underset{\underset{H}{|}}{\overset{\overset{CH_2OH}{|}}{C}} - COOH$$

**Exam Tip**
Remember that in hydrolysis a molecule of water is used, so for Q2 you need to make sure you've added two Hs and one O.

## Protein structure

Proteins are big, complicated molecules. They're much easier to explain if you describe their structure in four 'levels'. These levels are a protein's primary, secondary, tertiary and quaternary structures. The four structural levels of a protein are held together by different kinds of bonds.

### Primary structure

This is the sequence of amino acids in the polypeptide chain. Different proteins have different sequences of amino acids in their primary structure. A change in just one amino acid may change the structure of the whole protein. It is held together by the peptide bonds between the amino acids.

**Tip:** Remember, proteins are polymers of amino acids (see previous page).

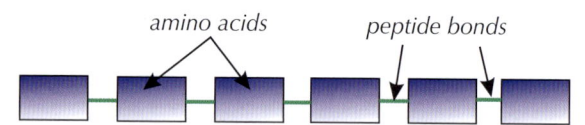

*Figure 4: A protein's primary structure.*

### Secondary structure

The polypeptide chain doesn't remain flat and straight. Hydrogen bonds form between the –NH and –CO groups of the amino acids in the chain. This makes it automatically coil into an alpha (α) helix or fold into a beta (β) pleated sheet — this is the secondary structure.

**Tip:** In a polypeptide chain the –NH and –CO groups are polar. The H atom in the N–H bond has a slightly positive charge and the O atom in the C=O bond has a slightly negative charge. This means hydrogen bonds can form between different amino acids in a chain.

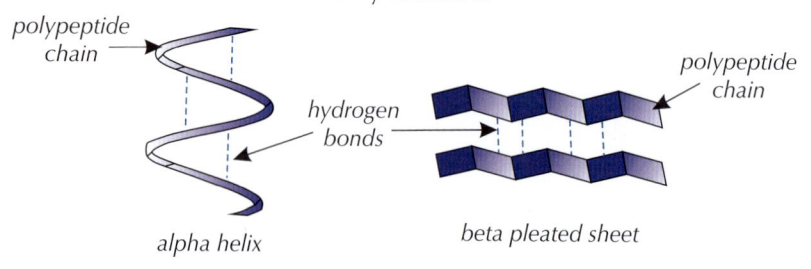

$$\overset{\delta-}{N}-\overset{\delta+}{H}----\overset{\delta-}{O}=\overset{\delta+}{C}$$

*Figure 5: A protein's secondary structure.*

## Tertiary structure

The coiled or folded chain of amino acids is often coiled and folded further. More bonds form between different parts of the polypeptide chain such as:

- **Ionic bonds** — these are attractions between negatively-charged R groups and positively-charged R groups on different parts of the molecule — see Figure 7.

- **Disulfide bonds** — whenever two molecules of the amino acid cysteine come close together, the sulfur atom in one cysteine bonds to the sulfur in the other cysteine, forming a disulfide bond — see Figure 6.

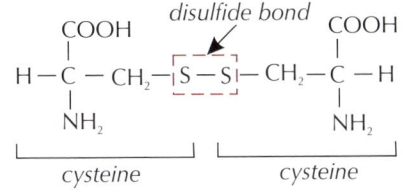

*Figure 6: A disulfide bond.*

- **Hydrophobic and hydrophilic interactions** — when hydrophobic (water-repelling) R groups are close together in the protein, they tend to clump together. This means that hydrophilic (water-attracting) R groups are more likely to be pushed to the outside, which affects how the protein folds up into its final structure — see Figure 7.

- **Hydrogen bonds** — these weak bonds form between slightly positively-charged hydrogen atoms in some R groups and slightly negatively-charged atoms in other R groups on the polypeptide chain — see Figure 7.

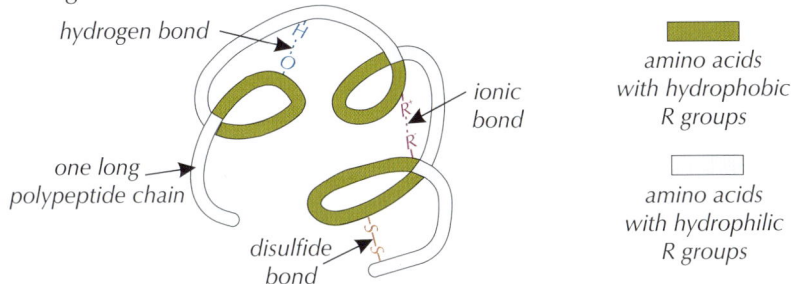

*Figure 7: Examples of bonding in a protein's tertiary structure.*

For proteins made from a single polypeptide chain, the tertiary structure forms their final 3D structure.

**Tip:** Remember, an R group is an amino acid's variable group. It's also called an amino acid's 'side chain'.

**Exam Tip**
Make sure you spell the name of a bond correctly in the exam, otherwise you won't get the mark.

**Tip:** Heating a protein to a high temperature will break up its ionic bonds, hydrophobic/hydrophilic interactions and hydrogen bonds. In turn this will cause a change in the protein's 3D shape.

## Quaternary structure

Some proteins are made of several different polypeptide chains held together by bonds. The quaternary structure is the way these polypeptide chains are assembled together.

- Example
  Haemoglobin is made of four polypeptide chains, bonded together — see Figure 9 on the next page.

The quaternary structure tends to be determined by the tertiary structure of the individual polypeptide chains being bonded together. Because of this, it can be influenced by all the bonds mentioned above. For proteins made from more than one polypeptide chain, the quaternary structure is the protein's final 3D structure.

**Tip:** Not all proteins have a quaternary structure — some are made of only one polypeptide chain.

## Investigating protein structure

Computer modelling can create 3D interactive images of proteins. This is really handy for investigating the different levels of structure in a protein molecule.

**Tip:** Figures 8, 10, 11 and 12 on the next page are examples of images of proteins made by computer modelling.

**Exam Tip**
You need to learn how the structures of haemoglobin, insulin and amylase (or another named enzyme) relate to their function.

*Figure 8:* A molecular model of haemoglobin.

**Tip:** It's the iron-containing haem groups in haemoglobin that bind to oxygen.

# Globular proteins

Globular proteins are round and compact. In a globular protein, the hydrophilic R groups on the amino acids tend to be pushed to the outside of the molecule. This is caused by the hydrophobic and hydrophilic interactions in the protein's tertiary structure (see previous page). This makes globular proteins soluble, so they're easily transported in fluids.

Globular proteins have a range of functions in living organisms.

### Example — Haemoglobin

Haemoglobin is a globular protein that carries oxygen around the body in red blood cells (see page 199). It's known as a **conjugated protein** — this means it's a protein with a non-protein group attached. The non-protein part is called a **prosthetic group**. Each of the four polypeptide chains in haemoglobin has a prosthetic group called haem. A haem group contains iron, which oxygen binds to.

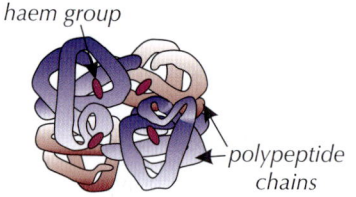

*Figure 9:* Haemoglobin's quaternary structure.

### Example — Insulin

Insulin is a hormone secreted by the pancreas. It helps to regulate the blood glucose level. Its solubility is important — it means it can be transported in the blood to the tissues where it acts. An insulin molecule consists of two polypeptide chains, which are held together by disulfide bonds. When they're in the pancreas, six of these molecules bind together to form a large, globular structure (see Figure 10).

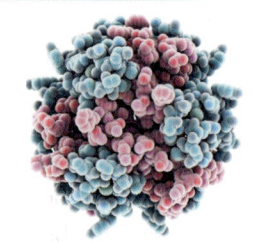

*Figure 10:* The quaternary structure of insulin.

### Example — Amylase

Amylase is an enzyme (see page 105) that catalyses the breakdown of starch in the digestive system. It is made of a single chain of amino acids. Its secondary structure contains both alpha-helix and beta-pleated sheet sections. Most enzymes are globular proteins.

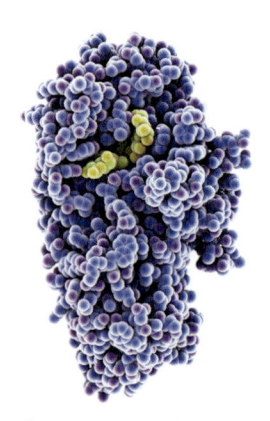

*Figure 11:* A molecular model of amylase.

# Fibrous proteins

Fibrous proteins are tough and rope-shaped. They're also insoluble and strong. They're structural proteins and are fairly unreactive (unlike many globular proteins). You need to know about these three fibrous proteins:

### Example — Collagen

Collagen is found in animal connective tissues, such as bone, skin and muscle. It is a very strong molecule. Minerals can bind to the protein to increase its rigidity, e.g. in bone.

*Figure 12:* A molecular model of collagen.

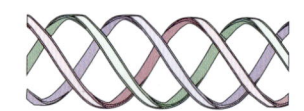

*Figure 13:* The structure of a collagen molecule.

Module 2: Section 2 Biological Molecules

### Example — Keratin
Keratin is found in many of the external structures of animals, such as skin, hair, nails, feathers and horns. It can either be flexible (as it is in skin) or hard and tough (as it is in nails).

### Example — Elastin
Elastin is found in elastic connective tissue, such as skin, large blood vessels and some ligaments. It is elastic, so it allows tissues to return to their original shape after they have been stretched.

*Figure 14: Keratin layers within a nail.*

## Practice Questions — Fact Recall

Q1  What are the monomers of proteins?

Q2  What is a polypeptide?

Q3  Draw the general structure of an amino acid.

Q4  What are the main five elements found in proteins?

Q5  What is the name of the bond that forms between amino acids?

Q6  What sort of reaction:
   a) links amino acids together?
   b) breaks amino acids apart?

Q7  Describe how the secondary structure of a protein is formed.

Q8  Look at the diagram of the polypeptide chain on the right.
   a) What level of a protein's structure does it show?
   b) Name the bonds labelled A-C.
   c) Describe how the bond labelled C is formed.

Q9  What is the quaternary structure of a protein?

Q10 Explain how the globular structure of haemoglobin makes it suited to its function.

Q11 What is a conjugated protein?

Q12 State two properties of a globular protein that are different to those of a fibrous protein.

Q13 a) What is the function of collagen?
   b) How is collagen suited to its function?

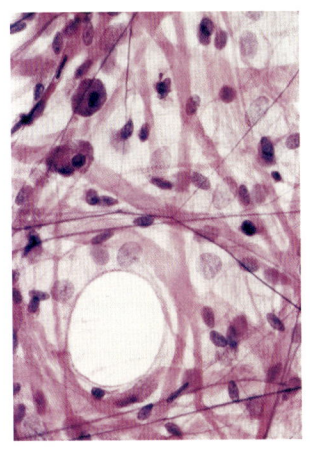

*Figure 15: Light micrograph showing elastin fibres (thin dark lines) and collagen (thicker pink lines) in connective tissue.*

Module 2: Section 2 Biological Molecules

**Learning Objectives:**

- Know the key inorganic ions that are involved in biological processes, including the correct symbols for:
  - Cations: calcium ions ($Ca^{2+}$), sodium ions ($Na^+$), potassium ions ($K^+$), hydrogen ions ($H^+$), and ammonium ions ($NH_4^+$).
  - Anions: nitrate ions ($NO_3^-$), hydrogencarbonate ions ($HCO_3^-$), chloride ions ($Cl^-$), phosphate ions ($PO_4^{3-}$), and hydroxide ions ($OH^-$).

**Specification Reference 2.1.2**

**Tip:** Children who don't receive enough calcium may develop rickets — a condition that causes the bones to become soft and weak.

**Tip:** An enzyme cofactor is a non-protein substance that is required for an enzyme's activity. There's more about enzyme cofactors on page 116.

**Tip:** Plants need nitrogen to produce chlorophyll (the green pigment found in leaves and stems). If a plant doesn't get enough nitrogen, its leaves will turn yellow.

# 6. Inorganic Ions

*Inorganic ions may be small, but they're essential for many biological processes. All the key inorganic ions you need to know about are on these two pages...*

## What are inorganic ions?

An ion is an atom (or group of atoms) that has an electric charge. An inorganic ion is one which doesn't contain carbon (although there are a few exceptions to this rule). Inorganic ions are really important in biological processes. The ones you need to know about are listed below and on the next page.

## Cations

An ion with a positive charge is called a cation.

| Name of cation | Chemical Symbol | Example(s) of roles in biological processes |
|---|---|---|
| Calcium | $Ca^{2+}$ | Involved in the transmission of nerve impulses and the release of insulin from the pancreas. Acts as a cofactor for many enzymes, e.g. those involved in blood clotting. Is important for bone formation. |
| Sodium | $Na^+$ | Important for generating nerve impulses, for muscle contraction and for regulating fluid balance in the body. |
| Potassium | $K^+$ | Important for generating nerve impulses, for muscle contraction and for regulating fluid balance in the body. Activates essential enzymes needed for photosynthesis in plant cells. |
| Hydrogen | $H^+$ | Affects the pH of substances (more $H^+$ ions than $OH^-$ ions in a solution creates an acid). Also important for photosynthesis reactions that occur in the thylakoid membranes inside chloroplasts (see p. 41) and respiration reactions that occur in the inner membrane of mitochondria (p. 41). |
| Ammonium | $NH_4^+$ | Absorbed from the soil by plants and is an important source of nitrogen (which is then used to make, e.g. amino acids, nucleic acids). |

74 Module 2: Section 2 Biological Molecules

# Anions

An ion with a negative charge is called an anion.

| Name of anion | Chemical Symbol | Example(s) of roles in biological processes |
|---|---|---|
| Nitrate | $NO_3^-$ | Absorbed from the soil by plants and is an important source of nitrogen (which is then used to make, e.g. amino acids, nucleic acids). |
| Hydrogencarbonate | $HCO_3^-$ | Acts as a buffer, which helps to maintain the pH of the blood. |
| Chloride | $Cl^-$ | Involved in the 'chloride shift' which helps to maintain the pH of the blood during gas exchange (see p. 202). Acts as a cofactor for the enzyme amylase (see p. 116). Also involved in some nerve impulses. |
| Phosphate | $PO_4^{3-}$ | Involved in photosynthesis and respiration reactions. Needed for the synthesis of many biological molecules, such as nucleotides (including ATP), phospholipids, and calcium phosphate (which strengthens bones). |
| Hydroxide | $OH^-$ | Affects the pH of substances (more $OH^-$ ions than $H^+$ ions in a solution creates an alkali). |

*Figure 1:* A plant with nitrogen deficiency.

**Tip:** Maintaining pH in the body is really important — a pH that is too high or too low will cause proteins (including enzymes) in the body to denature (see p. 110) and so lose their function.

**Tip:** ATP stands for adenosine triphosphate — its structure contains three phosphate groups (in blue below):

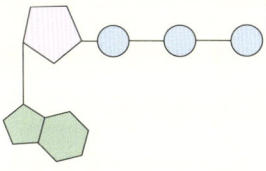

See p. 89 for more.

## Practice Question — Application

Q1 Which of the ions below acts as an enzyme cofactor for amylase?
    A  $Na^+$    B  $OH^-$    C  $Cl^-$    D  $K^+$

## Practice Questions — Fact Recall

Q1 Write the chemical symbol for each of the following:
    a) a hydrogen ion,
    b) an ammonium ion,
    c) a phosphate ion,
    d) a hydroxide ion.
Q2 Which ion is essential for forming strong bones?
Q3 Name two ions that are important for generating nerve impulses.
Q4 Give two sources of nitrogen for plants.
Q5 Name an ion that acts as a buffer in the blood.
Q6 What would be the effect of adding $OH^-$ ions to a solution?

**Exam Tip**
Make sure you know all the chemical symbols for the ions on these pages, as well as their names — some of them are trickier than others.

Module 2: Section 2 Biological Molecules

## Learning Objectives:

- Know how to carry out and interpret the results of the following chemical tests (all PAG9):
  - the biuret test for proteins,
  - the iodine test for starch,
  - the emulsion test for lipids,
  - the Benedict's test for reducing and non-reducing sugars,
  - reagent test strips for reducing sugars.
- Know how to use quantitative methods to determine the concentration of a chemical substance in a solution using:
  - colorimetry (PAG5),
  - biosensors.

**Specification Reference 2.1.2**

**Figure 1:** A negative (left) and positive (right) biuret test result.

**Tip:** If you're using dilute sodium hydroxide for this test, you'll need to wear safety goggles.

**Exam Tip**
When a question says 'suggest' you're not expected to know the exact answer — you're expected to use your knowledge to come up with a sensible answer.

# 7. Biochemical Tests for Molecules

The next few pages are all about tests you can do to find out if a substance contains proteins, carbohydrates or lipids. You never know when you might need to find out exactly what is in a food sample...

## Qualitative testing

PRACTICAL ACTIVITY GROUP 9

The next three pages are about qualitative testing, which is how you determine whether a substance is present in a sample or not. There are different qualitative tests for different biological molecules. You need to know how to do these tests and how to interpret the results. Don't forget to do a risk assessment before carrying out each one — see page 7 for the kinds of things you need to look out for.

## The biuret test for proteins

If you needed to find out if a substance contained protein you'd use the biuret test. There are two stages to this test.

1. The test solution needs to be alkaline, so first you add a few drops of sodium hydroxide solution.
2. Then you add some copper(II) sulfate solution.

If protein is present, the solution turns purple. If there's no protein, the solution will stay blue — see Figures 1 and 2. The colours can be fairly pale, so you might need to look carefully.

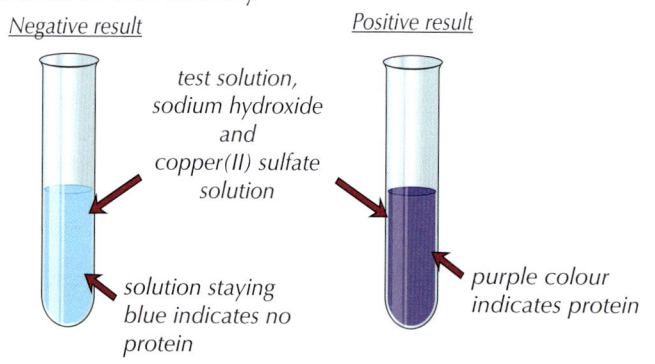

*Negative result* — test solution, sodium hydroxide and copper(II) sulfate solution — solution staying blue indicates no protein

*Positive result* — purple colour indicates protein

**Figure 2:** A positive and negative biuret test result.

### Practice Questions — Application

A biuret test was carried out to determine which liquids contained protein. The results of the experiment are shown in the table below.

| Liquid | Result |
|---|---|
| De-ionised water | Blue |
| Cow's milk | Blue |
| Orange juice | Purple |
| Orange squash | Blue |
| Goat's milk | Purple |

Q1  Which of the liquids in the table gave a positive test result?
Q2  Suggest why the scientist tested de-ionised water.

Module 2: Section 2  Biological Molecules

## The iodine test for starch

If you want to test for the presence of starch in a sample, you'll need to do the iodine test. Just add iodine dissolved in potassium iodide solution to the test sample. If starch is present, the sample changes from browny-orange to a dark, blue-black colour — see Figures 3 and 4. If there is no starch, it stays browny-orange.

**Exam Tip**
Make sure you always talk about iodine in potassium iodide solution, not just iodine.

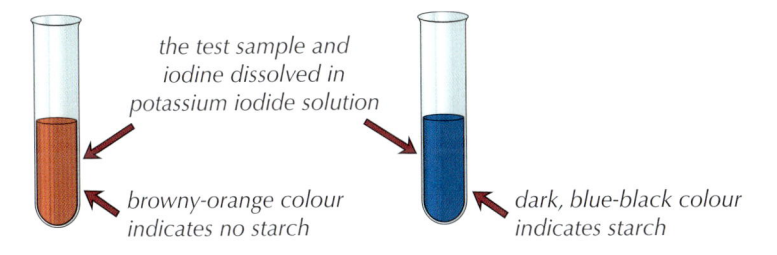

*Figure 3:* A negative (left) and positive (right) iodine test result.

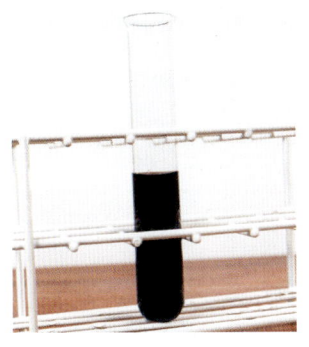

*Figure 4:* A dark blue-black colour indicates the presence of starch in an iodine test.

## The emulsion test for lipids

If you want to test for the presence of lipids in a sample, you'll need to do the emulsion test. To do this you shake the test substance with ethanol for about a minute, then pour the solution into water. If lipid is present, the solution will turn milky — see Figures 5 and 6. The more lipid there is, the more noticeable the milky colour will be. If there's no lipid, the solution will stay clear.

**Tip:** Ethanol is flammable, so make sure you do this test away from any open flames.

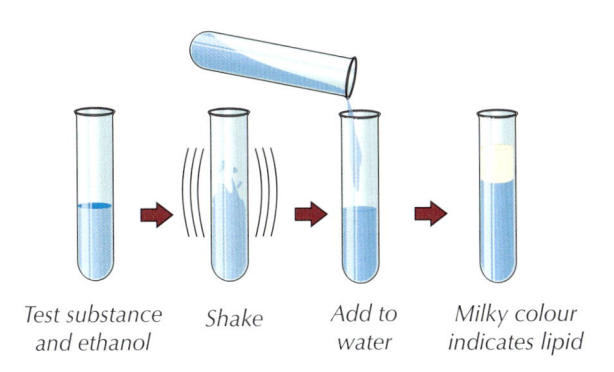

*Figure 5:* The emulsion test for lipids.

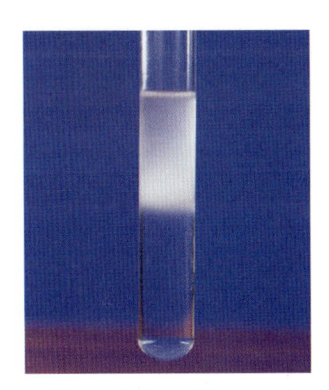

*Figure 6:* A positive result using the emulsion test.

## The Benedict's test for sugars

Sugar is a general term for monosaccharides and disaccharides. All sugars can be classified as reducing or non-reducing. To test for sugars you use the Benedict's test. The test differs depending on the type of sugar you are testing for.

### Reducing sugars

Reducing sugars include all monosaccharides (e.g. glucose) and some disaccharides (e.g. maltose and lactose). You add Benedict's reagent (which is blue) to a sample and heat it in a water bath that's been brought to the boil. If the test's positive it will form a coloured precipitate — solid particles suspended in the solution. The colour of the precipitate changes as shown in Figure 7 (see next page).

**Tip:** If the substance you want to test is a solid, you may have to prepare a solution of it before testing. You could do this by first crushing the solid with water and then filtering out the solid.

Module 2: Section 2 Biological Molecules 77

**Exam Tip**
Be careful with your wording when you're describing the Benedict's test — you need to say you <u>heat</u> the sample, you won't get a mark for saying you warm it.

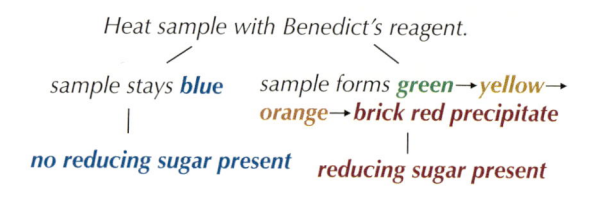

Heat sample with Benedict's reagent.
- sample stays **blue** → **no reducing sugar present**
- sample forms **green → yellow → orange → brick red precipitate** → **reducing sugar present**

*Figure 7: Benedict's test for reducing sugars.*

The higher the concentration of reducing sugar, the further the colour change goes — you can use this to compare the amount of reducing sugar in different solutions. (A more accurate way of doing this is to filter the solution and weigh the precipitate.)

### Non-reducing sugars

If the result of the reducing sugars test is negative, there could still be a non-reducing sugar present. To test for non-reducing sugars, like sucrose, first you have to break them down into monosaccharides. You do this by getting a new sample of the test solution (i.e. not the same one you've already added Benedict's reagent to) adding dilute hydrochloric acid and carefully heating it in a water bath that's been brought to the boil. You then neutralise it with sodium hydrogencarbonate. Then just carry out the Benedict's test as you would for a reducing sugar — see Figure 9.

**Tip:** Always use an excess of Benedict's solution — this makes sure that all the sugar reacts.

**Tip:** Be careful when taking the test tubes out of the water bath after the Benedict's test, as they could be hot.

Heat sample with Benedict's reagent.
- sample stays **blue** → **no reducing sugar present**
  - Heat a new sample with dilute hydrochloric acid then neutralise sample by adding sodium hydrogencarbonate. Heat sample with Benedict's reagent.
    - sample stays **blue** → **no non-reducing (or reducing) sugar present**
    - sample forms **green → yellow → orange → brick red precipitate** → **non-reducing sugar present**
- sample forms **green → yellow → orange → brick red precipitate** → **reducing sugar present**

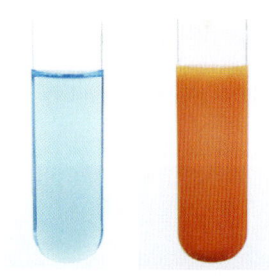

*Figure 8: A blue colour (left) indicates a negative Benedict's test result and a brick red colour (right) indicates a positive result.*

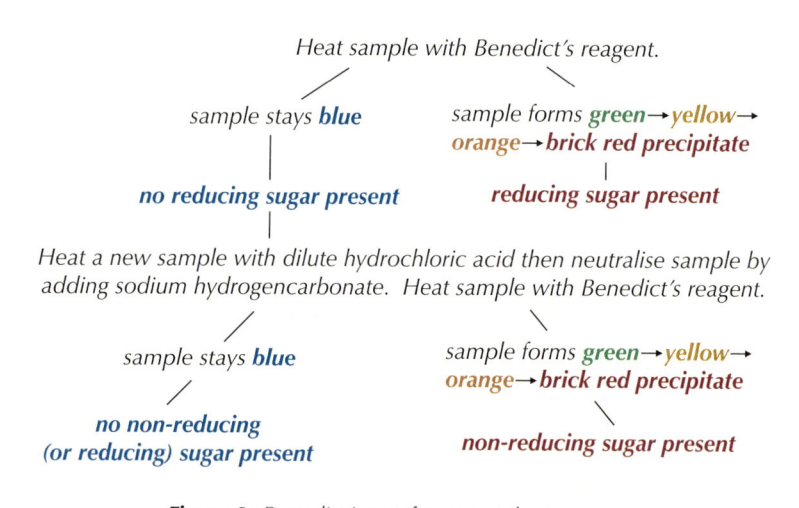

*Figure 9: Benedict's test for non-reducing sugars.*

### Practice Question — Application

**Q1** Samples from two different solutions, A and B, were heated with Benedict's reagent. The sample of solution A remained blue, while the sample of solution B formed a brick red precipitate. What conclusions can you draw from these results?

## Test strips for glucose

Glucose can also be tested for using test strips coated in a reagent. The strips are dipped in a test solution and change colour if glucose is present. The colour change can be compared to a chart to give an indication of the concentration of glucose present — see Figure 10. The strips are useful for testing a person's urine for glucose, which may indicate they have diabetes.

*Figure 10: A urine test strip being compared to a results chart. The result shows an elevated level of glucose.*

Module 2: Section 2  Biological Molecules

## Quantitative tests

Quantitative tests tell you the amount (i.e. concentration) of a substance that is present in a sample. You need to know how to use colorimetry to find out the concentration of a substance in a sample, as well as how a biosensor works.

## Colorimetry and the Benedict's test

**PRACTICAL ACTIVITY GROUP 5**

You can use Benedict's reagent and a colorimeter to get a quantitative estimate of how much glucose (or other reducing sugar) there is in a solution.

### What is a colorimeter?

A colorimeter is a device that measures the strength of a coloured solution by seeing how much light passes through it — see Figure 12. A colorimeter measures absorbance (the amount of light absorbed by the solution). The more concentrated the colour of the solution, the higher the absorbance is.

*Figure 11: A colorimeter is used to measure the amount of light absorbed by a substance.*

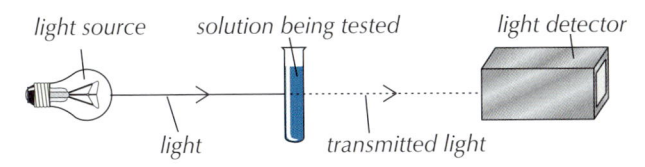

*Figure 12: A diagram showing how a colorimeter works.*

To find out the glucose concentration of an unknown solution, you first need to make up several solutions of known glucose concentrations, then measure the absorbance of these solutions, and finally plot these absorbances on a graph to make a calibration curve (see p. 80). You can then use the calibration curve to estimate the concentration of glucose in the unknown solution.

It's easiest to measure the concentration of the blue Benedict's solution that's left after the test (the paler the solution, the more glucose there was). So, the higher the glucose concentration, the lower the absorbance of the solution.

**Tip:** Don't forget to do a risk assessment before starting this experiment.

### Making known concentrations of glucose

You can make up glucose solutions of different, known concentrations using a serial dilution technique:

---
**Example**

This is how you'd make five serial dilutions with a dilution factor of 2, starting with an initial glucose concentration of 40 mM.

1. Line up five test tubes in a rack.
2. Add 10 cm³ of the initial 40 mM sucrose solution to the first test tube and 5 cm³ of distilled water to the other four test tubes (see Figure 13).
3. Then, using a pipette, draw 5 cm³ of the solution from the first test tube, add it to the distilled water in the second test tube and mix the solution thoroughly. You now have 10 cm³ of solution that's half as concentrated as the solution in the first test tube (it's 20 mM).
4. Repeat this process three more times to create solutions of 10 mM, 5 mM and 2.5 mM.

*Figure 13: How to make serial dilutions.*

**Tip:** You don't have to dilute solutions by a factor of 2. E.g. to dilute by a factor of 10, take 1 cm³ from your original sample and add it to 9 cm³ of water.

---

Module 2: Section 2 Biological Molecules

**Tip:** In the negative control, there's no glucose. If there's no glucose, none of the Benedict's reagent will react and so the solution will remain blue — this should give you the highest absorbance value.

**Tip:** In a centrifuge, solutions are spun at high speed so the precipitate is separated from the solution.

**Tip:** When you're handling cuvettes you need to wipe away any marks or moisture from the sides the light will be passing through. You should also gently tap the cuvette to remove any air bubbles.

**Tip:** Your teacher will show you how to calibrate the colorimeter you are using to zero.

## Measuring the absorbance of known solutions

Once you've got your glucose solutions, you need to find out the absorbance of each one. Here's how:

- Do a Benedict's test on each solution (plus a negative control of pure water). Use the same amount of Benedict's solution in each case.
- Remove any precipitate — either leave for 24 hours (so that the precipitate settles out) or centrifuge them.
- Use a colorimeter to measure the absorbance of the Benedict's solution remaining in each tube. The method is outlined below.

    1. Switch the colorimeter on and allow five minutes for it to stabilise. Then set up the colorimeter so you're using a red filter (or a wavelength of 630 nm).
    2. Add distilled water to a cuvette so it is three quarters full (a cuvette is a small container that fits inside a colorimeter). Put the cuvette into the colorimeter. Two of the cuvette's sides may be ridged or frosted — you need to make sure you put the cuvette into the colorimeter the correct way, so that the light will be passing through the clear sides. Calibrate the machine to zero.
    3. Next, use a pipette to transfer a sample of the solution from the first test tube to a clean cuvette — again it should be about three quarters full.
    4. Put the cuvette in the colorimeter and read and record the absorbance of the solution.
    5. Repeat steps 1-4 for the remaining solutions (using a clean pipette and cuvette each time).

## Making and using a calibration curve

To make a calibration curve, plot a graph of your results showing absorbance (on the *y*-axis) against glucose concentration (on the *x*-axis).
Then you can test the unknown solution in the same way as the known concentrations and use the calibration curve to find its concentration.

---
**Example** — Maths Skills

To find the glucose concentration of an unknown solution with an absorbance value of 0.5, you need to follow these steps:

1. Find 0.5 on the *y*-axis (vertical axis) of the calibration graph.
2. Read across from this value to the curve.
3. Read down from the curve to the *x*-axis.

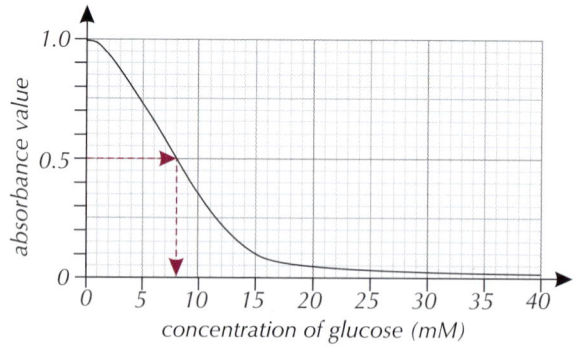

4. Read the concentration value from the *x*-axis.
    The unknown solution has a glucose concentration of **8 mM**.

## Biosensors

A biosensor is a device that uses a biological molecule, such as an enzyme (see page 105) to detect a chemical. The biological molecule produces a signal (e.g. a chemical signal), which is converted to an electrical signal by a transducer (another part of the biosensor). The electrical signal is then processed and can be used to work out other information.

### Example — Glucose biosensors

A glucose biosensor is used to determine the concentration of glucose in a solution. It does this using the enzyme glucose oxidase and electrodes. The enzyme catalyses the oxidation of glucose at the electrodes — this creates a charge, which is converted into an electrical signal by the electrodes (the transducer). The electrical signal is then processed to work out the initial glucose concentration.

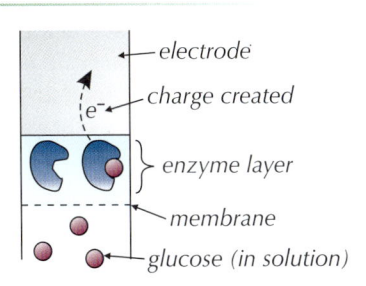

**Figure 14:** How a glucose biosensor works.

**Figure 15:** Glucose biosensors can be used to monitor blood sugar levels.

### Practice Question — Application

Q1 A student used a colorimeter to measure the absorbance of known concentrations of starch solution, after doing the iodine test on them. She then drew the calibration curve on the right. The student also carried out the iodine test on a solution with an unknown concentration of starch. The absorbance of the unknown solution was 0.85. Find the concentration of the solution using the calibration curve.

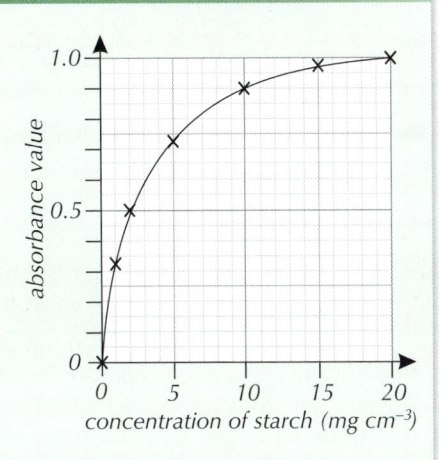

### Practice Questions — Fact Recall

Q1 The biuret test is used to test for proteins.
   a) What is added to the test solution to make it alkaline?
   b) What is added next to the solution?
   c) What would a positive test result look like?

Q2 Name a test to find out if starch is present in a sample or not.

Q3 Describe a test you could do to find out if a sample contains lipids, including what observation would indicate a positive result.

Q4 Describe how to test for reducing sugars and say what a positive and a negative result would look like.

Q5 a) What is a colorimeter?
   b) Assuming a calibration curve had already been created, describe how you would use a colorimeter and the calibration curve to measure the glucose concentration of an unknown solution.

Q6 Describe a biosensor and outline how it works.

Module 2: Section 2 Biological Molecules

## Learning Objectives:

- Understand the principles and use of paper and thin layer chromatography to separate biological molecules or compounds, including the calculation of retention ($R_f$) values using the formula:
$R_f$ = distance moved by the solute ÷ distance moved by the solvent.

- Be able to carry out practical investigations to analyse biological solutions using paper or thin layer chromatography (PAG6).

**Specification Reference 2.1.2**

*Figure 1: Plant pigments that have been separated by thin-layer chromatography.*

**Tip:** The pattern of spots you end up with is called a chromatogram.

**Tip:** The sample of mixture is also called a blot.

**Tip:** Don't forget to do a risk assessment before you do this experiment to identify all the safety precautions you need to take.

# 8. Separating Molecules

*Chromatography is a useful way of identifying what molecules you've got in a mixture, and you need to know all about it...*

## Chromatography

Chromatography is used to separate stuff in a mixture — once it's separated out, you can often identify the components. For example, chromatography can be used to separate out and identify biological molecules such as amino acids, carbohydrates, vitamins and nucleic acids.

There are quite a few different types of chromatography — you only need to know about paper chromatography and thin-layer chromatography.

### How does chromatography work?

All types of chromatography (including paper and thin-layer) have the same basic set up:

- A **mobile phase** — where the molecules can move.
  In both paper and thin-layer chromatography the mobile phase is a liquid solvent, such as ethanol or water.

- A **stationary phase** — where the molecules can't move.
  In paper chromatography the stationary phase is a piece of chromatography paper. In thin-layer chromatography the stationary phase is a thin (0.1-0.3 mm) layer of solid, e.g. silica gel, on a glass or plastic plate.

They all use the same basic principle:

- The mobile phase moves through or over the stationary phase.
- The components in the mixture spend different amounts of time in the mobile phase and the stationary phase.
- The components that spend longer in the mobile phase travel faster or further.
- The time spent in the different phases is what separates out the components of the mixture.

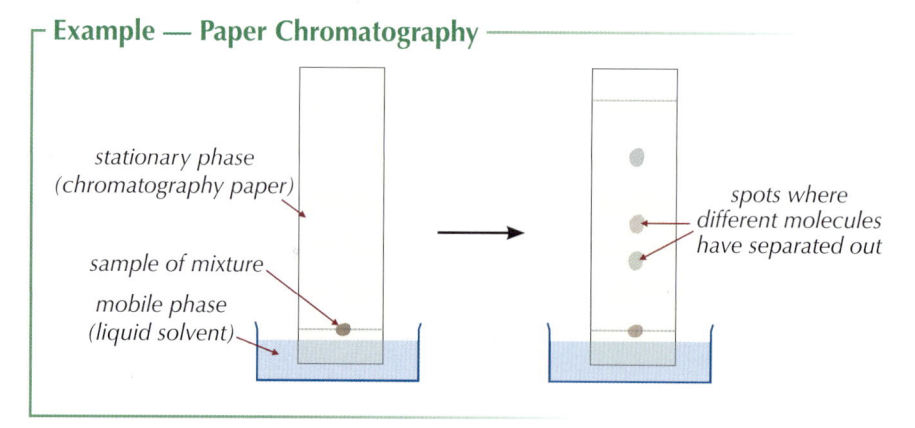

### Example — Paper Chromatography

- stationary phase (chromatography paper)
- sample of mixture
- mobile phase (liquid solvent)
- spots where different molecules have separated out

## Identifying unknown molecules

**PRACTICAL ACTIVITY GROUP 6**

In the exam you might be asked how chromatography can be used to identify the biological molecules in a mixture. An example of how paper chromatography can be used to identify amino acids in a mixture is shown on the next page.

Module 2: Section 2  Biological Molecules

### Example — Separating amino acids

You need to make sure you're wearing gloves, safety goggles and a lab coat throughout the experiment — the solvent used for amino acids is harmful and corrosive, and ninhydrin irritates the skin and eyes. The gloves will also prevent amino acids from your skin getting on the chromatography paper.

1. Draw a pencil line near the bottom of a piece of chromatography paper and put a concentrated spot of the mixture of amino acids on it. It's best to carefully roll the paper into a cylinder with the spot on the outside so it'll stand up.

2. Add a small amount of prepared solvent (a mixture of butan-1-ol, glacial ethanoic acid and water is usually used for amino acids) to a beaker and dip the bottom of the paper into it (not the spot). This should be done in a fume cupboard. Cover with a lid to stop the solvent evaporating — see Figure 2 (top).

3. As the solvent spreads up the paper, the different amino acids (solutes) move with it, but at different rates, so they separate out.

4. When the solvent's nearly reached the top, take the paper out and mark the solvent front with pencil. Then you can leave the paper to dry out before you analyse it (see below and next page).

5. Amino acids aren't coloured, which means you won't be able to see them on the paper. So before you can analyse them, you have to spray the paper with ninhydrin solution to turn the amino acids purple — see Figure 2 (bottom). This should also be done in a fume cupboard.

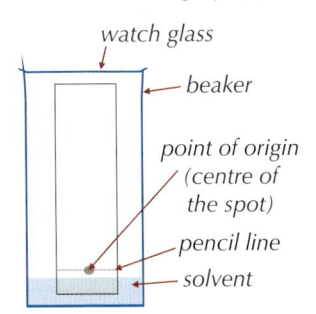

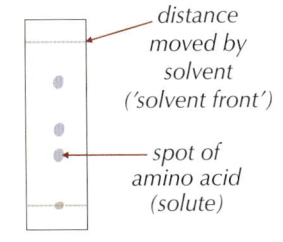

**Figure 2:** Setting up paper chromatography to separate amino acids (top) and the results (bottom).

**Tip:** A lot of chromatography solvents are highly flammable, so you shouldn't work with them near any open flames (e.g. from Bunsen burners).

**Tip:** Make sure you use a pencil (not a pen) to draw the line, and that the pencil line is above the solvent level.

**Tip:** Both the solvent and ninhydrin are volatile (evaporate easily) and are harmful if inhaled, so make sure you use them in a fume cupboard.

**Tip:** If you're trying to identify different biological molecules, the method will vary slightly (e.g. a different solvent might be used) but the basic principle will be the same.

**Tip:** You can't use ninhydrin to detect all biological molecules, only proteins and amino acids.

# $R_f$ values

Once the chromatogram is dry, you can use $R_f$ values to identify the separated molecules. An $R_f$ value is the ratio of the distance travelled by a solute to the distance travelled by the solvent. You can calculate it using this formula:

$$R_f \text{ value} = \frac{\text{distance moved by the solute}}{\text{distance moved by the solvent}}$$

When you're measuring how far a solute has travelled, you measure from the point of origin to the vertical centre of the spot (see Figure 3).

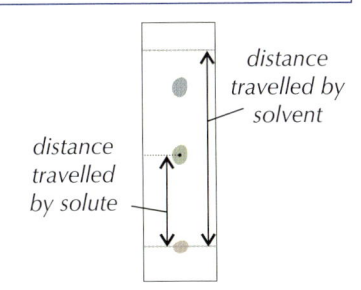

**Figure 3:** Diagram to show the distances to measure in order to work out the $R_f$ value of a solute on a chromatogram.

**Tip:** $R_f$ stands for 'retention (or retardation) factor'.

**Tip:** The substances in the sample mixture (e.g. amino acids) dissolve as the solvent passes over it, so they are called solutes.

Module 2: Section 2 Biological Molecules

**Tip:** You could also compare your chromatogram to the chromatogram of a known mixture and identify the components that way — if two solutes have travelled the same distance in the solvent, they will be the same molecule.

**Tip:** The stationary phase and solvent that you use will affect the $R_f$ value. Temperature can have an effect on the $R_f$ value as well. If you're looking up $R_f$ values, you need to check that they were recorded under the same conditions as your experiment.

---

### Example — Maths Skills

A solution containing a mixture of three amino acids is separated using paper chromatography.
The chromatogram is shown in Figure 4.
Calculate the $R_f$ value of solute X.

To find the $R_f$ value of solute X, all you have to do is stick the numbers into the formula:

$$R_f \text{ value} = \frac{\text{distance moved by the solute}}{\text{distance moved by the solvent}}$$

$$= 2.3 \text{ cm} \div 8.8 \text{ cm} = \mathbf{0.26}$$

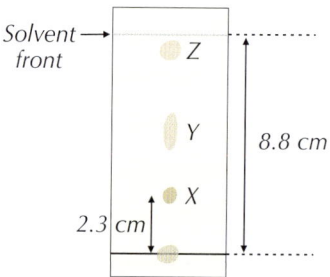

**Figure 4:** A sample chromatogram.

You can work out what was in a mixture by looking up the $R_f$ value of each solute in a database, or table, of known values.

### Example

**Figure 5 shows the $R_f$ values of five amino acids under the conditions used in the experiment above. Use the table to identify solute X.**

Solute X has an $R_f$ value of 0.26. Glycine also has an $R_f$ value of 0.26, so solute X must be glycine.

| Amino acid | $R_f$ value |
|---|---|
| Glycine | 0.26 |
| Alanine | 0.39 |
| Tyrosine | 0.46 |
| Valine | 0.61 |
| Leucine | 0.74 |

**Figure 5:** $R_f$ values of amino acids.

---

### Practice Question — Application

Q1 A student used paper chromatography to separate out a mixture of three amino acids. The chromatogram that she produced is shown on the right.
   a) Calculate the $R_f$ values of the three solutes, A, B and C.
   b) Use the table in Figure 5 to identify the solutes A, B and C.

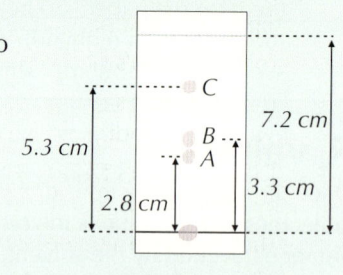

**Tip:** $R_f$ values are always between 0 and 1.

### Practice Questions — Fact Recall

Q1 What is chromatography used for?
Q2 What would be used for the mobile phase in paper chromatography?
Q3 Describe the stationary phase in thin-layer chromatography.
Q4 Give the formula for calculating $R_f$ values.

# Section Summary

Make sure you know...

- That water molecules are polar (they have a slight negative charge on one side and a slight positive charge on the other).
- That a hydrogen bond is a weak bond between a slightly positively-charged hydrogen atom in one molecule and a slightly negatively-charged atom in another molecule.
- The properties of water (high specific heat capacity, high latent heat of evaporation, very cohesive, lower density when solid, good solvent) and how they relate to the functions of water.
- That polymers are big molecules made from large numbers of smaller units called monomers.
- What is meant by a condensation reaction and a hydrolysis reaction, and how each one works.
- The chemical elements that make up carbohydrates, lipids and proteins.
- The molecular structures of the monosaccharides α-glucose and β-glucose, and how they differ.
- The molecular structure of ribose (a pentose monosaccharide) and how it differs from glucose (a hexose monosaccharide).
- That glycosidic bonds are formed between monosaccharides during condensation reactions to form disaccharides (e.g. maltose) and polysaccharides (e.g. amylose), and broken during hydrolysis reactions.
- The structure of starch (amylose and amylopectin), glycogen (long, branched chains of α-glucose) and cellulose (long, unbranched chains of β-glucose held together by hydrogen bonds to form microfibrils), and how their structures and properties are related to their functions.
- The structure of a triglyceride (one molecule of glycerol with three fatty acids) and a phospholipid (one molecule of glycerol, two fatty acids and a phosphate group) as examples of macromolecules.
- That ester bonds are formed between glycerol and fatty acids during condensation reactions (to form triglycerides) and are broken during hydrolysis reactions.
- The general structure of a saturated and an unsaturated fatty acid.
- How the properties of a triglyceride, phospholipid and cholesterol are related to their functions.
- The structure of an amino acid (carboxyl group, amino group and R group).
- That peptide bonds are formed between amino acids during condensation reactions (to form dipeptides and polypeptides) and broken during hydrolysis reactions.
- That a protein's primary structure is the sequence of amino acids, held together by peptide bonds.
- That a protein's secondary structure is an alpha (α) helix or beta (β) pleated sheet, held together by hydrogen bonding between the -NH and -CO groups of amino acids in the chain.
- That a protein's tertiary structure is the further coiling or folding of the polypeptide chain, held together by ionic bonds, disulfide bonds, hydrophobic and hydrophilic interactions, and hydrogen bonds.
- That a protein's quaternary structure is the way in which two or more polypeptide chains are assembled together.
- That haemoglobin (a conjugated protein), insulin and most enzymes (e.g. amylase) are globular proteins and how their structures relate to their functions.
- That collagen, keratin and elastin are fibrous proteins and how their properties relate to their functions.
- The key inorganic ions that are involved in biological processes, including their chemical symbols.
- How to test a substance for the presence of proteins (biuret test), starch (iodine test), lipids (emulsion test) and sugars (Benedict's test and reagent test strips) and interpret the results.
- How to use a colorimeter to determine the concentration of a substance (e.g. glucose) in a solution.
- How biosensors can be used to determine the concentration of a chemical substance (e.g. glucose).
- How to use paper and thin-layer chromatography to separate biological molecules in a solution.
- How to calculate retention ($R_f$) values from a chromatogram using the formula $R_f$ = distance moved by the solute ÷ distance moved by the solvent, and use $R_f$ values to identify molecules in a solution.

# Exam-style Questions

**1**   Photosynthesis is the process by which plants synthesise glucose from carbon dioxide and water using light as an energy source. Glucose is stored as starch in a plant.

**(a)**   A student investigating photosynthesis kept two plants, A and B, under different conditions. They tested a leaf from each plant for the presence of starch, using the iodine test. **Table 1.1** below shows the results of the test. Complete the table to show the observation from the iodine test on each of the leaves.

|        | Observation | Starch present |
|--------|-------------|----------------|
| Leaf A |             | Yes            |
| Leaf B |             | No             |

**Table 1.1**

*(2 marks)*

**(b)**   Amylose is one of the polysaccharides that forms starch.
   **(i)**   Name the other polysaccharide present in starch molecules.

*(1 mark)*

   **(ii)**   Describe the structure of amylose and explain how its structure makes it suited to its function.

*(3 marks)*

**(c)**   Cellulose is also a polysaccharide found in plants.
   **(i)**   Describe **three** ways in which cellulose differs from starch.

*(3 marks)*

**Fig. 1.1** shows a glucose molecule that makes up cellulose.

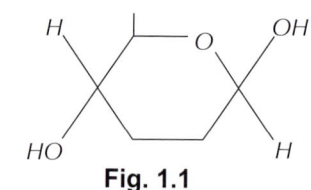

**Fig. 1.1**

   **(ii)**   Draw how two molecules of glucose link together to form part of a cellulose molecule.

*(1 mark)*

   **(iii)**   Describe how a cellulose molecule is broken apart into molecules of glucose.

*(3 marks)*

**2**   The human body contains many different proteins.
Each of these proteins has a primary, secondary and tertiary structure.

**(a)**   Describe the primary structure of a protein.

*(2 marks)*

**(b)** The tertiary structure of a protein is held in place by different types of bonds. Complete the following passage about these bonds.

To form the tertiary structure of a protein, ..................... bonds form between negatively and positively charged R groups on different parts of the polypeptide chain. Whenever two molecules of the amino acid cysteine come close together they can become joined by their sulfur atoms to form ..................... bonds. Weak bonds called ..................... bonds also form between slightly ..................... -charged hydrogen atoms in some R groups and slightly ..................... -charged atoms in other R groups on the polypeptide chain.

*(5 marks)*

**(c)** The biuret test can be used to test for the presence of protein in a urine sample. Describe how this test would be carried out, including what observations would indicate positive and negative results.

*(4 marks)*

**3** Plants use a variety of pigments in their leaves to capture sunlight for photosynthesis. A scientist uses thin-layer chromatography to separate out the photosynthetic pigments from a mixture obtained from plant leaves. **Fig. 3.1** shows the thin-layer chromatogram that he produces.

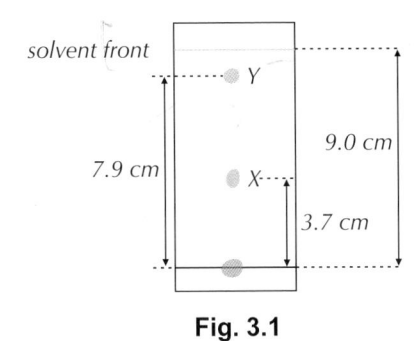

solvent front
Y
9.0 cm
7.9 cm
X
3.7 cm

**Fig. 3.1**

**(a)** Explain why the different pigments separate as they travel up the plate.

*(2 marks)*

**(b)** The equation for calculating $R_f$ values is given below.

$$R_f \text{ value} = \frac{\text{distance travelled by spot}}{\text{distance travelled by solvent}}$$

Calculate the $R_f$ value of **spot X**.

*(1 mark)*

Another scientist repeats the experiment above using the same mixture of pigments but the chromatogram does not give the same $R_f$ values.

**(c)** Suggest **two** possible variations in the method that could have produced these different results.

*(2 marks)*

# Module 2 — Section 3: Nucleotides and Nucleic Acids

**Learning Objectives:**
- Know the structure of a nucleotide as the monomer from which nucleic acids are made.
- Know the differences between DNA and RNA nucleotides, including the type of pentose sugar in each.
- Be able to identify the purines and pyrimidines in DNA and RNA nucleotides.
- Know the structure of ADP and ATP as phosphorylated nucleotides, comprising of a pentose sugar (ribose), a nitrogenous base (adenine) and inorganic phosphates.

**Specification Reference 2.1.3**

**Tip:** The structure of a nucleotide is the same in all living organisms.

**Tip:** Nucleic acids are an essential part of how characteristics are passed on from one generation to another (this is known as heredity).

**Tip:** A polynucleotide is a polymer made up of nucleotide monomers.

## 1. Nucleotides

*DNA and RNA are molecules that are essential for the function of living organisms and they're both made up of nucleotides...*

### Nucleotide structure

A nucleotide is a type of biological molecule. It's made from: a pentose sugar (that's a sugar with 5 carbon atoms), a nitrogenous (nitrogen-containing) base and a phosphate group (see Figure 1). All nucleotides contain the elements C, H, O, N and P.

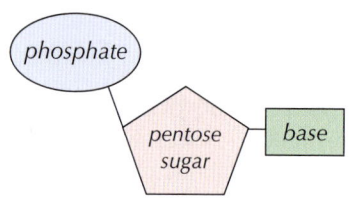

**Figure 1:** A nucleotide.

### Importance of nucleotides

Nucleotides are really important. For a start they're the monomers (see page 62) that make up DNA and RNA. DNA and RNA are both types of nucleic acid. They're found in all living cells. **DNA** is used to store genetic information — the instructions an organism needs to grow and develop. **RNA** is used to make proteins from the instructions in DNA.

There are also special types of nucleotide, such as ADP and ATP (see next page). They're used to store and transport energy in cells.

### DNA nucleotides

The nucleotides in DNA all contain the same pentose sugar called deoxyribose. (DNA stands for deoxyribonucleic acid.) Each DNA nucleotide also has the same phosphate group. The base on each nucleotide can vary though. There are four possible bases — adenine (A), thymine (T), cytosine (C) and guanine (G). Figure 2 shows the structure of a DNA nucleotide.

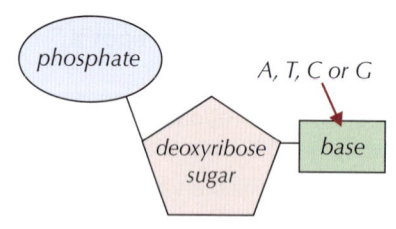

**Figure 2:** A DNA nucleotide.

A molecule of DNA contains two polynucleotide chains — each chain is made up of lots of nucleotides joined together. There's more on how polynucleotides form on page 91.

## RNA nucleotides

RNA (ribonucleic acid) contains nucleotides with a ribose sugar (not deoxyribose). Like DNA, an RNA nucleotide also has a phosphate group and one of four different bases. In RNA though, uracil replaces thymine as a base. An RNA molecule is made up of a single polynucleotide chain. Figure 3 shows the structure of a RNA nucleotide.

**Tip:** Remember, ribose is an example of a pentose sugar.

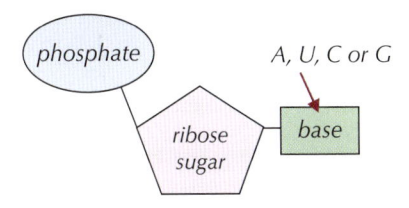

*Figure 3: A RNA nucleotide.*

## Purines and pyrimidines

There are two types of base present in DNA and RNA nucleotides — these are called **purines** and **pyrimidines**. Each of the bases present in DNA or RNA nucleotides can be classed as one of these types. Adenine and guanine are both purines. Cytosine, thymine and uracil are pyrimidines.

The difference between these types of bases is in their structures. A purine base contains two carbon-nitrogen rings joined together, whereas a pyrimidine base only has one carbon-nitrogen ring. So a pyrimidine base is smaller than a purine base (see Figure 4).

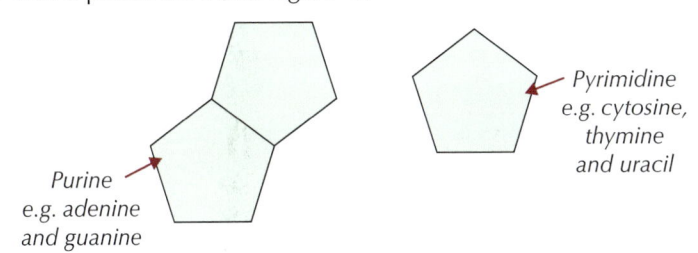

*Figure 4: Basic structures of a purine and a pyrimidine (not to scale).*

**Tip:** You can remember that cytosine and thymine are pyrimidines because of the 'y'.

## ADP and ATP

ADP and ATP are phosphorylated nucleotides. To phosphorylate a nucleotide, you add one or more phosphate groups to it. ADP (adenosine diphosphate) contains the base adenine, the sugar ribose and two phosphate groups (see Figure 5). ATP (adenosine triphosphate) contains the base adenine, the sugar ribose and three phosphate groups (see Figure 6).

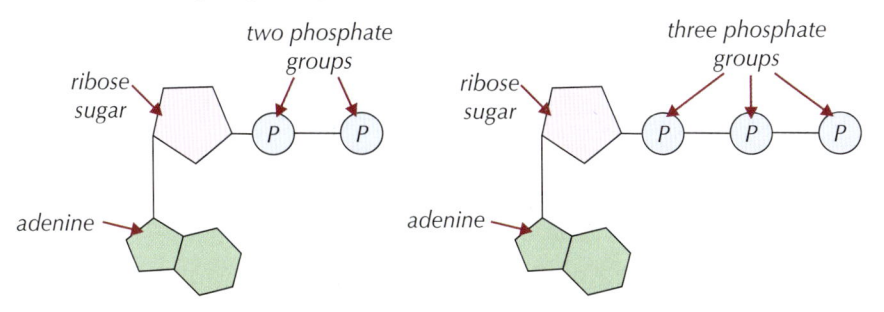

*Figure 5: A molecule of ADP.*

*Figure 6: A molecule of ATP.*

**Tip:** To remember the difference between adenosine diphosphate and adenosine triphosphate just remember 'di' means two and 'tri' means three. So adenosine diphosphate must contain two phosphate groups, and adenosine triphosphate must contain three phosphate groups.

Module 2: Section 3 Nucleotides and Nucleic Acids

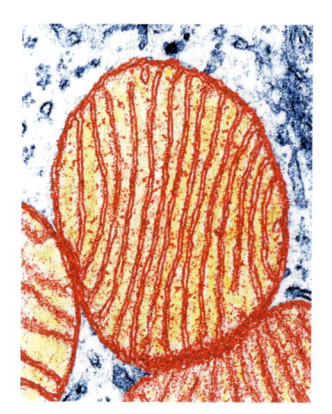

## Making and using ATP

Plant and animal cells release energy from glucose — this process is called respiration. A cell can't get its energy directly from glucose. So, in respiration, the energy released from glucose is used to make ATP and then molecules of ATP provide energy for chemical reactions in the cell.

ATP is synthesised from ADP and inorganic phosphate ($P_i$). The ADP is phosphorylated to form ATP and a phosphate bond is formed (see Figure 8).

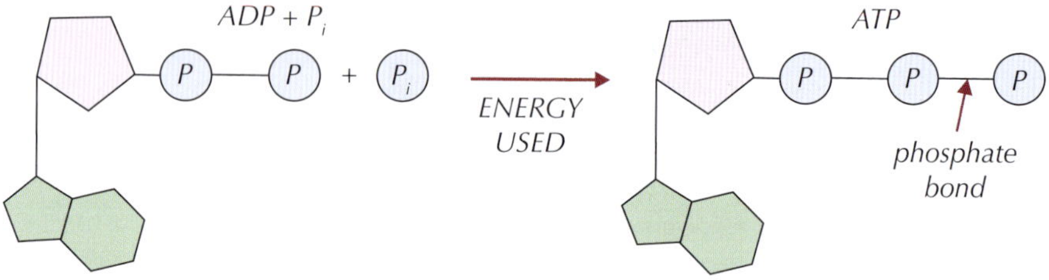

*Figure 7: A transmission electron micrograph showing mitochondria, the site of ATP synthesis in cells.*

*Figure 8: Synthesis of ATP from ADP and $P_i$.*

Energy is stored in the phosphate bond. When this energy is needed by a cell, ATP is broken back down into ADP and inorganic phosphate ($P_i$). Energy is released from the phosphate bond and used by the cell (see Figure 9).

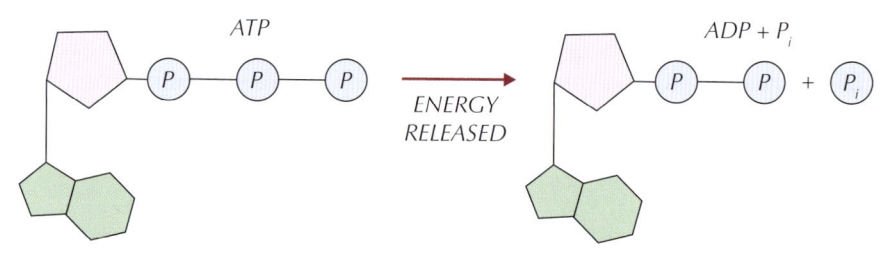

*Figure 9: Breakdown of ATP to form ADP and $P_i$.*

### Practice Questions — Fact Recall

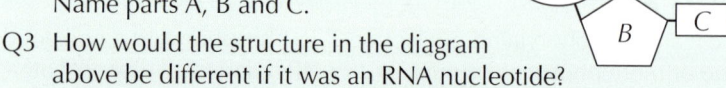

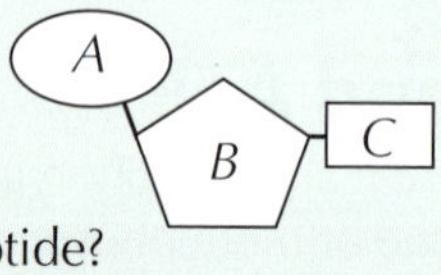

Q1  What is the name for the monomers that make up nucleic acids?
Q2  The diagram shows a DNA nucleotide. Name parts A, B and C.
Q3  How would the structure in the diagram above be different if it was an RNA nucleotide?
Q4  Name the purine bases that can be present in DNA and RNA.
Q5  Name the pyrimidines that can be present in RNA.
Q6  Outline the difference between the structure of a purine and a pyrimidine base.
Q7  What is added to a nucleotide to phosphorylate it?
Q8  Describe the structure of a molecule of ADP.

# 2. Polynucleotides and DNA

*DNA is actually two strings of nucleotides joined together...*

## Polynucleotide structure

Nucleotides join together to form **polynucleotides**. The nucleotides join up between the phosphate group of one nucleotide and the sugar of another via a condensation reaction (see page 62). This forms a **phosphodiester** bond (consisting of the phosphate group and two ester bonds). The chain of sugars and phosphates is known as the sugar-phosphate backbone (see Figure 1). Polynucleotides can be broken down into nucleotides again by breaking the phosphodiester bonds using hydrolysis reactions.

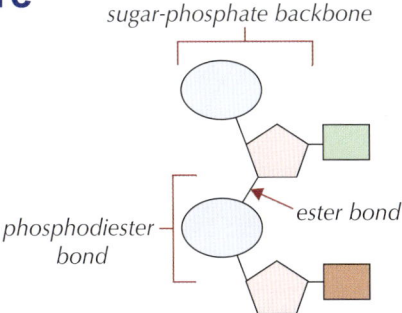

*Figure 1: Structure of a single polynucleotide strand.*

## DNA structure

DNA is composed of two polynucleotide strands joined together to form a double-helix shape. The two strands join together by hydrogen bonding between the bases. Each base can only join with one particular partner — this is called complementary base pairing. Adenine always pairs with thymine (A - T) and guanine always pairs with cytosine (G - C) — see Figure 2. This means that a purine (A or G) always pairs with a pyrimidine (T or C). Two hydrogen bonds form between A and T, and three hydrogen bonds form between C and G.

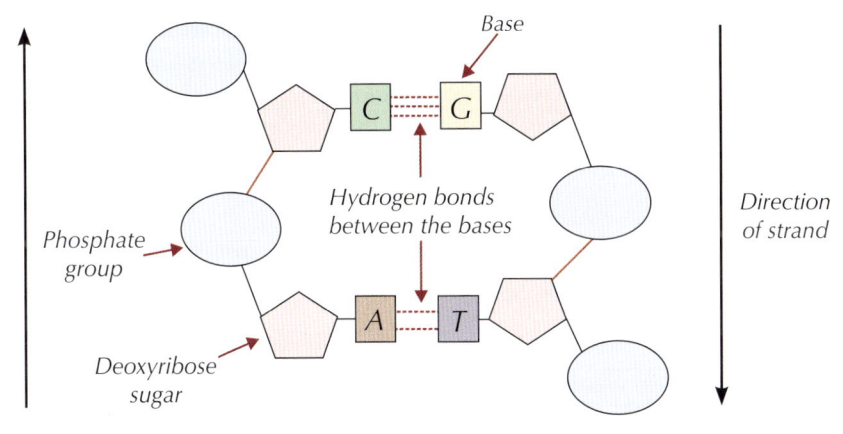

*Figure 2: Complementary base pairing in DNA molecules.*

The two polynucleotide strands are antiparallel — this means they run in opposite directions. Two antiparallel strands twist to form a DNA double-helix. Overall, the structure of a DNA molecule looks like the one in Figure 4 on the next page.

**Learning Objectives:**
- Understand the synthesis and breakdown of polynucleotides by the formation and breakage of phosphodiester bonds.
- Know the structure of DNA (deoxyribonucleic acid) including how hydrogen bonding between complementary base pairs (A to T, G to C) on two antiparallel DNA polynucleotides leads to the formation of a DNA molecule, and how the twisting of DNA produces its 'double-helix' shape.
- Be able to carry out practical investigations into the purification of DNA by precipitation (PAG9).

**Specification Reference 2.1.3**

**Tip:** If you're struggling to remember which base pairs with which, just think — you eat **A**pple **T**urnover with **G**loopy **C**ustard.

**Tip:** The two ends of a polynucleotide strand are different — one end has a phosphate group and the other has a hydroxyl (OH) group attached to the sugar. That's how you can tell which direction a strand is running in.

Module 2: Section 3 Nucleotides and Nucleic Acids

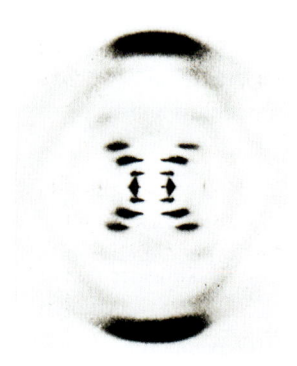

*Figure 3: X-ray diffraction picture of DNA. The cross of bands shows that the molecule is a helix.*

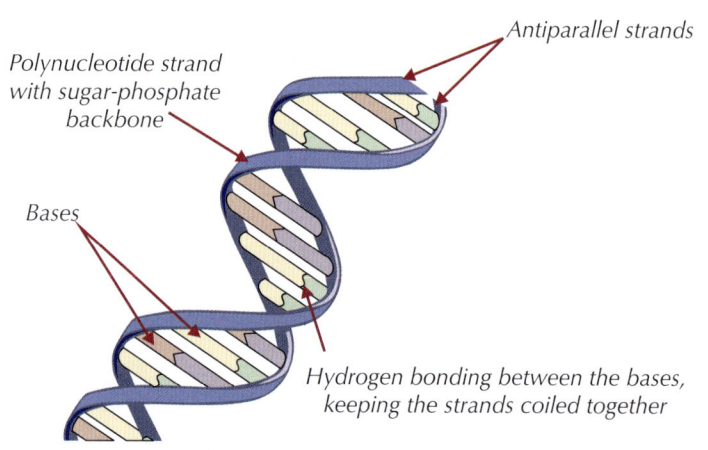

*Figure 4: The DNA double-helix.*

You can use computer modelling to investigate the structure of DNA and other nucleic acids. For example, the computer software RasMol can be used to produce graphical representations of molecules.

## Purifying DNA

**PRACTICAL ACTIVITY GROUP 9**

Scientists often need to extract a pure DNA sample from cells in order to analyse it, e.g. for use in forensics. DNA can be purified using a precipitation reaction. You need to know how to purify DNA by precipitation, so here's how to do it:

1. Break up the cells in your sample (e.g. some onion or tomato). You can do this using a blender for about 10 seconds.
2. Make up a solution of detergent (a dilute washing-up liquid will do), salt (sodium chloride) and distilled water.
3. Add the broken-up cells to a beaker containing the detergent solution — Figure 5.
4. Incubate the beaker in a water bath at 60 °C for 15 minutes (see Figure 5). Whilst in the water bath, the detergent in the mixture breaks down the cell membranes. The salt binds to the DNA and causes it to clump together. The temperature of the water bath should be high enough to stop enzymes in the cells from working properly and breaking down the DNA.
5. Once incubated, put your beaker in an ice bath to cool the mixture down (see Figure 5).

**Tip:** Remember to do a risk assessment before carrying out this experiment. For example, enzymes (see p. 105) can irritate the skin and may cause an allergic reaction so they need to be handled with care.

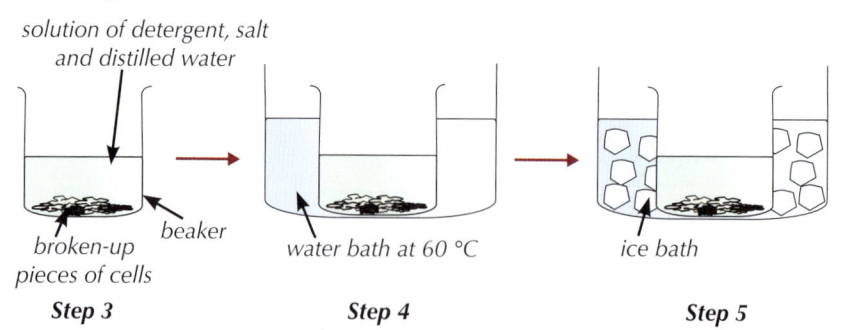

*Figure 5: Steps 3-5 in DNA purification.*

6. When it's cooled, filter the mixture using coffee filter paper (or gauze) and a funnel. Transfer a sample of your filtered mixture to a clean boiling tube and discard the contents of the filter paper.

Module 2: Section 3  Nucleotides and Nucleic Acids

7. Add protease enzymes to the filtered mixture. These will break down some proteins in the mixture, e.g. proteins bound to the DNA.
8. Slowly dribble some cold ethanol down the side of the tube, so that it forms a layer on top of the DNA-detergent mixture (see Figure 6).
9. If you leave the tube for a few minutes, the DNA will form a white precipitate (solid) (see Figure 6 and Figure 7), which you can remove from the tube using a glass rod (or a hooked instrument like a bent paper clip).

**Tip:** See pages 105-120 for more about enzymes.

**Tip:** You could also add RNase enzymes to the mixture to breakdown any RNA present. This would have to be added before the protease though to prevent the RNase (a protein) being destroyed by the protease.

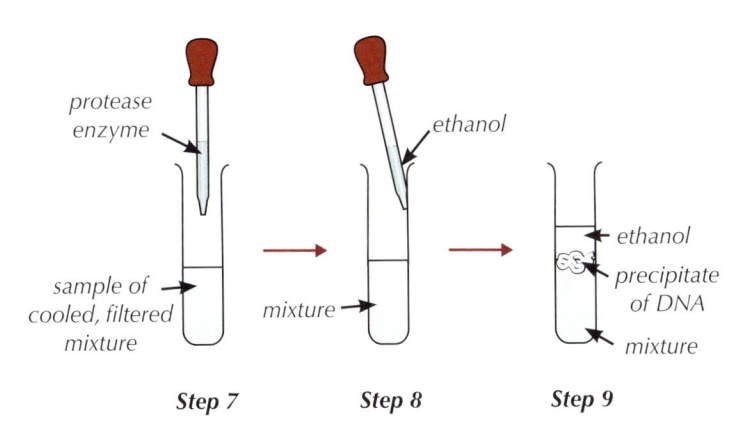

**Figure 6:** Steps 7-9 in DNA purification.

**Figure 7:** White precipitate of DNA formed after addition of ethanol during DNA purification.

## Practice Questions — Application

Q1 Here are the base sequences of two short stretches of DNA. For each one, write down the sequence of bases they would pair up with:
   a) ACTGTCGTAGTCGATGCTA
   b) TGCACCATGTGGTAAATCG

Q2 In a DNA purification experiment, some onion cells are broken up and then mixed together with salt, diluted washing-up liquid and distilled water. The mixture is then placed in a water bath at 30 °C for 15 minutes. Suggest what affect using this temperature might have on the result of the experiment.

Q3 Scientists analysed a section of double stranded DNA. There were 68 bases in total (34 base pairs) and 22 of the bases were adenine. How many of the bases were:
   a) thymine?   b) cytosine?   c) guanine?

## Practice Questions — Fact Recall

Q1 a) What type of bonds join nucleotides together in a polynucleotide?
   b) Which parts of the nucleotides are joined by these bonds?

Q2 Describe how a DNA double-helix is formed from two polynucleotide strands.

Q3 Describe how you could purify DNA from a sample of cells using a precipitation reaction.

**Exam Tip**
Questions on the structure of DNA are easy marks in the exam and they come up a lot. Make sure you know the structure inside out.

Module 2: Section 3 Nucleotides and Nucleic Acids

**Learning Objectives:**
- Understand semi-conservative DNA replication, including the roles of the enzymes helicase and DNA polymerase.
- Know the importance of replication in conserving genetic information with accuracy.
- Understand that random, spontaneous mutations can occur during replication.

**Specification Reference 2.1.3**

# 3. DNA replication

*DNA is able to replicate itself and does so regularly when cells are dividing.*

## Why does DNA replicate?

DNA copies itself before cell division (see p. 147) so that each new cell has the full amount of DNA. This is important for making new cells and for passing genetic information from generation to generation (see p. 147-154).

## How is DNA replicated?

A DNA molecule has a paired base structure (see page 91), which makes it easy for DNA to copy itself. Here's how it works:

**1** **DNA helicase** (an enzyme) breaks the hydrogen bonds between the two polynucleotide DNA strands. The helix unzips to form two single strands.

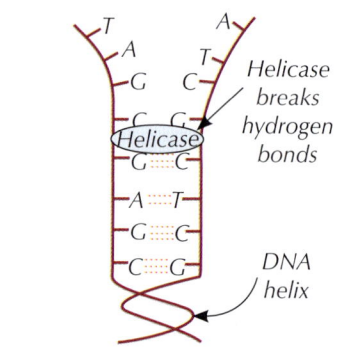

**2** Each original single strand acts as a template for a new strand. Free-floating DNA nucleotides join to the exposed bases on each original template strand by complementary base pairing — A with T and G with C.

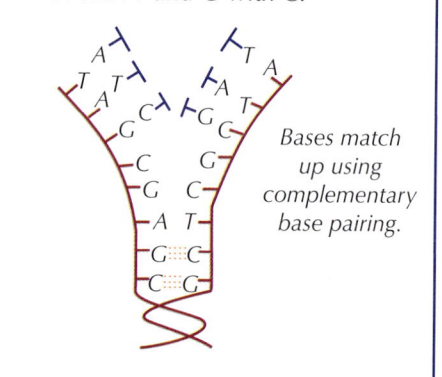

**3** The nucleotides on the new strand are joined together by the enzyme **DNA polymerase**. This forms the sugar-phosphate backbone. Hydrogen bonds form between the bases on the original and new strand.

The strands twist to form a double-helix. Each new DNA molecule contains one strand from the original DNA molecule and one new strand.

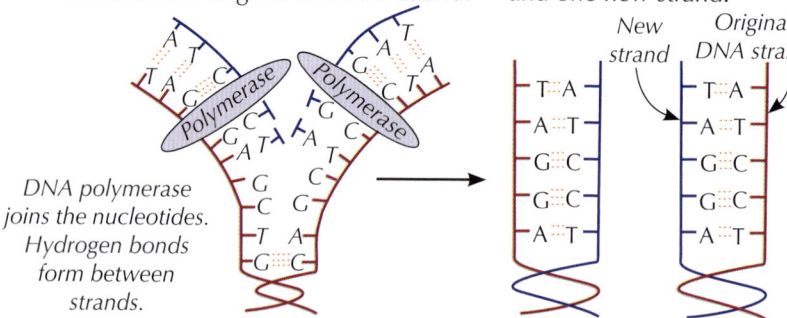

This type of copying is called **semi-conservative replication** because half of the strands in each new DNA molecule are from the original piece of DNA (i.e. the new molecule contains one old strand and one new strand).

**Tip:** Phosphodiester bonds form between the DNA nucleotides on the new strand (see page 91).

**Exam Tip**
If you're asked to describe the process of semi-conservative replication in the exam, you need to make sure you do it in the <u>correct order</u> or you won't get all the marks. Get the sequence clear in your head now.

Module 2: Section 3  Nucleotides and Nucleic Acids

# Accuracy of DNA replication

DNA replication is really accurate — it has to be, to make sure genetic information is conserved (stays the same) each time the DNA in a cell is replicated. Every so often though, a random, spontaneous mutation occurs. A mutation is any change to the DNA base sequence. Mutations don't always have an effect, but they can alter the sequence of amino acids in a protein. This can cause an abnormal protein to be produced. The abnormal protein might function better than the normal protein — or it might not work at all.

## Practice Question — Application

Q1 The evidence that DNA replicated semi-conservatively came from an experiment carried out by Meselson and Stahl. Their experiment used two isotopes of nitrogen — heavy nitrogen ($^{15}$N) and light nitrogen ($^{14}$N).

Two samples of bacteria were grown — one in a nutrient broth containing light nitrogen, and one in a broth with heavy nitrogen. As the bacteria reproduced, they took up nitrogen from the broth to help make new DNA. The bacteria that had been grown in the heavy nitrogen broth were then grown in a light nitrogen broth and left for one round of DNA replication.

At each stage of the experiment, the composition of the bacterial DNA was analysed. The results are shown in the table below.

|  | Bacteria grown in light nitrogen broth only | Bacteria grown in heavy nitrogen broth only | Bacteria grown in heavy nitrogen broth, then in light nitrogen broth |
|---|---|---|---|
| % of heavy nitrogen in one DNA molecule | 0 | 100 | 50 |
| % of light nitrogen in one DNA molecule | 100 | 0 | 50 |

a) DNA is copied by semi-conservative replication. Explain how the results shown in the table above provide evidence that DNA replicates semi-conservatively.

b) Scientists predicted that DNA could replicate semi-conservatively because of the paired base structure of a double-stranded DNA molecule. Explain how a paired base structure helps DNA to replicate semi-conservatively.

c) Suggest one way in which Meselson and Stahl may have made sure that their results were valid.

**Tip:** See page 5 for more about valid results.

## Practice Questions — Fact Recall

Q1 Which bonds need to break in a DNA molecule before replication can begin?

Q2 Describe the role of DNA polymerase in DNA replication.

Q3 Why is it important that DNA replication is accurate?

Q4 Mutations can occur during DNA replication. What is a mutation?

## Learning Objectives:

- Understand how a gene determines the sequence of amino acids in a polypeptide (the primary structure of a protein).
- Know the roles of messenger RNA (mRNA), transfer RNA (tRNA) and ribosomal RNA (rRNA).
- Understand the nature of the genetic code, including the triplet, non-overlapping degenerate and universal nature of the code.

**Specification Reference 2.1.3**

**Tip:** A triplet is a sequence of three bases as shown below.

bases on DNA
A T C T C A
DNA triplet

**Tip:** For more about ribosomes, see page 40.

**Tip:** There's more about transcription and translation on pages 99-101.

**Tip:** mRNA is copied from DNA — so its sequence is complementary to the DNA sequence. See page 99 for more.

# 4. Genes and Protein Synthesis

*DNA and RNA have starring roles in protein synthesis. Here's why...*

## Genes

DNA contains genes. A **gene** is a sequence of DNA nucleotides that codes for a polypeptide. The sequence of amino acids in a polypeptide forms the primary structure of a protein (see page 70).

Different proteins have a different number and order of amino acids. It's the order of nucleotide bases in a gene that determines the order of amino acids in a particular protein. Each amino acid is coded for by a sequence of three bases (called a **triplet**) in a gene. Different sequences of bases code for different amino acids. This is the genetic code — see next page for more. So the sequence of bases in a section of DNA is a template that's used to make proteins during protein synthesis.

## DNA, RNA and protein synthesis

DNA molecules are found in the nucleus of the cell, but the organelles that make proteins (ribosomes) are found in the cytoplasm. DNA is too large to move out of the nucleus, so a section is copied into mRNA (see Figure 1). This process is called **transcription**. The mRNA leaves the nucleus and joins with a ribosome in the cytoplasm, where it can be used to synthesise a protein. This process is called **translation**. Figure 1 summarises this.

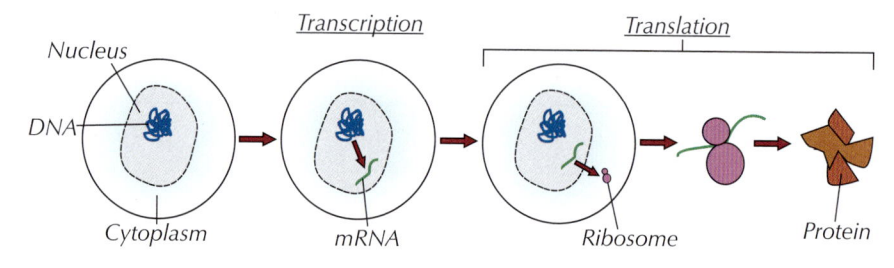

**Figure 1:** Making a protein from DNA.

## RNA

Remember, RNA is a single polynucleotide strand and it contains uracil (U) as a base instead of thymine (see page 89). Uracil always pairs with adenine during protein synthesis. RNA isn't all the same though. You need to know about:

### Messenger RNA (mRNA)

mRNA is a single polynucleotide strand (see Figure 2). It's made in the nucleus during transcription. mRNA carries the genetic code from the DNA in the nucleus to the cytoplasm, where it's used to make a protein during translation. In mRNA, groups of three adjacent bases are usually called **codons**.

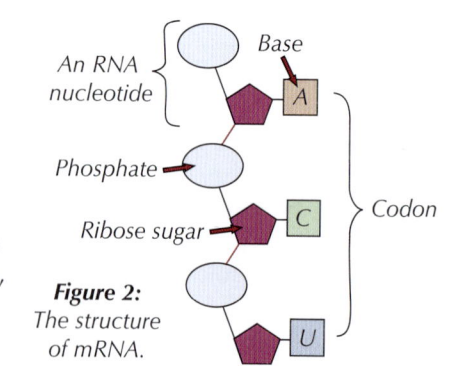

**Figure 2:** The structure of mRNA.

Module 2: Section 3 Nucleotides and Nucleic Acids

### Transfer RNA (tRNA)
tRNA is a single polynucleotide strand that's folded into a clover shape (see Figure 3). Hydrogen bonds between specific base pairs hold the molecule in this shape. Every tRNA molecule has a specific sequence of three bases at one end called an **anticodon**. They also have an amino acid binding site at the other end. tRNA is found in the cytoplasm where it's involved in translation. It carries the amino acids that are used to make proteins to the ribosomes.

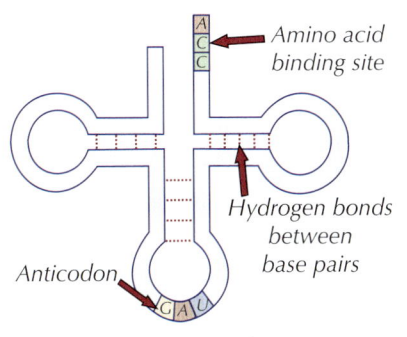

*Figure 3:* The structure of tRNA.

**Tip:** Transfer RNA is so called because it transfers amino acids to the ribosomes. There's more about this on pages 100-101.

**Tip:** Codons and anticodons are sometimes referred to as triplets.

### Ribosomal RNA (rRNA)
rRNA forms the two subunits in a ribosome, along with proteins (see Figure 4). The ribosome moves along the mRNA strand during protein synthesis. The rRNA in the ribosome helps to catalyse the formation of peptide bonds between the amino acids.

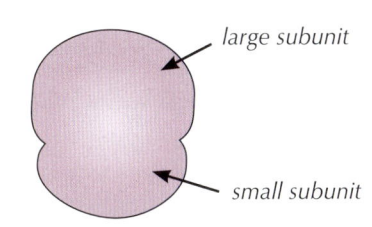

*Figure 4:* The structure of a ribosome.

**Tip:** Amino acids in a polypeptide are joined together by peptide bonds — see p. 69.

## The genetic code
The genetic code is the sequence of base triplets (codons) in DNA or mRNA, which codes for specific amino acids. In the genetic code, each base triplet is read in sequence, separate from the triplet before it and after it. Base triplets don't share their bases — the code is **non-overlapping**.

#### Examples

Order of bases on mRNA
G U C U C A U C A
Base triplet (codon)   Code read in sequence

| mRNA base triplet | Amino acid |
|---|---|
| GUC | valine |
| UCA | serine |

Order of amino acids in a protein: valine — serine — serine

Order of bases on mRNA
C U A U A C C A U
Code read in sequence

| mRNA base triplet | Amino acid |
|---|---|
| CUA | leucine |
| UAC | tyrosine |
| CAU | histidine |

Order of amino acids in a protein: leucine — tyrosine — histidine

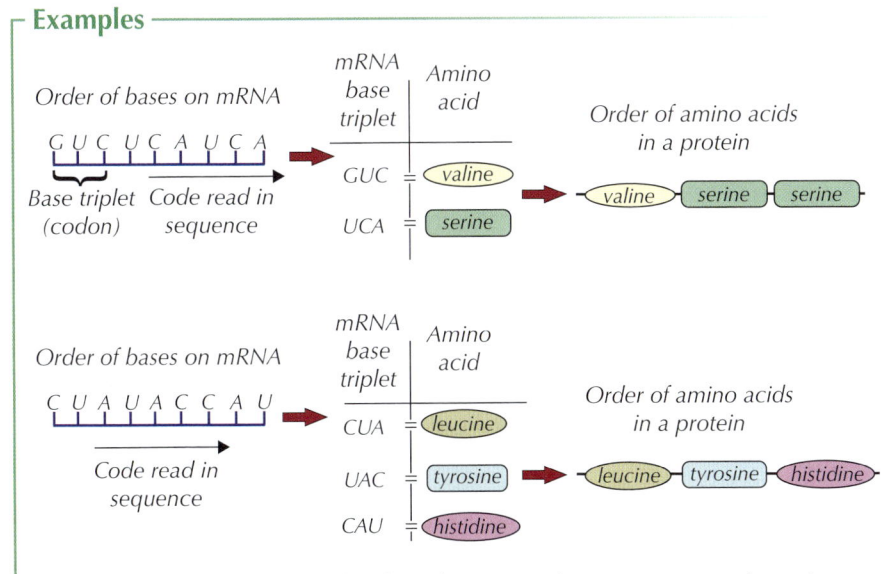

*Figure 5:* Examples to explain how the non-overlapping genetic code works.

**Exam Tip**
You'll be pleased to know you don't need to learn which base sequences code for which amino acids — all the information you need to answer any questions will be given to you in the exam.

**Tip:** Start and stop signals are also called start and stop codons.

The genetic code is also **degenerate** — there are more possible combinations of triplets than there are amino acids (20 amino acids but 64 possible triplets). This means that some amino acids are coded for by more than one base triplet, e.g. tyrosine can be coded for by UAU or UAC. Not all triplets code for amino acids though. For example, some triplets are used to tell the cell when to stop production of a protein — these are called stop signals. They're found at the end of the mRNA. E.g. UAG is a stop signal. (There are also start signals at the start of the mRNA which tell the cell when to start protein production, but these code for a specific amino acid called methionine.)

The genetic code is also **universal** — the same specific base triplets code for the same amino acids in all living things. E.g. UAU codes for tyrosine in all organisms.

### Practice Questions — Application

Q1 How many amino acids do the following mRNA sequences code for?
 a) GAUGGUUAUGACC
 b) UAUUGCGACCACAGAGAC
 c) ACGGACCAUAGGAGGUACUAUUGCGAUCA

The table below shows six amino acids and some of the codons that code for them:

| Amino acid: | His | Arg | Gly | Tyr | Cys | Asp |
|---|---|---|---|---|---|---|
| mRNA codon: | CAU/ CAC | AGA/ AGG | GGC/ GGU | UAC/ UAU | UGC/ UGU | GAC/ GAU |

**Exam Tip**
You won't always get information about mRNA codons and amino acids presented in a table like this in the exam, e.g. it could be in the form of a graph or diagram. Don't let that throw you though. The trick is to read the question carefully, then apply what you know.

Q2 Use the table to determine the amino acid sequence coded for by the following mRNA sequences:
 a) CAUUACUACAGAGGCUGCCAUAGAGGC
 b) AGGUACGACGACUGUCACGGUUAUCAC

Q3 Use the table to determine a mRNA sequence that could code for the following amino acid sequence:
 Asp - Tyr - Cys - Arg - Arg - Gly - Cys - Gly - Tyr - His - Gly - Asp

### Practice Questions — Fact Recall

Q1 What is the genetic code?
Q2 Name the molecule responsible for:
 a) carrying the genetic code from the nucleus to the cytoplasm.
 b) carrying the amino acids used to make proteins to the ribosomes.
Q3 What is the role of rRNA in the ribosome?
Q4 a) What is an mRNA codon?
 b) Describe the function of mRNA codons.
 c) What is another name for an mRNA codon?
Q5 Explain why the genetic code is thought of as:
 a) non-overlapping,
 b) universal.

# 5. Transcription and Translation

*Proteins are synthesised (made) using the instructions in DNA. Protein synthesis involves two main stages: transcription and translation.*

## Transcription

Transcription is the first stage of protein synthesis. During transcription an mRNA copy of a gene (a section of DNA) is made in the nucleus. Here's how:

### 1. RNA polymerase attaches to the DNA

Transcription starts when **RNA polymerase** (an enzyme) attaches to the DNA double-helix at the beginning of a gene.
The hydrogen bonds between the two DNA strands in the gene break, separating the strands, and the DNA molecule uncoils at that point. One of the strands is then used as a template to make an mRNA copy — see Figure 1.

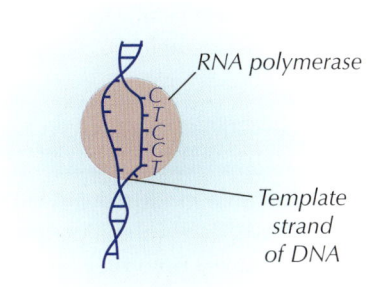

*Figure 1: RNA polymerase attaches to the DNA double-helix.*

### 2. Complementary mRNA is formed

The RNA polymerase lines up free RNA nucleotides alongside the template strand. Complementary base pairing means that the mRNA strand ends up being a complementary copy of the DNA template strand (except the base T is replaced by U in RNA). Once the RNA nucleotides have paired up with their specific bases on the DNA strand, they're joined together by RNA polymerase, forming an mRNA strand — see Figure 2.

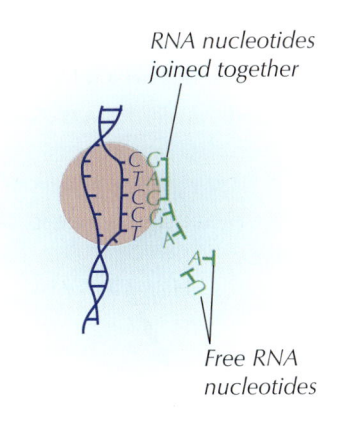

*Figure 2: A complementary mRNA strand starts to form.*

### 3. RNA polymerase moves down the DNA strand

The RNA polymerase moves along the DNA, assembling the mRNA strand. The hydrogen bonds between the uncoiled strands of DNA re-form once the RNA polymerase has passed by and the strands coil back into a double-helix — see Figure 3.

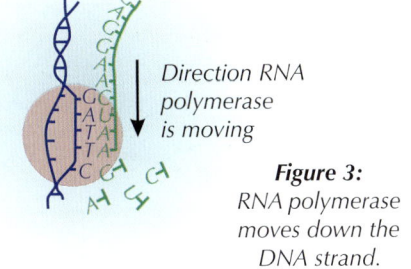

*Figure 3: RNA polymerase moves down the DNA strand.*

---

**Learning Objectives:**
- Understand the transcription and translation of genes resulting in the synthesis of polypeptides, including the role of RNA polymerase.

**Specification Reference 2.1.3**

**Tip:** In prokaryotes, the DNA strands are separated by RNA polymerase. In eukaryotes, the strands are separated by a complex of proteins including DNA helicase.

**Tip:** Free RNA nucleotides aren't bound to anything in the nucleus — they're just floating freely.

**Tip:** The DNA template strand is also called the antisense strand.

**Tip:** Here's an example of complementary base pairing:

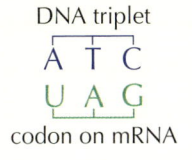

DNA triplet
A T C
U A G
codon on mRNA

**Tip:** It's easy to remember that RNA polymerase is involved in the making of mRNA. Don't confuse it with DNA polymerase, which is involved in the making of DNA (see page 94).

Module 2: Section 3  Nucleotides and Nucleic Acids   99

### 4. mRNA leaves the nucleus

When RNA polymerase reaches a stop codon, it stops making mRNA and detaches from the DNA. The mRNA moves out of the nucleus through a nuclear pore and attaches to a ribosome in the cytoplasm, where the next stage of protein synthesis takes place (see below).

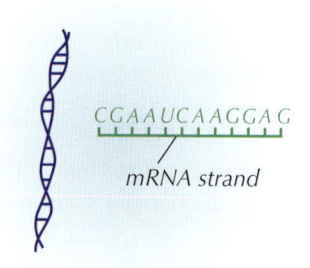

CGAAUCAAGGAG
mRNA strand

*Figure 4:* mRNA detaches from the DNA.

## Practice Question — Application

**Q1** α–amanitin is a deadly toxin produced by some mushrooms. It works by inhibiting RNA polymerase. What effect will this have on protein synthesis? Explain your answer.

# Translation

Translation is the second stage of protein synthesis. It takes place at the ribosomes in the cytoplasm. During translation, amino acids are joined together by a ribosome to make a polypeptide chain (protein), following the sequence of codons carried by the mRNA. Here's how it works:

The mRNA attaches itself to a ribosome and transfer RNA (tRNA) molecules carry amino acids to the ribosome.

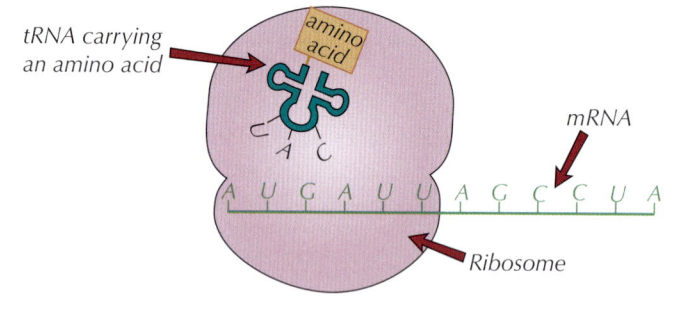

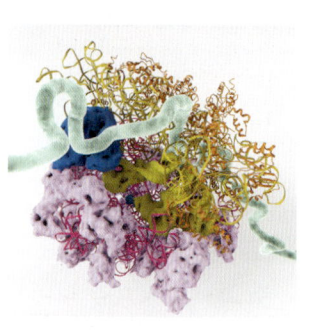

**Tip:** See pages 96-97 for more on the structures of mRNA and tRNA.

*Figure 5:* mRNA (turquoise) attached to a bacterial ribosome.

tRNA carrying an amino acid
mRNA
Ribosome

A tRNA molecule, with an anticodon that's complementary to the start codon on the mRNA, attaches itself to the mRNA by complementary base pairing. A second tRNA molecule attaches itself to the next codon on the mRNA in the same way.

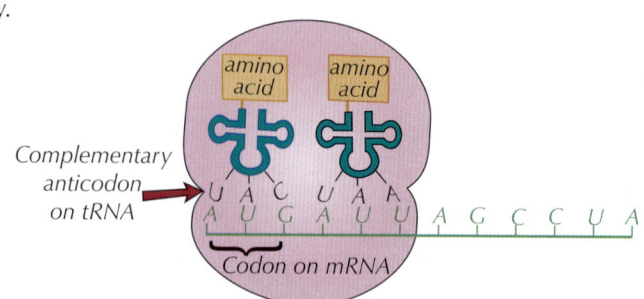

**Tip:** Here's an example of a tRNA anticodon complementary to a start codon on mRNA:

tRNA anticodon
U A C
A U G
codon on mRNA

Complementary anticodon on tRNA
Codon on mRNA

Ribosomal RNA (rRNA) in the ribosome catalyses the formation of a peptide bond between the two amino acids attached to the tRNA molecules. This joins the amino acids together. The first tRNA molecule moves away, leaving its amino acid behind.

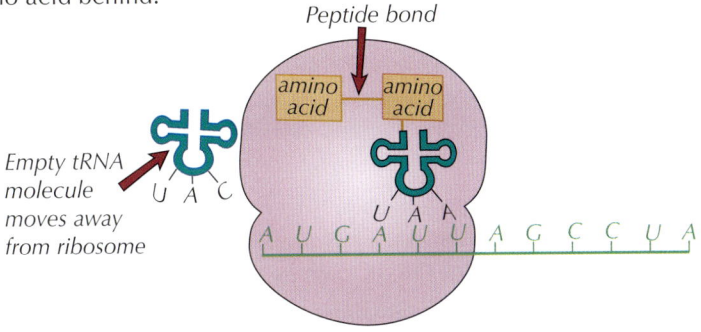

*Peptide bond*

*Empty tRNA molecule moves away from ribosome*

**Tip:** Once the amino acids are lined up in the correct order, the ribosome joins them together.

**Tip:** Ribosomes are actually complexes made up of rRNA (ribosomal RNA) and loads of different proteins. See page 97 for more about rRNA.

A third tRNA molecule binds to the next codon on the mRNA. Its amino acid binds to the first two and the second tRNA molecule moves away. This process continues, producing a chain of linked amino acids (a polypeptide chain), until there's a **stop codon** on the mRNA molecule.

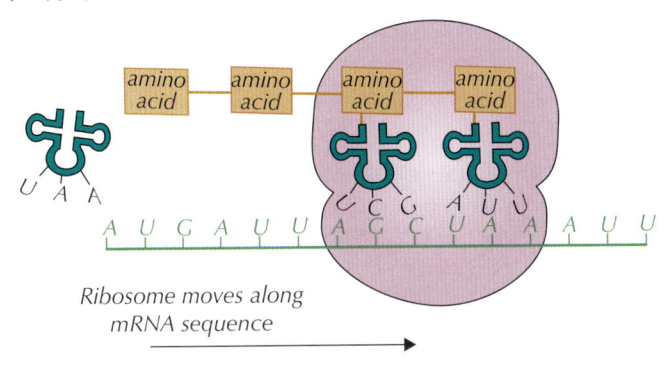

*Ribosome moves along mRNA sequence*

**Tip:** Protein synthesis happens this way in all eukaryotic cells (e.g. plants, animals and fungi). It's a bit different in prokaryotes (e.g. bacteria).

The polypeptide chain (protein) then moves away from the ribosome and translation is complete.

*Polypeptide chain*

**Tip:** Protein synthesis is also called polypeptide synthesis as it makes a polypeptide (protein).

## Practice Questions — Application

Q1 Diamond-Blackfan anaemia is an inherited condition caused by one of several gene mutations. The mutations can affect the function of the proteins that make up ribosomes. What effect could this have on protein synthesis? Explain your answer.

Q2 An error occurs during transcription that accidentally inserts a stop codon into the middle of an mRNA sequence. What effect could this have on the protein that is eventually produced? Explain your answer.

**Tip:** A mutation is any change to the DNA base sequence. See page 95 for more.

## Practice Questions — Fact Recall

Q1 What is produced during transcription?
Q2 What is RNA polymerase? Describe its role in protein synthesis.
Q3 What happens to the uncoiled strands of DNA once RNA polymerase has passed along them during transcription?

Module 2: Section 3 Nucleotides and Nucleic Acids

Q4 a) Explain how tRNA molecules pair up with mRNA.
   b) During which stage of protein synthesis does this happen?
   c) What feature on the mRNA strand results in the termination of protein synthesis?

## Section Summary

Make sure you know...

- That nucleotides are made up of a pentose sugar, a nitrogenous (nitrogen-containing) base (adenine, cytosine, guanine, thymine or uracil) and a phosphate group.
- That nucleotides are the monomers that make up nucleic acids, such as DNA and RNA.
- The differences between DNA and RNA nucleotides, including bases (RNA contains uracil instead of thymine) and type of pentose sugar (RNA contains ribose instead of deoxyribose).
- That there are two types of nitrogenous base in nucleotides, pyrimidines (cytosine, thymine and uracil) and purines (guanine and adenine), which have different structures.
- That ADP and ATP are both phosphorylated nucleotides made up of the base adenine and the sugar ribose, but that ADP contains two phosphate groups, while ATP contains three phosphate groups.
- That polynucleotides (polymers made up of nucleotides) are made by the formation of phosphodiester bonds, and are broken up by the breakage of these bonds.
- That DNA is made up of two antiparallel polynucleotide strands with hydrogen bonds between complementary base pairs (A and T, G and C).
- That the two antiparallel DNA strands twist together forming a double-helix.
- How to carry out an experiment to purify DNA using a precipitation reaction.
- Understand how semi-conservative DNA replication works and the roles that the enzymes DNA helicase and DNA polymerase play in this process.
- That the process of DNA replication is very accurate and that this is important for the conservation of genetic information.
- That random, spontaneous mutations can occur in DNA replication that alter DNA's base sequence.
- That a gene is a sequence of DNA nucleotides and how this sequence determines the order of amino acids in a polypeptide (which is a protein's primary structure).
- That each amino acid is coded for by a sequence of three bases called a triplet.
- That mRNA molecules carry the genetic code from the DNA in the nucleus to the cytoplasm, where it's used to make a protein during translation.
- That tRNA molecules carry amino acids to the ribosomes during translation.
- That rRNA in ribosomes catalyses the formation of peptide bonds between the amino acids.
- That the genetic code is the sequence of base triplets (codons) in DNA or mRNA which codes for specific amino acids.
- That the genetic code is non-overlapping (triplets don't share bases), degenerate (there are more possible combinations of triplets than there are amino acids) and universal (the same base triplets code for the same amino acids in all living things).
- That polypeptide (protein) synthesis involves the transcription and translation of genes.
- That transcription is the first stage of protein synthesis and involves the production of an mRNA copy of a gene in the nucleus.
- That during transcription the enzyme RNA polymerase attaches to the DNA double helix and the two DNA strands separate. RNA polymerase then lines up free RNA nucleotides alongside the DNA template strand and assembles the mRNA strand.
- That translation is the second stage of protein synthesis in which amino acids are joined together by ribosomes to make a polypeptide strand (protein) based on the order of codons in mRNA.

# Exam-style Questions

**1** Which of the following statements about semi-conservative replication is/are correct?

**Statement 1:** DNA helicase breaks hydrogen bonds between the two polynucleotide DNA strands.

**Statement 2:** DNA polymerase attaches to the original template strand by complementary base pairing.

**Statement 3:** Free-floating RNA nucleotides join to the exposed bases on each original template strand.

- **A** 1, 2 and 3
- **B** Only 1 and 2
- **C** Only 2 and 3
- **D** Only 1

*(1 mark)*

**2** Which of these statements correctly describes the components of a molecule of ATP?

- **A** Ribose, adenine and three phosphate groups.
- **B** Deoxyribose, thymine and three phosphate groups.
- **C** Deoxyribose, adenine and two phosphate groups.
- **D** Ribose, thymine and two phosphate groups.

*(1 mark)*

**3** Researchers have been studying a genetic disease with the aim of developing a treatment for it. The genetic disease is caused by the production of a specific enzyme.

**(a)** Part of the DNA sequence for the enzyme is shown in **Fig. 1.1**.

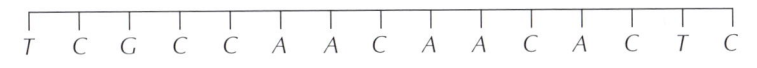

T C G C C A A C A A C A C T C

**Fig. 1.1**

State the complementary mRNA sequence to the sequence shown in **Fig. 1.1** **and** how many amino acids this DNA sequence would code for. (Assume there are no start or stop codons present).

*(2 marks)*

**(b)** The researchers are exploring a possible treatment for the genetic disease that would involve disrupting the process of translation.

**(i)** Name the organelle that mRNA attaches to during translation.

*(1 mark)*

**(ii)\*** Once mRNA has attached to this organelle, translation begins. Describe the process of translation from this point, including the roles of rRNA and tRNA.

*(6 marks)*

*The quality of your response will be assessed in this question.

**4 (a)** DNA is a polynucleotide.
State the **three** components that make up a DNA nucleotide.

*(3 marks)*

**(b) (i)** Urea is a weak alkali. Adding urea to a solution of double-stranded DNA will severely disrupt the hydrogen bonding in the DNA.
Explain what effect this will have on the structure of the DNA.

*(2 marks)*

**(ii)** Depurination of DNA results in the loss of purine bases.
Name the **two** DNA bases that would be lost during depurination.

*(2 marks)*

**(c) (i)** Use the most appropriate terms to complete the passage on DNA replication below.

Hydrogen bonds between the two polynucleotide strands break and the DNA double-helix ……………… to form two separate strands. Each original strand acts as a ……………… for the new strand. Free-floating DNA nucleotides join on to the exposed bases by ……………… base pairing — for example, thymine pairs with ……………… . The nucleotides on the new strands are then joined together by the enzyme ……………… ……………… and bonds form between the new and original strands.

*(5 marks)*

**(ii)** What is the name given to the method by which DNA replicates itself?

*(1 mark)*


**5** mRNA and DNA both play important roles in protein synthesis.
**(a)** Give **three** ways in which the structure of mRNA is different to the structure of DNA.

*(3 marks)*

**(b)** Describe the role of mRNA in protein synthesis.

*(2 marks)*

**(c)** DNA contains genes.
**(i)** Give the definition of a **gene**.

*(1 mark)*

**(ii)** Suggest how random, spontaneous mutations in a gene during DNA replication could affect the protein produced.

*(3 marks)*

**(d)** DNA carries the genetic code.
Explain why this code is described as being degenerate.

*(1 mark)*

Module 2: Section 3  Nucleotides and Nucleic Acids

# Module 2 Section 4: Enzymes

## 1. Action of Enzymes

*Enzymes are proteins that speed up the rate of chemical reactions. Without enzymes, bodily processes such as digestion would not happen.*

### Enzymes as biological catalysts

Enzymes speed up chemical reactions by acting as biological catalysts. A catalyst is a substance that speeds up a chemical reaction without being used up in the reaction itself — biological catalysts are those found in living organisms. They catalyse metabolic reactions — both at a cellular level (e.g. respiration) and for the organism as a whole (e.g. digestion in mammals).

Enzymes can affect structures in an organism (e.g. enzymes are involved in the production of collagen, an important protein in the connective tissues of animals) as well as functions (like respiration). Enzyme action can be **intracellular** — within cells, or **extracellular** — outside cells.

#### Example — Intracellular enzyme

Catalase is an enzyme that works inside cells to catalyse the breakdown of hydrogen peroxide to harmless oxygen ($O_2$) and water ($H_2O$).

Hydrogen peroxide ($H_2O_2$) is the toxic by-product of several cellular reactions. If left to build up, it can kill cells.

#### Examples — Extracellular enzymes

Amylase and trypsin both work outside cells in the human digestive system.

Amylase is found in saliva. It's secreted into the mouth by cells in the salivary glands. It catalyses the hydrolysis (breakdown, see page 62) of starch into maltose (a sugar) in the mouth.

Trypsin catalyses the hydrolysis of peptide bonds — turning big polypeptides into smaller ones (which then get broken down into amino acids by other enzymes). Trypsin is produced by cells in the pancreas and secreted into the small intestine.

### Enzyme structure

Enzymes are globular proteins (see page 72). They have an **active site**. The active site is the part of the enzyme where the **substrate** molecules (the substance that the enzyme interacts with) bind to. The active site has a specific shape, which is determined by the enzyme's tertiary structure (see page 71).

For the enzyme to work, the substrate has to fit into the active site (its shape has to be complementary). If the substrate shape doesn't match the active site, the reaction won't be catalysed (see Figure 1 on the next page). This means that enzymes are very specific and work with very few substrates — usually only one. When a substrate binds to an enzyme's active site, an **enzyme-substrate complex** is formed.

---

**Learning Objectives:**
- Know the role of enzymes in catalysing reactions that affect metabolism at a cellular and whole organism level.
- Understand that enzymes affect both structure and function.
- Understand the role of enzymes in catalysing both intracellular and extracellular reactions, including catalase as an example of an enzyme that catalyses intracellular reactions and amylase and trypsin as examples of enzymes that catalyse extracellular reactions.
- Understand the mechanism of enzyme action, with reference to:
  - the tertiary structure,
  - specificity,
  - the active site,
  - the lock and key hypothesis,
  - the induced-fit hypothesis,
  - enzyme-substrate complexes,
  - enzyme-product complexes,
  - product formation,
  - lowering of activation energy.

**Specification Reference 2.1.4**

**Tip:** Metabolic reactions are reactions that occur in living cells.

**Exam Tip**
When describing enzyme action you need to say the active site and the substrate have a complementary shape, rather than the same shape.

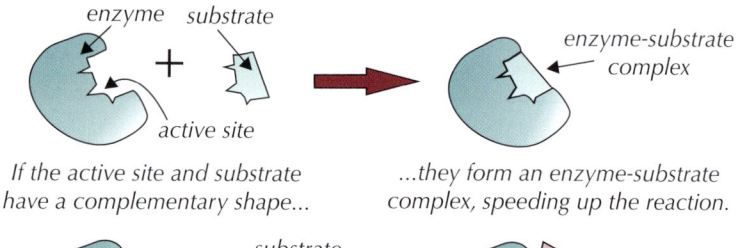

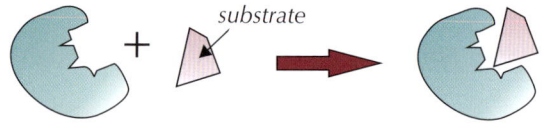

*If the active site and substrate have a complementary shape...*  ...they form an enzyme-substrate complex, speeding up the reaction.

*If the active site and substrate **do not** have a complementary shape...*  ...the substrate can't fit into the active site so the reaction **can't** be catalysed.

**Figure 1:** *An enzyme's active site has a complementary shape to the substrate.*

# How enzymes speed up reactions

In a chemical reaction, a certain amount of energy needs to be supplied to the chemicals before the reaction will start. This is called the **activation energy** — it's often provided as heat. Enzymes reduce the amount of activation energy that's needed (see Figure 2), often making reactions happen at a lower temperature than they could without an enzyme. This speeds up the rate of reaction.

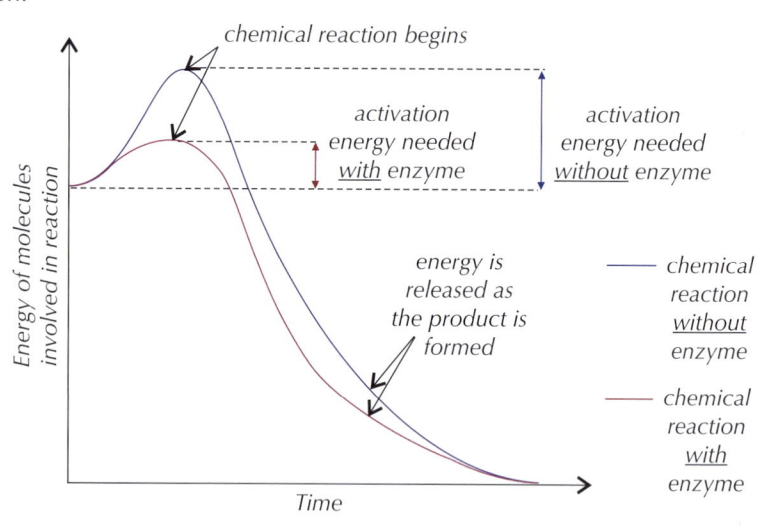

**Tip:** Understanding how enzymes function and the factors that affect them (see pages 109-111) has improved our knowledge about how biological processes work. This has allowed us to utilise enzymes in industrial processes, e.g. cellulase enzymes are used in the production of biofuels.

**Tip:** Imagine you have to get to the top of a mountain to start a chemical reaction. It would take a lot of energy to get to the top. An enzyme effectively reduces the height of the mountain, so it doesn't take as much energy to start the reaction.

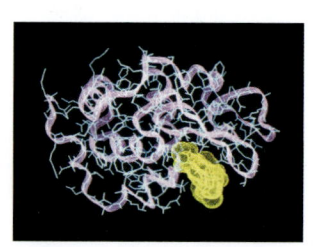

**Figure 2:** *A graph to show the activation energy needed for a reaction with and without an enzyme.*

When a substance binds to an enzyme's active site, an enzyme-substrate complex is formed (see Figure 1 above) — it's this that lowers the activation energy. Here are two reasons why:

- If two substrate molecules need to be joined, attaching to the enzyme holds them close together, reducing any repulsion between the molecules so they can bond more easily.
- If the enzyme is catalysing a breakdown reaction, fitting into the active site puts a strain on bonds in the substrate. This strain means the substrate molecule breaks up more easily.

**Figure 3:** *Computer model of an enzyme-substrate complex. The substrate (yellow) has bound to the enzyme's active site.*

Module 2: Section 4  Enzymes

# Models of enzyme action

Scientists now have a pretty good understanding of how enzymes work. As with most scientific theories, this understanding has changed over time.

*HOW SCIENCE WORKS*

## The 'lock and key' model

Enzymes are a bit picky — they only work with substrates that fit their active site. Early scientists studying the action of enzymes came up with the 'lock and key' model. This is where the substrate fits into the enzyme in the same way that a key fits into a lock — the active site and substrate have a complementary shape.

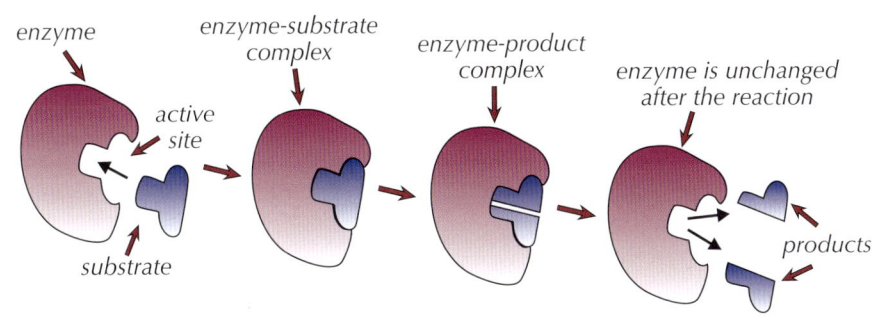

*Figure 4: The 'lock and key' model.*

**Tip:** An enzyme-product complex is formed when the substrate has been converted into its products, but they've not yet been released from the active site.

Scientists soon realised that the lock and key model didn't give the full story. The enzyme and substrate do have to fit together in the first place, but new evidence showed that the enzyme-substrate complex changed shape slightly to complete the fit. This locks the substrate even more tightly to the enzyme. Scientists modified the old lock and key model and came up with the 'induced fit' model.

**Tip:** The 'lock and key' model can also be called the 'lock and key' hypothesis, and the 'induced fit' model can also be called the 'induced fit' hypothesis.

## The 'induced fit' model

The 'induced fit' model helps to explain why enzymes are so specific and only bond to one particular substrate. The substrate doesn't only have to be the right shape to fit the active site, it has to make the active site change shape in the right way as well. This is a prime example of how a widely accepted theory can change when new evidence comes along. The 'induced fit' model is still widely accepted — for now, anyway.

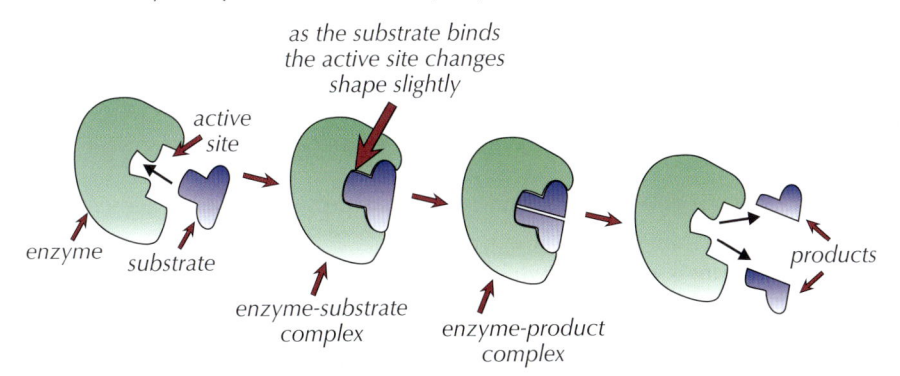

*Figure 5: The 'induced fit' model.*

**Tip:** The diagrams on this page show how enzymes break substrates down (e.g. one substrate molecule goes into the active site and two products come out). Enzymes can also catalyse synthesis reactions (e.g. two substrate molecules go into the active site, bind together and one product comes out).

Module 2: Section 4 **Enzymes**

## Practice Question — Application

**Q1** The enzyme maltase can be used in the industrial production of glucose syrup. It catalyses this reaction:

$$\text{maltose} \xrightarrow{\text{maltase}} \text{glucose}$$

An error in the process at a factory carrying out this industrial process meant that the enzyme sucrase, instead of maltase, was added to the maltose. Sucrase catalyses this reaction:

$$\text{sucrose} \xrightarrow{\text{sucrase}} \text{glucose}$$

No glucose was produced from this batch.

Using your knowledge of enzyme action, explain why no glucose was produced.

## Practice Questions — Fact Recall

**Q1** What is a catalyst?

**Q2** What term is used to describe an enzyme that acts:
  a) within cells?
  b) outside cells?

**Q3** a) Explain why the action of catalase is important to some cells.
  b) Is catalase an example of an intracellular or an extracellular enzyme?

**Q4** What reaction does amylase catalyse?

**Q5** a) What role does trypsin play in human digestion?
  b) Is trypsin an example of an intracellular or an extracellular enzyme?

**Q6** What determines the shape of an enzyme's active site?

**Q7** What is formed when a substrate binds with an active site?

**Q8** Look at the graph below.

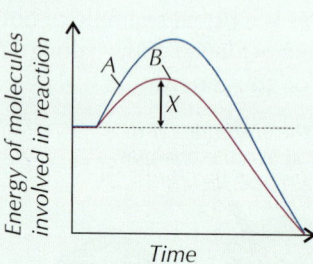

  a) Which line shows a reaction with the presence of an enzyme?
  b) What does the line labelled X represent?

**Q9** Explain, in terms of activation energy, why an enzyme enables reactions to happen at lower temperatures than they could without an enzyme.

**Q10** Describe the 'lock and key' model of enzyme action.

**Q11** What is the main difference between the 'lock and key' model and the 'induced fit' model?

Module 2: Section 4  Enzymes

# 2. Factors Affecting Enzyme Activity

*Enzymes are great at speeding up reactions, but there are several factors that affect how fast they work.*

## Temperature

Like any chemical reaction, the rate of an enzyme-controlled reaction increases when the temperature's increased. More heat means more kinetic energy, so molecules move faster. This makes the substrate molecules more likely to collide with the enzymes' active sites. The energy of these collisions also increases, which means each collision is more likely to result in a reaction. The rate of reaction continues to increase until the enzyme reaches its **optimum temperature** — this is the temperature at which the rate of an enzyme-controlled reaction is at its fastest.

But, if the temperature gets too high, the reaction stops. The rise in temperature makes the enzyme's molecules vibrate more. If the temperature goes above a certain level, this vibration breaks some of the bonds that hold the enzyme in shape. The active site changes shape and the enzyme and substrate no longer fit together. At this point, the enzyme is **denatured** — it no longer functions as a catalyst (see Figures 1 and 2).

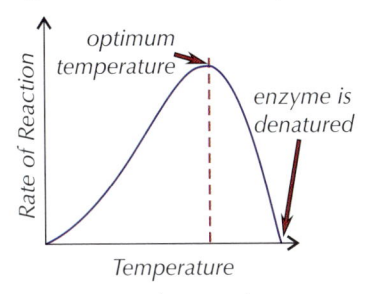

**Figure 1:** *Effect of temperature on the rate of an enzyme-controlled reaction.*

*Low temperatures* — At low temperatures the substrate fits into the active site.

*High temperatures* — At high temperatures the enzyme vibrates more. This breaks some of the bonds that hold it in shape. The active site changes shape and the substrate can no longer fit. The enzyme is denatured.

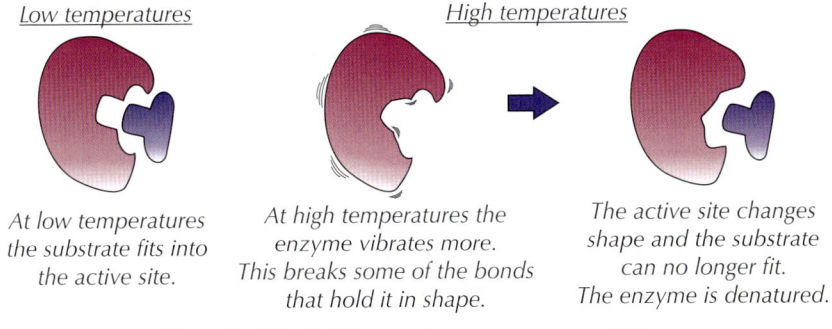

**Figure 2:** *Effect of temperature on enzyme activity.*

## The temperature coefficient (Q₁₀)

The temperature coefficient or $Q_{10}$ value for a reaction shows how much the rate of a reaction changes when the temperature is raised by 10 °C. You can calculate the $Q_{10}$ value using this equation:

$$Q_{10} = \frac{R_2 \text{ (rate at higher temperature)}}{R_1 \text{ (rate at lower temperature)}}$$

---

**Learning Objective:**
- Know the effects of pH, temperature, enzyme concentration and substrate concentration on enzyme activity, including reference to the temperature coefficient ($Q_{10}$), which is calculated using the formula: $Q_{10} = R_2 \div R_1$.

**Specification Reference 2.1.4**

**Tip:** Every enzyme has an optimum temperature. For most human enzymes it's around 37 °C but some enzymes, like those used in biological washing powders, can work well at 60 °C.

**Tip:** High temperatures break the weak bonds in an enzyme's tertiary structure, e.g. hydrogen bonds and ionic bonds. See page 71 for more on protein bonds.

**Exam Tip**
Make sure you don't say the enzyme's killed by high temperatures — it's <u>denatured</u>.

Module 2: Section 4 Enzymes 109

- **Example** — Maths Skills
  1. The graph on the right shows the rate of a reaction between 0 °C and 50 °C.
  2. Here's how to calculate the $Q_{10}$ value of the reaction using the rate at 30 °C and at 40 °C:

  $$Q_{10} = \frac{R_2}{R_1} = \frac{\text{rate at 40 °C}}{\text{rate at 30 °C}} = \frac{8}{4} = 2$$

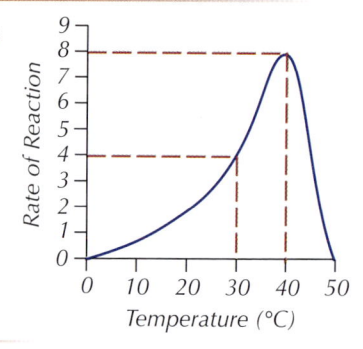

At temperatures before the optimum, a $Q_{10}$ value of 2 means that the rate doubles when the temperature is raised by 10 °C. A $Q_{10}$ value of 3 would mean that the rate trebles. Most enzyme-controlled reactions have a $Q_{10}$ value of around 2.

## pH

All enzymes have an optimum pH value — this is the pH at which the rate of an enzyme-controlled reaction is at its fastest. Most human enzymes work best at pH 7 (neutral), but there are exceptions. Pepsin, for example, works best at acidic pH 2, which is useful because it's found in the stomach. Above and below the optimum pH, the $H^+$ and $OH^-$ ions found in acids and alkalis can break the ionic bonds and hydrogen bonds that hold the enzyme's tertiary structure in place. This makes the active site change shape, so the enzyme is denatured.

**Exam Tip**
Don't forget — both a pH that's too high and one that's too low will denature an enzyme, not just one that's too high.

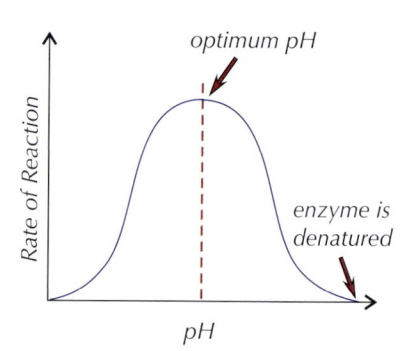

**Figure 3:** Effect of pH on the rate of an enzyme-controlled reaction.

## Enzyme concentration

The more enzyme molecules there are in a solution, the more likely a substrate molecule is to collide with one and form an enzyme-substrate complex. So increasing the concentration of the enzyme increases the rate of reaction.
    But, if the amount of substrate is limited, there comes a point when there's more than enough enzyme molecules to deal with all the available substrate, so adding more enzyme has no further effect.

**Tip:** The enzyme concentration graph initially shows a linear (straight line) relationship between the concentration and the rate of reaction. This means you can use the gradient of the line to work out how fast the rate is changing — see page 20 for more on finding a gradient.

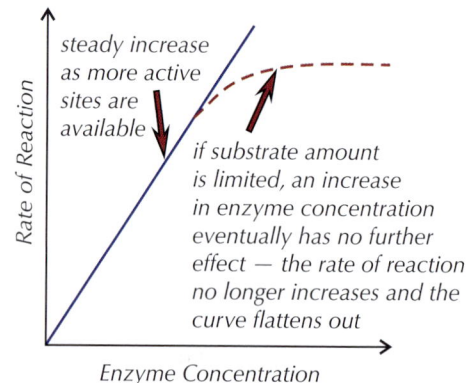

**Figure 4:** A graph to show the rate of an enzyme-controlled reaction against enzyme concentration.

Module 2: Section 4 Enzymes

## Substrate concentration

The higher the substrate concentration, the faster the reaction. More substrate molecules means a collision between substrate and enzyme is more likely, so more active sites will be occupied and more enzyme-substrate complexes will be formed. This is only true up until a 'saturation' point though. After that, there are so many substrate molecules that the enzymes have about as much as they can cope with (all the active sites are full), and adding more makes no difference — the enzyme concentration becomes the limiting factor.

Substrate concentration decreases with time during a reaction (unless more substrate is added to the reaction mixture), so if no other variables are changed, the rate of reaction will decrease over time too. This makes the initial rate of reaction (the reaction rate right at the start of the reaction, close to time 0) the highest rate of reaction.

**Figure 5:** A graph to show the rate of an enzyme-controlled reaction against substrate concentration.

*Labels on graph: steady increase as more substrate molecules are available; all active sites used — increase in substrate concentration has no further effect.*

**Tip:** The graphs showing how different factors affect enzyme activity show the rate of reaction (i.e. the speed of the reaction). When the line on the graph levels off it doesn't mean the reaction has stopped, just that it isn't going any faster.

**Tip:** A limiting factor is a variable that can slow down the rate of a reaction.

**Tip:** This graph shows how the substrate concentration decreases over the course of an enzyme-controlled reaction:

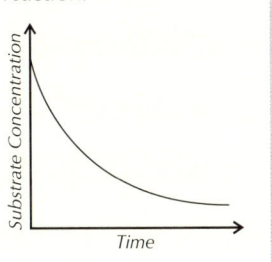

### Practice Question — Application

Q1 Hyperthermophilic bacteria are found in hot springs where temperatures reach 80 °C. Psychrotrophic bacteria are found in very cold environments. The graph on the right shows the rate of reaction for an enzyme from three different bacteria.
  a) Explain which curve on the graph shows the enzyme from:
     i) hyperthermophilic bacteria,
     ii) psychrotrophic bacteria.
  b) Explain what would happen to enzyme activity for each type of bacteria shown on the graph if they were put into an environment with a temperature range of 60-75 °C.

### Practice Questions — Fact Recall

Q1 Explain why an increase in temperature increases the rate of enzyme activity.
Q2 Explain how a very high temperature can stop an enzyme from working.
Q3 What would a temperature coefficient of 4 tell you about the effect of temperature on the rate of an enzyme-controlled reaction?
Q4 Give a factor other than temperature that can denature an enzyme.
Q5 Explain the effect of increasing the enzyme concentration on the rate of an enzyme-controlled reaction.
Q6 Explain what happens to the rate of an enzyme-controlled reaction when the substrate concentration is increased after the saturation point.

Module 2: Section 4  Enzymes

**Learning Objective:**
- Be able to investigate the effects of pH, temperature, enzyme concentration and substrate concentration on enzyme activity (PAG4).

**Specification Reference 2.1.4**

# 3. Enzyme-Controlled Reactions

*The rate of enzyme-controlled reactions can be determined by experiments.*

## Measuring rates of reactions

**PRACTICAL ACTIVITY GROUP 4**

You need to know how the effects of pH, temperature, enzyme concentration and substrate concentration can be investigated experimentally. Here are two ways of measuring the rate of an enzyme-controlled reaction:

1. You can measure how fast the product of the reaction appears and use this to compare the rate of reaction under different conditions.

### Example

Catalase catalyses the breakdown of hydrogen peroxide into water and oxygen. It's easy to measure the volume of oxygen produced and to work out how fast it's given off. In this investigation, temperature is the independent variable — the thing you change. The dependent variable (the thing you measure) will be the volume of oxygen produced. You need to control all the other variables that could affect the outcome of the investigation (i.e. keep them constant). That includes the pH, the enzyme concentration, the substrate concentration, etc.

Figure 1 below shows the apparatus you'll need. The oxygen released displaces the water from the measuring cylinder. (A stand and clamp would also be pretty useful to hold the cylinder upside down, as would a stopwatch and a water bath.)

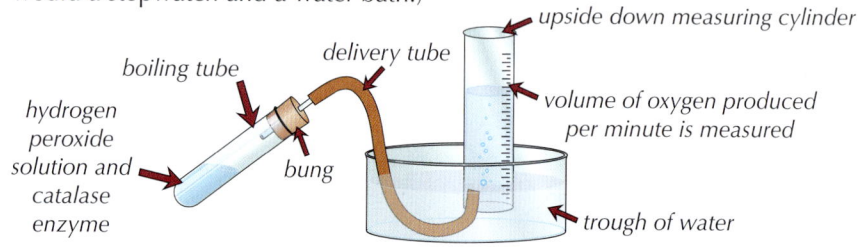

**Figure 1:** Apparatus needed for investigating the breakdown of hydrogen peroxide.

**Tip:** Don't forget to do a risk assessment before you do either of the experiments on these next two pages. You should always take basic safety precautions including wearing goggles and a lab coat.

Here's how to carry out the experiment:

1. Set up boiling tubes containing the same volume and concentration of hydrogen peroxide. To keep the pH constant, add equal volumes of a suitable buffer solution to each boiling tube.
2. Set up the rest of the apparatus as shown in the diagram.
3. Put each boiling tube in a water bath set to a different temperature (e.g. 10 °C, 20 °C, 30 °C and 40 °C) along with another tube containing catalase. Wait 5 minutes before moving onto the next step so the enzyme gets up to temperature.
4. Use a pipette to add the same volume and concentration of catalase to each boiling tube. Then quickly attach the bung and delivery tube.
5. Record how much oxygen is produced in the first minute (60 s) of the reaction. Use a stopwatch to measure the time.
6. Repeat the experiment at each temperature three times, and use the results to find a mean volume of oxygen produced.
7. Calculate the mean rate of reaction at each temperature by dividing the volume of oxygen produced by the time taken (i.e. 60 s). The units will be $cm^3 s^{-1}$.

**Tip:** A buffer solution is able to resist changes in pH when small amounts of acid or alkali are added.

**Tip:** A negative control reaction, i.e. a boiling tube not containing catalase, should also be carried out at each temperature.

Module 2: Section 4 Enzymes

2. You can measure how fast the substrate is broken down and use this to compare the rate of reaction under different conditions.

**Tip:** Which method you use to measure the rate of a reaction will normally depend on whether the product or the substrate is easier to test for.

### Example

The enzyme amylase catalyses the breakdown of starch to maltose. In this experiment, the independent variable is the concentration of amylase and the dependent variable is the time taken to break down starch to maltose. All other variables need to be controlled. Figure 2 below shows how the experiment can be set up. You'll need the apparatus shown in the diagram as well as a stopwatch.

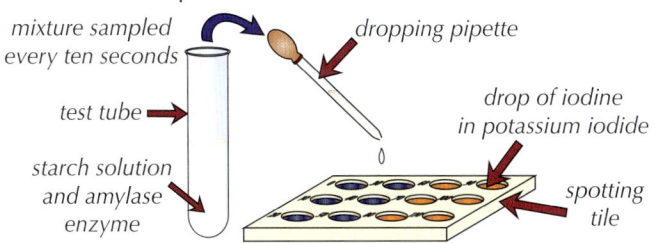

*Figure 2: Apparatus needed for investigating the breakdown of starch.*

1. Put a drop of iodine in potassium iodide solution into each well on a spotting tile. Label the wells to help you read your results.
2. Mix together a known concentration and volume of amylase and starch in a test tube.
3. Use a dropping pipette to put a drop of this mixture into one of the wells containing the iodine solution at regular intervals (e.g. every 10 seconds).
4. Observe the resulting colour. The iodine solution goes dark blue-black when starch is present but remains its normal browny-orange colour when there's no starch around.
5. You can see how fast amylase is working by recording how long it takes for the iodine solution to no longer turn blue-black when starch/amylase mixture is added — see Figure 3.

**Exam Tip**
You might have learnt different methods for measuring the rate of an enzyme-controlled reaction to those shown here and on the previous page — it doesn't matter which ones you revise, so long as you know them well enough to describe in the exam.

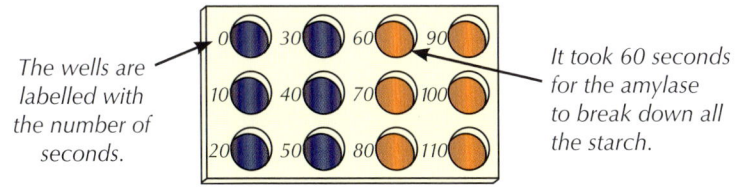

*Figure 3: Example results from investigating the breakdown of starch.*

The wells are labelled with the number of seconds. It took 60 seconds for the amylase to break down all the starch.

**Tip:** This experiment uses the starch test — see page 77.

6. Repeat the experiment using different concentrations of amylase.
7. Make sure that you also repeat the experiment three times at each amylase concentration and use your results to find the mean time taken.

## Variables

The experiments on this page and the previous one show you how you can investigate the effects of temperature and enzyme concentration on the rate of enzyme-controlled reactions.

You can also alter these experiments to investigate the effect of a different variable, such as pH (by adding a buffer solution with a different pH to each test tube or boiling tube) or substrate concentration (you could use serial dilutions to make substrate solutions with different concentrations). The key to experiments like this is to remember to only change one variable — everything else should stay the same.

**Tip:** There's more about controlling variables on page 5.

## Estimating the initial rate of reaction

You can use a **tangent** to estimate the initial rate of reaction from a graph. As you know from page 111, the initial rate of reaction is the rate of reaction right at the start of the reaction, close to time equals zero (t = 0) on the graph. To work out the initial rate of reaction carry out the following steps:

1. Draw a tangent to the curve at t = 0, using a ruler. Do this by positioning the ruler so it's an equal distance from the curve at both sides of where it's touching it. Here you'll have to estimate where the curve would continue if it carried on below zero. Then draw a line along the ruler.

2. Calculate the **gradient** of the tangent — this is the initial rate of reaction. The equation for the gradient of a straight line is:
Gradient = change in y axis ÷ change in x axis.

3. Finally, you need to work out the units of the rate. The units will vary depending on what was measured in the experiment. To work out the units of rate from a graph, divide the units of the y axis by the units of the x axis (which should always be time).

**Tip:** For more details on how to draw a tangent, see page 21.

**Tip:** If you're comparing the initial rate of reaction for two different reactions, you can work out the ratio of the rates to give you a quick and easy comparison. E.g. if the initial rate of a reaction at 30 °C is 1.2 $cm^3$ $s^{-1}$ and the initial rate at 60 °C is 3.0 $cm^3$ $s^{-1}$, you could write the ratio of the initial rates of reaction at 30 °C : 60 °C as 1 : 2.5. There's more about working out ratios on pages 13-14.

### Example — Maths Skills

The graph below shows the volume of product released by an enzyme-controlled reaction at 37 °C.

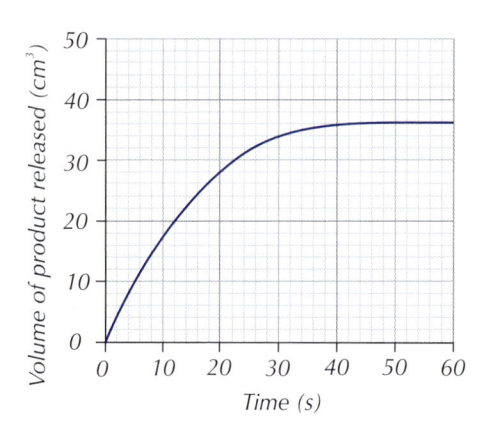

To work out the initial rate of reaction:

1. **Draw a tangent at t = 0.**
   (See the red line on the graph on the right.)

2. **Calculate the gradient of the tangent.**
   The gradient at t = 0 is:
   change in y ÷ change in x
   = 50 ÷ 18 = 2.8

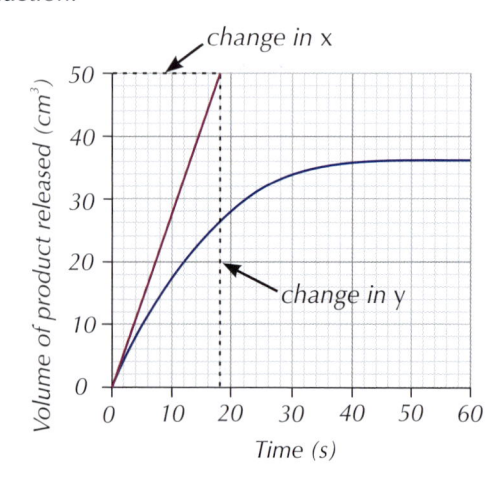

3. **Work out the units.**
   units of y ÷ units of x
   = $cm^3$ ÷ s = $cm^3$ $s^{-1}$

So the initial rate of reaction is **2.8 $cm^3$ $s^{-1}$**.

Module 2: Section 4 Enzymes

## Practice Questions — Application

**Q1** The graph below shows the increase in the concentration of product from an enzyme-catalysed reaction at 25 °C.

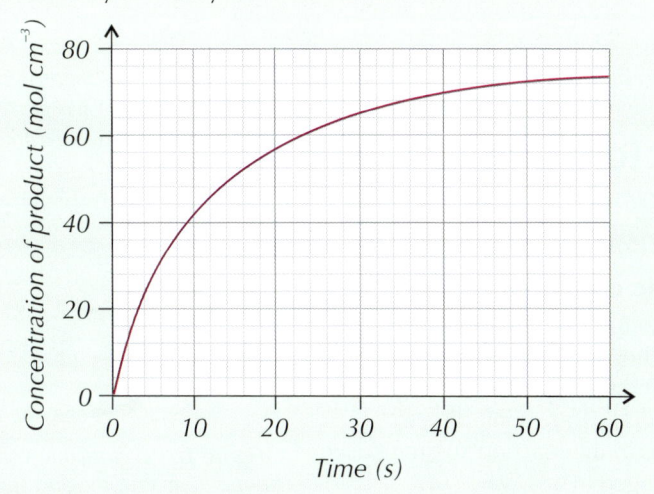

[Graph: Concentration of product (mol cm$^{-3}$) vs Time (s)]

Use this graph to calculate the initial rate of reaction.

**Q2** A group of students were investigating the effect of hydrogen peroxide concentration on the rate of breakdown of hydrogen peroxide by the enzyme catalase. They measured the volume of oxygen released by the reaction. Their results are shown in the graph below.

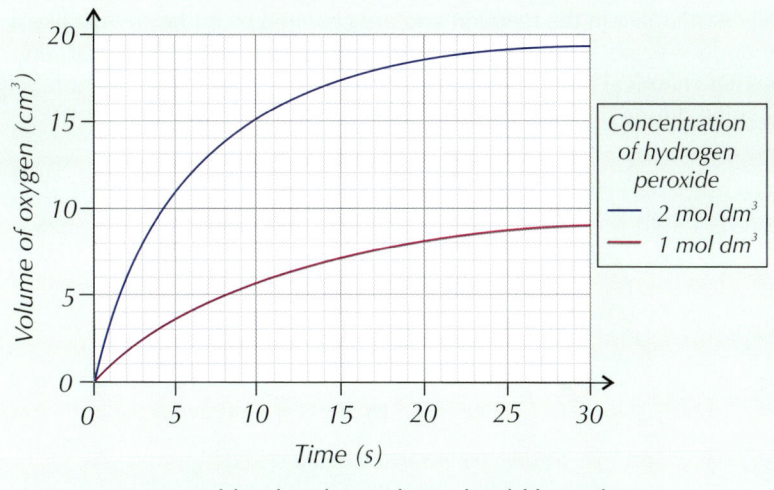

[Graph: Volume of oxygen (cm$^3$) vs Time (s), Concentration of hydrogen peroxide: 2 mol dm$^3$, 1 mol dm$^3$]

a) Name two variables that the students should keep the same during this investigation.
b) Calculate the ratio of the initial rates of reaction at 2 mol dm$^3$ : 1 mol dm$^3$ hydrogen peroxide. Write your answer in the form X : 1.

**Exam Tip**
Don't forget to add the correct units to your answer, or you may miss out on some easy marks.

## Practice Question — Fact Recall

**Q1** Describe how you could measure the rate of the breakdown of hydrogen peroxide by catalase at different temperatures, including the equipment you would use.

Module 2: Section 4 Enzymes

## Learning Objectives:

- Understand the need for coenzymes, cofactors and prosthetic groups in some enzyme-controlled reactions, including Cl⁻ as a cofactor for amylase, $Zn^{2+}$ as a prosthetic group for carbonic anhydrase and vitamins as a source of coenzymes.
- Understand the effects of inhibitors on the rate of enzyme-controlled reactions, including competitive and non-competitive and reversible and non-reversible inhibitors, with reference to the action of metabolic poisons and some medicinal drugs, and the role of product inhibition.
- Understand that some enzymes involved in metabolic pathways are synthesised as inactive precursors (covered at A level only).

**Specification Reference 2.1.4**

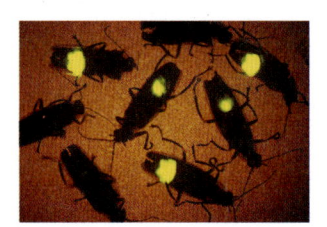

**Figure 3:** The chemical reaction that makes fireflies glow is catalysed by the enzyme luciferase and an organic cofactor, ATP.

### Exam Tip
You need to learn the Cl⁻ and $Zn^{2+}$ examples here for the exam.

# 4. Cofactors and Enzyme Inhibition

*Some substances might need to be present for an enzyme to work. But other substances can slow enzymes down or stop them working altogether.*

## Cofactors and coenzymes
Some enzymes will only work if there is another non-protein substance bound to them. These non-protein substances are called cofactors.

### Inorganic cofactors
Some cofactors are inorganic molecules or ions. They work by helping the enzyme and substrate to bind together (see Figure 1). They don't directly participate in the reaction so aren't used up or changed in any way.

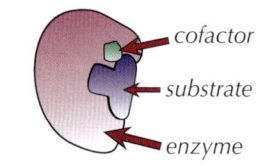

**Figure 1:** An inorganic cofactor bound to an enzyme and substrate.

> **Example**
> 
> Chloride ions (Cl⁻) are inorganic cofactors for the enzyme amylase.

### Organic cofactors (coenzymes)
Some cofactors are organic molecules — these are called coenzymes. They participate in the reaction and are changed by it (they're just like a second substrate, but they aren't called that). They often act as carriers, moving chemical groups between different enzymes. They're continually recycled during this process (see Figure 2).

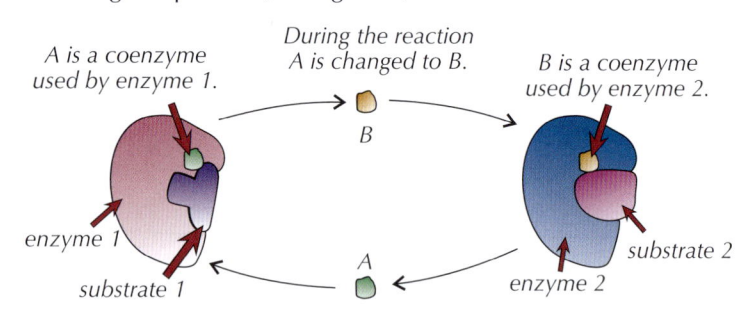

**Figure 2:** The recycling of coenzymes.

Vitamins are often sources of coenzymes. For example, the coenzyme NAD is derived from vitamin B3.

### Prosthetic Groups
If a cofactor is tightly bound to the enzyme, it's known as a prosthetic group.

> **Example**
>
> Zinc ions ($Zn^{2+}$) are a prosthetic group for carbonic anhydrase (an enzyme in red blood cells, which catalyses the production of carbonic acid from water and carbon dioxide). The zinc ions are a permanent part of the enzyme's active site.

116   Module 2: Section 4  Enzymes

# Enzyme inhibitors

Enzyme activity can be prevented by enzyme inhibitors — molecules that bind to the enzyme that they inhibit. Inhibition can be competitive or non-competitive.

## Competitive inhibitors

Competitive inhibitor molecules have a similar shape to that of substrate molecules. They compete with the substrate molecules to bind to the active site, but no reaction takes place. Instead they block the active site, so no substrate molecules can fit in it — see Figure 4.

How much the enzyme is inhibited depends on the relative concentrations of the inhibitor and substrate. If there's a high concentration of the inhibitor, it'll take up nearly all the active sites and hardly any of the substrate will get to the enzyme. But if there's a higher concentration of substrate, then the substrate's chances of getting to an active site before the inhibitor increase. So increasing the concentration of substrate will increase the rate of reaction (up to a point) — see Figure 5.

**Exam Tip**
Don't say that the inhibitor molecule and the substrate have the same shape — they have a <u>similar</u> shape.

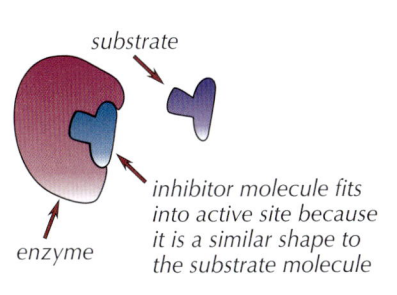

*Figure 4: Competitive inhibition.*

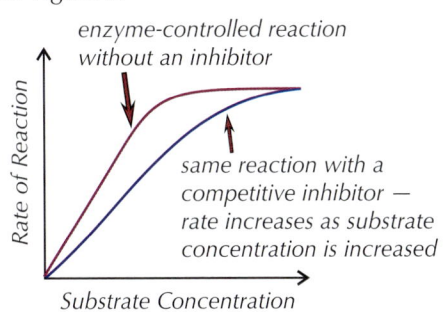

*Figure 5: Effect of a competitive inhibitor on the rate of an enzyme-controlled reaction.*

**Tip:** If you have a competitive inhibitor, increasing the concentration of substrate will reverse its effects — the substrate will out-compete the inhibitor for the active site.

## Non-competitive inhibitors

Non-competitive inhibitor molecules bind to the enzyme away from its active site. The site they bind to is known as the enzyme's allosteric site. This causes the active site to change shape so the substrate molecules can no longer bind to it — see Figure 6.

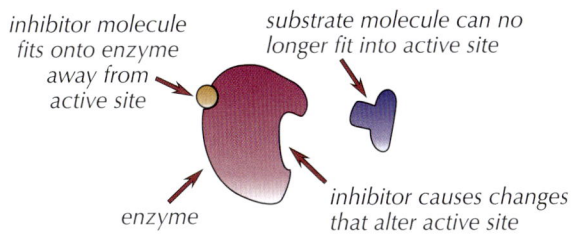

*Figure 6: Non-competitive inhibition.*

**Exam Tip**
When you're talking about shape change, always refer to the <u>active site</u> — don't just say the enzyme's changed shape.

Non-competitive inhibitor molecules don't 'compete' with the substrate molecules to bind to the active site because they are a different shape. Increasing the concentration of substrate won't make any difference — enzyme activity will still be inhibited.

*Figure 7: Effect of a non-competitive inhibitor on the rate of an enzyme-controlled reaction.*

Module 2: Section 4 Enzymes  117

### Reversible and non-reversible inhibition

Inhibitors can be reversible (not bind permanently to an enzyme) or non-reversible (bind permanently to an enzyme). Which one they are depends on the strength of the bonds between the enzyme and the inhibitor.

- If they're strong, covalent bonds, the inhibitor can't be removed easily and the inhibition is irreversible.
- If they're weaker hydrogen bonds or weak ionic bonds, the inhibitor can be removed and the inhibition is reversible.

**Tip:** A covalent bond is formed between two atoms that share electrons.

**Exam Tip**
This is exactly the kind of question you could get in the exam — enzyme-inhibition is a favourite with examiners, so make sure you know it inside out.

## Practice Questions — Application

**Q1** Methanol is broken down in the body into formaldehyde. The build up of formaldehyde can cause death. The enzyme that hydrolyses the reaction is alcohol dehydrogenase. The enzyme-substrate complex formed is shown on the right.

a) A diagram of ethanol is shown on the right. If someone had been poisoned with methanol, they could be helped by being given ethanol as soon as possible. Explain why.

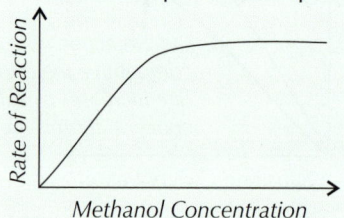

b) The graph shows the rate of the reaction with no ethanol present. Sketch a graph with the same axes showing the rate of reaction with the presence of ethanol.

**Q2** Scientists have identified a substance (substance A) that inhibits the enzyme glycogen phosphorylase. This enzyme is responsible for the breakdown of glycogen into glucose. Substance A inhibits glycogen phosphorylase by binding to it away from the active site.

a) Is substance A a competitive or non-competitve inhibitor? Explain your answer.

The scientists test the effect of substance A in a solution containing glycogen and glycogen phosphorylase. The graph on the right shows the rate of the reaction over time.

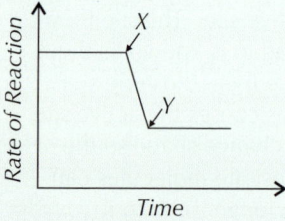

b) At point X the scientists increase the concentration of substance A in the test solution. Describe and explain the shape of the graph between points X and Y.

c) Explain which of the graphs below represents the effect of:
   i) increasing the glycogen concentration at point Z.
   ii) increasing the glycogen phosphorylase concentration at point Z.

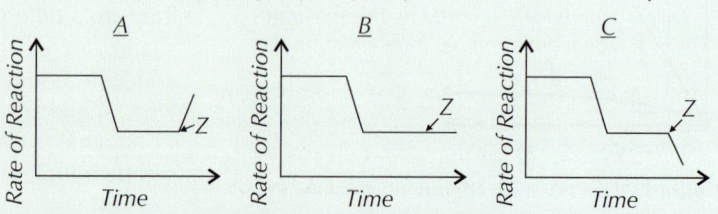

**Tip:** It might help you to jot down the role of each substance to answer these questions, e.g. glycogen = substrate, glucose = product, substance A = inhibitor.

Module 2: Section 4 Enzymes

## Drugs
Some medicinal drugs are enzyme inhibitors, for example:

### Examples
- Some antiviral drugs (drugs that stop viruses) — e.g. reverse transcriptase inhibitors are a class of antiviral developed to treat HIV. They work by inhibiting the enzyme reverse transcriptase, which catalyses the replication of viral DNA. This prevents the virus from replicating.
- Some antibiotics — e.g. penicillin inhibits the enzyme transpeptidase, which catalyses the formation of proteins in bacterial cell walls. This weakens the cell wall and prevents the bacterium from regulating its osmotic pressure. As a result the cell bursts and the bacterium is killed.

**Tip:** Human Immunodeficiency virus (HIV) is a virus that causes AIDS.

## Metabolic poisons
Metabolic poisons interfere with metabolic reactions (the reactions that occur in cells), causing damage, illness or death — they're often enzyme inhibitors. In the exam you might be asked to describe the action of one named poison.

### Examples
- Cyanide is a non-competitive, irreversible inhibitor of cytochrome c oxidase, an enzyme that catalyses respiration reactions. Cells that can't respire die.
- Malonate is a competitive inhibitor of succinate dehydrogenase (which also catalyses respiration reactions).
- Arsenic is a non-competitive inhibitor of pyruvate dehydrogenase, yet another enzyme that catalyses respiration reactions.

**Exam Tip**
It doesn't matter which metabolic poison you learn for the exam, so long as you know an example and can describe how it works.

## Product inhibition
Metabolic pathways are regulated by **end-product inhibition**. A metabolic pathway is a series of connected metabolic reactions. The product of the first reaction takes part in the second reaction — and so on. Each reaction is catalysed by a different enzyme. Many enzymes are inhibited by the product of the reaction they catalyse. This is known as product inhibition. End-product inhibition is when the final product in a metabolic pathway inhibits an enzyme that acts earlier on in the pathway — see Figure 8.

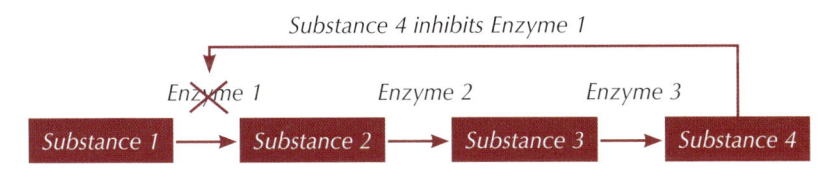

*Substance 4 inhibits Enzyme 1*

Substance 1 →(Enzyme 1)→ Substance 2 →(Enzyme 2)→ Substance 3 →(Enzyme 3)→ Substance 4

**Figure 8:** End-product inhibition

End-product inhibition is a nifty way of regulating the pathway and controlling the amount of end-product that gets made.

### Example
Phosphofructokinase is an enzyme involved in the metabolic pathway that breaks down glucose to make ATP. ATP inhibits the action of phosphofructokinase — so a high level of ATP prevents more ATP from being made.

Both product and end-product inhibition are reversible. So when the level of product starts to drop, the level of inhibition will start to fall and the enzyme can start to function again — this means that more product can be made.

## Enzyme inhibition to protect cells

Enzymes are sometimes synthesised as **inactive precursors** in metabolic pathways to prevent them causing damage to cells. Part of the precursor molecule inhibits its action as an enzyme. Once this part is removed (e.g. via a chemical reaction) the enzyme becomes active.

> **Example**
>
> Some proteases (which break down proteins) are synthesised as inactive precursors to stop them damaging proteins in the cell in which they're made.

### Practice Question — Application

Q1 The diagram below shows two interlinked metabolic pathways.

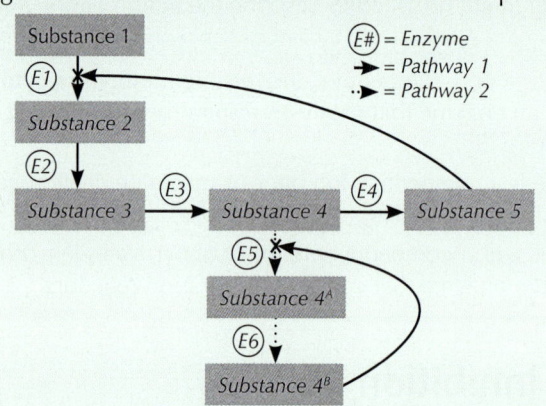

(E#) = Enzyme
→ = Pathway 1
⇢ = Pathway 2

a) Substance 4$^B$ is able to regulate its own production from substance 4 by inhibiting enzyme 5. What is this process called?

b) Suggest what immediate effect inhibition of enzyme 5 (in pathway 2) would have on the amount of substance 2 being produced (in pathway 1)? Explain your answer.

### Practice Questions — Fact Recall

Q1 What is a cofactor?

Q2 Describe how a coenzyme is recycled during an enzyme-controlled reaction.

Q3 What is a prosthetic group?

Q4 Where do the following molecules bind to an enzyme:
   a) a non-competitive inhibitor?   b) a competitive inhibitor?

Q5 State the bonds present between an enzyme and a:
   a) reversible inhibitor.            b) non-reversible inhibitor.

Q6 Name a poison that inhibits enzyme action and describe how it works.

Q7 Explain the method of enzyme inhibition that can be used to protect cells that synthesise potentially damaging enzymes.

# Section Summary

Make sure you know:
- That an enzyme is a biological catalyst (a substance that speeds up chemical reactions in living organisms without being used up in the reaction itself).
- That an enzyme can affect both the structure and function of an organism.
- That enzyme action may be intracellular (within cells) or extracellular (outside cells).
- That catalase is an enzyme that catalyses intracellular reactions and amylase and trypsin are enzymes that catalyse extracellular reactions.
- That enzymes are globular proteins with a specific tertiary structure and that the active site is the part of the enzyme that binds to a substrate to form an enzyme-substrate complex.
- That an enzyme's active site has a specific shape complementary to the shape of the substrate, and so enzymes will usually only work with one substrate.
- That the formation of an enzyme-substrate complex lowers the activation energy needed for a reaction, and the reasons why.
- That an enzyme-product complex is formed when the substrate has been converted into its products, but the products are still bound to the enzyme's active site.
- How to describe the 'lock and key' model and the 'induced fit' model of enzyme action.
- That increasing the temperature increases the rate of an enzyme-controlled reaction by:
  - increasing the kinetic energy of substrate and enzyme molecules, which increases the likelihood of a collision between them.
  - increasing the energy of collisions between substrate and enzyme molecules, which means collisions are more likely to result in a reaction.
- That enzymes have an optimum temperature and if the temperature becomes too high, the enzyme will become denatured.
- That the temperature coefficient ($Q_{10}$) value for a reaction shows how much the reaction rate changes in response to the temperature being raised by 10 °C and the formula is: $Q_{10} = R_2 \div R_1$.
- That enzymes have an optimum pH at which the rate of an enzyme-controlled reaction is at its fastest and that if the pH is too high or too low, the enzyme will become denatured.
- That increasing enzyme concentration will increase the rate of a reaction until the amount of substrate becomes the limiting factor.
- That increasing substrate concentration will increase the rate of a reaction until the saturation point is reached and all active sites are full (enzyme concentration is the limiting factor). And that over the course of a reaction substrate concentration will decrease, decreasing the rate of reaction.
- How to describe experiments that investigate the effects of pH, temperature, enzyme concentration and substrate concentration on the rate of an enzyme-controlled reaction.
- How to draw a tangent to a graph and use it to work out the initial rate of a reaction.
- That cofactors and coenzymes are non-protein substances needed to activate some enzymes, and are able to explain how they work. $Cl^-$ ions are an example of a cofactor (for amylase).
- That prosthetic groups are a type of cofactor that is tightly bound to an enzyme and that $Zn^{2+}$ ions are an example of a prosthetic group for the enzyme carbonic anhydrase.
- That competitive inhibitors have a similar shape to a substrate and inhibit enzymes by binding to the active site and that non-competitive inhibitors inhibit enzyme activity by binding to them away from the active site, causing the active site to change shape.
- That some enzyme inhibitors are reversible and some are irreversible, and are able to explain why.
- That some metabolic poisons and medicinal drugs work by inhibiting enzymes.
- That product inhibition is when a product inhibits the enzyme that has catalysed its formation and end-product inhibition is when the final product in a metabolic pathway inhibits an enzyme that acts earlier in the pathway.

# Exam-style Questions

**1** Apples contain a substance called catechol and the enzyme catecholase. When an apple is cut open and exposed to oxygen, the following chemical reaction takes place:

$$\text{catechol} + \tfrac{1}{2}O_2 \xrightarrow{\text{catecholase}} \text{benzoquinone} + H_2O$$

**(a) (i)** What effect do enzymes have on the activation energy of a reaction?

*(1 mark)*

**(ii)** Explain why enzymes have this effect.

*(2 marks)*

**(b) (i)*** Use the '**induced fit**' **model** of enzyme activity to explain how catecholase catalyses the reaction shown above.

In your answer you should make clear how the shape of the enzyme relates to its function.

*(6 marks)*

**(ii)** Name **another model** of enzyme action not mentioned in part **(i)** and describe how it differs to the induced fit model.

*(2 marks)*

**(c)** Benzoquinone has a brown colour and its production is responsible for the 'browning' of apples once they have been cut.

To reduce the browning of an apple once it has been cut, would it be best to store the apple at room temperature or in a fridge? Explain your answer.

*(4 marks)*

**(d)** Catecholase uses copper as a cofactor.

**(i)** Describe how copper enables catecholase to function.

*(3 marks)*

**(ii)** Give **two** differences between organic and inorganic cofactors.

*(2 marks)*

**(e)** Copper binds more easily to a chemical called PTU than it does to catecholase.

Suggest why the rate of apple browning would be **lower** in the presence of PTU.

*(3 marks)*

* The quality of your response will be assessed in this question.

**2** Triglycerides are a type of fat found in foods. In the stomach, gastric lipase acts as a catalyst to break triglycerides down into diglycerides and fatty acids.

$$\text{triglyceride} \xrightarrow{\text{gastric lipase}} \text{diglyceride} + \text{fatty acid}$$

**(a)** Fig. 2.1 shows the rate of reaction for gastric lipase at different pH values.

**(i)** What is the **optimum pH** of gastric lipase?

*(1 mark)*

**(ii)** At what pH value(s) is gastric lipase **denatured**? Give a reason for your answer.

*(2 marks)*

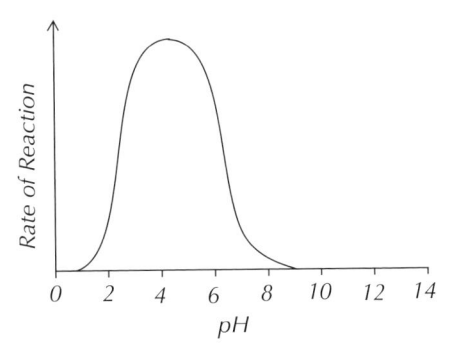

**Fig. 2.1**

**(iii)** Explain what happens when an enzyme is denatured by an extreme pH value.

*(3 marks)*

**(iv)** Suggest **two** variables you would control if you were investigating the activity of gastric lipase at different pH values.

*(2 marks)*

**(b)** The weight-loss drug, orlistat, stops triglycerides from being broken down. Orlistat is a competitive inhibitor of gastric lipase.

Fig. 2.2 shows the reaction with and without orlistat present.

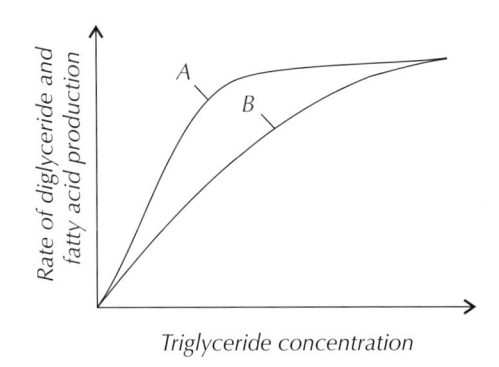

**Fig. 2.2**

**(i)** Which curve on Fig 2.2 shows the reaction **without** the presence of orlistat? Give a reason for your answer.

*(1 mark)*

**(ii)** Explain the action of orlistat in this reaction.

*(3 marks)*

Module 2: Section 4 **Enzymes**

# Module 2 Section 5: Biological Membranes

### Learning Objectives:
- Understand the roles of membranes at the surface of cells and within cells, including their role as:
  - partially permeable barriers between the cell and its environment, between organelles and the cytoplasm, and within organelles
  - sites of cell communication (cell signalling)
  - sites of chemical reactions.
- Know the fluid mosaic model of membrane structure and the roles of the following components:
  - phospholipids
  - cholesterol
  - proteins
  - glycolipids
  - glycoproteins.
- Understand the factors affecting membrane structure and permeability, including the effects of solvents and temperature.
- Know how to carry out practical investigations into factors affecting membrane structure and permeability (PAG5 and PAG8).

**Specification Reference 2.1.5**

## 1. Cell Membranes — The Basics

*Cell membranes are the boundaries of cells, but there's an awful lot more to them than that...*

### Membrane function
Cells (and many of the organelles inside them) are surrounded by membranes that have a wide range of functions. You need to be able to describe the functions of membranes at the cell surface, as well as those within cells.

#### Membranes at the cell surface (plasma membranes)
Plasma membranes are a barrier between the cell and its environment, controlling which substances enter and leave the cell. They're **partially permeable** — they let some molecules through but not others.

Substances can move across the plasma membrane by **diffusion**, **osmosis** or **active transport** (see pages 132-140). Plasma membranes also allow recognition by other cells (e.g. the cells of the immune system, see p. 230) and cell communication (sometimes called cell signalling, see p. 130).

#### Membranes within cells
The membranes around organelles (see p. 40-41) divide the cell into different compartments — they act as a barrier between the organelle and the cytoplasm. This makes different functions more efficient.

— Example —
The substances needed for respiration (like enzymes) are kept together inside a mitochondrion by the mitochondrion's outer membrane.

Membranes can form vesicles to transport substances between different areas of the cell (see pages 140-141).

— Example —
Proteins are transported in vesicles from the rough endoplasmic reticulum to the Golgi apparatus during protein synthesis.

Membranes within cells are also partially permeable so they can control which substances enter and leave the organelle.

— Example —
RNA (see page 96) leaves the nucleus via the nuclear membrane (also called the nuclear envelope). DNA is too large to pass through the partially permeable membrane, so it remains in the nucleus.

You can also get membranes within organelles — these act as barriers between the membrane contents and the rest of the organelle.

— Example —
Thylakoid membranes in chloroplasts (see p. 41) keep the components needed for the light-dependent reactions of photosynthesis together.

124 Module 2: Section 5 Biological Membranes

Membranes within cells can be the site of chemical reactions. The membranes of some organelles are folded, increasing their surface area and making chemical reactions more efficient.

> **Example**
> The inner membrane of a mitochondrion contains enzymes needed for respiration. It has a large surface area, which increases the number of enzymes present and makes respiration more efficient.

## Membrane structure

The structure of all membranes is basically the same. They're all composed of lipids (mainly a type called phospholipids), proteins and carbohydrates (usually attached to proteins or lipids).

In 1972, the **fluid mosaic model** was suggested to describe the arrangement of molecules in the membrane — see Figure 1. In the model, phospholipid molecules form a continuous, double layer (called a bilayer). This bilayer is 'fluid' because the phospholipids are constantly moving. Protein molecules are scattered through the bilayer, like tiles in a mosaic. Some proteins have a carbohydrate attached — these are called **glycoproteins**. Some lipids also have a carbohydrate attached — these are called **glycolipids**. Cholesterol molecules are also present within the bilayer.

**Tip:** For more on models and theories, see page 1.

**Tip:** The phospholipid bilayer is ~ 7 nm thick.

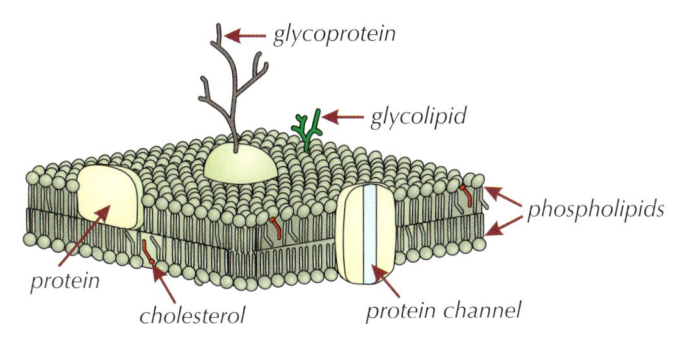

*Figure 1:* The fluid mosaic model of a cell membrane.

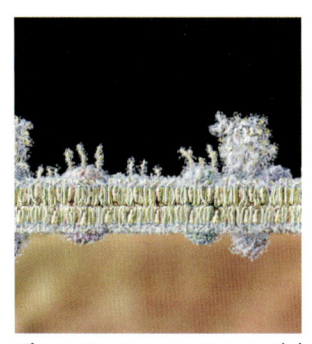

*Figure 2:* A computer model of the fluid mosaic model.

## Membrane components

There are five main components you need to know about:

### Phospholipids

Phospholipid molecules form a barrier to dissolved (water-soluble) substances. Phospholipids have a 'head' and a 'tail'. The head is **hydrophilic** — it attracts water. The tail is **hydrophobic** — it repels water. The molecules automatically arrange themselves into a bilayer — the heads face out towards the water on either side of the membrane (see Figure 3).

The centre of the bilayer is hydrophobic so the membrane doesn't allow water-soluble substances (like ions and polar molecules) to diffuse through it — it acts as a barrier to these dissolved substances. Fat-soluble substances, e.g. fat-soluble vitamins, dissolve in the bilayer and pass directly through the membrane.

**Tip:** A polar molecule has one end with a slightly positive charge and one end with a slightly negative charge. These charges are nowhere near as strong as the positive or negative charge on an ion, but they do help polar molecules to dissolve in water. Non-polar substances have no charges.

**Tip:** Water is actually a polar molecule, but it can diffuse (by osmosis) through the cell membrane because it's so small (see page 132).

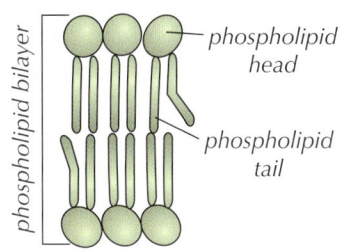

*Figure 3:* Phospholipid bilayer.

Module 2: Section 5 Biological Membranes

**Tip:** There's more on phospholipids and cholesterol on pages 67-68.

## Cholesterol

Cholesterol gives the membrane stability. It is a type of lipid that's present in all cell membranes (except bacterial cell membranes). Cholesterol molecules fit between the phospholipids (see Figure 4). At higher temperatures, they bind to the hydrophobic tails of the phospholipids, causing them to pack more closely together. This makes the membrane less fluid and more rigid. At lower temperatures, cholesterol prevents phospholipids from packing too close together, and so increases membrane fluidity. Cholesterol also has hydrophobic regions, so it's able to create a further barrier to polar substances moving through the membrane.

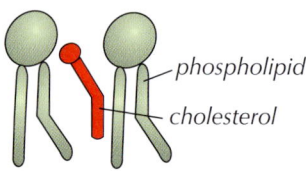

*Figure 4:* Cholesterol in the membrane.

**Tip:** Charged particles include ions and polar molecules.

## Proteins

Proteins control what enters and leaves the cell. Some proteins form channels in the membrane (see pages 139-140) — these allow small, charged particles through. Other proteins (called carrier proteins) transport larger molecules and charged particles across the membrane by active transport and facilitated diffusion (see pages 139-140). Proteins also act as receptors for molecules (e.g. hormones) in cell signalling (see page 130). When a molecule binds to the protein, a chemical reaction is triggered inside the cell.

**Tip:** A hydrogen bond is a weak bond that forms between a slightly positively-charged hydrogen atom in one molecule and a slightly negatively-charged atom or group in another molecule, e.g. oxygen.

## Glycolipids and glycoproteins

Glycolipids and glycoproteins stabilise the membrane by forming hydrogen bonds with surrounding water molecules. They act as receptors for messenger molecules in cell signalling and are sites where drugs, hormones and antibodies bind (see pages 130-131). They're also antigens — cell surface molecules involved in self-recognition and the immune response (see p. 230).

**Tip:** Remember, glyco<u>lipids</u> are carbohydrates attached to <u>lipids</u>, and glyco<u>proteins</u> are carbohydrates attached to <u>proteins</u>. <u>Glyco</u> is Greek for sweet or sugar and it refers to the carbohydrate bit.

### Practice Questions — Application

Q1 Suggest a function of each of the following membranes:
   a) the membrane surrounding a chloroplast.
   b) the membrane surrounding a bacterial cell.

Q2 Chloride ions (Cl⁻) need to pass through the plasma membrane to get inside the cell. How might they move across the membrane?

Q3 The protein content of a typical cell membrane is around 50%. In energy-releasing organelles, such as mitochondria, the amount rises to around 75%. Suggest a reason for this difference.

Module 2: Section 5 Biological Membranes

# Factors affecting membrane permeability

Anything that affects the structure of a cell membrane can affect its permeability. You need to know the effects that solvents and temperature can have on cell membranes.

## Solvents

The permeability of cell membranes depends on the solvent surrounding them. This is because some solvents (such as ethanol) dissolve the lipids in a cell membrane, so the membrane loses its structure. Some solvents increase membrane permeability more than others, e.g. ethanol increases membrane permeability more than methanol. Increasing the concentration of the solvent will also increase membrane permeability. For example, Figure 5 shows the effect of increasing alcohol concentration on membrane permeability.

**Tip:** A solvent is any substance (usually a liquid) that can dissolve other substances.

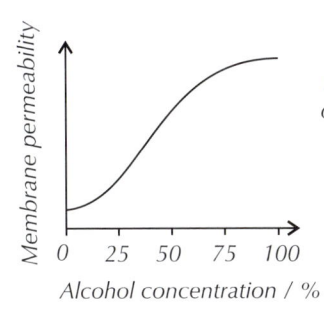

**Figure 5:** The effect of increasing alcohol concentration on membrane permeability.

## Temperature

Cell membranes are affected by temperature — it affects how much the phospholipids in the bilayer can move, which affects membrane structure and permeability.

- **Temperatures below 0 °C** — The phospholipids don't have much energy, so they can't move very much. They're packed closely together and the membrane is rigid. But channel proteins and carrier proteins in the membrane denature (lose structure and function), increasing the permeability of the membrane (see Point 1, Figure 6). Ice crystals may form and pierce the membrane, making it highly permeable when it thaws.

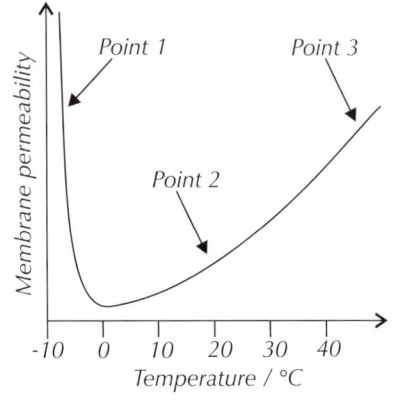

**Figure 6:** Graph to show the effect of temperature on membrane permeability.

**Tip:** You may remember from Module 2: Section 4 that proteins (e.g. enzymes) denature at high temperatures. Well, very cold temperatures (i.e. those below 0 °C) can cause proteins to denature too.

- **Temperatures between 0 and 45 °C** — The phospholipids can move around and aren't packed as tightly together — the membrane is partially permeable (see Point 2, Figure 6). As the temperature increases the phospholipids move more because they have more energy — this increases the permeability of the membrane.

- **Temperatures above 45 °C** — The phospholipid bilayer starts to melt (break down) and the membrane becomes more permeable. Water inside the cell expands, putting pressure on the membrane. Channel proteins and carrier proteins in the membrane denature so they can't control what enters or leaves the cell — this increases the permeability of the membrane (Point 3, Figure 6).

**Tip:** Think about what happens when you cook fruit or vegetables — as you apply heat, the food softens and liquid is released. This is partly because the cell membranes start to break down and become more permeable.

**Tip:** You should assess all safety risks before proceeding with this experiment. Be careful when using a scalpel — make sure you cut away from yourself and that the blade is clean and sharp.

# Investigating cell membrane permeability

You can investigate how different variables (e.g. solvent concentration and temperature) affect cell membrane permeability by doing experiments using beetroot. Beetroot cells contain a coloured pigment that leaks out — the higher the permeability of the membrane, the more pigment leaks out of the cell.

**PRACTICAL ACTIVITY GROUP 5**

**PRACTICAL ACTIVITY GROUP 8**

### Example — Investigating temperature

Here's how you could investigate the effect of temperature on beetroot membrane permeability:

1. Use a scalpel to carefully cut five equal sized pieces of beetroot. (Make sure you do your cutting on a cutting board.) Rinse the pieces to remove any pigment released during cutting.
2. Add the five pieces to five different test tubes, each containing 5 cm$^3$ of water. Use a measuring cylinder or pipette to measure the water.
3. Place each test tube in a water bath at a different temperature, e.g. 10 °C, 20 °C, 30 °C, 40 °C, 50 °C, for the same length of time (measured using a stopwatch).
4. Remove the pieces of beetroot from the tubes, leaving just the coloured liquid.

**Tip:** Place the tubes into the water bath gently to avoid splashing hot water on yourself. Use tongs to remove them after the experiment — they may be hot.

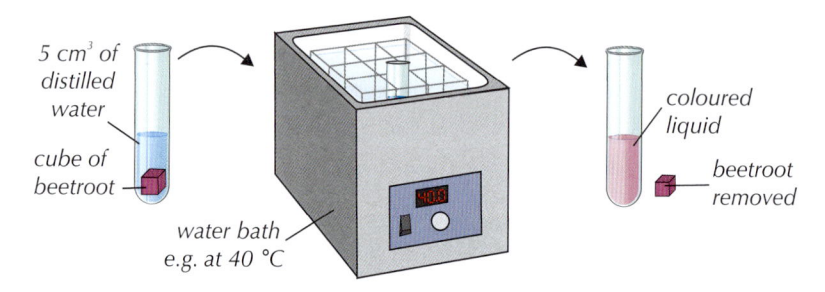

**Figure 7:** Investigating the effect of temperature on beetroot cell membrane permeability.

**Tip:** See page 79 for more on colorimeters.

5. Now you need to use a **colorimeter**. Firstly, switch the colorimeter on and allow five minutes for it to stabilise. Then set up the colorimeter so you're using a blue filter (or a wavelength of about 470 nm).
6. Add distilled water to a cuvette and then put it into the colorimeter. Calibrate the machine to zero — your teacher will show you how to do this.
7. Next, use a pipette to transfer a sample of the liquid from the first test tube to a clean cuvette.
8. Put the cuvette in the colorimeter and read and record the absorbance of the solution.
9. Repeat steps 7-8 for the liquids in the remaining four test tubes (using a clean pipette and cuvette each time).
10. You're now ready to analyse your results. Bear in mind that the higher the absorbance reading, the more pigment released, so the higher the permeability of the membrane.

**Tip:** Your cuvettes should be about three quarters full of the sample liquid (or water) before they go into the colorimeter.

Depending on the resources you have available, you may be able to connect the colorimeter to a computer and use software to collect the data and draw a graph of the results.

Module 2: Section 5  Biological Membranes

## Practice Questions — Application

Q1 Adjua leaves some frozen raspberries on a plate to defrost. When she returns, there's a red puddle on the plate around the fruit. Use your knowledge of cell membranes to explain what has happened.

Q2 An experiment was carried out to investigate the effect of increasing methanol concentration on the permeability of beetroot cell membranes. Beetroot cubes were soaked in varying concentrations of methanol for a set amount of time, then a colorimeter was used to read the absorbance of the liquid once the beetroot cubes had been removed. The results of the experiment were used to produce a graph.

a) Give four variables that should be controlled in this experiment.

b) Give two things that should be done with the colorimeter before it is used to measure the absorbance of the liquid samples.

c) Suggest which of the graphs below (A or B) was produced using the results of the experiment. Explain your answer.

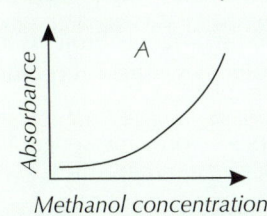

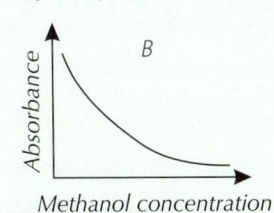

## Practice Questions — Fact Recall

Q1 Explain what is meant when a cell membrane is described as being 'partially permeable'.

Q2 Give three functions of membranes within cells.

Q3 Identify the structures labelled A-E in the diagram below.

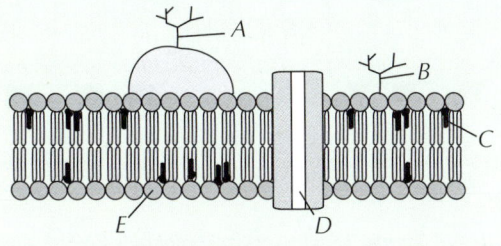

Q4 Explain the meaning of the terms 'hydrophilic' and 'hydrophobic'.

Q5 Explain why the plasma membrane is an effective barrier against water-soluble substances.

Q6 How does the plasma membrane control what enters and leaves the cell?

Q7 Give the function(s) of the following membrane components:

a) cholesterol,

b) glycoproteins and glycolipids.

Q8 Describe and explain what happens to the plasma membrane at temperatures above 45 °C.

**Exam Tip**
Not all diagrams of the fluid mosaic model look the same, so don't just memorise the pictures — make sure you learn what all the different components actually are, what they do and how they fit together.

**Learning Objectives:**

- Understand the role of membranes as sites of cell communication (cell signalling).
- Understand the role of membrane-bound receptors as sites where hormones and drugs can bind.

**Specification Reference 2.1.5**

# 2. Cell Membranes and Signalling

*The cells in your body all need to work together — and to do that, they need to communicate. The cell membrane plays a key role in this communication.*

## Cell signalling

Cells need to communicate with each other to control processes inside the body and to respond to changes in the environment. Cells communicate with each other by cell signalling, which uses messenger molecules.

Cell signalling starts when one cell releases a messenger molecule (e.g. a hormone). This molecule travels to another cell (e.g. in the blood). The messenger molecule is detected by the cell because it binds to a receptor on its cell membrane. The binding then triggers a change in the cell, e.g. a series of chemical signals is set off.

## Membrane receptors

The cell membrane is important in the signalling process. Proteins in the cell membrane act as receptors for messenger molecules. These receptor proteins are called 'membrane-bound receptors'.

Receptor proteins have specific shapes — only messenger molecules with a complementary shape can bind to them. Different cells have different types of receptors — they respond to different messenger molecules. A cell that responds to a particular messenger molecule is called a **target cell**. Figure 1 shows how messenger molecules are able to bind to target cells but not to non-target cells.

**Tip:** Complementary shapes fit together, e.g.

Non-complementary shapes don't fit together, e.g.

**Tip:** You don't just get a single type of receptor on each cell. Every cell type has a specific combination of many different receptors.

*Messenger molecule binds to receptor on target cell.*

*The messenger molecule can't bind to the receptor on non-target cells.*

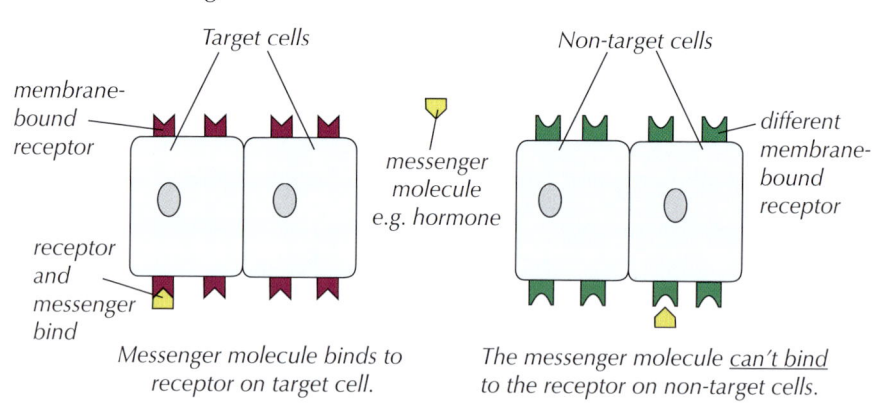

**Figure 1:** Messenger molecules and membrane-bound receptors.

### Hormones as messenger molecules

Many messenger molecules are hormones. Hormones work by binding to receptors in cell membranes and triggering a response in the cell.

---
**Example 1 — Glucagon**

Glucagon is a hormone that's released when there isn't enough glucose in the blood. It binds to receptors on liver cells, causing the liver cells to break down stores of glycogen to glucose.

---

Module 2: Section 5 Biological Membranes

### Example 2 — FSH
FSH is a hormone that's released by the pituitary gland during the menstrual cycle. It binds to receptors on cells in the ovaries, causing an egg to mature ready for ovulation.

**Tip:** A hormone can trigger different responses in different cells. For example, in men, FSH binds to cells in the testes and initiates the production of sperm.

## The role of drugs
Many drugs work by binding to receptors in cell membranes. They either trigger a response in the cell, or block the receptor and prevent it from working. Understanding how cells communicate using membrane-bound receptors is important in the development of medicinal drugs — the receptors can be used as sites for targeted action.

### Example 1 — Morphine
The body produces chemicals called endorphins, to relieve pain. Endorphins bind to opioid receptors in the brain and reduce the transmission of pain signals. Morphine is a drug used to relieve pain. It works by binding to the same opioid receptors as endorphins, also triggering a reduction in pain signals.

### Example 2 — Antihistamines
Cell damage causes the release of a chemical called histamine. Histamine binds to receptors on the surface of other cells and causes inflammation. Antihistamines work by blocking histamine receptors on cell surfaces. This prevents histamine from binding to the cell and stops inflammation.

## Practice Questions — Application
The diagrams below show a messenger molecule, its membrane-bound receptor and a molecule of an antagonistic drug. The drug inhibits the action of the messenger molecule.

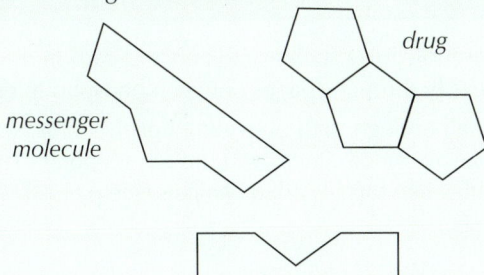

**Tip:** Don't worry if you're not sure what antagonistic means — all the information you need is given in the question. (But just so you know, an antagonistic molecule blocks the action of another molecule.)

Q1 Using the information in the diagrams and your own knowledge, explain how the drug works.

Q2 The diagram on the right shows a mutated version of the membrane-bound receptor. Explain why cells with only the mutated version of the receptor can't respond to the messenger molecule.

Q3 The messenger molecule is only able to produce a response in liver cells. Suggest why this is the case.

Module 2: Section 5 Biological Membranes

**Learning Objectives:**

- Understand the movement of molecules across membranes by diffusion (a passive method).
- Know how to carry out practical investigations into the factors affecting diffusion rates in model cells (PAG8).
- Understand that osmosis is the movement of water across a partially permeable membrane down a water potential gradient.
- Understand the effects that solutions of different water potential can have on plant and animal cells.
- Know how to carry out practical investigations into the effects of solutions of different water potential on plant and animal cells (PAG8).

**Specification Reference 2.1.5**

**Tip:** Particles are constantly moving about randomly using their own kinetic energy — this is how they are able to diffuse from one side of the membrane to the other.

**Tip:** Large molecules, ions and most polar substances need help to cross the plasma membrane — see pages 139-141.

# 3. Diffusion and Osmosis

*There are many ways substances move in and out of cells across the membrane. First up, diffusion and osmosis.*

## Diffusion

Diffusion is the net movement of particles (molecules or ions) from an area of higher concentration to an area of lower concentration — see Figure 1. Molecules will diffuse both ways, but the net movement will be to the area of lower concentration. This continues until particles are evenly distributed throughout the liquid or gas. The concentration gradient is the path from an area of higher concentration to an area of lower concentration. Particles diffuse down a concentration gradient.

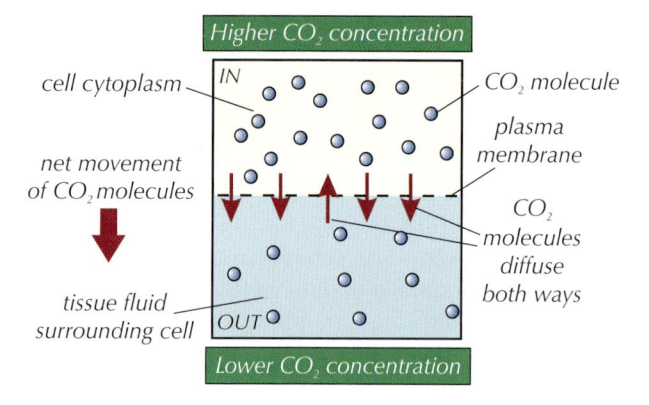

**Figure 1:** Diffusion of carbon dioxide across the plasma membrane.

Diffusion is a passive process — no energy is needed for it to happen. Particles can diffuse across plasma membranes, as long as they can move freely through the membrane.

**Examples**
- Small, non-polar molecules such as oxygen and carbon dioxide are able to diffuse easily through spaces between phospholipids.
- Water is also small enough to fit between phospholipids, so it's able to diffuse across plasma membranes even though it's polar. The diffusion of water molecules like this is called osmosis (see p. 134).

### Factors affecting the rate of diffusion

There are four main factors that affect the rate of diffusion:

- The concentration gradient — the higher it is, the faster the rate of diffusion.
- The thickness of the exchange surface — the thinner the exchange surface (i.e. the shorter the distance the particles travel), the faster the rate.
- The surface area — the larger the surface area (e.g. of the plasma membrane), the faster the rate of diffusion.
- The temperature — the warmer it is, the faster the rate of diffusion because the particles have more kinetic energy so they move faster.

Module 2: Section 5 Biological Membranes

# Investigating diffusion

You can investigate diffusion using model cells — these are materials that are used to represent real cells. Agar jelly is commonly used as a model cell because it has a similar consistency to the cytoplasm of a real cell.

Phenolphthalein is a chemical that can be used to investigate diffusion. It's a pH indicator — it's pink in alkaline solutions and colourless in acidic solutions. If you place cubes of agar jelly containing phenolphthalein and an alkali, such as sodium hydroxide, in an acidic solution and leave them for a while they'll eventually turn colourless as the acid diffuses into the agar jelly and neutralises the sodium hydroxide.

The following three examples show you how you can use agar jelly and phenolphthalein to investigate factors that affect the rate of diffusion:

## Example 1 — Concentration gradient

1. First, make up some agar jelly with phenolphthalein and dilute sodium hydroxide. This will make the jelly a lovely shade of pink.
2. Prepare 5 test tubes containing hydrochloric acid (HCl) in increasing concentrations, e.g. 0.2 M, 0.4 M, 0.6 M, 0.8 M, 1 M.
3. Using a scalpel, cut out 5 equal-sized cubes from the agar jelly.
4. Put one of the cubes into the first test tube and use a stopwatch to time how long it takes for the cube to turn colourless.
5. Then do the same for the rest of the test tubes of HCl using a new cube each time.

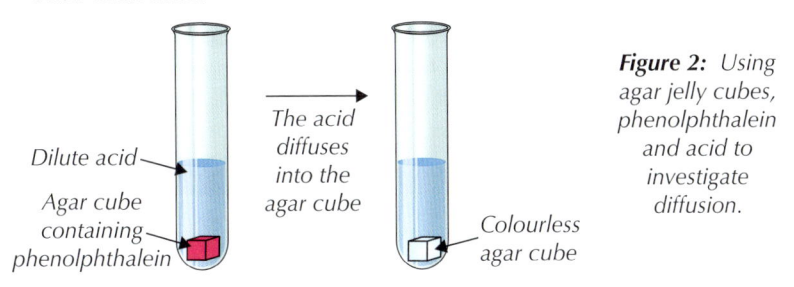

**Figure 2:** Using agar jelly cubes, phenolphthalein and acid to investigate diffusion.

You would expect the cube in the highest concentration of HCl to go colourless fastest, because the concentration gradient is the greatest (see previous page).

## Example 2 — Surface area

Prepare the agar jelly as in Example 1. Then cut it into different sized cubes and work out their surface area to volume ratio (see page 166). Time how long it takes each cube to go colourless when placed in the same concentration of HCl. You would expect the cube with the largest surface area to volume ratio to go colourless fastest.

## Example 3 — Temperature

Prepare the agar jelly as in Example 1 and cut into equal-sized cubes. Then prepare several boiling tubes containing the same concentration of HCl (and put the boiling tubes into water baths at different temperatures). When the HCl in each tube has reached the desired temperature, put a cube of the agar jelly into it and time how long it takes the cube to go colourless. You would expect the cube in the highest temperature to go colourless fastest.

---

**Tip:** Before you start your experiment, make sure you do a risk assessment and identify any hazards. You should wear safety goggles and a lab coat when working with acids.

**Exam Tip**
There are other ways to investigate diffusion in model cells. For example, a different substance could be used as the model cell (e.g. Visking tubing or gelatine cubes) and different pH indicators could be used (e.g. cresol red). Don't worry if you get a question in the exam that uses a different method or different equipment to what's used here — just apply what you know about diffusion to the context you're given.

**Tip:** Don't forget to repeat your experiment at least three times and calculate the mean of your results. This helps to reduce the effect of random errors, making your results more precise (see page 6).

**Tip:** Remember you only change the variable you are investigating — all the other variables should be kept constant (see page 5).

**Tip:** Don't increase the temperature above 65 °C or the agar jelly will start to melt.

### Practice Questions — Application

**Q1** The photograph on the right shows ink diffusing through a beaker of water. Explain what is happening to the ink molecules.

**Q2** Carbon dioxide is a waste product of respiration and must be removed from cells. How will each of the following affect the rate of diffusion of carbon dioxide across a plasma membrane? Explain your answer in each case.
  a) Increasing the thickness of the cell membrane.
  b) Increasing the number of folds in the cell membrane.
  c) Reducing the concentration of carbon dioxide outside of the cell.

**Q3** A student wants to carry out an experiment to investigate diffusion. Her teacher gives her some agar jelly dyed purple with potassium permanganate. Potassium permanganate turns colourless when it reacts with hydrochloric acid.
  a) Describe how the student could use the agar jelly to investigate the effect of temperature on diffusion.
  b) Describe what she should expect to see in the experiment.

## Osmosis

Osmosis is the diffusion of water molecules across a partially permeable membrane down a **water potential gradient**. This means water molecules move from an area of higher water potential (i.e. higher concentration of water molecules) to an area of lower water potential (i.e. lower concentration of water molecules) — see Figure 3.

Water potential is the potential (likelihood) of water molecules to diffuse out of or into a solution.

Pure water has a water potential of zero. Adding solutes to pure water lowers its water potential — so the water potential of any solution is always negative. The more negative the water potential, the stronger the concentration of solutes in the solution.

**Tip:** Water can also move across a membrane through protein channels (see pages 139-140) called aquaporins.

**Exam Tip**
You should always use the term <u>water potential</u> in the exam — never say water concentration.

**Tip:** Another way of looking at it is that pure water has the highest water potential and all solutions have a lower water potential than pure water.

**Exam Tip**
In the exam, you might get asked about experiments involving distilled water. Distilled water is water that's been purified, so it has a water potential of 0.

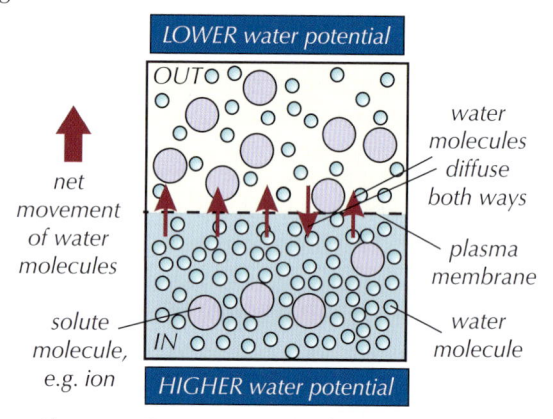

**Figure 3:** Osmosis across a plasma membrane.

--- Example ---
Glass A contains pure water — it's got a water potential of zero. Glass B contains a solution of orange squash. The orange squash molecules are a solute. They lower the concentration of the water molecules. This means that the water potential of the orange squash is lower than the water potential of pure water.

Module 2: Section 5 Biological Membranes

# Water potential and cells

Cells are affected by the water potential of the surrounding solution. Water moves in or out of a cell by osmosis. How much moves in or out depends on the water potential of the surrounding solution compared to that of the cell. Animal and plant cells behave differently in different solutions.

## Isotonic solutions

If two solutions have the same water potential they're said to be isotonic. Cells in an isotonic solution won't lose or gain any water — there's no net movement of water molecules because there's no difference in water potential between the cell and the surrounding solution. Both plant and animal cells will stay the same when placed in an isotonic solution — see Figure 4.

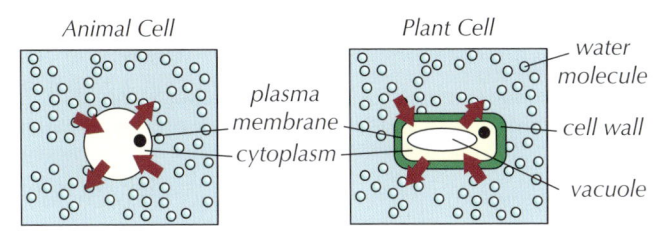

*No net movement of water.*
**Figure 4:** *Cells in isotonic solutions.*

**Tip:** A hypotonic solution would have a weaker concentration of solutes than the cell.

## Hypotonic solutions

If a cell is placed in a solution that has a higher water potential, water will move into the cell by osmosis. Solutions with a higher water potential compared with the inside of the cell are called hypotonic. An animal cell in a hypotonic solution will swell and could eventually burst (see Figure 5).

If a plant cell is placed in a hypotonic solution, the vacuole will swell and the contents of the vacuole and cytoplasm will push against the cell wall (see Figure 5). This causes the cell to become **turgid** (swollen). The cell won't burst because the inelastic cell wall is able to withstand the increase in pressure.

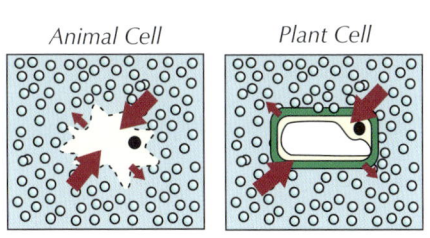

*Net movement of water into the cell.*
**Figure 5:** *Cells in hypotonic solutions.*

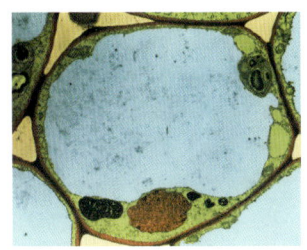

**Figure 6a:** *A turgid plant cell. The full vacuole (blue) is pushing against the cell wall.*

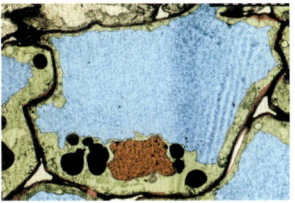

**Figure 6b:** *A flaccid plant cell. Water has left the vacuole.*

## Hypertonic solutions

If a cell is placed in a solution that has a lower water potential, water will move out of the cell by osmosis. Solutions with a lower water potential than the cell are called hypertonic. If an animal cell is placed in a hypertonic solution it will shrink (see Figure 7). If a plant cell is placed in a hypertonic solution it will become **flaccid** (limp). The cytoplasm and plasma membrane will eventually pull away from the cell wall (again, see Figure 7). This is called **plasmolysis**.

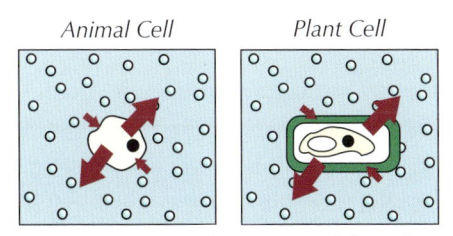

*Net movement of water out of the cell.*
**Figure 7:** *Cells in hypertonic solutions.*

**Tip:** A hypertonic solution would have a stronger concentration of solutes than the cell.

Module 2: Section 5 Biological Membranes

**Tip:** Before you start your investigation do a risk assessment so you are aware of any potential hazards.

**Tip:** You might also see M written as mol dm$^{-3}$.

**Tip:** You could also investigate the water potential of other plant cell types, such as carrot, using the same basic method.

**Tip:** See page 13 for more on calculating percentage change.

# Investigating the effect of water potential on plant cells

PRACTICAL ACTIVITY GROUP 8

You need to know how you could investigate the effect of solutions of different water potential on plant cells. The experiment described below is an example of an experiment you could do using potato cylinders and varying sucrose solutions. Remember, the higher the sucrose concentration, the lower the water potential.

## Method for the experiment

1. Prepare sucrose solutions of the following concentrations: 0.0 M, 0.2 M, 0.4 M, 0.6 M, 0.8 M, 1.0 M.
2. Use a cork borer to cut potatoes into identically sized cylinders, about 1 cm in diameter. Divide the cylinders into groups of three and measure the mass of each group using a mass balance.
3. Place one group into each of your sucrose solutions and leave the cylinders in the solutions for at least 20 minutes (making sure that they all get the same amount of time).
4. Remove the cylinders and pat them dry gently with a paper towel. Weigh each group again and record your results.
5. Calculate the percentage change in mass for each group.

### Examples — Maths Skills

To find the percentage change in mass, use the following formula:

$$\text{percentage change} = \frac{\text{final mass} - \text{initial mass}}{\text{initial mass}} \times 100$$

1. So, if you had a group of cylinders that weighed 13.2 g at the start of the experiment and 15.1 g at the end, the percentage change in mass would be...

$$\text{percentage change} = \frac{15.1 - 13.2}{13.2} \times 100 = \mathbf{14.4\%}$$

The positive result tells you the potato cylinders gained mass.

2. If you had another group of potato cylinders that weighed 13.3 g at the start of the experiment and 11.4 g at the end, the percentage change in mass would be...

$$\text{percentage change} = \frac{11.4 - 13.3}{13.3} \times 100 = \mathbf{-14.3\%}$$

The negative result tells you the potato cylinders lost mass.

The potato cylinders will gain water (and therefore mass) in solutions with a higher water potential than the cylinders, and lose water in solutions with a lower water potential.

**Figure 8:** Osmosis in carrot cells. The carrot on the left has been placed in salty water (low water potential) and the carrot on the right has been placed in pure water.

**Tip:** If you could see the potato cells under a microscope, you'd see them becoming turgid as the cylinder gains mass and plasmolysed as the cylinder loses mass (see previous page).

## Plotting a graph of your results

Next you can use your results to plot a graph. This helps you find the point at which the potato cells don't change in mass. At this point the cells must be in an isotonic solution, because the cells don't lose or gain water — so you can use your graph to find the water potential of the potato cells (see next page).

## Example — Maths Skills

The table shows results from the experiment. You can use the data to draw a scatter graph.

| concentration (M) | 0 | 0.2 | 0.4 | 0.6 | 0.8 | 1.0 |
|---|---|---|---|---|---|---|
| % change | 20 | 5 | -7 | -14 | -17 | -18 |

1. Draw your axes — don't forget to label them, including the units.
2. Plot the points carefully. You then need to draw a line of best fit through your points. In this case, draw a smooth curve passing through as many points as possible.
3. The point where the line of best fit crosses the x-axis is the point where the sucrose solution has the same water potential as the potato cells. Here it's around 0.27 M. You can look up the water potential for this concentration of sucrose solution in, e.g. a textbook.

This point is where the water potential of the sucrose solution is the same as the water potential of the potato cells.

**Tip:** There's more about plotting graphs and lines of best fit on page 19.

**Tip:** Don't forget to use a sensible scale so that your graph takes up at least half of your graph paper.

**Tip:** Put the independent variable, the concentration, on the x-axis and the dependent variable, the percentage change in mass, on the y-axis.

# Investigating the effect of water potential on animal cells

**PRACTICAL ACTIVITY GROUP 8**

You can investigate the effect of water potential on animal cells using chickens' eggs that have had their shells dissolved. The remaining membrane is partially permeable, so it's a good model for showing the effects of osmosis in animal tissue.

Here's an example of how you could do it:

### Example — Osmosis in chickens' eggs

1. Make up sodium chloride solutions of different concentrations, e.g. 0.2 M, 0.4 M, 0.6 M, 0.8 M, 1.0 M, and pour an equal volume into separate beakers.
2. Take your de-shelled eggs and carefully pat them with absorbent paper to remove any excess moisture.
3. Use a mass balance to weigh each egg, then record its mass in a table.
4. Place each egg in a different beaker, making sure that the sodium chloride solution is covering the whole egg (see Figure 9). Leave all the eggs for the same amount of time, e.g. 24 hours.
5. Remove the eggs, dry them and then weigh them again. Use your results to calculate the percentage change in mass for each egg (see previous page).
6. Plot a graph of your results (as shown above) and use it to see how solutions of different water potential (i.e. different sodium chloride solutions) affect the mass of the egg.

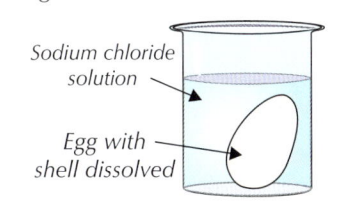

**Figure 9:** Investigating the effect of solutions of different water potential on animal cells.

**Tip:** Before you start, make sure you think through any safety issues and work out how you are going to minimise the risks. You should wear safety goggles for this practical in case any of the solutions are splashed in your eyes.

**Tip:** Your teacher will dissolve the shells in hydrochloric acid so the eggs are ready for you to use.

**Tip:** Water potential is usually measured in kilopascals (or kPa). It's actually a unit of pressure.

**Tip:** Remember, a higher water potential is closer to 0 (the water potential of pure water).

**Tip:** Visking tubing is a partially permeable membrane — it's used a lot in osmosis and diffusion experiments.

## Practice Questions — Application

Q1 Describe the net movement of water molecules in each of the following situations:
   a) Human cheek cells with a water potential of −300 kPa are placed in a salt solution with a water potential of −325 kPa.
   b) Apple slices with a water potential of −750 kPa are placed in a beaker of pure water.
   c) Orange squash with a water potential of −450 kPa is sealed in a length of Visking tubing and suspended in a solution of equal water potential.

Q2 Potato cells with a water potential of −350 kPa are placed in sucrose solutions with varying water potentials. The water potential of each solution is shown in the table below.

| Solution | Water potential |
|---|---|
| 1 | −250 kPa |
| 2 | −500 kPa |
| 3 | −1000 kPa |

   a) After 15 minutes, the potato cells in solution 1 have become turgid. Explain why this has happened.
   b) Predict what will happen to the cells in solutions 2 and 3. Explain your answers.

## Practice Questions — Fact Recall

Q1 What is diffusion?
Q2 Is diffusion an active or a passive process?
Q3 What types of molecules are able to diffuse through the plasma membrane of a cell?
Q4 Give four factors that affect the rate of diffusion.
Q5 What term is used to describe the diffusion of water molecules across a partially permeable membrane down a water potential gradient?
Q6 Define the term 'water potential'.
Q7 Describe and explain what will happen to each of the following:
   a) an animal cell placed in a hypotonic solution,
   b) a plant cell placed in a hypotonic solution,
   c) a plant cell placed in a hypertonic solution.

**Tip:** A hypotonic solution has a higher water potential than the cell. A hypertonic solution has a lower water potential than the cell.

# 4. Facilitated Diffusion and Active Transport

*The large size or charged nature of some molecules prevents them from being able to pass directly through a membrane. That's where facilitated diffusion and active transport come in...*

## Facilitated diffusion

Some larger molecules (e.g. amino acids, glucose) would diffuse extremely slowly through the phospholipid bilayer because they're so big. Charged particles, e.g. ions and polar molecules, would also diffuse slowly — that's because they're water soluble, and the centre of the bilayer is hydrophobic (see page 125). So to speed things up, large or charged particles diffuse through carrier proteins or channel proteins in the cell membrane instead — this is called facilitated diffusion.

Like diffusion, facilitated diffusion moves particles down a concentration gradient, from a higher to a lower concentration. It's also a passive process — it doesn't use energy. But unlike diffusion, there are two types of membrane protein involved — carrier proteins and channel proteins.

### Carrier proteins

Carrier proteins move large molecules (including polar molecules and ions) into or out of the cell, down their concentration gradient. Different carrier proteins facilitate the diffusion of different molecules.

**Example**

GLUT1 is a carrier protein found in almost all animal cells. It specifically helps to transport glucose across the plasma membrane.

Here's how carrier proteins work:
- First, a large molecule attaches to a carrier protein in the membrane.
- Then, the protein changes shape.
- This releases the molecule on the opposite side of the membrane — see Figure 1.

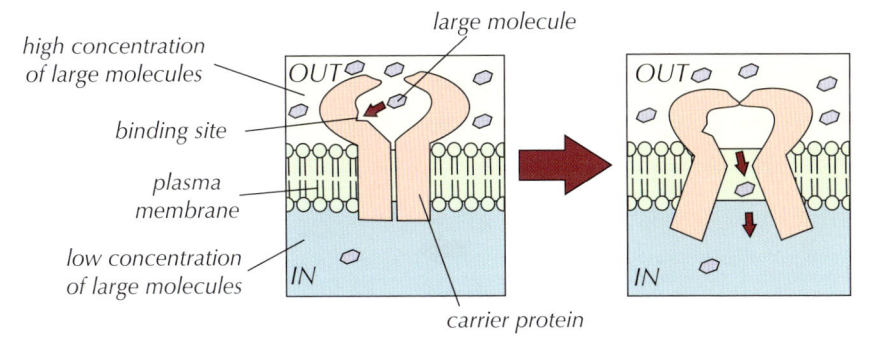

**Figure 1:** Movement of a molecule by a carrier protein.

### Channel proteins

Channel proteins form pores in the membrane for smaller ions and polar molecules to diffuse through, down their concentration gradient (see Figure 3 — next page). Different channel proteins facilitate the diffusion of different charged particles.

---

**Learning Objectives:**
- Understand the movement of molecules across membranes by facilitated diffusion (a passive method).
- Understand the movement of molecules across membranes by active transport, endocytosis and exocytosis (all processes that require adenosine triphosphate, ATP, as an immediate source of energy).

**Specification Reference 2.1.5**

**Tip:** Remember — small, non-polar substances and water can diffuse directly through the membrane.

**Exam Tip**
Always say <u>down</u> the concentration gradient in the exam, not across or along — or you won't get the marks.

**Tip:** Carrier proteins are sometimes called transport proteins.

Module 2: Section 5 Biological Membranes

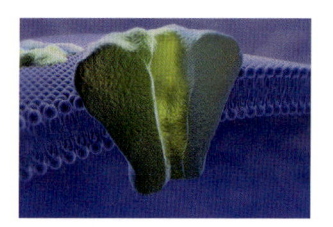

Figure 2: Computer model showing a cross-section of a channel protein in the phospholipid bilayer.

**Tip:** ATP stands for adenosine triphosphate (there's more about ATP on pages 89-90).

**Tip:** Most of the ATP in a cell is produced by aerobic respiration. Aerobic respiration takes place in the mitochondria and is controlled by enzymes.

**Exam Tip**
It's easy to get facilitated diffusion and active transport confused because they both use proteins to transport molecules. But active transport is the only one that uses energy (ATP) to do so.

**Tip:** Endocytosis and exocytosis (see next page) both require energy.

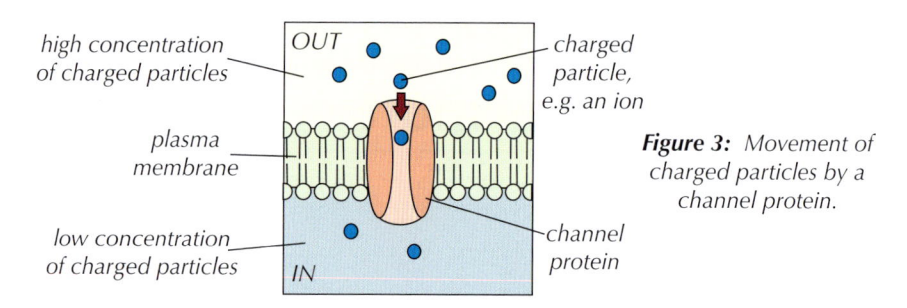

Figure 3: Movement of charged particles by a channel protein.

## Active transport

Active transport uses energy to move molecules and ions across plasma membranes, against a concentration gradient. This process involves carrier proteins and is pretty similar to facilitated diffusion — see Figure 4. A molecule attaches to the carrier protein, the protein changes shape and this moves the molecule across the membrane, releasing it on the other side. The only difference is that energy is used (from ATP — a common source of energy used in the cell), to move the solute against its concentration gradient.

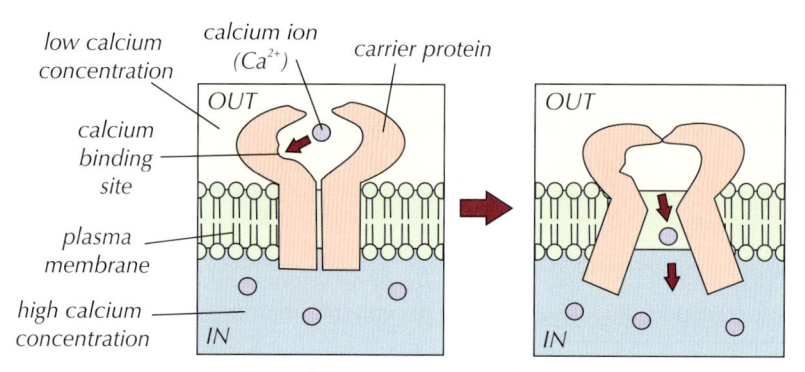

Figure 4: The active transport of calcium ions. (calcium ion $Ca^{2+}$)

## Endocytosis

Some molecules are way too large to be taken into a cell by carrier proteins, e.g. proteins, lipids and some carbohydrates. Instead a cell can surround a substance with a section of its plasma membrane. The membrane then pinches off to form a vesicle inside the cell containing the ingested substance — the substance has been taken in by endocytosis (see Figure 5).

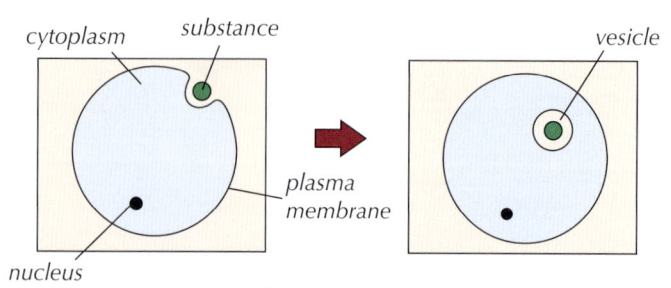

Figure 5: The process of endocytosis.

Some cells also take in much larger objects by endocytosis — for example, some white blood cells (mainly phagocytes, see page 230) use endocytosis to take in things like microorganisms and dead cells so that they can destroy them. Like active transport, this process uses ATP for energy.

Module 2: Section 5 Biological Membranes

# Exocytosis

Some substances produced by the cell (e.g. digestive enzymes, hormones, lipids) need to be released from the cell — this is done by exocytosis (see Figure 6). Vesicles containing these substances pinch off from the sacs of the Golgi apparatus and move towards the plasma membrane. The vesicles fuse with the plasma membrane and release their contents outside the cell. Some substances (like membrane proteins) aren't released outside the cell — instead they are inserted straight into the plasma membrane. Exocytosis also uses ATP as an energy source.

**Tip:** It can be easy to confuse endocytosis and exocytosis — so try to remember that <u>ex</u>ocytosis is used for things <u>ex</u>iting the cell.

*Vesicle buds off from Golgi apparatus.*
*Vesicle moves to plasma membrane.*
*Vesicle fuses with plasma membrane.*
*Contents of vesicle released outside the cell.*

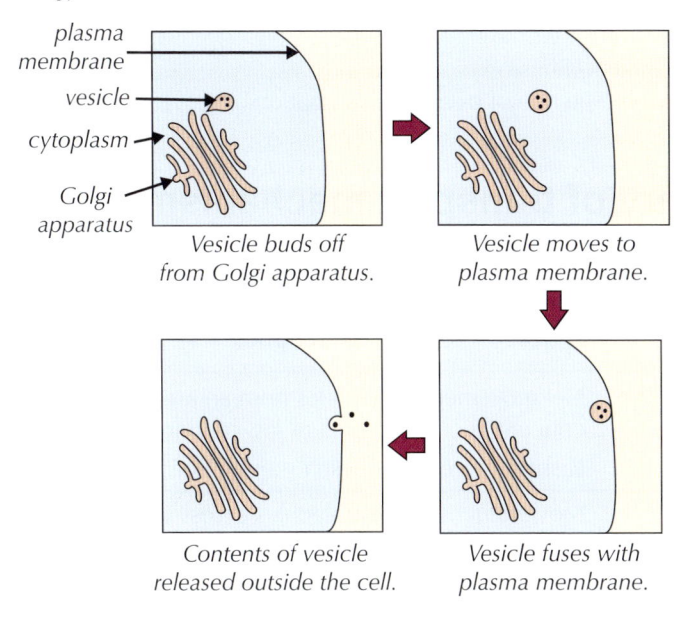

**Figure 6:** *The process of exocytosis.*

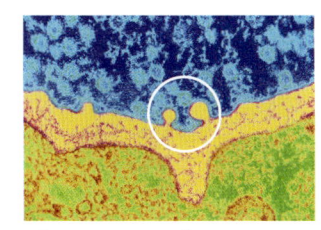

**Figure 7:** *Vesicles containing substances for secretion breaking through the plasma membrane (circled).*

**Tip:** There's more on vesicles and the Golgi apparatus on p. 41.

## Practice Questions — Application

Q1 The diagram below shows a gap between two neurones. Each neurone is surrounded by a membrane. Chemical messengers are secreted from the membrane of neurone 1 and travel across the gap to the membrane of neurone 2, where they bind with cell surface receptors.

a) Name structure Z.
b) Describe what is happening in steps A to C on the diagram.

Once the chemical messengers bind to the receptors, they cause sodium ions (Na⁺) to move across the membrane of neurone 2, down a concentration gradient.

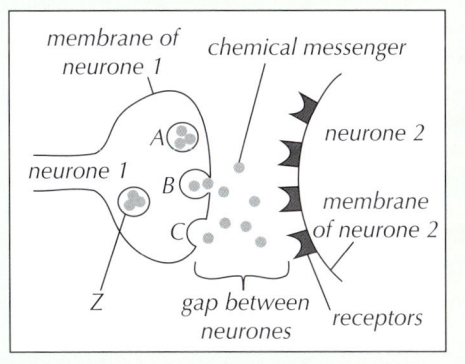

c) Suggest how the sodium ions might travel across the membrane.

**Exam Tip**
Always be specific about which membrane you're talking about in the exam — don't just say, 'fuses with the cell membrane', if what you mean is 'fuses with the cell surface (plasma) membrane'.

Module 2: Section 5 Biological Membranes

Q2  The overall equation for aerobic respiration can be written as:

glucose + oxygen → carbon dioxide + water + ATP

The graph below shows the relationship between the relative rates of oxygen consumption and the active transport of sodium ions across epithelial cells.

a) Describe the relationship shown by the graph and suggest an explanation for this relationship.

b) What effect would the rate of the facilitated diffusion of sodium ions have on the rate of oxygen consumption?

## Summary of transport mechanisms

You've covered a lot of different transport mechanisms in this section, so here's a handy table to help you remember the similarities and differences:

**Tip:** Understanding the different ways that substances are transported into our cells is really important in medicine. It helps scientists understand how different drugs get into our cells and could help them to develop new ways to administer drugs in the future.

**Exam Tip**
Make sure you know the definitions of each type of transport off by heart.

**Exam Tip**
Make sure you know what types of molecules (e.g. large/small, polar/non-polar/ionic) are moved by the different types of transport.

| Type of transport: | Description |
|---|---|
| **Diffusion** (see p. 132) | • Net movement of particles from an area of higher concentration to an area of lower concentration.<br>• Passive process — doesn't require energy. |
| **Osmosis** (see pages 134-135) | • Movement of water molecules across a partially permeable membrane down a water potential gradient, from an area of higher water potential to an area of lower water potential.<br>• Passive process — doesn't require energy. |
| **Facilitated diffusion** (see pages 139-140) | • Net movement of particles from an area of higher concentration to an area of lower concentration.<br>• Uses carrier proteins to aid the diffusion of large molecules (including ions and polar molecules) through the plasma membrane.<br>• Uses channel proteins to aid the diffusion of smaller ions and polar molecules through the plasma membrane.<br>• Passive process — doesn't require energy. |
| **Active transport** (see p. 140) | • Movement of molecules against a concentration gradient.<br>• Uses carrier proteins to transport molecules.<br>• Active process — requires energy (ATP). |
| **Endocytosis** (see p. 140) | • Movement of large molecules (e.g. proteins) or objects (e.g. dead cells) into a cell.<br>• The plasma membrane surrounds a substance and then pinches off to form a vesicle inside the cell.<br>• Active process — requires energy (ATP). |
| **Exocytosis** (see p. 141) | • Movement of molecules out of a cell.<br>• Vesicles fuse with the plasma membrane and release their contents.<br>• Active process — requires energy (ATP). |

Module 2: Section 5  Biological Membranes

## Practice Question — Application

Q1 Copy and complete the table to show which kind of transport could be used in each case. The first column has been done for you.

| Transport system | A plant cell taking in water | Calcium ions moving into a cell against a concentration gradient | A muscle cell taking in polar glucose molecules | A white blood cell taking in anthrax bacteria |
|---|---|---|---|---|
| Osmosis | ✓ | | | |
| Facilitated diffusion using channel proteins | ✓ | | | |
| Facilitated diffusion using carrier proteins | ✗ | | | |
| Active transport using carrier proteins | ✗ | | | |
| Endocytosis | ✗ | | | |
| Exocytosis | ✗ | | | |

**Tip:** Calcium ions are charged, but relatively small.

**Tip:** Glucose is a polar molecule, but it's also relatively large.

**Tip:** If you're struggling with this table, think carefully about the type of substance being transported in each case.

## Practice Questions — Fact Recall

Q1 Describe the difference between simple diffusion through a plasma membrane and facilitated diffusion through a plasma membrane.

Q2 Summarise the similarities and differences between facilitated diffusion and active transport.

Q3 Describe how the following are used to transport substances across a cell membrane:

a) carrier proteins,  b) channel proteins.

Q4 Describe the process of endocytosis.

Q5 Give an example of a substance that might be transported across a cell membrane by exocytosis.

# Section Summary

Make sure you know...

- That plasma membranes are partially permeable and have a range of functions including: controlling which substances enter and leave the cell, allowing recognition by other cells, and allowing cells to communicate.
- That membranes within cells are also partially permeable and have a range of functions including: surrounding an organelle and acting as a barrier between the organelle and the cytoplasm, controlling what substances enter and leave an organelle, acting as the site of chemical reactions, and (for membranes within organelles) acting as a barrier between the membrane contents and the rest of the organelle.
- The fluid mosaic model of cell membrane structure, including the roles of phospholipids (form a barrier to dissolved substances), cholesterol (regulates the fluidity), proteins (control what enters and leaves the cell, act as receptors), glycolipids and glycoproteins (stabilise the membrane, act as receptors/antigens).
- That some solvents, such as ethanol, dissolve the lipids in a cell membrane, causing it to lose its structure and become more permeable.
- That temperature influences how much the phospholipids in the bilayer of a cell membrane can move, affecting the membrane's structure and permeability.
- How to investigate the effect of a variable, such as solvent concentration or temperature, on cell membrane structure and permeability, e.g. by using cubes of beetroot.
- That cells communicate with each other through cell signalling using messenger molecules, and that messenger molecules bind to membrane-bound receptors on target cells.
- That membrane-bound receptors are sites where hormones and drugs bind.
- That diffusion is the passive movement of particles from an area of higher concentration to an area of lower concentration.
- That the rate of diffusion is affected by concentration gradient, thickness of the exchange surface, surface area and temperature.
- How to investigate the effect of a variable, such as concentration gradient, surface area or temperature, on the rate of diffusion in model cells, e.g. by using cubes of agar jelly and a pH indicator such as phenolphthalein.
- That osmosis is diffusion of water molecules across a partially permeable membrane down a water potential gradient, from an area of higher water potential to an area of lower water potential.
- How animal and plant cells behave in isotonic, hypotonic and hypertonic solutions.
- How to investigate the effect of water potential on plant and animal cells, e.g. by using potato cylinders or a chicken's egg with the shell dissolved and a range of sucrose or salt solutions.
- That facilitated diffusion (a passive process) uses carrier proteins and channel proteins to move large molecules and charged particles, e.g. ions and polar molecules, down a concentration gradient.
- That active transport uses carrier proteins and energy (from ATP) to actively move molecules against a concentration gradient.
- That cells can take in large substances by endocytosis using energy from ATP — the plasma membrane surrounds the substance and then pinches off, forming a vesicle inside the cell.
- That cells can secrete substances by exocytosis also using energy from ATP — vesicles containing substances for release outside the cell fuse with the plasma membrane, then release their contents.

# Exam-style Questions

1      Fig. 1.1 shows normal onion cells under a light microscope. The cytoplasm appears dark grey. Fig. 1.2 shows the same onion cells after they have been placed in a **weak salt solution**. The solution has a lower water potential than the onion cells.

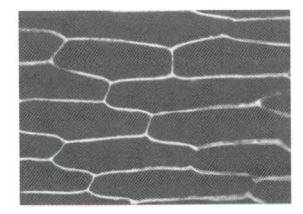

Fig. 1.1      Fig. 1.2

    (a) (i) Explain what is meant by the term water potential.

*(1 mark)*

        (ii) Describe and explain the changes seen between **Fig. 1.1** and **Fig. 1.2**.

*(3 marks)*

        (iii) Describe what might happen if animal cells were placed in a solution with a lower water potential than the cell contents.

*(1 mark)*

    (b) In **Fig. 1.2** it is possible to see the cells' plasma membranes.
        (i) Describe the fluid mosaic structure of the plasma membrane.

*(4 marks)*

        (ii) State **two** functions of the plasma membrane.

*(2 marks)*

2      Glucose is a product of digestion. It is also a relatively large polar molecule. Once glucose has been digested, it must be absorbed into the bloodstream from the cells of the small intestine. Part of the absorption process happens by facilitated diffusion.

    (a) (i) Suggest why facilitated diffusion is necessary for glucose to cross the plasma membranes of the intestinal cells.

*(3 marks)*

        (ii) Does this process require energy? Explain your answer.

*(1 mark)*

        (iii) State the type of molecule that facilitates the diffusion of glucose across plasma membranes in the small intestine, and briefly describe how it does so.

*(2 marks)*

    (b) Another stage of the absorption process uses active transport. Explain what is meant by the term active transport.

*(2 marks)*

Module 2: Section 5  Biological Membranes

**3**   A group of students investigated the water potential of potato cells.

They cut cubes of potato of the same size and shape, weighed them and placed a single cube into each of four different concentrations of sucrose solution. One cube was placed in pure water.

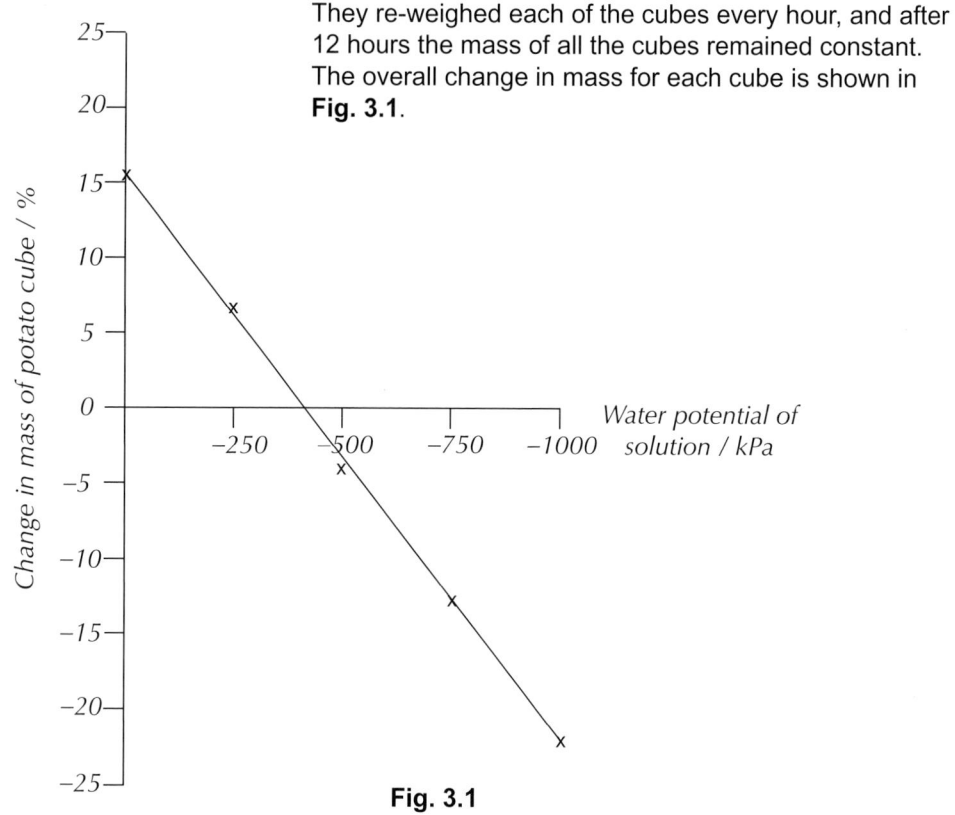

They re-weighed each of the cubes every hour, and after 12 hours the mass of all the cubes remained constant. The overall change in mass for each cube is shown in **Fig. 3.1**.

**Fig. 3.1**

**(a)** The students recorded the difference in mass between the cubes at the start and end of the experiment in grams, but plotted the overall change as a percentage. Suggest why the graph was plotted in this way.

*(1 mark)*

**(b)** What was the change in mass for the potato cube placed in pure water?

*(1 mark)*

**(c) (i)** Explain why the cubes in the **−500, −750** and **−1000 kPa** solutions lost mass.

*(2 marks)*

**(ii)** Use **Fig. 3.1** to estimate the water potential of the potato cells.

*(1 mark)*

**(d)** Suggest how the students could make their results more precise.

*(1 mark)*

**(e)** If the experiment was repeated with cubes that had a larger surface area, would you expect the mass of all the cubes to become constant before 12 hours, at 12 hours or after 12 hours? Explain your answer.

*(2 marks)*

# Module 2 Section 6: Cell Division and Cellular Organisation

## 1. The Cell Cycle and Mitosis

*We need new cells for growth and to replace damaged tissue, so our body cells need to be able to make more of themselves. They do this during the cell cycle.*

### The cell cycle

The cell cycle is the process that all body cells in multicellular organisms use to grow and divide. It starts when a cell has been produced by cell division and ends with the cell dividing to produce two identical cells.

The cell cycle consists of a period of cell growth and DNA replication, called **interphase**, and a period of cell division, called M phase. M phase involves **mitosis** (nuclear division) and **cytokinesis** (cytoplasmic division). Interphase (cell growth) is subdivided into three separate growth stages. These are called $G_1$, S and $G_2$ — see Figure 1.

The cell cycle is regulated by checkpoints. Checkpoints occur at key points during the cycle to make sure it's OK for the process to continue.

**G2 Checkpoint**
The cell checks whether all the DNA has been replicated without any damage. If it has, the cell can enter mitosis.

**M PHASE** (mitosis and cytokinesis)

**Metaphase Checkpoint** (see next page)

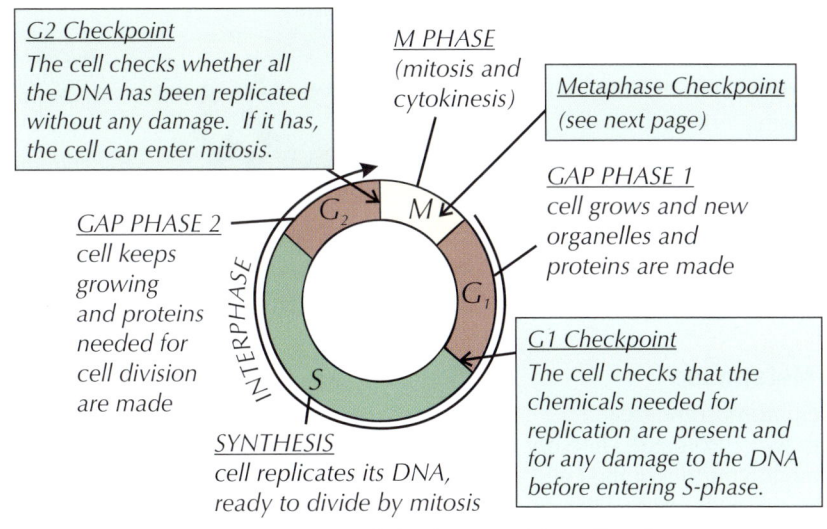

**GAP PHASE 2**
cell keeps growing and proteins needed for cell division are made

**GAP PHASE 1**
cell grows and new organelles and proteins are made

**G1 Checkpoint**
The cell checks that the chemicals needed for replication are present and for any damage to the DNA before entering S-phase.

**SYNTHESIS**
cell replicates its DNA, ready to divide by mitosis

*Figure 1: Stages and checkpoints of the cell cycle.*

### Interphase

During interphase the cell carries out normal functions, but also prepares to divide. The cell's DNA is unravelled and replicated, to double its genetic content. The organelles are also replicated so it has spare ones, and its ATP content is increased (ATP provides the energy needed for cell division).

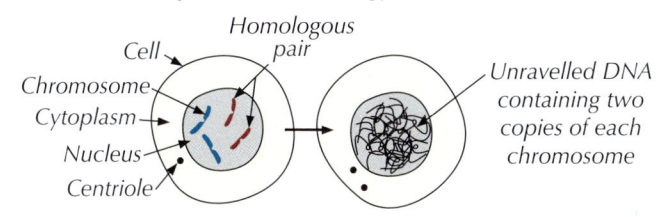

### Learning Objectives:

- Understand the cell cycle, including the processes taking place during interphase ($G_1$, S and $G_2$), mitosis and cytokinesis, leading to genetically identical cells.
- Know how the cell cycle is regulated, including an outline of the use of checkpoints to control the cycle.
- Understand the significance of mitosis in life cycles, including growth, tissue repair and asexual reproduction in plants, animals and fungi.
- Know the main stages of mitosis, including the changes in the nuclear envelope, chromosomes, chromatids, centromere, centrioles, spindle fibres and cell membrane.
- Be able to recognise sections of plant tissue showing the cell cycle and stages of mitosis.
- Be able to prepare and examine stained sections and squashes of plant tissue, in order to produce labelled diagrams showing the cell cycle and stages of mitosis observed (PAG1).

**Specification Reference 2.1.6**

*Figure 2: Interphase in bluebell cells.*

**Tip:** You could remember the order of the phases in mitosis (**p**rophase, **m**etaphase, **a**naphase, **t**elophase) by using, '**p**urple **m**ice **a**re **t**asty'.

# Mitosis

There are two types of cell division — mitosis and meiosis (see p. 151 for more on meiosis). Mitosis is the form of cell division that occurs during the cell cycle. It's needed for the growth of multicellular organisms (like us) and for repairing damaged tissues. Some animals, plants and fungi also use it to reproduce asexually (without sex). Mitosis is really one continuous process, but it's described as a series of division stages — prophase, metaphase, anaphase and telophase.

## The structure of chromosomes in mitosis

Before we go into the detail of mitosis, you need to know more about the structure of chromosomes. As mitosis begins, the chromosomes are made of two strands joined in the middle by a **centromere**. The separate strands are called **chromatids**. Two strands on the same chromosome are called **sister chromatids**. There are two strands because each chromosome has already made an identical copy of itself during interphase. When mitosis is over, the chromatids end up as one-strand chromosomes in the new daughter cells.

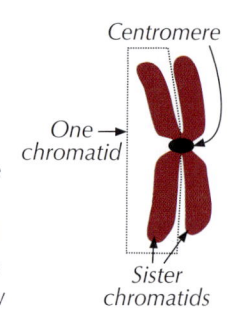

### 1. Prophase

The chromosomes condense, getting shorter and fatter. Tiny bundles of protein called **centrioles** start moving to opposite ends of the cell, forming a network of protein fibres across it called the **spindle**. The **nuclear envelope** (the membrane around the nucleus) breaks down and chromosomes lie free in the cytoplasm.

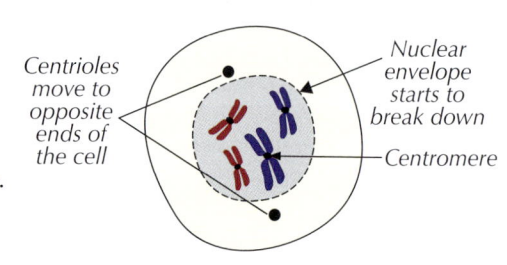

*Figure 3: Prophase in bluebell cells.*

### 2. Metaphase

The chromosomes (each with two chromatids) line up along the middle of the cell (at the spindle equator) and become attached to the spindle by their centromere. At the metaphase checkpoint, the cell checks that all the chromosomes are attached to the spindle before mitosis can continue.

*Figure 4: Metaphase in bluebell cells.*

### 3. Anaphase

The centromeres divide, separating each pair of sister chromatids. The spindles contract, pulling chromatids to opposite ends of the cell, centromere first.

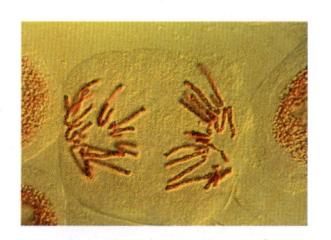

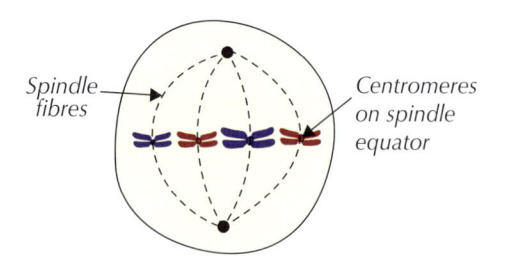

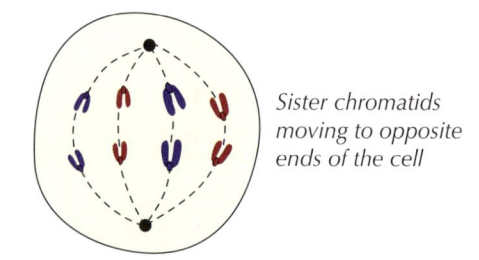

*Figure 5: Anaphase in bluebell cells.*

Module 2: Section 6 Cell Division and Cellular Organisation

## 4. Telophase

The chromatids reach the opposite poles on the spindle. They uncoil and become long and thin again. They're now called chromosomes again. A nuclear envelope forms around each group of chromosomes, so there are now two nuclei.

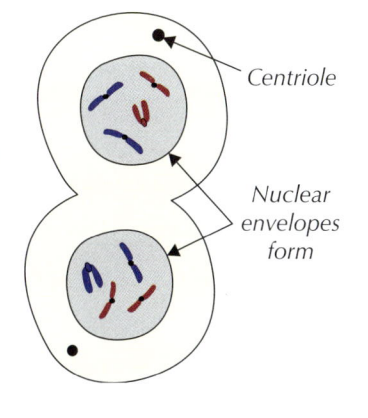

*Figure 6: Telophase in bluebell cells.*

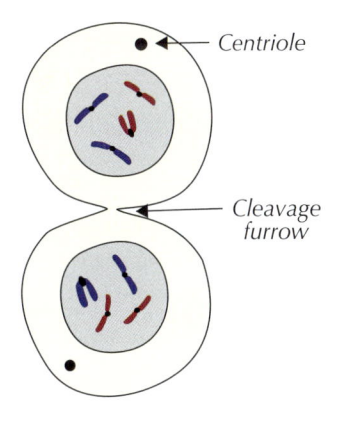

### Cytokinesis

The cytoplasm divides. In animal cells, a cleavage furrow forms to divide the cell membrane. There are now two daughter cells that are genetically identical to the original cell and to each other. Cytokinesis usually begins in anaphase and ends in telophase. It's a separate process to mitosis.

# Investigating mitosis

**PRACTICAL ACTIVITY GROUP 1**

You can stain chromosomes so you can see them under a microscope. This means you can watch what happens to them during mitosis. To do this, you need to stain the specimen, put it on a microscope slide and examine it under a microscope — see pages 52-54 for more details of how to do these things.

Figure 7 shows some plant root tip cells on a 'squash' microscope slide, viewed under a light microscope. Squashes like this can be made by treating the very tips of growing roots in hydrochloric acid, then breaking them open and spreading the cells thinly on a microscope slide using a mounted needle. A few drops of stain are then added to the spread out cells before they are physically squashed beneath a coverslip. When you look at the slide under the light microscope, you should be able to see cells at different stages of the cell cycle and mitosis. You need to be able to recognise, draw and label each stage.

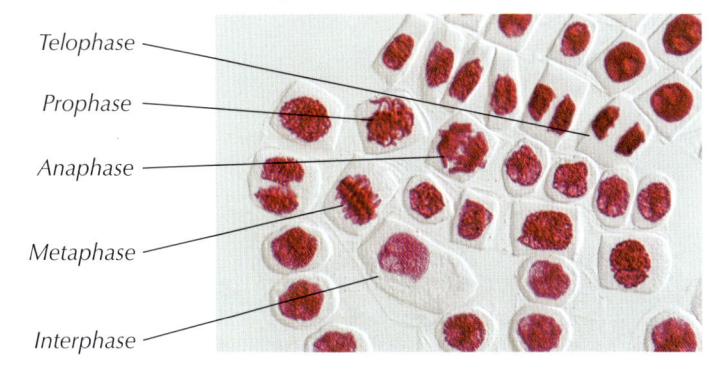

*Figure 7: Stained plant root cells on a squash microscope slide.*

**Tip:** If you do carry out an experiment like this make sure you're wearing safety goggles and a lab coat before you start. You should also wear gloves when using stains.

**Tip:** Different stains you can use for this include toluidine blue O, ethano-orcein and Feulgen stain. Make sure you carry out a risk assessment (see p. 7) before you do this experiment, including assessing the specific risks for the particular staining technique you're using.

**Tip:** You can recognise cells in interphase because the chromosomes will be spread out and not condensed.

Module 2: Section 6 Cell Division and Cellular Organisation

## Practice Question — Application

Q1  Mitosis takes place during M phase of the cell cycle.

a) Copy and complete the table below to show the different stages involved in mitosis and the order that they occur in.

| Stage of Mitosis | Step Number |
|---|---|
|  | 3 |
|  |  |
| Prophase | 1 |
| Metaphase |  |

b) The images below show mitosis occurring in three onion cells.

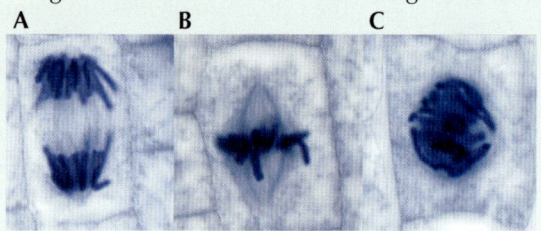

A  B  C

Which cell (A-C) is undergoing the following:
i) metaphase?
ii) prophase?

c) Describe the stage of mitosis shown by cell A.

## Practice Questions — Fact Recall

Q1  What is the cell cycle?
Q2  During which period of the cell cycle does cell growth occur?
Q3  Why is DNA is checked during interphase?
Q4  Why is mitosis needed?
Q5  Describe what happens during prophase.
Q6  During which stage of mitosis do chromosomes line up along the centre of a cell?
Q7  During which stage of mitosis are chromatids pulled to opposite ends of the cell?
Q8  How does an animal cell divide by cytokinesis?
Q9  How many cells are produced during mitosis?
Q10 In mitosis, a parent cell divides to produce genetically different daughter cells. True or false?

# 2. Sexual Reproduction and Meiosis

*Some organisms reproduce using mitosis. Other organisms produce offspring through sexual reproduction, so they need gametes (sex cells) — and these are made by meiosis. It's way less confusing than it sounds, promise...*

## Sexual reproduction

Gametes are the sperm cells in males and egg cells in females. In sexual reproduction two gametes join together at fertilisation to form a zygote, which divides and develops into a new organism.

Normal body cells have the **diploid number (2n)** of chromosomes — meaning each cell contains two of each chromosome (a pair), one from the mum and one from the dad. The chromosomes that make up each pair are the same size and have the same genes, although they could have different versions of those genes (called alleles). These pairs of matching chromosomes are called **homologous chromosomes**.

**Example**

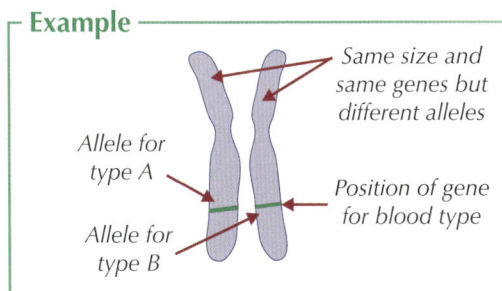

*Figure 1: Diagram showing a pair of homologous chromosomes.*

Gametes have a **haploid (n) number** of chromosomes — there's only one copy of each chromosome. At fertilisation, a haploid sperm fuses with a haploid egg, making a cell with the normal diploid number of chromosomes. Half these chromosomes are from the father (the sperm) and half are from the mother (the egg). The diploid cell produced by fertilisation is called a zygote.

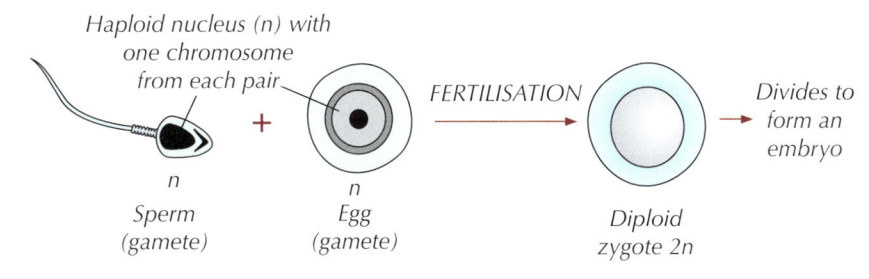

*Figure 2: Diagram to show fertilisation.*

## What is meiosis?

Meiosis is a type of cell division that happens in the reproductive organs to produce gametes. Meiosis involves a reduction division. Cells that divide by meiosis are diploid to start with, but the cells that are formed from meiosis are haploid — the chromosome number halves. Cells formed by meiosis are all genetically different because each new cell ends up with a different combination of chromosomes.

---

**Learning Objectives:**
- Understand what homologous chromosomes are.
- Understand the significance of meiosis in life cycles, including the production of haploid cells.
- Know the main stages of meiosis, including:
  - interphase
  - prophase 1
  - metaphase 1
  - anaphase 1
  - telophase 1
  - prophase 2
  - metaphase 2
  - anaphase 2
  - telophase 2
- Understand the mechanisms of genetic variation by crossing over and independent assortment.

**Specification Reference 2.1.6**

**Exam Tip**
Make sure you know what a homologous pair of chromosomes is for the exam.

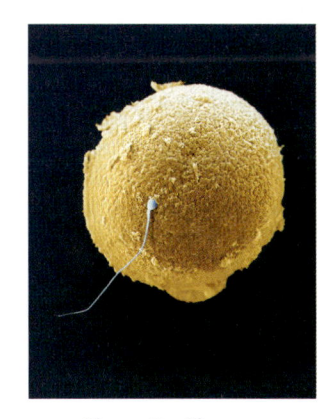

*Figure 3: Electron micrograph of a sperm fertilising an egg.*

Module 2: Section 6 Cell Division and Cellular Organisation

**Tip:** You've come across interphase before — it also takes place before mitosis (see page 147).

### Interphase

The whole of meiosis begins with interphase. During interphase, the cell's DNA unravels and replicates to produce double-armed chromosomes called sister chromatids (see p. 148).

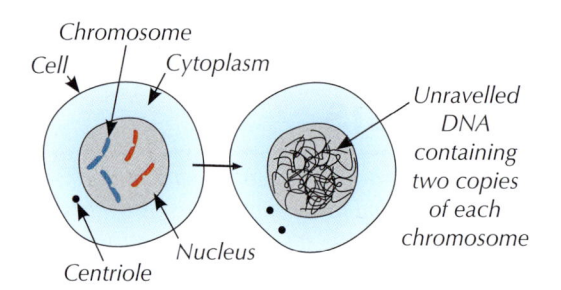

# Meiosis 1

Meiosis involves two divisions — meiosis 1 and meiosis 2. After interphase, the cells enter meiosis 1. Meiosis 1 is the reduction division (it halves the chromosome number). There are four similar stages to each division in meiosis called prophase, metaphase, anaphase and telophase. Here's what happens during each of those stages in meiosis 1:

### Prophase 1

The chromosomes condense, getting shorter and fatter. **Homologous chromosomes** pair up — number 1 with number 1, 2 with 2, 3 with 3 etc. Crossing-over occurs (see next page). Just like in mitosis, centrioles start moving to opposite ends of the cell, forming the spindle fibres. The nuclear envelope (the membrane around the nucleus) breaks down.

**Tip:** If you need a reminder about what centrioles and spindle fibres are, take a look back at prophase in mitosis on page 148.

### Metaphase 1

The homologous pairs line up across the centre of the cell and attach to the spindle fibres by their centromeres.

### Anaphase 1

The spindles contract, pulling the pairs apart (one chromosome goes to each end of the cell).

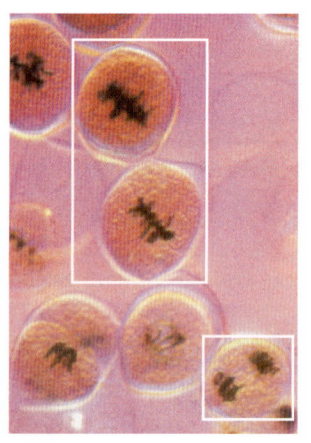

**Figure 4:** Light micrograph of cells undergoing meiosis. The highlighted cells in the centre are in metaphase 1. The bottom right cell is in anaphase 1.

### Telophase 1

A nuclear envelope forms around each group of chromosomes. Cytokinesis (division of the cytoplasm) occurs and two haploid daughter cells are produced.

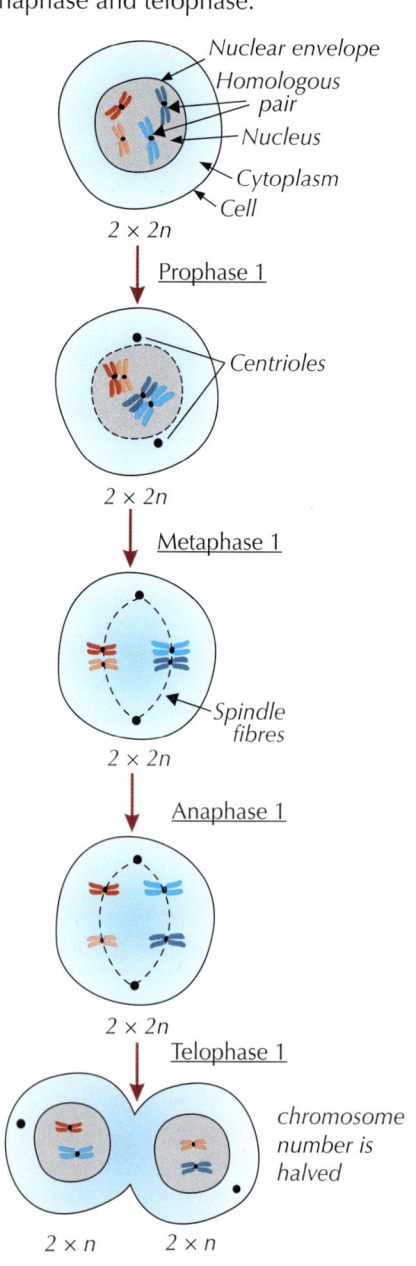

**Tip:** We've only shown 4 chromosomes here for simplicity. Humans actually have 46 (23 homologous pairs).

Module 2: Section 6 Cell Division and Cellular Organisation

# Meiosis 2

The two daughter cells undergo prophase 2, metaphase 2, anaphase 2, telophase 2 (and cytokinesis) — these are pretty much the same as the stages in meiosis 1, except with half the number of chromosomes. In anaphase 2, the sister chromatids are separated — each new daughter cell inherits one chromatid from each chromosome. Four haploid daughter cells are produced.

*End of meiosis 1 = two haploid daughter cells*

2 x n  *STAGES OF MEIOSIS 2*  2 x n

n    n    n    n

*End of meiosis 2 = four haploid daughter cells*

**Tip:** Unlike in prophase 1, there is no pairing up of homologous chromosomes in prophase 2. This is because the pairs have already been split up by the end of meiosis 1.

*Figure 5: Chromatids separating during meiosis 2.*

# Genetic variation

Genetic variation is the differences that exist between individuals' genetic material. The reason meiosis is important is that it creates genetic variation — it makes gametes that are all genetically different. Then during fertilisation, any egg can fuse with any sperm, which also creates variation. This means new individuals have a new mixture of alleles, making them genetically unique.

# Creating genetic variation in gametes

There are two main events during meiosis that lead to genetic variation:

### 1. Crossing over of chromatids

During prophase 1 of meiosis 1, homologous pairs of chromosomes come together and pair up. The chromatids twist around each other and bits of chromatids swap over. The chromatids still contain the same genes but now have a different combination of alleles — see Figure 6.

*Chromatids of one chromosome* → *Crossing over occurs between chromatids* → *Chromatids now have a new combination of alleles*

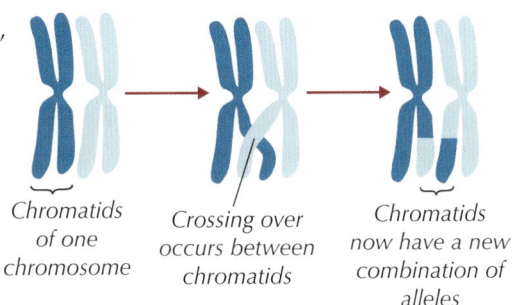

**Figure 6:** *Crossing over.*

**Tip:** Crossing over is also known as recombination.

MEIOSIS 1

*The chromosomes of homologous pairs come together*

*Prophase 1 — chromatids cross over*

*One chromosome from each homologous pair ends up in each cell*

The crossing over of chromatids in meiosis 1 means that each of the four daughter cells formed from meiosis 2 contain chromatids with different alleles — see Figure 7.

MEIOSIS 2

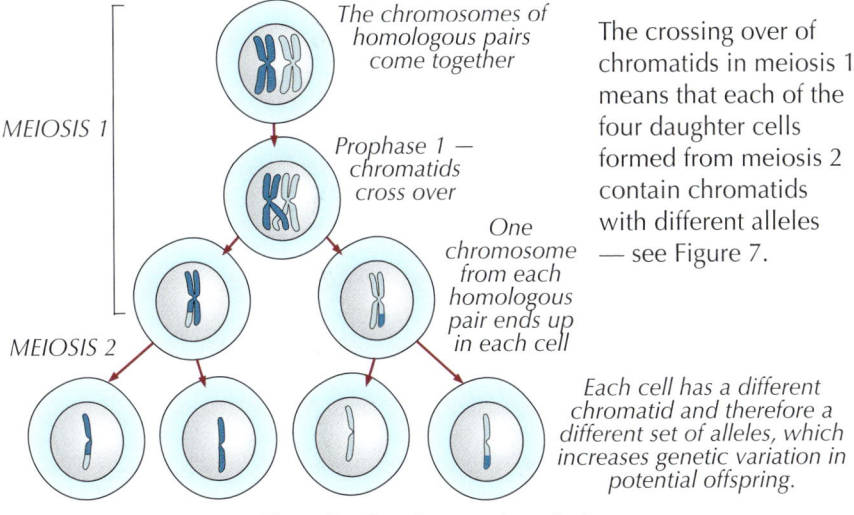

*Each cell has a different chromatid and therefore a different set of alleles, which increases genetic variation in potential offspring.*

**Figure 7:** *Crossing over in meiosis.*

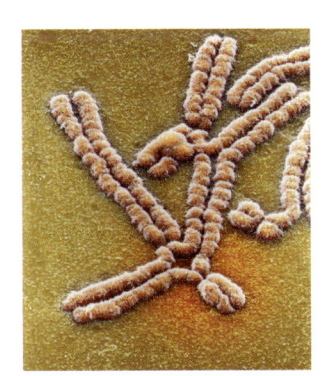

*Figure 8: Electron micrograph showing crossing over occurring in cells.*

Module 2: Section 6 Cell Division and Cellular Organisation    153

## 2. Independent assortment of chromosomes

Remember that each homologous pair of chromosomes in your cells is made up of one chromosome from your mum (maternal) and one chromosome from your dad (paternal). When the homologous pairs line up in metaphase 1 and are separated in anaphase 1, it's completely random which chromosome from each pair ends up in which daughter cell, so the four daughter cells produced by meiosis have completely different combinations of those maternal and paternal chromosomes. This is called independent assortment (separation) of the chromosomes. This 'shuffling' of chromosomes leads to genetic variation in any potential offspring.

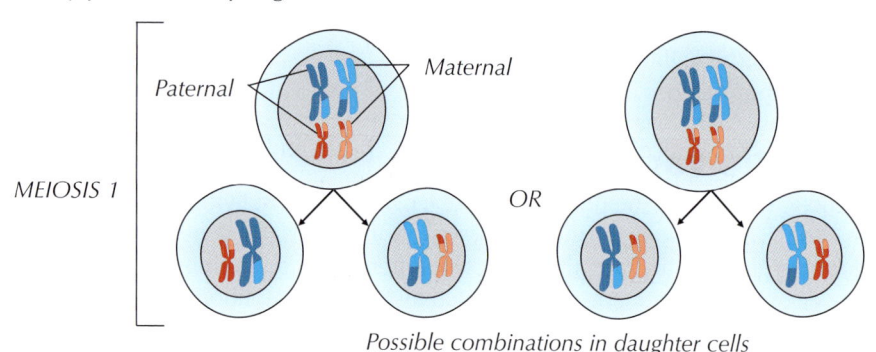

*Figure 9:* Independent assortment of chromosomes.

### Practice Questions — Application

**Q1** For each of the following cells, state which stage of meiosis 1 or 2 the cell is in (e.g. prophase 1).
a)    b)    c)    d)

**Tip:** To answer Q1 you need to look at the number of chromosomes as well as what is happening to them in each cell.

**Q2** The diagram to the right shows two homologous chromosomes. The red cross marks a point at which crossing-over can occur. Draw the chromosomes as they would be if crossing-over occurred at this point.

### Practice Questions — Fact Recall

**Q1** Are the following haploid or diploid:
   a) normal body cells?   b) gametes?   c) zygotes?

**Q2** During meiosis 1, describe what happens in:
   a) prophase,   b) metaphase,   c) anaphase,   d) telophase.

**Q3** Briefly describe what happens during meiosis 2.

**Q4** a) What are the two main events in meiosis that lead to genetic variation?
   b) Describe how each of these processes works.

# 3. Stem Cells and Differentiation

*All multicellular organisms stem from, err, stem cells. Every cell in your body was produced from a stem cell. So was every cell in every other multicellular organism's body. So they're pretty important.*

## Stem cells

Multicellular organisms are made up of many different cell types that are **specialised** for their function, e.g. liver cells, muscle cells and white blood cells. All these specialised cell types originally came from stem cells. Stem cells are **unspecialised** cells — they can develop into different types of cell. All multicellular organisms have some form of stem cell.

### Example

In humans, stem cells are found in early embryos and in a few places in adults. In the first few days of an embryo's life, any of its cells can develop into any type of human cell — they're all stem cells. In adults, stem cells are found in a few places (e.g. bone marrow), but they're not as flexible — they can only develop into a limited range of cells (see below).

## Differentiation

Stem cells divide to become new cells, which then become specialised. The process by which a cell becomes specialised for its job is called **differentiation** (see Figure 1). Stem cells are also able to divide to produce more undifferentiated stem cells, i.e. they can renew themselves.

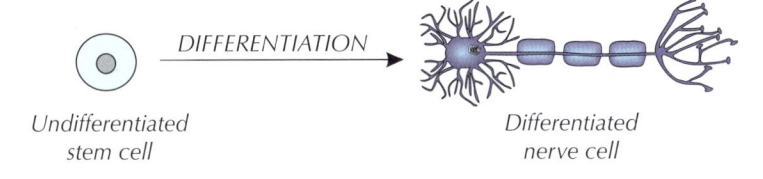

**Figure 1:** *Diagram showing stem cell differentiation.*

In animals, adult stem cells are used to replace damaged cells.

### Example

Bones are living organs, containing nerves and blood vessels. The main bones of the body have marrow in the centres. Here, adult stem cells divide and differentiate to replace worn out blood cells — **erythrocytes** (red blood cells) and **neutrophils** (white blood cells that help to fight infection).

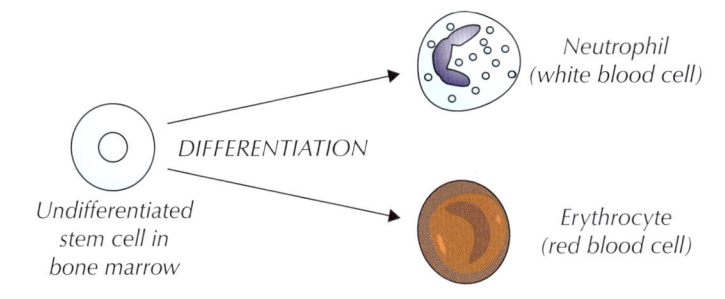

**Figure 2:** *Diagram showing how a stem cell in the bone marrow can differentiate into a neutrophil or erythrocyte.*

### Learning Objectives:

- Understand the features and differentiation of stem cells, including that they are a renewing source of undifferentiated cells.
- Know that erythrocytes and neutrophils are derived from stem cells in bone marrow.
- Know that xylem vessels and phloem sieve tubes are produced from meristems.
- Understand the potential uses of stem cells in research and medicine including:
  - the repair of damaged tissues,
  - the treatment of neurological conditions such as Alzheimer's and Parkinson's,
  - research into developmental biology.
- Know how cells of multicellular organisms are specialised for particular functions, including erythrocytes, neutrophils, squamous and ciliated epithelial cells, sperm cells, palisade cells, root hair cells and guard cells.

**Specification Reference 2.1.6**

**Figure 3:** *Bone marrow stem cells (left) can differentiate into red blood cells (right).*

Module 2: Section 6 Cell Division and Cellular Organisation

Plants are always growing, so stem cells are needed to make new shoots and roots throughout their lives. Stem cells in plants can differentiate into various plant tissues.

### Example
In plants, stem cells are found in the meristems (parts of the plant where growth can take place). In the root and stem, stem cells of the vascular cambium divide and differentiate to become **xylem vessels** and **phloem sieve tubes**.

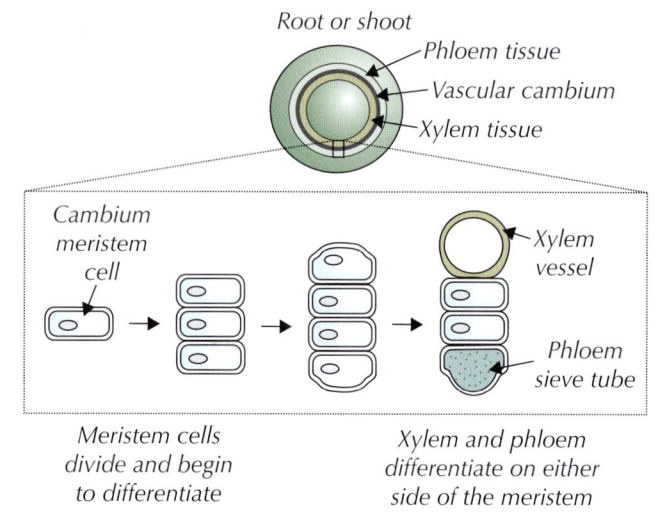

**Figure 4:** The differentiation of stem cells in the meristem into xylem and phloem.

> **Exam Tip**
> Make sure you know the example from the previous page of bone marrow stem cells differentiating into blood cells and this example of meristem cells differentiating into xylem and phloem for the exam — you could be tested on them.

> **Tip:** There's more about the function of xylem and phloem on p. 206.

## Stem cells and medicine

Stem cells can develop into different specialised cell types, so they have a huge potential for use in medicine. Scientists think they could be used to repair damaged tissues (like the heart) and treat neurological disorders (like **Alzheimer's** and **Parkinson's**).

### Examples
- Heart disease is a big problem in many countries. If it results in heart tissue becoming damaged, the body is unable to sufficiently replace the damaged cells. Researchers are currently trying to develop ways of using stem cells to make replacement heart cells to repair the damaged tissue.
- With Alzheimer's, nerve cells in the brain die in increasing numbers. This results in severe memory loss. Researchers are hoping to use stem cells to regrow healthy nerve cells in people with Alzheimer's.
- Patients with Parkinson's suffer from tremors that they can't control. The disease causes the loss of a particular type of nerve cell found in the brain. These cells release a chemical called dopamine, which is needed to control movement. Transplanted stem cells may help to regenerate the dopamine-producing cells.

> **Exam Tip**
> You could get asked about how stem cells can be used to repair all sorts of damaged tissues — you won't necessarily get asked about repairing heart tissue. Don't worry though — the principles for repairing different tissues are the same.

Stem cells are also used by scientists researching developmental biology, i.e. how organisms grow and develop. Studying stem cells can help us to understand more about things like developmental disorders and cancer.

# Specialised cells

Once cells differentiate, they have a specific function. Their structure is adapted to perform that function. You need to know how the following cell types, found in multicellular organisms, are specialised for their functions:

## Examples — Animal cells

**Erythrocytes** (red blood cells) carry oxygen in the blood. The biconcave disc shape provides a large surface area for gas exchange. They have no nucleus so there's more room for haemoglobin (see p. 199), the protein that carries oxygen.

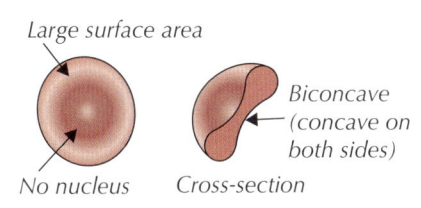

*Large surface area*
*No nucleus*
*Biconcave (concave on both sides)*
*Cross-section*

**Neutrophils** (a type of white blood cell) defend the body against disease. Their flexible shape allows them to engulf foreign particles or pathogens (see p. 230). The many lysosomes in their cytoplasm contain digestive enzymes to break down the engulfed particles.

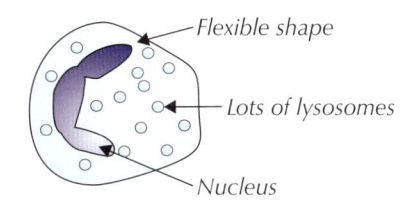

*Flexible shape*
*Lots of lysosomes*
*Nucleus*

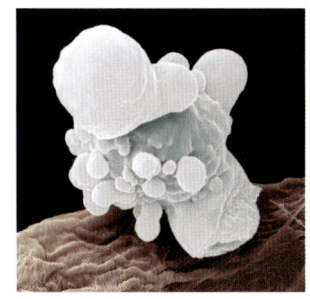

**Figure 5:** A scanning electron micrograph of a white blood cell.

**Epithelial cells** cover the surfaces of organs. The cells are joined by interlinking cell membranes and a membrane at their base. Ciliated epithelia (e.g. in the airways) have cilia that beat to move particles away. Other epithelia (e.g. in the small intestine) have microvilli — folds in the cell membrane that increase the cell's surface area. Squamous epithelia (e.g. in the lungs) are very thin to allow efficient diffusion of gases.

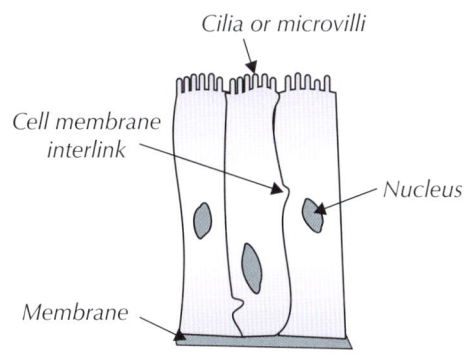

*Cilia or microvilli*
*Cell membrane interlink*
*Nucleus*
*Membrane*

**Tip:** Cells that have cilia on them are called ciliated cells — the tissue is called ciliated epithelium.

**Figure 6:** Epithelial cells (pinkish-brown) with cilia (yellow) in the airways.

**Sperm cells** (male sex cells) have a flagellum (tail) so they can swim to the egg (female sex cell). They also have lots of mitochondria to provide the energy to swim. The acrosome contains digestive enzymes to enable the sperm to penetrate the surface of the egg.

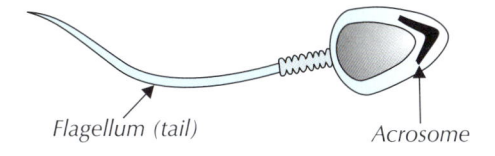

*Flagellum (tail)*
*Acrosome*

**Figure 7:** Scanning electron micrograph of a sperm cell.

Module 2: Section 6 Cell Division and Cellular Organisation

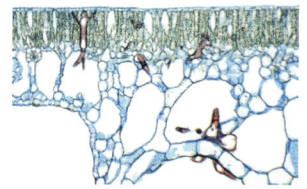

*Figure 8: The band of green cells at the top of this water lily leaf are palisade mesophyll cells.*

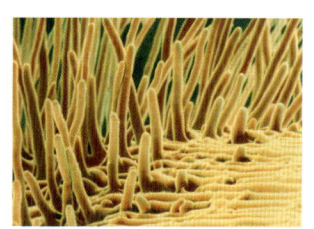

*Figure 9: Scanning electron micrograph of the root hairs on a cress root.*

**Exam Tip**
Any of the animal cell or plant cell examples on p. 157-158 could come up in the exam, so make sure you learn them.

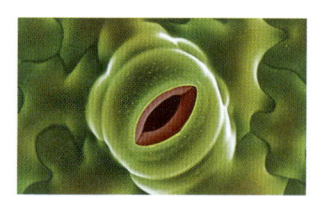

*Figure 10: Turgid guard cells (red) open the stoma in a tobacco leaf.*

**Exam Tip**
You could be given diagrams or photos of erythrocytes, neutrophils, epithelial cells, sperm cells, palisade mesophyll cells, root hair cells and guard cells in the exam. Don't worry if they don't look exactly like the ones on these pages — they will still have the same adaptations.

## Examples — Plant cells

**Palisade mesophyll cells** in leaves do most of the photosynthesis. They contain many chloroplasts, so they can absorb a lot of sunlight. The walls are thin, so carbon dioxide can easily diffuse into the cell.

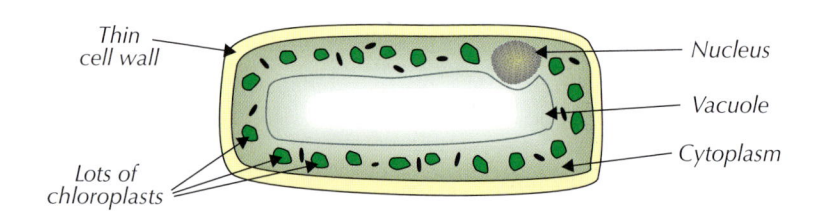

*Thin cell wall — Nucleus — Vacuole — Cytoplasm — Lots of chloroplasts*

**Root hair cells** absorb water and mineral ions from the soil. They have a large surface area for absorption and a thin, permeable cell wall, for entry of water and ions. The cytoplasm contains extra mitochondria to provide the energy needed for active transport (see p. 140).

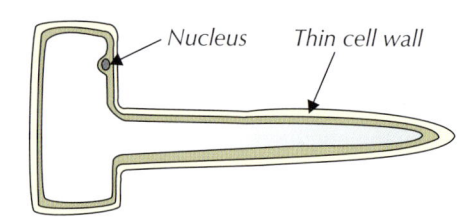

*Nucleus — Thin cell wall*

**Guard cells** are found in pairs, with a gap between them to form a stoma. This is one of the tiny pores in the surface of the leaf used for gas exchange. In the light, guard cells take up water (into their vacuoles) and become turgid. Their thin outer walls and thickened inner walls force them to bend outwards, opening the stomata. This allows the leaf to exchange gases for photosynthesis.

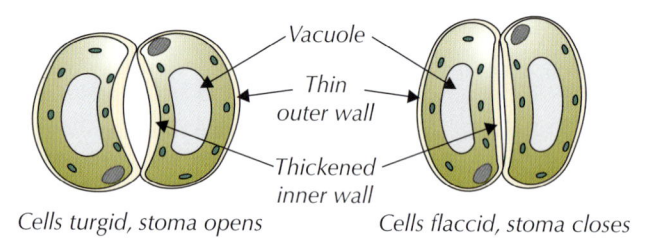

*Vacuole — Thin outer wall — Thickened inner wall*

*Cells turgid, stoma opens — Cells flaccid, stoma closes*

## Practice Questions — Application

**Q1** The cornea is the exposed transparent component that covers the front of the eye. The cornea has its own supply of stem cells known as limbal stem cells, which are located at its edge. As the outside of the cornea is exposed, it is quite susceptible to damage.
  a) Suggest the advantage of the cornea having its own supply of stem cells.
  b) Limbal stem cells are a type of adult stem cell. Suggest why most types of adult stem cell are unlikely to be suitable for the treatment of Alzheimer's.

Module 2: Section 6  Cell Division and Cellular Organisation

Q2 The photograph below shows epithelial cells of the small intestine.

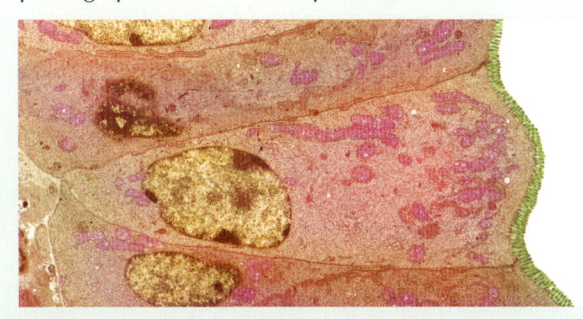

With reference to the photograph above, give one way in which epithelial cells are adapted to their function.

## Practice Questions — Fact Recall

Q1 What is a stem cell?

Q2 Define the term differentiation.

Q3 a) What are:
   i) erythrocytes?
   ii) neutrophils?
   b) Where in the body are the stem cells that differentiate into erythrocytes and neutrophils found?

Q4 Briefly describe the formation of xylem and phloem from stem cells in the root of a plant.

Q5 Describe how stem cells could be used to treat heart disease.

Q6 Describe how stem cells could be used to treat Parkinson's disease.

Q7 Describe one adaptation of the following to their function:
   a) erythrocytes,
   b) neutrophils.

Q8 What is the function of:
   a) palisade mesophyll cells?
   b) root hair cells?

Q9 Describe how guard cells are adapted to their function.

### Learning Objectives:

- Understand the organisation of cells into tissues, organs and organ systems.
- Know squamous and ciliated epithelia, cartilage, muscle, xylem and phloem as examples of tissues.

**Specification Reference 2.1.6**

# 4. Tissues, Organs and Systems

*As you saw on pages 157-158, there are loads of different types of specialised cells. These cells are grouped together to make up tissues, organs and organ systems, which perform particular functions. To understand how a whole organism operates, you need to understand how cells, tissues, organs and organ systems work together.*

## Tissues

A tissue is a group of cells (plus any extracellular material secreted by them) that are specialised to work together to carry out a particular function. A tissue can contain more than one cell type.

### Animal tissues

You need to know the following examples of animal tissues:

---
**Examples — Animal Tissues**

**Squamous epithelium tissue** is a single layer of flat cells lining a surface. It's found in many places in the body, including the alveoli in the lungs, and provides a thin exchange surface for substances to diffuse across quickly.

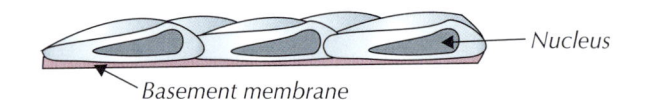

**Tip:** Epithelium is a tissue that forms a covering or a lining.

**Ciliated epithelium** is a layer of cells covered in cilia (see p. 42). It's found on surfaces where things need to be moved — in the trachea for instance, where the cilia waft mucus along (see p. 171).

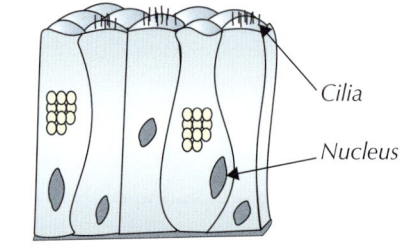

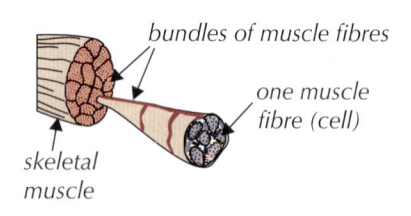

**Figure 1:** Scanning electron micrograph of skeletal muscle, showing muscle fibres (shown in red).

**Muscle tissue** is made up of bundles of elongated cells called muscle fibres. There are three different types of muscle tissue: smooth (e.g. found lining the stomach wall), cardiac (found in the heart) and skeletal (which you use to move). They're all slightly different in structure.

**Cartilage** is a type of connective tissue found in the joints. It also shapes and supports the ears, nose and windpipe. It's formed when cells called chondroblasts secrete an extracellular matrix (a jelly-like substance containing protein fibres), which they become trapped inside.

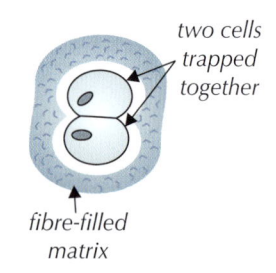

---

Module 2: Section 6 Cell Division and Cellular Organisation

## Plant tissues

You also need to know these two examples of plant tissues:

### Examples — Plant Tissues

**Xylem tissue** is a plant tissue with two jobs — it transports water around the plant, and it supports the plant. It contains hollow xylem vessel cells (which are dead) and living parenchyma cells.

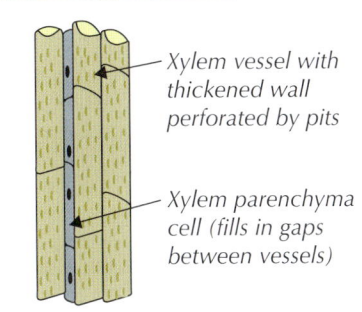

- Xylem vessel with thickened wall perforated by pits
- Xylem parenchyma cell (fills in gaps between vessels)

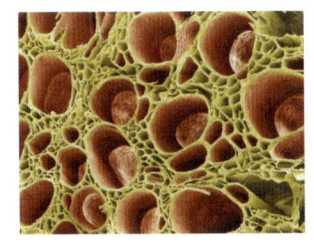

**Phloem tissue** transports sugars around the plant. It's arranged in tubes and is made up of sieve cells, companion cells, and some ordinary plant cells. Each sieve cell has end walls with holes in them, so that sap can move easily through them. These end walls are called sieve plates.

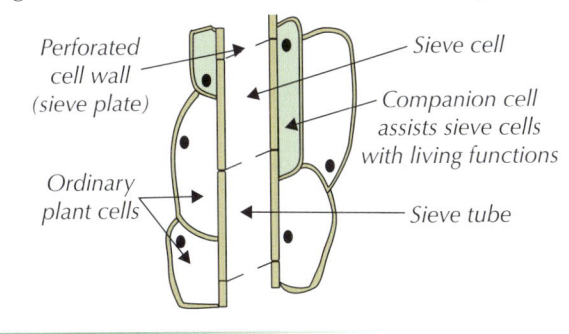

- Perforated cell wall (sieve plate)
- Sieve cell
- Companion cell assists sieve cells with living functions
- Ordinary plant cells
- Sieve tube

*Figure 2:* Xylem tissue in a small root. The xylem vessels are brown and the parenchyma cells green.

**Exam Tip**
Take a look at pages 206-208 for more on xylem and phloem.

# Organs

An organ is a group of different tissues that work together to perform a particular function.

### Examples

The **lungs** are an animal organ which carry out gas exchange. They contain squamous epithelium tissue (in the alveoli) and ciliated epithelium tissue (in the bronchi etc.). They also have elastic connective tissue and vascular tissue (in the blood vessels).

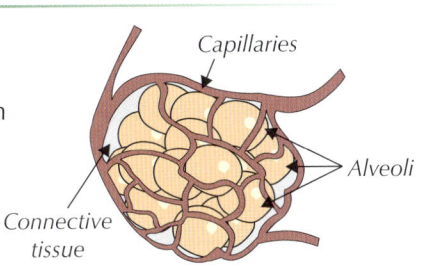

- Capillaries
- Alveoli
- Connective tissue

**Tip:** Gas exchange is the exchange of gases (oxygen and carbon dioxide) between an organism and its environment. There's loads more about it on pages 171-178.

The **leaf** is a plant organ which carries out gas exchange and photosynthesis. It contains palisade tissue, as well as epidermal tissue (to prevent water loss from the leaf), and xylem and phloem tissues in the veins.

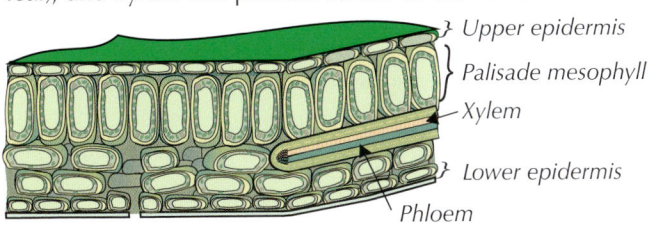

- Upper epidermis
- Palisade mesophyll
- Xylem
- Lower epidermis
- Phloem

*Figure 3:* The cross section of a taro leaf. The palisade mesophyll is bright green and the xylem and phloem are grey.

Module 2: Section 6 Cell Division and Cellular Organisation

## Organ systems

Organs work together to form organ systems — each system has a particular function.

### Examples

The **respiratory system** is made up of all the organs, tissues and cells involved in gas exchange. The lungs, trachea, larynx, nose, mouth and diaphragm are all part of the respiratory system.

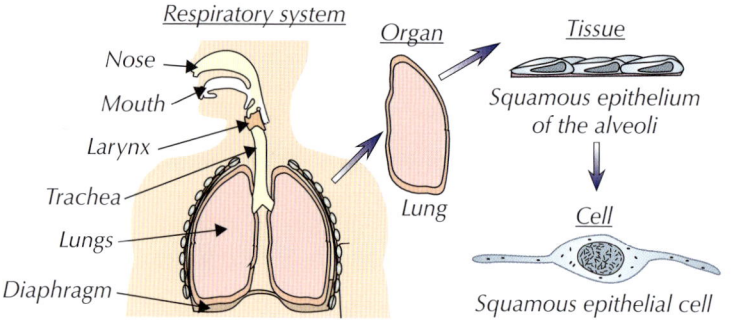

*Respiratory system*: Nose, Mouth, Larynx, Trachea, Lungs, Diaphragm

*Organ*: Lung → *Tissue*: Squamous epithelium of the alveoli → *Cell*: Squamous epithelial cell

The **circulatory system** is made up of the organs involved in blood supply. The heart, arteries, veins and capillaries are all parts of this system.

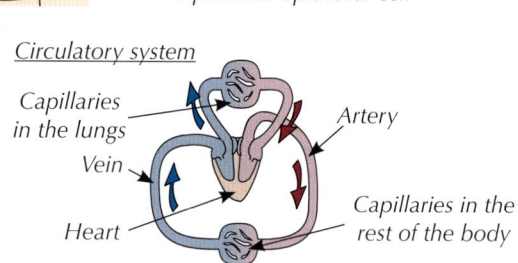

*Circulatory system*: Capillaries in the lungs, Vein, Heart, Artery, Capillaries in the rest of the body

**Exam Tip**
Make sure you know the definition of tissues, organs and organ systems really well. You could be asked to apply your knowledge to lots of different examples in the exam — and it's easy marks if you've got the definitions straight in your head.

**Tip:** For more on the function of the circulatory system take a look at page 185.

### Practice Question — Application

Q1 The picture below is a transmission electron micrograph of a type of plant tissue.

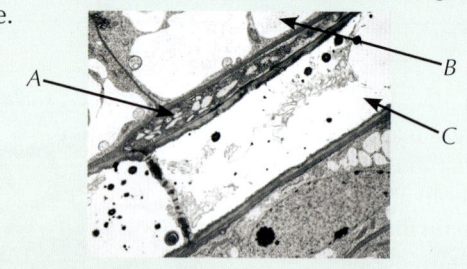

a) Name the cells labelled A - C.
b) What is this type of plant tissue called?

### Practice Questions — Fact Recall

Q1 What is a tissue?
Q2 Tissues can't contain more than one type of cell. True or false?
Q3 Explain why the following are defined as tissues:
   a) squamous epithelium,
   b) ciliated epithelium.
Q4 Describe the basic structure of muscle tissue.
Q5 What is cartilage?

Module 2: Section 6  Cell Division and Cellular Organisation

Q6  Give two examples of plant tissues.
Q7  What is an organ?
Q8  What is an organ system?
Q9  Give an example of an organ system and explain why it is classed as an organ system.

## Section Summary

Make sure you know:
- That most of the cell cycle is taken up by interphase — a period of cell growth, consisting of $G_1$, S and $G_2$ phases, during which the cell's genetic material is copied and checked for DNA damage.
- That a small percentage of the cell cycle is taken up by mitosis and cytokinesis, which produce two genetically identical daughter cells.
- How the cell cycle is regulated by checkpoints.
- That mitosis is needed for the growth of multicellular organisms and tissue repair.
- That some animals, plants and fungi also use mitosis to reproduce asexually.
- The stages of mitosis — prophase (chromosomes condense, the spindle forms and the nuclear envelope breaks down), metaphase (chromosomes line up along the centre of the cell and attach to the spindle), anaphase (the spindles contract, pulling chromatids to opposite ends of the cell) and telophase (chromatids reach the opposite ends of the cell and uncoil and a nuclear envelope forms).
- That cytokinesis is where the cytoplasm of a cell divides.
- How to prepare and examine stained sections and squashes of plant tissue, in order to produce labelled diagrams of cells at different stages of the cell cycle and mitosis.
- That the term 'homologous pair of chromosomes' refers to a pair of matching chromosomes.
- That gametes are produced by meiosis (a type of cell division that produces four genetically different cells). These gametes are haploid (they only have one copy of each chromosome).
- That in sexual reproduction two haploid gametes join together at fertilisation to form a diploid zygote (it has two copies of each chromosome). This then divides and develops into a new organism.
- The main stages of meiosis — interphase, prophase 1, metaphase 1, anaphase 1, telophase 1, prophase 2, metaphase 2, anaphase 2 and telophase 2.
- How genetic variation can be caused by independent assortment of chromosomes and crossing over.
- That stem cells are unspecialised cells that can develop into different types of cell and can also replicate themselves, so are a renewing source of undifferentiated cells.
- That differentiation is the process by which a cell becomes specialised.
- That erythrocytes and neutrophils are derived from stem cells in bone marrow and xylem and phloem are produced from stem cells found in meristems.
- That stem cells have a huge potential in medicine and could be used to repair damaged tissues or treat neurological conditions such as Parkinson's and Alzheimer's. They're also used in developmental biology research.
- How erythrocytes, neutrophils, ciliated and squamous epithelial cells and sperm cells in animals, and palisade mesophyll cells, root hair cells and guard cells in plants are specialised for their functions.
- That a tissue is a group of cells (plus any extracellular material secreted by them) that are specialised to carry out a particular function.
- These examples of tissues — squamous epithelium, ciliated epithelium, muscle tissue, cartilage, xylem tissue and phloem tissue.
- That an organ is a group of different tissues that work together to perform a particular function and that organ systems are organs which work together for a particular function.
- How cells, tissues, organs and organ systems work together so multicellular organisms can function.

# Exam-style Questions

**1**      **Fig. 1.1** shows changes in the mass of a cell and its DNA during the cell cycle.

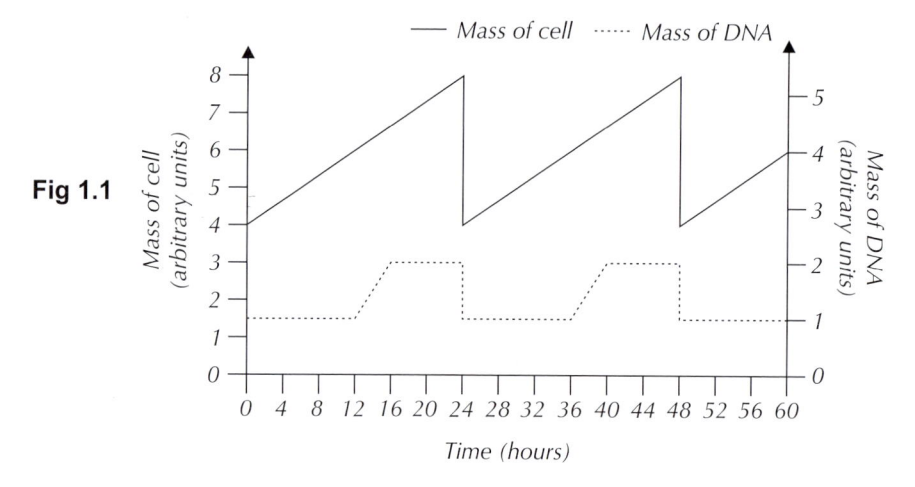

**Fig 1.1**

    **(a)**     During which hours does synthesis take place? Explain your answer.

*(2 marks)*

    **(b)**     At which hours does mitosis take place? Explain your answer.

*(2 marks)*

    **(c)**     Describe what is happening within the cell between 0 and 24 hours.

*(4 marks)*

    **(d) (i)**     How many cell divisions are shown on the graph? Explain your answer.

*(2 marks)*

          **(ii)**     At what time will the next cell division take place?

*(1 mark)*

    **(e) (i)**     Telophase is a phase of mitosis. Describe what happens during telophase in animal cells.

*(2 marks)*

          **(ii)**     Give **three** reasons why mitosis is important for organisms.

*(3 marks)*

**2**      A doctor was studying a sperm sample using a microscope. He observed that a large proportion of the sperm cells in the sample had abnormally shaped tails.

    **(a)**     Explain why the patient whose sample the doctor was studying may experience reduced fertility.

*(2 marks)*

    **(b)**     Other than having a tail, give **two** other ways in which sperm cells are adapted for their function.

*(2 marks)*

Module 2: Section 6    Cell Division and Cellular Organisation

**3** Water enters the plant through its root hair cells and is transported around the plant in the xylem. **Fig. 3.1** on the right shows some root hair cells on the root of a plant.

Fig 3.1

(a) Give **two** ways in which the structure of a root hair cell is specialised for its role.
*(2 marks)*

(b) (i) Stem cells differentiate into xylem cells. Where are these stem cells found?
*(1 mark)*

(ii) Explain why xylem can be considered a tissue.
*(2 marks)*

**4** **Fig 4.1** shows the average DNA content of a group of cells that are undergoing meiosis:

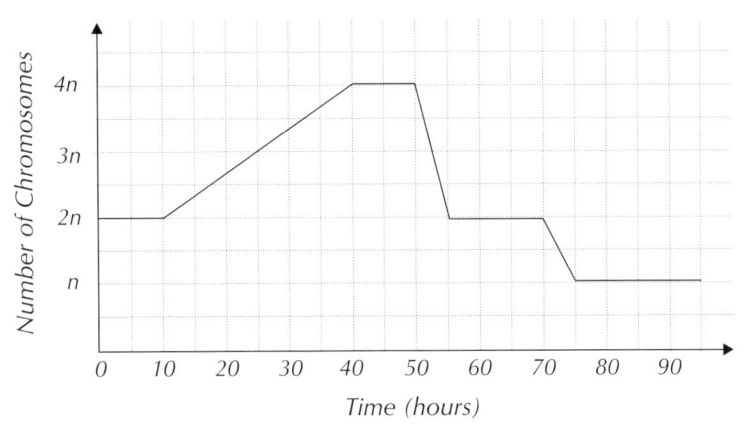

Fig 4.1

(a) Explain what is happening:

(i) between 10 hours and 40 hours.
*(1 mark)*

(ii) between 40 hours and 50 hours.
*(1 mark)*

(iii) between 50 hours and 55 hours.
*(1 mark)*

(iv) between 70 hours and 75 hours.
*(1 mark)*

(b) (i) Describe how daughter cells produced by meiosis differ to their parent cell.
*(2 marks)*

(ii) Explain how crossing over during meiosis can give rise to genetic variation.
*(3 marks)*

Module 2: Section 6 **Cell Division and Cellular Organisation**

# Module 3  Section 1: Exchange and Transport

## 1. Specialised Exchange Systems

*Every organism has substances it needs to take in and others it needs to get rid of in order to survive. An organism's size and surface area affect how quickly this is done.*

**Learning Objectives:**
- Understand the need for specialised exchange surfaces, including the effects of metabolic activity, surface area to volume ratio (SA:V), and the different characteristics of single-celled and multicellular organisms.
- Know that surface area to volume ratio can be calculated using the formula: ratio = surface area ÷ volume.
- Know the features of an efficient exchange surface, including:
  - increased surface area – root hair cells
  - thin layer – alveoli
  - good blood supply/ventilation to maintain gradient – gills/alveolus.

**Specification Reference 3.1.1**

### Exchange of substances with the environment

Every organism, whatever its size, needs to exchange things with its environment. Cells need to take in things like oxygen and glucose for aerobic respiration and other metabolic reactions. They also need to excrete waste products like carbon dioxide and urea. How easy the exchange of substances is depends on the organism's surface area to volume ratio.

### Surface area : volume ratios

Before going into the effects of surface area : volume ratios, you need to understand a bit more about them. Smaller organisms have bigger surface area : volume ratios than larger organisms. This is shown in the example below.

---

**Example — Maths Skills**

A mouse has a bigger surface area relative to its volume than a hippo. This can be hard to imagine, but you can prove it mathematically.

Imagine these animals as cubes...

The mouse could be represented by a cube measuring 1 cm × 1 cm × 1 cm.

Its volume is: $1 \times 1 \times 1 = 1$ cm$^3$

Its surface area is: $6 \times 1 \times 1 = 6$ cm$^2$

So the mouse has a surface area : volume ratio of **6 : 1**.

"cube mouse"

Compare this to a cube hippo measuring 2 cm × 4 cm × 4 cm.

Its volume is: $2 \times 4 \times 4 = 32$ cm$^3$

Its surface area is:

$2 \times 4 \times 4 = 32$ cm$^2$
(top and bottom surfaces of cube)

$+ 4 \times 2 \times 4 = 32$ cm$^2$
(four sides of the cube)

Total surface area = 64 cm$^2$

So the hippo has a surface area : volume ratio of 64 : 32 or **2 : 1**.

"cube hippo"

The cube mouse's surface area is six times its volume, but the cube hippo's surface area is only twice its volume. Smaller animals have a bigger surface area compared to their volume.

---

**Figure 1:** *A hippo (top) has a small surface area : volume ratio. A mouse (bottom) has a large surface area : volume ratio.*

To calculate the surface area to volume ratio (i.e. to express it as a single value rather than a ratio), you just divide the surface area by the volume.

166  Module 3: Section 1  Exchange and Transport

## Calculating volume and surface area

You might be asked to calculate volume or surface area in the exam. For example, you could be asked to calculate the volume or surface area of a cell.

### Example — Maths Skills

*Bacillus* are rod-shaped bacteria — as shown in Figure 2.

To calculate the volume of this cell, you need to split the bacterium into parts: the cylindrical centre and the hemispheres on either end.

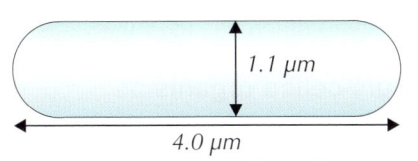

**Figure 2:** A *Bacillus* cell.

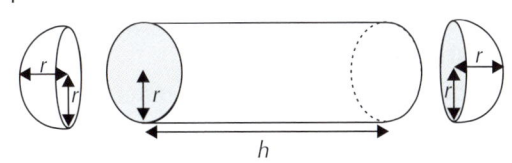

1. Start by calculating the volume of the cylinder. The formula you need is **πr²h** or **π × radius² × height**. First find the radius, then the height:
   radius (r) = 1.1 ÷ 2         height (h) = 4.0 − 0.55 − 0.55
   = **0.55 μm**                    = **2.9 μm**

   Then use them to calculate the volume of the cylinder:
   Volume of a cylinder = πr²h
   = π × 0.55² × 2.9 = **2.755...**

2. Now find the volume of the two hemispheres. The formula for the volume of a sphere is $\frac{4}{3}\pi r^3$.

   A sphere is made of two hemispheres, so the total volume of the two hemispheres = $\frac{4}{3} \pi \times 0.55^3$
   = **0.696...**

3. Finally, add the volume of the cylinder and the two hemispheres together to find the total volume of the cell:
   Total volume = 2.755... + 0.696...
   = **3.5 μm³** (2 s.f.)

### Practice Question — Application

**Q1** Below are three 3D shapes of different sizes (not drawn to scale).

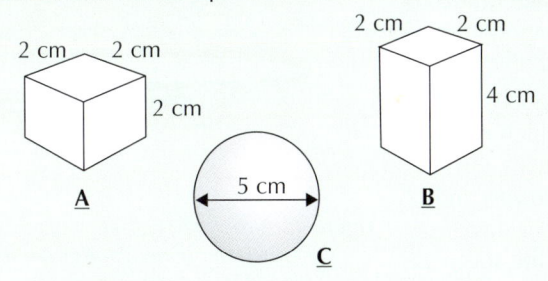

A: cube 2 cm × 2 cm × 2 cm
B: cuboid 2 cm × 2 cm × 4 cm
C: sphere, 5 cm diameter

a) For each 3D shape work out its:
   i) surface area.
   ii) volume.
   iii) surface area : volume ratio.
b) Which 3D shape has the greatest surface area : volume ratio?

---

**Exam Tip**
If you're asked to calculate a surface area to volume ratio in the exam, always give your answer in its simplest form, e.g. 2 : 1 rather than 64 : 32.

**Exam Tip**
If an exam question requires you to calculate the surface area or volume of a sphere or cylinder, you'll be given the formula to use in the question. However, it's a good idea to learn the formulae for the area and circumference of a circle and the surface area and volume of other 3D shapes (e.g. cuboids), in case you're asked to calculate one in the exam.

**Tip:** The radius (*r*) of a circle is the distance from any point on the outer edge of the circle to its centre. It's half the diameter (*d*).

**Tip:** Remember that volume is given in units cubed (e.g. μm³) and surface area is given in units squared (μm²).

**Tip:** The formula for calculating the surface area of a sphere is 4πr².

**Tip:** A good way to compare two ratios (e.g. 7 : 2 and 3 : 1) is to get the last figure in each ratio to be 1 (e.g. 7 : 2 would become 3.5 : 1). Then you can easily see which ratio is the largest (e.g. 3.5 : 1 is a bigger ratio than 3 : 1).

Module 3: Section 1 Exchange and Transport

## Specialist exchange surfaces

An organism needs to supply every one of its cells with substances like glucose and oxygen (for respiration). It also needs to remove waste products from every cell to avoid damaging itself. Single-celled organisms exchange substances differently to multicellular organisms.

### Single-celled organisms

In single-celled organisms, substances can diffuse directly into (or out of) the cell across the cell surface membrane. The diffusion rate is quick because of the short distances the substances have to travel and because single-celled organisms have a relatively high surface area : volume ratio.

### Multicellular organisms

In multicellular organisms, diffusion across the outer membrane is too slow, for three reasons:

1. Some cells are deep within the body — there's a big distance between them and the outside environment.
2. Larger animals have a low surface area to volume ratio — it's difficult to exchange enough substances to supply a large volume of animal through a relatively small outer surface.
3. Multicellular organisms have a higher metabolic rate than single-celled organisms, so they use up oxygen and glucose faster.

So rather than using straightforward diffusion to absorb and excrete substances, multicellular organisms need specialised **exchange surfaces** (like the alveoli in the lungs, see next page).

**Tip:** Remember, diffusion is the net movement of particles down a concentration gradient from an area of higher concentration to an area of lower concentration — see page 132 for more.

**Tip:** There's more on factors affecting the rate of diffusion on p. 132.

## Special features of exchange surfaces

Exchange surfaces have special features to improve their efficiency, such as...

### 1. A large surface area

Most exchange surfaces have a large surface area to increase their efficiency.

#### Example — Root hair cells

The cells on plant roots grow into long 'hairs' which stick out into the soil. Each branch of a root will be covered in millions of these microscopic hairs.

This gives the roots a large surface area, which helps to increase the rate of absorption of water (by osmosis) and mineral ions (by active transport) from the soil.

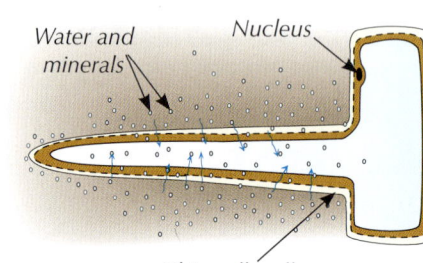

*Figure 4:* A root hair cell, showing the absorption of water and mineral ions from the soil.

*Figure 3:* An electron micrograph of a root tip from a poppy plant, showing how root hair cells (white) increase the surface area of the root.

### 2. They're thin

Exchange surfaces are usually thin to decrease the distance that the substances being exchanged have to travel over, and so improve efficiency. Some are only one cell thick.

### Example — Alveoli

The alveoli are the gas exchange surface in the lungs. Each alveolus is made from a single layer of thin, flat cells called the alveolar epithelium.

Oxygen ($O_2$) diffuses out of the alveolar space into the blood. Carbon dioxide ($CO_2$) diffuses in the opposite direction.

The thin alveolar epithelium helps to decrease the distance over which $O_2$ and $CO_2$ diffusion takes place, which increases the rate of diffusion (see p. 132).

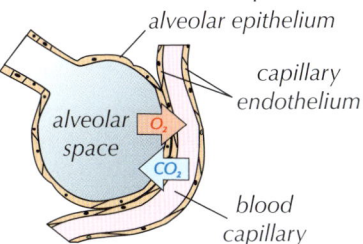

**Figure 5:** *Diagram of an alveolus, showing the thin alveolar epithelium.*

## 3. A good blood supply and/or ventilation

Another key feature of exchange surfaces is that they have a good blood supply and/or are well ventilated to increase efficiency.

**Tip:** For more on ventilation, see p. 174.

### Example — Alveoli

The alveoli are surrounded by a large capillary network, giving each alveolus its own blood supply. The blood constantly takes oxygen away from the alveoli, and brings more carbon dioxide.

The lungs are also ventilated (you breathe in and out) so the air in each alveolus is constantly replaced.

These features help to maintain concentration gradients of $O_2$ and $CO_2$. Figure 7 sums this up nicely.

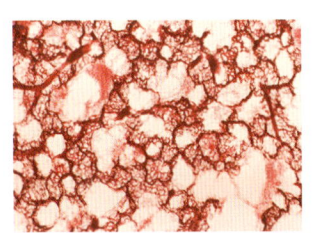

**Figure 6:** *A light micrograph of capillaries surrounding alveoli.*

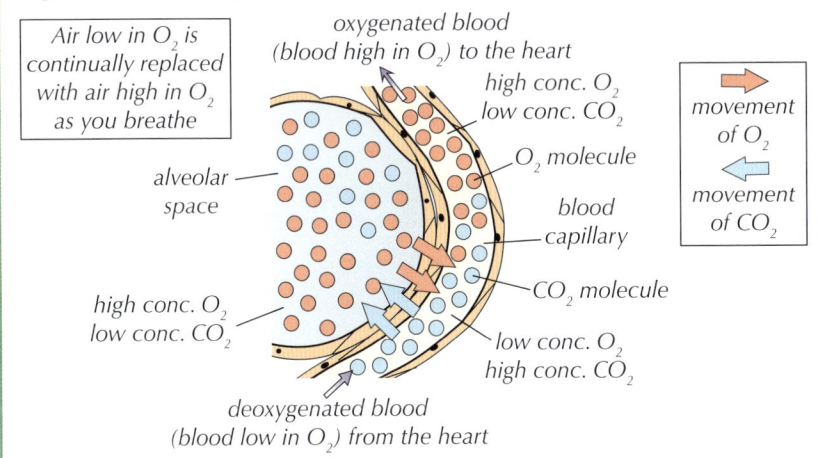

**Figure 7:** *Diagram showing how $O_2$ moves from an area of high concentration (inside the alveolus) to an area of low concentration (in the deoxygenated blood).*

### Example — Gills

The gills are the gas exchange surface in fish. In the gills, $O_2$ and $CO_2$ are exchanged between the fish's blood and the surrounding water.

Fish gills contain a large network of capillaries — this keeps them well-supplied with blood. They're also well-ventilated — fresh water constantly passes over them.

These features help to maintain a concentration gradient of $O_2$ — increasing the rate at which $O_2$ diffuses into the blood.

**Tip:** There's more on how a concentration gradient is maintained in fish gills on p. 177.

Module 3: Section 1 Exchange and Transport

## Practice Questions — Application

Q1 A mountain climber is climbing at altitude, where there's less oxygen. Suggest how this will affect gas exchange in the alveoli.

Q2 One of the effects of severe obesity is that the sufferer cannot fully inhale. Suggest the effect this would have on the rate of diffusion of oxygen.

Q3 The pictures below show light micrographs of healthy lung tissue (top) and diseased lung tissue from a patient with emphysema (bottom). The alveoli appear white.

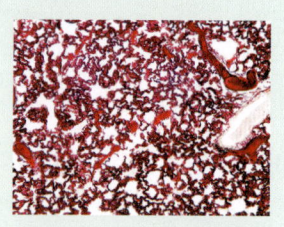

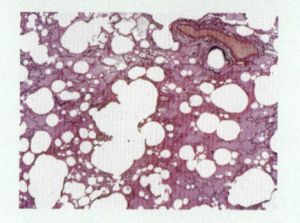

a) Describe the main difference between the healthy lung tissue and the diseased lung tissue.

b) Use your answer to part a) to explain why people with emphysema have a lower level of oxygen in the blood than normal.

**Tip:** To answer Q3 b) here, think about the factors that increase the efficiency of an exchange surface (see pages 168-169). Then decide what factor has been affected in the diseased lung tissue.

## Practice Questions — Fact Recall

Q1 a) Name two substances an animal needs to take in from its environment.

b) Name two substances an animal needs to release into its environment.

Q2 Explain three reasons why diffusion is too slow in multicellular organisms for them to absorb and excrete substances in this way.

Q3 a) Describe an example where a large surface area increases the efficiency of an exchange system.

b) Other than having a large surface area, give two features that improve the efficiency of exchange surfaces.

Q4 Explain what makes fish gills efficient exchange surfaces.

# 2. Gas Exchange in Mammals

*Multicellular organisms need a gaseous exchange system to survive. The gaseous exchange system in mammals is based around the lungs.*

## Gas exchange

In mammals, the lungs are gas exchange organs. They help to get oxygen into the blood (for respiration) and to get rid of carbon dioxide (made by respiring cells) from the body.

### Structure of the gaseous exchange system

As you breathe in, air enters the trachea (windpipe). The trachea splits into two bronchi — one bronchus leading to each lung. Each bronchus then branches off into smaller tubes called bronchioles. The bronchioles end in small 'air sacs' called alveoli — see Figure 1. This is where gases are exchanged (see page 169). There are lots of alveoli in the lungs to provide a large surface area for diffusion. The ribcage, intercostal muscles and diaphragm all work together to move air in and out (see page 174).

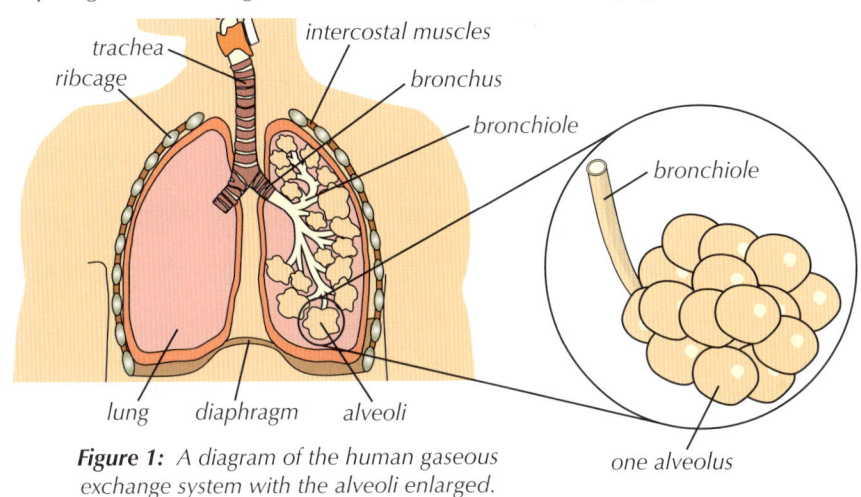

**Figure 1:** A diagram of the human gaseous exchange system with the alveoli enlarged.

**Learning Objective:**
- Know the structures and functions of the components of the mammalian gaseous exchange system, including the distribution and functions of the following in the trachea, bronchi, bronchioles and alveoli:
  - cartilage,
  - ciliated epithelium,
  - goblet cells,
  - smooth muscle,
  - elastic fibres.

  **Specification Reference 3.1.1**

**Tip:** There are actually three layers of intercostal muscles. You need to know about two of them (the internal and external intercostal muscles — see p. 174) for your exam. We've only shown one layer here for simplicity.

## Key features of the gaseous exchange system

The gaseous exchange system is made up of different cells and tissues. These help it to exchange gases efficiently:

### Goblet cells

Goblet cells (lining the airways) secrete mucus (see Figure 2). The mucus traps microorganisms and dust particles in the inhaled air, stopping them from reaching the alveoli.

**Figure 2:** Goblet cell secreting mucus.

### Cilia

The cilia are hair-like structures on the surface of epithelial cells lining the airways. They beat the mucus secreted by the goblet cells — see Figure 3. This moves the mucus (plus the trapped microorganisms and dust) upward away from the alveoli towards the throat, where it's swallowed. This helps prevent lung infections.

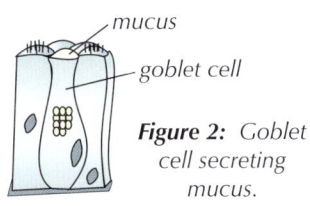

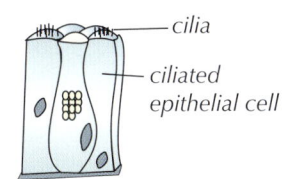

**Figure 3:** Ciliated epithelium.

**Figure 4:** An electron micrograph of ciliated cells (pink) and goblet cells (green) in the bronchus.

Module 3: Section 1 Exchange and Transport

**Tip:** Blood vessels are also made up of elastic fibres and smooth muscle — see page 188.

### Elastic fibres
Elastic fibres in the walls of the trachea, bronchi, bronchioles and alveoli help the process of breathing out (see page 174). On breathing in, the lungs inflate and the elastic fibres are stretched. Then, the fibres recoil to help push the air out when exhaling.

### Smooth muscle
Smooth muscle in the walls of the trachea, bronchi and bronchioles (except the smallest bronchioles) allows their diameter to be controlled. During exercise the smooth muscle relaxes, making the tubes wider. This means there's less resistance to airflow and air can move in and out of the lungs more easily.

### Cartilage
Rings of cartilage in the walls of the trachea and bronchi provide support. It's strong but flexible — it stops the trachea and bronchi collapsing when you breathe in and the pressure drops (see p. 174).

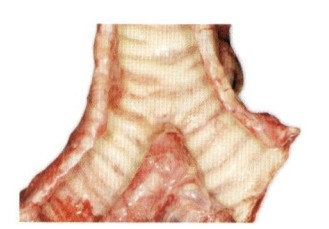

**Figure 5:** Cartilage rings (cream) in the trachea.

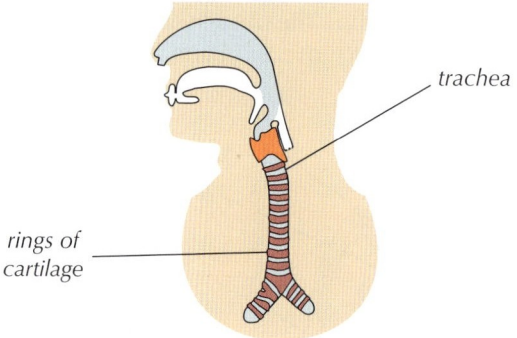

**Figure 6:** A diagram showing the rings of cartilage in the trachea.

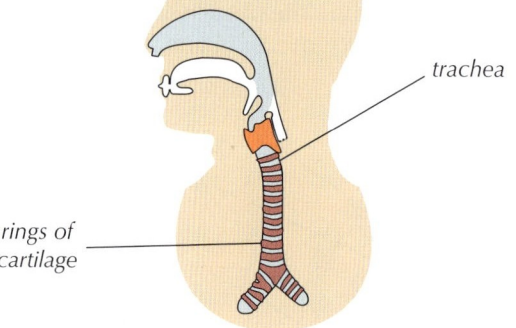

## Distribution of features in the gaseous exchange system
You need to know the distribution of the features described above and on the previous page for the exam. This is illustrated in Figure 8 and summarised in the table on the next page (Figure 9).

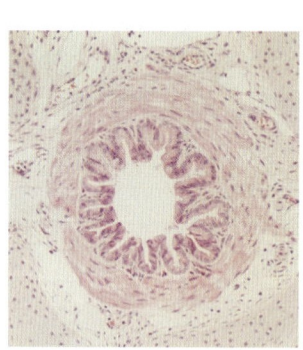

**Figure 7:** Cross-section of a bronchiole. The dark pink folds are ciliated epithelium. The pink ring around it is smooth muscle.

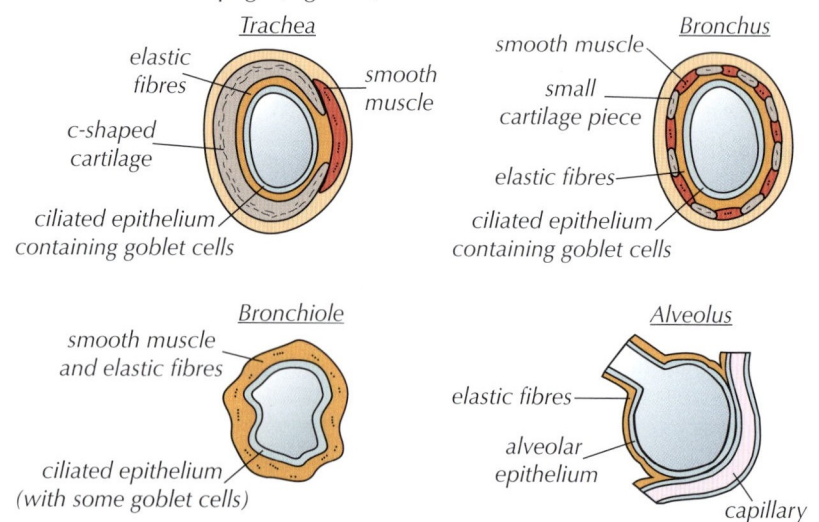

**Figure 8:** Cross-sections of structures in the mammalian gaseous exchange system.

| Part of the lung | Cartilage | Smooth muscle | Elastic fibres | Goblet cells | Epithelium |
|---|---|---|---|---|---|
| Trachea | large C-shaped pieces | ✓ | ✓ | ✓ | ciliated |
| Bronchi | smaller pieces | ✓ | ✓ | ✓ | ciliated |
| Larger bronchiole | none | ✓ | ✓ | ✓ | ciliated |
| Smaller bronchiole | none | ✓ | ✓ | ✗ | ciliated |
| Smallest bronchiole | none | ✗ | ✓ | ✗ | no cilia |
| Alveoli | none | ✗ | ✓ | ✗ | no cilia |

*Figure 9:* Table summarising the distribution of features in the mammalian gaseous exchange system.

## Practice Question — Application

Q1 The light micrograph below shows a cross-section through part of the gaseous exchange system.

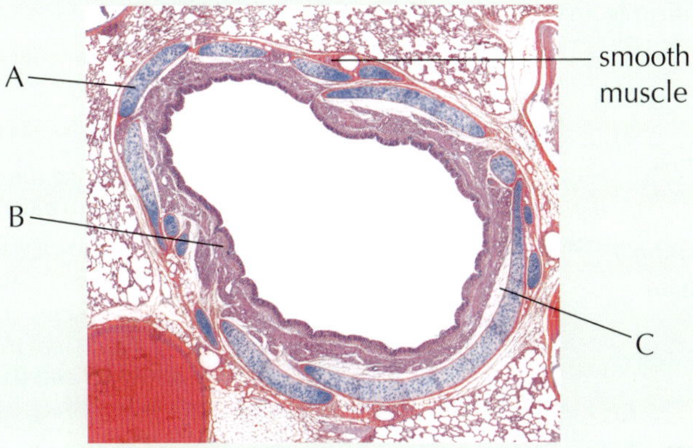

a) Name the part of the gaseous exchange system shown in the picture.
b) Name the components labelled A - C.

**Exam Tip**
You might get a picture or diagram to interpret in the exam that doesn't look exactly like what you've learnt (e.g. the light micrograph on the left). If this happens, don't panic — all the key features will still be there, you'll just have to apply your knowledge to find them.

## Practice Questions — Fact Recall

Q1 In the mammalian gaseous exchange system, what is the function of:
a) goblet cells?  b) cilia?

Q2 Describe the function and distribution of elastic fibres in the gaseous exchange system of mammals.

Q3 Where in the airways is smooth muscle found?

Q4 Describe the difference between the distribution of cartilage in the trachea and in the bronchi.

Module 3: Section 1 Exchange and Transport

**Learning Objectives:**
- Understand the mechanism of ventilation in mammals, including the function of the ribcage, intercostal muscles (internal and external) and diaphragm.
- Understand the relationship between vital capacity, tidal volume, breathing rate and oxygen uptake, including analysis and interpretation of primary and secondary data, e.g. from a data logger or spirometer (PAG10).

**Specification Reference 3.1.1**

# 3. Ventilation in Mammals

*Breathing is pretty important, both for life and for the exam...*

## What is ventilation?
Ventilation consists of inspiration (breathing in) and expiration (breathing out). It's controlled by the movements of the diaphragm, intercostal muscles and ribcage.

### Inspiration
- The external intercostal and diaphragm muscles contract.
- This causes the ribcage to move upwards and outwards and the diaphragm to flatten, increasing the volume of the thorax (the space where the lungs are).
- As the volume of the thorax increases the lung pressure decreases (to below atmospheric pressure).
- This causes air to flow into the lungs — see Figure 1.
- Inspiration is an active process — it requires energy.

**Figure 1:** Diagram showing what happens during inspiration.

air flows in
thorax volume increases, air pressure decreases
external intercostal muscles contract, causing ribs to move outwards and upwards
diaphragm muscles contract, causing diaphragm to move downwards and flatten

**Tip:** Air always flows from areas of <u>high</u> pressure to areas of <u>low</u> pressure.

### Expiration
- The external intercostal and diaphragm muscles relax.
- The ribcage moves downwards and inwards and the diaphragm becomes curved again.
- The thorax volume decreases, causing the air pressure to increase (to above atmospheric pressure).
- Air is forced out of the lungs — see Figure 2.
- Normal expiration is a passive process — it doesn't require energy.
- Expiration can be forced though (e.g. if you want to blow out the candles on your birthday cake). During forced expiration, the internal intercostal muscles contract, to pull the ribcage down and in.

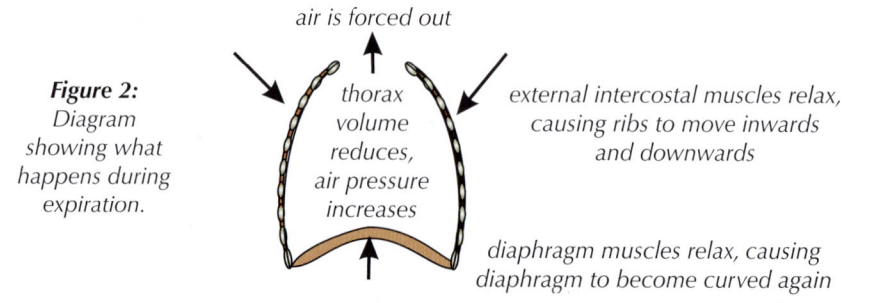

**Tip:** It's the movement of the ribcage and diaphragm and the resulting change in lung pressure that causes air to flow in and out — not the other way round.

**Figure 2:** Diagram showing what happens during expiration.

air is forced out
thorax volume reduces, air pressure increases
external intercostal muscles relax, causing ribs to move inwards and downwards
diaphragm muscles relax, causing diaphragm to become curved again

**Tip:** Remember, when the diaphragm contracts, it's flat. When it relaxes, it bulges upwards. Think of it like trying to hold your stomach in — you contract your muscles to flatten your stomach and relax to release it.

Module 3: Section 1 Exchange and Transport

# Spirometers

A spirometer is a machine that can be used to investigate breathing. It can give readings of:

- **Tidal volume** (TV) — the volume of air in each breath. This is usually about 0.4 dm$^3$.
- **Vital capacity** — the maximum volume of air that can be breathed in or out.
- **Breathing rate** — how many breaths are taken per unit time (usually per minute).
- **Oxygen uptake** — the rate at which a person uses up oxygen (e.g. the number of dm$^3$ used per minute).

**Tip:** dm$^3$ is short for decimetres cubed — it's the same as litres.

## How to use a spirometer

A spirometer has an oxygen-filled chamber with a movable lid (see Figure 4). The person using the spirometer breathes through a tube connected to the oxygen chamber. As the person breathes in and out, the lid of the chamber moves up and down. These movements are recorded by a pen attached to the lid of the chamber — this writes on a rotating drum, creating a **spirometer trace**. Or the spirometer can be hooked up to a motion sensor — this will use the movements to produce electronic signals, which are picked up by a **data logger**. The soda lime in the tube the subject breathes into absorbs carbon dioxide.

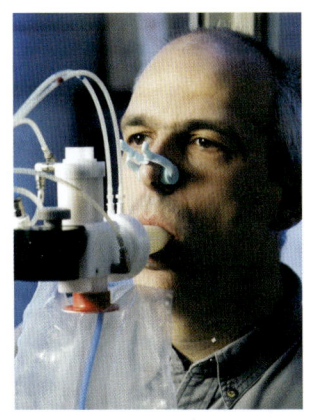

*Figure 3: A person using a spirometer.*

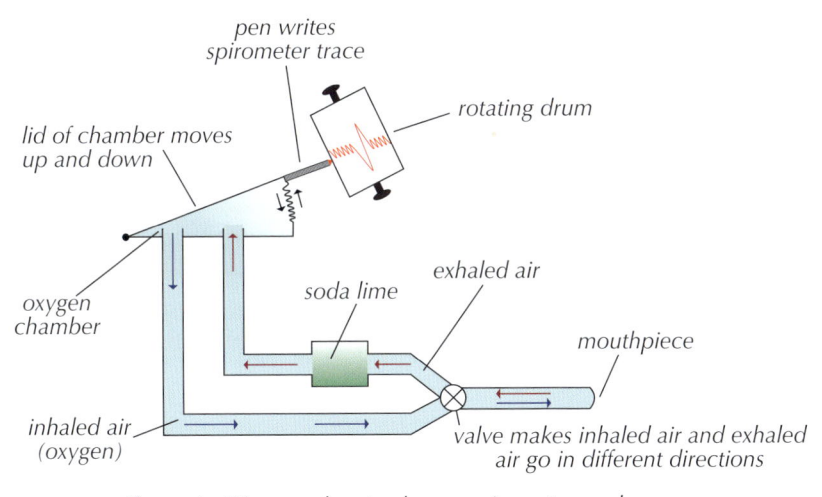

*Figure 4: Diagram showing how a spirometer works.*

The total volume of gas in the chamber decreases over time. This is because the air that's breathed out is a mixture of oxygen and carbon dioxide. The carbon dioxide is absorbed by the soda lime — so there's only oxygen in the chamber which the subject inhales from. As this oxygen gets used up by respiration, the total volume decreases.

To get a valid reading from a spirometer, the person using it must wear a nose clip — this ensures that they can only breathe in and out through their mouth (and so all the air they breathe goes through the spirometer). The machine must also be airtight.

**Tip:** Make sure you carry out a risk assessment before carrying out this experiment. E.g. using a spirometer can be dangerous as you're continually breathing in the same air that you just breathed out — so you need to make sure there's enough oxygen in the chamber.

# Analysing data from spirometers

In the exam, you might have to work out breathing rate, tidal volume, vital capacity and oxygen uptake from a spirometer trace. There's an example of how to do this on the next page.

**Exam Tip**
Sometimes, you'll see oxygen *consumption* written rather than oxygen *uptake*. They both mean the same thing.

Module 3: Section 1 Exchange and Transport

**Tip:** A line sloping upwards on this spirometer trace indicates that the person using it is breathing out (and so the volume of gas in the spirometer is increasing).

A line sloping down indicates that the person is breathing in.

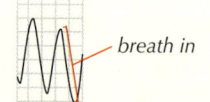

The longer the line, the deeper the breath in or out.

### Example — Maths Skills

The graph below shows a spirometer trace.

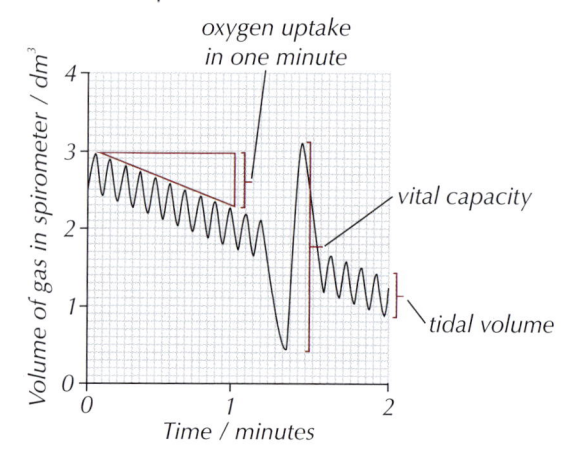

- In this trace, the breathing rate in the first minute is 10 breaths per minute (there are 10 'peaks' in the first minute).
- The tidal volume may change from time to time, but in this trace it's about 0.5 dm³.
- The graph shows a vital capacity of 2.65 dm³.
- Oxygen uptake is the decrease in the volume of gas in the spirometer chamber. It can be read from the graph by taking the average slope of the trace. In this case, it drops by 0.7 dm³ in the first minute — so oxygen uptake is 0.7 dm³/min.

**Exam Tip**
Make sure you look carefully at the axes of any graph you get in the exam. For example, it could be the volume of gas in the lungs, not the spirometer, that's plotted on the y-axis.

### Practice Questions — Application

Look at the spirometer trace below.
It was recorded from a healthy 17 year old student at rest.

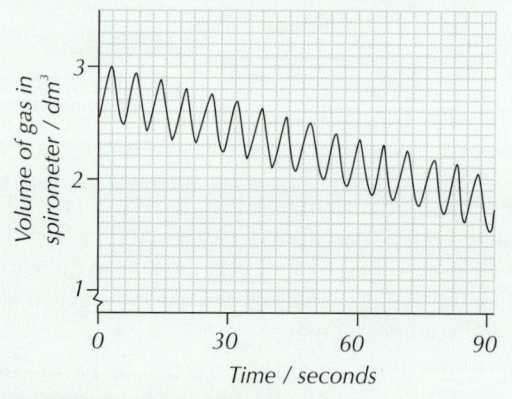

Q1  What is the student's tidal volume?
Q2  Work out the breathing rate of this student. Give your answer in breaths per minute.
Q3  Explain why the volume of gas in the spirometer drops over time.

Module 3: Section 1 Exchange and Transport

# 4. Gas Exchange in Fish and Insects

*Gas exchange systems in fish and insects are quite different to those in mammals.*

## Gas exchange in fish

There's a lower concentration of oxygen in water than in air. So fish have special adaptations to get enough of it. In a fish, the gas exchange surface is the gills.

### Structure of gills

Water, containing oxygen, enters the fish through its mouth and passes out through the gills. Each gill is made of lots of thin plates called **gill filaments** or **primary lamellae** which give a big surface area for exchange of gases (and so increase the rate of diffusion). The gill filaments are covered in lots of tiny structures called **gill plates** or **secondary lamellae**, which increase the surface area even more — see Figure 1. Each gill is supported by a gill arch. The gill plates have lots of blood capillaries and a thin surface layer of cells to speed up diffusion between the water and the blood.

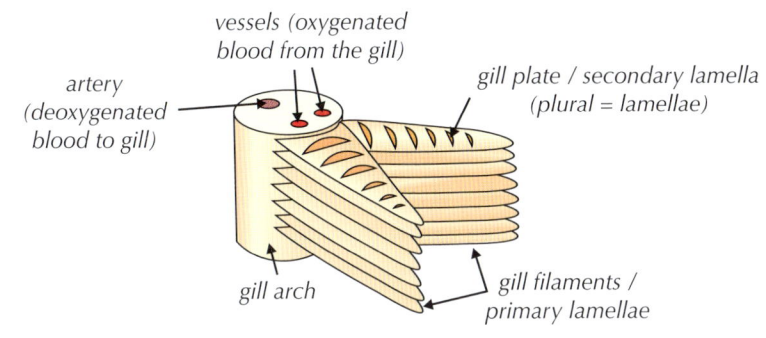

**Figure 1:** A section of a fish's gill.

### The counter-current system

In the gills of a fish, blood flows through the gill plates in one direction and water flows over in the opposite direction — see Figure 3. This is called a counter-current system. The counter-current system means that the water with a relatively high oxygen concentration always flows next to blood with a lower concentration of oxygen. This in turn means that a steep concentration gradient is maintained between the water and the blood — so as much oxygen as possible diffuses from the water into the blood.

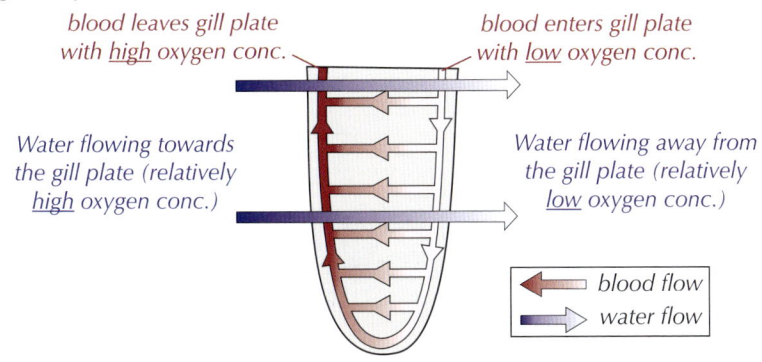

**Figure 3:** The counter-current system across a gill plate.

---

**Learning Objective:**
- Understand the mechanisms of ventilation and gas exchange in bony fish and insects, including:
  - bony fish – changes in volume of the buccal cavity and the functions of the operculum, gill filaments and gill lamellae (gill plates); countercurrent flow
  - insects – spiracles, trachea, thoracic and abdominal movement to change body volume, exchange with tracheal fluid.

**Specification Reference 3.1.1**

**Tip:** You might've thought the slits on the side of a fish's head were its gills, but in fact the actual gills are inside the fish. Those slits just let out water that has flowed over the gills.

**Figure 2:** The gills inside a mackerel.

**Tip:** Bony fish include salmon and cod. Unsurprisingly, they have a skeleton made of bone — not all fish do.

## Ventilation in fish

You need to know how fish gills are ventilated in bony fish. First, the fish opens its mouth, which lowers the floor of the buccal cavity (the space inside the mouth). The volume of the buccal cavity increases, decreasing the pressure inside the cavity. Water is then sucked in to the cavity — see Figure 5. When the fish closes its mouth, the floor of the buccal cavity is raised again. The volume inside the cavity decreases, the pressure increases, and water is forced out of the cavity across the gill filaments.

Each gill is covered by a bony flap called the **operculum** (which protects the gill). The increase in pressure forces the operculum on each side of the head to open, allowing water to leave the gills.

*Figure 4: Perch head showing operculum.*

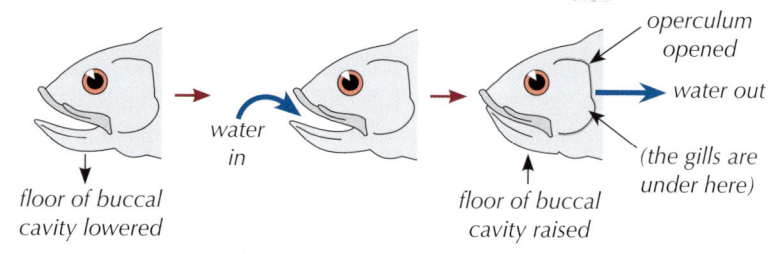

*Figure 5: Diagram showing the mechanism of ventilation in fish.*

**Tip:** In some bony fish, the operculum bulges out (increasing the volume of the cavity behind the operculum) just after the floor of the buccal cavity lowers. This contributes to the decrease in pressure that causes water to enter the fish's mouth.

## Gas exchange and ventilation in insects

Terrestrial insects have microscopic air-filled pipes called tracheae which they use for gas exchange. Air moves into the tracheae through pores on the surface called spiracles. Oxygen travels down the concentration gradient towards the cells. Carbon dioxide from the cells moves down its own concentration gradient towards the spiracles to be released into the atmosphere. The tracheae branch off into smaller tracheoles which have thin, permeable walls and go to individual cells. The tracheoles also contain fluid, which oxygen dissolves in. The oxygen then diffuses from this fluid into body cells. Carbon dioxide diffuses in the opposite direction.

Insects use rhythmic abdominal movements to change the volume of their bodies and move air in and out of the spiracles. When larger insects are flying, they use their wing movements to pump their thoraxes too.

**Tip:** Terrestrial insects are just insects that live on land.

**Tip:** Tracheae is the plural of trachea.

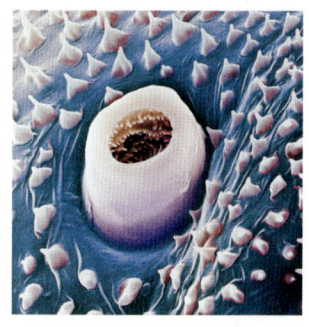

*Figure 6: A spiracle on the surface of a garden tiger moth caterpillar.*

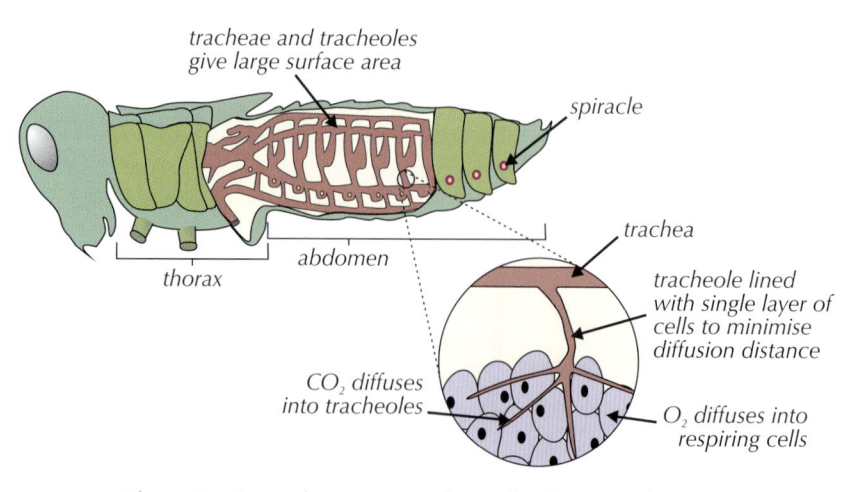

*Figure 7: Gas exchange across the tracheal system of an insect.*

Module 3: Section 1 Exchange and Transport

## Practice Questions — Application

Q1  In polluted water the dissolved oxygen concentration is lower than it is in clean water. Explain how this would affect gas exchange across the gills of a fish.

Q2  The graph below shows how the relative oxygen concentrations of blood and water change with distance along a gill plate.

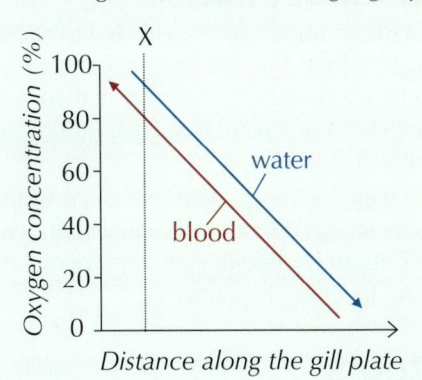

*Graph: Oxygen concentration (%) vs Distance along the gill plate. Two lines labelled 'water' and 'blood' both decreasing; vertical dashed line marked X near the start.*

a) What happens to the oxygen concentration of blood as it moves along the gill plate?

b) What happens to the oxygen concentration of water as it moves along the gill plate?

c) What is the oxygen concentration of the blood at distance X on the graph?

d) Use evidence from the graph to explain why the oxygen concentration of the blood increases straight after point X.

**Exam Tip**
If you're asked to interpret data from a graph in the exam, use specific values in your answer where you can.

## Practice Questions — Fact Recall

Q1  Describe the structure of fish gills.

Q2  Describe how the 'counter-current' system in fish aids gas exchange.

Q3  Describe how the gills of bony fish are ventilated.

Q4  What is an operculum?

Q5  What happens to the operculum during ventilation in fish?

Q6  How does air get into an insect's tracheae?

Q7  Describe how carbon dioxide moves out of an insect's cells into the atmosphere.

Q8  Give two ways in which larger insects can increase the movement of air in and out of their spiracles.

**Learning Objectives:**
- Know how to dissect, examine and draw the gaseous exchange system of a bony fish and/or insect trachea (PAG2).
- Know how to examine microscope slides to show the histology of exchange surfaces.

**Specification Reference 3.1.1**

# 5. Dissecting Gas Exchange Systems

*Here's your chance to see what gas exchange systems really look like inside...*

## Carrying out dissections

As part of your A-Level in biology, you're expected to carry out some dissections, including the dissection of the gaseous exchange system in a bony fish and/or insect trachea, a dissection of a mammalian heart (see page 192) and a dissection of the stems of a plant (see page 209). You could also be asked about dissections in your exams.

The next two pages cover gaseous exchange system dissections in bony fish and insect tracheae. Whatever the dissection, you're expected to know how to carry it out safely and ethically. You might also need to record your observations using labelled diagrams.

## Dissection tools

**Figure 1:** Common dissection tools. (Scalpel, Tweezers (or forceps), Dissecting scissors, Dissecting pin)

**Figure 2:** A wax-filled dissection tray.

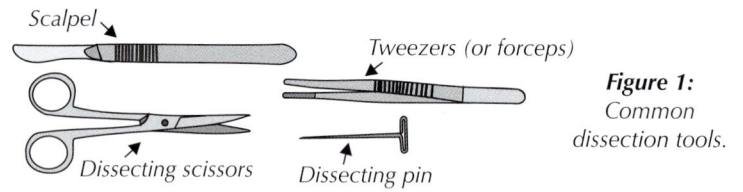

Figure 1 shows some of the tools that you might need to use for your dissections. Scalpels have a very sharp detachable blade and can be used for making very fine cuts. Dissecting scissors are also used for precise cutting. They are safer to use than scalpels (because the blades are less likely to snap under pressure) and it can be easier to avoid damaging the tissue underneath when using scissors. Dissecting pins can be used with a wax-filled dissection tray (see Figure 2) to pin a specimen in place during the dissection. Tweezers are useful for holding and manipulating the smaller parts of the specimen.

Your dissecting tools (e.g. scalpels, dissecting scissors) should all be clean, sharp and free from rust — blunt tools don't cut well and can be dangerous.

**Tip:** Always follow your teacher's safety instructions when working with dissection tools.

**Tip:** Make sure that you assess all the risks involved in this dissection before you start.

## Dissecting fish gills

**PRACTICAL ACTIVITY GROUP 2**

Fish dissection is messy, so make sure you're wearing an apron or lab coat, and gloves. Then follow these steps:

1) Place your chosen fish (something like a perch or salmon works well) in a dissection tray or on a cutting board.
2) Push back the operculum and use scissors to carefully remove the gills. Cut each gill arch through the bone at the top and bottom. They should look a bit like Figure 3.
3) If you look closely, you should be able to see the gill filaments.
4) Finish off by drawing the gill and labelling it.

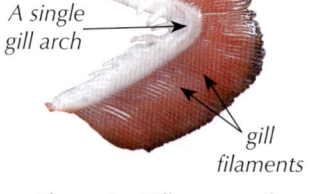

**Figure 3:** Gills removed from a bony fish. (A single gill arch, gill filaments)

Module 3: Section 1 Exchange and Transport

# Dissecting insects

Big insects like grasshoppers or cockroaches are usually best for dissecting because they're easier to handle. For dissection, you'll need to use an insect that's been humanely killed fairly recently.

**PRACTICAL ACTIVITY GROUP 2**

1. First fix the insect to a dissecting board. You can put dissecting pins through its legs to hold it in place.
2. To examine the tracheae, you'll need to carefully cut and remove a piece of exoskeleton (the insect's hard outer shell) from along the length of the insect's abdomen — see Figure 4.
3. Use a syringe to fill the abdomen with saline solution. You should be able to see a network of very thin, silvery-grey tubes — these are the tracheae. They look silver because they're filled with air.
4. You can mount the tracheae on a wet mount microscope slide and examine them under a light microscope (see pages 53-54). Again, the tracheae will appear silver or grey. You should also be able to see rings of chitin in the walls of the tracheae — these are there for support (like the rings of cartilage in a human trachea).

**Tip:** Some live insects, e.g. grasshoppers, can cause allergic reactions in some people. They need to be handled very carefully. A full risk assessment should be carried out before doing this dissection.

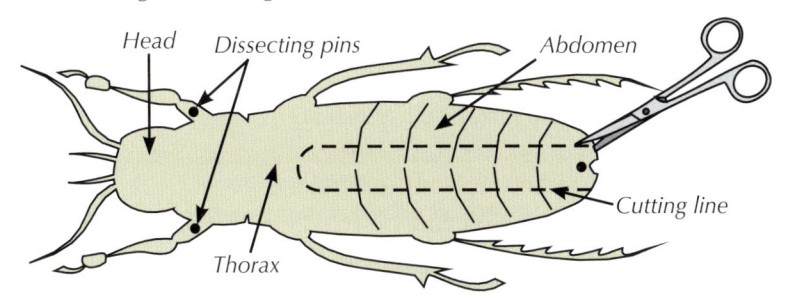

*Figure 4:* How to remove a piece of exoskeleton from an insect abdomen.

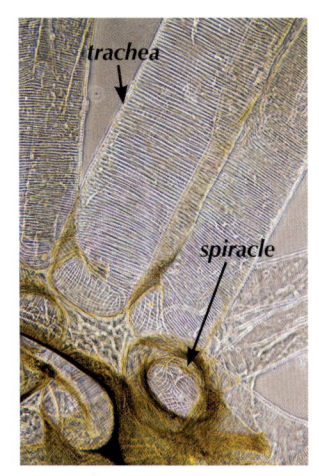

*Figure 5:* Light microscope image of part of a silkworm showing the spiracles, chitin rings and silver/grey tracheae.

## Practice Question — Application

**Q1** A student was dissecting a grasshopper to examine the tracheae. As part of the protocol, she used scissors to remove a piece of exoskeleton from the insect's abdomen and then filled the abdomen with saline solution.

a) Give a possible reason for why she used scissors rather than a scalpel to remove the piece of exoskeleton.

b) Describe what the tracheae would look like when the abdomen was filled with saline solution.

c) When examining the tracheae under a light microscope, she noticed that the walls of the tracheae had lots of ring shaped structures along their length. What are these rings and what is their function?

**Tip:** Dissecting animals can give you a better understanding of their anatomy, but there are some ethical issues involved. E.g. there are concerns that the animals used are not always raised in a humane way — they may be subject to overcrowding, extremes of temperature or lack of food — and they may not be killed humanely either. If animals (e.g. insects) are raised in school for dissection, it's important to make sure they are looked after properly and killed humanely to minimise any suffering or distress.

**HOW SCIENCE WORKS**

## Practice Questions — Fact Recall

**Q1** What are dissection pins used for?
**Q2** Why might you use tweezers when carrying out a dissection?
**Q3** When carrying out a dissection on a bony fish, where would you expect to find the gills?

Module 3: Section 1 Exchange and Transport

# Section Summary

Make sure you know...

- How to work out the surface area : volume ratios of simple organisms, e.g. by using simple known shapes.
- That a value for a surface area to volume ratio can be calculated using the formula:
  ratio = surface area ÷ volume.
- That single-celled organisms exchange substances with their environment by direct diffusion through their cell surface membranes, and that the rate of diffusion is quick because of the organisms' high surface area : volume ratios.
- That multicellular organisms can't exchange substances by direct diffusion across their outer membranes because it would be too slow — some cells are deep within the body, larger animals have a low surface area : volume ratio and multicellular organisms have a higher metabolic rate, so need more oxygen and glucose faster. Instead, they have specialised exchange surfaces.
- That all exchange surfaces are adapted for efficient exchange including having a large surface area (e.g. root hair cells), being thin (often only one cell thick, e.g. alveoli) and having a good blood supply and/or ventilation to maintain a steep concentration gradient (e.g. alveoli, gills).
- The structures of the mammalian gaseous exchange system.
- The functions of parts of the mammalian gaseous exchange system, including:
  - that goblet cells lining the airways secrete mucus, and cilia sweep it away from the alveoli (removing trapped microorganisms and dust),
  - that elastic fibres in the walls of the airways and the alveoli stretch and recoil to help the process of breathing out,
  - that smooth muscle allows the diameter of the airways to be controlled,
  - that cartilage provides the trachea and bronchi with support.
- How to describe the distribution of goblet cells, ciliated epithelium, elastic fibres, smooth muscle and cartilage in the mammalian gaseous exchange system.
- How the ribcage, diaphragm and intercostal muscles all work together during ventilation.
- That tidal volume is the volume of air in each breath, vital capacity is the maximum volume of air that can be breathed in or out, breathing rate is how many breaths are taken per unit time (e.g. per minute) and oxygen uptake is the rate at which a person uses up oxygen.
- How a spirometer can be used to measure tidal volume, vital capacity, breathing rate and oxygen uptake, and how a data logger can be used to capture the information.
- How to interpret data from a spirometer trace.
- How gas exchange in bony fish works, including the structure of gills (gill filaments and gill plates) and the counter-current system (where blood flows through the gill plates in one direction and water flows over the gill plates in the opposite direction, to maintain a steep concentration gradient of oxygen between the water and blood).
- How ventilation works in bony fish — the changes in volume and pressure in the buccal cavity which cause water to be sucked in and then forced out, and the role of the operculum.
- How gas exchange works in insects — that air enters tracheae through spiracles and oxygen travels down its concentration gradient towards the cells, and carbon dioxide travels down its concentration gradient towards the spiracles.
- How insects use rhythmic abdominal movements and/or their wing movements during flying to change the volume of their bodies and pump air in and out for ventilation.
- How to carry out dissections of gaseous exchange systems in fish and insects and make labelled diagrams of your observations.
- How to observe dissected insect gaseous exchange systems under a light microscope, using a wet mount microscope slide.

# Exam-style Questions

**1** Breathing involves the processes of inspiration (breathing in) and expiration (breathing out).

(a) Use the most appropriate terms to complete the passage on inspiration below.

During inspiration, the diaphragm and external .......................... muscles .......................... . This causes the .......................... to move upwards and outwards and the diaphragm to flatten, increasing the .......................... of the thorax. As this happens, lung .......................... decreases to below that of the atmosphere, causing air to flow into the lungs.

*(5 marks)*

(b) The volume of air in each breath is known as the tidal volume. What is the **maximum volume** of air that can be breathed in or out known as?

*(1 mark)*

(c) A spirometer is a machine used to investigate breathing. A spirometer trace of a person at rest is shown in **Fig. 1.1**.

(i) What happened between points A and B?

*(1 mark)*

(ii) Use **Fig. 1.1** to work out the person's breathing rate.

*(1 mark)*

(iii) Suggest how the appearance of this trace would differ if the volume of gas in the spirometer was recorded instead of the volume of gas in the lungs. Explain your answer.

*(4 marks)*

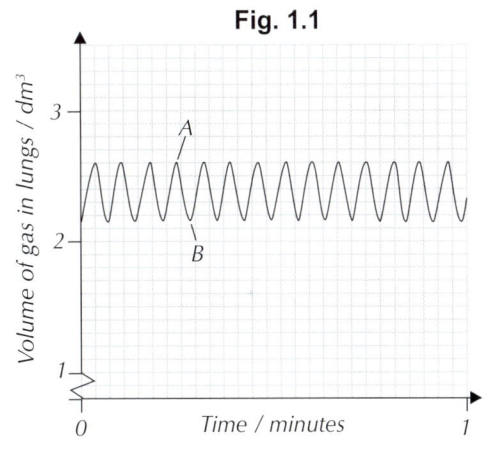

**Fig. 1.1**

(d) Suggest **one** thing that could be done to obtain a more **precise** measurement of the person's tidal volume.

*(1 mark)*

**2** Fig. 2.1 shows a spherical bacterium with a radius of 0.7 μm.

(a) Give the surface area to volume ratio of this bacterium. Use the following formulae: surface area of a sphere = $4\pi r^2$, volume of a sphere = $\frac{4}{3}\pi r^3$.

*(1 mark)*

**Fig. 2.1**

0.7 μm

(b) Explain why this bacterium doesn't have a gaseous exchange system.

*(3 marks)*

Module 3: Section 1 Exchange and Transport

3   **Fig. 3.1** shows a scanning electron micrograph of alveoli in a healthy human lung (left) and in a diseased lung (right). The magnification is x 60.

Fig. 3.1

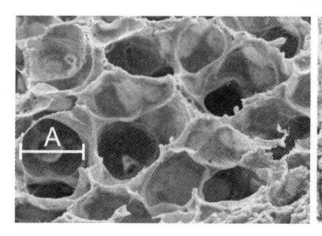

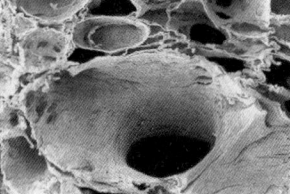

(a) Calculate the actual width of the labelled alveolus, A.
Give your answer in μm.
*(2 marks)*

(b) Describe **one** difference between the healthy alveoli and the diseased alveoli, and explain what effect this would have on gaseous exchange in the alveoli.
*(3 marks)*

(c) Oxygen tents contain a higher percentage of oxygen than normal air.
Suggest how being in an oxygen tent might benefit a patient with emphysema.
*(2 marks)*

4   **Fig. 4.1** shows a cross section of the mammalian trachea.

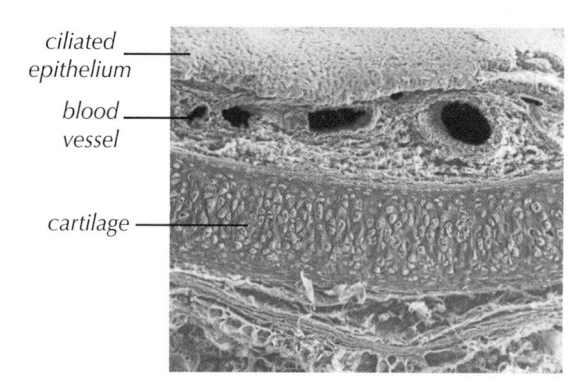

Fig. 4.1

(a) Describe the function of the cilia on ciliated epithelial cells.
*(1 mark)*

(b) (i) Give **one** function of cartilage in the trachea.
*(1 mark)*

(ii) Where else in the mammalian gaseous exchange system is cartilage found?
*(1 mark)*

(c) Give **one** other feature of the trachea **not** labelled in **Fig 4.1** and describe its function.
*(2 marks)*

Module 3: Section 1  Exchange and Transport

# Module 3 Section 2: Transport in Animals

## 1. Circulatory Systems

*All multicellular organisms need to transport materials around the body. Transport systems can vary depending on the organism — we humans have a transport system called the circulatory system.*

### Why do multicellular organisms need a transport system?

As you saw on page 168, single-celled organisms can get substances that they need by diffusion across their outer membrane. If you're multicellular though, it's a bit harder to supply all your cells with everything they need — multicellular organisms are relatively big and they have a low surface area to volume ratio and a higher **metabolic rate** (the speed at which chemical reactions take place in the body). A lot of multicellular organisms (e.g. mammals) are also very active. This means that a large number of cells are all respiring very quickly, so they need a constant, rapid supply of glucose and oxygen. Carbon dioxide (a waste product of respiration) also needs to be removed from cells quickly.

To make sure that every cell has a good enough supply of useful substances and has its waste products removed, multicellular organisms need a transport system. The circulatory system in mammals uses blood to carry glucose and oxygen around the body. It also carries hormones, antibodies (to fight disease) and waste products (like $CO_2$).

### Single and double circulatory systems

Not all organisms have the same type of circulatory system — some have a single circulatory system, e.g. fish, and others have a double circulatory system, e.g. mammals.

#### Single circulatory system

In a single circulatory system, blood only passes through the heart once for each complete circuit of the body.

— Example ————————————————————

Fish have a single circulatory system. The heart pumps blood to the gills (to pick up oxygen) and then on through the rest of the body (to deliver the oxygen) in a single circuit.

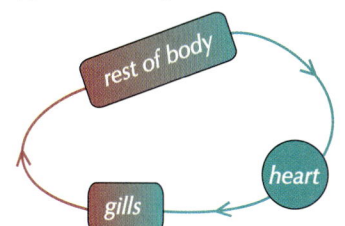

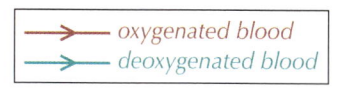

→ oxygenated blood
→ deoxygenated blood

---

**Learning Objectives:**
- Understand why multicellular animals need transport systems in terms of their size, surface area to volume ratio (SA:V) and metabolic rate.
- Know the different types of circulatory systems, including:
  - single (in fish)
  - double (in mammals)
  - closed (in fish and mammals)
  - open (in insects).

**Specification Reference 3.1.2**

**Exam Tip**
Remember, multicellular organisms have a small <u>surface area to volume ratio</u> — just writing they have a small surface area won't get you full marks in the exam.

**Exam Tip**
You need to learn all the examples in this topic for your exams.

**Exam Tip**
If you're asked to define a single or double circulatory system, writing that the blood travels through the heart once/twice isn't enough. You need to say it does this for <u>each complete circuit</u> of the body too.

### Double circulatory system
In a double circulatory system, the blood passes through the heart twice for each complete circuit of the body.

**Example**

Mammals have a double circulatory system. The heart is divided down the middle, so it's really like two hearts joined together. The right side of the heart pumps blood to the lungs (to pick up oxygen). From the lungs it travels to the left side of the heart, which pumps it to the rest of the body. When blood returns to the heart, it enters the right side again.

So, our circulatory system is really two linked loops. One sends blood to the lungs — this is called the pulmonary system, and the other sends blood to the rest of the body — this is called the systemic system.

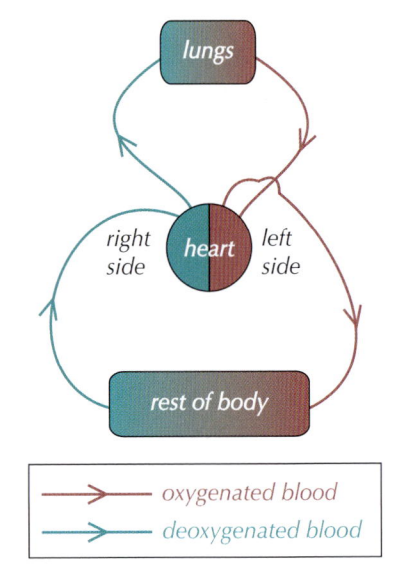

The advantage of the mammalian double circulatory system is that the heart can give the blood an extra push between the lungs and the rest of the body. This makes the blood travel faster, so oxygen is delivered to the tissues more quickly.

**Tip:** The right and left sides of the heart are reversed in the diagram because it's the right and left of the person the heart belongs to.

## Closed and open circulatory systems
Some organisms have a closed circulatory system and some have an open circulatory system.

### Closed circulatory system
All vertebrates (e.g. fish and mammals) have a closed circulatory system. In a closed circulatory system, the blood is enclosed inside blood vessels.

**Example**

In fish, the heart pumps blood into arteries. These branch out into millions of capillaries. Substances like oxygen and glucose diffuse from the blood in the capillaries into the body cells, but the blood stays inside the blood vessels as it circulates. Veins take the blood back to the heart.

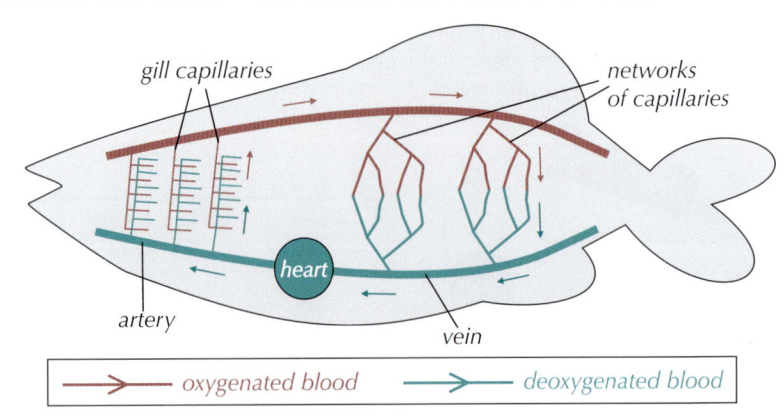

**Tip:** Although this example is about fish, the circulation of blood through the various different types of blood vessel is the same in other organisms with a closed circulatory system (see page 188 for more about blood vessels).

Module 3: Section 2  Transport in Animals

## Open circulatory system

Some invertebrates (e.g. insects) have an open circulatory system. In an open circulatory system, blood isn't enclosed in blood vessels all the time. Instead, it flows freely through the body cavity.

### Example

An insect's heart is segmented. It contracts in a wave, starting from the back, pumping the blood into a single main artery. That artery opens up into the body cavity. The blood flows around the insect's organs, gradually making its way back into the heart segments through a series of valves.

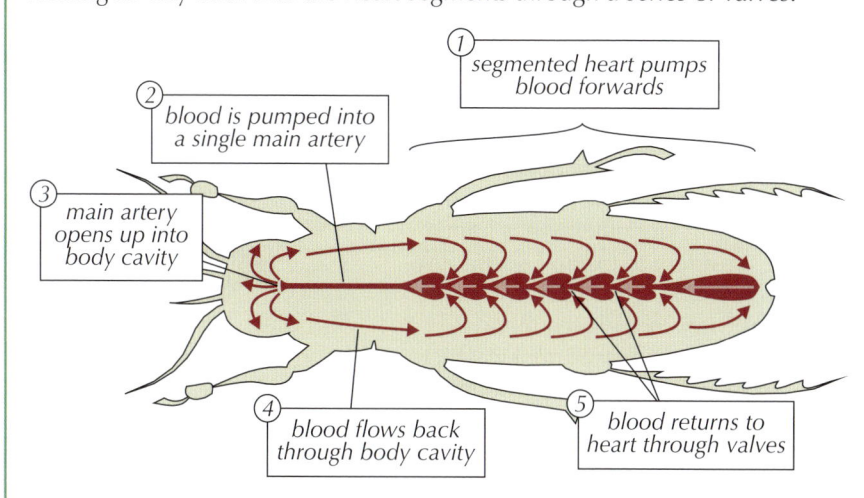

1. segmented heart pumps blood forwards
2. blood is pumped into a single main artery
3. main artery opens up into body cavity
4. blood flows back through body cavity
5. blood returns to heart through valves

The circulatory system supplies the insect's cells with nutrients, and transports things like hormones around the body. It doesn't supply the insect's cells with oxygen though — this is done by a system of tubes called the tracheal system.

**Tip:** Insects need to be relatively small to supply all their cells with the things they need. Useful substances in their blood have to diffuse through the whole body cavity — if they were bigger, they wouldn't be able to supply all their cells properly.

**Tip:** For more about the insect tracheal system see page 178.

### Practice Questions — Fact Recall

Q1 Give two reasons why multicellular organisms need transport systems.
Q2 Name a group of animals that has a double circulatory system.
Q3 Explain why the circulatory system of a fish is described as:
   a) a single circulatory system,
   b) a closed circulatory system.
Q4 Explain why the insect circulatory system is described as an open circulatory system.

**Exam Tip**
Make sure you read the question properly — if you're asked what a closed circulatory system is, don't answer with the definition of a double circulatory system because you've misread the question.

Module 3: Section 2 Transport in Animals

**Learning Objectives:**
- Know the structure and functions of arteries, arterioles, capillaries, venules and veins, including the distribution of different tissues within the vessel walls.
- Be able to describe how tissue fluid is formed from plasma, with reference to hydrostatic pressure and oncotic pressure.
- Be able to explain the differences in the composition of blood, tissue fluid and lymph.

**Specification Reference 3.1.2**

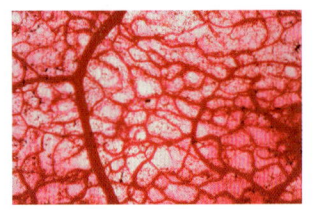

*Figure 2: A light micrograph of capillaries.*

**Tip:** Veins and some large venules contain valves. None of the other types of blood vessels do.

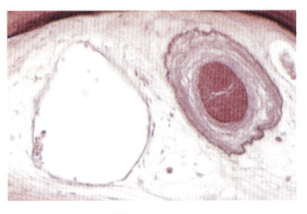

*Figure 4: A light micrograph of a cross-section through a vein (left) and an artery (right).*

**Tip:** Arteries are the 'way art' (way out) of the heart, and veins are the 'vey in' (way in).

# 2. Blood Vessels

*As you know, mammals have a closed circulatory system, which means our blood is enclosed in blood vessels (see p. 186). There are five different types of blood vessels...*

## Types of blood vessel

The five types of blood vessel that you need to know about are arteries, arterioles, capillaries, venules and veins.

### Arteries
Arteries carry blood from the heart to the rest of the body. Their walls are thick and muscular and have elastic tissue to stretch and recoil as the heart beats, which helps maintain the high pressure. The inner lining (endothelium) is folded, allowing the artery to expand — this also helps it to maintain the high pressure. All arteries carry oxygenated blood except for the pulmonary arteries, which take deoxygenated blood to the lungs.

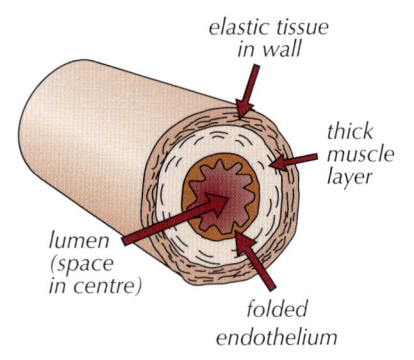

*Figure 1: The structure of an artery.* (elastic tissue in wall, thick muscle layer, lumen (space in centre), folded endothelium)

### Arterioles
Arteries branch into arterioles, which are much smaller than arteries. Like arteries, arterioles have a layer of smooth muscle, but they have less elastic tissue. The smooth muscle allows them to expand or contract, thus controlling the amount of blood flowing to tissues.

### Capillaries
Arterioles branch into capillaries, which are the smallest of the blood vessels. Substances like glucose and oxygen are exchanged between cells and capillaries, so they're adapted for efficient diffusion, e.g. their walls are only one cell thick.

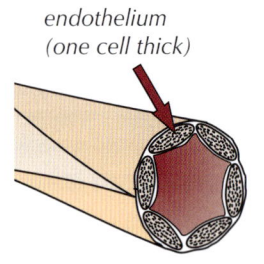

*Figure 3: The structure of a capillary.* (endothelium (one cell thick))

### Venules
Capillaries connect to venules, which have very thin walls that can contain some muscle cells. Venules join together to form veins.

### Veins
Veins take blood back to the heart under low pressure. They have a wider lumen than equivalent arteries, with very little elastic or muscle tissue. Veins contain valves to stop the blood flowing backwards (see p. 192). Blood flow through the veins is helped by contraction of the body muscles surrounding them. All veins carry deoxygenated blood (because oxygen has been used up by body cells), except for the pulmonary veins, which carry oxygenated blood to the heart from the lungs.

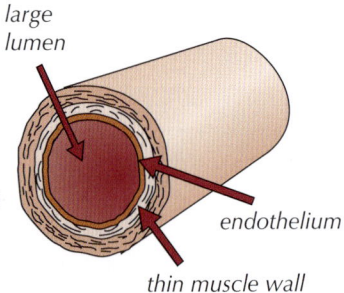

*Figure 5: The structure of a vein.* (large lumen, endothelium, thin muscle wall)

Module 3: Section 2 Transport in Animals

## Tissue fluid

Tissue fluid is the fluid that surrounds cells in tissues. It's made from substances that leave the blood plasma, e.g. oxygen, water and nutrients. (Unlike blood, tissue fluid doesn't contain red blood cells or big proteins, because they're too large to be pushed out through the capillary walls.) Cells take in oxygen and nutrients from the tissue fluid, and release metabolic waste into it. In a capillary bed (the network of capillaries in an area of tissue), substances move out of the capillaries, into the tissue fluid, by pressure filtration.

### Pressure filtration

At the start of the capillary bed, nearest the arteries, the **hydrostatic pressure** inside the capillaries is greater than the hydrostatic pressure in the tissue fluid. This difference in hydrostatic pressure forces fluid out of the capillaries and into the spaces around the cells, forming tissue fluid. As fluid leaves, the hydrostatic pressure reduces in the capillaries — so the hydrostatic pressure is much lower at the end of the capillary bed that's nearest to the venules.

As water leaves the capillaries, the concentration of plasma proteins in the capillaries increases and the water potential decreases. Plasma proteins in the capillaries generate a form of pressure called **oncotic pressure** — so at the venule end of the capillary bed there's a high oncotic pressure and a low water potential. Because the water potential in the capillaries is lower than the water potential in the tissue fluid, some water re-enters the capillaries from the tissue fluid at the venule end by osmosis — see Figure 6.

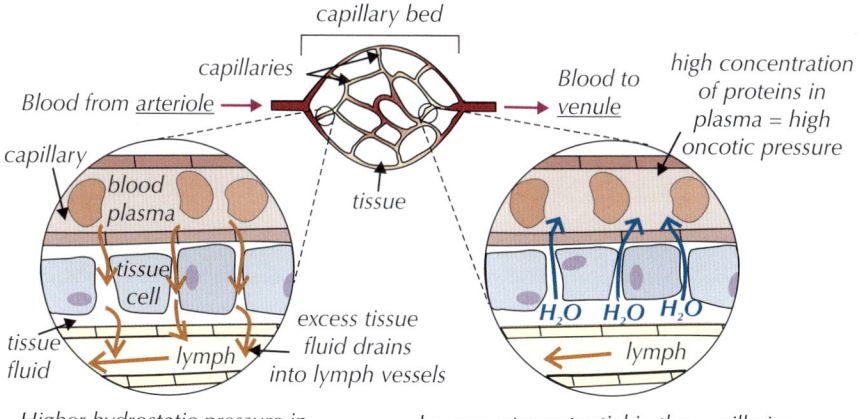

**Exam Tip**
Don't write in the exam that tissue fluid doesn't contain any proteins — it still contains some, just not big ones.

**Tip:** Hydrostatic pressure is the pressure exerted by a liquid.

**Tip:** Water potential is the likelihood of water molecules to diffuse out of or into a solution — see page 135.

**Tip:** Blood plasma is just the liquid that carries everything in the blood.

**Tip:** Pressure is highest at the start of a capillary bed nearest the arterioles — this is caused by the left ventricle contracting and sending the blood out of the heart, through the arteries and arterioles, at high pressure.

*Higher hydrostatic pressure in capillaries than in tissue fluid — fluid is forced out of capillary.*

*Lower water potential in the capillaries than in tissue fluid — some water re-enters capillary by osmosis.*

**Figure 6:** *The movement of fluid between capillaries and tissue cells.*

## Lymph vessels

Not all of the tissue fluid re-enters the capillaries at the vein end of the capillary bed — some excess tissue fluid is left over. This extra fluid eventually gets returned to the blood through the **lymphatic system** — a kind of drainage system, made up of lymph vessels (see Figure 7 — next page).

The smallest lymph vessels are the lymph capillaries. Excess tissue fluid passes into lymph vessels. Once inside, it's called **lymph**. Valves in the lymph vessels stop the lymph going backwards (see Figure 8 — next page). Lymph gradually moves towards the main lymph vessels in the thorax (chest cavity). Here, it's returned to the blood, near the heart.

**Tip:** Don't get the effect of hydrostatic pressure and that of osmosis mixed up — at the arteriole end of a capillary bed, the fluid is forced out of the capillaries by hydrostatic pressure. However, at the venule end of a capillary bed, water moves into the capillaries by osmosis. See p. 134-135 for more on osmosis.

Module 3: Section 2  Transport in Animals   189

**Tip:** The lymphatic system is also part of the immune system.

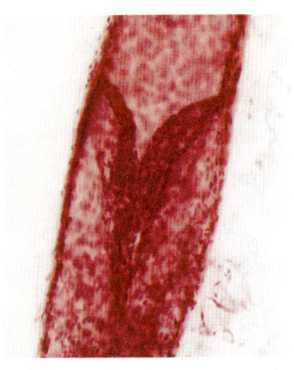

*Figure 8:* Light micrograph of a lymph vessel containing a valve. Here the valve allows lymph to move from top to bottom only.

**Tip:** Platelets are small fragments of cells that play an important role in blood clotting.

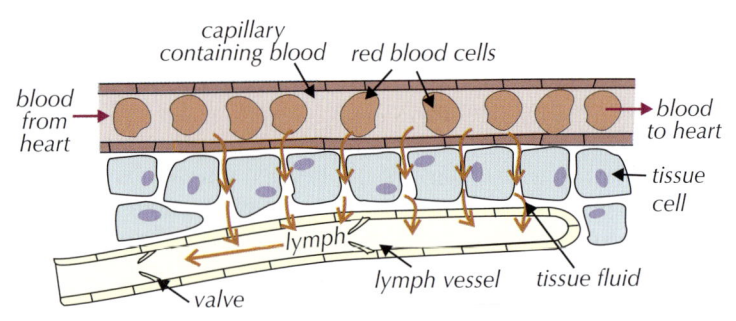

*Figure 7:* Tissue fluid draining into lymph vessels.

## Blood, tissue fluid and lymph

So, tissue fluid is formed from blood, and lymph is formed from tissue fluid — you need to know the differences in the composition of these three fluids.

| | Blood | Tissue fluid | Lymph | Comment |
|---|---|---|---|---|
| Red blood cells | ✓ | ✗ | ✗ | Red blood cells are too big to get through capillary walls into tissue fluid. |
| White blood cells | ✓ | very few | ✓ | Most white blood cells are in the lymph system. They only enter tissue fluid when there's an infection. |
| Platelets | ✓ | ✗ | ✗ | Only present in tissue fluid if the capillaries are damaged. |
| Proteins | ✓ | very few | only antibodies | Most plasma proteins are too big to get through capillary walls. |
| Water | ✓ | ✓ | ✓ | Tissue fluid and lymph have a higher water potential than blood. |
| Dissolved solutes | ✓ | ✓ | ✓ | Solutes (e.g. salt) can move freely between blood, tissue fluid and lymph. |

**Tip:** For this application question, think about how the concentration of protein in the blood affects the water potential of the capillary.

### Practice Question — Application

Q1  Albumin is a protein found in the blood. Hypoalbuminemia is a condition where the level of albumin in the blood is very low. It causes an increase in tissue fluid, which can lead to swelling. Explain how hypoalbuminemia causes an increase in tissue fluid.

### Practice Questions — Fact Recall

Q1  Explain how the structure of each of the following blood vessels is related to its function:
 a) artery,   b) capillary,   c) vein.
Q2  Explain how the structure of an arteriole differs from an artery.
Q3  Which type of blood vessel connects capillaries to veins?
Q4  What is tissue fluid?
Q5  Explain the movement of fluid at the arteriole end of a capillary bed.
Q6  Where does excess tissue fluid drain into?
Q7  a) Give two differences between blood and tissue fluid.
 b) Give one difference between tissue fluid and lymph.

# 3. Heart Basics

*You've seen on p. 186 that mammals like you and I have a double circulatory system. Well, now you need to know about the pump that keeps the blood flowing nicely through the system. Introducing the mammalian heart...*

## External and internal structure of the heart

Figures 1 and 2 below show the external and internal structure of the heart. The heart consists of two muscular pumps. The right side of the heart pumps deoxygenated blood to the lungs and the left side pumps oxygenated blood to the rest of the body.

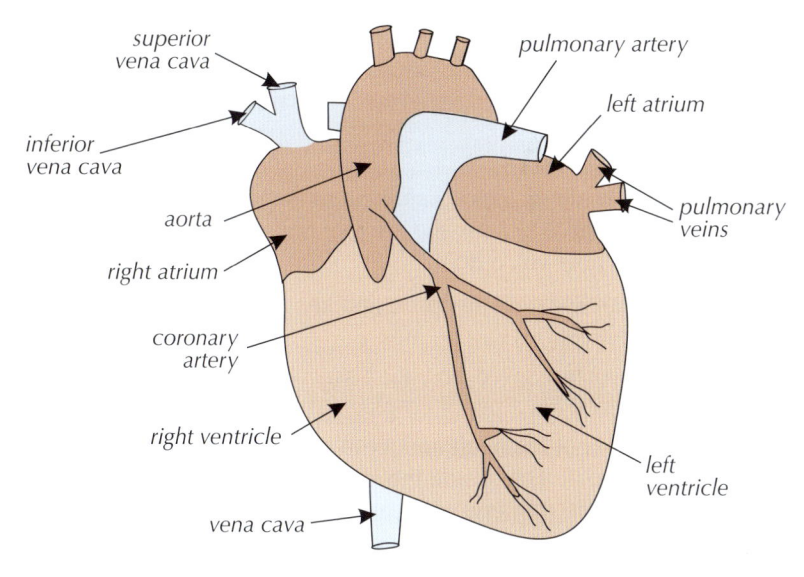

**Figure 1:** *The external structure of the heart.*

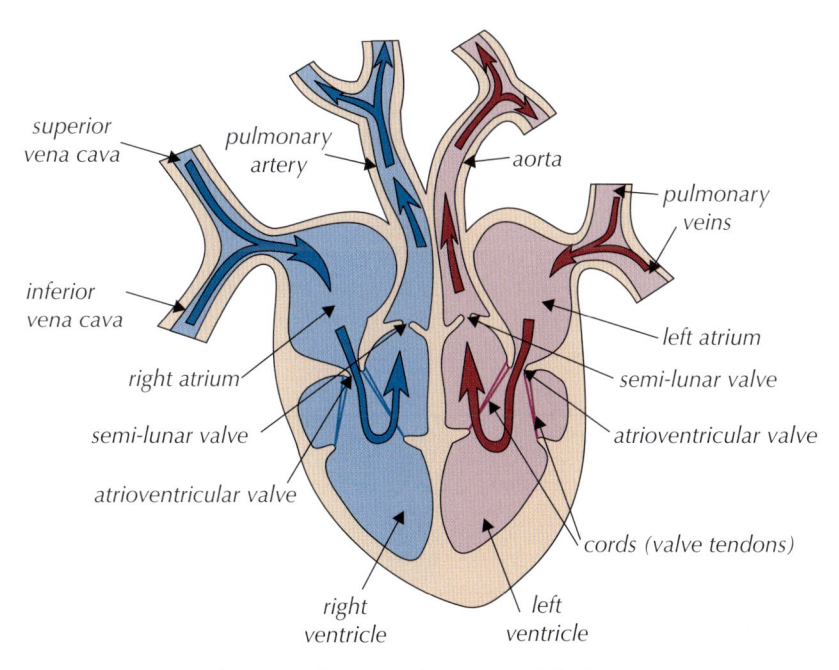

**Figure 2:** *The internal structure of the heart.*

---

**Learning Objectives:**

- Know the external and internal structure of the mammalian heart.
- Be able to dissect, examine and draw the external and internal structure of a mammalian heart (PAG2).
- Understand what happens during the cardiac cycle, including the role of the valves and the pressure changes that occur in the heart and associated vessels.
- Know how to calculate cardiac output using the formula: cardiac output = heart rate × stroke volume.

**Specification Reference 3.1.2**

**Tip:** The left ventricle wall is thicker and more muscular than the right, to push blood all the way round the body. Also, the ventricles have thicker walls than the atria because they have to push blood out of the heart.

**Tip:** There's more about how the atrioventricular valves and semi-lunar valves work on the next page.

Module 3: Section 2 **Transport in Animals**   191

**Exam Tip**
Make sure you don't get the atrioventricular valves mixed up with the semi-lunar valves when answering exam questions — you won't get a mark for writing the wrong name.

## Heart valves

The **atrioventricular** (**AV**) **valves** link the atria to the ventricles, and the **semi-lunar** (**SL**) **valves** link the ventricles to the pulmonary artery and aorta — they all stop blood flowing the wrong way.

The valves only open one way — whether they're open or closed depends on the relative pressure of the heart chambers. If there's higher pressure behind a valve, it's forced open, but if pressure is higher in front of the valve it's forced shut — see Figure 3. This means that the flow of blood is unidirectional — it only flows in one direction.

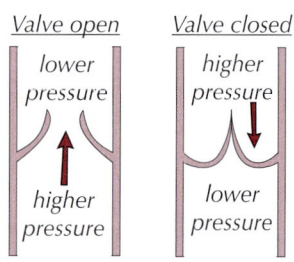

*Valve open*: lower pressure / higher pressure
*Valve closed*: higher pressure / lower pressure

**Figure 3:** Diagram showing how heart valves open and close.

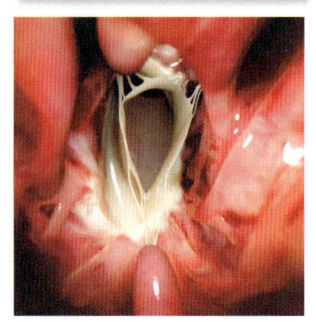

**Figure 4:** A heart valve.

**Tip:** Remember to carry out a risk assessment before you begin your dissection. You need to be very careful when using scalpels — they're really sharp.

## Heart dissection

You need to be able to dissect and examine a mammalian heart. You need to be able to draw the internal and external structure too. This is how you'd do it:

PRACTICAL ACTIVITY GROUP 2

1. Make sure you are wearing an apron and lab gloves because heart dissections can be messy.
2. Place the heart you are given on your dissecting tray. You're likely to be given a pig or cow's heart.
3. Look at the outside of the heart and try to identify the four main vessels attached to it. Feel inside the vessels to help you — remember arteries are thick and rubbery, whereas veins are much thinner.
4. Identify the right and left atria, the right and left ventricles and the coronary arteries. Draw a sketch of the outside of the heart and label it.
5. Using a clean scalpel, carefully cut along the lines shown on Figure 6 to look inside each ventricle. You could measure and record the thickness of the ventricle walls and note any differences between them.
6. Next, cut open the atria and look inside them too. Note whether the atria walls are thicker or thinner than the ventricle walls.
7. Then find the atrioventricular valves, followed by the semi-lunar valves. Look at the structure of the valves and see if you can see how they only open one way. Draw a sketch to show the valves and the inside of the ventricles and atria.
8. Make sure you wash your hands and disinfect all work surfaces once you've completed your dissection.

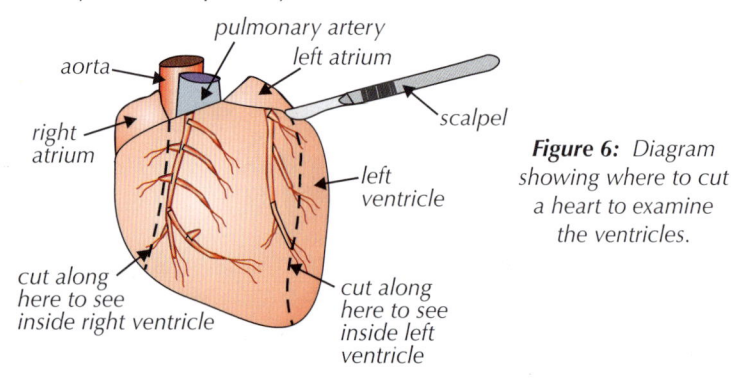

**Tip:** See page 180 for more information on dissections and the tools you might need to use.

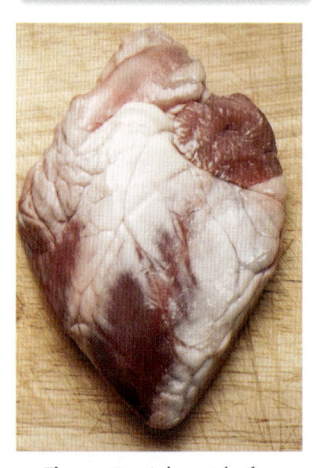

**Figure 5:** A heart before dissection. The fat on the outside may make it hard to see the openings of the blood vessels — you might have to find them with your fingers.

**Figure 6:** Diagram showing where to cut a heart to examine the ventricles.

(Labels: aorta, pulmonary artery, left atrium, scalpel, right atrium, left ventricle, cut along here to see inside right ventricle, cut along here to see inside left ventricle)

192   Module 3: Section 2   Transport in Animals

# The cardiac cycle

The cardiac cycle is an ongoing sequence of contraction and relaxation of the atria and ventricles that keeps blood continuously circulating round the body. The volumes of the atria and ventricles change as they contract and relax, altering the pressure in each chamber. This causes valves to open and close, which directs the blood flow through the heart. If you listen to a human heartbeat you can hear a 'lub-dub' sound. The first 'lub' sound is caused by the atrioventricular valves closing (see stage 2 below). The second 'dub' sound is caused by the semi-lunar valves closing (see stage 3 below). The cardiac cycle can be simplified into these three stages:

**Tip:** Cardiac contraction is also called systole, and relaxation is called diastole.

## 1. Ventricles relax, atria contract

The ventricles are relaxed. The atria contract, decreasing the volume of the chambers and increasing the pressure inside the chambers. This pushes the blood into the ventricles through the atrioventricular valves. There's a slight increase in ventricular pressure and chamber volume as the ventricles receive the ejected blood from the contracting atria.

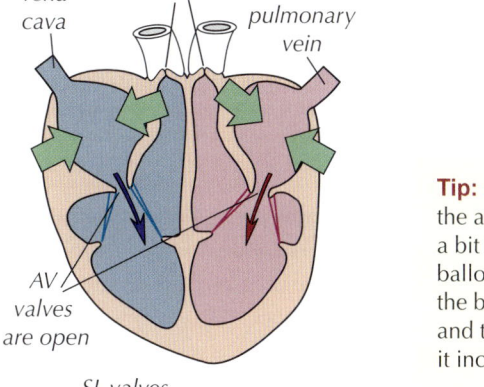

**Tip:** Contraction of the atria or ventricles is a bit like squeezing a balloon — the size of the balloon decreases and the pressure inside it increases.

## 2. Ventricles contract, atria relax

The atria relax. The ventricles contract (decreasing their volume), increasing their pressure.
The pressure becomes higher in the ventricles than the atria, which forces the AV valves shut to prevent back-flow. The pressure in the ventricles is also higher than in the aorta and pulmonary artery, which forces open the SL valves and blood is forced out into these arteries.

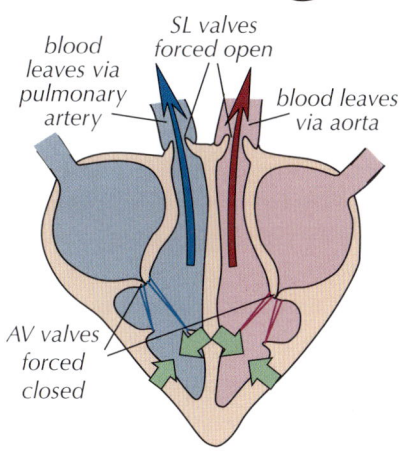

**Tip:** Remember that if there's a higher pressure in front of a valve it's forced shut and if there's a higher pressure behind a valve it's forced open (see previous page).

## 3. Ventricles relax, atria relax

The ventricles and the atria both relax. The higher pressure in the pulmonary artery and aorta closes the SL valves to prevent back-flow into the ventricles. Blood returns to the heart and the atria fill again due to the higher pressure in the vena cava and pulmonary vein. In turn this starts to increase the pressure of the atria. As the ventricles continue to relax, their pressure falls below the pressure of the atria and so the AV valves open. This allows blood to flow passively (without being pushed by atrial contraction) into the ventricles from the atria. The atria contract, and the whole process begins again.

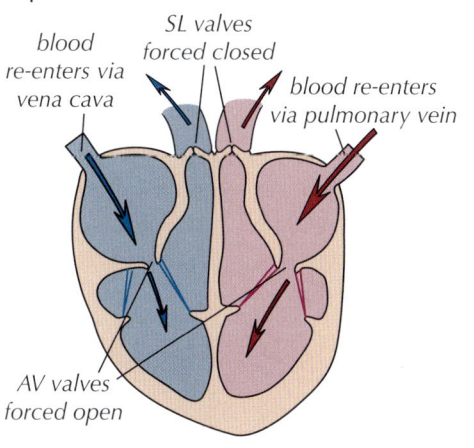

**Exam Tip**
When writing about the cardiac cycle in the exam, make sure you always name the valves. You should also make sure you name them in full at least once before abbreviating them.

Module 3: Section 2 Transport in Animals

**Tip:** You can rearrange this formula if you need to find the heart rate or stroke volume — a formula triangle like this might help:

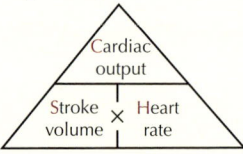

```
      Cardiac
      output
   ─────────────
   Stroke × Heart
   volume   rate
```

To use a formula triangle, put your finger over the bit of the triangle that corresponds to what you want to find, then read off the correct formula.

# Calculating cardiac output

In the exam you could be asked to calculate cardiac output. Cardiac output is the volume of blood pumped by the heart per minute (measured in $cm^3$ $min^{-1}$). It's calculated using this formula:

> cardiac output = heart rate × stroke volume

- **Heart rate** — the number of beats per minute (bpm).
- **Stroke volume** — the volume of blood pumped during each heartbeat, measured in $cm^3$.

**Example — Maths Skills**

Calculate your **cardiac output** if you have a stroke volume of 70 $cm^3$ and a heart rate of 75 bpm.

cardiac output = heart rate × stroke volume
= 75 × 70 = **5250 $cm^3$ $min^{-1}$**

## Practice Questions — Application

The diagram below shows pressure changes in one cardiac cycle.

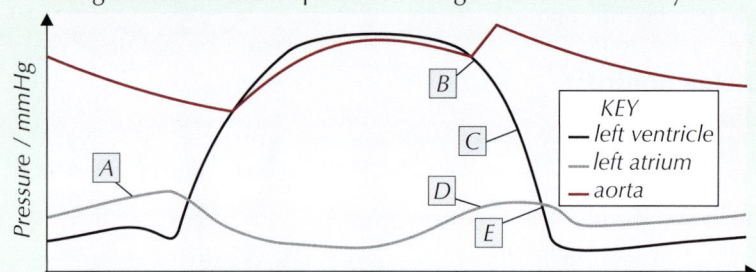

**Tip:** mmHg is a unit of measurement for pressure. It means millimetres of mercury.

**Tip:** To answer the questions on the right you need to be able to link the pressure changes in the left ventricle, left atrium and aorta to each of the three stages of the cardiac cycle.

Q1  Why is the atrial pressure increasing at point A?
Q2  Explain whether the semi-lunar valve is open or closed at point B.
Q3  Why is the ventricular pressure decreasing at point C?
Q4  Why is the atrial pressure increasing at point D?
Q5  Explain whether the atrioventricular valve is open or closed at point E.

## Practice Questions — Fact Recall

Q1  Which side of the heart pumps deoxygenated blood?
Q2  The diagram on the right shows the external structure of the heart. Name the structures labelled A to H.
Q3  a) Name the valves that link the ventricles to the aorta and pulmonary artery.
    b) What is the function of these valves?
Q4  What is the cardiac cycle?
Q5  When the atria contract, describe the pressure and volume changes that take place in the atria.
Q6  What is the formula for calculating cardiac output?

**Tip:** Remember, as the volume in a chamber decreases, the pressure increases.

Module 3: Section 2 Transport in Animals

# 4. Electrical Activity of The Heart

*You don't have to remember to send electrical impulses to your heart muscle to make it contract — it happens automatically. This electrical activity can be captured on electrocardiograms, which can help to diagnose heart problems.*

## Control of heartbeat

Cardiac muscle is 'myogenic' — this means that it can contract and relax without receiving signals from nerves. This pattern of contractions controls the regular heartbeat.

The process starts in the **sino-atrial node (SAN)**, which is in the wall of the right atrium. The SAN is like a pacemaker — it sets the rhythm of the heartbeat by sending regular waves of electrical activity over the atrial walls. This causes the right and left atria to contract at the same time. A band of non-conducting collagen tissue prevents the waves of electrical activity from being passed directly from the atria to the ventricles. Instead, these waves of electrical activity are transferred from the SAN to the **atrioventricular node (AVN)**.

The AVN is responsible for passing the waves of electrical activity on to the bundle of His. But, there's a slight delay before the AVN reacts, to make sure the ventricles contract after the atria have emptied. The **bundle of His** is a group of muscle fibres responsible for conducting the waves of electrical activity to the finer muscle fibres in the right and left ventricle walls, called the **Purkyne tissue**. The Purkyne tissue carries the waves of electrical activity into the muscular walls of the right and left ventricles, causing them to contract simultaneously, from the bottom up.

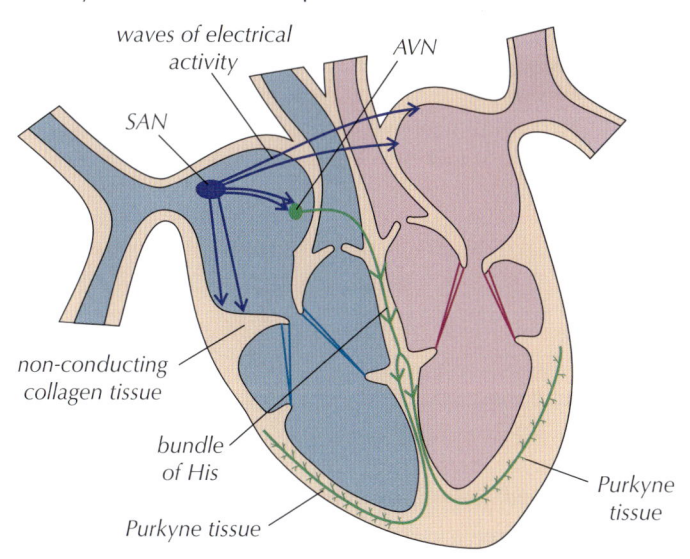

**Figure 1:** The pathway of electrical activity in the heart.

## Electrocardiographs

A doctor can check someone's heart function using an electrocardiograph — a machine that records the electrical activity of the heart. The heart muscle depolarises (loses electrical charge) when it contracts, and repolarises (regains charge) when it relaxes. An electrocardiograph records these changes in electrical charge using electrodes placed on the chest.

**Learning Objectives:**
- Know how heart action is initiated and coordinated, including the myogenic nature of cardiac muscle and the roles of the sino-atrial node (SAN), atrio-ventricular node (AVN) and Purkyne tissue.
- Understand the use of electrocardiograms (ECGs) and be able to interpret ECG traces for normal and abnormal heart activity, e.g. tachycardia, bradycardia, ectopic heartbeat and fibrillation.

**Specification Reference 3.1.2**

**Exam Tip**
The waves of electrical activity initiated by the SAN are also called waves of excitation. Never write that they are 'signals', 'messages' or just 'electricity'.

**Exam Tip**
Make sure you learn where the different structures are in the heart — you could miss out on easy marks in the exam if you don't.

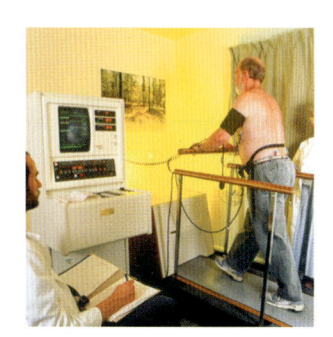

**Figure 2:** A patient exercising whilst linked up to an electrocardiograph.

Module 3: Section 2 Transport in Animals

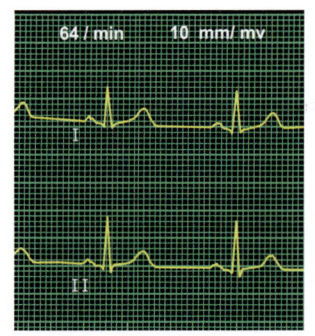

**Figure 3:** An ECG of a healthy heartbeat.

**Tip:** ECGs are produced on a standard grid where each little square represents 0.04 s.

**Exam Tip**
Make sure you learn the names of the different waves and what causes them — you may have to interpret an ECG in the exam.

**Exam Tip**
This formula only works if the time taken for one heartbeat is in seconds — check the units of any values you're given in the exam.

**Exam Tip**
The normal heart rate range for an adult at rest is 60 to 100 beats per minute (bpm). So if you work out heart rate in the exam and get a value way outside this range (e.g. 5 bpm), you know you need to do your calculation again.

**Tip:** This resting heart rate is outside the normal range — it's too fast. If a person's heart rate is consistently too fast, it may mean they have a heart problem — see the next page.

### Electrocardiograms (ECGs)
The trace produced by an electrocardiograph is called an electrocardiogram, or ECG. A normal ECG looks like this:

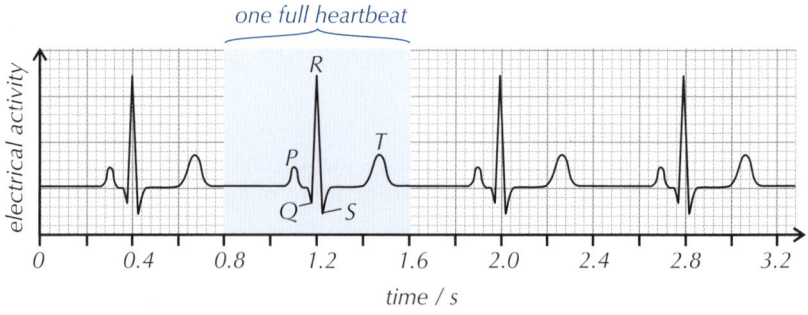

The **P wave** is caused by contraction (depolarisation) of the atria. The main peak of the heartbeat, together with the dips at either side, is called the **QRS complex** — it's caused by contraction (depolarisation) of the ventricles. The **T wave** is due to relaxation (repolarisation) of the ventricles. The height of the wave indicates how much electrical charge is passing through the heart — a bigger wave means more electrical charge, so (for the P and R waves) a bigger wave means a stronger contraction.

## Calculating heart rate
Your heart rate is the number of beats per unit time — usually beats per minute (bpm). You can use an ECG to work out a person's heart rate by using the following equation:

heart rate (bpm) = 60 ÷ time taken for one heartbeat (s)

### Examples — Maths Skills

1. To find out the heart rate shown on the ECG below, first you need to find the time taken for one heartbeat. You can do this by working out the time between one wave (e.g. the R wave) and the next.

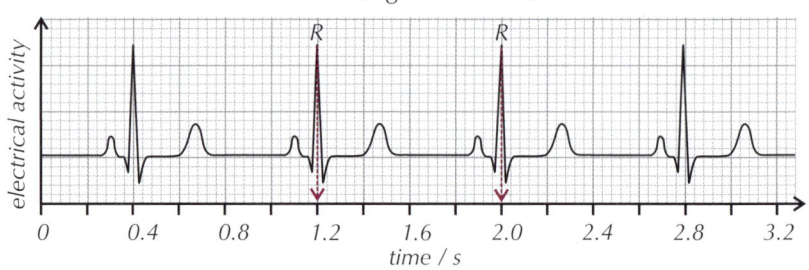

   Here, one heartbeat lasts (2 − 1.2) = 0.8 s
   Heart rate = 60 ÷ time taken for one heartbeat
   = 60 ÷ 0.8 = **75 bpm**

2. Here, the time taken for one heartbeat is worked out using the time between one S wave and the next.
   One heartbeat lasts
   (0.92 − 0.34) = 0.58 s
   Heart rate = 60 ÷ 0.58 = **103 bpm**

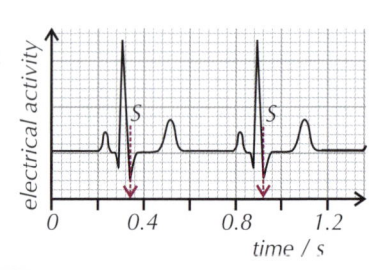

Module 3: Section 2 Transport in Animals

# Diagnosing heart problems

Doctors compare their patients' ECGs with a normal trace. This helps them to diagnose any heart problems.

## Examples

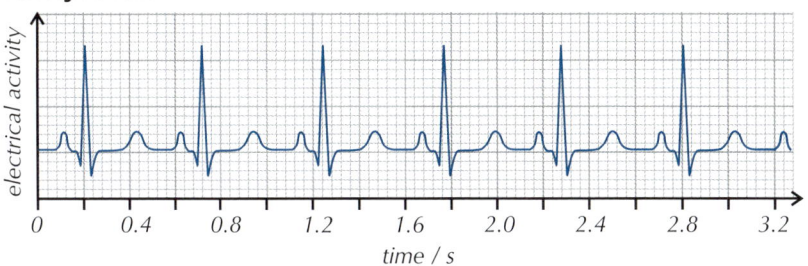

### Tachycardia

This heartbeat is too fast — around 120 beats per minute. It's called **tachycardia**. That might be OK during exercise, but at rest it shows that the heart isn't pumping blood efficiently.

### Bradycardia

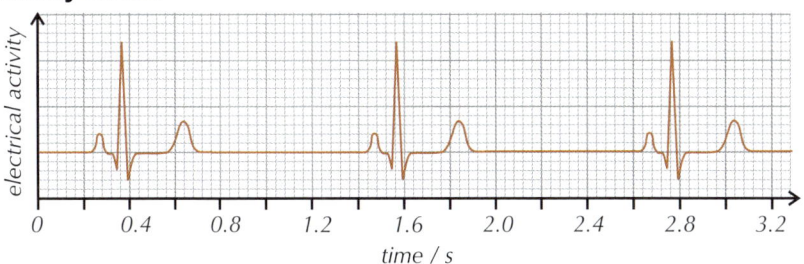

This heartbeat is too slow — 50 beats per minute. A heartbeat below 60 beats per minute is called **bradycardia**. A heart rate this slow is normal in some people (e.g. trained athletes) but in others it can indicate a problem with the electrical activity of the heart, e.g. there may be something preventing impulses from the SAN being passed on properly.

### Ectopic heartbeat

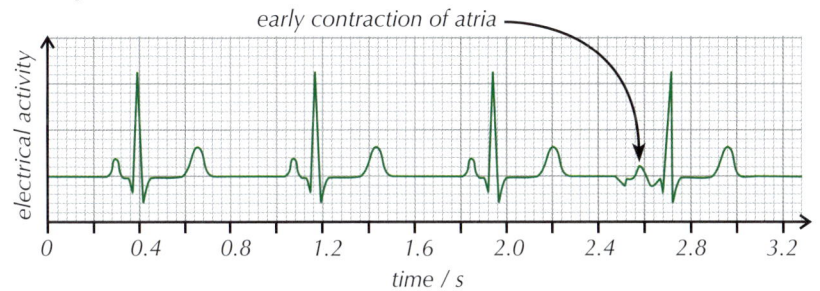

The 4th heartbeat on this ECG is an **ectopic heartbeat** — an 'extra' heartbeat that interrupts the regular rhythm. Here it's caused by an earlier contraction of the atria than in the previous heartbeats (you can see that the P wave is different and that it comes earlier than it should). However, it can be caused by early contraction of the ventricles too. Then you would see a taller and wider QRS complex, sometimes without the P wave before it. Occasional ectopic heartbeats in a healthy person don't cause a problem.

---

**Exam Tip**
Don't be thrown in the exam if you get shown an ECG that doesn't look exactly like one of these examples — they can look different depending on the exact nature of the heart problem. Just identify the different waves and apply your knowledge of how the heartbeat is coordinated to answer the question.

**Exam Tip**
In the exam the y-axis of an ECG may be labelled 'potential difference'. Don't let this put you off — just focus on what the question is asking you.

**Exam Tip**
You might be asked to find the differences between an ECG of normal heart activity and one of abnormal heart activity. To do this look for any differences between the P waves, QRS complexes and T waves, for example, look at their duration and height. Then relate this to what these waves are caused by. E.g. a longer T wave means the ventricles have a longer relaxation/rest period.

Module 3: Section 2 Transport in Animals

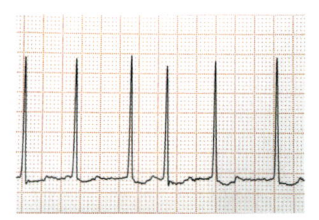

**Figure 4:** *An ECG showing atrial fibrillation.*

**Fibrillation**

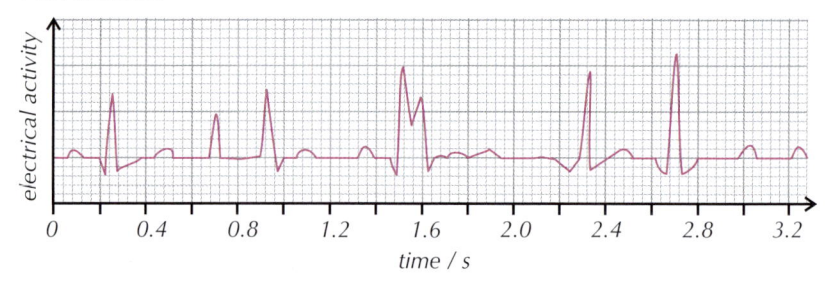

**Fibrillation** is a really irregular heartbeat. The atria or ventricles completely lose their rhythm and stop contracting properly. It can result in anything from chest pain and fainting to lack of pulse and death.

## Practice Questions — Application

Below are an ECG of a person with a normal heart rate (A) and an ECG of a person with an abnormal heart rate (B).

A = Normal ECG

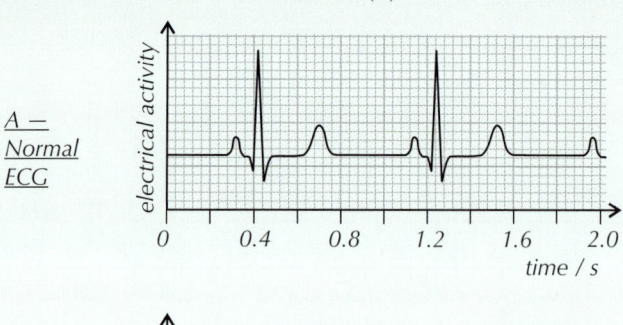

B = Abnormal ECG

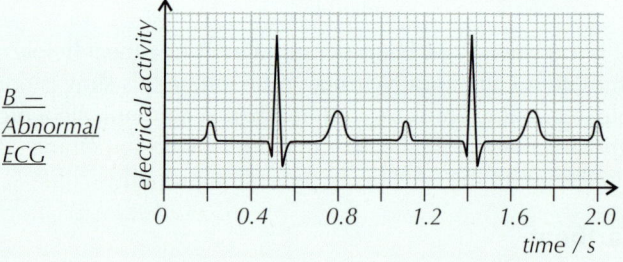

**Exam Tip**
Always show your working for calculation questions — you can still pick up marks for correct working, even if you get the final answer wrong or misread values off a graph.

**Tip:** Remember, the units for heart rate are usually beats per minute (bpm).

Q1 Work out the heart rate shown on:  a) ECG A   b) ECG B.
Q2 Describe two differences between the heartbeats shown by ECG A and ECG B.

## Practice Questions — Fact Recall

Q1 a) What does SAN stand for, in relation to the heart?
   b) What is the function of the SAN?
Q2 Name the tissue that prevents electrical signals passing directly from the atria to the ventricles.
Q3 Describe the role of the bundle of His.
Q4 Describe the role of the Purkyne tissue.
Q5 a) What does ECG stand for?
   b) Give an example of a heart problem that an ECG can be used to diagnose.

# 5. Haemoglobin

*Lots of organisms have haemoglobin in their blood to transport oxygen.*

## Haemoglobin and oxyhaemoglobin

Human haemoglobin is found in red blood cells — its role is to carry oxygen around the body. Haemoglobin is a large protein with a quaternary structure (see pages 71 and 72 for more) — it's made up of more than one polypeptide chain (four of them in fact). Each chain has a haem group which contains iron and gives haemoglobin its red colour (see Figure 1). Each molecule of human haemoglobin can carry four oxygen molecules.

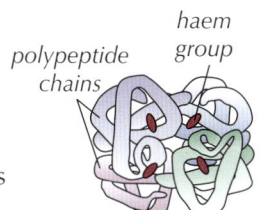

**Figure 1:** *Human haemoglobin.*

In the lungs, oxygen joins to the iron in haemoglobin to form **oxyhaemoglobin**. This is a reversible reaction — near the body cells, oxygen leaves oxyhaemoglobin and it turns back to haemoglobin (see Figure 2). When an oxygen molecule joins to haemoglobin it's referred to as **association** or **loading**, and when oxygen leaves oxyhaemoglobin it's referred to as **dissociation** or **unloading**.

$$Hb + 4O_2 \underset{unloading}{\overset{loading}{\rightleftharpoons}} HbO_8$$

haemoglobin   oxygen                        oxyhaemoglobin

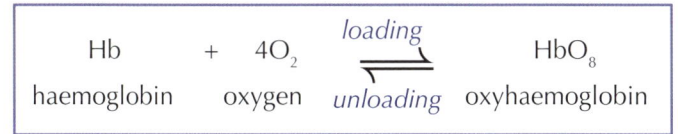

**Figure 2:** *The association and dissociation of oxyhaemoglobin.*

## Affinity for oxygen and pO$_2$

Affinity for oxygen means the tendency a molecule has to bind with oxygen. Haemoglobin's affinity for oxygen varies depending on the conditions it's in — one of the conditions that affects it is the **partial pressure of oxygen (pO$_2$)**.

pO$_2$ is a measure of oxygen concentration. The greater the concentration of dissolved oxygen in cells, the higher the partial pressure. As pO$_2$ increases, haemoglobin's affinity for oxygen also increases:

- Oxygen loads onto haemoglobin to form oxyhaemoglobin where there's a high pO$_2$.
- Oxyhaemoglobin unloads its oxygen where there's a lower pO$_2$.

Oxygen enters blood capillaries at the alveoli in the lungs. Alveoli have a high pO$_2$ so oxygen loads onto haemoglobin to form oxyhaemoglobin. When cells respire, they use up oxygen — this lowers the pO$_2$. Red blood cells deliver oxyhaemoglobin to respiring tissues, where it unloads its oxygen. The haemoglobin then returns to the lungs to pick up more oxygen. Figure 3 summarises this process.

*Alveoli in lungs*
- HIGH oxygen concentration
- HIGH pO$_2$
- HIGH affinity
- Oxygen LOADS

*Respiring tissue*
- LOW oxygen concentration
- LOW pO$_2$
- LOW affinity
- Oxygen UNLOADS

**Figure 3:** *Oxygen loading and unloading in the body.*

---

**Learning Objectives:**

- Know the role of haemoglobin in the transportation of oxygen around the body.
- Understand that oxygen molecules bind reversibly to haemoglobin.
- Recognise the oxygen dissociation curves for human adult and fetal haemoglobin, and understand the significance of the different affinities for oxygen.
- Understand the changes to the dissociation curve at different carbon dioxide concentrations (the Bohr effect).
- Know the role of haemoglobin in the transportation of carbon dioxide to the lungs.
- Understand how carbonic anhydrase, haemoglobinic acid, HCO$_3^-$ and the chloride shift are involved in the transport of oxygen and carbon dioxide by haemoglobin.

**Specification Reference 3.1.2**

**Tip:** Haemoglobin is sometimes shortened to Hb.

**Tip:** Red blood cells can also be called erythrocytes.

## Dissociation curves

An oxygen dissociation curve shows how saturated the haemoglobin is with oxygen at any given partial pressure. The affinity of haemoglobin for oxygen affects how saturated the haemoglobin is:

**Tip:** 100% saturation means every haemoglobin molecule is carrying the maximum of 4 molecules of oxygen.

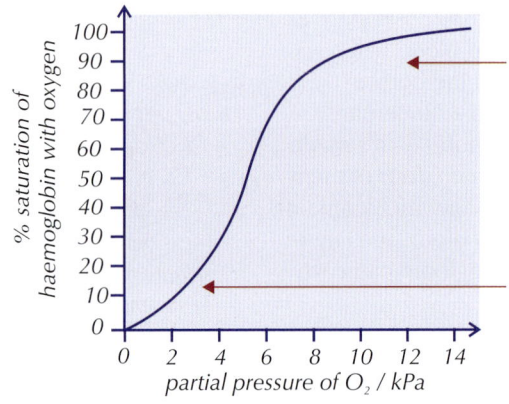

**Tip:** 0% saturation means none of the haemoglobin molecules are carrying any oxygen.

Where $pO_2$ is high (e.g. in the lungs), haemoglobin has a high affinity for oxygen, so it has a high saturation of oxygen.

Where $pO_2$ is low (e.g. in respiring tissues), haemoglobin has a low affinity for oxygen, so it has a low saturation of oxygen.

*Figure 4: Dissociation curve for adult haemoglobin.*

Weirdly, the saturation of haemoglobin can also affect the affinity — this is why the graph is 'S-shaped' and not a straight line. When haemoglobin combines with the first $O_2$ molecule, its shape alters in a way that makes it easier for other molecules to join too. But as the haemoglobin starts to become saturated, it gets harder for more oxygen molecules to join. As a result, the curve has a steep bit in the middle where it's really easy for oxygen molecules to join, and shallow bits at each end where it's harder — see Figure 5. When the curve is steep, a small change in $pO_2$ causes a big change in the amount of oxygen carried by the haemoglobin.

**Tip:** Different organisms have different types of haemoglobin with different oxygen transporting capacities — it depends on things like where they live, how active they are and their size. Having a particular type of haemoglobin is an adaptation that helps the organism to survive in a particular environment.

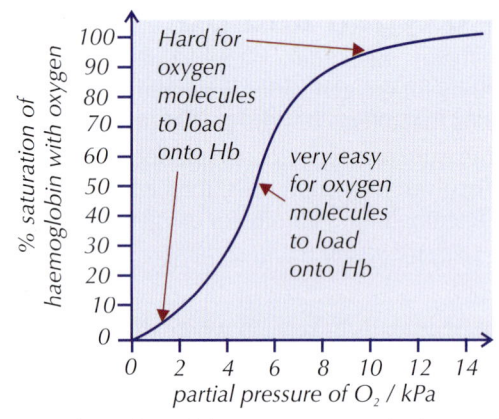

**Tip:** kPa (kilopascal) is a unit used to measure pressure.

*Figure 5: The S-shaped dissociation curve for haemoglobin.*

## Fetal haemoglobin

Adult haemoglobin and fetal haemoglobin have different affinities for oxygen. Fetal haemoglobin has a higher affinity for oxygen than adult haemoglobin (the fetus's blood is better at absorbing oxygen than its mother's blood). This is really important because the fetus gets oxygen from its mother's blood across the placenta.

By the time the mother's blood reaches the placenta, its oxygen saturation has decreased because some has been used up by the mother's body. The placenta has a low $pO_2$, so adult oxyhaemoglobin will unload its oxygen (adult oxyhaemoglobin will dissociate).

Module 3: Section 2  Transport in Animals

For the fetus to get enough oxygen to survive its haemoglobin has to have a higher affinity for oxygen than adult haemoglobin. This means fetal haemoglobin takes up oxygen (becomes more saturated) in lower $pO_2$ than adult haemoglobin — see Figure 6. If its haemoglobin had the same affinity for oxygen as adult haemoglobin, its blood wouldn't be saturated enough.

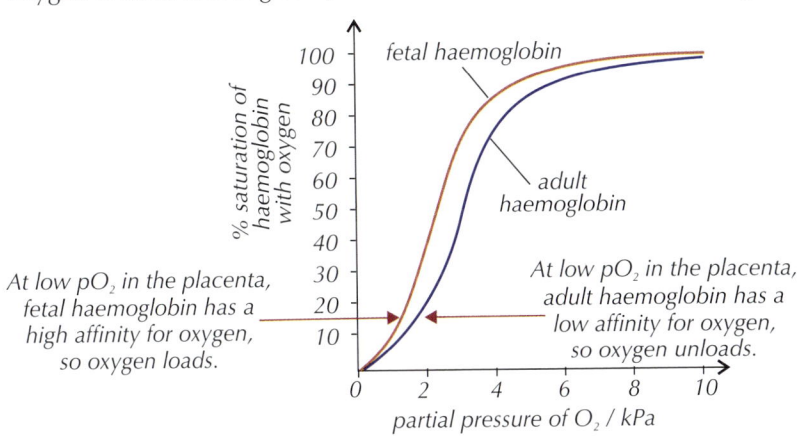

**Tip:** The placenta acts like a fetus's lungs — the fetal haemoglobin has a higher affinity for oxygen (than adult haemoglobin), so it becomes more saturated with $O_2$ at the placenta.

**Exam Tip**
If you're asked to draw a dissociation curve for feta**l** haemoglobin, make sure you draw it to the **l**eft of adult haemoglobin curve.

*Figure 6:* The dissociation curve for adult haemoglobin and fetal haemoglobin.

## Carbon dioxide concentration

The **partial pressure of carbon dioxide (pCO$_2$)** is a measure of the concentration of $CO_2$ in a cell. To complicate matters, $pCO_2$ also affects oxygen unloading. Haemoglobin gives up its oxygen more readily at a higher $pCO_2$. It's a cunning way of getting more $O_2$ to cells during activity.

When cells respire they produce carbon dioxide, which raises the $pCO_2$. This increases the rate of oxygen unloading — the dissociation curve 'shifts' right (but it is still the same shape). The saturation of blood with oxygen is lower for a given $pO_2$, meaning that more oxygen is being released — see Figure 7. This is called the **Bohr effect**.

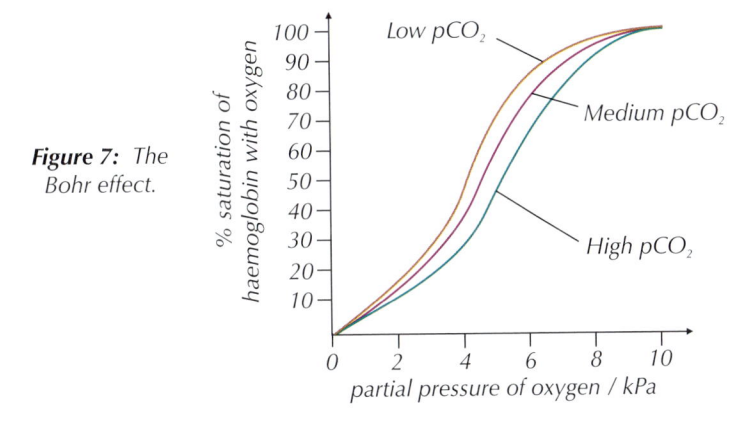

**Tip:** Active cells need more oxygen for aerobic respiration. The word equation for aerobic respiration is: glucose + oxygen → carbon dioxide + water + energy.

**Tip:** When dissociation curves are being compared, the further left the curve is, the higher the haemoglobin's affinity for oxygen is.

*Figure 7:* The Bohr effect.

**Tip:** The Boh**r** effect shifts the oxygen dissociation curve to the **r**ight.

### Explanation of the Bohr effect
The reason for the Bohr effect is linked to how $CO_2$ affects blood pH. Most of the $CO_2$ from respiring tissues diffuses into red blood cells. Here it reacts with water to form **carbonic acid**, catalysed by the enzyme **carbonic anhydrase**. The rest of the $CO_2$, around 10%, binds directly to haemoglobin and is carried to the lungs. The carbonic acid dissociates (splits up) to give hydrogen ions (H$^+$) and hydrogencarbonate ions (**HCO$_3^-$**) — see Figure 8 on the next page.

**Tip:** Hydrogencarbonate ions can also be called bicarbonate ions.

Module 3: Section 2 Transport in Animals

**Tip:** pH is a measure of the H⁺ ion concentration of a solution. An acidic solution has a low pH and a high concentration of H⁺ ions.

**Tip:** More $CO_2$ is released from actively respiring tissues, which causes the dissociation of more $O_2$.

PLASMA | RED BLOOD CELLS

carbon dioxide (+ water) $CO_2$ (+ $H_2O$) —carbonic anhydrase→ carbonic acid $H_2CO_3$ → hydrogen ions + hydrogencarbonate ions $H^+$    $HCO_3^-$

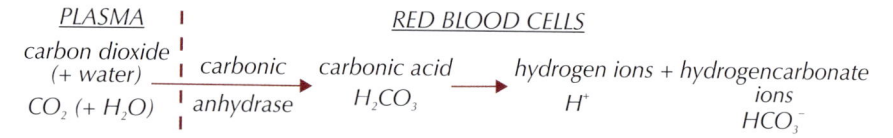

**Figure 8:** The formation and splitting of carbonic acid.

This increase in H⁺ ions causes oxyhaemoglobin to unload its oxygen so that haemoglobin can take up the H⁺ ions. This forms a compound called **haemoglobinic acid** — see Figure 9. (This process also stops the H⁺ ions from increasing the cell's acidity — the haemoglobin 'mops up' the H⁺ ions.) The $HCO_3^-$ ions diffuse out of the red blood cells and are transported in the blood plasma. To compensate for the loss of $HCO_3^-$ ions from the red blood cells, chloride ions (Cl⁻) diffuse into the red blood cells (see Figure 9). This is called the **chloride shift** and it maintains the balance of charge between the red blood cell and the plasma.

PLASMA | RED BLOOD CELLS

hydrogen ions + oxyhaemoglobin → haemoglobinic acid + oxygen
$H^+$    $HbO_8$    HHb    $4O_2$

Cl⁻ → 
← $HCO_3^-$
chloride shift

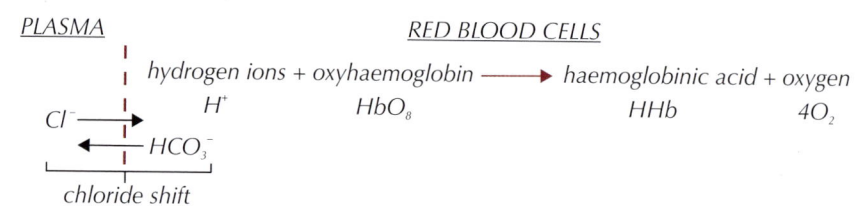

**Figure 9:** The chloride shift and the unloading of oxygen in red blood cells.

When the blood reaches the lungs the low $pCO_2$ causes some of the $HCO_3^-$ ions and H⁺ ions to recombine into $CO_2$ (and water). The $CO_2$ then diffuses into the alveoli and is breathed out.

### Practice Questions — Application

The graph on the right shows a dissociation curve for adult haemoglobin.

Q1 Copy the graph and draw another dissociation curve to represent fetal haemoglobin.

Q2 Explain why you have drawn the dissociation curve for fetal haemoglobin in this way.

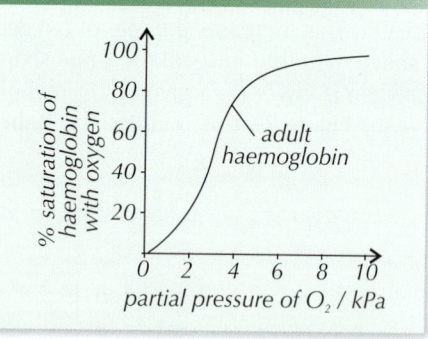

### Practice Questions — Fact Recall

Q1 What does oxygen load onto haemoglobin to form?

Q2 Where in the body would you find cells with a high $pO_2$? Explain your answer.

Q3 What is shown on an oxygen dissociation curve?

Q4 State the main advantage of the Bohr effect.

Q5 Describe the shift that the Bohr effect would have on a dissociation curve for normal adult haemoglobin.

Q6 Name the enzyme that converts $CO_2$ to carbonic acid.

Q7 a) What happens to carbonic acid in red blood cells?
   b) How does this lead to the unloading of oxygen?

Q8 What is the chloride shift?

Module 3: Section 2 Transport in Animals

# Section Summary

Make sure you know...

- That due to their large size, high metabolic rate and small surface area to volume ratio, multicellular organisms need a transport system to supply their cells with useful substances and to take away waste.
- That fish have a single circulatory system (blood only passes through the heart once for each complete circuit of the body) and that mammals have a double circulatory system (blood passes through the heart twice for each complete circuit of the body).
- That fish and mammals have a closed circulatory system (the blood is enclosed inside blood vessels) and that insects have an open circulatory system (the blood isn't always enclosed in blood vessels).
- The structures of arteries, arterioles, capillaries, venules and veins including the distribution of different tissues within the walls of the vessels.
- That the function of arteries and arterioles is to carry blood away from the heart (under high pressure), that capillaries are the site for the exchange of substances between the cells and the blood, and that venules and veins carry blood back to the heart under low pressure.
- How tissue fluid is formed — high hydrostatic pressure at the arteriole end of the capillary bed forces water and small molecules out of the capillaries into the spaces around the tissues.
- That the high oncotic pressure (and low water potential) at the venule end of the capillary bed causes some water to be reabsorbed back into the capillaries from the tissue fluid.
- That tissue fluid is formed from blood, and lymph is formed from tissue fluid, and the differences in the composition of blood, tissue fluid and lymph.
- The external and internal structure of the heart, including the superior and inferior vena cava, pulmonary artery, aorta, pulmonary vein, right atrium, left atrium, semi-lunar valves, atrioventricular valves, cords, right ventricle, left ventricle and coronary artery.
- How to safely dissect and examine a mammalian heart and draw the external and internal structure.
- The stages of the cardiac cycle, including the roles of the semi-lunar and atrioventricular valves and the pressure changes that occur in the heart and associated vessels during the cycle.
- That cardiac output is the volume of blood pumped by the heart per minute and is calculated using the formula: cardiac output = heart rate × stroke volume.
- That cardiac muscle is myogenic and the roles of the following structures in controlling the heartbeat: sino-atrial node, atrioventricular node, bundle of His, Purkyne tissue.
- How to interpret and explain electrocardiogram (ECG) traces of normal and abnormal heart activity, such as tachycardia, bradycardia, ectopic heartbeat and fibrillation.
- That the role of haemoglobin is to carry oxygen around the body.
- That oxygen binds reversibly with haemoglobin forming oxyhaemoglobin.
- That a dissociation curve shows how saturated haemoglobin is at any given partial pressure.
- That the fetal dissociation curve is shifted left from the adult dissociation curve — fetal haemoglobin has a higher affinity for oxygen than adult haemoglobin, allowing it to pick up the oxygen from adult oxyhaemoglobin at the placenta.
- That an increase in carbon dioxide concentration ($pCO_2$) increases the rate of oxygen unloading and the dissociation curve shifts right — this is called the Bohr effect.
- That some of the $CO_2$ that enters red blood cells is transported to the lungs by haemoglobin.
- The explanation behind the Bohr effect — $CO_2$ in red blood cells is converted to carbonic acid by carbonic anhydrase, carbonic acid splits into hydrogen ions ($H^+$) and hydrogencarbonate ions ($HCO_3^-$), and this increase in hydrogen ions causes oxyhaemoglobin to unload oxygen so that haemoglobin can take up the hydrogen ions (forming haemoglobinic acid).
- That the chloride shift is the movement of chloride ions ($Cl^-$) from the plasma into red blood cells to compensate for the loss of $HCO_3^-$.

# Exam-style Questions

1. Which of the following statements about ECG traces is/are correct?

   **Statement 1:** A longer QRS complex may indicate a problem with the Purkyne tissue.

   **Statement 2:** A higher P wave indicates a stronger contraction of the atria.

   **Statement 3:** The T wave is caused by contraction of the ventricles.

   A   1, 2 and 3
   C   Only 2 and 3
   B   Only 1 and 2
   D   Only 1

   *(1 mark)*

2. **Fig. 2.1** is a diagram of the internal structure of the mammalian heart. The valves are shown but not labelled.

   (a) Describe and explain where the blood is flowing **into** in **Fig. 2.1**.

   *(3 marks)*

   (b) Name the valves that connect the atria to the ventricles and describe their function.

   *(2 marks)*

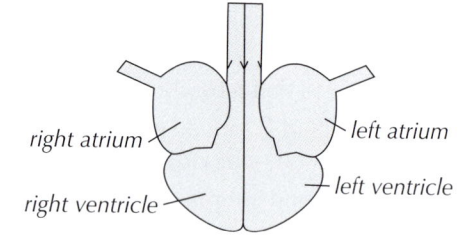

   **Fig. 2.1**

   (c) Mammals have a double circulatory system, which is why the heart is divided down the middle.

   (i) Explain what is meant by a double circulatory system.

   *(1 mark)*

   (ii) Describe how the mammalian double circulatory system works and suggest the advantage to mammals of having this system.

   *(3 marks)*

3. **Fig. 3.1** shows two oxygen dissociation curves for the same man.

   One curve was produced based on blood tests when he was watching television and the other was produced based on blood tests immediately after a bike ride.

   (a) Which curve was produced after the bike ride? Explain your answer.

   *(2 marks)*

   **Fig. 3.1**

   (b) What name is given to the effect shown on the graph?

   *(1 mark)*

   (c) Explain why more $HCO_3^-$ ions would have been released from the man's red blood cells following his bike ride compared to when he was watching television.

   *(3 marks)*

**4** Some people suffer from a disease called third-degree atrioventricular block — the waves of electrical activity from the sino-atrial node (SAN) are not relayed to the atrioventricular node (AVN). A pacemaker can be fitted to take over this role. **Fig. 4.1** shows a heart with a pacemaker attached.

(a) From **Fig. 4.1**, identify which labels correspond to the following structures by writing a letter from A to G in the table.

| AVN | |
| --- | --- |
| Right ventricle | |
| Pulmonary vein | |

*(3 marks)*

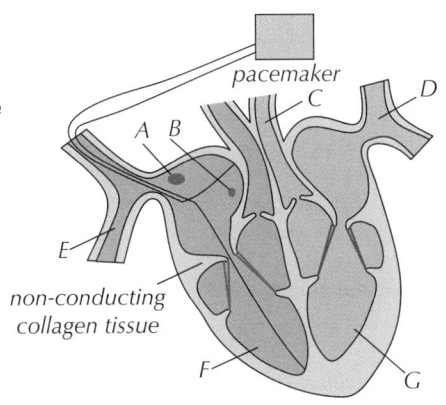

**Fig. 4.1**

(b) What is the purpose of the non-conducting collagen tissue shown on the diagram?
*(1 mark)*

(c) Explain why the pacemaker must be programmed to have a delay between receiving waves of electrical activity from the SAN and activating the AVN.
*(1 mark)*

(d) Describe the passage of the waves of electrical activity from the AVN to rest of the heart, causing the ventricles to contract.
*(3 marks)*

**5** **Fig 5.1** shows part of the circulatory system of a mammal. The arrows show the direction of blood flow.

(a) (i) Which vessel in **Fig 5.1**, **X**, **Y** or **Z**, transports blood at the highest pressure? Explain your answer.
*(1 mark)*

**Fig. 5.1**

(ii) State **three** ways in which the structure of blood vessel **X** differs from the structure of blood vessel **Y**.
*(3 marks)*

(b) The liver is surrounded by a capillary bed and tissue fluid. Describe how tissue fluid is formed.
*(2 marks)*

(c) State **two** ways in which blood is different from lymph.
*(2 marks)*

Module 3: Section 2 Transport in Animals

# Module 3 — Section 3: Transport in Plants

**Learning Objectives:**
- Understand why multicellular plants need transport systems in terms of their size, surface area to volume ratio (SA:V) and metabolic rate.
- Know the structure and function of the vascular system in the roots, stems and leaves of herbaceous dicotyledonous plants, including the structure and function of xylem vessels, sieve tube elements and companion cells.
- Be able to examine and draw stained sections of plant tissue to show the distribution of xylem and phloem (PAG1).
- Be able to dissect stems, both longitudinally and transversely, and examine them to demonstrate the position and structure of xylem vessels (PAG2).

**Specification Reference 3.1.3**

## 1. Xylem and Phloem

*Humans have one transport system — the circulatory system. Plants go one better and have two transport systems — the xylem and the phloem...*

### Why do plants need transport systems?
Plants need substances like water, minerals and sugars to live. They also need to get rid of waste substances. Like animals, plants are multicellular so have a small surface area to volume ratio (SA:V, see page 166). They are also relatively big so have a high metabolic rate. Exchanging substances by direct diffusion (from the outer surface to the cells) would be too slow to meet their metabolic needs. So plants need transport systems to move substances to and from individual cells quickly.

### Location of xylem and phloem tissues
There are two types of tissue involved in transport in plants. **Xylem tissue** transports water and mineral ions in solution. These substances move up the plant from the roots to the leaves. **Phloem tissue** mainly transports sugars (also in solution) both up and down the plant.

Xylem and phloem make up a plant's vascular system. They are found throughout a plant and they transport materials to all parts. Where they're found in each part is connected to the xylem's other function, which is support. The position of the xylem and phloem in the root, stem and leaf are shown in the transverse cross-sections below (see Figures 1-3). Transverse means the sections are cut through each structure at a right angle to its length.

**Tip:** Plants also need carbon dioxide, but this enters at the leaves (where it's needed).

**Tip:** These diagrams all show the xylem and phloem in 'herbaceous dicotyledonous plants' — flowering plants without a woody stem.

### Roots
In a root, the xylem and phloem are in the centre to provide support for the root as it pushes through the soil — see Figure 1.

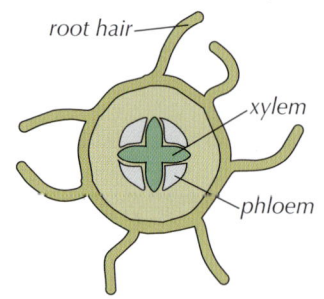

*Figure 1: Transverse cross-section of a root.*

### Stem
In the stems, the xylem and phloem are near the outside to provide a sort of 'scaffolding' that reduces bending — see Figure 2.

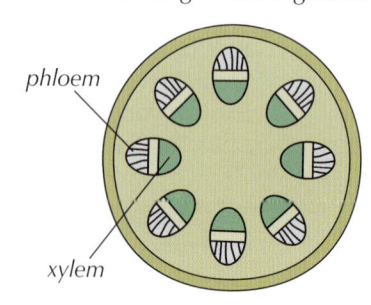

*Figure 2: Transverse cross-section of a stem.*

### Leaves
In a leaf, xylem and phloem make up a network of veins which support the thin leaves — see Figure 3.

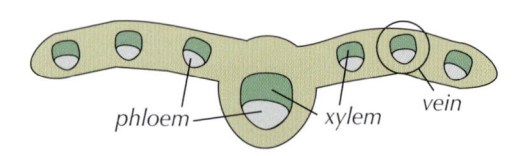

*Figure 3: Transverse cross-section of a leaf.*

You can also get longitudinal cross-sections. These are taken along the length of a structure. For example, Figure 4 shows where the xylem and phloem are located in a typical stem.

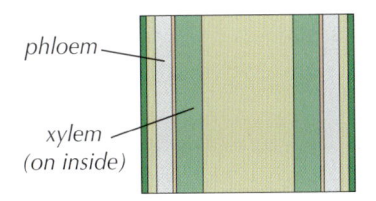

*Figure 4:* Longitudinal cross-section of a stem.

## Adaptations of xylem vessels

Xylem is a tissue made from several different cell types (see page 161). You need to learn about xylem vessels — the part of xylem tissue that actually transports the water and ions.

Xylem vessels are very long, tube-like structures formed from cells (vessel elements) joined end to end — see Figure 5. There are no end walls on these cells, making an uninterrupted tube that allows water to pass up through the middle easily. The cells are dead, so they contain no cytoplasm.

The cell walls are thickened with a woody substance called **lignin**, which helps to support the walls and stops them collapsing inwards. Lignin can be deposited in xylem walls in different ways, e.g. in a spiral or as distinct rings. Being deposited in these patterns allows flexibility and prevents the stem from breaking. The amount of lignin increases as the cell gets older.

Water and mineral ions move into and out of the vessels through small **pits** in the walls where there's no lignin. This is how other types of cells are supplied with water.

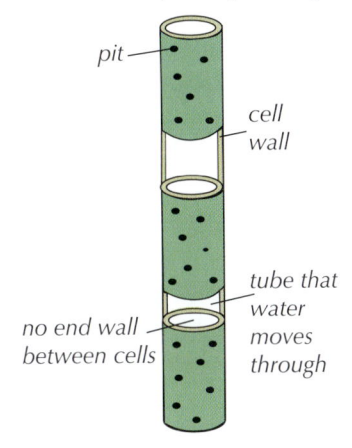

*Figure 5:* A xylem vessel with internal detail showing.

**Exam Tip**
Remember to write that lignin supports the xylem walls, not the whole plant.

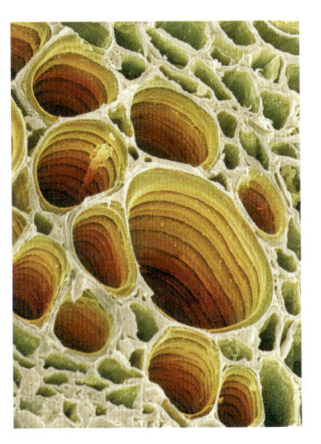

*Figure 6:* An SEM image of xylem vessels — the lignin that supports the vessels is clearly visible (orange).

## Adaptations of phloem tissue

Phloem tissue transports **solutes** (dissolved substances), mainly sugars like sucrose, round plants. Like xylem, phloem is formed from cells arranged in tubes. But, unlike xylem, it's purely a transport tissue — it isn't used for support as well. Phloem tissue contains phloem fibres, phloem parenchyma, sieve tube elements and companion cells. Sieve tube elements and companion cells are the most important cell types in phloem for transport (see Figures 8 and 9 — next page).

### Sieve tube elements

These are living cells that form the tube for transporting sugars through the plant. They are joined end to end to form sieve tubes. The 'sieve' parts are the end walls, which have lots of holes in them to allow solutes to pass through. Unusually for living cells, sieve tube elements have no nucleus, a very thin layer of cytoplasm and few organelles. The cytoplasm of adjacent cells is connected through the holes in the sieve plates.

**Tip:** Phloem tissue also transports small amounts of amino acids, certain ions and plant hormones — but mainly sugars.

Module 3: Section 3 Transport in Plants

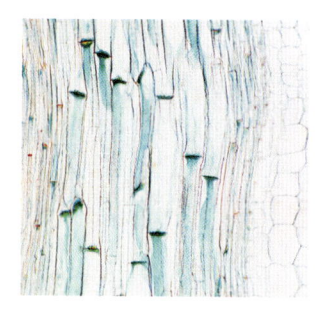

**Figure 7:** Phloem vessels in a Cucurbita plant. The sieve cells are stained blue and the sieve plates are dark green.

**Figure 8:** Phloem tissue — longitudinal cross-section.

**Figure 9:** Phloem tissue — transverse view.

**Tip:** The active transport of solutes requires energy — see page 140 for more details.

### Companion cells

The lack of a nucleus and other organelles in sieve tube elements means that they can't survive on their own. So there's a companion cell for every sieve tube element (see Figures 8 and 9). Companion cells carry out the living functions for both themselves and their sieve cells. For example, they provide the energy for the active transport of solutes.

## Examination of stained plant tissue

**PRACTICAL ACTIVITY GROUP 1**

**Tip:** You could look at a section of plant tissue you've prepared yourself — there's more on this on the next page.

You might have to look at stained sections of plant tissue under a light microscope and examine them to identify the distribution of the xylem and phloem tissue. The distribution of these tissues will depend on the part of the plant you are looking at. Look back at Figures 1-3 on page 206 to see how the distribution changes in the root, stem and leaf. Be aware that when you look at real plant tissue, the distribution won't be as clear cut as in the diagrams and you'll be able to see lots of other plant cells as well — it might take you a little while to figure out what you're looking at.

The cells will look different depending on what stain has been used on the sample. For example, staining with toluidine blue O (TBO) will make the lignin in the walls of the xylem cells blue-green. The phloem cells and the rest of the tissue will generally appear varying shades of pink and purple.

**Tip:** With a light microscope you won't be able to see all of the organelles in your sample — you might see some of the bigger ones in some cells (e.g. nuclei, chloroplasts) depending on the magnification and the stain you are using.

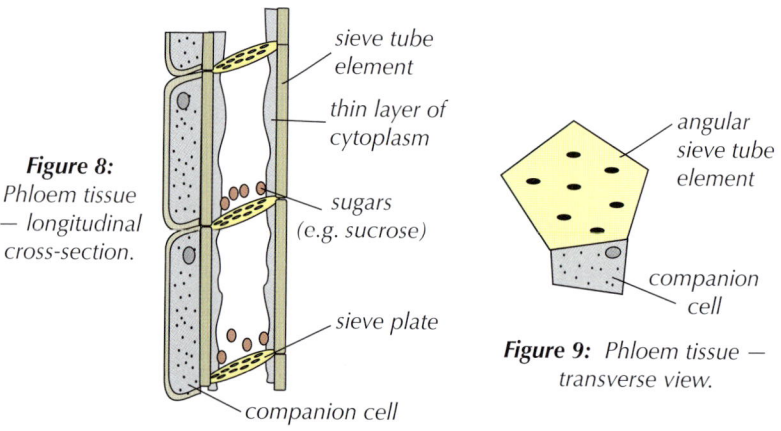

You need to be able to draw the sections you examine. Make your drawings as clear as possible — think about the relative size and position of the structures you draw and add clear labels to show what you've identified. You should also include the magnification you viewed the sample at.

#### Example

The picture on the right shows a transverse cross-section of a buttercup root viewed under a light microscope. As you can see, the xylem vessels are arranged in a rough cross shape. You might also notice that most of the xylem vessels have a wider diameter than the phloem vessels (you'll probably find this is the case for many cross-sections you look at).

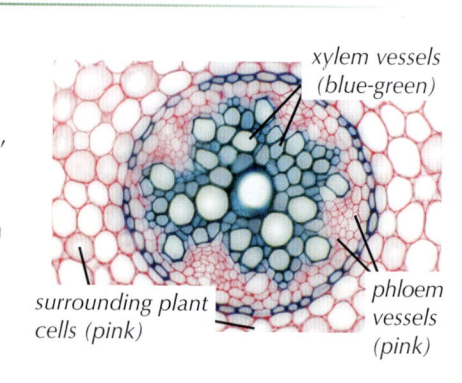

Module 3: Section 3 Transport in Plants

# Plant dissection

You need to know how to dissect a plant stem and prepare the tissue in order to examine the position and the structure of the xylem vessels under a light microscope. You can do this using the following method:

**PRACTICAL ACTIVITY GROUP 2**

---
### Example

1. Use a scalpel (or razor blade) to cut a cross-section of the stem (transverse or longitudinal). Cut the sections as thinly as possible — thin sections are better for viewing under a microscope. You might need to use tweezers to hold the stem still whilst you are cutting.
2. Use tweezers to gently place the cut sections in water until you come to use them. This stops them from drying out.
3. Add a drop of water to a microscope slide, add the plant section and carefully add one or two drops of a stain, e.g. toluidine blue O (TBO), and leave for about one minute.
4. Carefully apply a cover slip so you have created a wet mount (see page 53).
5. View the specimen under a light microscope and draw a labelled diagram of what you observe (see previous page).

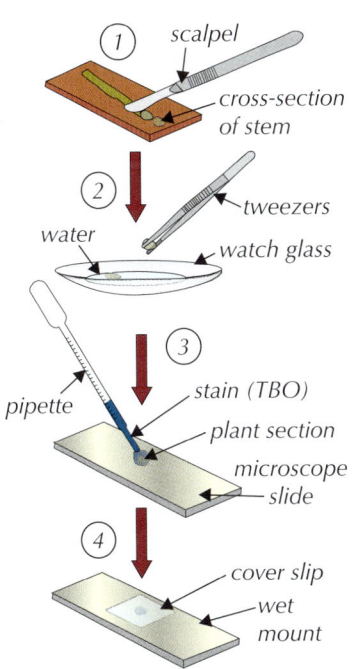

---

**Tip:** As with all practicals you do, make sure you have carried out a risk assessment before you begin. Pay particular attention to safety when working with sharp blades and remember you should wear gloves and eye protection when working with stains.

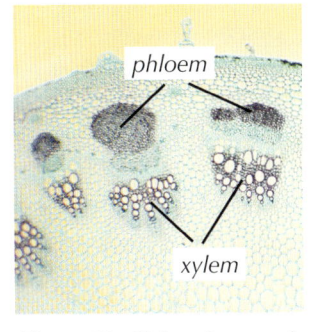

**Figure 10:** Light micrograph of a transverse cross-section through a stem showing xylem and phloem tissue.

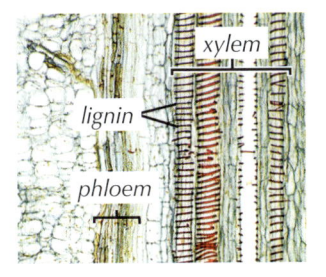

**Figure 11:** Light micrograph of a longitudinal cross-section through a stem showing xylem and phloem tissue.

## Practice Questions — Application

**Q1** The photo on the right is a light micrograph of a transverse cross-section through a leaf. The labels are pointing to the xylem and phloem tissue.
Which label, W or X, is pointing to phloem tissue? Give a reason for your answer.

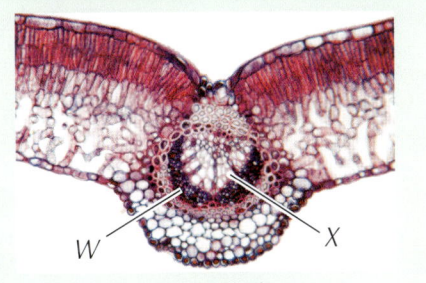

**Q2** Figure A below is an SEM image of phloem tissue in a plant stem. Figure B below is an SEM image of xylem vessels in an ash tree.

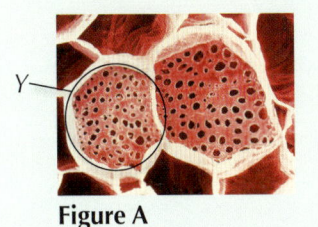

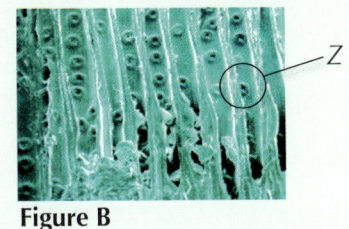

**Figure A**  **Figure B**

a) Name structure Y in Figure A.
b) Name structure Z in Figure B and describe its function.

**Tip:** Microscopes pop up everywhere in Biology — SEM stands for scanning electron microscope. (You learnt about these on page 49.)

Module 3: Section 3 Transport in Plants

## Practice Questions — Fact Recall

Q1 Explain why plants can't exchange substances by direct diffusion.

Q2 The outline below represents a transverse cross-section of a plant's stem. Copy the outline and draw in the position of the xylem and phloem.

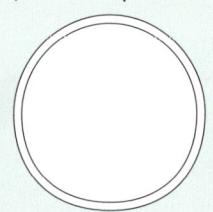

Q3 The diagram below shows the cross-section of a root.

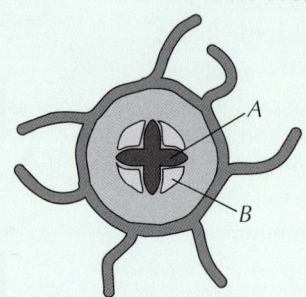

Name the structures labelled A and B.

Q4 What do xylem vessels transport?

Q5 Name the substance present in the xylem vessel walls that prevents them collapsing.

Q6 What is the main substance phloem tissue transports?

Q7 a) Are sieve tube elements living cells or dead cells?

b) Give two ways that sieve tube elements differ from normal plant cells.

Q8 Briefly describe the function of companion cells.

Q9 Briefly describe how you could dissect and examine a plant stem.

**Tip:** Look back at the diagrams on page 206 if you're struggling to remember how xylem and phloem tissue are distributed in different parts of a plant.

# 2. Water Transport

*Plants are pretty clever when it comes to transporting water. They can take it up from their roots to their leaves against the force of gravity. Let's see how they manage that...*

## How does water enter a plant?

Water has to get from the soil, through the root and into the xylem to be transported around the plant. Water enters through root hair cells and then passes through the root **cortex**, including the **endodermis**, to reach the xylem — see Figure 1.

Water is drawn into the roots via **osmosis**. Water always moves from areas of higher water potential to areas of lower water potential — it goes down a water potential gradient. The soil around roots generally has a high water potential (i.e. there's lots of water there) and leaves have a lower water potential (because water constantly evaporates from them). This creates a water potential gradient that keeps water moving through the plant in the right direction, from roots (high) to leaves (low) — see Figure 2.

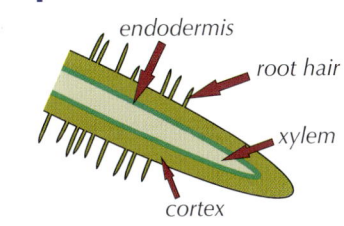

**Figure 1:** Cross-section of a root.

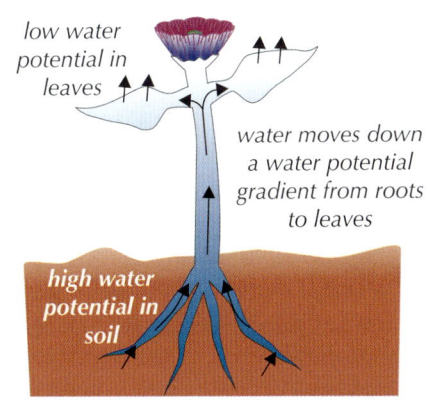

**Figure 2:** Water potential gradient up a plant.

## Water transport through the root

Water travels through the roots (via the root cortex) into the xylem by two different pathways:

### The symplast pathway

The symplast pathway (see Figure 3) goes through the living parts of cells — the cytoplasm. The cytoplasm of neighbouring cells connects through **plasmodesmata** (small channels in the cell walls). Water moves through the symplast pathway via osmosis.

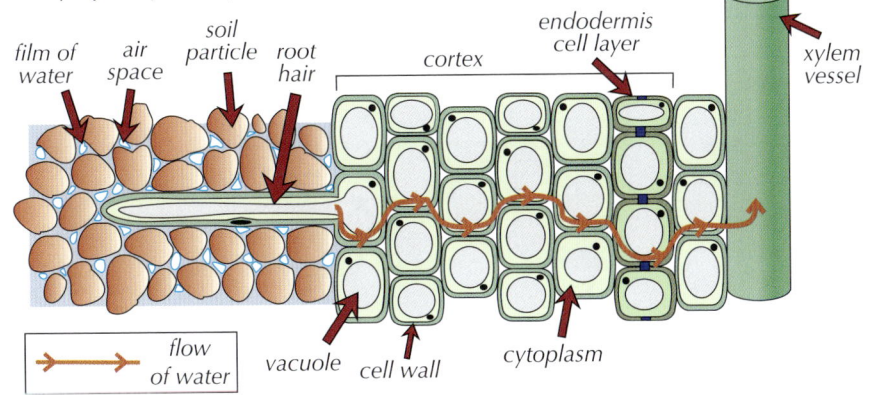

**Figure 3:** The symplast pathway.

**Figure 4:** Root hairs on a cress root.

### Learning Objectives:

- Know how water is transported into a plant, through the plant and to the air surrounding the leaves in terms of water potential.
- Know details of the pathways taken by water as it is transported through a plant.
- Understand the mechanisms of water movement in a plant, in terms of the transpiration stream, cohesion and adhesion.

**Specification Reference 3.1.3**

**Tip:** Remember, osmosis is the diffusion of water molecules across a partially permeable membrane, from an area of higher water potential to an area of lower water potential — see p. 134.

Module 3: Section 3 Transport in Plants

**Tip:** Both pathways are used, but the main one is the apoplast pathway because it provides the least resistance.

### The apoplast pathway

The apoplast pathway (see Figure 5) goes through the non-living parts of the cells — the cell walls. The walls are very absorbent and water can simply diffuse through them, as well as passing through the spaces between them. The water can carry solutes and move from areas of high hydrostatic pressure to areas of low hydrostatic pressure (i.e. along a pressure gradient). This is an example of mass flow (see page 218).

When water in the apoplast pathway gets to the endodermis cells in the root, its path is blocked by a waxy strip in the cell walls, called the **Casparian strip**. Now the water has to take the symplast pathway. This is useful, because it means the water has to go through a plasma (cell-surface) membrane. Cell membranes are partially permeable and are able to control whether or not substances in the water get through (see p. 124). Once past this barrier, the water moves into the xylem.

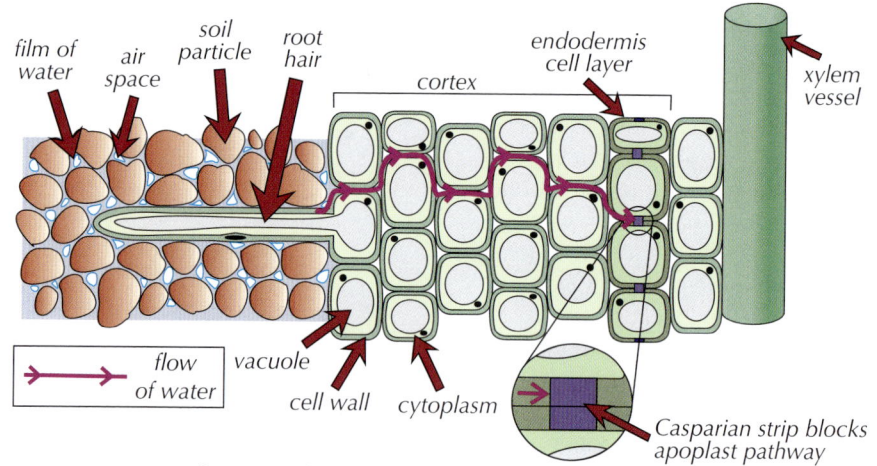

**Exam Tip**
If you're asked to identify the endodermis from a diagram, look for which layer of cells has the Casparian strip.

**Figure 5:** The apoplast pathway.

**Tip:** Water passes from the xylem into the leaf cells by osmosis (down its water potential gradient — see p. 134).

**Tip:** 'Stomata' is plural, 'stoma' is singular.

**Exam Tip**
Don't call stomata 'pores' in the exam — use the scientific term.

**Exam Tip**
Don't be put off in the exam if you come across the term 'mesophyll cells' — they're just a type of leaf cell.

# Water transport through the leaves

Xylem vessels transport the water all around the plant. At the leaves, water leaves the xylem and moves into the cells mainly by the apoplast pathway. Water evaporates from the cell walls into the spaces between cells in the leaf. When the **stomata** (tiny pores in the surface of the leaf) open, water evaporates — it diffuses out of the leaf (down the water potential gradient) into the surrounding air — see Figure 6. The evaporation of water from a plant's surface is called **transpiration** (see p. 214).

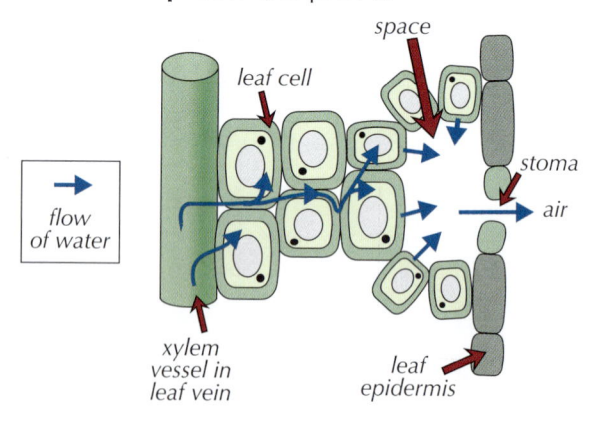

**Figure 6:** Water loss from a leaf.

Module 3: Section 3 Transport in Plants

## Water movement up a plant

The movement of water from roots to leaves is called the **transpiration stream**. The mechanisms that move the water include cohesion, tension and adhesion.

### Cohesion and tension

Cohesion and tension help water move up plants, from roots to leaves, against the force of gravity (see Figure 7).

1. Water evaporates from the leaves at the 'top' of the xylem (transpiration).
2. This creates a tension (suction), which pulls more water into the leaf.
3. Water molecules are cohesive (they stick together) so when some are pulled into the leaf others follow. This means the whole column of water in the xylem, from the leaves down to the roots, moves upwards.
4. Water enters the stem through the root cortex cells.

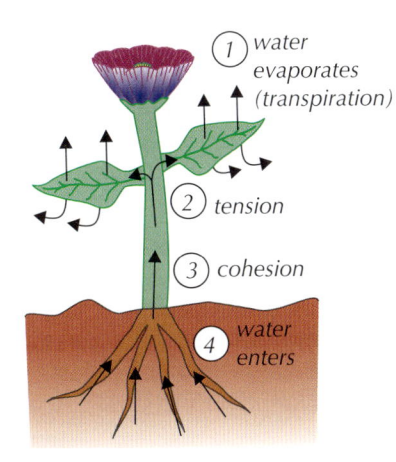

*Figure 7: Water movement up a plant.*

**Tip:** Air bubbles can form in the xylem, which block the column of water, preventing water from reaching the cells. Without enough water the cells become flaccid (see page 135) and the plant wilts.

**Tip:** Water movement up a plant increases as the transpiration rate increases — see p. 214.

**Tip:** Cohesion and tension allow the mass flow of water over long distances up the stem.

### Adhesion

Adhesion is also partly responsible for the movement of water. As well as being attracted to each other, water molecules are attracted to the walls of the xylem vessels. This helps water to rise up through the xylem vessels.

---

### Practice Questions — Application

The diagram below shows a section through a root.

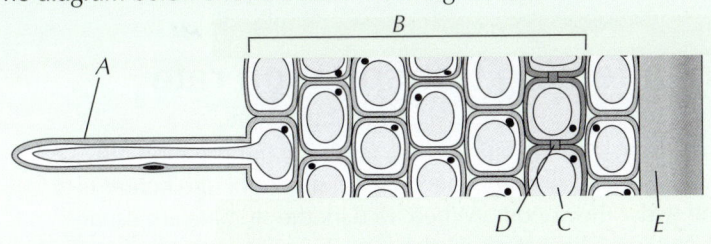

Answer the following questions about the diagram.

Q1 What type of cell is cell A?
Q2 Which cell layer is the endodermis — B or C?
Q3 Name structure D.
Q4 If structure E was blocked, suggest what effect this may have on the plant.

### Practice Questions — Fact Recall

Q1 Briefly describe the pathway of water from the soil into the xylem.
Q2 Describe how water moves through the symplast and apoplast pathways.
Q3 What is transpiration?
Q4 What is the transpiration stream?
Q5 Explain adhesion in terms of water movement in the xylem.

**Exam Tip**
Don't get transpiration mixed up with the transpiration stream — they are two different processes.

**Learning Objectives:**

- Understand the process of transpiration and how it happens as a consequence of gaseous exchange.
- Know how environmental factors affect transpiration rate.
- Be able to carry out investigations to estimate transpiration rates using a potometer (PAG5 and PAG11).
- Know how some plants are adapted to the availability of water in their environment, including xerophytes (e.g. cacti and marram grass) and hydrophytes (e.g. water lilies).

Specification Reference 3.1.3

# 3. Transpiration

*Transpiration was introduced on the previous couple of pages, but unfortunately there's loads more you need to know about it...*

## Why does transpiration happen?

So you know that transpiration is the evaporation of water from a plant's surface, especially the leaves. But I bet you didn't know it happens as a result of **gas exchange**.

A plant needs to open its stomata to let in carbon dioxide so that it can produce glucose (by photosynthesis). But this also lets water out — there's a higher concentration of water inside the leaf than in the air outside, so water moves out of the leaf down the water potential gradient when the stomata open. So transpiration's really a side effect of the gas exchange needed for photosynthesis.

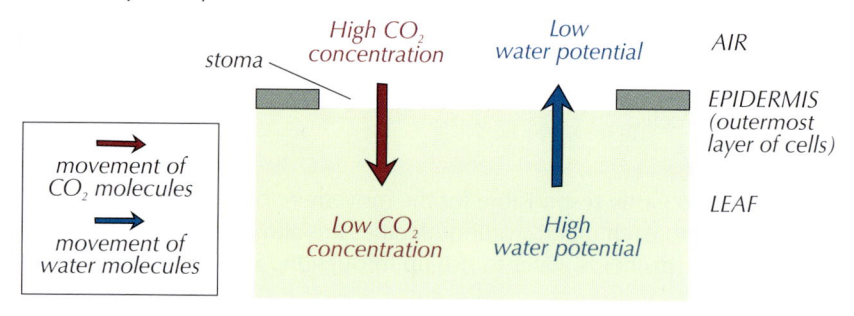

**Figure 1:** Simplified diagram to show gas exchange and water loss from a leaf.

**Tip:** Water moves from areas of higher water potential to areas of lower water potential — it moves down the water potential gradient.

**Tip:** Stomata are found on both sides of most leaves but they are usually more numerous on the underside — this reduces the amount of water lost through transpiration.

**Tip:** The rate of transpiration can fluctuate at different times of day, e.g. because the humidity is higher or lower.

## Factors affecting transpiration rate

There are four main factors that affect transpiration rate:

1. **Light intensity** — the lighter it is the faster the transpiration rate. This is because the stomata open when it gets light (the lighter it gets, the wider they open). When it's dark the stomata are usually closed, so there's little transpiration.

2. **Temperature** — the higher the temperature the faster the transpiration rate. Warmer water molecules have more energy so they evaporate from the cells inside the leaf faster. This increases the water potential gradient between the inside and outside of the leaf, making water diffuse out of the leaf faster.

3. **Humidity** — the lower the humidity, the faster the transpiration rate. If the air around the plant is dry, the water potential gradient between the leaf and the air is increased, which increases transpiration rate.

4. **Wind** — the windier it is, the faster the transpiration rate. Lots of air movement blows away water molecules from around the stomata. This increases the water potential gradient, which increases the rate of transpiration.

Module 3: Section 3  Transport in Plants

# Estimating transpiration rate — potometers

PRACTICAL ACTIVITY GROUP 5
PRACTICAL ACTIVITY GROUP 11

A potometer is a special piece of apparatus used to estimate transpiration rates. It actually measures water uptake by a plant, but it's assumed that water uptake by the plant is directly related to water loss by the leaves. You can use it to estimate how different factors affect the transpiration rate.

**Tip:** Transpiration rate isn't exactly the same as water uptake by a plant — some water is used for photosynthesis and to support the plant, and some water is produced during respiration.

## Using a potometer
The steps for using a potometer are listed below. As with all experiments you do, make sure you've carried out a risk assessment before you begin.

1. Cut a shoot underwater to prevent air from entering the xylem. Cut it at a slant to increase the surface area available for water uptake.
2. Assemble the potometer in water (see Figure 2) and insert the shoot under water, so no air can enter.
3. Remove the apparatus from the water but keep the end of the capillary tube submerged in a beaker of water.
4. Check that the apparatus is watertight and airtight.
5. Dry the leaves, allow time for the shoot to acclimatise and then shut the tap.
6. Remove the end of the capillary tube from the beaker of water until one air bubble has formed, then put the end of the tube back into the water.
7. Record the starting position of the air bubble.
8. Start a stopwatch and record the distance moved by the bubble per unit time, e.g. per hour. The rate of air bubble movement is an estimate of the transpiration rate.
9. Remember, only change one variable (e.g. temperature) at a time. All other conditions (e.g. light intensity, humidity) must be kept constant.

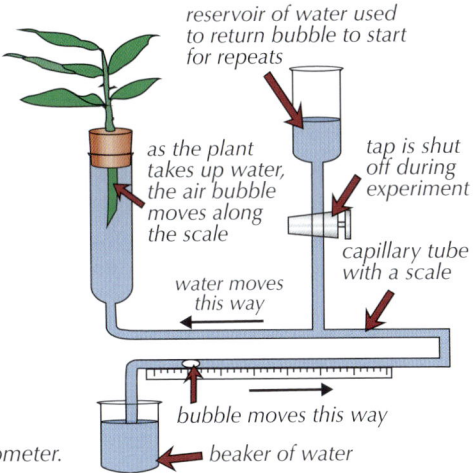

**Tip:** You can use a potometer to test the effect of different factors on transpiration rate, e.g. by using a fan to increase air movement or a lamp to increase light intensity etc. You could also investigate the role of stomata by preventing water from escaping from them (e.g. by coating the underside of the leaf with petroleum jelly).

**Tip:** The air bubble is sometimes called the air-water meniscus.

**Tip:** When estimating the rate of transpiration by measuring water uptake, you need to carry out repeats to improve the precision of your results and to help identify any anomalies in your data. (See pages 6 and 10 for more.)

**Figure 2:** A potometer.

## Adaptations in xerophytic plants

**Xerophytes** are plants like cacti and marram grass (which grows on sand dunes). They're adapted to live in dry climates. Their adaptations prevent them losing too much water by transpiration.

**Tip:** The thick, waxy layer on the epidermis of a plant is called a cuticle.

### Example — Cacti
- Cacti have a thick, waxy layer on the epidermis — this reduces water loss by evaporation because the layer is waterproof (water can't move through it).
- They have spines instead of leaves — this reduces the surface area for water loss.
- Cacti also close their stomata at the hottest times of the day when transpiration rates are the highest.

**Figure 3:** Cacti spines.

Module 3: Section 3 Transport in Plants 215

*Figure 4: Marram grass.*

### Example — Marram grass

- Marram grass has stomata that are sunk in pits, so they're sheltered from the wind. This traps moist air in the pits and helps to slow transpiration down by lowering the water potential gradient.
- It also has a layer of 'hairs' on the epidermis — this also traps moist air round the stomata, which reduces the water potential gradient between the leaf and the air, slowing transpiration down.
- In hot or windy conditions marram grass plants roll their leaves — again this traps moist air, slowing down transpiration. It also reduces the exposed surface area for losing water and protects the stomata from wind.
- Like cacti, marram grass has a thick, waxy layer on the epidermis to reduce water loss by evaporation.

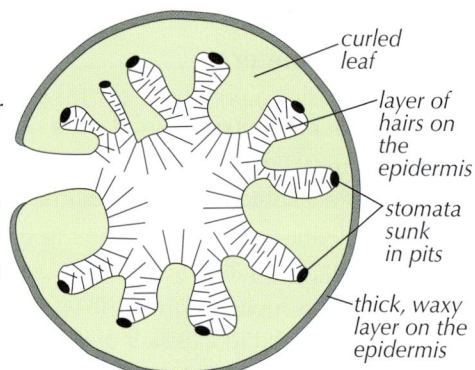

*Figure 5: Cross-section through a marram grass leaf.*

## Adaptations in hydrophytic plants

**Hydrophytes** are plants like water lilies, which live in aquatic habitats. As they grow in water, they don't need adaptations to reduce water loss (like xerophytes), but they do need adaptations to help them cope with a low oxygen level. Here are some adaptations of hydrophytes...

- Air spaces in the tissues help the plants to float and can act as a store of oxygen for use in respiration. For example, water lilies have large air spaces in their leaves (see Figure 8). This allows the leaves to float on the surface of the water, increasing the amount of light they receive. Air spaces in the roots and stems allow oxygen to move from the floating leaves down to parts of the plant that are underwater.
- Stomata are usually only present on the upper surface of floating leaves. This helps maximise gas exchange.
- Hydrophytes often have flexible leaves and stems — these plants are supported by the water around them, so they don't need rigid stems for support. Flexibility helps to prevent damage by water currents.

*Figure 6: Water lilies.*

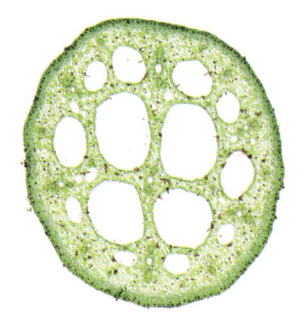

*Figure 7: Light micrograph of a transverse cross-section through a water lily stem showing large air spaces (white circles).*

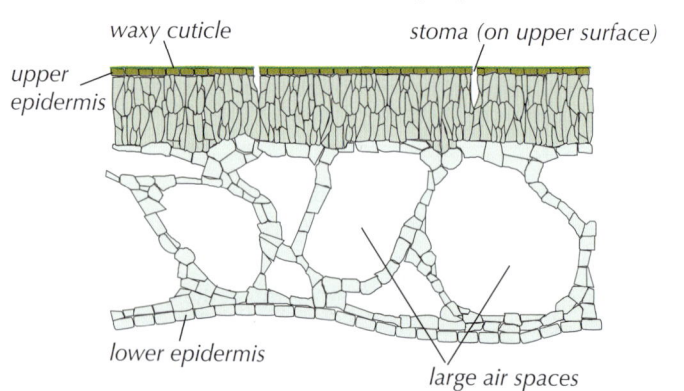

*Figure 8: Transverse cross-section through a leaf from a water lily.*

Module 3: Section 3 Transport in Plants

## Practice Questions — Application

Q1 The photographs below show sections of leaves from two different plants.

A    B

Which leaf belongs to a xerophyte? Explain your answer.

Q2 A potometer was used to test the effect of temperature on transpiration rate. The test was repeated 3 times. The results are shown in the table.

| Temperature (°C) | Distance moved by the bubble in 10 minutes (mm) |||
|---|---|---|---|
| | Test 1 | Test 2 | Test 3 |
| 10 | 15 | 12 | 14 |
| 20 | 19 | 16 | 19 |
| 30 | 25 | 22 | 23 |

a) Calculate the mean result for each temperature. Give your answers to one decimal place.

b) Plot a graph of the mean results and use it to estimate the distance the bubble would move in ten minutes at 25 °C.

c) Describe and explain the results of the experiment.

Q3 The plant *Eichhornia crassipes* is causing problems in many parts of the world as, left uncontrolled, it can completely cover the surface of large bodies of water where it grows.

a) Suggest whether *Eichhornia crassipes* is a xerophyte or a hydrophyte. Give a reason for your answer.

b) With reference to the stems and leaves, suggest and explain how *Eichhornia crassipes* may be adapted to its habitat.

**Exam Tip**
If you're asked in the exam to give your answer to one decimal place, make sure you round it up or down correctly — otherwise you won't get the marks.

## Practice Questions — Fact Recall

Q1 What process is transpiration a consequence of?

Q2 Explain how wind affects transpiration rate.

Q3 Other than wind, give three factors that affect transpiration rate.

Q4 When using a potometer to estimate transpiration rate, what assumption is made?

Q5 Describe and explain three adaptations that cacti have to reduce water loss.

Q6 Give an example of a hydrophyte.

Module 3: Section 3 Transport in Plants

**Learning Objectives:**

- Understand the mechanism of translocation as an energy-requiring process transporting assimilates, especially sucrose, between sources (e.g. leaves) and sinks (e.g. roots and meristems).
- Know how assimilates are removed at the sink.
- Know the details of active loading at the source.

**Specification Reference 3.1.3**

**Tip:** Assimilates are substances that become incorporated into the plant tissue.

**Exam Tip**
Make sure you learn what the terms 'source' and 'sink' mean — you could be tested on them in the exam.

**Tip:** Sugars are transported as sucrose because sucrose is both soluble and metabolically inactive — so it doesn't get used up during transport.

**Tip:** The phloem transports solutes up and down a plant, from sources to sinks. (See pages 206-208 for more on the phloem.)

# 4. Translocation

*The phloem transports dissolved substances (like sugars) around the plant to where they're needed. Scientists still aren't sure exactly how this movement works, but they do have a hypothesis...*

## What is translocation?

Translocation is the movement of dissolved substances (e.g. sugars like sucrose, and amino acids) to where they're needed in a plant. Dissolved substances are sometimes called **assimilates**. Translocation is an energy-requiring process that happens in the phloem.

Translocation moves substances from 'sources' to 'sinks'. The **source** of a substance is where it's made (so it's at a high concentration there). The **sink** is the area where it's used up (so it's at a lower concentration there).

─ Example ─
The source for sucrose is usually the leaves (where it's made following photosynthesis), and the sinks are the other parts of the plant, e.g. food storage organs and meristems (areas of growth) in the roots, stems and leaves.

Some parts of a plant can be both a sink and a source.

─ Example ─
Sucrose can be stored in the roots. During the growing season, sucrose is transported from the roots to the leaves to provide the leaves with energy for growth. In this case, the roots are the source and the leaves are a sink.

Enzymes maintain a concentration gradient from the source to the sink by changing the dissolved substances at the sink (e.g. by breaking them down or making them into something else). This makes sure there's always a lower concentration at the sink than at the source.

─ Examples ─
In potatoes, sucrose is converted to starch in the sink areas, so there's always a lower concentration of sucrose at the sink than inside the phloem. This makes sure a constant supply of new sucrose reaches the sink from the phloem.

In other sinks, enzymes such as invertase break down sucrose into glucose (and fructose) for use by the plant — again this makes sure there's a lower concentration of sucrose at the sink.

## The mass flow hypothesis

Scientists still aren't certain exactly how the dissolved substances (solutes) are transported from source to sink by translocation. The best supported theory is the mass flow hypothesis:

### 1. Source

Active transport is used to actively load the solutes (e.g. sucrose from photosynthesis) into the sieve tubes of the phloem at the source (e.g. the leaves). There's more on this on the next two pages. This lowers the water potential inside the sieve tubes, so water enters the tubes by osmosis from the xylem and companion cells. This creates a high pressure inside the sieve tubes at the source end of the phloem — see Figure 1 on the next page.

218 Module 3: Section 3 Transport in Plants

## 2. Sink

At the sink end, solutes are removed from the phloem to be used up. This usually happens by diffusion (a passive process) because the solutes are at a higher concentration in the phloem than they are in the surrounding tissue at the sink. The removal of solutes increases the water potential inside the sieve tubes, so water also leaves the tubes by osmosis. This lowers the pressure inside the sieve tubes — see Figure 1.

## 3. Flow

The result is a pressure gradient from the source end to the sink end. This gradient pushes solutes along the sieve tubes towards the sink. When they reach the sink the solutes will be used (e.g. in respiration) or stored (e.g. as starch).

The higher the concentration of sucrose at the source, the higher the rate of translocation.

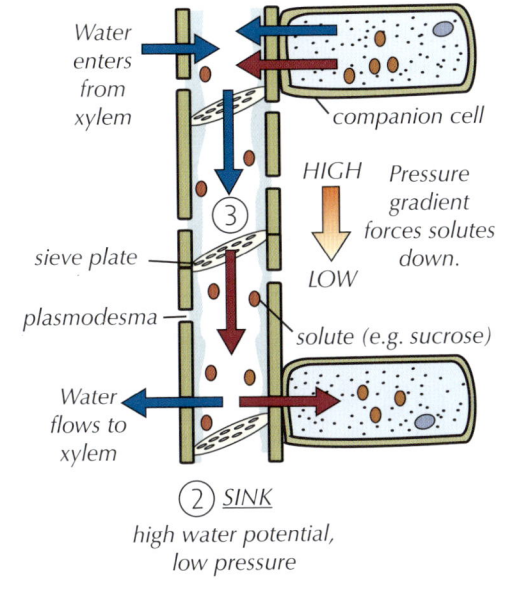

**Figure 1:** How the mass flow hypothesis works.

① SOURCE — low water potential, high pressure
② SINK — high water potential, low pressure

**Tip:** There's more about sieve plates and companion cells on pages 207-208.

**Tip:** Once they've left the phloem cells, the solutes are transported to cells in the sink via the symplast or apoplast pathways (see pages 211-212).

**Tip:** Make sure you know the differences between transport in the xylem and phloem — transport in the phloem can take place in both directions, uses living cells and doesn't rely on cohesion or adhesion. Transport in the xylem happens in just one direction (from roots to leaves), in non-living cells and relies on cohesion and adhesion to move the column of water.

# Active loading

Active loading is used at the source to move substances into the companion cells from surrounding tissues, and from the companion cells into the sieve tubes, against a concentration gradient. The concentration of sucrose is usually higher in the companion cells than the surrounding tissue cells, and higher in the sieve tube cells than the companion cells (see Figure 2).

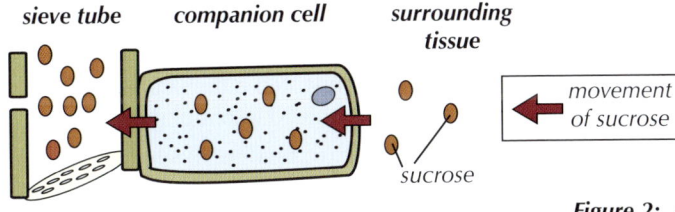

**Figure 2:** Active loading of sucrose against its concentration gradient.

**Tip:** Active transport uses energy to move substances against their concentration gradient — see page 140.

Sucrose is moved to where it needs to go using active transport and co-transport proteins. Co-transport proteins are a type of carrier protein that bind two molecules at a time. The concentration gradient of one of the molecules is used to move the other molecule against its own concentration gradient. In active loading, $H^+$ ions are used to move sucrose against its concentration gradient. The steps and Figure 3 on the next page tell you how it works.

**Tip:** Carrier proteins are found in cell membranes — they're used to transport substances across the membrane (see page 139 for more).

Module 3: Section 3 Transport in Plants

1. In the companion cell, ATP is used to actively transport hydrogen ions (H⁺) out of the cell and into surrounding tissue cells (see Figure 3). This sets up a concentration gradient — there are more H⁺ ions in the surrounding tissue than in the companion cell.
2. An H⁺ ion binds to a co-transport protein in the companion cell membrane and re-enters the cell (down the concentration gradient). A sucrose molecule binds to the co-transport protein at the same time. The movement of the H⁺ ion is used to move the sucrose molecule into the cell, against its concentration gradient.
3. Sucrose molecules are then transported out of the companion cells and into the sieve tubes by the same process.

**Tip:** This diagram looks complicated but the process is really quite simple. Just remember an H⁺ ion is actively transported against its concentration gradient so it can be co-transported back again, this time down its concentration gradient and taking sucrose with it.

**Tip:** Companion cells contain many mitochondria, which means they can make lots of ATP for active loading.

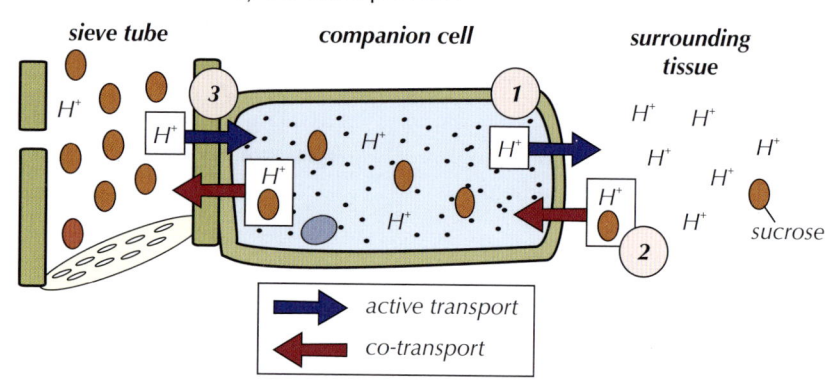

**Figure 3:** Active transport and co-transport in the active loading of sucrose.

ATP is one of the products of respiration. The breakdown of ATP supplies the initial energy needed for the active transport of the H⁺ ions.

### Practice Questions — Application

**Tip:** Aphids are small insects that feed on the sap carried in the phloem of a plant.

Q1 An investigation into pressure in the phloem was carried out using aphids. The aphids were allowed to pierce the phloem of a plant, then their bodies were removed leaving the mouthparts behind, allowing the sap to run out. A higher pressure means that the sap flows out more quickly.

Would you expect sap to flow out more quickly when aphids were placed near the leaves or at the bottom of the stem? Explain your answer.

Q2 A scientist conducts an experiment in which a metabolic inhibitor (which stops ATP production) is introduced into a plant.

Explain how this would affect the active loading of sucrose into the phloem at the source and the process of translocation.

### Practice Questions — Fact Recall

Q1 Define translocation.
Q2 What is the difference between a source and a sink in a plant?
Q3 Using the mass flow hypothesis:
   a) explain why water enters the sieve tubes in the roots,
   b) explain why water leaves the sieve tubes at the sink.
Q4 What is active loading?

# Section Summary

Make sure you know...

- That plants are multicellular, have a small surface area to volume ratio and have a relatively high metabolic rate, so they need a transport system to move substances to and from individual cells — direct diffusion would be too slow to support their metabolic rate.
- That plants have two transport systems — the xylem (which transports water and mineral ions) and the phloem (which mainly transports sugars) and how they are distributed in the roots, stems and leaves of a plant.
- How xylem vessels are adapted for transporting water and mineral ions — they're made up of cells with no end walls (so water can easily pass up through the middle), the cells are dead (so they contain no cytoplasm), their walls are lignified (which helps to support the xylem walls and give flexibility) and they contain pits (which is how other types of cell are supplied with water).
- How sieve tube elements in phloem tissue are adapted for transporting solutes — they're joined end to end (to form sieve tubes), they have no nucleus, a thin layer of cytoplasm and few organelles, and they contain sieve plates with holes (which allow solutes to pass through from one cell to another).
- That companion cells in the phloem carry out the living functions for themselves and the sieve cells.
- How to examine and draw stained sections of plant tissue, showing the distribution of xylem and phloem.
- How to dissect stems, both longitudinally and transversely, and examine them to locate the position and structure of xylem vessels.
- That water is transported into, around and out of a plant by moving down a water potential gradient — from an area of high water potential in the soil surrounding the roots to an area of lower water potential in air surrounding the leaves.
- How water moves through a plant following the symplast pathway (via the cytoplasm of cells) and the apoplast pathway (via the cell walls).
- How water passes out of the leaves to the surrounding air — down a water potential gradient through the stomata.
- That the transpiration stream is the movement of water from roots to leaves and how cohesion and tension, and adhesion move water up the xylem.
- That transpiration is the evaporation of water from a plant's surface and occurs as a result of gas exchange — as stomata open to let carbon dioxide in, water is let out.
- How transpiration rate is affected by light, temperature, humidity and wind.
- How to use a potometer to estimate transpiration rates.
- How xerophytic plants (e.g. cacti and marram grass) are adapted to living in dry climates — cacti have a thick, waxy layer on the epidermis, spines instead of leaves and close their stomata at the hottest times of the day. Marram grass has stomata that are sunk in pits, a layer of hairs on the epidermis, can roll its leaves in hot or windy conditions and has a thick, waxy layer on the epidermis.
- How hydrophytes (e.g. water lilies) are adapted to live in aquatic habitats and cope with low oxygen levels — they have air spaces in their tissues, stomata on the upper surface of their leaves and flexible leaves and stems.
- That translocation is the movement of assimilates (e.g. sucrose) in a plant, from their source (where they're produced) to their sink (where they're used up).
- The mechanism of translocation — solutes are actively loaded into the sieve tubes at the source and diffuse out of the sieve tubes at the sink. This addition and removal of solutes affects the water potential inside the sieve tubes, which results in a pressure gradient from source to sink — this gradient pushes assimilates along the sieve tubes to where they're needed.
- How solutes are actively loaded from surrounding tissue cells into the phloem at the source — the process involves the active transport of $H^+$ ions and then the co-transport of $H^+$ ions and solutes.

# Exam-style Questions

**1**    **Fig 1.1** shows the passage of water through part of a plant's root. Which of the following statements about **Fig. 1.1** is correct?

     **A**    ATP is required for the transport of water through the cells shown.

     **B**    The water travels via the symplast pathway until it is stopped by the Casparian strip.

     **C**    The rate of the water movement will decrease as it gets darker.

     **D**    The cells shown have a lower water potential than cells in the leaves.

*(1 mark)*

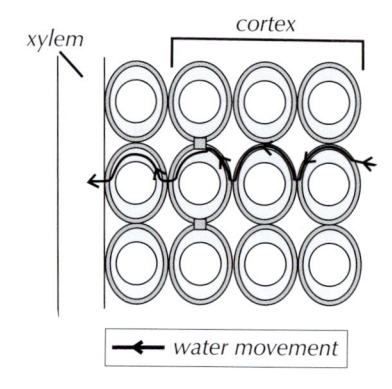

**Fig. 1.1**

**2**    **Fig. 2.1** and **Fig 2.2** show transverse cross-sections through two different plants. One is from *Potamogeton*, a plant found in ponds, and the other is from *Clematis*, a common garden plant.

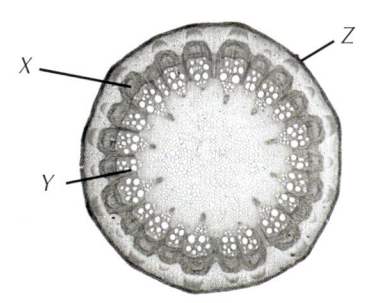

**Fig. 2.1** 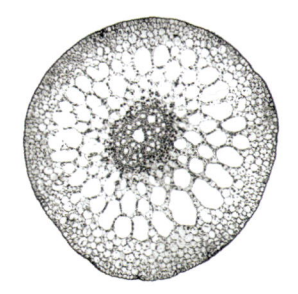      **Fig. 2.2**

**(a)**    Which letter (X, Y or Z) on **Fig. 2.1** shows xylem tissue?

*(1 mark)*

**(b)**    From which region of the plant has the section shown in **Fig 2.1** been taken from? Give a reason for your answer.

*(1 mark)*

**(c)**    A longitudinal cross-section of the stem of a *Clematis* plant would reveal the presence of lignin. Explain the function of this substance in a plant stem.

*(2 marks)*

**(d)**    Which cross-section (**Fig 2.1** or **Fig 2.2**) shows the *Potamogeton*? Give a reason for your answer.

*(1 mark)*

**(e)**    Other than features that can be identified on the cross-section, suggest **one** way in which *Potamogeton* may be adapted to its environment.

*(1 mark)*

Module 3: Section 3   Transport in Plants

**3** A student used a potometer to investigate the effect of light intensity on transpiration rate. Her results are shown in **Fig. 3.1**.

(a) (i) Using **Fig 3.1**, work out the rate of bubble movement for a light intensity of **1.5 arbitrary units**. Give your answer in mm min$^{-1}$.

*(2 marks)*

(ii) Using your knowledge of cohesion and tension, explain the results shown by the graph.

*(4 marks)*

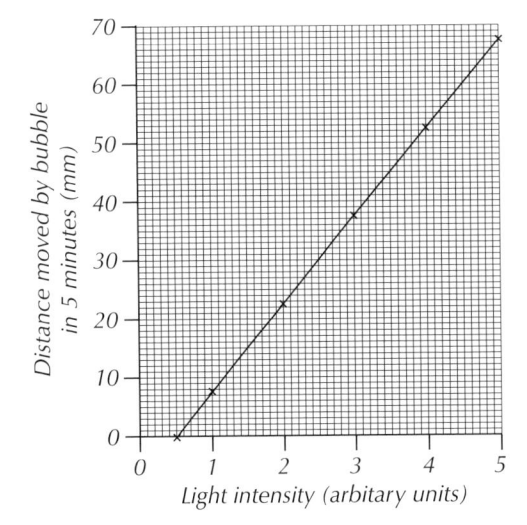

Fig. 3.1

(b) Suggest what negative control should be used for this investigation.

*(1 mark)*

(c) Explain how and why transpiration occurs.

*(2 marks)*

(d) The experiment was repeated in a more humid environment. Suggest how this would affect the results. Explain your answer.

*(2 marks)*

**4** Fig 4.1 shows a section of the phloem in a plant.

(a) (i) Name structure **A** and describe its function.

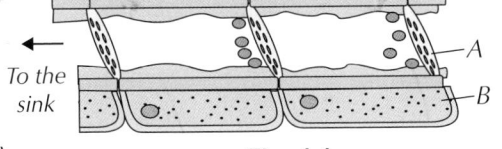

*(2 marks)*

Fig. 4.1

(ii) Describe and explain the function of cell **B**.

*(2 marks)*

(b) Explain why lots of ATP is needed at the source end of the phloem.

*(1 mark)*

(c) Give **two** parts of plants that are common sinks.

*(2 marks)*

(d)* The mass flow hypothesis is the best supported theory to describe the mechanism of translocation.

Based on this mechanism, determine whether the pressure inside the phloem's sieve tubes would be greatest at the sink end or at the source end and explain the reason for the difference in pressure.

*(6 marks)*

*The quality of your response will be assessed in this question.

# Module 4 — Section 1: Disease and the Immune System

### Learning Objectives:
- Know the different types of pathogen that can cause communicable diseases in plants and animals including:
  - bacteria: tuberculosis (TB), bacterial meningitis, ring rot,
  - viruses: HIV/AIDS, influenza, tobacco mosaic virus,
  - fungi: black sigatoka, ring worm, athlete's foot,
  - Protoctista: malaria, potato/tomato late blight.
- Understand the means of transmission of animal and plant communicable pathogens, including direct and indirect transmission, with reference to vectors, spores and living conditions (e.g. climate, social factors).

**Specification Reference 4.1.1**

**Tip:** You might have heard communicable diseases referred to as infectious diseases.

**Exam Tip**
Make sure you learn all the diseases on this page, what organisms they affect and the type of pathogen that causes each of them. You could get tested on them directly in the exam.

## 1. Pathogens and Communicable Diseases

*There are many different types of pathogens that can cause diseases in plants or animals. Here are a few that you need to know about for your exams...*

## What is disease?

Disease is a condition that impairs the normal functioning of an organism. Both plants and animals can get diseases. A **pathogen** is an organism that causes disease. Types of pathogen include bacteria, viruses, fungi and protoctists (a type of single-celled eukaryotic organism).

### Communicable diseases

A **communicable disease** is a disease that can spread between organisms. You need to learn all the communicable diseases in the table below, as well as the pathogens that cause them:

| Disease: | Affects: | Bacterium | Virus | Fungus | Protoctist |
|---|---|---|---|---|---|
| Tuberculosis (TB) | Animals, typically humans and cattle | ✔ | | | |
| Bacterial meningitis | Humans | ✔ | | | |
| Ring rot | Potatoes, tomatoes | ✔ | | | |
| HIV/AIDS | Humans | | ✔ | | |
| Influenza | Animals, including humans | | ✔ | | |
| Tobacco mosaic virus (TMV) | Plants | | ✔ | | |
| Black sigatoka | Banana plants | | | ✔ | |
| Ringworm | Cattle | | | ✔ | |
| Athlete's foot | Humans | | | ✔ | |
| Potato/tomato late blight | Potatoes/tomatoes | | | | ✔ |
| Malaria | Animals, including humans | | | | ✔ |

(Pathogen Responsible)

# Transmission of disease

Communicable diseases can be spread from one organism to another by direct or indirect transmission.

## Direct transmission

Direct transmission is when a disease is transmitted directly from one organism to another. Direct transmission can happen in several ways, including: droplet infection (coughing or sneezing tiny droplets of mucus or saliva directly onto someone), sexual intercourse, or touching an infected organism.

**Examples**
- HIV can be transmitted directly between humans via sexual intercourse. The virus can also be transmitted directly from a mother to her unborn child through the placenta.
- Athlete's foot can be spread via touch.

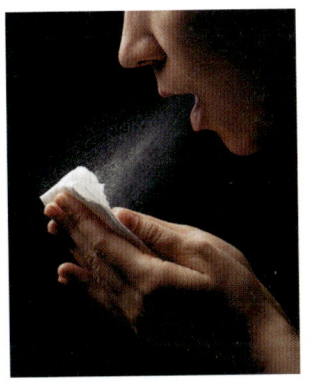

*Figure 1: Influenza can be directly transmitted by sneezing.*

## Indirect transmission

Indirect transmission is when a disease is transmitted from one organism to another via an intermediate. Intermediates include air, water, food or another organism (known as a **vector**).

**Examples**
- Potato/tomato late blight is spread when spores are carried between plants — first in the air, then in water.
- Malaria is spread between humans (and other animals) via mosquitoes — insects that feed on blood. The mosquitoes act as vectors — they don't cause malaria themselves, they just spread the protoctists that cause it.

**Tip:** Spores are the cells that some organisms use to reproduce asexually, including some protoctists and all fungi.

**Tip:** A vector is an organism that spreads disease by carrying pathogens from one host to another.

# Factors affecting transmission

Living conditions, social factors and climate affect the transmission of disease.

## Living conditions

Overcrowded living conditions increase the transmission of many communicable diseases.

**Example**
Tuberculosis (TB) is spread directly via droplet infection (see above). It's also spread indirectly because the bacteria can remain in the air for long periods of time and infect new people. The risk of TB infection is increased when lots of people live crowded together in a small space.

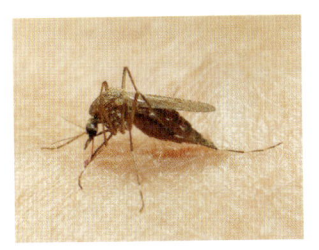

*Figure 2: A mosquito feeding on human blood.*

## Social factors

In humans, social factors (such as income, occupation and the area where a person lives) can also increase the transmission of communicable diseases.

**Examples**
The risk of HIV infection is high in places where there's limited access to:
- good healthcare — people are less likely to be diagnosed and treated for HIV, and the most effective anti-HIV drugs are less likely to be available, so the virus is more likely to be passed on to others.
- good health education — to inform people about how HIV is transmitted and how it can be avoided, e.g. through safe-sex practices like using condoms.

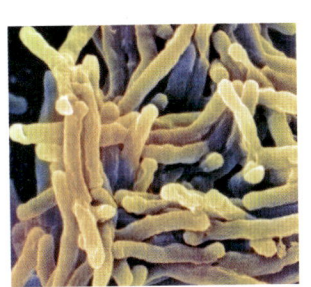

*Figure 3: An SEM of Mycobacterium tuberculosis.*

Module 4: Section 1 Disease and the Immune System

**Figure 4:** *Tomatoes infected with late blight.*

**Figure 5:** *Leaf of a tobacco plant showing damage caused by the tobacco mosaic virus.*

### Climate

Climate can also affect the spread of communicable diseases.

--- Examples ---
- Potato/tomato late blight is especially common during wet summers because the spores need water to spread (see previous page).
- Malaria is most common in tropical countries, which are humid and hot. This is because these are the ideal conditions for mosquitoes (the malaria vectors) to breed.

## Practice Questions — Application

**Q1** Tobacco mosaic virus (TMV) is a virus that infects a wide range of plants, causing a characteristic mottled or mosaic effect on the leaves (see Figure 5). The virus enters plant cells through small wounds. It is present in the sap of infected plants, but can also contaminate seed coats (the protective coating on the seed).
  a) Suggest one way that TMV could be transmitted directly between plants.
  b) Suggest one way that TMV could be transmitted indirectly between plants.

**Q2** Ringworm produces spores that can spread between cattle either directly or indirectly.
  a) Why might ringworm spread faster between cattle housed indoors rather than in a field?
  b) A farmer uses the same brush to groom all of his prize-winning cattle, which could transfer spores between cows. Is this an example of direct or indirect transmission?
  c) Ringworm can be transmitted to humans via direct contact. Suggest one way of minimising the risk of transmission from an infected cow to the farmer.

**Q3** Tuberculosis (TB) usually affects the lungs. It's spread via droplet infection and through the air in poorly ventilated spaces. The disease can be treated with antibiotics but treatment takes several months and patients do not always finish the course.

Suggest two ways to prevent the spread of TB from a person with symptoms of TB infection to uninfected members of the public.

## Practice Questions — Fact Recall

**Q1** What is a pathogen?
**Q2** What is a communicable disease?
**Q3** What type of plant can be affected by black sigatoka?
**Q4** What type of pathogen causes athlete's foot?
**Q5** Give an example of a disease caused by a protoctist.
**Q6** Give one way a disease can be transmitted directly.
**Q7** What is a vector?
**Q8** Why is transmission of HIV more likely in countries where there is limited access to good health care?
**Q9** Why is malaria more common in countries with a hot, humid climate?

Module 4: Section 1 Disease and the Immune System

# 2. Defence Against Pathogens

*Both animals and plants have several methods of protecting themselves against infection.*

## Barriers to infection

Pathogens need to enter an organism in order to cause disease. Animals and plants have evolved defences to protect themselves from pathogens gaining entry.

## Animal defences

Most animals, including humans, have a range of primary, non-specific defences against pathogens. These include:

### The skin

This acts as a physical barrier, blocking pathogens from entering the body. It also acts as a chemical barrier by producing chemicals that are antimicrobial (which destroy or slow the growth of microorganisms) and can lower pH, inhibiting the growth of pathogens.

**Examples**
- Skin cells secrete fatty acids, such as oleic acid, that can kill some bacteria. Fatty acids also lower the pH of the skin, creating an acidic environment that is difficult for pathogens to colonise.
- Skin cells also secrete lysozyme, an enzyme which catalyses the breakdown of carbohydrates in the cell walls of some bacteria.

### Mucous membranes

These protect body openings that are exposed to the environment (such as the mouth, nostrils, ears, genitals and anus). Some membranes secrete mucus — a sticky substance that traps pathogens and contains antimicrobial enzymes.

**Example — The gas-exchange system**
If you breathe in air that contains pathogens, most of them will be trapped in mucus lining the lung epithelium (the outer layer of cells in the passages to the lungs). These cells also have cilia (hair-like structures) that beat and move the mucus up the trachea to the throat and mouth, where it's removed — see Figure 2. There's loads more about this on page 171.

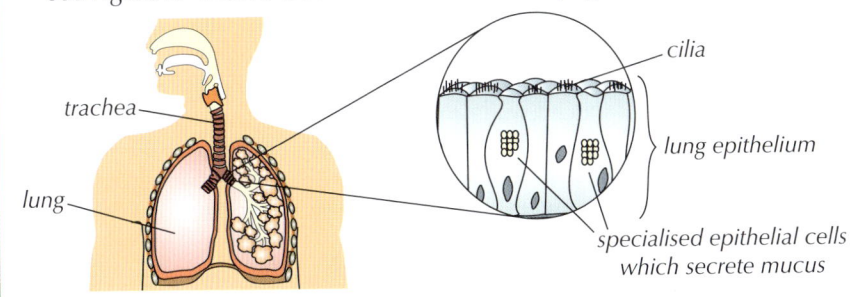

**Figure 2:** A diagram of the gas-exchange system.

### Blood clotting

A blood clot is a mesh of protein (fibrin) fibres. Blood clots plug wounds to prevent pathogen entry and blood loss. They're formed by a series of chemical reactions that take place when platelets (fragments of cells in the blood) are exposed to damaged blood vessels.

---

**Learning Objectives:**
- Recall the primary non-specific defences against pathogens in animals, including the skin, mucous membranes, blood clotting, inflammation, wound repair and expulsive reflexes.
- Recall plant defences against pathogens, including production of chemicals and plant responses that limit the spread of the pathogen (e.g. callose deposition).

**Specification Reference 4.1.1**

**Tip:** Non-specific means they work in the same way for all pathogens. There's more on non-specific and specific responses on page 230.

**Figure 1:** An electron micrograph of lung epithelium cells. The cilia are shown in blue.

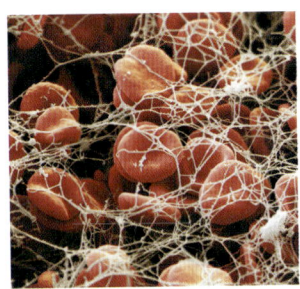

**Figure 3:** An electron micrograph of a blood clot.

Module 4: Section 1 Disease and the Immune System

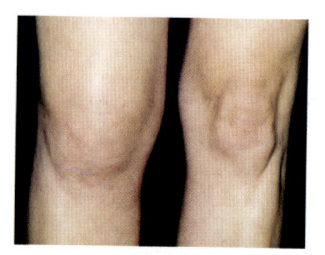

*Figure 4: Swelling of the knee (on the left) due to a sports injury.*

### Inflammation
The signs of inflammation include swelling, pain, heat and redness. It can be triggered by tissue damage — the damaged tissue releases molecules which increase the permeability of the blood vessels, so they start to leak fluid into the surrounding area. This causes swelling and helps to isolate any pathogens that may have entered the damaged tissue. The molecules also cause vasodilation (widening of the blood vessels), which increases blood flow to the affected area. This makes the area hot and brings white blood cells to the area to fight off any pathogens that may be present.

### Wound repair
The skin is able to repair itself in the event of injury and re-form a barrier against pathogen entry. The surface is repaired by the outer layer of skin cells dividing and migrating to the edges of the wound. The tissue below the wound then contracts to bring the edges of the wound closer together. It is repaired using collagen fibres — too many collagen fibres and you'll end up with a scar.

### Expulsive reflexes
Expulsive reflexes include coughing and sneezing. A sneeze happens when the mucous membranes in the nostrils are irritated by things such as dust or dirt. A cough stems from irritation in the respiratory tract. Both coughing and sneezing are an attempt to expel foreign objects, including pathogens, from the body. They happen automatically.

If pathogens make it past these defences, they'll have the animal's immune system to deal with — see pages 230-232.

*Figure 5: Woman coughing.*

## Plant defences
Like animals, plants have defences against infection by pathogens. These include:

### Physical plant defences
Most plant leaves and stems have a waxy cuticle, which provides a physical barrier against pathogen entry. It may also stop water collecting on the leaf, which could reduce the risk of infection by pathogens that are transferred between plants in water.

Plant cells themselves are surrounded by cell walls. These form a physical barrier against pathogens that make it past the waxy cuticle.

Plants also produce a polysaccharide called callose. Callose gets deposited between plant cell walls and plasma membranes during times of stress, e.g. pathogen invasion. Callose deposition may make it harder for pathogens to enter cells. Callose deposition at the plasmodesmata (small channels in the cell walls) may limit the spread of viruses between cells — see Figure 7.

*Figure 6: Waxy surface of a cabbage leaf.*

**Tip:** Plasmodesmata connect the cytoplasm of neighbouring cells, so they can easily transfer substances between them (see page 211).

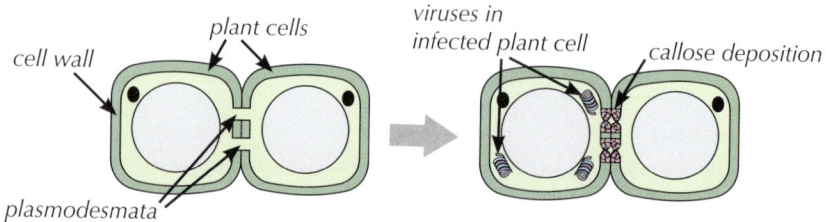

*Figure 7: Callose deposition between two plant cells.*

Module 4: Section 1 Disease and the Immune System

## Chemical plant defences

Plants don't just rely on physical defences. They also produce antimicrobial chemicals (including antibiotics, see page 242) which kill pathogens or inhibit their growth.

### Examples

- Some plants produce chemicals called saponins. These are thought to destroy the cell membranes of fungi and other pathogens.
- Plants also produce chemicals called phytoalexins, which inhibit the growth of fungi and other pathogens.

Other chemicals secreted by plants are toxic to insects — this reduces the amount of insect-feeding on plants and therefore reduces the risk of infection by plant viruses carried by insect vectors.

*Figure 8:* Quinoa seeds coated in saponins (white).

### Practice Questions — Application

Q1 Tuberculosis is caused by the bacterium *Mycobacterium tuberculosis*, which can be spread through the air. Describe the non-specific defence that would be encountered by *M. tuberculosis* if it entered the lungs of a healthy person.

Q2 Patients with severe burns are susceptible to infection from usually harmless bacteria. Explain why this is the case.

Q3 Aphids are small insects that feed by sucking sap from a plant. Suggest why a plant that has an aphid infestation may be more susceptible to infection.

### Practice Questions — Fact Recall

Q1 Describe how the skin acts as a chemical barrier against pathogens.
Q2 What is a blood clot?
Q3 What is the purpose of inflammation in the area surrounding damaged tissue?
Q4 Give an example of an expulsive reflex.
Q5 Name two physical defences that a plant cell has against pathogens.
Q6 a) Why might callose deposition occur in a plant cell?
    b) State two places where callose deposition can occur.
Q7 What is the purpose of phytoalexins produced by plants?

**Learning Objectives:**

- Recall the structure and mode of action of phagocytes, including neutrophils and antigen-presenting cells and the roles of cytokines, opsonins, phagosomes and lysosomes.

- Be able to give an outline of the action of opsonins.

- Recall the structure, different roles and modes of action of T lymphocytes in the specific immune response, including clonal selection and clonal expansion, T helper cells, T killer cells and T regulatory cells.

- Recall the structure, different roles and modes of action of B lymphocytes in the specific immune response, including plasma cells.

- Understand the significance of cell signalling (reference to interleukins).

- Be able to examine and draw cells observed in blood smears.

**Specification Reference 4.1.1**

**Tip:** Opsonins work in different ways. Some hide the negative charges on the membrane of the pathogen, making it easier for the negatively-charged phagocyte to get closer to the pathogen.

# 3. The Immune System

*The body's primary defences keep most pathogens away... but if any sneak through, the immune system is there to keep us safe.*

## The immune response

If a pathogen gets past the primary defences and enters the body, the immune system will respond. An immune response is the body's reaction to a foreign **antigen**. Antigens are molecules (usually proteins or polysaccharides) found on the surface of cells. When a pathogen (like a bacterium) invades the body, the antigens on its cell surface are identified as foreign, which activates cells in the immune system.

The immune response involves specific and non-specific stages. The **non-specific response** happens in the same way for all microorganisms — whatever foreign antigens they have. The **specific response** is antigen-specific — it is aimed at specific pathogens. It involves white blood cells called T and B lymphocytes.

## The main stages of the immune response

### 1. Phagocytosis

A **phagocyte** is a type of white blood cell that carries out phagocytosis (engulfment of pathogens). They're found in the blood and in tissues and carry out a non-specific immune response. Here's how they work:

- A phagocyte recognises the antigens on a pathogen.
- The cytoplasm of the phagocyte moves round the pathogen, engulfing it. This may be made easier by the presence of **opsonins** — molecules in the blood that attach to foreign antigens to aid phagocytosis.
- The pathogen is now contained in a **phagosome** (a type of vesicle, see page 41) in the cytoplasm of the phagocyte.
- A **lysosome** (an organelle that contains digestive enzymes) fuses with the phagosome. The enzymes break down the pathogen.
- The phagocyte then presents the pathogen's antigens. It sticks the antigens on its surface to activate other immune system cells. When a phagocyte does this it is acting as an **antigen-presenting cell** (APC).

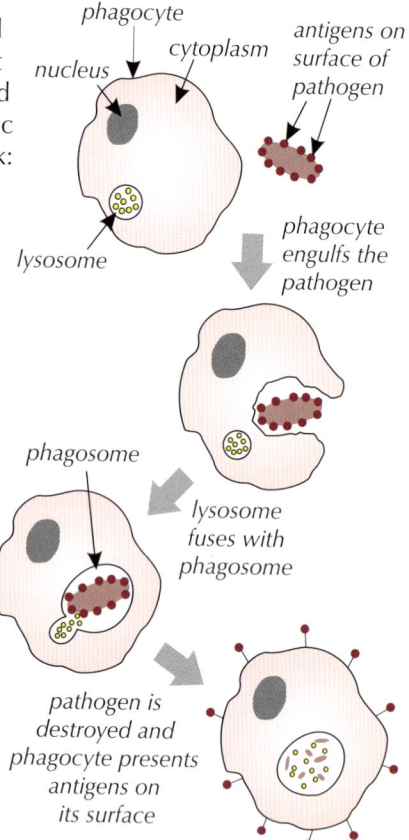

*Figure 1: The process of phagocytosis and antigen presentation.*

**Neutrophils** are a type of phagocyte. They're the first white blood cells to respond to a pathogen inside the body. Neutrophils move towards a wound in response to signals from **cytokines** (proteins that act as messenger molecules — see page 130). The cytokines are released by cells at the site of the wound.

230 | Module 4: Section 1 Disease and the Immune System

## 2. T lymphocyte activation

A T lymphocyte is another type of white blood cell. Its surface is covered with receptors. The receptors bind to antigens presented by APCs (see Figure 3).

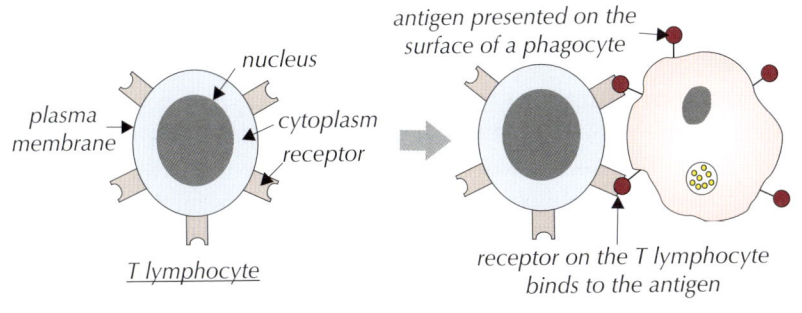

*Figure 3: Activation of a T lymphocyte.*

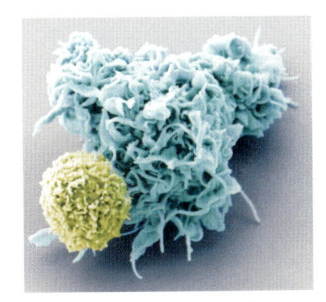

*Figure 2: A SEM of a T lymphocyte (yellow) binding to a phagocytic cell (blue).*

Each T lymphocyte has a different receptor on its surface. When the receptor on the surface of a T lymphocyte meets a complementary antigen, it binds to it — so each T lymphocyte will bind to a different antigen. This process activates the T lymphocyte and is known as **clonal selection**. The activated T lymphocyte then undergoes **clonal expansion** — it divides to produce clones of itself.

**Tip:** A complementary antigen means its shape fits into the shape of the receptor.

Different types of activated T lymphocytes carry out different functions:

- **T helper cells** release substances to activate B lymphocytes (see below) and T killer cells.
- **T killer cells** attach to and kill cells that are infected with a virus.
- **T regulatory cells** suppress the immune response from other white blood cells. This helps to stop immune system cells from mistakenly attacking the host's body cells.

Some activated T lymphocytes become **memory cells** (see page 236).

## 3. B lymphocyte activation and plasma cell production

B lymphocytes are also a type of white blood cell (see Figure 4). They're covered with **antibodies** — proteins that bind antigens to form an **antigen-antibody complex**.

Each B lymphocyte has a different shaped antibody on its membrane, so different ones bind to different shaped antigens (see Figure 5).

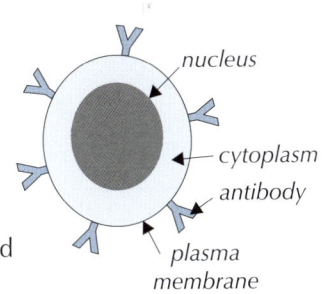

*Figure 4: A B lymphocyte.*

**Tip:** T lymphocytes and B lymphocytes are sometimes just called T cells and B cells.

Antibody A will bind to antigen A, as they have complementary shapes.

Antibody A will not bind to antigen B, as they don't have complementary shapes.

*Figure 5: Complementary binding between antibodies and antigens.*

**Exam Tip**
Never say that antigens and antibodies have the 'same shape' or a 'matching shape' — you need to use the phrase 'complementary shape'.

Module 4: Section 1 Disease and the Immune System

When the antibody on the surface of a B lymphocyte meets a complementary antigen, it binds to it — so each B lymphocyte will bind to a different antigen. This, together with substances released from helper T cells, activates the B lymphocyte. This process is another example of clonal selection. The activated B lymphocyte then divides, by mitosis, into plasma cells (see below) and memory cells (see p. 236). This is another example of clonal expansion.

**Tip:** The B lymphocyte divides by mitosis, so that all the cells produced are genetically identical. This means that they all produce identical antibodies specific to the pathogen.

### 4. Antibody production
Plasma cells are clones of the B lymphocyte (they're identical to the B lymphocyte). They secrete loads of the antibody, specific to the antigen, into the blood. These antibodies will bind to the antigens on the surface of the pathogen to form lots of antigen-antibody complexes. This is the signal for the immune system to attack and destroy the pathogen. There's lots more on the structure of antibodies and how they help to clear an infection in the next topic (pages 234-235).

## Cell signalling and the immune response
Cell signalling is basically how cells communicate. A cell may release (or present) a substance that binds to the receptors on another cell — this causes a response of some kind in the other cell.

**Tip:** See page 130 for more on cell signalling.

Cell signalling is really important in the immune response because it helps to activate all the different types of white blood cells that are needed.

— **Example** —
T helper cells release interleukins (a type of cytokine) that bind to receptors on B lymphocytes. This activates the B lymphocytes — the T helper cells are signalling to the B lymphocytes that there's a pathogen in the body.

## Blood smears
As the name suggests, a blood smear is a sample of blood smeared over a microscope slide. Stains are added to the sample to make the different cells easy to see. You need to be able to examine and draw cells observed in a blood smear — see Figure 6. When looking at a blood smear you're likely to see red blood cells, white blood cells and platelets (tiny fragments of cells involved in blood clotting). Some types of white blood cell have granules in their cytoplasm (so they look grainy) and other types don't.

**Tip:** See page 52 for more on staining microscope images.

— **Example** —

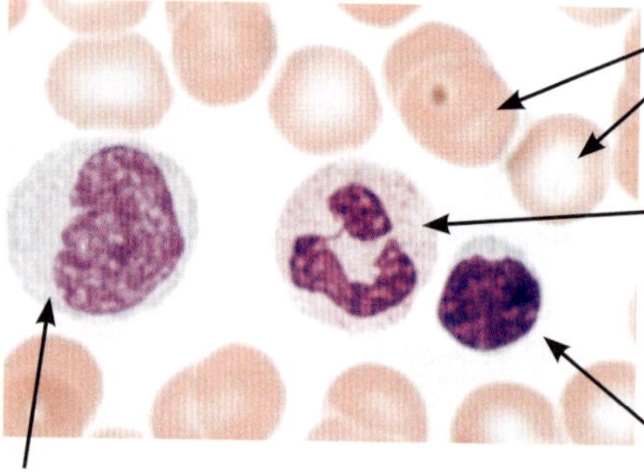

Most of the cells are red blood cells (see page 157). They're easy to spot because they don't have a nucleus.

This is a neutrophil. Its nucleus looks like three interconnected blobs — the posh way of saying this is that the nucleus is 'multi-lobed'. The cytoplasm of a neutrophil is grainy.

This is a monocyte. It's the biggest white blood cell and a type of phagocyte. It has a kidney-bean shaped nucleus and a non-grainy cytoplasm.

This is a lymphocyte. It's much smaller than the neutrophil. The nucleus takes up most of the cell and there's very little cytoplasm to be seen (it's not grainy either). You can't tell whether this is a T lymphocyte or a B lymphocyte under a light microscope.

**Figure 6:** Light micrograph of a blood smear and how to interpret it.

## Practice Questions — Application

Q1 Look at the blood smear below.

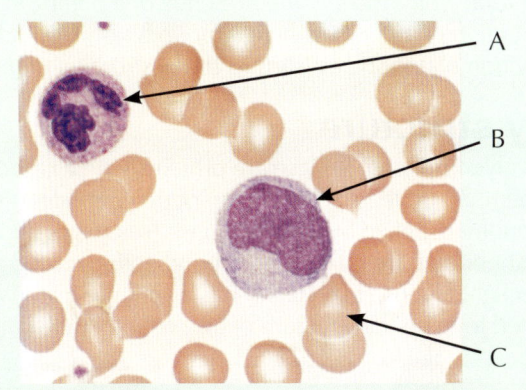

a) Name the cells A, B and C.
b) What is the role of cell A in a non-specific immune response?

Q2 AIDS is an immune system disorder caused by the human immunodeficiency virus. The virus infects and destroys T lymphocytes, so the number that work properly gradually falls. AIDS patients often suffer from opportunistic infections — infections that wouldn't normally cause too much of a problem in a healthy person. Common ones are tuberculosis, pneumonia and an infection of the brain called toxoplasmosis. Explain why AIDS patients suffer from opportunistic infections.

Q3 Rheumatic fever is a disease where the immune system attacks cells in the heart. It's often triggered by an infection with the bacterium *Streptococcus pyogenes*. Antigens on the surface of *S. pyogenes* have a very similar shape to antigens on the surface of heart cells. Suggest why *S. pyogenes* infection can lead to rheumatic fever.

**Tip:** Antigens aren't just found on pathogens — your body cells have antigens on them too.

## Practice Questions — Fact Recall

Q1 What is an immune response?
Q2 What are antigens?
Q3 Define phagocytosis.
Q4 What is a phagosome?
Q5 What is the role of a lysosome during phagocytosis?
Q6 What proteins signal for neutrophils to move towards a wound?
Q7 Describe how a phagocyte that has captured a pathogen activates T lymphocytes.
Q8 What are the functions of T lymphocytes and plasma cells?
Q9 Draw a flow diagram showing the four main stages of the immune response.
Q10 Give an example of cell signalling being used during an immune response.

**Learning Objectives:**

- Recall the structure and general functions of antibodies.
- Be able to give an outline of the actions of agglutinins and anti-toxins.

**Specification Reference 4.1.1**

# 4. Antibodies

*In the previous topic you saw how the presence of a pathogen in the body led to the production of antibodies by B lymphocytes. Now it's time to see how the production of antibodies leads to the destruction of the pathogen.*

## Antibody structure

Antibodies are glycoproteins — these are proteins with a carbohydrate group attached. Remember, proteins are made up of polypeptides — chains of amino acid monomers linked by peptide bonds (see pages 69-73 for more on proteins). Antibodies are made of four polypeptide chains — two heavy chains and two light chains. Each chain has a variable region and a constant region. You need to learn the structure of an antibody molecule (see Figure 1).

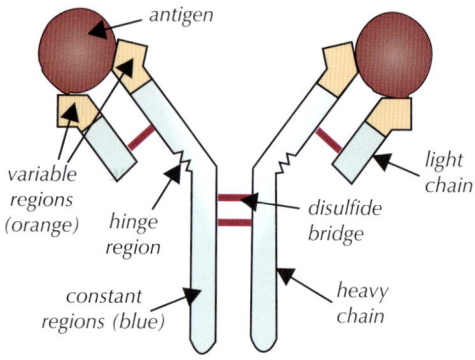

**Figure 1:** Antibody structure.

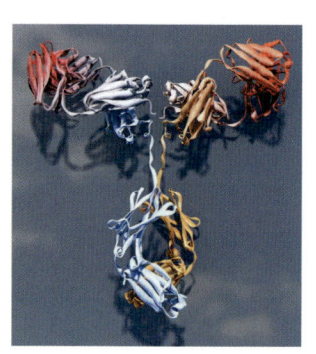

**Figure 2:** A molecular model of an antibody.

The **variable regions** of the antibody form the antigen-binding sites. The shape of the variable region is complementary to a particular antigen. The variable regions differ between antibodies. The **hinge region** allows flexibility when the antibody binds to the antigen. The **constant regions** allow binding to receptors on immune system cells, e.g. phagocytes. The constant region is the same (i.e. it has the same sequence of amino acids) in all antibodies. Disulfide bridges (a type of bond) hold the polypeptide chains of the protein together.

**Tip:** Antibodies need variable regions so that they can recognise and bind to different antigens. If all antibodies recognised the same pathogen they wouldn't be very useful.

## The role of antibodies in clearing infections

Antibodies help to clear an infection in three main ways:

### 1. Agglutinating pathogens

Each antibody has two binding sites, so an antibody can bind to two pathogens at the same time — the pathogens become clumped together. Phagocytes then bind to the antibodies and phagocytose a lot of pathogens all at once (see Figure 4). Antibodies that behave in this way are known as **agglutinins**.

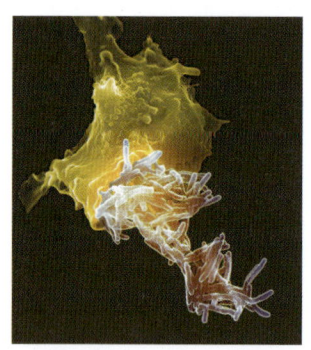

**Figure 3:** A phagocyte (yellow) engulfing a clump of bacteria that has been agglutinated by antibodies.

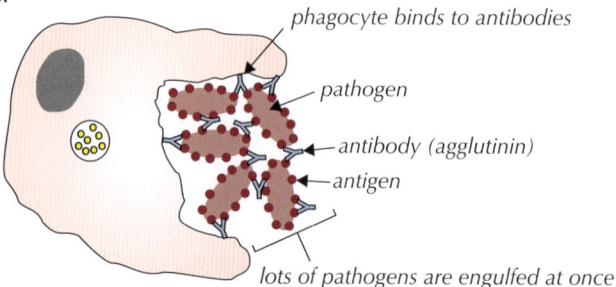

**Figure 4:** Agglutination of pathogens by antibodies.

Module 4: Section 1 Disease and the Immune System

## 2. Neutralising toxins

Like antigens, toxins have different shapes. Antibodies called **anti-toxins** can bind to the **toxins** produced by pathogens. This prevents the toxins from affecting human cells, so the toxins are neutralised (inactivated). The toxin-antibody complexes are also phagocytosed (see Figure 5).

**Tip:** Different pathogens cause damage in different ways. Not all pathogens produce toxins, so this mode of action will only be useful against some pathogens.

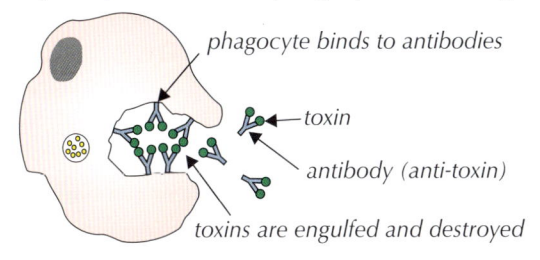

*Figure 5: Neutralisation of toxins by antibodies.*

## 3. Preventing the pathogen binding to human cells

When antibodies bind to the antigens on pathogens, they may block the cell-surface receptors that the pathogens need to bind to the host cells. This means the pathogen can't attach to or infect the host cells (see Figure 6).

**Exam Tip**
You need to be able to describe all three ways in which antibodies can work, so make sure you read these two pages carefully.

**Tip:** Host cells are cells in the organism that have been infected by the pathogen.

**No Antibodies**
The pathogens can bind to and infect host cells.

**Antibodies**
The pathogens are coated in antibodies and can't bind to host cells.

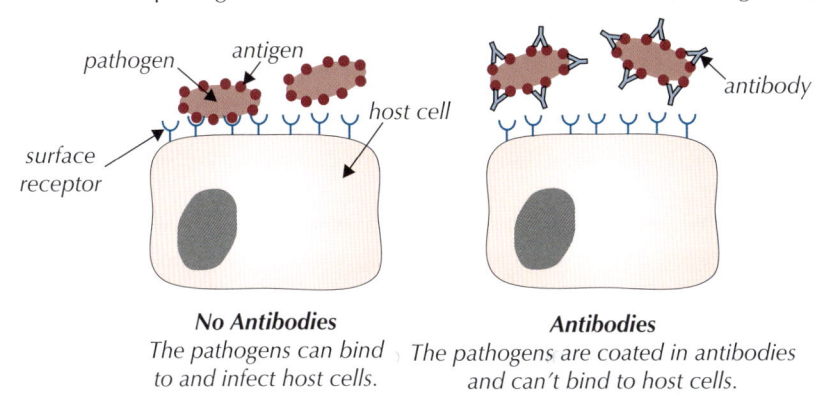

*Figure 6: Antibodies preventing pathogens from binding to human cells.*

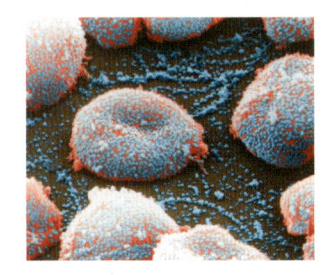

*Figure 7: Flu virus particles (blue) attached to red blood cells (red). If these flu virus particles were bound by antibodies they would not be able to bind to the surface of the red blood cells.*

### Practice Question — Application

Q1  If someone is bitten by a poisonous snake or spider, they will be given antivenom. Antivenom contains anti-toxins against the toxins in the poison. Using your knowledge of antibodies, explain how antivenom works.

### Practice Questions — Fact Recall

Q1  Give the functions of the following regions of an antibody:
   a) The variable region.
   b) The hinge region.
   c) The constant region.

Q2  How many binding sites do antibodies have, and why is it useful for them to have this number?

Q3  Give three ways in which antibodies can help defend the body against pathogens.

Module 4: Section 1  Disease and the Immune System

**Learning Objective:**
- Understand the primary and secondary immune responses, including the roles of T memory cells and B memory cells.

**Specification Reference 4.1.1**

# 5. Primary and Secondary Immune Responses

*There's more than one type of immune response...*

## The primary immune response

When a pathogen enters the body for the first time, the antigens on its surface activate the immune system. This is called the primary response. The primary response is slow because there aren't many B lymphocytes that can make the antibody needed to bind to the pathogen. Eventually the body will produce enough of the right antibody to overcome the infection. Meanwhile the infected person will show symptoms of the disease.

After being exposed to an antigen, both T and B lymphocytes produce **memory cells**. These memory cells remain in the body for a long time. Memory T lymphocytes remember the specific antigen and will recognise it a second time around. Memory B lymphocytes record the specific antibodies needed to bind to the antigen. The person is now **immune** — their immune system has the ability to respond quickly to a second infection.

**Tip:** Being immune doesn't mean you'll never be infected by that pathogen again — it just means that if it gets into your body a second time your immune system quickly kills it before you get ill.

## The secondary immune response

If the same pathogen enters the body again, the immune system will produce a quicker, stronger immune response — the secondary response (see Figure 1). Clonal selection happens faster. Memory B lymphocytes divide into plasma cells that produce the right antibody to the antigen. Memory T lymphocytes are activated and divide into the correct type of T lymphocytes to kill the cell carrying the antigen. The secondary response often gets rid of the pathogen before you begin to show any symptoms.

**Tip:** The secondary response only happens if it's the same pathogen. If it's a different pathogen you just get another primary response.

**Tip:** The secondary response is always faster than the primary response. This is shown by a steeper line in graphs of blood antibody concentration against time.

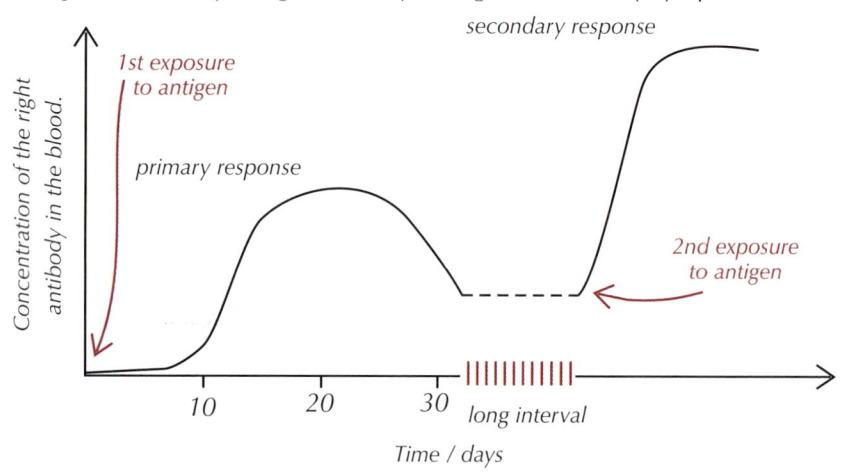

**Figure 1:** A graph of antibody concentration against time since antigen exposure.

## Maintaining immunity

Memory B and T lymphocytes only have a limited lifespan. This means that someone who is immune to a particular pathogen won't always stay immune forever — once all of the memory B and T lymphocytes have died, that person may be susceptible to attack by the pathogen again. Immunity can be maintained by being continually exposed to the pathogen, so you continue to make more and more memory B and T lymphocytes.

**Tip:** This is why some vaccines require booster shots later on (e.g. after several years) — to maintain the numbers of memory T and B cells. See pages 238-240 for more on vaccines.

236  Module 4: Section 1  Disease and the Immune System

### Example
People who live in malarial areas and who are constantly exposed to the malaria pathogen will build up a limited immunity to malaria. But if they move away from the malarial area, they'll have no further exposure to the pathogen and eventually they may lose the immunity they have. If they then returned to a malarial area, they would undergo a primary immune response when they encountered the malaria pathogen again.

## Comparing the two responses
In the exam you might be asked to compare and contrast the primary and secondary immune response — basically say how they're similar and say how they're different. This is summarised in the table below:

|  | Primary response | Secondary response |
|---|---|---|
| Pathogen | Enters for 1st time | Enters for 2nd time |
| Speed of response | Slow | Fast |
| Cells activated | B and T lymphocytes | Memory cells |
| Symptoms | Yes | No |

**Exam Tip:** If you're asked to compare and contrast the primary and secondary responses in the exam, make sure you talk about similarities as well as differences. The similarities are, e.g. both are triggered by invasion of the body by a pathogen, both ultimately get rid of the pathogen and both involve the production of antibodies.

### Practice Questions — Application
The graph below shows the immune responses of two mice exposed to a pathogen. Both mice were exposed on day 0 of the experiment.

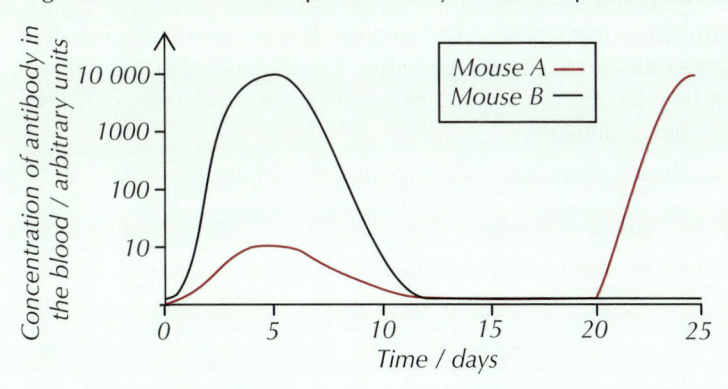

Q1 How much antibody did each mouse have in its blood on day 5?
Q2 Which mouse was already immune to the pathogen? Explain your answer.
Q3 a) On which day was Mouse A exposed to the pathogen again?
   b) Describe what happened to Mouse A's immune system after it was exposed again.

**Tip:** Don't get the primary response mixed up with primary defences (see pages 227-228).

### Practice Questions — Fact Recall
Q1 Why is the primary immune response slower than a secondary immune response?
Q2 Why does immunity not always last forever?
Q3 Give three differences (other than the speed) between a primary and a secondary immune response.

Module 4: Section 1 Disease and the Immune System

**Learning Objectives:**
- Understand the differences between active and passive immunity, and between natural and artificial immunity, and recall examples of each type of immunity.
- Understand autoimmune diseases, including an appreciation of the term 'autoimmune disease' and a named example, e.g. arthritis, lupus.
- Understand the principles of vaccination and the role of vaccination programmes in the prevention of epidemics, including routine vaccinations and reasons for changes to vaccines and vaccination programmes (including global issues).

**Specification Reference 4.1.1**

**Tip:** Don't get active and passive immunity mixed up. Just remember that in <u>active</u> immunity your body is <u>actively</u> doing something — it's producing antibodies.

**Tip:** T regulatory cells (p. 231) usually protect against autoimmune disease by suppressing any immune response to self-antigens.

# 6. Immunity and Vaccinations

*After you've been infected once by a pathogen you'll be immune to it, but being infected in the first place can be pretty unpleasant. Vaccination can make you immune without the being ill part.*

## Active and passive immunity

Immunity can be active or passive:

### Active immunity
This is the type of immunity you get when your immune system makes its own antibodies after being stimulated by an antigen. There are two different types of active immunity:

1. **Natural** — this is when you become immune after catching a disease. E.g. if you have measles as a child, you shouldn't be able to catch it again in later life.
2. **Artificial** — this is when you become immune after you've been given a vaccination containing a harmless dose of antigen (see next page).

### Passive immunity
This is the type of immunity you get from being given antibodies made by a different organism — your immune system doesn't produce any antibodies of its own. Again, there are two types:

1. **Natural** — this is when a baby becomes immune due to the antibodies it receives from its mother, through the placenta and in breast milk.
2. **Artificial** — this is when you become immune after being injected with antibodies from someone else. E.g. if you contract tetanus you can be injected with antibodies against the tetanus toxin, collected from blood donations.

In the exam you might have to compare and contrast these types of immunity:

| Active Immunity | Passive Immunity |
| --- | --- |
| Requires exposure to antigen | No exposure to antigen |
| It takes a while for protection to develop | Protection is immediate |
| Protection is long-term | Protection is short-term |
| Memory cells are produced | Memory cells aren't produced |

## Autoimmune diseases

Sometimes, an organism's immune system isn't able to recognise self-antigens — antigens present on the organism's own cells. When this happens, the immune system treats the self-antigens as foreign antigens and launches an immune response against the organism's own tissues. A disease resulting from this abnormal immune response is known as an **autoimmune disease**.

### Example — Lupus
Lupus is caused by the immune system attacking cells in the connective tissues. This damages the tissues and causes painful inflammation (see page 228). Lupus can affect the skin and joints, as well as organs such as the heart and lungs.

Module 4: Section 1 Disease and the Immune System

### Example — Rheumatoid arthritis
Rheumatoid arthritis is caused by the immune system attacking cells in the joints. Again, this causes pain and inflammation.

Autoimmune diseases are usually chronic (long-term). They can often be treated, but not cured.

## Vaccination
While your B lymphocytes are busy dividing to build up their numbers to deal with a pathogen (i.e. the primary response — see page 236), you suffer from the disease. Vaccination can help avoid this.

Vaccines contain substances that cause your body to produce memory cells against a particular pathogen, without the pathogen causing disease. This means you become immune without getting any symptoms. The substances in the vaccine may be antigens, which could be free or attached to a dead or attenuated (weakened) pathogen. The substances can also be other molecules, such as mRNA (see p.96) designed to code for antigens found on a pathogen. When the mRNA enters the body cells, it provides the instructions needed for cells to produce these antigens, which triggers memory cells to be made.

Vaccines may be injected or taken orally. The disadvantages of taking a vaccine orally are that it could be broken down by enzymes in the gut or the molecules of the vaccine may be too large to be absorbed into the blood. Sometimes booster vaccines are given later on (e.g. after several years) to make sure that more memory cells are produced.

Epidemics (mass outbreaks of disease) can be prevented if a large percentage of the population is vaccinated. That way, even people who haven't been vaccinated are unlikely to get the disease, because there's no one to catch it from. This is called **herd immunity** — see Figure 3.

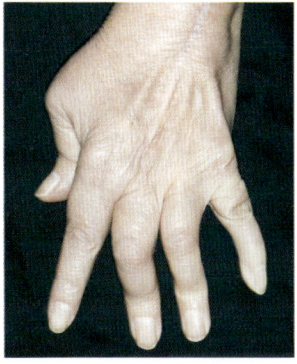

*Figure 1:* Inflamed joints in the hand caused by rheumatoid arthritis.

**Tip:** Attenuated viruses have usually been genetically or chemically modified so that they can't produce toxins or attach to and infect host cells.

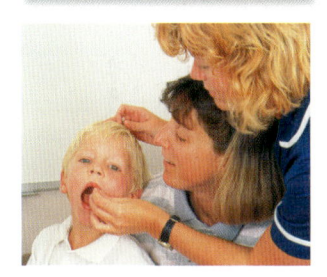

*Figure 2:* A boy being given an oral vaccination for polio.

**Tip:** Herd immunity means not everyone needs to be vaccinated. As long as enough people get the vaccine, the pathogen won't be able to spread and even non-vaccinated people will be protected.

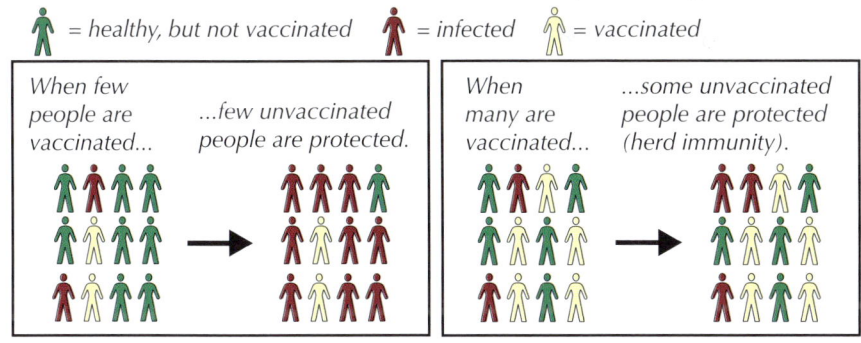

*Figure 3:* Herd immunity

Vaccination is not the same as immunisation. Vaccination is the administration of a substance designed to stimulate the immune system. Immunisation is the process by which you develop immunity. Vaccination causes immunisation.

### Routine vaccines
Routine vaccines are offered to everybody. They include:
- **the MMR** — protects against measles, mumps and rubella. The MMR is usually given to children as an injection at around a year old, and again before they start school. It contains attenuated measles, mumps and rubella viruses.
- **the meningitis C vaccine** — protects against the bacteria that cause meningitis C. It is first given as an injection to babies at 3 months. Boosters are then given to 1-year-olds and teenagers.

# Changing vaccines and vaccination programmes

Vaccinating against a disease isn't always straightforward. For example, some sneaky pathogens can change their surface antigens. This means that when you're infected, the memory cells produced following a vaccination will not recognise the different antigens. So the immune system has to start from scratch and carry out a primary response against these new antigens. For this reason, a vaccine and vaccination programme may have to change regularly.

## Example — The influenza virus

The influenza (flu) vaccine changes every year. That's because the antigens on the surface of the influenza virus change regularly, forming new strains of the virus. Memory cells produced from vaccination with one strain of the flu will not recognise other strains with different antigens. The strains are immunologically distinct.

**Exam Tip**
You need to learn this example for the exam.

**Tip:** Pathogens of the same type that have different surface antigens are often referred to as strains.

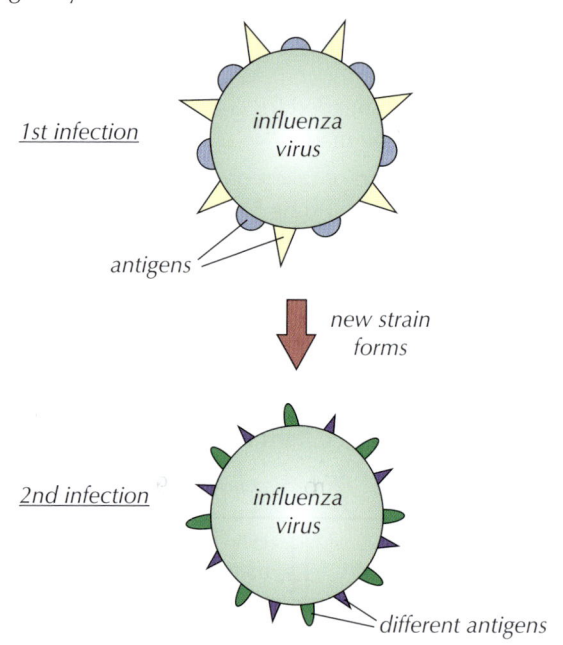

*Figure 4: Changing antigens in the influenza virus.*

*Figure 5: A TEM of an influenza virus.*

Every year there are different strains of the influenza virus circulating in the population, so a different vaccine has to be made. Laboratories collect samples of these different strains, and organisations, such as the WHO (World Health Organisation) and CDC (Centre for Disease Control), test the effectiveness of different influenza vaccines against them.

New vaccines are developed and one is chosen every year that is the most effective against the recently circulating influenza viruses. Governments and health authorities then implement a programme of vaccination using this most suitable vaccine. This is a good example of how society uses science to inform decision making.

Sometimes people are given a vaccine that protects them from a strain causing an epidemic in another country — this helps stop the strain from spreading globally.

## Practice Questions — Application

Q1 Which of the following is an example of artificial active immunity?
   A  Becoming immune to chickenpox after receiving antibodies through the placenta.
   B  Becoming immune to meningitis C after receiving a vaccine.
   C  Becoming immune to swine flu after catching the disease.
   D  Becoming immune to diphtheria after receiving an injection of antibodies against the diphtheria toxin.

Q2 Whooping cough is an infection of the respiratory system. The graph below shows the number of cases of whooping cough in Scotland between 1960 and 1999, and the vaccine uptake from the 1970s to 1999.

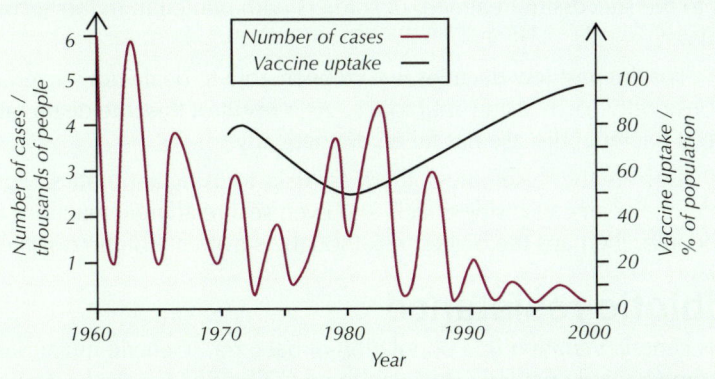

a) What percentage of the population were vaccinated in 1990?
b) How many cases of whooping cough were there in 1965?
c) The whooping cough vaccine was introduced in Scotland in the 1950s. Describe and explain the overall trend in the number of cases of whooping cough from 1960 to 1975.

**Exam Tip**
Always pay attention to the units on the axes — on the graph on the left, the y-axis is number of cases in thousands of people, so in 1963 there weren't 6 cases — there were 6000.

**Tip:** When reading off graphs with multiple scales, double-check you've got the right one. If you're struggling to read off the answer, draw lines on the graph to help you.

## Practice Questions — Fact Recall

Q1 Define the terms active and passive immunity.
Q2 a) What is an autoimmune disease?
   b) What causes this type of disease?
Q3 What causes the symptoms of lupus?
Q4 Other than lupus, give another example of an autoimmune disease.
Q5 How do vaccines give people immunity?
Q6 What is herd immunity?
Q7 Explain why a new vaccine against flu has to be developed every year.

Module 4: Section 1  Disease and the Immune System

### Learning Objectives:

- Understand the benefits and risks of using antibiotics to manage bacterial infection.
- Know that the wide use of antibiotics began following the discovery of penicillin in the mid-20th century.
- Understand the increase in bacterial resistance to antibiotics (examples to include *Clostridium difficile* and MRSA) and its implications.
- Understand possible sources of medicines, including examples of microorganisms and plants (and so the need to maintain biodiversity).
- Understand the potential for personalised medicines and synthetic biology.

**Specification Reference 4.1.1**

# 7. Antibiotics and Other Medicines

*Medical intervention, such as antibiotics, can be used to support the body's natural defences against pathogens.*

## Antibiotics

**Antibiotics** are chemicals that kill or inhibit the growth of bacteria. They're used by humans as drugs to treat bacterial infections. They're useful because they can usually target bacterial cells without damaging human body cells. Penicillin was the first antibiotic to be isolated (by Alexander Fleming, in 1928). Antibiotic use became widespread from the mid-twentieth century — partly thanks to the successful treatment of soldiers with penicillin in the Second World War.

For the past few decades, we've been able to deal with bacterial infections pretty easily using antibiotics. As a result of this, the death rate from infectious bacterial disease has fallen dramatically.

Despite their usefulness, there are risks to using antibiotics. For example, they can cause side effects and even severe allergic reactions in some people. Perhaps the biggest risk though, is from antibiotic resistance...

## Antibiotic resistance

There is genetic variation in a population of bacteria. Genetic mutations make some bacteria naturally resistant to an antibiotic. For the bacterium, this ability to resist an antibiotic is a big advantage. It's better able to survive in a host who's being treated with antibiotics to get rid of the infection, and so it lives for longer and reproduces many more times. This leads to the **allele** for antibiotic resistance being passed on to lots of offspring. It's an example of natural selection — see Figure 1. This is how antibiotic resistance spreads and becomes more common in a population of bacteria over time.

**Tip:** Antibiotics are used to treat bacterial infections in animals too.

**Tip:** An allele is a version of a gene — see page 276.

**Tip:** There's more about natural selection on pages 287-288.

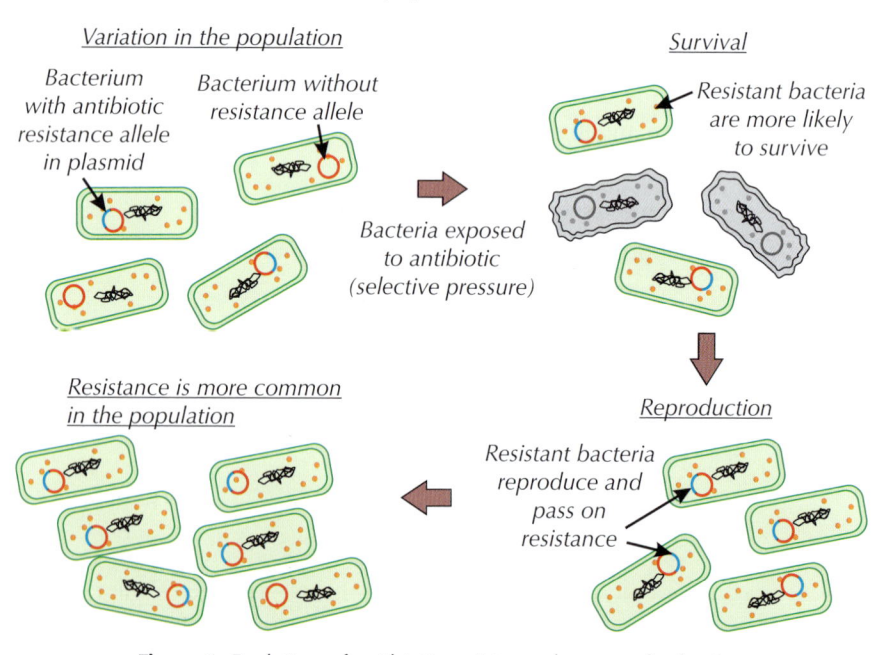

**Figure 1:** *Evolution of antibiotic resistance by natural selection.*

242    Module 4: Section 1   Disease and the Immune System

## Problems with antibiotic resistance

Antibiotic resistance is a problem for people who become infected with these bacteria, because you can't easily get rid of them with antibiotics. Increased use of antibiotics means that antibiotic resistance is increasing. 'Superbugs' that are resistant to most known antibiotics are becoming more common. This means we are less able to treat some potentially life-threatening bacterial infections. You need to know about these antibiotic-resistant bacteria:

#### Examples
- **MRSA** (meticillin-resistant *Staphylococcus aureus*) causes serious wound infections and is resistant to several antibiotics, including meticillin (which used to be called methicillin).
- ***Clostridium difficile*** infects the digestive system, usually causing problems in people who have already been treated with antibiotics. It is thought that the harmless bacteria that are normally present in the digestive system are killed by the antibiotics, which *C. difficile* is resistant to. This allows *C. difficile* to flourish. *C. difficile* produces a toxin, which causes severe diarrhoea, fever and cramps.

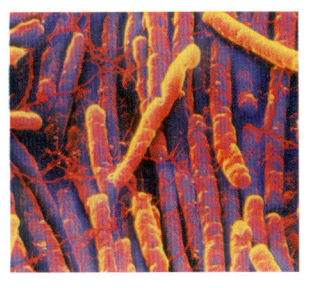

*Figure 2: SEM of* Clostridium difficile *bacteria (rod-shaped cells).*

### Preventing antibiotic resistance

Developing new antibiotics and modifying existing ones are two ways of overcoming the current problem of antibiotic resistance. This isn't easy though.

To reduce the likelihood of antibiotic resistance developing in the first place, doctors are being encouraged to reduce their use of antibiotics, e.g. not to prescribe them for minor infections and not to prescribe them to prevent infections (except in patients with already weak immune systems, e.g. the elderly or people with HIV). Patients are advised to take all of the antibiotics they're prescribed to make sure the infection is fully cleared and all the bacteria have been killed (which reduces the likelihood of a population of antibiotic-resistant bacteria developing).

**Tip:** MRSA and *Clostridium difficile* infections are most common in hospitals, where many antibiotics are used and patients who are already ill have weakened immune systems.

## Sources of medicines

Scientists need to be constantly developing new drugs to target resistant strains of pathogens, as well as developing drugs for diseases that are currently incurable.

Many medicinal drugs are manufactured using natural compounds found in plants, animals or microorganisms.

#### Examples
- Penicillin is obtained from a fungus.
- Some cancer drugs are made using soil bacteria.
- Daffodils are grown to produce a drug used to treat Alzheimer's disease.

Only a small proportion of organisms have been investigated so far, so it's possible that plants or microorganisms exist that contain compounds that could be used to treat currently incurable diseases, such as AIDS. Others may produce new antibiotics.

Possible sources of drugs need to be protected by maintaining the **biodiversity** (the variety of different species) on Earth. If we don't protect them, some species could die out before we get a chance to study them. Even organisms that have already been studied could still prove to be useful sources of medicines as new techniques are developed for identifying, purifying and testing compounds.

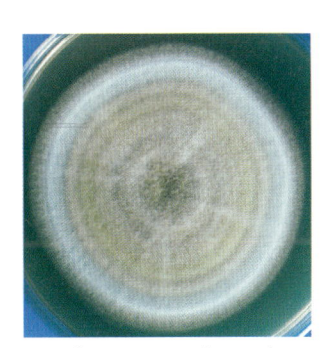

*Figure 3: A colony of* Penicillium chrysogenum *fungus growing on an agar plate. This fungus produces penicillin.*

Module 4: Section 1 Disease and the Immune System

# Future of medicine

The future of medicine looks very high-tech...

## Personalised medicine

Your genes determine how your body responds to certain drugs. Different people respond to the same drug in different ways — which makes certain drugs more effective for some people than others. This is where personalised medicines come in.

Personalised medicines are medicines that are tailored to an individual's DNA. The theory is that if doctors have your genetic information, they can use it to predict how you will respond to different drugs and only prescribe the ones that will be most effective for you. Scientists hope that by studying the relationship between someone's genetic make-up and their responsiveness to drugs, more effective drugs can be produced in the future.

## Synthetic biology

Synthetic biology involves using technology to design and make things like artificial proteins, cells and even microorganisms. It has applications in lots of different areas, including medicine.

— Example —
Scientists are looking at engineering bacteria to destroy cancer cells, while leaving healthy body cells intact.

**Tip:** Drugs taken to prevent rejection of a transplanted organ can also make patients more at risk of infection by suppressing immune responses.

### Practice Questions — Application

Q1 When, approximately, did antibiotic use become widespread?
 A Mid-19th century
 B Late-19th century
 C Early-20th century
 D Mid-20th century

Q2 Transplant patients are more at risk of infection. Why might rising antibiotic resistance lead to high death rates in transplant patients?

Q3 In 2000, a strain of *Clostridium difficile* emerged that is resistant to fluoroquinolones, a widely used group of antibiotics.
 a) Outline how this strain of *C. difficile* may have evolved by natural selection.
 b) *C. difficile* infections are most common in hospitalised patients. Suggest why the bacteria are able to establish an infection in this case.
 c) Outline two strategies that are designed to reduce the likelihood of antibiotic resistance developing in populations of bacteria.

### Practice Questions — Fact Recall

Q1 What are antibiotics?
Q2 What was the first antibiotic to be discovered?
Q3 Give an example of an antibiotic-resistant bacterium, other than *C. difficile*.
Q4 What type of microorganism is penicillin derived from?
Q5 What are personalised medicines?
Q6 What is synthetic biology?

# Section Summary

Make sure you know...

- That a pathogen is an organism that can cause disease.
- That a communicable disease is a disease that can be spread between organisms.
- About the following communicable diseases (including the organisms they are caused by and affect):
  - Tuberculosis, bacterial meningitis and ring rot are caused by bacteria.
  - HIV/AIDS, influenza and tobacco mosaic virus are caused by viruses.
  - Black sigatoka, ring worm and athlete's foot are caused by fungi.
  - Malaria and potato/tomato late blight are caused by protoctists.
- How communicable diseases can be transferred between organisms by direct transmission (directly from one organism to another) or indirect transmission (from one organism to another via an intermediate, such as spores or a vector).
- How transmission of pathogens can be affected by living conditions, climate and social factors.
- The primary non-specific defences against pathogens in animals, including the skin, mucous membranes, blood clotting, inflammation, wound repair and expulsive reflexes.
- The primary non-specific defences against pathogens in plants, including waxy cuticles, cell walls and callose deposition (physical barriers) and the production of chemicals (against pathogens and vectors).
- The structure of phagocytes and the process of phagocytosis (engulfment of pathogens).
- The roles of opsonins, phagosomes, lysosomes, antigen-presenting cells (APCs), neutrophils and cytokines in phagocytosis.
- The structure of T lymphocytes, how they are activated (clonal selection) and divide to produce clones (clonal expansion), and the roles of different types — T helper cells, T killer cells and T regulatory cells in an immune response.
- The structure of B lymphocytes, and how they are activated and divide to produce plasma cells and memory cells.
- That cells communicate by signalling using substances such as interleukins.
- How to examine and draw cells observed in blood smears.
- The structure of antibodies (proteins that bind to antigens), including constant and variable regions.
- How antibodies clear infections by agglutinating pathogens, neutralising toxins and preventing pathogens from binding to cells.
- What the primary immune response and secondary immune response are and how they work, including the role of memory cells in secondary immune responses.
- The similarities and differences between active, passive, natural and artificial immunity, including examples of each type of immunity.
- What an 'autoimmune disease' is and a named example of one (e.g. lupus or rheumatoid arthritis).
- How vaccines make people immune to disease by stimulating memory cell production.
- The role of vaccines in preventing epidemics, by creating herd immunity.
- What routine vaccinations are and why vaccines or vaccination programmes may change.
- The benefits (reducing death rates from bacterial disease) and risks (side effects, allergic reactions and increasing antibiotic resistance) of using antibiotics to manage bacterial infection.
- That widespread use of antibiotics began in the mid-20th century, following the discovery of penicillin.
- How bacteria develop antibiotic resistance by natural selection, including *Clostridium difficile* and MRSA as examples of antibiotic-resistant bacteria.
- Possible sources for medicines, including microorganisms and plants.
- Why it's important, in terms of drug development, to maintain biodiversity.
- What personalised medicine and synthetic biology are, and their potential in the future.

# Exam-style Questions

**1** Which of the communicable diseases below is caused by a fungus?

    **A** malaria

    **B** tomato late blight

    **C** ring rot

    **D** ringworm

*(1 mark)*

**2** Tuberculosis (TB) is an infectious disease. More than one million people worldwide die from tuberculosis every year.

  **(a)** Identify the type of pathogen that causes TB.

*(1 mark)*

  **(b)** **Fig. 1.1** shows the number of reported cases of TB in the UK between 2000 and 2009.

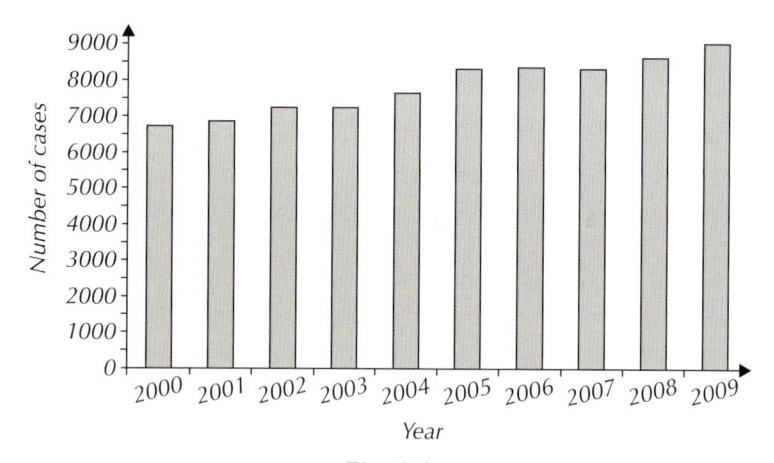

**Fig. 1.1**

    **(i)** Describe the trend in the number of reported TB cases in the UK between 2000 and 2009.

*(1 mark)*

    **(ii)** Calculate the approximate percentage increase in the number of cases of reported TB in the UK between 2003 and 2009. Show your working.

*(2 marks)*

    **(iii)** A newspaper headline states that "The number of TB cases in England is predicted to rise by 33% by the year 2018". Discuss this claim using the information in the graph.

*(3 marks)*

**3** In 1918 there was a worldwide outbreak of influenza called 'Spanish flu'. The virus responsible was the **H1N1** strain — it had type 1 haemagglutinin (H1) and type 1 neuraminidase (N1) antigens on its surface.

**(a)** When someone is infected with Spanish flu their immune system responds. The first stage of this response involves the phagocytosis of virus particles.

**(i)*** Describe the sequence of steps in phagocytosis.

*(6 marks)*

**(ii)** What is the role of opsonins in phagocytosis?

*(1 mark)*

**(iii)** Outline the main stages of the immune response after phagocytosis.

*(5 marks)*

**(b)** Spanish flu circulated the globe for over a year. Explain why survivors of the Spanish flu did not contract it when exposed for a second time.

*(2 marks)*

**(c)** In 1957 there was another outbreak of influenza called 'Asian flu'. It was caused by the **H2N2** strain of influenza. Explain why survivors of the Spanish flu may have contracted Asian flu.

*(3 marks)*

**(d)** Every year new flu vaccines are developed. These contain antigens to multiple strains of influenza. Suggest why this is the case.

*(1 mark)*


**4** Diphtheria is an infectious disease caused by a pathogenic species of bacteria. Cases of diphtheria are now very rare since the introduction of a vaccination in the early 1940s.

**(a) (i)** Explain how having a vaccination leads to the formation of memory B lymphocytes.

*(3 marks)*

**(ii)** Explain why individuals who don't have a particular vaccine will still gain some protection from the introduction of the vaccine.

*(2 marks)*

**(b)** Memory B lymphocytes differentiate into plasma cells which produce antibodies.

**(i)** Name the **three** main regions of an antibody and give the function of each region.

*(3 marks)*

**(ii)** Tick the boxes to show which **three** of the following are functions of antibodies.

| Agglutinating pathogens | | Activating memory T lymphocytes | |
|---|---|---|---|
| Killing pathogens directly | | Mutating pathogen DNA | |
| Neutralising toxins | | Stopping pathogens binding to cells | |

*(3 marks)*

*The quality of your response will be assessed in this question.

Module 4: Section 1 **Disease and the Immune System**

# Module 4 Section 2: Biodiversity

## Learning Objectives:

- Understand how biodiversity may be considered at different levels, including habitat biodiversity (e.g. sand dunes, woodland, meadows, streams), species biodiversity (species richness and species evenness) and genetic biodiversity (e.g. different breeds within a species).
- Know how sampling is used in measuring the biodiversity of a habitat and the importance of sampling the range of organisms in a habitat.
- Be able to carry out practical investigations collecting random and non-random samples in the field (PAG3).
- Know how sampling can be carried out, including random and non-random sampling (e.g. opportunistic, stratified and systematic).
- Know how to measure species richness and species evenness in a habitat.
- Be able to use and interpret Simpson's Index of Diversity ($D$) to calculate the biodiversity of a habitat, using the formula:
  $D = 1 - (\Sigma(n/N)^2)$
  and know the significance of both high and low values of $D$.

**Specification Reference 4.2.1**

# 1. Investigating Biodiversity

*Biodiversity is an important indicator of a habitat's health — the higher the biodiversity of the habitat, the healthier that habitat is. You can work out a habitat's biodiversity using a bit of data and a nifty little equation...*

## Biodiversity

The term 'biodiversity' refers to the variety of living organisms in an area. It can be considered at three different levels:

### 1. Habitat diversity

A habitat is the area inhabited by a species. It includes the physical factors, like the soil and temperature range, and the living (biotic) factors, like availability of food or the presence of predators. Habitat diversity is the number of different habitats in an area.

#### Examples
- A coastal area could contain many different habitats — beaches, sand dunes, mudflats, salt marshes, etc.
- A river valley could contain meadows, agricultural fields, streams, woodland, etc.

### 2. Species diversity

A species is a group of similar organisms able to reproduce to give fertile offspring. Species diversity is the number of different species (species richness) and the abundance of each species (species evenness) in an area.

#### Example
A woodland could contain many different species of plants, insects, birds and mammals.

### 3. Genetic diversity

Genetic diversity is the variation of alleles (versions of a gene) within a species or a population of a species.

#### Examples
- Human blood type is determined by a gene with three different alleles.
- The variation in alleles within the dog species gives rise to different breeds, such as a Labrador or poodle.

## Collecting data on biodiversity

Collecting data on biodiversity usually means finding out the number of different species in a habitat or the number of individuals in each species. In most cases though, it'd be too time-consuming to count every individual organism in a habitat. Instead, a **sample** of the population is taken. Estimates about the whole habitat are based on the sample.

# Random sampling

To make sure the sample isn't biased, it should be random. For example, if you were looking at plant species in a field you could pick random sample sites by dividing the field into a grid using measuring tapes and use a random number generator to select coordinates — see Figure 1. Doing this makes sure that each sample site has the same **probability** of being chosen.

*Non-random sampling*

*Only look at a small area of the field.*

*Random sampling*

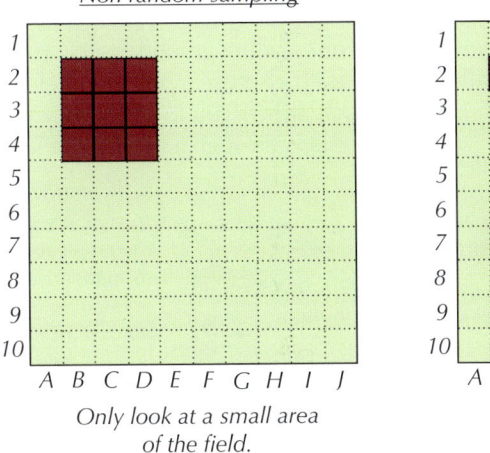

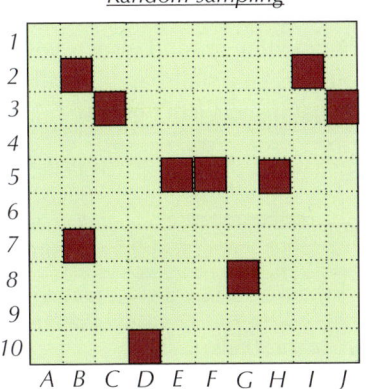

*Randomly select squares in the field.*

**Figure 1:** *Diagram to show non-random sampling by picking a small area (left) and random sampling using a random number generator (right).*

To ensure any variation observed in the sample isn't just due to chance, it's important to analyse the results statistically. This allows you to be more confident that the results are true and therefore will reflect what's going on in the whole population.

# Non-random sampling

Sometimes it's necessary to take a non-random sample. For example, when there's a lot of variety in the distribution of species in the habitat and you want to make sure that all the different areas are sampled or that all the different species are sampled. There are three types of non-random sampling:

### 1. Systematic sampling
This is when samples are taken at fixed intervals, often along a line.

> **Example**
> If you were looking at plant species in a field, quadrats (square frames that you place on the ground) could be placed along a line (called a **transect**) from an area of shade in the corner to the middle of the field — see Figure 2. Each quadrat would then be a sample site.

### 2. Opportunistic sampling
This is when samples are chosen by the investigator. It's used because it is simple to carry out, but the data will be biased.

### 3. Stratified sampling
This is when different areas in a habitat are identified and sampled separately in proportion to their part of the habitat as a whole.

> **Example**
> A heathland may have patches of gorse in it — the heath and gorse areas would be sampled separately according to how much of each there was in the habitat.

**Tip:** A sample is biased if it doesn't represent the population as a whole. For example, if you were looking at the average height of students in a school but only measured the heights of people from one particular class, the sample would be biased.

**Tip:** The chance of something happening is the possibility it will occur. Probability is a measure of how likely events are to happen.

**Tip:** A random number generator will give you coordinates at random, e.g. C3, E5, etc. Then you just take your samples from these coordinates.

**Tip:** You can also make sure your samples are random by taking samples at different times of the day and in different weather conditions.

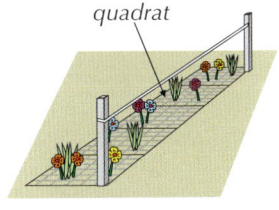

**Figure 2:** *Quadrats placed along a transect line. This type of transect is called a belt transect.*

Module 4: Section 2 Biodiversity

**Tip:** You'll need to do a risk assessment before you carry out an investigation into biodiversity. The risks of working outdoors are quite different to ones you'd face in the lab and they'll vary depending on the environment you're working in.

*Figure 3: Pitfall traps like this one can be used to catch ground-dwelling insects.*

**Tip:** When you collect data on biodiversity you can damage the environment (e.g. by trampling plants) and disturb animals. It's a good idea to find ways of minimising this when you plan your investigation. It's also worth having a think about any ethical issues your investigation might raise, e.g. whether catching animals will cause them distress.

**Tip:** If you're sampling mobile organisms you should make sure they can't escape before you count them and that you don't count individuals more than once.

**Tip:** Carrying out repeats and calculating a mean will make your estimate more precise. See page 6 for more.

# Estimating biodiversity using samples:

PRACTICAL ACTIVITY GROUP 3

1. Choose a site to sample, e.g. a small area within the habitat being studied. You could choose this site randomly or non-randomly (see previous page).

2. Record the number of different species or count the number of individuals of each species. How you do this depends on what you're counting.

### Examples

For crawling ground insects you could use a pitfall trap (a small pit that insects can't get out of).

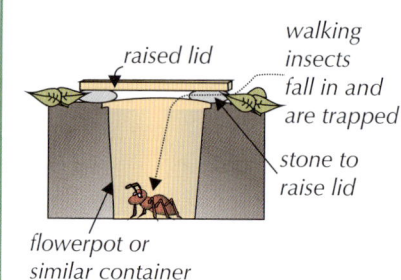

For crawling ground insects you could also use a pooter (a device that allows you to safely suck small insects through a tube into a jar).

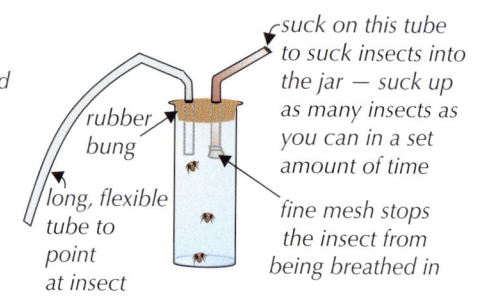

For small organisms that live in soil or leaf litter you could use a Tullgren funnel — a sample of soil or leaf litter is put on a mesh filter at the top of a funnel and a light shone down onto it. The light acts as a heat source and dries out the soil/leaf litter, so organisms move away from it and fall into the beaker. The mesh holds the soil/leaf litter in place but lets the small organisms pass through.

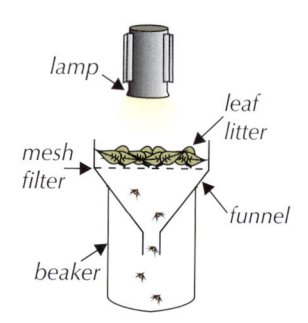

For some aquatic organisms you could use kick sampling — you gently kick the sediment at the bottom of a stream for a set amount of time, then hold a net downstream of where you've kicked and collect the organisms that have been disturbed.

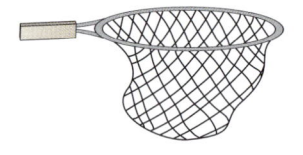

For organisms living in long grass you could use a sweep net — you stand still and sweep the net once from left to right through the grass, then quickly sweep the net up and turn the contents of the net into a collecting tray.

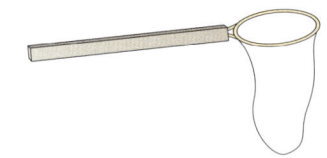

3. Repeat the process — take as many samples as possible. This gives a better indication of the whole habitat. All your samples should be chosen in the same way as your first sample — so if you started with a random sample, all your other samples should be random too.

4. The number of individuals for the whole habitat can then be estimated by calculating the mean for the data collected in each sample and multiplying it by the size of the whole habitat.

5. When sampling different habitats and comparing them, always use the same sampling technique. E.g. if you're using a series of pitfall traps you should make sure they're set up in the same way and left for the same length of time. If you're using a Tullgren funnel, keep the light source the same distance from the top of the funnel and keep it there for the same amount of time, e.g. 2 days.

There are lots of different practical investigations you could do using this method.

### Example
You could investigate the impact of mowing on the biodiversity of your school playing field by sampling a mowed and an un-mowed field. Calculate the biodiversity for each field using Simpson's Index (see next page).

## Species richness and species evenness

**Species richness** is the number of different species in an area. The higher the number of species, the greater the species richness. It's measured by taking random samples of a habitat and counting the number of different species (see previous two pages).

**Species evenness** is a measure of the relative abundance of each species in an area. The more similar the population size of each species, the greater the species evenness. It's measured by taking random samples of a habitat, and counting the number of individuals of each different species.

The greater the species richness and evenness in an area, the higher the biodiversity. The lower the species richness and evenness, the lower the biodiversity.

**Exam Tip**
If you're asked to define species richness in the exam, you need to say it's the <u>number</u> of species in an area — if you talk about variety or amount you won't get the mark.

**Tip:** A low species evenness means that one or two species dominate a habitat — other species are only present in low numbers or are not present at all.

### Example
Habitat X and habitat Y both contain two different species and 30 individual organisms.

|  | Habitat X | Habitat Y |
|---|---|---|
| No. organisms in species 1 | 28 | 15 |
| No. organisms in species 2 | 2 | 15 |
| Total | 30 | 30 |

There are two species in each habitat so the species richness in the two habitats is the same — 2. However, in habitat Y the individual organisms are more evenly distributed between the different species — there are 15 organisms of each species, compared to 28 organisms in species 1 and just 2 organisms in species 2 in habitat X. Habitat Y has greater species evenness. This suggests that habitat Y has a higher biodiversity.

**Tip:** Abundance is the number of individuals. Distribution means where the individuals are found.

## Simpson's Index of Diversity

Species richness and species evenness are simple ways of measuring diversity. But species that are present in a habitat in very small numbers shouldn't be treated the same as those with bigger populations. This is where Simpson's Index of Diversity comes in.

Module 4: Section 2 Biodiversity

**Tip:** Change has a big effect on habitats with a low index of diversity because there aren't many species present. If one of only a few species gets wiped out, e.g. by a new predator, it makes a much bigger difference to a habitat than if one of many species gets wiped out.

**Exam Tip**
If you're asked to work out a Simpson's Index of Diversity in the exam, remember that the answer should be between 0 and 1. So if you get a negative number or a number greater than 1, then you've made a mistake.

**Tip:** You need to work out the $(n/N)^2$ bit for each different species and then add them all together.

**Exam Tip**
The numbers in this table have been rounded to 3 significant figures. In the exam, round your answers to the same number of significant figures used in the question (unless you're told otherwise).

Simpson's Index of Diversity (D) is a useful way of measuring species diversity. It's calculated using an equation that takes into account both species richness and species evenness. You calculate Simpson's Index of Diversity using the following formula:

$$D = 1 - \left( \sum \left( \frac{n}{N} \right)^2 \right)$$

Where...
$n$ = Total number of organisms in one species
$N$ = Total number of all organisms
$\Sigma$ = 'Sum of' (i.e. added together)

Simpson's Index of Diversity is always a value between 0 and 1. The closer the index is to one, the more diverse the habitat and the greater its ability to cope with change (e.g. the appearance of a new predator). Low index values suggest the habitat is more easily damaged by change, making it less stable. The greater the species richness and evenness, the higher the value of Simpson's Index.

### Example — Maths Skills

There are 3 different species of flower in this field — a red species, a white and a blue. There are 3 of the red species, 5 of the white and 3 of the blue.
There are 11 organisms altogether, so $N = 11$.
So the index of diversity for this field is:

$$D = 1 - \left( \left(\frac{3}{11}\right)^2 + \left(\frac{5}{11}\right)^2 + \left(\frac{3}{11}\right)^2 \right) = 1 - (0.07 + 0.21 + 0.07)$$
$$= 1 - 0.35 = \mathbf{0.65}$$

The field has an index of diversity of 0.65, which is fairly high.

Calculating the Index of Diversity can get quite tricky. If you've got a lot of data you might find it easier to plug the numbers into a table — that way you can make sure you don't miss out any steps.

### Example — Maths Skills

A student investigates the diversity of fish species in her local pond. She finds 46 fish of 6 different species. To help her calculate Simpson's Index of Diversity for the pond she draws the following table.

| Species | n (total number of organisms in species) | $\frac{n}{N}$ | $\left(\frac{n}{N}\right)^2$ |
|---|---|---|---|
| A | 1 | 1 / 46 | 0.000473 |
| B | 6 | 6 / 46 | 0.0170 |
| C | 2 | 2 / 46 | 0.00189 |
| D | 15 | 15 / 46 | 0.106 |
| E | 3 | 3 / 46 | 0.00425 |
| F | 19 | 19 / 46 | 0.171 |
| | N (total number of all organisms) = 46 | | $\sum \left(\frac{n}{N}\right)^2 = 0.301$ |

She then uses the numbers from the table to calculate the Index:

$$D = 1 - 0.301 = \mathbf{0.699}$$

Module 4: Section 2 Biodiversity

## Practice Questions — Application

**Q1** An environmental officer is investigating the population of fish in a lake using a net. She sweeps the net through the water to catch fish.

Suggest two ways in which the environmental officer could standardise the method she uses to collect her data to ensure her results are repeatable.

**Q2** The table below shows the number of individuals of each species of insect found in two ponds.

| Species | Number of individuals found in Pond A | Number of individuals found in Pond B |
|---|---|---|
| Damselfly | 3 | 13 |
| Dragonfly | 5 | 5 |
| Stonefly | 2 | 7 |
| Water boatman | 3 | 2 |
| Crane fly | 1 | 18 |
| Pond skater | 4 | 9 |

a) Which pond has the greatest species evenness? Explain your answer.

b) Use the data provided in the table and the formula given below to calculate the Index of Diversity to 3 significant figures for:

i) Pond A,　　ii) Pond B.

$$D = 1 - (\Sigma(n/N)^2)$$
where $N$ = total number of all organisms
and $n$ = total number of organisms in one species.

c) Would the two ponds be likely to cope with the introduction of a new species of predator? Explain your answer.

**Tip:** Standardise means make the same. Repeatable means that if the same person repeats the experiment using the same method and equipment, they will get the same results.

**Exam Tip**
You can use a calculator to help you with this question — you'll be allowed to take one into the exam with you.

**Exam Tip**
If you've got time at the end of the exam, always go back over any calculation questions and check the answer — it's easy to make a silly mistake somewhere and lose marks.

## Practice Questions — Fact Recall

**Q1** Define the following terms:
a) biodiversity,　　b) habitat,　　c) species.

**Q2** Name and describe three levels at which biodiversity can be considered.

**Q3** Sampling can be random or non-random.
a) Explain why it is important to take random samples when collecting data on biodiversity.
b) Give an example of when you might choose to take a non-random sample instead of a random sample.
c) Give three examples of non-random sampling methods.

**Q4** Define the following terms:
a) species richness,　　b) species evenness.

**Q5** Name two things needed to calculate Simpson's Index of Diversity.

**Q6** What does a high Simpson's Index of Diversity value indicate?

**Exam Tip**
It's really important you've got the meaning of terms like species, habitat, biodiversity, species richness and species evenness fixed in your brain. It'll make any biodiversity questions a lot easier to understand.

**Learning Objectives:**
- Understand how genetic biodiversity may be assessed, including calculations of genetic diversity within isolated populations, such as zoos (captive breeding), rare breeds and pedigree animals.
- Be able to calculate the percentage of gene variants (alleles) in a genome, using the formula: proportion of polymorphic gene loci = number of polymorphic gene loci ÷ total number of loci.

**Specification Reference 4.2.1**

**Tip:** A <u>pedigree animal</u> is one that has been bred purely from animals of the same breed. A <u>rare breed</u> is usually a breed of farm animal that's not used in large-scale farming.

**Tip:** The individuals in an isolated population can only breed with each other. This increases the risk of inbreeding, which is why genetic diversity tends to be low in isolated populations.

**Tip:** Loci is the plural of locus. Polymorphic gene loci are those points on a chromosome that can have more than one allele.

# 2. Genetic Diversity

*Genetic diversity is a measure of the biodiversity within a species. Measuring genetic diversity is important in helping us to understand the survivability of different species. Greater genetic diversity is linked to a greater ability to adapt and survive.*

## Importance of genetic diversity

You know from page 248 that genetic diversity is the variation of alleles within a species (or within a population of a species). You can do calculations to work out the genetic diversity of a population. This is important because if a population has low genetic diversity, they might not be able to adapt to a change in the environment and the whole population could be wiped out by a single event (e.g. a disease).

Populations in which genetic diversity may be low include isolated populations, such as those bred in captivity (e.g. in zoos), populations of pedigree animals and rare breeds. Calculations can be used to monitor the genetic diversity of these populations over time and efforts can be made to increase the genetic diversity of the population if needed.

### Example

Breeding programmes in zoos are very closely managed to maximise genetic diversity. Databases are kept up to date with the details of each animal on the breeding programme. It is then decided which animals should be paired for breeding and these animals are transferred between the zoos that hold them. This helps to reduce inbreeding (breeding between closely related individuals) which reduces genetic diversity.

## What is polymorphism?

You know that alleles are different versions of a gene. Alleles of the same gene are always found at the same point (called a **locus**) on a chromosome. Polymorphism describes a locus that has two or more alleles (see Figure 1).

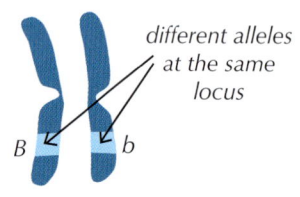

**Figure 1:** Diagram to show polymorphism at a gene locus.

## Assessing genetic diversity

Genetic polymorphism is used to measure genetic diversity. Working out the proportion of **polymorphic gene loci** in a population gives you a measure of genetic diversity. There's a nifty formula you can use:

$$\text{proportion of polymorphic gene loci} = \frac{\text{number of polymorphic gene loci}}{\text{total number of loci}}$$

Module 4: Section 2 Biodiversity

## Example 1 — Maths Skills

100 genes are sampled in a population. 40 of the genes are polymorphic. Work out the proportion of polymorphic gene loci.

$$\text{proportion of polymorphic gene loci} = \frac{40}{100} = \mathbf{0.4}$$

## Example 2 — Maths Skills

55 of the genes sampled in a population are polymorphic, out of 170 genes sampled in total. Work out the percentage of genes that have alleles.

The number of genes that have alleles is just another way of saying 'the proportion of gene loci that are polymorphic', so start by using the same formula as before:

$$\text{proportion of polymorphic gene loci} = \frac{55}{170} = 0.32$$

Then multiply the answer by 100 to convert the proportion to a percentage.

$$\text{percentage of genes that have alleles} = 0.32 \times 100 = \mathbf{32\%}$$

**Exam Tip**
Read the question carefully to check whether you're being asked for the proportion or the percentage. If you're asked for the percentage, first work out the proportion and then multiply your answer by 100.

### Practice Questions — Application

Q1 The genetic diversity of a population of gorillas in a zoo is monitored. Of the 80 genes sampled, 12 were found to be polymorphic.
   a) Calculate the proportion of polymorphic gene loci.
   b) Suggest one way the zoo could increase the genetic diversity of its gorilla population.
   c) Explain why the zoo might want to increase the genetic diversity of the population.

Q2 Two species of frog are studied to determine their genetic diversity. In species A, 66 of the genes sampled are polymorphic out of 90 genes sampled in total. In species B, 42 of the genes sampled are polymorphic out of the 90 genes sampled in total.
   a) Calculate the percentage of genes that have alleles in species A.
   b) Calculate the percentage of genes that have alleles in species B.
   c) Suggest which of these species is more likely to be able to adapt to a change in the environment. Explain your answer.

*Figure 2: Gorilla thinking about how to increase his species' genetic diversity.*

### Practice Questions — Fact Recall

Q1 What is a polymorphic gene locus?
Q2 Describe how you can assess the genetic diversity of a population.
Q3 Give the formula you can use to work out the proportion of polymorphic gene loci.

Module 4: Section 2 Biodiversity

**Learning Objective:**

- Understand the factors affecting biodiversity, including human population growth, agriculture (monoculture) and climate change.

**Specification Reference 4.2.1**

# 3. Factors Affecting Biodiversity

*Remember, biodiversity can be considered at the level of habitat diversity, species diversity or genetic diversity (see page 248). Many of the things humans do affect biodiversity...*

## Human population growth

The human population of the planet has grown hugely in the last couple of centuries and is continuing to rise. This is decreasing biodiversity because of the following factors:

### 1. Habitat loss

As the human population grows, we need to develop more land for housing and to produce food. This development is destroying habitats.

**Example**

There is deforestation in the Amazon to make way for grazing and agriculture. This decreases habitat diversity. With fewer habitats for organisms to live in, species diversity also decreases.

*Figure 1: View of deforested land in the Ecuadorian rainforest.*

### 2. Over-exploitation

A greater demand for resources (such as food, water and energy) means a lot of resources are being used up faster than they can be replenished. This can destroy habitats or it can affect species directly.

**Example**

Industrial fishing can deplete the populations of certain fish species and may even cause extinction (a species to die out). This decreases genetic diversity within populations, as well as decreasing species diversity (as a result of extinction).

**Tip:** The factors described on this page and the next two can all affect biodiversity at a local or a global level.

### 3. Urbanisation

Sprawling cities and major road developments can isolate species, meaning populations are unable to interbreed and genetic diversity is decreased.

**Example**

Populations of some animals, for example snakes, living in areas isolated by roads show a lower genetic diversity than populations living in areas of continuous habitat. This is thought to be because the isolated animals are unable to migrate and breed as they usually would.

### 4. Pollution

As the human population grows, we're producing more waste and more pollution. High levels of pollutants can kill species or destroy habitats.

**Examples**

- High levels of fertiliser flowing into a river from nearby fields can lead to a decrease in fish species in that river. This decreases biodiversity.
- Some of the gases that are released from factories and cars cause acid rain, which can lower the pH of rivers, lakes and soil. Many aquatic organisms can't survive below a certain pH.

Module 4: Section 2 Biodiversity

# Monoculture

In order to feed an ever growing number of people, large areas of land are devoted to monoculture — the growing of a single variety of a single crop.

**Example**
In Africa, large areas of land are used for palm oil plantations.

This leads to a decline in biodiversity because of the following factors:

## 1. Habitat loss
Habitats are lost as land is cleared to make way for the large fields, reducing habitat diversity. This is not just the case on land. Marine fish farms are often built in locations that are ideal for wild fish and other marine life.

**Example**
Mangrove forests are areas of trees that grow in tropical and sub-tropical coastal regions. They are rich in biodiversity and provide a habitat for a wide variety of plant and animal species. One of the biggest threats to mangrove forests comes from clearance to make space for shrimp farms.

## 2. Loss of local plants and animals
Local and naturally occurring plants and animals are seen as weeds and pests, and so are destroyed with pesticides and herbicides, reducing species diversity.

**Example**
Use of herbicides on corn farms in the USA kills the local milkweed plant, which is the main source of food for the monarch butterfly. Monarch butterfly numbers are decreasing, which may partly be as a result of this.

**Figure 2:** *Mangrove forest in Asia.*

## 3. Loss of heritage varieties
Heritage (traditional) varieties of crops are lost because they don't make enough money and so are not planted any more, which reduces species diversity.

# Climate change and global biodiversity

Climate change is a significant long-term change in an area's climate, e.g. its average temperature or rainfall patterns. It occurs naturally, but the scientific consensus is that the climate change we're experiencing at the moment is caused by humans increasing emissions of greenhouse gases (such as carbon dioxide). Greenhouse gases cause global warming (increasing global average temperature), which causes other types of climate change, e.g. changing rainfall patterns. Climate change can affect biodiversity by:

## Changing environmental conditions
Climate change will affect the environmental conditions in different areas of the world in different ways — some places will get warmer, some colder, some wetter and others drier. All of these changes are likely to affect global biodiversity.

One reason for this is that most species need a particular climate to survive, so a change in climate may mean that an area that was previously inhabitable becomes uninhabitable (and vice versa). This may cause an increase or decrease in the range of some species (the area in which they live). This could increase or decrease biodiversity.

**Tip:** The Earth is heated by the Sun. Greenhouses gases in the atmosphere absorb most of the energy that would otherwise be radiated out into space, and re-radiate it back to Earth. This keeps us warm. But too much greenhouse gas means too much heat is absorbed and re-radiated back to Earth, so we're getting warmer.

**Example**

The southern range limit of the Sooty Copper Butterfly has moved 60 miles north in recent decades.

Changing environmental conditions may force some species to migrate to a more suitable area, causing a change in species distribution. Migrations usually decrease biodiversity in the areas the species migrate from, and increase biodiversity in the areas they migrate to. If there isn't a suitable habitat to migrate to, the species is a plant and can't migrate, or if the change is too fast, the species may become extinct. This will decrease biodiversity.

**Exam Tip**
Make sure you use the correct scientific terms in the exam — for example, talk about species not being <u>adapted</u> to a new climate rather than not liking the new climate.

**Example**

Corals die if water temperature changes by just one or two degrees. In 1998 a coral reef near Panama was badly damaged because the water temperature had increased — at least one species of coral became extinct as a result.

## Practice Question — Application

Q1 A study was carried out to investigate the effect of temperature on the changing distribution of subtropical plankton species in the north Atlantic. Data collected on global sea surface temperature and plankton distribution are shown in the figures below.

**Figure A:** Graph to show changing global sea-surface temperature.

**Tip:** Plankton are small organisms, such as algae, which are found drifting in water.

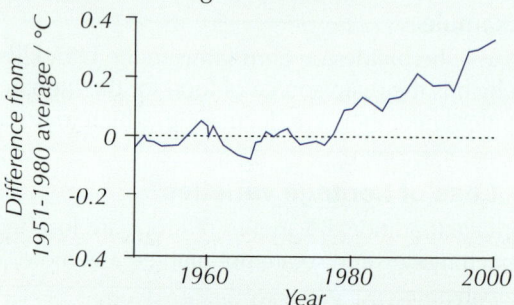

**Figure B:** Diagram to show subtropical plankton distribution.

■ subtropical plankton

**Tip:** Don't be put off by the question having two different types of data source — just look at each one carefully and compare the trends they show.

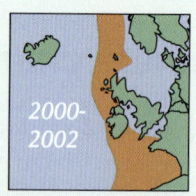

a) Describe the data shown in Figure A and Figure B.
b) What conclusion can be drawn from this information?
c) Explain why the study can't conclude that the change in sea-surface temperature caused the change in plankton distribution.
d) Plankton are an important food source for many other marine organisms. Suggest how the change in plankton distribution may have affected biodiversity in the north Atlantic.

## Practice Questions — Fact Recall

Q1 Describe one way in which human population growth affects biodiversity.
Q2 Describe how monoculture affects biodiversity.

Module 4: Section 2 Biodiversity

# 4. Biodiversity and Conservation

*As you saw on the previous few pages, several factors cause the loss of biodiversity — but luckily we have ways of conserving species. Maintaining biodiversity is important for many reasons, but the main ones are ecological, economic and aesthetic.*

## Ecological reasons to maintain biodiversity

The ecological reasons for maintaining biodiversity are all down to the complex relationships between organisms and their environments.

### Protecting species

An ecosystem is all the organisms living in an area and all the non-living conditions, e.g. temperature. Organisms in an ecosystem are **interdependent** — they depend on each other to survive. This means that the loss of just one species can have pretty drastic effects on an ecosystem, such as:

- Disruption of food chains.

> **Example**
> Some species of bear feed on salmon, which feed on herring. If the number of herring decline it can affect both the salmon and the bear populations.

- Disruption of nutrient cycles.

> **Example**
> Decomposers like worms improve the quality of soil by recycling nutrients. If worm numbers decline, soil quality will be affected. This will affect the growth of plants and the amount of food available to animals.

There are some species on which many of the other species in an ecosystem depend and without which the ecosystem would change dramatically — these are called **keystone species**. Keystone species tend to have a relatively low population size but a huge effect on the environment. Keystone species are often predators, keeping the population of prey in check.

> **Example**
> The wolf is a keystone species in America. Wolf populations were eliminated in most American states during the 20th century. Without the wolves to hunt them, elk populations increased, leading to overgrazing. This led to the loss of plant species, as well as the loss of species that depend on those plants such as beavers and songbirds. The situation has since been reversed in some national parks.

Keystone species can also be modifiers — maintaining the environment needed for the ecosystem (e.g. beavers building dams), or hosts — plants that provide a particular environment, such as palm trees.

### Maintaining genetic resources

Genetic resources refer to any material from plants, animals or microorganisms, containing genes, that we find valuable. Genetic resources could be crops, plants used for medicines, microorganisms used in industrial processes, or animal breeds. We need to maintain genetic resources for several reasons (see next page).

---

**Learning Objectives:**

- Understand the ecological reasons for maintaining biodiversity, including protecting keystone species (interdependence of organisms) and maintaining genetic resources.
- Understand the economic reasons for maintaining biodiversity, including reducing soil depletion from continuous monoculture.
- Understand the aesthetic reasons for maintaining biodiversity, including protecting landscapes.
- Understand *in situ* conservation methods for maintaining biodiversity, including the importance of marine conservation zones and wildlife reserves.
- Understand *ex situ* methods of maintaining biodiversity including the importance of seed banks, botanic gardens and zoos.
- Know of international and local conservation agreements made to protect species and habitats, including the Convention on International Trade in Endangered Species (CITES), the Rio Convention on Biological Diversity (CBD) and the Countryside Stewardship Scheme (CSS).

**Specification Reference 4.2.1**

- Genetic resources provide us with a variety of everyday products, such as:

  **Examples**
  - Food and drink — plants and animals are the source of almost all food and some drinks.
  - Clothing — a lot of fibres and fabrics are made from plants and animals (e.g. cotton from plants and leather from animals).
  - Drugs — many are made from compounds from plants (e.g. the painkiller morphine is made from poppies).
  - Fuels — we use a number of organisms to produce renewable fuels, including ethanol and biogas. Fossil fuels are non-renewable (they'll run out), so other sources are of major economic importance.
  - Other industrial materials — a huge variety of other materials are produced from plant and animal species, including wood, paper, dyes, adhesives, oils, rubber and chemicals such as pesticides.

- Genetic resources also allow us to adapt to changes in the environment.

  **Example**
  Climate change (see page 257) may mean that some crops won't be able to grow in the same areas as they do now, e.g. there might be droughts in those areas. However, we may be able to use genes from a plant that's resistant to drought to genetically engineer a drought-resistant crop — that's if we have such genetic resources to choose from.

**Tip:** It's important to conserve all the organisms we currently use to make products, as well as those we don't currently use — they may provide us with new products in the future, e.g. new medicine.

## Economic reasons to maintain biodiversity

Many of the genetic resources described above are important to the global economy. Products derived from plant and animal species are traded on a local and global scale. There are also other economic reasons for maintaining biodiversity, such as:

### Reducing soil depletion

Monoculture is growing a single variety of a single crop (see p. 257). Continuous monoculture involves planting the same crop in the same field without interruption. So, for example, a corn crop will be planted in a field and when that crop is harvested, another corn crop will be planted pretty much straight away. Continuous monoculture causes soil depletion because the nutrients required by the crop are gradually used up. (In more traditional farming methods crops are rotated with other types of crops, so that the nutrients and organic matter are replaced.) The economic costs of soil depletion include increased spending on fertilisers (to artificially replace nutrients) and decreased yields (in the long run and if fertilisers are not used).

**Tip:** 'Yield' is the amount of a crop produced.

## Aesthetic reasons to maintain biodiversity

Biodiversity brings joy to millions of people. Areas rich in biodiversity provide pleasant, attractive landscapes that people can enjoy. By maintaining biodiversity we protect these beautiful landscapes. The more biodiversity in an area, the more visitors the area is likely to attract — this also has economic advantages.

> **Example**
> At the end of the 19th century the National Trust, a conservation charity, was founded with the aim of saving the nation's heritage and open spaces. It now owns and protects many areas of outstanding natural beauty, including parts of the Lake District in Cumbria.

*Figure 1: Wastwater in the Lake District is owned and cared for by the National Trust.*

### Practice Question — Application
A prairie is a large area of grassland, common in North America. Prairie dogs are small rodents that live in networks of underground burrows on prairies. They are a food source for several larger animals and birds of prey. The burrows they dig provide nests for other species, such as the burrowing owl, and their digging helps to circulate air through the soil, maintaining soil quality for plant growth. Prairie dogs are considered to be a keystone species.

Q1 Explain why prairie dogs are considered to be a keystone species and suggest what effects their removal would have on the prairie ecosystem.

*Figure 2: A prairie dog.*

## Maintaining biodiversity through conservation

Biodiversity can be maintained through conservation — the protection and management of species and habitats. Conservation is important to ensure the survival of **endangered species** — species which are at risk of extinction because of a low population, or a threatened habitat. A species that is critically endangered is likely to become extinct because its population size is too small.

**Exam Tip**
If you're asked to define 'critically endangered' in the exam, make sure you emphasise that the species is <u>likely</u> to die out.

## Types of conservation
There are two main types of conservation:

### 1. *In situ* conservation
*In situ* conservation means conservation on site — it involves protecting species in their natural habitat. Methods of *in situ* conservation include:

- Establishing protected areas such as national parks and wildlife reserves (also known as nature reserves) — habitats and species are protected in these areas by restricting urban development, industrial development and farming. A similar idea has been introduced to sea ecosystems with Marine Conservation Zones, where human activities (like fishing) are controlled.
- Controlling or preventing the introduction of species that threaten local biodiversity. For example, grey squirrels are not native to Britain. They compete with the native red squirrel and have caused a population decline. So they're controlled in some areas.
- Protecting habitats — e.g. controlling water levels to conserve wetlands and coppicing (trimming trees) to conserve woodlands. This allows organisms to continue living in their natural habitat.
- Restoring damaged areas — such as a coastline polluted by an oil spill.

Module 4: Section 2 Biodiversity

**Tip:** There are lots of laws that help to conserve biodiversity. For example, European Protected Species are legally protected throughout Europe.

- Promoting particular species — this could be by protecting food sources or nesting sites.
- Giving legal protection to endangered species, e.g. making it illegal to kill them.

### Advantages and disadvantages

The advantage of *in situ* conservation is that often both the species and their habitat are conserved. This means that larger populations can be protected and it's less disruptive than removing organisms from their habitats. The chances of the population recovering are also greater than with *ex situ* methods (see below). But it can be difficult to control some factors that are threatening a species (such as poaching, predators, disease or climate change).

**Tip:** Remember, in *in situ* conservation species stay *in* their natural habitat, whereas in *ex situ* conservation species *exit* their natural habitat.

## 2. *Ex situ* conservation

*Ex situ* conservation means conservation off site — it involves protecting a species by removing part of the population from a threatened habitat and placing it in a new location. *Ex situ* conservation is often a last resort. Methods of *ex situ* conservation include:

- Relocating an organism to a safer area, e.g. some white rhinos have been relocated from the Congo to Kenya because they were in danger from poachers who kill them for their ivory.
- Breeding organisms in captivity then reintroducing them to the wild when they are strong enough, e.g. sea eagles have been reintroduced to Britain through a captive breeding programme. Breeding is carried out in animal sanctuaries and zoos.
- Botanic gardens are controlled environments used to grow a variety of rare plants for the purposes of conservation, research, display and education. Endangered plant species as well as species that are extinct in the wild can be grown and reintroduced into suitable habitats.
- Seed banks — seeds can be frozen and stored in seed banks for over a century without losing their fertility. Seed banks provide a useful source of seeds if natural reserves are destroyed, for example by disease or other natural disasters.

*Figure 3:* Sea eagles have been reintroduced to Britain.

*Figure 4:* Lots of threatened plant species are preserved at the Royal Botanic Gardens.

**Tip:** When species are conserved *ex situ*, it's important to make sure that there is enough genetic variation in the population to improve their chances of, e.g. surviving a disease.

### Advantages and disadvantages

The advantages of *ex situ* conservation are that it can be used to protect individual animals in a controlled environment — things like predation and hunting can be managed more easily. Competition for resources can be reduced, and it's possible to check on the health of individuals and treat them for diseases. Breeding can also be manipulated, e.g. through the use of reproductive hormones and IVF. Finally, it can be used to reintroduce species that have left an area.

But, there are disadvantages — usually only a small number of individuals can be cared for. It can be difficult and expensive to create and sustain the right environment. In fact, animals that are habituated (used to) human contact may be less likely to exhibit natural behaviour and may be more likely to catch a disease from humans. *Ex situ* conservation is usually less successful than *in situ* methods — many species can't breed successfully in captivity, or don't adapt to their new environment when moved to a new location.

Module 4: Section 2 Biodiversity

# Conservation and international cooperation

Conservation is much more likely to be successful when countries work together. For example, some endangered species are found in lots of countries, so it'd be pointless making hunting a species illegal in one country if poachers could just go and hunt them in another. Information about threats to biodiversity needs to be shared and countries need to decide on conservation methods and implement them together. Here are a couple of examples of successful international cooperation:

### Rio Convention on Biological Diversity (CBD)

The Rio Convention on Biological Diversity is an international agreement that aims to develop international strategies on the conservation of biodiversity and how to use animal and plant resources in a sustainable way. The convention made it part of international law that conserving biodiversity is everyone's responsibility. It also provides guidance to governments on how to conserve biodiversity.

**Tip:** Using resources in a sustainable way means they'll still be around for future generations to use.

### CITES Agreement

CITES (Convention on International Trade in Endangered Species) is an agreement designed to increase international cooperation in regulating trade in wild animal and plant specimens. The member countries all agreed to make it illegal to kill endangered species. The agreement helps to conserve species by limiting trade through licensing, and by making it illegal to trade in products made from endangered animals (such as rhino ivory and leopard skins). It's also designed to raise awareness of threats to biodiversity through education.

#### Example
Between 1979 and 1989 the number of African elephants dropped from around 1.3 million to around 600 000 because they were being hunted for their ivory tusks. In 1989, the CITES banned ivory trade to end the demand for elephant tusks so that fewer elephants would be killed for their tusks. The population of elephants in Kenya has doubled since 1989 and elephant populations in some countries, like Botswana, have been downgraded to a less endangered status.

*Figure 5: A decline in elephant populations due to hunting for their ivory tusks has led to a ban on the sale of ivory.*

## Local conservation agreements

Whilst international cooperation is important, schemes at the local level are vital too. Here is an example from the UK:

### The Countryside Stewardship Scheme (CSS)

The Countryside Stewardship Scheme was introduced in 1991. Some of its aims were to conserve wildlife and biodiversity, and to improve and extend wildlife habitats by promoting specific management techniques to landowners. The Government offered 10-year agreements to pay landowners who followed the management techniques they were suggesting. For example, to regenerate hedgerows, to leave grassy margins around the edges of fields where wildflowers could grow, and to graze upland areas to keep down bracken. In the year 2000, there were 10 000 agreements in England. Since the introduction of the scheme, various species have begun to rebuild in numbers, including birds such as the stone curlew, black grouse and bittern.

*Figure 6: An Australian Northern Quoll.*

**Tip:** Take a look back at the start of the topic if you need a reminder about economic reasons for conservation.

## Practice Questions — Application

Q1 The Northern Quoll is an endangered species in Australia. The population has declined due to the cane toad which was introduced to control a pest in sugarcane fields. Some conservationists are exploring preserving the Northern Quoll *in situ* by eradicating cane toads, whereas others are considering conserving them in a nature reserve. Sugarcane is an important crop in Australia.

a) i) Suggest an advantage of *in situ* over *ex situ* conservation of the Northern Quoll.

ii) Suggest an advantage of *ex situ* over *in situ* conservation of the Northern Quoll.

b) Suggest the potential economic impact of the *in situ* conservation of the Northern Quoll.

## Practice Questions — Fact Recall

Q1 Describe the ecological reasons why it is important to maintain biodiversity.

Q2 Give one:
a) economic reason for maintaining biodiversity.
b) aesthetic reason for maintaining biodiversity.

Q3 What is conservation?

Q4 a) Define *in situ* conservation.
b) Give two examples of methods used in *in situ* conservation.

Q5 a) Define *ex situ* conservation.
b) Give two examples of methods used in *ex situ* conservation.
c) Give one disadvantage of *ex situ* conservation over *in situ* conservation.

Q6 What is the Rio Convention on Biological Diversity (CBD)?

Q7 What is the CITES agreement?

Q8 Give two examples of management techniques suggested in the Countryside Stewardship Scheme (CSS).

## Section Summary

Make sure you know:
- That biodiversity can be explored at the levels of habitat biodiversity (the number of different habitats in an area), species diversity (the number of different species and the abundance of each species in an area) and genetic diversity (the variation of alleles within a species or a population of a species).
- How to use sampling as a way of collecting data on biodiversity without having to count each individual organism in a habitat.
- That sampling can be random or non-random and that practical investigations can be carried out in the field by collecting random and non-random samples.
- How to carry out random sampling by using a grid and a random number generator, so that each random sample site has the same probability of being chosen.

- How to carry out non-random sampling to ensure all different areas in a habitat are sampled, including how to use systematic, opportunistic and stratified sampling.
- The different techniques that can be used to collect samples of organisms, including the use of pitfall traps, pooters, Tullgren funnels, kick sampling and sweep nets.
- That species richness refers to the number of different species in an area and is measured by taking random samples of a habitat and counting the number of different species.
- That species evenness is a measure of the relative abundance of each species in an area and is measured by taking random samples of a habitat and counting the number of individuals of each different species.
- How to calculate Simpson's Index of Diversity using the formula: $D = 1 - (\Sigma(n/N)^2)$
- That habitats with a high Index of Diversity (a value close to 1) have a high biodiversity.
- That habitats with a low Index of Diversity (a value close to 0) are less stable and have a lower ability to cope with change, e.g. the introduction of a new predator, than areas of high biodiversity.
- That it is important to measure genetic diversity within isolated populations, e.g. zoos, rare breed populations and populations of pedigree animals.
- How to calculate genetic biodiversity using the formula: proportion of polymorphic gene loci = number of polymorphic gene loci ÷ total number of loci, and how to convert this into a percentage.
- That human population growth has affected biodiversity through habitat loss, over-exploitation, urbanisation and pollution.
- That monoculture has affected biodiversity through habitat loss, loss of local plants and animals and loss of heritage varieties.
- That climate change has affected biodiversity through changing environmental conditions.
- That maintaining biodiversity is important for ecological reasons (including protecting keystone species and maintaining genetic resources), economic reasons (including reducing soil depletion caused by continuous monoculture) and aesthetic reasons (including protecting landscapes).
- That *in situ* conservation involves protecting species in their natural habitat, whereas *ex situ* conservation involves protecting a species by moving part of a population from a threatened habitat and placing it in a new location.
- That *in situ* conservation includes establishing protected areas, such as wildlife reserves and marine conservation zones.
- That *ex situ* conservation includes breeding organisms in captivity (e.g. in zoos), then reintroducing them to the wild, and conserving organisms in botanic gardens and seed banks.
- That the Rio Convention on Biological Diversity (CBD) is an international agreement that aims to develop international strategies in the conservation of biodiversity and how to use animal and plant resources in a sustainable way.
- That the CITES (Convention on International Trade in Endangered Species) is an agreement designed to increase international cooperation in regulating trade in wild animal and plant specimens.
- That the Countryside Stewardship Scheme (CSS) is a local agreement to conserve wildlife and biodiversity by promoting specific management techniques to landowners.

# Exam-style Questions

**1** Domestic sheep are all members of the species *Ovis aries*. There are over 200 breeds of domestic sheep. The existence of these different breeds is an example of which type of diversity?

    **A** habitat diversity

    **B** genetic diversity

    **C** species diversity

    **D** breeding diversity

*(1 mark)*

**2** A student is investigating the species diversity of insects in a 500 m² area of woodland.

The student sampled the insect population by arranging a series of covered pitfall traps in the ground. The student arranged the traps in a straight line along the edge of the woodland and left them overnight before coming back to count the insects she had caught.

**(a)** Explain what is meant by the term 'species diversity'.

*(2 marks)*

**(b)** Give **two** reasons why the student did not obtain a representative sample of insects living in the woodland.

*(2 marks)*

**(c)** The student found that the woodland had a low species evenness.
What does a low species evenness tell you about a habitat?

*(1 mark)*

**(d)** The student wants to compare the species diversity of insects in the woodland with the species diversity of insects on her local common.

Suggest **one** thing the student must do when sampling insects on the common to ensure that her findings from both habitats are comparable.

*(1 mark)*

**3\*** Polar bears are a keystone species that play an important role in the maintenance of the Arctic ecosystem. They use the ice sheets that surround the Arctic shoreline to hunt for their main prey, seals. This helps to keep the populations of seals in check and also provides leftover food for scavengers such as the Arctic fox and Arctic birds.

Suggest and explain the effect climate change might have on the population of polar bears and the effect this might have on the Arctic ecosystem.

*(6 marks)*

\*The quality of your response will be assessed in this question.

**4** A company wishes to clear part of a wood next to a town and build a new housing estate on the land. A study was conducted on the trees found in the town centre and in the wood. The results are shown in **Fig. 4.1**.

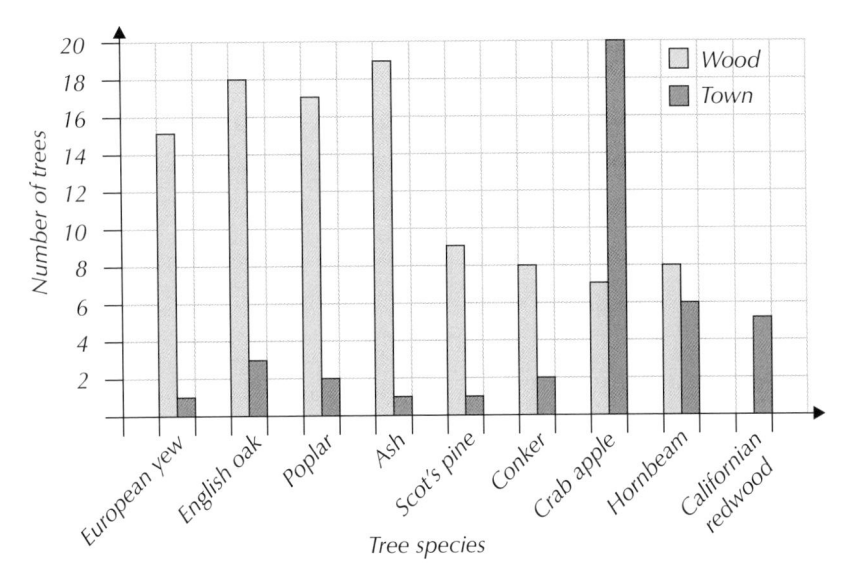

**Fig. 4.1**

**(a)** Simpson's Index of Diversity can be calculated using the following equation:

$$D = 1 - (\sum (n/N)^2)$$

where $n$ = Total number of organisms in one species
$N$ = Total number of all organisms

Use the data in **Fig. 4.1** and the formula provided above to calculate Simpson's Index of Diversity for trees in the wood and in the town.

*(4 marks)*

**(b)** Explain what your answers to part **(a)** tell you about the town habitat and the woodland habitat.

*(2 marks)*

**(c)** The company discovers that the wood supports a small population of red squirrels, which are an endangered species.

Suggest **two** conservation measures that could be undertaken to protect the wood's red squirrel population if the development project goes ahead.

*(2 marks)*

# Module 4 Section 3: Classification and Evolution

### Learning Objectives:
- Understand the biological classification of species, including the taxonomic hierarchy of domain, kingdom, phylum, class, order, family, genus and species.
- Understand the binomial system of naming species and the advantage of such a system.
- Know the features used to classify organisms into the five kingdoms: Prokaryotae, Protoctista, Fungi, Plantae, Animalia.
- Understand the relationship between classification and phylogeny.

Specification Reference 4.2.2

**Tip:** There's more on domains on page 273.

**Exam Tip**
You need to learn the names and order of the taxonomic groups. If you're struggling to remember the order, try this mnemonic...

<u>D</u>aft <u>K</u>ids <u>P</u>refer <u>C</u>hips <u>O</u>ver <u>F</u>loppy <u>G</u>reen <u>S</u>pinach.

## 1. Classification Basics

*Scientists group organisms together to make them easier to study.*

### What is classification?

Classification is the act of arranging organisms into groups based on their similarities and differences. This makes it easier for scientists to identify them and to study them. **Taxonomy** is the study of classification. There are a few different classification systems in use, but they all involve placing organisms into groups in a **taxonomic hierarchy**.

In the hierarchy you need to know about, there are eight levels of groups (called taxonomic groups). Similar organisms are first sorted into one of three very large groups called domains, e.g. animals, plants and fungi are in the Eukarya domain. Similar organisms are then sorted into slightly smaller groups called kingdoms, e.g. all animals are in the animal kingdom (Animalia). Similar organisms from that kingdom are then grouped into a phylum. Similar organisms from each phylum are then grouped into a class, and so on down the eight levels of the taxonomic hierarchy. This is illustrated in Figure 1.

Domain
Kingdom
Phylum
Class
Order
Family
Genus
Species

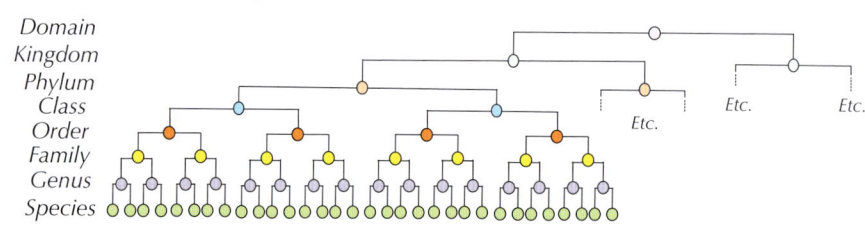

**Figure 1:** *A diagram illustrating the eight taxonomic groups used in classification.*

**Example — the classification of humans**
Domain = *Eukarya*, Kingdom = *Animalia*, Phylum = *Chordata*,
Class = *Mammalia*, Order = *Primates*, Family = *Hominidae*,
Genus = *Homo*, Species = *sapiens*.

As you move down the hierarchy, there are more groups at each level but fewer organisms in each group. The hierarchy ends with species — the groups that contain only one type of organism (e.g. humans, dogs, *E. coli* and about 50 million other living species).

### Naming species

The nomenclature (naming system) used for classification is called the **binomial system** — all organisms are given one internationally accepted scientific name in Latin that has two parts.

The first part of the name is the genus name and has a capital letter. The second part is the species name and begins with a lower case letter. Names are always written in *italics* (or they're <u>underlined</u> if they're handwritten).

**Examples**
Humans are *Homo sapiens* — the genus is *Homo* and the species is *sapiens*.
Dogs are *Canis familiaris* — the genus is *Canis* and the species is *familiaris*.
Cats are *Felis catus* — the genus is *Felis* and the species is *catus*.

The binomial system helps to avoid the confusion of using common names.

**Example**
Americans call a type of bird cockatoos and Australians call them flaming galahs, but it's the same bird. If the correct scientific name is used — *Eolophus roseicapillus* — there's no confusion.

**Tip:** In Latin names the genus is often shortened to the first letter. E.g. *E. coli* is short for *Escherichia coli* — *Escherichia* is the genus and *coli* is the species.

## The five kingdoms
The five kingdom classification system is a bit old now (see page 273), but you still need to learn these five kingdoms and the general characteristics of the organisms in each of them:

### Prokaryotae
**Example:** bacteria
**Features:** prokaryotic, unicellular (single-celled), no nucleus, less than 5 μm

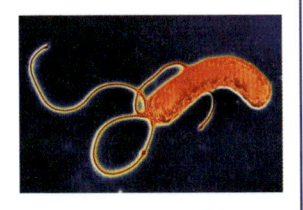

**Tip:** Remember, prokaryotes don't have a nucleus, eukaryotes do. There's more on the differences between prokaryotes and eukaryotes on page 46.

### Protoctista
**Examples:** algae, protozoa
**Features:** eukaryotic cells, usually live in water, single-celled or simple multicellular organisms

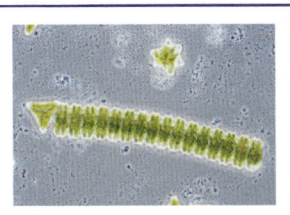

**Exam Tip**
Make sure you can spell the names of the different kingdoms — Latin words are tricky, but if you get them wrong, the examiners might not know what you mean and you could miss out on marks. Watch out for Prot**oct**ista in particular.

### Fungi
**Examples:** moulds, yeasts, mushrooms
**Features:** eukaryotic, chitin cell wall, saprotrophic (absorb substances from dead or decaying organisms), single-celled or multicellular organisms

### Plantae
**Examples:** mosses, ferns, flowering plants
**Features:** eukaryotic, multicellular, cell walls made of cellulose, can photosynthesise, contain chlorophyll, autotrophic (produce their own food)

**Tip:** Plants are also known as photoautotrophs — they produce their own food using light.

### Animalia
**Examples:** nematodes (roundworms), molluscs, insects, fish, reptiles, birds, mammals
**Features:** eukaryotic, multicellular, no cell walls, heterotrophic (consume plants and animals)

**Exam Tip**
Always use the proper scientific terms where you can — e.g. write 'autotrophic' not 'produces own food' in the exam.

Module 4: Section 3 Classification and Evolution

**Tip:** Sharing a common ancestry means that you have some of the same ancestors (relatives from previous generations). Some organisms share more recent common ancestors than others.

# Phylogeny

Evolution is the gradual change in organisms over time — see page 287. It has led to a huge variety of different organisms on Earth, all of which share a common ancestry. **Phylogeny** is the study of the evolutionary history of groups of organisms. Phylogeny tells us who's related to whom and how closely related they are. This can be shown on a phylogenetic tree, like the one in Figure 2.

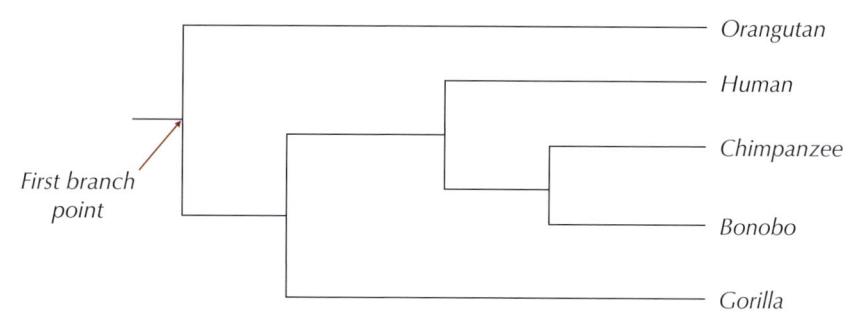

*Figure 2: Phylogenetic tree of the Hominidae family.*

This tree shows the relationship between members of the Hominidae family (great apes and humans). The first branch point represents a common ancestor of all the family members. This ancestor is now extinct. Orangutans were the first group to diverge (evolve to become a different species) from this common ancestor. Each of the following branch points represents another common ancestor from which a different group diverged. Gorillas diverged next, then humans, closely followed by bonobos and chimpanzees.

According to phylogenetics, a **species** is the smallest group that shares a common ancestor — in other words, the end of a branch on a phylogenetic tree. Closely related species diverged away from each other most recently. E.g. humans and chimpanzees are closely related, as they diverged very recently. You can see this because their branches are close together. Humans and orangutans are more distantly related, as they diverged longer ago, so their branches are further apart.

Classification systems now take into account phylogeny when arranging organisms into groups. Classifying organisms in this way is known as **cladistics**.

*Figure 3: Orangutans, chimps and gorillas are all closely related.*

**Tip:** The groups at the ends of the branches on this phylogenetic tree aren't actually individual species (e.g. sharks are a group of several different species). That's because the tree has been simplified — if it continued to species level, it would be huge.

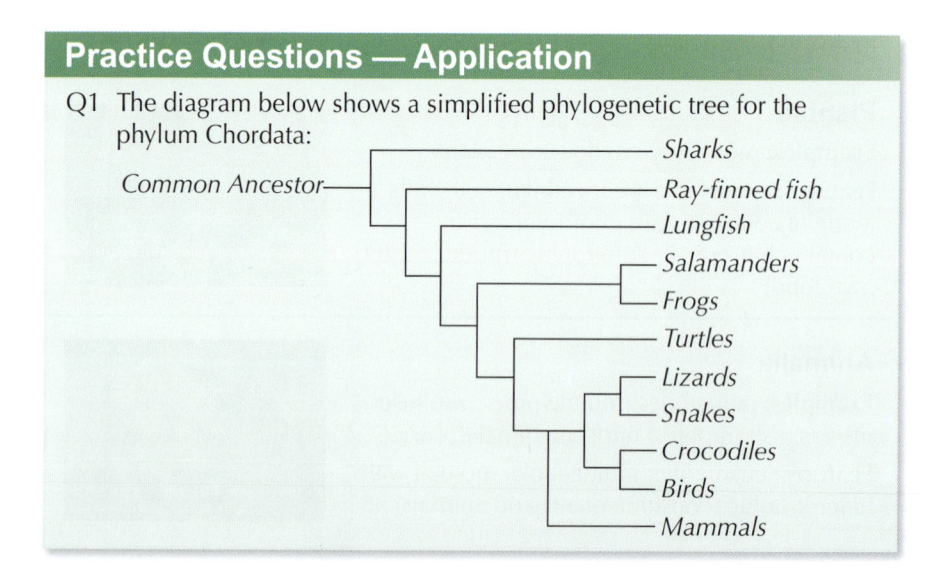

## Practice Questions — Application

Q1  The diagram below shows a simplified phylogenetic tree for the phylum Chordata:

270   Module 4: Section 3   Classification and Evolution

a) Which group was first to diverge from the common ancestor?
b) Are frogs more closely related to salamanders or turtles?
c) To which other group are:
   (i) birds most closely related?
   (ii) snakes most closely related?

Q2 Donkeys are part of the phylum Chordata.
The binomial name for donkeys is *Equus asinus*.
Complete the table below for the classification of the donkey.

| Taxonomic Group | |
|---|---|
| | Eukarya |
| Kingdom | Animalia |
| | |
| Class | Mammalia |
| Order | Perrisodactyla |
| Family | Equidae |
| | |
| | |

**Tip:** It might surprise you that some organisms are closely related — but just because you can't see a similarity in their features doesn't mean the phylogenetic tree is wrong.

## Practice Questions — Fact Recall

Q1 What is classification?
Q2 Describe how organisms are named using the binomial system.
Q3 Give three characteristics of the kingdom Plantae.
Q4 According to phylogenetics, what is a species?

**Learning Objectives:**
- Recall the use of similarities in observable features in original classification.
- Recall the evidence that has led to new classification systems (such as the three domains of life, which clarifies relationships), including the more recent use of similarities in biological molecules and other genetic evidence.
- Know the details of the three domains and a comparison of the kingdom and domain classification systems.

**Specification Reference 4.2.2**

**Tip:** Molecular evidence is sometimes referred to as biochemical evidence.

**Tip:** There's more on DNA bases on page 88.

# 2. The Evolution of Classification Systems

*Classification systems aren't set in stone. Like living organisms, they evolve...*

## Evidence for classification

Early classification systems only used observable features (things you can see) to place organisms into groups. Observable features can be anatomical (structural), e.g. how many legs an organism has, or behavioural, e.g. whether an organism lives in groups. But this method has problems. Scientists don't always agree on the relative importance of different features and groups based solely on physical features may not show how related organisms are.

--- Example ---
Sharks and whales look quite similar and they both live in the sea. But they're not actually closely related — sharks are cartilaginous fish (meaning they have skeletons made of cartilage instead of bone), whereas whales are vertebrate mammals (they have a backbone) — they're from two completely different classes.

Classification systems are now based on observable features along with other evidence. This evidence tells us how similar, and therefore how closely related, organisms are. The types of evidence taxonomists look at include embryological evidence (the similarities in the early stages of an organism's development), fossil evidence and molecular evidence.

### Molecular evidence

Gathering molecular evidence involves analysing the similarities in proteins and DNA. More closely related organisms will have more similar molecules. You can compare things like how DNA is stored and the sequence of DNA bases.

--- Example ---
The diagram below shows part of the DNA base sequence for gene X in three different species...

Species A:   ATTGTCTGATTGGTGCTAGTCGTCGATGCTAGGTCG

Species B:   ATTGT<u>A</u>TGATTGGTGCTAGTCG<u>G</u>CGATGCTAGGTCG

Species C:   ATTG<u>A</u>TTGA<u>AA</u>GG<u>A</u>GCTA<u>C</u>TCGT<u>A</u>GAT<u>ATA</u>AGG<u>GGT</u>

There are 13 differences between the base sequences in species A and C, but only 2 differences between the base sequences in species A and B. This suggests that species A and B are more closely related than A and C.

You can also compare the sequence of amino acids in proteins from different organisms.

--- Example ---
Cytochrome C is a short protein found in many species. The more similar the amino acid sequence of cytochrome C in two different species, the more closely related the species are likely to be.

## Changing the classification of organisms

New technologies (e.g. new DNA analysis techniques, better microscopes) can result in new discoveries being made. Scientists can share their new discoveries in meetings and scientific journals. How organisms are classified is continually revised to take account of any new findings that scientists discover.

**Tip:** There's more on how and why scientists share their findings on page 2.

— Example —
Skunks were classified in the family Mustelidae until molecular evidence revealed their DNA sequence was significantly different to other members of that family. So they were reclassified into the family Mephitidae.

## Five kingdoms vs three domains

The five kingdom classification system shown on page 269 has now been replaced with the three domain system. In the older system, the largest groups were the five kingdoms — all organisms were placed into one of these groups (see Figure 1).

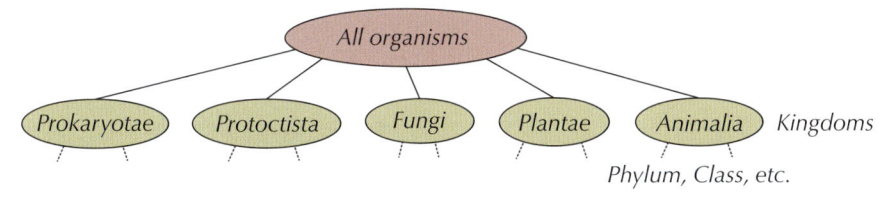

**Figure 1:** A diagram illustrating the top tier of the five kingdom system.

In 1990, the three domain system was proposed. This new system has three domains — large superkingdoms that are above the kingdoms in the taxonomic hierarchy (see Figure 2).

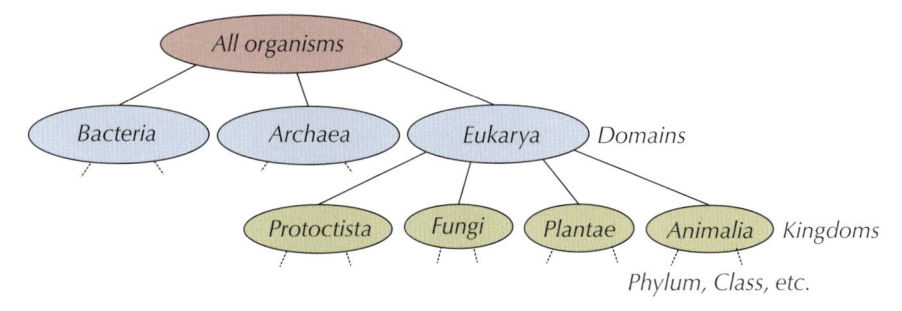

**Figure 2:** A diagram illustrating the top two tiers of the three domain system.

In the three domain system, organisms that were in the kingdom Prokaryotae (which contains unicellular organisms without a nucleus) are separated into two domains — the Archaea and Bacteria. Organisms with cells that contain a nucleus are placed in the domain Eukarya (this includes four of the five kingdoms). The lower hierarchy stays the same — Kingdom, Phylum, Class, Order, Family, Genus, Species. The three domain system was proposed because of new evidence, mainly molecular.

— Examples —
The Prokaryotae were reclassified into two domains because new evidence showed large differences between the Archaea and Bacteria.

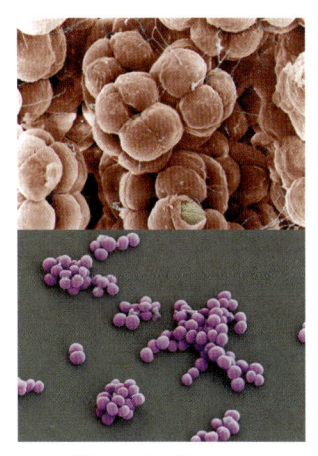

**Figure 3:** Electron micrographs of an Archaea species (top) and a Bacteria species (bottom). Archaea and Bacteria often look very similar, but are biochemically different.

Module 4: Section 3 Classification and Evolution     273

The new evidence included:

**Molecular evidence**:

The enzyme RNA polymerase (needed to make RNA) is different in Bacteria and Archaea. Archaea, but not Bacteria, have similar histones (proteins that bind to DNA) to Eukarya.

**Cellular evidence**:

The bonds of the lipids (see page 66) in the cell membranes of Bacteria and Archaea are different. The development and composition of flagellae (see page 42) are also different.

Most scientists now agree that Archaea and Bacteria evolved separately and that Archaea are more closely related to Eukarya than Bacteria. The three domain system reflects how different the Archaea and Bacteria are.

The development of the three domain system is an example of how scientific knowledge is always changing and improving (see page 2).

## Practice Questions — Application

The graph below illustrates the sequence of a small stretch of DNA in 3 different species:

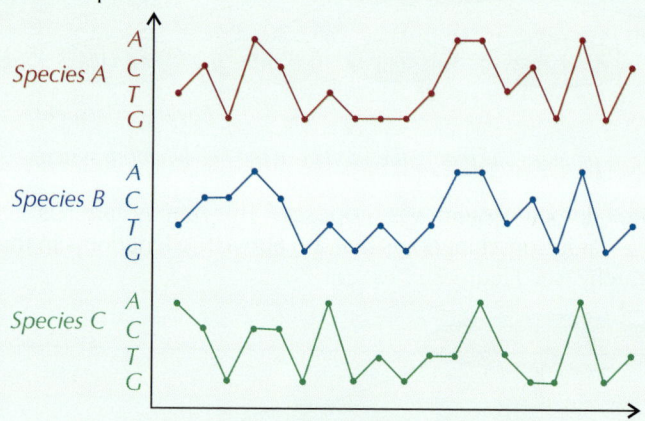

*Distance along gene sequence (bp)*

**Tip:** The distance along the gene sequence on the diagram is given as 'bp' — base pairs.

Q1 Using the graph, write down the base sequence for this stretch of DNA in each of the three species.

Q2 In how many places do the base sequences of species A and B differ?

Q3 In how many places do the base sequences of species A and C differ?

Q4 Is species A more closely related to species B or species C? Explain your answer.

Q5 To which of the two species is species C most closely related? Explain your answer.

## Practice Questions — Fact Recall

Q1 Explain how proteins can be used to help classify organisms.

Q2 Describe the three domain system of classification.

Q3 Describe one piece of evidence that led to Prokaryotes being reclassified.

# 3. Variation

*All organisms vary — it's what makes each and every one of us unique.*

## What is variation?

Variation is the differences that exist between individuals. Every individual organism is unique — even clones (such as identical twins) show some variation. It can occur:

### Within species

Variation within a species is called **intraspecific** variation.

**Example**
Individual European robins weigh between 16 g and 22 g and show some variation in many other characteristics including length, wingspan, colour and beak size.

### Between species

The variation between different species is called **interspecific** variation.

**Example**
The lightest species of bird is the bee hummingbird, which weighs around 1.6 g on average. The heaviest species of bird is the ostrich, which can weigh up to 160 kg (100 000 times as much).

**Learning Objectives:**
- Understand the different types of variation, including intraspecific and interspecific variation.
- Know the differences between continuous and discontinuous variation, including examples of a range of characteristics found in plants, animals and microorganisms.
- Understand both genetic and environmental causes of variation.

**Specification Reference 4.2.2**

## Continuous variation

Continuous variation is when the individuals in a population vary within a range — there are no distinct categories.

**Examples**

**Animals**
- Height — humans can be any height within a range (e.g. 139 cm, 175 cm, 185.9 cm, etc.), not just tall or short — see Figure 1.
- Mass — humans can be any mass within a range.
- Milk yield — cows can produce any volume of milk within a range.

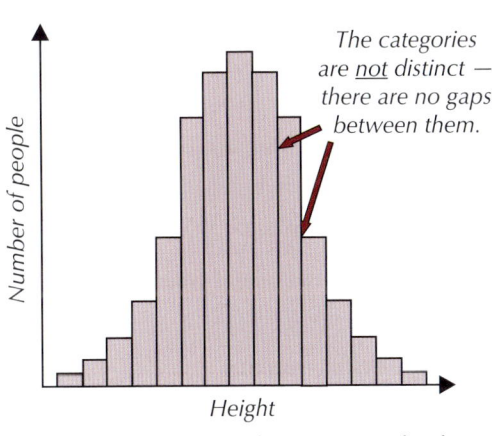

**Figure 1:** *Graph to show an example of continuous variation in humans.*

The categories are *not* distinct — there are no gaps between them.

**Plants**
- Surface area of leaves — the surface area of each of a tree's leaves can be any value within a range.
- Mass — the mass of the seeds from a flower head varies within a range.

**Microorganisms**
- Width — the width of *E. coli* bacteria varies within a range.
- Length — the length of the flagellum (see p. 42) can vary within a range.

**Tip:** Don't get inter- and intra-specific variation mixed up. If you're struggling, just remember — int**er** means diff**er**ent species and intr**a** means the s**a**me species.

**Tip:** Continuous variation can be shown by continuous data. The continuous data for height in humans is quantitative — this means it has values that can be measured with a number.

Module 4: Section 3 Classification and Evolution

**Tip:** Blood group is an example of discontinuous variation with <u>qualitative</u> data — this is data that doesn't contain any numbers.

*Figure 2: Pea seeds can be wrinkled or smooth.*

**Exam Tip**
It's worth learning the examples on this page and on page 275, as well as the meanings of continuous and discontinuous variation.

## Discontinuous variation
Discontinuous variation is when there are two or more distinct categories — each individual falls into only one of these categories, and there are no intermediates.

### Examples
**Animals**
- Blood group — humans can be group A, B, AB or O (see Figure 3).

**Plants**
- Colour — courgettes are either yellow, dark green or light green.
- Seed shape — some pea plants have smooth seeds and some have wrinkled seeds.

**Microorganisms**
- Antibiotic resistance — bacteria are either resistant or not.
- Pigment production — some types of bacteria can produce a coloured pigment, some can't.

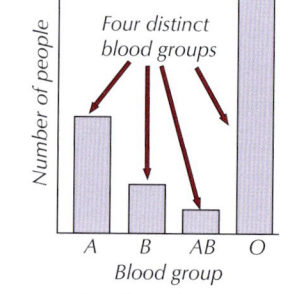

*Figure 3: Graph to show an example of discontinuous variation in humans.*

## Causes of variation
Variation can be caused by genetic factors, environmental factors or a combination of both.

### Genetic factors
Different species have different genes. Individuals of the same species have the same genes, but different versions of them (called **alleles**). The alleles an organism has make up its **genotype**. The differences in genotype result in variation in **phenotype** — the characteristics displayed by an organism.

#### Examples
Variation caused by genetic factors includes:
- Eye colour in humans (which can be blue, green, grey, brown),
- Blood type in humans (O, A, B or AB),
- Antibiotic resistance in bacteria.

You inherit your genes from your parents. This means variation caused by genetic factors is inherited.

### Environmental factors
Variation can also be caused by differences in the environment, e.g. climate, food, lifestyle. Characteristics controlled by environmental factors can change over an organism's life.

#### Examples
Variation caused only by environmental factors includes accents and whether people have pierced ears.

### Both genetic and environmental factors
Genetic factors determine the characteristics an organism's born with, but environmental factors can influence how some characteristics develop.

**Tip:** Most characteristics of an organism are determined by both genes and the environment.

Module 4: Section 3 Classification and Evolution

- Examples
  - Height — genes determine how tall an organism can grow (e.g. tall parents tend to have tall children). But diet or nutrient availability affect how tall an organism actually grows.
  - Flagellum — genes determine if a microorganism can grow a flagellum, but some will only start to grow them in certain environments, e.g. if metal ions are present.

## Practice Question — Application

Q1 A twin study was performed to determine whether head circumference is influenced mainly by environmental factors or by genetic factors. 25 pairs of identical twins were selected for the study and the mean difference in the head circumference of each pair was calculated. The same was done for 25 pairs of non-identical twins and 25 pairs of unrelated individuals of the same age. The results are shown on the right.

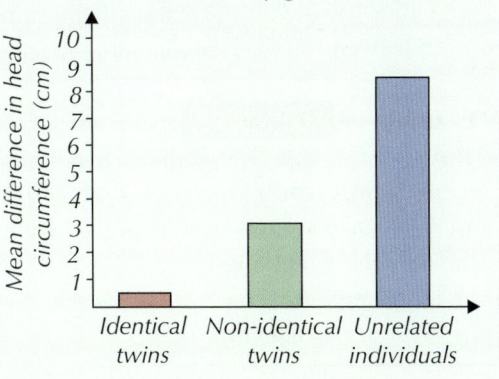

a) Is head circumference an example of continuous or discontinuous variation?
b) Describe the data.
c) Do you think that genetic or environmental factors have a larger effect on head circumference? Explain your answer.

A similar study was performed on adults to determine the effects of genetic and environmental factors on activity levels. Pairs of identical twins, pairs of non-identical twins and pairs of unrelated individuals of the same age were asked to wear a pedometer and the mean difference in steps taken per day was recorded. The results are shown on the right.

d) Explain what the results show about the role of genetics in determining activity levels.

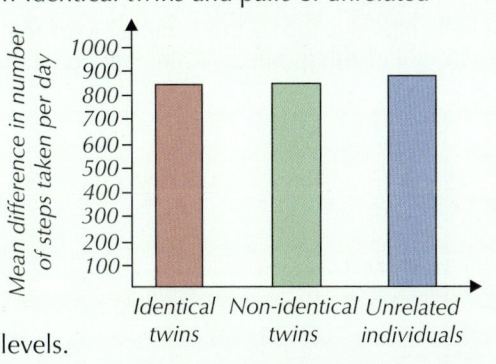

## Practice Questions — Fact Recall

Q1 What is: a) intraspecific variation? b) interspecific variation?
Q2 Describe the difference between continuous variation and discontinuous variation. Give an example of each.
Q3 Give one example of a characteristic that is influenced by both genetic factors and environmental factors.

## Learning Objectives:
- Be able to use standard deviation to measure the spread of a set of data.
- Be able to use the Spearman's rank correlation coefficient to consider the relationship of data.

**Specification Reference 4.2.2**

# 4. Investigating Variation

*To investigate variation, you usually take samples of a population. There's more on taking samples on page 249.*

## Mean and standard deviation

You can use the mean and standard deviation to measure how much variation there is in a sample.

### Mean

The mean is an average of the values collected in a sample. Find it using this formula:

$$\text{mean} = \frac{\text{total of all the values in your data}}{\text{the number of values in your data}}$$

### Example — Maths Skills

The heights of different seedlings in a group are: 6 cm, 4 cm, 7 cm, 6 cm, 5 cm, 8 cm, 7 cm, 5 cm, 7 cm and 9 cm.

To calculate the mean, add all of the heights together and divide by the number of seedlings:

Mean height = (6 + 4 + 7 + 6 + 5 + 8 + 7 + 5 + 7 + 9) ÷ 10 = 64 ÷ 10
= **6.4 cm**

**Tip:** When you calculate the mean, check that it's within the range of values that you used in the calculation. If the mean isn't within the range, you know you've calculated it wrong. E.g. the mean here should be between 4 and 9 cm.

The mean can be used to tell if there is variation between samples.

### Examples

- The mean height of a species of tree in woodland A = 26 m, woodland B = 32 m and woodland C = 35 m. So the mean height varies.
- The mean number of leaves on a clover plant in field X = 3, field Y = 3 and field Z = 3. So the mean number of leaves does not vary.

Most samples will include values either side of the mean, so you end up with a bell-shaped graph — this is called a **normal distribution** (see Figure 1). A normal distribution is symmetrical about the mean.

**Tip:** Normal distribution (symmetrical):

Not a normal distribution (skewed):

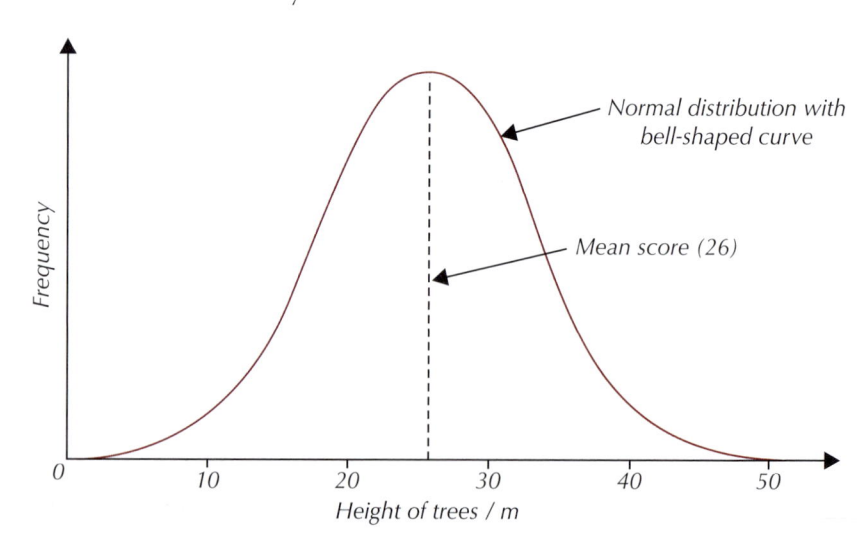

**Figure 1:** The height of trees in woodland A.

Module 4: Section 3 Classification and Evolution

## Standard deviation

The standard deviation tells you how much the values in a single sample vary. It's a measure of the spread of values about the mean. Sometimes you'll see the mean written as, for example, 9 ± 3. This means that the mean is 9 and the standard deviation is 3, so most of the values are spread between 6 and 12.

Both of the graphs in Figure 2 show a normal distribution. However, the values in a sample can vary a little or a lot:

*Here, all the values are similar and close to the mean — the data varies little, so the graph is steep and the standard deviation is small.*

*Here, the values vary a lot, so the graph is fatter and the standard deviation is large.*

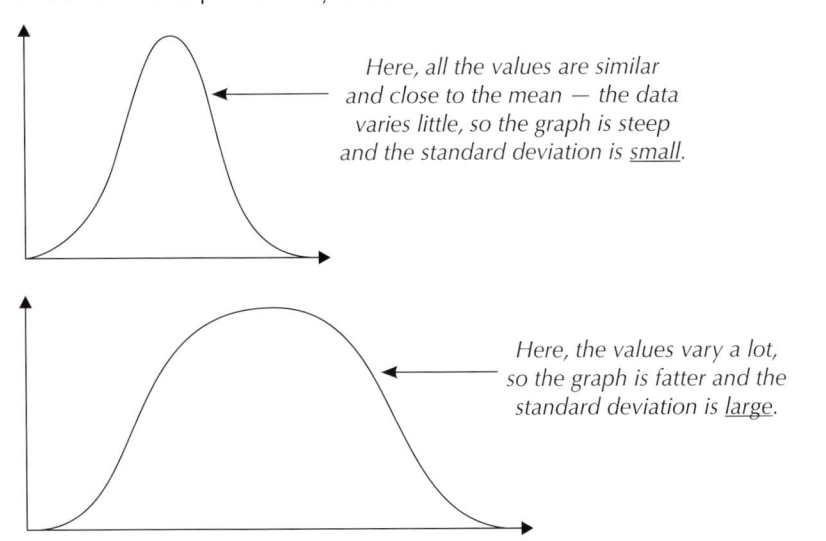

**Figure 2:** *A normal distribution curve with a small standard deviation (top) and with a large standard deviation (bottom).*

**Exam Tip**
You won't get marks for describing the standard deviation as the spread of results — it's the spread of values about the mean.

---Example---

Height of trees in woodland A:
mean = 26,
standard deviation = 3

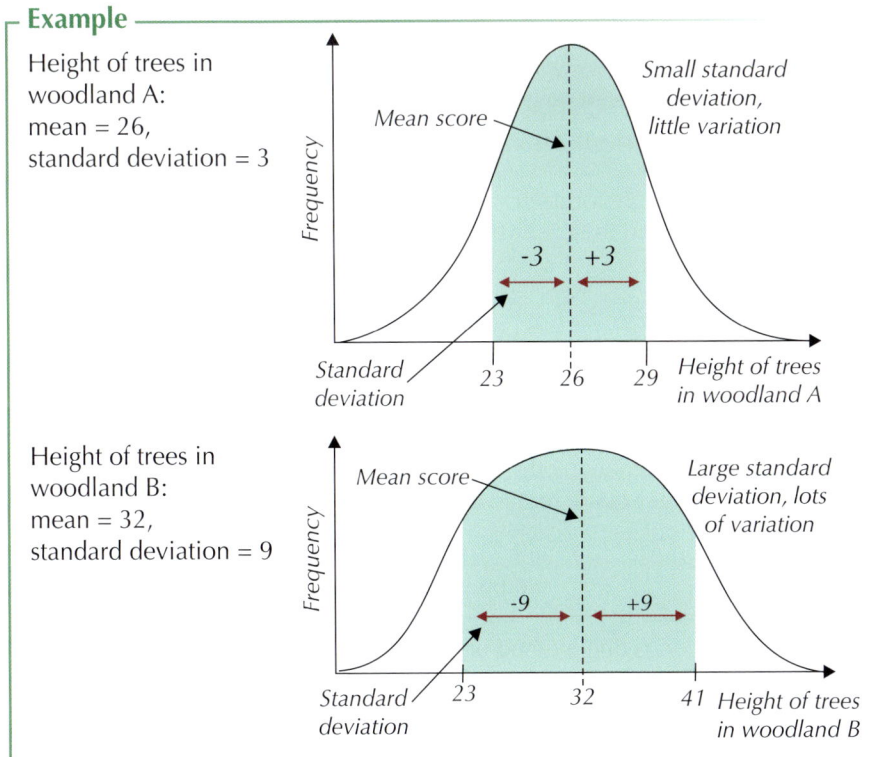

Height of trees in woodland B:
mean = 32,
standard deviation = 9

So the trees are generally taller in woodland B, but there's a greater variation in height compared to woodland A.

**Exam Tip**
You need to know how to interpret data that includes standard deviations for your exam.

**Tip:** Values with a larger standard deviation show greater variation.

Module 4: Section 3 Classification and Evolution

## Calculating standard deviation

Figure 3 shows the formula for finding the standard deviation of a group of values:

**Tip:** Standard deviation (S) can also be represented by the Greek letter sigma: 'σ'.

*'S' just stands for standard deviation.*

*This symbol is sigma — it means 'sum of'.*

*'x' stands for a value in the data set, and 'x̄' is the mean. So '$(x - \bar{x})^2$' means "take away the mean from the value, then square the result".*

$$S = \sqrt{\frac{\sum (x - \bar{x})^2}{n - 1}}$$

*Square root sign*

*'n' stands for the number of values.*

**Figure 3:** *Explanation of the formula for standard deviation.*

---

**Example — Maths Skills**

The table below shows the height of four different trees in a forest.

| Tree | Height (m) |
|------|-----------|
| A | 22 |
| B | 27 |
| C | 26 |
| D | 29 |

To find the standard deviation:

- Write out the equation:

$$S = \sqrt{\frac{\sum (x - \bar{x})^2}{n - 1}}$$

- Work out the mean height of the trees, $\bar{x}$:

  $(22 + 27 + 26 + 29) \div 4 = \mathbf{26}$

- Work out $(x - \bar{x})^2$ for each value of $x$. For each tree height in the table, you need to take away the mean, then square the answer:

  A: $(22 - 26)^2 = (-4)^2 = \mathbf{16}$   B: $(27 - 26)^2 = 1^2 = \mathbf{1}$
  C: $(26 - 26)^2 = 0^2 = \mathbf{0}$     D: $(29 - 26)^2 = 3^2 = \mathbf{9}$

- Add up all these numbers to find $\sum (x - \bar{x})^2$:

  $16 + 1 + 0 + 9 = \mathbf{26}$

- Divide this number by the number of values, $n$, minus 1. Then take the square root to get the answer:

  $26 \div 3 = 8.66...$

  $\sqrt{8.66...} = \mathbf{2.94 \text{ to 2 s.f.}}$

---

Standard deviation is one method of calculating the dispersion of data. Another method of calculating dispersion is by looking at the range — see page 11. This is simply the difference between the highest and lowest figures in the data. Standard deviation is more useful than the range because it takes into account all the values in the data set, whereas the range only uses two. This makes the range more likely to be affected by an anomalous result (an unusually high or low value in the data set) than standard deviation.

**Tip:** There's more on anomalous results on page 10.

## Practice Questions — Application

**Q1** The graph below shows the wing spans of two different species of bird, both of which live in the same area of woodland.

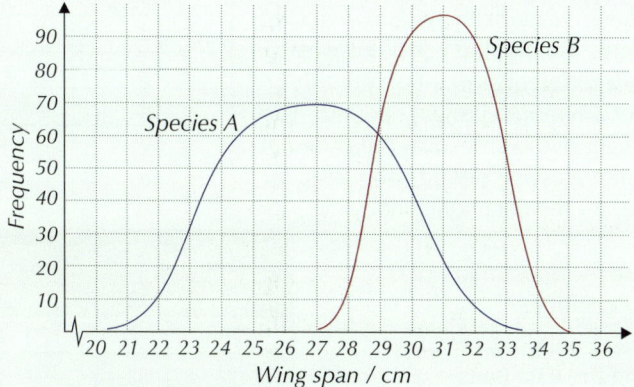

a) i) Describe the data.
   ii) Which species shows a greater variation in wingspan? Explain your answer.
   iii) Suggest a reason for the difference in wingspan between species A and B. Give a reason for your answer.
b) How much longer is species B's mean wing span than species A's? Give your answer as a percentage.

**Q2** The table on the right shows the length of five rainbow boa snakes measured by conservationists investigating the effect of habitat loss on the well-being of the species. Using the formula below, calculate the standard deviation of this data.

$$s = \sqrt{\frac{\sum (x - \bar{x})^2}{n - 1}}$$

| Snake | length (cm) |
|-------|-------------|
| A     | 177         |
| B     | 182         |
| C     | 190         |
| D     | 187         |
| E     | 191         |

**Exam Tip**
Always show your working in calculation questions — don't just guess an answer. You could pick up marks for using the correct method, even if your final answer is wrong.

# Correlations in variation

If you need to work out whether there's a correlation (relationship) between a genetic or environmental factor and variation in a particular characteristic, you can calculate the **Spearman's rank correlation coefficient** ($r_s$). As well as telling you whether or not the two variables are related, $r_s$ will tell you how strongly they're related. It uses the formula:

$$r_s = 1 - \frac{6\sum d^2}{n(n^2 - 1)}$$

where '$d$' is the 'difference in rank between data pairs' and '$n$' is the total number of data pairs

**Tip:** Spearman's rank is a type of statistical test — see page 16 for more. See page 23 for more on correlations.

The result of the test is a number between -1 and +1. If the figure is -1, then there is a perfect negative correlation between the two variables. If the figure is +1, then there's a perfect positive correlation. The closer the figure is to 0, the weaker the correlation is. It'll all become clear with an example...

### Example — Maths Skills

A team of biologists investigated how different amounts of rainfall affect the height of a particular crop.

**Tip:** The amount of rainfall received by a crop is an environmental factor. The height of the crop shows continuous variation.

Module 4: Section 3 Classification and Evolution

In a laboratory facility, they prepared 7 test fields of the crop, where all conditions needed for plant growth could be controlled. All conditions except the amount of rainfall (simulated with a sprinkler system) were kept constant. Each of the test fields was exposed to a different amount of monthly rainfall over a 6 month growing period. The average height of the crops was measured at the end of the growing period. The table on the right shows the data collected.

| Monthly Rainfall (mm) | Average height of crop (cm) |
|---|---|
| 20 | 20.1 |
| 30 | 22.3 |
| 40 | 19.9 |
| 50 | 25.7 |
| 60 | 36.3 |
| 70 | 45.2 |
| 80 | 58.1 |

**Tip:** A data pair consists of the two corresponding figures for each variable. E.g. 20 mm monthly rainfall and an average crop height of 20.1 cm make up one data pair.

To calculate the Spearman's rank correlation coefficient:

1. First, rank both sets of data, keeping the data pairs together. The highest value for each variable is given the rank of 1, the second highest value is ranked 2, etc.

| Monthly Rainfall (mm) | Rank | Average height of crop (cm) | Rank |
|---|---|---|---|
| 20 | 7 | 20.1 | 6 |
| 30 | 6 | 22.3 | 5 |
| 40 | 5 | 19.9 | 7 |
| 50 | 4 | 25.7 | 4 |
| 60 | 3 | 36.3 | 3 |
| 70 | 2 | 45.2 | 2 |
| 80 | 1 | 58.1 | 1 |

2. Then work out the difference in rank between the two values in each data pair (d) and square it to calculate $d^2$.

| Monthly Rainfall (mm) | Rank | Average height of crop (cm) | Rank | Difference between ranks (d) | $d^2$ |
|---|---|---|---|---|---|
| 20 | 7 | 20.1 | 6 | 1 | 1 |
| 30 | 6 | 22.3 | 5 | 1 | 1 |
| 40 | 5 | 19.9 | 7 | 2 | 4 |
| 50 | 4 | 25.7 | 4 | 0 | 0 |
| 60 | 3 | 36.3 | 3 | 0 | 0 |
| 70 | 2 | 45.2 | 2 | 0 | 0 |
| 80 | 1 | 58.1 | 1 | 0 | 0 |

**Tip:** A positive correlation means that as one variable increases, so does the other. A negative correlation means that as one variable increases, the other decreases. See page 23 for more.

3. Now count the number of data pairs (n). There are 7 data pairs here, so n = 7.

4. Now you can put all this information into the Spearman's rank formula:

$$r_s = 1 - \frac{6\sum d^2}{n(n^2 - 1)} = 1 - \frac{6(1 + 1 + 4 + 0 + 0 + 0 + 0)}{7(7^2 - 1)}$$

$$= 1 - \frac{6 \times 6}{7 \times 48} = 1 - \frac{36}{336}$$

$$= \mathbf{0.893} \text{ (3 s.f.)}$$

Because the figure is positive and close to 1, this suggests that there is a positive correlation between monthly rainfall and the average height of this crop.

**Tip:** You usually come up with the null hypothesis before you start your investigation — but we've explained how to calculate the correlation coefficient first here for clarity.

Once you've got your result, you need to find out if it's statistically significant or not. First, you need to come up with a **null hypothesis**. When you're investigating correlations, the null hypothesis should always be that there is no correlation between the factors you're investigating — even if you expect that there will be. So the null hypothesis for the example above could be "there is no correlation between monthly rainfall and the average height of this crop".

The result of the Spearman's rank test allows you to decide whether the null hypothesis can be rejected. To determine whether the null hypothesis can be rejected, you consult a table of **critical values** (see Figure 4).

The result is compared to the critical value at p = 0.05, which corresponds to *n* for the data you're looking at (in this case, 7). This value represents the point at which the correlation you're investigating would occur 95 out of 100 times, so there's only a 5% chance that the correlation is down to chance. You can reject the null hypothesis if the result of your test is higher than this value. If your result is a negative number, you ignore the minus sign when comparing it to the critical value. In this example, the Spearman's rank correlation coefficient (0.893) is higher than the relevant critical value, so the null hypothesis can be rejected. The result is statistically significant and the positive correlation is unlikely to be due to chance.

| n | p = 0.05 |
|---|---|
| 7 | 0.786 |
| 8 | 0.738 |
| 9 | 0.700 |
| 10 | 0.648 |
| 11 | 0.618 |
| 12 | 0.587 |

**Figure 4:** A table of critical values for the Spearman's rank test.

**Tip:** When you're checking your result against the critical value, always make sure that you use the right critical value for the number of data pairs that you've investigated.

**Tip:** If your result is not statistically significant, it means the correlation could just be down to chance.

## Practice Question — Application

Q1 A group of scientists were investigating whether the average milk yield of a herd of cows is affected by the amount of space each cow in the herd has in a field. Herds of 30 cows were kept in different sized fields for a month, where they had different amounts of space per cow. Each day, each cow was milked and the volume of milk it produced was recorded. An average daily milk yield was then calculated for each herd of cows from each of the different sized fields. The results are shown in the table on the right.

| Space per cow (km²) | Average Daily Milk Yield (dm³) |
|---|---|
| 0.004 | 32.1 |
| 0.005 | 36.2 |
| 0.006 | 37.4 |
| 0.007 | 34.3 |
| 0.008 | 36.7 |
| 0.009 | 38.9 |
| 0.010 | 37.6 |
| 0.011 | 33.4 |

a) Using the formula on the right, calculate the Spearman's rank correlation coefficient for this data.

$$r_s = 1 - \frac{6\Sigma d^2}{n(n^2 - 1)}$$

b) Using the table of critical values in Figure 4 above, determine whether the null hypothesis "there is no correlation between the average daily milk yield of a herd of cows and the amount of space per cow in a field" should be accepted or rejected.

**Exam Tip**
Don't let the context put you off. In your exam, the background information you get given could be about anything. Just pick out the information that you need and carry out the test like in the example.

## Practice Questions — Fact Recall

Q1 How do you calculate a mean?
Q2 What shape is the graph of a data set with a normal distribution?
Q3 What does standard deviation measure?

**Learning Objectives:**
- Know the different types of adaptations of organisms to their environment, including anatomical, physiological and behavioural adaptations.
- Understand why organisms from different taxonomic groups may show similar anatomical features, including the marsupial mole and placental mole.

**Specification Reference 4.2.2**

**Tip:** Organisms that are well adapted to their environment have a selective advantage over less well adapted organisms.

*Figure 1: When American possums feel threatened, they 'play dead' to escape attack.*

*Figure 2: An otter's streamlined body helps it to move easily through water.*

# 5. Adaptations

*Variation gives some organisms an advantage over others...*

## What are adaptations?
All the variation between and within species means that some organisms are better adapted to their environment than others. Being adapted to an environment means an organism has features that increase its chances of survival and reproduction, and also the chances of its offspring reproducing successfully. These features are called **adaptations** and can be behavioural, physiological and anatomical (see below).

Adaptations develop because of evolution by natural selection (see page 287). In each generation, the best-adapted individuals are more likely to survive and reproduce — passing on the alleles for their adaptations to their offspring. Individuals that are less well adapted are more likely to die before reproducing.

## Types of adaptations
There are three main types of adaptations that you need to know about.

### 1. Behavioural adaptations
These are ways an organism acts that increase its chance of survival.

**Examples**
- Possums sometimes 'play dead' — if they're being threatened by a predator they play dead to escape attack. This increases their chance of survival.
- Scorpions dance before mating — this makes sure they attract a mate of the same species, increasing the likelihood of successful mating.

### 2. Physiological adaptations
These are processes inside an organism's body that increase its chance of survival.

**Examples**
- Brown bears hibernate — they lower their rate of metabolism (all the chemical reactions taking place in their body) over winter. This conserves energy, so they don't need to look for food in the months when it's scarce — increasing their chance of survival.
- Some bacteria produce antibiotics — these kill other species of bacteria in the area. This means there's less competition, so they're more likely to survive.

### 3. Anatomical (structural) adaptations
These are structural features of an organism's body that increase its chance of survival.

**Examples**
- Otters have a streamlined shape — making it easier to glide through the water. This makes it easier for them to catch prey and escape predators, increasing their chance of survival.
- Whales have a thick layer of blubber (fat) — this helps to keep them warm in the cold sea. This increases their chance of survival in places where their food is found.

## Practice Question — Application

Q1 The common pipistrelle bat lives throughout Britain on farmland, or in open woodland, hedgerows and urban areas. It feeds by flying and catching insects in the air.

a) Some adaptations of the common pipistrelle bat are shown in the table below. Put a tick to show whether each adaptation is behavioural, physiological or anatomical.

|  | | Behavioural | Physiological | Anatomical |
|---|---|---|---|---|
| Adaptation | Light, flexible wings | | | |
| | Male bats make mating calls to attract females | | | |
| | Bats lower their metabolism to hibernate over winter | | | |

b) For each of the adaptations in the table above, suggest how it helps the common pipistrelle bat to survive.

**Exam Tip**
Read any information you're given in the exam carefully — it's there to help you answer the question.

# Convergent Evolution

Organisms from different taxonomic groups may have similar features even though they're not closely related — for example, whales and sharks (see page 272). This is usually because the organisms have evolved in similar environments and to fill similar ecological niches. When two species evolve similar characteristics independently of one another (because they've adapted to live in similar environments) it's called **convergent evolution**.

There are examples of convergent evolution between the distantly-related marsupial and placental mammals.

**Tip:** For a reminder about what a taxonomic group is, take a look at page 268.

## Marsupial and placental mammals

There are three different groups of mammals. Most mammals are placental mammals, while some are marsupials (and a very few are egg-laying monotremes).

Marsupials are found mainly in Australia and the Americas. They diverged from placental mammals many millions of years ago and have been evolving separately ever since. There are a few distinct differences between marsupial mammals (e.g. kangaroos) and placental mammals (e.g. humans):

| Marsupial Mammals | Placental Mammals |
|---|---|
| Have a short gestation period (pregnancy). | Have a longer gestation period. |
| Don't develop a full placenta. | Develop a placenta during pregnancy, which allows the exchange of nutrients and waste products between the fetus and the mother. |
| Are born early in their development and climb into their mother's pouch. Here they become attached to a teat and receive milk while they continue to develop. | Are born more fully developed. |

*Figure 3:* The offspring of marsupials like this kangaroo are born earlier on in development than placental mammals. They climb into their mother's pouch, where they continue to develop.

Module 4: Section 3 Classification and Evolution

Although marsupial and placental mammals have been evolving separately for many millions of years, the evolution of some species has converged.

### Example

There are many different species of mole. Most are placental moles, but there are also two species of marsupial mole.

Marsupial moles and placental moles aren't closely related — they evolved independently on different continents. They do share similar anatomical features though, e.g. they look alike (see Figure 4). That's because they've both evolved to live in similar environments. Both types of mole live in tunnels in the ground and they burrow to reach their food supply (e.g. earthworms, insects and other invertebrates). Their adaptations to this lifestyle include:

- Small or nonexistent eyes because they don't need to be able to see underground.
- No external ears, to keep a streamlined head for burrowing.
- Scoop-shaped and powerful front paws, which are good for digging.
- Claws that are specialised for digging.
- A tube shaped body and cone shaped head, which makes it easier to push through sand or soil.

**Figure 4:** *A marsupial mole (eating a gecko, top) and a placental mole (bottom). These moles have independently evolved to have similar features.*

### Exam Tip
Make sure that you learn the example of marsupial and placental moles as animals that have similar adaptations but aren't closely related. It might come up in the exam.

## Practice Question — Application

Q1 Brushtail possums and ring-tailed lemurs are both animals that spend a significant amount of time in trees. Despite not being closely related both have evolved opposable thumbs, which can move independently of other digits. This improves the possums' and lemurs' grips. Most animals do not have opposable thumbs.
   a) What type of adaptation are opposable thumbs?
   b) Suggest why brushtail possums and ring-tailed lemurs have independently evolved opposable thumbs.

## Practice Questions — Fact Recall

Q1 Why is it helpful for an organism to be adapted to its environment?
Q2 What is a physiological adaptation?
Q3 List five adaptations shared by both marsupial and placental moles and explain how each one is linked to the moles' lifestyle.

# 6. The Theory of Evolution

*Evolution is the slow and continual change of organisms from one generation to the next. Darwin and Wallace came up with a neat little theory to explain it...*

## Darwin's contribution

Scientists use theories to attempt to explain their observations — Charles Darwin was no exception. Darwin made four key observations about the world around him.

### Darwin's observations:
1. Organisms produce more offspring than survive.
2. There's variation in the characteristics of members of the same species.
3. Some of these characteristics can be passed on from one generation to the next.
4. Individuals that are best adapted to their environment are more likely to survive.

### Natural selection

Darwin wrote the **theory of evolution by natural selection** to explain his observations. His theory was that:

- Individuals within a population show variation in their phenotypes (their characteristics).
- Selection pressures (environmental factors such as predation, disease and competition) create a struggle for survival.
- Individuals with better adaptations (characteristics that give a selective advantage, e.g. being able to run away from predators faster) are more likely to survive and have reproductive success — in other words, they reproduce and pass on their advantageous adaptations to their offspring.
- Over time, the proportion of the population possessing the advantageous adaptations increases.
- Over generations this leads to evolution as the favourable adaptations become more common in the population.

We now know that genes determine many of an organism's characteristics and that individuals show variations in their phenotypes partly as a result of genetic variation, i.e. the different alleles they have. When an organism with advantageous characteristics reproduces, the alleles that determine those characteristics may be passed on to its offspring.

### Example — peppered moths
- Peppered moths show variation in colour — there are light ones (with alleles for light colour) and dark ones (with alleles for dark colour).
- Before the 1800s there were more light moths than dark moths.
- During the 1800s, pollution had blackened many of the trees that the moths lived on.
- Dark coloured moths were now better adapted to this environment — they were better camouflaged from predators, so would be more likely to survive, reproduce and pass on the alleles for their dark colouring to their offspring.
- During this time the number of dark moths increased and the alleles for dark colour became more common in the population.

**Learning Objectives:**
- Know the contribution of Darwin and Wallace in formulating the theory of evolution by natural selection.
- Understand the mechanism by which natural selection can affect the characteristics of a population over time and appreciate that genetic variation, selection pressure and reproductive success (or failure) results in an increased proportion of the population possessing the advantageous characteristic(s).
- Know the evidence for the theory of evolution by natural selection, including fossil, DNA and molecular evidence.

**Specification Reference 4.2.2**

**Tip:** The opposite is also true — organisms without advantageous adaptations are less likely to survive and reproduce.

**Tip:** When Darwin published his theory in 1859, he didn't know about genes and alleles.

*Figure 1: Two colours of peppered moth on tree bark.*

Module 4: Section 3 Classification and Evolution    287

Tip: Natural selection is one process by which evolution occurs.

## Wallace's contribution

Alfred Russel Wallace, a scientist working at the same time as Darwin, played an important part in developing the theory of evolution by natural selection. He independently came up with the idea of natural selection and wrote to Darwin about it. He and Darwin published their papers on evolution together and acknowledged each other's work — although they didn't always agree about the mechanisms involved in natural selection.

Wallace's observations provided lots of evidence to support the theory of evolution by natural selection. For example, he realised that warning colours are used by some species (e.g. butterflies) to deter predators from eating them and that this was an example of an advantageous adaptation that had evolved by natural selection.

Unfortunately for Wallace, it wasn't until Darwin published his famous book 'On the Origin of Species' that other scientists began to pay attention to the theory. In this book Darwin gave lots of evidence to support the theory and expanded on it. For example, he wrote about all the species that he had observed during his voyage to South America and the Galápagos Islands in the 1830s. The book is partly why Darwin is usually better remembered than Wallace — even though Wallace helped to come up with the theory.

## Evidence to support evolution

There's plenty of evidence to support evolution, such as...

### Fossil record evidence

Fossils are the remains of organisms preserved in rocks. By arranging fossils in chronological (date) order, gradual changes in organisms can be observed that provide evidence of evolution.

Tip: The evidence supporting evolution isn't always perfect, e.g. there are sometimes gaps in the fossil record. This is because fossils don't always form and when they do, they can be easily damaged or destroyed.

— Example —
The fossil record of the horse shows a gradual change in characteristics, including increasing size, lengthening of the limbs and hoof development.

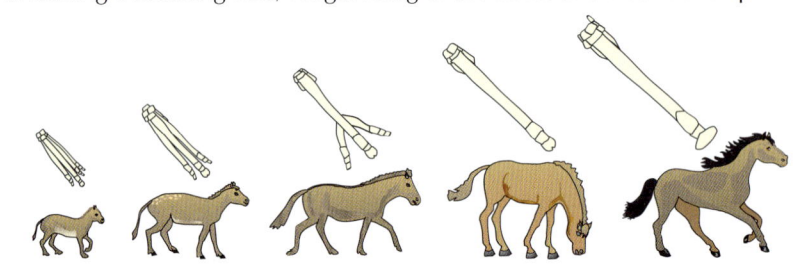

**Figure 2:** *Suggested evolution of the horse.*

### Molecular evidence — DNA

The theory of evolution suggests that all organisms have evolved from shared common ancestors. Closely related species diverged (evolved to become different species) more recently.

Tip: There's more on DNA base sequences on pages 97-98.

Evolution is caused by gradual changes in the base sequence of organisms' DNA. So, organisms that diverged away from each other more recently should have more similar DNA, as less time has passed for changes in the DNA sequence to occur. This is exactly what scientists have found.

> **Example**
> Humans, chimps and mice all evolved from a common ancestor. Humans and mice diverged a long time ago, but humans and chimps diverged quite recently. The DNA base sequence of humans and chimps is 94% the same, but human and mouse DNA is only 85% the same.

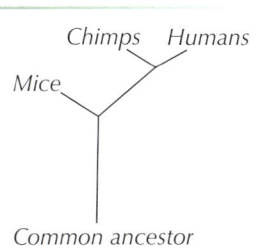

In eukaryotes, most DNA is found in the cell nucleus. But scientists don't just analyse nuclear DNA to find out about evolutionary relationships. Eukaryotic organisms also have DNA in their mitochondria, so scientists can also look at differences in mitochondrial DNA to see how closely related organisms are.

## Molecular evidence — proteins and other molecules

In addition to DNA, the similarities in other molecules provide evidence. Scientists compare the sequence of amino acids in proteins, and compare antibodies. Organisms that diverged away from each other more recently have more similar molecules, as less time has passed for changes in proteins and other molecules to occur.

### Practice Questions — Application

Q1 The cytochrome C protein is found in almost all living organisms. Suggest how scientists might use cytochrome C to provide evidence for evolution.

Q2 There are many different species of rat snake, all found in different habitats and with slightly different colourings. The black rat snake lives in wooded habitats and has a dark, brown-black colouring (see Figure 3). Describe how natural selection could explain the evolution of a rat snake with black colouring in a wooded habitat.

**Figure 3:** A black rat snake climbing up a tree.

### Practice Questions — Fact Recall

Q1 State two observations made by Darwin that led him to develop his theory of evolution.

Q2 What are selection pressures?

Q3 Name the scientist who published a paper on the theory of evolution by natural selection at the same time as Darwin.

Q4 Explain how the following can provide evidence for evolution:
a) the fossil record,  b) DNA.

Module 4: Section 3 Classification and Evolution

**Learning Objective:**
- Understand how evolution in some species has implications for human populations, including the evolution of pesticide resistance in insects and drug resistance in microorganisms.
  **Specification Reference 4.2.2**

# 7. More on Evolution

*When pests and pathogens evolve to become resistant to the substances we use to control them, it can have serious implications for humans.*

## The evolution of pesticide resistance

Pesticides are chemicals that kill pests (e.g. insects that damage crops). Scientists have observed the evolution of pesticide resistance in many species of insect.

### Examples
- Some populations of mosquito have evolved resistance to the pesticide DDT.
- Some populations of pollen beetles (which damage the crop oilseed rape) are resistant to pyrethroid pesticides.

**Tip:** The pesticide is acting as a <u>selection pressure</u>. Its presence determines which alleles become more common in the population, i.e. the alleles for pesticide resistance.

The evolution of pesticide resistance can be explained by natural selection:
- There is variation in a population of insects. Genetic mutations make some insects naturally resistant to a pesticide.
- If the population of insects is exposed to that pesticide, only the individuals with resistance will survive to reproduce.
- The alleles which cause the pesticide resistance will be passed on to the next generation. Over many generations, the population will evolve to become more resistant to the chemical.

**Tip:** Mutations are changes to the DNA base code (see p. 95). They can produce new alleles, e.g. alleles for pesticide resistance.

### Example — DDT resistance in mosquitoes

DDT was first used to kill malaria-carrying mosquitoes around the time of WWII. In the 1950s, DDT-resistant mosquitoes began to appear in areas of widespread DDT use. Here's what happened:
- Genetic mutations gave some mosquitoes an allele that made them naturally resistant to DDT.
- When a mosquito population was exposed to DDT, mosquitoes without the allele for DDT resistance were killed, but individuals with the allele survived, reproduced and passed on the allele to the next generation.
- Over many generations, DDT resistance became widespread in mosquito populations that had been exposed to DDT.

### The implications of pesticide resistance for humans

Crop infestations with pesticide-resistant insects are harder to control — some insects are resistant to lots of different pesticides. It takes farmers a while to figure out which pesticide will kill the insect and in that time all the crop could be destroyed.

**Tip:** Beneficial insects include natural pest predators (e.g. ladybirds), as these feed on pest species, removing them from the crop.

If the insects are resistant to specific pesticides (ones that only kill that insect), farmers might have to use broader pesticides (those that kill a range of insects), which could kill beneficial insects. And if disease-carrying insects (e.g. mosquitoes) become pesticide-resistant, the spread of disease could increase.

A population of insects could also evolve resistance to all pesticides in use. To prevent this, new pesticides need to be produced. This takes time and costs money.

# The evolution of drug resistance

You might remember from page 242 that scientists have observed the evolution of antibiotic resistance in many species of bacteria, e.g. MRSA. Other pathogens have evolved resistance to specific drugs too.

**Tip:** Antibiotic resistance is becoming a huge problem. See page 243 for more.

### Example
Some of the protoctists that cause malaria are resistant to several drugs used to treat malaria.

## The implications of drug resistance for humans

Infections caused by drug-resistant microorganisms are harder to treat — especially if the microorganism is resistant to lots of different drugs. It can take doctors a while to figure out which drugs will get rid of the infection, and in that time the patient could become very ill or die.

There could come a point where a pathogen has become resistant to all the drugs we currently use against it. To prevent this, new drugs need to be developed. This takes time and costs a lot of money.

## Practice Question — Application

Q1 *P. falciparum* is a species of protoctist that causes malaria. Between the 1950s and 1990s, malaria caused by *P. falciparum* was most commonly treated with the drug chloroquine. During this period, *P. falciparum* developed widespread resistance to chloroquine.

a) Suggest how *P. falciparum* evolved to become resistant to chloroquine.

b) Some populations of *P. falciparum* are now resistant to multiple anti-malarial drugs. Explain the implications this may have for:
   i) people infected with malaria,
   ii) the drug companies that make anti-malarial drugs.

## Section Summary

Make sure you know...
- That organisms can be classified into a taxonomic hierarchy consisting of the following eight groups: domain, kingdom, phylum, class, order, family, genus, species.
- That the binomial system is used to give each organism a two part scientific (Latin) name — the first part is the name of the organism's genus and the second part is the name of its species — and that this helps to avoid the confusion of using common names.
- The defining features of the Prokaryotae, Protoctista, Fungi, Plantae and Animalia kingdoms.
- That phylogeny is the study of the evolutionary history of groups of organisms (i.e. how closely related they are) and that it can be used to help classify organisms.
- That classification systems were originally based only on observable features, but that scientists now use a range of different evidence to classify organisms (including similarities in DNA base sequences and similarities in biological molecules, such as proteins).
- The similarities and differences between the 'three domain' and 'five kingdom' classification systems.

- That the three domain classification system was introduced because of new molecular evidence.
- That variation is the differences that exist between individuals and that it can occur within a species (intraspecific variation) or between species (interspecific variation).
- That continuous variation is where the individuals in a population vary within a range — there are no distinct categories.
- That discontinuous variation is where there are two or more distinct categories and each individual falls into only one of these categories.
- How to describe the differences between continuous and discontinuous variation using examples from plants, animals and microorganisms.
- That variation can be caused by genetic factors, environmental factors or a combination of both.
- How to use standard deviation to measure the amount of variation in a sample (how spread out the data is either side of the mean).
- How to use the Spearman's rank correlation coefficient to determine whether there is significant correlation between two variables.
- That an adaptation is a feature that increases an organism's chances of survival and reproduction, and also the chances of its offspring reproducing successfully.
- That adaptations can be behavioural, physiological or anatomical (structural).
- The reasons why organisms from different taxonomic groups may show similar anatomical features even though they're not closely related, including the example of marsupial moles and placental moles.
- The contributions of Charles Darwin and Alfred Russel Wallace to the theory of evolution by natural selection.
- How natural selection affects the characteristics of a population over time — including the roles of genetic variation, selection pressure and reproductive success.
- That fossil evidence, along with DNA and other molecular evidence, provides support for evolution.
- How insects evolving resistance to pesticides and microorganisms evolving resistance to drugs has implications for humans.

# Exam-style Questions

**1** The organism *Halobacterium salinarum* is classified as Archaea under the three domain system.

(a) Fill in the blanks in the table below to show how *H. salinarum* is classified.

| Domain | Archaea |
|---|---|
| Kingdom | Euryarchaeota |
| Phylum | Euryarchaeota |
|  | Halobacteria |
| Order | Halobacteriales |
|  | Halobacteriaceae |
|  |  |
| Species |  |

*(2 marks)*

(b) Under the five kingdom classification system, *H. salinarum* would have been classified as Prokaryotae.

   (i) Give **two** characteristics of the Prokaryotae kingdom.

*(2 marks)*

   (ii) Explain why the three domain system does **not** contain the Prokaryotae kingdom.

*(2 marks)*

   (iii) Give **one** similarity between the three domain classification system and the five kingdom classification system.

*(1 mark)*

**2** The **RuBisCO gene** is found in all plants.

When a new species of plant is being classified, this gene is often compared with the gene in other species to determine evolutionary relatedness.

(a) Describe how a scientist could compare the RuBisCO gene in two different species of plant to determine how closely related they are.

*(2 marks)*

(b) Why is the RuBisCO gene useful for determining relationships between plant species?

*(1 mark)*

(c) The RuBisCO gene codes for an enzyme. Describe how a scientist could compare the RuBisCO enzyme in two different species of plant to determine how closely related they are.

*(2 marks)*

(d) Classification of plants was originally based only on observable features. Explain why taxonomists now consider other evidence when classifying plant species.

*(2 marks)*

Module 4: Section 3 Classification and Evolution

**3** **Fig. 3.1** shows the use of an anti-aphid pesticide on a farm and the number of aphids found on the farm over a period of time.

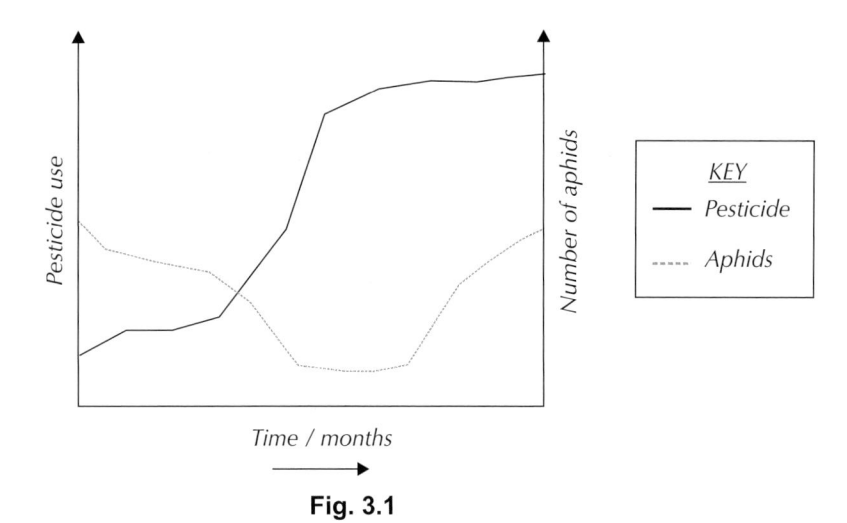

**Fig. 3.1**

(a) (i) Describe the changes shown in the data in **Fig. 3.1**.

*(3 marks)*

(ii) Explain how the changes you described in **part i)** may have occurred.

*(4 marks)*

(b) Suggest **one** implication these changes may have for the farmer.

*(2 marks)*

**4** The bat *Anoura fistulata* has a very long tongue (up to one and a half times the length of its body).

The tongue enables the bat to feed on the nectar inside a deep tubular flower found in the forests of Ecuador.

(a) The bat's tongue is an **anatomical** adaptation to feeding on deep flowers.

(i) What is an adaptation?

*(2 marks)*

(ii) Give **two** other types of adaptation an organism can have to its environment.

*(2 marks)*

(b) Describe how natural selection can explain the evolution of *Anoura fistulata's* long tongue.

*(4 marks)*

(c) A team of biologists were trying to determine how recently *Anoura fistulata* diverged from another species of bat. Explain how molecular evidence could be used to determine how recently the species diverged from each other.

*(4 marks)*

# Module 5 Section 1: Communication and Homeostasis

## 1. Communication Basics

*In order to survive, organisms need to respond to what's going on around them. Communication systems make sure information gets passed on from one part of the organism to another.*

### Responding to the environment

Animals increase their chances of survival by responding to changes in their external environment, e.g. by avoiding harmful environments such as places that are too hot or too cold. They also respond to changes in their internal environment to make sure that the conditions are always optimal for their metabolism (all the chemical reactions that go on inside them). Plants also increase their chances of survival by responding to changes in their environment. Any change in the internal or external environment, e.g. a change in temperature, light intensity or pressure, is called a **stimulus**.

### Receptors and effectors

Receptors detect stimuli. They are specific — they only detect one particular stimulus, e.g. pressure, light or glucose concentration. There are many different types of receptor that each detect a different type of stimulus, e.g. pressure receptors only detect pressure. Some receptors are cells, e.g. photoreceptors are receptor cells that connect to the nervous system. Some receptors are proteins on cell surface membranes, e.g. glucose receptors are proteins found in the cell membranes of some pancreatic cells.

Effectors are cells that bring about a response to a stimulus, to produce an effect. Effectors include muscle cells and cells found in glands, e.g. the pancreas. Receptors and effectors play an important role in communicating information from one part of an organism to another. This makes sure that the activities of different organs are coordinated to keep the organism working effectively.

### Cell signalling

To produce a response, receptors need to communicate with effectors and effectors may need to communicate with other cells. This happens via cell signalling. Cell signalling can occur between adjacent (nearby) cells or between distant cells. For example, cells in the nervous system communicate by secreting chemicals called neurotransmitters, which send signals to adjacent cells, such as other nerve cells or muscle cells. The hormonal system works by cells releasing chemicals called hormones, which travel in the blood and act as signals to distant cells. Cell-surface receptors allow cells to recognise the chemicals involved in cell signalling.

**Learning Objectives:**
- Be able to outline the need for communication systems in multicellular organisms, including the need for animals and plants to respond to changes in the internal and external environment and to coordinate the activities of different organs.
- Know that cells communicate with each other by a process called cell signalling and that this occurs between adjacent cells and between distant cells.

**Specification Reference 5.1.1**

**Tip:** There's much more about how receptors work on pages 297-298.

**Tip:** The nervous system and hormonal system are 'communication systems'.

### Practice Questions — Fact Recall

Q1 Why is it important that organisms respond to stimuli?
Q2 Give one reason why communication systems are needed in multicellular organisms.
Q3 What is cell signalling?

**Learning Objectives:**
- Know the structures and functions of sensory, motor and relay neurones.
- Understand the roles of mammalian sensory receptors in converting different types of stimuli into nerve impulses.
- Be able to outline the roles of sensory receptors (e.g. Pacinian corpuscle) in responding to specific types of stimuli and their roles as transducers.

**Specification Reference 5.1.3**

# 2. The Nervous System

*The nervous system passes on information from one part of an organism to another using nerve impulses. It's a very fast form of communication.*

## Neurones

The nervous system is made up of a complex network of cells called neurones. There are three main types of neurone:

1. **Sensory neurones** transmit nerve impulses from receptors to the central nervous system (CNS) — the brain and spinal cord.
2. **Motor neurones** transmit nerve impulses from the CNS to effectors.
3. **Relay neurones** transmit nerve impulses between sensory neurones and motor neurones.

### Structure of neurones

All neurones have a cell body with a nucleus (plus cytoplasm and all the other organelles you usually get in a cell). The cell body has extensions that connect to other neurones — dendrites and dendrons carry nerve impulses towards the cell body (dendrites are smaller branches of a dendron), and axons carry nerve impulses away from the cell body. You need to learn the structures of sensory, motor and relay neurones:

- Sensory neurones have short dendrites and one long dendron to carry nerve impulses from receptor cells to the cell body, and one short axon that carries nerve impulses from the cell body to the CNS.

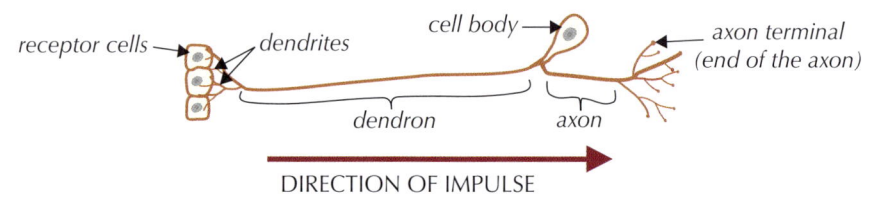

**Tip:** Dendrites and dendrons carry information towards the cell body, axons carry it away from the cell body.

- Motor neurones have many short dendrites that carry nerve impulses from the CNS to the cell body, and one long axon that carries nerve impulses from the cell body to effector cells.

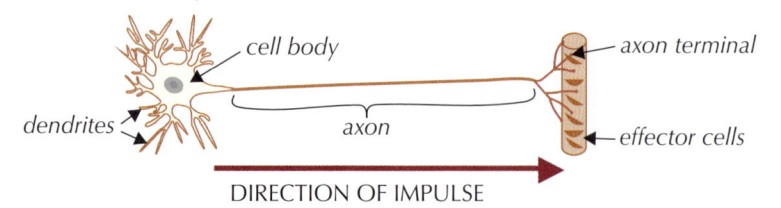

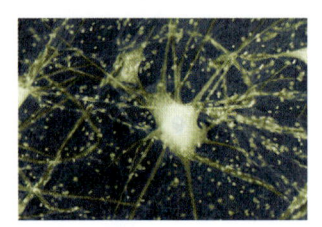

**Tip:** This is a non-myelinated motor neurone — see page 303 for the structure of a myelinated one.

- Relay neurones have many short dendrites that carry nerve impulses from sensory neurones to the cell body, and one axon that carries nerve impulses from the cell body to motor neurones.

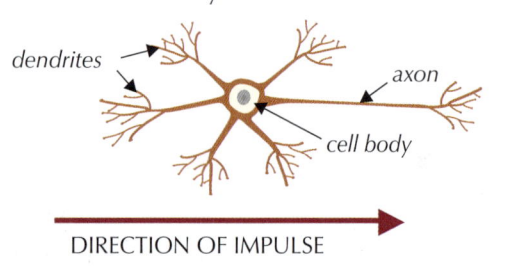

**Figure 1:** *A light micrograph of a motor neurone — many dendrites can be seen extending from the cell body.*

**Tip:** Relay neurones transmit nerve impulses through the CNS.

Module 5: Section 1 Communication and Homeostasis

# Nervous communication

A stimulus is detected by receptor cells and a nerve impulse is sent along a sensory neurone. When a nerve impulse reaches the end of a neurone chemicals called neurotransmitters take the information across the gap (called a synapse) to the next neurone, which then sends a nerve impulse (see pages 305-306). The CNS processes the information, decides what to do about it and sends impulses along motor neurones to an effector (see Figure 2).

**Tip:** Nerve impulses are electrical impulses. They're also called action potentials.

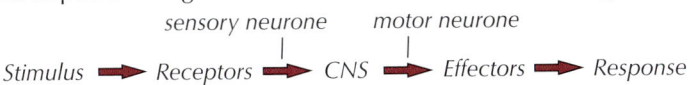

Stimulus ➡ Receptors ➡ CNS ➡ Effectors ➡ Response
(sensory neurone between Receptors and CNS; motor neurone between CNS and Effectors)

**Figure 2:** *The pathway of nervous communication.*

--- Example ---
A real-life example of nervous communication is when you see a friend waving to you and you wave back in response:
- **Stimulus** — you see a friend waving.
- **Receptors** — light receptors (photoreceptors) in your eyes detect the wave. The electrical impulse is carried by a sensory neurone to the CNS.
- **CNS** — processes information and decides what to do about it. An electrical impulse is sent along a motor neurone.
- **Effectors** — muscle cells are stimulated by the motor neurone.
- **Response** — muscles contract to make your arm wave.

# Sensory receptors

Different stimuli have different forms of energy, e.g. light energy or chemical energy. But your nervous system only sends information in the form of nerve impulses (electrical impulses). Sensory receptors convert the energy of a stimulus into electrical energy. They act as **transducers** — something that converts one form of energy into another.

Here's a bit more about how receptor cells that communicate information via the nervous system work...

**Tip:** Sensory receptors are cells. There are other types of receptors, such as proteins on cell surface membranes, but they work in a different way.

## The resting potential

When a nervous system receptor is in its resting state (not being stimulated), there's a difference in charge between the inside and the outside of the cell — the inside is negatively charged relative to the outside (see Figure 3). This means there's a **voltage** across the membrane. Voltage is also known as the **potential difference**. The potential difference when a cell is at rest is called its **resting potential**. The resting potential is generated by ion pumps and ion channels (see p. 300).

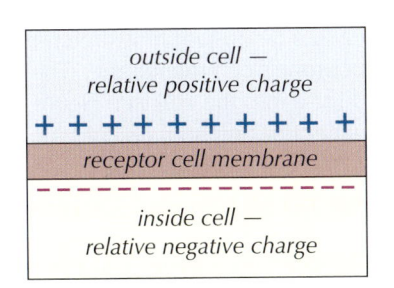

outside cell — relative positive charge
+ + + + + + + + + + +
receptor cell membrane
– – – – – – – – – – –
inside cell — relative negative charge

**Figure 3:** *Relative charges either side of a receptor cell membrane at rest.*

## The generator potential

When a stimulus is detected, the cell membrane is excited and becomes more permeable, allowing more ions to move in and out of the cell — altering the potential difference. The change in potential difference due to a stimulus is called the **generator potential**.

**Tip:** An ion is a particle with a positive or negative electrical charge, e.g. sodium ions ($Na^+$).

Module 5: Section 1  Communication and Homeostasis

A bigger stimulus excites the membrane more, causing a bigger movement of ions and a bigger change in potential difference — so a bigger generator potential is produced (see Figure 4).

**Tip:** Potential difference across a cell membrane is usually measured in millivolts (mV).

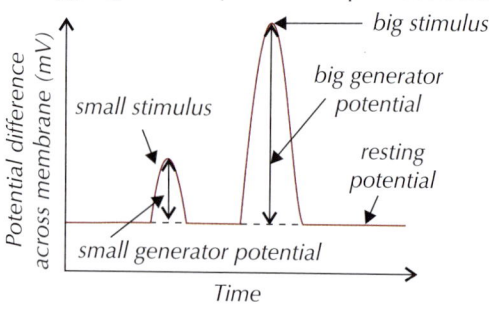

**Figure 4:** The bigger stimulus produces the bigger generator potential.

## The action potential

If the generator potential is big enough it'll trigger an action potential (nerve impulse) along a neurone. An action potential is only triggered if the generator potential reaches a certain level called the **threshold level**. If the stimulus is too weak the generator potential won't reach the threshold, so there's no action potential (see Figure 5).

**Tip:** There's much more on action potentials on pages 301-302.

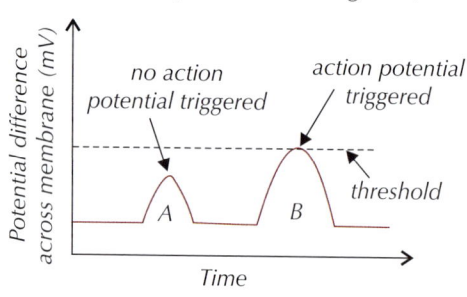

**Figure 5:** Generator potential not reaching the threshold (A) and reaching the threshold (B).

**Tip:** Pacinian corpuscles only respond to mechanical stimuli, not to any other type of stimulus — this is a good example of how receptors only respond to specific stimuli.

**Tip:** Stretch-mediated sodium ion channels get their name because they only open and let sodium ions pass through when they're stretched.

─ Example ─
Pacinian corpuscles are mechanoreceptors — they detect mechanical stimuli, e.g. pressure and vibrations. They're found in your skin. They contain the end of a sensory neurone, called a sensory nerve ending. The sensory nerve ending is wrapped in lots of layers of connective tissue called lamellae.

When a Pacinian corpuscle is stimulated, e.g. by a tap on the arm, the lamellae are deformed and press on the sensory nerve ending. This causes deformation of stretch-mediated sodium channels in the sensory neurone's cell membrane. The sodium ion channels open and sodium ions diffuse into the cell (see Figure 6), creating a generator potential. If the generator potential reaches the threshold, it triggers an action potential.

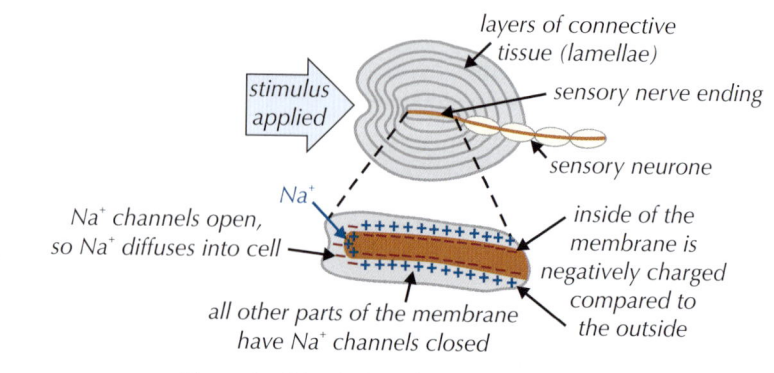

**Figure 6:** Stimulation of a Pacinian corpuscle.

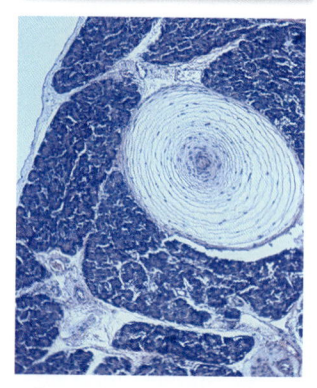

**Figure 7:** Light micrograph showing a section of a Pacinian corpuscle at rest.

298   Module 5: Section 1   Communication and Homeostasis

## Practice Questions — Application

For a particular receptor cell, an action potential is triggered when the generator potential reaches −60 mV.

**Q1** What name is given to the value at which an action potential will be triggered?

**Q2** The graph below shows generator potentials in the receptor cell.

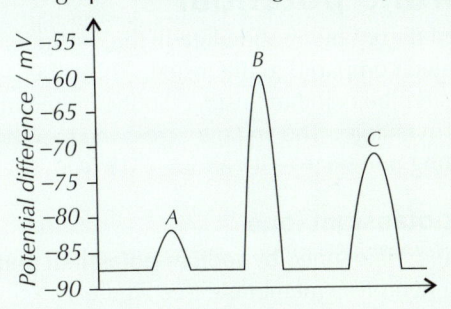

a) Which curve shows a generator potential that would trigger an action potential? Give a reason for your answer.

b) What is the resting potential of this receptor cell?

## Practice Questions — Fact Recall

**Q1** What is the function of:
   a) a sensory neurone?
   b) a motor neurone?
   c) a relay neurone?

**Q2** The diagram on the right shows a non-myelinated motor neurone. Name the structures labelled A-D.

**Q3** Give two structural differences between a sensory neurone and a motor neurone.

**Q4** Describe the pathway of nervous communication from stimulus to response.

**Q5** Why are sensory receptors described as 'transducers'?

**Q6** Explain how a generator potential is produced.

**Q7** Explain how a bigger stimulus causes a bigger generator potential than a smaller stimulus.

**Q8** Describe the response of a Pacinian corpuscle stimulated by a tap on the arm.

**Exam Tip**
Questions on the structure of neurones are easy marks, so make sure you learn the structures of each type of neurone really well.

Module 5: Section 1 Communication and Homeostasis

**Learning Objectives:**
- Understand how the resting potential is established and maintained.
- Understand the generation and transmission of nerve impulses in mammals, including how an action potential is generated (with reference to positive feedback) and transmitted in a myelinated neurone.
- Understand the significance of the frequency of impulse transmission.
- Understand the differences in structure and function of myelinated and non-myelinated neurones.

**Specification Reference 5.1.3**

# 3. The Nervous Impulse

*Nervous impulses are the electrical charges transmitted along a neurone. They're created by the movement of sodium and potassium ions across a neurone cell membrane.*

## The resting membrane potential

In a neurone's resting state (when it's not being stimulated), the outside of the membrane is positively charged compared to the inside. This is because there are more positive ions outside the cell than inside. So the membrane is polarised — there's a difference in charge. The voltage across the membrane when it's at rest is called the resting potential — it's about −70 mV.

### Movement of sodium and potassium ions

The resting potential is created and maintained by **sodium-potassium pumps** and **potassium ion channels** in a neurone's membrane (see Figure 1).

- Sodium-potassium pumps use **active transport** to move three sodium ions (Na⁺) out of the neurone for every two potassium ions (K⁺) moved in. ATP is needed to do this.
- Potassium ion channels allow **facilitated diffusion** of potassium ions (K⁺) out of the neurone, down their concentration gradient.

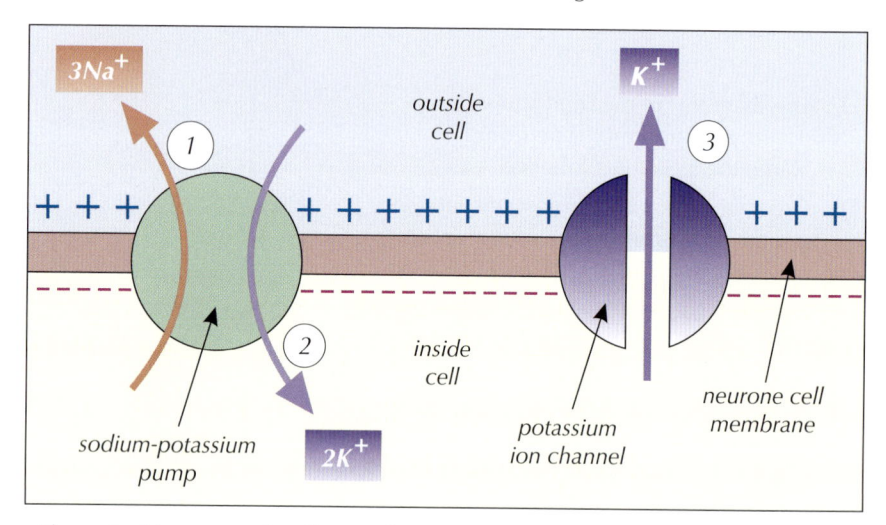

**Figure 1:** *Movement of sodium and potassium ions across a resting cell membrane.*

1. The sodium-potassium pumps move sodium ions out of the neurone, but the membrane isn't permeable to sodium ions, so they can't diffuse back in. This creates a sodium ion **electrochemical gradient** (a concentration gradient of ions) because there are more positive sodium ions outside the cell than inside.
2. The sodium-potassium pumps also move potassium ions in to the neurone.
3. When the cell's at rest, most potassium ion channels are open. This means that the membrane is permeable to potassium ions, so some diffuse back out through potassium ion channels.

Even though positive ions are moving in and out of the cell, in total more positive ions move out of the cell than enter. This makes the outside of the cell positively charged compared to the inside.

**Tip:** The neurone cell membrane also has sodium ion channels (see next page), but these are closed when the cell's at rest.

**Tip:** Remember, sodium-potassium pumps are SOPI — Sodium Out, Potassium In.

# Action potentials

When a neurone is stimulated, sodium ion channels in the cell membrane open. If the stimulus is big enough, it'll trigger a rapid change in potential difference. This causes the cell membrane to become **depolarised** (it's no longer polarised). The sequence of events that happens is known as an action potential — see Figure 2.

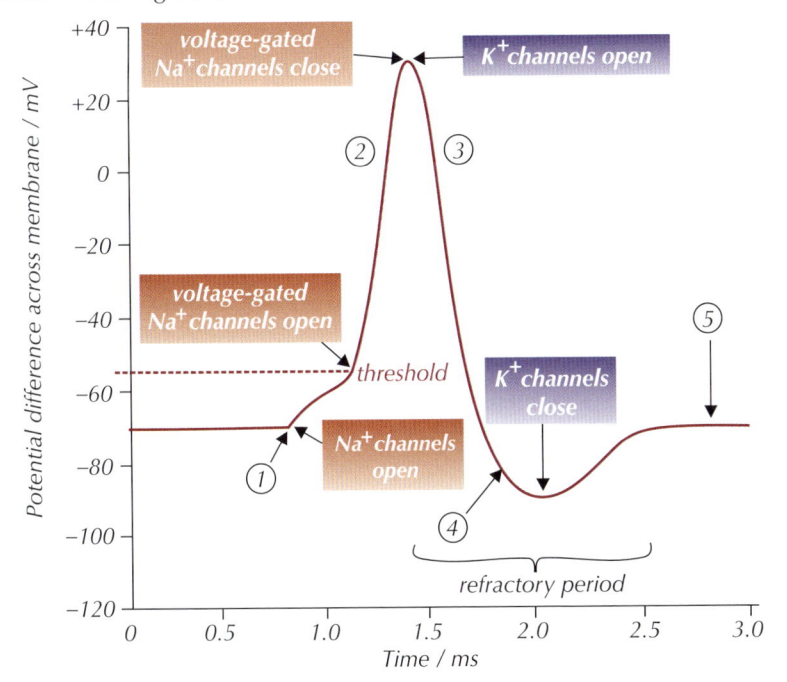

*Figure 2:* A graph to show the changes in potential difference across a neurone cell membrane during an action potential.

**Exam Tip**
You don't have to learn the mV values given here — they're only approximate and vary from neurone to neurone. Don't be thrown in the exam if you're given a graph with different values.

**Tip:** Voltage-gated ion channels are channels that only open at a certain voltage.

1. **Stimulus** — this excites the neurone cell membrane, causing sodium ion channels to open. The membrane becomes more permeable to sodium, so sodium ions diffuse into the neurone down the sodium ion electrochemical gradient. This makes the inside of the neurone less negative.

2. **Depolarisation** — if the potential difference reaches the threshold (around −55 mV), voltage-gated sodium ion channels open and more sodium ions diffuse into the neurone. This is positive feedback (see page 316).

3. **Repolarisation** — at a potential difference of around +30 mV the sodium ion channels close and voltage-gated potassium ion channels open. The membrane is more permeable to potassium so potassium ions diffuse out of the neurone down the potassium ion concentration gradient. This starts to get the membrane back to its resting potential. This is negative feedback (see pages 315-316).

4. **Hyperpolarisation** — potassium ion channels are slow to close so there's a slight 'overshoot' where too many potassium ions diffuse out of the neurone. The potential difference becomes more negative than the resting potential (i.e. less than −70 mV).

5. **Resting potential** — the ion channels are reset. The sodium-potassium pump returns the membrane to its resting potential by pumping sodium ions out and potassium ions in, and maintains the resting potential until the membrane's excited by another stimulus.

**Tip:** The graph below shows when the sodium ion channels (orange) are open during an action potential (dotted line):

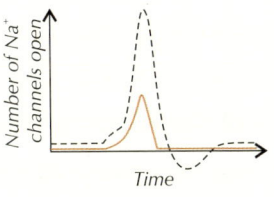

And this graph shows when the potassium ion channels (blue) are open:

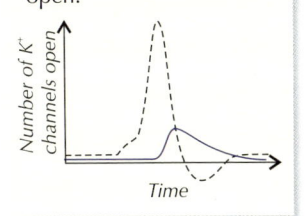

Module 5: Section 1 Communication and Homeostasis

### The refractory period

After an action potential, the neurone cell membrane can't be excited again straight away. This is because the ion channels are recovering and they can't be made to open — sodium ion channels are closed during repolarisation and potassium ion channels are closed during hyperpolarisation. This period of recovery is called the refractory period (see Figure 3).

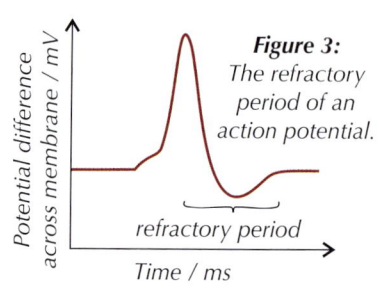

*Figure 3: The refractory period of an action potential.*

The refractory period acts as a time delay between one action potential and the next. This makes sure that action potentials don't overlap but pass along as discrete (separate) impulses. The refractory period also makes sure action potentials are unidirectional (they only travel in one direction).

## Waves of depolarisation

When an action potential happens, some of the sodium ions that enter the neurone diffuse sideways. This causes sodium ion channels in the next region of the neurone to open and sodium ions diffuse into that part. This causes a wave of depolarisation to travel along the neurone. The wave moves away from the parts of the membrane in the refractory period because these parts can't fire an action potential.

**Tip:** A wave of depolarisation is like a Mexican wave travelling through a crowd — sodium ions rushing inwards causes a wave of activity along the membrane.

**Tip:** The electrical impulse can be said to 'propagate' along the neurone. This just describes the wave-like movement of the action potential.

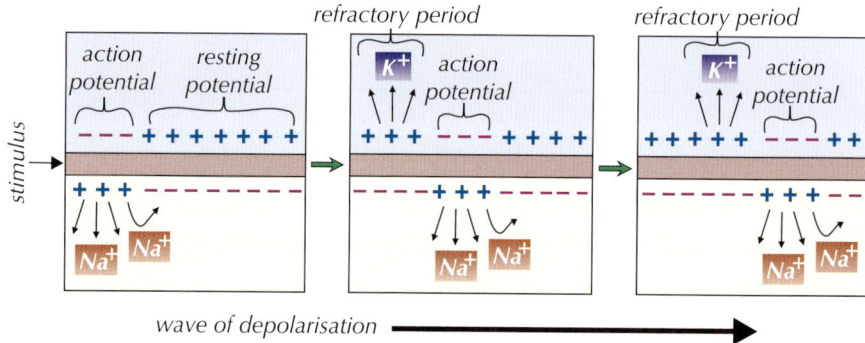

*Figure 4: The movement of ions across a neurone cell membrane during a wave of depolarisation.*

## Frequency of impulses

Once the threshold is reached, an action potential will always fire with the same change in voltage, no matter how big the stimulus is. If the threshold isn't reached, an action potential won't fire (see Figure 5). This is the **all-or-nothing** nature of action potentials.

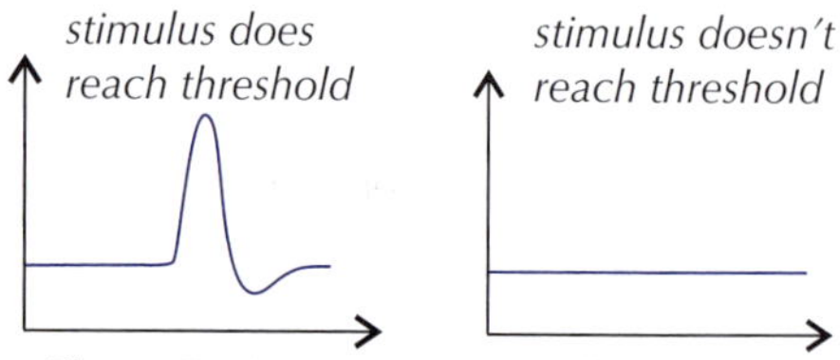

A bigger stimulus won't cause a bigger action potential but it will cause them to fire more frequently (see Figure 6). So if the brain receives a high frequency of action potentials, it interprets this as a big stimulus and responds accordingly.

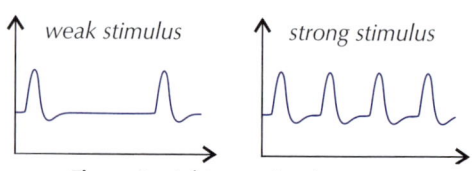

**Tip:** The all-or-nothing principle stops the brain from getting over-stimulated by not responding to very small stimuli.

*Figure 5: An action potential only fires if the stimulus reaches the threshold.*

*Figure 6: A bigger stimulus causes more frequent action potentials.*

302 Module 5: Section 1 Communication and Homeostasis

# Speed of conduction

Three factors affect the speed of conduction of action potentials:

## 1. Myelination

Some neurones are myelinated — they have a **myelin sheath** (see Figure 8). The myelin sheath is an electrical insulator. In the peripheral nervous system (see p. 353), the myelin sheath is made of a type of cell called a **Schwann cell**, which is wrapped around the axon (and/or dendron). Between the Schwann cells are tiny patches of bare membrane called the **nodes of Ranvier**. Sodium ion channels are concentrated at the nodes of Ranvier.

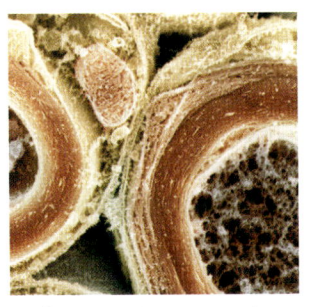

*Figure 7: A cross-section through a myelinated neurone. The myelin sheath (orange/brown) surrounds the axon (dark brown).*

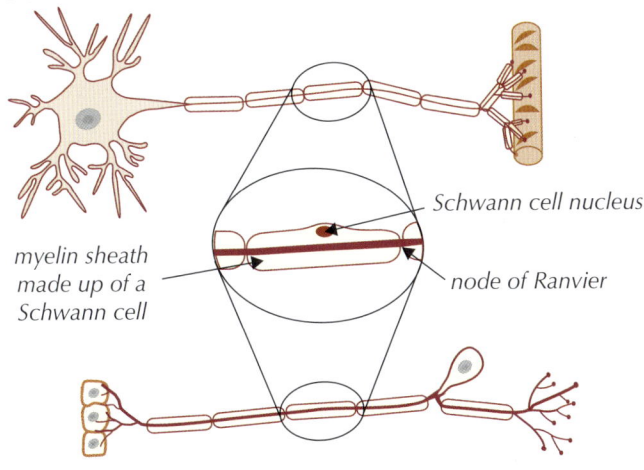

*Figure 8: Structure of a myelinated motor neurone (top) and a myelinated sensory neurone (bottom), with the myelin sheath enlarged.*

### Saltatory conduction

In a myelinated neurone, depolarisation only happens at the nodes of Ranvier (where sodium ions can get through the membrane). The neurone's cytoplasm conducts enough electrical charge to depolarise the next node, so the impulse 'jumps' from node to node. This is called saltatory conduction and it's really fast — see Figure 9.

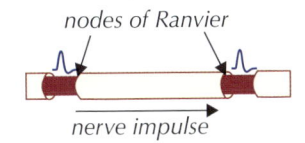

*Figure 9: Saltatory conduction along a myelinated neurone.*

In a non-myelinated neurone, the impulse travels as a wave along the whole length of the axon membrane (see Figure 10). This is slower than saltatory conduction (although it's still pretty quick).

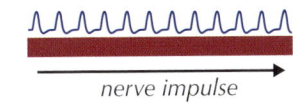

*Figure 10: Conduction along a non-myelinated neurone.*

## 2. Axon diameter

Action potentials are conducted quicker along axons with bigger diameters because there's less resistance to the flow of ions than in the cytoplasm of a smaller axon. With less resistance, depolarisation reaches other parts of the neurone cell membrane quicker.

## 3. Temperature

The speed of conduction increases as the temperature increases too, because ions diffuse faster. The speed only increases up to around 40 °C though — after that the proteins begin to denature and the speed decreases.

**Exam Tip**
You need to know the structure and function of neurones — both the myelinated ones (like those in Figure 8) and the non-myelinated ones (see page 296).

**Tip:** In the central nervous system, the myelin sheath is formed from cells called oligodendrocytes.

**Tip:** Long neurones, like a motor neurone from your spinal cord to your foot, are myelinated to speed up the conduction of action potentials.

**Tip:** If you imagine a Mexican wave travelling through a crowd, then saltatory conduction is like every tenth person doing the wave instead of everyone doing the wave — so it travels much faster.

**Tip:** The pumps and channels that move ions across the membrane are proteins, so these will denature at high temperatures.

Module 5: Section 1 Communication and Homeostasis

**Tip:** Remember, the potential difference is the voltage across the membrane.

## Practice Questions — Application

The graph below shows the changes in potential difference across a neurone cell membrane during an action potential.

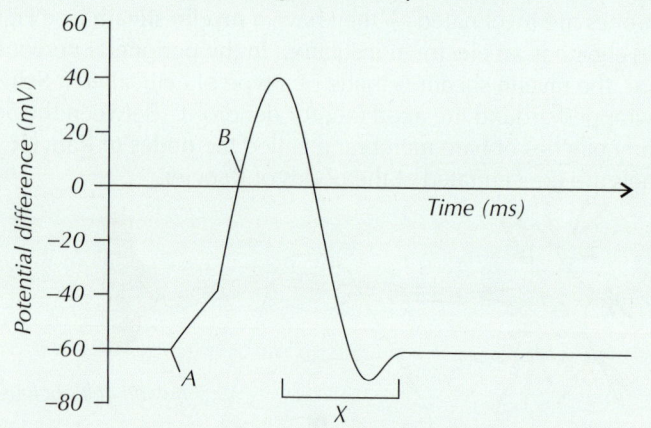

Q1  Describe the different events occurring at points A and B.
Q2  What is the threshold level for this action potential?
Q3  What is the resting potential of this neurone cell membrane?
Q4  a) Explain the shape of the curve during the period marked X.
    b) What name is given to the period marked X?
Q5  How would the graph look if a bigger stimulus triggered the action potential? Explain your answer.

**Exam Tip**
Always be clear in your exam answers as to whether you're talking about sodium ions ($Na^+$) or potassium ions ($K^+$) — don't just write 'sodium', 'potassium' or 'ions'.

**Exam Tip**
In your exam, be careful not to use phrases like 'ions move across the membrane' — you need to make it clear whether they're moving into or out of the cell.

## Practice Questions — Fact Recall

Q1  Which two proteins in a neurone's cell membrane are responsible for creating and maintaining the resting membrane potential?
Q2  Following a stimulus, explain how the opening of sodium ion channels affects the potential difference across a neurone cell membrane.
Q3  a) Describe and explain the movement of sodium ions if the potential difference across a neurone cell membrane reaches the threshold level.
    b) What type of feedback is this an example of?
Q4  a) After an action potential, why can't the neurone cell membrane be excited again straight away?
    b) What two effects does this have on the conduction of action potentials along a neurone?
Q5  Explain how waves of depolarisation are produced.
Q6  Describe the structure of a myelinated neurone in the peripheral nervous system.
Q7  How does conduction along a myelinated neurone differ compared to conduction along a non-myelinated neurone?
Q8  Give two factors, other than myelination, that affect the conduction of action potentials.

Module 5: Section 1  Communication and Homeostasis

# 4. Synapses

*If you've ever wondered how information passes from one neurone to the next, now's your chance to find out...*

**Learning Objectives:**
- Know the structure of synapses, including the structure of a cholinergic synapse.
- Understand the role of synapses in neurotransmission, including the action of neurotransmitters at the synapse, the effect of excitatory and inhibitory synapses, and the importance of synapses in summation and control.

**Specification Reference 5.1.3**

## Synapses and neurotransmitters

A synapse is the junction between a neurone and another neurone, or between a neurone and an effector cell, e.g. a muscle or gland cell. The tiny gap between the cells at a synapse is called the synaptic cleft. The presynaptic neurone (the one before the synapse) has a swelling called a synaptic knob. This contains synaptic vesicles filled with chemicals called neurotransmitters.

When an action potential reaches the end of a neurone it causes neurotransmitters to be released into the synaptic cleft. They diffuse across to the postsynaptic membrane (the one after the synapse) and bind to specific receptors. When neurotransmitters bind to receptors they might trigger an action potential (in a neurone), cause muscle contraction (in a muscle cell), or cause a hormone to be secreted (from a gland cell).

Neurotransmitters are removed from the cleft so the response doesn't keep happening, e.g. they're taken back into the presynaptic neurone or they're broken down by enzymes (and the products are taken into the neurone).

### Cholinergic synapses

There are different types of synapses, each with a slightly different structure that relates to their function. You need to learn the structure of a **cholinergic synapse** — see Figure 2. A cholinergic synapse uses the neurotransmitter **acetylcholine** (**ACh**) which binds to receptors called cholinergic receptors.

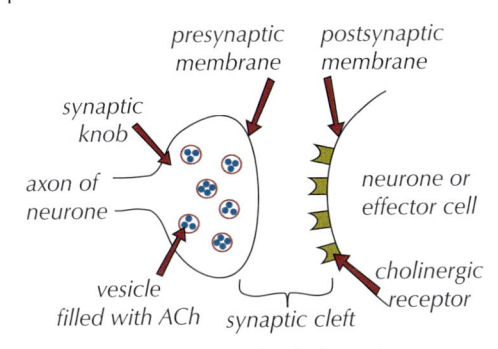

**Figure 2:** The structure of a cholinergic synapse.

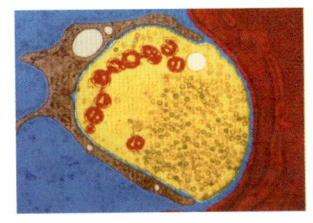

**Figure 1:** A synaptic knob (yellow) containing vesicles (large red circles).

## Synaptic transmission

This is how a nerve impulse is transmitted across a cholinergic synapse:

### 1. Arrival of an action potential

An action potential arrives at the synaptic knob of the presynaptic neurone. The action potential stimulates voltage-gated calcium ion channels in the presynaptic neurone to open. Calcium ions ($Ca^{2+}$) diffuse into the synaptic knob. (They're pumped out afterwards by active transport.)

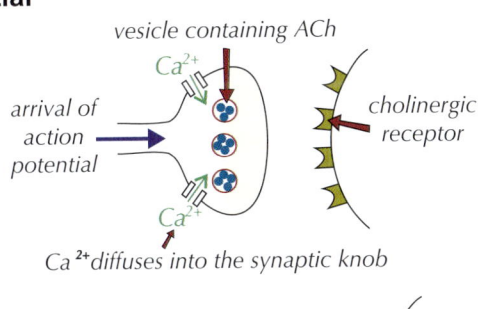

*$Ca^{2+}$ diffuses into the synaptic knob*

**Tip:** Remember, voltage-gated ion channels are channels that only open when the potential difference across a membrane reaches a certain voltage.

### 2. Fusion of the vesicles

The influx of calcium ions into the synaptic knob causes the synaptic vesicles to move to the presynaptic membrane. They then fuse with the presynaptic membrane. The vesicles release ACh into the synaptic cleft by **exocytosis**.

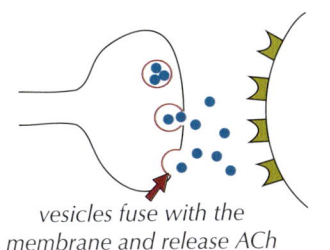

*vesicles fuse with the membrane and release ACh*

Module 5: Section 1 Communication and Homeostasis

### 3. Diffusion of ACh

ACh diffuses across the synaptic cleft and binds to specific cholinergic receptors on the postsynaptic membrane. This causes sodium ion channels in the postsynaptic neurone to open. The influx of sodium ions into the postsynaptic neurone causes depolarisation. An action potential on the postsynaptic membrane is generated if the threshold is reached. ACh is removed from the synaptic cleft so the response doesn't keep happening. It's broken down by an enzyme called acetylcholinesterase (AChE) and the products are re-absorbed by the presynaptic neurone and used to make more ACh.

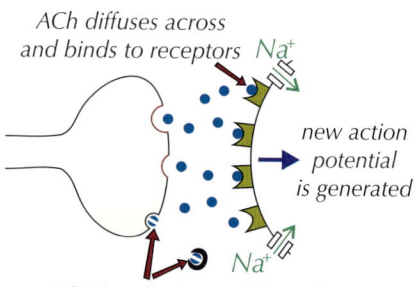

**Tip:** Look back at page 301 if you need a reminder of how action potentials are generated.

ACh diffuses across and binds to receptors Na$^+$

new action potential is generated

AChE breaks down ACh and the products are re-absorbed

## Disruption of synaptic transmission

Because synapses use chemical communication, they can be affected by chemicals like drugs, toxins or poisons. For example, some chemicals are the same shape as neurotransmitters so they mimic their action at receptors (these drugs are called agonists). This means more receptors are activated.

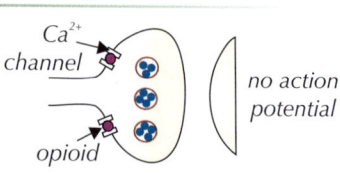

**Exam Tip**
Don't worry, you don't have to learn the action of any specific drug or toxin for your exam. But examiners like to test your knowledge of synapses, e.g. by asking about how drugs or toxins would affect their activity, so make sure you understand these examples.

--- Example ---
Nicotine mimics acetylcholine. It binds to certain types of cholinergic receptors in the brain.

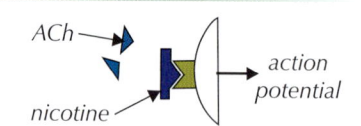

ACh → action potential
nicotine

Some chemicals block receptors so they can't be activated by neurotransmitters. This means fewer receptors (if any) can be activated.

--- Example ---
Curare blocks the effects of acetylcholine by blocking certain cholinergic receptors at neuromuscular junctions, so muscle cells can't be stimulated. This results in the muscle being paralysed.

ACh → no action potential
curare

Some chemicals inhibit the enzyme that breaks down neurotransmitters (they stop it from working). This means there are more neurotransmitters in the synaptic cleft to bind to receptors and they're there for longer.

**Tip:** The nervous system uses lots of different neurotransmitters, not just acetylcholine. You'll come across ones called dopamine and noradrenaline too.

--- Example ---
Nerve gases stop acetylcholine from being broken down in the synaptic cleft. This can lead to loss of muscle control.

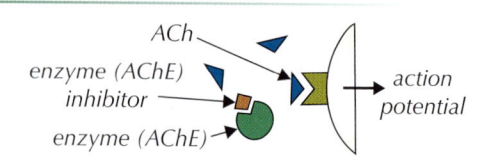

ACh
enzyme (AChE) inhibitor → action potential
enzyme (AChE)

Some chemicals inhibit the release of neurotransmitters from the presynaptic neurone so fewer receptors are activated.

--- Example ---
Opioids block calcium ion channels in the presynaptic neurone. This means fewer vesicles fuse with the presynaptic membrane so less neurotransmitter is released.

Ca$^{2+}$ channel → no action potential
opioid

Module 5: Section 1 Communication and Homeostasis

> **Practice Question — Application**
>
> Q1  Acetylcholine (ACh) is involved in many functions in the body, including saliva production. Carbachol is a drug that binds and activates cholinergic receptors. Predict the effect of carbachol on saliva production and explain your answer.

**Exam Tip**
Don't worry if you've never heard of particular drug names — all the information you need to answer the question will be in the question itself.

# Roles of synapses

Synapses play vital roles in the nervous system. The way they work affects how information is passed on throughout the body.

### Excitatory and inhibitory synapses

Neurotransmitters can be excitatory, inhibitory or both. Excitatory neurotransmitters depolarise the postsynaptic membrane, making it fire an action potential if the threshold is reached (see pages 305-306). Inhibitory neurotransmitters hyperpolarise the postsynaptic membrane (make the potential difference more negative), preventing it from firing an action potential. A synapse where excitatory neurotransmitters are released from the presynaptic membrane following an action potential is called an **excitatory synapse**. A synapse where inhibitory neurotransmitters are released is an **inhibitory synapse**.

**Tip:** Acetylcholine is an excitatory neurotransmitter at cholinergic synapses in the CNS and at neuromuscular junctions (see p. 371). But it's an inhibitory neurotransmitter at cholinergic synapses in the heart. When it binds to receptors here, it can cause potassium ion channels to open on the postsynaptic membrane, hyperpolarising it.

### Divergence and convergence

When one neurone connects to many neurones information can be dispersed to different parts of the body. This is called **synaptic divergence** (see Figure 3). When many neurones connect to one neurone information can be amplified (made stronger). This is called **synaptic convergence** (see Figure 4).

one neurone releases neurotransmitters... ...to many neurones

many neurones release neurotransmitters... ... to one neurone

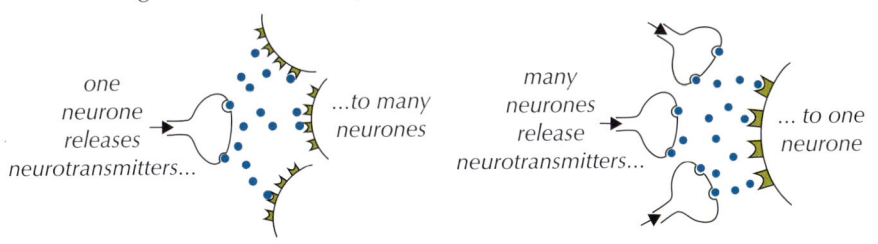

**Figure 3:** Synaptic divergence.

**Figure 4:** Synaptic convergence.

**Tip:** Synaptic <u>d</u>ivergence is when information from one neurone <u>d</u>ivides, and synaptic <u>c</u>onvergence is when information from many neurones <u>c</u>omes together.

### Summation

If a stimulus is weak, only a small amount of neurotransmitter will be released from a neurone into the synaptic cleft. This might not be enough to excite the postsynaptic membrane to the threshold level and stimulate an action potential. Summation is where the effect of neurotransmitters released from many neurones (or one neurone that's stimulated a lot in a short period of time) is added together. It means synapses accurately process information, finely tuning the response. There are two types of summation:

1. **Spatial summation** is where two or more presynaptic neurones converge and release their neurotransmitters at the same time onto the same postsynaptic neurone. The small amount of neurotransmitter released from each of these neurones can be enough altogether to reach the threshold in the postsynaptic neurone and trigger an action potential — see Figure 5 on the next page. Stimuli might arrive from different sources, but spatial summation allows signals from multiple stimuli to be coordinated into a single response.

**Tip:** Summation is where the <u>sum</u> total of lots of smaller impulses triggers an action potential.

Module 5: Section 1  Communication and Homeostasis

**Tip:** Remember, only excitatory neurotransmitters can trigger an action potential (see previous page).

*Figure 5: One presynaptic neurone only releases a few neurotransmitters (left) but three presynaptic neurones release enough to trigger an action potential (right).*

If some neurones release an inhibitory neurotransmitter then the total effect of all the neurotransmitters might be no action potential — see Figure 6.

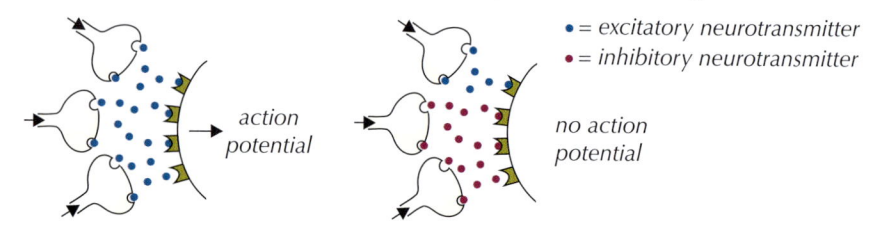

*Figure 6: If some presynaptic neurones release inhibitory neurotransmitters, it might prevent an action potential from being triggered (right).*

2. **Temporal summation** is where two or more nerve impulses arrive in quick succession from the same presynaptic neurone. This makes an action potential more likely because more neurotransmitter is released into the synaptic cleft — see Figure 7.

**Tip:** Impulses have to follow each other very quickly, otherwise the neurotransmitter will be removed from the cleft before it's reached a level high enough to trigger an action potential.

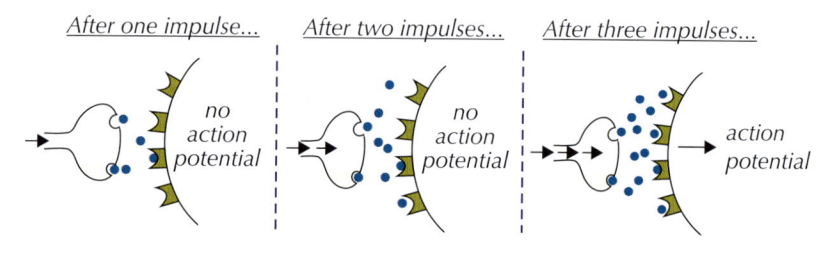

*Figure 7: The effects of temporal summation at a synapse.*

## Unidirectional transmission

Synapses make sure impulses are unidirectional — the nervous impulse can only travel in one direction. This is because neurotransmitters are only released from presynaptic neurones and receptors for neurotransmitters are only on the postsynaptic membranes.

**Tip:** Don't get the presynaptic and postsynaptic neurones mixed up — remember 'pre' means before and 'post' means after.

### Practice Questions — Fact Recall

Q1 At a cholinergic synapse in the CNS:
  a) Describe and explain the movement of calcium ions following the arrival of an action potential at a presynaptic neurone.
  b) Explain how acetylcholine (ACh) leaves the presynaptic neurone and can cause an action potential in the postsynaptic neurone.

Q2 Explain the purpose of:
  a) synaptic divergence,     b) synaptic convergence.

Q3 Explain how an action potential may be more likely as a result of:
  a) spatial summation,     b) temporal summation.

# Exam-style Questions

1     **Fig 1.1** shows five action potentials recorded across the membrane of a myelinated axon.

   **(a) (i)** Explain why the action potentials don't overlap.

*(3 marks)*

**Fig. 1.1**

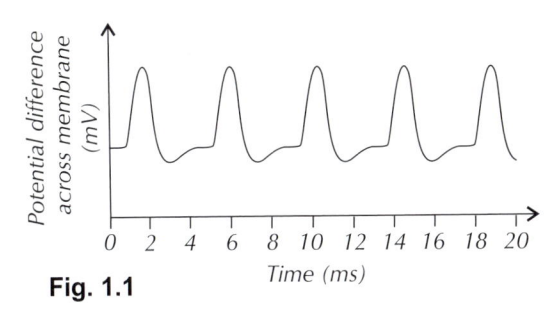

     **(ii)** If the action potentials continue at the same frequency, calculate the number of action potentials along the axon in 500 ms.

*(2 marks)*

   **(b)**  **Fig. 1.2** shows the neurone cell membrane at two different times during one action potential.

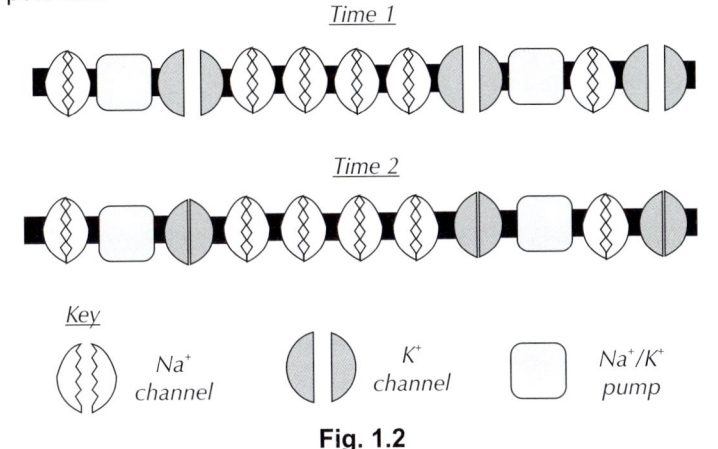

Time 1

Time 2

Key: Na⁺ channel, K⁺ channel, Na⁺/K⁺ pump

**Fig. 1.2**

     **(i)*** Describe the stages of the action potential that are occurring at Times 1 and 2. Use evidence from **Fig. 1.2** to support your answer.

*(6 marks)*

The neurone cell membrane shows **sodium-potassium (Na⁺/K⁺) pumps**.

     **(ii)** Describe the movement of sodium and potassium ions across a sodium-potassium pump.

*(3 marks)*

     **(iii)** Explain why a sodium-potassium pump is needed by the neurone cell membrane after Time 2.

*(2 marks)*

   **(c)** Saxitoxin is a chemical that blocks **voltage-gated sodium ion channels**. Use your knowledge of action potentials to explain the effect that saxitoxin is likely to have upon the nervous system.

*(2 marks)*

\* The quality of your response will be assessed in this question.

**2** Fig. 2.1 shows the structure of a myelinated motor neurone.

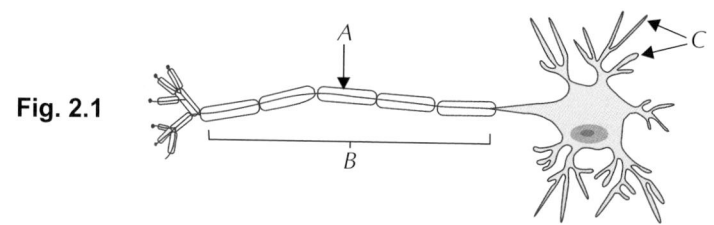

Fig. 2.1

(a) (i) Name the type of cell that forms structure **A**.

*(1 mark)*

(ii) Complete the table to give the names of the structures labelled **B** and **C** and their functions.

|   | Structure | Function |
|---|-----------|----------|
| B |           |          |
| C |           |          |

*(4 marks)*

(b) Sensory and relay neurones differ in structure and function to motor neurones.
(i) Give the **function** of a sensory neurone.

*(1 mark)*

(ii) Give the **function** of a relay neurone.

*(1 mark)*

(c) Guillain-Barré syndrome is an auto-immune disease whereby the myelin sheath around certain neurones is damaged.

Use your knowledge of myelination to explain how Guillain-Barré syndrome can result in muscle weakness and paralysis.

*(2 marks)*

**3** A neuromuscular junction is a specialised synapse between a motor neurone and a muscle cell. It uses **acetylcholine** as a neurotransmitter.

(a) Explain how an action potential along a motor neurone results in acetylcholine being released at the neuromuscular junction.

*(4 marks)*

(b) An action potential is more likely if two or more nerve impulses arrive in quick succession from the same presynaptic neurone.
(i) What is the name given to this effect?

*(1 mark)*

(ii) Explain why this effect makes an action potential in the muscle cell more likely.

*(5 marks)*

(c) The drug tubocurarine blocks receptors at neuromuscular junctions.
Doctors use this drug as an anaesthetic as it temporarily paralyses muscles.
Suggest how tubocurarine works.

*(4 marks)*

# 5. The Hormonal System and Glands

*Like the nervous system, the hormonal system is a form of cell signalling that helps us to respond to our environment.*

## What is the hormonal system?

The hormonal system sends information as chemical signals. It's made up of glands (called endocrine glands) and hormones. **Endocrine glands** are groups of cells that are specialised to secrete hormones, e.g. the pancreas secretes insulin. **Hormones** are 'chemical messengers'. Many hormones are proteins or peptides, e.g. insulin. Some hormones are steroids, e.g. progesterone.

Hormones are secreted when an endocrine gland is stimulated. Glands can be stimulated by a change in concentration of a specific substance (sometimes another hormone). They can also be stimulated by electrical impulses.

### Hormonal communication

Hormones diffuse directly into the blood, then they're taken around the body by the circulatory system. They diffuse out of the blood all over the body but each hormone will only bind to specific receptors for that hormone, found on the membranes of some cells, called **target cells**. Tissue that contains target cells is called **target tissue**. The hormones trigger a response in the target cells (the effectors).

Stimulus ➡ Receptors ➡ Hormone ➡ Effectors ➡ Response

**Figure 1:** The pathway of hormonal communication.

---
**Example**

A real-life example of hormonal communication is the process the body uses to increase blood glucose concentration when it's lower than normal:

- **Stimulus** — low blood glucose concentration.
- **Receptors** — receptors on pancreas cells detect the low blood glucose concentration.
- **Hormone** — the pancreas releases the hormone glucagon into the blood.
- **Effectors** — target cells in the liver detect glucagon and convert glycogen into glucose.
- **Response** — glucose is released into the blood, so glucose concentration increases.

---

## Action of hormones

A hormone is called a **first messenger** because it carries the chemical message the first part of the way, from the endocrine gland to the receptor on the target cells. When a hormone binds to its receptor it activates an enzyme in the cell membrane. The enzyme catalyses the production of a molecule inside the cell called a signalling molecule — this molecule signals to other parts of the cell to change how the cell works.

The signalling molecule is called a **second messenger** because it carries the chemical message the second part of the way, from the receptor to other parts of the cell. Second messengers activate a cascade (a chain of reactions) inside the cell.

---

**Learning Objectives:**

- Understand endocrine communication by hormones, including the secretion of hormones into the blood, transport by the blood and detection by target cells or tissues.
- Know the action of hormones in cell signalling, including adrenaline (first messenger), activation of adenylyl cyclase, and cyclic AMP (second messenger).
- Know the structure and functions of the adrenal glands, including the hormones secreted by the cortex and medulla and their functions.
- Understand the histology of the pancreas, including the endocrine tissues.
- Be able to examine and draw stained sections of the pancreas to show the histology of the endocrine tissues (PAG1).

**Specification References 5.1.4, 5.1.5**

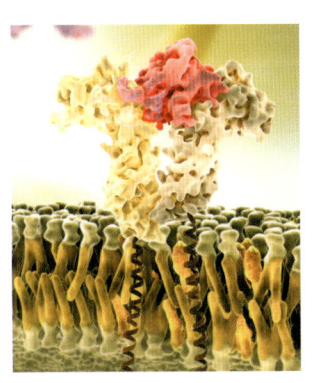

**Figure 2:** A growth hormone molecule (pink) bound to a growth hormone receptor (yellow and beige) in the membrane of the target cell.

Module 5: Section 1 Communication and Homeostasis

**Tip:** The release of adrenaline also has an effect on heart rate — there's more about this on page 357.

### Adrenaline

Adrenaline is a hormone that's secreted from your adrenal glands (see below). It's secreted when there's a low concentration of glucose in your blood, when you're stressed and when you're exercising. Adrenaline gets the body ready for action by making more glucose available for muscles to respire, e.g. by activating glycogenolysis (the breakdown of glycogen to glucose — see p. 322).

Adrenaline is a first messenger. It binds to specific receptors in the cell membranes of many cells, e.g. liver cells. When adrenaline binds it activates an enzyme in the membrane called adenylyl cyclase. Activated adenylyl cyclase catalyses the production of a second messenger called cyclic AMP (cAMP) from ATP. cAMP activates a cascade, e.g. a cascade of enzyme reactions makes more glucose available to the cell by catalysing the breakdown of glycogen into glucose — see Figure 3.

**Tip:** Lots of cells in the body have receptors for adrenaline. The cascade that's activated is not the same in every type of cell and the second messenger isn't always cAMP, so adrenaline affects different tissues in different ways.

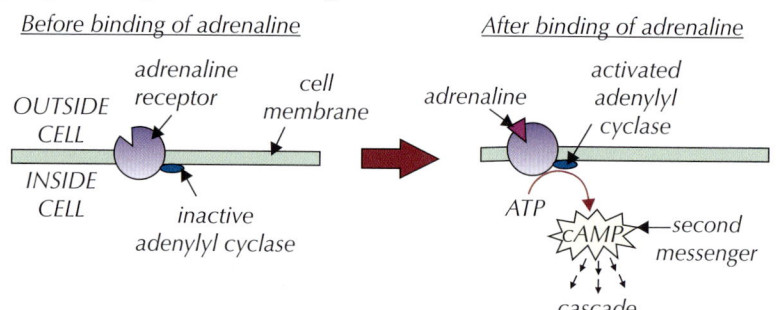

*Figure 3: Diagram showing the action of adrenaline as a first messenger and cAMP as a second messenger.*

## Adrenal glands

The adrenal glands are endocrine glands that are found just above your kidneys. Each adrenal gland has an outer part called the cortex and an inner part called the medulla (see Figure 4). The cortex and the medulla have different functions and the hormones they secrete produce different responses. For example, they play different roles in our response to stress, producing effects which help to prepare the body for the '**fight or flight**' response (see page 357).

**Tip:** The <u>m</u>edulla is the name given to the <u>m</u>iddle of an organ. The <u>c</u>ortex is the <u>o</u>uter layer.

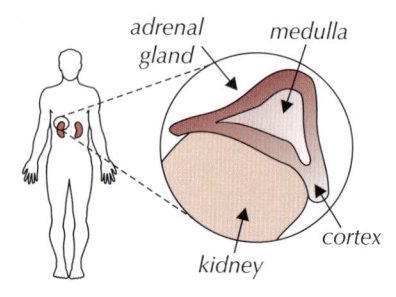

*Figure 4: The location and structure of an adrenal gland.*

### The cortex

The cortex secretes **steroid hormones**, e.g. it secretes cortisol and aldosterone when you're stressed. These hormones have a role in both the short-term and the long-term responses to stress. Their effects include:

**Tip:** Cortisol, aldosterone, adrenaline and noradrenaline work together to control your response to stress. See the next page for more on the roles of adrenaline and noradrenaline.

- stimulating the breakdown of proteins and fats into glucose. This increases the amount of energy available so the brain and muscles can respond to the situation.
- increasing blood volume and pressure by increasing the uptake of sodium ions and water by the kidneys.
- suppressing the immune system.

312 | Module 5: Section 1 Communication and Homeostasis

### The medulla
The medulla secretes **catecholamine hormones** (modified amino acids), e.g. it secretes adrenaline and noradrenaline when you're stressed. These act to make more energy available in the short-term by increasing heart and breathing rate, causing cells to break down glycogen into glucose and constricting some blood vessels so that blood is diverted to the brain and muscles.

## The pancreas
The pancreas is a gland that's found below the stomach. You need to know about its endocrine function. The areas of the pancreas that contain endocrine tissue are called the **islets of Langerhans**. They're found in clusters around blood capillaries and they secrete hormones directly into the blood. They're made up of two types of cell, alpha (α) cells and beta (β) cells (see Figure 5). α cells secrete a hormone called glucagon and β cells secrete a hormone called insulin. Glucagon and insulin help to control blood glucose concentration (see p. 322).

**Tip:** One of the learning objectives is to understand the histology of the pancreas — this just means its structure as seen under a microscope.

**Tip:** See page 324 for more detail on the structure of beta cells.

**Figure 5:** The location of α and β cells in the islets of Langerhans.

Figure 6 shows what you might see if you looked at a stained section of pancreatic tissue under a light microscope.

PRACTICAL ACTIVITY GROUP 1

**Tip:** See pages 52-55 for more on how to use a light microscope to examine and draw a section.

- The purple stained cells are the β cells.
- The islets of Langerhans (endocrine tissue) appear as paler patches in amongst all the other cells.
- If you look closely you can see pink stained cells — these are α cells.

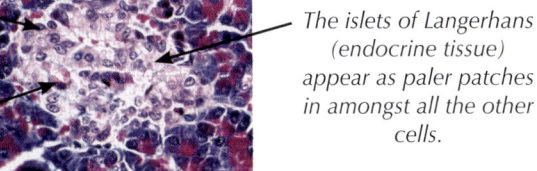

**Figure 6:** Light micrograph of a section of pancreatic tissue.

**Tip:** You can only differentiate between α and β cells if a special stain has been used to make them different colours, e.g. chrome haematoxylin and phloxine.

### Practice Questions — Application
Read the passage below and then answer the questions that follow on the next page.

> When a baby sucks on its mother's nipple, electrical impulses are sent from the nipple via the central nervous system to the mother's posterior pituitary gland, which is stimulated to secrete oxytocin into the blood. Oxytocin binds to specific receptors on myoepithelial cells, found in the epithelial tissue of mammary glands in the mother's breast. This causes contraction of the myoepithelial cells, which in turn causes milk to be secreted via milk ducts, out of the mother's nipple.

Q1  Copy and complete the table below by naming the molecules and structures involved in the pathway of communication described on the previous page.

| Molecule / Structure | Name |
|---|---|
| Hormone | |
| Target cells | |
| Target tissue | |
| Endocrine gland | |

Q2  It can take several minutes from when the baby starts sucking its mother's nipple to when milk is released. Suggest why this is.

## Practice Questions — Fact Recall

Q1  What is an endocrine gland?

Q2  Give two types of stimuli that trigger hormone secretion.

Q3  Once a hormone is in the bloodstream, why doesn't it affect every cell in the body?

Q4  When adrenaline binds to receptors in the cell membrane of liver cells, it activates the enzyme adenylyl cyclase. This then catalyses the production of a second messenger inside the cell.
   a) What is the name of the second messenger produced?
   b) What effect does the second messenger have inside the cell?
   c) What is the first messenger in this example?

Q5  The adrenal glands have an inner part and an outer part.
   a) Name both parts.
   b) Explain the role that the inner part plays when the body is stressed.

Q6  The image below shows a light micrograph of a section through the pancreas. The yellow tissue contains α and β cells.

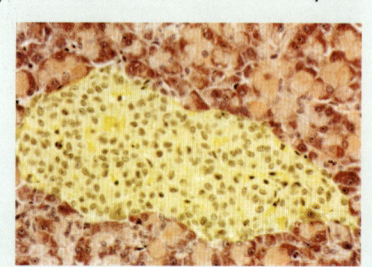

   a) What is the name of the yellow tissue shown in the micrograph?
   b) Name the hormone secreted by:
      i)  α cells,
      ii) β cells.

**Exam Tip**
Make sure you read questions in the exam carefully — e.g. if you're asked to give two examples of something make sure you give two. You'll miss out on marks if you only give one and waste time if you give more than two.

# 6. Homeostasis Basics

*The body has some pretty clever systems to control its internal environment...*

**Learning Objectives:**
- Understand the principles of homeostasis.
- Know the differences between receptors and effectors in homeostasis.
- Know the differences between negative feedback and positive feedback.

**Specification Reference 5.1.1**

## What is homeostasis?

Changes in your external environment can affect your internal environment — the blood and tissue fluid that surrounds your cells. Homeostasis is the maintenance of a constant internal environment. It involves control systems that keep your internal environment roughly constant (within certain limits). Keeping your internal environment constant is vital for cells to function normally and to stop them being damaged.

It's particularly important to maintain the right core body temperature. This is because temperature affects enzyme activity, and enzymes control the rate of metabolic reactions (chemical reactions in living cells).

### Temperature

The rate of metabolic reactions increases when the temperature's increased. More heat means more kinetic energy, so molecules move faster. This makes the substrate molecules more likely to collide with the enzymes' active sites. The energy of these collisions also increases, which means each collision is more likely to result in a reaction.

But, if the temperature gets too high (e.g. over 40 °C), the reaction essentially stops. The rise in temperature makes the enzyme's molecules vibrate more. If the temperature goes above a certain level, this vibration breaks some of the hydrogen bonds that hold the enzyme in its 3D shape. The active site changes shape and the enzyme and substrate no longer fit together. At this point, the enzyme is denatured — it no longer functions as a catalyst (see Figure 1).

If body temperature is too low enzyme activity is reduced, slowing the rate of metabolic reactions. The highest rate of enzyme activity happens at their optimum temperature — about 37 °C in humans (see Figure 1).

**Tip:** As well as maintaining core body temperature, it's also important to maintain the right concentration of glucose in the blood (see page 322), so there's always enough available for respiration.

**Tip:** When an enzyme is denatured the reaction may still happen but it'll be too slow for the body's needs.

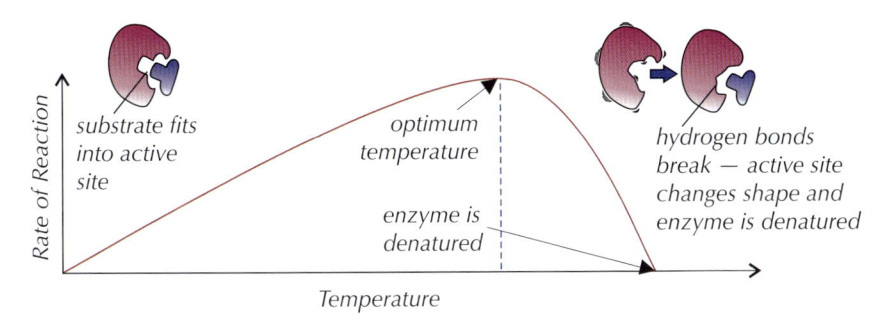

**Figure 1:** Effect of temperature on the rate of a metabolic reaction.

## Negative feedback

Homeostatic systems involve receptors, a communication system and effectors. Receptors detect when a level is too high or too low, and the information's communicated via the nervous system or the hormonal system to effectors. The effectors respond to counteract the change — bringing the level back to normal. The mechanism that restores the level to normal is called a **negative feedback mechanism** — see Figure 2 (on the next page).

**Tip:** The 'level' in Figure 2 refers to something inside the body that needs to be controlled, e.g. temperature level, blood glucose level.

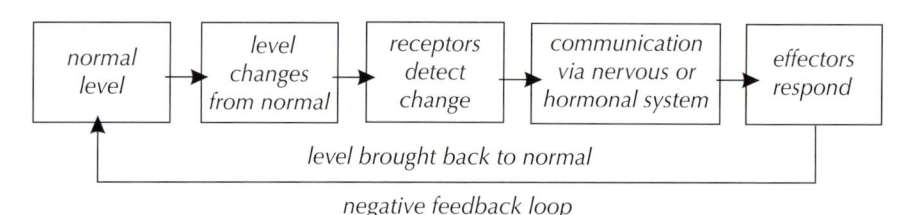

normal level → level changes from normal → receptors detect change → communication via nervous or hormonal system → effectors respond

level brought back to normal

negative feedback loop

**Figure 2:** A negative feedback mechanism.

Negative feedback keeps things around the normal level.

### Example
Body temperature is usually kept within 0.5 °C above or below 37 °C.

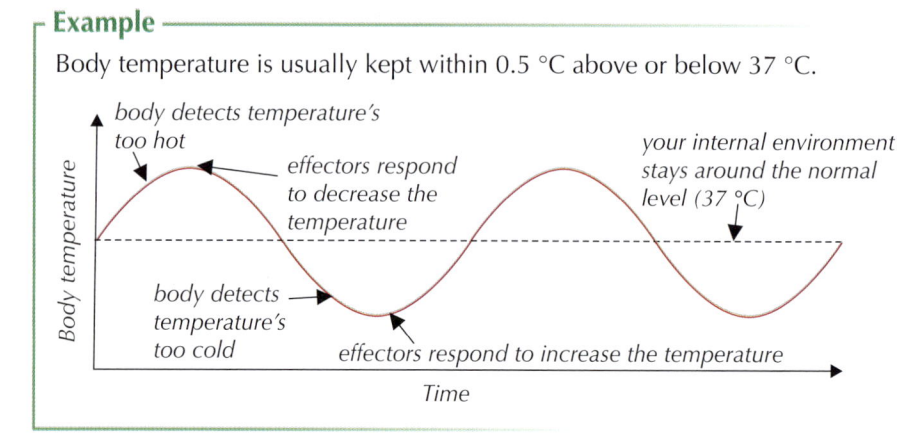

*body detects temperature's too hot*
*effectors respond to decrease the temperature*
*your internal environment stays around the normal level (37 °C)*
*body detects temperature's too cold*
*effectors respond to increase the temperature*

Body temperature vs Time

**Tip:** There are various ways in which effectors respond to change body temperature in mammals — see pages 319-320 for more.

Negative feedback only works within certain limits though — if the change is too big then the effectors may not be able to counteract it, e.g. a huge drop in body temperature caused by prolonged exposure to cold weather may be too large to counteract.

## Positive feedback

Some changes trigger a positive feedback mechanism, which amplifies the change. The effectors respond to further increase the level away from the normal level. The mechanism that amplifies a change away from the normal level is called a **positive feedback mechanism** — see Figure 3.

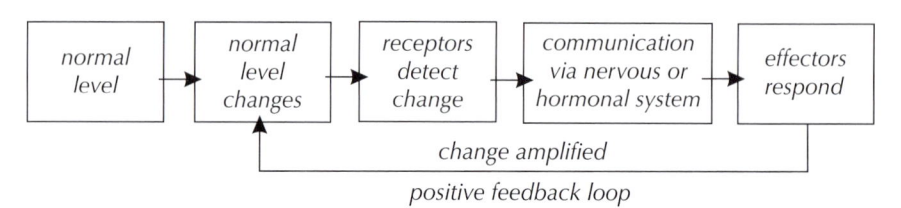

normal level → normal level changes → receptors detect change → communication via nervous or hormonal system → effectors respond

change amplified

positive feedback loop

**Figure 3:** A positive feedback mechanism.

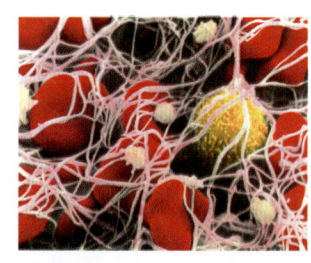

**Figure 4:** At a site of injury, more and more platelets (shown above as small, green balls) are produced to form a clot as part of a positive feedback mechanism.

Positive feedback isn't involved in homeostasis because it doesn't keep your internal environment constant. Positive feedback is useful to rapidly activate processes in the body.

### Example
During the formation of a blood clot after an injury, platelets become activated and release a chemical — this triggers more platelets to be activated, and so on. This means platelets very quickly form a blood clot at the injury site. (The process ends with negative feedback, when the body detects the blood clot has been formed.)

## Practice Questions — Application

**Q1** Read the following two passages about control systems in the body:

Passage A
A high blood concentration of carbon dioxide lowers the pH of the blood. Chemoreceptors in the blood vessels detect this change and send signals to the brain to increase the respiration rate.

Passage B
When oestrogen concentration is high it stimulates the anterior pituitary gland to release LH. LH stimulates the ovaries to release more oestrogen.

**Tip:** Oestrogen and LH are both hormones — you don't need to know anything about their effects in the body to answer the question.

For each passage, state whether it's an example of negative or positive feedback and explain your answer.

**Q2** When low blood calcium concentration is detected, the secretion of parathyroid hormone (PTH) from the parathyroid gland is stimulated. When high blood calcium concentration is detected, the secretion of the hormone calcitonin, from the thyroid gland, is stimulated. These two hormones work via negative feedback mechanisms to control the blood calcium concentration. Their effects are shown on the graph.

**Tip:** Parathyroid and thyroid glands are found in the neck.

a) Suggest an explanation for the shape of the graph between:
   i) A and B.
   ii) C and D.

b) Suggest what could happen to the blood calcium concentration of someone who has had a parathyroid gland removed. Explain your answer.

## Practice Questions — Fact Recall

**Q1** What is homeostasis?

**Q2** Explain why it is important for the body to maintain its internal temperature within normal limits.

**Q3** The diagram below shows a negative feedback loop. Describe what happens in the missing labels, A-C.

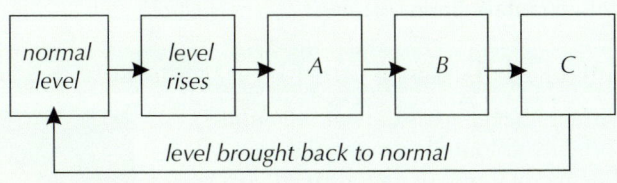

normal level → level rises → A → B → C → level brought back to normal

*negative feedback loop*

**Q4** Describe how positive feedback mechanisms differ from negative feedback mechanisms.

**Learning Objectives:**
- Understand the behavioural responses involved in temperature control in ectotherms.
- Understand the physiological and behavioural responses involved in temperature control in endotherms, including peripheral temperature receptors, the role of the hypothalamus and effectors in skin and muscles.

**Specification Reference 5.1.1**

# 7. Control of Body Temperature

*Some organisms can control their body temperature internally. Many different mechanisms allow them to do this and they're controlled by the brain.*

## Temperature control in ectotherms and endotherms

Animals are classed as either ectotherms (e.g. reptiles, fish) or endotherms (e.g. mammals, birds), depending on how they control their body temperature.

### Ectotherms

Ectotherms can't control their body temperature internally — they control their temperature by changing their behaviour.

**Example**

A lizard is an ectotherm. When its internal temperature drops, a lizard will move to find a warmer area such as a place in the sunshine. When its internal temperature gets too high, it will move to somewhere cooler such as a burrow beneath the sand.

This means the internal temperature of ectotherms depends on the external temperature (their surroundings).

Ectotherms have a variable metabolic rate because they can't keep their internal temperature constant. They generate very little heat themselves. This means the activity level of ectotherms depends on the external temperature too — they're more active at higher temperatures and less active at lower temperatures.

### Endotherms

Endotherms control their body temperature internally by homeostasis, as well as by altering their behaviour.

**Example**

An elephant is an endotherm. Its temperature is mainly controlled internally by homeostasis, but it may also change its behaviour to control its temperature. For example, it may wallow in mud or flap its ears to help it cool down.

This means that, compared to ectotherms, the internal temperature of endotherms is less affected by the external temperature (within certain limits).

Endotherms have a constantly high metabolic rate because they can keep their internal temperature constant. They generate a lot of heat from metabolic reactions. This means the activity level of endotherms is largely independent of the external temperature — they can be active at any temperature (within certain limits).

**Figure 1:** *A lizard basking in the sun to warm up.*

**Tip:** In ectotherms, respiration and other metabolic reactions happen faster in warmer weather. This means in warmer weather more energy is available for faster movement, etc., so ectotherms are more active in warmer weather.

### Practice Questions — Application

Q1 On a thermal image, areas of heat radiation appear brightly coloured. On the right is a thermal image of a mouse and a snake.

a) What can you conclude about the temperature of the external environment when the image was taken? Explain your answer.

b) Would you expect the mouse or the snake to be more active at the time the image was taken? Explain your answer.

Q2 In an experiment, the internal temperatures of a chuckwalla and a hoatzin were recorded over a range of external temperatures controlled by a heat source. The organisms were kept in enclosed environments with a heat source. The results are shown in the table below.

| | Temperature (°C) | | | | |
|---|---|---|---|---|---|
| External | 20 | 24 | 28 | 32 | 38 |
| Chuckwalla | 26.7 | 30.4 | 37.7 | 40.1 | 43.2 |
| Hoatzin | 38.5 | 38.7 | 38.8 | 39.0 | 38.9 |

a) Use information from the table to explain which organism is an ectotherm and which is an endotherm.

b) Will the metabolic reactions of the chuckwalla or the hoatzin be most affected during this investigation? Explain your answer.

**Exam Tip**
Don't be thrown in the exam by names of unfamiliar organisms — just concentrate on what the question's asking you.

# Mechanisms to change body temperature

Mammals use different mechanisms to reduce or increase their body temperature.

**Tip:** Remember, mammals are endotherms.

## Mechanisms to reduce body temperature

1. **Sweating** — more sweat is secreted from sweat glands when the body's too hot. The water in sweat evaporates from the surface of the skin and takes heat from the body. The skin is cooled.

2. **Hairs lie flat** — mammals have a layer of hair that provides insulation by trapping air (air is a poor conductor of heat). When it's hot, erector pili muscles relax so the hairs lie flat. Less air is trapped, so the skin is less insulated and heat can be lost more easily.

3. **Vasodilation** — when it's hot, arterioles near the surface of the skin dilate (this is called vasodilation). More blood flows through the capillaries in the surface layers of the dermis. This means more heat is lost from the skin by radiation and the temperature is lowered.

**Tip:** Heat radiation is the transfer of heat energy to surroundings by infrared radiation.

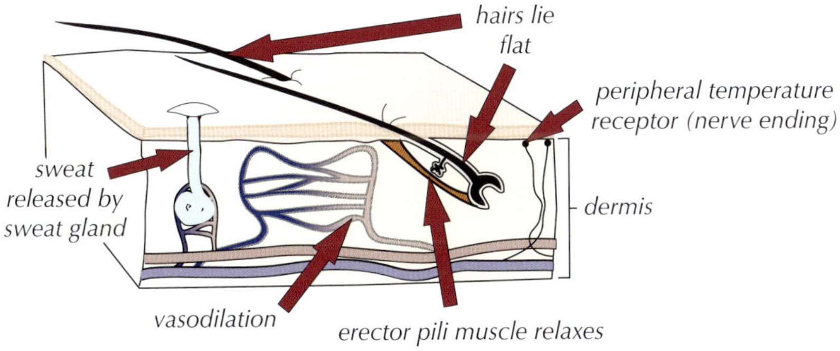

**Tip:** Changes in temperature are detected by thermoreceptors — see next page.

*Figure 2:* Mechanisms to reduce body temperature in a mammal.

## Mechanisms to increase body temperature

1. **Shivering** — when it's cold, muscles contract in spasms. This makes the body shiver and more heat is produced from increased respiration.

2. **Hormones** — the body releases adrenaline and thyroxine. These increase metabolism and so more heat is produced.

**Tip:** The products of respiration are $CO_2$, water and energy (heat) — see p. 391 for more.

Module 5: Section 1 Communication and Homeostasis

**Tip:** These three mechanisms are all ways to conserve heat, whereas the previous two mechanisms (shivering and hormones) actually produce heat.

3. **Much less sweat** — less sweat is secreted from sweat glands when it's cold, reducing the amount of heat loss.
4. **Hairs stand up** — erector pili muscles contract when it's cold, which makes the hairs stand up. This traps more air and so prevents heat loss.
5. **Vasoconstriction** — when it's cold, arterioles near the surface of the skin constrict (this is called vasoconstriction) so less blood flows through the capillaries in the surface layers of the dermis. This reduces heat loss.

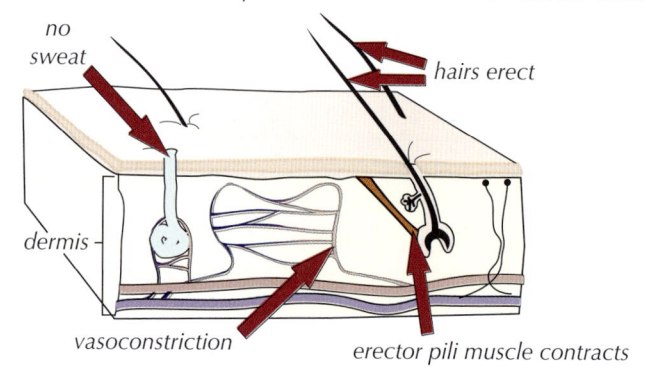

*Figure 3:* Mechanisms to increase body temperature in a mammal.

# Control of body temperature by the hypothalamus

Body temperature in mammals is maintained at a constant level by a part of the brain called the **hypothalamus**. The hypothalamus receives information about both internal and external temperature from **thermoreceptors** (temperature receptors):

- Thermoreceptors in the hypothalamus detect internal temperature (the temperature of the blood).
- Thermoreceptors in the skin (called peripheral temperature receptors) detect external temperature (the temperature of the skin).

Thermoreceptors send impulses along sensory neurones to the hypothalamus, which sends impulses along motor neurones to effectors (e.g. skeletal muscles, or sweat glands and erector pili muscles in the skin). The effectors respond to restore the body temperature back to normal.

**Tip:** Control of body temperature is called thermoregulation.

**Tip:** The levels of some things in our body are controlled by the nervous system (like body temperature here) and others are controlled by the hormonal system.

### Rise in body temperature

When thermoreceptors detect body temperature is too high, they send impulses to the hypothalamus, which sends impulses to effectors. Effectors respond to increase heat loss from the body (e.g. sweat glands produce sweat) and to reduce the amount of heat that's produced by the body. Body temperature then returns to normal — see Figure 4.

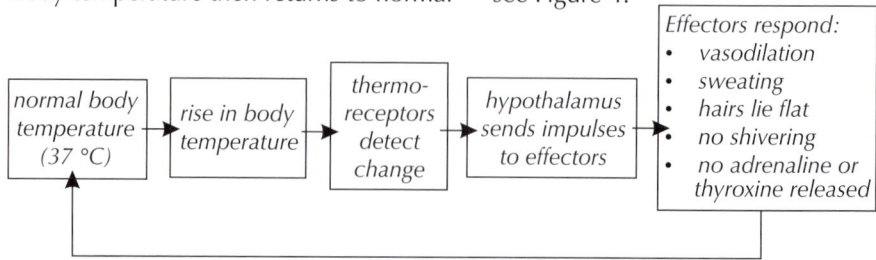

**Tip:** When you feel hot (e.g. when you exercise) you might find yourself sweaty and red-faced — this is just your body's (unattractive) response to the rise in internal body temperature.

Effectors respond:
- vasodilation
- sweating
- hairs lie flat
- no shivering
- no adrenaline or thyroxine released

normal body temperature (37 °C) → rise in body temperature → thermoreceptors detect change → hypothalamus sends impulses to effectors → [Effectors respond]

body temperature falls

*Figure 4:* Negative feedback mechanism activated by a rise in body temperature.

Module 5: Section 1   Communication and Homeostasis

## Fall in body temperature

When thermoreceptors detect body temperature is too low, they send impulses to the hypothalamus, which sends impulses to effectors. Effectors respond to produce more heat (e.g. adrenaline and thyroxine are released to increase metabolism) and to conserve it. Body temperature then returns to normal — see Figure 5 below.

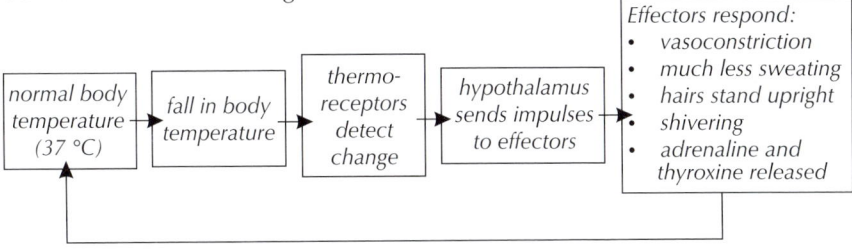

**Tip:** When you feel cold you might notice yourself shivering and raised hairs on your arms — this is your body's response to increase your internal body temperature.

```
normal body          fall in body      thermo-          hypothalamus      Effectors respond:
temperature    →    temperature   →   receptors   →    sends impulses →   • vasoconstriction
(37 °C)                                detect           to effectors       • much less sweating
  ↑                                    change                              • hairs stand upright
  |                                                                        • shivering
  |                                                                        • adrenaline and
  |_____        thyroxine released
                              body temperature rises
```

**Figure 5:** Negative feedback mechanism activated by a fall in body temperature.

### Practice Questions — Application

Q1  If a person spends a long time in a hot bath, their skin might appear pink when they get out. Explain the role of the nervous system in this response.

Q2  When blood glucose concentration gets low, the brain receives signals which stimulate feelings of hunger. Assuming activity levels are the same, is a person likely to feel hungry more quickly in a hot or cold external environment? Explain your answer.

Q3  The effects of some sympathomimetic drugs, such as cocaine, include vasoconstriction and an increase in muscular activity. In hot weather people who have taken cocaine are at risk of hyperthermia (their internal body temperature becomes dangerously high). Suggest why this occurs.

**Tip:** To answer question 2, think about how metabolism is affected when the body has to produce heat.

**Tip:** An increase in muscular activity will increase the rate of respiration.

### Practice Questions — Fact Recall

Q1  How is body temperature controlled in:
  a) an ectotherm?
  b) an endotherm?

Q2  How do the metabolic rates of an ectotherm and an endotherm differ?

Q3  Explain how sweat glands are important for controlling body temperature.

Q4  Describe two mechanisms that the body uses to increase heat production and explain how they work.

Q5  Describe how arterioles near the skin surface respond when low temperatures are detected by thermoreceptors.

Q6  What part of a mammal's brain controls body temperature?

Q7  Describe how the brain receives information about the external temperature of the body.

Q8  Briefly describe how the nervous system returns internal body temperature to normal following a fall in body temperature.

### Learning Objectives:

- Understand how blood glucose concentration is regulated, including the action of insulin and glucagon as an example of negative feedback, and the role of the liver.
- Know how insulin secretion is controlled, with reference to potassium channels and calcium channels in the beta cells of the pancreas.
- Know the differences between Type 1 and Type 2 diabetes mellitus, including their causes and the treatments used for each.
- Know the potential treatments for diabetes mellitus, including the use of insulin produced by genetically modified bacteria and the potential use of stem cells.

Specification Reference 5.1.4

**Tip:** Liver cells are also called hepatocytes.

**Tip:** Glycogen is a polysaccharide made up of branched chains of α-glucose — for more, see page 65.

### Exam Tip
Take care not to write 'a cells' and 'b cells' instead of 'α cells' and 'β cells'. Read through your answers before the end of the exam to catch easy mistakes like this.

# 8. Control of Blood Glucose Concentration

*Blood glucose concentration is under tight control by a hormonal system. If this control system doesn't work properly it may result in diabetes.*

## Glucose concentration in the blood

All cells need a constant energy supply to work — so blood glucose concentration must be carefully controlled. The concentration of glucose in the blood is normally around 90 mg per 100 cm$^3$ of blood. It's monitored by cells in the **pancreas**. Blood glucose concentration rises after eating food containing carbohydrate. It falls after exercise, as more glucose is used in respiration to release energy.

## Hormonal control of blood glucose concentration

The hormonal system (see p. 311) controls blood glucose concentration using two hormones called insulin and glucagon. They're both secreted by clusters of cells in the pancreas called the **islets of Langerhans** (see page 313). The islets of Langerhans contain **beta (β) cells** and **alpha (α) cells**. β cells secrete insulin into the blood. α cells secrete glucagon into the blood. Insulin and glucagon act on effectors, which respond to restore the blood glucose concentration to the normal level.

### Insulin

Insulin lowers blood glucose concentration when it's too high. It binds to specific receptors on the cell membranes of liver cells and muscle cells and increases the permeability of cell membranes to glucose, so the cells take up more glucose.

Insulin also activates enzymes that convert glucose into glycogen. Liver and muscle cells are able to store glycogen in their cytoplasm, as an energy source. The process of forming glycogen from glucose is called **glycogenesis** (see Figure 1). Insulin also increases the rate of respiration of glucose, especially in muscle cells.

activated by insulin
↓
glycogenesis
GLUCOSE ⟶ GLYCOGEN

**Figure 1:** *The process of glycogenesis.*

### Glucagon

Glucagon raises blood glucose concentration when it's too low. It binds to specific receptors on the cell membranes of liver cells and activates enzymes that break down glycogen into glucose. The process of breaking down glycogen is called **glycogenolysis**.

Glucagon also promotes the formation of glucose from glycerol and amino acids. The process of forming glucose from non-carbohydrates is called **gluconeogenesis** (see Figure 2). Glucagon also decreases the rate of respiration of glucose in cells.

GLYCEROL
AMINO ACIDS ⟶ GLUCOSE ⟵ GLYCOGEN
gluconeogenesis       glycogenolysis
↑                     ↑
activated by glucagon

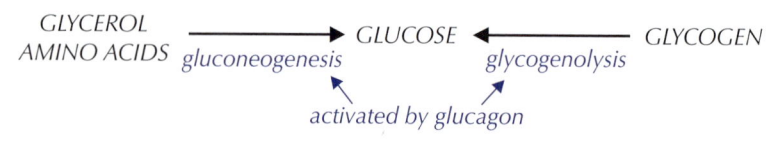

**Figure 2:** *The processes of glycogenolysis and gluconeogenesis.*

# Negative feedback mechanisms and glucose concentration

Negative feedback mechanisms keep blood glucose concentration normal.

## Rise in blood glucose concentration

When the pancreas detects blood glucose concentration is too high, the β cells secrete insulin and the α cells stop secreting glucagon. Insulin then binds to receptors on liver and muscle cells (the effectors). The liver and muscle cells respond to decrease the blood glucose concentration, e.g. glycogenesis is activated (see previous page). Blood glucose concentration then returns to normal.

**Tip:** 'Genesis' means 'making' — so glyco<u>genesis</u> means making glycogen.

normal blood glucose concentration → rise in blood glucose concentration → pancreas detects change → pancreas secretes insulin, stops glucagon secretion → Liver and muscle cells respond:
• cells take up more glucose
• glycogenesis is activated
• cells respire more glucose

↓ blood glucose concentration falls ↑

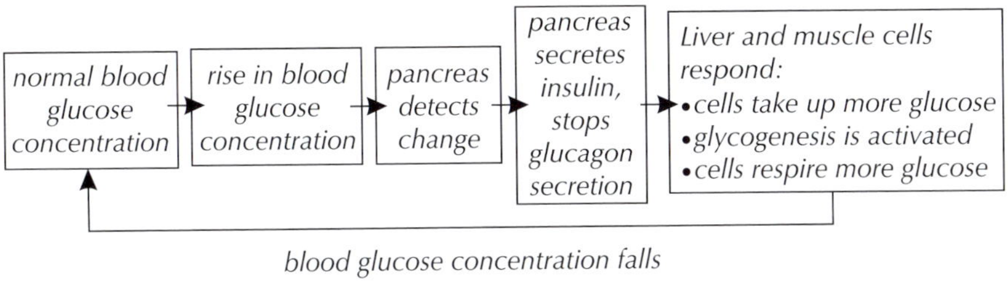

*Figure 3:* Negative feedback mechanism activated by a rise in blood glucose.

## Fall in blood glucose concentration

When the pancreas detects blood glucose is too low, the α cells secrete glucagon and the β cells stop secreting insulin. Glucagon then binds to receptors on liver cells (the effectors). The liver cells respond to increase the blood glucose concentration, e.g. glycogenolysis is activated (see previous page). Blood glucose concentration then returns to normal.

**Tip:** 'Lysis' means 'splitting' — so glycogeno<u>lysis</u> means splitting glycogen.

normal blood glucose concentration → fall in blood glucose concentration → pancreas detects change → pancreas secretes glucagon, stops insulin secretion → Liver cells respond:
• glycogenolysis is activated
• gluconeogenesis is activated
• cells respire less glucose

↓ blood glucose concentration rises ↑

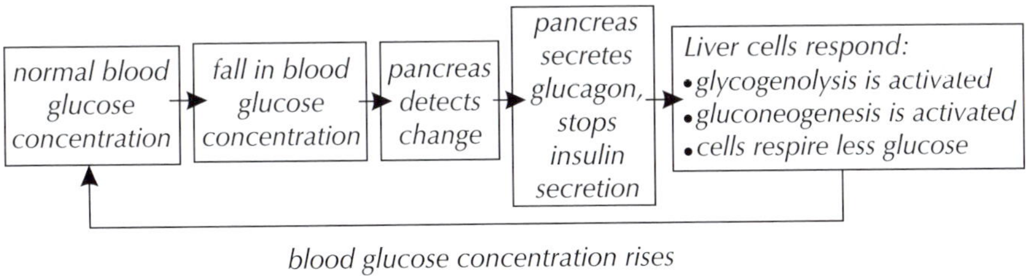

*Figure 4:* Negative feedback mechanism activated by a fall in blood glucose.

**Tip:** 'Neo' means 'new' — so gluco<u>neo</u>genesis means making new glucose.

### Practice Questions — Application

Q1 Adrenaline activates glycogenolysis. What effect will adrenaline have on blood glucose concentration?

Q2 After eating a big bowl of pasta describe how a person's blood glucose concentration will change and explain how their body returns it back to normal.

Q3 Von Gierke's disease is a glycogen storage disease. It's caused by an enzyme deficiency, which means the processes of glycogenolysis and gluconeogenesis can't work properly. Explain why someone with von Gierke's disease might suffer from hypoglycaemia if they don't eat regularly.

**Tip:** <u>Hypo</u>glycaemia is a condition where blood glucose concentration is abnormally <u>low</u>. (And <u>hyper</u>glycaemia is a condition where blood glucose concentration is abnormally <u>high</u>.)

Module 5: Section 1 Communication and Homeostasis

**Tip:** The β cell is similar to a sensory receptor cell. When it's at rest (not being stimulated) its membrane is polarised — see page 297.

**Tip:** You should be familiar with the functions of the organelles inside an animal cell from Module 2: Section 1.

# Control of insulin secretion by beta cells

β cells contain insulin stored in vesicles. They have potassium ion (K⁺) channels and calcium ion (Ca²⁺) channels in their membrane (see Figure 5). When the blood glucose concentration is around the normal level (or lower), the K⁺ channels are open and the Ca²⁺ channels are closed. Potassium ions diffuse out of the cell through the open K⁺ channels, which makes the inside of the cell membrane more negatively charged compared to the outside. This is because there are more positive ions outside the cell than inside — the membrane is polarised.

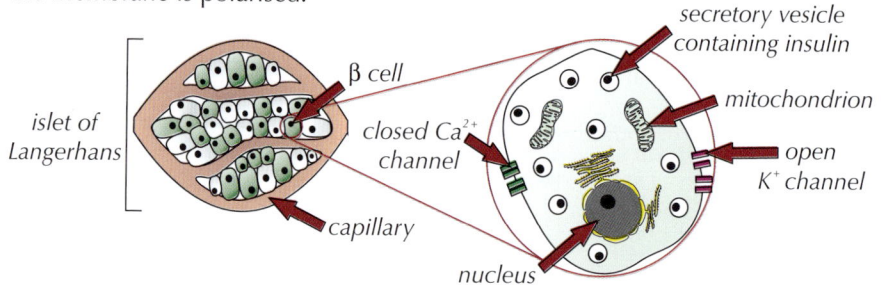

**Figure 5:** Diagram showing location of β cells in the islets of Langerhans, with the structure of a β cell enlarged.

When the β cell detects a high blood glucose concentration, changes within the cell result in the secretion of insulin. Here's how it happens:

### 1. High blood glucose concentration detected

When blood glucose concentration is high, more glucose enters the β cells by facilitated diffusion. More glucose in a β cell causes the rate of respiration to increase, making more ATP.

**Tip:** Facilitated diffusion means particles (e.g. glucose molecules) diffuse across a membrane with the help of carrier proteins or channel proteins in the plasma membrane.

### 2. Potassium ion channels close

The rise in ATP triggers the potassium ion channels in the β cell plasma membrane to close. This means potassium ions (K⁺) can't get through the membrane — so they build up inside the cell. This makes the inside of the β cell less negative because there are more positively-charged potassium ions inside the cell — so the plasma membrane of the β cell is depolarised.

### 3. Calcium ion channels open

Depolarisation triggers calcium ion channels in the membrane to open, so calcium ions diffuse into the β cell. This causes the vesicles to move to and fuse with the β cell plasma membrane, releasing insulin by exocytosis.

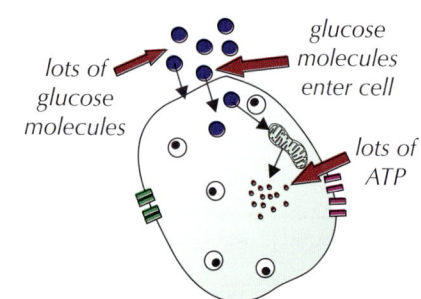

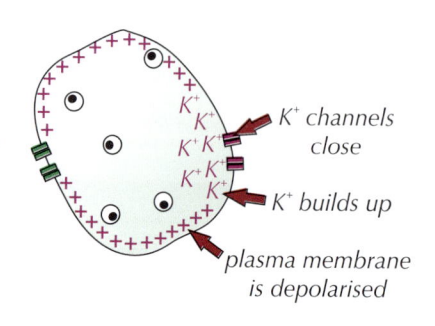

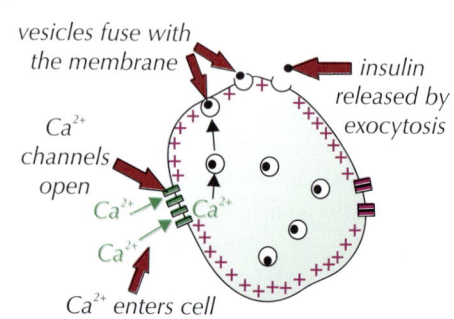

**Tip:** The calcium ion channels are voltage-gated — they open at a certain voltage.

324   Module 5: Section 1   Communication and Homeostasis

# Diabetes

Diabetes mellitus is a condition where blood glucose concentration can't be controlled properly. There are two types: Type 1 diabetes and Type 2 diabetes.

## Type 1 diabetes

Type 1 diabetes is an auto-immune disease, in which the body attacks and destroys the β cells in the islets of Langerhans. This means people with Type 1 diabetes don't produce any insulin. After eating, the blood glucose concentration rises and stays high, which can result in death if left untreated. The kidneys can't reabsorb all this glucose, so some of it's excreted in the urine.

Type 1 diabetes usually develops in children or young adults. A person's risk of developing Type 1 diabetes is slightly increased if there's a close family history of the disease.

**Tip:** An auto-immune disease is where a person's immune system mistakes their own cells for pathogens, so it starts to attack them.

### Treating Type 1 diabetes

Type 1 diabetes is treated with insulin therapy. For most people with Type 1 diabetes this involves having regular insulin injections throughout the day. For some people it involves using an insulin pump — a machine that continuously delivers insulin into the body via a tube inserted beneath the skin.

Some people have been successfully treated by having islet cell transplantation — they receive healthy islet cells from a donor so their pancreas can produce some insulin (although they usually still need some additional insulin therapy).

Whatever type of treatment they have, people with Type 1 diabetes need to regularly monitor their blood glucose concentration and think carefully about their diet and level of activity. Eating a healthy, balanced diet reduces the amount of insulin that needs to be injected, so people with Type 1 diabetes often have a carefully planned diet so that they can manage the amount of glucose they are taking in. Doing regular exercise reduces the amount of insulin that needs to be injected by using up blood glucose.

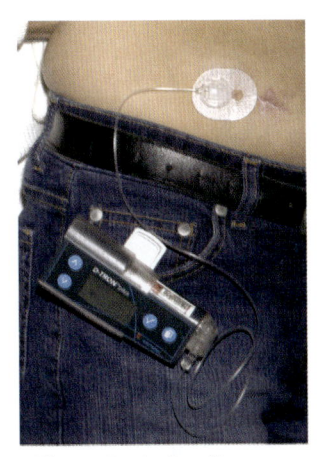

*Figure 6: An insulin pump attached to a person's abdomen.*

## Type 2 diabetes

Type 2 diabetes occurs when the β cells don't produce enough insulin or when the body's cells don't respond properly to insulin. Cells don't respond properly because the insulin receptors on their membranes don't work properly, so the cells don't take up enough glucose. This means the blood glucose concentration is higher than normal.

Type 2 diabetes is usually acquired later in life than Type 1, and it's often linked with obesity. The risk of developing Type 2 diabetes is also increased in people from certain ethnic groups, e.g. African or Asian, and in people with a close family history of the disease.

### Treating Type 2 diabetes

Type 2 diabetes is initially managed through lifestyle changes. Eating a healthy, balanced diet, getting regular exercise and losing weight if needed can help prevent the onset of Type 2 diabetes as well as control the effects.

If blood glucose concentration can't be controlled through lifestyle changes alone, then medication may be prescribed. There are some examples of this medication on the next page.

**Tip:** Type 2 diabetes is becoming increasingly common in the UK. This has been linked to increasing levels of obesity, a move towards more unhealthy diets and low levels of physical activity.

**Examples**
- Metformin — This is usually the first medicine to be prescribed. Metformin acts on liver cells to reduce the amount of glucose that they release into the blood. It also acts to increase the sensitivity of cells to insulin so more glucose can be taken up with the same amount of insulin.
- Sulfonylureas (e.g. gliclazide) — These stimulate the pancreas to produce more insulin.
- Thiazolidinediones (e.g. pioglitazone) — These also make the body cells more sensitive to insulin.

In some people with Type 2 diabetes, these types of medication are not enough to control blood glucose concentration so insulin therapy is used in addition or instead.

## Practice Questions — Application

In an experiment, the blood glucose concentrations of a person with Type 2 diabetes and a person without diabetes were recorded at regular intervals in a 150 minute time period. 15 minutes into the experiment a glucose drink was given. The normal range for blood glucose concentration in a healthy individual is between 82 and 110 mg per 100 cm³. The results of the experiment are shown on the graph below.

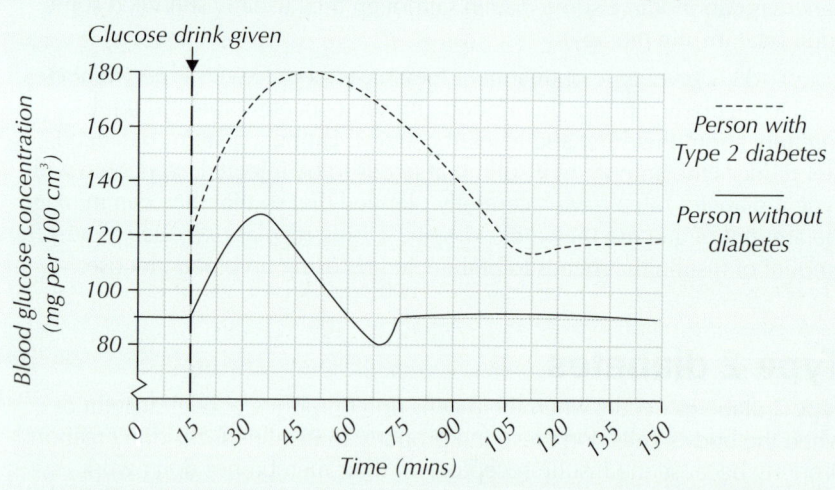

**Exam Tip**
If you get given a graph in the exam it's a good idea to look at it carefully and try and work out what it is showing before you start answering the questions. It sounds obvious, but if you just jump straight in you might miss something important.

**Tip:** Think about the causes of the two different types of diabetes for Q2.

Q1 Explain why the blood glucose concentration of the person with Type 2 diabetes takes longer to decrease after they take the glucose drink than the person without diabetes.

Q2 Suggest how the blood glucose concentration of a person with Type 1 diabetes would differ from the person with Type 2 diabetes after having the glucose drink.

Q3 Suggest what time insulin is released in the person without diabetes. Explain your answer.

Q4 Blood glucose concentration continues to rise after the release of insulin. Why is this?

Q5 Explain how negative feedback works to increase the blood glucose concentration in the person without diabetes between 65 and 75 minutes.

Module 5: Section 1 Communication and Homeostasis

## Insulin from GM bacteria

Insulin used to be extracted from animal pancreases (e.g. pigs and cattle), to treat people with Type 1 diabetes. But nowadays, human insulin can be made by genetically modified (GM) bacteria (see p. 520). Using GM bacteria to produce insulin is much better for many reasons, for example:

- Producing insulin using GM bacteria is cheaper than extracting it from animal pancreases.
- Larger quantities of insulin can be produced using GM bacteria.
- GM bacteria make human insulin. This is more effective than using pig or cattle insulin (which is slightly different to human insulin) and it's less likely to trigger an allergic response or be rejected by the immune system.
- Some people prefer insulin from GM bacteria for ethical or religious reasons. E.g. some vegetarians may object to the use of animals, and some religious people object to using insulin from pigs.

**Tip:** GM bacteria have had a gene from another organism inserted into them, so that they'll produce the protein coded for by that gene.

## Curing diabetes

Your body is made up of many different types of cells that are specialised for their function, e.g. liver cells, β cells. All specialised cells originally came from stem cells. Stem cells are unspecialised cells — they have the ability to develop into any type of cell.

Using stem cells could potentially cure diabetes. Stem cells could be grown into β cells, which would then be implanted into the pancreas of a person with Type 1 diabetes. This means the person would be able to make insulin as normal. This treatment is still being developed but, if it's effective, it'll cure people with Type 1 diabetes — they won't need insulin therapy anymore.

**Tip:** Look back at Module 2 if you need to remind yourself about stem cells.

### Practice Questions — Fact Recall

Q1 Give three ways in which insulin reduces blood glucose concentration.

Q2 Name the process that converts glucose to glycogen.

Q3 Name and describe two processes activated by glucagon.

Q4 In the pancreas, potassium ion channels and calcium ion channels in β cell membranes open and close in response to blood glucose concentration.
   a) State whether the channels are opened or closed when the blood glucose concentration is around the normal level.
   b) State what happens to the channels when the blood glucose concentration is high.

Q5 a) What is Type 1 diabetes?
   b) Describe how Type 1 diabetes can be treated with insulin therapy.
   c) Give another way that Type 1 diabetes can be treated and describe what this involves.

Q6 Describe the different ways that Type 2 diabetes can be treated.

Q7 Give three advantages of using genetically modified bacteria to produce insulin rather than using animal pancreases.

Q8 Describe how stem cells may be able to cure Type 1 diabetes.

**Exam Tip**
There are lots of similar sounding words in this section so you need to make sure you get your spelling spot on in the exam, e.g. if you write 'glycogon' the examiner won't know whether you mean glucagon or glycogen so you won't get the marks.

# Section Summary

Make sure you know...

- That multicellular organisms need communication systems to respond to changes in their internal and external environment and to coordinate the activities of different organs.
- That cell signalling allows communication between adjacent cells and distant cells.
- That sensory neurones have short dendrites, long dendrons and short axons, and transmit nerve impulses from receptors to the central nervous system (CNS).
- That motor neurones have short dendrites and long axons, and transmit nerve impulses from the CNS to effectors.
- That relay neurones have short dendrites and one axon, and transmit nerve impulses between sensory neurones and motor neurones.
- That sensory receptors act as transducers as they convert the energy of a stimulus into electrical energy, and that they respond to specific stimuli, e.g. Pacinian corpuscles respond to touch.
- How a resting membrane potential is established and maintained by sodium-potassium pumps and potassium ion channels in a neurone's cell membrane.
- That when sodium ion channels in a neurone's cell membrane open, the membrane becomes more permeable to sodium ions and that this causes depolarisation (the potential difference of the membrane becomes more positive), resulting in an action potential if the threshold level is reached.
- That voltage-gated sodium ion channels open when the potential difference reaches the threshold level in an example of positive feedback and that they close again as voltage-gated potassium ion channels open during repolarisation.
- That the slow closure of potassium ion channels allows too many potassium ions to leave the neurone, causing a period of 'hyperpolarisation', but that the sodium-potassium pump returns the membrane back to its resting potential.
- That an action potential is transmitted along a neurone in a wave of depolarisation.
- That if the threshold is reached, an action potential will always fire with the same change in voltage and if the threshold isn't reached there'll be no action potential.
- The structure of a myelinated neurone.
- That action potentials are passed more quickly along myelinated than unmyelinated neurones because impulses are only conducted at the nodes of Ranvier (where sodium channels are concentrated).
- The structure of a synapse, e.g. a cholinergic synapse includes a synaptic knob, vesicles filled with acetylcholine (ACh), a synaptic cleft and specific cholinergic receptors on the postsynaptic membrane.
- That the arrival of an action potential at the presynaptic neurone triggers voltage-gated calcium channels to open, so calcium ions diffuse into the synaptic knob causing vesicles to fuse with the presynaptic membrane. Neurotransmitters diffuse across the synaptic cleft to bind to receptors on the postsynaptic membrane. This causes sodium ion channels to open and the influx of sodium ions triggers an action potential if the threshold is reached.
- The roles of synapses in the nervous system, including excitatory synapses (in which neurotransmitters depolarise the postsynaptic membrane), inhibitory synapses (in which neurotransmitters hyperpolarise the postsynaptic membrane), synaptic divergence (one neurone connecting to many neurones), synaptic convergence (many neurones connecting to one neurone), spatial summation (two or more presynaptic neurones releasing their neurotransmitters at the same time onto the same postsynaptic neurone), temporal summation (two or more nerve impulses arriving in quick succession from the same presynaptic neurone) and unidirectional transmission (impulses only travelling in one direction).
- That communication by the hormonal system involves the secretion of hormones (chemical messengers) into the blood by endocrine glands (groups of cells that are specialised to secrete hormones), transport by the blood and detection by target cells (cells that contain receptors for certain hormones) or target tissues (tissues that contain target cells).

- That a first messenger (e.g. adrenaline) activates an enzyme (e.g. adenylyl cyclase) in a cell membrane and this catalyses the production of a second messenger inside a cell (e.g. cAMP) from ATP, which activates a cascade inside the cell (e.g. catalysing the breakdown of glycogen into glucose).
- That the cortex of an adrenal gland secretes steroid hormones, e.g. cortisol, which are involved in both the short-term and the long-term responses to stress and the medulla secretes catecholamine hormones, e.g. adrenaline, which are involved in the short-term response to stress.
- The histology of the pancreas — it contains endocrine tissue called the islets of Langerhans, which contains α and β cells.
- How to examine and draw a section of pancreatic tissue using a light microscope.
- That homeostasis is the maintenance of a constant internal environment and that homeostatic systems involve receptors, which detect when a level is too high or too low, and effectors, which respond to counteract the change.
- That negative feedback is a mechanism that restores a level to normal, whereas positive feedback is a mechanism that amplifies a change away from the normal level.
- That ectotherms control their body temperature by changing their behaviour, and endotherms control their body temperature internally by homeostasis, as well as by altering their behaviour.
- How endotherms control their body temperature internally with communication via peripheral temperature receptors, the hypothalamus and effectors in skin and muscles (e.g. thermoreceptors in the skin detect changes in temperature and send impulses to the hypothalamus, which sends impulses to effectors to respond in a negative feedback mechanism).
- That insulin lowers blood glucose concentration when it's too high by binding to receptors on liver and muscle cells, causing cells to take up and respire more glucose and activating glycogenesis (the process of forming glycogen from glucose).
- That glucagon raises blood glucose concentration when it's too low by binding to receptors on liver cells and activating glycogenolysis (the process of breaking down glycogen) and gluconeogenesis (the process of forming glucose from non-carbohydrates), and causing the cells to respire less glucose.
- That the actions of insulin and glucagon in regulating glucose concentration are examples of negative feedback.
- That insulin secretion from β cells in the pancreas happens when blood glucose concentration is high and more glucose molecules enter the β cells. This increases the rate of respiration and increases ATP production, which causes potassium ion channels to close, depolarising the β cell membranes. This causes calcium ion channels to open and allows calcium ions to enter the cells, which causes vesicles to move to and fuse with the cell membranes so that insulin is released by exocytosis.
- That Type 1 diabetes is an auto-immune disease that causes the body to be unable to produce insulin.
- That Type 1 diabetes can be treated with insulin therapy (regular insulin injections or attachment to an insulin pump) or islet cell transplantation (receiving healthy islet cells from a donor) alongside a healthy, balanced diet and exercise.
- That Type 2 diabetes occurs when the β cells in the pancreas don't produce enough insulin or the body's cells don't respond properly to insulin.
- That Type 2 diabetes can be managed through lifestyle changes (eating a healthy, balanced diet and getting regular exercise), medication and insulin therapy (if necessary).
- That insulin can nowadays be produced by genetically modified bacteria and this has many advantages over using insulin from animals (e.g. it's cheaper, larger quantities can be produced, it's more effective as it makes human insulin, people may prefer it for religious or ethical reasons).
- That it may be possible to grow stem cells into β cells and insert these into the pancreas of someone with Type 1 diabetes, as a potential way of curing the disease.

# Exam-style Questions

1     Which of the following statements is **not** correct?
      A    People with Type 1 diabetes don't produce insulin.
      B    Type 1 diabetes can be controlled by eating a healthy, balanced diet.
      C    Type 2 diabetes is usually acquired later in life than Type 1 diabetes.
      D    People with Type 2 diabetes don't produce enough insulin or don't respond properly to insulin.

*(1 mark)*

2     The 'fight or flight' response is important for a person's survival. Adrenaline is one hormone that is involved in this response.

   (a)    During times of danger, more adrenaline will be secreted into a person's bloodstream from their adrenal glands. Where in the adrenal glands is adrenaline released from?

*(1 mark)*

   (b)    Describe how adrenaline triggers a cascade inside a cell.

*(3 marks)*

   (c)    One effect of a cascade triggered by adrenaline is the breakdown of glycogen into glucose.

      (i)    What name is given to this process?

*(1 mark)*

      (ii)    Which hormone also produces this response?

*(1 mark)*

3     β cells respond to changes in blood glucose concentration as part of a negative feedback mechanism.

   (a)    What is a negative feedback mechanism?

*(1 mark)*

   (b)    **Fig. 3.1** shows a diagram of a cell in the body of someone who has recently eaten a meal high in carbohydrates (which are broken down to glucose).

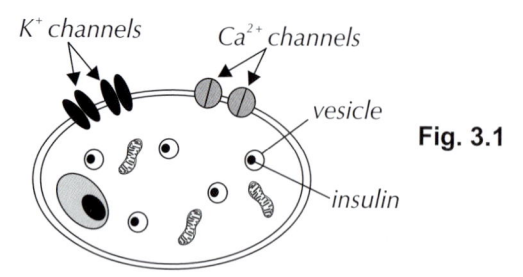

      (i)    Name the type of cell shown in **Fig. 3.1**.

*(1 mark)*

(ii) The potassium ion channels are **closed** in **Fig. 3.1**. Describe and explain the events that have caused these channels to close.

*(3 marks)*

(iii) When the potassium ion channels are closed, potassium ions can't diffuse through the membrane, which causes them to build up inside the cell. Explain how this leads to the release of insulin from the vesicle.

*(4 marks)*

(c) One of the effects of insulin release is **glycogenesis**.
What is meant by glycogenesis?

*(1 mark)*

4 The activity levels of a squirrel and a tortoise living in the same area were recorded over a 20 hour period. The temperature of the external environment in the test period was also recorded. The results are shown in **Fig. 4.1**.

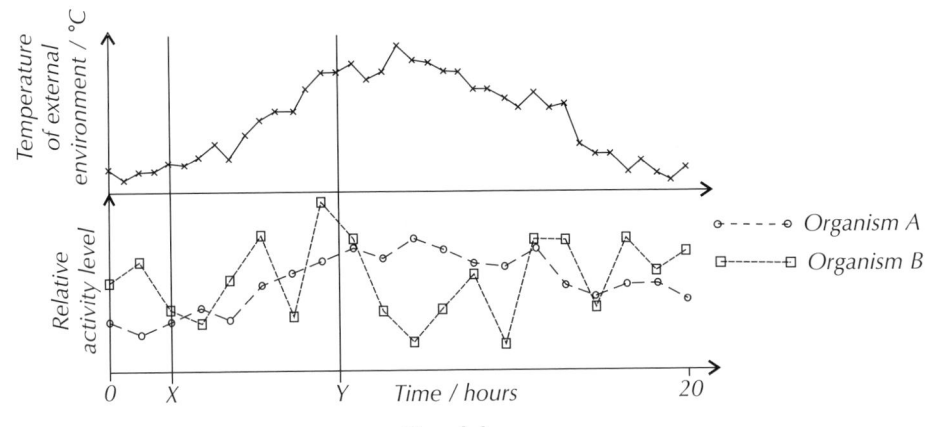

**Fig. 4.1**

(a) Describe the activity levels of the organisms in relation to temperature.

*(2 marks)*

(b) Tortoises are ectotherms, squirrels are endotherms.
 (i) Which organism, **A** or **B**, is the tortoise? Explain your answer.

*(1 mark)*

 (ii) Squirrels have a much wider geographical range than tortoises. Suggest why this is.

*(2 marks)*

(c) (i) It was observed that the hairs on the squirrel were standing up at point **X**. Explain how and why this response came about.

*(4 marks)*

 (ii) The squirrel has mechanisms that work to reduce its body temperature. Describe and explain **two** of these mechanisms that may occur at point **Y** in **Fig. 4.1**.

*(4 marks)*

# Module 5  Section 2: Excretion

## Learning Objectives:
- Know what is meant by excretion and its importance in maintaining metabolism and homeostasis, including the removal of metabolic wastes (such as carbon dioxide and nitrogenous waste) from the body.
- Know the gross structure and the histology of the mammalian liver.
- Be able to examine and draw stained sections to show the histology of liver tissue (PAG1).
- Know the functions of the mammalian liver, including its roles in:
  - the formation of urea (including an outline of the ornithine cycle),
  - detoxification,
  - the storage of glycogen.

**Specification Reference 5.1.2**

**Tip:** 'Hepatic' means anything to do with the liver. For example, the hepatic artery is the artery supplying the liver with blood.

**Tip:** Don't get the hepatic vein and hepatic portal vein mixed up — remember, the hepatic portal vein brings the products of digestion to the liver.

# 1. The Liver and Excretion

*Excretion is all about removing waste. Without it, the waste products our cells produce would build up inside us — not good. The main organs involved in excretion are the liver and the kidneys. Let's kick off with the liver...*

## What is excretion?
All the chemical reactions that happen in your cells make up your **metabolism**. Metabolism produces waste products — substances that aren't needed by the cells, such as carbon dioxide and nitrogenous (nitrogen-containing) waste. Many of these products are toxic, so if they were allowed to build up in the body they would cause damage, e.g. by affecting other metabolic reactions. This is where excretion comes in. Excretion is the removal of the waste products of metabolism from the body.

### Example
Carbon dioxide is a waste product of respiration. Too much in the blood is toxic, so it's removed from the body by the lungs (e.g. in mammals) or gills (e.g. in fish). The lungs and gills act as excretory organs.

Excreting waste products from the body maintains normal metabolism. It also maintains **homeostasis** (see page 315) by helping to keep the levels of certain substances in the blood roughly constant.

## The liver
One of the functions of the liver is to break down metabolic waste products and other substances that can be harmful, like drugs and alcohol. They're broken down into less harmful products that can then be excreted.

You need to learn all the different veins, arteries and ducts connected to the liver. These are listed below and shown in Figure 1.

- The hepatic artery supplies the liver with oxygenated blood from the heart, so the liver has a good supply of oxygen for respiration, providing plenty of energy.
- The hepatic vein takes deoxygenated blood away from the liver.
- The hepatic portal vein brings blood from the duodenum and ileum (parts of the small intestine), so it's rich in the products of digestion. This means any ingested harmful substances are filtered out and broken down straight away.
- The bile duct takes bile (a substance produced by the liver to emulsify fats) to the gall bladder to be stored.

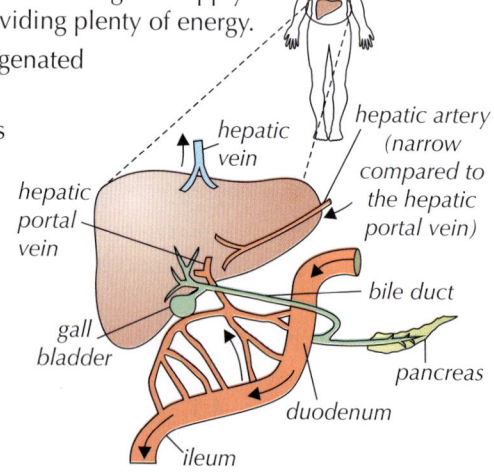

**Figure 1:** *The location of the liver in the body and its associated blood vessels.*

## Liver histology

The liver is made up of liver lobules — cylindrical structures made of cells called hepatocytes that are arranged in rows radiating out from the centre (see Figure 2). Each lobule has a central vein in the middle that connects to the hepatic vein. Many branches of the hepatic artery, hepatic portal vein and bile duct are also found connected to each lobule (only one of each is shown in Figure 2).

**Figure 2:** *Structure of liver lobules in the liver.*

The hepatic artery and the hepatic portal vein are connected to the central vein by capillaries called sinusoids (see Figure 5). Blood runs through the sinusoids, past the hepatocytes that remove harmful substances and oxygen from the blood. The harmful substances are broken down by the hepatocytes into less harmful substances that then re-enter the blood. The blood runs to the central vein, and the central veins from all the lobules connect up to form the hepatic vein. Cells called Kupffer cells are also attached to the walls of the sinusoids. They remove bacteria and break down old red blood cells. Hepatocytes produce bile and secrete it into tubes called bile canaliculi. These tubes drain into the bile ducts. The bile ducts from all the lobules eventually connect up and leave the liver.

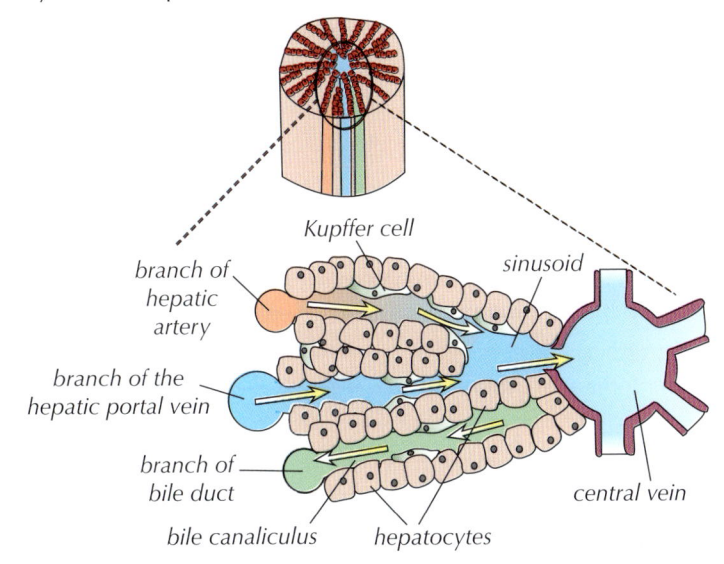

**Figure 5:** *Enlarged diagram of a liver lobule, showing the sinusoid and hepatocytes radiating out from the central vein.*

**Tip:** The histology of the liver just means its structure as seen under a microscope.

**Tip:** Remember, the liver receives two blood supplies — oxygenated blood from the heart and blood from the digestive system.

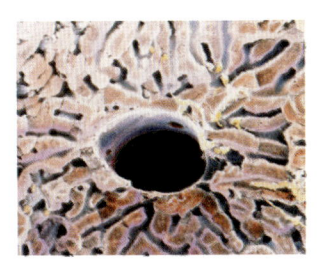

**Figure 3:** *An electron micrograph of a liver lobule, showing the sinusoids (grey tracks) between the hepatocytes (pink), radiating out from the cental vein (the black hole).*

**Tip:** Kupffer cells are liver macrophages — a type of white blood cell that carries out phagocytosis (engulfing and digesting pathogens such as bacteria).

**Figure 4:** *An electron micrograph of a Kupffer cell attached to the wall of a sinusoid.*

Module 5: Section 2 Excretion

**Tip:** Be careful when handling slides — they can shatter very easily.

### Examining liver tissue under a microscope

You need to know what liver tissue looks like under a light microscope and be able to identify and draw the different structures that you see. Before examination, a sample of liver tissue is placed on a microscope slide. The sample is stained so the cells are easier to see.

**Tip:** Tissue samples to be viewed under the microscope are commonly stained with haematoxylin and eosin.

#### Example

Figure 6 shows an example of what liver tissue looks like under a light microscope — it shows a section through one of the liver's many lobules.

This large white circular shape is the central vein.

These white spaces are the sinusoids.

These cells that radiate out from the central vein are the hepatocytes. The red dots are the nuclei.

**Tip:** See page 333 for the functions of all these structures.

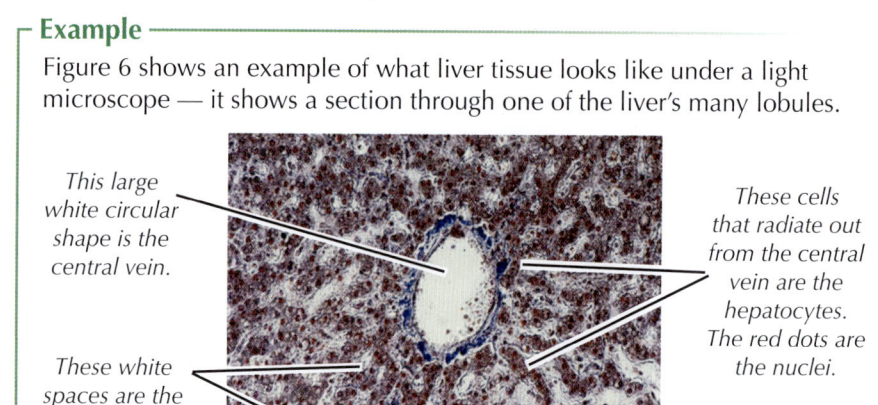

**Figure 6:** Light micrograph of a stained section of liver tissue.

**Tip:** All amino acids share the same basic structure, shown below:

$$\begin{array}{c} R \\ | \\ H_2N - C - COOH \\ | \\ H \end{array}$$

Each amino acid has an amino group (-NH$_2$), containing nitrogen. The variable R group can be any hydrocarbon.

## Deamination and the ornithine cycle

One of the liver's most important roles is getting rid of excess amino acids produced by eating and digesting protein. Amino acids contain nitrogen in their amino groups. Nitrogenous substances can't usually be stored by the body. This means excess amino acids can be damaging to the body, so they must be used by the body (e.g. to make proteins) or be broken down and excreted. Here's how excess amino acids are broken down in the liver:

1. First, the nitrogen-containing amino groups (-NH$_2$) are removed from any excess amino acids, forming ammonia (NH$_3$) and organic acids — this process is called **deamination**.

$$\text{amino acids} \xrightarrow{\text{deamination}} \text{ammonia} + \text{organic acids}$$

2. The organic acids can be respired to give ATP or converted to carbohydrate and stored as glycogen.

3. Ammonia is too toxic for mammals to excrete directly, so it's combined with CO$_2$ in the **ornithine cycle** to create urea and water (see next page).

$$\text{ammonia} + \text{carbon dioxide} \longrightarrow \text{urea} + \text{water}$$

**Tip:** Glycogen stored in the liver is important in the control of blood glucose level (see page 322 for more).

4. The urea is released from the liver into the blood. The kidneys then filter the blood and remove the urea as urine (see pages 337-339), which is excreted from the body.

**Tip:** Figure 7 on the next page summarises the processes of deamination and the ornithine cycle.

334    Module 5: Section 2   Excretion

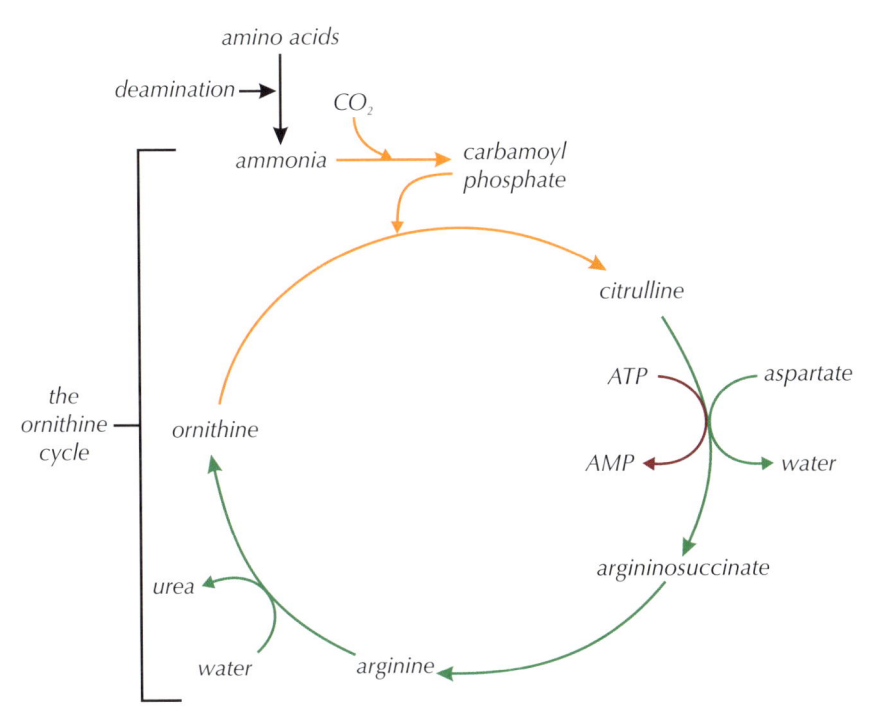

*Figure 7: Deamination and the ornithine cycle. The part of the ornithine cycle in orange happens in the mitochondria of liver cells and the part in green happens in the cytoplasm.*

**Tip:** You don't need to worry too much about the names of the chemicals involved in the process of converting ammonia to urea. The important thing to remember in the ornithine cycle is that ammonia from deamination is combined with carbon dioxide to produce urea and water.

**Tip:** Ornithine and citrulline are amino acids. These are too big to diffuse quickly through the mitochondrial membrane so require carrier proteins to move them across via facilitated diffusion or active transport.

## Detoxification

The liver also breaks down other harmful substances, like alcohol, drugs and unwanted hormones. They're broken down into less harmful compounds that can then be excreted from the body — this process is called detoxification. Some of the harmful products broken down by the liver include:

### Alcohol (ethanol)
Alcohol is a toxic substance that can damage cells. It's broken down by the liver into ethanal, which is then broken down into a less harmful substance called acetic acid. Excess alcohol over a long period can lead to cirrhosis of the liver — this is when the cells of the liver die and scar tissue blocks blood flow.

### Paracetamol
Paracetamol is a common painkiller that's broken down by the liver. Excess paracetamol in the blood can lead to liver and kidney failure.

### Insulin
Insulin is a hormone that controls blood glucose concentration (see page 322). Insulin is also broken down by the liver as excess insulin can cause problems with blood sugar levels.

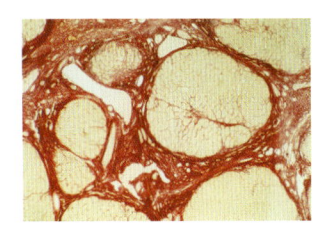

*Figure 8: Light micrograph of a liver tissue with cirrhosis. The lobules (pale yellow circles) are surrounded by fibrous scar tissue (red).*

## Glycogen storage

The body needs glucose for energy. The liver converts excess glucose in the blood to glycogen in a process called glycogenesis (see p. 322). The glycogen is then stored as granules in the liver cells until the glucose is needed for energy.

Module 5: Section 2 Excretion

**Exam Tip**
Don't panic in the exam if you're given the name of something like an enzyme or a disease that you don't recognise. Just apply your knowledge of how the ornithine cycle works normally and you'll be able to work out the answer.

## Practice Questions — Application

Argininosuccinate synthetase (AS) is an enzyme which catalyses the conversion of citrulline to argininosuccinate in the ornithine cycle, as shown in the diagram below. If there's an AS deficiency then ammonia builds up in the blood, which can be fatal.

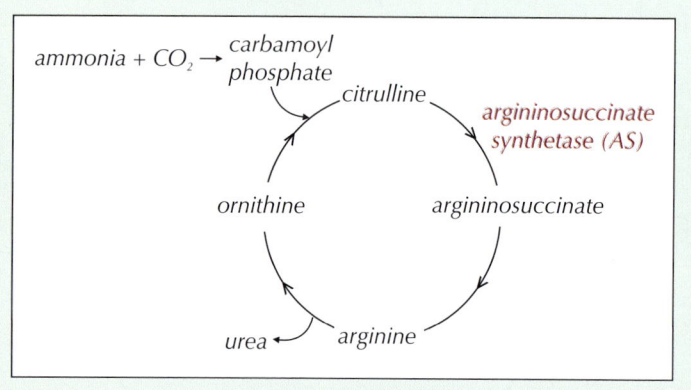

ammonia + $CO_2$ → carbamoyl phosphate → citrulline → argininosuccinate synthetase (AS) → argininosuccinate → arginine → urea → ornithine →

Q1 a) Predict whether there would be a high or a low level of argininosuccinate in the blood of a person with AS deficiency. Explain why.
   b) Predict whether there would be a high or a low level of citrulline in the blood of a person with AS deficiency. Explain why.

Q2 AS deficiency can be treated by eating a low protein diet. Explain how this treatment works.

**Tip:** To answer Q2 think about where the ammonia entering the ornithine cycle is coming from.

## Practice Questions — Fact Recall

Q1 Define the term 'excretion'.
Q2 Give two waste products of metabolism that need to be removed from the body.
Q3 Why is excretion important for homeostasis?
Q4 Where does blood from the hepatic portal vein come from?
Q5 Which blood vessel do the central veins in liver lobules connect to?
Q6 What are sinusoids?
Q7 Name the features labelled X and Y on the light micrograph of a cross-section through a liver lobule on the right.
Q8 Briefly describe how urea is formed, starting with the breakdown of excess amino acids.
Q9 What is detoxification?
Q10 Briefly describe how the liver processes excess glucose in the blood.

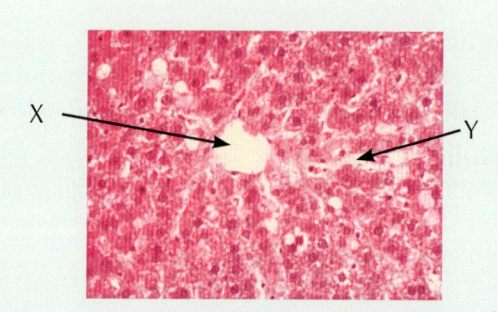

# 2. The Kidneys and Excretion

*One of the main functions of the kidneys is to excrete waste products, e.g. urea produced by the liver.*

## Excretion of waste products

Blood enters the kidney through the renal artery and then passes through capillaries in the cortex of the kidneys. As the blood passes through the capillaries, substances are filtered out of the blood and into long tubules that surround the capillaries. This process is called **ultrafiltration** (see below). Useful substances (e.g. glucose) are reabsorbed back into the blood from the tubules in the medulla and cortex — this is called **selective reabsorption** (see next page). The remaining unwanted substances (e.g. urea) pass along the tubules, then along the ureter to the bladder, where they're expelled as urine. The filtered blood passes out of the kidneys through the renal vein.

You need to learn the structure of the kidneys (see Figure 1).

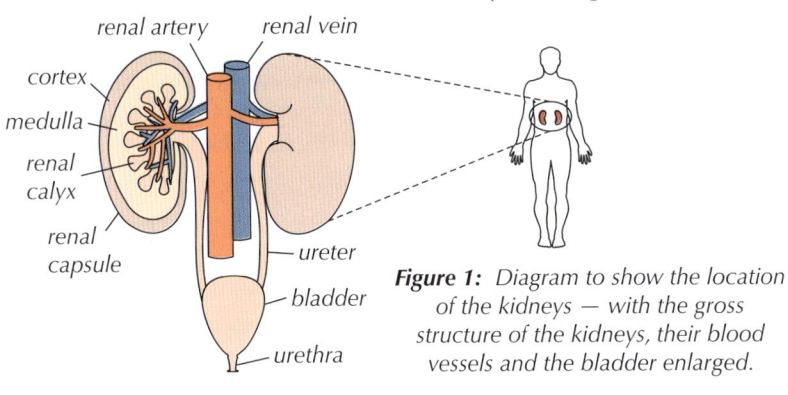

**Figure 1:** Diagram to show the location of the kidneys — with the gross structure of the kidneys, their blood vessels and the bladder enlarged.

## The nephrons

The long tubules along with the bundle of capillaries where the blood is filtered are called nephrons — there are around one million nephrons in each kidney.

### Ultrafiltration

Blood from the renal artery enters smaller arterioles in the cortex. Each arteriole splits into a structure called a glomerulus — a bundle of capillaries looped inside a hollow ball called a Bowman's capsule (see Figure 3). This is where ultrafiltration takes place.

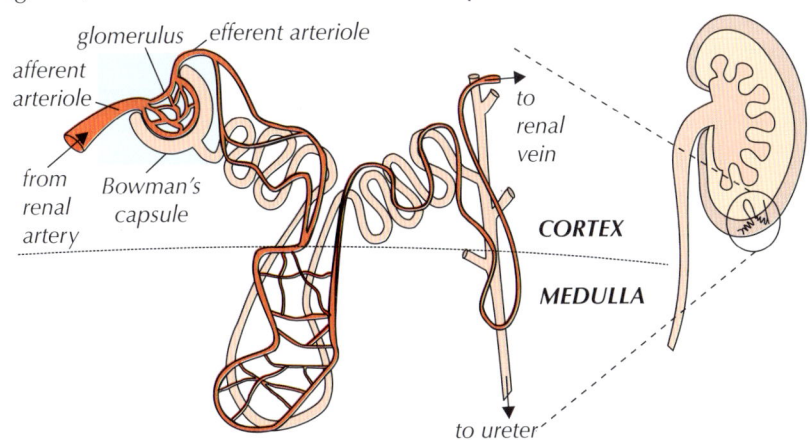

**Figure 3:** The location and structure of one nephron. Ultrafiltration takes place in the glomerulus and Bowman's capsule (highlighted in blue).

---

**Learning Objectives:**

- Know the functions of the mammalian kidney.
- Know the gross structure and histology of the mammalian kidney, including the detailed structure of a nephron and its associated blood vessels.
- Know the mechanisms of action of the mammalian kidney, including the processes of ultrafiltration, selective reabsorption and the production of urine.
- Be able to examine and draw stained sections of kidney tissue to show the histology of nephrons (PAG1).
- Know how to dissect, examine and draw the external and internal structure of the kidney (PAG2).

**Specification Reference 5.1.2**

**Tip:** The kidneys also play a role in the control of the water potential of the blood (see p. 342-344).

**Tip:** 'Renal' means anything to do with the kidneys.

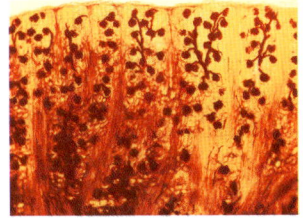

**Figure 2:** Light micrograph of a section through the cortex, showing the glomeruli (tiny balls) and the vessels that supply them.

Module 5: Section 2 Excretion    337

**Tip:** The kidneys are involved in removing toxic waste from the body — so they have an important role in homeostasis (see p. 315).

The arteriole that takes blood into each glomerulus is called the afferent arteriole, and the arteriole that takes the filtered blood away from the glomerulus is called the efferent arteriole (see Figure 3 on the previous page). The efferent arteriole is smaller in diameter than the afferent arteriole, so the blood in the glomerulus is under high pressure. The high pressure forces liquid and small molecules in the blood out of the capillary and into the Bowman's capsule.

The liquid and small molecules pass through three layers to get into the Bowman's capsule and enter the nephron tubule — the capillary endothelium, a membrane (called the basement membrane) and the epithelium of the Bowman's capsule (see Figure 4).

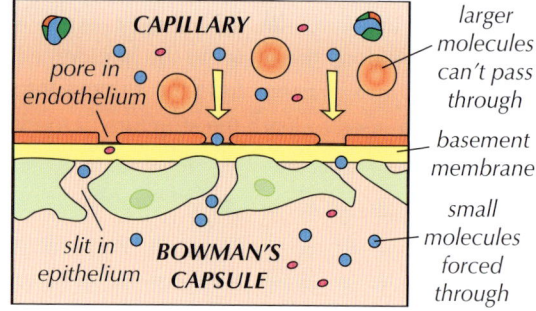

**Tip:** The cells that make up the epithelium of the Bowman's capsule are called podocytes.

**Figure 4:** Diagram to show the three layers separating the glomerular capillary and the Bowman's capsule.

**Tip:** The filtrate can also be called the tubular fluid.

Larger molecules like proteins and blood cells can't pass through and stay in the blood. The liquid and small molecules, now called **filtrate**, pass along the rest of the nephron and useful substances are reabsorbed along the way — see below. Finally, the filtrate flows through the collecting duct and passes out of the kidney along the ureter.

### Selective reabsorption

Selective reabsorption of the useful substances takes place as the filtrate flows along the proximal convoluted tubule (PCT), through the loop of Henle, and along the distal convoluted tubule (DCT) — see Figure 5. Useful substances leave the tubules of the nephrons and enter the capillary network that's wrapped around them.

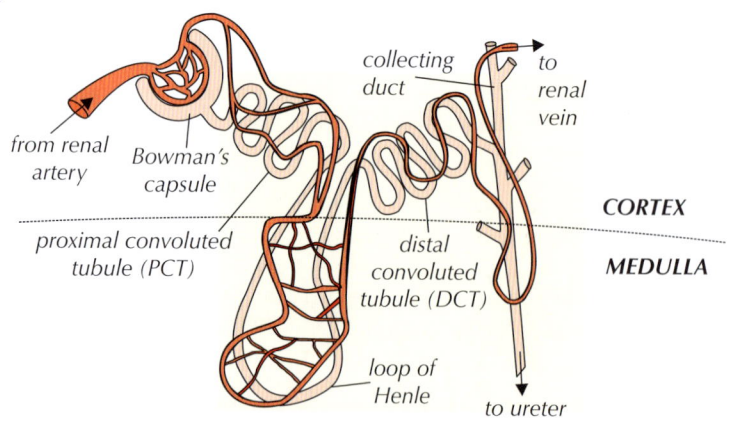

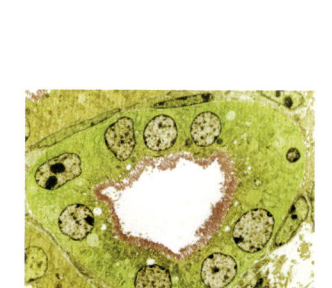

**Figure 6:** Electron micrograph of a cross-section through the proximal convoluted tubule (PCT). Microvilli (shown in reddish-brown) line the inside of the tubule, increasing the surface area for reabsorption.

**Figure 5:** Diagram to show the structure of one nephron. Selective reabsorption takes place in the areas highlighted in yellow.

The epithelium of the wall of the PCT has microvilli to provide a large surface area for the reabsorption of useful materials from the filtrate (in the tubules) into the blood (in the capillaries). Useful solutes like glucose, amino acids, vitamins and some salts are reabsorbed along the PCT by **active transport** and **facilitated diffusion**. Some urea is also reabsorbed by diffusion.

Water enters the blood by **osmosis** because the water potential of the blood is lower than that of the filtrate. Water is reabsorbed from the loop of Henle, DCT and the collecting duct (see p. 342). The filtrate that remains is urine, which passes along the ureter to the bladder.

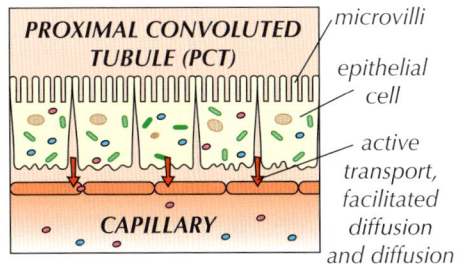

**Figure 7:** Epithelial wall of the proximal convoluted tubule (PCT).

**Tip:** Water potential basically describes the tendency of water to move from one area to another. Water will move from an area of higher water potential to an area of lower water potential — it moves down the water potential gradient.

### Urine

Urine is usually made up of water and dissolved salts, urea and other substances such as hormones and excess vitamins. Urine doesn't usually contain proteins or blood cells as they're too big to be filtered out of the blood. Glucose, amino acids and vitamins are actively reabsorbed back into the blood (see previous page), so they're not usually found in the urine either.

**Tip:** The volume of water in urine varies depending on how much you've drunk (see p. 342). The amount of urea also varies depending on how much protein you've eaten (see p. 334).

## Kidney histology

PRACTICAL ACTIVITY GROUP 1

You need to be able to look at stained kidney tissue under a light microscope and identify and draw what you see. You'll see different parts of the nephron depending on whether you're looking at the cortex or the medulla region of the kidney.

#### Examples

- The light micrograph below shows a stained section of tissue from the **cortex** of the kidney.

  This bundle of capillaries is the glomerulus.

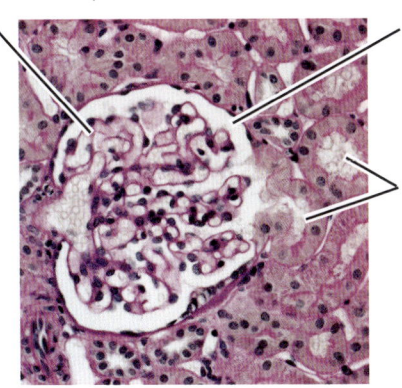

  The white area around the glomerulus is the Bowman's capsule.

  These circular areas are the PCTs and DCTs. They are surrounded by squamous epithelial cells — the purple blobs are the nuclei.

**Tip:** Make sure you're aware of any potential hazards before you start looking at tissue samples.

- The light micrograph below shows a stained section of tissue from the **medulla** of the kidney.

  The loops of Henle are surrounded by capillaries — the red dots here are red blood cells in the capillaries.

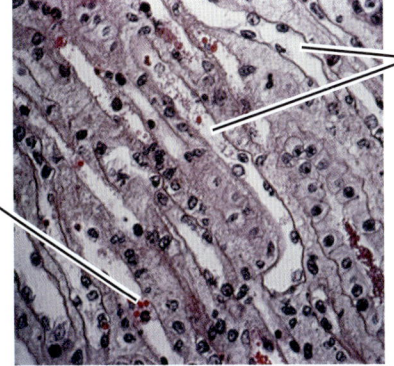

  These white areas are the loops of Henle.

**Tip:** You may also see collecting ducts in the medulla.

Module 5: Section 2 Excretion

**Tip:** It's important to do a risk assessment before you start this practical. Be careful with sharp dissection instruments and make sure you wash your hands thoroughly once you have finished.

# Kidney dissection

**PRACTICAL ACTIVITY GROUP 2**

You need to know how to dissect a mammalian kidney and examine and draw the external and internal structure. For this dissection you'll need a mammal's kidney (e.g. from a sheep, pig or cow), a dissecting tray, a scalpel, an apron and lab gloves.

## External examination

1. Look at the outside of the kidney — it's covered with a thin, strong membrane called the renal capsule.
2. Beneath the renal capsule is the outside of the cortex.
3. You'll notice that part of the kidney is indented — this is the renal hilum and you'll probably see tubes coming from here.
4. Have a look at the tubes and see if you can identify them as the renal vein, renal artery and ureter. You might need to look inside the blood vessels to identify them — the wall of the artery will be thicker than the wall of the vein. The ureter is likely to have the most adipose (fatty) tissue around it.
5. Draw a sketch of the outside of the kidney and add clear labels (see Figure 8).

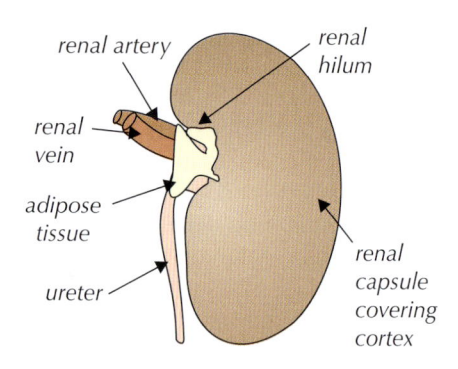

**Figure 8:** A diagram showing the external features of a kidney.

**Tip:** Make sure you use a sharp pencil when drawing your sketch and try to use one smooth line to draw the outline of features rather than lots of sketchy lines. You don't need to colour in or shade your diagrams.

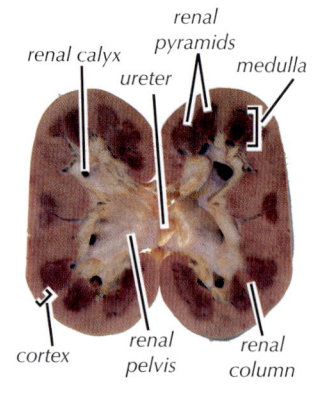

**Figure 9:** A kidney cut in half lengthways to show the internal structures.

## Internal examination

1. Cut the kidney in half lengthways from one side. Split it open and have a look at the structures inside.
2. You should notice that the cortex appears dense and grainy and is a lighter shade than the medulla.
3. In the medulla you will find many cone-shaped structures — these are renal pyramids. They appear stripy because they contain straight sections of nephrons (loops of Henle and collecting ducts).
4. In-between the pyramids are renal columns.
5. You may see hollow cavities leading from the base of the renal pyramids — these are the renal calyces (singular is a renal calyx).
6. These lead to a larger hollow structure called the renal pelvis, which connects to the ureter.
7. Draw a sketch to show the structures you see inside the kidney (see Figure 10). Don't forget to add labels.

**Tip:** Your completed diagram should show the different structures in the correct proportions. It might be difficult to see the structures clearly — use Figures 9 and 10 to help you identify what you're looking at.

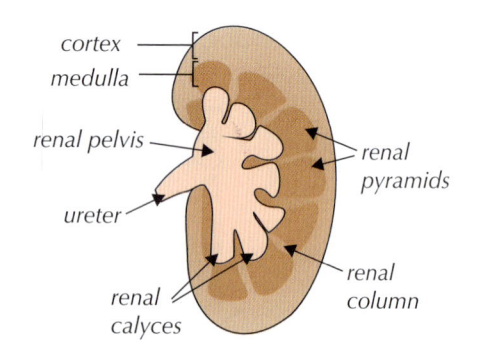

**Figure 10:** A diagram showing the internal structures of a kidney.

## Practice Questions — Application

**Q1** The kidneys filter the blood in order to produce urine. The flow diagram below shows the sequence of urine production. Name the missing structures, A to D.

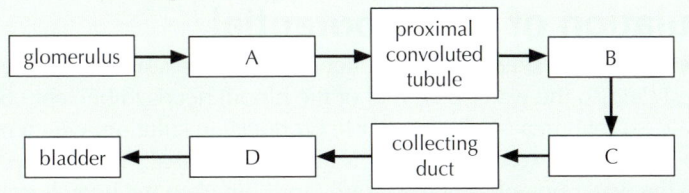

glomerulus → A → proximal convoluted tubule → B → C → collecting duct → D → bladder

**Q2** The diagram below shows an electron micrograph of a cross-section of the barrier between the Bowman's capsule and the blood supply.

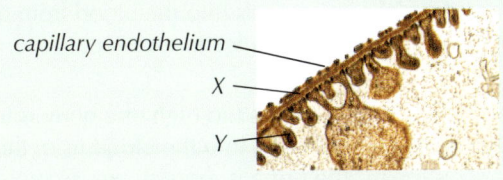

*capillary endothelium*
X
Y

a) Name the structures labelled X and Y.
b) Hereditary nephrotic syndrome is an inherited disease which affects the structure of the barrier shown above, resulting in the presence of large amounts of protein in the urine (proteinuria). Suggest why hereditary nephrotic syndrome causes proteinuria.

**Exam Tip**
Don't be put off by long words or unfamiliar diseases in your exams — the examiners just want you to apply what you know to an unfamiliar context.

## Practice Questions — Fact Recall

**Q1** The diagram below shows a glomerulus and surrounding structures.

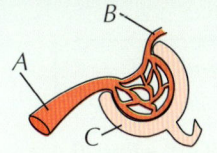

a) Name blood vessel A.
b) Name the structure labelled C.
c) Vessel A has a larger diameter than vessel B. Explain why this is important in the process of ultrafiltration.

**Q2** Name three substances that are reabsorbed in the proximal convoluted tubule.

**Q3** Name the structures labelled X, Y and Z on the diagram of a dissected kidney on the right.

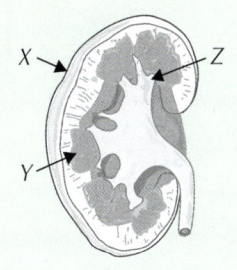

**Q4** If you were examining the internal structure of a kidney:
a) explain how you could differentiate between the renal vein, renal artery and ureter.
b) describe what you would expect to see in the medulla region.

Module 5: Section 2 Excretion

**Learning Objectives:**
- Know the functions of the mammalian kidney.
- Understand the control of the water potential of the blood, including the roles of:
  - osmoreceptors in the hypothalamus,
  - the posterior pituitary gland,
  - ADH and its effect on the walls of the collecting ducts.

**Specification Reference 5.1.2**

**Tip:** For more on reabsorption in the nephrons, see pages 338-339.

**Tip:** Figure 1 is explained in detail on the next page.

**Tip:** Na$^+$ is a sodium ion and Cl$^-$ is a chloride ion. These ions help establish the water potential that drives the reabsorption of water from the filtrate back into the blood.

# 3. The Kidneys and Water Potential

*As well as helping out with excretion, the kidneys also play a major role in regulating the blood's water potential — they're pretty busy organs...*

## Regulation of water potential

Water is essential to keep the body functioning, so the amount of water in the blood (and so the water potential of the blood) needs to be kept constant. Mammals excrete urea (and other waste products) in solution, which means water is lost during excretion. Water is also lost in sweat. The kidneys regulate the water potential of the blood (and urine), so the body has just the right amount of water:

- If the water potential of the blood is too low (the body is dehydrated), more water is reabsorbed by osmosis into the blood from the tubules of the nephrons. This means the urine is more concentrated, so less water is lost during excretion.
- If the water potential of the blood is too high (the body is too hydrated), less water is reabsorbed by osmosis into the blood from the tubules of the nephrons. This means the urine is more dilute, so more water is lost during excretion (see next page).

Regulation of the water potential of the blood takes place in the middle and last parts of the nephron — the loop of Henle, the distal convoluted tubule (DCT) and the collecting duct (see below). The volume of water reabsorbed is controlled by hormones (see next page).

## The loop of Henle

The loop of Henle is made up of two 'limbs' — the descending limb and the ascending limb. They help set up a mechanism called the countercurrent multiplier mechanism — see Figure 1. It's this mechanism that helps to reabsorb water back into the blood.

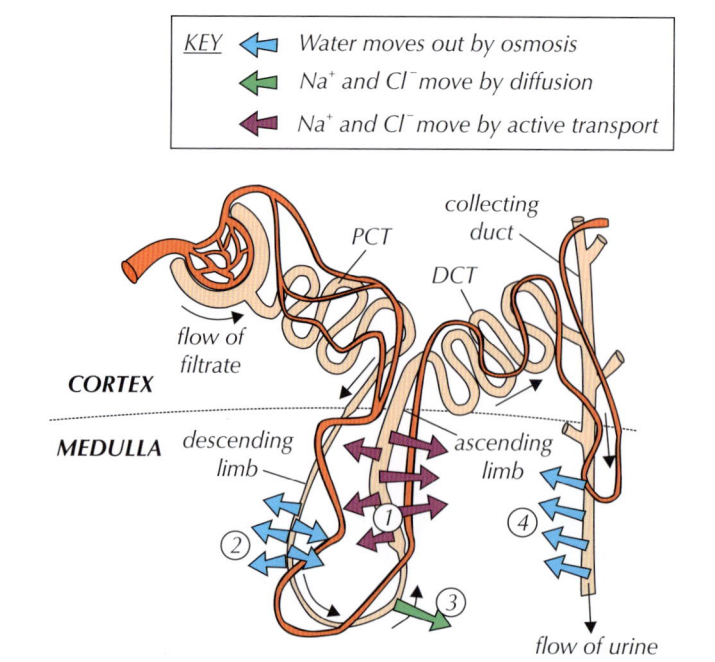

**Figure 1:** The countercurrent multiplier mechanism.

342 Module 5: Section 2 Excretion

Here's how the countercurrent multiplier mechanism works:

1. Near the top of the ascending limb, Na⁺ and Cl⁻ ions are actively pumped out into the medulla. The ascending limb is impermeable to water, so the water stays inside the tubule. This creates a low water potential in the medulla, because there's a high concentration of ions.
2. Because there's a lower water potential in the medulla than in the descending limb, water moves out of the descending limb into the medulla by osmosis. This makes the filtrate more concentrated (the ions can't diffuse out — the descending limb isn't permeable to them). The water in the medulla is reabsorbed into the blood through the capillary network.
3. Near the bottom of the ascending limb Na⁺ and Cl⁻ ions diffuse out into the medulla, further lowering the water potential in the medulla. (The ascending limb is impermeable to water, so it stays in the tubule.)
4. The first three stages massively increase the ion concentration in the medulla, which lowers the water potential. This causes water to move out of the collecting duct by osmosis. As before, the water in the medulla is reabsorbed into the blood through the capillary network.

The volume of water reabsorbed from the collecting duct into the capillaries is controlled by changing the permeability of the collecting duct (see below).

**Tip:** Remember, water moves down the water potential gradient, from a region of higher water potential to an area of lower water potential.

### Loop of Henle length in different animals

Different animals have different length loops of Henle. The longer an animal's loop of Henle, the more water they can reabsorb from the filtrate. When there's a longer ascending limb, more ions are actively pumped out into the medulla, which creates a really low water potential in the medulla. This means more water moves out of the nephron and collecting duct into the capillaries, giving very concentrated urine. Animals that live in areas where there's little water usually have long loops to save as much water as possible.

- Examples
  - The fennec fox, desert kangaroo rat and camel (see Figure 2) live in hot, dry environments such as deserts. As a result they have evolved long loops of Henle, which enable them to produce small volumes of concentrated urine in order for them to conserve water.
  - In contrast, frogs and toads don't have a loop of Henle at all, so they can't produce concentrated urine. This is because they live in a wet environment, so they don't have to conserve water.

*Figure 2:* The fennec fox (top), desert kangaroo rat (middle) and camel (bottom) all have long loops of Henle.

## Antidiuretic hormone (ADH)

The water potential of the blood is monitored by cells called **osmoreceptors** in a part of the brain called the **hypothalamus**. When the osmoreceptors are stimulated by a low water potential in the blood, the hypothalamus sends nerve impulses to the **posterior pituitary gland** to release a hormone called antidiuretic hormone (ADH) into the blood.

ADH molecules bind to receptors on the plasma membranes of cells in the DCT and the collecting duct. When this happens, protein channels called aquaporins are inserted into the plasma membrane. These channels allow water to pass through via osmosis, making the walls of the DCT and collecting duct more permeable to water. This means more water is reabsorbed from these tubules into the medulla and into the blood by osmosis. A small amount of concentrated urine is produced, which means less water is lost from the body.

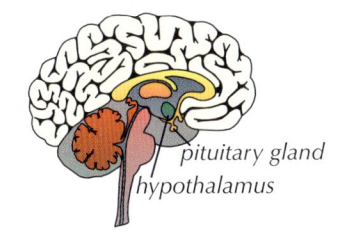

*Figure 3:* Location of the hypothalamus and the pituitary gland in the brain.

Module 5: Section 2 Excretion     343

ADH changes the water content of the blood when it's too low or too high:

**Tip:** Diuresis is when lots of dilute urine is produced. Antidiuretic hormone is so called because it causes a small amount of concentrated urine to be produced (the opposite of diuresis).

### Dehydration — blood water content is too low

Dehydration is what happens when you lose water, e.g. by sweating during exercise, so the water content of the blood needs to be increased:
- The water content of the blood drops, so its water potential drops.
- This is detected by osmoreceptors in the hypothalamus.
- The posterior pituitary gland is stimulated to release more ADH into the blood.
- More ADH means that the DCT and collecting duct are more permeable, so more water is reabsorbed into the blood by osmosis.
- A small amount of highly concentrated urine is produced and less water is lost.

### Hydration — blood water content is too high

**Tip:** Like many hormones, ADH is a protein. Once it's had its effect, it travels in the bloodstream to the liver where it's broken down (see page 334).

If you're hydrated, you've taken in lots of water, so the water content of the blood needs to be reduced:
- The water content of the blood rises, so its water potential rises.
- This is detected by the osmoreceptors in the hypothalamus.
- The posterior pituitary gland releases less ADH into the blood.
- Less ADH means that the DCT and collecting duct are less permeable, so less water is reabsorbed into the blood by osmosis.
- A large amount of dilute urine is produced and more water is lost.

### Practice Questions — Application

Q1 A runner is dehydrated whilst running on a hot, sunny day. He left his drink at home and is producing a lot of sweat during his run.
  a) Why is the runner dehydrated?
  b) How does the runner's body detect that he is dehydrated?
  c) The runner's posterior pituitary gland releases antidiuretic hormone (ADH). Explain what effect ADH has on the distal convoluted tubule and the collecting duct of the runner's kidneys.
  d) When he returns home, he rehydrates by drinking a sports drink containing sodium and chloride ions. Explain how the presence of these ions helps the runner's kidneys to conserve water.

Q2 Exercise-associated hyponatremia (EAH) is a condition experienced by some athletes who drink excessive amounts of fluid when competing in endurance events like marathons. The condition affects the balance of fluid in cells and is potentially fatal if it affects the brain cells.
  a) Explain what normally happens when a person consumes too much fluid.
  b) Athletes who experience EAH are often unable to suppress their ADH production. Explain why this can cause problems if they have consumed too much fluid.

### Practice Questions — Fact Recall

Q1 Which limb of the loop of Henle is impermeable to water?
Q2 Explain why a longer loop of Henle allows more concentrated urine to be produced.

# 4. Kidney Failure

*If things start going wrong with the kidneys, it can cause big problems...*

## What is kidney failure?

Kidney failure is when the kidneys can't carry out their normal functions because they don't work properly. Kidney failure can be detected by measuring the **glomerular filtration rate** (**GFR**) — this is the rate at which blood is filtered from the glomerulus into the Bowman's capsule. A rate lower than the normal range indicates the kidneys aren't working properly. Kidney failure can be caused by many things, including kidney infections and high blood pressure.

### Kidney infections

Kidney infections can cause inflammation (swelling) of the kidneys, which can damage the cells. This interferes with filtering in the Bowman's capsules, or with reabsorption in the other parts of the nephrons.

### High blood pressure

High blood pressure can damage the glomeruli. The blood in the glomeruli is already under high pressure but the capillaries can be damaged if the blood pressure gets too high. This means larger molecules like proteins can get through the capillary walls and into the urine.

## Problems arising from kidney failure

Kidney failure causes lots of problems:

### Examples

- Waste products that the kidneys would normally remove (e.g. urea) begin to build up in the blood. Too much urea in the blood causes weight loss and vomiting.
- Fluid starts to accumulate in the tissues because the kidneys can't remove excess water from the blood. This causes parts of the body to swell, e.g. the person's legs, face and abdomen can swell up.
- The balance of electrolytes (ions) in the body becomes, well, unbalanced. The blood may become too acidic, and an imbalance of calcium and phosphate can lead to brittle bones. Salt build-up may cause more water retention.
- Long-term kidney failure causes anaemia — a lack of haemoglobin in the blood.

If the problems caused by kidney failure can't be controlled, it can eventually lead to death.

## Treating kidney failure

When the kidneys can no longer function (i.e. they've totally failed), a person is unable to survive without treatment. There are two main treatment options — renal dialysis or a kidney transplant (see the next page).

---

**Learning Objectives:**
- Know the effects of kidney failure and the problems that arise, including the effect on glomerular filtration rate (GFR) and electrolyte balance.
- Know the potential treatments for kidney failure, including the use of renal dialysis (haemodialysis and peritoneal dialysis) and kidney transplants.

**Specification Reference 5.1.2**

**Tip:** Kidney failure is also called renal failure.

**Exam Tip:** Kidney failure can cause all kinds of health problems — make sure you learn these examples for your exams.

Module 5: Section 2 Excretion

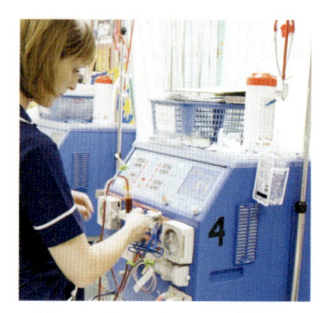

*Figure 1: A haemodialysis machine, which acts as an artificial kidney.*

### Renal dialysis
Renal dialysis is where a patient's blood is filtered. There are two types:

#### 1. Haemodialysis
In haemodialysis the patient's blood is passed through a dialysis machine — the blood flows on one side of a partially permeable membrane and dialysis fluid flows on the other side (see Figure 2). The blood and dialysis fluid flow in opposite directions in order to maintain a steep concentration gradient between the two fluids, to increase the rate of diffusion.

During haemodialysis, waste products and excess water and ions diffuse across the membrane into the dialysis fluid, removing them from the blood. Blood cells and larger molecules like proteins are prevented from leaving the blood.

One of the problems with haemodialysis is that patients can feel increasingly unwell between haemodialysis sessions because waste products and fluid starts to build up in their blood. Also, each session takes three to five hours, and patients need two or three sessions a week, usually in hospital. This is quite expensive and is pretty inconvenient for the patient.

**Tip:** During a haemodialysis session, an anticoagulant is added to the blood to prevent it from clotting in the machine. Towards the end of the session no more anticoagulant is added, to allow the blood to clot as normal once the session has finished.

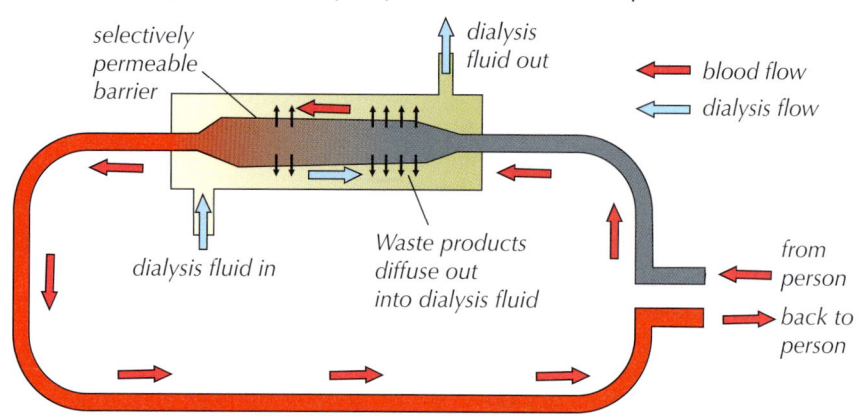

*Figure 2: A simplified diagram showing blood flow and dialysis flow in a haemodialysis machine.*

#### 2. Peritoneal dialysis
Before a patient can have peritoneal dialysis for the first time, an operation is needed to insert a tube that goes from outside the patient's body into their abdominal cavity (the space in the body where the intestines, stomach, kidneys, etc. are found). The abdominal cavity is lined with a membrane called the peritoneum. During peritoneal dialysis, dialysis fluid is put through the tube into the abdominal cavity (see Figure 3). The fluid remains in the body while waste products from the patient's blood diffuse out of capillaries and across the peritoneum into the dialysis fluid. After several hours, there's an exchange — the fluid inside the body is drained out, and a fresh lot of dialysis fluid is put in. This fluid is left there until the next exchange.

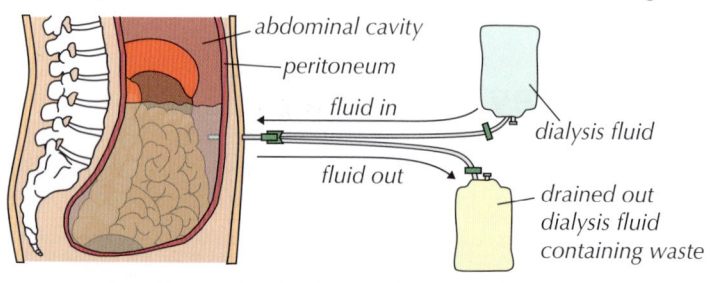

*Figure 3: Diagram showing how peritoneal dialysis is carried out.*

Module 5: Section 2 Excretion

Peritoneal dialysis can be carried out by the patient at home — this either involves around four exchanges a day or else the dialysis can be carried out by a machine overnight. The main downsides of peritoneal dialysis compared to haemodialysis are that there's a risk of infection around the site of the tube and the patient doesn't have any dialysis-free days.

There are disadvantages to both types of renal dialysis, but dialysis can keep a person alive until a transplant is available (see below), and it's a lot less risky than having the major surgery involved in a transplant.

### Kidney transplant

A kidney transplant is where a new kidney is implanted into a patient's body to replace a damaged kidney. The new kidney has to be from a person with the same blood and tissue type. They're often donated from a living relative, as people can survive with only one kidney. They can also come from other people who've recently died — organ donors.

Transplants have a lot of advantages over dialysis. For example, it's cheaper to give a person a transplant than keep them on dialysis for a long time. Having a kidney transplant is more convenient for a person than having regular dialysis sessions, and patients don't have the problem of feeling unwell between dialysis sessions.

However, there are also disadvantages to having a kidney transplant. These include the fact that the patient will have to undergo a major operation, which is risky. There's also the risk that the immune system may reject the transplant. This means that the patient has to take drugs to suppress it.

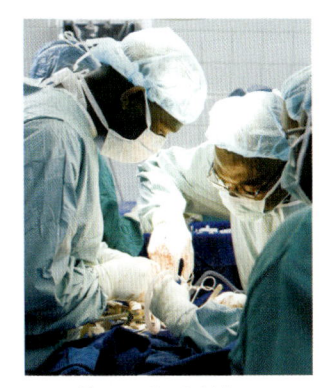

**Figure 4:** *A kidney transplant is a risky but potentially life saving operation for a patient with kidney failure.*

### Practice Questions — Application

Q1  A patient has kidney failure and is having haemodialysis while he waits for a transplant.
   a) In haemodialysis, why must the blood and the dialysis fluid flow in opposite directions?
   b) The patient is old and weak. Suggest one reason why his doctor may be concerned about him having a kidney transplant.

Q2  A hospital patient is found to have a GFR of 5200 cm$^3$ hour$^{-1}$, which is lower than the normal range. Tests revealed the patient had 0 mg of glucose in their urine and a blood glucose concentration of 0.9 mg cm$^{-3}$.
   a) Using the patient's GFR, calculate the rate at which glucose is reabsorbed back into their blood. Give your answer in mg min$^{-1}$.
   b) What could have caused a lower GFR than normal?

**Exam Tip:**
In your exams you might be asked to weigh up the positive and negative aspects of a treatment such as renal dialysis or a kidney transplant — so make sure you know both sides of the story.

### Practice Questions — Fact Recall

Q1  How can kidney failure be detected?
Q2  Explain how kidney infections can cause problems with reabsorption in the nephrons.
Q3  Give two problems that can result from kidney failure.
Q4  Explain how haemodialysis can help to restore the electrolyte balance of the blood.
Q5  Give two disadvantages of using peritoneal dialysis to treat kidney failure.

**Learning Objective:**

- Know how excretory products can be used in medical diagnosis, including the use of urine samples in diagnostic tests, with reference to:
  - using monoclonal antibodies in pregnancy testing,
  - testing for anabolic steroids and drugs.

**Specification Reference 5.1.2**

**Tip:** Even though hCG is a protein hormone, it's small enough to pass from the blood into the filtrate at the Bowman's capsule (see page 338 for more).

**Tip:** Antibodies are proteins that bind to antigens (molecules found on the surface of cells) to form an antigen-antibody complex. In a pregnancy test, the hCG antibodies in the test strip will bind to the antigens on the hCG in the urine.

# 5. Detecting Chemicals

*Urine is made by filtering the blood, so you can have a look at what's in a person's blood by testing their urine. Urine samples can be used for medical purposes such as testing for pregnancy and drug use.*

## Human chorionic gonadotropin (hCG)

Human chorionic gonadotropin (hCG) is a hormone that is only found in the urine of pregnant women. This means you can test if a woman is pregnant by looking for hCG.

### Testing for pregnancy

- A stick is used with an application area that contains monoclonal antibodies for hCG bound to a coloured bead (blue). Monoclonal antibodies are all identical to each other.
- When urine is applied to the application area any hCG will bind to the antibody on the beads.
- The urine moves up to the test strip, carrying the beads with it.
- The test strip has antibodies to hCG stuck in place (immobilised).
- If there is hCG present the test strip turns blue because the immobilised antibody binds to any hCG attached to the blue beads, concentrating the blue beads in that area. If no hCG is present, the beads will pass through the test area without binding to anything, and so it won't go blue.

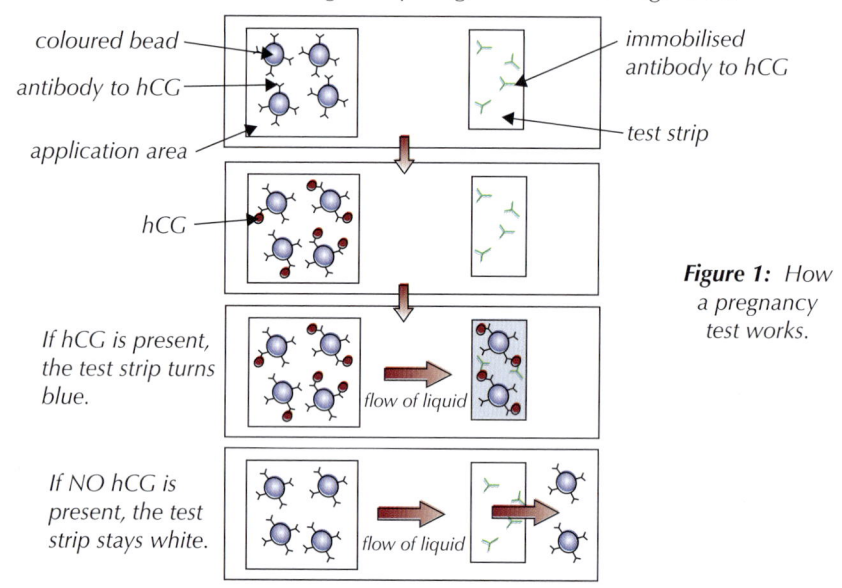

**Figure 1:** How a pregnancy test works.

*Figure 2: A lab technician testing a urine sample for hCG.*

## Anabolic steroids

Anabolic steroids are drugs that build up muscle tissue. Testosterone is an anabolic steroid, and there are other common ones, such as Nandrolone. Some athletes are banned from taking anabolic steroids. This is to try to stop the misuse of steroids that can have dangerous side-effects, such as liver damage. Also, it's considered unfair for some athletes to use steroids.

However, there are some athletes who continue to take steroids, as there is an increasing pressure on elite athletes to perform well (e.g. for sponsorship deals, etc.). Taking steroids can have positive effects on performance, such as increased strength and power owing to the build up of athletes' muscle tissue.

Module 5: Section 2 Excretion

### Testing for steroids

Steroids are removed from the blood in the urine, so athletes regularly have their urine tested for steroids (or the products made when they're broken down) by a technique called gas chromatography/mass spectrometry (GC/MS). In gas chromatography the urine sample is vaporised (turned into a gas) and passed through a column containing a polymer. Different substances move through the column at different speeds, so substances in the urine sample separate out.

Once the substances have separated out, a mass spectrometer converts them into ions, then separates the ions depending on their mass and charge. The results are analysed by a computer and by comparing them with the results of known substances it's possible to tell which substances were in the urine sample.

## Recreational drugs

Sometimes people have their urine tested to see if they've been using recreational drugs such as cannabis, ecstasy or cocaine. For example, some employers can carry out drug tests on their employees. Testing for these drugs usually starts with test strips, which contain antibodies that the drug being tested for (or the products made when it's broken down) will bind to.

A sample of urine is applied to the test strip and if a certain amount of the drug (or its products) is present a colour change will occur, indicating a positive result. If this first test shows a positive result, a sample of the urine is usually sent for further testing to confirm which drugs have been used. This second test uses GC/MS (just like the test for steroids).

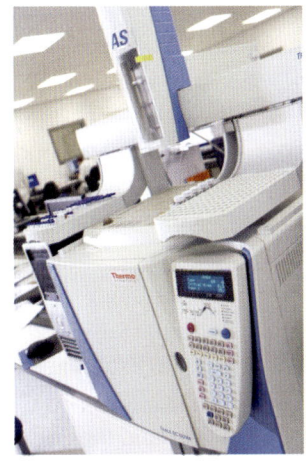

*Figure 3:* Gas chromatography/mass spectrometry machine used to test for the presence of steroids in an athlete's urine.

---

### Practice Questions — Application

An employer carries out a five panel drug test on all potential employees before hiring them. The test screens for five different types of illegal drugs: amphetamines, cocaine, opiates, phencyclidine and marijuana. It consists of five test strips, one for each type of drug. The results are indicated by coloured lines appearing on the test strips.

Q1 Suggest why five different test strips are needed to screen for the five different types of drugs.

Q2 a) Some prescribed drugs, e.g. codeine, can produce a false positive on the opiates test strip. Suggest why this might be the case.

b) If a strip tests positive for opiates, suggest what else could be done with the sample to confirm whether the potential employee has taken illegal drugs.

**Tip:** A false positive occurs when a test produces a positive result, when in truth the result should be negative.

---

### Practice Questions — Fact Recall

Q1 Which hormone is detected in a pregnancy test?

Q2 A pregnancy test uses antibodies bound to a blue bead. What colour will the test strip turn in a negative pregnancy test?

Q3 a) What technique is used to test a urine sample for the presence of anabolic steroids?

b) Briefly explain how this technique works.

# Section Summary

Make sure you know...

- That excretion is the removal of waste products of metabolism (e.g. carbon dioxide and nitrogenous waste) from the body. This helps to maintain normal metabolism and homeostasis by keeping the levels of certain substances in the blood roughly constant.
- The gross structure of the liver, including the hepatic artery, hepatic vein, hepatic portal vein and bile duct.
- The histology of the liver, including the liver lobules, hepatocytes, sinusoids, central vein, Kupffer cells and canaliculi.
- How to examine and draw a stained section of liver tissue.
- The liver's role in the formation of urea — this process involves the deamination of excess amino acids, and the conversion of ammonia and carbon dioxide into urea and water via the ornithine cycle.
- That the liver breaks down substances such as alcohol, paracetamol and insulin into less harmful substances in a process known as detoxification.
- That the liver converts excess glucose into glycogen and stores it as granules in its cells until it is needed for energy.
- That one of the main functions of the kidney is to excrete waste products.
- The gross structure of the kidney, including the kidney cortex and medulla, renal calyx, renal capsule, renal artery, renal vein and ureter.
- The detailed structure of the nephron and its associated blood vessels, including the afferent arteriole, glomerulus, Bowman's capsule, efferent arteriole, proximal convoluted tubule (PCT), loop of Henle, distal convoluted tubule (DCT) and collecting duct.
- How urine is formed through the processes of ultrafiltration and selective reabsorption.
- How the kidney reabsorbs water as it travels through the loop of Henle, the distal convoluted tubule and the collecting duct.
- How to examine and draw a stained section of kidney tissue to show the histology of nephrons.
- How to dissect a mammalian kidney, and examine and draw its external and internal structure.
- That one of the functions of the kidney is to aid the control of the water potential of the blood.
- That the water potential of the blood is monitored by osmoreceptors in the hypothalamus, and how the release of antidiuretic hormone (ADH) from the posterior pituitary gland is used to control the reabsorption of water in the kidneys.
- The problems arising from kidney failure including the effect on glomerular filtration rate (GFR) and electrolyte balance.
- The potential treatment options available to patients with kidney failure (haemodialysis, peritoneal dialysis and kidney transplants).
- How monoclonal antibodies are used to test urine samples for the presence of human chorionic gonadotropin (hCG) and therefore pregnancy in women.
- How antibodies and gas chromatography/mass spectrometry are used to test urine samples for the presence of anabolic steroids and drugs.

# Exam-style Questions

**1** The following statements describe the development of a positive result in a pregnancy test. They are not in the correct order.

1. hCG binds to mobile antibodies and coloured beads.
2. Urine is applied to a test stick.
3. A colour change is visible to the user.
4. hCG binds to immobilised antibodies.
5. Antibodies for hCG bound to coloured beads are applied to a test stick.

Which is the correct order for the development of a positive result in a pregnancy test?

**A** 2, 1, 3, 5, 4    **B** 2, 5, 4, 1, 3    **C** 5, 2, 3, 1, 4    **D** 5, 2, 1, 4, 3

*(1 mark)*

**2 (a)** **Fig. 2.1** is an electron micrograph showing a section through a proximal convoluted tubule of a kidney.

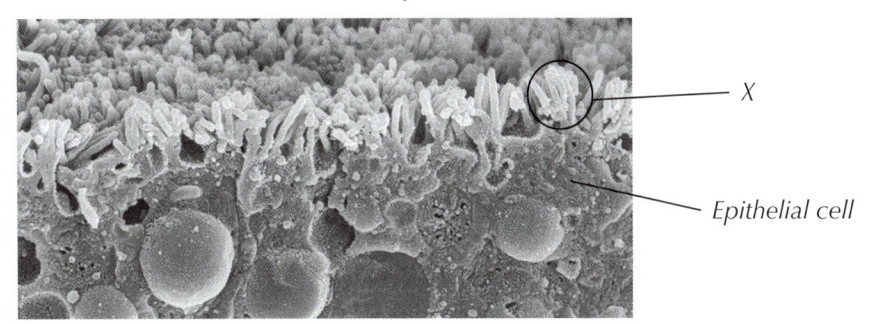

**Fig. 2.1**

Name the structure labelled **X** on **Fig. 2.1** and explain how this structure helps the epithelial cells of the proximal convoluted tubule to carry out their function.

*(3 marks)*

**(b)** **Fig. 2.2** shows a nephron.

**(i)** What name is given to structure **A**?

*(1 mark)*

**(ii)** Which **two** letters (**A** to **F**) indicate the locations where antidiuretic hormone (ADH) acts?

*(1 mark)*

**Fig. 2.2**

**(iii)** Explain how a longer structure **D** can result in animals producing urine that is more concentrated.

*(4 marks)*

**3 (a)** The tubular fluid to blood plasma concentration ratio (TF/P ratio) is an index used to measure how well the kidney is working. If substances are able to pass freely from the glomerulus into the Bowman's capsule they will have a TF/P ratio of 1.0, as their concentration in the plasma is the same as in the initial tubular fluid.

(i) Complete **Table 3.1** to show which of the following substances will have a TF/P ratio of 1.0 in a healthy kidney. The first two have been done for you.

| Substance | TF/P ratio of 1.0 |
|---|---|
| glucose | ✓ |
| serum albumin (protein) | X |
| sodium ions (Na⁺) |  |
| urea |  |
| red blood cells |  |

Table 3.1

*(2 marks)*

(ii) The TF/P ratio of the protein serum albumin is normally less than 1.0 in a healthy kidney, meaning that the concentration of serum albumin is higher in the plasma than the tubular fluid. Explain why this is the case.

*(1 mark)*

(iii) Kidney failure can be caused by high blood pressure. Suggest why high blood pressure may result in a TF/P ratio of 1.0 for the protein serum albumin.

*(3 marks)*

**(b)** A patient has kidney failure as a result of high blood pressure.

(i) Tests reveal that the patient's glomerular filtration rate (GFR) is 1200 $cm^3$ $hr^{-1}$. The patient reabsorbs 98.2% of her filtrate. Calculate the amount of urine the patient produces each day. Give your answer in $cm^3$ $day^{-1}$.

*(3 marks)*

(ii) The patient's doctor prescribes diuretics to reduce her blood pressure. Diuretics can reduce the amount of Na⁺ that is reabsorbed by the nephron. Suggest how diuretics can be used to decrease blood pressure.

*(5 marks)*

**(c)** Over time, waste products such as urea build up in the patient's body. Urea is a result of the breakdown of amino acids by the liver.

(i) Name the blood vessel in which urea leaves the liver.

*(1 mark)*

(ii) The production of urea involves the ornithine cycle. Outline how the ornithine cycle is involved in urea production.

*(2 marks)*

(iii) Suggest **one** possible health problem the patient may experience as a result of the accumulation of urea in her blood.

*(1 mark)*

# Module 5 Section 3: Animal Responses

## 1. The Nervous System

*You might remember the nervous system from Section 1 — you need to know more about it here. Firstly here's a recap on animal communication systems...*

### Responding to the environment

You might remember from page 295 that animals increase their chances of survival by responding to changes in their external environment, e.g. by avoiding harmful environments such as places that are too hot or too cold. They also respond to changes in their internal environment to make sure that the conditions are always optimal for their metabolism (all the chemical reactions that go on inside them). Any change in the internal or external environment is called a **stimulus**. Animals continuously need to respond to stimuli — this is a complex process often involving coordination between the nervous system, hormonal system and muscles.

### Receptors and effectors

Receptors detect stimuli and effectors bring about a response to a stimulus. Effectors include muscle cells and cells found in glands, e.g. the pancreas. Receptors communicate with effectors via the nervous system or the hormonal (endocrine) system, or sometimes using both. The nervous and hormonal systems coordinate the response.

### Structure of the nervous system

The nervous system is split into two main structural systems — the **central nervous system** (**CNS**) and the **peripheral nervous system**. The CNS is made up of the brain and spinal cord, whereas the peripheral nervous system is made up of the neurones that connect the CNS to the rest of the body.

The peripheral nervous system has two different functional systems — the **somatic** and **autonomic** nervous systems. The somatic nervous system controls conscious activities, e.g. running and playing video games. The autonomic nervous system controls unconscious activities, e.g. digestion and heart rate.

The autonomic nervous system is split into the sympathetic and parasympathetic nervous systems, which have opposite effects on the body. The sympathetic nervous system is the 'fight or flight' system that gets the body ready for action. Sympathetic neurones release the neurotransmitter noradrenaline. The parasympathetic system is the 'rest and digest' system that calms the body down. Parasympathetic neurones release the neurotransmitter acetylcholine.

The structure of the nervous system is summarised in Figure 1.

> CNS
> |
> peripheral nervous system
> → somatic nervous system
> → autonomic nervous system
>    → sympathetic nervous system
>    → parasympathetic nervous system

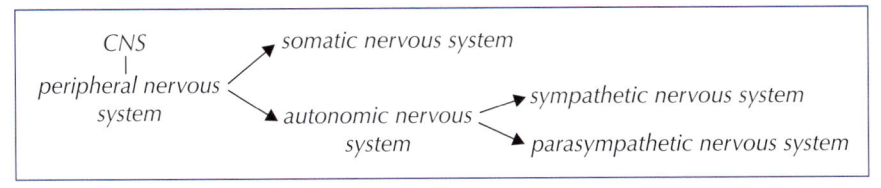

**Figure 1:** *Organisation of the nervous system.*

---

**Learning Objectives:**
- Know the organisation of the mammalian nervous system, including:
  - the structural organisation of the nervous system into the central and peripheral systems,
  - the functional organisation into the somatic and autonomic nervous systems.
- Know the gross structure of the human brain and the functions of its parts, including the cerebrum, hypothalamus, medulla oblongata, cerebellum and pituitary gland.
- Know what a reflex action is and understand the survival value of reflex actions, including the blinking reflex and knee-jerk reflex.

**Specification Reference 5.1.5**

**Exam Tip**
Figures 2 and 3 below show cross sections through the brain. You won't always see the brain from this view though — in the exam you might be asked to locate structures when looking at the brain from a different direction, e.g. from below or from the front.

**Tip:** The hypothalamus is also involved in the control of the water potential of the blood (see pages 343-344).

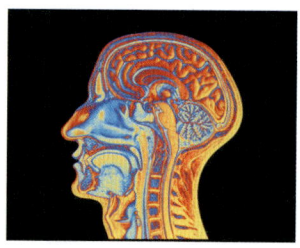

*Figure 3: MRI scan showing a section through the head. The cerebrum is the highly folded structure at the top (orange). The cerebellum (blue) lies below the cerebrum at the back of the head.*

# The brain

The brain is part of the central nervous system. You need to know the location and function of the five brain structures listed below and shown in Figure 2.

### 1. Cerebrum
The cerebrum is the largest part of the brain. It's divided into two halves called cerebral hemispheres. The cerebrum has a thin outer layer called the cerebral cortex, which is highly folded. The cerebrum is involved in vision, hearing, learning and thinking.

### 2. Hypothalamus
The hypothalamus is found just beneath the middle part of the brain. It automatically maintains body temperature at the normal level. It also produces hormones that control the pituitary gland (see below).

### 3. Medulla oblongata
The medulla oblongata is at the base of the brain, at the top of the spinal cord. It automatically controls breathing rate and heart rate.

### 4. Cerebellum
The cerebellum is underneath the cerebrum and it also has a folded cortex. It's important for muscle coordination, posture and coordination of balance.

### 5. Pituitary gland
The pituitary gland is found beneath (and is controlled by) the hypothalamus. It releases hormones and stimulates other glands, e.g. the adrenal glands (see p. 357), to release their hormones.

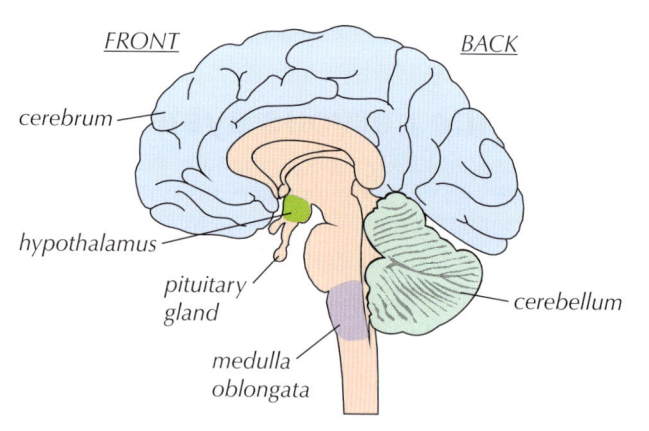

*Figure 2: Structures of the brain.*

## Practice Questions — Application

Q1 The image to the right shows the human brain viewed from the front.
   a) Name structure A.
   b) Name structure B.
   c) Give one function of each of the following brain structures:
      i) structure A,
      ii) medulla oblongata,
      iii) hypothalamus.

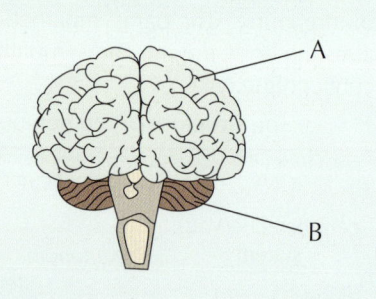

Module 5: Section 3 Animal Responses

Q2 Dyspraxia is a condition which has been linked to an abnormally developed cerebellum. People with dyspraxia may have difficulty with tasks such as throwing and catching, and may often fall over. Suggest why having an abnormally developed cerebellum could cause these symptoms.

**Tip:** Nervous impulses that involve the conscious brain are voluntary responses — you have to think about them. Reflex actions don't involve the conscious brain so they're involuntary responses — your body responds without thinking about it first.

# Reflex actions

A reflex action is where the body responds to a stimulus without making a conscious decision to respond. This is because the pathway of communication doesn't involve conscious parts of the brain — instead it goes through unconscious parts of the brain or the spinal cord. Because you don't have to spend time deciding how to respond, information travels really fast from receptors to effectors. Reflex actions are protective — they help organisms to avoid damage to the body because the response happens so quickly.

The pathway of communication linking receptors to effectors in a reflex action typically involves three neurones — a sensory neurone, a relay neurone and a motor neurone (see Figure 4).

**Tip:** See page 296 for more about the structure and function of the different types of neurone.

Stimulus → Receptors → CNS (relay neurone in unconscious part of brain or spinal cord) → Effectors → Response

(sensory neurone | motor neurone)

**Tip:** Not all reflex actions involve a relay neurone — see the knee-jerk example on the next page.

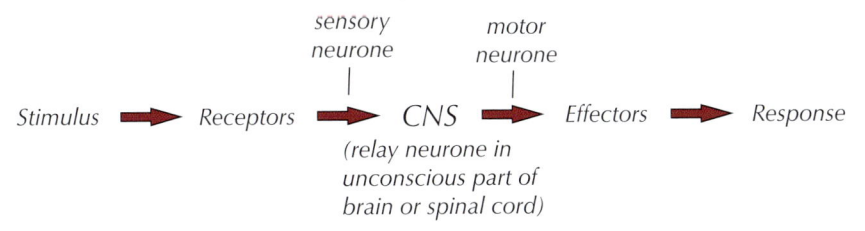

*Figure 4: The pathway of nervous communication in a reflex action.*

Animals have lots of different reflexes to help them survive:

**Exam Tip**
You need to learn details of the blinking reflex and the knee-jerk reflex for your exams.

### Example — Blinking reflex

When your body detects something that could damage your eye, you automatically blink — you quickly close your eyelid to protect your eye, then open your eyelid again.
For example, you blink if your eye is touched:

- **Stimulus** — something touches your eye.
- **Receptors** — sensory nerve endings in the cornea (front part of the eye) detect the touch stimulus. A nerve impulse is sent along the sensory neurone to a relay neurone in the CNS.
- **CNS** — the impulse is then passed from the relay neurone to motor neurones.

**Tip:** The blinking reflex can also occur because of other stimuli, e.g. hearing a sudden loud noise or a flash of bright light.

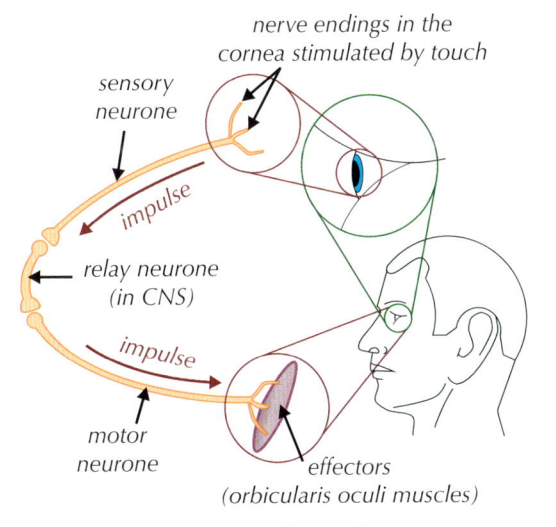

*Figure 6: The pathway of nervous communication in the blinking reflex.*

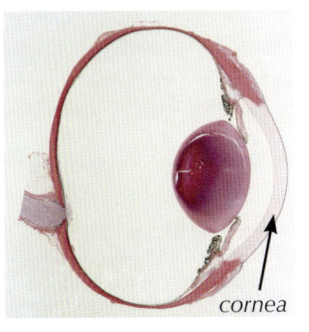

*Figure 5: Light micrograph of a cross-section of a human eye showing the cornea (light pink).*

Module 5: Section 3 Animal Responses    355

**Tip:** If there's a relay neurone involved in the reflex arc then it's possible to override the reflex, e.g. in the blinking reflex your brain could tell your eye to withstand the touch.

- **Effectors** — the motor neurones send impulses to the orbicularis oculi muscles that move your eyelids.
- **Response** — these muscles contract causing your eyelids to close quickly and prevent your eye from being damaged.

### Example — Knee-jerk reflex

The knee-jerk reflex works to quickly straighten your leg if the body detects your quadriceps is suddenly stretched. It helps to maintain posture and balance. For example, if your knees buckle after landing from a jump, the reflex causes your quadriceps to contract to keep you upright. This is how it works:

**Tip:** The quadriceps is a group of four muscles at the front of your thigh.

**Stimulus** — your quadriceps muscle is stretched.

**Receptors** — stretch receptors in the quadriceps muscle detect that the muscle is being stretched. A nerve impulse is passed along a sensory neurone.

**CNS** — the sensory neurone communicates directly with a motor neurone in the spinal cord (there is no relay neurone involved).

**Effectors** — the motor neurone carries the nerve impulse to the quadriceps muscle.

**Response** — the quadriceps muscle contracts so the lower leg moves forward quickly.

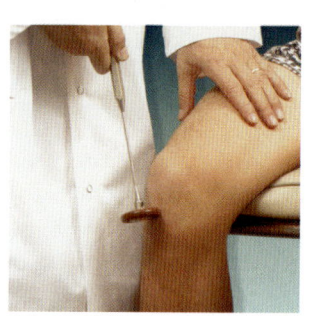

*Figure 8:* You can test your knee-jerk reflex by quickly hitting your patellar tendon (just below your knee cap) when your leg is bent.

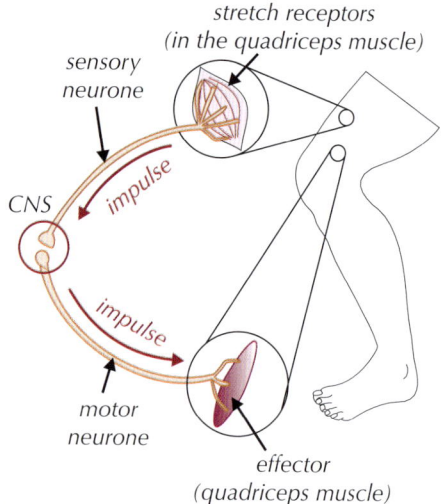

*Figure 7:* The pathway of nervous communication in the knee-jerk reflex.

**Tip:** Remember that although the knee-jerk reflex doesn't involve a relay neurone, it still involves the CNS (spinal cord).

### Practice Question — Application

Q1 When your hand touches a hot surface, you automatically and quickly withdraw your hand away from the source of heat.
   a) What two pieces of information tell you that the sentence above is describing a reflex action?
   b) The reflex action described involves three neurones. Describe the pathway of nervous communication that occurs in this example.

### Practice Questions — Fact Recall

Q1 What two structures is the central nervous system made up of?
Q2 What is the overall role of the autonomic nervous system?
Q3 Name the gland located just below the hypothalamus and describe its function.
Q4 Where is the medulla oblongata located?
Q5 What is a reflex action?
Q6 Describe the pathway of nervous communication in the blinking reflex when it's triggered by something touching the eye.

**Exam Tip**
The medulla <u>oblongata</u> always refers to the brain structure. (The inner part of some structures, e.g. the adrenal glands, is called the medulla.)

Module 5: Section 3 Animal Responses

# 2. 'Fight or Flight' Response and Heart Rate

*For many animal responses it's really important that the nervous and hormonal systems work together. The 'fight or flight' response and the control of heart rate are good examples of how nerves and hormones coordinate a response.*

## The 'fight or flight' response

When an organism is threatened (e.g. by a predator) it responds by preparing the body for action (e.g. for fighting or running away). This response is called the 'fight or flight' response. Nerve impulses from sensory neurones arrive at the hypothalamus (see page 354), activating both the hormonal (endocrine) system and the sympathetic nervous system.

The pituitary gland is stimulated to release a hormone called ACTH. This causes the cortex of the adrenal gland to release steroidal hormones, which have a range of effects on the body, helping it to respond to stress both in the short and long-term (see page 312).

The sympathetic nervous system is activated, triggering the release of adrenaline from the medulla region of the adrenal gland. The sympathetic nervous system and adrenaline produce a faster response than the hormones secreted by the cortex of the adrenal gland. Their effects include:

- Heart rate is increased and the heart contracts with more force, causing blood to be pumped around the body faster.
- The muscles around the bronchioles relax, causing the airways to widen, so breathing is deeper.
- The intercostal muscles and diaphragm also contract faster and with more strength, increasing the rate and depth of breathing.
- Glycogen is converted into glucose via glycogenolysis (see page 322), so more glucose is available for muscles to respire.
- Muscles in the arterioles supplying the skin and gut constrict, and muscles in the arterioles supplying the heart, lungs and skeletal muscles dilate — so blood is diverted from the skin and gut to the heart, lungs and skeletal muscles. This increases blood flow to skeletal muscles (e.g. in the legs), making them ready for action.
- Erector pili muscles in the skin contract — this makes hairs stand on end so the animal looks bigger.

## Control of heart rate — the nervous system

There's a small mass of tissue in the wall of the right atrium of the heart called the sino-atrial node (SAN). The SAN generates electrical impulses that cause the cardiac muscles to contract. The rate at which the SAN fires (i.e. heart rate) is unconsciously controlled by the cardiovascular centre in the medulla oblongata (a structure in the brain — see page 354).

Animals need to alter their heart rate to respond to internal stimuli, e.g. to prevent fainting due to low blood pressure or to make sure the heart rate is high enough to supply the body with enough oxygen.

---

**Learning Objectives:**
- Understand how the 'fight or flight' response to environmental stimuli in mammals is coordinated by the nervous and endocrine systems.
- Know the effects of nervous mechanisms and hormones on heart rate.
- Be able to monitor physiological functions, for example by taking pulse rate measurements before, during and after exercise, or by using sensors to record electrical activity in the heart (PAG11).
- Be able to use Student's t-test to compare the means of data values of two sets of data.

**Specification Reference 5.1.5**

**Tip:** What happens in the 'fight or flight' response brings together topics from different areas of Biology — heart rate, breathing, glycogenolysis, muscle contraction, etc. This makes it an ideal topic for a synoptic exam question. For more on synoptic questions, see the 'Exam Help' section (pages 571-573).

**Tip:** Remember, it's the autonomic nervous system that's involved in the control of heart rate (see page 353).

Internal stimuli are detected by pressure receptors and chemical receptors:

- There are pressure receptors called baroreceptors in the aorta and the carotid arteries. They're stimulated by high and low blood pressure.
- There are chemical receptors called chemoreceptors in the aorta, the carotid arteries and in the medulla oblongata. They monitor the oxygen level in the blood and also carbon dioxide and pH (which are indicators of $O_2$ level).

Nerve impulses from receptors are sent to the cardiovascular centre along sensory neurones. The cardiovascular centre processes the information and sends impulses to the SAN along motor neurones.

**Tip:** The carotid arteries are major arteries in the neck.

### Control of heart rate in response to different stimuli

**1. High blood pressure**

Baroreceptors detect high blood pressure and send impulses along sensory neurones to the cardiovascular centre, which sends impulses along parasympathetic neurones. These secrete acetylcholine, which binds to receptors on the SAN. This causes the heart rate to slow down in order to reduce blood pressure back to normal.

**2. Low blood pressure**

Baroreceptors detect low blood pressure and send impulses along sensory neurones to the cardiovascular centre, which sends impulses along sympathetic neurones. These secrete noradrenaline, which binds to receptors on the SAN. This causes the heart rate to speed up in order to increase blood pressure back to normal.

**Tip:** The effectors in all of these situations are the cardiac muscles of the heart.

**3. High blood $O_2$, low $CO_2$ or high blood pH levels**

Chemoreceptors detect chemical changes in the blood and send impulses along sensory neurones to the cardiovascular centre, which sends impulses along parasympathetic neurones. These secrete acetylcholine, which binds to receptors on the SAN. This causes the heart rate to decrease in order to return oxygen, carbon dioxide and pH levels back to normal.

**Tip:** Low blood $O_2$, high $CO_2$ or low blood pH levels are a result of increased respiration.

**4. Low blood $O_2$, high $CO_2$ or low blood pH levels**

Chemoreceptors detect chemical changes in the blood and send impulses along sensory neurones to the cardiovascular centre, which sends impulses along sympathetic neurones. These secrete noradrenaline, which binds to receptors on the SAN. This causes the heart rate to increase in order to return oxygen, carbon dioxide and pH levels back to normal.

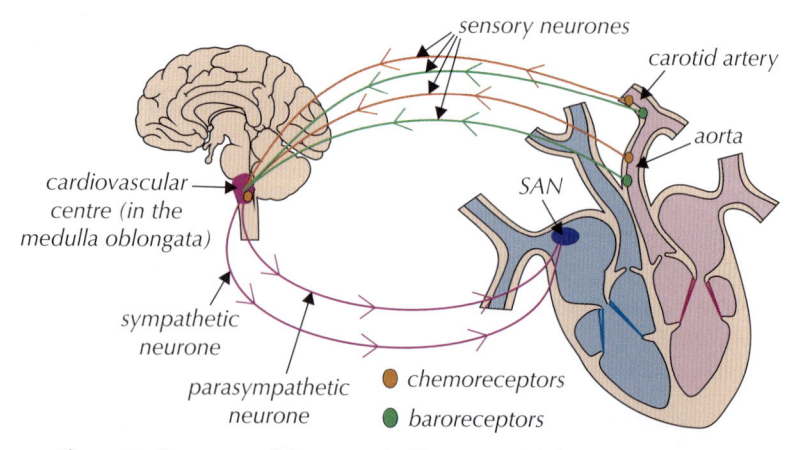

*Figure 1:* Summary of the control of heart rate by the nervous system.

Module 5: Section 3 Animal Responses

# Control of heart rate — the hormonal system

When an organism is threatened the adrenal glands release adrenaline. Adrenaline binds to specific receptors in the heart. This causes the cardiac muscle to contract more frequently and with more force, so heart rate increases and the heart pumps more blood.

**Tip:** The hormonal system is also known as the endocrine system.

**Tip:** Remember, adrenaline is released when the 'fight or flight' system is activated.

## Practice Questions — Application

Q1 Anaemia is a condition in which the oxygen carrying capacity of the blood is reduced. Use your knowledge of the nervous control of heart rate to explain why a person with anaemia is likely to have a more rapid heart rate than someone without anaemia.

Q2 A man is driving when a child runs out onto the road in front of him. He manages to swerve and avoid the child. Immediately afterwards he finds that his heart is beating fast and his breathing rate has increased.

   a) What response is the man experiencing and what is the purpose of this response?

   b) Name the branch of the autonomic nervous system responsible for the response.

   c) The table below shows some other responses that the man's body makes. Copy and complete the table, stating if each response is increased or decreased as a result of the incident.

| Response | Increased or decreased? |
| --- | --- |
| strength of contraction of heart muscle | |
| depth of breathing | |
| blood supply to the gut | |
| blood supply to the skeletal muscles | |
| blood glucose level | |
| blood supply to the skin | |

# Investigating heart rate

**PRACTICAL ACTIVITY GROUP 11**

You can investigate how different factors affect your heart rate. For example, you could investigate the effect of exercise on heart rate. When you exercise, your rate of respiration increases. This reduces the pH and the oxygen level in the blood and increases the carbon dioxide level. Chemoreceptors detect these changes and cause heart rate to increase to bring the levels back to normal.

**Tip:** If you have any medical conditions that might affect your ability to participate in exercise, make sure you have carefully considered the risks before starting this experiment. You might want to investigate a different effect instead (see below).

### Example

Before you start, make sure you know how to measure your heart rate. Find your pulse in your wrist by placing your index and middle finger where the base of your thumb meets your forearm. Count the number of beats in 15 seconds and then multiply by four to get the number of beats per minute. Then:

1. Measure your heart rate at rest and record it in a table.
2. Do some gentle exercise, such as stepping on and off a step for 5 minutes. Immediately afterwards, measure your heart rate again.

**Tip:** You could also measure other effects on heart rate in a similar way. For example, you could test the effect of a loud noise or the effect of anxiety (by doing something that makes you nervous).

3. Return to a resting position. Measure your heart rate every minute until it returns to the starting rate. Record how long it takes to return to normal.

You would expect your heart rate to increase after this exercise. But if you wanted to find out whether this exercise caused a **significant** increase in heart rate you could collect more results (e.g. by repeating exactly the same experiment using other people) and then carrying out a statistical test.

### Heart rate monitors

The investigation in the example above used pulse measurements to monitor heart rate, but you could use an electronic heart rate monitor instead.

There are different types of electronic heart rate monitors, but the ones you're likely to use consist of a chest strap and a wrist monitor. The chest strap contains electrodes (sensors) which detect the electrical activity of the heart (through the skin) as it beats. The data is picked up by the electrodes and then transmitted wirelessly to the wrist monitor, which displays the data as a heart rate in beats per minute (bpm).

There are several advantages of using an electronic heart rate monitor over manually taking your pulse. For example, a monitor can measure your heart rate as you are exercising and keep a continual record of how it changes, whereas manual pulse measurements must be done at intervals.

## Using Student's t-test

Student's t-test is a statistical test used to find out whether there is a significant difference in the means of two data sets. The value obtained is compared to a critical value, which helps you decide how likely it is that the results or 'differences in the means' were due to chance.

Student's t-test can be used to determine whether a particular variable, such as exercise, has a significant effect on heart rate or whether any results observed were just due to chance. There are quite a lot of steps involved when performing Student's t-test. The easiest way to understand it is to follow through an example:

### Example — Maths Skills

In an investigation into the effect of regular, intense exercise on resting heart rate, 16 volunteers were divided into two equal groups. One group received six months of endurance training (Set 1) and the other group did not (Set 2). The resting heart rates of both groups were then measured. The results are shown in Figure 3. Use Student's t-test to determine whether endurance training has a significant effect on resting heart rate.

**Figure 3:** Table of results.

|            | Resting heart rate at end of test period (bpm) |    |    |    |    |    |    |    |
|------------|----|----|----|----|----|----|----|----|
| Data set 1 | 67 | 72 | 65 | 61 | 75 | 78 | 65 | 69 |
| Data set 2 | 89 | 68 | 78 | 70 | 67 | 82 | 94 | 76 |

1. Firstly, you need to identify the **null hypothesis**. This is always that the means for the two sets of data are going to be exactly the same, i.e. there is no significant difference between them.
   - So here the null hypothesis is that there is no significant difference between the mean resting heart rate of people who received endurance training and those who did not.

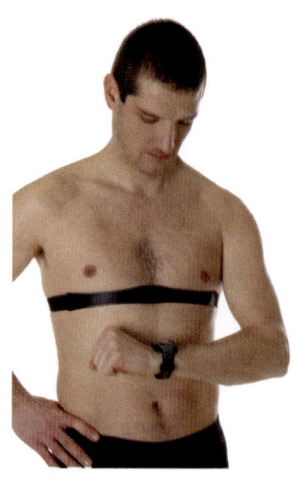

*Figure 2: A man using a heart rate monitor with chest strap and wrist monitor.*

**Tip:** Make sure the monitor is clean before each use by wiping the sensors, e.g. with a mild detergent — dirty electrodes can give poor readings.

**Tip:** You can also get electronic heart rate monitors that are just worn on the wrist and don't use a chest strap — these just measure pulse rate and tend to be less accurate than ones that use a chest strap (although they may be more comfortable).

**Tip:** The Student's t-test equation used in this example (on the next page) is used to compare the means of two groups of different individuals. There is a different equation that you can use for paired data (data that includes two measurements for each person, e.g. before and after endurance training).

2. Next you need to calculate the **mean** for each data set.
   - Data set 1: $\bar{x}$ = (67 + 72 + 65 + 61 + 75 + 78 + 65 + 69) ÷ 8 = **69**
   - Data set 2: $\bar{x}$ = (89 + 68 + 78 + 70 + 67 + 82 + 94 + 76) ÷ 8 = **78**

3. Then you need to calculate the **standard deviation** of each data set. For this you'll need to use the following formula:

   $$s = \sqrt{\frac{\Sigma(x - \bar{x})^2}{n - 1}}$$

   where, s = standard deviation, Σ = sum of,
   x = a value in the data set,
   $\bar{x}$ = mean of the data set,
   n = number of values in the data set.

   - So start by working out $(x - \bar{x})^2$ for each value of x (each heart rate in the data set). For each heart rate, you need to take away the mean for that data set and then square the answer:

     Data set 1:
     $(67 - 69)^2 = 4$
     $(72 - 69)^2 = 9$
     $(65 - 69)^2 = 16$
     $(61 - 69)^2 = 64$
     $(75 - 69)^2 = 36$
     $(78 - 69)^2 = 81$
     $(65 - 69)^2 = 16$
     $(69 - 69)^2 = 0$

     Data set 2:
     $(89 - 78)^2 = 121$
     $(68 - 78)^2 = 100$
     $(78 - 78)^2 = 0$
     $(70 - 78)^2 = 64$
     $(67 - 78)^2 = 121$
     $(82 - 78)^2 = 16$
     $(94 - 78)^2 = 256$
     $(76 - 78)^2 = 4$

   - Add up all these numbers to find $\Sigma(x - \bar{x})^2$:
     Data set 1: **226**, Data set 2: **682**

   - Divide this number by the number of values in the data set minus 1 then find the square root to get the standard deviation:
     Data set 1: $s = \sqrt{(226 ÷ 7)} = $ **5.7**
     Data set 2: $s = \sqrt{(682 ÷ 7)} = $ **9.9**

4. Now you've found the mean and standard deviation of each data set, you need to use this **Student's t-test formula** to calculate your t value:

   $$t = \frac{\bar{x}_1 - \bar{x}_2}{\sqrt{(s_1^2 / n_1) + (s_2^2 / n_2)}}$$

   $\bar{x}$ = mean
   s = standard deviation
   n = number of values in data set
   $_1$ or $_2$ = data set being referred to

   - $t = \dfrac{69 - 78}{\sqrt{(5.7^2 / 8) + (9.9^2 / 8)}} = $ **-2.2** (to 1 d.p.)

   You can ignore the minus sign and just use a t value of 2.2.

5. Next, calculate the **degrees of freedom** by doing $(n_1 + n_2) - 2$. Remember, n is the number of values in each data set.
   - So here, degrees of freedom = (8 + 8) − 2 = **14**

6. Finally, look up the values for t in a **table of critical values** (see Figure 4, next page). If the value obtained for the t-test is greater than the critical value at a probability (or P value) of 5% or less (≤ 0.05), then you can be 95% confident that the difference is significant and not due to chance. You'd reject the null hypothesis.
   - You need to find the critical value at 14 degrees of freedom at p = 0.05.

**Tip:** Remember, to do a t-test like this, you will need two sets of data.

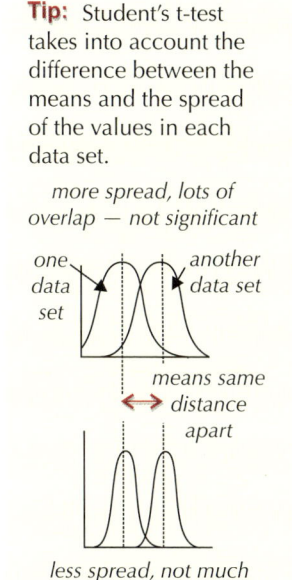

**Tip:** Student's t-test takes into account the difference between the means and the spread of the values in each data set.

*more spread, lots of overlap — not significant*

*means same distance apart*

*less spread, not much overlap — significant*

**Tip:** You may see vertical lines at either side of the top row of this formula, i.e. $|\bar{x}_1 - \bar{x}_2|$. This is just telling you that you're finding the numerical difference of whatever's between the lines (so if you get a negative answer you can just ignore the sign).

**Tip:** If the result of your statistical test is greater than the critical value at a P value of less than 2% (< 0.02), or even 1%, you can be even more confident that the difference is significant.

The critical value from the table is **2.145**. The *t* value of **2.2** that you have just calculated is greater than this critical value. This means that the null hypothesis can be rejected and you can say that the mean resting heart rate for the group that received endurance training was significantly lower after six months than for the group that did not receive training.

| degrees of freedom | critical *t* values | | | |
|---|---|---|---|---|
| 12 | 1.356 | 1.782 | 2.179 | 2.681 |
| 13 | 1.350 | 1.771 | 2.160 | 2.650 |
| 14 | 1.345 | 1.761 | 2.145 | 2.624 |
| 15 | 1.341 | 1.753 | 2.131 | 2.602 |
| probability that result is due to chance only | 0.2 (20%) | 0.1 (10%) | 0.05 (5%) | 0.02 (2%) |

***Figure 4:*** *Table of critical values.*

Abridged from Statistical Tables for Biological Agricultural and Medical Research, R.A Fisher and F. Yates (6th ed.) © 1963 Reprinted by permission of Pearson Business

**Exam Tip**
You'll be given a table of critical values in the exam.

## Practice Question — Application

Q1 An experiment was carried out on the effect of caffeine on heart rate. Fourteen volunteers were given an electronic heart rate monitor. The volunteers were split into two equal groups. One group was given a capsule containing caffeine and the other was given a placebo. After one hour, the heart rate of each volunteer was recorded. The results are shown in the table on the right.

| Heart rate after 1 hour (bpm) | |
|---|---|
| Caffeine | No caffeine |
| 71 | 58 |
| 90 | 72 |
| 82 | 65 |
| 76 | 67 |
| 88 | 60 |
| 85 | 74 |
| 66 | 78 |

a) Explain how an electronic heart rate monitor (that uses a chest strap) can be used to measure heart rate.

b) Using the formulae for standard deviation and Student's t-test and the table of critical values below, determine whether caffeine has a significant effect on heart rate at a 95% confidence level.

$$s = \sqrt{\frac{\sum(x - \bar{x})^2}{n - 1}}$$

$$t = \frac{\bar{x}_1 - \bar{x}_2}{\sqrt{(s_1^2 / n_1) + (s_2^2 / n_2)}}$$

| degrees of freedom | critical *t* values | | | |
|---|---|---|---|---|
| 12 | 1.356 | 1.782 | 2.179 | 2.681 |
| 13 | 1.350 | 1.771 | 2.160 | 2.650 |
| 14 | 1.345 | 1.761 | 2.145 | 2.624 |
| 15 | 1.341 | 1.753 | 2.131 | 2.602 |
| P value | 0.2 | 0.1 | 0.05 | 0.02 |

Abridged from Statistical Tables for Biological Agricultural and Medical Research, R.A Fisher and F. Yates (6th ed.) © 1963 Reprinted by permission of Pearson Business

**Tip:** Caffeine is a drug that affects the nervous system.

**Tip:** A placebo is a substance that looks like the real drug being tested, but doesn't contain the drug. It has no physical effects on the person taking it.

**Tip:** Remember:
$s$ = standard deviation,
$\Sigma$ = the sum of,
$\bar{x}$ = mean of a data set,
$x$ = values in data set,
$n$ = number of values in a data set, and
$_1$ or $_2$ = data set being referred to.

**Exam Tip**
You might not have to carry out all the steps involved in Student's t-test in the exam — still it's good to take the time to practice the full method as you never know what you'll get asked to do in the exam.

## Practice Questions — Fact Recall

Q1 Which part of the brain coordinates the 'fight or flight' response?

Q2 a) What type of receptor detects a fall in blood pressure?

b) Where are these receptors located in the body?

Q3 What effect do impulses from parasympathetic neurones have on heart rate?

Q4 Briefly describe how you could investigate the effect of a loud noise on heart rate.

# 3. Muscle Contraction

*Muscles are effectors — they contract in response to nervous impulses in order to bring about a response. You need to know their structure and how it enables them to contract.*

## Movement

The CNS (brain and spinal cord) coordinates muscular movement — it receives sensory information and decides what kind of response is needed. If the response needed is movement, the CNS sends nervous impulses along motor neurones to tell skeletal muscles to contract. Skeletal muscle (also called striated, striped or voluntary muscle) is the type of muscle you use to move, e.g. the biceps and triceps move the lower arm.

## Skeletal muscle

Skeletal muscle is made up of large bundles of long cells, called muscle fibres. The cell membrane of muscle fibre cells is called the sarcolemma. Bits of the sarcolemma fold inwards across the muscle fibre and stick into the sarcoplasm (a muscle cell's cytoplasm). These folds are called transverse (T) tubules and they help to spread electrical impulses throughout the sarcoplasm so they reach all parts of the muscle fibre — see Figure 2.

A network of internal membranes called the sarcoplasmic reticulum runs through the sarcoplasm. The sarcoplasmic reticulum stores and releases calcium ions that are needed for muscle contraction. Muscle fibres have lots of mitochondria to provide the ATP that's needed for muscle contraction. They are multinucleate (contain many nuclei) and have lots of long, cylindrical organelles called **myofibrils**. Myofibrils are made up of proteins and are highly specialised for contraction.

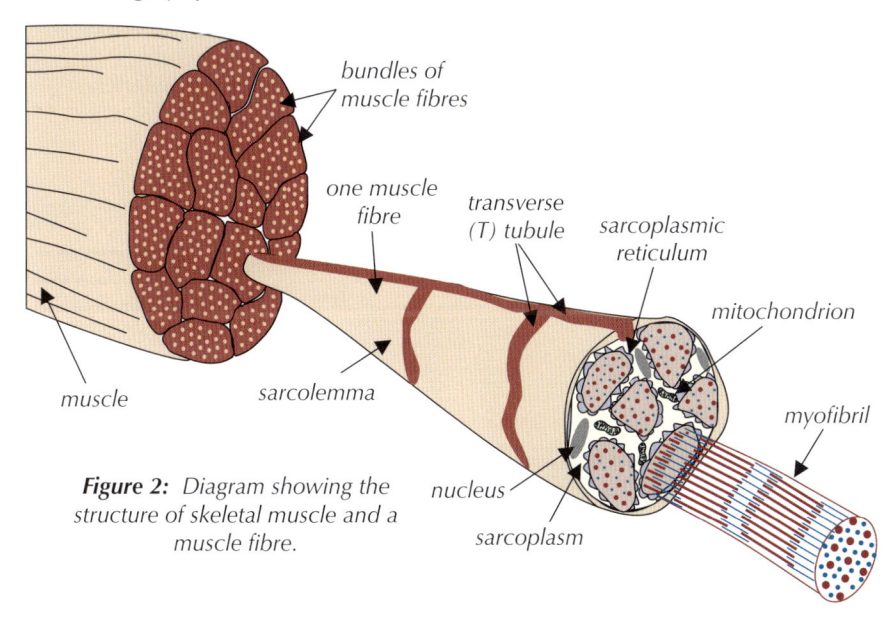

### Learning Objectives:
- Know the structure of mammalian muscle.
- Know the mechanism of muscular contraction, including the sliding filament model of muscular contraction and the role of ATP.
- Know how the supply of ATP is maintained in muscles by creatine phosphate.
- Know the structural and functional differences between skeletal, involuntary and cardiac muscle.
- Be able to examine stained sections or photomicrographs of skeletal muscle (PAG1).

**Specification Reference 5.1.5**

**Tip:** You also have other types of muscle in your body — the structures of these muscle types are covered on pages 369-370.

**Figure 1:** A scanning electron micrograph of a section of muscle fibre with myofibrils (pink and yellow) bundled together.

**Figure 2:** Diagram showing the structure of skeletal muscle and a muscle fibre.

## Myofibrils

Myofibrils contain bundles of thick and thin myofilaments that move past each other to make muscles contract. The thick myofilaments are made of the protein **myosin** and the thin myofilaments are made of the protein **actin**.

Module 5: Section 3 Animal Responses

**Tip:** There's more detail on the way myosin and actin work in muscle contraction on pages 365-367.

**Tip:** To remember which band is which, think: d**a**rk = **A**-bands and l**i**ght = **I**-bands.

If you look at a myofibril under an electron microscope, you'll see a pattern of alternating dark and light bands (see Figures 3 and 4). Dark bands contain the thick myosin filaments and some overlapping thin actin filaments — these are called A-bands. Light bands contain thin actin filaments only — these are called I-bands.

A myofibril is made up of many short units called **sarcomeres**. The ends of each sarcomere are marked with a Z-line. In the middle of each sarcomere is an M-line. The M-line is the middle of the myosin filaments. Around the M-line is the H-zone. The H-zone only contains myosin filaments.

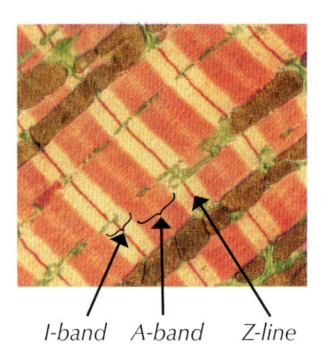

**Figure 4:** A transmission electron micrograph of myofibrils showing the banding of myosin (red) and actin (yellow).

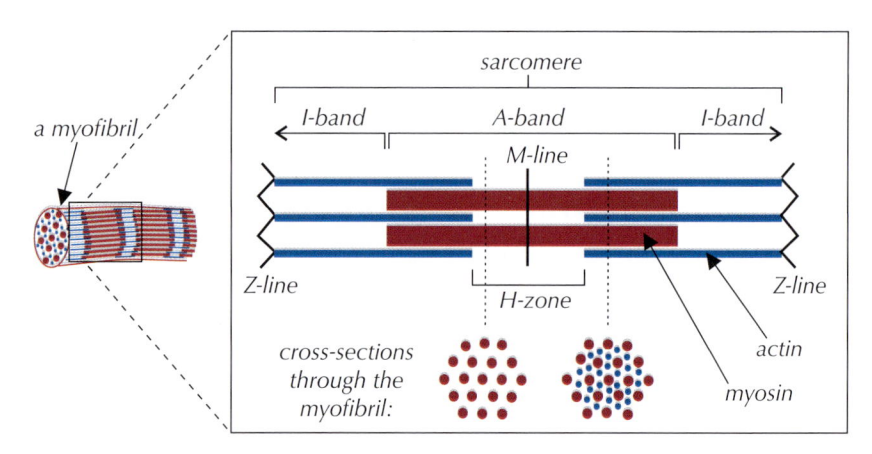

**Figure 3:** The structure of a sarcomere — a unit of a myofibril.

## The sliding filament model

Muscle contraction is explained by the sliding filament model. This is where myosin and actin filaments slide over one another to make the sarcomeres contract — the myofilaments themselves don't contract. The simultaneous contraction of lots of sarcomeres means the myofibrils and muscle fibres contract. Sarcomeres return to their original length as the muscle relaxes.

**Tip:** <u>A</u> bands are the only ones that stay the <u>sa</u>me length.

The Z-lines get closer together — the sarcomeres get shorter.

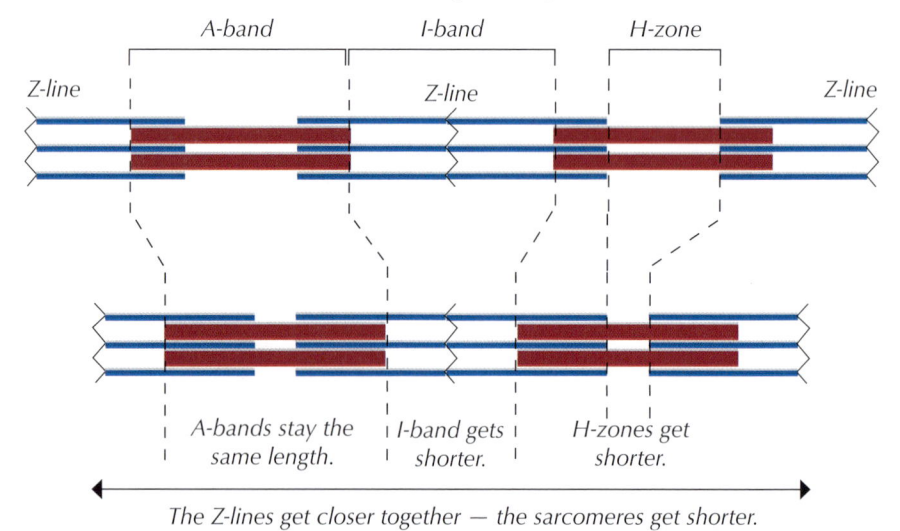

**Figure 5:** Sarcomeres during relaxation (top) and contraction (bottom).

364 Module 5: Section 3 Animal Responses

## Practice Questions — Application

**Q1** Cross-sections from three different sites along a sarcomere are shown below.

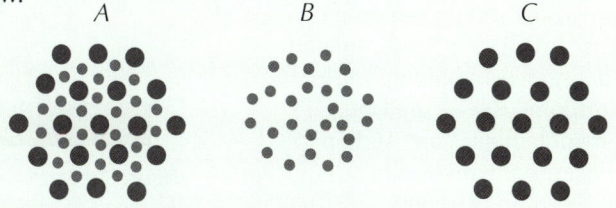

A    B    C

Which cross-section(s) could be from:
a) an I-band?
b) an M-line?
c) an A-band?
d) a Z-line?

**Tip:** The diagrams in Q1 might look a bit odd at first, but with a bit of logical thinking you should be able to work out the answers. It might help if you sketch out the sarcomere structure with the bands on, so you can see what's happening.

**Q2** The lengths of three different sections of a sarcomere were measured when a rabbit muscle was relaxed. These values are given in the first column of the table below. Work out which other set of values in the table (options 1-3) shows the lengths of the sections when the muscle was contracted. Explain your answer.

|        | Relaxed (μm) | Option 1 (μm) | Option 2 (μm) | Option 3 (μm) |
|--------|--------------|---------------|---------------|---------------|
| A-band | 1.5          | 1.5           | 1.2           | 1.5           |
| I-band | 0.8          | 0.5           | 0.5           | 1             |
| H-zone | 0.7          | 0.2           | 0.7           | 0.2           |

# Myosin and actin filaments

Muscle contraction involves myosin and actin filaments sliding over one another. Here's a bit more detail about the two types of filament:

### Myosin filaments
Myosin filaments have globular heads that are hinged, so they can move back and forth. Each myosin head has a binding site for actin and a binding site for ATP — see Figure 6.

### Actin filaments
Actin filaments have binding sites for myosin heads, called actin-myosin binding sites. Two other proteins called **tropomyosin** and **troponin** are found between actin filaments. These proteins are attached to each other (troponin holds tropomyosin in place) and they help myofilaments move past each other (see Figure 6).

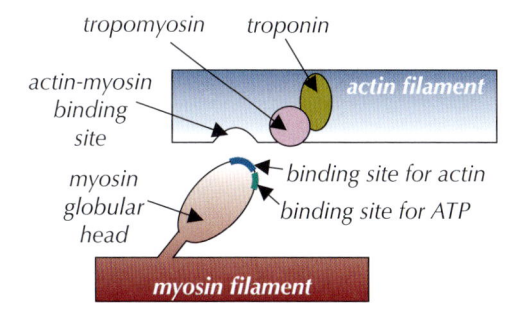

**Figure 6:** The structure of myosin and actin filaments.

**Tip:** Figure 6 has been simplified — troponin and tropomyosin are actually joined in a long chain that coils round the actin filament.

Module 5: Section 3 Animal Responses    365

## Binding sites in resting muscles

For myosin and actin filaments to slide past each other, the myosin head needs to bind to the actin-myosin binding site on the actin filament. In a resting (unstimulated) muscle the actin-myosin binding site is blocked by tropomyosin — see Figure 7. This means myofilaments can't slide past each other because the myosin heads can't bind to the actin filaments.

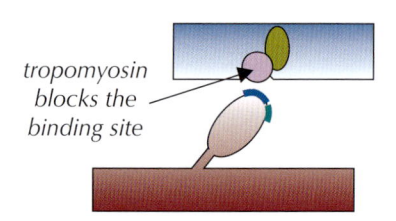

*Figure 7: Actin and myosin filaments in resting muscle.*

## Muscle contraction

### Arrival of an action potential

**Tip:** Depolarisation makes the sarcolemma less negative than when it's at rest. See page 302 for more on depolarisation.

When an action potential from a motor neurone stimulates a muscle cell, it depolarises the sarcolemma. Depolarisation spreads down the T-tubules to the sarcoplasmic reticulum. This causes the sarcoplasmic reticulum to release stored calcium ions ($Ca^{2+}$) into the sarcoplasm. This influx of calcium ions into the sarcoplasm triggers muscle contraction.

**Tip:** If you can't remember your sarcolemma from your sarcoplasmic reticulum then take a look back at page 363.

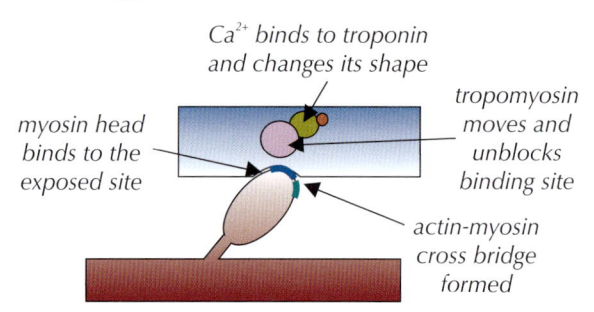

*Figure 8: Formation of an actin-myosin cross bridge.*

Calcium ions bind to troponin, causing it to change shape. This pulls the attached tropomyosin out of the actin-myosin binding site on the actin filament. This exposes the binding site, which allows the myosin head to bind. The bond formed when a myosin head binds to an actin filament is called an **actin-myosin cross bridge** — see Figure 8.

### Movement of the actin filament

Calcium ions also activate the enzyme ATPase, which breaks down ATP (into ADP + Pi) to provide the energy needed for muscle contraction. The energy released from ATP moves the myosin head to the side, which pulls the actin filament along in a kind of rowing action (see Figure 9).

**Tip:** The movement of the myosin head to the side is called a 'power stroke'.

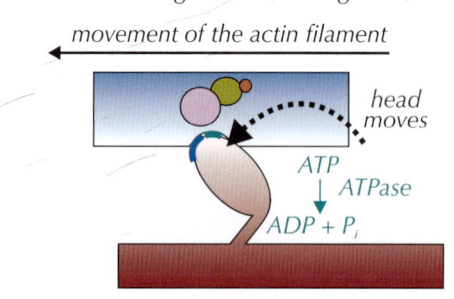

*Figure 9: Movement of the myosin head.*

## Breaking of the cross bridge

ATP also provides the energy to break the actin-myosin cross bridge, so the myosin head detaches from the actin filament after it's moved. The myosin head then returns to it's starting position, and reattaches to a different binding site further along the actin filament — see Figure 10. A new actin-myosin cross bridge is formed and the cycle is repeated (attach, move, detach, reattach to new binding site...).

Many actin-myosin cross bridges form and break very rapidly, pulling the actin filament along — which shortens the sarcomere, causing the muscle to contract. The cycle will continue as long as calcium ions are present and bound to troponin.

**Tip:** As the actin filaments are being moved along, the I-bands are getting shorter and the Z-lines are moving closer together.

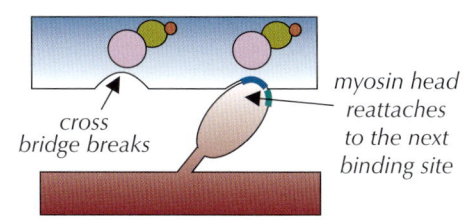

*Figure 10: Myosin head forms a new actin-myosin cross bridge.*

## Return to resting state

When the muscle stops being stimulated, calcium ions leave their binding sites on the troponin molecules and are moved by active transport back into the sarcoplasmic reticulum (this needs ATP too). The troponin molecules return to their original shape, pulling the attached tropomyosin molecules with them. This means the tropomyosin molecules block the actin-myosin binding sites again — see Figure 11.

Muscles aren't contracted because no myosin heads are attached to actin filaments (so there are no actin-myosin cross bridges). The actin filaments slide back to their relaxed position, which lengthens the sarcomere.

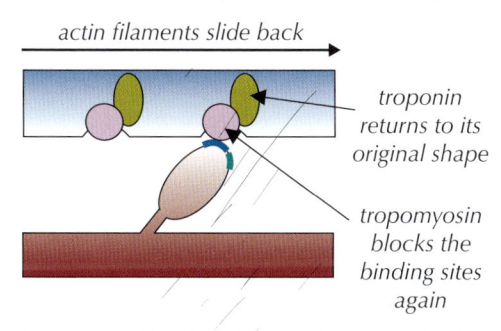

*Figure 11: Blocking of the actin-myosin binding sites as the muscle returns to its resting state.*

### Practice Questions — Application

**Q1** Cardiac muscle in the heart has some similarities to skeletal muscle, for example, it has both actin and myosin filaments. Patients who suffer from heart failure may be given positive inotropic agents — these are substances which increase the level of calcium ions in the cytoplasm of muscle cells.

Use your knowledge of muscle contraction to explain why this treatment may be used.

**Exam Tip**
Remember, it's dead easy to lose marks in the exam by rushing headlong into answering a question without reading it through properly first. Take your time — make sure you understand any information in a table or a graph before attempting the question.

Q2 The graph below shows the calcium ion concentration in the sarcoplasm of a muscle fibre over time.

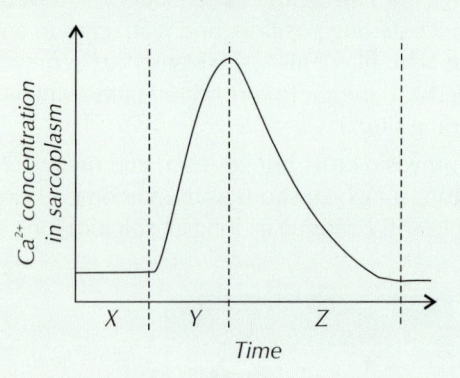

a) During what time period (X, Y or Z):
   i) is the muscle fibre the longest length? Explain your answer.
   ii) would $Ca^{2+}$ ions be bound to troponin? Explain your answer.
   iii) would ATPase be activated? Explain your answer.
b) Describe the movement of calcium ions during time period Z.
c) Describe the event that causes an increase in $Ca^{2+}$ ions in the sarcoplasm at the beginning of time period Y.

## Energy for muscle contraction

So much energy is needed when muscles contract that ATP gets used up very quickly. ATP has to be continually generated so exercise can continue — this happens in three main ways:

### 1. Aerobic respiration

Most ATP is generated via oxidative phosphorylation in the cell's mitochondria. Aerobic respiration only works when there's oxygen so it's good for long periods of low-intensity exercise, e.g. a long walk.

**Tip:** There's more on aerobic respiration on pages 413-418 and anaerobic respiration on pages 420-421.

### 2. Anaerobic respiration

ATP is made rapidly by glycolysis. The end product of glycolysis is pyruvate, which is converted to lactate by lactate fermentation. Lactate can quickly build up in the muscles and cause muscle fatigue (where the muscles can't contract as forcefully as they could do previously). Anaerobic respiration is good for short periods of hard exercise, e.g. a 400 m sprint.

### 3. ATP-creatine phosphate (ATP-CP) system

ATP is made by phosphorylating ADP — adding a phosphate group taken from CP. The equation for this is shown in Figure 12. CP is stored inside cells and the ATP-CP system generates ATP very quickly. CP runs out after a few seconds so it's used during short bursts of vigorous exercise, e.g. a tennis serve. The ATP-CP system is anaerobic (it doesn't need oxygen) and it's alactic (it doesn't form any lactate).

**Tip:** Many activities use a combination of these systems.

$$ADP + CP \rightarrow ATP + C \text{ (creatine)}$$

**Figure 12:** *Phosphorylation of ADP by CP.*

# Types of muscle

There are three types of muscle in the body — you need to know about the structural and functional differences between them.

## Skeletal muscle (also called voluntary muscle)

Skeletal muscle contraction is controlled consciously (you have to voluntarily decide to contract it). It's made up of many muscle fibres — these are multinucleate (have many nuclei) and can be many centimetres long.

Some muscle fibres contract very quickly — they're used for speed and strength but fatigue (get tired) quickly. Some muscle fibres contract slowly and fatigue slowly — they're used for endurance and posture.

### Examining skeletal muscle under the microscope

You need to know how to examine a stained section of skeletal muscle under a light microscope or examine a photomicrograph of one.

**PRACTICAL ACTIVITY GROUP 1**

**Tip:** Make sure you do a risk assessment before starting this practical.

#### Example

This is a photomicrograph of a section through skeletal muscle tissue. The key features that you're likely to see when you look at any stained section of skeletal muscle tissue are pointed out.

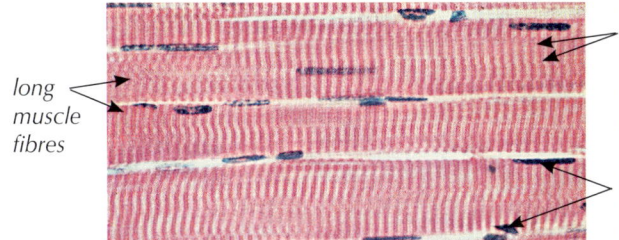

- long muscle fibres
- cross-striations (alternating darker and lighter pink stripes — these are the A-bands and I-bands, see page 364)
- many nuclei in each muscle fibre (stained blue)

*Figure 13:* Features of skeletal muscle tissue seen under a light microscope.

**Tip:** Stained sections or photomicrographs you're given to look at might not look quite like this — it depends on which stain has been used. For example, using a different stain could cause the features to appear different colours.

## Involuntary muscle (also called smooth muscle)

Involuntary muscle contraction is controlled unconsciously (it'll contract automatically without you deciding to). Involuntary muscle is also called smooth muscle because it doesn't have the striped appearance of voluntary muscle. It's found in the walls of your hollow internal organs, e.g. the gut, the blood vessels. Your gut smooth muscles contract to move food along (peristalsis) and your blood vessel smooth muscles contract to reduce the flow of blood.

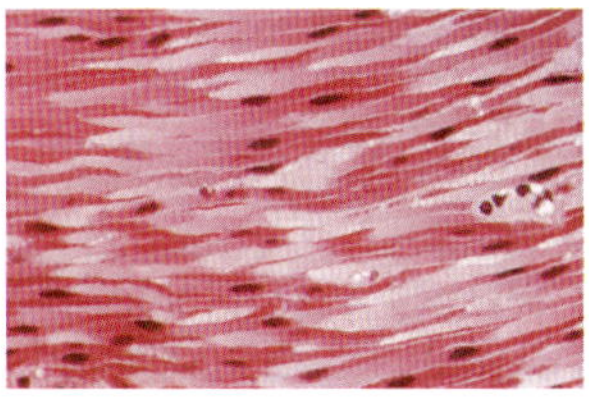

Each muscle fibre is uninucleate (has one nucleus). The muscle fibres are spindle-shaped with pointed ends, and they're only about 0.2 mm long (see Figure 15). The muscle fibres contract slowly and don't fatigue.

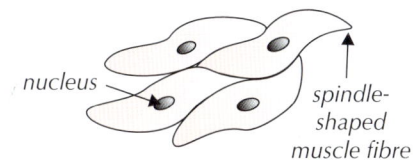

- nucleus
- spindle-shaped muscle fibre

*Figure 15:* The structure of involuntary muscle.

*Figure 14:* A light micrograph of a section through involuntary muscle tissue.

## Cardiac muscle (heart muscle)

Cardiac muscle contracts on its own — it's myogenic. It's found in the walls of your heart and its function is to pump blood around the body. It's made of muscle fibres connected by intercalated discs, which have low electrical resistance so nerve impulses pass easily between cells. The muscle fibres are branched to allow nerve impulses to spread quickly through the whole muscle (see Figure 16, on the next page).

**Tip:** Remember, the rate of contraction of cardiac muscle is controlled involuntarily by the autonomic nervous system (see page 353).

Module 5: Section 3 Animal Responses

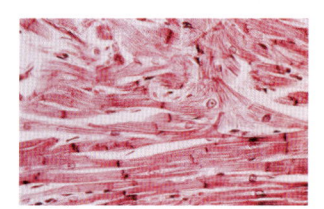

**Figure 17:** A light micrograph of a section through cardiac muscle tissue.

Each cardiac muscle fibre is uninucleate. The muscle fibres are shaped like cylinders and they're about 0.1 mm long. You can see some cross-striations under a microscope but the striped pattern isn't as strong as it is in skeletal muscle. The muscle fibres contract rhythmically and don't fatigue.

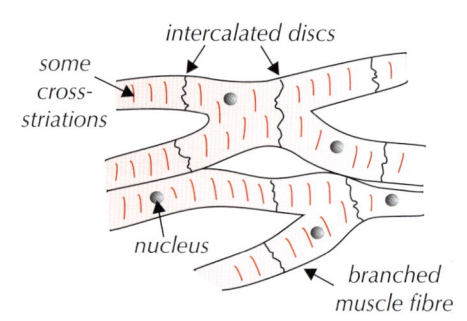

**Figure 16:** The structure of cardiac muscle.

## Practice Questions — Fact Recall

Q1 What are the roles of the following structures within muscle fibres:
 a) transverse T-tubules?
 b) sarcoplasmic reticulum?
 c) mitochondria?

Q2 Describe the structure of an A-band in a myofibril and describe its appearance under an electron microscope.

Q3 What is the sliding filament model of muscle contraction?

Q4 Name the two proteins found between actin filaments that help myofilaments slide past each other.

Q5 Explain how calcium ions in the sarcoplasm allow the formation of actin-myosin cross bridges.

Q6 Describe the role of ATP in muscle contraction.

Q7 a) Give one advantage and one disadvantage of generating ATP via the ATP-creatine phosphate (ATP-CP) system.
 b) Give two other ways in which ATP can be generated.

Q8 Copy and complete the table below to show the structural differences between the three types of muscle fibres.

|  | Skeletal | Involuntary | Cardiac |
| --- | --- | --- | --- |
| Number of nuclei |  |  |  |
| Length |  |  |  |
| Shape of muscle fibres |  |  |  |
| Are cross-striations visible under a light microscope? |  |  |  |

Q9 Describe the function of cardiac muscle.

**Tip:** Remember — skeletal muscle is voluntary muscle, involuntary muscle is smooth muscle and cardiac muscle is heart muscle.

# 4. Nerve Impulses and Muscle Contraction

*When electrical impulses arrive at muscle cells they trigger the contraction of the muscle by depolarising the cells. This electrical activity can be monitored.*

## Neuromuscular junctions

A neuromuscular junction is a synapse between a motor neurone and a muscle cell. Neuromuscular junctions work in the same way as synapses between neurones — they release neurotransmitters, which trigger depolarisation in the postsynaptic cell (see pages 305-306). Depolarisation of a muscle cell always causes it to contract (if the threshold level is reached). Neuromuscular junctions use the neurotransmitter acetylcholine (ACh), which binds to receptors called nicotinic cholinergic receptors (see Figure 1). Acetylcholinesterase (AChE) stored in clefts on the postsynaptic membrane is released to break down acetylcholine after use.

**Learning Objectives:**
- Understand the action of neuromuscular junctions.
- Know how to monitor muscle contraction and fatigue using sensors to record electrical activity (PAG10 and PAG11).

**Specification Reference 5.1.5**

**Tip:** Synapses are covered in Section 1 — see pages 305-308.

**Tip:** Acetylcholinesterase (AChE) is an enzyme.

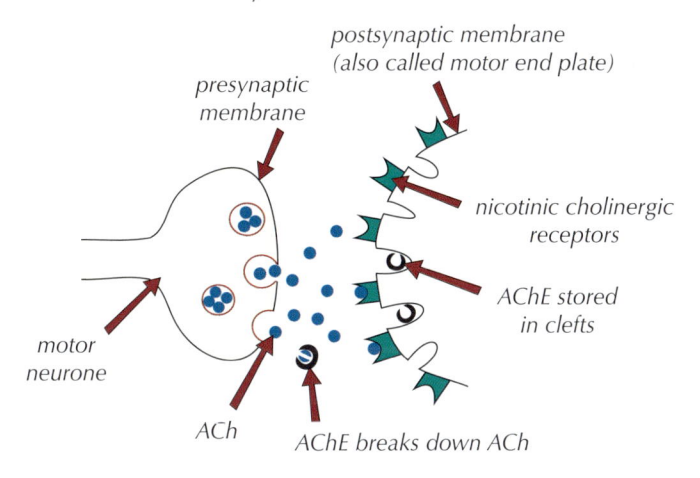

*Figure 1: The structure of a neuromuscular junction.*

### The effect of chemicals

Sometimes a chemical (e.g. a drug) may block the release of the neurotransmitter or affect the way it binds to the receptors on the postsynaptic membrane. This may prevent the action potential from being passed on to the muscle, so the muscle won't contract.

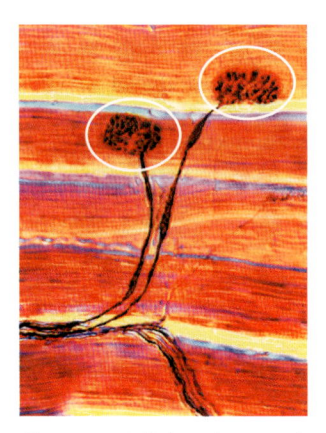

*Figure 2: A light micrograph showing neuromuscular junctions (circled) on skeletal muscle.*

--- Example ---
Pancuronium bromide is a non-depolarising, neuromuscular blocking drug. It competes against ACh for the nicotinic cholinergic receptors, binding to them so that the action of ACh is blocked and the muscle cell does not depolarise. It is used during surgery because it relaxes the muscles.

The action of pancuronium bromide can be reversed by inhibiting the action of AChE so that the concentration of ACh increases. This means it can out-compete the drug for available nicotinic cholinergic receptors.

Chemicals that affect the action of neurotransmitters at neuromuscular junctions can be fatal if they affect the muscles involved in breathing, e.g. the diaphragm and intercostal muscles. If they can't contract, ventilation can't take place and the organism can't respire aerobically.

**Tip:** The dosage of drugs used to relax muscles during surgery and other medical procedures is very carefully controlled. Also the patient is monitored closely to ensure they are getting enough oxygen.

Module 5: Section 3 Animal Responses

**Tip:** Make sure you carry out a risk assessment before you begin this practical. You should move any liquids away from the electrical equipment and ensure your hands are dry if you're connecting or disconnecting the electrodes.

**Tip:** The area of skin where the electrodes are to be attached should be clean — this aids the conductance of the signal.

**Tip:** A motor unit is made up of a motor neurone and all the muscle fibres that it connects to.

**Tip:** Muscle fatigue has been linked to muscle cells having an insufficient supply of ATP. This could be due to a lack of oxygen, glucose or creatine phosphate, which limits the rate at which ATP can be regenerated.

**Tip:** The EMG may look different depending on how the data from the electrodes is processed by the computer software being used.

# Detecting electrical activity

PRACTICAL ACTIVITY GROUP 10
PRACTICAL ACTIVITY GROUP 11

If you have access to specialist equipment you may be able to investigate muscle contraction and fatigue by monitoring the electrical activity that occurs. Remember, muscles contract in response to nervous impulses — these are electrical signals.

Electrical signals in muscles can be detected by electrodes (sensors) placed on the skin. The electrodes are connected to a computer to allow the electrical signals to be monitored. The procedure is called electromyography and the reading it generates is called an electromyogram (EMG).

To carry out the procedure:

1. First of all you need to attach two electrodes to places on the muscle that you want to record from — in this example we will use the biceps muscle in the arm. A third electrode goes on an inactive point (such as the bony wrist area) to act as a control (see Figure 3).

2. Switch off any other electrical equipment that you don't need as this generates 'noise' that interferes with the electrical signal from the muscle.

3. Connect the electrodes to an amplifier and a computer. (An amplifier increases the strength of the electrical signals from the muscle.)

4. Keep the muscle relaxed. You should see a straight line on the electromyogram.

5. Then contract the muscle by bending your arm. You should see spikes in the graph as motor units are activated to contract the muscle (see Figure 4).

6. If you then lift a weight, the amplitude (height) of the trace on the graph will increase — there are more electrical signals because more motor units are required to lift the weight.

7. If you continue to hold the weight, your muscle will begin to fatigue. This means that the muscle can no longer contract as forcefully as it could previously. On the electromyogram you will see the amplitude of the trace increase further. This is because your brain is trying to activate more motor units to generate the force needed to hold the weight up.

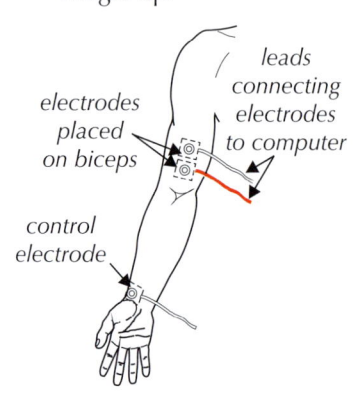

**Figure 3:** Diagram showing where to place the electrodes to monitor electrical activity in the biceps.

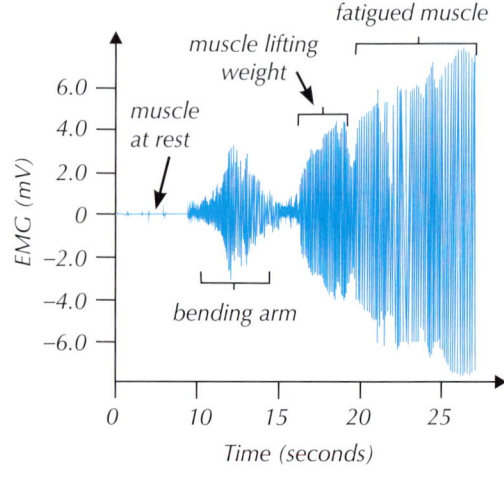

**Figure 4:** Example of an electromyogram (EMG).

Module 5: Section 3 Animal Responses

## Practice Questions — Application

Q1  Myasthenia gravis is an autoimmune disease in which the receptors at neuromuscular junctions are gradually destroyed. Suggest what symptoms a sufferer might have and explain your answer.

Q2  Galantamine is a drug that inhibits the enzyme AChE. Predict the effect of galantamine at a neuromuscular junction and explain your answer.

Q3  The graph below is an electromyogram (EMG) taken from an athlete's forearm. The athlete was asked to pick up a series of weights.

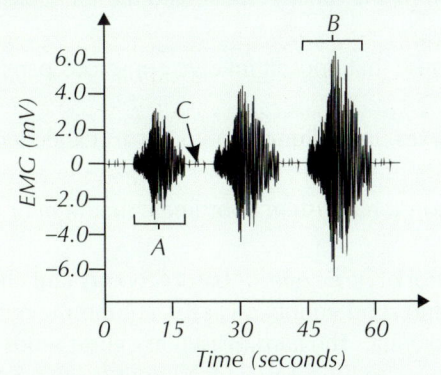

**Tip:** An autoimmune disease is where a person's immune system mistakes their own cells for pathogens, so it starts to attack them.

**Tip:** mV stands for millivolts.

a)  Suggest what is happening at point C.

b)  Suggest an explanation for the electrical activity shown on the graph during time period A compared with that during time period B.

c)  The researcher would like to use electromyography to help athletes train by monitoring the point at which their muscles start to fatigue. She asks the athlete to hold a weight up for as long as he can. Describe and explain what the researcher would expect to see on the EMG trace as the athlete's muscle becomes fatigued.

## Practice Questions — Fact Recall

Q1  What is a neuromuscular junction?

Q2  Which neurotransmitter is used at neuromuscular junctions?

Q3  How is neurotransmitter removed from a neuromuscular junction?

Q4  Briefly explain why chemicals that block neurotransmitters at a neuromuscular junction can be fatal.

Q5  Briefly explain how sensors that monitor electrical activity can be used to monitor muscle contraction.

Module 5: Section 3 Animal Responses

# Section Summary

Make sure you know:
- That the mammalian nervous system is split into the central nervous system (brain and spinal cord) and the peripheral nervous system (the neurones that connect the CNS to the rest of the body).
- That the peripheral nervous system is split into the somatic nervous system (which controls conscious activities) and the autonomic nervous system (which controls unconscious activities).
- The functions of the cerebrum (vision, hearing, learning, thinking), the hypothalamus (controlling body temperature and producing hormones that control the pituitary gland), the medulla oblongata (controlling breathing and heart rate), the cerebellum (muscle coordination, posture, balance) and the pituitary gland (releasing hormones and stimulating other glands), and the locations of these structures in the brain.
- That a reflex action is a rapid, involuntary response that doesn't involve conscious parts of the brain and helps to protect the body from damage.
- The pathway of nervous communication in reflexes, including the blinking and knee-jerk reflexes, and how they help to protect the body.
- How the sympathetic nervous system and the hormonal system coordinate the 'fight or flight' to an external stimulus, e.g. a perceived threat.
- How the nervous system is involved in the control of heart rate — baroreceptors and chemoreceptors detect changes in blood pressure or chemistry and send impulses via the autonomic nervous system to the cardiovascular centre in the medulla oblongata. The cardiovascular centre sends signals via sympathetic neurones or parasympathetic neurones to the SAN, which controls heart rate.
- That the hormonal system is also involved in the control of heart rate, and that adrenaline increases heart rate and causes the heart to pump more blood.
- How to investigate physiological functions, such as the effect of exercise on heart rate, by manually recording pulse rate or by using an electrical heart rate monitor.
- How to use Student's t-test to compare the means of two sets of data and to determine whether results are significant.
- That skeletal muscle is made of large bundles of long multinucleate cells called muscle fibres.
- The sliding filament model of muscle contraction — myosin and actin filaments slide over one another to make the sarcomeres contract (the myofilaments themselves don't contract).
- How actin, myosin, calcium ions and ATP work together to make a myofibril contract.
- That energy from ATP is used for muscle contraction and that ATP generation involves aerobic respiration, anaerobic respiration and the ATP-creatine phosphate (ATP-CP) system.
- The structural and functional differences between skeletal (voluntary) muscle, involuntary (smooth) muscle and cardiac (heart) muscle.
- How to examine stained sections or photomicrographs of skeletal muscle.
- That a neuromuscular junction is a synapse between a motor neurone and a muscle cell.
- That neuromuscular junctions use the neurotransmitter acetylcholine (ACh), which binds to nicotinic cholinergic receptors. This triggers depolarisation in the postsynaptic cell. Acetylcholinesterase (AChE) stored in clefts on the postsynaptic membrane is released to break down acetylcholine after use.
- How to use sensors that record electrical activity to monitor muscle contraction and fatigue.

# Exam-style Questions

**1** Which row correctly describes the pathway of nervous communication in response to low blood pressure?

| | Locations of receptors that detect low blood pressure | Source of the impulses sent to the heart along motor neurones | Neurotransmitter secreted by motor neurones | Effect on heart rate |
|---|---|---|---|---|
| A | carotid arteries, aorta | medulla oblongata | noradrenaline | increase |
| B | medulla oblongata, aorta | hypothalamus | acetylcholine | decrease |
| C | carotid arteries, aorta | hypothalamus | noradrenaline | decrease |
| D | medulla oblongata, aorta | medulla oblongata | acetylcholine | increase |

*(1 mark)*

**2** **Fig. 2.1** shows a cross-section through the human brain.

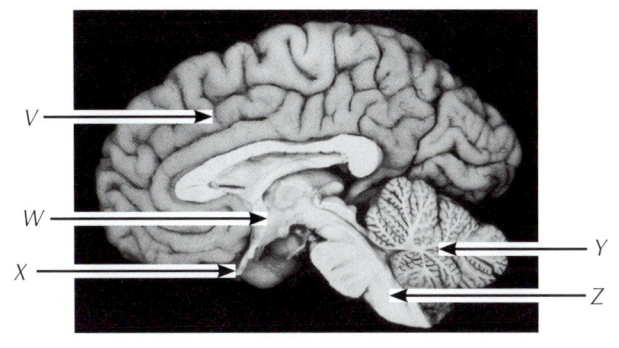

**Fig. 2.1**

**(a)** Name the part of the brain labelled **Z** in **Fig. 2.1** and give its function.

*(2 marks)*

**(b)** Ataxia is condition which can cause difficulty with walking and balance.

**(i)** Suggest the letter of the part of the brain that is often not functioning properly in people with ataxia.

*(1 mark)*

**(ii)** People with ataxia may also experience difficulty with fine motor skills such as writing. Using this evidence, suggest which part of the peripheral nervous system ataxia affects. Give a reason for your answer.

*(1 mark)*

**(iii)** People with ataxia may still show normal reflex actions.
Suggest why this might be the case.

*(1 mark)*

**(iv)** A symptom of ataxia can be muscle spasticity, in which a person can experience involuntary and sustained muscle contractions. This symptom can be treated with a drug called trihexyphenidyl, which competes with acetylcholine for receptors on motor end plates. Explain why trihexyphenidyl could relieve muscle spasticity.

*(3 marks)*

Module 5: Section 3 Animal Responses

**3** Effective control of a person's heart rate is important for their survival. Heart rate is controlled by the hormonal system and the nervous system.

(a) (i) During times of danger, more adrenaline will be secreted into a person's bloodstream. Where is adrenaline released from?

*(1 mark)*

(ii) Give **two** ways in which adrenaline affects the heart.

*(2 marks)*

(iii) Describe and explain how blood vessels are affected by adrenaline.

*(3 marks)*

(b) Heart rate is a measure of how quickly cardiac muscle contracts. Describe the structure of cardiac muscle.

*(2 marks)*

**4** A bodybuilder lifts weights to increase the size of the muscles in his arms. **Fig. 4.1** shows part of a myofibril in the biceps muscle when it is **contracted**.

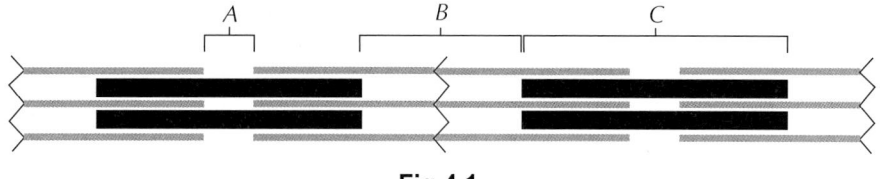

**Fig 4.1**

(a) Name the sections of the myofibril labelled **A-C** in **Fig. 4.1**.

*(3 marks)*

(b) For each of the sections **A-C**, state how it will appear when the biceps relaxes, compared to how it appears in **Fig. 4.1**.

*(2 marks)*

(c) A myofibril contains myosin filaments.
(i) Describe the structure of a myosin filament.

*(3 marks)*

(ii)* Describe the role of the myosin filament and ATP in muscle contraction.

*(6 marks)*

The bodybuilder manages to lift an extremely heavy weight with a short burst of explosive power. He can only sustain the lift for a few seconds.

(d) (i) Describe how ATP is likely to be generated in the bodybuilder's arm muscles when he lifts the heavy weight.

*(2 marks)*

(ii) Give **one** advantage of ATP being generated in this way.

*(1 mark)*

(e) Give **three structural** differences between a muscle fibre in the bodybuilder's biceps and a muscle fibre in the walls of his blood vessels.

*(3 marks)*

*The quality of your response will be assessed in this question.

# Module 5 — Section 4: Plant Responses and Hormones

# 1. Plant Responses

*Plants need to respond to stimuli in order to survive. These next few pages are all about what makes plants grow the way that they do...*

## Responses to stimuli

Plants, like animals, increase their chances of survival by responding to changes in their environment.

**Examples**
- They sense the direction of light and grow towards it to maximise light absorption for photosynthesis.
- They sense gravity, so their roots and shoots grow in the right direction.
- Climbing plants have a sense of touch, so they can find things to climb and reach the sunlight.

The examples given above are all tropisms (see next page). Plants are also more likely to survive if they respond to **abiotic stress** and **herbivory**.

## Abiotic stress

Abiotic stress is anything that's potentially harmful to a plant that's natural, but nonliving, like a drought (water stress). Plants can respond to abiotic stress, e.g. some respond to extreme cold by producing their own form of antifreeze.

**Example**
Carrots produce antifreeze proteins at low temperatures — the proteins bind to ice crystals and lower the temperature that water freezes at, stopping more ice crystals from growing.

## Herbivory

Herbivory is when plants are eaten by animals (including insects). Plants have chemical defences that they can use against herbivory. For example, they can produce toxic chemicals in response to being eaten.

**Examples**
- **Alkaloids** — these are chemicals with bitter tastes, noxious smells or poisonous characteristics that deter or kill herbivores, e.g. tobacco plants produce the alkaloid nicotine in response to tissue damage. Nicotine is highly poisonous to many insects.
- **Tannins** — these taste bitter, and in some herbivores (e.g. cattle, sheep) they can bind to proteins in the gut, making the plant hard to digest. Both of these things deter animals from eating the plant.

Some plants release **pheromones** in response to herbivory. Pheromones are signalling chemicals that produce a response in other organisms.

**Examples**
- Some plants release alarm pheromones into the air in response to herbivore grazing. This can cause nearby plants that detect these chemicals to start making chemical defences such as tannins.

---

**Learning Objectives:**
- Be able to explain the different types of plant responses, including:
  - the response to abiotic stress,
  - the response to herbivory, e.g. chemical defences (such as alkaloids, tannins and pheromones) and folding in response to touch (*Mimosa pudica*),
  - the range of tropisms in plants.
- Know about the roles of plant hormones.
- Be able to carry out practical investigations into phototropism and geotropism (PAG11).

**Specification Reference 5.1.5**

**Tip:** Herbivores are animals that eat plants.

*Figure 1: A leaf of M. pudica folding up after one of its leaflets has been touched.*

**Exam Tip**
Make sure you remember the name of the touch-sensitive *Mimosa pudica*. It could come up as an example in your exam.

**Tip:** A positive tropism is growth towards the stimulus and a negative tropism is growth away from it.

*Figure 4: A radish seedling showing positive phototropism.*

*Figure 7: A radish seedling showing negative geotropism.*

- When corn plants are being eaten by caterpillars, they can produce pheromones which attract parasitic wasps. These wasps then lay their eggs in the caterpillars (eww), which eventually kills them.

Other plants are able to fold up in response to being touched.

**Example**
If a single leaflet (a mini leaf-shaped structure that makes up part of a leaf) of the plant *Mimosa pudica* is touched, a signal spreads through the whole leaf, causing it to quickly fold up. It's thought that this could help protect *Mimosa pudica* against herbivory in a variety of ways, e.g. it may help to knock off any small insects feeding on the plant. It may also scare off animals trying to eat it.

## Tropisms

A **tropism** is the response of a plant to a directional stimulus (a stimulus coming from a particular direction). Plants respond to stimuli by regulating their growth. A positive tropism is growth towards the stimulus, whereas a negative tropism is growth away from the stimulus.

### Phototropism

Phototropism is the growth of a plant in response to light. Shoots are positively phototropic and grow towards light (see Figure 2). Roots are negatively phototropic and grow away from light (see Figure 3).

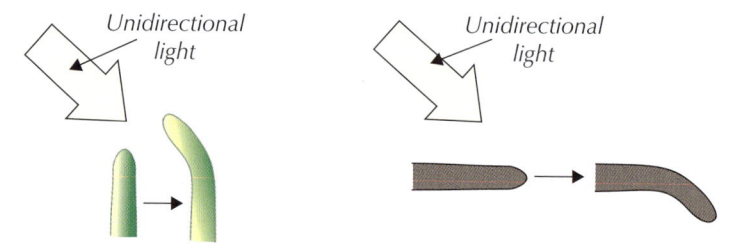

*Figure 2: Phototropism in shoots.*

*Figure 3: Phototropism in roots.*

### Geotropism

Geotropism is the growth of a plant in response to gravity. Shoots are negatively geotropic and grow upwards (see Figure 5). Roots are positively geotropic and grow downwards (see Figure 6).

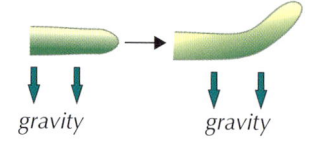

*Figure 5: Geotropism in shoots.*

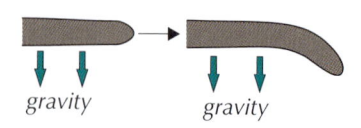

*Figure 6: Geotropism in roots.*

### Other tropisms

There are some other tropisms that you might come across.

**Examples**
- Hydrotropism — plant growth in response to water. Roots are positively hydrotropic.
- Thermotropism — plant growth in response to temperature.
- Thigmotropism — plant growth in response to contact with an object.

Module 5: Section 4  Plant Responses and Hormones

# Growth hormones

Plants respond to some stimuli using growth hormones — these are chemicals that speed up or slow down plant growth. Growth hormones are produced in the growing regions of the plant (e.g. shoot tips and root tips) and they move to where they're needed in the other parts of the plant.

A growth hormone called **gibberellin** stimulates seed germination, stem elongation, side shoot formation and flowering (there's more about gibberellin on page 384).

Growth hormones called **auxins** stimulate the growth of shoots by cell elongation. Auxins are produced in the tips of shoots in flowering plants and diffuse backwards to stimulate the cell just behind the tips to elongate — this is where cell walls become loose and stretchy, so the cells get longer (see Figure 8). If the tip of a shoot is removed, no auxin will be available and the shoot stops growing. Auxins stimulate growth in shoots but high concentrations inhibit growth in roots.

**Tip:** Growth hormones are also called growth substances.

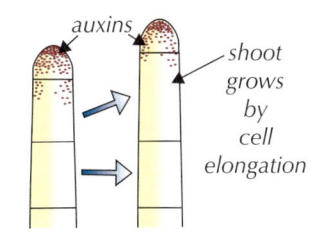

*Figure 8: Effect of auxins on shoot growth.*

## Indoleacetic acid (IAA)

Indoleacetic acid (IAA) is an important auxin that's produced in the tips of shoots and roots in flowering plants. It's moved around the plant to control tropisms — it moves by diffusion and active transport over short distances, and via the phloem over long distances. This results in different parts of the plant having different amounts of IAA. The uneven distribution of IAA means there's uneven growth of the plant.

**Tip:** You should remember the phloem from Module 3. It's a tissue which transports sugars around a plant. For more, see pages 206-208.

### Example — phototropism

IAA moves to the more shaded parts of the shoots and roots, so there's uneven growth.

IAA moves to this side — cells elongate and the shoot bends towards the light.

IAA moves to this side — growth is inhibited so the root bends away from the light.

**Tip:** Remember, root growth is <u>inhibited</u> by high concentrations of IAA. The opposite is true in shoots — high concentrations of IAA <u>promote</u> shoot growth.

### Example — geotropism

IAA moves to the underside of shoots and roots, so there's uneven growth.

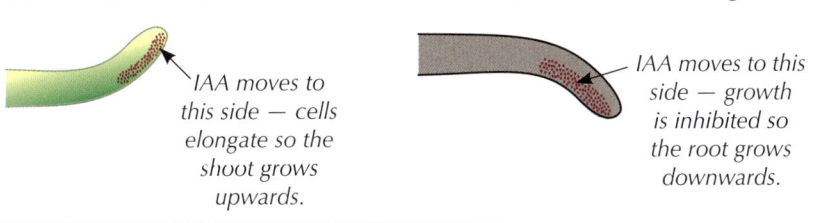

IAA moves to this side — cells elongate so the shoot grows upwards.

IAA moves to this side — growth is inhibited so the root grows downwards.

**Tip:** Remember, geotropism is the growth of a plant in response to gravity.

**Tip:** Make sure you do a risk assessment before you carry out any practical work as part of these investigations.

**Tip:** Using shoots that are roughly the same height and planting them in the same type of soil is to try and control other variables in the experiment that aren't being investigated. Doing this increases the validity of your results.

**Tip:** Three shoots are used for each preparation to give some repeats. Doing repeats helps to make the results more precise by reducing the effect of random error.

# Practical investigations into phototropism

There are lots of experiments that you can do to investigate how plant shoots respond to light. Here's an example:

1. Take nine wheat shoots that are roughly equal in height and plant them in individual pots in the same type of soil.
2. Next, prepare the shoots as follows (see Figure 9):
   - Cover the tips of three shoots with a foil cap (shoot A).
   - Leave three shoots without foil (shoot B).
   - Wrap the bases of the final three shoots with foil, leaving only the tip exposed (shoot C).
3. Set up the shoots in front of a light source. Make sure that the shoots are all the same distance from the light source and experience the same intensity of light. You should also make sure that all other variables, including temperature and exposure to moisture, are controlled (e.g. by growing all the shoots in the same propagator and watering them all equally).
4. Leave the shoots to grow for two days.
5. After they've been left for 2 days, record the amount of growth (in mm) and the direction of growth of your shoots. This gives you both quantitative and qualitative data.

**Figure 9:** Preparation of wheat shoots.

You would expect to see some results like the ones shown in Figure 10. The shoots with exposed tips (B and C) should have grown towards the light source (positive phototropism). Covering the tip with a foil cap (shoot A) prevents growth towards the light — it's the tip (where IAA is produced) that's most sensitive to light and because it's covered the shoot should have continued to grow straight up. Covering the base of the shoot with foil (shoot C) should still allow the tip to grow towards the light.

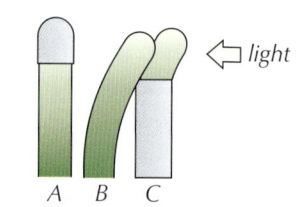

**Figure 10:** Wheat shoots at the end of the investigation.

# Practical investigations into geotropism

There are lots of ways you could investigate geotropism. Here's one of them:

1. Line three Petri dishes with moist (but not soaking wet) cotton wool. You should use the same volume of water and the same amount of cotton wool in each dish.
2. Space out 10 cress seeds on the surface of the cotton wool in each dish (see Figure 11) and push each seed down into the wool slightly.
3. Tape a lid onto each dish and wrap each one in foil, making sure there are no gaps. The dishes are wrapped in foil to prevent any light reaching the seeds — this would affect your results because shoots from the germinating seeds would grow towards any light entering the dish (due to phototropism).

**Tip:** Using the same volume of water and the same amount of cotton wool in each dish is another example of controlling variables. It helps to ensure that all of the germinating seeds are exposed to the same amount of water and growing medium.

**Figure 11:** Cress seeds arranged on cotton wool in a Petri dish.

4. Choose somewhere you can leave the dishes where the temperature is likely to be warmish and pretty constant, e.g. a cupboard. Don't put your dishes somewhere that's too cold (i.e. less than room temperature) otherwise your seeds might not germinate.

5. Next, you need to set up your dishes so they're placed at different angles (see Figure 12):

- Prop one dish upright at a 90° angle (A in Figure 12) — label it and mark which way is 'up' (or 'down'). To keep your dish upright, attach it to a wooden block using tape — you could use a different object as long as it's heavy enough to stop the dish falling over.
- Place another dish on a slope at a 45° angle (B). As with dish A, use tape to attach the plate to the wooden block to stop it moving.
- Place the third dish (C) on a flat, horizontal surface.

Don't forget to label your dishes carefully, so you know which way up each one was when you come to unwrap the dishes at the end of the experiment.

**Tip:** When you're growing plants from seeds in an experiment always check the conditions they need to germinate. Seeds usually come with details of the conditions needed for successful germination, e.g. what temperature they should be kept at.

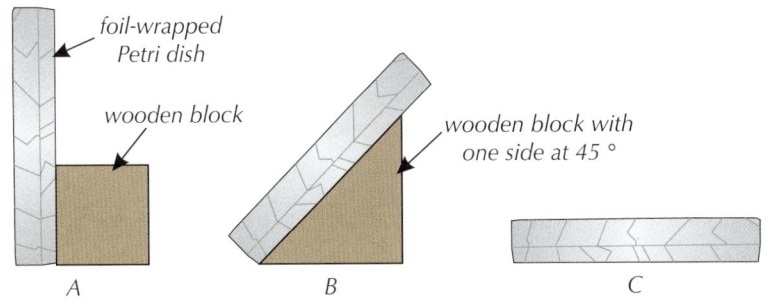

*Figure 12:* Petri dishes arranged at different angles.

6. Leave the seeds for 4 days.
7. After the 4 days, unwrap each dish and note direction of the shoot and root growth of the cress seedlings.

You should find that whatever angle the dishes were placed at, the shoots have all grown away from gravity (negative geotropism) and the roots have grown towards gravity (positive geotropism).

**Tip:** In this investigation you could get quantitative data by measuring the amount of growth of the shoots and roots and the angle of their growth.

## Practice Questions — Application

Q1  An experiment was carried out to investigate the role of auxin in shoot growth. Eight shoots, equal in height and mass, had their tips removed. Sponges soaked in glucose and either auxin or water were then placed where the tips should be. Four shoots were then placed in the dark (experiment A) and the other four shoots were exposed to a light source, directed at them from the right (experiment B):

**Tip:** Remember, growth hormones are produced in shoot tips. So by removing the tips, any auxin already present is removed.

Module 5: Section 4 Plant Responses and Hormones

After two days the amount of growth (in mm) and direction of growth was recorded. The results are shown in the table below.

|  | Growth | | | |
|---|---|---|---|---|
|  | Shoot A | Shoot B | Shoot C | Shoot D |
| Experiment A (dark) | 6 mm, right | 6 mm, left | 6 mm, straight | 1 mm, straight |
| Experiment B (light) | 8 mm, right | 8 mm, right | 8 mm, right | 3 mm, straight |

a) Why did shoot A bend to the right in experiment A?
b) Explain why shoot C grew straight in experiment A.
c) Why did shoots A, B and C grow to the right in experiment B?
d) What was the purpose of Sponge D in both experiments?
e) Suggest why the sponges in experiment A were soaked in glucose.

Q2 Thigmotropism is a plant growth response to touch.
a) In the diagram on the right, does the shoot display positive or negative thigmotropism?
b) Is the concentration of auxins, such as IAA, likely to be highest at the point labelled X or Y? Explain why.

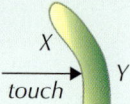

## Practice Questions — Fact Recall

Q1 What is meant by the term 'abiotic stress'?
Q2 Give an example of a plant response to herbivory.
Q3 What is a negative tropism?
Q4 What name is given to the growth of a plant in response to light?
Q5 What parts of a plant produce growth hormones?
Q6 Do auxins stimulate or inhibit growth in roots?
Q7 Name one example of an auxin.
Q8 Auxins travel around a plant to control tropisms.
    a) How do auxins move over short distances?
    b) How do auxins move over long distances?
Q9 Explain how the distribution of auxins affects the growth of:
    a) shoots in response to light.
    b) roots in response to gravity.

# 2. The Effects of Plant Hormones

*As you've seen, plant hormones are involved in tropisms. It's not just tropisms though — hormones are responsible for loads of other effects in plants too...*

## Auxins and apical dominance

The shoot tip at the top of a flowering plant is called the apical bud. Auxins stimulate the growth of the apical bud and inhibit the growth of side shoots from lateral buds. This is called **apical dominance** — the apical bud is dominant over the lateral buds (see Figure 1).

Apical dominance prevents side shoots from growing — this saves energy and prevents side shoots from the same plant competing with the shoot tip for light. Because energy isn't being used to grow side shoots, apical dominance allows a plant in an area where there are loads of other plants to grow tall very fast, past the smaller plants, to reach the sunlight.

If you remove the apical bud then the plant won't produce auxins, so the side shoots will start growing by cell division and cell elongation (see Figure 2). However, if you replace the tip with a source of auxin, side shoot development is inhibited. This demonstrates that apical dominance is controlled by auxin (see Figure 3).

**Figure 1:** Apical dominance.

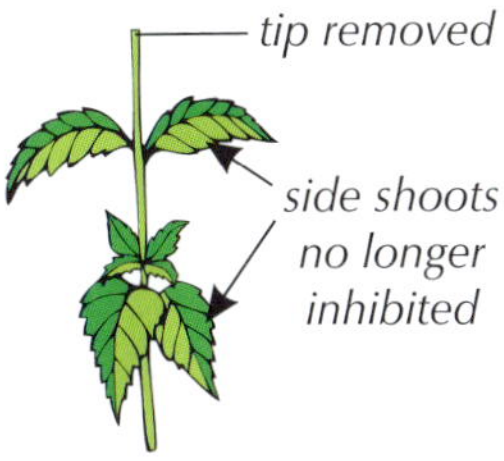

**Figure 2:** Inhibition of apical dominance by removing the apical bud.

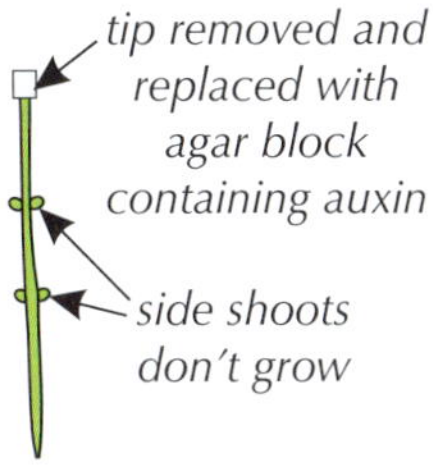

**Figure 3:** Return of apical dominance when apical bud replaced by an auxin source.

Auxins become less concentrated as they move away from the apical bud to the rest of the plant. If a plant grows very tall, the bottom of the plant will have a low auxin concentration so side shoots will start to grow near the bottom.

## Investigating the role of auxins in apical dominance

**PRACTICAL ACTIVITY GROUP 11**

Scientists have demonstrated the role of auxins in apical dominance in experiments like the one below. You could also do this experiment yourself:

1. Plant 30 plants of the same type (e.g. pea plants) that are a similar age, height and weight in pots containing the same type of soil.
2. Count and record the number of side shoots growing from the main stem of each plant. These might be tricky to spot — they may be located where the stalks of leaves join to the main stem.
3. For 10 plants, remove the tip of the shoot and apply a paste containing auxins to the top of the stem.
4. For another 10 plants, remove the tip of the shoot and apply a paste without auxins to the top of the stem.

### Learning Objectives:

- Be able to carry out practical investigations into the effect of plant hormones on growth (PAG11).
- Understand the experimental evidence for the role of auxins in the control of apical dominance.
- Understand the experimental evidence for the role of gibberellin in the control of seed germination and stem elongation.
- Be able to explain the roles of plant hormones, including their role in seed germination, leaf loss in deciduous plants and stomatal closure.
- Be able to explain the commercial use of plant hormones, including the use of hormones to control ripening, the use of hormonal weed killers and rooting powders.

**Specification Reference 5.1.5**

**Figure 4:** The redwood tree displays apical dominance and grows tall enough to reach the sunlight in a thick forest.

Module 5: Section 4 Plant Responses and Hormones

**Tip:** Remember to do a risk assessment before starting practical work.

**Tip:** It's really important that you keep the conditions the same for each plant — if you don't, you can't be sure what's actually causing your results.

**Tip:** *HOW SCIENCE WORKS* Experiments can provide evidence to support an idea. For example, the results of this experiment support the idea that auxins are involved in apical dominance. One piece of evidence can't confirm a theory is true though. See pages 1-3 for more on this.

5. Leave the final 10 plants as they are — these are your untreated controls. Remember, you always need to have controls (e.g. without the hormone, untouched) for comparison — so you know the effect you see is likely to be due to the hormone and not any other factor.
6. Leave your plants to grow for six days. You need to keep all the plants in the same conditions — the same light intensity, water, etc. This makes sure any variables that may affect your results are controlled, which makes your experiment valid.
7. After six days, count the number of side shoots growing from the main stem of each of your plants.

You might get results like these:

|  | average number of side shoots per plant ||
|---|---|---|
|  | start of experiment | end of experiment |
| untreated plants (control group) | 4 | 5 |
| tips removed, auxin paste applied | 4 | 5 |
| tips removed, paste without auxins applied | 4 | 9 |

The results in the table show that removing the tips of shoots caused extra side shoots to grow, but removing tips and applying auxins prevented extra side shoots from growing. The results suggest auxins inhibit the growth of side shoots — providing evidence that auxins are involved in apical dominance.

## Gibberellins

Gibberellins are growth hormones that are produced in young leaves and in seeds. They stimulate seed germination, stem elongation, side shoot formation and flowering.

Gibberellins stimulate the stems of plants to grow by stem elongation — this helps plants to grow very tall. If a dwarf variety of a plant is treated with gibberellin, it will grow to the same height as the tall variety. Unlike auxins, gibberellins don't inhibit plant growth in any way.

Gibberellins stimulate seed germination by triggering the breakdown of starch into glucose in the seed. The plant embryo in the seed can then use the glucose to begin respiring and release the energy it needs to grow. Gibberellins are inhibited (and so seed germination is prevented) by the hormone abscisic acid.

**Figure 5:** *Gibberellins play an important role in the germination and stem elongation of corn seeds.*

### Auxins and gibberellins

Auxins and gibberellins sometimes work together to affect plant growth. They're often **synergistic** — this means that they work together to have a really big effect.

— Example —
Auxins and gibberellins work together to help plants grow very tall.

Auxins and gibberellins are sometimes **antagonistic** — this means they oppose each other's actions.

— Example —
Gibberellins stimulate the growth of side shoots but auxins inhibit the growth of side shoots.

Module 5: Section 4 Plant Responses and Hormones

# Investigating the role of gibberellins in stem elongation

**PRACTICAL ACTIVITY GROUP 11**

Scientists have done lots of experiments to provide evidence for the role of gibberellins in plant growth.

> **Example**
> Scientists have produced genetically altered seeds that are unable to produce gibberellins. These seeds are unable to germinate unless they are given gibberellins.

There are many different ways of investigating the role of gibberellins in **stem elongation**. Here's an example of how you could do it:

1. Plant 40 plants (e.g. dwarf pea plants) that are a similar age, height and mass in pots containing the same type of soil.
2. Leave 20 plants to grow, watering them all in the same way and keeping all other conditions the same. These plants are your negative controls.
3. Leave the other 20 plants to grow in the same conditions, except water them with a dilute solution of gibberellin (e.g. 100 mg dm$^{-3}$ gibberellin).
4. Let all the plants grow for 28 days.
5. Every 7 days measure the length of the stem of each plant. Calculate the mean stem length for the plants watered normally and the plants watered with gibberellin.

You might get results a bit like these:

| time / days | mean stem length / cm | |
|---|---|---|
| | plants watered normally | plants watered with gibberellin |
| 0 | 14 | 14 |
| 7 | 15 | 17 |
| 14 | 18 | 27 |
| 21 | 19 | 38 |
| 28 | 23 | 46 |

**Tip:** It's a good idea to wear gloves when handling soils. This will help prevent you coming into contact with any microorganisms present in the soil.

**Tip:** Remember, negative controls are used to check that only the independent variable (i.e. watering with gibberellin) is affecting the dependent variable (i.e. growth of plant stems).

**Tip:** mg dm$^{-3}$ means milligram per decimetre cubed (or 0.001 g per cubic decimetre). One cubic decimetre is equivalent to one litre.

You can use your results to calculate the growth rate of plants:

- Plants watered normally:
  Mean growth in 28 days = 23 cm − 14 cm = 9 cm
  Mean rate of growth over 28 days = 9 cm ÷ 28 days
  = **0.32 cm/day** or **0.32 cm day$^{-1}$**

- Plants watered with gibberellin:
  Mean growth in 28 days = 46 cm − 14 cm = 32 cm
  Mean rate of growth over 28 days = 32 cm ÷ 28 days
  = **1.14 cm day$^{-1}$**

The results in the table and the growth rates calculated show that stems grow more when watered with a dilute solution of gibberellin. This provides evidence that gibberellin stimulates stem elongation.

# Leaf loss in deciduous plants

Deciduous plants are plants that lose their leaves in winter. Losing their leaves helps plants to conserve water (lost from leaves) during the cold part of the year, when it might be difficult to absorb water from the soil (the soil water may be frozen), and when there's less light for photosynthesis.

**Tip:** The technical term for leaf loss is abscission.

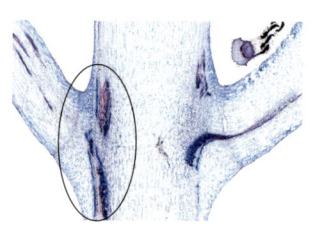

*Figure 6: Light micrograph of a developing abscission layer (dark purple, circled) between a plant's leaf stalk and stem.*

Leaf loss is triggered by the shortening day length in the autumn and is controlled by hormones:

- **Auxins inhibit leaf loss** — auxins are produced by young leaves. As the leaf gets older, less auxin is produced, leading to leaf loss.
- **Ethene stimulates leaf loss** — ethene is produced by ageing leaves. As the leaves get older, more ethene is produced. A layer of cells (called the abscission layer — see Figure 6) develops at the bottom of the leaf stalk (where the leaf joins the stem). The abscission layer separates the leaf from the rest of the plant. Ethene stimulates the cells in the abscission layer to expand, breaking the cell walls and causing the leaf to fall off.

Auxins are antagonistic (work in opposition) to ethene.

## Stomatal closure

Plants need to be able to close their stomata in order to reduce water loss through **transpiration**. They do this using guard cells. Guard cells are found either side of a stomatal pore. When the guard cells are full of water, they are plump and turgid and the pore is open. When the guard cells lose water, they become flaccid, making the pore close (see Figure 7).

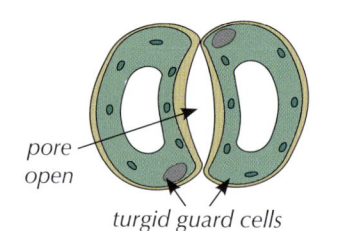

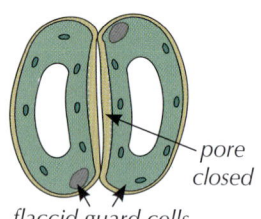

**Tip:** You covered transpiration in Module 3: Section 3. As a reminder, it's the evaporation of water from a plant's surface, especially the leaves.

**Tip:** You met water potential in Module 2: Section 5. It's the likelihood of water molecules to diffuse into or out of solution. If you raise the water potential of a solution, then water is more likely to move out of it, via osmosis.

*Figure 7: Guard cell turgidity causes the opening and closing of stomata.*

The plant hormone **abscisic acid** (**ABA**) is able to trigger stomatal closure:

1. ABA binds to receptors on the guard cell membranes. This causes specific ion channels to open, which allows calcium ions to enter the cytosol from the vacuole.
2. The increased concentration of calcium ions in the cytosol causes other ion channels to open. These ion channels allow ions (such as potassium ions) to leave the guard cells, raising the water potential of the cells.
3. Water then leaves the guard cells by osmosis.
4. The guard cells become flaccid and the stomata close.

## Commercial uses of plant hormones

Plant hormones have several different commercial applications. E.g. the fruit industry uses plant hormones to control how different fruits develop.

### Ethene

Ethene stimulates enzymes that break down cell walls, break down chlorophyll and convert starch into sugars. This makes the fruit soft, ripe and ready to eat.

--- Example ---
Bananas are harvested and transported before they're ripe because they're less likely to be damaged this way. They're then exposed to ethene on arrival so they all ripen at the same time on the shelves and in people's homes.

*Figure 8: Unripe bananas (top) can be exposed to ethene so that they ripen (bottom).*

Module 5: Section 4 Plant Responses and Hormones

## Auxins

Auxins are also used commercially by farmers and gardeners.

### Examples

- Auxins are used in selective weedkillers (herbicides) — they make weeds produce long stems instead of lots of leaves. This makes the weeds grow too fast, so they can't get enough water or nutrients, so they die.
- Auxins are used as rooting hormones (e.g. in rooting powder) — they make a cutting (part of the plant, e.g. a stem cutting) grow roots. The cutting can then be planted and grown into a new plant. Many cuttings can be taken from just one original plant and treated with rooting hormones, so lots of the same plant can be grown quickly and cheaply from just one plant.

*Figure 9:* Auxins enable cuttings to grow roots and grow into new plants.

### Practice Questions — Application

A student is investigating the effect of watering plants with different concentrations of gibberellin on plant height. She plants 60 plants and over the following 6 weeks she waters 20 of the plants with water, 20 of the plants with a 50 mg dm$^{-3}$ gibberellin solution and the remaining 20 plants with a 100 mg dm$^{-3}$ gibberellin solution. She grows all the plants under the same conditions.

Q1 The student chooses plants of the same type with similar characteristics. Explain why she does this.

Q2 Which set of plants would you expect to have the longest average stem length at the end of the 6 weeks? Explain your answer.

Q3 One of the plants has an initial stem length of 8 cm. By the end of the experiment it has grown to 26 cm.
   a) Calculate the average growth rate of this plant. Give your answer in cm day$^{-1}$ and to 2 d.p.
   b) Calculate the percentage increase in growth.

**Tip:** Make sure you know how to calculate percentage increases. A percentage change (i.e. a percentage increase or decrease) can be calculated using the formula shown below:

$$\frac{\text{final value} - \text{original value}}{\text{original value}} \times 100$$

### Practice Questions — Fact Recall

Q1 Apical dominance prevents side shoots from growing. Explain the advantage of this in plants.

Q2 Describe how gibberellins stimulate seed germination.

Q3 a) Why do deciduous plants lose their leaves in winter?
   b) What role do auxins play in leaf loss?
   c) What effect does ethene have on the abscission layer?

Q4 Stomata can close to help reduce water loss from a plant.
   a) Which type of cells are found either side of a stomatal pore and control its opening and closure?
   b) Name a hormone which can trigger stomatal closure.

Q5 Describe how ethene can be used to ripen fruit.

## Section Summary

Make sure you know:

- That to increase their chances of survival, plants need to respond to stimuli in their environment, and that these stimuli include abiotic (natural, but nonliving) stresses and herbivory (being eaten by animals, including insects).
- That plant responses to herbivory include the production of chemical defences (such as alkaloids, tannins and pheromones) and folding in response to touch (as seen in *Mimosa pudica*).
- That plants exhibit a range of different tropisms, including phototropism (growth in response to light) and geotropism (growth in response to gravity).
- That growth hormones (e.g. auxins and gibberellin) coordinate how a plant responds to changes in its environment, e.g. indoleacetic acid (IAA) moves to shaded parts of shoots and roots to control growth in response to the direction of light and gravity.
- How to carry out practical investigations looking at phototropism and geotropism (PAG11).
- That apical dominance is when the apical bud (the shoot tip at the top of a flowering plant) inhibits the growth of side shoots from lateral buds and that this occurs because auxins produced by the shoot tip inhibit the development of these lateral buds.
- How to carry out practical investigations into the effect of plant hormones on growth (PAG11).
- About experimental evidence that supports the role of auxins in the control of apical dominance.
- That gibberellins stimulate the stems of plants to elongate and that they stimulate seeds to germinate by triggering the breakdown of starch into glucose in the seed.
- About experimental evidence that supports the role of gibberellin in the control of seed germination and stem elongation.
- That auxins inhibit leaf loss and ethene stimulates leaf loss in deciduous plants.
- That abscisic acid (ABA) can trigger the closure of stomata by causing guard cells to become flaccid.
- How plant hormones are used commercially, e.g. ethene is used to control when fruit ripens, auxins are used as selective weedkillers and as rooting hormones.

# Exam-style Questions

**1** The following statements describe steps in the closure of stomata triggered by the hormone abscisic acid (ABA). They are **not** in the correct order.

1. Calcium ions enter the cytosol of the guard cell.
2. The water potential of the cell increases.
3. Potassium ions leave the guard cell.
4. Water leaves the guard cells by osmosis.
5. The guard cells become flaccid.
6. ABA binds to receptors on guard cell membranes.

Which option states the correct order of events in the closure of stomata?

A   1, 3, 6, 5, 4, 2     C   5, 2, 1, 3, 4, 6
B   6, 1, 3, 2, 4, 5     D   6, 1, 2, 3, 5, 4

*(1 mark)*

**2** Scientists took three Goosegrass seedlings and planted them in individual pots with soil taken from the same source. They let each seedling grow for 15 days in the conditions shown in **Fig. 2.1**.

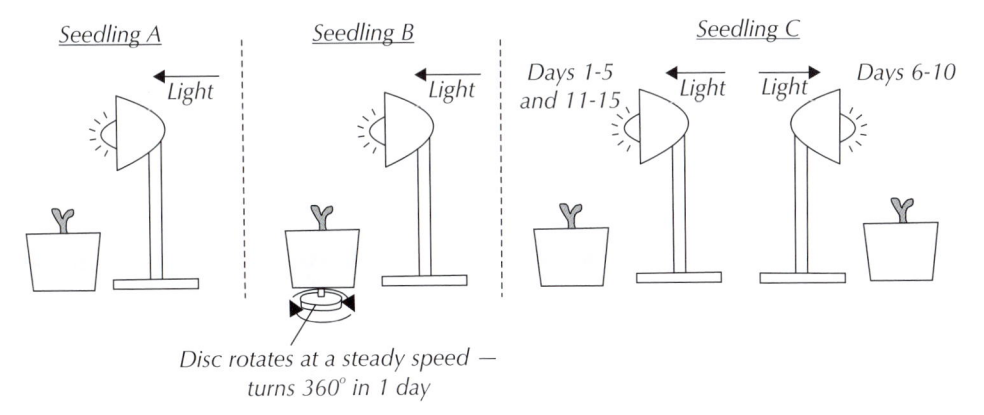

Fig. 2.1

**(a)** Suggest what response the scientists were testing with this experiment.

*(1 mark)*

**(b)** The scientists didn't include a control in their experiment. Describe the conditions that should have been used for a seedling acting as a control.

*(2 marks)*

**(c)** Suggest why the scientists used soil taken from the same source for all the seedlings.

*(1 mark)*

**(d)** Describe and explain the pattern of growth in the three plants that you would expect to see by the end of the experiment.

*(3 marks)*

**(e)** Explain the role of growth hormones in controlling the direction of growth in this experiment.

*(3 marks)*

**3** Part of a gardener's job is to maintain the size and shape of plants being grown in a commercial greenhouse.
**Fig. 3.1** shows a plant that is growing in the greenhouse.

Buds are labelled with the numbers **1-5** and the dashed line labelled **X** is a location where the stem could be cut.

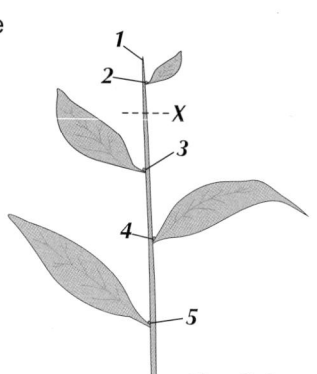

**(a)** State the name that can be used to describe buds **2-5**.

*(1 mark)*

**(b) (i)** The gardener removes bud **1** from the plant. Explain the effect this would have on the growth of the plant.

*(2 marks)*

**Fig. 3.1**

**(ii)** A gel containing auxins was applied to the exposed shoot tip after the removal of bud **1**. Explain the effect this would have on the growth of the plant.

*(1 mark)*

**(iii)** Suggest another commercial use for the auxin-containing gel.

*(1 mark)*

**(c)** In a different greenhouse, tomatoes are being grown. They were all planted at the same time but the fruits on some plants are more developed than others. Before harvesting all tomato plants are exposed to ethene gas for 24 hours. Suggest why this is done.

*(1 mark)*

**4** Insects are feeding on the leaves of a plant. In response, the plant releases defensive chemicals, which generates a response in nearby plants.

**(a)** Suggest what the plant has released.

*(1 mark)*

**(b)** Some plants produce tannins in response to being eaten. Explain how these chemicals can act as a deterrent to herbivory.

*(1 mark)*

**(c)** Suggest why manipulation of plant defence chemicals is an active area of research for scientists investigating ways to minimise crop damage caused by herbivory.

*(1 mark)*

# Module 5 Section 5: Photosynthesis

## 1. Storing and Releasing Energy

*Energy is required for all life processes. This means that being able to store and release energy is really important for plants and animals.*

### Why is energy important?
Living things need energy for biological processes to occur.

**Examples**
- Plants need energy for things like photosynthesis, active transport (e.g. to take in minerals via their roots), DNA replication and cell division.
- Animals need energy for things like muscle contraction, maintenance of body temperature, active transport, DNA replication and cell division.
- Microorganisms need energy for things like DNA replication, cell division, protein synthesis and sometimes motility (movement).

Without energy, these biological processes would stop and the plant, animal or microorganism would die.

### Photosynthesis and energy
Plants can make their own food (glucose). They do this using photosynthesis. Photosynthesis is the process where energy from light is used to make glucose from water ($H_2O$) and carbon dioxide ($CO_2$). (The light energy is converted to chemical energy in the form of glucose — $C_6H_{12}O_6$.) The overall equation is:

$$6CO_2 + 6H_2O + \text{Energy} \longrightarrow C_6H_{12}O_6 + 6O_2$$

Energy is stored in the glucose until the plants release it by respiration. Animals can't make their own food. So, they obtain glucose by eating plants (or other animals), then respire the glucose to release energy.

### Respiration and energy
Living cells release energy from glucose — this process is called respiration. This energy is used to power all the biological processes in a cell. There are two types of respiration:

- **Aerobic respiration** — respiration using oxygen.
- **Anaerobic respiration** — respiration without oxygen.

Aerobic respiration produces carbon dioxide and water, and releases energy. The overall equation is:

$$C_6H_{12}O_6 + 6O_2 \longrightarrow 6CO_2 + 6H_2O + \text{Energy}$$

## ATP
As you learned in Module 2, ATP (adenosine triphosphate) is the immediate source of energy in a cell.

A cell can't get its energy directly from glucose. So, in respiration, the energy released from glucose is used to make ATP. ATP is made from the nucleotide base adenine, combined with a ribose sugar and three phosphate groups (see Figure 1). It carries energy around the cell to where it's needed.

**Learning Objectives:**
- Understand the need for cellular respiration, including examples of why plants, animals and microorganisms need to respire.
- Understand the interrelationship between the processes of photosynthesis and respiration, including the relationship between the raw materials and products of the two processes.

**Specification References 5.2.1, 5.2.2**

**Tip:** The glucose made in photosynthesis by plants is needed for use in respiration in both plants and animals.

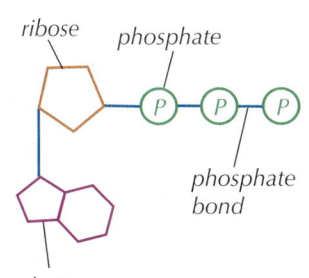

*Figure 1: The structure of adenosine triphosphate (ATP). It consists of adenine, ribose and three phosphate groups.*

**Tip:** Inorganic phosphate (P$_i$) is just the fancy name for a single phosphate.

ATP is synthesised from ADP (adenosine diphosphate) and inorganic phosphate (P$_i$) using energy from an energy-releasing reaction, e.g. the breakdown of glucose in respiration. The energy is stored as chemical energy in the phosphate bond (see Figure 2). The enzyme **ATP synthase** catalyses this reaction.

**Tip:** Adenosine <u>di</u>phosphate has <u>two</u> phosphates. Adenosine <u>tri</u>phosphate has <u>three</u> phosphates.

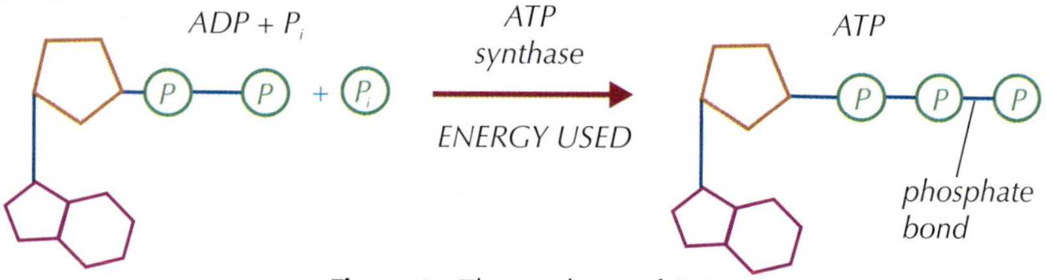

**Figure 2:** The synthesis of ATP.

This process is known as **phosphorylation** — adding phosphate to a molecule. ADP is phosphorylated to ATP.

ATP then diffuses to the part of the cell that needs energy. Here, it's broken down back into ADP and inorganic phosphate (P$_i$). Chemical energy is released from the phosphate bond and used by the cell. **ATPase** catalyses this reaction.

**Tip:** In a cell there's a constant cycle between ADP and P$_i$, and ATP. This allows energy to be stored and released as it's needed.

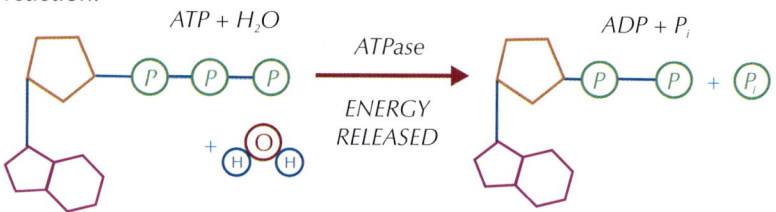

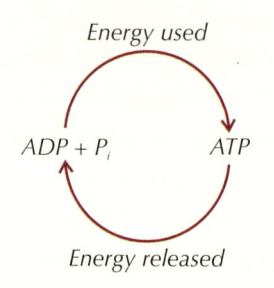

**Figure 3:** The breakdown of ATP.

This process is known as **hydrolysis**. It's the splitting (lysis) of a molecule using water (hydro).

## ATP's properties

ATP has specific properties that make it a good energy source.

- ATP stores or releases only a small, manageable amount of energy at a time, so no energy is wasted.
- It's a small, soluble molecule so it can be easily transported around the cell.
- It's easily broken down, so energy can be easily released.
- It can transfer energy to another molecule by transferring one of its phosphate groups.
- ATP can't pass out of the cell, so the cell always has an immediate supply of energy.

**Tip:** It's important to remember that ATP doesn't make energy — it's a store of energy. Energy is used to make ATP, then it's released when ATP is hydrolysed to ADP and P$_i$.

## The compensation point

Plants carry out both photosynthesis and respiration. Both processes can occur at the same time and at different rates. The rate at which photosynthesis takes place is partly dependent on the light intensity of the environment that the plant is in (see page 402).

There's a particular level of light intensity at which the rate of photosynthesis exactly matches the rate of respiration. This is called the **compensation point** for light intensity.

**Tip:** The products of photosynthesis (e.g. O$_2$) can be used as reactants in respiration and vice versa. Reactants can also come from elsewhere (e.g. O$_2$ can come from air).

One way to work out the compensation point for a plant is to measure the rate at which oxygen is produced and used by a plant at different light intensities. Because photosynthesis produces oxygen and respiration uses it, in this case, the compensation point is the light intensity at which oxygen is being used as quickly as it is produced (see the example below). The rate of $CO_2$ production and use could also be measured — photosynthesis uses $CO_2$ and respiration produces it.

**Tip:** The compensation point is different for different species of plants.

### Example — Maths Skills

The graph below shows the net oxygen generation by a plant grown in a controlled environment under different light intensities. When the rate of oxygen production equals the rate of oxygen usage, oxygen generation is zero. This is the compensation point.

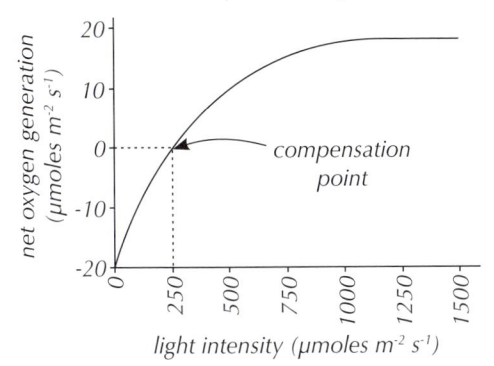

In this example, the compensation point occurs at a light intensity of 250 µmoles $m^{-2}$ $s^{-1}$.

**Exam Tip**
Graphs showing the compensation point won't always show oxygen generation. If you haven't seen the factors used on the scales of the graph before, don't panic. Just remember that the compensation point is the point at which photosynthesis and respiration are occurring at the same rate and apply your knowledge to work it out from the graph you've been given.

## Practice Question — Application

Q1 The graph on the right shows the $CO_2$ uptake of a plant over the course of a day in early spring.

a) Give the times when compensation points occur.

b) Suggest and explain why the compensation points occur at these particular times.

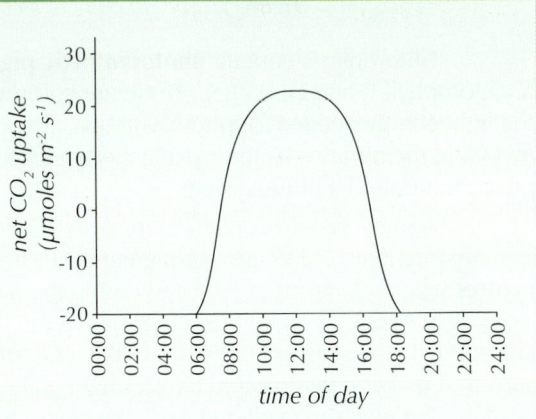

## Practice Questions — Fact Recall

Q1 Name three biological processes in plants that need energy.
Q2 Outline the relationship between the raw materials and products of photosynthesis and respiration.
Q3 What is the function of ATP?
Q4 Describe the structure of a molecule of ATP.
Q5 a) What is ATP broken down into by ATPase?
   b) By what process is ATP broken down?

Module 5: Section 5 Photosynthesis

### Learning Objectives:

- Know the structure of a chloroplast and the sites of the two main stages of photosynthesis.
- Know the components of a chloroplast including outer membrane, lamellae, grana, thylakoid, stroma and DNA.
- Understand the importance of photosynthetic pigments in photosynthesis, including reference to light harvesting systems and photosystems.
- Understand the light-dependent stage of photosynthesis, including how energy from light is harvested and used to drive the production of chemicals which can be used as a source of energy for other metabolic processes (ATP and reduced NADP), with reference to electron carriers and cyclic and non-cyclic photophosphorylation. Also understand the role of water in this stage.
- Understand the chemiosmotic theory, including the electron transport chain, proton gradients and ATP synthase in photophosphorylation.

**Specification References 5.2.1, 5.2.2**

# 2. Photosynthesis and the Light-dependent Reaction

*In photosynthesis, light energy is used to make glucose. It involves a series of reactions, but before we get stuck into it you need to know a bit of background information...*

## Chloroplasts

Photosynthesis takes place in the chloroplasts of plant cells. Chloroplasts are small, flattened organelles found in plant cells (see Figure 1). They have a double membrane called the chloroplast envelope. Thylakoids (fluid-filled sacs) are stacked up in the chloroplast into structures called grana (singular = granum). The grana are linked together by bits of thylakoid membrane called lamellae (singular = lamella).

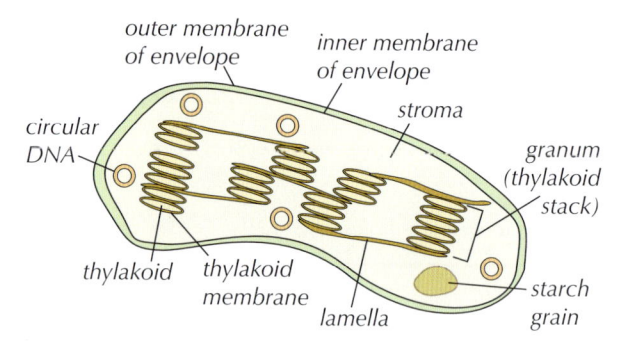

**Figure 1:** The structure of a chloroplast.

Chloroplasts contain **photosynthetic pigments** (e.g. chlorophyll a, chlorophyll b and carotene). These are coloured substances that absorb the light energy needed for photosynthesis. The pigments are found in the thylakoid membranes — they're attached to proteins. The protein and pigment is called a **photosystem**.

A photosystem contains two types of photosynthetic pigments — primary pigments and accessory pigments. Primary pigments are **reaction centres** where electrons are excited during the light-dependent reaction (see pages 396-397) — in most chloroplasts the primary pigment is chlorophyll a. Accessory pigments make up **light-harvesting systems**. These surround reaction centres and transfer light energy to them to boost the energy available for electron excitement to take place. There are two photosystems used by plants to capture light energy. Photosystem I (or PSI) absorbs light best at a wavelength of 700 nm and photosystem II (PSII) absorbs light best at 680 nm.

Contained within the inner membrane of the chloroplast and surrounding the thylakoids is a gel-like substance called the stroma — see Figure 1. It contains enzymes, sugars and organic acids. Chloroplasts have their own DNA. It's found in the stroma and is often circular. There can be multiple copies in each chloroplast. Carbohydrates produced by photosynthesis and not used straight away are stored as starch grains in the stroma.

# Redox reactions

Redox reactions are reactions that involve **oxidation** and **reduction**. They occur in photosynthesis (and in respiration) so it's really important that you get your head round them:

- If something is reduced it has gained electrons (e⁻), and may have gained hydrogen or lost oxygen.
- If something is oxidised it has lost electrons, and may have lost hydrogen or gained oxygen.
- Oxidation of one molecule always involves reduction of another molecule.

**Tip:** One way to remember electron and hydrogen movement is OILRIG. **O**xidation **I**s **L**oss, **R**eduction **I**s **G**ain.

# Coenzymes

A coenzyme is a molecule that aids the function of an enzyme. They usually work by transferring a chemical group from one molecule to another. A coenzyme used in photosynthesis is **NADP**. NADP transfers hydrogen from one molecule to another — this means it can reduce (give hydrogen to) or oxidise (take hydrogen from) a molecule.

**Tip:** When hydrogen is transferred between molecules, electrons are transferred too.

# The stages of photosynthesis

There are actually two stages that make up photosynthesis — the light-dependent reaction and the light-independent reaction. The next few pages are all about the light-dependent reaction, but before we get into all that you need to know how the two stages link together.

*Figure 2: A cross-sectional image of two chloroplasts.*

### 1. The light-dependent reaction

As the name suggests, this reaction needs light energy — see Figure 3. It takes place in the thylakoid membranes of the chloroplasts. Here, light energy is absorbed by photosynthetic pigments in the photosystems and converted to chemical energy. The light energy is used to add a phosphate group to ADP to form ATP, and to reduce NADP to form reduced NADP. (Reduced NADP is an energy-rich molecule because it can transfer hydrogen, and so electrons, to other molecules.) ATP transfers energy and reduced NADP transfers hydrogen to the light-independent reaction. During the process water ($H_2O$) is oxidised to oxygen ($O_2$).

**Tip:** Reduced NADP is also written as NADPH — it's NADP that's gained a hydrogen. Remember OILRIG — reduction is gain.

### 2. The light-independent reaction (the Calvin cycle)

As the name suggests, this reaction doesn't use light energy directly. (But it does rely on the products of the light-dependent reaction.) It takes place in the stroma of the chloroplast — see Figure 3. Here, the ATP and reduced NADP from the light-dependent reaction supply the energy and hydrogen to make glucose from $CO_2$.

**Tip:** See pages 399-400 for loads more information on the Calvin cycle.

*Figure 3: How the light-dependent and light-independent reactions link together in a chloroplast.*

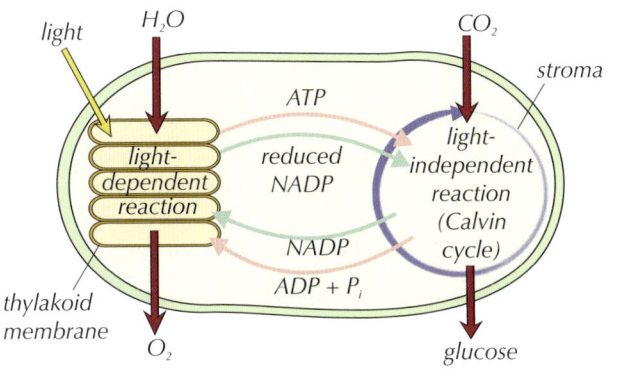

**Tip:** The light-independent reaction can take place in the dark. However, it needs the products of the light-dependent reaction (ATP and reduced NADP) so in reality it only continues for a little while after it gets dark.

Module 5: Section 5 Photosynthesis

*Photosynthesis Map*

*The light-dependent reaction*

You are here

*The light-independent reaction*

# The light-dependent reaction

In the light-dependent reaction, the light energy absorbed by the photosystems is used for three things:

1. Making ATP from ADP and inorganic phosphate. This is called **photophosphorylation** — it's the process of adding phosphate to a molecule using light.
2. Making reduced NADP from NADP.
3. Splitting water into protons (H⁺ ions), electrons and oxygen. This is called **photolysis** — it's the splitting (lysis) of a molecule using light (photo) energy.

The light-dependent reaction actually includes two types of photophosphorylation — non-cyclic and cyclic. Each of these processes has different products and is explained on the next couple of pages.

## Non-cyclic photophosphorylation

Non-cyclic photophosphorylation produces ATP, reduced NADP and oxygen ($O_2$). To understand the process you need to know that the photosystems in the thylakoid membranes (see page 394) are linked by **electron carriers**. Electron carriers are proteins that transfer electrons. The photosystems and electron carriers form an **electron transport chain** — a chain of proteins through which excited electrons flow. There are several processes going on all at once in non-cyclic photophosphorylation — they're shown in the diagrams below and on the next page.

**Tip:** Not all of the electron carriers are shown in these diagrams.

### 1. Light energy excites electrons in chlorophyll

Light energy is absorbed by PSII. The light energy excites electrons in chlorophyll. The electrons move to a higher energy level (i.e. they have more energy — see Figure 4). These high-energy electrons move along the electron transport chain to PSI.

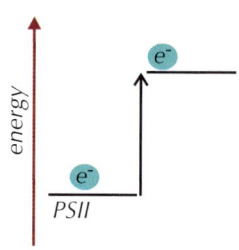

**Figure 4:** Light energy excites electrons in PSII, moving them to a higher energy level.

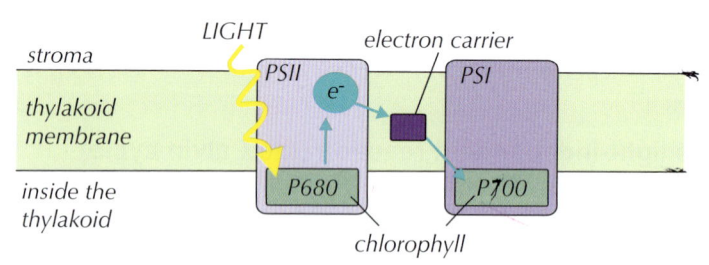

**Tip:** If too much light energy has been absorbed, plants release some of the excess energy by emitting fluorescent light. This is called chlorophyll fluorescence.

### 2. Photolysis of water produces protons, electrons and oxygen

As the excited electrons from chlorophyll leave PSII to move along the electron transport chain, they must be replaced. Light energy splits water into protons (H⁺ ions), electrons and oxygen. (So the oxygen in photosynthesis comes from water.) The reaction is: $H_2O \longrightarrow 2H^+ + \frac{1}{2}O_2$

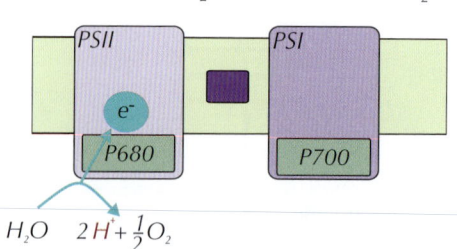

**Tip:** The $O_2$ produced from the photolysis of water is really important. It diffuses out of the chloroplast and eventually into the atmosphere for us to breathe. Good old plants.

Module 5: Section 5 Photosynthesis

## 3. Energy from the excited electrons makes ATP

The excited electrons lose energy as they move along the electron transport chain (see Figure 5). This energy is used to transport protons (H⁺ ions) into the thylakoid, via membrane proteins called proton pumps, so that the thylakoid has a higher concentration of protons than the stroma. This forms a proton gradient across the membrane. Protons move down their concentration gradient, into the stroma, via an enzyme called ATP synthase. The energy from this movement combines ADP and inorganic phosphate ($P_i$) to form ATP.

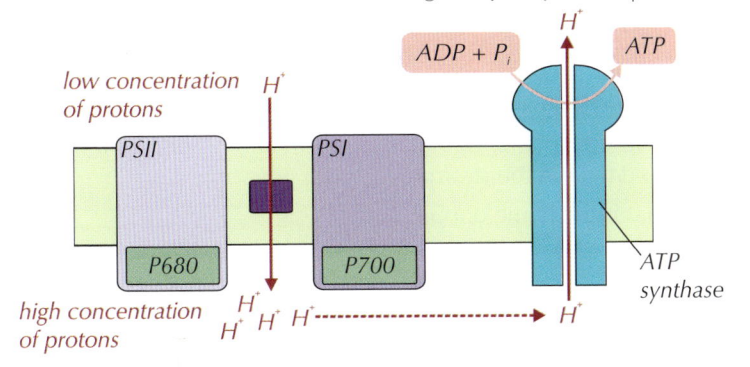

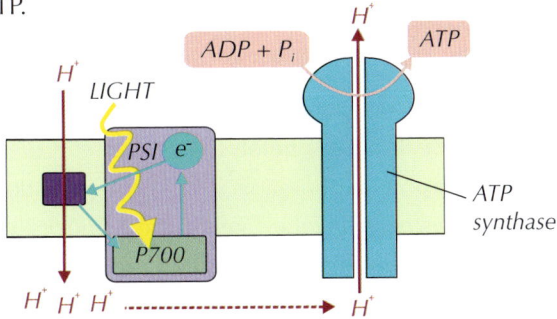

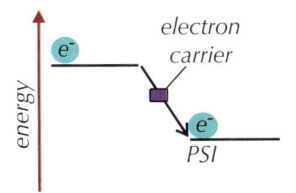

**Figure 5:** The excited electrons lose energy as they pass down the electron transport chain.

**Tip:** The process of electrons flowing down the electron transport chain and creating a proton gradient across the membrane to drive ATP synthesis is called chemiosmosis. It's described by the chemiosmotic theory.

## 4. Energy from the excited electrons generates reduced NADP

Light energy is absorbed by PSI, which excites the electrons again to an even higher energy level (see Figure 6). Finally, the electrons are transferred to NADP, along with a proton from the stroma, to form reduced NADP.

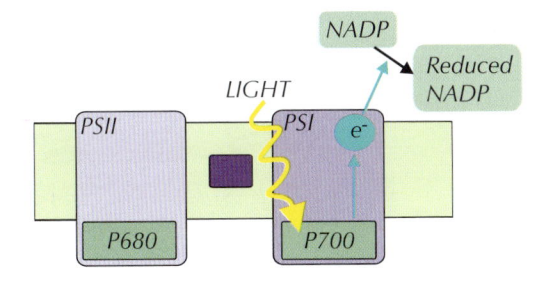

**Tip:** Remember a 'proton' is just another word for a hydrogen ion (H⁺).

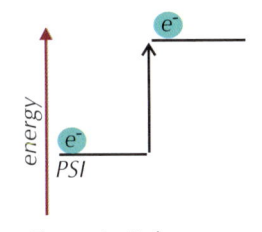

**Figure 6:** Light energy excites electrons in PSI to an even higher energy level.

**Tip:** The ATP and reduced NADP made here in the light-dependent reaction are really important for use later on in the light-independent reaction (see pages 399-400).

# Cyclic photophosphorylation

Cyclic photophosphorylation only produces ATP and only uses PSI. It's called 'cyclic' because the electrons from the chlorophyll molecule aren't passed onto NADP, but are passed back to PSI via electron carriers. This means the electrons are recycled and can repeatedly flow through PSI. This process doesn't produce any reduced NADP or oxygen — it only produces small amounts of ATP.

**Tip:** ATP is formed in the same way in cyclic photophosphorylation as in non-cyclic photophosphorylation — by the movement of protons across the thylakoid membrane.

Module 5: Section 5 Photosynthesis

## Practice Questions — Application

This diagram on the right shows a process in the light-dependent reaction.

Tip: Tempting as it is, you need to be able to answer this question without looking back at the last couple of pages.

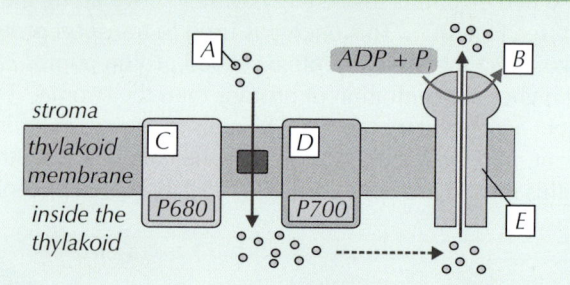

Q1 The object labelled A in the diagram is transported across the thylakoid membrane, so that its concentration is higher in the thylakoid than in the stroma.
   a) What is the name of object A?
   b) Explain why it is important that the concentration of object A is higher inside the thylakoid than in the stroma.
Q2 What is the name of structure C?
Q3 Which structure, C or D, is involved in cyclic photophosphorylation?
Q4 What does cyclic photophosphorylation produce?

## Practice Questions — Fact Recall

Q1 The diagram on the right shows a chloroplast. Label the parts A-I.

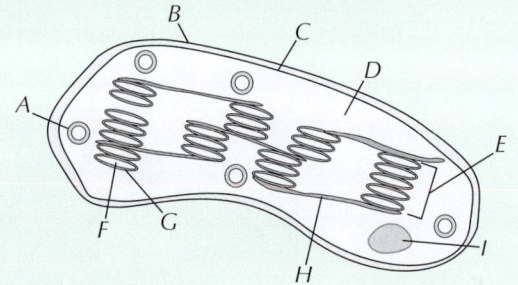

Q2 a) What are photosynthetic pigments?
   b) Name the primary photosynthetic pigment in most chloroplasts.
Q3 What are light-harvesting systems and what is their purpose?
Q4 What are the two photosystems used by plants called?
Q5 NADP is a coenzyme used in photosynthesis. What chemical group does it transfer between molecules?
Q6 Where in the chloroplast does the light-dependent reaction occur?
Q7 Which products of the light-dependent reaction are needed in the light-independent reaction?
Q8 What is photophosphorylation?
Q9 What is the electron transport chain?
Q10 a) Name the products of the photolysis of water.
    b) What is the purpose of photolysis in the light-dependent reaction?
Q11 Name the photosystem(s) involved in and the product(s) of:
    a) non-cyclic photophosphorylation,
    b) cyclic photophosphorylation.

Tip: Make sure you get your head round what happens in cyclic and non-cyclic phosphorylation (see previous two pages) — don't get them mixed up.

# 3. Light-independent Reaction

*The light-independent reaction is the second (and final, phew) stage of photosynthesis. It uses the products of the light-dependent reaction (ATP and reduced NADP) to make organic substances for the plant.*

## The Calvin cycle

The light-independent reaction is also called the Calvin cycle. It takes place in the stroma of the chloroplasts. It makes a molecule called **triose phosphate** from carbon dioxide ($CO_2$) and **ribulose bisphosphate** (a 5-carbon compound). Triose phosphate can be used to make glucose and other useful organic substances. There are a few steps in the cycle, and it needs ATP and $H^+$ ions to keep it going. The reactions are linked in a cycle (see Figure 1), which means the starting compound, ribulose bisphosphate, is regenerated.

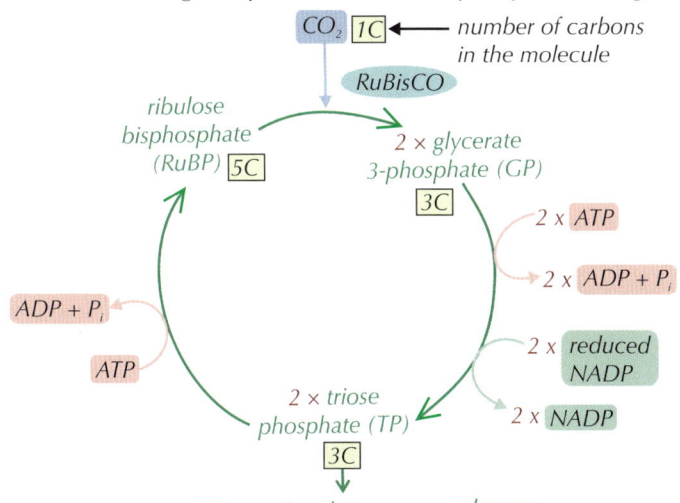

**Learning Objectives:**
- Understand the fixation of carbon dioxide and the light-independent stage of photosynthesis, including how the products of the light-dependent stage are used in the light-independent stage (Calvin cycle) to produce triose phosphate (TP) with reference to ribulose bisphosphate (RuBP), ribulose bisphosphate carboxylase (RuBisCO) and glycerate 3-phosphate (GP).
- Know the uses of triose phosphate (TP), including as a starting material for the synthesis of carbohydrates, lipids and amino acids, and the recycling of TP to regenerate the supply of RuBP.

**Specification Reference 5.2.1**

*Figure 1: One turn of the Calvin cycle.*

Here's what happens at each stage in the cycle:

### 1. Formation of glycerate 3-phosphate

Carbon dioxide enters the leaf through the stomata and diffuses into the stroma of the chloroplast. Here, it's combined with ribulose bisphosphate (RuBP), a 5-carbon compound. This gives an unstable 6-carbon compound, which quickly breaks down into two molecules of a 3-carbon compound called **glycerate 3-phosphate** (GP). **Ribulose bisphosphate carboxylase** (RuBisCO) catalyses the reaction between carbon dioxide and RuBP.

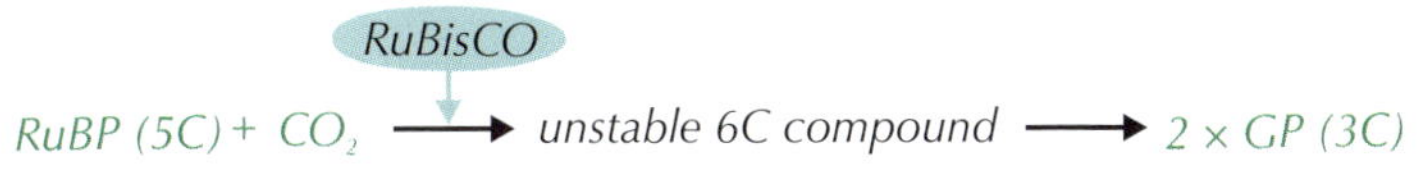

$$RuBP\ (5C) + CO_2 \xrightarrow{RuBisCO} \text{unstable 6C compound} \longrightarrow 2 \times GP\ (3C)$$

**Tip:** The Calvin cycle is also called carbon dioxide fixation, because carbon from $CO_2$ is 'fixed' into an organic molecule.

### 2. Formation of triose phosphate

The 3-carbon compound GP is reduced to a different 3-carbon compound called triose phosphate (TP). ATP (from the light-dependent reaction) provides the energy to do this. This reaction also requires $H^+$ ions, which come from reduced NADP (also from the light-dependent reaction). Reduced NADP is recycled to NADP (for use in the light-dependent reaction again). Triose phosphate is then converted into many useful organic compounds, e.g. glucose (see pages 400-401).

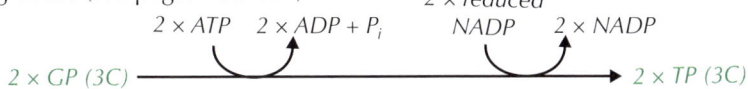

*Photosynthesis Map*

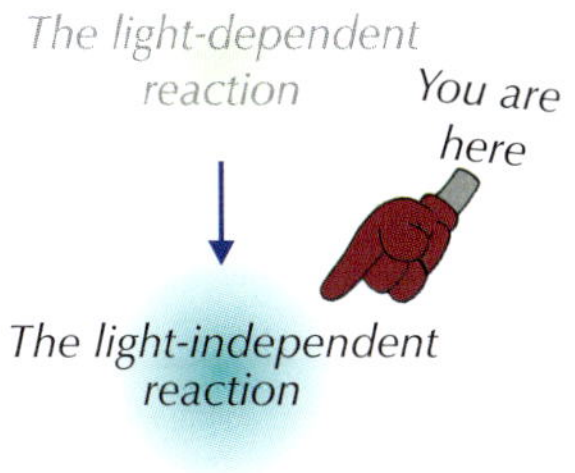

*The light-dependent reaction*

*You are here*

*The light-independent reaction*

Module 5: Section 5 Photosynthesis

**Tip:** Useful organic compounds have more than one carbon atom, e.g. glucose has six carbon atoms. This means the cycle has to turn more than once to make them — see below.

**Tip:** It's really important that RuBP is regenerated. If it wasn't then glycerate 3-phosphate wouldn't be formed, the Calvin cycle would stop and photosynthesis would be unable to continue.

### 3. Regeneration of ribulose bisphosphate

Five out of every six molecules of TP produced in the cycle aren't used to make useful organic compounds, but to regenerate RuBP. Regenerating RuBP uses the rest of the ATP produced by the light-dependent reaction.

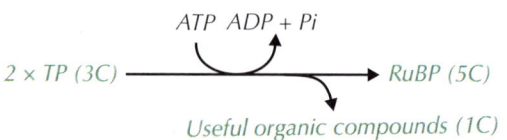

$$2 \times TP\ (3C) \xrightarrow{ATP \rightarrow ADP + Pi} RuBP\ (5C)$$

Useful organic compounds (1C)

## Hexose sugars

A hexose sugar is a monosaccharide that has six carbon atoms, e.g. glucose (see Figure 2). One hexose sugar is made by joining two molecules of triose phosphate (TP) together. Hexose sugars can be used to make larger carbohydrates (see next page).

The Calvin cycle needs to turn six times to make one hexose sugar. The reason for this is that three turns of the cycle produces six molecules of triose phosphate (because two molecules of TP are made for every one $CO_2$ molecule used). Five out of six of these TP molecules are used to regenerate ribulose bisphosphate (RuBP). This means that for three turns of the cycle only one TP is produced that's used to make a hexose sugar.

As a hexose sugar has six carbons, two TP molecules are needed to form one hexose sugar. This means the cycle must turn six times to produce two molecules of TP that can be used to make one hexose sugar — see Figure 3. Six turns of the cycle need 18 ATP and 12 reduced NADP from the light-dependent reaction.

This might seem a bit inefficient, but it keeps the cycle going and makes sure there's always enough RuBP ready to combine with carbon dioxide taken in from the atmosphere.

**Figure 2:** The structure of glucose, a hexose sugar.

**Exam Tip**
If you're asked in the exam to work out how many turns of the Calvin cycle are needed to produce a certain number of hexose sugars you need to remember that five out of every six TP molecules are used to regenerate RuBP.

**Tip:** Six turns of the Calvin cycle produce 12 GP molecules because one turn produces 2 GP, so 6 × 2 = 12 GP.

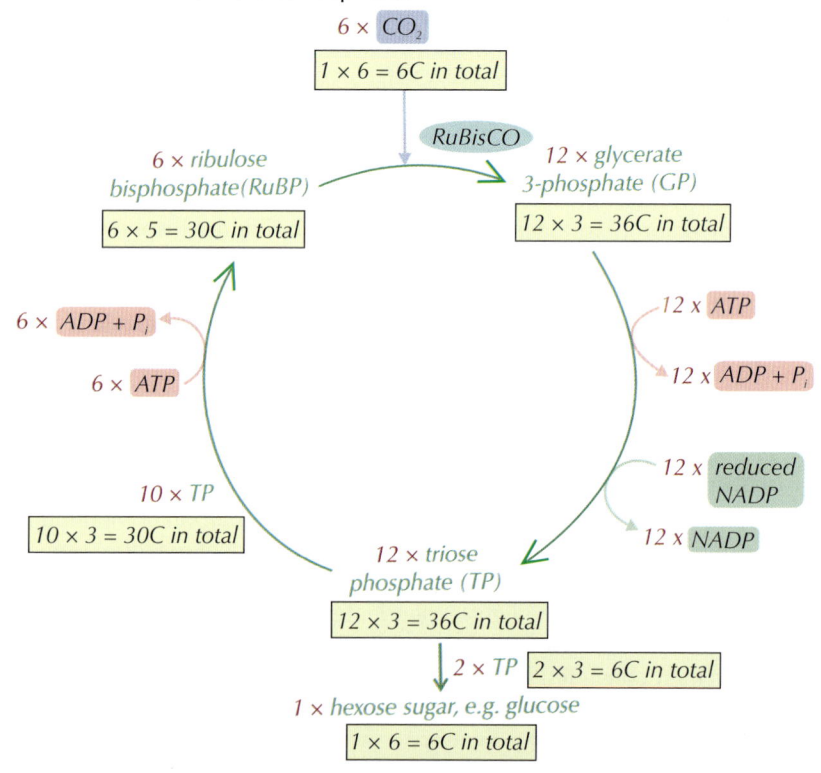

**Figure 3:** Six turns of the Calvin cycle.

- 6 × $CO_2$ | 1 × 6 = 6C in total
- 6 × ribulose bisphosphate (RuBP) | 6 × 5 = 30C in total
- RuBisCO
- 12 × glycerate 3-phosphate (GP) | 12 × 3 = 36C in total
- 12 × ATP
- 12 × ADP + $P_i$
- 12 × reduced NADP
- 12 × NADP
- 12 × triose phosphate (TP) | 12 × 3 = 36C in total
- 6 × ADP + $P_i$
- 6 × ATP
- 10 × TP | 10 × 3 = 30C in total
- 2 × TP | 2 × 3 = 6C in total
- 1 × hexose sugar, e.g. glucose | 1 × 6 = 6C in total

Module 5: Section 5 Photosynthesis

# Carbohydrates, lipids and amino acids

The Calvin cycle is the starting point for making all the organic substances a plant needs. Triose phosphate (TP) and glycerate 3-phosphate (GP) molecules are used to make carbohydrates, lipids and amino acids:

- **Carbohydrates** — hexose sugars are made from two triose phosphate molecules (see the previous page) and larger carbohydrates (e.g. sucrose, starch, cellulose — see Figure 4) are made by joining hexose sugars together in different ways.
- **Lipids** — these are made using glycerol, which is synthesised from triose phosphate, and fatty acids, which are synthesised from glycerate 3-phosphate.
- **Amino acids** — some amino acids are made from glycerate 3-phosphate.

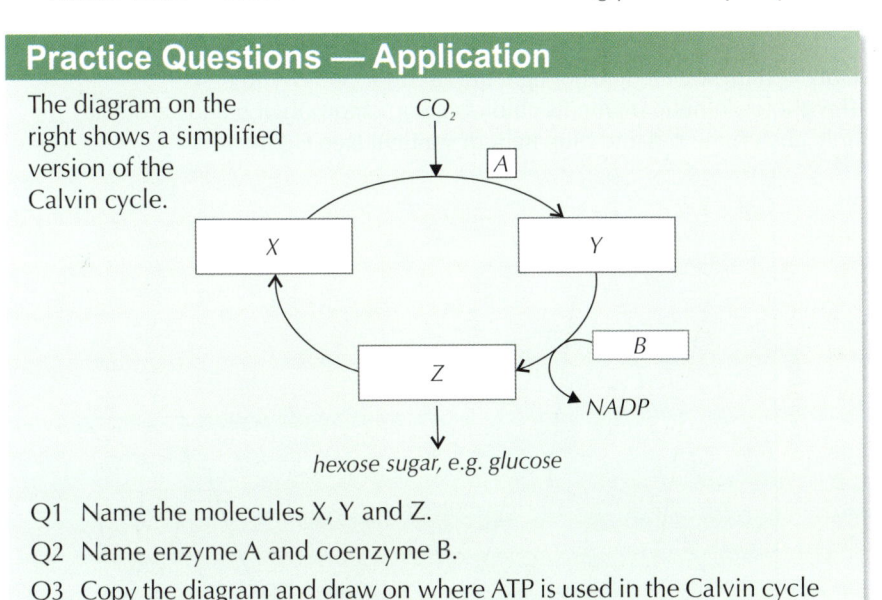

*Figure 4: Cellulose strands in a plant cell wall made from hexose sugars.*

**Tip:** The Calvin cycle can be summarised as follows:
*Inputs*
$CO_2$
ATP
Reduced NADP

*Outputs*
Organic substances
RuBP

## Practice Questions — Application

The diagram on the right shows a simplified version of the Calvin cycle.

Q1 Name the molecules X, Y and Z.
Q2 Name enzyme A and coenzyme B.
Q3 Copy the diagram and draw on where ATP is used in the Calvin cycle (including how many molecules of ATP are used).

**Exam Tip**
Don't panic if you get a diagram of the Calvin cycle in the exam that doesn't look exactly the same as the one on the previous page (e.g. it might have extra or fewer stages) — as long as you remember the key points then you'll be fine.

## Practice Questions — Fact Recall

Q1 What is the role of carbon dioxide in the Calvin cycle?
Q2 a) Write out an equation that shows how two molecules of triose phosphate are formed.
    b) Is this reaction an oxidation or reduction reaction?
Q3 Describe the role of ATP in the Calvin cycle.
Q4 If six molecules of triose phosphate (TP) are produced by the Calvin cycle, how many of these will be used to regenerate ribulose bisphosphate?
Q5 To make one hexose sugar:
    a) How many turns of the Calvin cycle are needed?
    b) How many molecules of ATP are needed?
    c) How many molecules of reduced NADP are needed?
Q6 Describe how the products of the Calvin cycle are used to make the following organic substances:
    a) large carbohydrates,   b) lipids,   c) some amino acids.

**Exam Tip**
If you're asked to 'discuss the fate' of a molecule in the Calvin cycle, you just need to write about what happens to it.

**Learning Objectives:**

- Understand factors affecting photosynthesis, including limiting factors in photosynthesis with reference to carbon dioxide concentration, light intensity and temperature, and the implications of water stress (stomatal closure).
- Understand the effect on the rate of photosynthesis, and on levels of GP, RuBP and TP, of changing carbon dioxide concentration, light intensity and temperature.

**Specification Reference 5.2.1**

**Tip:** If you exposed a plant to only green light, there would be little or no photosynthesis because most of the green light is reflected rather than being absorbed. This is why plants look green.

**Tip:** The width of the opening of stomata is called the stomatal aperture.

**Tip:** Remember: stomata are pores in the epidermis of a plant which allow gas exchange.

# 4. Limiting Factors in Photosynthesis

*There are optimum conditions for photosynthesis. If you're a budding gardener then these pages are for you...*

## Optimum conditions for photosynthesis

The ideal conditions for photosynthesis vary from one plant species to another. Most plants in temperate climates, like in the UK, would be happy with the conditions below and on the next page.

### 1. High light intensity of a certain wavelength

Light is needed to provide the energy for the light-dependent reaction — the higher the intensity of the light, the more energy it provides. Only certain wavelengths of light are used for photosynthesis. The photosynthetic pigments chlorophyll a, chlorophyll b and carotene only absorb the red and blue light in sunlight (see Figure 1).

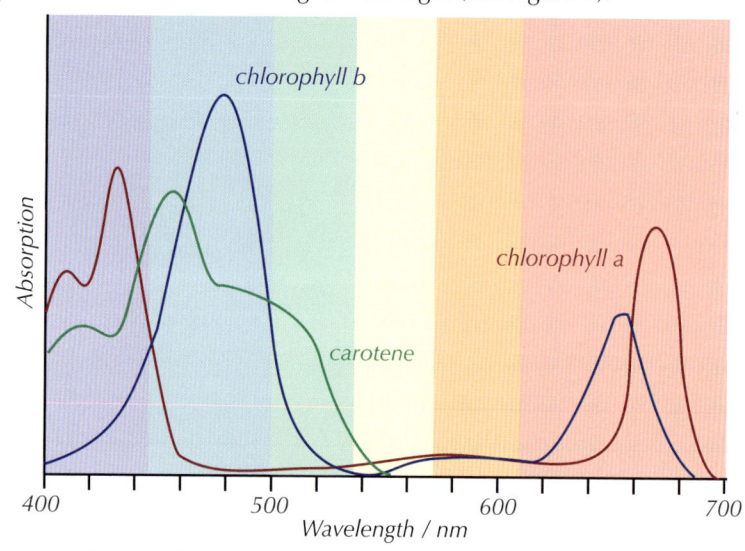

**Figure 1:** *The wavelengths of light absorbed by chlorophylls a and b, and carotene.*

### 2. Temperature around 25 °C

Photosynthesis involves enzymes (e.g. ATP synthase, RuBisCO). If the temperature falls below 10 °C the enzymes become inactive, but if the temperature is more than 45 °C they may start to **denature** (lose structure and function). Also, at high temperatures:

- Stomata close to avoid losing too much water. This causes photosynthesis to slow down because less carbon dioxide enters the leaf when the stomata are closed.
- The thylakoid membranes may be damaged. This could reduce the rate of the light-dependent stage reactions by reducing the number of sites available for electron transfer.
- The membrane around the chloroplast could be damaged, which could cause enzymes important in the Calvin cycle to be released into the cell. This would reduce the rate of the light-independent stage reactions.
- Chlorophyll could be damaged. This would reduce the amount of pigment that can absorb light energy, which would reduce rate of the light-dependent stage reactions.

Module 5: Section 5 Photosynthesis

## 3. Carbon dioxide at 0.4%

Carbon dioxide makes up 0.04% of the gases in the atmosphere. Increasing this to 0.4% gives a higher rate of photosynthesis, but any higher and the stomata start to close.

# Limiting factors of photosynthesis

Light, temperature and carbon dioxide can all limit photosynthesis. All three of these things need to be at the right level to allow a plant to photosynthesise as quickly as possible. If any one of these factors is too low or too high, it will limit photosynthesis (slow it down). Even if the other two factors are at the perfect level, it won't make any difference to the speed of photosynthesis as long as that factor is at the wrong level.

**Tip:** A limiting factor is a variable that can slow down the rate of a reaction.

— Examples —————
- On a warm, sunny, windless day, it's usually carbon dioxide that's the limiting factor.
- At night it's usually the light intensity that's the limiting factor.

However, any of these factors could become the limiting factor, depending on the environmental conditions. The graphs below and on the next page show the effect of each limiting factor on the rate of photosynthesis:

*Figure 2:* As night falls, light intensity begins to limit the rate of photosynthesis.

— Examples —————

### Light intensity

Between points A and B, the rate of photosynthesis is limited by the light intensity. So as the light intensity increases, so can the rate of photosynthesis. Point B is the **saturation point** — increasing light intensity after this point makes no difference, because something else has become the limiting factor. The graph now levels off.

**Tip:** The saturation point is where a factor is no longer limiting the reaction — something else has become the limiting factor.

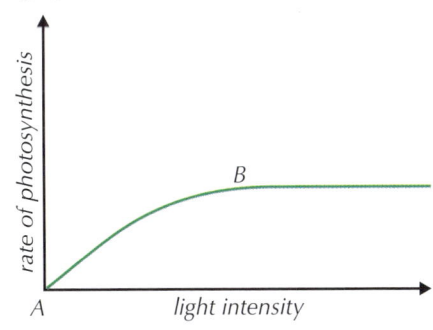

### Temperature

Both these graphs level off when light intensity is no longer the limiting factor. The graph at 25 °C levels off at a higher point than the one at 15 °C, showing that temperature must have been a limiting factor at 15 °C.

**Tip:** As each of the graphs level off, it doesn't mean that photosynthesis has stopped — it means that the rate of photosynthesis is not increasing anymore.

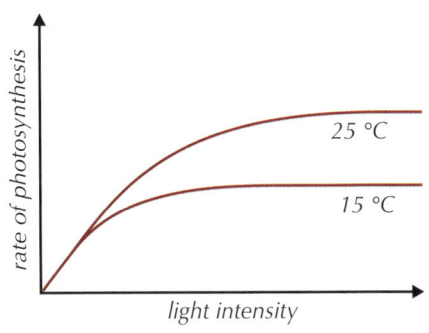

Module 5: Section 5 Photosynthesis    403

### Carbon dioxide concentration

Both these graphs level off when light intensity is no longer the limiting factor. The graph at 0.4% carbon dioxide ($CO_2$) levels off at a higher point than the one at 0.04%, so carbon dioxide concentration must have been a limiting factor at 0.04% carbon dioxide. The limiting factor here isn't temperature because it's the same for both graphs (25 °C).

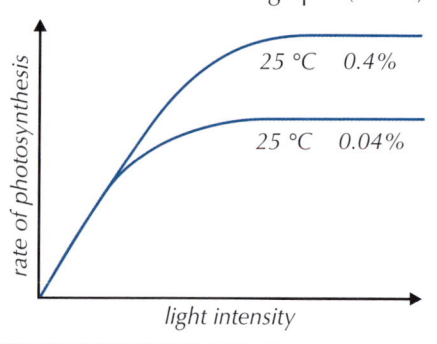

**Tip:** A greenhouse is the same thing as a glasshouse.

*Figure 3: Lamps in greenhouses provide light at night.*

## Water stress

Water stress can also affect photosynthesis. When plants don't have enough water, their stomata will close to preserve what little water they do have, leading to less $CO_2$ entering the leaf for the Calvin cycle and slowing photosynthesis down.

## Increasing plant growth

Commercial growers (e.g. farmers) know the factors that limit photosynthesis and therefore limit plant growth. This means they can create an environment where plants get the right amount of everything that they need, which increases growth and so increases yield. Growers create optimum conditions in **glasshouses**, as shown in Figure 4.

| Limiting Factor | Management in Glasshouse |
|---|---|
| Carbon dioxide concentration | Carbon dioxide is added to the air, e.g. by burning a small amount of propane in a carbon dioxide generator. |
| Light | Light can get in through the glass. Lamps provide light at night time. |
| Temperature | Glasshouses trap heat energy from sunlight, which warms the air. Heaters and cooling systems can also be used to keep a constant optimum temperature. |

*Figure 4: Techniques used by growers to create optimum conditions in a glasshouse.*

## Limiting factors and the Calvin cycle

Light intensity, temperature and $CO_2$ concentration all affect the rate of photosynthesis, which means they affect the levels of glycerate 3-phosphate (GP), ribulose bisphosphate (RuBP) and triose phosphate (TP) in the Calvin cycle.

## Light intensity

In low light intensities, the products of the light-dependent stage (reduced NADP and ATP) will be in short supply (see Figure 5). This means that conversion of GP to TP and RuBP is slow. So the level of GP will rise as it's still being made, but it isn't being used up as quickly. The levels of TP and RuBP will fall as they're used up to make GP, but aren't being remade as quickly — see Figure 6.

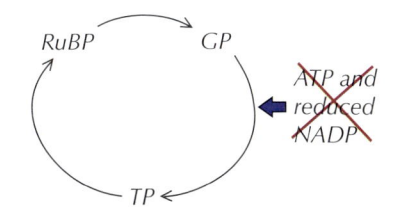

**Figure 5:** The effect of low light intensity on the Calvin cycle.

**Tip:** See pages 399-400 for how GP, TP and RuBP are made in the Calvin cycle.

**Tip:** Light intensity doesn't affect the Calvin cycle directly because light isn't needed for the reactions of the Calvin cycle. However, the Calvin cycle does depend on the products from the light-dependent reaction, so it is indirectly affected by light intensity.

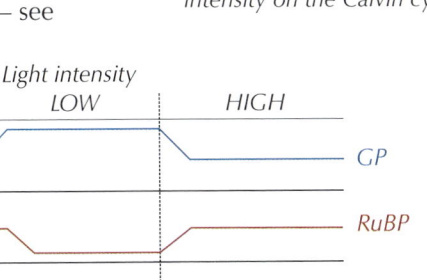

**Figure 6:** The effect of light intensity on the levels of GP, RuBP and TP.

## Temperature

All the reactions in the Calvin cycle are catalysed by enzymes (e.g. RuBisCO). At low temperatures, all of the reactions will be slower as the enzymes work more slowly. This means the levels of RuBP, GP and TP will fall. GP, TP and RuBP are affected in the same way at very high temperatures, because the enzymes will start to denature (see Figure 7).

**Figure 7:** The effect of temperature on the Calvin cycle.

**Tip:** Unlike light intensity, temperature does affect the Calvin cycle directly because it affects enzyme activity.

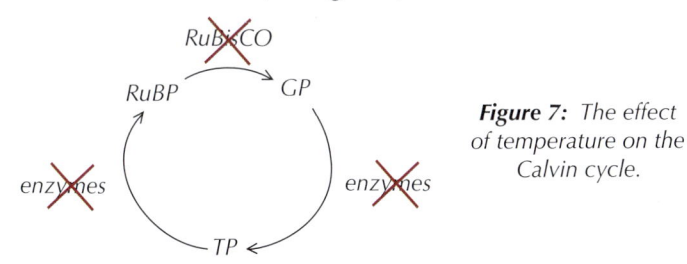

## Carbon dioxide concentration

At low $CO_2$ concentrations, conversion of RuBP to GP is also slow as there's less $CO_2$ to combine with RuBP to make GP — see Figure 8. So the level of RuBP will rise as it's still being made, but isn't being used up. The levels of GP and TP will fall as they're used up to make RuBP, but aren't being remade.

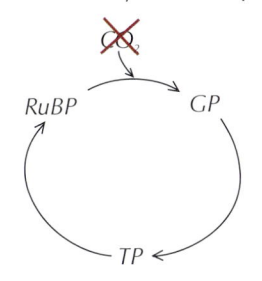

**Figure 8:** The effect of low $CO_2$ concentration on the Calvin cycle.

Module 5: Section 5 Photosynthesis

## Practice Questions — Application

**Q1** A farmer grows two tomato crops — one in a greenhouse and the other outside. He records the average plant height each week for seven weeks. The results are shown in the graph below.

a) For each tomato crop, calculate the percentage difference in the average plant height between week two and week five.

b) Describe three ways in which the farmer may have created ideal conditions in the greenhouse in order to increase photosynthesis.

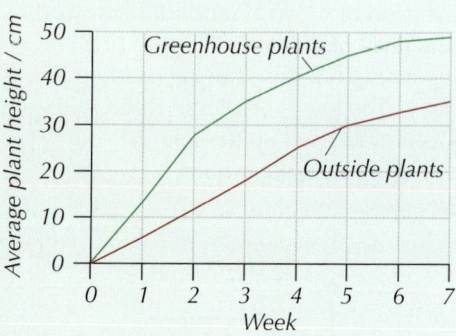

**Q2** Technicians at a plant-growing company were trying to reduce the running costs of their greenhouses. In one greenhouse, they reduced the amount of water used to water the plants by 40%. In a second greenhouse, they replaced the paraffin heaters that they used to heat the greenhouse with electric heaters, which maintained the same temperature, but were cheaper to run. The changes resulted in slower growth of the plants in the greenhouses, due to a reduced rate of photosynthesis.

a) Suggest why reducing the amount of water given to the plants could result in a reduced rate of photosynthesis.

b) Suggest why replacing the paraffin heaters with electric heaters could result in a reduced rate of photosynthesis.

**Q3** a) Jen has two house plants. She puts plant A under a light with a wavelength of 520 nm and plant B under a light with a wavelength of 480 nm. All other conditions the two plants are kept in are the same. After 4 weeks she measures the height of both plants. Which plant do you think was tallest? Explain your answer.

b) Jen keeps another house plant in her conservatory, which gets sun throughout the day and can reach temperatures of 40 °C. She regularly waters the plant but it's beginning to die. Suggest why this might be and explain your answer.

**Tip:** Look back at page 402 for a recap on the wavelengths of light used for photosynthesis.

## Practice Questions — Fact Recall

**Q1** Explain why a low light intensity decreases the rate of the Calvin cycle, even though it's a light-independent reaction.

**Q2** Describe how the following would affect the concentration of RuBP in the Calvin cycle:
a) low light intensity,
b) low temperature,
c) low concentration of $CO_2$.

# 5. Photosynthesis Experiments

*You need to know how to carry out two types of experiment related to different aspects of photosynthesis for your exams.*

## Investigating the pigments in leaves

All plants contain several different photosynthetic pigments in their leaves. Each pigment absorbs a different wavelength of light, so having more than one type of pigment increases the range of wavelengths of light that a plant can absorb. In addition to photosynthetic pigments, some plants also have other pigments in their leaves, which play other essential roles, e.g. protecting the leaves from excessive UV radiation. Different species of plants contain different proportions and mixtures of pigments.

**PRACTICAL ACTIVITY GROUP 6**

A sample of pigments can be extracted from the leaves of a plant and separated using thin-layer chromatography (TLC). You can then identify the pigments present in the sample by calculating their **$R_f$ values**. An $R_f$ value is the distance a substance has moved through the stationary phase in relation to the solvent. Each pigment has a specific $R_f$ value, under specific conditions, which can be looked up in a database.

### Example

Like all types of chromatography, TLC involves a mobile phase (in this case a liquid solvent) and a stationary phase (in TLC, this is a chromatography plate — a solid plate of glass or plastic with a thin layer of gel, which the pigments can travel through, on top). Here's how you do it:

1. Grind up several leaves (spinach works nicely) with some anhydrous sodium sulfate, then add a few drops of propanone.
2. Transfer the liquid to a test tube, add some petroleum ether and gently shake the tube. Two distinct layers will form in the liquid — the top layer is the pigments mixed in with the petroleum ether.
3. Transfer some of the liquid from the top layer into a second test tube with some anhydrous sodium sulfate.
4. Draw a horizontal pencil line near the bottom of a chromatography plate. Build up a concentrated spot of the liquid from step 3 on the line by applying several drops, ensuring each one is dry before the next is added. This is the point of origin.
5. Once the point of origin is completely dry, put the plate into a glass beaker with some prepared solvent (e.g. a mixture of propanone, cyclohexane and petroleum ether) — just enough so that the point of origin is a little bit above the solvent. Put a lid on the beaker and leave the plate to develop. As the solvent spreads up the plate, the different pigments (solutes) move with it, but at different rates — so they separate.

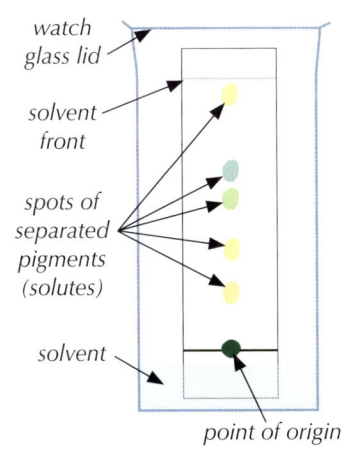

**Figure 2:** *Diagram showing plant pigments separated by thin layer chromatography.*

### Learning Objectives:
- Be able to use thin layer chromatography (TLC) to separate photosynthetic pigments (PAG6).
- Be able to carry out practical investigations into factors affecting the rate of photosynthesis (PAG11).

**Specification Reference 5.2.1**

**Tip:** Make sure you carry out a risk assessment before you do this experiment. Be especially aware of the hazards involved with using propanone, petroleum ether and the chromatography solvent, which are toxic and highly flammable.

**Tip:** It's best to do steps 2 and 5 in a fume cupboard as the chemicals used are volatile (evaporate easily) and the vapours are hazardous.

**Figure 1:** *Plant pigments that have been separated by thin-layer chromatography.*

Module 5: Section 5 Photosynthesis

**Tip:** The pattern of spots you end up with is called a chromatogram.

**Tip:** $R_f$ values are always between 0 and 1.

**Tip:** The stationary phase and solvent that you use will affect the $R_f$ value. If you're looking up $R_f$ values, you need to check that they were recorded under the same conditions as your experiment.

6. When the solvent has nearly reached the top, take the plate out and mark the solvent front (the furthest point the solvent has reached) with a pencil and leave the plate to dry in a well-ventilated place.

7. There should be several new coloured spots on the chromatography plate between the point of origin and the solvent front. These are the separated pigments. You can calculate their $R_f$ values and look them up in a database to identify what the pigments are.
You can calculate the $R_f$ value using this formula:

$$R_f \text{ value} = \frac{\text{distance moved by the solute}}{\text{distance moved by the solvent}}$$

### Practice Question — Application

**Q1** A scientist uses thin-layer chromatography to separate out the photosynthetic pigments from a mixture obtained from plant leaves. The chromatogram that he produces is shown on the right.

a) Calculate the $R_f$ value of spot Y.

b) The scientist carried out the same experiment using paper chromatography. Suggest why the $R_f$ values he obtained were different to those calculated from his first experiment.

(Diagram labels: solvent front, Y, 9.00 cm, 7.90 cm, X, 3.47 cm)

## Investigating the rate of photosynthesis

Canadian pondweed (*Elodea*) can be used to measure the effect of light intensity, temperature and $CO_2$ concentration on the rate of photosynthesis. The rate at which oxygen is produced by the pondweed can be easily measured and this corresponds to the rate of photosynthesis.

**PRACTICAL ACTIVITY GROUP 11**

**Tip:** Make sure you think about and address the risks involved in this experiment before you begin. Pond water can be an infection risk, so make sure you cover any cuts and grazes, and wash your hands well after you've finished the experiment.

— **Example** —

The apparatus below is used to measure the effect of light intensity on photosynthesis.

(Diagram labels: light source, ruler, syringe, $O_2$ bubble, water in capillary tube, clamp, small $O_2$ bubbles, Canadian pondweed, water, ruler to vary distance from plant)

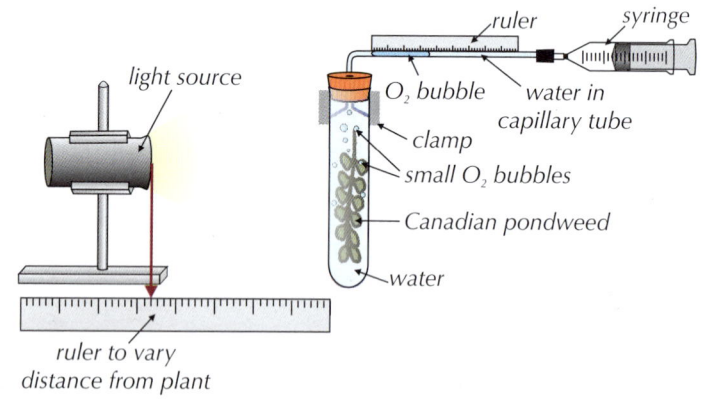

Here's how the experiment works:

1. A source of white light is placed at a specific distance from the pondweed.

408   Module 5: Section 5   Photosynthesis

2. The pondweed is left to photosynthesise for a set amount of time. As it photosynthesises, the oxygen released will collect in the capillary tube.
3. At the end of the experiment, the syringe is used to draw the gas bubble in the tube up alongside a ruler and the length of the gas bubble is measured. This is proportional to the volume of $O_2$ produced.
4. Any variables that could affect the results should be controlled, e.g. temperature, the time the weed is left to photosynthesise.
5. The experiment is repeated and the average length of gas bubble is calculated, to make the results more precise.
6. The whole experiment is then repeated with the light source placed at different distances from the pondweed.

**Tip:** To work out the exact volume of $O_2$ produced, you also need to know the radius of the capillary tube.

The apparatus used in this experiment can be adapted to measure the effect of temperature and $CO_2$ on photosynthesis, e.g. the test tube of pondweed is put into a beaker of water at a set temperature and $CO_2$ is bubbled into the test tube (then the experiment's repeated with different temperatures of water / concentrations of $CO_2$).

**Tip:** The volume of $O_2$ can also be measured by counting the number of small $O_2$ bubbles released by the pondweed, but this is less accurate.

### Practice Question — Fact Recall
Q1 Describe an experiment involving pondweed that could be used to determine the effect of light intensity on the rate of photosynthesis. (Make sure you include a brief description of the apparatus.)

### Section Summary
Make sure you know...
- That plants, animals and microorganisms need energy to power biological processes (e.g. photosynthesis, active transport, DNA replication, cell division, muscle contraction, maintenance of body temperature and protein synthesis).
- That plants are able to produce their own food, but animals can't make their own food and so rely on eating plants or other animals.
- That in photosynthesis, light energy is used to produce complex organic molecules such as glucose.
- That plants and animals release energy from the products of photosynthesis by respiration.
- That ATP is the immediate source of energy in a cell. It is used to carry out biological processes.
- That ATP consists of the base adenine, a ribose sugar and three phosphate groups.
- What a plant's compensation point is and how to work it out using a suitable graph.
- That photosynthesis takes place in the chloroplasts of plants.
- That a photosynthetic pigment is a coloured substance that absorbs light energy in photosynthesis.
- That a photosystem contains primary pigments, which are reaction centres for the light-dependent stage of photosynthesis, and accessory pigments, which surround reaction centres and transfer light energy to them to boost the energy available for electron excitement to take place.
- That photosynthesis has two stages — the light-dependent reaction (which takes place in the thylakoid membranes) and the light-independent reaction (which takes place in the stroma).

Module 5: Section 5 Photosynthesis

- That the light-dependent reaction includes non-cyclic photophosphorylation and cyclic photophosphorylation. In both processes, light energy is absorbed by the chlorophyll in photosystems and used to excite electrons. As the electrons move down the electron transport chain they lose energy, which is used to generate a proton gradient across the thylakoid membrane. The subsequent movement of protons down their concentration gradient is used to produce ATP. This method of ATP production is called chemiosmosis, which is described by the chemiosmotic theory. In non-cyclic photophosphorylation, reduced NADP is also produced.
- That the protons and electrons needed for the light-dependent reaction come from the photolysis of water — the splitting of water using light, which also produces oxygen. It happens in non-cyclic photophosphorylation.
- That in the light-independent reaction, carbon dioxide ($CO_2$) enters the Calvin cycle, where it is combined with ribulose bisphosphate (RuBP) to form two molecules of glycerate 3-phosphate (GP). These two molecules of GP are then reduced to two molecules of triose phosphate (TP) using ATP and reduced NADP from the light-dependent reaction. Five out of every six molecules of TP are used to regenerate RuBP (allowing the Calvin cycle to continue), while the remaining TP is used to produce organic substrates such as carbohydrates, lipids and amino acids.
- That a limiting factor is a variable that can slow down the rate of a reaction. The limiting factors of photosynthesis are light intensity, temperature and carbon dioxide concentration. Water stress can also play a role.
- How the limiting factors of photosynthesis affect the concentrations of GP, RuBP and TP in the Calvin cycle.
- How photosynthetic pigments can be separated using thin layer chromatography.
- That photosynthetic pigments separated by thin layer chromatography can be identified by calculating their $R_f$ values and comparing them to a database.
- That the rate of photosynthesis can be investigated by measuring the effect of changing light intensity, temperature and $CO_2$ concentration on the rate of oxygen production in pondweed.

# Exam-style Questions

**1** Plants use photosynthesis to produce glucose.

   **(a)** Photosynthesis occurs in the chloroplasts.
       **Fig. 1.1** shows the structure of a chloroplast.

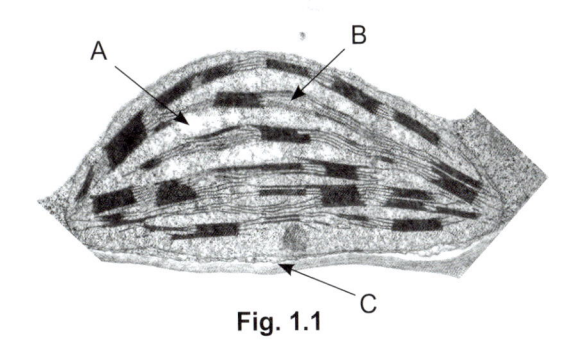

**Fig. 1.1**

     **(i)** Identify the structures labelled **A – C**.

*(3 marks)*

     **(ii)** Which of the structures **A – C** is the site of the light-independent reaction of photosynthesis?

*(1 mark)*

   **(b)** Chloroplasts contain photosynthetic pigments, which are organised into photosystems. Photosystems contain primary and accessory pigments.

       What is the purpose of each these types of photosynthetic pigment in a photosystem?

*(2 marks)*

   **(c)** Glucose is synthesised from a 3-carbon compound produced in the light-independent reaction of photosynthesis.

     **(i)*** Describe how this 3-carbon compound is produced.

*(6 marks)*

     **(ii)** Only one out of six of the 3-carbon compounds produced in the light-independent reaction is converted into glucose. Describe what happens to the other five.

*(2 marks)*

   **(d)** The glucose generated in photosynthesis is used to make ATP.
       Name the process in which glucose is used to make ATP.

*(1 mark)*

*The quality of your response will be assessed in this question.

**2** DNIP is an artificial hydrogen acceptor that can be used to measure the rate of photosynthesis. When DNIP is reduced it turns from blue to colourless. In the presence of NADP, DNIP is reduced first. A scientist used DNIP to investigate the rate of photosynthesis in plant chloroplasts under three different conditions. The results are shown below.

| Tube | Condition | Colour after 24 hours |
|---|---|---|
| A | Unboiled chloroplasts kept in the dark | blue |
| B | Unboiled chloroplasts kept in the light | colourless |
| C | Boiled chloroplasts kept in the light | blue |

(a) Explain the result for tube B.

*(3 marks)*

(b) Explain the results for tubes A and C.

*(2 marks)*

(c) Describe the role of reduced NADP in the light-independent reaction of photosynthesis.

*(2 marks)*

**3** A student carried out a study into the effect of different factors on the rate of photosynthesis in a certain species of plant. He calculated the rate of photosynthesis by measuring how much oxygen was released by the plants over a period of time.

(a) Is this an accurate way of calculating the rate of photosynthesis? Explain your answer.

*(1 mark)*

(b) The student carried out three experiments in his study — the results of which are shown in **Fig. 3.1**. In each experiment the plants had an adequate supply of water.

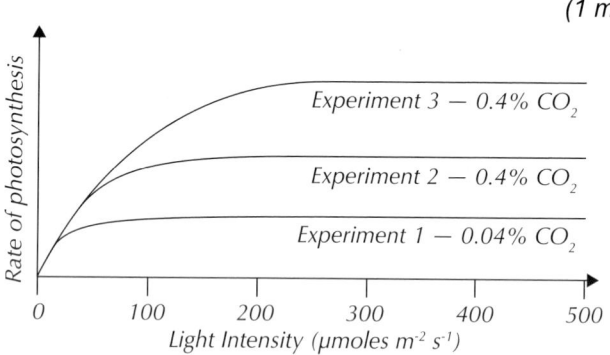

Graph showing Rate of photosynthesis vs Light Intensity ($\mu$moles $m^{-2}$ $s^{-1}$) from 0 to 500. Three curves:
- Experiment 3 — 0.4% $CO_2$ (highest plateau)
- Experiment 2 — 0.4% $CO_2$ (middle plateau)
- Experiment 1 — 0.04% $CO_2$ (lowest plateau)

**Fig. 3.1**

(i) Describe and explain the results of experiment 1.

*(3 marks)*

(ii) What is the limiting factor of photosynthesis in experiment 2? Explain your answer.

*(2 marks)*

(c) The student extended experiment 2 by measuring the amount of RuBP and TP produced by the plant over time. After 5 minutes, the student lowered the $CO_2$ concentration of the plants to 0.04%. Describe and explain what effect the lowering of $CO_2$ concentration had on the levels of RuBP and TP in the plants.

*(2 marks)*

Module 5: Section 5 Photosynthesis

# Module 5 Section 6: Respiration

## 1. Aerobic Respiration

*Respiration is the process that allows cells to produce ATP from glucose. The next few pages are about aerobic respiration — respiration using oxygen.*

### Mitochondria
Most of the reactions in respiration take place in the mitochondria. You covered the mitochondrial structure in Module 2, but you might want to refresh your memory of it before you start this page — see Figure 1.

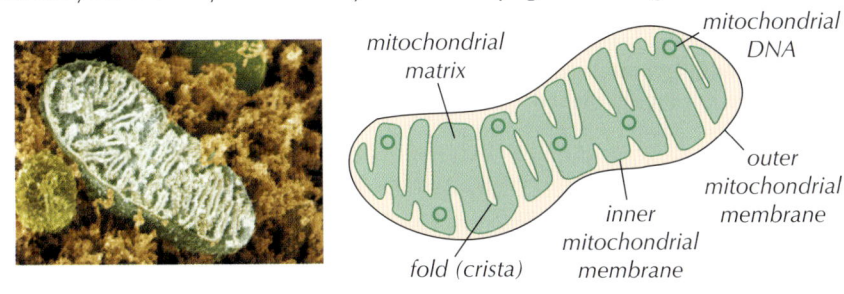

**Figure 1:** *A mitochondrion in a nerve cell (left) and mitochondrial structure (right).*

### Coenzymes
As you saw in photosynthesis, a coenzyme is a molecule that aids the function of an enzyme by transferring a chemical group from one molecule to another. Coenzymes used in respiration include **NAD**, **coenzyme A** and **FAD**. NAD and FAD transfer hydrogen from one molecule to another. This means they can reduce (give hydrogen to) or oxidise (take hydrogen from) a molecule. Coenzyme A transfers acetate between molecules (see page 415).

### Aerobic respiration
There are four stages in aerobic respiration:
1. Glycolysis.
2. The link reaction.
3. The Krebs cycle.
4. Oxidative phosphorylation.

The first three stages are a series of reactions. The products from these reactions are used in the final stage to produce loads of ATP. The first stage happens in the cytoplasm of cells and the other three stages take place in the mitochondria.
 All cells use glucose to respire, but organisms can also break down other complex organic molecules (e.g. fatty acids, amino acids), which can then be respired.

---

**Learning Objectives:**
- Know the structure and components of a mitochondrion, including the inner and outer mitochondrial membranes, cristae, matrix and mitochondrial DNA.
- Understand the importance of coenzymes in cellular respiration, with reference to NAD, FAD and coenzyme A.
- Know the process and site of glycolysis
- Know the link reaction and its site in the cell.
- Know the process and site of the Krebs cycle.
- Understand the importance of decarboxylation, dehydrogenation, the reduction of NAD and FAD, and substrate level phosphorylation in the Krebs cycle.
- Know the process and site of oxidative phosphorylation.
- Understand the chemiosmotic theory, including the electron transport chain, proton gradients and ATP synthase in oxidative phosphorylation.

**Specification Reference 5.2.2**

**Tip:** The plural of crista is cristae.

*Aerobic Respiration Map*

*Glycolysis* ← You are here

↓

*Link Reaction*

↓

*Krebs Cycle*

↓

*Oxidative Phosphorylation*

**Tip:** Remember the first part of OILRIG, (page 395) — oxidation is loss, so when triose phosphate is oxidised it loses hydrogen.

**Tip:** Reduced NAD is also called NADH.

**Tip:** Glycolysis takes place in the cytoplasm of cells because glucose can't cross the outer mitochondrial membrane. Pyruvate can cross this membrane, so the rest of the reactions in respiration occur within the mitochondria.

# Stage 1 — Glycolysis

Glycolysis makes **pyruvate** from glucose. Glycolysis involves splitting one molecule of glucose (with 6 carbons — 6C) into two smaller molecules of pyruvate (3C). The process happens in the cytoplasm of cells. Glycolysis is the first stage of both aerobic and anaerobic respiration and doesn't need oxygen to take place — so it's an anaerobic process.

There are two stages in glycolysis — phosphorylation and oxidation. First, ATP is used to phosphorylate glucose to triose phosphate. Phosphorylation is the process of adding phosphate to a molecule. Then triose phosphate is oxidised, releasing ATP. Overall there's a net gain of 2 ATP.

## 1. Phosphorylation

Glucose is phosphorylated by adding a phosphate from a molecule of ATP. This creates one molecule of hexose phosphate and a molecule of ADP. Hexose phosphate is phosphorylated by ATP to form hexose bisphosphate and another molecule of ADP. Then, hexose bisphosphate is split up into 2 molecules of triose phosphate.

glucose 6C ← number of carbons in the molecule

ATP → $P_i$ → ADP

hexose phosphate 6C

ATP → $P_i$ → ADP

hexose bisphosphate 6C

↓

2 × triose phosphate 3C

## 2. Oxidation

Triose phosphate is oxidised (loses hydrogen), forming 2 molecules of pyruvate. NAD collects the hydrogen ions, forming 2 reduced NAD. 4 ATP are produced, but 2 were used up in stage one, so there's a net gain of 2 ATP.

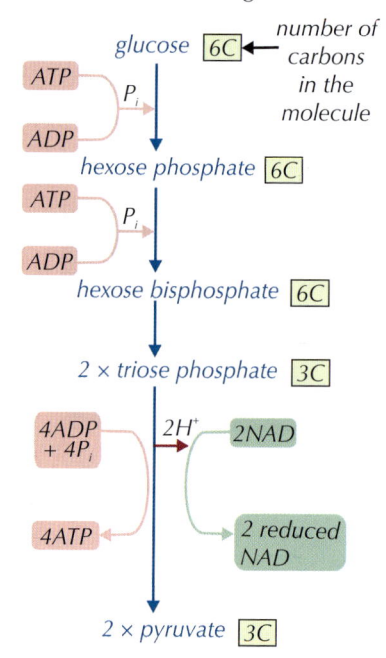

4ADP + 4$P_i$ → 2$H^+$ → 2NAD

4ATP → 2 reduced NAD

2 × pyruvate 3C

## The products of glycolysis

Here's what happens to all the products of glycolysis...

| Products from glycolysis | Where it goes |
| --- | --- |
| 2 reduced NAD | To oxidative phosphorylation |
| 2 pyruvate | To the link reaction |
| 2 ATP (net gain) | Used for energy |

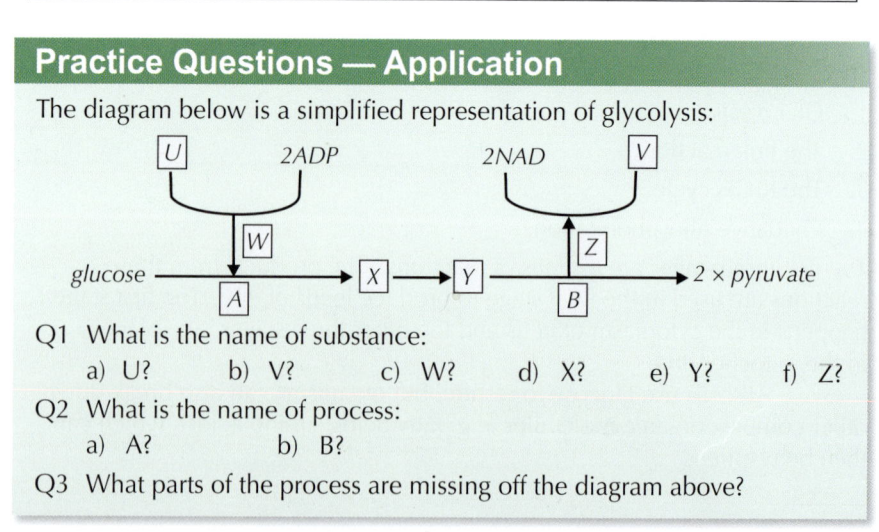

### Practice Questions — Application

The diagram below is a simplified representation of glycolysis:

glucose → [A] → W → [X] → Y → [B] → 2 × pyruvate

U, 2ADP feed into W; 2NAD, V feed around Z

**Q1** What is the name of substance:
   a) U?   b) V?   c) W?   d) X?   e) Y?   f) Z?

**Q2** What is the name of process:
   a) A?   b) B?

**Q3** What parts of the process are missing off the diagram above?

Module 5: Section 6 Respiration

## Stage 2 — The link reaction

Pyruvate is actively transported into the matrix of the mitochondria. Here, the link reaction converts pyruvate to acetyl coenzyme A. Pyruvate is **decarboxylated**, so one carbon atom is removed from pyruvate in the form of carbon dioxide. NAD is reduced to NADH — it collects hydrogen from pyruvate, changing pyruvate into acetate. Acetate is combined with coenzyme A (CoA) to form acetyl coenzyme A (acetyl CoA). No ATP is produced in this reaction.

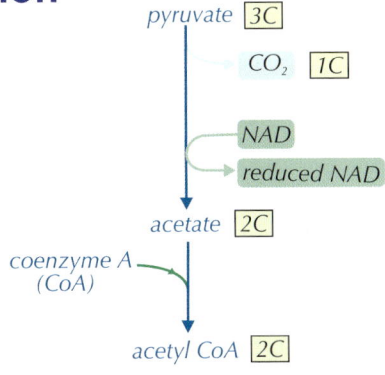

**Tip:** Decarboxylation is the removal of carbon dioxide from a molecule.

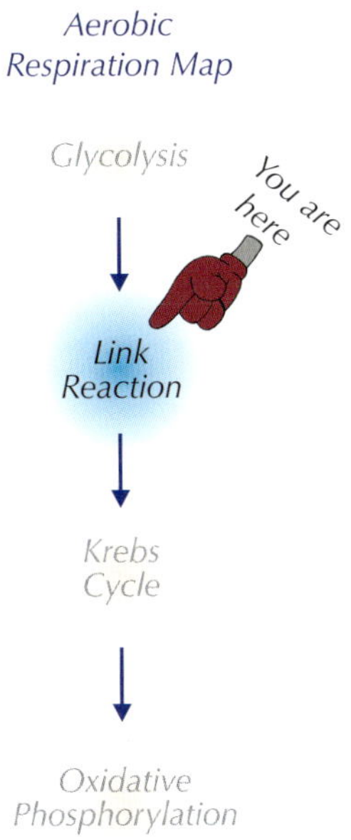

*Aerobic Respiration Map*

### The products of the link reaction

Two pyruvate molecules are made for every glucose molecule that enters glycolysis. This means the link reaction and the third stage (the Krebs cycle) happen twice for every glucose molecule.

Here's what happens to the products of two link reactions (i.e. for one glucose molecule):

| Products from two link reactions | Where it goes |
|---|---|
| 2 acetyl coenzyme A | To the Krebs cycle |
| 2 carbon dioxide | Released as a waste product |
| 2 reduced NAD | To oxidative phosphorylation |

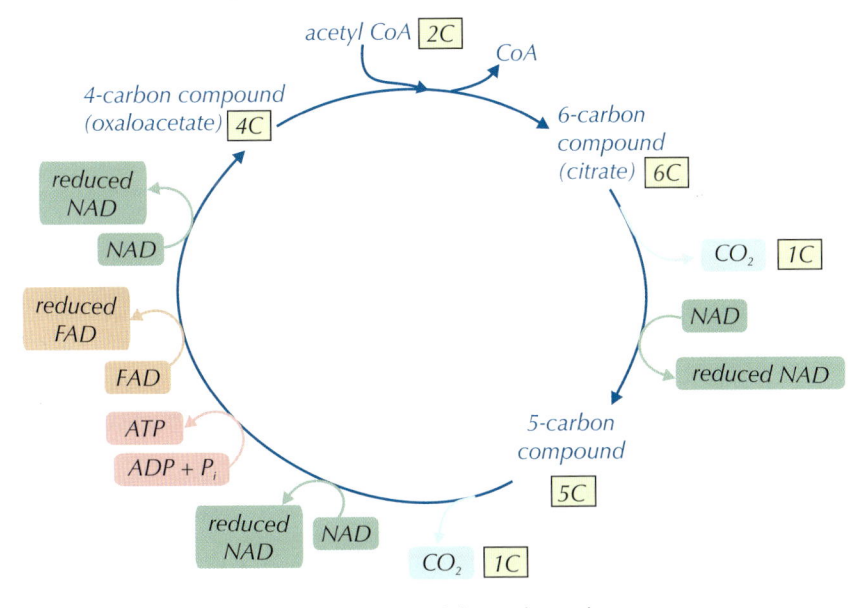

## Stage 3 — The Krebs cycle

The Krebs cycle produces reduced coenzymes and ATP. It involves a series of oxidation-reduction reactions, which take place in the matrix of the mitochondria. The cycle happens once for every pyruvate molecule, so it goes round twice for every glucose molecule.

*Aerobic Respiration Map*

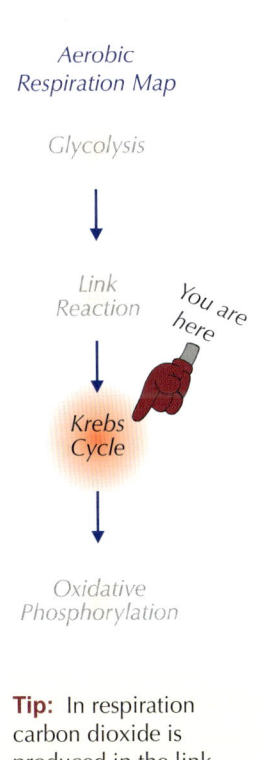

**Figure 2:** One turn of the Krebs cycle.

**Tip:** In respiration carbon dioxide is produced in the link reaction and the Krebs cycle.

Module 5: Section 6 Respiration

Here's what happens at each stage in the Krebs cycle:

### 1. Formation of citrate

The acetyl group from acetyl CoA (produced in the link reaction) combines with oxaloacetate to form citrate (citric acid). This is catalysed by citrate synthase. Coenzyme A goes back to the link reaction to be used again.

oxaloacetate (4C) + acetyl CoA (2C) → citrate (6C) (releasing CoA)

**Tip:** Coenzyme A transfers acetate between molecules (see page 413 for a reminder on coenzymes).

### 2. Formation of a 5-carbon compound

The 6C citrate molecule is converted to a 5C molecule. Decarboxylation occurs, where carbon dioxide is removed. **Dehydrogenation** also occurs. The hydrogen is used to produce reduced NAD from NAD.

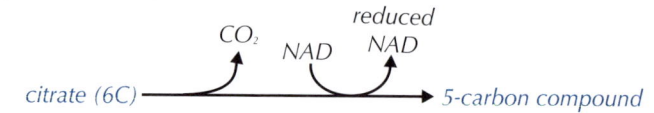

citrate (6C) → 5-carbon compound (releasing $CO_2$, using NAD, producing reduced NAD)

**Tip:** Dehydrogenation is the removal of hydrogen from a molecule.

### 3. Regeneration of oxaloacetate

The 5C molecule is then converted to a 4C molecule. (There are some intermediate compounds formed during this conversion, but you don't need to know about them.) Decarboxylation and dehydrogenation occur, producing one molecule of reduced FAD and two of reduced NAD. ATP is produced by the direct transfer of a phosphate group from an intermediate compound to ADP. When a phosphate group is directly transferred from one molecule to another it's called **substrate-level phosphorylation**. Citrate has now been converted into oxaloacetate.

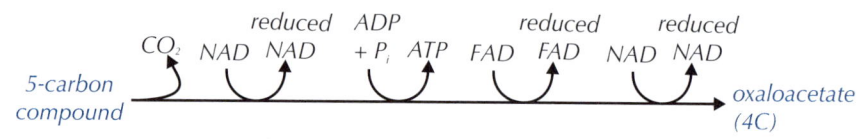

5-carbon compound → oxaloacetate (4C) (releasing $CO_2$, NAD → reduced NAD, ADP + $P_i$ → ATP, FAD → reduced FAD, NAD → reduced NAD)

**Tip:** See previous page if you can't remember what decarboxylation is.

**Tip:** Remember, reduced NAD may be written as NADH. Reduced FAD may also be written as $FADH_2$. Don't worry, they still mean the same things.

### The products of the Krebs cycle

Some products of the Krebs cycle are reused, some are released and others are used for the next stage of respiration — oxidative phosphorylation.

| Product from one Krebs cycle | Where it goes |
| --- | --- |
| 1 coenzyme A | Reused in the next link reaction |
| Oxaloacetate | Regenerated for use in the next Krebs cycle |
| 2 carbon dioxide | Released as a waste product |
| 1 ATP | Used for energy |
| 3 reduced NAD | To oxidative phosphorylation |
| 1 reduced FAD | To oxidative phosphorylation |

**Tip:** The table only shows the products of <u>one</u> turn of the Krebs cycle. The cycle turns <u>twice</u> for one glucose molecule, so one glucose molecule produces twice as much as what's shown in the table.

**Tip:** Remember that the Krebs cycle is just that... a cycle — some of its products need to be recycled for the process to continue.

## Practice Questions — Application

Q1 The diagram below shows part of the Krebs cycle:

oxaloacetate → citrate → 5C-intermediate

a) How many carbon atoms do oxaloacetate and citrate each have?

b) What happens to turn the 5C-intermediate back into oxaloacetate?

Q2 If six molecules of glucose were respired, how many molecules of $CO_2$ would be produced from the Krebs cycle?

Q3 Fats can be broken down and converted into acetyl coenzyme A. Explain how this allows fats to be respired.

# Stage 4 — Oxidative phosphorylation

Oxidative phosphorylation is the process where the energy carried by electrons, from reduced coenzymes (reduced NAD and reduced FAD), is used to make ATP. (The whole point of the previous stages is to make reduced NAD and reduced FAD for the final stage.)

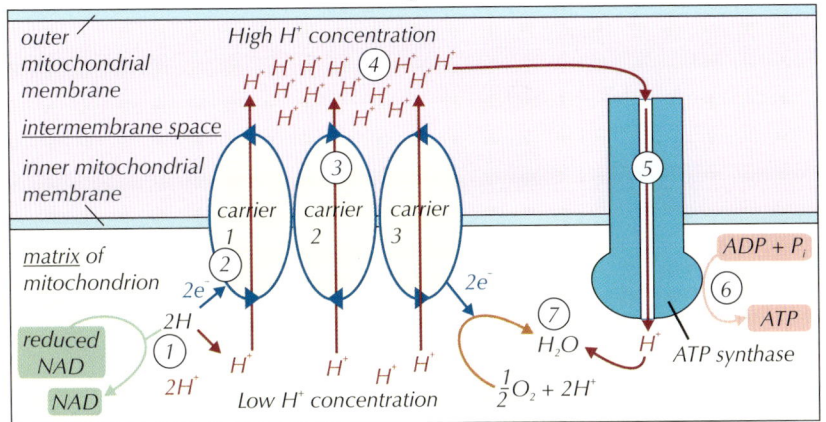

The numbers in the diagram above correspond to these steps:
1. Hydrogen atoms are released from reduced NAD and reduced FAD as they're oxidised to NAD and FAD. The hydrogen atoms split into protons ($H^+$) and electrons ($e^-$).
2. The electrons move along the **electron transport chain** (made up of three electron carriers), losing energy at each carrier (see Figure 3). The electron transport chain is located in the inner mitochondrial membrane. This membrane is folded into cristae, which increases the membrane's surface area to maximise respiration.
3. This energy is used by the electron carriers to pump protons from the mitochondrial matrix into the intermembrane space (the space between the inner and outer mitochondrial membranes).
4. The concentration of protons is now higher in the intermembrane space than in the mitochondrial matrix — this forms an electrochemical gradient (a concentration gradient of ions).
5. Protons move down the electrochemical gradient, back into the mitochondrial matrix, via ATP synthase.
6. This movement drives the synthesis of ATP from ADP and inorganic phosphate ($P_i$). This process of ATP production driven by the movement of $H^+$ ions across a membrane (due to electrons moving down an electron transport chain) is called chemiosmosis (which is described by the **chemiosmotic theory**).
7. In the mitochondrial matrix, at the end of the transport chain, the protons, electrons and oxygen (from the blood) combine to form water. Oxygen is said to be the **final electron acceptor**.

## Practice Questions — Application

Antimycin A inhibits carrier 2 in the electron transport chain of oxidative phosphorylation.

**Q1** If antimycin A was added to isolated mitochondria, what state (oxidised or reduced) would carriers 1 and 3 be in after its addition? Explain your answers.

**Q2** Suggest why antimycin A can be used as a fish poison.

*Aerobic Respiration Map*

*Glycolysis*
↓
*Link Reaction*
↓
*Krebs Cycle*     You are here
↓
*Oxidative Phosphorylation*

**Tip:** Oxidative phosphorylation takes place in the inner mitochondrial membrane.

**Tip:** The regenerated coenzymes from the electron transport chain are reused in the Krebs cycle.

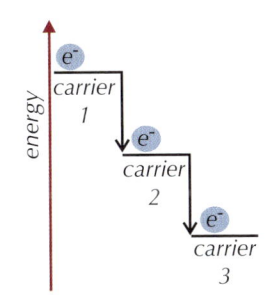

**Figure 3:** As electrons move along the electron transport chain, they lose energy.

**Tip:** The job of a carrier is to transfer electrons. When a carrier receives electrons it's reduced and when it passes on electrons it becomes oxidised again.

Module 5: Section 6 Respiration

## Stages of aerobic respiration

Glycolysis, the link reaction and the Krebs cycle are basically a series of reactions which produce ATP, reduced NAD, reduced FAD and $CO_2$. The reduced coenzymes (NAD and FAD) are then used in oxidative phosphorylation, to produce loads more ATP. The overall process is shown below:

**Tip:** Don't forget oxygen's role in respiration. It's the final electron acceptor in the electron transport chain in oxidative phosphorylation (see previous page).

**Tip:** Remember that the whole purpose of respiration is to produce ATP to fuel biological processes. That's why it's happening continuously in plant and animal cells, and microorganisms.

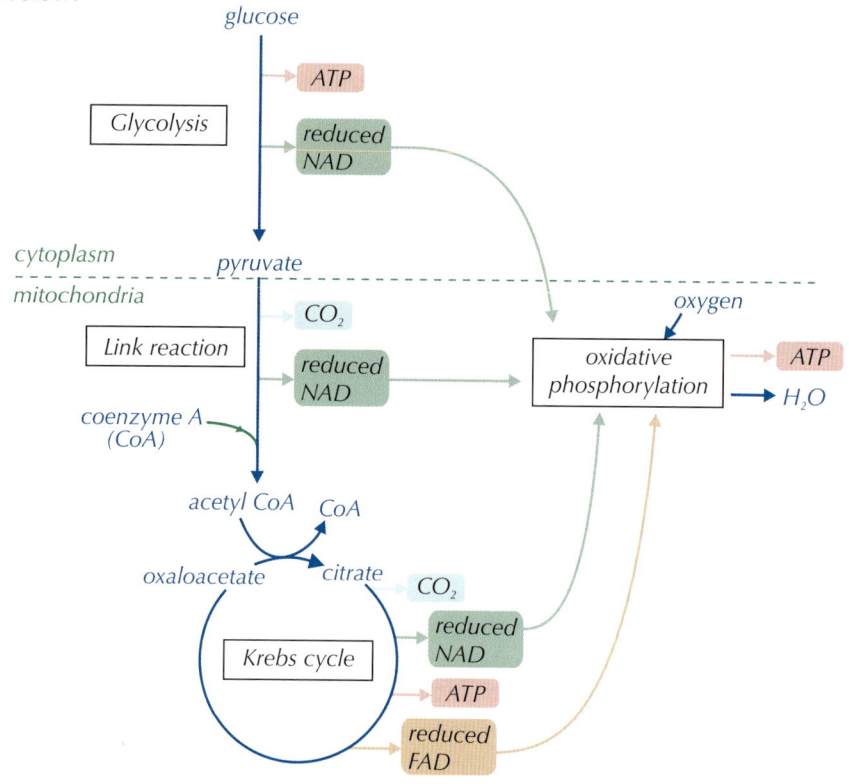

## Aerobic respiration and ATP

As you know, oxidative phosphorylation makes ATP using energy from the reduced coenzymes — 2.5 ATP are made from each reduced NAD and 1.5 ATP are made from each reduced FAD.

The table below shows that a cell can make 32 ATP from one molecule of glucose in aerobic respiration. (Remember, one molecule of glucose produces 2 pyruvate, so the link reaction and Krebs cycle happen twice.)

**Tip:** For each molecule of glucose, 28 molecules of ATP are produced by oxidative phosphorylation (i.e. that's the ATP made from reduced NAD and reduced FAD).

| Stage of respiration | Molecules produced | Number of ATP molecules |
|---|---|---|
| Glycolysis | 2 ATP | 2 |
| Glycolysis | 2 reduced NAD | 2 × 2.5 = 5 |
| Link Reaction (×2) | 2 reduced NAD | 2 × 2.5 = 5 |
| Krebs cycle (×2) | 2 ATP | 2 |
| Krebs cycle (×2) | 6 reduced NAD | 6 × 2.5 = 15 |
| Krebs cycle (×2) | 2 reduced FAD | 2 × 1.5 = 3 |
| | | Total ATP = **32** |

Module 5: Section 6 Respiration

## Practice Questions — Fact Recall

**Q1** Where in the cell does glycolysis take place?

**Q2** What is ATP used for in glycolysis?

**Q3** How is pyruvate transported into the mitochondria?

**Q4** Where in the mitochondria does the link reaction take place?

**Q5** a) In the link reaction, pyruvate is converted into acetate. Describe how this happens.

b) The second stage of the link reaction relies on coenzyme A. What is the role of coenzyme A in the link reaction?

c) State what happens to the products of the link reaction.

**Q6** During the Krebs cycle ATP is produced by the direct transfer of a phosphate group from an intermediate compound to ADP. What name is given to this process?

**Q7** After each turn of the Krebs cycle, what happens to:

a) coenzyme A?    b) oxaloacetate?

**Q8** During oxidative phosphorylation, what happens to electrons as they move down the electron transport chain?

**Q9** What is chemiosmosis?

**Q10** What is said to be the final electron acceptor in oxidative phosphorylation?

**Q11** Give one example of a decarboxylation reaction in respiration.

**Q12** Draw out the table below and fill it in with crosses to show where the following substances are made in respiration.

| Substance | Glycolysis | Link reaction | Krebs cycle | Oxidative phosphorylation |
|---|---|---|---|---|
| ATP | | | | |
| reduced NAD | | | | |
| reduced FAD | | | | |
| $CO_2$ | | | | |

**Exam Tip**
You really need to know this stuff for your exam. If you find you're struggling to answer a question go back to the relevant page and make sure you really understand what's going on.

**Learning Objectives:**

- Understand the process of anaerobic respiration in eukaryotes, including anaerobic respiration in mammals and yeast and the benefits of being able to respire anaerobically.
- Know why anaerobic respiration produces a much lower yield of ATP than aerobic respiration.

**Specification Reference 5.2.2**

**Tip:** Some bacteria carry out lactate fermentation too.

**Tip:** Remember, NAD is needed to oxidise triose phosphate to pyruvate in glycolysis — see page 414.

# 2. Anaerobic Respiration

*How cells respire aerobically is covered on pages 413-418. This page is all about how cells respire anaerobically.*

## What is anaerobic respiration?

Anaerobic respiration is a type of respiration that doesn't use oxygen. Like aerobic respiration, it starts with glycolysis. However, unlike aerobic respiration it doesn't involve the link reaction, the Krebs cycle or oxidative phosphorylation.

There are two types of anaerobic respiration — alcoholic fermentation and lactate fermentation. These two processes are similar, because they both take place in the cytoplasm, they both produce two ATP per molecule of glucose and they both start with glycolysis (which produces pyruvate). They differ in which organisms they occur in and what happens to the pyruvate (see below).

## Lactate fermentation

Lactate fermentation occurs in mammals and produces lactate. Reduced NAD (from glycolysis) transfers hydrogen to pyruvate to form lactate and NAD — see Figure 1. NAD can then be reused in glycolysis. The production of lactate regenerates NAD. Glycolysis needs NAD in order to take place. This means glycolysis can continue even when there isn't much oxygen around, so a small amount of ATP can still be produced to keep some biological processes going.

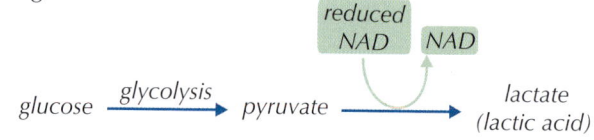

glucose →(glycolysis)→ pyruvate →(reduced NAD → NAD)→ lactate (lactic acid)

**Figure 1:** *The reactions of lactate fermentation.*

Our cells can tolerate a high level of lactate (and the coinciding low pH conditions) for short periods of time. For example, during short periods of hard exercise, when they can't get enough ATP from aerobic respiration. However, too much lactate is toxic and is removed from the cells into the bloodstream. The liver takes up lactate from the bloodstream and converts it back into glucose in a process called gluconeogenesis (see p. 322).

## Alcoholic fermentation

Alcoholic fermentation occurs in yeast cells and produces ethanol. $CO_2$ is removed from pyruvate to form ethanal. Reduced NAD (from glycolysis) transfers hydrogen to ethanal to form ethanol and NAD — see Figure 3. NAD can then be reused in glycolysis. The production of ethanol also regenerates NAD so glycolysis can continue when there isn't much oxygen around.

**Figure 2:** *Yeast cells can respire anaerobically using alcoholic fermentation.*

**Tip:** Alcoholic fermentation also occurs in plants.

glucose →(glycolysis)→ pyruvate →($CO_2$)→ ethanal →(reduced NAD → NAD)→ ethanol

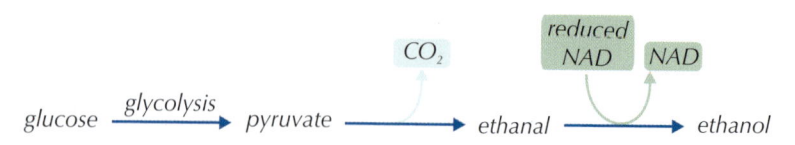

**Figure 3:** *The reactions of alcoholic fermentation.*

Module 5: Section 6  Respiration

# Anaerobic respiration and ATP

The ATP yield from anaerobic respiration is always lower than from aerobic respiration. This is because anaerobic respiration only includes one energy-releasing stage (glycolysis), which only produces 2 ATP per glucose molecule. The energy-releasing reactions of the Krebs cycle and oxidative phosphorylation need oxygen, so they can't occur during anaerobic respiration.

**Tip:** Aerobic respiration produces 32 ATP per molecule of glucose — see page 418.

## Practice Questions — Application

Q1 Kate is competing in a 100 m sprint. Towards the end of the race her body cannot supply oxygen to the muscle cells in her legs quickly enough.
   a) Will Kate's muscle cells begin respiring aerobically or anaerobically towards the end of the race?
   b) How many molecules of ATP are produced per molecule of glucose by this type of respiration?
   c) Write out the word equation for this reaction.

Q2 The diagram below shows the two fates of glucose in anaerobic conditions.

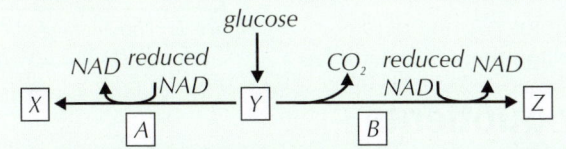

   a) What is the name of substance:
      i) X?   ii) Y?   iii) Z?
   b) Which process, A or B:
      i) is lactate fermentation?
      ii) happens in plant cells?
      iii) can happen in bacterial cells?
   c) How many molecules of ATP are made by each of these processes?

## Practice Questions — Fact Recall

Q1 Where in the cell does anaerobic respiration take place?
Q2 Give one similarity between aerobic respiration and anaerobic respiration.
Q3 In which organisms do the following occur:
   a) lactate fermentation?   b) alcoholic fermentation?
Q4 Describe what happens to pyruvate in lactate fermentation.
Q5 Describe what happens to ethanal in alcoholic fermentation.
Q6 a) If aerobic respiration produces 32 ATP per molecule of glucose, how many fewer ATP molecules does anaerobic respiration produce?
   b) Explain why anaerobic respiration gives a lower yield of ATP than aerobic respiration.

**Learning Objectives:**
- Know the difference in relative energy values of carbohydrates, lipids and proteins as respiratory substrates.
- Understand the use and interpretation of the respiratory quotient (RQ), including calculating the respiratory quotient using the formula:

$$RQ = \frac{CO_2\ produced}{O_2\ consumed}$$

**Specification Reference 5.2.2**

# 3. Respiratory Substrates

*Glucose isn't the only molecule that can be respired...*

## What is a respiratory substrate?

Any biological molecule that can be broken down in respiration to release energy is called a respiratory substrate. Cells respire glucose, but they also respire other carbohydrates, lipids and proteins — these are all respiratory substrates. Different respiratory substrates enter respiration at different points. Glucose enters right at the beginning — at the start of glycolysis. Proteins and lipids enter respiration at the Krebs cycle.

### Energy values of respiratory substrates

Different respiratory substrates release different amounts of energy when they're respired — as shown by their different energy values in Figure 1. Lipids have the highest energy value, followed by proteins, then carbohydrates. This is because most ATP is made in oxidative phosphorylation, which requires hydrogen atoms from reduced NAD and reduced FAD. This means that respiratory substrates that contain more hydrogen atoms per unit of mass cause more ATP to be produced when respired. Lipids contain the most hydrogen atoms per unit of mass, followed by proteins and then carbohydrates.

| Respiratory Substrate | Average Energy Value (kJ g⁻¹) |
|---|---|
| Carbohydrates | 15.8 |
| Lipids | 39.4 |
| Proteins | 17.0 |

*Figure 1: The average energy values of different respiratory substrates.*

## Respiratory quotients

When an organism respires a specific respiratory substrate, the respiratory quotient (RQ) can be worked out. The respiratory quotient is the volume of carbon dioxide produced when that substrate is respired, divided by the volume of oxygen consumed, in a set period of time. You calculate it using these equations:

$$RQ = \frac{\text{Volume of } CO_2 \text{ released}}{\text{Volume of } O_2 \text{ consumed}} \quad \text{or} \quad RQ = \frac{\text{Molecules of } CO_2 \text{ released}}{\text{Molecules of } O_2 \text{ consumed}}$$

**Exam Tip:** The two equations on the left mean the same thing. The volume of gas is equal to the number of molecules of that gas. In the exam you'll get the equation written in terms of volumes, but the other equation may be easier to use, as shown below.

**Exam Tip:** Make sure you know how to calculate a respiratory quotient — it could come up in the exam.

---- Example ----

You can work out the RQ for cells that only respire glucose.
First you need the basic equation for aerobic respiration:

$$C_6H_{12}O_6 + 6O_2 \rightarrow 6CO_2 + 6H_2O + \text{energy}$$

From the equation you can see that for every six molecules of oxygen consumed, six molecules of carbon dioxide are released.
So, you just need to plug these numbers into the RQ equation:

$$RQ \text{ for glucose} = \frac{\text{Molecules of } CO_2 \text{ released}}{\text{Molecules of } O_2 \text{ released}} = \frac{6}{6} = 1$$

Respiratory quotients have been worked out for the respiration of other respiratory substrates — see Figure 2. Lipids and proteins have an RQ value lower than one because more oxygen is needed to oxidise fats and lipids than to oxidise carbohydrates.

| Respiratory substrate | RQ |
|---|---|
| Lipids (triglycerides) | 0.7 |
| Proteins or amino acids | 0.9 |
| Carbohydrates | 1 |

*Figure 2: The respiratory quotients of different respiratory substrates.*

**Tip:** Oleic acid is a fatty acid. Fatty acids make up triglycerides (lipids), so you would expect oleic acid to have an RQ of about 0.7 looking at Figure 2. Like other lipids, oleic acid enters respiration at the Krebs cycle.

422  Module 5: Section 6  Respiration

## Example
Oleic acid ($C_{18}H_{34}O_2$) is a fatty acid that can be respired. The equation for aerobic respiration using oleic acid is:

$$2C_{18}H_{34}O_2 + 51O_2 \rightarrow 36CO_2 + 34H_2O + \text{energy}$$

So, the RQ for oleic acid = $\dfrac{\text{Molecules of } CO_2 \text{ released}}{\text{Molecules of } O_2 \text{ released}} = \dfrac{36}{51} = 0.71$

# Uses of the respiratory quotient

You can work out the respiratory quotient for a whole organism as well as a particular substrate. The respiratory quotient for a whole organism is an average of all the respiratory quotients for all the different molecules the organism is respiring. You can work it out by directly measuring the volume of oxygen consumed and the volume of carbon dioxide released, and then putting these figures into the equation on the previous page.

The respiratory quotient for an organism is useful because it tells you what kind of respiratory substrate an organism is respiring and what type of respiration it's using (aerobic or anaerobic).

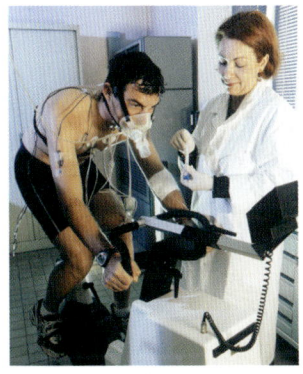

**Figure 3:** *This equipment measures $O_2$ intake and $CO_2$ output, which could be used to calculate the RQ of the man during exercise.*

**Tip:** Don't forget, carbohydrates have an RQ of 1, lipids have an RQ of about 0.7 and proteins have an RQ of around 0.9.

## Examples
- Under normal conditions the usual RQ for humans is between 0.7 and 1.0. An RQ in this range shows that some fats (lipids) are being used for respiration, as well as carbohydrates like glucose. Protein isn't normally used by the body for respiration unless there's nothing else.
- High RQs (greater than 1) mean that an organism is short of oxygen, and is having to respire anaerobically as well as aerobically.
- Plants sometimes have a low RQ. This is because the $CO_2$ released in respiration is used for photosynthesis (so it's not measured).

### Practice Questions — Application

Q1 The equation for the respiration of a mystery molecule is:
$$C_{57}H_{104}O_6 + 80O_2 \rightarrow 57CO_2 + 52H_2O$$
a) Calculate the respiratory quotient of the mystery molecule.
b) Suggest whether this molecule is a carbohydrate, a protein or a lipid. Explain your answer.

Q2 Robert consumes about 250 ml of $O_2$ per minute and releases around 180 ml of $CO_2$.
a) Calculate Robert's respiratory quotient.
b) Robert eats a bowl of pasta for lunch. After lunch, Robert's respiratory quotient increases to nearly 1. Suggest why.

**Tip:** The equation for calculating RQ is:
$$\dfrac{\text{Volume of } CO_2 \text{ released}}{\text{Volume of } O_2 \text{ consumed}}$$

**Tip:** Don't forget — you can use either the volumes of $CO_2$ and $O_2$, or the number of molecules of these gases, to work out the RQ.

### Practice Questions — Fact Recall

Q1 What is a respiratory substrate?
Q2 Explain why lipids have a higher energy value than carbohydrates or proteins.
Q3 Which have the highest RQ — lipids, proteins or carbohydrates?
Q4 Why are the respiratory quotients of organisms useful?

Module 5: Section 6 Respiration

## Learning Objectives:

- Be able to carry out practical investigations into respiration rates in yeast, under aerobic and anaerobic conditions (PAG4, PAG11).

- Be able to carry out practical investigations into the effect of factors such as temperature, substrate concentration and different respiratory substrates on the rate of respiration (PAG4, PAG10, PAG11).

**Specification Reference 5.2.2**

**Tip:** Make sure you think about and address all the risks involved in the experiments on pages 424-427 before you carry them out.

**Tip:** A buffer solution is able to resist changes in pH when small amounts of acid or alkali are added.

**Tip:** The yeast will only respire aerobically until the oxygen trapped in the tube is all used up. If you wanted to run the experiment for more time or with more yeast or glucose, you could use a conical flask that can trap more oxygen.

**Tip:** To calculate the rate of $CO_2$ production, divide the total volume of $CO_2$ produced at a particular temperature by the number of minutes the apparatus was left for.

# 4. Respiration Experiments

*These pages give you some experiments that you could use to carry out investigations into the respiration rates of organisms.*

## Investigating the respiration rates of yeast

Yeast are single-celled organisms that can be grown in culture. They can respire aerobically when plenty of oxygen is available and anaerobically when oxygen isn't available. Both aerobic and anaerobic respiration (see page 420) in yeast produce $CO_2$. So the rate of $CO_2$ production gives an indication of the yeast's respiration rate. One way to measure $CO_2$ production is by using a gas syringe to collect the $CO_2$ as shown in the methods below:

**PRACTICAL ACTIVITY GROUP 4**

**PRACTICAL ACTIVITY GROUP 11**

### Example — Aerobic Respiration

1. Put a known volume and concentration of substrate solution (e.g. glucose) in a test tube.
2. Add a known volume of buffer solution to keep the pH constant. (Choose the optimum pH for the yeast you're testing — usually 4-6.)
3. Place the test tube in a water bath set to 25 °C. This ensures that the temperature stays constant throughout the experiment. Leave it there for 10 minutes to allow the temperature of the substrate to stabilise.
4. Add a known mass of dried yeast (e.g. *Saccharomyces cerevisiae*) to the test tube and stir for two minutes.
5. After the yeast has dissolved into the solution, put a bung with a tube attached to a gas syringe in the top of the test tube. The gas syringe should be set to zero.
6. Start a stop watch as soon as the bung has been put in the test tube.
7. As the yeast respire, the $CO_2$ formed will travel up the tube and into the gas syringe, which is used to measure the volume of $CO_2$ released.
8. At regular time intervals (e.g. every minute), record the volume of $CO_2$ that is present in the gas syringe. Do this for a set amount of time (e.g. 10 minutes).
9. A control experiment should also be set up, where no yeast is present. No $CO_2$ should be formed without the yeast.
10. Repeat the experiment three times. Use your data to calculate the mean rate of $CO_2$ production.

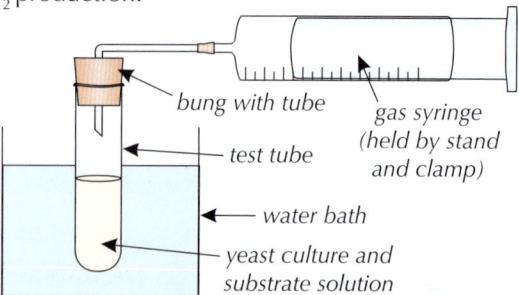

**Figure 1:** Diagram showing how apparatus can be set up to measure aerobic respiration in yeast.

## Example — Anaerobic Respiration

1. Set up the apparatus according to steps 1-4 of the experiment on the previous page.
2. After the yeast has dissolved into the substrate solution, trickle some liquid paraffin down the inside of the test tube so that it settles on and completely covers the surface of the solution. This will stop oxygen getting in, which will force the yeast to respire anaerobically.
3. Put a bung, with a tube attached to a gas syringe, in the top of the test tube. The gas syringe should be set to zero.
4. Perform steps 6-10 from the method on the previous page.

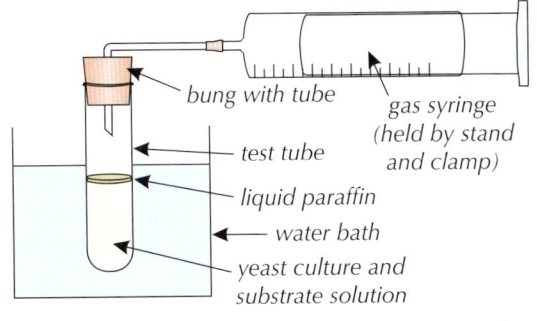

**Figure 2:** *Diagram showing how apparatus can be set up to measure anaerobic respiration in yeast.*

Labels: bung with tube; gas syringe (held by stand and clamp); test tube; liquid paraffin; water bath; yeast culture and substrate solution

**Tip:** To test that the gas produced is definitely $CO_2$, connect the yeast and substrate solution to a test tube of limewater rather than a gas syringe. The limewater will turn cloudy in the presence of $CO_2$.

**Tip:** You could look up published results about the rate of respiration in yeast and see how they compare to yours. If there are any differences, you could try and work out what caused them and how you could improve the way you carried out your own experiment.

The only difference between these experiments is the presence or absence of oxygen, so you can directly compare your results for both experiments with each other to find out how the respiration rate of yeast under aerobic and anaerobic conditions differs.

You can also easily adapt these methods to investigate the effects of variables, such as temperature, substrate concentration and the use of different respiratory substrates (e.g. sucrose), on the respiration rate. For example, to investigate the effect of different temperatures on the respiration rate, you could perform the experiment with the test tubes in water baths set at different temperatures.

### Practice Question — Application

Q1 A scientist is investigating the effect of pH on aerobic respiration in two different species of yeast. The mean rate of $CO_2$ production is indicative of the respiration rate. Her results are shown in the graph below.

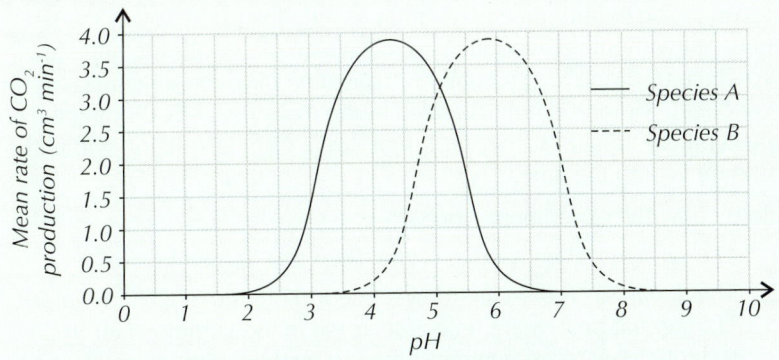

*Graph: Mean rate of $CO_2$ production ($cm^3$ $min^{-1}$) vs pH, showing Species A (solid line) peaking around pH 4–4.5 at ~3.9, and Species B (dashed line) peaking around pH 6 at ~3.5.*

a) Describe an experiment the scientist could have done to obtain the results shown in the graph.

b) The results show that each species has a different optimum pH. Suggest an explanation for this.

**Tip:** Negative controls are used to check that only the independent variable is affecting the dependent variable. Negative controls aren't expected to have any effect on the experiment.

**Tip:** Before doing this experiment, you need to think about the ethical issues involved, as well as any safety issues. You must treat the woodlice with respect and ensure that they're not harmed or distressed unnecessarily. *(HOW SCIENCE WORKS)*

**Tip:** Wear eye protection when working with potassium hydroxide and make sure that the woodlice don't come into contact with it.

**Figure 4:** A respirometer set up to measure the rate of respiration by germinating peas (left). Glass beads are being used as a control (right).

c) At pH 5.5, how much faster is the mean rate of $CO_2$ production by species B than species A? Give your answer as a percentage.

d) The scientist also carried out the same experiment using boiled yeast of each species. Explain why.

## Using a respirometer to measure oxygen consumption

PRACTICAL ACTIVITY GROUP **4**
PRACTICAL ACTIVITY GROUP **10**
PRACTICAL ACTIVITY GROUP **11**

**Respirometers** can be used to indicate the rate of aerobic respiration by measuring the amount of oxygen consumed by an organism over a period of time. The example below shows how a respirometer can be used to measure the respiration rate of woodlice. You could also use it to measure the respiration rate of other small organisms or of plant seeds.

— **Example** —

The apparatus is set up as shown below:

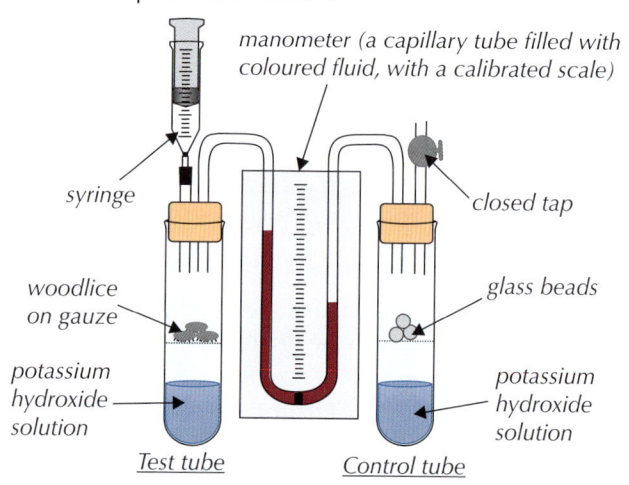

*(Diagram labels: manometer (a capillary tube filled with coloured fluid, with a calibrated scale); syringe; closed tap; woodlice on gauze; glass beads; potassium hydroxide solution; potassium hydroxide solution; Test tube; Control tube)*

**Figure 3:** Diagram showing how a respirometer can be set up to measure oxygen consumption.

Each tube contains potassium hydroxide solution, which absorbs carbon dioxide. The control tube is set up in exactly the same way as the test tube, but without the woodlice, to make sure the results are only due to the woodlice respiring (e.g. it contains beads that have the same mass as the woodlice). Coloured fluid is added to the manometer by dipping the end of the capillary tube into a beaker full of fluid. Capillary action will make the fluid move into the tube.

Here's how the experiment works:

1. The syringe is then used to set the fluid to a known level.
2. The apparatus is then left for a set period of time (e.g. 20 minutes). During that time, there'll be a decrease in the volume of air in the test tube, due to oxygen consumption by the woodlice (all the $CO_2$ produced is absorbed by the potassium hydroxide). The decrease in the volume of air will reduce the pressure in the tube and cause the coloured liquid in the manometer to move towards the test tube.

Module 5: Section 6 **Respiration**

3. The distance moved by the liquid in a given time is measured. This value can then be used to calculate the volume of oxygen taken in by the woodlice per minute. (You also need to know the diameter of the capillary tube in the manometer to do this.)
4. Any variables that could affect the results are controlled and kept the same (e.g. volume of potassium hydroxide and mass of woodlice).
5. To produce more precise results, the experiment is repeated and a mean volume of $O_2$ is calculated.

**Tip:** This experiment has some limitations. For example, it can be difficult to accurately read the meniscus of the fluid in the manometer.

**Tip:** You can use a respirometer to investigate the effect of different factors on the rate of respiration by changing the independent variable.

## Using sensors and data loggers

Respirometers can be set up with an electronic oxygen sensor to measure the oxygen concentration inside the respirometer chamber at set intervals and also with data loggers to automatically record the data measured by the sensor. Using technology like this reduces the chance of human error when it comes to recording data. The data collected by the data logger can be put into data analysis software, which can help you to analyse your data and draw conclusions from your experiment.

### Practice Questions — Fact Recall

Q1 If you were measuring anaerobic respiration in yeast, why would you add a layer of liquid paraffin to the yeast solution in the test tube before sealing the tube with a rubber bung?

Q2 Suggest a negative control experiment that could be included when measuring the rate of respiration of yeast in a test tube.

Q3 In a respirometer, what is the function of the potassium hydroxide solution?

Q4 If you were using a respirometer to measure the oxygen consumed by germinating peas with a mass of 10 g, what mass of glass beads would you have in the control tube?

### Section Summary

Make sure you know...
- The structure and components of a mitochondrion, including the inner and outer mitochondrial membranes, cristae, mitochondrial matrix and mitochondrial DNA.
- That NAD and FAD are coenzymes that transfer hydrogen between molecules during respiration and that coenzyme A is a coenzyme that transfers acetate between molecules during respiration.
- That there are four stages of aerobic respiration — glycolysis, the link reaction, the Krebs cycle and oxidative phosphorylation.
- That glycolysis happens in the cytoplasm of a cell, and that the link reaction and the Krebs cycle occur in the mitochondrial matrix.
- That in glycolysis, ATP is used to phosphorylate glucose to hexose bisphosphate. Hexose bisphosphate then splits into two molecules of triose phosphate, which are then oxidised to pyruvate. There is a net gain of two ATP and two reduced NAD, per molecule of glucose. That in the link reaction, pyruvate is converted to acetate (via decarboxylation and the reduction of NAD). Then acetate is combined with coenzyme A to form acetyl coenzyme A.

- That in the Krebs cycle, acetyl coenzyme A (a 2C molecule) combines with oxaloacetate (4C) to produced citrate (6C). Citrate is decarboxylated and dehydrogenated to produce a 5-carbon compound, which is then used to regenerate oxaloacetate. During these reactions reduced NAD, reduced FAD, ATP and $CO_2$ are produced.
- That ATP is produced in the Krebs cycle by substrate-level phosphorylation — a phosphate group is directly transferred from an intermediate molecule to ADP.
- That oxidative phosphorylation occurs in the inner mitochondrial membrane.
- That oxidative phosphorylation uses electrons from reduced NAD and reduced FAD to make ATP. Electrons travel down the electron transport chain (which is made up of three electron carriers), losing energy at each carrier. This energy is used to form a proton gradient across the inner mitochondrial membrane. The protons then move down the concentration gradient through ATP synthase, making ATP by chemiosmosis (as described by the chemiosmotic theory).
- That oxygen is the final electron acceptor in aerobic respiration.
- That there are two types of anaerobic respiration (lactate fermentation and alcoholic fermentation) and the similarities between them — they both happen in the cytoplasm, they both produce 2 ATP per glucose molecule and they both start with glycolysis.
- The differences between lactate fermentation and alcoholic fermentation — lactate fermentation occurs in mammals and produces lactate, and alcoholic fermentation occurs in yeast cells and produces ethanol.
- That anaerobic respiration allows glycolysis to continue even when there's not much oxygen around, meaning that some ATP is still produced and some biological processes can continue.
- That anaerobic respiration produces a much lower yield of ATP than aerobic respiration because it only includes one energy releasing stage (glycolysis), which only produces 2 ATP per glucose molecule.
- That a respiratory substrate is any molecule that can be broken down in respiration to release energy.
- That lipids, carbohydrates and proteins have different relative energy values as respiratory substrates.
- How to calculate respiratory quotients.
- How to use the respiratory quotient of a whole organism to determine what respiratory substrates the organism is respiring or what type of respiration it is using.
- How to carry out investigations into respiration rates in yeast under aerobic and anaerobic conditions.
- How to carry out investigations into the effects of different factors on the rate of respiration.
- How to investigate an organism's respiration rate using a respirometer.

# Exam-style Questions

1  Petite mutants are yeast cells that have mutations in genes that are important for mitochondrial function. They are called petite mutants because they grow and divide to form unusually small colonies when grown in medium with a low glucose concentration. **Fig. 1.1** below shows the structure of a mitochondrion from a normal yeast cell and **Fig. 1.2** shows a mitochondrion from a petite mutant.

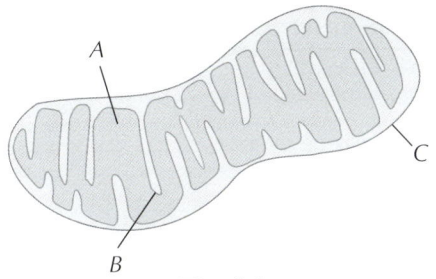

Fig. 1.1 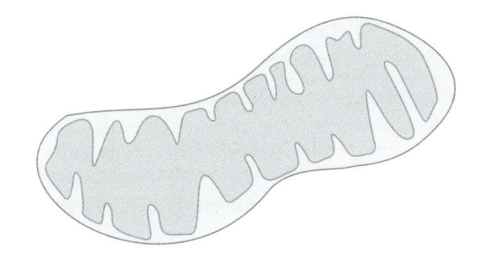            Fig. 1.2

(a) (i) Name structures **A**, **B** and **C** in Fig. 1.1.

*(3 marks)*

(ii) State how the structure of the mitochondrion in **Fig. 1.2** differs from that in **Fig. 1.1**.

*(1 mark)*

(b) (i) Petite mutants lack functioning mitochondria but they can still produce ATP by glycolysis. Explain why.

*(1 mark)*

(ii) Hexose bisphosphate is an intermediate compound in glycolysis. Describe how hexose bisphosphate is formed from a molecule of glucose.

*(3 marks)*

(iii) Describe the role of coenzyme NAD in glycolysis.

*(2 marks)*

(c) Normal yeast cells can respire a range of different respiratory substrates, including glycerol ($C_3H_8O_3$). The equation for the respiration of glycerol is:

$$2C_3H_8O_3 + 7O_2 \rightarrow 6CO_2 + 8H_2O$$

The respiratory quotient (RQ) is defined as:

$$RQ = \frac{\text{Volume of } CO_2 \text{ released}}{\text{Volume of } O_2 \text{ consumed}}$$

Calculate the respiratory quotient of glycerol.

*(2 marks)*

Module 5: Section 6 Respiration        429

**2** The link reaction is a stage of aerobic respiration.
Which row correctly describes the link reaction?

|   | Site of reaction | Fate of NAD | Decarboxylation occurs? | Product of reaction |
|---|---|---|---|---|
| A | mitochondrial matrix | NAD is oxidised | yes | pyruvate |
| B | inner mitochondrial membrane | NAD is reduced | no | pyruvate |
| C | inner mitochondrial membrane | NAD is oxidised | no | acetyl CoA |
| D | mitochondrial matrix | NAD is reduced | yes | acetyl CoA |

*(1 mark)*

**3** **Fig. 3.1** shows a simplified version of the Krebs cycle.

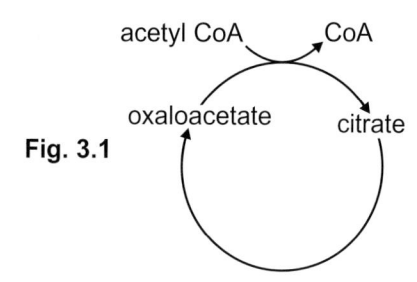

Fig. 3.1

Which row correctly shows the number of molecules of by-products produced as citrate is reconverted into oxaloacetate?

|   | $CO_2$ | reduced NAD | reduced FAD | ATP |
|---|---|---|---|---|
| A | 3 | 1 | 0 | 2 |
| B | 2 | 3 | 1 | 1 |
| C | 2 | 1 | 1 | 2 |
| D | 0 | 2 | 2 | 1 |

*(1 mark)*

**4** In oxidative phosphorylation hydrogen atoms are released from reduced NAD and reduced FAD.

**(a) (i)** Describe the reactions in respiration in which these reduced coenzymes are produced.

*(5 marks)*

**(ii)** The hydrogen atoms split up into hydrogen ions and electrons.
Describe the movement of electrons in oxidative phosphorylation.

*(3 marks)*

**(b)** DNP is an uncoupler. This means it carries $H^+$ ions from the intermembrane space back into the matrix of mitochondria during oxidative phosphorylation. Describe **and** explain the effect that DNP would have on the production of ATP in animal cells.

*(4 marks)*

# Module 6 Section 1: Cellular Control

## 1. Regulating Gene Expression

*In cells, genes are transcribed and then translated into proteins. This process is tightly controlled. When you think about it, it needs to be — the proteins that the genes code for determine all sorts, from the structure of the cell to the regulation of metabolic reactions.*

### Controlling gene expression

All the cells in an organism carry the same genes (DNA), but the structure and function of different cells varies. This is because not all the genes in a cell are expressed (transcribed and used to make a functional protein) — they are selectively switched on or off. Because cells show different gene expression, different proteins are made and these proteins modify the cell — they determine the cell structure and control cell processes (including the expression of more genes, which produce more proteins).

Gene expression (and therefore protein synthesis) can be controlled at the **transcriptional**, **post-transcriptional** and **post-translational** level. This happens via a number of different mechanisms.

### Transcriptional level control

Gene expression can be controlled at the transcriptional level by altering the rate of transcription of genes. E.g. increased transcription produces more mRNA, which can be used to make more protein. This is controlled by **transcription factors** — proteins that bind to DNA and switch genes on or off by increasing or decreasing the rate of transcription. Factors that start transcription are called **activators** and those that stop transcription are called **repressors**.

The shape of a transcription factor determines whether it can bind to DNA or not, and can sometimes be altered by the binding of some molecules, e.g. certain hormones and sugars. This means the amount of some molecules in an environment or a cell can control the synthesis of some proteins by affecting transcription factor binding.

- In eukaryotes, transcription factors bind to specific DNA sites near the start of their target genes (see Figure 1) — these are the genes they control the expression of.

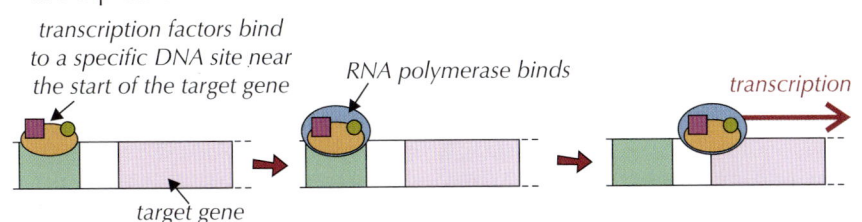

*Figure 1: Diagram to show a transcription factor activating transcription.*

- In prokaryotes control of gene expression often involves transcription factors binding to **operons** (see next page).

**Learning Objectives:**
- Be able to explain the regulatory mechanisms that control gene expression at:
  - the transcriptional level (including transcription factors in eukaryotes and the *lac* operon),
  - post-transcriptional level (including the editing of primary mRNA and the removal of introns to produce mature mRNA),
  - post-translational level (including the activation of proteins by cyclic AMP).

**Specification Reference 6.1.1**

**Tip:** You'll have covered transcription and translation in Module 2 of your course.

**Tip:** It's easy to remember what activators and repressors do — it's all in the name. Activators <u>activate</u> transcription and repressors <u>repress</u> transcription.

## Operons

An operon is a section of DNA that contains a cluster of **structural genes** that are all transcribed together, as well as **control elements** and sometimes a **regulatory gene** — see Figure 2.

The structural genes code for useful proteins, such as enzymes. The control elements include a **promoter** (a DNA sequence located before the structural genes that RNA polymerase binds to) and an **operator** (a DNA sequence that transcription factors bind to). The regulatory gene codes for an activator or a repressor.

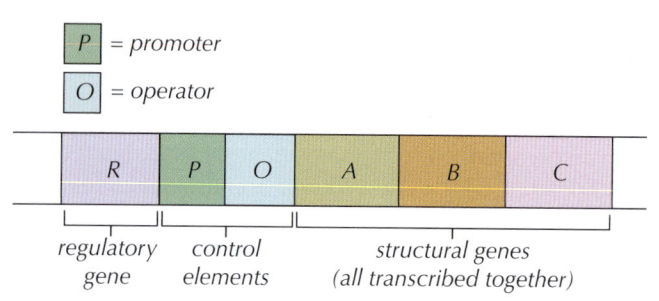

P = promoter
O = operator

| R | P | O | A | B | C |

regulatory gene | control elements | structural genes (all transcribed together)

**Figure 2:** Diagram to show the basic structure of a prokaryotic operon.

### Example — the *lac* operon in *E. coli*

**Exam Tip**
You need to learn this example for your exam.

*E. coli* is a bacterium that respires glucose, but it can use lactose if glucose isn't available. The genes that produce the enzymes needed to respire lactose are found on an operon called the *lac* operon. The *lac* operon has three structural genes — lacZ, lacY and lacA, which produce proteins that help the bacteria digest lactose (including β-**galactosidase** and **lactose permease**). Here's how it works:

**Lactose NOT present**

The regulatory gene (lacI) produces the lac repressor, which is a transcription factor that binds to the operator site when there's no lactose present. This blocks transcription because RNA polymerase can't bind to the promoter.

**Tip:** By binding to the operator, the lac repressor blocks RNA polymerase from binding to the promoter and beginning transcription.

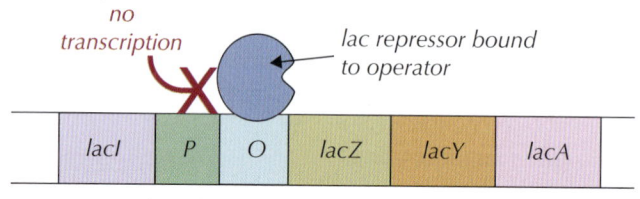

no transcription — lac repressor bound to operator

| lacI | P | O | lacZ | lacY | lacA |

lacZ, lacY and lacA aren't transcribed

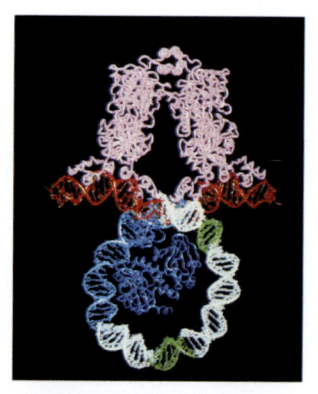

**Lactose present**

When lactose is present, it binds to the repressor, changing the repressor's shape so that it can no longer bind to the operator site. RNA polymerase can now begin transcription of the structural genes.

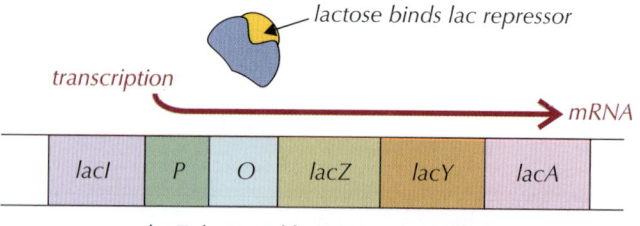

lactose binds lac repressor

transcription → mRNA

| lacI | P | O | lacZ | lacY | lacA |

lacZ, lacY and lacA are transcribed

**Figure 3:** Molecular model of the lac repressor (pink) binding to DNA.

Module 6: Section 1 Cellular Control

## Post-transcriptional level control

Control of gene expression can also take place after genes have been transcribed. After transcription, mRNA in eukaryotic cells is edited — that's because genes in eukaryotic DNA contain sections that don't code for amino acids. These sections of DNA are called **introns**. All the bits that do code for amino acids are called **exons**.

During transcription the introns and exons are both copied into mRNA. mRNA strands containing introns and exons are called **primary mRNA transcripts** (or pre-mRNA). Introns are removed from primary mRNA strands by a process called splicing — introns are removed and the exons are joined together to form **mature mRNA** strands (see Figure 4). This takes place in the nucleus. The mature mRNA then leaves the nucleus for the next stage of protein synthesis (translation).

**Tip:** In prokaryotes, mRNA is produced directly from DNA without splicing taking place. There's no need for splicing because there are no introns in prokaryotic DNA.

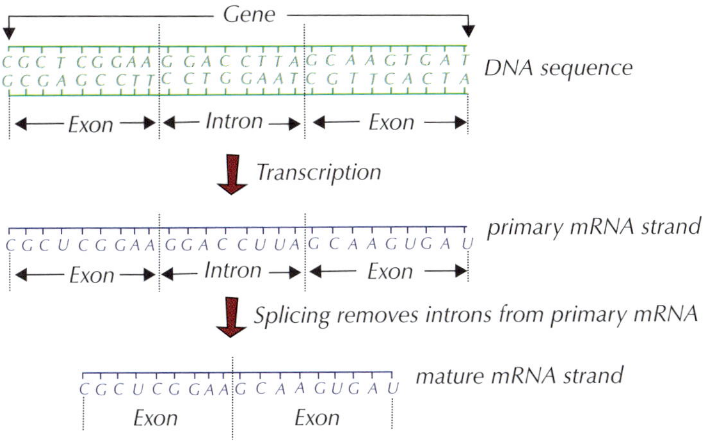

**Tip:** The primary mRNA strand shown here is complementary to the bottom strand of the DNA sequence (the DNA template strand):

CGCUC...
GCGAG...

**Figure 4:** *Primary mRNA is spliced to produce mature mRNA.*

## Post-translational level control

Some proteins aren't functional straight after they have been synthesised (i.e. after translation) — they need to be activated to work (become a functional protein). Like protein synthesis, protein activation is also controlled by molecules, e.g. hormones and sugars.

### cAMP

Some molecules that control protein activation work by binding to cell membranes and triggering the production of **cyclic AMP** (cAMP) inside the cell. cAMP then activates proteins inside the cell by altering their three-dimensional (3D) structure. For example, altering the 3D structure can change the active site of an enzyme, making it become more or less active.

**Tip:** The control molecules (e.g. hormones) bind to specific protein receptors in the cell membrane.

#### Example — activation of protein kinase A (PKA) by cAMP

PKA is an enzyme made of four subunits. When cAMP isn't bound, the four units are bound together and are inactive. When cAMP binds, it causes a change in the enzyme's 3D structure, releasing the active subunits — PKA is now active.

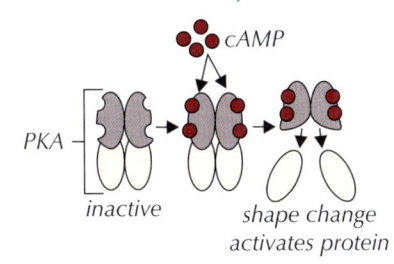

**Tip:** cAMP is a second messenger — it relays the message from the control molecule to the inside of the cell (see pages 311-312).

Module 6: Section 1 Cellular Control

## Practice Questions — Application

In the presence of lactose, normal *E. coli* produce the enzyme β-galactosidase, which is coded for by a structural gene on the *lac* operon. In the absence of lactose, β-galactosidase is not produced.

An experiment was carried out in which different *E. coli* mutants were isolated and grown in media containing either lactose or glucose. The mutants had mutations (changes in their DNA base sequence), which meant they behaved differently to normal *E. coli*.

To detect whether the bacteria produced working β-galactosidase, a chemical that turns yellow in the presence of active β-galactosidase was added to the medium. The bacteria were left for some time, after which the colour was recorded and the production of mRNA (that codes for β-galactosidase) was measured. The results are shown in the table below.

**Tip:** There's more on mutations on pages 438-440.

| Medium | Mutant | mRNA | Colour |
|---|---|---|---|
| Glucose | Normal | No | No yellow |
| Lactose | Normal | Yes | Yellow |
| Glucose | Mutant 1 | Yes | Yellow |
| Lactose | Mutant 1 | Yes | Yellow |
| Glucose | Mutant 2 | No | No yellow |
| Lactose | Mutant 2 | Yes | No yellow |

**Tip:** Remember, variables are quantities that have the potential to change. There's more about variables on p. 3.

Q1 Suggest three variables that should have been controlled in this experiment.

Q2 Explain why normal *E. coli* bacteria were included in this test.

Q3 Describe and suggest an explanation for:
 a) the Mutant 1 results,
 b) the Mutant 2 results.

Q4 A different group of scientists also carried out the experiment using the same method and *E. coli* mutants. They achieved very similar results. What does this suggest about the results of this experiment?

## Practice Questions — Fact Recall

Q1 a) What is a transcription factor?
 b) Explain what the two types of transcription factor do.
 c) Describe where transcription factors bind in eukaryotic gene expression.

Q2 Describe the function of the following parts of an operon:
 a) structural genes,
 b) control elements,
 c) a regulatory gene.

Q3 Describe how the *lac* operon controls protein production in *E. coli* when lactose is not present.

Q4 In eukaryotes, mRNA is edited before translation. What is the result of this?

Q5 Describe how molecules like hormones control protein activation.

Module 6: Section 1 Cellular Control

# 2. Body Plans

*The development of an organism follows a careful plan, controlled by proteins. Some of these proteins activate (start) or repress (stop) transcription of developmental genes. Other proteins cause unneeded cells to break down and die.*

## Body plans and Hox genes

A body plan is the general structure of an organism.

> **Example**
>
> The *Drosophila* fruit fly has various body parts (head, abdomen, etc.) that are arranged in a particular way — this is its body plan.

Proteins control the development of a body plan — they help set up the basic body plan so that everything is in the right place, e.g. legs grow where legs should grow. The proteins that control body plan development are coded for by genes called **Hox genes**.

> **Example**
>
> Two Hox gene clusters control the development of the *Drosophila* body plan — one controls the development of the head and anterior thorax (yellow in Figure 1) and the other controls the development of the posterior thorax and abdomen (red in Figure 1).

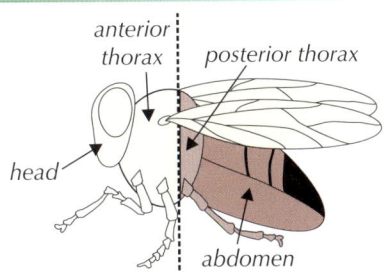

**Figure 1:** Body plan of a *Drosophila*.

Similar Hox genes are found in animals, plants and fungi, which means that body plan development is controlled in a similar way in flies, mice, humans, etc. Hox genes have regions called **homeobox sequences**, which are highly conserved — this means that these sequences have changed very little during the evolution of different organisms that possess these homeobox sequences.

### How do Hox genes control development?

**Homeobox sequences** code for a part of the protein called the **homeodomain**. The homeodomain binds to specific sites on DNA, enabling the protein to work as a transcription factor (see page 431). The proteins bind to DNA at the start of developmental genes, activating or repressing transcription and so altering the production of proteins involved in the development of the body plan (see Figure 3).

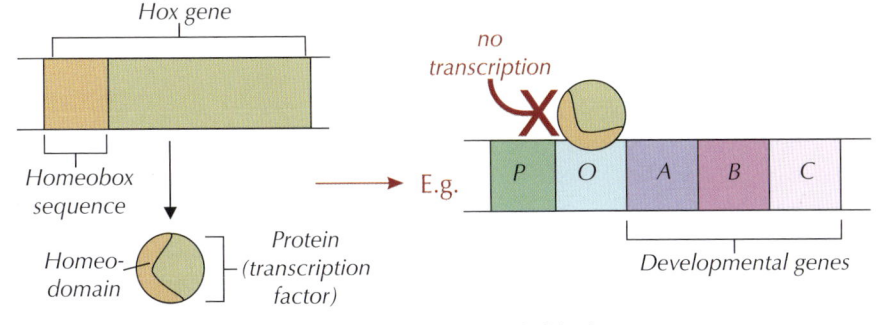

**Figure 3:** Diagram to show how a protein coded for by a Hox gene may act as a transcription factor to repress the transcription of developmental genes.

**Learning Objectives:**
- Be able to explain the genetic control of the development of body plans in different organisms.
- Know that homeobox gene sequences in plants, animals and fungi are similar and highly conserved.
- Understand the role of Hox genes in controlling body plan development.
- Understand the importance of mitosis and apoptosis as mechanisms controlling the development of body form.
- Appreciate that the genes which regulate the cell cycle and apoptosis are able to respond to internal and external cell stimuli, e.g. stress.

**Specification Reference 6.1.1**

**Tip:** *Drosophila* are 'model organisms' — scientists use them to study how genes control development, then apply their findings to other, more complex animals (like humans).

**Figure 2:** A mutation in a Hox gene has caused this *Drosophila* to grow legs in place of antennae. This shows that Hox genes are important in development.

Module 6: Section 1 Cellular Control    435

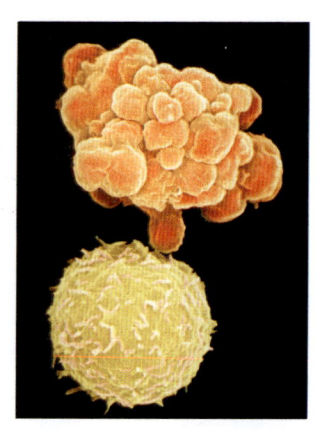

*Figure 5: A normal white blood cell (bottom) and one undergoing apoptosis (top). The cell membrane of the apoptotic cell has formed blebs (round blobs).*

## Mitosis and apoptosis

Both mitosis (part of the cell cycle where one cell divides to form two daughter cells) and apoptosis are involved in the development of body plans.

### What is apoptosis?

Some cells die and break down as a normal part of development. This is a highly controlled process called **apoptosis**, or programmed cell death. Once apoptosis has been triggered the cell is broken down in a series of steps. These steps are shown in Figure 4.

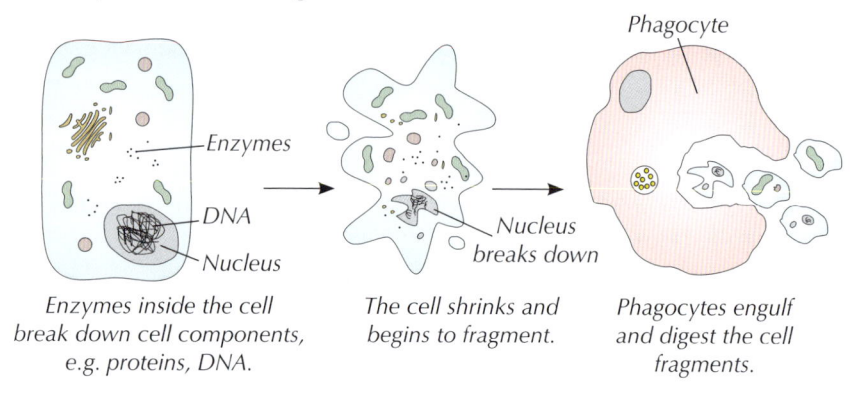

Enzymes inside the cell break down cell components, e.g. proteins, DNA.

The cell shrinks and begins to fragment.

Phagocytes engulf and digest the cell fragments.

*Figure 4: The main steps in apoptosis.*

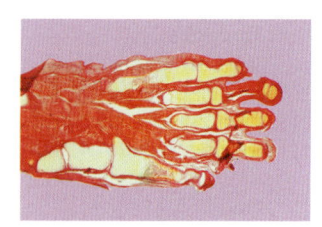

*Figure 6: Light micrograph of a developing human hand. You can still see the connecting tissue between the fingers that would eventually undergo apoptosis.*

### The roles of mitosis and apoptosis in development

Mitosis and differentiation create the bulk of the body parts and then apoptosis refines the parts by removing unwanted structures.

**Examples**
- When hands and feet first develop in humans, the digits (fingers and toes) are connected. They're only separated when cells in the connecting tissue undergo apoptosis.
- As tadpoles develop into frogs, their tail cells are removed by apoptosis.
- An excess of nerve cells are produced during the development of the nervous system. Nerve cells that aren't needed undergo apoptosis.

During development, genes that control mitosis and genes that control apoptosis are switched on and off in appropriate cells. This means that some new cells are produced whilst some cells die, and the correct body plan develops.

### Responses of genes that regulate the cell cycle and apoptosis

The genes that regulate progression through the cell cycle (e.g. cells undergoing mitosis) and apoptosis can respond to both internal and external stimuli.

**Examples**
- An internal stimulus could be DNA damage. If DNA damage is detected during the cell cycle, this can result in the expression of genes which cause the cycle to be paused and can even trigger apoptosis.
- An external stimulus, such as stress caused by a lack of nutrient availability, could result in gene expression that prevents cells from undergoing mitosis. Gene expression which leads to apoptosis being triggered can also be caused by an external stimulus such as attack by a pathogen.

*Figure 7: A developing tadpole. The tail will be lost as the cells undergo apoptosis.*

Module 6: Section 1 Cellular Control

## Practice Questions — Application

Q1 It is thought that the process of apoptosis may play a role in plant development.
   a) What is the end result of apoptosis?
   b) Suggest how apoptosis may affect plant development.

Q2 Several studies have been carried out into the development of the plant *Arabidopsis thaliana*.

   It has been found that a change to the base sequence of the ag-1 gene affects flower development in *Arabidopsis thaliana* — the change causes petals to grow in place of stamens (the long, thin structures that produce pollen).

   a) Using the information given above, explain why ag-1 is classed as a Hox gene.
   b) Ag-1 contains a homeobox sequence. Explain how a homeobox sequence helps to control an organism's development.
   c) Explain why studying *Arabidopsis thaliana* could help scientists to understand development in a wide range of organisms, not just plants.

**Tip:** *Arabidopsis thaliana* is a member of the mustard family. It's widely used as a model organism in research into plant genetics. This is due to its relatively small genome (most of which has been sequenced) and short life cycle (the time it takes to develop from a seed to a mature plant).

*Figure 8:* Arabidopsis thaliana.

## Practice Questions — Fact Recall

Q1 What is a body plan?
Q2 Name the genes that control the development of a body plan.
Q3 Explain why development of body plans is similar in animals, plants and fungi.
Q4 Outline the process of apoptosis.
Q5 Explain how mitosis is involved in the development of body plans.
Q6 State the two types of stimuli that genes regulating the cell cycle and apoptosis can respond to and give an example of each.

## Learning Objectives:

- Recall types of gene mutations and their possible effects on protein function and production, including substitution, insertion or deletion of one or more nucleotides.
- Be able to explain the possible effects of these gene mutations (i.e. beneficial, neutral or harmful).

**Specification Reference 6.1.1**

# 3. Gene Mutations

*Genes are pretty awesome. However, their base sequences can sometimes be mutated, changing the protein that gets produced.*

## What are mutations?

Any change to the base (nucleotide) sequence of DNA is called a **mutation**. The types of mutations that can occur include:

- **Substitution** — one or more bases are swapped for another base, e.g. ATGCCT becomes AT*T*CCT (G is swapped for T).
- **Deletion** — one or more bases are removed, e.g. ATGCCT becomes ATCT (GC is removed).
- **Insertion** — one or more bases are added, e.g. ATGCCT becomes ATG*A*CCT (A is added).

The order of DNA bases in a gene determines the order of amino acids in a particular protein. If a mutation occurs in a gene, the primary structure (amino acid chain) of the protein it codes for could be altered.

**Tip:** Mutations can occur spontaneously (e.g. through errors in DNA replication), but exposure to mutagenic agents (e.g. UV light, ionising radiation and certain chemicals) may increase the rate at which mutations occur.

### Example

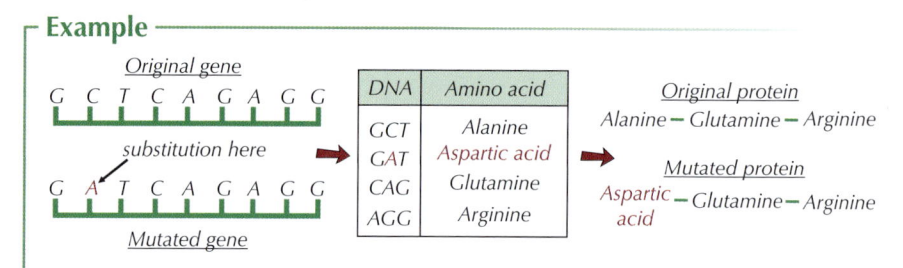

*Original gene*
G C T C A G A G G

*substitution here*

G **A** T C A G A G G

*Mutated gene*

| DNA | Amino acid |
|---|---|
| GCT | Alanine |
| GAT | Aspartic acid |
| CAG | Glutamine |
| AGG | Arginine |

*Original protein*
Alanine – Glutamine – Arginine

*Mutated protein*
Aspartic acid – Glutamine – Arginine

A change in the primary structure may change the final 3D shape of the protein so it doesn't work properly, e.g. active sites in enzymes may not form properly, meaning that substrates can't bind to them. Mutations might also result in a protein not being produced at all (see page 440).

**Tip:** For a protein with a single polypeptide chain, the final 3D shape is called the tertiary structure.

## Frameshift mutations

Some mutations can have a huge effect on the base sequence of a gene. For example, adding or deleting a base changes the number of bases present, causing a shift in all the base triplets that follow. This is called a frameshift mutation — when an insertion or deletion changes the way the rest of the base sequence is read. The earlier a frameshift mutation appears in the base sequence, the more amino acids are affected and the greater the mutation's effect on the protein.

**Tip:** If the number of bases added or removed is a multiple of three, it won't cause a frameshift mutation because the triplets that follow the mutation will still be read correctly. So a deletion of three bases might actually affect a protein less seriously than the deletion of one base.

### Examples

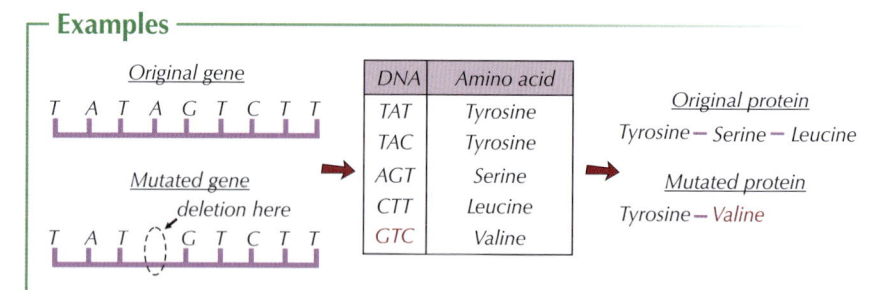

*Original gene*
T A T A G T C T T

*Mutated gene*
*deletion here*
T A T G T C T T

| DNA | Amino acid |
|---|---|
| TAT | Tyrosine |
| TAC | Tyrosine |
| AGT | Serine |
| CTT | Leucine |
| GTC | Valine |

*Original protein*
Tyrosine – Serine – Leucine

*Mutated protein*
Tyrosine – Valine

Module 6: Section 1 Cellular Control

*Original gene*
T A T A G T C T T

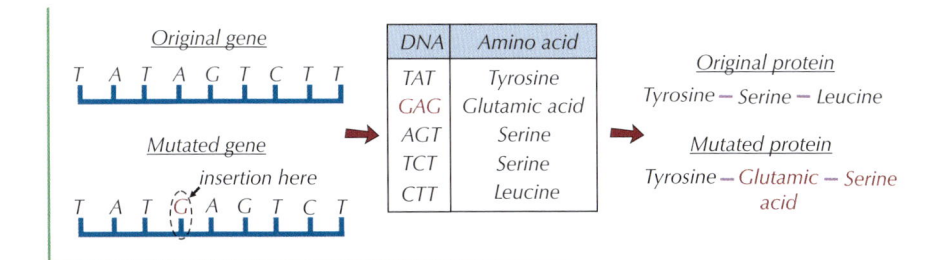

*Mutated gene*
insertion here
T A T G A G T C T

| DNA | Amino acid |
|-----|------------|
| TAT | Tyrosine |
| GAG | Glutamic acid |
| AGT | Serine |
| TCT | Serine |
| CTT | Leucine |

*Original protein*
Tyrosine — Serine — Leucine

*Mutated protein*
Tyrosine — Glutamic — Serine
acid

**Exam Tip**
You could be asked to predict how much a mutation will affect a protein's structure. Just remember that a frameshift mutation affects more amino acids than a substitution mutation, so it will have a bigger overall effect on the protein's structure.

## Mutations that don't affect an organism

Different mutations affect proteins in different ways. Some mutations can have a **neutral** effect on a protein's function. They may have a neutral effect because:

- The mutation changes a base in a triplet, but the amino acid that the triplet codes for doesn't change. This happens because some amino acids are coded for by more than one triplet.

  — Example —
  Both TAT and TAC code for tyrosine, so if TAT is changed to TAC the amino acid won't change.

- The mutation produces a triplet that codes for a different amino acid, but the amino acid is chemically similar to the original so it functions like the original amino acid.

  — Example —
  Arginine (AGG) and lysine (AAG) are coded for by similar triplets — a substitution mutation can swap the amino acids. But this mutation could have a neutral effect on a protein as the amino acids are chemically similar.

- The mutated triplet codes for an amino acid not involved with the protein's function.

  — Example —
  If the affected amino acid is located far away from an enzyme's active site, the protein will work as it normally does.

A neutral effect on protein function won't affect an organism overall.

**Tip:** A substitution mutation is more likely to have a neutral effect on a protein than a frameshift mutation because it only affects one amino acid.

## Mutations that do affect an organism

Some mutations do affect a protein's function — they can make a protein more or less active, e.g. by changing the shape of an enzyme's active site. If protein function is affected it can have a **beneficial** or **harmful** effect on the whole organism.

### Mutations with beneficial effects

These have an advantageous effect on an organism, i.e. they increase its chance of survival.

— Example —
Some bacterial enzymes break down certain antibiotics. Mutations in the genes that code for these enzymes could make them work on a wider range of antibiotics. This is beneficial to the bacteria because antibiotic resistance can help them to survive.

**Tip:** Just to confuse things, some mutations alter a protein's function, but the effect is neither harmful nor beneficial to the whole organism. This means that the mutation doesn't affect the organism's chances of survival.

Module 6: Section 1 Cellular Control

**Tip:** Natural selection is the process by which heritable characteristics in a population change over time due to selection pressures. If an individual has an allele which increases their chance of survival (which could have arisen by mutation), it's more likely to reproduce and pass on this advantageous allele to its offspring. So the frequency of this allele is likely to increase from generation to generation — see page 471.

Mutations that are beneficial to the organism are passed on to future generations by the process of natural selection.

## Mutations with harmful effects

These have a disadvantageous effect on an organism, i.e. they decrease its chance of survival.

### Examples

- Cystic fibrosis (CF) can be caused by a deletion of three bases in the gene that codes for the CFTR (cystic fibrosis transmembrane conductance regulator) protein. The mutated CFTR protein folds incorrectly, so it's broken down. This leads to excess mucus production, which affects the lungs of CF sufferers.
- Certain mutations in the BRCA1 gene can increase the risk of developing breast cancer. BRCA1 produces a protein that helps to repair breaks in DNA. But mutations in the BRCA1 gene itself can result in a very short protein that can't do its job. This may lead to uncontrolled cell division and the development of cancer.

Mutations can also affect whether or not a protein is produced. E.g. if a mutation occurs at the start of a gene, so that RNA polymerase can't bind to it and begin transcription, the protein coded for by the gene won't be made. The loss of production of a protein can have harmful effects — some genetic disorders are caused by this.

### Example

The HBB gene codes for the beta-globin protein, which is a component of haemoglobin. The genetic disorder beta thalassaemia can be caused by a mutation in the region of the HBB gene where transcription is initiated. A mutation in this region leads to little or no production of beta-globin, which leads to low levels of haemoglobin. As a result, red blood cell development is disrupted and less oxygen can be transported to the body's cells.

**Tip:** Beta thalassaemia can have some severe symptoms. These include weakness, shortness of breath, abnormal bone development and growth problems (i.e. children failing to grow at a normal rate).

## Practice Questions — Application

The table below shows some amino acids and the base triplets that code for them. The following letters represent part of the DNA base sequence of a gene:

CTTCATGATACA

Look at the four mutated base sequences below.

Mutation A: CTCCATGATACA
Mutation B: CTTCATCATACA
Mutation C: CTTATGATACA
Mutation D: CTTTATCATGATACA

| Base Triplet(s) | Amino Acid |
|---|---|
| GAT | Asp |
| CAT | His |
| ATA | Ile |
| CTT/CTC | Leu |
| ATG | Met |
| ACA | Thr |
| TAT | Tyr |

Q1 For each of the base sequences:
   a) State the type of mutation that has taken place.
   b) Give the amino acid sequence coded for by the mutated gene.
Q2 Explain which mutation is likely to have:
   a) the least serious effect on the structure of the protein produced,
   b) the most serious effect on the structure of the protein produced.

**Exam Tip**
If you're asked how a mutation affects protein structure in the exam, don't fall into the trap of only writing about how the mutation will change the base sequence. Make sure you make it clear how the altered base sequence will affect both the amino acid sequence and the protein's structure.

Module 6: Section 1 Cellular Control

## Practice Questions — Fact Recall

Q1 What is a mutation?

Q2 Give three ways in which a mutation may have a neutral effect on the protein produced by a gene.

Q3 Explain how a mutation may be beneficial to an organism.

Q4 Give one example of how a mutation can lead to a protein not being produced.

## Section Summary

Make sure you know...

- That there are regulatory mechanisms that control gene expression (and therefore protein synthesis) at three different levels: the transcriptional level, the post-transcriptional level and the post-translational level.
- That at the transcriptional level, the control of gene expression in eukaryotes involves transcription factors, and in prokaryotes (e.g. bacteria) it often involves operons (sections of DNA that contain structural genes, control elements and sometimes a regulatory gene).
- How the *lac* operon in *E. coli* controls the production of the enzymes needed to respire lactose — the genes that code for the enzymes are only switched on (transcribed) in the presence of lactose.
- That at the post-transcriptional level, gene expression is controlled by the editing of primary mRNA. Introns are removed from primary mRNA (by a process called splicing) to produce mature mRNA.
- That the post-translational control of gene expression includes some proteins being activated before they can work. An example of this is the activation of proteins by cyclic AMP (cAMP) — cAMP activates proteins by altering their 3D structure.
- That a body plan is the general structure of an organism.
- That the development of the body plan in animals, plants and fungi is controlled in a similar way, by a similar group of genes called Hox genes.
- That the homeobox sequences within Hox genes are very similar in animals, plants and fungi, and these sequences have changed very little during evolution.
- How Hox genes and the homeobox sequences they contain control the development of body plans by regulating transcription.
- That apoptosis (programmed cell death) is a highly controlled process that leads to cells being broken down in stages.
- How mitosis and apoptosis are important mechanisms involved in the development of different parts of the body — mitosis (and cell differentiation) creates the bulk of body parts and then apoptosis can refine these parts by removing unwanted structures.
- That the genes that regulate the cell cycle (including mitosis) and apoptosis are able to respond to internal cell stimuli (e.g. DNA damage) and external stimuli (e.g. stress).
- That gene mutations are changes to the base (nucleotide) sequence of DNA. These can affect protein function by altering the amino acid sequence (primary structure), and whether a protein is produced at all.
- That substitution mutations involve one base being swapped for another, insertion mutations involve one or more nucleotides being added, and deletion mutations involve one or more nucleotides being removed.
- How gene mutations can have neutral, beneficial or harmful effects on an organism.

# Exam-style Questions

**1** Which of the following statements is/are true?

**Statement 1:** The homeobox sequences found in Hox genes are highly conserved.

**Statement 2:** Mutations in Hox genes can cause developmental abnormalities.

**Statement 3:** Identical Hox genes are found in all living things.

A   1, 2 and 3
B   Only 1 and 2
C   Only 2 and 3
D   Only 1

*(1 mark)*

**2** Glucagon is a hormone involved in the regulation of the blood glucose level in humans. It controls protein activation in a cell via the secondary messenger cAMP.

(a) Glucagon is a protein.
How is the order of amino acids in glucagon determined?

*(1 mark)*

(b) Suggest how glucagon could control the activation of a protein via cAMP.

*(2 marks)*

(c) cAMP is also involved in the regulation of the *lac* operon in *E. coli*.

When the concentration of glucose is low, cAMP activates the protein CRP. CRP helps RNA polymerase bind to the promoter at the start of the operon.

Explain how this helps *E. coli* to continue respiring when the concentration of glucose is low, but lactose is present.

*(3 marks)*

**3** A mutation in the APC gene is found in the majority of colon cancers.
The mutation prevents the protein produced from carrying out its function.

(a) Mutations that result in a non-functioning APC protein are usually caused by **base deletions**.
Explain how the deletion of a single base could result in a non-functioning protein.

*(3 marks)*

(b) Explain why a single-base **substitution** in a gene may have a less serious effect on the gene's protein structure than a single-base deletion.

*(2 marks)*

(c) Mutations in the APC gene that lead to the development of colon cancer have a harmful effect on a person. Explain how other mutations may have a **neutral effect** on an organism.

*(4 marks)*

Module 6: Section 1  Cellular Control

# Module 6 Section 2: Patterns of Inheritance

## 1. Types and Causes of Variation

*You might remember learning about variation in Module 4... Here it is again, but you need to know it in a bit more detail now.*

### Continuous variation
Continuous variation is when the individuals in a population vary within a range — there are no distinct categories.

**Examples**
- Height — humans can be any height within a range (e.g. 139 cm, 175 cm, 185.9 cm, etc.), not just tall or short — see Figure 1.
- Waist circumference — humans can have any waist size within a range.
- Fur length — dogs can have any length of fur within a range.

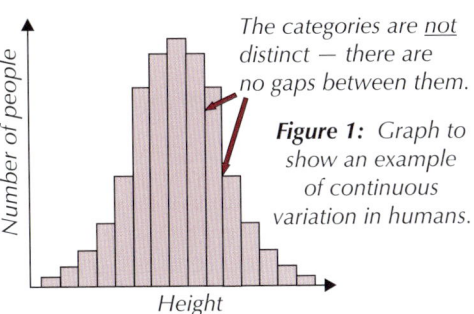

*The categories are not distinct — there are no gaps between them.*

**Figure 1:** Graph to show an example of continuous variation in humans.

Continuous variation can be shown by continuous data. Continuous data is quantitative — this means it has values that can be measured with a number.

### Discontinuous variation
Discontinuous variation is when there are two or more distinct categories — each individual falls into only one of these categories, there are no intermediates.

**Examples**
- Blood group — humans can be group A, B, AB or O (see Figure 2).
- Violet flower colour — violets can either be coloured or white.
- Tongue-rolling ability — you can either roll your tongue or you can't.

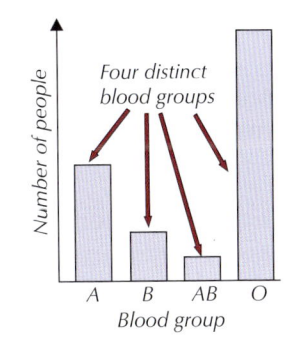

*Four distinct blood groups*

**Figure 2:** Graph to show an example of discontinuous variation in humans.

Discontinuous variation can be shown by qualitative data — this is data that doesn't contain any numbers.

### Phenotypic variation
Phenotypic variation is the variation in an organism's **phenotype** (i.e. the characteristics it displays, see page 446). Phenotypic variation is influenced by different factors — see next page.

**Learning Objectives:**
- Understand the genetic basis of continuous and discontinuous variation, including reference to the number of genes that influence each type of variation.
- Be able to explain how sexual reproduction can lead to genetic variation within a species, including meiosis and the random fusion of gametes at fertilisation.
- Understand the contribution of both environmental and genetic factors to phenotypic variation.
- Recall examples of both genetic and environmental contributions to phenotypic variation, e.g. diet in animals and etiolation or chlorosis in plants as environmental examples.

**Specification Reference 6.1.2**

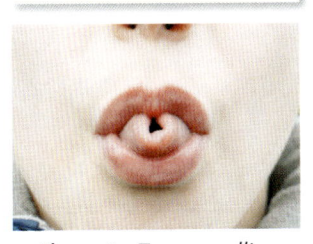

**Figure 3:** Tongue-rolling ability is an example of a characteristic that shows discontinuous variation.

**Tip:** Characteristics are sometimes described as phenotypic traits.

### 1. Genotype

Different species have different genes. Individuals of the same species have the same genes, but different **alleles** (versions of genes). The genes and alleles of an organism make up its genotype (see page 446).

Sexual reproduction leads to variation in genotypes within a species. **Meiosis** makes gametes with a unique assortment of alleles through crossing-over and the independent assortment of chromosomes. The random fusion of gametes during fertilisation also increases genetic variation in the offspring. Differences in genotype result in phenotypic variation.

> **Example**
> Human blood group — there are three different blood group alleles, which result in four different blood groups.

**Tip:** You'll have covered how meiosis leads to genetic variation back in Module 2 — have a look back at pages 151-154 if you need a reminder of how it works.

Inherited characteristics that show continuous variation are usually influenced by many genes — these characteristics are said to be **polygenic**.

> **Example**
> Human skin colour is polygenic — it comes in loads of different shades of colour.

**Tip:** 'Poly' means 'many' and 'mono' means 'one' — so 'polygenic' means 'many genes' and 'monogenic' means 'one gene'. Simple.

Inherited characteristics that show discontinuous variation are usually influenced by only one gene (or a small number of genes). Characteristics controlled by only one gene are said to be **monogenic**.

> **Example**
> Violet flower colour (either coloured or white) is controlled by only one gene.

**Tip:** Blood group is also a monogenic characteristic. It's only controlled by one gene (there just happen to be a few different alleles of that gene — see page 452 for more on this).

### 2. The environment

Phenotypic variation can also be caused by differences in the environment, e.g. climate, food, lifestyle. Characteristics controlled by environmental factors can change over an organism's life.

> **Examples**
> - Etiolation — this is when plants grow abnormally long and spindly because they're not getting enough light.
> - Chlorosis — this is when plants don't produce enough chlorophyll and turn yellow (see Figure 4). It's caused by several environmental factors, e.g. a lack of magnesium in soil.

*Figure 4:* Chlorosis of a camellia plant due to iron deficiency.

### 3. Genotype and the environment

Genotype tends to influence the characteristics an organism is born with, but environmental factors can influence how some characteristics develop. Most phenotypic variation is caused by the combination of genotype and environmental factors. Phenotypic variation influenced by both usually shows continuous variation.

> **Example 1 — Body mass in animals**
> Body mass is partly genetic but it's also strongly influenced by environmental factors, like diet. For example, if your diet doesn't contain enough of the right nutrients, your body mass is likely to be lower than that determined by your genes. Body mass varies within a range, so it's continuous variation.

## Example 2 — Height of pea plants

Pea plants come in tall and dwarf forms (discontinuous variation, see Figure 5), which is determined by genotype. However, the exact height of the tall and dwarf plants varies (continuous variation) because of environmental factors (e.g. light intensity and water availability affect how tall a plant grows).

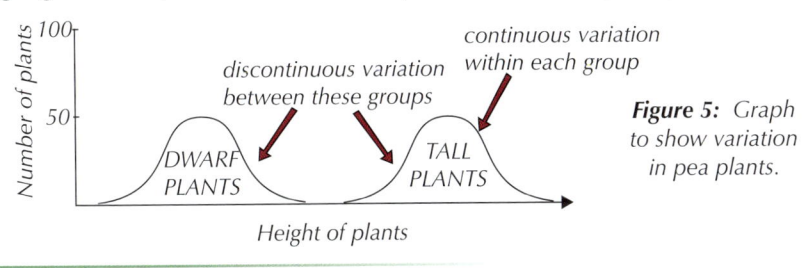

**Figure 5:** Graph to show variation in pea plants.

## Practice Questions — Application

**Q1** MAOA is an enzyme that breaks down monoamines in humans. Low levels of MAOA have been linked to mental health problems. MAOA production is controlled by a single gene, but taking anti-depressants or smoking tobacco can reduce the amount produced.

a) Is MAOA production monogenic or polygenic?

b) Patient X has mental health problems linked to low MAOA levels. Are these problems likely to be due to the patient's genotype, the environment or both? Explain your answer.

**Tip:** Monoamines are a type of chemical with one amine group ($NH_2$).

**Q2** A study was conducted into how temperature affects the percentage germination of seeds of one type of plant. Seeds of three different genotypes of the plant were each grown at three different temperatures, and the mean percentage germination was recorded. The results are shown in the graph below.

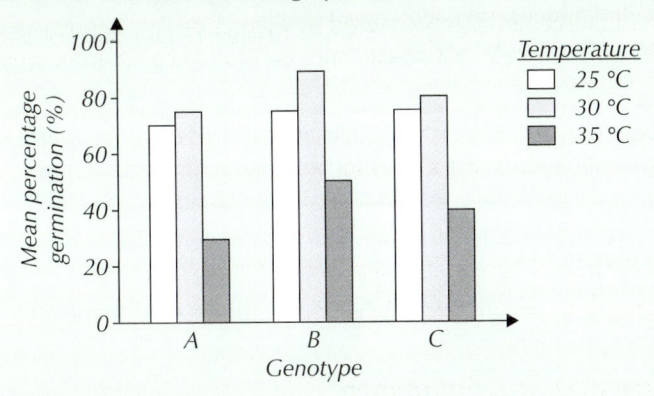

What can be concluded about the influence of genotype and environmental factors on the mean percentage germination of seeds? Give evidence from the study to support your answer.

## Practice Questions — Fact Recall

**Q1** Are traits that show continuous variation usually monogenic or polygenic?

**Q2** What is etiolation?

**Q3** What type of variation do traits that are influenced by both genotype and the environment tend to show?

Module 6: Section 2 Patterns of Inheritance

# 2. Genetic Terms

*Inheritance is all about how you got the genes you have and how likely you are to pass them on to your children. To help you understand the rest of this section, you really need to get to grips with the basic terms described below.*

## Basic terms and definitions

### Genes and alleles

**Tip:** 'Codes for' means 'contains the instructions for'.

A **gene** is a sequence of bases on a DNA molecule that codes for a protein (polypeptide) which results in a characteristic.

You can have one or more versions of the same gene. These different versions are called **alleles**. The order of bases in each allele is slightly different — that's because each allele codes for different versions of the same characteristic. Alleles are represented using letters.

**Tip:** A base is a nitrogen-containing molecule that forms part of a DNA nucleotide.

- Examples
  - There are many different alleles for eye colour. The allele for brown eyes is shown using a B, and the allele for blue eyes uses b.
  - Pea plants have a gene for seed shape. The allele for a round seed shape is shown using R, and the allele for wrinkled seed shape uses r.

Most plants and animals, including humans, have two alleles of each gene, one from each parent. That's because we inherit one copy of each chromosome of a pair from our parents. The allele of each gene is found at a fixed position, called a **locus**, on each chromosome in a pair (see Figure 1).

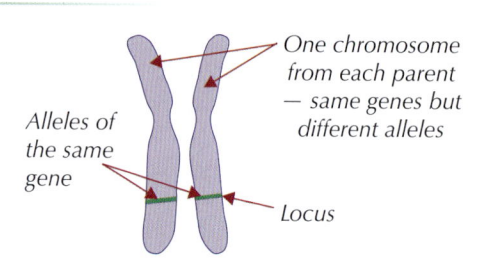

**Figure 1:** Diagram showing a locus on a pair of chromosomes.

### Genotype

The genotype of an organism is the alleles it has. This could be a list of all its alleles but usually it's just the alleles for one characteristic at a time.

- Examples
  - One person may have the genotype BB for eye colour and another person Bb.
  - One pea plant might have the genotype RR for seed shape and another pea plant rr.

### Phenotype

**Tip:** The phenotype of an organism can't always be seen. E.g. your metabolic rate (how fast your metabolic reactions are) is a phenotype but you can't see it.

The phenotype of an organism is the characteristics the alleles produce.

- Examples
  - One person may have brown eyes and another may have blue eyes.
  - One pea plant may have round seeds and another may have wrinkled seeds.

### Homozygous and heterozygous

If an organism carries two copies of the same allele it's said to be homozygous. If an organism carries two different alleles then it's heterozygous.

### Examples
- The genotypes BB and bb are homozygous and the genotype Bb is heterozygous.
- The genotypes RR and rr are homozygous and the genotype Rr is heterozygous.

**Exam Tip**
You don't need to learn these examples for the exam — they're just here to help you understand the different terms.

### Dominant and recessive alleles
An allele whose characteristic appears in the phenotype even when there's only one copy is called a dominant allele. Dominant alleles are shown by a capital letter. Recessive alleles are those whose characteristics only appear in the phenotype if two copies are present. They're shown by lower case letters.

### Examples
- The allele for brown eyes, B, is dominant, so if a person's genotype is Bb or BB they'll have brown eyes. The allele for blue eyes, b, is recessive, so a person will only have blue eyes if their genotype is bb.
- The allele for round seed shape, R, is dominant, so if a pea plant's genotype is Rr or RR it will have round seeds. The allele for wrinkled seed shape, r, is recessive, so a pea plant will only have wrinkled seeds if its genotype is rr.

### Codominant alleles
Some alleles are both expressed in the phenotype because neither one is recessive. They are said to be codominant alleles.

### Examples
- Horses can have alleles for white hair or coloured hair. Neither allele is recessive, so a horse with one copy of each allele will have a roan coat — a coat with a mixture of white hairs and coloured hairs.
- The alleles for haemoglobin are codominant because they're both expressed in the phenotype (see page 450).

*Figure 2: A horse with a roan coat.*

### Carrier
A carrier is a person carrying an allele which is not expressed in the phenotype but that can be passed on to offspring.

### Example
Cystic fibrosis is an inherited disease caused by a mutation in the CFTR gene. It's a recessive disease, so both CFTR alleles have to be mutated for someone to get the disease. If someone has one mutated CFTR allele and one normal CFTR allele, they won't have cystic fibrosis but they will be a carrier of the disease.

**Tip:** If two carriers of cystic fibrosis have a child, there's a 1 in 4 chance that the child will be born with cystic fibrosis.

### Practice Questions — Application
- Q1 In owl monkeys, the allele T codes for a tufted tail and t codes for a non-tufted tail. For each of the following genotypes, give the owl monkey's phenotype: A — Tt, B — TT, C — tt.
- Q2 The yellow colour pea seed allele is dominant to the green allele.
    - a) What would be the phenotype of a pea seed with the genotype Yy?
    - b) Give the genotype of a homozygous pea seed that's yellow.
    - c) Give the genotype of a green pea seed.

**Exam Tip**
Make sure you can answer these questions before you move on. If you don't understand these genetic terms now, you'll struggle with the rest of the section.

Module 6: Section 2 Patterns of Inheritance

**Learning Objective:**
- Be able to use genetic diagrams to show patterns of inheritance, including monogenic inheritance and codominance.

**Specification Reference 6.1.2**

**Tip:** Monogenic inheritance is sometimes called monohybrid inheritance.

*Figure 1a:* Photo of a fruit fly with normal wings.

*Figure 1b:* Photo of a fruit fly with vestigial wings.

**Tip:** The first set of offspring is called the $F_1$ generation.

**Tip:** A monogenic cross with two homozygous parents will <u>always</u> produce <u>all heterozygous</u> offspring in the $F_1$ generation.

# 3. Genetic Diagrams — Monogenic Crosses

*Genetic diagrams show how alleles could be passed on to the next generation.*

## What are genetic diagrams?

The body cells of individuals have two alleles for each gene. Gametes (sex cells) contain only one allele for each gene. When gametes from two parents fuse together, the alleles they contain form the genotype of the offspring produced.

Genetic diagrams show the possible genotypes of offspring, so they can be used to predict the genotypes and phenotypes of the offspring that would be produced if two parents are crossed (bred). You need to know how to use genetic diagrams to predict the results of various crosses, including **monogenic crosses**.

## Monogenic inheritance

Monogenic inheritance is the inheritance of a characteristic controlled by a single gene. Monogenic crosses show the likelihood of the different alleles of that gene (and so different versions of the characteristic) being inherited by offspring of particular parents. The example below shows how wing length can be inherited in fruit flies.

---

**Example**

The allele for normal wings is dominant, so it's shown by a capital letter N. Any flies that have even one N allele will have normal wings. The allele for vestigial (little) wings is recessive, so it's shown by the letter n. Only flies that have two n alleles will have vestigial wings.

The genetic diagram in Figure 2 shows a cross between one homozygous parent with normal wings (NN) and one homozygous parent with vestigial wings (nn). The normal winged parent can only produce gametes with the allele for normal wings (N). The vestigial winged parent can only produce gametes with the allele for vestigial wings (n).

Here's how to draw a genetic diagram for this cross:

**Step 1:** Make sure you're clear what the letters mean.

**Step 2:** Show the parents' genotype at the top.

**Step 3:** The middle circles show the possible gametes. Put one of each letter into a circle.

**Step 4:** The lines show all the possible ways the gametes could combine. Fill in the possible combinations in the bottom boxes.

N — normal wings allele
n — vestigial (little) wings allele

NN **x** nn — Parents' genotypes

(N) (N) (n) (n) — Gametes' alleles

Nn  Nn  Nn  Nn — Possible genotypes of $F_1$ offspring

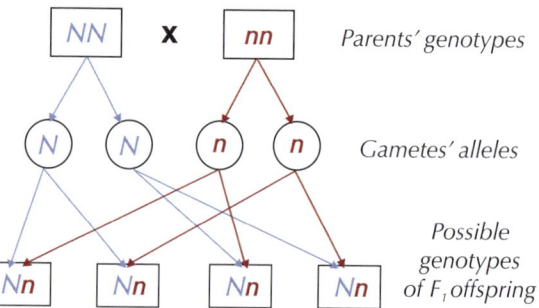

*Figure 2:* Genetic diagram showing a single generation monogenic cross between homozygous parents.

All offspring produced are heterozygous (Nn), as one allele is inherited from each parent.

Module 6: Section 2 Patterns of Inheritance

The genetic diagram in Figure 3 shows a cross between two parents from the $F_1$ generation (both heterozygous). Just follow the same steps as on the previous page, but this time the gametes produced by each $F_1$ offspring may contain the allele for either normal (N) or vestigial wings (n).

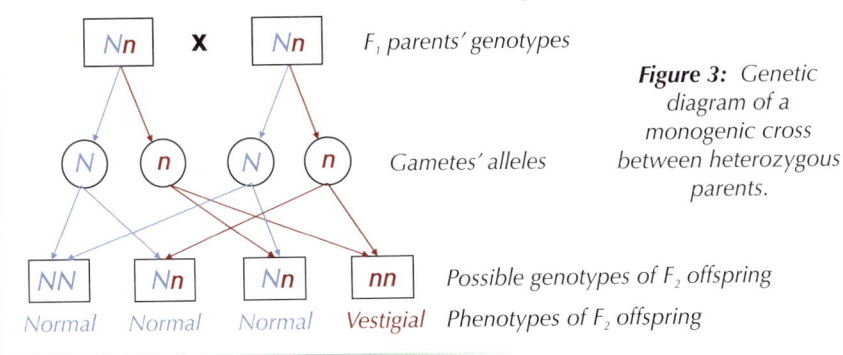

Nn × Nn — $F_1$ parents' genotypes

Gametes' alleles: N, n, N, n

Possible genotypes of $F_2$ offspring: NN, Nn, Nn, nn
Phenotypes of $F_2$ offspring: Normal, Normal, Normal, Vestigial

**Figure 3:** Genetic diagram of a monogenic cross between heterozygous parents.

**Exam Tip**
If you draw a genetic diagram in the exam and you use letters that haven't been given to you in the question, you'll need to include a key to explain what those letters mean.

**Tip:** The second set of offspring is called the $F_2$ generation.

## Phenotypic ratios
The phenotypic ratio is the ratio of different phenotypes in the offspring. Genetic diagrams allow you to predict the phenotypic ratios in $F_1$ and $F_2$ offspring.

**Example — Maths Skills**
Using the example above, there's a 75% chance the $F_2$ offspring will have the normal wings phenotype (genotype NN or Nn) and a 25% chance they'll have the vestigial wings phenotype (genotype nn). So you'd expect a 3 : 1 ratio of normal : vestigial wings in the offspring. This is the phenotypic ratio.

Usually whenever you do a monogenic cross with two heterozygous parents you get a 3 : 1 ratio of dominant : recessive characteristics. However, sometimes you won't get the expected (predicted) phenotypic ratio. This can be because of linkage (see pages 455-458) epistasis (see pages 460-462).

**Tip:** The 3 : 1 ratio is only an expected ratio. In practice, the phenotypic ratio in the offspring will probably be slightly different to this anyway, just by chance.

# Punnett squares
A Punnett square is just another way of showing a genetic diagram. The Punnett squares below show the same crosses from p. 448 and above.

**Example**

**Step 1:** Work out the alleles the gametes would have.

Parents' genotypes: NN, nn
Gametes' alleles: N, N, n, n

| Gametes' alleles | N | N |
|---|---|---|
| n | Nn | Nn |
| n | Nn | Nn |

Possible genotypes of $F_1$ offspring

**Step 2:** Cross the parents' gametes to show the possible genotypes of the $F_1$ generation — all heterozygous, Nn.

| Gametes' alleles | N | n |
|---|---|---|
| N | NN | Nn |
| n | Nn | nn |

Possible genotypes of $F_2$ offspring

Normal : vestigial
3 : 1
Ratio of phenotypes in $F_2$ offspring

**Step 3:** Cross the gametes of the $F_1$ generation to show the possible genotypes of the $F_2$ generation. The Punnett square shows a 75% chance that offspring will have normal wings and a 25% chance that they'll have vestigial wings, i.e. a 3 : 1 ratio.

**Exam Tip**
It's up to you whether you draw a diagram or a Punnett square in the exam, whichever you find easier. The steps are the same, so just take your time and go through it carefully.

Module 6: Section 2 Patterns of Inheritance

# Monogenic inheritance of codominant alleles

Occasionally, alleles show codominance — both alleles are expressed in the phenotype, and neither one is recessive. One example in humans is the allele for sickle-cell anaemia, a genetic disorder caused by a mutation in the haemoglobin gene. It causes red blood cells to be sickle (crescent) shaped.

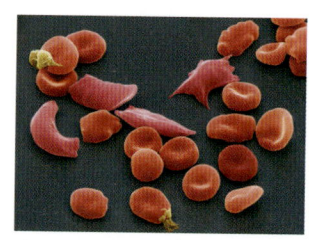

*Figure 4: A coloured scanning electron micrograph (SEM) of normal red blood cells (red) and sickle-shaped cells (pink).*

### Example

People who are homozygous for normal haemoglobin ($H^N H^N$) don't have the disease. People who are homozygous for sickle haemoglobin ($H^S H^S$) have sickle-cell anaemia — all their blood cells are sickle shaped. People who are heterozygous ($H^N H^S$) have an in-between phenotype, called the sickle-cell trait — they have some normal haemoglobin and some sickle haemoglobin. The two alleles are codominant because they're both expressed in the phenotype.

The genetic diagram in Figure 5 shows the possible offspring from crossing two parents with sickle-cell trait (heterozygous).

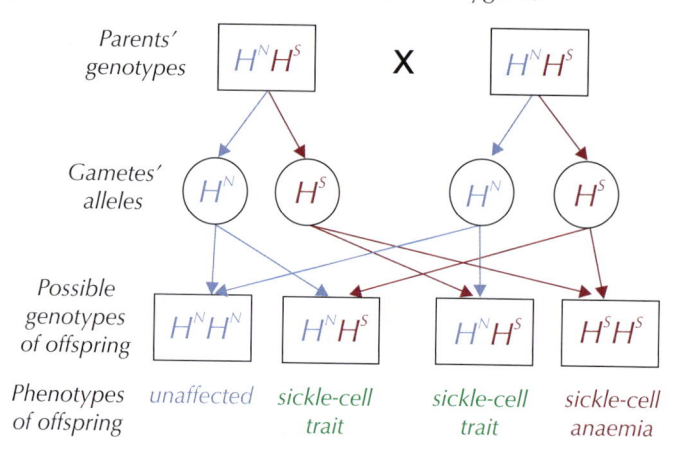

*Figure 5: Genetic diagram showing a monogenic cross of codominant alleles.*

This cross has produced a 1 : 2 : 1 phenotypic ratio of unaffected : sickle-cell trait : sickle-cell anaemia, or unaffected homozygous : heterozygous : disorder homozygous.

**Tip:** When alleles show codominance they're represented in a slightly different way to normal — you show the main gene as a normal capital letter (H) and then the alleles as superscript capitals ($H^S$ or $H^N$), because neither is recessive.

**Tip:** A codominant cross where one parent is homozygous for one allele and the other parent homozygous for the other allele will produce all heterozygous offspring in the $F_1$ generation. E.g. for the sickle-cell trait:

|  | $H^N$ | $H^N$ |
|---|---|---|
| $H^S$ | $H^N H^S$ | $H^N H^S$ |
| $H^S$ | $H^N H^S$ | $H^N H^S$ |

Usually, whenever you do a monogenic cross involving codominant alleles with two heterozygous parents, you get a 1 : 2 : 1 phenotypic ratio of homozygous for one allele : heterozygous : homozygous for the other allele.

### Practice Questions — Application

**Q1** The allele for tall pea plants is dominant over the allele for dwarf pea plants. Give the possible genotype(s) of offspring produced if a homozygous tall pea plant is crossed with a homozygous dwarf pea plant. Show your working.

**Q2** In dogs, the allele for curly hair (H) is dominant over the allele for smooth hair (h). A cross between two dogs that are heterozygous for curly hair results in eight puppies. How many of those puppies would you expect to have curly hair? Show your working.

**Tip:** In these questions, where you're not given letters to use for a genetic diagram, just choose sensible ones yourself, e.g. T for tall dominant allele and t for dwarf recessive allele.

450 | Module 6: Section 2 Patterns of Inheritance

Q3  A couple decide to have a child. One of the couple has sickle-cell anaemia (genotype $H^SH^S$) and the other is homozygous normal for the sickle-cell gene (genotype $H^NH^N$).
  a) Draw a genetic diagram to show that the child will be a carrier of the sickle-cell allele ($H^NH^S$).
  b) The child grows up and has children with an individual with the sickle-cell trait. What is the probability that any of these children will have sickle-cell anaemia? Show your working.

Q4  Polydactyly is a genetic disorder where a baby is born with extra fingers or toes. The disorder is caused by a dominant allele. What is the probability of a baby being born with the condition if a person heterozygous for the disorder and a person without the disorder have a child? Show your working.

Q5  In one organism, the alleles for skin colour show codominance. Any organisms that are homozygous with blue alleles are blue in colour. Organisms that are homozygous with yellow alleles are yellow in colour. Heterozygous organisms are yellow and blue striped. What colour ratio of organisms would be produced if a heterozygous parent was crossed with a homozygous blue parent? Show your working.

**Exam Tip**
If you're asked to find the probability of something, you can write it as a fraction (e.g. ¾), a decimal (e.g. 0.75) or a percentage (e.g. 75%).

**Tip:** Make sure you really know your definitions, especially homozygous, heterozygous, genotype and phenotype (see pages 446-447).

## Practice Questions — Fact Recall

Q1  What is monogenic inheritance?
Q2  Define the term 'phenotypic ratio'.
Q3  What are codominant alleles?
Q4  Predict the phenotypic ratio for:
  a) a monogenic cross <u>not</u> involving codominant alleles with two heterozygous parents,
  b) a monogenic cross involving codominant alleles with two heterozygous parents.

Module 6: Section 2  Patterns of Inheritance

**Learning Objective:**
- Be able to use genetic diagrams to show patterns of inheritance, including multiple alleles, and dihybrid inheritance.

**Specification Reference 6.1.2**

# 4. Genetic Diagrams — Multiple Allele and Dihybrid Crosses

*Multiple allele crosses aren't much different to the monogenic crosses you've already come across. They still only involve one gene, it's just the gene can have more than two alleles. If you want to, you can also use genetic diagrams to look at the inheritance of two genes simultaneously — this is called a dihybrid cross.*

## Multiple allele crosses

Inheritance is more complicated when there are more than two alleles of the same gene (multiple alleles).

--- Example ---

In the ABO blood group system in humans there are three alleles for blood type:
- $I^O$ is the allele for blood group O.
- $I^A$ is the allele for blood group A.
- $I^B$ is the allele for blood group B.

Allele $I^O$ is recessive. Alleles $I^A$ and $I^B$ are codominant — people with genotype $I^A I^B$ will have blood group AB.

Figure 1 shows a cross between a heterozygous person with blood group A and a heterozygous person with blood group B.

**Tip:** Recessive blood groups are normally really rare, but it just so happens that loads of people in Britain are descended from people who were $I^O I^O$, so O's really common.

Parents' genotypes: $I^A I^O$ × $I^B I^O$ (Heterozygous Blood group A × Heterozygous Blood group B)

Gametes' alleles: $I^A$, $I^O$, $I^B$, $I^O$

Possible genotypes of offspring: $I^A I^B$, $I^A I^O$, $I^B I^O$, $I^O I^O$

Phenotypes of offspring: Group AB, Group A, Group B, Group O

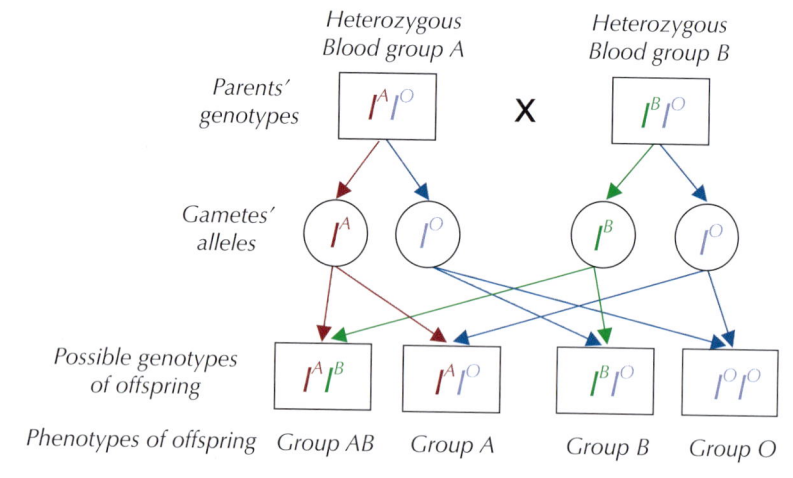

**Figure 1:** *Genetic diagram showing the inheritance of blood group.*

Any offspring could have one of four different blood groups (A, B, O or AB). So the expected phenotypic ratio is 1 : 1 : 1 : 1.

## Dihybrid crosses

**Tip:** Monogenic crosses (see p. 448) look at the inheritance of one characteristic only.

Dihybrid inheritance is the inheritance of two characteristics, which are controlled by different genes. Each of the two genes will have different alleles. **Dihybrid crosses** can be used to show the likelihood of offspring inheriting certain combinations of the two characteristics from particular parents. The example on the next page is a dihybrid cross showing how seed shape and colour are inherited in pea plants.

Module 6: Section 2 Patterns of Inheritance

## Example

As you saw on page 446, the gene for seed shape has two alleles. The allele for round seeds (R) is dominant and the allele for wrinkled seeds (r) is recessive. The seed colour gene also has two alleles. The allele for a yellow seed (Y) is dominant and the allele for a green seed (y) is recessive.

The genetic diagram in Figure 3 shows a cross between two heterozygous parents — both have round and yellow seeds (RrYy).

Here's how to draw a genetic diagram for this cross:

**Step 1:** Make sure you're clear what the letters mean.

> R — round seeds      Y — yellow seeds
> r — wrinkled seeds   y — green seeds

*Figure 2: Pea seeds can be wrinkled or round.*

**Tip:** See page 447 for a reminder of what dominant and recessive alleles are.

**Step 2:** Work out the alleles the gametes would have.

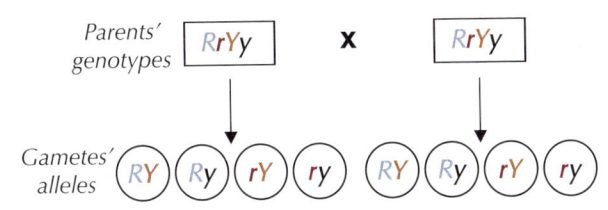

Parents' genotypes: RrYy × RrYy

Gametes' alleles: RY, Ry, rY, ry    RY, Ry, rY, ry

**Tip:** You could never get a gamete that contained both the alleles for a particular gene (e.g. Rr or Yy) because the homologous chromosomes that contain these alleles are separated during meiosis.

**Step 3:** Cross the parents' gametes to show the possible offspring.

|      | RY   | Ry   | rY   | ry   |
|------|------|------|------|------|
| RY   | RRYY | RRYy | RrYY | RrYy |
| Ry   | RRYy | RRyy | RrYy | Rryy |
| rY   | RrYY | RrYy | rrYY | rrYy |
| ry   | RrYy | Rryy | rrYy | rryy |

Round and yellow seeds
= RRYY, RrYY, RrYy, RRYy = 9

Round and green seeds
= RRyy, Rryy = 3

Wrinkled and yellow seeds
= rrYY, rrYy = 3

Wrinkled and green seeds
= rryy = 1

Phenotypic ratio: 9 : 3 : 3 : 1

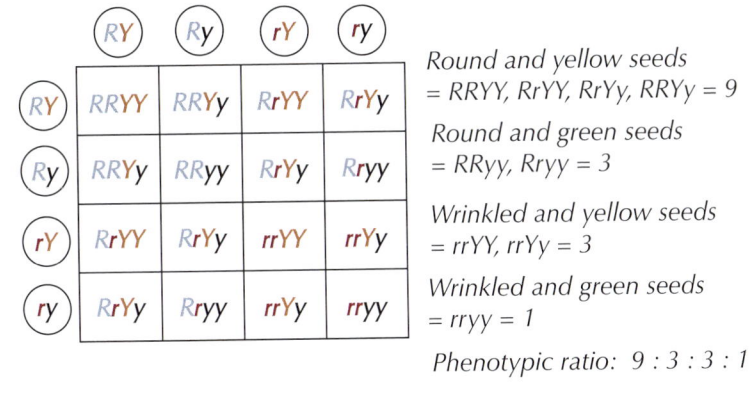

*Figure 3: Genetic diagram showing a dihybrid cross between two heterozygous parents.*

Usually, whenever you do a dihybrid cross with two heterozygous parents you get a 9 : 3 : 3 : 1 phenotypic ratio of dominant both : dominant first, recessive second : recessive first, dominant second : recessive both.

**Tip:** A dihybrid cross between a homozygous dominant parent and a homozygous recessive parent (e.g. RRYY × rryy) will produce all heterozygous offspring in the $F_1$ generation.

Module 6: Section 2 **Patterns of Inheritance**

## Practice Questions — Application

**Tip:** Q1 involves a monogenic cross with multiple alleles.

**Q1** The striping pattern of cats can be determined by three alleles — Ta for Abyssinian, T for the mackerel phenotype and tb for blotched. Abyssinian is dominant to both of the other alleles, mackerel is dominant to blotched only and blotched is recessive to all. (So the dominance of the alleles is Ta > T > tb.)
What are the possible striping patterns of offspring if a TaT cat and a tbtb cat breed together?

**Q2** The colour of one species of moth is controlled by three alleles — pale typical (m), darkly mottled insularia (M') and nearly black melanic (M). The table below shows all possible genotype combinations and their phenotypic outcomes.

| Genotype | Phenotype |
|---|---|
| mm | Typical |
| MM | Melanic |
| M'M' | Insularia |
| mM | Melanic |
| mM' | Insularia |
| MM' | Melanic |

a) Describe the dominance of the different alleles.

b) A homozygous melanic and a typical pale moth breed. Show all the possible results of this cross.

**Q3** In tomato plants, the allele for round fruit (F) is dominant to the allele for pear-shaped fruit (f). The allele for red fruit colour (R) is dominant to the allele for yellow fruit colour (r).

a) Two tomato plants, heterozygous for fruit shape and colour, are crossed. Draw a Punnett square for this cross.

b) What is the expected ratio of round, red tomatoes to pear-shaped, yellow tomatoes?

**Q4** In cattle, the alleles for black colouring (B) and polled (no horns) (P) are dominant and the alleles for red colouring (b) and horns (p) are recessive.

a) A black bull with no horns (BBPP) is crossed with a red cow with horns. What would the phenotypic ratio of the $F_1$ generation be?

b) Use a genetic diagram to show the expected phenotypic ratio in the offspring of a cross between two heterozygous black cattle with no horns.

## Practice Questions — Fact Recall

**Q1** How many genes are involved in a multiple allele cross?
**Q2** What is dihybrid inheritance?
**Q3** Predict the phenotypic ratio of the offspring for a dihybrid cross <u>not</u> involving codominant alleles with two heterozygous parents.

# 5. Linkage

*There are two types of gene linkage, and they can both affect the phenotypic ratios of monogenic and dihybrid crosses. You can use this variation from the expected ratios to identify that genes are linked.*

## Inheritance of sex-linked characteristics

The genetic information for biological sex is carried on two sex chromosomes. In mammals, females have two X chromosomes (XX) and males have one X chromosome and one Y chromosome (XY).

Figure 1 is a genetic diagram that shows how sex is inherited. From this you can see that the probability of having male offspring is 50% and the probability of having female offspring is 50%.

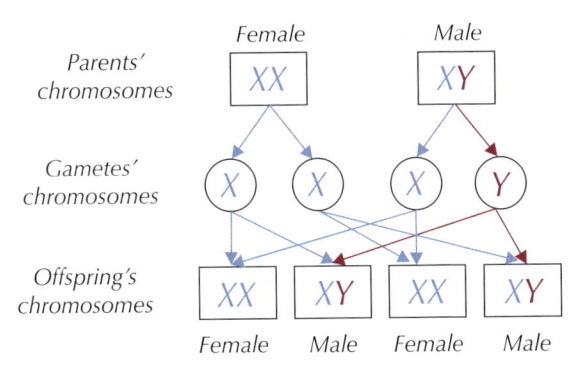

**Figure 1:** *Genetic diagram showing the inheritance of sex.*

Some characteristics are **sex-linked**. That means the alleles that code for them are located on a sex chromosome. The Y chromosome is smaller than the X chromosome and carries fewer genes. So most genes on the sex chromosomes are only carried on the X chromosome (called X-linked genes).

As males only have one X chromosome they often only have one allele for sex-linked genes. So because they only have one copy they express the characteristic of this allele even if it's recessive. This makes males more likely than females to show recessive phenotypes for genes that are sex-linked.

Genetic disorders caused by faulty alleles located on sex chromosomes include colour blindness and haemophilia. The faulty alleles for both of these disorders are carried on the X chromosome and so are called X-linked disorders. Y-linked disorders do exist but are less common.

---
**Example**

Figure 2 on the next page shows a genetic diagram for colour blindness. Colour blindness is a sex-linked disorder caused by a faulty allele carried on the X chromosome. As it's sex-linked both the chromosome and the allele are represented in the genetic diagram, e.g. $X^n$, where X represents the X chromosome and n the faulty allele for colour vision. The Y chromosome doesn't have an allele for colour vision so is just represented by Y.

Females would need two copies of the recessive allele to be colour blind, while males only need one copy. This means colour blindness is much rarer in women than men. Females with one copy of the recessive allele are said to be **carriers**.

---

**Learning Objectives:**
- Be able to explain linkage.
- Be able to use genetic diagrams to show patterns of inheritance, including sex linkage.
- Be able to use phenotypic ratios to identify linkage (autosomal and sex linkage).

**Specification Reference 6.1.2**

**Tip:** In mammals, males are <u>heterogametic</u> — they have two different kinds of sex chromosomes (X and Y). Females are <u>homogametic</u> — they have only one kind of sex chromosome (X).

**Tip:** Remember, a carrier is a person carrying an allele which is not expressed in the phenotype but that can be passed on to offspring. Males can't be carriers of X-linked disorders because they only have one copy of each chromosome, so if they have the allele they have the disease — whether it's recessive or not.

**Tip:** The faulty allele for colour vision is represented by a lower case 'n', so you know it's a recessive allele.

Module 6: Section 2 Patterns of Inheritance

**Exam Tip**
Always read the question carefully — if it only asks you for the F₁ genotypes, don't write about anything else in your answer. It wastes time and you might lose marks.

**Tip:** This cross isn't any harder than the simple monogenic ones you saw on pages 448-450. Just follow the same steps to work out all the possible combinations of gametes and what they would mean.

**Tip:** If a colour-blind female and an unaffected male had children, the predicted ratio of offspring without colour-blindness : offspring with colour-blindness would be 1 : 1 — all male offspring would be colour-blind, and all female offspring would be carriers.

Here's how to draw a Punnett square for the sex-linked cross between a carrier female and an unaffected male:

**Step 1:** Make sure you're clear what the letters mean. You need to show X and Y chromosomes too this time. You usually show them as a capital X and Y and then have the genes as superscript letters.

N — normal colour vision allele
n — faulty colour vision allele
X — female    Y — male

Carrier female: $X^N X^n$
Unaffected male: $X^N Y$

**Step 2:** Work out the alleles the gametes would have.

Gametes' alleles: $X^N$, $X^n$, $X^N$, Y

**Step 3:** Cross the parents' gametes to show the possible offspring.

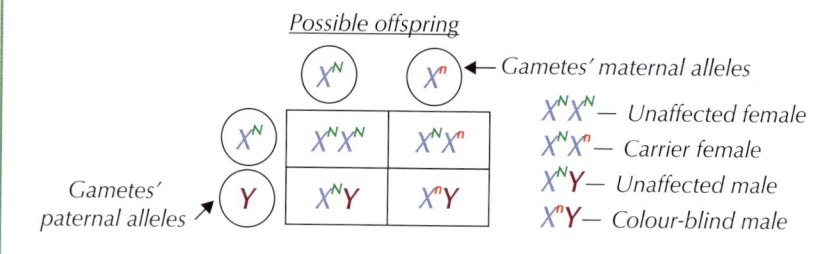

$X^N X^N$ — Unaffected female
$X^N X^n$ — Carrier female
$X^N Y$ — Unaffected male
$X^n Y$ — Colour-blind male

**Figure 2:** Punnett square showing the inheritance of colour-blindness.

In the example above there's a 3 : 1 ratio of offspring without colour blindness : offspring with colour-blindness. But when a female carrier and a male without colour-blindness have children (as in this example), only their male offspring are at risk of being colour-blind. So you can also say that there's a predicted 2 : 1 : 1 ratio — of female offspring without colour-blindness : male offspring without colour-blindness : male offspring with colour-blindness.

This ratio will change if a female carrier ($X^N X^n$) and a male with colour-blindness ($X^n Y$) have children. The predicted ratio will then be 1 : 1 — of offspring with colour-blindness : offspring without colour-blindness. The ratio will be the same for offspring of each sex (see Figure 3). You only end up with this predicted ratio for a monogenic F₂ cross with a sex-linked characteristic.

Carrier female: $X^N X^n$
Colour-blind male: $X^n Y$

$X^N X^n$ — Carrier female
$X^n X^n$ — Colour-blind female
$X^N Y$ — Unaffected male
$X^n Y$ — Colour-blind male

Possible genotypes of offspring: $X^N X^n$, $X^N Y$, $X^n X^n$, $X^n Y$

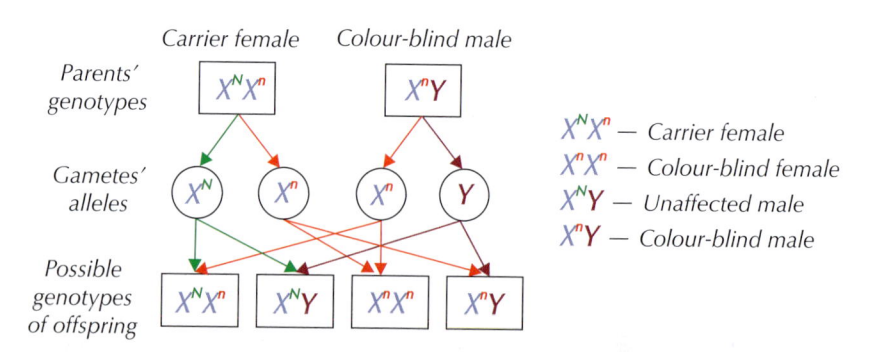

**Figure 3:** Genetic diagram showing the inheritance of colour-blindness in an F₂ cross.

Module 6: Section 2  Patterns of Inheritance

# Linkage of autosomal genes

**Autosome** is the fancy name for any chromosome that isn't a sex chromosome. Autosomal genes are the genes located on the autosomes. Genes on the same autosome are said to be **linked** — that's because they'll stay together during the independent assortment of chromosomes in meiosis I, and their alleles will be passed on to the offspring together. The only reason this won't happen is if crossing over splits them up first. The closer together two genes are on the autosome, the more closely they are said to be linked. This is because crossing over is less likely to split them up.

**Tip:** Independent assortment is the random division of homologous (paired) chromosomes into separate daughter cells during meiosis. Crossing over is when two homologous chromosomes 'swap bits'. It happens in meiosis I before independent assortment. You'll have learnt about both of these in Module 2: Section 6.

*A pair of X-shaped autosomes.*

Genes A, B and C are all linked. Genes A and B are more closely linked than genes A and C.

Crossing over occurs.

Genes A and B stay together, but are split up from gene C.

**Figure 4a:** Autosomal genes being split up during crossing over.

Autosome pair after crossing over has occurred.

Genes A and B end up in the same daughter cell — they will be inherited together by the offspring.

parent cell

daughter cells

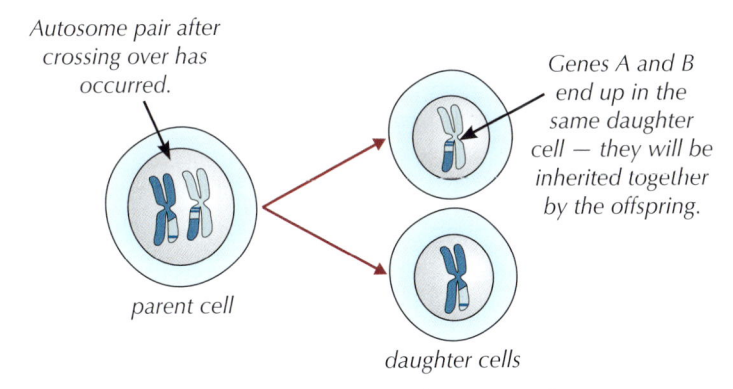

**Figure 4b:** Independent assortment of autosomes during meiosis I.

If two genes are autosomally linked, you won't get the phenotypic ratio you expect in the offspring of a cross.

### Example

In a dihybrid cross between two heterozygous parents you'd expect a 9 : 3 : 3 : 1 ratio in the offspring. Instead, the phenotypic ratio is more likely to be that expected for a monogenic cross between two heterozygous parents (3 : 1) because the two autosomally-linked alleles are inherited together. This means that a higher proportion of the offspring will have their parents' (heterozygous) genotype and phenotype.

**Tip:** There's more about the expected phenotypic ratios for dihybrid and monogenic crosses on pages 449 and 453.

So you can use the predicted phenotypic ratio to identify autosomal linkage — see next page.

Module 6: Section 2 Patterns of Inheritance

**Tip:** Crossing the offspring with one of the parents is known as a back cross.

**Tip:** Watch out — a 1 : 1 : 1 : 1 ratio is expected here because the cross is between a homozygous parent and a heterozygous parent not two heterozygous parents (which would be a 9 : 3 : 3 : 1 ratio).

― **Example** ―

A scientist was investigating autosomal linkage between the genes for eye colour and wing length in fruit flies. The gene for normal wings (N) is dominant to the gene for vestigial wings (n) and the gene for red eyes (R) is dominant to the gene for purple eyes (r).

The first cross the scientist carried out was between flies homozygous dominant for both normal wings and red eyes (NNRR) and flies homozygous recessive for both vestigial wings and purple eyes (nnrr). The resulting offspring were all heterozygous for normal wings and red eyes (NnRr).

The second cross the scientist carried out was between these offspring (NnRr) and the flies homozygous recessive for vestigial wings and purple eyes (nnrr). He expected a 1 : 1 : 1 : 1 ratio as shown in Figure 5:

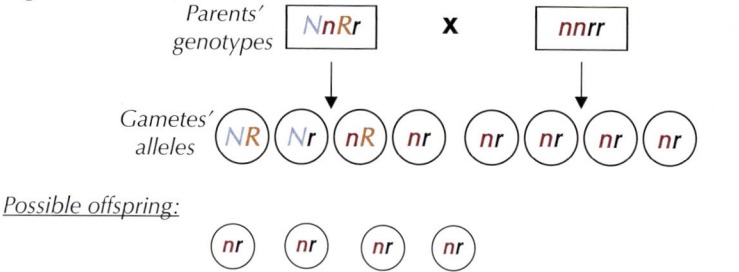

Parents' genotypes: NnRr × nnrr

Gametes' alleles: (NR) (Nr) (nR) (nr)    (nr) (nr) (nr) (nr)

*Possible offspring:*

|    | nr   | nr   | nr   | nr   |
|----|------|------|------|------|
| NR | NnRr | NnRr | NnRr | NnRr | normal wings, red eyes = 4
| Nr | Nnrr | Nnrr | Nnrr | Nnrr | normal wings, purple eyes = 4
| nR | nnRr | nnRr | nnRr | nnRr | vestigial wings, red eyes = 4
| nr | nnrr | nnrr | nnrr | nnrr | vestigial wings, purple eyes = 4

Phenotypic ratio: 1 : 1 : 1 : 1

**Figure 5:** *Genetic diagram showing the expected phenotypic ratio for a dihybrid cross between one heterozygous parent and one homozygous parent.*

However, the results the scientist got for the NnRr × nnrr cross showed an 8 : 1 : 1 : 8 ratio, as in the table:

|                                | Number of offspring |
|--------------------------------|---------------------|
| Normal wings, red eyes (NnRr)  | 1216 |
| Normal wings, purple eyes (Nnrr) | 152 |
| Vestigial wings, red eyes (nnRr) | 148 |
| Vestigial wings, purple eyes (nnrr) | 1184 |

Phenotypic ratio = 8 : 1 : 1 : 8

**Tip:** To give the ratio 1216 : 152 : 148 : 1184 in its simplest form, divide each number by the smallest number in the ratio (i.e. 148).

In order for the NnRr and nnrr genotypes to be so common in the offspring, the NR alleles and the nr alleles in the NnRr parent must have been linked. This means that the NnRr parent produced mostly NR and nr gametes. Some Nr and nR gametes were still made due to crossing over, but there were fewer Nnrr and nnRr offspring overall. As a result, a higher proportion of the offspring have their parents' phenotypes.

**Exam Tip**
In the exam you might get some genetic cross results that show linkage and have to explain them.

## Practice Questions — Application

Q1 Fragile X syndrome is an X-linked dominant disorder. A male and female, each with Fragile X syndrome, have a child. The female is heterozygous for the disorder. Give the possible genotypes and phenotypes of the child.

Q2 Hypertrichosis pinnae (extremely hairy ears) was once thought to be a Y-linked characteristic. If this were true, why might a father with 'bald' ears whose child has hairy ears, be suspicious of his wife?

Q3 Duchenne muscular dystrophy is a form of muscular dystrophy that causes muscle breakdown and difficulties walking and breathing. It is caused by a recessive X-linked allele. What is the probability of having a child with Duchenne muscular dystrophy if a normal male has a child with a carrier female?

Q4 In corn plants, the allele for glossy leaves (G) is dominant to the gene for normal leaves (g) and the gene for branching of ears (B) is dominant to the gene for no branching (b). A cross is carried out between a plant that is heterozygous for glossy leaves and branching of ears (GgBb) and a plant that is homozygous recessive for normal leaves and no branching (ggbb).

a) Use a genetic diagram to work out the expected phenotypic ratio in the offspring.

b) The results of the cross are shown in the table below.

|  | Number of offspring |
|---|---|
| Glossy leaves, lots of branching (GgBb) | 126 |
| Glossy leaves, no branching (Ggbb) | 81 |
| Normal leaves, lots of branching (ggBb) | 74 |
| Normal leaves, no branching (ggbb) | 133 |

What is the observed phenotypic ratio in the offspring?

c) Suggest why the observed ratio differs from the expected ratio.

*Figure 6:* A photo showing normal leaves and no branching in two ears of corn.

## Practice Questions — Fact Recall

Q1 What is the probability of having a female child?
Q2 Some characteristics are sex-linked. What does this mean?
Q3 Why are X-linked disorders more common in males than females?
Q4 What is an autosome?
Q5 Why are genes on the same autosome said to be linked?

**Learning Objectives:**
- Be able to explain epistasis.
- Be able to use phenotypic ratios to identify epistasis.

**Specification Reference 6.1.2**

# 6. Epistasis

*Just like linkage, epistasis affects the phenotypic ratios of dihybrid crosses.*

## What is epistasis?

Many different genes can control the same characteristic — they interact to form the phenotype. This can be because the allele of one gene masks (blocks) the expression of the alleles of other genes — this is called **epistasis**.

### Example 1 — Widow's peak

In humans a widow's peak (see Figure 1) is controlled by one gene and baldness by others. If you have the alleles that code for baldness, it doesn't matter whether you have the allele for a widow's peak or not, as you have no hair. The baldness genes are epistatic to the widow's peak gene, as the baldness genes mask the expression of the widow's peak gene.

### Example 2 — Flower colour

Flower pigment in a plant is controlled by two genes. Gene 1 codes for a yellow pigment (Y is the dominant yellow allele) and gene 2 codes for an enzyme that turns the yellow pigment orange (R is the dominant orange allele). If you don't have the Y allele it won't matter if you have the R allele or not as the flower will be colourless. Gene 1 is epistatic to gene 2 as it can mask the expression of gene 2.

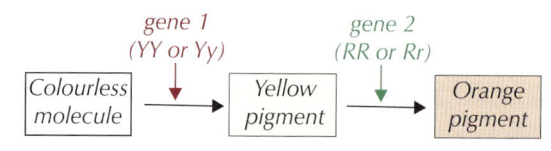

```
              gene 1              gene 2
             (YY or Yy)          (RR or Rr)
                ↓                    ↓
 Colourless  ──────→   Yellow   ──────→   Orange
 molecule              pigment            pigment
```

**Figure 1:** *A man with a widow's peak (a V-shaped hair growth). If this man were bald, you wouldn't be able to tell whether he had a widow's peak or not.*

**Tip:** Epistatic genes are usually at different loci (different positions on chromosomes).

## Phenotypic ratios for epistatic genes

Crosses involving epistatic genes don't result in the expected phenotypic ratios, e.g. if you cross two heterozygous orange flowered plants (YyRr) from the example above you wouldn't get the expected 9 : 3 : 3 : 1 phenotypic ratio for a normal dihybrid cross.

The phenotypic ratio you would expect to get from a dihybrid cross involving an epistatic allele depends on whether the epistatic allele is recessive or dominant.

### Recessive epistatic alleles

If the epistatic allele is recessive then two copies of it will mask (block) the expression of the other gene. If you cross a homozygous recessive parent with a homozygous dominant parent you will produce a 9 : 3 : 4 phenotypic ratio of dominant both : dominant epistatic, recessive other : recessive epistatic in the $F_2$ generation.

**Tip:** Remember the $F_1$ generation is the first generation and the $F_2$ generation is the second generation.

### Example

The flower colour example above is an example of a recessive epistatic allele. If a plant is homozygous recessive for the epistatic gene (yy) then it will be colourless, masking the expression of the orange gene. So if you cross homozygous parents you should get a 9 : 3 : 4 ratio of orange : yellow : white in the $F_2$ generation. You can check the phenotypic ratio is right using a genetic diagram — see Figure 2 on the next page.

Module 6: Section 2 **Patterns of Inheritance**

**Key:**

| Y — yellow pigment | R — orange pigment |
|---|---|
| y — no yellow pigment | r — no orange pigment |

**F₁ cross:** YYRR x yyrr ⟶ All YyRr

**F₂ cross:**

Parents' genotypes: YyRr x YyRr

Gametes' alleles: YR, Yr, yR, yr × YR, Yr, yR, yr

Possible offspring genotypes:

|  | YR | Yr | yR | yr |
|---|---|---|---|---|
| **YR** | YYRR | YYRr | YyRR | YyRr |
| **Yr** | YYRr | YYrr | YyRr | Yyrr |
| **yR** | YyRR | YyRr | yyRR | yyRr |
| **yr** | YyRr | Yyrr | yyRr | yyrr |

Orange = YYRR, YYRr, YyRR, YyRr = 9

Yellow = Yyrr, YYrr = 3

White = yyRR, yyRr, yyrr = 4

Phenotypic ratio: 9 : 3 : 4

*Figure 2: Genetic diagram of a dihybrid cross with two heterozygous parents, involving a recessive epistatic gene.*

**Tip:** All of the F₁ offspring have to have the genotype YyRr because the only gametes you can get from the parents are YR and yr.

**Tip:** You should be familiar with Punnett squares by now but if not, see page 449 for a recap.

**Tip:** This is a dihybrid cross because you're looking at the inheritance of two genes.

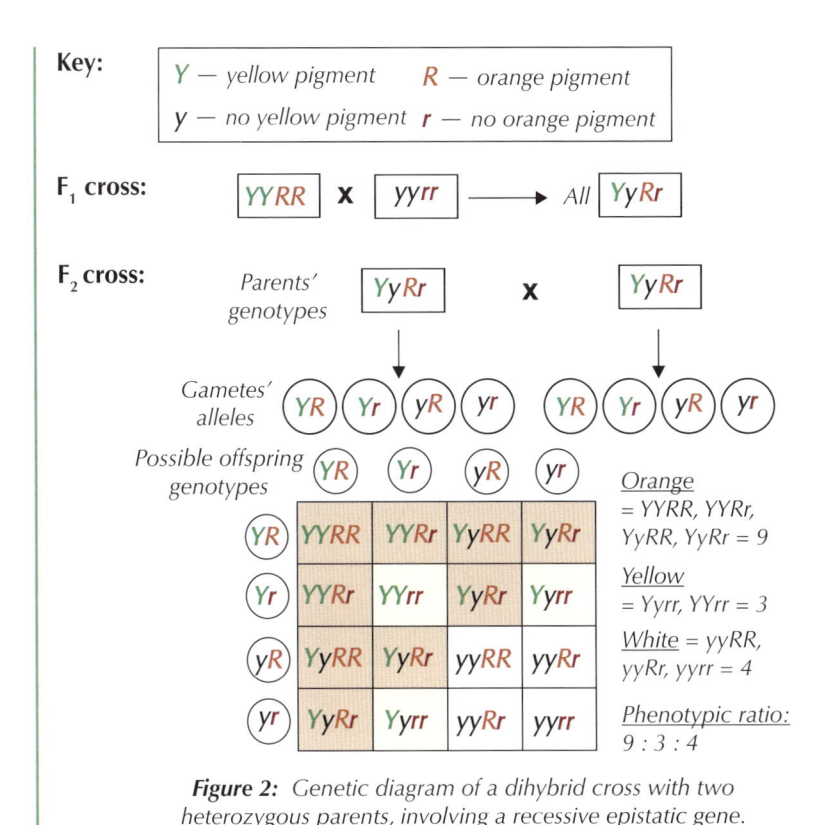

## Dominant epistatic alleles

If the epistatic allele is dominant, then having at least one copy of it will mask (block) the expression of the other gene. Crossing a homozygous recessive parent with a homozygous dominant parent will produce a 12 : 3 : 1 phenotypic ratio of dominant epistatic : recessive epistatic, dominant other : recessive both in the F₂ generation.

### Example

Squash colour is controlled by two genes — the colour epistatic gene (W/w) and the yellow gene (Y/y). The no-colour, white allele (W) is dominant over the coloured allele (w), so WW or Ww will be white and ww will be coloured. The yellow gene has the dominant yellow allele (Y) and the recessive green allele (y). So if the plant has at least one W, then the squash will be white, masking the expression of the yellow gene.

*Colour epistatic gene* → *Yellow gene* → *Squash colour*

- coloured allele (ww) → yellow allele (YY or Yy) → Yellow
- coloured allele (ww) → green allele (yy) → Green
- white allele (WW or Ww) → White

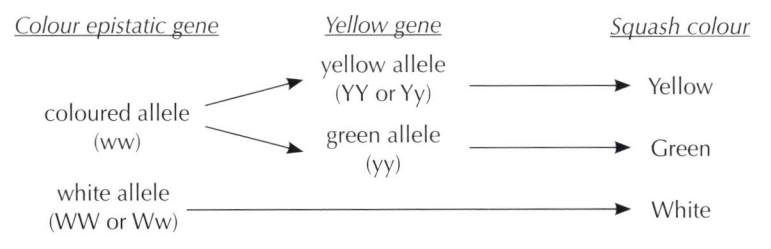

*Figure 3: Diagram to show how squash colour is controlled by two genes.*

So if you cross wwyy with WWYY, you'll get a 12 : 3 : 1 ratio of white : yellow : green in the F₂ generation. The genetic diagram to prove it is shown in Figure 5 (see next page).

**Exam Tip:** Make sure you know the difference between dominant and recessive epistatic alleles. The phenotypic ratios you'd expect to get are different for each.

*Figure 4: These squash are yellow in colour so they must have the genotype wwYY or wwYy.*

Module 6: Section 2 Patterns of Inheritance 461

**Key:**  W — white    w — coloured    Y — yellow    y — green

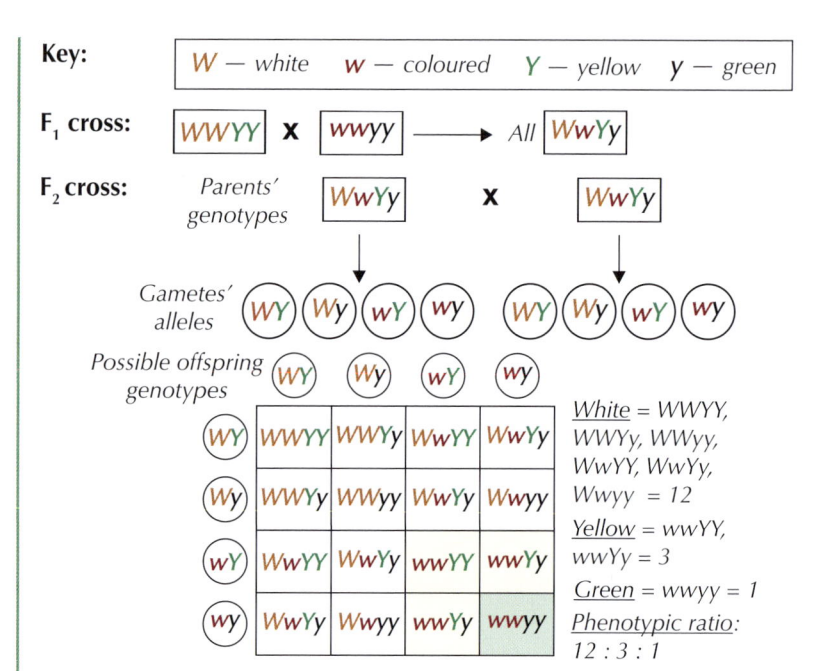

**F₁ cross:** WWYY × wwyy ⟶ All WwYy

**F₂ cross:** Parents' genotypes: WwYy × WwYy

Gametes' alleles: WY, Wy, wY, wy    WY, Wy, wY, wy

Possible offspring genotypes:

|    | WY   | Wy   | wY   | wy   |
|----|------|------|------|------|
| WY | WWYY | WWYy | WwYY | WwYy |
| Wy | WWYy | WWyy | WwYy | Wwyy |
| wY | WwYY | WwYy | wwYY | wwYy |
| wy | WwYy | Wwyy | wwYy | wwyy |

<u>White</u> = WWYY, WWYy, WWyy, WwYY, WwYy, Wwyy = 12
<u>Yellow</u> = wwYY, wwYy = 3
<u>Green</u> = wwyy = 1
<u>Phenotypic ratio</u>: 12 : 3 : 1

**Figure 5:** *Genetic diagram of a dihybrid cross with two heterozygous parents, involving a dominant epistatic gene.*

**Exam Tip**
If you set your crosses out like this in the exam, it'll help you keep track of what you're doing and it'll help the examiner follow your working out.

**Figure 6:** *Chocolate and black coated Labrador retrievers.*

## Practice Questions — Application

**Q1** Coat colour in Labrador retrievers is controlled by two genes. Gene 1 controls whether the dog can express dark pigment in its coat (E) or not (e). Gene 1 is epistatic over gene 2, which controls whether the dark pigment is black (B) or chocolate (b). Dogs that can't express dark pigment in their coat are yellow (golden) in colour.
  a) Write down all the possible genotypes for:
    i) a black Labrador,    ii) a chocolate Labrador,
    iii) a yellow Labrador.
  b) Describe and explain the phenotypic ratio produced in the $F_2$ generation if a black Labrador retriever (EEBB) breeds with a yellow Labrador retriever (eebb).

**Q2** Petal colour in a species of flower is controlled by this pathway:

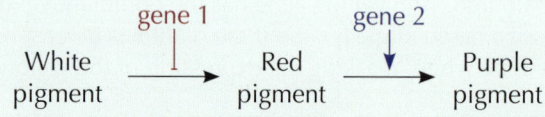

White pigment —gene 1⊣→ Red pigment —gene 2→ Purple pigment

Gene 1 codes for a protein that prevents the formation of the red pigment. This means the dominant allele for gene 1 (W) causes the petals to be white and the recessive allele (w) causes red pigment to be made. Gene 2 codes for a protein that turns the red pigment into purple pigment. This means the dominant allele for gene 2 (P), causes the petals to be purple and the recessive allele (p) causes the petals to stay red. When a white flower (WWPP) is crossed with a red flower (wwpp), 48 white flowers, 12 purple flowers and 4 red flowers are produced in the $F_2$ generation.
  a) Is this an example of dominant or recessive epistasis?
  b) Explain the phenotypic ratio shown by the cross.
  c) Draw a genetic diagram to show this cross.

Module 6: Section 2 Patterns of Inheritance

# 7. The Chi-Squared Test

*OK, it's time for a bit of maths. The chi-squared test can be a bit tricky to get your head around, but it might pop up in the exam so make sure you spend some time working through the next few pages.*

## What is the chi-squared test?

The chi-squared ($\chi^2$) test is a statistical test that's used to see if the results of an experiment support a theory. First, the theory is used to predict a result — this is called the expected result. Then, the experiment is carried out and the actual result is recorded — this is called the observed result.

To see if the results support the theory you have to make a hypothesis called the **null hypothesis**. The null hypothesis is always that there's no significant difference between the observed and expected results. Your experimental result will usually be a bit different from what you expect, but you need to know if the difference is just due to chance, or because your theory is wrong. The $\chi^2$ test is then carried out and the outcome either supports or rejects the null hypothesis.

### Using the chi-squared test

You can use the $\chi^2$ test in genetics to test theories about the inheritance of characteristics.

--- Example — inheritance of wing length experiment ---

**Theory:** Wing length in fruit flies is controlled by a single gene with two alleles (monogenic inheritance). The dominant allele (N) gives normal wings, and the recessive allele (n) gives vestigial wings.

**Expected results:** With monogenic inheritance, if you cross a homozygous dominant parent with a homozygous recessive parent, you'd expect a 3 : 1 phenotypic ratio of normal : vestigial wings in the $F_2$ generation.

**Observed results:** The experiment (of crossing a homozygous dominant parent with a homozygous recessive parent) is carried out on fruit flies and the number of offspring in the $F_2$ generation with normal and vestigial wings is counted.

**Null hypothesis:** There's no significant difference between the observed and expected results.

**Chi-squared test:** To find out if the results are significant you first need to calculate the **chi-squared value** (see below) and then compare it to the **critical value** (see page 465). If the $\chi^2$ test shows the observed and expected results are not significantly different, then we are unable to reject the null hypothesis — the data supports the theory that wing length is controlled by monogenic inheritance.

## Calculating the chi-squared value

Chi-squared ($\chi^2$) is calculated using this formula:

$$\chi^2 = \sum \frac{(O - E)^2}{E}$$

O = observed result
E = expected result
$\Sigma$ = the sum of...

The best way to understand the $\chi^2$ test is to work through an example — there's one for testing the wing length of fruit flies, as explained above, on the next page.

**Learning Objective:**
- Be able to use the chi-squared ($\chi^2$) test to determine the significance of the difference between observed and expected results.

**Specification Reference 6.1.2**

**Tip:** A theory is a possible explanation for something and a hypothesis is a specific testable statement. See page 1 for more on this.

**Tip:** See pages 448-450 for a recap on monogenic inheritance.

*Figure 1: Karl Pearson — the English statistician who developed the chi-squared test.*

**Exam Tip**
You don't need to learn the formula for chi-squared — it'll be given to you in the exam.

Module 6: Section 2 Patterns of Inheritance 463

## Example — Maths Skills

Homozygous dominant flies (NN) are crossed with homozygous recessive flies (nn) and 160 offspring are produced in the $F_2$ generation.

1. First the number of offspring expected (E) for each phenotype (out of a total of 160) is worked out using this equation:

   $$E = \text{total no. of offspring} \div \text{ratio total} \times \text{predicted ratio}$$

   A 3 : 1 phenotypic ratio of normal : vestigial wings is expected, so the ratio total is 3 + 1 = 4. Here are the expected results:

   | Phenotype | Ratio | Expected result (E) |
   |---|---|---|
   | Normal wings | 3 | 160 ÷ 4 × 3 = 120 |
   | Vestigial wings | 1 | 160 ÷ 4 × 1 = 40 |

   **Tip:** This isn't the only way to work out the expected results. If you're taught a different way in class, stick with whichever method you find easiest.

2. Then the actual number of offspring observed with each phenotype (out of the 160 offspring) is recorded, e.g. 111 with normal wings:

   | Phenotype | Ratio | Expected result (E) | Observed result (O) |
   |---|---|---|---|
   | Normal wings | 3 | 120 | 111 |
   | Vestigial wings | 1 | 40 | 49 |

3. The results are used to work out $\chi^2$, taking it one step at a time:

   a. First calculate O − E (subtract the expected result from the observed result) for each phenotype.

   | Phenotype | Ratio | Expected result (E) | Observed result (O) | O − E |
   |---|---|---|---|---|
   | Normal wings | 3 | 120 | 111 | 111 − 120 = −9 |
   | Vestigial wings | 1 | 40 | 49 | 49 − 40 = 9 |

   b. Then the resulting numbers are squared:

   | Phenotype | Ratio | Expected result (E) | Observed result (O) | O − E | (O − E)² |
   |---|---|---|---|---|---|
   | Normal wings | 3 | 120 | 111 | −9 | −9² = 81 |
   | Vestigial wings | 1 | 40 | 49 | 9 | 9² = 81 |

   **Tip:** Don't forget — if you multiply a negative number by a negative number you get a positive number. So $-9^2$ ($-9 \times -9$) is 81 and not −81.

   c. These figures are divided by the expected results:

   | Phenotype | Ratio | Expected result (E) | Observed result (O) | O − E | (O − E)² | $\frac{(O-E)^2}{E}$ |
   |---|---|---|---|---|---|---|
   | Normal wings | 3 | 120 | 111 | −9 | 81 | 81 ÷ 120 = 0.675 |
   | Vestigial wings | 1 | 40 | 49 | 9 | 81 | 81 ÷ 40 = 2.025 |

   **Exam Tip**
   Make sure you divide (O − E)² by E and not O. It's easy to get these two mixed up when you're under pressure in the exam.

   d. Finally, the numbers are added together to get $\chi^2$.

   | Phenotype | Ratio | Expected result (E) | Observed result (O) | O − E | (O − E)² | $\frac{(O-E)^2}{E}$ |
   |---|---|---|---|---|---|---|
   | Normal wings | 3 | 120 | 111 | −9 | 81 | 0.675 |
   | Vestigial wings | 1 | 40 | 49 | 9 | 81 | 2.025 |

   $$\sum \frac{(O-E)^2}{E} = 0.675 + 2.025 = \boxed{2.7}$$

   **Tip:** Remember you need to work out (O − E)² ÷ E for each phenotype first, then add all the numbers together.

# The critical value

To find out whether there is a significant difference between your observed and expected results you need to compare your $\chi^2$ value to a critical value. The critical value is the value of $\chi^2$ that corresponds to a 0.05 (5%) level of probability that the difference between the observed and expected results is due to chance.

## Finding the critical value

In the exam you might be given the critical value or asked to work it out from a table.

**Example — Maths Skills**

Figure 2 below is a chi-squared table — this shows a range of probabilities that correspond to different critical values for different **degrees of freedom** (explained below). Biologists normally use a **probability level** (P value) of 0.05 (5%), so you only need to look in that column.

| degrees of freedom | no. of classes | Critical values |||||| 
|---|---|---|---|---|---|---|---|
| 1 | 2 | 0.46 | 1.64 | 2.71 | 3.84 | 6.64 | 10.83 |
| 2 | 3 | 1.39 | 3.22 | 4.61 | 5.99 | 9.21 | 13.82 |
| 3 | 4 | 2.37 | 4.64 | 6.25 | 7.82 | 11.34 | 16.27 |
| 4 | 5 | 3.36 | 5.99 | 7.78 | 9.49 | 13.28 | 18.47 |
| probability that result is due to chance only | | 0.50 (50%) | 0.20 (20%) | 0.10 (10%) | 0.05 (5%) | 0.01 (1%) | 0.001 (0.1%) |

*Abridged from Statistical Tables for Biological, Agricultural and Medical Research, R.A Fisher and F. Yates (6th ed.) © 1963 Reprinted by permission of Pearson Business*

**Figure 2:** A chi-squared table.

In order to find the critical value for the wing length experiment:

- First, the degrees of freedom for the experiment are worked out — this is the number of classes (number of phenotypes) minus one. There were two phenotypes, so the degrees of freedom = 2 − 1 = **1**.
- Next, the critical value corresponding to the degrees of freedom (1 in this case) and a probability level of 0.05 is found in the table. By following the arrows in Figure 2 you can see that the critical value is **3.84**.

**Exam Tip**
The table of critical values you get given in the exam might look a bit different to this, but don't panic. It'll still contain all the information you need to answer the question.

**Tip:** Remember, the two phenotypes for the wing length experiment are normal wings and vestigial wings.

## Comparing the $\chi^2$ value to the critical value

If your $\chi^2$ value is larger than (or equal to) the critical value, then there is a significant difference between the observed and expected results (something other than chance is causing the difference) — and the null hypothesis can be rejected. If your $\chi^2$ value is smaller than the critical value, then there is no significant difference between the observed and expected results — the null hypothesis can't be rejected. This is summarised in Figure 3.

> $\chi^2$ value ≥ critical value = rejection of the null hypothesis
> $\chi^2$ value < critical value = failure to reject the null hypothesis

**Figure 3:** Possible outcomes of a chi-squared test.

**Tip:** In this kind of statistical test, you can never prove that the null hypothesis is true — you can only 'fail to reject it'. This just means that the evidence doesn't give you a reason to think the null hypothesis is wrong.

**Example — Maths Skills**

The chi-squared value of 2.7 is smaller than the critical value of 3.84. This means that there's no significant difference between the observed and expected results. We've failed to reject the null hypothesis — so the theory that wing length in fruit flies is controlled by monogenic inheritance is supported.

**Tip:** If the $\chi^2$ value had been bigger than 3.84 then something else must have been affecting wing length — like epistasis or sex linkage.

Module 6: Section 2 Patterns of Inheritance

## Practice Questions — Application

**Q1** The critical value for a chi-squared test is 5.99. Explain whether or not the difference between the observed and expected results would be significant if the calculated chi-squared value was:

　a) 6.20,　　　　　　　　　　b) 4.85.

**Q2** Fruit flies can have grey bodies or ebony bodies. The allele for grey bodies is dominant over the allele for ebony bodies. If two heterozygous parents are crossed, you would expect a 3 : 1 phenotypic ratio of grey : ebony offspring. When this cross was carried out, 64 offspring were produced, 45 of which had grey bodies and the rest were ebony. Copy and complete the table below to calculate the chi-squared value for this experiment.

| Phenotype | Ratio | Expected result (E) | Observed result (O) | O – E | (O – E)² | (O – E)²/E |
|---|---|---|---|---|---|---|
| Grey body | 3 | | 45 | | | |
| Ebony body | 1 | | | | | |

$$\chi^2 = \Sigma \frac{(O - E)^2}{E} =$$

**Exam Tip**
You won't always be told the observed number of offspring for both phenotypes. You can work out the number of offspring for the phenotype you don't know by taking the number you do know away from the total.

For the following questions, you may need to use the $\chi^2$ table below:

| Degrees of freedom | \multicolumn{6}{c}{Probability (p)} |
|---|---|---|---|---|---|---|
| | 0.50 | 0.20 | 0.10 | 0.05 | 0.01 | 0.001 |
| 1 | 0.46 | 1.64 | 2.71 | 3.84 | 6.64 | 10.83 |
| 2 | 1.39 | 3.22 | 4.61 | 5.99 | 9.21 | 13.82 |
| 3 | 2.37 | 4.64 | 6.25 | 7.82 | 11.34 | 16.27 |
| 4 | 3.36 | 5.99 | 7.78 | 9.49 | 13.28 | 18.47 |

probability levels ←
critical values

**Tip:** Remember the degrees of freedom are just the number of classes minus one (n – 1).

**Q3** A student is looking at the inheritance of pea shape (round vs. wrinkled) and pea colour (green vs. yellow) in pea plants. His theory is that this is a simple case of dihybrid inheritance with no linkage or epistasis involved. He predicts that if this is the case, when two heterozygous plants are crossed, there will be a 9 : 3 : 3 : 1 ratio in the offspring. To test his theory, the student carries out this cross and looks at the phenotypes of the 128 offspring produced.

Some of his results are shown in the table below. His null hypothesis is that there is no significant difference between the observed and expected results.

a) Copy and complete the table to calculate $\chi^2$ for this experiment:

| Phenotype | Ratio | Expected result (E) | Observed result (O) | O – E | (O – E)² | (O – E)²/E |
|---|---|---|---|---|---|---|
| Round, green | 9 | | 74 | | | |
| Round, yellow | 3 | | 21 | | | |
| Wrinkled, green | 3 | | | | | |
| Wrinkled, yellow | 1 | | 7 | | | |

$$\chi^2 = \Sigma \frac{(O - E)^2}{E} =$$

**Exam Tip**
In the exam, you could be given a table like this to fill in. If you're not given a table, the easiest way to calculate $\chi^2$ would be to draw a table like this yourself and work through it step by step.

b) Find the critical value for this experiment and explain whether the null hypothesis can be rejected or not.

*Abridged from Statistical Tables for Biological Agricultural and Medical Research, R.A Fisher and F. Yates (6th ed.) © 1963 Reprinted by permission of Pearson Business*

Module 6: Section 2 Patterns of Inheritance

Q4  A scientist comes up with the following theory:

> 'Height in plants is controlled by a single gene with two alleles. The dominant allele gives tall plants. The recessive allele gives dwarf plants.'

The scientist predicts that if this theory is true, when a homozygous recessive plant is crossed with a homozygous dominant plant you will get a 3 : 1 ratio of tall : dwarf in the $F_2$ generation. The scientist then comes up with a null hypothesis and carries out the cross. Of the 52 $F_2$ offspring produced, 9 were dwarf.

a) What should the scientist's null hypothesis be?

b) The formula for calculating chi-squared is:

$$\chi^2 = \Sigma \frac{(O - E)^2}{E}$$

Use the chi-squared test to explain whether or not the results of the scientist's experiment support his theory.

**Tip:** Remember to check whether the ratio and number of offspring of each phenotype in the question refer to the $F_1$ or the $F_2$ generation.

Q5  A flower can have red, white or pink flowers. If this is an example of codominance and two heterozygous plants were crossed, you would expect a 1 : 2 : 1 ratio of red : pink : white flowers in the offspring. This cross was performed and of the 160 offspring produced, 92 had pink flowers, 24 had red flowers and 44 had white flowers. The null hypothesis is that there is no significant difference between the observed and expected results.

a) The formula for calculating chi-squared is:

$$\chi^2 = \Sigma \frac{(O - E)^2}{E}$$

Use the chi-squared test to show that this is unlikely to be an example of codominance.

b) If the determination of flower colour in this plant involved recessive epistasis a 9 : 3 : 4 phenotypic ratio of pink flowers : red flowers : white flowers would be expected. Using the chi-squared test, show that recessive epistasis is likely to be involved. (The null hypothesis is that there is no significant difference between the observed and expected results.)

**Exam Tip**
You can take a calculator in the exam to help you do these kinds of questions.

**Tip:** There's more about recessive epistasis on pages 460-461.

# Section Summary

Make sure you know...

- That characteristics which show continuous variation are usually polygenic (influenced by many genes), while characteristics that display discontinuous variation are usually monogenic (influenced by one gene).
- That both genotype and the environment contribute to phenotypic variation.
- That genetic variation is generated during meiosis via crossing-over and the independent assortment of chromosomes, and during fertilisation via the random fusion of gametes.
- That examples of environmental contributions to phenotypic variation include diet in animals, and that etiolation and chlorosis in plants are variations in phenotype caused by environmental factors.
- That there can be one or more versions of the same gene and that these are called alleles.
- That most plants and animals have two alleles for each gene and that each one is found at a fixed position (called a locus) on each chromosome in a pair.
- That the genotype of an organism is what alleles it has and that the phenotype of an organism is the characteristics the alleles produce.
- That if an organism has two different alleles for the same characteristic it's heterozygous, but if it has two copies of the same allele it's homozygous.
- That an allele can be dominant (its characteristic is always shown in the phenotype), recessive (its characteristic is only shown in the phenotype if there are two copies of it) or codominant (where two alleles are both shown in the phenotype).
- That a carrier is a person carrying an allele which is not expressed in the phenotype but that can be passed on to offspring.
- How to use genetic diagrams to show the inheritance of a single gene (monogenic inheritance) and the inheritance of codominant alleles.
- That the phenotypic ratio is the ratio of phenotypes in the offspring and that the typical phenotypic ratio for a monogenic cross between two heterozygous parents is 3 : 1 of dominant : recessive characteristic and the typical phenotypic ratio for a cross between two heterozygous parents involving codominant alleles is 1 : 2 : 1 of homozygous for one allele : heterozygous : homozygous for the other allele.
- How to use genetic diagrams showing crosses involving multiple alleles and showing the inheritance of two characteristics controlled by different genes (dihybrid inheritance).
- That a typical phenotypic ratio for a dihybrid cross between two heterozygous parents is 9 : 3 : 3 : 1 (dominant both : dominant first, recessive second : recessive first, dominant second : recessive both).
- How to use genetic diagrams to show the inheritance of sex-linked characteristics (the alleles that code for them are located on sex chromosomes) and recognise that sex linkage alters expected phenotypic ratios in the offspring of crosses.
- How to identify genes linked on autosomes (chromosomes that aren't sex chromosomes) and recognise that autosomal linkage alters expected phenotypic ratios in the offspring of crosses.
- That epistasis is when the allele of one gene masks the expression of the alleles of other genes.
- What recessive epistasis is and that when the epistatic allele is recessive, crossing a homozygous recessive parent with a homozygous dominant parent will produce a 9 : 3 : 4 phenotypic ratio of dominant both : dominant epistatic, recessive other : recessive epistatic in the $F_2$ generation.
- What dominant epistasis is and that when the epistatic allele is dominant, crossing a homozygous recessive parent with a homozygous dominant parent will produce a 12 : 3 : 1 phenotypic ratio of dominant epistatic : recessive epistatic, dominant other : recessive both in the $F_2$ generation.
- How to calculate the chi-squared ($\chi^2$) value for an experiment, how to find the critical value from a chi-squared table and how to use these values to determine whether the difference between observed and expected results is significant or not, and whether or not to reject the null hypothesis.

# Exam-style Questions

**1** In mice, the allele for wild-type speckled coat colour, agouti (A), is dominant to the allele for solid coloured fur (a).

(a) Several pairs of heterozygous agouti mice are crossed, producing 256 offspring.
Assuming this is a normal case of monogenic inheritance, with no linkage involved, how many of the offspring would you expect to have the agouti coat colour?
*(1 mark)*

(b) The alleles for coat colour (A and a) are actually controlled by another gene (P). If a mouse is homozygous recessive for this gene, it is unable to produce any pigmentation and so will be albino.
Give the possible genotype(s) that will produce the albino phenotype.
*(1 mark)*

(c) A student produces a genetic diagram to show the phenotypic ratio produced in the F$_2$ generation if a homozygous dominant mouse (PPAA) breeds with a homozygous recessive mouse (ppaa). His results are shown in **Table 1.1** below.

**Table 1.1**

|     | PA   | pA   | Pa   | pa   |
|-----|------|------|------|------|
| PA  | PPAA | PpAA | PPAa | PpAa |
| pA  | PpAA | ppAA | PpAa | ppAa |
| Pa  | PPAa | PpAa | PPaa | Ppaa |
| pa  | PpAa | ppAa | Ppaa | ppaa |

The student concludes that this cross produces a phenotypic ratio of 9 : 3 : 3 : 1. This is incorrect. Give the phenotypic ratio that would be expected from this cross and explain why the student's conclusion is wrong.
*(3 marks)*

**2** Yeast cells can convert substance 1 to substance 3 via the enzyme pathway shown in **Fig. 2.1**. Two different gene loci control the pathway and each has two alleles. Having the dominant versions of alleles A and B means that the yeast cell will produce enzymes A and B as shown in **Fig. 2.1**.

Fig. 2.1  Substance 1 →(Enzyme A, allele A)→ Substance 2 →(Enzyme B, allele B)→ Substance 3

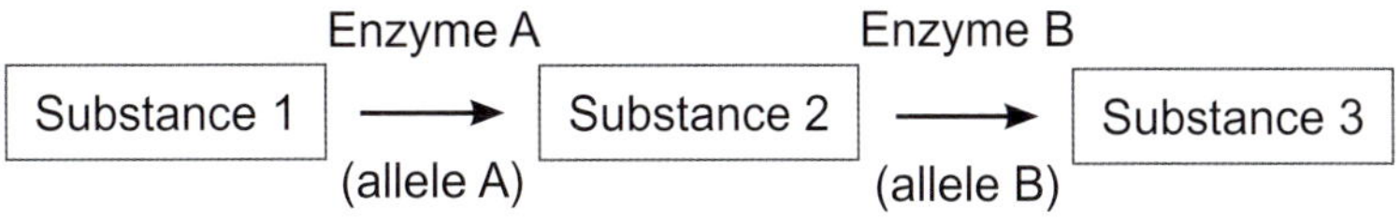

Yeast cells that lack either enzyme A or enzyme B cannot convert substance 1 to substance 3 and so cannot grow in media containing substance 1.

(a) Complete **Table 2.1** by putting a tick (✓) or a cross (✗) in the correct boxes below to show whether or not yeast cells with the following genotypes could grow on substance 1. The first one has been done for you

**Table 2.1**

| Genotype | Growth on substance 1 |
|---|---|
| AaBb | ✓ |
| aaBb | |
| AAbb | |
| AABb | |

*(1 mark)*

(b) Some of the cells that could not grow on substance 1 will grow if supplied with substance 2. Suggest why (with reference to their genotype).

*(3 marks)*

(c) Yeast cells with genotype AaBb were crossed with yeast cells homozygous recessive for both alleles. Draw a genetic diagram to show the expected ratio of offspring genotypes for this cross. Predict the percentage of $F_1$ cells that would not be able to grow in medium containing substance 1.

*(4 marks)*

3  Haemophilia is a sex-linked genetic disorder. It is caused by a faulty allele on the X-chromosome. The faulty allele ($X^h$) is recessive to the normal allele ($X^H$). A study was carried out into the inheritance of haemophilia. The phenotypes of children in families where the mother was a carrier of the disease (genotype $X^H X^h$) and the father was a haemophiliac (genotype $X^h Y$) were recorded.

(a) Draw a genetic diagram to show why a 1 : 1 : 1 : 1 phenotypic ratio of haemophiliac male : haemophiliac female : carrier female : unaffected male was expected in the results of this study.

*(3 marks)*

(b) Of the 272 children in this study, 130 were boys and 142 were girls. 61 of the boys and 70 of the girls had haemophilia. A chi-squared test was used to analyse the results.

(i) Calculate the chi-squared value ($\chi^2$) for this study.

$$\chi^2 = \sum \frac{(O - E)^2}{E}$$

O = observed result
E = expected result

*(3 marks)*

(ii) Use your calculated value of $\chi^2$ and **Table 3.1** to determine whether or not the difference between the observed and expected results is significant.

| Degrees of freedom | Probability (P) | | | | | |
|---|---|---|---|---|---|---|
| | 0.50 | 0.20 | 0.10 | 0.05 | 0.01 | 0.001 |
| 1 | 0.46 | 1.64 | 2.71 | 3.84 | 6.64 | 10.83 |
| 2 | 1.39 | 3.22 | 4.61 | 5.99 | 9.21 | 13.82 |
| 3 | 2.37 | 4.64 | 6.25 | 7.82 | 11.34 | 16.27 |

**Table 3.1**

Abridged from Statistical Tables for Biological Agricultural and Medical Research, R.A Fisher and F. Yates (6th ed.) © 1963 Reprinted by permission of Pearson Business

*(1 mark)*

# Module 6 Section 3: Evolution

# 1. Evolution by Natural Selection and Genetic Drift

*You might remember evolution from Module 4. It's caused by the variation in alleles within a species.*

## Alleles and evolution

The complete range of alleles present in a population is called the **gene pool**. How often an allele occurs in a population is called the **allele frequency**. It's usually given as a percentage of the total population, e.g. 35%, or a decimal, e.g. 0.35. The frequency of an allele in a population changes over time — this is evolution.

## Evolution by natural selection

Evolution may take place by the process of natural selection. Here's how it works:

- Individuals within a population vary because they have different alleles. New alleles are usually generated by **mutations** in genes.
- Predation, disease and competition (selection pressures) create a struggle for survival.
- Because individuals vary, some are better adapted to the selection pressures than others.
- Individuals that have an allele that increases their chance of survival (an advantageous allele) are more likely to survive, reproduce and pass on the advantageous allele than individuals with other alleles.
- This means that a greater proportion of the next generation inherit the advantageous allele.
- They, in turn, are more likely to survive, reproduce and pass on their genes. So the frequency of the advantageous allele increases from generation to generation.

An allele is only advantageous with the right selection pressure. Without a selection pressure, natural selection won't take place.

## Evolution and the environment

Whether the environment is changing or stable affects which characteristics are selected for by natural selection.

### Selection in a stable environment

When the environment isn't changing much, individuals with alleles for characteristics towards the middle of the range are more likely to survive and reproduce. This is called **stabilising selection** and it reduces the range of possible phenotypes.

---

**Learning Objective:**
- Understand the factors that can affect the evolution of a species, to include stabilising and directional selection, genetic drift, genetic bottlenecks and the founder effect.

**Specification Reference 6.1.2**

**Tip:** A population is a group of organisms of the same species living in a particular area.

**Tip:** Genetic variation is generated by meiosis (see page 444) and mutations.

**Tip:** A selection pressure is anything that affects an organism's chance of survival and reproduction.

**Exam Tip**
If you're asked to describe the process of natural selection in the exam, it's important to make it clear that it takes place <u>over many generations</u>.

## Example

In any mammal population there's a range of fur length. In a stable climate, having fur at the extremes of this range reduces the chances of surviving as it's harder to maintain the right body temperature, so mammals with very short or very long fur have a selective disadvantage. Mammals with alleles for average fur length are the most likely to survive, reproduce and pass on their alleles. These mammals have a selective advantage, so these alleles for average fur length increase in frequency.

Over time, the proportion of the population with average fur length increases and the range of fur lengths decreases — as shown in Figure 1. In the offspring graph the range of fur lengths has decreased, which results in a narrower graph. The proportion with average length fur has increased, resulting in a taller graph in the average fur length region.

**Tip:** The breeding population is just the animals that are surviving, reproducing and passing on their alleles.

**Exam Tip**
Here the data is shown as a graph, but you could be given a table of data in your exam.

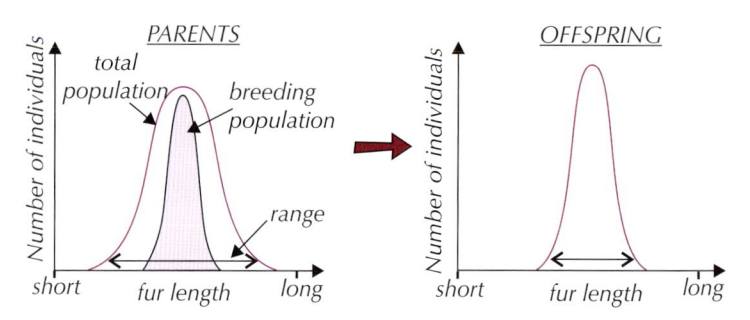

**Figure 1:** Graphs that show stabilising selection across generations.

## Selection in a changing environment

When there's a change in the environment, individuals with alleles for characteristics of an extreme type are more likely to survive and reproduce. This is called **directional selection**.

**Tip:** If a species can't adapt to changes in its environment, then its numbers may decrease and it may become extinct.

### Example

If the environment becomes very cold, individual mammals with alleles for long fur length will find it easier to maintain the right body temperature than animals with short fur length. They have a selective advantage, so they're more likely to survive, reproduce and pass on their alleles. Over time the frequency of alleles for long fur length increases — see Figure 2. In the offspring graph, the average fur length (dotted line) has moved towards the extreme, longer end.

**Tip:** With data that shows <u>stabilising</u> selection, the mean <u>stays</u> in the middle. With data that shows <u>directional</u> selection, the mean moves in one <u>direction</u> or the other.

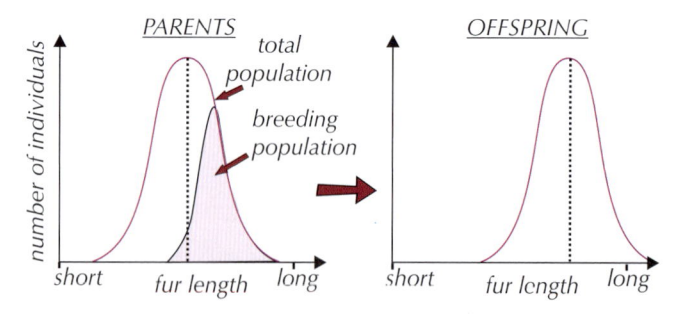

**Figure 2:** Graphs that show directional selection across generations.

Module 6: Section 3  Evolution

# Evolution via genetic drift

Natural selection is just one process by which evolution occurs. Evolution also occurs due to genetic drift — this just means that instead of environmental factors affecting which individuals survive, breed and pass on their alleles, chance dictates which alleles are passed on.
Here's how it works:

- Individuals within a population show variation in their genotypes (e.g. A and B, see Figure 3).
- By chance, the allele for one genotype (B) is passed on to the offspring more often than others. So the number of individuals with the allele increases.
- If by chance the same allele is passed on more often again and again, it can lead to evolution as the allele becomes more common in the population.

genotype A (4), genotype B (4) → genotype A (3), genotype B (5) → genotype A (1), genotype B (7)

**Figure 3:** *Diagram to show genetic drift in a population.*

**Exam Tip**
Don't confuse genetic drift with natural selection in the exam. In natural selection, characteristics become more common if they increase an organism's likelihood of survival. In genetic drift, they become more common by chance.

## Genetic drift and population size

Natural selection and genetic drift work alongside each other to drive evolution, but one process can drive evolution more than the other depending on the population size. Evolution by genetic drift usually has a greater effect in smaller populations where chance has a greater influence. In larger populations any chance variations in allele frequency tend to even out across the whole population.

**Tip:** Genetic drift tends to cause the genetic diversity of a population to decrease. Lack of genetic diversity may make species less able to adapt to future changes in their environment, so genetic drift can be a problem for small populations.

### Example — the evolution of human blood groups

Different Native American tribes show different blood group frequencies. For example, the Blackfeet tribe are mainly group A, but Navajos are mainly group O. Blood group doesn't affect survival or reproduction, so the differences aren't due to evolution by natural selection. In the past, human populations were much smaller and were often found in isolated groups. The blood group differences were due to evolution by genetic drift — by chance the allele for blood group O was passed on more often in the Navajo tribe, so over time this allele and blood group became more common.

## Genetic bottlenecks

A genetic bottleneck is an event (such as a natural disaster) that causes a big reduction in a population's size, leading to a reduction in the gene pool. Evolution by genetic drift has a greater effect if there's a genetic bottleneck.

**Tip:** The gene pool is the complete range of alleles in a population.

### Example

The mice in a large population are either black or grey. The coat colour doesn't affect their survival or reproduction. A large flood hits the population and the only survivors are grey mice and one black mouse. Grey becomes the most common colour due to genetic drift (see Figure 4 on the next page).

**Tip:** Disease and habitat destruction by humans can also act as genetic bottlenecks.

Module 6: Section 3 Evolution

**Tip:** The flood is the genetic bottleneck here — it's significantly reduced the size of the mouse population.

*Generation 1*
Black: 7
Grey: 7
Allele frequencies similar for grey and black mice.

Breeding →

*Generation 2*
Black: 6
Grey: 8
The allele frequencies are about the same as Generation 1.

↓ Flood

*Generation 3*
Black: 2
Grey: 7
The population recovers, but most of the mice are now grey.

← Genetic drift

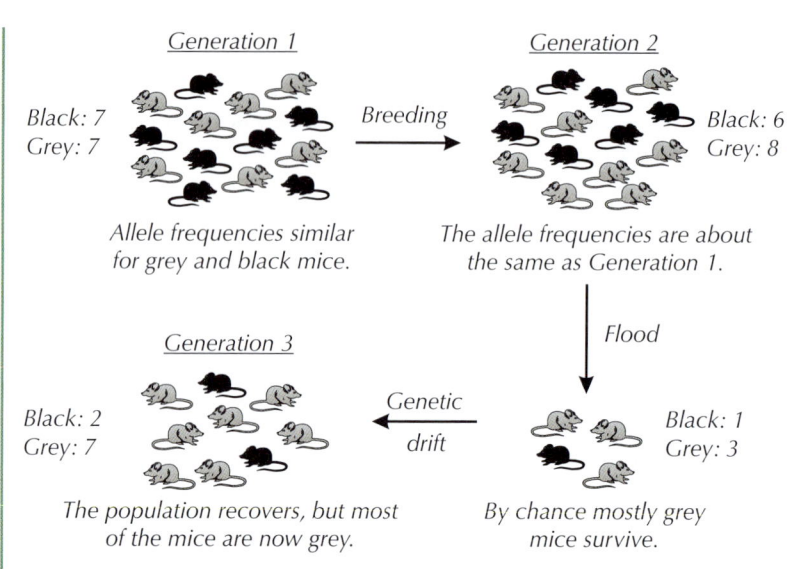

Black: 1
Grey: 3
By chance mostly grey mice survive.

**Figure 4:** *An example of a genetic bottleneck in a mouse population.*

### The founder effect

The founder effect describes what happens when just a few organisms from a population start a new population and there are only a small number of different alleles in the initial gene pool. Here's how it works:

- Individuals within a population show variation in their genotypes (see Figure 5).
- Some of these individuals start a new population. By chance these individuals mostly have one particular genotype (e.g. the blue genotype).
- Without any further 'gene flow' (i.e. the introduction of new alleles from outside the population) the new population will grow with reduced genetic variation. As the population is small, it's more heavily influenced by genetic drift than a larger population.

**Tip:** The brown genotype in Figure 5 could represent carriers of a genetic disorder. It's easy to see why the founder effect can lead to an unusually high incidence of a certain genetic disorder within a population, if the allele for it is present in the founding population.

*Original population*
Coloured circles show different genotypes.

*Original population*
Maintains a high level of genetic diversity.

*Founder population*
A small group splits off to form a new population.

*New population*
Genetic diversity is greatly reduced. Genotype frequencies are very different to the original population.

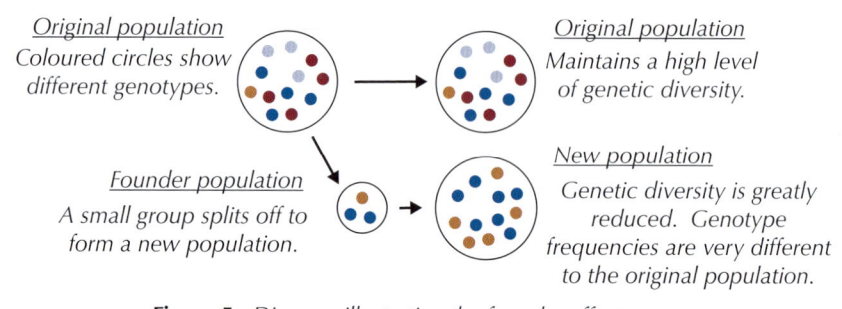

**Figure 5:** *Diagram illustrating the founder effect.*

The founder effect can occur as a result of migration leading to geographical separation or if a new colony is separated from the original population for another reason, such as religion.

---
**Example**

The Amish population of North America are all descended from a small number of Swiss who migrated there. The population shows little genetic diversity. They have remained isolated from the surrounding population due to their religious beliefs, so few new alleles have been introduced. The population has an unusually high incidence of certain genetic disorders.

## Practice Questions — Application

**Q1** Flowers of a plant species can be purple, pink or white. Each colour is coded for by a different allele. The graphs below show the frequencies of these alleles in two populations of the plant species.

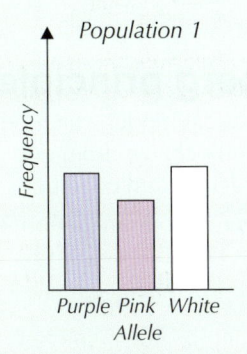

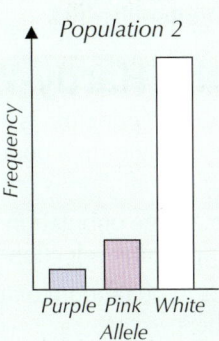

a) Describe the differences in allele frequencies between the two populations.
b) Explain how genetic drift could have led to the allele frequencies shown in Population 2.
c) Which is likely to be the smaller population, 1 or 2? Give a reason for your answer.

**Q2** The frequency of an allele involved in fur colouring was calculated for two populations of woodland mammal found in the north and south of a large forest. The results are shown in the table below. In 1999 a fire destroyed thousands of square miles of trees in the north of the forest.

a) The allele frequency for the southern population peaked in 2000. Suggest an explanation for this.
b) The allele is involved in the production of dark fur. Use this information to explain how natural selection might have accounted for the results for the northern population.

| Year | Allele frequency | |
|---|---|---|
| | North | South |
| 1994 | 0.31 | 0.17 |
| 1996 | 0.33 | 0.17 |
| 1998 | 0.33 | 0.19 |
| 2000 | 0.48 | 0.32 |
| 2002 | 0.52 | 0.24 |

**Tip:** Take your time looking at any data you're given — make sure you really understand what the table in Q2 is showing you before you attempt to answer the questions.

**Tip:** To help you answer Q2 b), think about how the fire might change the forest environment.

## Practice Questions — Fact Recall

**Q1** Explain what is meant by the following terms:
  a) gene pool,
  b) allele frequency.
**Q2** How are allele frequency and evolution related?
**Q3** Explain why variation is needed for evolution to take place.
**Q4** How does a stable environment affect selection?
**Q5** What is a genetic bottleneck and how does it influence evolution?
**Q6** Explain why the founder effect can lead to an increased incidence of genetic disease.

Module 6: Section 3 Evolution

**Learning Objective:**
- Be able to use the equations for the Hardy-Weinberg principle ($p + q = 1$ and $p^2 + 2pq + q^2 = 1$) to calculate allele frequencies in populations.

**Specification Reference 6.1.2**

# 2. The Hardy-Weinberg Principle

*A little bit of maths now... but I promise it's not too bad. Basically, you can work out allele and genotype frequencies for a whole population — which is more useful than it sounds.*

## What is the Hardy-Weinberg principle?

The Hardy-Weinberg principle is a mathematical model which predicts that the frequencies of alleles in a population won't change from one generation to the next. But this prediction is only true under certain conditions:

- It has to be a large population where there's no immigration, emigration, mutations or natural selection (see page 471).
- There needs to be random mating — all possible genotypes can breed with all others.

The Hardy-Weinberg equations (see below) are based on this principle. They can be used to estimate the frequency of particular alleles and genotypes within populations. If frequencies do change between generations in a large population then immigration, emigration, natural selection or mutations have happened.

## The Hardy-Weinberg equations

There are two Hardy-Weinberg equations — one is used for working out allele frequency and the other one is usually used when you're dealing with genotype frequencies.

### Allele frequency

The total frequency of all possible alleles for a characteristic in a certain population is 1.0. So the frequencies of the individual alleles (the dominant one and the recessive one) must add up to 1.0. Here's that idea in an equation:

$$p + q = 1$$

Where...
$p$ = the frequency of the dominant allele
$q$ = the frequency of the recessive allele

**Tip:** If the frequencies for two alleles add up to more than one, they're not alleles for the same gene (characteristic). If they come to less than one, there are more than two alleles for that gene.

### Genotype frequency

The total frequency of all possible genotypes for one characteristic in a certain population is 1.0. So the frequencies of the individual genotypes must add up to 1.0. But remember there are three genotypes — homozygous recessive, homozygous dominant and heterozygous. Here's the second equation:

$$p^2 + 2pq + q^2 = 1$$

Where...
$p^2$ = frequency of homozygous dominant genotype
$2pq$ = frequency of heterozygous genotype
$q^2$ = frequency of homozygous recessive genotype

**Tip:** Remember, homozygous dominant means two copies of the dominant allele (e.g. BB), homozygous recessive means two copies of the recessive allele (e.g. bb) and heterozygous means one copy of each allele (e.g. Bb). See pages 446-447.

## Uses of the Hardy-Weinberg principle

The best way to understand how to use the principle and the equations is to follow through some examples — like the ones on the next page...

## Predicting allele frequency

You can figure out the frequency of one allele if you know the frequency of the other:

### Example — Maths Skills

- A species of plant has either red or white flowers. Allele R (red) is dominant and allele r (white) is recessive. If the frequency of R is 0.4 in Population X, what is the frequency of r?
- You know the frequency of one allele and just need to find the frequency of the other using $p + q = 1$ (where $p$ = dominant allele, R, and $q$ = recessive allele, r). So:  $p + q = 1$
  $R + r = 1$
  $0.4 + r = 1$
  $r = 1 - 0.4 = 0.6$

So the frequency of the r allele in Population X is 0.6.

You can also figure out allele frequencies if you're given information about genotype (or phenotype) frequencies:

### Example — Maths Skills

- There are two alleles for flower colour (R and r), so there are three possible genotypes — RR, Rr and rr. If the frequency of genotype RR is 0.56 in Population Y, what is the allele frequency of r?
- You know that RR is the homozygous dominant genotype, so RR = $p^2$. You also know that the allele frequency for R = $p$, so:
  $p^2 = 0.56$
  $p = \sqrt{0.56} = 0.75$, so R = 0.75

You also know that $p + q = 1$, where $p$ = the dominant allele, R, and $q$ = the recessive allele, r. So:  $p + q = 1$
  $R + r = 1$
  $0.75 + r = 1$
  $r = 1 - 0.75 = 0.25$

So the frequency of the r allele (white) in Population Y is 0.25.

**Tip:** Remember, genotype is the alleles an organism has (e.g. Rr) and phenotype is the characteristics the alleles produce (e.g. red flowers). See page 446 for more.

**Exam Tip**
You'll be allowed to take a calculator into the exam to help you with calculations like these.

## Predicting genotype frequency

Here you're after genotype, so it's $p^2$, $q^2$ or $2pq$ you need to find:

### Example — Maths Skills

- If there are two alleles for flower colour (R and r), there are three possible genotypes — RR, Rr and rr. In Population Z, the frequency of genotype RR is 0.34 and the frequency of genotype Rr is 0.27. Find the frequency of rr in Population Z.
- $p^2 + 2pq + q^2 = 1$, where $p^2$ = homozygous dominant genotype, RR, $2pq$ = heterozygous genotype, Rr, and $q^2$ = homozygous recessive genotype, rr. So:  $p^2 + 2pq + q^2 = 1$
  RR + Rr + rr = 1
  0.34 + 0.27 + rr = 1
  rr = 1 − 0.34 − 0.27 = 0.39

So the frequency of the rr genotype in Population Z is 0.39.

**Tip:** The more examples you practise, the more confident you'll be at working out allele and genotype frequencies when it comes to your exam.

Module 6: Section 3 Evolution

**Exam Tip**
It's easier than it might seem to decide which equation to use. If you're given one allele frequency and asked to find the other it's the simple equation. If you know two out of the three genotype frequencies, you can find the other frequency using the big equation. For anything else you'll probably need to use a combination of equations.

**Tip:** There's more on carriers on page 447.

### Predicting the percentage of a population that has a certain genotype

You're looking at genotype again, so it's ultimately something to do with $p^2$, $q^2$ or $2pq$. But you might have to use a combination of equations to get there:

#### Example — Maths Skills

- The frequency of cystic fibrosis (genotype ff) in the UK is currently approximately 1 birth in every 2500. Use this information to estimate the percentage of people in the UK that are cystic fibrosis carriers (Ff).
- To do this you need to find the frequency of the heterozygous genotype Ff, i.e. $2pq$, using both equations. (You can't just use the big one as you only know one of the three genotypes — $q^2$.)

**First calculate q:**
Frequency of cystic fibrosis (homozygous recessive, ff) is 1 in 2500
$$ff = q^2 = \frac{1}{2500} = 0.0004. \text{ So } q = \sqrt{0.0004} = 0.02$$

**Next calculate p:**
Use $p + q = 1$, rearranged: $p = 1 - q = 1 - 0.02 = 0.98$

**Then calculate 2pq:**
$2pq = 2 \times p \times q = 2 \times 0.98 \times 0.02 = 0.039$

The frequency of genotype Ff is 0.039, so the percentage of the UK population that are carriers is $0.039 \times 100 = 3.9\%$.

### Practice Questions — Application

Q1 In a human population, the allele frequency for the recessive albino allele is measured over generations as shown in the table below.

a) Calculate the frequency of the pigmented (non-albino) allele in generation 1.
b) Calculate the frequency of the heterozygous genotype in generation 1.
c) Does the Hardy-Weinberg principle apply to this population? Explain your answer.

| Generation | Allele frequency |
|---|---|
| 1 | 0.10 |
| 4 | 0.07 |
| 7 | 0.03 |

Q2 ADA deficiency is an inherited metabolic disorder caused by a recessive allele. The recessive allele frequency in a population is 0.16. What is the frequency of the homozygous dominant genotype in the same population?

Q3 Seed texture in pea plants is controlled by two alleles, the dominant round allele and the recessive wrinkled allele. 31% of a population have wrinkled seeds. What percentage of the population have a heterozygous genotype?

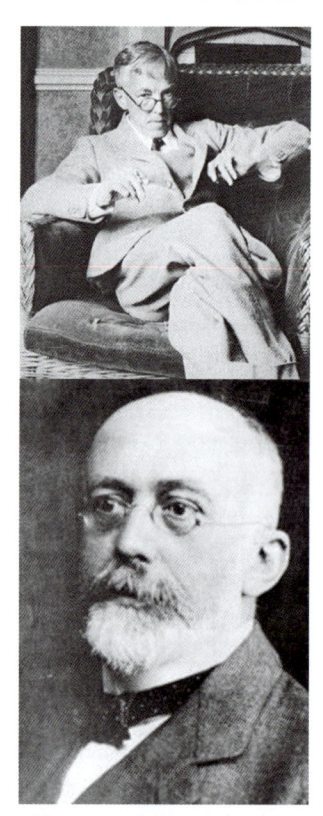

**Figure 1:** G H Hardy (top) and Wilhelm Weinberg (bottom) actually came up with the ideas behind the Hardy-Weinberg principle independently from one another.

### Practice Questions — Fact Recall

Q1 Describe the Hardy-Weinberg principle and the conditions under which it is true.
Q2 Write down the two Hardy-Weinberg equations and describe what each component represents.

# 3. Artificial Selection

*Selection for particular characteristics happens naturally in populations as a result of environmental factors — but it can also happen artificially when humans get involved...*

## What is artificial selection?

Artificial selection is when humans select individuals in a population to breed together to get desirable traits. Here are two examples:

### 1. Modern dairy cattle

Modern dairy cows have been produced through artificial selection. One of the characteristics that has been selected for is a high milk yield. Here's how it's done:

- Farmers select a female with a very high milk yield and a male whose mother had a very high milk yield and breed these two together.
- Then they select the offspring with the highest milk yields and breed them together.
- This is continued over several generations until a very high milk-yielding cow is produced.

Other characteristics selected for in dairy cows include:

- a high milk quality (rich and creamy),
- a long lactation period (so the cow produces milk for longer),
- large udders (to make milking easier),
- resistance to mastitis (inflammation of the udders) and other diseases,
- a calm temperament.

Artificial selection has been taking place for hundreds of years but it's been made much easier by modern techniques, e.g. artificial insemination and IVF give farmers more control over which cows reproduce. Animal cloning (see pages 515-518) allows farmers to produce genetically identical copies of their best cows, so they can be certain of the offspring's characteristics.

### 2. Bread wheat

Bread wheat (*Triticum aestivum*) is the plant from which flour is produced for bread-making. It produces a high yield of wheat because of artificial selection by humans:

- Wheat plants with a high wheat yield (e.g. large ears) are bred together.
- The offspring with the highest yields are then bred together.
- This is continued over several generations to produce a plant that has a very high yield.

Large ears × Large ears → Breed → Very large ears

Other characteristics selected for in bread wheat include:

- a higher tolerance of the cold than other wheat varieties,
- short stalks (so they don't collapse under the weight of the ears),
- uniform stalk heights (to make harvesting easier).

Techniques such as plant cloning (see pages 511-514) can be useful in the artificial selection of crop plants.

---

**Learning Objectives:**

- Understand the principles of artificial selection and its uses, including examples of selective breeding in plants and animals.
- Understand the importance of maintaining a resource of genetic material for use in selective breeding, including wild types.
- Understand the ethical considerations surrounding the use of artificial selection, including a consideration of the more extreme examples of the use of artificial selection to 'improve' domestic species, e.g. dog breeds.

**Specification Reference 6.1.2**

**Tip:** Artificial selection is also called selective breeding.

**Figure 1:** *The large ears of* Triticum aestivum.

Module 6: Section 3 Evolution

## Problems with artificial selection

Artificial selection is really useful, but it has downsides too.

### Reducing the gene pool

Artificial selection means that only organisms with similar traits and therefore similar alleles are bred together. This leads to a reduction in the number of alleles in the gene pool. A reduced gene pool could cause us problems in the future — for example, if a new disease appears, there's less chance of the alleles that could offer resistance to that disease being present in the population. Artificial selection could also mean that potentially useful alleles are accidentally lost from the population when other alleles are being selected for.

This means it's important to maintain resources of genetic material for use in the future, for example by preserving the original 'wild type' organisms that haven't undergone any artificial selection.

### Problems for organisms

Artificial selection can exaggerate certain traits, leading to health problems for the organisms involved. A reduced gene pool can also result in an increased incidence of genetic disease.

#### Examples

Modern pedigree dog breeds are all descended from a single wolf-like ancestor. Each breed has gone through many generations of artificial selection to produce the dogs we know today. Pedigree dogs such as Pugs and French Bulldogs have been bred to have flat, squashed up faces. This trait has become so exaggerated that many of these dogs now suffer breathing problems as a result.

There's a high incidence of hereditary deafness in certain dog breeds, including Dalmatians and English Bull Terriers. The cause of this is not fully understood, but there is evidence to suggest that deafness is linked to genes affecting pigmentation in these dogs.

*Figure 2: Pugs and Dalmatians can both suffer health problems as a result of selective breeding.*

Problems like these mean that there are ethical issues surrounding the use of artificial selection. For example, many people don't think it's fair to keep artificially selecting traits in dogs that cause them health problems.

**Tip:** There are ethical arguments for artificial selection too — it can make food production more efficient, which means more people can be fed using fewer resources, and it makes food production cheaper, which is important in parts of the world where people struggle to afford food. Make sure you can weigh up the benefits and the costs of artificial selection.

### Practice Questions — Fact Recall

Q1 Define artificial selection.
Q2 a) Describe how large udders may have been selected for in modern dairy cows.
   b) Apart from large udders, give one other characteristic that could be artificially selected for in dairy cows.
Q3 Outline an example of selective breeding in plants.
Q4 Describe two potential problems associated with selective breeding.

# 4. Speciation

*The next few pages cover what a species is and how a new one is formed...*

## What is speciation?

A **species** is defined as a group of similar organisms that can reproduce to give fertile offspring. Speciation is the development of a new species. It occurs when populations of the same species become **reproductively isolated** — changes in allele frequencies cause changes in phenotype that mean they can no longer breed together to produce fertile offspring.

## Allopatric speciation

Populations can become reproductively isolated through a combination of geographical isolation and natural selection — this is called **allopatric speciation**. Geographical isolation happens when a physical barrier, e.g. a flood or an earthquake, divides a population of a species, causing some individuals to become separated from the main population. Populations that are geographically isolated will experience slightly different conditions. For example, there might be a different climate on each side of the physical barrier. Because the environment is different for each population, different characteristics will become more common due to natural selection (because there are different selection pressures):

- Because different characteristics will be advantageous on each side, the allele frequencies will change in each population, e.g. if one allele is more advantageous on one side of the barrier, the frequency of that allele on that side will increase.
- Mutations will take place independently in each population, also changing the allele frequencies.
- The changes in allele frequencies will lead to changes in phenotype frequencies, e.g. the advantageous characteristics (phenotypes) will become more common on that side.

Eventually, individuals from different populations will have changed so much that they won't be able to breed with one another to produce fertile offspring — they'll have become reproductively isolated. The two groups will have become separate species — see Figure 2.

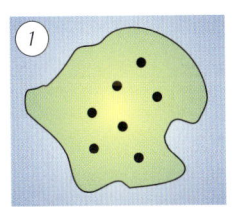

### Learning Objective:
- Understand the role of isolating mechanisms in the evolution of new species, to include geographical mechanisms (allopatric speciation) and reproductive mechanisms (sympatric speciation).

**Specification Reference 6.1.2**

**Tip:** Geographical isolation is also known as ecological isolation.

**Exam Tip**
It's important to use the correct terminology in the exam, so make sure you understand and can use terms such as 'allele frequency', 'geographical isolation', 'allopatric speciation' and 'sympatric speciation' (coming up on the next page).

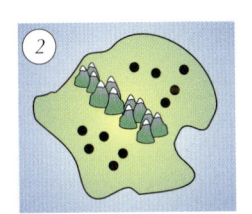

*Population of individuals*
● = individual organism

*Physical barriers stop interbreeding between populations.*

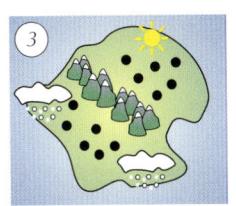

*Populations adapt to new environments.*

*Allele and phenotype frequency change leading to the development of new species.*

**Figure 2:** Diagram showing how geographical isolation could lead to reproductive isolation and so speciation.

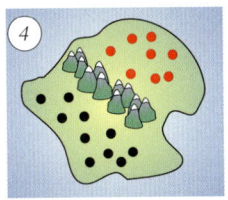

**Figure 1:** Four species of 'Darwin's finches'. These are often seen as a classic example of speciation.

Module 6: Section 3 Evolution

**Tip:** Don't confuse geographical isolation with reproductive isolation. Populations that are geographically isolated are physically separated, but may still be able to reproduce if brought back together. Geographical isolation can lead to reproductive isolation if natural selection significantly changes the allele frequencies in the two separated populations.

# How does reproductive isolation occur?

Reproductive isolation occurs because the changes in the alleles and phenotypes of the two populations prevent them from successfully breeding together. These changes include:

- Seasonal changes — individuals from the same population develop different flowering or mating seasons, or become sexually active at different times of the year.
- Mechanical changes — changes in genitalia prevent successful mating.
- Behavioural changes — a group of individuals develop courtship rituals that aren't attractive to the main population.

# Sympatric speciation

A population doesn't have to become geographically isolated to become reproductively isolated. Random mutations could occur within a population, resulting in the changes mentioned above, preventing members of that population breeding with other members of the species. Speciation without geographical isolation is called sympatric speciation.

**Tip:** Reproductive isolation is necessary for sympatric or allopatric speciation to take place.

It's generally thought that sympatric speciation is pretty rare, as it's difficult for a section of a population to become completely reproductively isolated from the rest of the population without being geographically isolated too (as is the case with allopatric speciation).

**Tip:** Polyploidy can be a mechanism of reproductive isolation.

### Example

Most eukaryotic organisms are diploid — they have two sets of homologous (matched) chromosomes in their cells. Sometimes, mutations can occur that increase the number of chromosomes. This is known as polyploidy. Individuals with different numbers of chromosomes can't reproduce sexually to give fertile offspring — so if a polyploid organism emerges in a diploid population, the polyploid organism will be reproductively isolated from the diploid organisms. If the polyploid organism then reproduces asexually, a new species could develop. Polyploidy can only lead to speciation if it doesn't prove fatal to the organism and more polyploid organisms can be produced. It's more common in plants than animals.

**Exam Tip**
Make sure you're clear on the difference between sympatric and allopatric speciation, and can remember which is which. If it helps, you could think of **S**ympatric speciation happening in the **S**ame place, and **A**llopatric speciation occurring in populations that are **A**way from each other.

### Practice Questions — Application

Q1 African elephants have been traditionally classified as one species, *Loxodonta africana*. However, recent research suggests that there are actually two separate species of African elephant, one living in a savannah (grassland) habitat and one living in forested areas. The two populations are thought to have separated from each other several million years ago when a drier climate caused some elephants to move out of the forests and onto the savannah.

Using your knowledge of speciation, describe how the two separate species of African elephant may have evolved.

Q2 *Rhagoletis pomonella* is a species of fly from North America. Historically, *R. pomonella* flies laid their eggs in hawthorn fruits, but when apples were introduced to North America, some started to lay their eggs inside apples. There are now two separate populations of *R. pomonella* — one laying its eggs inside apples and the other laying its eggs inside hawthorn fruits. The flies only tend to mate on fruit of the same species that they hatched in. Some scientists think this could be the beginning of speciation.

   a) Describe how you could test whether the two populations of *R. pomonella* had become different species.
   b) What kind of speciation would this be an example of? Explain your answer.

## Practice Questions — Fact Recall

Q1 Explain what is meant by the following terms:
   a) reproductive isolation,
   b) geographic isolation,
   c) speciation.

Q2 Describe the difference between allopatric speciation and sympatric speciation.

Q3 Suggest three changes that could lead to a population becoming reproductively isolated.

# Section Summary

Make sure you know...

- That evolution is a change in allele frequencies in a population over time, and can occur due to natural selection and genetic drift.
- Why variation is essential for natural selection — because organisms vary, some individuals will be better adapted to selection pressures than others. These organisms are more likely to survive, reproduce and pass on their beneficial alleles than others. This will increase the frequency of the beneficial allele in the population over many generations.
- That in a stable environment, selection will favour alleles for characteristics towards the middle of the range (stabilising selection).
- That in a changing environment, selection will favour alleles for characteristics of an extreme type (directional selection).
- That in evolution by genetic drift, alleles become more common in a population by chance.
- That genetic drift has a bigger effect in small populations than in large populations.
- That genetic bottlenecks occur when a population shrinks rapidly, e.g. due to a natural disaster.
- That the founder effect describes what happens when a few organisms from a population start a new population so there is only a small number of different alleles in the initial gene pool.
- That genetic bottlenecks and the founder effect make populations more susceptible to genetic drift.
- That the Hardy-Weinberg principle predicts that allele frequencies in a population won't change between one generation and the next, provided that certain conditions are met.
- How to use the Hardy-Weinberg equations ($p + q = 1$ and $p^2 + 2pq + q^2 = 1$) to calculate allele and genotype frequencies.
- How artificial selection is used to produce plants and animals with desirable traits.
- Why preserving 'wild type' organisms is important for maintaining resources of genetic material for use in the future.
- That there are ethical considerations concerning the use of artificial selection.
- That speciation is the development of a new species and it happens when populations of the same species become reproductively isolated (unable to interbreed to produce fertile offspring).
- That allopatric speciation can occur when populations of the same species are geographically isolated and differences in the gene pools develop that eventually lead to reproductive isolation.
- That sympatric speciation occurs when a random mutation causes reproductive isolation without geographic isolation.
- The different ways in which reproductive isolation can occur.

# Exam-style Questions

**1** A species of insectivorous bird usually breeds in mid-April, although there is variation between individuals in breeding date. Individuals that breed earlier in the year have difficulties finding sufficient food to feed their young, and the offspring of individuals that breed later are less likely to survive the following winter.

**(a)** State the kind of selection that is acting on this species.

*(1 mark)*

**(b)** It is thought that climate change may cause the insects that this species feeds on to increase in abundance earlier in the year. Describe and explain the possible effect of this selective pressure on the bird species.

*(2 marks)*

**2** Chickens that are farmed for their meat are known as broiler chickens. Broiler chickens grow faster than normal chickens, so can be slaughtered at a younger age, are more efficient at converting food into body mass, and produce a higher proportion of breast meat. However, their rapid growth to large sizes means broiler chickens are more vulnerable to cardiovascular problems than normal chickens, and can have problems with walking.

**(a) (i)** State the name of the process by which farmers developed broiler chickens from normal chickens.

*(1 mark)*

**(ii)** Describe how this process may have occurred.

*(2 marks)*

**(b)** Discuss the ethical issues around the development of broiler chickens for meat.

*(3 marks)*

**3** A forest is home to a population of a species of flightless beetle. A new motorway is built, separating an area of woodland from the main body of the forest, and isolating a small population of the beetle from the larger population in the main forest. The beetles will not cross open spaces, due to increased visibility to predators, so the motorway acts as a barrier between the two populations. There is no immigration into either woodland from the wider area.

Scientists study the two populations, collecting data on the size and colour of individuals, and how likely they are to survive (which they estimate from recapture rates). Over time, they notice that the beetles in the small fragment of woodland have evolved to become significantly smaller than the beetles in the main body of the forest. The size of the beetles in the main body of the forest remains unchanged.

**(a)** Suggest two possible mechanisms for this evolutionary change.

*(2 marks)*

**(b)** Describe how the scientists could distinguish between these two mechanisms using the data they have collected.

*(2 marks)*

**4** The Amish population of North America descended from a small group of migrants. They live isolated from the surrounding population, and it is rare for people to migrate into the Amish community.

The Amish population has an unusually high incidence of genetic disorders, including a rare form of dwarfism called Ellis-van Creveld syndrome, which can lead to health problems and death in childhood.

(a) Ellis-van Creveld syndrome is caused by a recessive allele (e). In some Amish communities, the frequency of Ellis-van Creveld syndrome may be as high as 5 births in every 1000.
The Hardy-Weinberg equations are:

$$p + q = 1$$
$$p^2 + 2pq + q^2 = 1$$

Use the Hardy-Weinberg equations to calculate the percentage of these communities that are **carriers** of Ellis-van Creveld syndrome (genotype Ee). Show your working. Give your answer to **two decimal places**.

*(2 marks)*

(b) What process is likely to have led to the high frequency of the Ellis-van Creveld allele in some Amish communities? Give a reason for your answer.

*(2 marks)*

**5** In the early 1970s, ten lizards of the species *Podarcis sicula* were introduced to the island of Pod Mrcaru in the Adriatic Sea from the nearby island of Pod Kopiste. Pod Mrcaru has denser vegetation than Pod Kopiste.

Thirty-six years later, researchers returned to the islands. They found that *P. sicula* on Pod Kopiste ate a diet mainly consisting of insects, whilst the diet of *P. sicula* on Pod Mrcaru had changed to include a high proportion of plant material. The *P. sicula* lizards on Pod Mrcaru had larger heads than the *P. sicula* on Pod Kopiste, and were able to bite with more force. *P. sicula* lizards on Pod Mrcaru had also developed chambers in their intestines, which are associated with fermenting cellulose in order to produce fatty acids, and which were absent in *P. sicula* from Pod Kopiste.

(a)* Explain how the differences between lizards on the two islands may have arisen in the 36 years since their introduction to Pod Mrcaru.

*(9 marks)*

(b) It is possible that these changes may be early stages of speciation.
  (i) State the name for this kind of speciation.

*(1 mark)*

  (ii) State what would need to occur for these two populations to become separate species.

*(1 mark)*

\* The quality of your response will be assessed in this question.

# Module 6  Section 4: Manipulating Genomes

## 1. Common Techniques

*There are many techniques that can be used to do things like copy, cut out and separate fragments of DNA. This allows us to study and alter genes. You might not get much opportunity to use the techniques involved, but you do need to know the theory behind a few of the more common ones...*

### Techniques for studying genes

There are lots of techniques used to study genes and their function — you need to learn some of these techniques for the exam. They include:

- The polymerase chain reaction (PCR) (see below).
- Cutting out DNA fragments using restriction enzymes (see p. 488-489).
- Gel electrophoresis (see pages 489-490).

These techniques are also used in DNA profiling (see page 492), genetic engineering (see pages 493-494), gene therapy (see pages 499-500) and DNA sequencing (see pages 501-506).

### The polymerase chain reaction

The polymerase chain reaction (PCR) can be used to select a fragment of DNA (containing the gene or bit of DNA you're interested in) and amplify it to produce millions of copies in just a few hours. PCR has several stages and is repeated over and over to make lots of copies. Here's how it works:

**Learning Objectives:**
- Understand the principles of the polymerase chain reaction (PCR) and its application in DNA analysis.
- Understand the use of restriction enzymes.
- Understand the principles and uses of electrophoresis for separating nucleic acid fragments or proteins.
- Know how to carry out electrophoresis (PAG6).

**Specification Reference 6.1.3**

### Step 1
A reaction mixture is set up that contains the DNA sample, free nucleotides, **primers** and **DNA polymerase**. Primers are short pieces of DNA that are complementary to the bases at the start of the fragment you want. DNA polymerase is an enzyme that creates new DNA strands.

### Step 2
The DNA mixture is heated to 95 °C to break the hydrogen bonds between the two strands of DNA. DNA polymerase doesn't denature even at this high temperature — this is important as it means many cycles of PCR can be carried out without having to use new enzymes each time. The mixture is then cooled to 50-65 °C so that the primers can bind (anneal) to the strands.

**Tip:** The techniques described over the next few pages will turn up again in the rest of the section, so make sure you're familiar with them now.

**Tip:** We've only shown very small pieces of DNA to make the diagrams easier to follow, but real genes are much longer. (Real primers are longer too, but not as big as genes.)

**Tip:** DNA polymerase is called a thermostable enzyme because it doesn't denature at high temperatures.

Module 6: Section 4  Manipulating Genomes

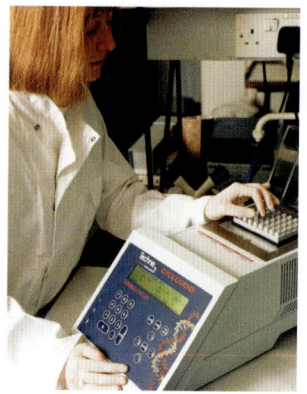

*Figure 1: Scientist using a programmable PCR machine.*

### Step 3
The reaction mixture is heated to 72 °C, so DNA polymerase can work. The DNA polymerase lines up free DNA nucleotides alongside each template strand. Complementary base pairing means new complementary strands are formed.

### Step 4
Two new copies of the fragment of DNA are formed and one cycle of PCR is complete. Then the cycle starts again — the mixture is heated to 95 °C and this time all four strands (two original and two new) are used as templates.

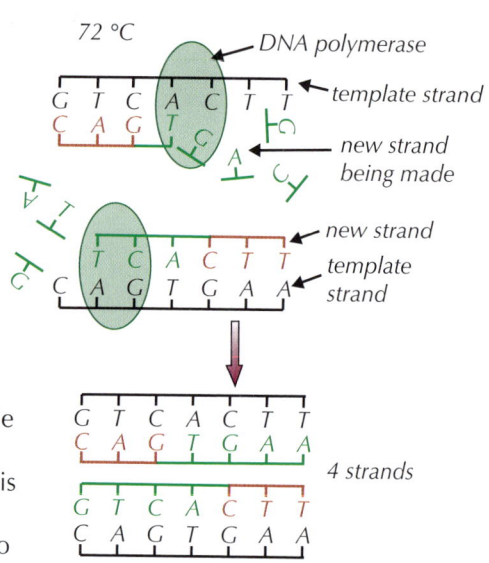

As shown below, each PCR cycle doubles the amount of DNA, e.g. 1st cycle = 2 × 2 = 4 DNA fragments, 2nd cycle = 4 × 2 = 8 DNA fragments and so on.

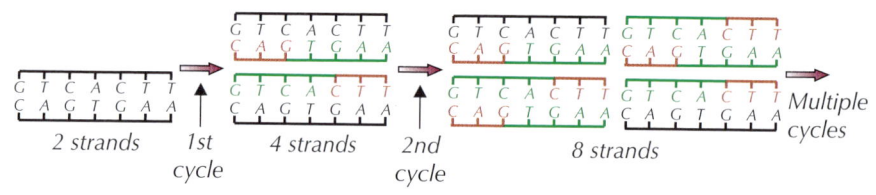

**Tip:** PCR produces lots of identical copies of DNA, so it can be used to clone genes outside of a living organism — this is called *in vitro* cloning.

**Tip:** Restriction enzymes are also known as restriction endonucleases.

## Using restriction enzymes

As well as PCR, another way to get a DNA fragment from an organism's DNA is by using restriction enzymes. Here's how they work:

Some sections of DNA have **palindromic sequences** of nucleotides. These sequences consist of antiparallel base pairs (base pairs that read the same in opposite directions) — see Figure 2.

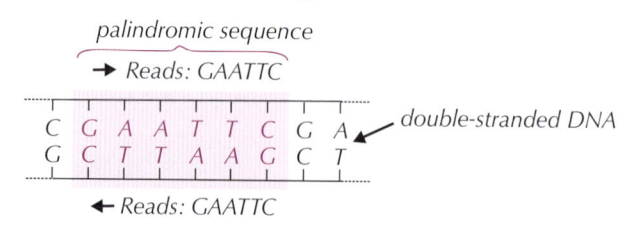

*Figure 2: A palindromic DNA sequence.*

Restriction enzymes recognise specific palindromic sequences (known as **recognition sequences**) and cut (digest) the DNA at these places. Different restriction enzymes cut at different specific recognition sequences, because the shape of the recognition sequence is complementary to an enzyme's active site.

**Tip:** Remember, the active site is where an enzyme's substrate binds. In this case, the recognition sequence is the substrate molecule.

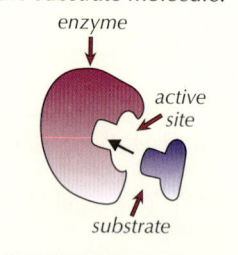

**Examples**
- The restriction enzyme *Eco*RI cuts at GAATTC.
- The restriction enzyme *Hind*III cuts at AAGCTT.

If recognition sequences are present at either side of the DNA fragment you want, you can use restriction enzymes to separate it from the rest of the DNA — see Figure 3. The DNA sample is incubated with the specific restriction enzyme, which cuts the DNA fragment via a hydrolysis reaction. Sometimes the cut leaves **sticky ends** — small tails of unpaired bases at each end of the fragment. Sticky ends can be used to bind (anneal) the DNA fragment to another piece of DNA that has sticky ends with complementary sequences (there's more about this on pages 493-494).

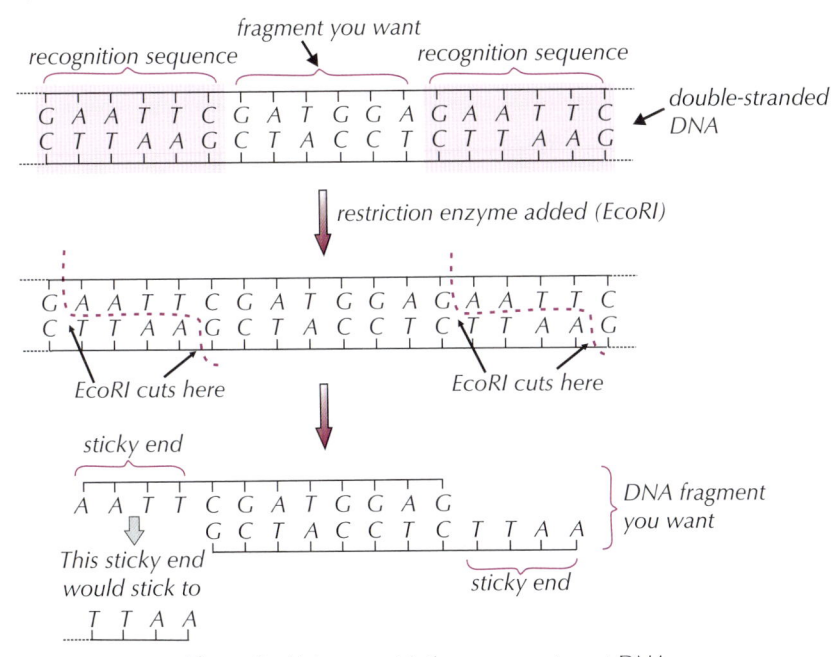

*Figure 3: Using a restriction enzyme to cut DNA.*

**Tip:** You won't always find the same restriction enzyme site either side of the fragment you want. E.g. you might get an *Eco*RI site on one side and a *Hind*III on the other, so you'd have to incubate the DNA sample with both enzymes to cut the piece you're after.

# Electrophoresis

PRACTICAL ACTIVITY GROUP 6

Electrophoresis is a procedure that uses an electrical current to separate out DNA fragments, RNA fragments or proteins depending on their size. Here's how you can carry out electrophoresis in the lab using samples of fragmented DNA — there are three main stages involved.

**Tip:** You'll need to carry out a risk assessment before doing any electrophoresis. It should include making sure your hands are dry before handling any electrical equipment.

## Stage 1

Electrophoresis is commonly performed using agarose gel that has been poured into a gel tray and left to solidify. A row of wells is created at one end of the gel. To perform electrophoresis, firstly you need to put the gel tray into a gel box (or tank). You need to make sure the end of the gel tray with the wells is closest to the negative electrode on the gel box. Then add buffer solution to the reservoirs at the sides of the gel box so that the surface of the gel becomes covered in the buffer solution (see Figure 4).

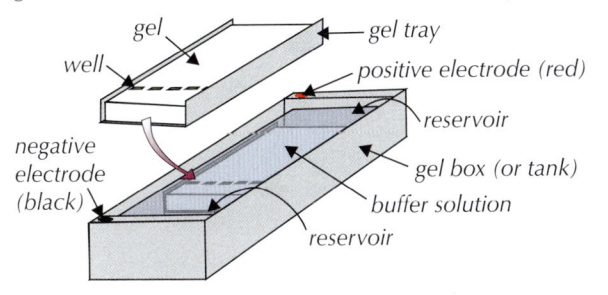

*Figure 4: Setting up a gel tray and gel box for electrophoresis.*

Module 6: Section 4 Manipulating Genomes

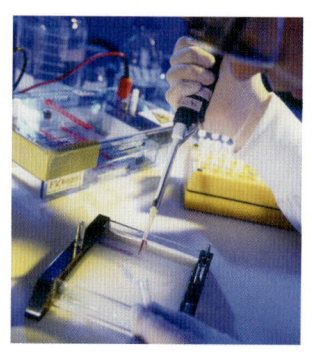

*Figure 6: A scientist loading a DNA sample into a gel.*

**Tip:** Electrophoresis forms the basis of DNA profiling — a process that can be used to determine how closely related (genetically similar) two or more organisms are.

### Stage 2

Take your fragmented DNA samples and, using a micropipette, add the same volume of loading dye to each — loading dye helps the samples to sink to the bottom of the wells and makes them easier to see.

Next add a set volume (e.g. 10 µl) of a DNA sample to the first well. You have to be really careful when adding the samples to the wells — make sure the tip of your micropipette is in the buffer solution and just above the opening of the well (see Figure 5). Don't stick the tip of the micropipette too far into the well or you could pierce the bottom of it.

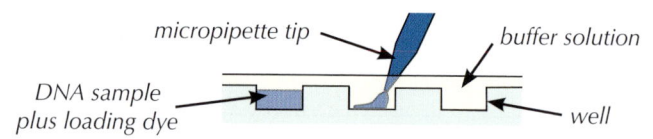

*Figure 5: Adding the DNA samples (with loading dye) to the wells in the gel.*

Then repeat this process and add the same volume of each of your other DNA samples to other wells in the gel. Use a clean micropipette tip each time. Make sure you record which DNA sample you have added to each well.

### Stage 3

Put the lid on the gel box and connect the leads from the gel box to the power supply. Then turn on the power supply and set it to the required voltage, e.g. 100 V. This causes an electrical current to be passed through the gel.

DNA fragments are negatively charged, so they'll move through the gel towards the positive electrode at the far end of the gel (called the anode). Small DNA fragments move faster and travel further through the gel, so the DNA fragments will separate according to size.

Let the gel run for about 30 minutes (or until the dye is about 2 cm from the end of the gel), then turn off the power supply. Remove the gel tray from the gel box and tip off any excess buffer solution. Wearing gloves, stain the DNA fragments by covering the surface of the gel with a staining solution then rinsing the gel with water. The bands of the different DNA fragments will now be visible (see Figure 7).

**Tip:** The size (length) of DNA fragments is measured in bases, e.g. ATCC = 4 bases or base pairs (bp) or nucleotides, 1000 bases is one kilobase (1 kb).

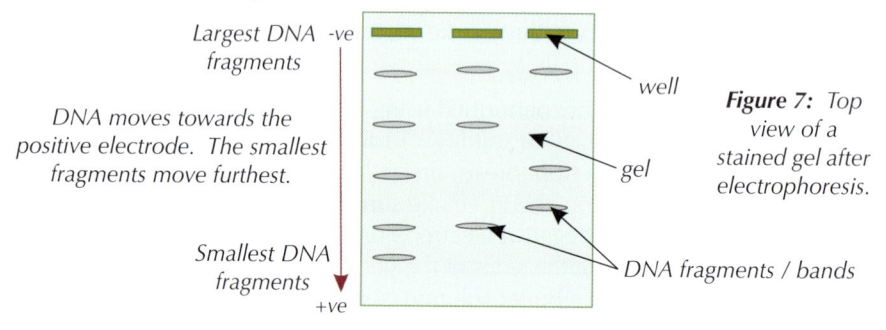

*Figure 7: Top view of a stained gel after electrophoresis.*

### Electrophoresis with RNA fragments and proteins

Electrophoresis can be carried out on RNA fragments following the same basic method as for DNA fragments.

However, proteins can be positively charged or negatively charged so, before they undergo electrophoresis, they're mixed with a chemical that denatures the proteins so they all have the same charge. Electrophoresis of proteins has many uses, e.g. to identify the proteins present in urine or blood samples, which may help to diagnose disease.

Module 6: Section 4 **Manipulating Genomes**

## Practice Questions — Application

**Q1** The following DNA fragment is being copied using PCR. The arrows mark the start of each DNA strand.

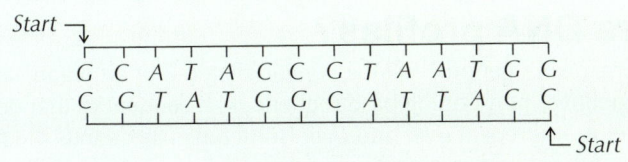

```
Start ↴
G C A T A C C G T A A T G G
C G T A T G G C A T T A C C
                        ↑ Start
```

a) The scientist carrying out the PCR uses primers that are four bases long. Give the sequences of the primers he will need to use to copy the DNA fragment.

b) The scientist carries out six cycles of PCR. How many single strands of DNA will he have once the six cycles are complete?

**Q2** Using information from the table below, describe and explain how restriction enzymes could be used to cut this DNA sequence:

CAGGATCCTCCTTACATAGTGAATTCATGC

| Restriction enzyme | Recognition sequence |
|---|---|
| BamHI | GGATCC |
| HindIII | AAGCTT |
| EcoRI | GAATTC |

**Tip:** Restriction enzymes are used a lot in gene technology to cut DNA fragments, so make sure you can answer Q2 — they'll pop up again, I promise.

**Q3** Below is part of a method for carrying out electrophoresis. A tray containing a prepared gel has already been added to a gel box and covered with buffer solution.

- Using a micropipette, add the same volume of loading dye to each DNA sample.
- Add 10 μl of each DNA sample (plus loading dye) to each well in the gel, so there is one sample in each well.
- Record which DNA sample has been added to each well.

a) Why is loading dye added to the DNA samples?

b) Describe how you could make sure that the DNA sample is successfully transferred to the well without being contaminated.

c) What are the next steps needed to make the DNA fragments move through the gel?

## Practice Questions — Fact Recall

**Q1** What does PCR stand for?
**Q2** Explain what is meant by the term 'palindromic sequence'.
**Q3** What are sticky ends? Why are they useful?
**Q4** Where would the longest DNA fragments be found in a gel — at the top (near the negative electrode) or at the bottom (near the positive electrode)?
**Q5** What do you need to do to samples of proteins before they can undergo electrophoresis?
**Q6** Give an example of a use for the electrophoresis of proteins.

Module 6: Section 4 Manipulating Genomes

**Learning Objective:**
- Know the principles of DNA profiling and its uses, including in forensics and analysis of disease risk.

**Specification Reference 6.1.3**

# 2. DNA Profiling

*Techniques for studying genes and their functions are actually very useful...*

## What are DNA profiles?
Some of an organism's genome (all the genetic material in an organism) consists of repetitive, non-coding base sequences — sequences that don't code for proteins and repeat over and over (sometimes thousands of times). The number of times these non-coding sequences are repeated differs from person to person, so the length of these sequences in nucleotides differs too.

The number of times a sequence is repeated at different, specific places (loci) in a person's genome (and so the number of nucleotides there) can be analysed using electrophoresis. This creates a DNA profile. The probability of two individuals having the same DNA profile is very low because the chance of two individuals having the same number of sequence repeats at each locus in DNA is very low.

### Use in forensic science
Forensic scientists use DNA profiling to compare samples of DNA collected from crime scenes (e.g. DNA from blood, semen, skin cells, saliva, hair etc.) to samples of DNA from possible suspects, to link them to crime scenes. The DNA is isolated from all the collected samples (from the crime scene and from the suspects). PCR (see pages 487-488) is used to amplify multiple areas containing different sequence repeats — primers are used to bind to either side of these repeats and so the whole repeat is amplified. The PCR products are run on an electrophoresis gel and the DNA profiles produced are compared to see if any match (i.e. if they have the same pattern of bands on the gel). If the samples match, it links a person to the crime scene.

**Tip:** Electrophoresis could also be used in this way to see if two DNA samples have come from the same species (i.e. the more similar the pattern of bands, the more likely the samples are from the same species).

**— Example —**
This gel shows that the DNA profile from suspect C matches that from the crime scene, linking them to the crime scene. All four bands match, so suspect C has the same number of repeats (nucleotides) at four different places.

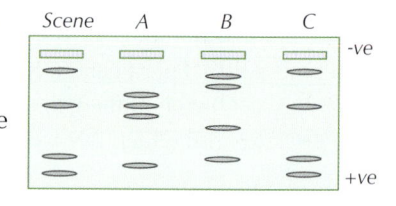

**Tip:** In DNA profiling in the UK, the results from ten different loci (plural for locus) are analysed. The chances of two DNA profiles matching by chance is up to 1 in a billion.

### Use in medical diagnosis
In medical diagnosis, a DNA profile can refer to a unique pattern of several alleles. It can be used to analyse the risk of genetic disorders. It's useful when the specific mutation isn't known or where several mutations could have caused the disorder, because it identifies a broader, altered genetic pattern.

**— Example —**
Preimplantation genetic haplotyping (PGH) screens embryos created by IVF for genetic disorders before they're implanted into the uterus. The faulty regions of the parents' DNA are used to produce DNA profiles, which are compared to the DNA profile of the embryo. If the profiles match, the embryo has inherited the disorder. It can be used to screen for cystic fibrosis, Huntington's disease etc.

---

**Practice Question — Fact Recall**

Q1 Describe how DNA profiling can be used in forensic science.

# 3. Genetic Engineering

*Genetic engineering uses gene technologies to alter organisms' DNA.*

## What is genetic engineering?

Genetic engineering is the manipulation of an organism's DNA. Organisms that have had their DNA altered by genetic engineering are called **transformed organisms**. These organisms have **recombinant DNA** — DNA formed by joining together DNA from different sources.

Genetic engineering involves extracting a gene from one organism and then inserting it into another organism (often one that's a different species). Genes can also be manufactured (e.g. by PCR) instead of extracted from an organism. The organism with the inserted gene will then produce the protein coded for by that gene.

An organism that has been genetically engineered to include a gene from a different species is sometimes called a **transgenic organism**. There's more on transgenic organisms on pages 495-497.

## Genetic engineering — the process

You need to know how genetic engineering is carried out.
There are three parts to the process:

### Part 1 — Obtaining DNA containing the desired gene

The first step is to get hold of a DNA fragment that contains the desired gene (i.e. the gene you're interested in). The fragment can be isolated from another organism using restriction enzymes.

### Part 2 — Making recombinant DNA

The next step is to insert the DNA fragment into **vector DNA** — a vector is something that's used to transfer DNA into a cell. Vectors can be **plasmids** (small, circular molecules of DNA in bacteria) or **bacteriophages** (viruses that infect bacteria). The vector DNA is isolated, then restriction enzymes and **DNA ligase** (an enzyme) are used to stick the DNA fragment and vector DNA together. Here's how it works:

**Step 1**
The vector DNA is isolated.

**Step 2**
The vector DNA is cut open using the same restriction enzyme that was used to isolate the DNA fragment containing the desired gene. This means that the sticky ends of the vector DNA are complementary to the sticky ends of the DNA fragment containing the gene.

**Step 3**
The vector DNA and DNA fragment are mixed together with DNA ligase. DNA ligase joins the sugar-phosphate backbones of the two bits of DNA. This process is called ligation.

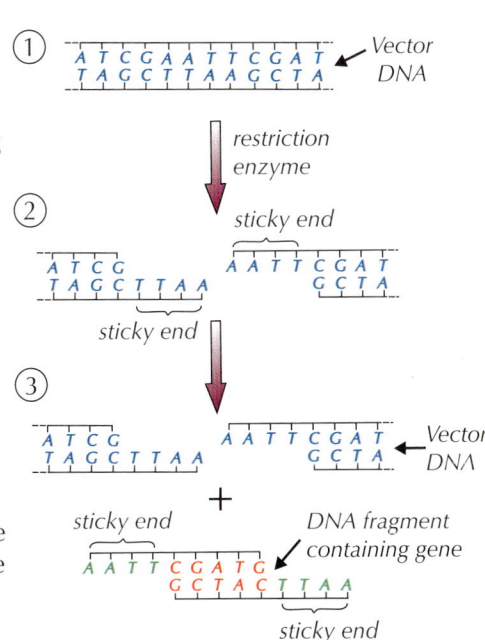

### Learning Objectives:

- Know the principles of genetic engineering, including the isolation of genes from one organism and the placing of these genes into another organism using suitable vectors.
- Understand the techniques used in genetic engineering, including the use of restriction enzymes, plasmids and DNA ligase to form recombinant DNA with the desired gene, and electroporation.

**Specification Reference 6.1.3**

**Tip:** Remember, restriction enzymes recognise specific palindromic sequences in the base pairs and cut the DNA at these points — see page 488-489 for more.

Module 6: Section 4 **Manipulating Genomes**

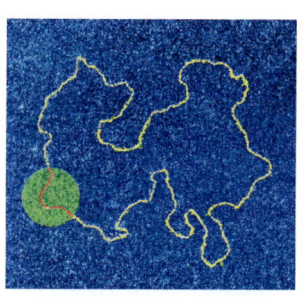

*Figure 1: Recombinant plasmid DNA. The DNA fragment containing the desired gene is highlighted red.*

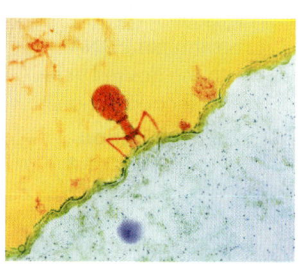

*Figure 2: This isn't an alien spaceship — it's actually a bacteriophage (orange) injecting its viral DNA into an E. coli bacterium (blue).*

**Step 4**
The new combination of bases in the DNA (vector DNA + DNA fragment) is called recombinant DNA.

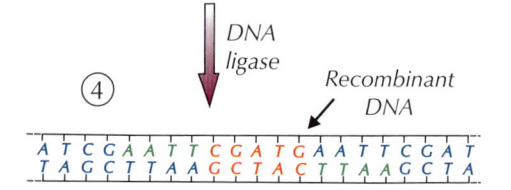

**Part 3 — Transforming cells**
The vector with the recombinant DNA is used to transfer the gene into the bacterial cells (called **host cells**). If a plasmid vector is used, the host cells have to be persuaded to take in the plasmid vector and its DNA.

— Example ——
A suspension of the bacterial cells is mixed with the plasmid vector and placed in a machine called an electroporator. The machine is switched on and an electrical field is created in the mixture, which increases the permeability of the bacterial cell membranes and allows them to take in the plasmids. This technique is called **electroporation**.

With a bacteriophage vector, the bacteriophage will infect the host bacterium by injecting its DNA into it — see Figure 2. The phage DNA (with the desired gene in it) then integrates into the bacterial DNA.

Cells that take up the vectors containing the desired gene are genetically engineered, so are called transformed.

### Practice Question — Application

Q1 A scientist is studying the role of a protein in cancer progression. He transformed some *E. coli* cells with recombinant DNA containing the gene that codes for this protein.

a) A DNA fragment containing the desired gene was made using restriction enzymes. Describe and explain how the recombinant DNA was produced using this fragment.

b) Name a technique that could be used to increase the likelihood of the *E. coli* cells taking up the recombinant DNA.

### Practice Questions — Fact Recall

Q1 What is genetic engineering?

Q2 What is the name given to DNA that has been formed by joining together DNA fragments from different sources?

Q3 a) Describe the role of a vector in genetic engineering.
   b) Give two different types of vectors.

Q4 Explain why it is important to cut open the vector DNA with the same restriction enzyme that was used to isolate the DNA fragment containing the desired gene.

Q5 Describe the role of DNA ligase in genetic engineering.

# 4. Genetically Modified Organisms

*Genetic engineering can be used to produce transformed organisms. These organisms are made to benefit humans in different ways. However, there can be negative ethical issues with this type of technology...*

## Creating insect-resistant plants

One way in which plants can be genetically manipulated is by having a gene inserted into their cells which makes them resistant to insect pests.

### Example

Soybeans are an important food source across the world, but yields of soybeans can be greatly reduced by insect pests that feed on the soybean plants.

Scientists have successfully genetically modified soybean plants to include a gene originally found in the bacteria *Bacillus thuringiensis* (Bt). The gene codes for a protein that is toxic to some of the insects that feed on soybean plants.

**Step 1**
To genetically modify a soybean plant, the desired gene can be isolated from Bt using restriction enzymes and inserted into a plasmid taken from the bacterium *Agrobacterium tumefaciens*.

**Step 2**
The plasmid is put back into *A. tumefaciens*.

**Step 3**
The soybean plant cells are then deliberately infected with the transformed bacteria. The desired gene gets inserted into the soybean plant cells' DNA, creating a genetically modified (GM) plant.

*plasmid + gene from Bt*

*Cut with the same restriction enzymes to give complementary sticky ends*

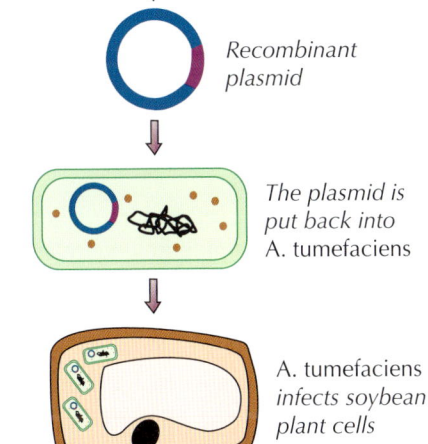

*Recombinant plasmid*

*The plasmid is put back into A. tumefaciens*

*A. tumefaciens infects soybean plant cells*

### Ethical issues

There are positive ethical issues concerning GM soybean plants — for example, they will reduce the amount of chemical pesticides that farmers use on their crops, which can harm the environment. GM plants can also be designed to be more nutritious.

But there are also negative ethical issues to consider. For example, farming GM soybean plants may encourage monoculture (where only one type of crop is planted). Monoculture decreases biodiversity and could leave the whole crop vulnerable to disease, because all the plants are genetically identical. There is also a risk that GM soybean plants could interbreed with wild plants creating 'superweeds' — weeds that are resistant to herbicides.

---

**Learning Objectives:**
- Understand the positive and negative ethical issues relating to the genetic manipulation of animals, plants and microorganisms including:
  - insect resistance in genetically modified soya, 'pharming' (i.e. genetically modified animals to produce pharmaceuticals) and genetically modified pathogens for research,
  - issues relating to patenting and technology transfer, e.g. making genetically modified seed available to poor farmers.

  **Specification Reference 6.1.3**

**Tip:** Genetically modified organisms are also known as genetically engineered or transformed organisms.

**Tip:** Biodiversity describes the variety of living organisms in an area. Monoculture reduces biodiversity by reducing the number of plant species in an area. This in turn reduces the number of other species, e.g. insects, that the area can support.

Module 6: Section 4 Manipulating Genomes

## Producing drugs from animals

Many pharmaceuticals (medicinal drugs) are produced using genetically modified organisms, such as animals. This is called 'pharming'.

**Example**

Hereditary antithrombin deficiency is a disorder that makes blood clots more likely to form in the body. The risk of developing blood clots in people with this disorder can be reduced with infusions of the protein antithrombin.

Scientists have developed a way to produce high yields of this protein using goats (see Figure 1).

1. DNA fragments that code for production of human antithrombin in the mammary glands are extracted.
2. The DNA fragments are injected into a goat embryo.
3. The embryo is implanted into a female goat.
4. When the offspring is born it is tested to see if it can produce the antithrombin protein.
5. If it does, selective breeding is used to produce a herd of goats that produce antithrombin in their milk.

The protein is extracted from the milk and used to produce a drug (ATryn®) that can be given to people with hereditary antithrombin deficiency.

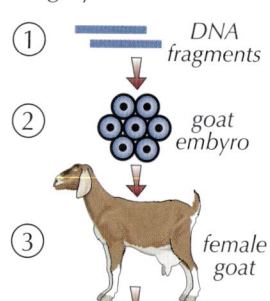

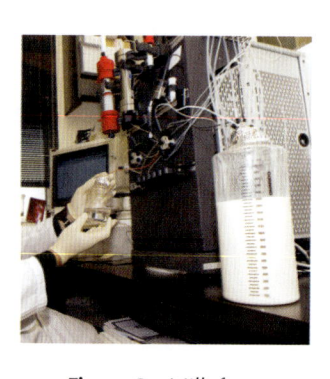

**Figure 2:** Milk from genetically modified cows, created to produce human growth hormone.

**Figure 1:** Diagram to show how antithrombin is produced from goats.

### Ethical issues

There are positive ethical issues with 'pharming'— drugs made this way can be made in large quantities compared to other methods of production. This can make them more available to more people.

However, the creation of genetically modified animals raises negative ethical issues. For example, there is concern that manipulating an animal's genes could cause harmful side-effects for the animal, and that using an animal in this way is enforcing the idea that animals are merely 'assets' that can be treated however we choose.

## Using pathogens for research

Scientists are carrying out research into genetically engineered pathogens (microorganisms that cause disease, such as viruses) in order to find treatments for disease.

**Example**

Scientists found that tumour cells have receptors on their membranes for the poliovirus — so the poliovirus will recognise and attack them. By genetically engineering the poliovirus to inactivate the genes that cause poliomyelitis, scientists can use it to attack and kill cancer cells without causing disease. This may lead to a treatment for cancer.

**Tip:** Poliomyelitis is the disease caused by the poliovirus.

Module 6: Section 4 Manipulating Genomes

## Ethical issues

The genetic modification of pathogens to help cure disease has obvious positive ethical issues — for example, it could mean that previously untreatable diseases can now be treated, reducing the suffering they would cause. However, there are many possible negative ethical issues as well:

- Some people are worried that the scientists researching the pathogens could become infected with the live pathogen and potentially cause a mass outbreak of disease.
- Some people are concerned that the genetically modified version of a pathogen could revert back to its original form and cause an outbreak of disease.
- Some people worry that in the wrong hands, knowledge of how to genetically engineer dangerous pathogens could be used maliciously to create agents for biowarfare.

Researchers using live pathogens have to follow strict protocols, which makes the chance of any of these things happening very, very low.

**Tip:** Biowarfare means deliberately attacking humans or other organisms using biological substances that can poison or cause disease.

# Ownership of GM organisms

Many scientists around the world are working on techniques to improve and advance genetic engineering. Scientists working for different institutions often share their knowledge and skills in this field so that, globally, beneficial genetically modified products can be created at a faster rate. The sharing of knowledge, skills and technology like this is called **technology transfer**.

Although they share information, a group of scientists or the company they work for may want to obtain legal protection for their genetically modified products, e.g. by getting a patent. This means, by law, they can control who uses the product and how for a set period of time.

## Ethical issues

This raises some positive ethical issues — it means that the owner of the patent will get money generated from selling the product. This encourages scientists to compete to be the first to come up with a new, beneficial genetic engineering idea, so we get genetically engineered products faster.

But the process raises many negative ethical issues too. For example, farmers in poorer countries may not be able to afford patented genetically modified seeds. Even if they can afford seeds for one year, some patents mean that they are not legally allowed to plant and grow any of the seeds from that crop without paying again. Many people think this is unfair and that the big companies that own the patents should relax the rules to help farmers in poorer countries.

*Figure 3:* Genetically modified cotton (Bt cotton), created to be resistant to insect pests, such as the cotton bollworm, is now widely grown in India.

Module 6: Section 4 Manipulating Genomes

**Tip:** The bacterium *A. tumefaciens* is a tool used to produce many transformed plants because of how it can transfer DNA into plant cells.

*Figure 4: Genetically modified Golden Rice (right) compared to normal white rice (left).*

**Exam Tip**
If you're asked to discuss the ethical issues surrounding genetic engineering in the exam, make sure you think about both sides of the debate. That means writing about both the positive and negative ethical issues.

## Practice Questions — Application

Q1 Golden Rice is a variety of transformed rice. It contains one gene from maize and one gene from a soil bacterium, which together enable the rice to produce beta-carotene. The beta-carotene is used by our bodies to produce vitamin A.
   a) Explain how Golden Rice could have been created.
   b) Suggest how Golden Rice may benefit humans.

Q2 People with Type 1 diabetes need to inject insulin to regulate their blood glucose concentration. Insulin used to be obtained from the pancreases of dead animals, such as pigs. However, the technology is now available to use genetically engineered bacteria to manufacture human insulin.

Suggest some positive ethical issues raised by the production of genetically modified insulin.

Q3 A 'pharming' company own the patent for the production of various human proteins in the milk of farm animals. They have produced genetically modified sheep that make the protein alpha-1-antitrypsin. This protein is lacking in sufferers of some lung diseases, such as hereditary emphysema.
   a) Explain how the sheep could have been genetically modified to produce the protein.
   b) Suggest why the company have taken out a patent for making the product.

## Practice Questions — Fact Recall

Q1 a) Why have scientists genetically modified soybean plants to be resistant to insect pests?
   b) Which bacterium is the gene in the genetically modified soybean plants taken from?
   c) Explain how the gene makes the plant insect-resistant.

Q2 a) What is pharming?
   b) Discuss the ethical issues surrounding pharming.

Q3 Give one advantage of carrying out research into genetically engineered pathogens.

Q4 What is meant by the term 'technology transfer'?

Q5 Give one negative issue faced by farmers in poor countries who farm with genetically modified seeds.

Module 6: Section 4 Manipulating Genomes

# 5. Gene Therapy

*There is a chance that in the future we'll be able to treat genetic disorders at the source — by using gene therapy to alter the mutations that have caused them.*

## How does gene therapy work?

**Genetic disorders** are inherited disorders caused by abnormal genes or chromosomes, e.g. cystic fibrosis. Gene therapy could be used to cure these disorders — it isn't being used widely yet but there is a form of somatic gene therapy available, and other treatments are undergoing clinical trials.

Gene therapy involves altering alleles inside cells to cure genetic disorders. How you do this depends on whether the disorder is caused by a mutated dominant allele or two mutated recessive alleles.

- If it's caused by two mutated recessive alleles you can add a working dominant allele to make up for them — you 'supplement' the faulty ones.
- If it's caused by a mutated dominant allele you can 'silence' the dominant allele (e.g. by sticking a bit of DNA in the middle of the allele so it doesn't work any more).

To get the 'new' allele (DNA) inside the cell, the allele is inserted into cells using vectors (see pages 493-494). A range of different vectors can be used, e.g. altered viruses, plasmids or liposomes (spheres made of lipid).

## Types of gene therapy

There are two types of gene therapy:

### 1. Somatic therapy

This involves altering the alleles in body cells, particularly the cells that are most affected by the disorder.

> **Example**
> Cystic fibrosis (CF) is a genetic disorder that's very damaging to the respiratory system, so somatic therapy for CF targets the epithelial cells lining the lungs.

Somatic therapy doesn't affect the individual's sex cells (sperm or eggs) though, so any offspring could still inherit the disease.

### 2. Germ line therapy

This involves altering the alleles in the sex cells. This means that every cell of any offspring produced from these cells will be affected by the gene therapy and they won't inherit the disease. Germ line therapy in humans is currently illegal though.

## Positive ethical issues of gene therapy

There are positive ethical issues surrounding gene therapy:

- Gene therapy could prolong the lives of people with life-threatening genetic disorders.
- Gene therapy could give people with genetic disorders a better quality of life if it helps to ease symptoms.
- Germ line therapy would allow the carriers of genetic disorders to conceive a baby without that disorder.
- Germ line therapy could decrease the number of people that suffer from genetic disorders and cancer, which is beneficial for individuals and society as a whole (as fewer people will require treatment).

---

**Learning Objectives:**
- Understand the principles of, and potential for, gene therapy in medicine.
- Know the differences between somatic cell gene therapy and germ line cell gene therapy.
- Understand the positive and negative ethical issues relating to the genetic manipulation of animals (including humans).

**Specification Reference 6.1.3**

**Tip:** If you can't remember the difference between dominant and recessive alleles, check out page 447.

**Tip:** Cancers are also caused by mutations. It's possible that some cancers could be treated using gene therapy in the future.

Module 6: Section 4 **Manipulating Genomes**

**Tip:** Gene expression is when genes are transcribed and translated into proteins (see pages 431-433). If a gene is overexpressed, this means that too much of the protein it codes for gets made.

## Negative ethical issues of gene therapy

There are also negative ethical issues surrounding gene therapy:
- The technology could potentially be used in ways other than for medical treatment, such as for treating the cosmetic effects of ageing.
- There's the potential to do more harm than good by using the technology (e.g. risk of overexpression of genes — see below).
- There's concern that gene therapy is expensive — some people believe that health service resources could be better spent on other treatments that have passed clinical trials.

## Disadvantages of gene therapy

There other potential disadvantages of gene therapy too:
- The body could identify vectors as foreign bodies and start an immune response against them.
- An allele could be inserted into the wrong place in the DNA, possibly causing more problems, e.g. cancer.
- An inserted allele could get overexpressed, producing too much of the missing protein, and so causing other problems.
- The effects of the treatment may be short-lived in somatic therapy.
- The patient might have to undergo multiple treatments with somatic therapy.
- It might be difficult to get the allele into specific body cells.

### Practice Questions — Application

Haemophilia B is caused by a mutation in the gene for the blood clotting factor IX (FIX). Sufferers usually have FIX levels less than 1% of normal values, causing frequent bleeding and often early death. Increasing levels to greater than 1% can greatly improve patient health. Treatment usually involves FIX injections multiple times a week, which is expensive and inconvenient. A trial has investigated the use of somatic gene therapy to treat haemophilia B. Six patients were injected with a virus carrying the normal FIX gene. Some results are shown on the right.

Q1 Explain the role of the virus.
Q2 Calculate the average maximum FIX level after gene therapy.
Q3 Was the trial a success? Give evidence to support your answer.
Q4 Describe the positive ethical issues of this treatment.

| Patient | Maximum FIX level (% of normal) after therapy |
|---------|----------------------------------------------|
| 1 | 2 |
| 2 | 2 |
| 3 | 3 |
| 4 | 4 |
| 5 | 8 |
| 6 | 12 |

### Practice Questions — Fact Recall

Q1 Define the term 'gene therapy'.
Q2 Describe the difference between somatic gene therapy and germ line gene therapy.

Module 6: Section 4 **Manipulating Genomes**

# 6. Sequencing Genes and Genomes

*Gene sequencing means finding out the order of bases in a gene. Genome sequencing means finding out the order of bases in all of an organism's DNA.*

## DNA sequencing

DNA can be sequenced by the **chain termination method** — this was one of the first methods used to determine the order of bases in a section of DNA (gene). Here's how it works:

### Step 1
A mixture of the following is added to four separate tubes:
- A single-stranded DNA template — the DNA to be sequenced.
- DNA polymerase — the enzyme that joins DNA nucleotides together.
- Lots of DNA primer — short pieces of DNA (see page 487).
- Free nucleotides — lots of free A, T, C and G nucleotides.
- A fluorescently-labelled modified nucleotide — like a regular nucleotide, but once it's added to a DNA strand, no more bases are added after it. A different modified nucleotide is added to each tube (these are called A*, T*, C*, G*).

### Step 2
The tubes undergo PCR (see pages 487-488), which produces many strands of DNA. The strands are different lengths because each one terminates at a different point depending on where the modified nucleotide was added. For example, look at Figure 1 below — in tube A (with the modified adenine nucleotide A*) sometimes A* is added to the DNA at point 4 instead of A, stopping the addition of any more bases (the strand is terminated). Sometimes A is added at point 4, then A* is added at point 5. Sometimes A is added at point 4, A again at point 5, G at point 6 and A* is added at point 7. So strands of three different lengths (4 bases, 5 bases and 7 bases) all ending in A* are produced.

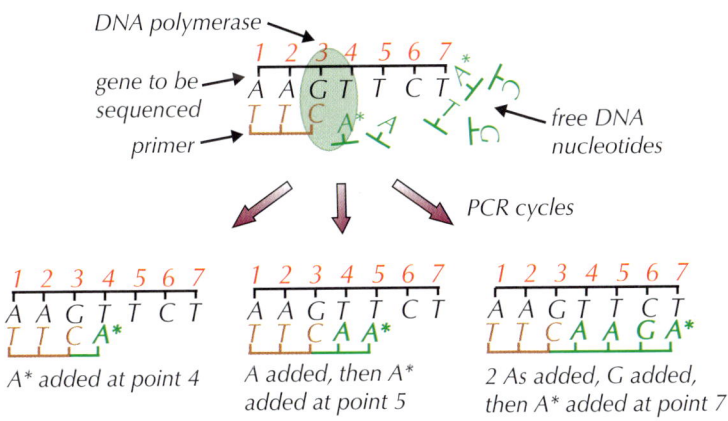

**Figure 1:** DNA sequencing example showing what happens in Tube A, which contains A*.

### Learning Objectives:
- Understand the principles of DNA sequencing and the development of new DNA sequencing techniques, including the rapid advancements of the techniques used in sequencing, which have increased the speed of sequencing and allowed whole genome sequencing, e.g. high-throughput sequencing.
- Understand how gene sequencing has allowed for the sequences of amino acids in polypeptides to be predicted.
- Understand how gene sequencing has allowed for the development of synthetic biology.
- Understand how gene sequencing has allowed for genome-wide comparisons between individuals and between species.
- Understand how bioinformatics and computational biology are contributing to biological research into genotype-phenotype relationships, epidemiology and searching for evolutionary relationships.

**Specification Reference 6.1.3**

**Tip:** In this example, A* can't be added at, e.g., point 3 because A doesn't pair with G in complementary base pairing.

Module 6: Section 4 Manipulating Genomes

**Tip:** Remember, the smallest (shortest) DNA fragments travel the furthest through the gel — towards the positive electrode.

### Step 3
The DNA fragments in each tube are separated by electrophoresis and visualised under UV light (because of the fluorescent label). The complementary base sequence can be read from the gel (see Figure 2). The smallest nucleotide (e.g. one base) is at the bottom of the gel. Each band after this represents one more base added. So by reading the bands from the bottom of the gel upwards, you can build up the DNA sequence one base at a time.

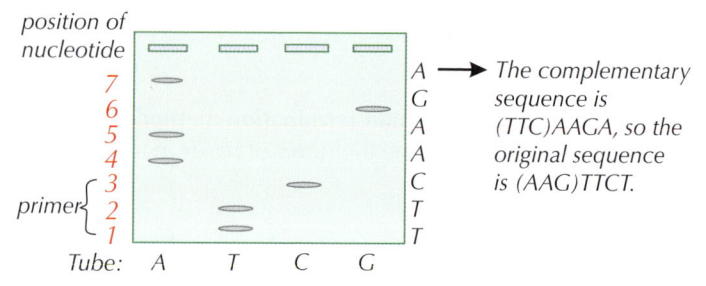

*Figure 2: An example of a DNA sequencing gel.*

The complementary sequence is (TTC)AAGA, so the original sequence is (AAG)TTCT.

*Figure 3: An actual DNA sequencing gel being analysed under UV light.*

## Genome sequencing
The chain-termination method can only be used for DNA fragments up to about 750 bp long. So if you want to sequence the entire genome (all the DNA) of an organism using this method, you need to chop it up into smaller pieces first. The smaller pieces are sequenced and then put back in order to give the sequence of the whole genome. Here's how it's done:

### Step 1
A genome is cut into smaller fragments (about 100 000 bp) using restriction enzymes — see Figure 4a.

### Step 2
The fragments are inserted into **bacterial artificial chromosomes** (**BACs**) — these are man-made plasmids. Each fragment is inserted into a different BAC.

### Step 3
The BACs are then inserted into bacteria — each bacterium contains a BAC with a different DNA fragment.

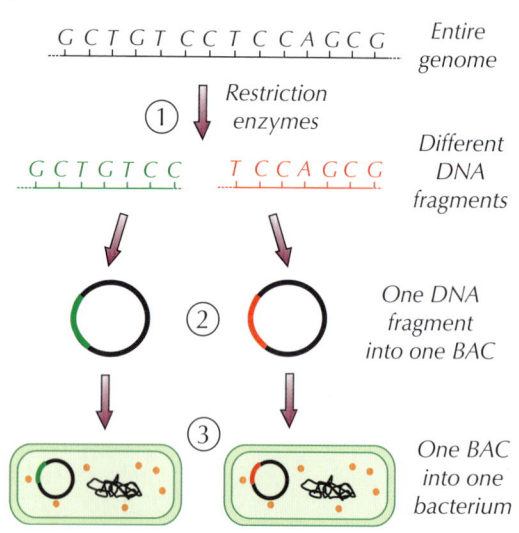

*Figure 4a: Genome sequencing — the first three stages.*

**Tip:** Genomes vary massively in size — the human genome is about 3 billion bases long, the zebra fish genome is about 1 billion bp, and the HIV genome is only around 9700 bp long. The size of the genome equates roughly to the number of genes. So humans have about 21 000 genes, zebra fish have about 16 000 genes and HIV has 9 genes.

### Step 4
The bacteria divide, creating colonies of cloned (identical) cells that all contain a specific DNA fragment — see Figure 4b (on the next page). Together the different colonies make a complete **genomic DNA library**.

### Step 5
DNA is extracted from each colony and cut up using restriction enzymes, producing overlapping pieces of DNA.

Module 6: Section 4 **Manipulating Genomes**

### Step 6
Each piece of DNA is sequenced, using the chain-termination method.
### Step 7
The pieces are put back in order to give the full sequence from that BAC (using powerful computer systems).
### Step 8
Finally the DNA fragments from all the BACs are put back in order, by computers, to complete the entire genome.

**Tip:** A DNA library stores DNA fragments from one organism in colonies of bacteria — a bit like the way a reading library stores books in a building.

**Tip:** An organism's genome is all the genetic information it has, not just chromosomal DNA. It can include plasmid DNA in bacteria and mitochondrial DNA in humans and other animals.

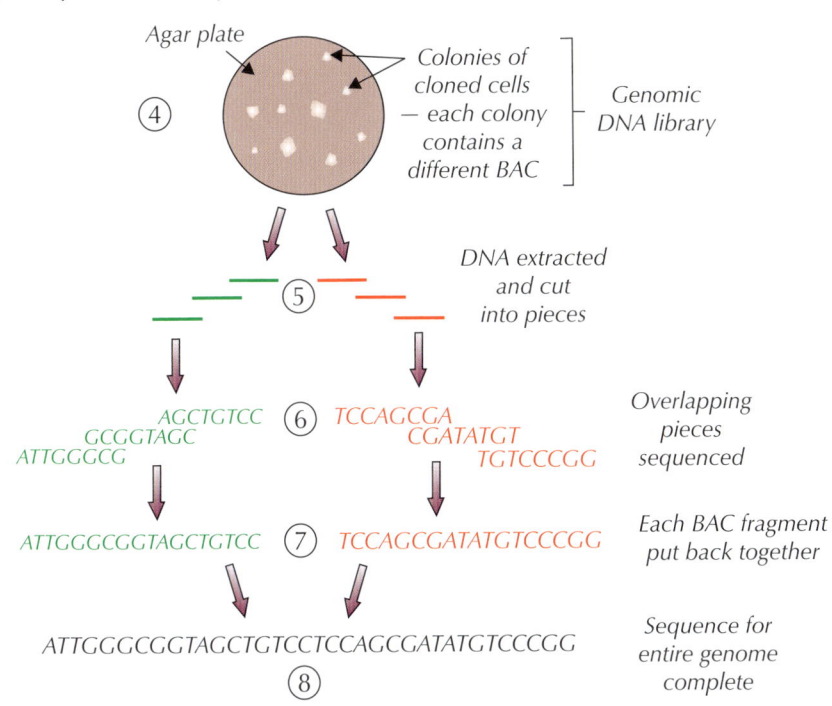

*Figure 4b:* Genome sequencing — the final five stages.

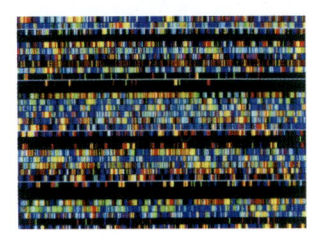

*Figure 5:* Computer screen display of part of the human genome sequence. The four different bases are represented by bands of different colours.

## Advances in sequencing

Continued research and improvements in modern technology have led to rapid advancements in the field of gene sequencing. The chain-termination technique described on the previous two pages is still commonly used but it has become automated and is faster — nowadays the tube contains all the modified nucleotides, each with a different coloured fluorescent label, and a machine reads the sequence for you. So instead of running a gel manually and determining the sequence from that, the sequence is read automatically by a computer (see Figure 6).

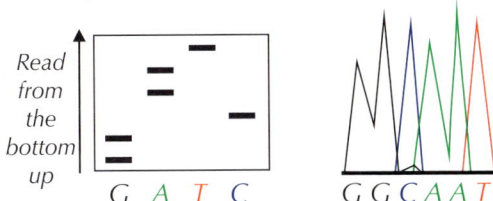

*Figure 6:* A DNA sequencing gel (left) and an automated DNA sequence computer read-out (right).

Further advances in the field have also led to **high-throughput sequencing** — techniques that can sequence a lot faster than original methods (e.g. up to 1000 times more bases in a given time), at a fraction of the cost. For example, the chain-termination technique has been made high-throughput by new technology allowing up to 384 sequences to be run in parallel.

There are several other, newer methods of high-throughput sequencing being used too, some of which don't use electrophoresis.

### Example — Pyrosequencing

High-throughput pyrosequencing is a recently developed technique.

**Figure 7:** These high-throughput DNA sequencers can sequence 400-600 million bases over a 10-hour run. This makes them very useful for sequencing the entire genome of an organism.

#### Step 1
A section of DNA is cut into fragments, split into single strands and then a strand from each fragment is attached to a small bead.

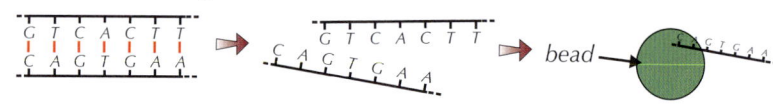

#### Step 2
PCR is used to amplify the DNA fragments on each bead.

#### Step 3
Then each bead is put into a separate well.

#### Step 4
Next, free nucleotides added to the wells attach to the DNA strands via complementary base pairing. The four different types of nucleotides are added to the wells one after the other, over and over again for 100 cycles.

#### Step 5
The wells also contain specific enzymes, which cause light to be emitted when a nucleotide is added to the DNA strand. More than one nucleotide can be added at a time if the bases are the same, so the intensity of the light can vary.

#### Step 6
Computers analyse the occurrence and intensities of the light emitted in the different wells, after each type of nucleotide is added, and process this information to interpret the DNA sequence.

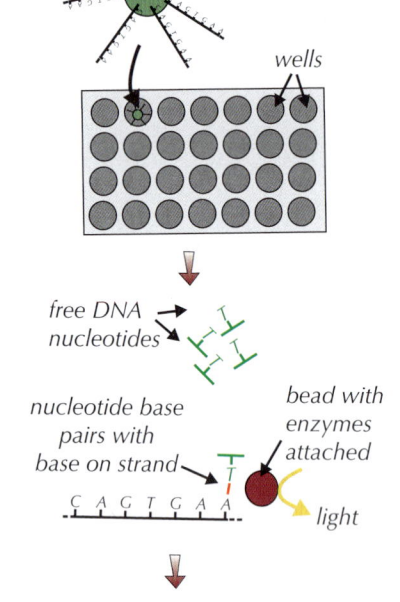

*A snapshot of the wells after one type of nucleotide has been added...*

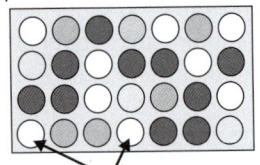

*bright spots indicate where the nucleotide joins the DNA strand*

This technique can sequence around 400 million bases in a ten-hour period (which is super fast compared to older techniques).

With newer, faster techniques such as pyrosequencing available, scientists can now sequence whole genomes much more quickly.

504    Module 6: Section 4 Manipulating Genomes

# Sequencing and synthetic biology

You might remember from Module 2 that amino acids are coded for by triplets of bases in a gene. This means that by sequencing a gene, the sequence of amino acids that a gene codes for and so the primary structure of a polypeptide can be predicted. This has allowed us to create biological molecules from scratch and so has led to the development of an area of biology called 'synthetic biology'.

Synthetic biology is a large field that includes building biological systems from artificially made molecules (e.g. proteins) to see whether they work in the way we think they do, and redesigning biological systems to perform better and include new molecules. It also includes designing new biological systems and molecules that don't exist in the natural world, but could be useful to humans, e.g. energy products (fuels) and drug products.

**Tip:** Synthetic biology is different from genetic engineering — genetic engineering involves the direct transfer of DNA from one organism to another, whereas in synthetic biology DNA is created from scratch.

### Example
Artemisinin is an antimalarial drug — until recently we got artemisinin by extracting it from a plant. Using synthetic biology, scientists have created all the genes responsible for producing a precursor to artemisinin. They've successfully inserted these genes into yeast cells, so we can now use yeast to help produce artemisinin.

# Sequencing and comparing genomes

Gene sequences and whole genome sequences can be compared between organisms of different species and between organisms of the same species. This is a complicated process which is made easier with the use of computers — it involves **computational biology** (using computers to study biology, e.g. to create computer simulations and mathematical models) and **bioinformatics** (developing and using computer software that can analyse, organise and store biological data).

There are many reasons why biological research can involve comparison of gene sequences and genomes:

### Studying genotype-phenotype relationships
Sometimes it's useful to be able to predict an organism's phenotype by analysing its genotype.

### Example
Marfan syndrome is a genetic disorder caused by a mutation of the FBN1 gene. The position and nature of the mutation on the gene affects what symptoms a person with Marfan syndrome will experience (e.g. they could get a number of problems associated with their vision, cardiovascular system or muscles). Scientists have sequenced the FBN1 gene of many people with Marfan syndrome and documented this along with details of their phenotype. Bioinformatics has allowed the scientists to compare all the data and identify genotype-phenotype correlations — this could help in the treatment of Marfan syndrome by using gene sequencing to predict what health problems the person is likely to face.

### Epidemiological studies

Epidemiology is the study of health and disease within a population — it considers the distribution of a disease, its causes and its effects. Some gene mutations have been linked to a greater risk of disease (e.g. mutations in the BRCA1 gene are linked to breast cancer). Computerised comparisons between the genomes of people that have a disease and those that don't can be used to detect particular mutations that could be responsible for the increased risk of disease.

### Understanding evolutionary relationships

All organisms evolved from shared common ancestors (relatives). Closely related species evolved away from each other more recently and so share more DNA. Whole genomes of different species can be sequenced and then analysed using computer software to tell us how closely related different species are. E.g. the genomes of humans and chimpanzees are about 94% similar. Comparing the genomes of members of the same species can also tell us about evolutionary relationships.

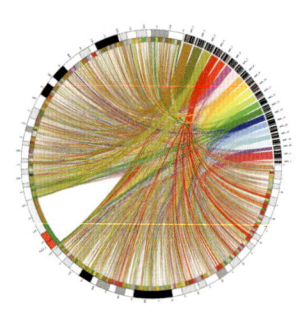

*Figure 8: A circular genome map used to visually compare the sequence of one human chromosome with the entire mouse genome. The coloured lines connect genes that have evolved from common ancestor genes.*

---Example---
When different groups of early humans separated and moved to different parts of the world, their genomes changed in slightly different ways. By using computers to compare the genomes of people from different parts of the world, it's possible to build up a picture of early human migration.

### Practice Question — Application

Scientists have found a large femur (thigh) bone from an unknown animal species in a swamp. They decide to sequence the bone's DNA, so they can establish what species the bone came from.

Q1 a) The scientists use a non-automated method to sequence the bone's DNA that involves four separate test tubes. What do they need to add to each tube?

b) Describe the next steps the scientists need to take to sequence the bone's DNA.

The DNA sequencing gel obtained from the DNA of the bone and three reference samples are shown below.

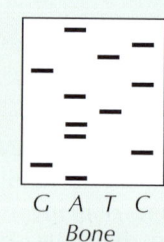

**Tip:** Remember that the sequence that you can read from the gel is the complementary sequence to the original reference sample of DNA.

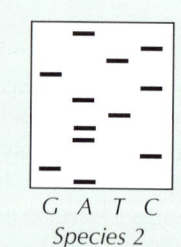

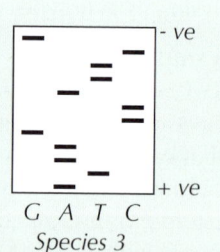

c) Give the original DNA sequence of the reference sample from Species 1.

d) Which species did the bone come from? Explain your answer.

## Practice Questions — Fact Recall

Q1  The chain termination method can be used to sequence DNA.
   a) What do you need to do before you can use this method to sequence an entire genome? Explain why.
   b) When sequencing an entire genome in this way, what are the man-made plasmids called that the DNA fragments are inserted into?

Q2  a) What are high-throughput sequencing techniques?
   b) Name a high-throughput sequencing technique.

Q3  Describe how DNA sequencing has allowed the development of synthetic biology.

Q4  Give two fields of biology where computers are used to aid the comparison of gene and genome sequences.

Q5  Describe how DNA sequencing can be used in epidemiological studies.

Q6  How can DNA sequencing help us understand evolutionary relationships between species?

## Section Summary

Make sure you know...

- That millions of identical copies of a DNA fragment can be made using the polymerase chain reaction (PCR).
- That fragments of DNA can be isolated using restriction enzymes. These enzymes recognise and cut DNA at different, specific palindromic sequences (called recognition sequences).
- That DNA fragments, RNA fragments or proteins can be run on an electrophoresis gel to separate them according to size (length).
- How to carry out electrophoresis.
- That an organism's genome contains repetitive, non-coding base sequences.
- That electrophoresis can be used to analyse the number of times a non-coding sequence is repeated in a person's genome, creating a DNA profile for that individual. DNA profiles can be used in forensics and to analyse the risk of genetic disorders.
- That genetic engineering involves isolating a gene from one organism, and placing the gene into another organism, using a vector, and that it produces transformed organisms.
- The techniques involved in genetic engineering — using restriction enzymes to isolate a DNA fragment containing a desired gene, creating recombinant DNA from the DNA fragment and vector DNA using DNA ligase, and using electroporation to get bacteria to take up the vector and produce transformed cells (cells that have taken up the recombinant DNA).
- That soybean plants can be genetically modified to be resistant to insects, and the ethical issues relating to this, including positive issues (e.g. reducing the amount of harmful chemical pesticides used on the crops) and negative issues (e.g. encouraging monoculture, which decreases biodiversity).
- How 'pharming' (producing drugs from genetically modified organisms, such as animals) works, and the ethical issues relating to this, including positive issues (e.g. being able to make the drugs more available by producing them in large quantities) and negative issues (e.g. that the manipulation of an animal's genes could cause harmful side-effects for the animal).

- That pathogens are genetically engineered for research into treatments for disease, and the ethical issues relating to this, including positive issues (e.g. the ability to treat previously untreated diseases) and negative issues (e.g. the possibility of a mass outbreak of the disease).
- What technology transfer is, and why scientists or companies may patent genetically modified products.
- The ethical issues surrounding patenting and technology transfer, including the issues of making genetically modified seed available to farmers in poorer countries.
- That gene therapy involves altering defective alleles inside body cells (somatic gene therapy) or sex cells (germ line gene therapy), to attempt to treat or cure genetic disorders.
- The positive and negative ethical issues raised by gene therapy.
- That DNA sequencing is used to determine the order of bases in a section of DNA (e.g. a fragment of a gene) and that the chain termination method is one way this can be carried out.
- That whole genomes can be sequenced using bacterial artificial chromosomes (BACs) and the chain termination method.
- That advancements in sequencing techniques, such as high-throughput sequencing, have increased the speed of sequencing so that whole genome sequencing can happen much more quickly.
- That gene sequencing allows the amino sequences of amino acids to be predicted.
- That gene sequencing has allowed for the development of synthetic biology in which biological molecules can be made from scratch.
- That the results of whole genome sequencing can be used to compare genomes between and within species.
- How computational biology and bioinformatics are contributing to biological research into genotype-phenotype relationships, epidemiology and the understanding of evolutionary relationships.

# Exam-style Questions

1. The following steps describe processes involved in genetic engineering. They are **not** in the correct order.

    1. DNA ligase joins the sugar-phosphate backbones together.
    2. The desired DNA fragment is isolated using restriction enzymes.
    3. The plasmid is cut open using restriction enzymes.
    4. The bacterial cells take in the plasmid.
    5. Bacterial cells are mixed with the plasmid and placed in an electroporator.
    6. The DNA fragment and plasmid are mixed together with DNA ligase.

    Which of these is the correct order for producing genetically engineered cells?

    A   5, 3, 2, 1, 4, 6
    B   2, 3, 6, 1, 5, 4
    C   5, 4, 6, 3, 2, 1
    D   2, 5, 4, 3, 6, 1

    *(1 mark)*

2. A prize-winning racehorse has been stolen from its stables. Police suspect it has been taken to a stud farm where it has previously gone to breed. The police have obtained DNA samples from four similar-looking horses at the stud farm and used them to produce DNA profiles to compare against a DNA profile from the stolen animal. The DNA profiles are shown in **Fig. 2.1**.

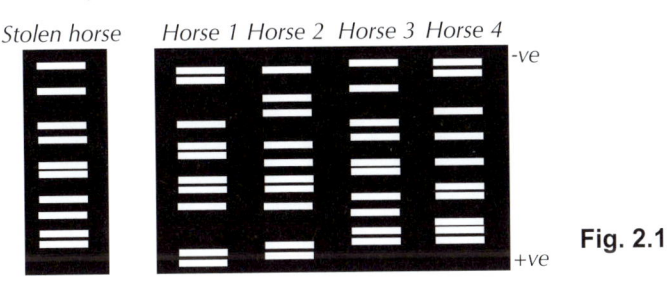

    Fig. 2.1

    (a) Describe and explain how the DNA profiles have been produced from the DNA samples.

    *(4 marks)*

    (b) Use your understanding of the biology behind DNA profiling technology to explain why the chances of two DNA profiles matching by chance are so small.

    *(3 marks)*

    (c) Is the stolen animal at the stud farm? Explain your answer.

    *(1 mark)*

    (d) Give **one** other use for DNA profiling technology other than in forensic science.

    *(1 mark)*

Module 6: Section 4 Manipulating Genomes

**3** An organic soybean farmer is concerned that his crop of non-GM soybean plants may have become cross-contaminated with a gene (called a transgene) from nearby GM soybean plants. One way to find out if the farmer's soybean plants contain the transgene is to first take a DNA sample from one of his plants and then use PCR to obtain DNA fragments of the region of DNA that would contain the transgene.

(a) Explain how the process of PCR works.

*(5 marks)*

The next step is to compare the DNA fragments produced to those from a sample of the GM soybean plant tissue, using gel electrophoresis. The GM soybean plant acts as a positive control.

(b) What would the gel show if the farmer's soybean plant did have the transgene?

*(1 mark)*

(c) What could be used as a negative control in this experiment?

*(1 mark)*

(d) Apart from cross-contamination, suggest and explain **one** other negative ethical issue associated with growing genetically modified plants.

*(2 marks)*

**4** A study was carried out to investigate the effectiveness of gene therapy in patients with X-linked severe combined immunodeficiency disease (SCID). SCID is an inherited disorder that affects the immune system. It is caused by a mutation in the IL2RG gene.

Ten patients were treated with a virus vector carrying a correct version of the IL2RG gene. After gene transfer, the patients' immune systems were monitored for at least three years and noted as functional (good) or not. Their health was also monitored for the same time. **Fig. 4.1** shows the results.

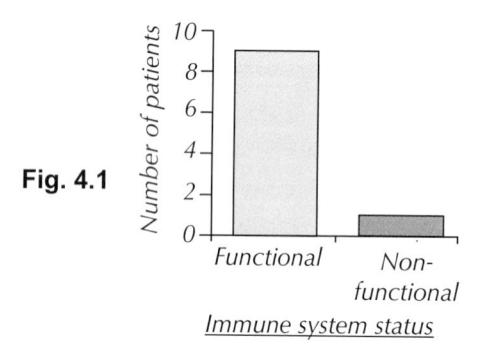

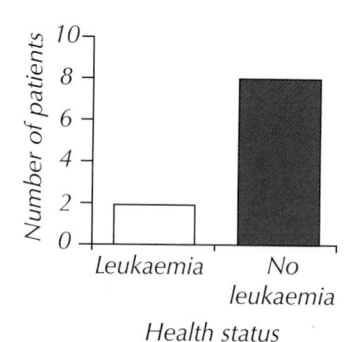

Fig. 4.1

(a) Besides viruses, give **one** other example of a type of vector they could have used.

*(1 mark)*

(b) (i) Describe the results shown in **Fig. 4.1**.

*(2 marks)*

(ii) Suggest **two** ways the study could be improved.

*(2 marks)*

(c) Outline **one** negative issue that may be raised by using gene therapy.

*(1 mark)*

# Module 6 Section 5: Cloning and Biotechnology

## 1. Plant Cloning

*Some plants produce clones naturally, but they can also be cloned artificially.*

### What is cloning?
Cloning is the process of producing genetically identical cells or organisms from the cells of an existing organism. Cloning can occur naturally in some plants and animals, but it can also be carried out artificially.

#### Vegetative propagation
Some plants can produce natural clones by vegetative propagation — this is the production of plant clones from non-reproductive tissues, e.g. roots, leaves and stems. It's a type of asexual reproduction. There are many different natural vegetative propagation methods used by plants:

**Examples**
- Rhizomes — These are stem structures that grow horizontally underground away from the parent plant. They have 'nodes' from which new shoots and roots can develop. An example of a plant that uses rhizomes is bamboo.
- Stolons — Also called runners, these are pretty similar to rhizomes. The main difference is that they grow above the ground, on the surface of the soil. New shoots and roots can either develop from nodes (like in rhizomes) or form at the end of the stolon. An example of a plant that uses stolons is the strawberry (see Figure 1).
- Suckers — These are shoots that grow from sucker buds (undeveloped shoots) present on the shallow roots of a parent plant. An example of a plant that uses suckers is the elm tree.
- Tubers — These are large underground plant structures that act as a food store for the plant. They're covered in 'eyes'. Each eye is able to sprout and form a new plant. An example of a plant that uses tubers is the potato.
- Bulbs — These are also underground food stores used by some plants. New bulbs are able to develop from the original bulb and form new individual plants. An example of a plant that uses bulbs is the onion.

#### Vegetative propagation in horticulture and agriculture
Horticulturists (plant growers) and farmers can exploit a plant's natural ability to produce clones. By manipulating the way in which a plant grows, they can induce vegetative propagation, so they get natural clones of the parent plant. There are several different methods they can use to do this:

**Examples**
- They can take cuttings (see next page).
- They can use grafting — joining the shoot of one plant to the growing stem and root of another plant.
- They can use layering — bending a stem of a growing plant downwards so it enters the soil and grows into a new plant.

---

**Learning Objectives:**

- Know that plants produce natural clones and that plant clones can be produced for use in horticulture, including examples of how natural plant clones are produced (various forms of vegetative propagation).
- Know how to dissect a selection of plant material to produce cuttings as an example of a simple cloning technique (PAG2).
- Know how artificial clones of plants are produced by tissue culture and micropropagation.
- Know the arguments for and against artificial cloning in plants and be able to evaluate the uses of plant cloning in horticulture and agriculture.

**Specification Reference 6.2.1**

*Figure 1: Stolons (runners) of strawberry plants.*

**Tip:** Farmers can use cloning methods to ensure they get uniform crops — as clones are genetically identical, any beneficial characteristics will be present in each crop plant.

**Tip:** Make sure you assess any risks before you start this experiment. Be particularly careful with sharp tools (e.g. scalpels) and be aware that some plants (e.g. chrysanthemums) can be irritants to skin, so it's best that you wear gloves if handling plants like these.

## Producing clones from cuttings

**PRACTICAL ACTIVITY GROUP 2**

Growing plants from cuttings is a really simple way to make clones of a parent plant. You need to know how to dissect plant material in order to produce clones using this method.

Here's how a cutting can be taken and grown from a stem:

1. Use a scalpel or sharp secateurs to take a cutting, between 5 cm and 10 cm long, from the end of a stem of your parent plant.
2. Remove the leaves from the lower end of your cutting (if there are any), leaving just one at the tip.
3. Dip the lower end of the cutting in rooting powder, which contains hormones that induce root formation.
4. Then plant your cutting in a pot containing a suitable growth medium (e.g. well-drained compost).
5. Provide your cutting with a warm and moist environment by either covering the whole pot with a plastic bag or by putting it in a propagator (a specialised piece of kit that provides these conditions — see Figure 3).
6. When your cutting has formed its own roots and is strong enough, you can plant it elsewhere to continue growing.

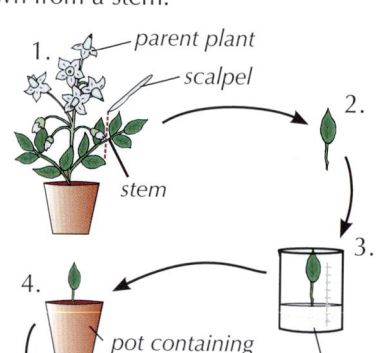

**Figure 3:** Plants in a propagator.

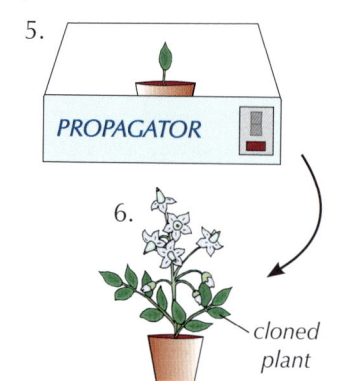

**Figure 2:** Example of how to produce a cloned plant from a stem cutting.

You can also take cuttings from other parts of a plant, such as a root or leaf:

### Examples

- To take a root cutting, cut a piece of root from the plant with a straight cut using a scalpel or secateurs. Then remove the uncut end of the root with a slanted cut. Dip the end of the cutting in rooting powder and plant it in a suitable growth medium. Then follow steps 5 and 6 from the method above.
- A popular type of leaf cutting (known as a split vein cutting) involves removing a complete leaf and scoring the large veins on the lower leaf surface using a scalpel (see Figure 4). You then put it on top of the growth medium with the broken veins facing down and then follow steps 5 and 6 from above. A new plant should form from each break in the veins.

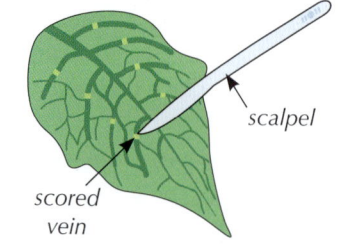

**Figure 4:** How to prepare a leaf for a split vein cutting.

Module 6: Section 5 Cloning and Biotechnology

# Tissue culture

Tissue culture is an artificial way of cloning plants — i.e. it's different from vegetative propagation, which is regarded as a 'natural' way to produce clones. Here's how tissue culture is carried out:

1. Cells are taken from the original plant that's going to be cloned. Cells from the stem and root tips are used because they're stem cells — like in humans, plant stem cells can develop into any type of cell.

2. The cells are sterilised to kill any microorganisms — bacteria and fungi compete for nutrients with the plant cells, which decreases their growth rate.

3. The cells are placed on a culture medium containing organic nutrients (like glucose and amino acids) and a high concentration of plant hormones (such as auxins, see p. 379). This is carried out under aseptic conditions (see p. 527). The cells divide to produce a mass of undifferentiated cells. The mass can be subdivided to produce lots of plants very quickly (see below).

4. When the cells have divided and grown into a small plant they're taken out of the medium and planted in soil — they'll develop into plants that are genetically identical to the original plant.

**Figure 5:** *The process of using tissue culture to clone a plant.*

**Tip:** Take a look back at what you learnt about stem cells in Module 2.

**Tip:** Plant hormones are included to help promote plant growth.

## Uses of tissue culture

Tissue culture is used to clone plants that don't readily reproduce or are endangered or rare.

### Example

A number of British orchid species are now endangered in the UK. It's very difficult to reproduce orchids using seeds because it can take a long time for the plants to produce flowers, they have a very specialised mechanism of pollination and the seeds usually need a specific fungus present in order to germinate. But many have been successfully reproduced using tissue culture.

It's also used to grow whole plants from genetically engineered plant cells.

**Figure 6:** *A lady's slipper orchid — one of the species of orchid which is critically endangered in the UK.*

## Micropropagation

Micropropagation is when tissue culture is used to produce lots of cloned plants very quickly. Cells are taken from developing cloned plants and subcultured (grown on another fresh culture medium) — repeating this process creates large numbers of clones (see Figure 8). This technique is used extensively in horticulture and agriculture, e.g. to produce fields full of a crop that has been genetically engineered to be pest-resistant.

**Tip:** See pages 493-494 for lots more on genetic engineering.

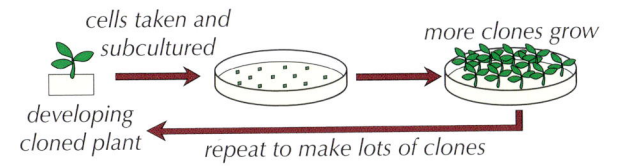

**Figure 8:** *Micropropagation of cloned plants.*

**Figure 7:** *Micropropagation.*

Module 6: Section 5 Cloning and Biotechnology 513

**Tip:** Agriculture and horticulture both involve cultivating plants — agriculture generally relates to farming (i.e. using land to grow crops for human use or consumption) whereas horticulture can involve the cultivation of any plant for any purpose, but usually on a smaller scale, e.g. for gardening.

# Arguments for and against artificial plant cloning

You need to be able to evaluate the uses of tissue culture in agriculture and horticulture — this handy list of arguments for and against tissue culture should help you.

## Arguments for
- Desirable genetic characteristics (e.g. high fruit production) are always passed on to clones. This doesn't always happen when plants reproduce sexually.
- Tissue culture allows plants to be reproduced in any season because the environment is controlled.
- Less space is required by tissue culture than would be needed to produce the same number of plants by conventional growing methods.
- It produces lots of plants quickly compared to the time it would take to grow them from seeds.

## Arguments against
- Undesirable genetic characteristics (e.g. producing fruit with lots of seeds) are always passed on to clones.
- Cloned plant populations have no genetic variability, so a single disease could kill them all.
- Production costs of tissue culture are very high due to high energy use and the training of skilled workers, so it's unsuitable for small scale production.
- Contamination by microorganisms during tissue culture can be disastrous and result in complete loss of the plants being cultured.

**Tip:** The advantages and disadvantages of cloning plants are similar to the advantages and disadvantages of cloning animals, which are covered on pages 517-518.

## Practice Questions — Application

Q1 A florist has discovered a wild flower that has an unusual pattern on its petals. She wants to reproduce the flower so she can sell it.
  a) Name and briefly describe a method which could be used to produce a large number of clones of the plant very quickly.
  b) Explain why producing clones of the plant might be better than reproducing the flower sexually.

Q2 Strawberry plants can reproduce by vegetative propagation. When they are growing well, runners extend from their stems.
  Gardeners can use the runners to reproduce their strawberry plants. Give two disadvantages of reproducing strawberry plants in this way, rather than from seeds.

**Tip:** To help you answer Q2, think about whether using seeds is an example of asexual or sexual reproduction.

## Practice Questions — Fact Recall

Q1 What is vegetative propagation?
Q2 Suggest a method for providing a warm and moist environment for a cutting once it has been transferred to a pot of growth medium.
Q3 Name three parts of a plant that can be dissected to produce a cutting.
Q4 Give two situations where cloning a plant using tissue culture might be useful.

# 2. Animal Cloning

**Learning Objectives:**
- Know how natural clones are produced in animal species, e.g. twins formed by embryo splitting.
- Know how artificial clones in animals can be produced by artificial embryo twinning or by enucleation and somatic cell nuclear transfer (SCNT).
- Know the arguments for and against artificial cloning in animals, and be able to evaluate the uses of animal cloning (including examples of cloning used in agriculture and medicine, and issues of longevity of cloned animals).

**Specification Reference 6.2.1**

*Scientists have been able to clone animals for quite a while now, but the process has advantages and disadvantages. Read on to find out more...*

## Natural animal clones

Animal clones can be produced naturally as a result of sexual reproduction. During sexual reproduction, once an egg has been fertilised, it's possible for it to split during the very early stages of development and develop into multiple embryos with the same genetic information. The embryos can develop as normal to produce offspring that are all genetically identical — they are clones. For example, identical twins are natural clones.

## Artificial animal clones

It's possible for scientists to produce clones of animals. You need to know how animals can be artificially cloned using the artificial embryo twinning and somatic cell nuclear transfer methods.

### Artificial embryo twinning

This type of artificial cloning is similar to what happens when animal clones form naturally. Figure 1 shows how this is done in cows, but the same technique can be used for other animals:

1. An egg cell is extracted from a female cow and fertilised in a Petri dish.
2. The fertilised egg is left to divide at least once, forming an embryo *in vitro* (outside a living organism).
3. Next, the individual cells from the embryo are separated and each is put into a separate Petri dish. Each cell divides and develops normally, so an embryo forms in each Petri dish.
4. The embryos are then implanted into female cows, which act as surrogate mothers.
5. The embryos continue to develop inside the surrogate cows, and eventually the offspring are born. They're all genetically identical to each other.

**Tip:** The process could also be done using an early embryo extracted from a pregnant animal, rather than using an embryo created in a lab.

**Tip:** Artificial embryo twinning and SCNT (see next page) involve the clone developing inside a surrogate animal. The vast majority of animals that have been successfully cloned are mammals — scientists would need to adapt the methods to clone animals that don't naturally develop inside a parent (e.g. birds, reptiles).

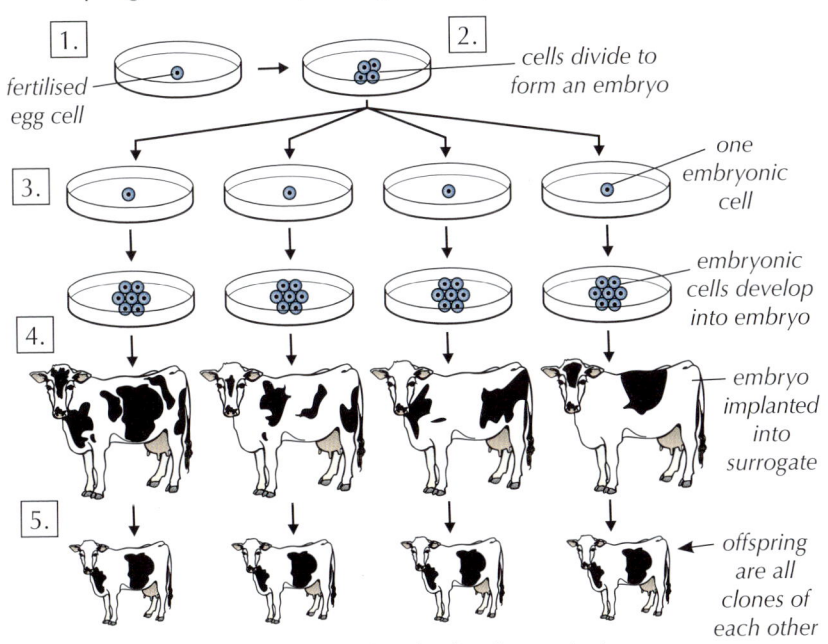

**Figure 1:** *The process of artificial embryo twinning.*

Module 6: Section 5 Cloning and Biotechnology 515

### Somatic cell nuclear transfer (SCNT)

This method is a bit more high-tech than artificial embryo twinning. Figure 3 shows how it's done with sheep (but again the principles are the same for other animals):

1. A **somatic cell** (any cell that isn't a reproductive cell) is taken from sheep A. The nucleus is extracted and kept.
2. An oocyte (immature egg cell) is taken from sheep B. Its nucleus is removed to form an **enucleated** oocyte.
3. The nucleus from sheep A is inserted into the enucleated oocyte — the oocyte from sheep B now contains the genetic information from sheep A.
4. The nucleus and the enucleated oocyte are fused together and stimulated to divide (e.g. by electrofusion, where an electrical current is applied). This produces an embryo.
5. Then the embryo is implanted into a surrogate mother and eventually a lamb is born that's a clone of sheep A.

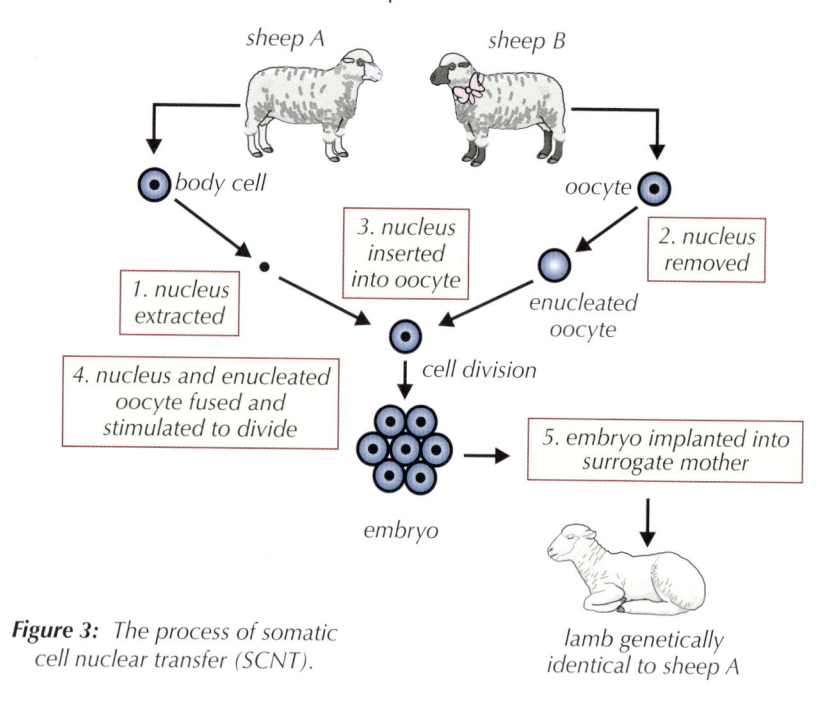

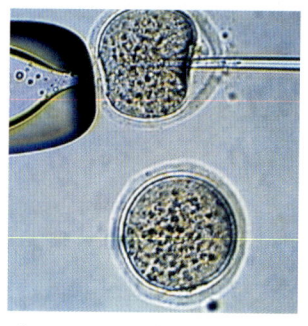

*Figure 2:* Nuclear transfer — here the nucleus of an adult mouse cell is being injected into an enucleated mouse oocyte (top, centre).

**Tip:** Producing a clone by SCNT can involve up to three different sheep (the nucleus donor, the egg donor and the surrogate mother), but the clone will only have genetic information from the nucleus donor.

*Figure 3:* The process of somatic cell nuclear transfer (SCNT).

# Uses of animal cloning

Animal cloning has many uses. Here are a few to take a look at:

- Scientists use cloned animals for research purposes.

### Example

In the field of medicine they can test new drugs on cloned animals. They're all genetically identical, so the variables that come from genetic differences (e.g. the likelihood of developing cancer) are removed.

- Cloning can be used in agriculture so farmers can increase the number of animals with desirable characteristics to breed from.

### Example

A prize-winning cow with high milk production could be cloned.

Module 6: Section 5 Cloning and Biotechnology

- Animals that have been genetically modified (see page 496) to produce a useful substance that they wouldn't normally produce could be cloned to produce lots of identical animals that all produce the same substance.

  **Example**
  A goat that has been genetically modified to produce a beneficial protein in its milk could be cloned.

- Cloning can also be used to save endangered animals from extinction by cloning new individuals.

  **Example**
  The European mouflon is a species of wild sheep which is currently endangered. Scientists have successfully cloned a European mouflon and it's hoped that this could help save the species.

Cloning doesn't have to be used to make whole animals. Sometimes scientists only want the cloned **embryonic stem cells**. These cells are harvested from young embryos and have the potential to become any cell type, so scientists think they could be used to replace damaged tissues in a range of diseases, e.g. heart disease, spinal cord injuries, degenerative brain disorders like Parkinson's disease. If replacement tissue is made from cloned embryonic stem cells that are genetically identical to the patient's own cells, it won't be rejected by their immune system.

**Tip:** In order to help save species from extinction, scientists freeze cells from animals alive today. Then, if the species ever becomes critically endangered or even extinct in the future, it may be possible to use these frozen cells to produce more of the animals (e.g. by cloning).

*Figure 4:* Two wild mouflon in Austria.

## Arguments for and against animal cloning

You might have to evaluate the uses of animal cloning, so you need to be aware of the arguments for and against the process:

### Arguments for
- Desirable genetic characteristics are always passed on to clones (e.g. high milk production in cows). This doesn't always happen with sexual reproduction because of processes such as independent assortment and crossing-over, which generate genetic variation during meiosis. So if a farmer had a cow that produced a lot of milk, the only way he could guarantee that his calves would also produce a lot of milk would be to clone the cow.
- Infertile animals can be reproduced, so if a farmer's prize winning cow was infertile for any reason, they could still reproduce it.
- Animals can be cloned at any time — you wouldn't have to wait until a breeding season to get new animals.
- Increasing the population of endangered species helps to preserve biodiversity.
- Cloning can help us develop new treatments for disease, which could mean less suffering for some people.

**Tip:** You learned about meiosis in Module 2.

### Arguments against
- Animal cloning is very difficult, time-consuming and expensive.
- There's no genetic variability in cloned populations, so undesirable genetic characteristics (e.g. a weak immune system) are always passed on to clones. This means that all of the cloned animals in a population are susceptible to the same diseases. Potentially, a single disease could wipe them all out.

**Exam Tip**
If you're asked to write about the advantages and disadvantages of animal cloning in the exam, make sure you write a balanced account of both — or you could lose marks.

Module 6: Section 5 Cloning and Biotechnology

*Figure 5: Dolly the sheep.*

**Tip:** Reproductive cloning of humans (to produce a full human being) is currently illegal in the UK. Cloning to produce a source of stem cells is allowed under licence. There's more on how society uses science to make decisions on page 4.

- Some evidence suggests that clones may not live as long as natural offspring. Some think this is unethical.

  **Example**

  Dolly the sheep was a clone generated by somatic cell nuclear transfer. It took 277 nuclear transfer attempts before Dolly was finally born, which shows just how difficult it is to successfully clone an animal. The average life expectancy of sheep the same breed as Dolly is 11-12 years but Dolly had to be put down at the age of six after developing a lung disease and arthritis.

- Using cloned human embryos as a source of stem cells is controversial. The embryos are usually destroyed after the embryonic stem cells have been harvested — some people believe that doing this is destroying a human life.

### Practice Questions — Application

**Q1** A scientist wants to clone some mice for use in a drug trial.
  a) Describe how he could use artificial embryo twinning to produce several cloned mice.
  b) Suggest why cloned mice are wanted for the drug trial, rather than mice produced via sexual reproduction.

**Q2** The diagram below shows the early stages of a process used to clone a dog:

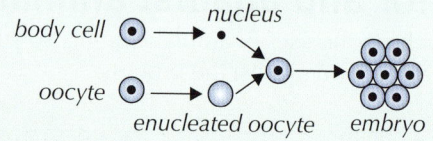

  a) What is this process called?
  b) Describe what would happen in the rest of this process.

### Practice Questions — Fact Recall

**Q1** Explain how natural animal clones occur.
**Q2** Explain why animal clones may be used in agriculture.
**Q3** Other than agriculture, give an example of how cloned animals may be useful.
**Q4** Give three arguments for and three arguments against animal cloning.

Module 6: Section 5 Cloning and Biotechnology

# 3. Biotechnology — The Use of Microorganisms

*The biotechnology industry is pretty big these days — it's used to produce loads of useful products. This topic looks at what biotechnology is and how microorganisms can be used in biotechnological processes.*

## What is biotechnology?

Biotechnology is the industrial use of living organisms (or parts of living organisms, see below) to produce food, drugs and other products.

The living organisms used are mostly microorganisms (bacteria and fungi). Here are a few reasons why:

- Their ideal growth conditions can be easily created — microorganisms will generally grow successfully as long as they have the right nutrients, temperature, pH, moisture levels and availability of gases (e.g. some need oxygen).
- Due to their short life-cycle, they grow rapidly under the right conditions, so products can be made quickly.
- They can grow on a range of inexpensive materials — this makes them economical to use.
- They can be grown at any time of the year.

### Enzymes in biotechnology

As well as whole living organisms, biotechnology also uses parts of living organisms (such as enzymes) to make products.

> **Example**
> Lactase (the enzyme that breaks down lactose) is prepared from *Aspergillus* fungi and is used in the production of lactose-free products (see page 531).

Enzymes used in industry can be contained within the cells of microorganisms — these are called intracellular enzymes. Enzymes are also used that aren't contained within cells — these are called isolated enzymes. Some are secreted naturally by microorganisms (called extracellular enzymes), but others have to be extracted. Naturally secreted enzymes are cheaper to use because it can be expensive to extract enzymes from cells.

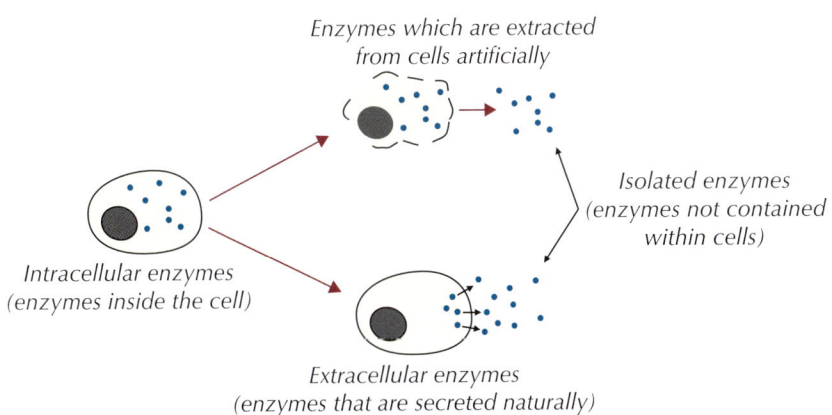

**Figure 1:** The different types of enzyme used in the biotechnology industry.

---

**Learning Objectives:**

- Understand the reasons why microorganisms are used in biotechnology, for example, their simple growth requirements, short life-cycle and economic advantages.
- Know how microorganisms are used in biotechnological processes, including brewing, baking, cheese making, yoghurt production, penicillin production, insulin production and bioremediation.
- Know the advantages and disadvantages of using microorganisms to make food for human consumption, including bacterial and fungal sources.

**Specification Reference 6.2.1**

**Tip:** Remember — enzymes are proteins that catalyse reactions in living organisms.

**Tip:** You can find out how isolated enzymes are used in biotechnology on page 531.

# Uses of microorganisms in biotechnology

Microorganisms are used in a wide variety of industrial processes.
You need to know how microorganisms are used in the following processes:

## Brewing (making beer)

To make beer, yeast (e.g. *Saccharomyces cerevisiae*) is added to a type of grain (such as barley) and other ingredients. The yeast respires anaerobically using the glucose from the grain and produces ethanol (alcohol) and $CO_2$. (When anaerobic respiration produces ethanol, the process is called fermentation.)

## Baking

Yeast is also the organism that makes bread rise. The $CO_2$ produced by fermentation of sugars in the dough makes sure it doesn't stay flat. Many flat breads, like tortillas, are made without yeast.

## Cheese making

Cheese production used to rely on a substance called rennet. Rennet contains the enzyme chymosin, which clots the milk — a key process in cheese making. Traditionally we used to get chymosin by extracting rennet from the lining of calves' stomachs, but now chymosin can be obtained from yeast cells that have been genetically modified to produce the enzyme. Cheese making also involves lactic acid bacteria (e.g. *Lactobacillus* and *Streptococcus*). These bacteria convert the lactose in milk into lactic acid, which makes it turn sour and contributes to it solidifying. The production of blue cheeses also involves the addition of fungi to make the characteristic blue veins.

*Figure 2: Rennet being added to milk to make cheese.*

## Yoghurt production

Just like cheese making, yoghurt production involves the use of lactic acid bacteria to clot the milk and cause it to thicken. This creates a basic yoghurt product and then any flavours and colours are added.

## Penicillin production

In times of stress, fungi from the *Penicillium* genus produce an antibiotic, penicillin, to stop bacteria from growing and competing for resources. Penicillin is one of the most common antibiotics used in medicine, so we produce it on a massive scale. The fungus (usually *Penicillium chrysogenum*) is grown under stress in industrial fermenters (see page 523) and the penicillin produced is collected and processed to be used in medicine.

*Figure 3: Penicillium fungus — this fungus produces penicillin.*

## Insulin production

Insulin is a hormone that's crucial for treating people with Type 1 diabetes. Insulin is made by genetically modified bacteria, which have had the gene for human insulin production inserted into their DNA. These bacteria are grown in an industrial fermenter on a massive scale and the insulin produced is collected and purified.

**Tip:** Bioremediation can also be carried out by introducing new bacteria to the environment that needs cleaning up, although this is less common.

## Bioremediation

Bioremediation is a posh name for the process of using organisms (usually microorganisms) to remove pollutants, like oil and pesticides, from contaminated sites. Most commonly, pollutant-removing bacteria that occur naturally at a site are provided with extra nutrients and enhanced growing conditions to allow them to multiply and thrive. These bacteria break down the pollutants into less harmful products, cleaning up the area.

**Example**
In 1989 an oil tanker spilled around 40 million litres of crude oil into the sea near the port of Valdez on the southern coast of Alaska. Scientists found that microorganisms present in the area could naturally biodegrade (break down) the oil. They discovered that the growth rate of these microorganisms could be greatly increased with the use of fertiliser (a substance containing nutrients). Therefore, large amounts of fertiliser were added to the water to clean up the oil more quickly.

## Pros and cons of using microorganisms in food production

As you can see from the previous page, microorganisms play a key role in the production of lots of different foods. Some microorganisms can also be grown as a source of protein (called single-cell protein), which can act as a valuable food source for humans and other animals. Examples of microorganisms used to make single-cell protein include the fungus *Fusarium venenatum* (which is used to make the popular meat substitute Quorn™) and the bacteria *Methylophilus methylotrophus* (which is used to produce animal feed).

There are advantages and disadvantages of producing food for human consumption using microorganisms.

### Advantages
- Microorganisms used to make single-cell protein can be grown using many different organic substrates, including waste materials such as molasses (a by-product of sugar processing). Production of single-cell protein could actually be used as a way of getting rid of waste products.
- Microorganisms can be grown quickly, easily and cheaply. Production costs are low because microorganisms have simple growth requirements, can be grown on waste products and less land is required in comparison to growing crops or rearing livestock.
- Microorganisms can be cultured anywhere if you have the right equipment. This means that a food source could be readily produced in places where growing crops and rearing livestock is difficult (e.g. very hot or cold climates). This could help tackle malnutrition in developing countries.
- Single-cell protein is also often considered a healthier alternative to animal protein.

### Disadvantages
- Because the conditions needed to grow the desired microorganism are also ideal for other microorganisms, a lot of effort has to go into making sure that the food doesn't get contaminated with unwanted bacteria, which could be dangerous to humans or spoil the food.
- People may not like the idea of eating food that has been grown using waste products.
- Single-cell protein doesn't have the same texture or flavour as real meat.
- If single-cell protein is consumed in high quantities, health problems could be caused due to the high levels of uric acid released when the large amounts of amino acids are broken down.

**Figure 4:** A selection of meat substitute products made from single-cell protein.

**Tip:** An organic substrate is a carbon-containing substance that can be used as an energy source by an organism.

## Practice Questions — Application

Q1  Land that used to be the location of a large chemical factory was being redeveloped into a housing estate. Over the course of the use of the land as a factory site, the soil had become contaminated with several harmful chemical pollutants that posed a risk to humans and wildlife. Before the development could go ahead, the soil had to be decontaminated.

Suggest and explain a biotechnological method that could be used to help clean up the contaminants from the soil.

Q2  It is possible that single-cell protein could be used as a valuable food source in some developing countries, such as India, where the climate can be very hot and the population size is increasing very quickly.

a)  Suggest why it may be advantageous to use single-cell protein as a food source in parts of India, rather than relying on food from crops and livestock.

b)  Suggest two arguments against producing single-cell protein on a large scale so it can be used as a human food source in developing countries, such as India.

**Tip:** To answer Q2a, think about the strains that a hot climate and rapidly growing population could put on conventional food production.

## Practice Questions — Fact Recall

Q1  What is biotechnology?

Q2  Give three reasons why biotechnology mostly uses microorganisms.

Q3  Explain how microorganisms are used in:
 a) brewing,
 b) baking,
 c) cheese making,
 d) yoghurt production,
 e) penicillin production,
 f) insulin production.

# 4. Biotechnology — Culturing Microorganisms

**Learning Objectives:**
- Understand the importance of manipulating the growing conditions in batch and continuous fermentation in order to maximise the yield of product required.
- Understand the standard growth curve of a microorganism in a closed culture and know how to estimate the number of individual organisms there will be in a culture using the formula $N = N_0 \times 2^n$.
- Know how to culture microorganisms effectively, using aseptic techniques (PAG7).
- Be able to carry out practical investigations into the factors affecting the growth of microorganisms (PAG7).

**Specification Reference 6.2.1**

*If you want to use microorganisms for a particular industrial process, you have to grow them first. This topic tells you how.*

## Fermentation vessels

Biotechnology uses **cultures** of microorganisms. A culture is a population of one type of microorganism that's been grown under controlled conditions. Cultures are grown in large containers called fermentation vessels (see Figure 1) to either obtain lots of the microorganism (e.g. for production of single-celled protein — see page 521) or to collect lots of a useful product that the microorganism makes.

There are two main methods for culturing microorganisms — **batch fermentation** and **continuous fermentation**. Batch fermentation is where microorganisms are grown in individual batches in a fermentation vessel — when one culture ends it's removed and then a different batch of microorganisms is grown in the vessel. This is known as a **closed culture** — see next page. Continuous fermentation is where microorganisms are continually grown in a fermentation vessel without stopping. Nutrients are put in and waste products taken out at a constant rate.

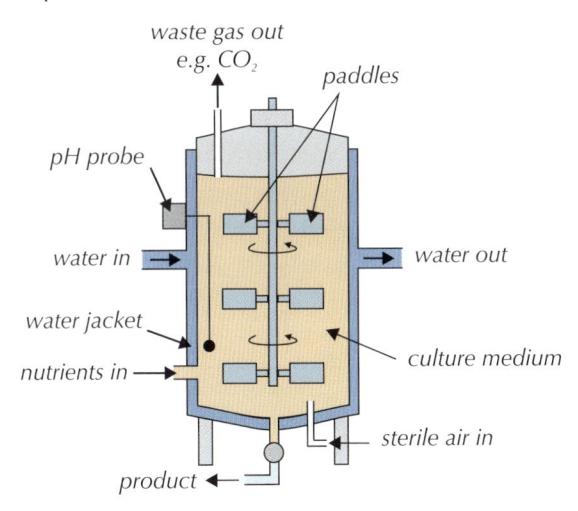

**Figure 1:** A typical fermentation vessel.

**Figure 2:** A vessel for the fermentation of yeast.

**Tip:** Extremes of pH can denature (deactivate) enzymes.

The conditions inside the fermentation vessels are kept at the optimum for growth — this maximises the yield of microorganisms and desirable products. The factors that need to be controlled in a fermentation vessel are explained below and on the next page.

### pH
The pH is monitored by a pH probe and kept at the optimum level. This increases the product yield because enzymes can work efficiently, so the rate of reaction is kept as high as possible.

### Temperature
The temperature is kept at the optimum level by a water jacket that surrounds the vessel. This increases the product yield because enzymes can work efficiently, so the rate of reaction is kept as high as possible.

Module 6: Section 5 Cloning and Biotechnology

**Tip:** If you didn't have paddles stirring the medium, the nutrients would all sink to the bottom and the nutrient concentration wouldn't be the same throughout the vessel.

### Oxygen supply
The volume of oxygen is kept at the optimum level for respiration by pumping in sterile air when needed. This increases the product yield because microorganisms can always respire to provide the energy for growth.

### Nutrient concentration
Microorganisms are kept in contact with fresh medium by paddles that circulate the medium around the vessel. This increases the product yield because microorganisms can always access the nutrients needed for growth.

### Contamination
Vessels are sterilised between uses with superheated steam to kill any unwanted organisms and make sure the next culture is not contaminated. This increases the product yield because the microorganisms aren't competing with other organisms.

## Closed cultures

A **closed culture** is when growth takes place in a vessel that's isolated from the external environment — extra nutrients aren't added and waste products aren't removed from the vessel during growth.

**Tip:** If a culture isn't isolated from the external environment it's called an open culture.

### Growth curves
In a closed culture, such as in batch fermentation, a population of microorganisms follows a **standard growth curve**. This growth curve has four phases (see Figure 3).

**Tip:** The growth curve for continuous fermentation looks like this:

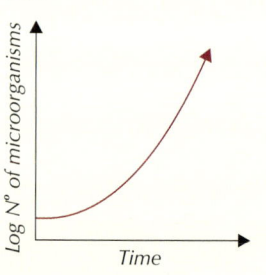

*[Graph: Log N° of microorganisms vs Time, showing exponentially increasing curve]*

There's no stationary or decline phase because it's an open culture — nutrients are constantly being added and waste is constantly being removed. So the microorganisms don't run out of food and waste can't build up to toxic levels.

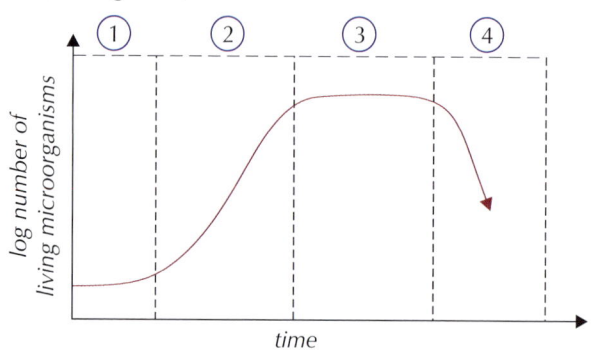

*[Graph: log number of living microorganisms vs time, showing four phases labelled 1, 2, 3, 4 — standard S-curve with decline at end]*

**Figure 3:** *The standard growth curve of a population of microorganisms in a closed culture.*

Here's what's happening in each of the four phases:

1. **Lag phase** — the population size increases very slowly because the microorganisms have to make enzymes and other molecules before they can reproduce. This means the reproduction rate is low.

2. **Exponential (log) phase** — the population size increases quickly because the culture conditions are at their most favourable for reproduction (lots of food and little competition). The number of microorganisms doubles at regular intervals.

3. **Stationary phase** — the population size stays level because the death rate of the microorganisms equals their reproductive rate. Microorganisms die because there's not enough food and poisonous waste products build up.

4. **Decline phase** — the population size falls because the death rate is greater than the reproductive rate. This is because food is very scarce and waste products are at toxic levels.

### Exam Tip
Make sure you learn what each of the four phases are called, what the growth curve looks like during each phase and why the curve has the shape it does.

Interpreting a standard growth curve can involve a bit of maths (see p. 525-526).

# Estimating the number of cells in a culture

During the exponential growth phase, the number of cells in a culture of microorganisms doubles at regular intervals. You can work out how many cells will be present in a population (N) after a certain number of divisions using this formula:

$N_0$ is the initial number of cells — $N = N_0 \times 2^n$ — $n$ is the number of divisions

**Tip:** The generation time is the time between divisions — the time taken for the cells to divide and reproduce.

### Example — Maths Skills

For a particular species of bacteria, the cells divide approximately every 30 minutes during the exponential growth phase. There are 300 bacterial cells present at the start of the exponential growth phase. Estimate how many cells are present after 7 hours (assuming the culture remains in the exponential growth phase during this time).

- First work out how many divisions will have taken place. 7 hours is 420 minutes, so in 7 hours there will be 420 ÷ 30 = 14 divisions.

- Then put the information into the formula:
  number of cells in population = $N_0 \times 2^n$ = $300 \times 2^{14}$
  = 4915200 cells = **4.9 × 10⁶ cells**

**Exam Tip**
The number of cells in a culture of microorganisms can be very large, so it's not uncommon to see values in standard form. Before the exam make sure you've brushed up on your maths skills and are comfortable interpreting numbers in standard form.

# Using logarithms in growth curves

Due to the rapid growth rate of microorganisms, the number of cells present after the exponential growth phase can vary massively from the number present at the beginning. This means that plotting the number of cells in a culture over time would be really difficult to do on a normal (linear) scale, because the y-axis would have to cover a really wide range of values.

To get around this problem, logarithms ('logs') are used. The log of a number tells you how many times 10 has been multiplied by 10 to give you that number (see Figure 4).

| Number | Power of 10 | Log value |
|---|---|---|
| 10 | 10¹ | 1 |
| 100 | 10² | 2 |
| 1000 | 10³ | 3 |
| 10 000 | 10⁴ | 4 |

**Figure 4:** Table showing how log values are derived.

You can calculate the log of a number using the log button on your calculator. All you do is press log, then the number you're using, then equals. Once the number of cells in a culture has been converted to logs, the growth curve is much easier to plot.

**Tip:** The log explained here is actually $\log_{10}$ (log to the base of 10). You can get logs to the base of other numbers too, but $\log_{10}$ is most commonly used.

**Tip:** Different calculators work differently so make sure you know how to calculate logs on yours.

### Example

A scientist recorded the number of cells present in a bacterial culture during its exponential growth phase. She converted the number of cells to log values to give a much narrower range of values, which are easier to plot on a graph (see Figure 5).

| Time (mins) | Nº of cells | Log Nº of cells |
|---|---|---|
| 0 | 12 | 1.08 |
| 20 | 25 | 1.40 |
| 40 | 46 | 1.66 |
| 60 | 97 | 1.99 |
| 80 | 189 | 2.28 |
| 100 | 388 | 2.59 |

**Figure 5:** Graph of log number of cells against time.

**Tip:** This is what the graph in the example on the right would look like if the actual number of cells were plotted, rather than their logs:

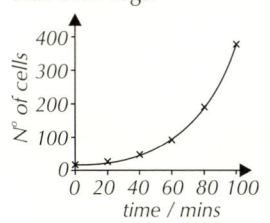

You can see it would be really hard to read values accurately from the y-axis because the scale is so small.

Module 6: Section 5 Cloning and Biotechnology

## Interpreting data values from a logarithmic scale

When you see microbial growth data presented on a logarithmic scale, the units on the y-axis may tell you the total number of cells rather than the log values. This makes it easier to work out how many cells are present at a given time, but you have to be careful because the smaller increments on the y-axis are not evenly spaced.

---

**Example — Maths Skills**

The graph below shows the growth of a bacterial culture over six hours. The graph is drawn with a logarithmic scale.
Estimate how many bacteria per cm³ were in the culture after four hours.

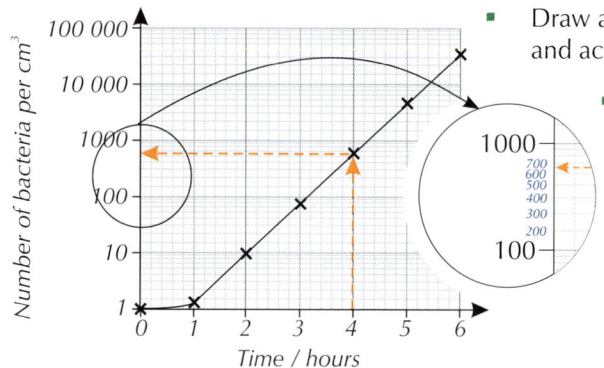

- Draw a line up from 4 hours and across to the y-axis.
- The large square between 100 and 1000 is divided into nine sections, so the scale must be going up by 100 bacteria for each of those sections.
- The line meets the y-axis between 600 and 700, so there were approximately **650 bacteria per cm³** after 4 hours.

---

**Tip:** If you work out the number of cells present at two time points on a growth curve, you can use them to work out the rate of growth during that time period. To do this you need to work out the gradient of the line (or of a tangent to the line if the line's curved) between your two time points. This is the formula to use:

$$\text{Gradient} = \frac{\text{Change in } y}{\text{Change in } x}$$

If only the log values are shown on the y-axis, it's still possible to work out how many cells are present at a given time by finding the **antilog**. To do this you need to use the $10^x$ button on your calculator. Simply press this, then enter the log value at your chosen time. When you press equals, you'll get the number of cells.

**Tip:** Sometimes, the antilog is referred to as the reverse log or inverse log.

**Tip:** $10^x$ is usually found written above the log button on a calculator (it's a second function of log). But again, different calculators work differently so make sure you know how to use yours.

---

**Example — Maths Skills**

The graph below shows part of a growth curve for a closed bacterial culture.

Estimate how many bacterial cells are present after 4 hours.

- You can see from the graph that at 4 hours, the log number of bacterial cells is 4.7.
- To get the actual number of bacterial cells, you need to calculate the antilog using your calculator:

$10^{4.7} = $ **50 118 cells** present at 4 hours.

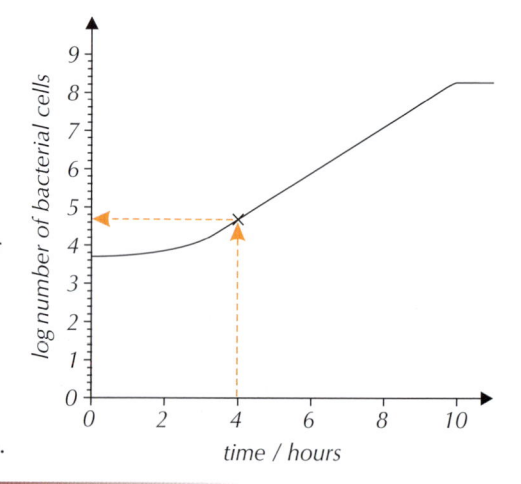

**Tip:** You should round estimations down to a whole number, because you can't get parts of cells.

526    Module 6: Section 5   Cloning and Biotechnology

# Culturing microorganisms in the lab

Cultures of microorganisms can be grown in the lab. A common way to do this is on an agar plate — a sterile Petri dish containing agar jelly. Nutrients can be added to the agar to help improve the growing conditions. The microorganisms you use are likely to be provided in a liquid broth (a mixture of distilled water and nutrients). To culture the microorganisms, use a sterile implement like a wire inoculation loop to transfer some of the sample to the plate. A pipette could also be used to transfer the sample, which could then be gently spread across the whole surface of the agar using a glass or plastic spreader. The plates then need to be incubated to allow the microorganisms to grow.

**PRACTICAL ACTIVITY GROUP 7**

**Tip:** There are lots of risks associated with culturing microorganisms. Make sure you've carried out a full risk assessment and know all about using aseptic techniques before you start.

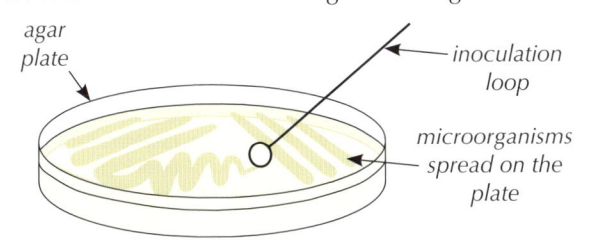

*Figure 6: An agar plate being used to culture microorganisms.*

**Tip:** Microorganisms can also be cultured in a broth, as well as on agar plates.

## Aseptic techniques

An important part of culturing microorganisms is using aseptic techniques. These are used to prevent contamination of cultures by unwanted microorganisms, which may affect the growth of the microorganism being cultured. Contaminated cultures in laboratory experiments give imprecise results and may be hazardous to health. Contamination on an industrial scale can be very costly because entire cultures may have to be thrown away. Below are some important aseptic techniques that you should follow when culturing microorganisms in the lab:

*Figure 7: A scientist transferring a microorganism to a Petri dish.*

**Tip:** Your teacher may recommend other aseptic techniques you need to follow.

### Examples

- Regularly disinfect work surfaces to minimise contamination.
- Work near a Bunsen flame. Hot air rises, so any microorganisms in the air should be drawn away from your culture.
- Sterilise the instrument used to transfer cultures before and after each use, e.g. sterilise a wire inoculation loop by passing it through a hot Bunsen burner flame for 5 seconds. This will kill any microorganisms on the instrument. Pre-sterilised plastic instruments should only be used once and then safely discarded.
- If you're using broth, briefly pass the neck of the broth container through a Bunsen burner flame just after it's opened and just before it's closed — this causes air to move out of the container, preventing unwanted organisms from falling in.
- Minimise the time that the agar plate is open and put the lid on as soon as possible. This reduces the chance of airborne microorganisms contaminating the culture. You could even work in an inoculation cabinet (a chamber that has a flow of sterile air inside it).
- Sterilise all glassware before and after use, e.g. in an autoclave (a machine which steams equipment at high pressure).
- Wear a lab coat and, if needed, gloves. Tie long hair back to prevent it from falling into anything.

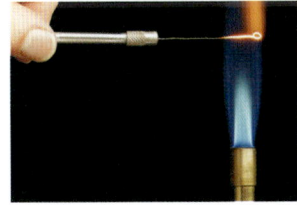

*Figure 8: An inoculation loop being sterilised in a Bunsen burner.*

Module 6: Section 5 Cloning and Biotechnology

**Tip:** Again, make sure you carry out a full risk assessment before you carry out this practical and follow aseptic techniques throughout the investigation.

# Investigating factors that affect the growth of microorganisms

PRACTICAL ACTIVITY GROUP 7

You can investigate the effects of different factors on the growth of microorganisms by growing them on agar plates under different conditions. The example below shows how you can investigate the effect of temperature on the growth of bacteria (although the same method can be used for other microorganisms, such as fungi).

### Example

1. You should be supplied with a sample of bacteria (e.g. *E. coli*) in broth. Using a sterile pipette, add the same volume (e.g. 0.1 cm³) of your sample to each of six agar plates. Discard your pipette safely after use (e.g. if it's a glass pipette, put it into a beaker of disinfectant while you are working and then into an autoclave once you've finished).

**Tip:** You could also use another tool such as a sterile cotton swab to spread the broth on the plate — make sure you're aware of the aseptic techniques required for whatever tool you're using.

2. Spread the broth across the entire surface of the agar using a sterile plastic spreader (see Figure 9). Discard the spreader safely after use.

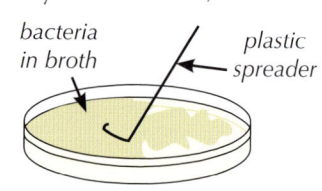

3. Put the lids on the agar plates and tape them shut.

**Figure 9:** Bacteria being spread onto an agar plate.

4. Place three plates in a fridge at 4 °C and put three in an incubator at 25 °C. If you don't have access to an incubator, just leave the plates at room temperature, somewhere where the temperature is most likely to remain constant. The plates should be incubated upside down. This stops any condensation forming on the lid from dropping onto the agar.

**Tip:** Don't completely seal the Petri dish with tape before incubation — it will prevent oxygen from entering the dish, which may encourage the growth of anaerobic disease-causing bacteria. Don't open the dish after incubation.

5. Put another lidded agar plate in each of the two different temperature locations — these plates should be uncultured (i.e. you shouldn't have added any bacteria to them). These plates will act as negative controls.

6. Leave all the plates for the same amount of time (e.g. 24 hours) then observe the results.

**Tip:** A negative control is not expected to have any effect on the experiment — see page 3 for more.

7. If bacterial growth has occurred, you should see colonies of bacteria on the surface of the agar (see Figure 10).

**Figure 10:** Colonies of bacteria present on an agar plate after incubation.

**Tip:** A colony is a large group of microorganisms, which usually originate from a single cell, living closely together on the agar. Colonies are visible to the naked eye.

8. Count the number of colonies that have formed on each plate and record your results in a table.

9. Work out the mean number of colonies formed at each temperature.

You might find that you have so many colonies that they overlap and you can't count them. If this happens, try making serial dilutions of your bacteria in broth and plate them on agar — this should give you a more manageable number of colonies because there will be fewer bacteria present in the solution to begin with.

**Tip:** Serial dilutions are a set of dilutions that decrease in concentration by the same factor each time.

Module 6: Section 5 Cloning and Biotechnology

The experiment on the previous page can be adapted to investigate the effects of different factors on the growth of microorganisms. For example, you could:

- investigate the effect of pH by adding buffers at different pH levels to the broth.
- investigate the effects of nutrient availability by using different preparations of agar, which contain different nutrients.

You could also investigate the growth of microorganisms directly in broth (without the need to plate the broth on agar) using a spectrophotometer. This is a machine that measures the turbidity (cloudiness) of the broth. Higher turbidity means that more cells are present and, therefore, more replication has taken place.

### Practice Questions — Application

Q1 Turbidity is a measure of the cloudiness of a liquid. The more bacteria in a liquid, the cloudier it will be. A scientist grew two different species of bacteria in liquid broth to see which species grew more quickly at room temperature. She measured the turbidity of the samples over time to track the bacterial growth. The results are shown in the graph.

   a) Suggest a suitable negative control for this experiment and explain why it should be used.

   b) Describe two aseptic techniques that the scientist would need to carry out in the preparation of the broth.

   c) Explain why it is important to use aseptic techniques when working with cultures of microorganisms in the lab.

   d) Describe the differences between the growth curves of each species of bacteria and suggest an explanation for them.

Q2 Kindi was working with a species of bacteria that had been isolated from a highly acidic environment. She wanted to test the ability of the species to grow at higher pH levels. Suggest a suitable experiment that she could perform to measure the species' growth performance at pH 3, pH 5 and pH 7.

**Tip:** Take a look back at page 524 if you need a reminder about the different phases on a microbial culture's growth curve.

### Practice Questions — Fact Recall

Q1 What is a culture?
Q2 State three things that are controlled in a fermentation vessel.
Q3 Explain what is meant by 'a closed culture'.
Q4 a) Name the four phases on the growth curve of a population of microorganisms in a closed culture.
   b) Describe and explain what is happening during each phase.

Module 6: Section 5 Cloning and Biotechnology

## Learning Objectives:

- Understand the different methods of immobilising enzymes for use in biotechnology.
- Be able to evaluate the uses of immobilised enzymes in biotechnology — examples could include:
  - lactase for the hydrolysis of lactose to glucose and galactose,
  - penicillin acyclase for the formation of semi-synthetic penicillins (to which some penicillin-resistant organisms are not resistant),
  - glucoamylase for the conversion of dextrins to glucose,
  - glucose isomerase for the conversion of glucose to fructose,
  - aminoacyclase for production of pure samples of L-amino acids,
  - nitrilase for the conversion of acrylonitrile to acrylamide (for use in the plastics industry).

**Specification Reference 6.2.1**

### Exam Tip
If you get asked about advantages and disadvantages of using immobilised enzymes in the exam, be specific — e.g. for an advantage, don't just say they're more economical than free enzymes, give the reasons why.

# 5. Immobilised Enzymes

*As you know from page 519, enzymes can be pretty important in biotechnology. Enzymes are often immobilised for use in industrial processes. These pages explain how and why immobilised enzymes are used.*

## Immobilising isolated enzymes

Isolated enzymes used in industry can become mixed in with the products of a reaction. The products then need to be separated from this mixture, which can be complicated and costly. This is avoided in large-scale production by using **immobilised enzymes** — enzymes that are attached to an insoluble material so they can't become mixed with the products. There are three main ways that enzymes are immobilised:

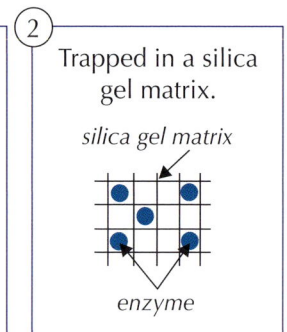

1. Encapsulated in jelly-like alginate beads, which act as a semi-permeable membrane. 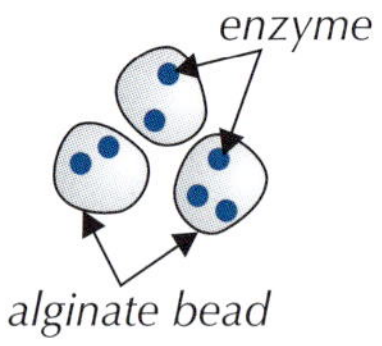
2. Trapped in a silica gel matrix.
3. Covalently bonded to cellulose or collagen fibres.

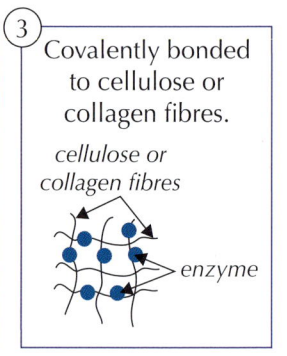

In industry, the substrate solution for a reaction is run through a column of immobilised enzymes (see Figure 1). The active sites of the enzymes are still available to catalyse the reaction but the solution flowing out of the column will only contain the desired product.

Here are some of the advantages and disadvantages of using immobilised enzymes in industry:

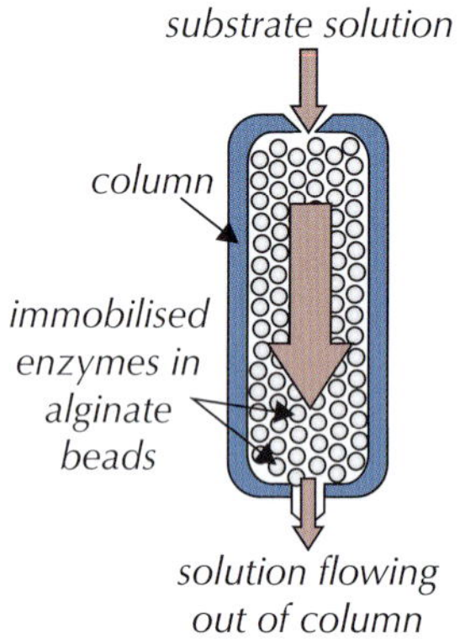

### Advantages
- Columns of immobilised enzymes can be washed and reused — this reduces the cost of running a reaction on an industrial scale because you don't have to keep buying new enzymes.
- The product isn't mixed with the enzymes — no money or time is spent separating them out.
- Immobilised enzymes are more stable than free enzymes — they're less likely to denature (become inactive) in high temperatures or extremes of pH.

### Disadvantages
- Extra equipment is required, which can be expensive to buy.
- Immobilised enzymes are more expensive to buy than free enzymes, so coupled with the equipment costs, they're not always economical for use in smaller-scale production.
- The immobilisation of the enzymes can sometimes lead to a reduction in the enzyme activity because they can't freely mix with their substrate.

**Figure 1:** A column of immobilised enzymes.

# Uses of immobilised enzymes

Immobilised enzymes are used in a wide range of industrial processes. Here are just a few examples of industrial processes that use them and the particular enzyme that they make use of:

## Conversion of lactose to glucose and galactose
Some people are unable to digest lactose (a sugar found in milk) because they don't produce enough (or any) of the enzyme lactase. Lactase breaks lactose down into glucose and galactose via a hydrolysis reaction. Industrially, fresh milk can now be passed over immobilised lactase to produce lactose-free milk for use in the production of lactose-free dairy products.

## Production of semi-synthetic penicillins
Penicillin is a useful antibiotic, but some bacteria have become penicillin resistant. Semi-synthetic penicillins can now be produced, which have the same antibiotic properties as natural penicillin, but are effective against penicillin-resistant organisms. Immobilised penicillin acylase enzyme is used in their production.

## Conversion of dextrins to glucose
Glucose and glucose syrup are used in massive amounts in industry, e.g. they're used in the food industry to sweeten and thicken foods. Glucose can be derived from starchy foods, such as corn and potatoes, with the help of immobilised enzymes. Starch breaks down into dextrins (carbohydrate products), which are then broken down into glucose by the immobilised enzyme glucoamylase.

## Conversion of glucose to fructose
Fructose is a sugar that's much sweeter than glucose. It's used as a sweetener in food — using fructose rather than glucose means that less sugar is needed to obtain the same level of sweetness in our foods. Immobilised glucose isomerase is used to convert glucose to fructose on an industrial scale.

## Production of pure samples of L-amino acids
Amino acids have two chemical forms (isomers) — L or D. Most amino acids utilised by the body need to be in the L form. Scientists are able to chemically synthesise amino acids, but end up with a mix of L and D forms. The enzyme aminoacylase separates them. Immobilised aminoacylase is used for the industrial production of pure samples of L-amino acids, which can be used for many purposes in the production of animal and human food, as well as in dietary supplements.

## Conversion of acrylonitrile to acrylamide
Acrylamide is a chemical that is typically used in industry to produce synthetic polymers (e.g. plastics), which have a wide range of uses. For example, acrylamide is involved in the production of the polymer that's used in disposable nappies to make them super-absorbent. In industry, immobilised nitrilase is used to convert acrylonitrile (a man-made chemical) to acrylamide.

> **Exam Tip**
> The examples on this page should give you an idea of how immobilised enzymes are used, but there are loads more examples. You won't necessarily get asked about one of the examples on this page, so you need to be prepared to apply your knowledge of immobilised enzymes in your exam, even if you've never heard of the enzyme or process in the question before.

**Figure 2:** *A field of* Brassica napus. *Rapeseed oil is made from the seeds of this plant.*

## Practice Questions — Application

Q1  A scientist wants to remove all of the protein from a sample. He decides to use a protease enzyme, but since the enzyme is a protein itself it can't be left in the sample at the end. Suggest how the scientist could overcome this problem.

Q2  Biodiesel is an alternative fuel to diesel that can be produced from animal, vegetable or plant oils, such as rapeseed oil. Immobilised lipase enzymes are often used in its production.
   a) Give two economical advantages of using immobilised lipase enzymes to produce large amounts of biodiesel, rather than free lipase.
   b) Using immobilised lipase for small-scale biodiesel production does not have the same economic advantages as production on a large scale. Suggest why.

## Practice Questions — Fact Recall

Q1  Give the three main ways that enzymes can be immobilised.

Q2  How do columns of immobilised enzymes work to produce a desired product?

Q3  Give three examples of immobilised enzymes and the industrial processes they are each used in.

# Section Summary

Make sure you know...

- That cloning is the process of producing genetically identical cells or organisms from the cells of an existing organism.
- That vegetative propagation is the natural production of plant clones from non-reproductive tissues.
- That plants produce natural clones via different methods of vegetative propagation (e.g. rhizomes, stolons/runners, suckers, tubers, bulbs) and that plant growers also use methods of vegetative propagation to produce clones (e.g. growing cuttings, grafting, layering).
- How to dissect plant material (e.g. the stem, roots or leaves) to produce cuttings, which can then be grown to produce plant clones.
- How plants can be artificially cloned using tissue culture and micropropagation (which is used to produce a large number of clones very quickly).
- The advantages and disadvantages of artificially cloning plants in agriculture and horticulture.
- How natural animal clones (e.g. twins) are produced — a fertilised egg splits in the very early stages of development and develops into multiple identical embryos, which leads to offspring that are clones.
- How artificial animal clones can be made by artificial embryo twinning and somatic cell nuclear transfer (SCNT).
- How artificial cloning of animals can be used, e.g. in agriculture and medicine.
- The arguments for and against the artificial cloning of animals.
- That biotechnology is the industrial use of living organisms to produce food, drugs and other products.
- That the organisms used in biotechnology are mostly microorganisms because their ideal growth conditions can be easily created, they have a short life-cycle so grow quickly under the right conditions, they can grow on inexpensive materials so are economical and they can be grown at any time of the year.
- The roles that microorganisms play in brewing, baking, cheese making, yoghurt production, penicillin production, insulin production and bioremediation.
- The advantages and disadvantages of using microorganisms to produce food for human consumption, e.g. foods made from single-cell protein.
- How microorganisms can be produced on an industrial scale for use in biotechnology using fermentation vessels.
- How growing conditions (i.e. pH, temperature, oxygen supply, nutrient concentration and contamination risk) in batch and continuous fermentation can be manipulated to maximise the yield of the desired product.
- What the standard growth curve for a population of microorganisms in a closed culture looks like, and what's happening during the lag, exponential (log), stationary and decline phases.
- How to estimate the number of individuals that will be present in a culture of microorganisms using the formula $N = N_0 \times 2^n$, where '$N_0$' is the initial number of cells in the culture and '$n$' is the number of divisions that there has been.
- How to culture microorganisms, and the aseptic techniques that need to be used when doing so.
- How to carry out an investigation into the effect of factors such as temperature, pH and nutrient availability on the growth of microorganisms.
- How enzymes can be immobilised for use in biotechnology.
- The advantages and disadvantages of using immobilised enzymes for industrial processes.

# Exam-style Questions

**1**  A group of scientists are manufacturing insulin for use in the treatment of diabetes.

**(a)**  The researchers genetically modify bacteria to produce the human insulin protein and grow the cells by continuous fermentation in the fermentation vessel shown in **Fig. 1.1**.

**(i)** Identify **three** features of the fermentation vessel in **Fig. 1.1** which help to increase the yield of protein produced. For each feature explain how it helps to increase the yield.

*(3 marks)*

**(ii)** Explain why it's important that the air entering the fermentation vessel is sterile.

*(2 marks)*

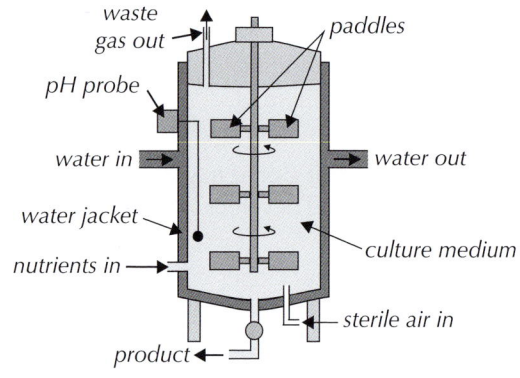

**Fig. 1.1**

**(b)**  The growth curve of the bacterial population is shown in **Fig. 1.2**. It has been plotted on a logarithmic scale.

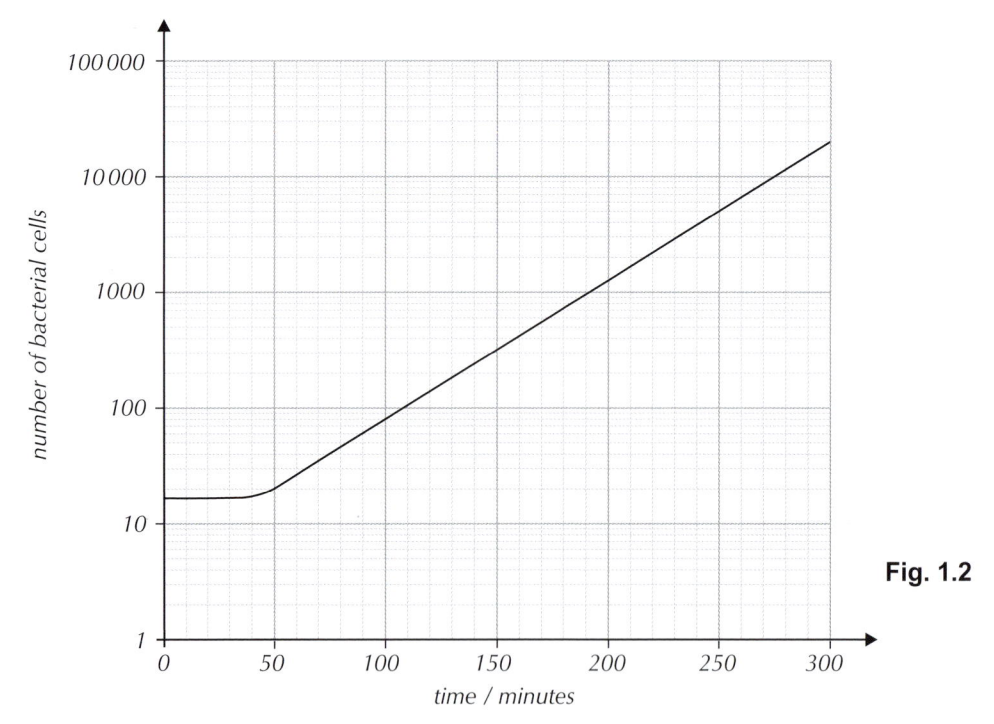

**Fig. 1.2**

**(i)** Using **Fig. 1.2**, estimate the time between each cellular division of the bacteria during the exponential growth phase.

*(1 mark)*

(ii) Explain why there is no increase in the number of bacterial cells between 0 and 40 minutes.

*(1 mark)*

(iii) Sketch out the growth curve you would expect to see if the bacteria had been grown by **closed culture**.

*(1 mark)*

(iv) Explain the differences between the growth curve of a bacterial population in a closed culture and the growth curve in **Fig. 1.2**.

*(4 marks)*

(c) The scientists believe that, in the future, diabetes could be cured using cloning to produce embryonic stem cells from the patient's own cells. Describe how embryonic stem cells could be produced from a human body cell using somatic cell nuclear transfer.

*(4 marks)*

2   Plant cloning can occur naturally via vegetative propagation or can be carried out artificially with human intervention. Both produce genetically identical copies of the parent plant.

(a) Name and describe **two** natural methods of vegetative propagation used by plants to produce clones of themselves.

*(2 marks)*

(b) A gardener wants to take cuttings to produce a clone of his blueberry plant. Describe how he could produce a clone from a cutting from a stem of the plant.

*(3 marks)*

(c) A company decides to use tissue culture to produce clones of the gardener's blueberry plant after the normal growing season has ended.

(i) When performing tissue culture, explain why the cells that are removed from the original plant are usually taken from the stem and root tips.

*(2 marks)*

(ii) In addition to being able to produce plants out of season, give **two** further advantages of cloning plants.

*(2 marks)*

(d) When inspecting clones grown from the same culture, a scientist working for the company notices that one of the clones has a bacterial infection.

(i) Suggest why this could be major problem.

*(1 mark)*

(ii) An antibiotic against the bacteria causing the infection is produced by a fungus. The fungus can be cultured using batch fermentation or continuous fermentation. Explain **two** reasons why fungi are commonly used in the biotechnology industry.

*(2 marks)*

# Module 6 Section 6: Ecosystems

## Learning Objectives:

- Know that ecosystems are dynamic systems that range in size and are influenced by both biotic and abiotic factors.
- Be able to give named examples of biotic and abiotic factors for a variety of ecosystems of different sizes (e.g. a rock pool, a playing field and a large tree).
- Understand how biomass is transferred through ecosystems.
- Understand the efficiency of biomass transfers between trophic levels.
- Know how biomass transfers between trophic levels can be measured.
- Know how human activities can manipulate the transfer of biomass through ecosystems.

**Specification Reference 6.3.1**

**Tip:** A consumer is an organism that eats other organisms, e.g. animals and birds.

**Tip:** A producer is an organism that produces organic molecules using sunlight energy, e.g. all plants are producers.

# 1. Ecosystems and Energy Flow

*You need to know what an ecosystem is and how energy flows through it. You also need to learn a whole load of ecology-based definitions — so it's probably time to stop reading this introduction and get started...*

## What is an ecosystem?

An **ecosystem** is all the organisms living in a certain area and all the non-living conditions (factors) found there. It's a dynamic system — this means it's changing all the time. An ecosystem includes both **biotic** and **abiotic factors**:

- Biotic factors are the living features of an ecosystem, for example, the presence of predators or food.
- Abiotic factors are the non-living features of an ecosystem, such as the temperature, rainfall, shape of the land (topology) and soil nutrient availability. In an aquatic ecosystem these may also include the pH and salinity (salt content) of the water.

The place where an organism lives within an ecosystem is known as its **habitat** — for example, a rocky shore on a lake, or a field.

### The impact of biotic and abiotic factors

Ecosystems cover different areas. They can be small, e.g. a pond, or large, e.g. an entire forest. Whatever size they are, ecosystems are influenced by biotic and abiotic factors. Here are some examples:

#### Example — Rock pools

- Biotic factors — Seaweed can be a food source for **consumers** such as limpets that graze on this **producer**. Intense competition for food (such as seaweed) can limit the number of organisms that are present in a small rock pool ecosystem.
- Abiotic factors — Rock pools are heavily influenced by the tides. At high tide they are completely submerged by the ocean so experience similar abiotic factors (e.g. pH, salinity, temperature, etc.) to the ocean ecosystem. However, at low tide they experience more extreme abiotic conditions (e.g. higher salinity and temperatures) — only some organisms can tolerate these conditions.

#### Example — Playing field

- Biotic factors — Producers include grass and other plants such as daisies, clover and dandelions. The large amount of these plants might attract a large number of organisms that use them as a food source (e.g. rabbits, caterpillars).
- Abiotic factors — Rainfall and sunlight affect the growth of the producers in the ecosystem. In a very wet year, the soil may become waterlogged, making it difficult for plants to grow. Poor plant growth may decrease the number of consumers the ecosystem is able to support.

### Example — Large tree

- Biotic factors — Insects, such as caterpillars, can use the leaves of a tree as a source of food. However, if they consume all the leaves on a tree (defoliation) they can slow tree growth and even lead to its death.
- Abiotic factors — Drought conditions (e.g. when there are prolonged periods of very low rainfall) can negatively impact the growth of a tree. In severe cases it can result in the whole tree (or parts of it) dying.

*Figure 1:* A caterpillar eating the leaves on a tree is an example of a biotic factor.

## Energy transfer through ecosystems

The main route by which energy enters an ecosystem is photosynthesis (e.g. by plants, see page 391). (Some energy enters sea ecosystems when bacteria use chemicals from deep sea vents as an energy source.) During photosynthesis plants convert sunlight energy into a form that can be used by other organisms. Plants are called producers (see previous page). They store energy as **biomass**. Biomass is the mass of living material, e.g. the mass of plant material. After producers store sunlight energy as biomass, you can then think of the following energy transfers through ecosystems as biomass transfers.

Energy is transferred through the living organisms of an ecosystem when organisms eat other organisms. Producers are eaten by organisms called **primary consumers**. Primary consumers are then eaten by **secondary consumers** and secondary consumers are eaten by **tertiary consumers**. Primary consumers are mainly herbivores (plant-eaters). Secondary and tertiary consumers eat other animals, so they're known as carnivores (or carnivorous organisms).

**Food chains** and **food webs** show how energy is transferred through an ecosystem. Food chains show simple lines of energy transfer, and food webs show lots of food chains in an ecosystem and how they overlap — there's an example of each below. A **trophic level** is a stage in a food chain that's occupied by a particular group of organisms, e.g. producers are the first trophic level in a food chain.

**Tip:** Remember, the <u>primary</u> consumer is the <u>first</u> consumer in a food chain, the <u>secondary</u> consumer is the <u>second</u> consumer in the food chain, and the <u>tertiary</u> consumer is the <u>third</u> consumer.

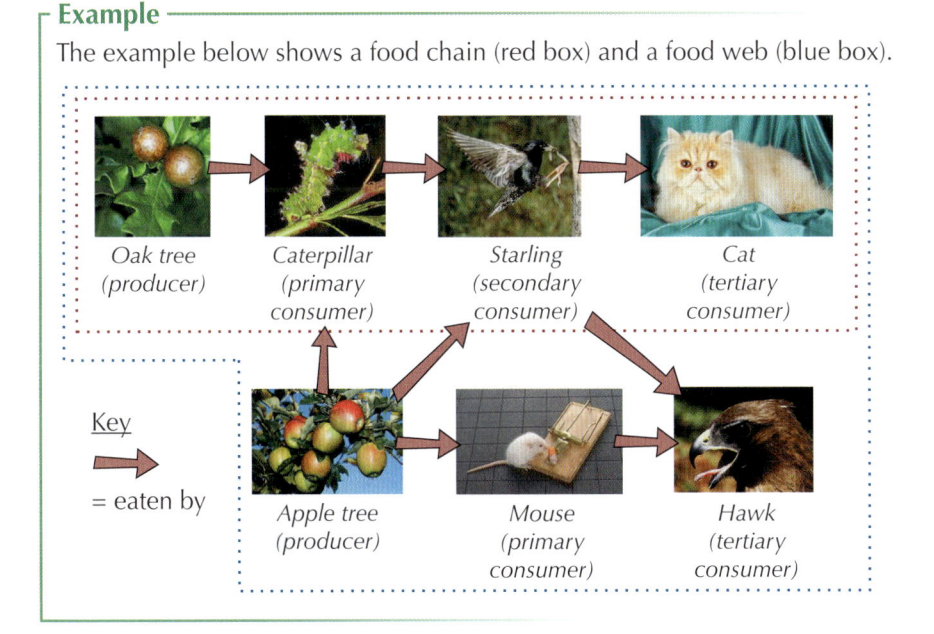

### Example

The example below shows a food chain (red box) and a food web (blue box).

Oak tree (producer) → Caterpillar (primary consumer) → Starling (secondary consumer) → Cat (tertiary consumer)

Key: → = eaten by

Apple tree (producer) → Mouse (primary consumer) → Hawk (tertiary consumer)

**Tip:** The arrows in a food chain show you the direction of energy flow.

Module 6: Section 6 Ecosystems

Energy locked up in the things that can't be eaten (e.g. bones, faeces) gets recycled back into the ecosystem by **decomposers** — organisms that break down dead or undigested organic material, e.g. bacteria and fungi.

## Calculating energy transfer

Not all the energy (e.g. from sunlight or food) that's available to the organisms in a trophic level is transferred to the next trophic level — around 90% of the total available energy is lost in various ways. Some of the available energy (60%) is never taken in by the organisms in the first place. Reasons for this include:

- Plants can't use all the light energy that reaches their leaves, e.g. some is the wrong wavelength, some is reflected, and some passes straight through the leaves.
- Some sunlight can't be used because it hits parts of the plant that can't photosynthesise, e.g. the bark of a tree.
- Some parts of food, e.g. roots or bones, aren't eaten by organisms so the energy isn't taken in — they pass to decomposers.
- Some parts of food are indigestible so pass through organisms and come out as waste, e.g. faeces — this also passes to decomposers.

The rest of the available energy (40%) is taken in (absorbed) — this is called the **gross productivity**. But not all of this is available to the next trophic level either. 30% of the total energy available (75% of the gross productivity) is lost to the environment when organisms use energy produced from respiration for movement or body heat. This is called **respiratory loss**.

This means that only 10% of the total energy available (25% of the gross productivity) becomes biomass (e.g. it's stored or used for growth) — this is called the **net productivity**. Net productivity (or biomass) is the amount of energy that's available to the next trophic level. The flow of energy transfer continues at the next trophic level — the process starts again from the beginning (see Figure 3).

**Tip:** When light energy from the sun is 'lost', this doesn't mean it disappears — it's just converted into different forms of energy.

**Tip:** The photosynthetic pigments in plants only absorb the blue and red wavelengths of light in sunlight, see page 402.

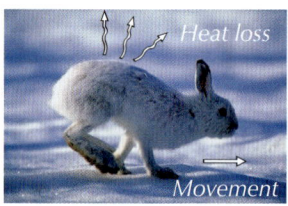

*Figure 2: Respiratory loss from a rabbit.*

**Tip:** The net productivity of the first organism in a food chain (e.g. a plant) is called the net primary productivity. Factors that affect the rate of photosynthesis (e.g. light intensity, temperature, etc. — see pages 402-404) will affect the net primary productivity of food chains.

**Tip:** The percentages used are general figures — real values for a given ecosystem will vary.

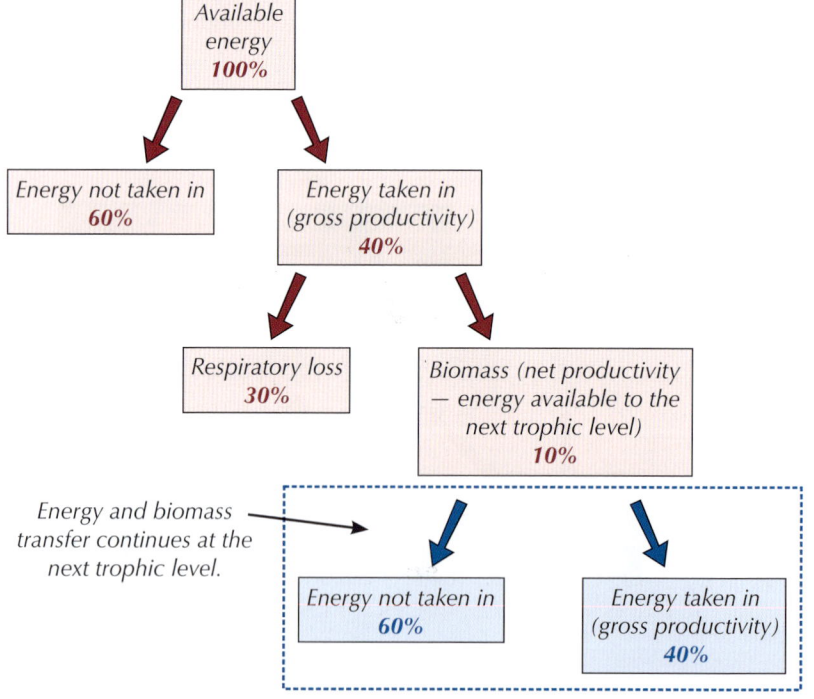

*Figure 3: Diagram showing energy transfer in a typical food chain.*

538    Module 6: Section 6 Ecosystems

Net productivity can be worked out with a simple calculation.
Here's how it's calculated:

> net productivity = gross productivity − respiratory loss

### Example — Maths Skills

Rabbits feed on grass which contains 20 000 kJm$^{-2}$yr$^{-1}$ of energy. However, they don't take in 12 000 kJm$^{-2}$yr$^{-1}$ of the energy available to them. You can use this information to work out the rabbits' gross productivity.

> gross productivity = energy available − energy not taken in
> = 20 000 − 12 000
> = **8000 kJm$^{-2}$yr$^{-1}$**

The rabbits lose 6000 kJm$^{-2}$yr$^{-1}$ using energy from respiration. You can use this to calculate the net productivity of the rabbits:

> net productivity = gross productivity − respiratory loss
> = 8000 − 6000
> = **2000 kJm$^{-2}$yr$^{-1}$**

So 2000 kJm$^{-2}$yr$^{-1}$ is available to the next trophic level.

**Tip:** The unit kJm$^{-2}$yr$^{-1}$ just means kilojoules per square metre per year.

**Tip:** In this example, the rabbits take in 8000 kJm$^{-2}$yr$^{-1}$ of energy.

## Efficiency of energy transfer

To find out how efficient the transfer of energy is between two trophic levels you need to work out the percentage efficiency of energy transfer. If you know the amount of energy available to a trophic level (net productivity of the previous trophic level) and the net productivity of that trophic level, you can work it out using this equation:

> % efficiency of energy transfer = $\dfrac{\text{net productivity of trophic level}}{\text{net productivity of previous trophic level}} \times 100$

### Example — Maths Skills

Following on from the example above, the rabbits receive 20 000 kJm$^{-2}$yr$^{-1}$ from the grass, and their net productivity is 2000 kJm$^{-2}$yr$^{-1}$.
So the percentage efficiency of energy transfer is:

> (2000 ÷ 20 000) × 100 = **10%**

**Tip:** This just shows that 10% of the energy available in the grass is passed on to the rabbit.

The efficiency of energy transfer is not the same throughout a food chain — as you move up a food chain, energy transfer generally becomes more efficient. Different amounts of energy are lost at different stages for different reasons, as shown in the table on the next page.

Even though the efficiency of energy transfer tends to increase as you move up the food chain, energy is still lost at each trophic level — so the more stages there are in a food chain, the more energy is lost overall. This energy loss limits the number of organisms that can exist in a particular ecosystem.

**Exam Tip**
Don't forget — the efficiency of energy transfer usually <u>increases</u> with increasing trophic level.

Module 6: Section 6  Ecosystems

Tip: Remember, energy that's used for growth and reproduction isn't lost — it becomes biomass in an organism.

Tip: The more digestible an organism's food, the more energy the organism can absorb from it. This means less is egested as waste (undigested) products.

| Stage of food chain | Efficiency of energy transfer | Reason |
|---|---|---|
| Sun to producer | Low, around 2-3% | Not all the light energy that plants receive can be absorbed (see page 538) and some energy that is absorbed is then lost during photosynthesis. |
| Producer to consumer | 5-10% | Energy transfer is less efficient from producer to consumer (i.e. to herbivores) than from consumer to consumer (i.e. to carnivores). This is because plants contain a greater proportion of indigestible material (e.g. cellulose within plant cell walls) than animals (which contain a large proportion of relatively digestible meat). |
| Consumer to consumer | High, around 15-20% | |

It might also be helpful to calculate how efficient organisms in one trophic level are at converting what they eat into energy for the next trophic level. You can work it out like this:

$$\frac{\text{energy transferred}}{\text{energy intake}} \times 100$$

Here, energy transferred means the net productivity of the trophic level.

## Measuring the efficiency of energy transfer

To calculate the efficiency of energy transfer between trophic levels, you need to know the net productivity of each trophic level. This means measuring the amount of energy in each trophic level. To measure the energy of the organisms in one trophic level, first you calculate the amount of energy or biomass in a sample of the organisms.

You can measure the amount of energy in an organism by measuring its **dry mass** (its biomass). To do this, you need to dry the organism out — this is done by heating it up to 80 °C until all the water in it has evaporated. You then weigh the organism. Remember, energy is stored as biomass, so it indicates how much energy an organism contains.

Tip: An organism's mass before it has been dried is called its wet mass.

Then you multiply the results from the sample to get an estimate of the energy in one trophic level.

Tip: This method of measuring energy transfer may not be very ethical, so ecologists more commonly use existing data to estimate values.

─ Examples ─

- A field of grass measures 10 000 m². To find the amount of energy in the whole field you could find the amount of energy in a 1 m² sample of grass, then multiply this figure by 10 000.
- Twenty rabbits live in the field of grass. To find the amount of energy in the rabbit population, you could find the amount of energy in one rabbit, then multiply this figure by 20.

Tip: A population is all the organisms of one species in a habitat.

The difference in energy between the trophic levels is the amount of energy transferred.

There are problems with this method though. For example, the consumers (rabbits) might have taken in energy from sources other than the producer measured (grass). This means the difference between the two figures calculated wouldn't be an accurate estimate of the energy transferred between only those two organisms. For an accurate estimate you'd need to include all the individual organisms at each trophic level.

# Controlling energy flow through ecosystems

Farmers try to reduce the amount of energy lost from food chains in order to increase productivity. They use farming methods that make the transfer of energy between trophic levels more efficient:

### Herbicides
Herbicides kill weeds that compete with agricultural crops for energy. Reducing competition means crops receive more energy, so they grow faster and become larger, increasing productivity.

### Fungicides
Fungicides kill fungal infections that damage agricultural crops. The crops use more energy for growth and less for fighting infection, so they grow faster and become larger, increasing productivity.

### Insecticides
Insecticides kill insect pests that eat and damage crops. Killing insect pests means less biomass is lost from crops, so they grow to be larger, which means productivity is greater.

### Natural predators
Natural predators introduced to the ecosystem eat the pest species, e.g. ladybirds eat greenfly. This means the crops lose less energy and biomass, increasing productivity.

### Fertilisers
Fertilisers are chemicals that provide crops with minerals needed for growth, e.g. nitrates. Crops use up minerals in the soil as they grow, so their growth is limited when there aren't enough minerals. Adding fertiliser replaces the lost minerals, so more energy from the ecosystem can be used to grow, increasing the efficiency of energy conversion.

### Rearing livestock intensively
Rearing livestock intensively involves controlling the conditions they live in and when they're slaughtered, so more of their energy is used for growth and less is used for other activities — the efficiency of energy conversion is increased so more biomass is produced and productivity is increased.

- **Examples**
  - Animals may be kept in warm, indoor pens where their movement is restricted. Less energy is wasted keeping warm and moving around.
  - Animals may be given feed that's higher in energy than their natural food. This increases the energy input, so more energy is available for growth.
  - Animals may be slaughtered before they reach adulthood. Young animals use a greater amount of their energy for growth, so this means more energy is transferred to their biomass.

**Tip:** All these methods try to increase (or prevent the loss) of an organism's biomass, which increases the amount of energy available to the next trophic level.

**Tip:** Restricting an animal's movement means they respire less, which lowers their respiratory loss.

*Figure 4: Battery farmed hens are an example of intensively reared livestock.*

The benefits of these methods are that more food can be produced in a shorter space of time, often at lower cost. However, enhancing productivity by intensive rearing raises ethical issues. For example, some people think the conditions intensively reared animals are kept in cause the animals pain, distress or restricts their natural behaviour, so it shouldn't be done.

### Practice Questions — Application

**Q1** In a food chain mussels have a gross productivity of 22 861 kJm$^{-2}$yr$^{-1}$ and a respiratory loss of 17 000 kJm$^{-2}$yr$^{-1}$.
  a) Calculate the net productivity of the mussels.

The mussels provide food for crayfish which have a net productivity of 627 kJm$^{-2}$yr$^{-1}$.
  b) Calculate the efficiency of energy transfer between the mussels and the crayfish.

**Q2** The diagram below shows the net productivity in a food chain. Use the diagram to answer the following questions.

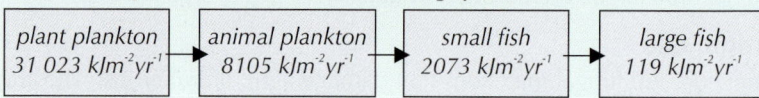

| plant plankton 31 023 kJm$^{-2}$yr$^{-1}$ | → | animal plankton 8105 kJm$^{-2}$yr$^{-1}$ | → | small fish 2073 kJm$^{-2}$yr$^{-1}$ | → | large fish 119 kJm$^{-2}$yr$^{-1}$ |

  a) The total amount of energy taken in by the small fish is 8072 kJm$^{-2}$yr$^{-1}$. Calculate how much energy the small fish lose through respiration.
  b) The respiratory loss of the large fish is 450 kJm$^{-2}$yr$^{-1}$. Calculate the gross productivity of the large fish. Give your answer in standard form in kJkm$^{-2}$yr$^{-1}$.
  c) Give one reason why the gross productivity of the large fish is less than the net productivity of the small fish.
  d) Calculate the percentage efficiency of energy transfer between each stage of the food chain.

**Exam Tip**
You might have to do calculations like these in the exam, so make sure you know the equations for net productivity and the efficiency of energy transfer. Look back to page 539 for a reminder.

**Exam Tip**
If you're asked to do a calculation, always check the question to see if it specifies what units you should give your answer in.

### Practice Questions — Fact Recall

**Q1** Describe what is meant by the biotic factors in an ecosystem.
**Q2** Give an example of an abiotic factor that might affect:
  a) a rock pool,
  b) a playing field,
  c) a large tree.
**Q3** Define the term: a) producer,   b) consumer.
**Q4** What is the main route by which energy enters an ecosystem?
**Q5** What name is given to the amount of energy taken in by an organism?
**Q6** Is energy transfer more efficient to herbivores or to carnivores? Explain your answer.
**Q7** Give one method that can be used to measure the amount of energy in a sample of organic material.
**Q8** Give two examples of farming methods that increase the transfer of energy through an ecosystem. Explain how each of the methods work.

Module 6: Section 6  Ecosystems

# 2. Recycling in Ecosystems

*Photosynthesis is the main way that energy enters an ecosystem — it's how energy from sunlight is used to make carbon compounds, and so it's where the carbon cycle begins...*

## The carbon cycle

All organisms need carbon to make essential compounds, e.g. plants use $CO_2$ (carbon dioxide) in photosynthesis to make glucose. The carbon cycle is how carbon moves through living organisms and the non-living environment. The cycle includes processes that involve organisms (photosynthesis, respiration, and decomposition) and also chemical and physical processes such as combustion and weathering:

**Figure 1:** The carbon cycle.

### Photosynthesis
Carbon (in the form of $CO_2$ from air and water) is absorbed by plants when they carry out photosynthesis — it becomes carbon compounds in plant tissues. Carbon is passed on to primary consumers when they eat the plants. It's passed on to secondary and tertiary consumers when they eat other consumers.

### Decomposition
All living organisms die and are broken down by microorganisms called **decomposers**, e.g. bacteria and fungi. Decomposers secrete enzymes which break down the carbon compounds (e.g. starch) in dead organic material. The decomposers then absorb the products of digestion (e.g. maltose) for use in respiration. Feeding on dead organic matter is called **saprobiontic nutrition** (see Figure 2).

### Respiration
Carbon is returned to the air (and water) as all living organisms (including the decomposers) carry out respiration, which produces $CO_2$.

### Combustion
If dead organic matter ends up in places where there aren't any decomposers, e.g. deep oceans or bogs, its carbon compounds can be turned into fossil fuels over millions of years (by heat and pressure). The carbon in fossil fuels (e.g. oil and coal) is released when they're burnt — this is called combustion.

---

**Learning Objectives:**
- Understand the role of recycling within ecosystems.
- Know the importance of the carbon cycle, including the role of organisms (photosynthesis, decomposition and respiration) and physical and chemical effects in the cycling of carbon within ecosystems.
- Know the role of decomposers and roles of microorganisms in recycling nitrogen within ecosystems, including *Rhizobium*, *Azotobacter*, *Nitrosomonas* and *Nitrobacter*.

**Specification Reference 6.3.1**

**Tip:** $CO_2$ diffuses into the air spaces within a leaf (via stomata), and then into the plant cells — they don't absorb carbon compounds through their roots.

**Figure 2:** Fungi (white areas) have begun decomposing these slices of bread.

**Tip:** Microorganisms that carry out saprobiontic nutrition are called saprobionts.

Module 6: Section 6 Ecosystems    543

**Tip:** The Earth's crust is made up of huge plates called tectonic plates. Currents in the molten rocks below the plates cause them to move slowly around and collide with one another. At some plate boundaries (where two plates meet), one plate is forced under the other.

*Figure 3: Weathering has formed these ridges and clefts on this limestone pavement.*

**Tip:** The carbon and nitrogen cycles show that carbon and nitrogen are recycled and can be reused by organisms. This recycling within the environment helps maintain balance in ecosystems.

### Release from volcanoes

As well as coal, other types of rock can be formed from dead organic matter deposited on the sea floor. For example, rocks such as limestone and chalk are mainly composed of calcium carbonate ($CaCO_3$). This comes from marine organisms like crabs, mussels, sea urchins and coral that utilise this compound in their development, e.g. to form shells.

One way carbon can be returned to the atmosphere from these rocks is by them being drawn down deep into the Earth's crust by the movement of tectonic plates. There they undergo chemical changes and release carbon dioxide, which is returned to the atmosphere by volcanoes.

### Weathering

The rocks can also eventually become land, which is then weathered (broken down by exposure to the atmosphere). This can happen chemically by rainwater (which is naturally slightly acidic due to the $CO_2$ dissolved in it) and physically, e.g. by plant roots, animals, etc. Chemical weathering causes mineral ions and bicarbonate ions ($HCO_3^-$) to be released from the rock into solution and enter groundwater, from where they are transported into rivers and the oceans. There they combine to form carbon-containing compounds such as $CaCO_3$.

### Release from and absorption into the ocean

$CO_2$ can also dissolve directly into the oceans from the atmosphere and be transported in the ocean by deep underwater currents (a physical process). $CO_2$ can remain in these slow-moving currents for hundreds of years before returning to the surface and being released back into the atmosphere.

## The nitrogen cycle

Plants and animals need nitrogen to make proteins and nucleic acids (DNA and RNA) for growth. The atmosphere's made up of about 78% nitrogen, but plants and animals can't use it in that form — they need bacteria to convert it into nitrogen compounds first. The nitrogen cycle shows how nitrogen is converted into a usable form and then passed on between different living organisms and the non-living environment. The nitrogen cycle includes food chains (nitrogen is passed on when organisms are eaten), and four different processes that involve bacteria — nitrogen fixation, ammonification, nitrification and denitrification:

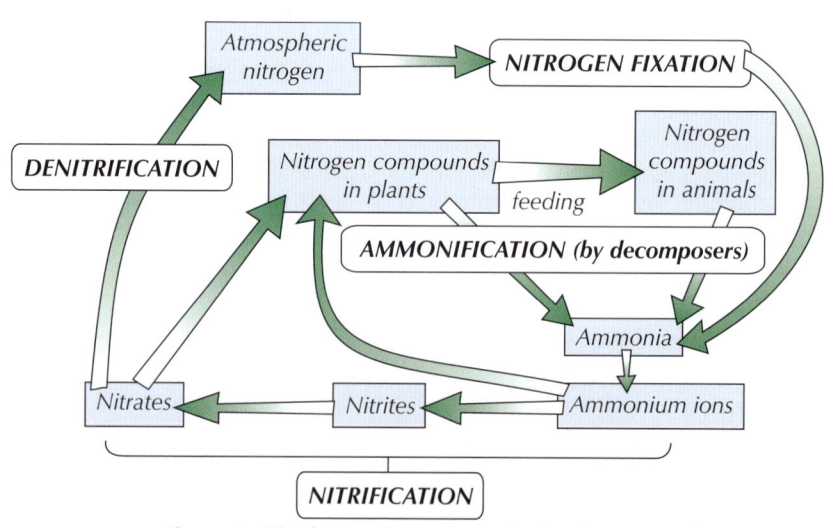

*Figure 4: The four main processes in the nitrogen cycle.*

Module 6: Section 6  Ecosystems

## Nitrogen fixation

Nitrogen fixation is when nitrogen gas in the atmosphere is converted to ammonia by bacteria such as *Rhizobium* and *Azotobacter*. The ammonia can then be used by plants. *Rhizobium* are found inside root nodules (growths on the roots — see Figure 5) of leguminous plants (e.g. peas, beans and clover). They form a **mutualistic relationship** with the plants — they provide the plant with nitrogen compounds and the plant provides them with carbohydrates. *Azotobacter* are found living in the soil. They don't form mutualistic relationships with plants.

*Figure 5:* Pink nodules of Rhizobium *on plant roots.*

**Tip:** A mutualistic relationship is where two organisms are dependent on one another, with both of them benefitting.

## Ammonification

Ammonification is when nitrogen compounds from dead organisms are turned into ammonia by decomposers, which goes on to form ammonium ions. Animal waste (urine and faeces) also contains nitrogen compounds. These are also turned into ammonia by decomposers and go on to form ammonium ions.

## Nitrification

Nitrification is when ammonium ions in the soil are changed into nitrogen compounds that can then be used by plants (nitrates). First nitrifying bacteria called *Nitrosomonas* change ammonium ions into nitrites. Then other nitrifying bacteria called *Nitrobacter* change nitrites into nitrates.

## Denitrification

Denitrification is when nitrates in the soil are converted into nitrogen gas by denitrifying bacteria — they use nitrates in the soil to carry out respiration and produce nitrogen gas. This happens under anaerobic conditions (where there's no oxygen), e.g. in waterlogged soils.

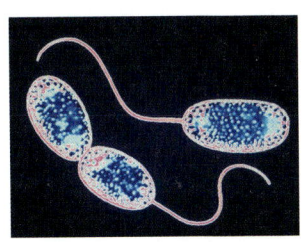

*Figure 6:* Nitrobacter *bacteria.*

## Other ways for nitrogen to enter an ecosystem

Not all of the usable nitrogen in an ecosystem has come from nitrogen fixation by bacteria. Other ways that nitrogen gets into an ecosystem is by lightning (which also fixes atmospheric nitrogen) or by artificial fertilisers (they're produced from atmospheric nitrogen on an industrial scale in the Haber process).

### Practice Questions — Fact Recall

Q1 Describe how organisms contribute to the movement of carbon through the carbon cycle.

Q2 Explain where the carbon released during combustion comes from.

Q3 Describe the role of weathering in the carbon cycle.

Q4 Describe how carbon is absorbed into the oceans.

Q5 Give one reason why plants and animals need nitrogen.

Q6 Copy and complete the table below about processes in the nitrogen cycle.

| Name of process | Bacteria responsible |
|---|---|
| Nitrogen fixation | |
| Ammonification | |
| Nitrification | |
| Denitrification | |

Q7 Describe the process of ammonification.

Q8 Name the process by which nitrates in the soil are converted into nitrogen gas by bacteria.

**Exam Tip**
You need to know the microorganisms involved at each stage in the nitrogen cycle, so make sure you get them straight in your head now.

**Learning Objective:**

- Understand the process of primary succession in the development of an ecosystem, including succession from pioneer species to a climax community and deflected succession.

**Specification Reference 6.3.1**

**Tip:** Remember, biotic conditions (factors) are the living features of an ecosystem, e.g. the plant and animal communities. Abiotic conditions (factors) are the non-living features, such as light, $CO_2$ and water availability.

# 3. Succession

*The types of organisms found in an environment change over time — and the environment itself changes too. This is due to a process called succession.*

## What is succession?

**Succession** is the process by which an ecosystem (see page 536) changes over time. Succession happens in a series of stages. At each stage, the species in an area slowly change the environmental conditions (for example, by making the soil more fertile), making those conditions more suitable for other species. This means that the **biotic conditions** change as the **abiotic conditions** change, causing one community of organisms to be succeeded (replaced) by another. There are two main types of succession — primary succession (see below) and secondary succession (see page 548).

## Primary succession

Primary succession happens on land that's been newly formed or exposed, e.g. where a volcano has erupted to form a new rock surface, or where sea level has dropped exposing a new area of land. There's no soil or organic material to start with, e.g. just bare rock.

### Pioneer stage of succession

Primary succession starts when species colonise a new land surface. Seeds and spores are blown in by the wind and begin to grow. The first species to colonise the area are called **pioneer species**. The abiotic conditions are hostile (harsh) and only pioneer species can grow because they're specialised to cope with the harsh conditions.

---- Examples ----

**Hostile abiotic conditions**

- There is limited water available because there's no soil to retain water.
- There are few minerals or nutrients because there's no soil.
- There may be high light intensity, exposure to wind and rain, and fluctuating temperatures because the area is directly exposed to the Sun and the elements.

**Pioneer species**

- Marram grass can grow on sand dunes near the sea because it has deep roots to get water and can tolerate the salty environment (see Figure 1).
- Lichens are organisms usually made up of a fungus and an alga. They're able to survive in rocky conditions because the fungus secretes acids which erode the rock, releasing minerals.
- Shrubs of the *Calligonum* genus are pioneer species that can grow in areas that experience periodic drought.

---

*Figure 1: Marram grass is able to grow in hostile conditions on sand dunes.*

**Tip:** The pioneer species help to stabilise an environment — they make it possible for other species to grow there.

The pioneer species change the abiotic conditions — they die and microorganisms decompose the dead organic material (humus). This forms a basic soil. This makes conditions less hostile, e.g. the basic soil helps to retain water, which means new organisms can move in and grow. The new organisms then die and are decomposed, adding more organic material, making the soil deeper and richer in minerals such as nitrates. Nitrogen-fixing bacteria turn nitrogen from the atmosphere into ammonia, which can then be used by plants (see page 545). This means larger plants like shrubs can start to grow in the deeper soil, which retains even more water and contains more nutrients.

## Later stages of succession

At each stage, different plants and animals that are better adapted for the improved conditions move in, out-compete the plants and animals that are already there, and become the dominant species in the ecosystem. The dominant species are the ones which cause the most change to the abiotic environment, making it more suitable for other species.

As succession goes on, the ecosystem becomes more complex. New species move in alongside existing species, which means the species diversity increases. Plants create more habitats for animals, the abiotic conditions become less hostile and the amount of biomass increases.

Eventually these changes result in a **climax community** — the ecosystem is supporting the largest and most complex community of plants and animals it can. It won't change much more — it's in a steady state.

**Tip:** You learnt about species diversity in Module 4: Section 2 — it's the number of different species and the abundance of each species in an area.

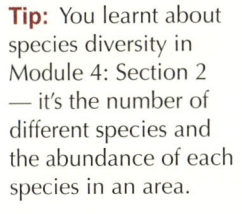

**Tip:** A community is all the populations of different species found in a habitat.

### Example — primary succession

1. Bare rock lacks soil, is exposed to strong winds and has periods of drought. Lichens (the pioneer species) are able to survive because they can grow in cracks to avoid the wind, break down rock to release minerals and are adapted to survive periods of drought.

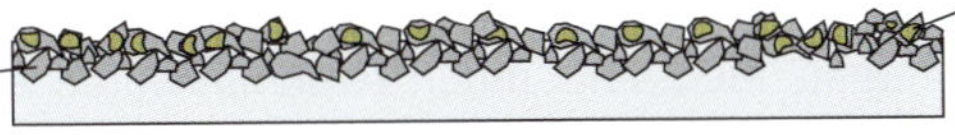

2. The lichens die and are decomposed helping to form a thin soil, which thickens as more organic material is formed. This means other species such as mosses can grow.

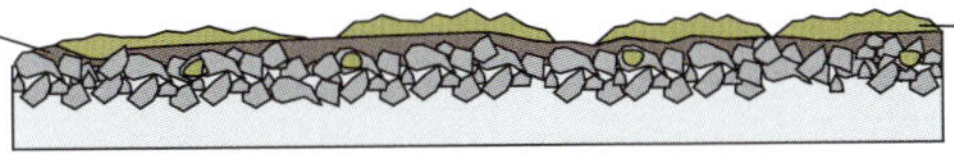

3. Larger plants that need more water can move in as the soil deepens, e.g. grasses and small flowering plants. The soil continues to deepen as the larger plants die and are decomposed.

**Figure 2:** Lichens (orange and white) have adaptations that allow them to live on bare rock.

4. Shrubs, ferns and small trees begin to grow, out-competing the grasses and smaller plants to become the dominant species. Diversity increases.

**Tip:** Primary succession also happens on sand dunes, salt marshes and even in lakes.

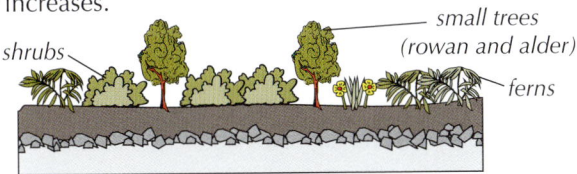

5. Finally, the soil is deep and rich enough in nutrients to support large trees. These become the dominant species, and the climax community is formed.

Module 6: Section 6  Ecosystems    547

*Figure 3: Secondary succession following a forest fire.*

*Figure 4: The climax community in many parts of Britain is deciduous woodland.*

*Figure 5: The climax community in most of Greenland is arctic tundra.*

**Tip:** 'Remains viable for' means how long the plant seeds are capable of germinating (sprouting).

## Secondary succession

Secondary succession happens on land that's been cleared of all the plants, but where the soil remains, e.g. after a forest fire or where a forest has been cut down by humans. The established community of species is usually destroyed, but without too much disturbance to the soil. It can occur during any stage (including the climax community) after the pioneer stage.

The process of secondary succession is similar to primary succession, but because there's already a soil layer, secondary succession starts at a later stage — and the pioneer species are larger plants, e.g. shrubs.

## Climatic climax communities

Which species make up the climax community depends on what the climate's like in an ecosystem. The climax community for a particular climate is called its **climatic climax**.

### Examples

- In a temperate climate, e.g. the UK, there's plenty of available water, mild temperatures and not much change between the seasons. The climatic climax will contain large trees because they can grow in these conditions once deep soils have developed (see Figure 4).
- In a polar climate there's not much available water, temperatures are low and there are massive changes between the seasons. Large trees won't ever be able to grow in these conditions, so the climatic climax contains only herbs or shrubs, but it's still the climax community (see Figure 5).

### Practice Questions — Application

A team analysed data on ecological changes in part of a national park. Their results are shown in the graph below.

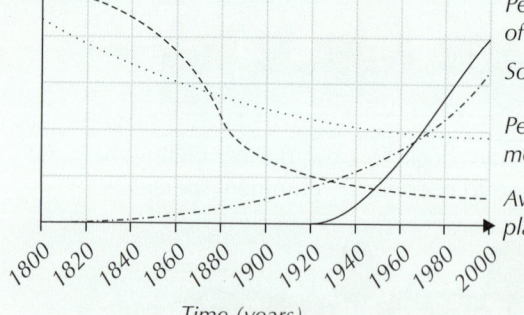

*Graph showing (curves labelled):*
- *Percentage cover of tree species*
- *Soil moisture content*
- *Percentage fluctuation around mean ground temperature*
- *Average length of time dominant plant seeds remain viable for*

*x-axis: Time (years), 1800 to 2000*

Q1 What type of succession is shown on the graph? Explain your answer.

Q2 Describe the characteristics of the dominant plant community between 1800 and 1860.

Q3 Describe and suggest an explanation for the change shown in the average length of time dominant plant seeds remain viable for.

Q4 During what time period would you expect to see a high percentage of plants whose seeds require high light intensity for germination? Explain your answer.

Q5 Describe and suggest an explanation for the change in the soil moisture content shown on the graph.

Module 6: Section 6 Ecosystems

# Preventing and deflecting succession

Human activities can prevent succession, stopping the normal climax community from developing. When succession is stopped artificially like this, the climax community is called a **plagioclimax**.

### Example
The management of a nature reserve in Dorset prevents the growth of large trees on areas of the land. This keeps the land as heathland and is done to protect some of the small reptiles that inhabit the area — if large trees were allowed to grow, other species of animals would move into the area which would out-compete the reptiles. The nature reserve is a plagioclimax.

Deflected succession is when succession is prevented by human activity, but the plagioclimax that develops is one that's different to any of the natural stages of the ecosystem — the path of succession has been deflected from its natural course.

### Example
A regularly mown grassy field won't develop woody plants, even if the climate of the ecosystem could support them. The growing points of the woody plants are cut off by the lawnmower, so larger plants can't establish themselves — only the grasses can survive being mowed, so the climax community is a grassy field. A grassy field isn't a natural stage — there should also be things like small flowering plants, so succession has been deflected.

*Figure 6:* Succession is prevented at a nature reserve in Dorset, creating a plagioclimax.

**Tip:** Grazing and burning have the same effect as mowing.

## Practice Questions — Fact Recall

Q1 What is succession?
Q2 Which type of succession happens in areas with no soil?
Q3 What name is given to the first species to colonise an area in primary succession?
Q4 What is a climax community?
Q5 Suggest an event that could cause secondary succession.
Q6 What is a climatic climax community?
Q7 What is a plagioclimax?

**Exam Tip**
You need to be able to use the correct ecological terms (like primary succession and climax community) in your exam.

Module 6: Section 6 Ecosystems 549

**Learning Objectives:**
- Know how sampling and recording methods can be used to determine the distribution and abundance of organisms in a variety of ecosystems.
- Know how the distribution and abundance of organisms in an ecosystem can be measured (PAG3).

**Specification Reference 6.3.1**

# 4. Investigating Ecosystems

*You need to be able to investigate populations of organisms. There are loads of ways of doing this. Whichever method you use, you need to make sure your samples are random...*

## Abundance and distribution

Investigating populations of organisms involves looking at the abundance and distribution of species in a particular area.

**PRACTICAL ACTIVITY GROUP 3**

### Abundance

Abundance is the number of individuals of one species in a particular area. The abundance of motile organisms and plants can be estimated by simply counting the number of individuals in samples taken. **Percentage cover** can also be used to measure the abundance of plants — this is how much of the area you're investigating is covered by a species (see next page).

### Distribution

Distribution is where a particular species is within the area you're investigating.

## Sampling

Most of the time it would be too time-consuming to measure the number of individuals and the distribution of every species in the entire area you're investigating, so instead you take samples:

1. Choose an area to sample — a small area within the area being investigated.
2. Samples should be random to avoid bias, e.g. by picking random sample sites (see below).
3. Use an appropriate technique to take a sample of the population (see next two pages).
4. Repeat the process, taking as many samples as possible in the time you have available. This gives a more precise estimate for the whole area.
5. The number of individuals for the whole area can then be estimated by taking an average of the data collected in each sample and multiplying it by the size of the whole area. The percentage cover for the whole area can be estimated by taking the average of all the samples.

**Tip:** You'll have learnt more about random sampling in Module 4.

**Tip:** When you are recording species it's important to identify them correctly. An identification key (a tool that allows you to identify species by their features) can help you do this.

**Tip:** Using tables of random numbers is another way of generating random numbers.

### Random sampling

If you were investigating populations in a field, you could pick random sample sites by dividing the field into a grid and using a random number generator and a random letter generator to select coordinates. This will give you coordinates at random, e.g. B7, E5, etc. (see Figure 1). Then you just take your samples from these coordinates.

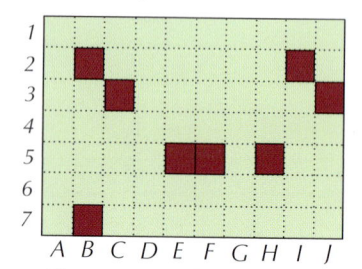

**Figure 1:** *Randomly selected squares in a field.*

## Methods for investigating populations

There are lots of different methods for studying populations of organisms, but you need to choose the most suitable one to use — this depends on the type of organism and its habitat. **Quadrats** and **transects** can be used for studying non-motile (sessile) organisms, e.g. plants and corals, or slow-moving organisms like limpets.

**Tip:** Remember, you need to be aware of any safety issues before carrying out an investigation.

550    Module 6: Section 6   Ecosystems

On the other hand, if you're studying more motile animals, like birds and insects, nets and traps are more appropriate.

## Frame quadrats

A frame quadrat is a square frame divided into a grid of 100 smaller squares by strings attached across the frame — see Figure 2.

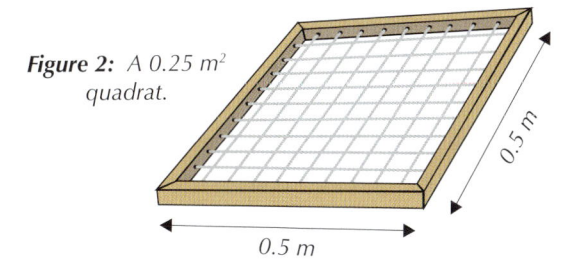

**Figure 2:** A 0.25 m² quadrat.

**Tip:** Putting your quadrat down where you happen to be standing, or even chucking it over your shoulder, doesn't count as taking a random sample. You're best off using a random number generator to select the coordinates to take your samples from.

Quadrats are placed on the ground at different points within the area you're investigating. This can be done by selecting random coordinates (see previous page). The number of individuals of each species is recorded in each quadrat.

The percentage cover of a species can also be measured by counting how much of the quadrat is covered by the species — you count a square if it's more than half-covered (see Figure 4). Percentage cover is a quick way to investigate populations and you don't have to count all the individual plants.

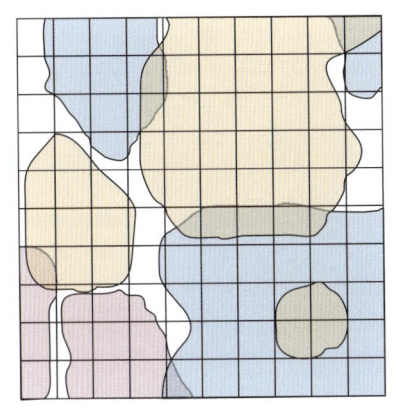

**Figure 4:** Measuring percentage cover using a quadrat.

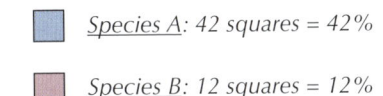

Species A: 42 squares = 42%

Species B: 12 squares = 12%

Species C: 47 squares = 47%

**Figure 3:** Quadrats can be used to measure the abundance of plant species in a field.

Frame quadrats are useful for quickly investigating areas with plant species that fit within a small quadrat — most frame quadrats are 1 m by 1 m. Areas with larger plants and trees need very large quadrats. Large quadrats aren't always in a frame — they can be marked out with a tape measure.

## Point quadrats

A point quadrat is a horizontal bar on two legs with a series of holes at set intervals along its length (see Figure 5). Point quadrats are placed on the ground at random points within the area you're investigating. Pins are dropped through the holes in the frame and every plant that each pin touches is recorded. If a pin touches several overlapping plants, all of them are recorded. The number of individuals of each species is recorded in each quadrat.

**Tip:** A problem with point quadrats is that very small or rare species may be missed.

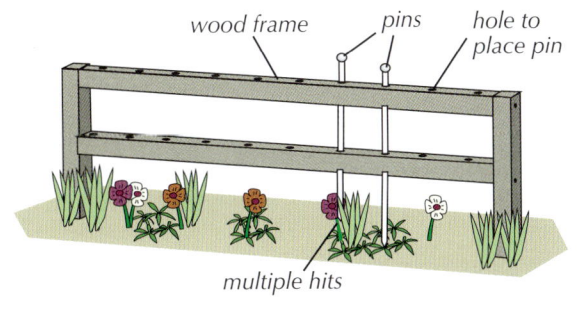

**Figure 5:** A point quadrat.

Module 6: Section 6 Ecosystems

The percentage cover of a species can also be measured by calculating the number of times a pin has touched a species as a percentage of the total number of pins dropped. Point quadrats are especially useful in areas where there's lots of dense vegetation close to the ground.

## Transects

You can use lines called transects to help find out how plants are distributed across an area, e.g. how the distribution of a plant species changes from a hedge towards the middle of a field. There are three types of transect:

- **Line transects** — a tape measure is placed along the transect and the species that touch the tape measure are recorded.
- **Belt transects** — data is collected along the transect using frame quadrats placed next to each other.
- **Interrupted transects** — instead of investigating the whole transect of either a line or a belt, you can take measurements at intervals. E.g. by placing point quadrats at right angles to the direction of the transect at set intervals along its length, such as every 2 m.

**Tip:** Transects can be used in many different ecosystems, not just fields. For example, along a beach or in a woodland.

**Tip:** Line transects are quick to carry out but a belt transect will give more data (as it covers a wider area). An interrupted belt transect is a good compromise between the two — it's quicker than a belt transect and gives more information than a line transect.

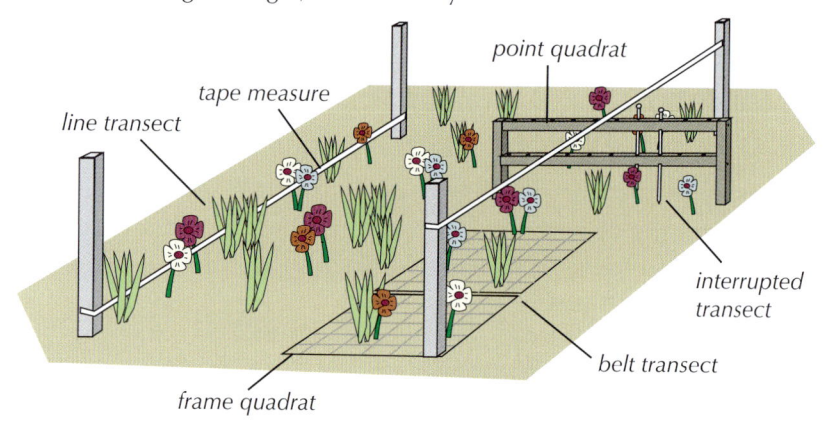

**Figure 6:** A line transect, a belt transect and an interrupted transect.

## Capturing motile organisms

If you're investigating motile organisms, you'll need to use equipment to capture them. The best method of capturing organisms will depend on what you're studying.

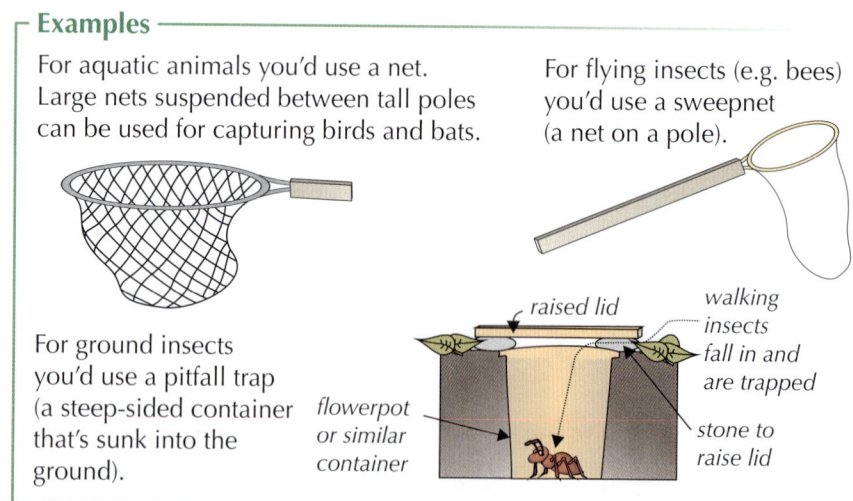

**Tip:** You could encounter lots of different risks working outdoors. Remember, you need to do a risk assessment before carrying out any investigations.

### Examples

For aquatic animals you'd use a net. Large nets suspended between tall poles can be used for capturing birds and bats.

For flying insects (e.g. bees) you'd use a sweepnet (a net on a pole).

For ground insects you'd use a pitfall trap (a steep-sided container that's sunk into the ground).

## Practice Questions — Application

Q1 A student is investigating the abundance of daisies in a field.
   a) She decides to use a frame quadrat to measure the percentage cover of daisies in the field. Describe how she could do this.
   b) Describe how the student could take random samples using a frame quadrat.

Q2 A scientist has been investigating the effect of salt spray from a road adjacent to an inland field. Her results are shown below.

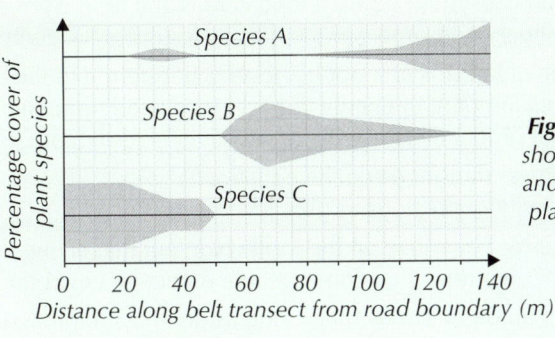

**Figure 7:** Kite diagram showing the distribution and abundance of three plant species in a field.

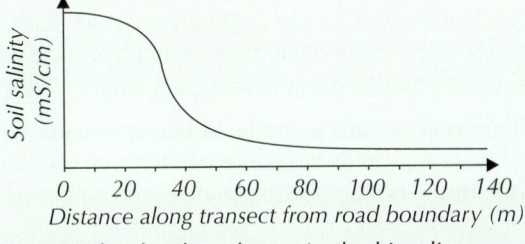

**Figure 8:** Graph showing the change in soil salinity in a field.

**Tip:** A kite diagram shows the distribution and abundance of organisms along a transect. The thickness of the kite shape shows the abundance — the thicker the kite shape, the more organisms there are.

   a) Describe the data shown in the kite diagram and the graph.
   b) One of the plant species is normally found in coastal areas. Which species is this likely to be, A, B or C? Explain your answer.
   c) The scientist is unable to prove that salt spray from the road is responsible for the absence of species B between 0 and 20 m from the road using the data shown above. Explain why.

## Practice Questions — Fact Recall

Q1 What is meant by the terms:
   a) abundance?
   b) distribution?

Q2 a) Why would an ecologist investigating the abundance of a species in an area take samples?
   b) Why is it important that these samples are taken at random?

Q3 Describe how a point quadrat would be used to investigate the abundance of a plant species in a field.

Q4 Explain the difference between a line transect and a belt transect.

Q5 Describe what you would use a pitfall trap for.

# Section Summary

Make sure you know:

- That an ecosystem is all the organisms living in a certain area and all the non-living conditions (factors) found there, and that it's a dynamic system — it's changing all the time.
- That biotic factors (e.g. the presence of predators and food) are all the living features of an ecosystem and that abiotic factors (e.g. temperature, soil) are all the non-living features of an ecosystem.
- The biotic and abiotic factors that affect ecosystems of different sizes, for example a rock pool, a playing field and a large tree.
- That biomass (stored energy) is transferred in an ecosystem through food chains and food webs from producers to primary consumers, then to secondary consumers and tertiary consumers by feeding.
- That not all of the energy that's available to the organisms in a trophic level is transferred to the next trophic level and that you can work out the total amount of energy that can be passed from one trophic level to the next using the equation: net productivity = gross productivity − respiratory loss.
- How to work out percentage efficiency of biomass transfer using the equation:
  (net productivity of trophic level ÷ net productivity of previous trophic level) × 100
- That the efficiency of biomass transfer increases as you move up the food chain but that energy is still lost at each level, and this limits the number of organisms that can exist in a particular environment.
- That you can measure the amount of energy in an organism by measuring its dry mass (biomass) and that you can use this to measure biomass transfers between trophic levels.
- That farming activities such as using herbicides, fungicides, insecticides, natural predators, fertilisers and intensively rearing livestock can increase the efficiency of energy transfer through an ecosystem.
- That the carbon cycle is important because all organisms need carbon to make essential compounds.
- That organisms play an important role in the carbon cycle — carbon in the air becomes carbon compounds in plants by photosynthesis, these carbon compounds are passed on through the food chain by feeding and are broken down by microorganisms during decomposition, and carbon is released back into the atmosphere by respiration.
- That physical and chemical processes also have a role in the carbon cycle and that they eventually return carbon to the atmosphere through combustion, weathering and via volcanoes.
- The four main processes of the nitrogen cycle and the microorganisms involved: nitrogen fixation (*Rhizobium*, *Azotobacter*), ammonification, nitrification (*Nitrosomonas*, *Nitrobacter*) and denitrification.
- That succession is the process by which an ecosystem changes over time, and how this happens.
- That succession begins with a pioneer species and ends with a climax community.
- That at each stage in succession, species change the abiotic conditions, so that the environment becomes more suitable for other species, increasing species diversity.
- That human activities can artificially stop succession from occurring, or can deflect succession from its natural course, leading to the formation of a plagioclimax.
- How samples of populations can be taken and recorded to investigate the distribution and abundance of organisms in different ecosystems.
- How the abundance and distribution of organisms can be measured using different methods such as frame quadrats, point quadrats, line transects, belt transects and interrupted transects.

# Exam-style Questions

**1** Fig. 1.1 below shows the carbon cycle.

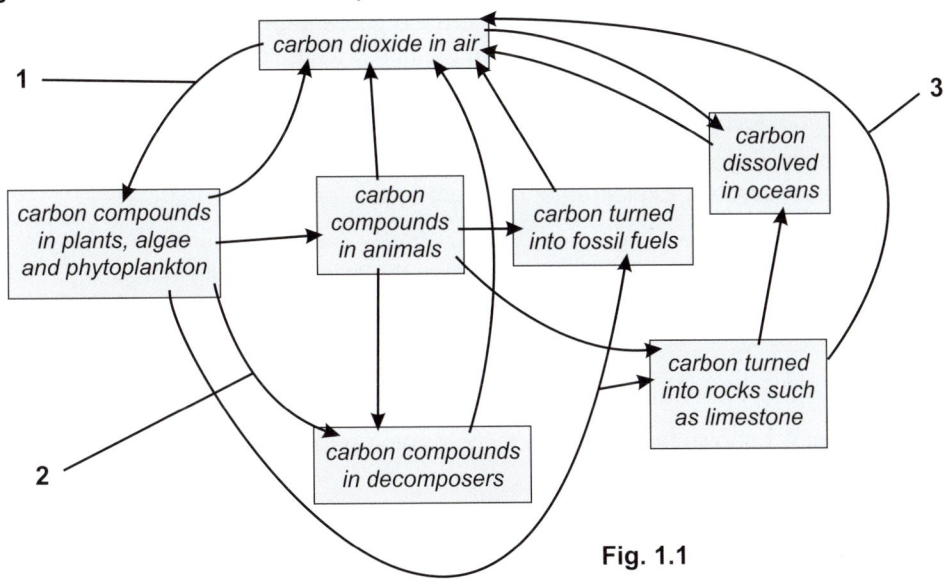

Fig. 1.1

Which of the following numbered processes is the result of action by organisms?

A   Only 1

B   Only 1 and 2

C   Only 2 and 3

D   1, 2 and 3

*(1 mark)*

**2** The process of primary succession leads to the development of ecosystems. Which of the following statements about primary succession is/are correct?

1   Primary succession starts on land where there is no soil or organic material.

2   Pioneer species make the abiotic conditions in an ecosystem less hostile.

3   The climax community is the largest and most complex community an ecosystem can support.

A   Only 1

B   Only 1 and 2

C   Only 2 and 3

D   1, 2 and 3

*(1 mark)*

**3** A team of scientists are investigating the distribution of marsh marigolds across a field that is directly next to a stream.

**(a) (i)** Suggest and describe a method the scientists could use to investigate the distribution of marsh marigolds.

*(2 marks)*

**(ii)** The team decide they want to record the percentage cover of marsh marigolds. Describe how they could measure the percentage cover **and** give **two** advantages of measuring species abundance this way.

*(3 marks)*

**(b)** Abiotic factors were investigated at the same places as the data on marsh marigolds was recorded. Explain what is meant by the term 'abiotic factors'.

*(1 mark)*

**(c)** Sheep frequently graze in the field that the scientists are investigating. Explain how this may result in deflected succession.

*(2 marks)*

**4** Fig. 4.1 shows the net productivity of some organisms in a food web. All the figures are in $kJm^{-2}yr^{-1}$.

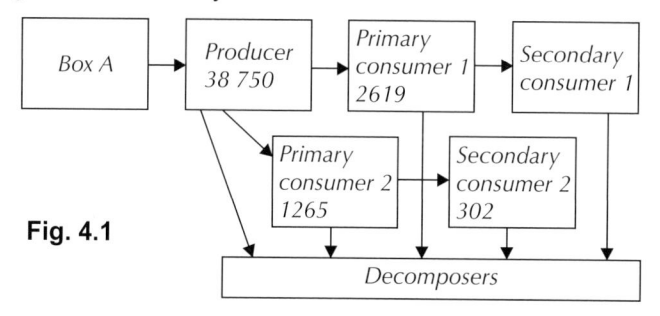

```
┌───────┐   ┌──────────┐   ┌─────────────┐   ┌─────────────┐
│ Box A │──▶│ Producer │──▶│  Primary    │──▶│ Secondary   │
│       │   │  38 750  │   │ consumer 1  │   │ consumer 1  │
└───────┘   └──────────┘   │    2619     │   │             │
                 │  │      └─────────────┘   └─────────────┘
                 │  │            │                  │
                 │  ▼      ┌─────────────┐   ┌─────────────┐
                 │         │  Primary    │──▶│ Secondary   │
                 │         │ consumer 2  │   │ consumer 2  │
                 │         │    1265     │   │    302      │
                 │         └─────────────┘   └─────────────┘
                 │               │                  │
                 ▼               ▼                  ▼
            ┌──────────────────────────────────────────────┐
            │                Decomposers                   │
            └──────────────────────────────────────────────┘
```

**Fig. 4.1**

**(a)** What source of energy is represented by Box A?

*(1 mark)*

**(b)** 476 $kJm^{-2}yr^{-1}$ of biomass energy is lost from primary consumer 1 to the decomposers. The respiratory loss of secondary consumer 1 is 1571 $kJm^{-2}yr^{-1}$. Calculate the net productivity of secondary consumer 1.

*(2 marks)*

**(c)** Give **two** reasons why the energy absorbed by secondary consumer 2 will not equal 1265 $kJm^{-2}yr^{-1}$.

*(2 marks)*

**(d)** Calculate the difference in the percentage efficiency of energy transfer between the producer and primary consumer 1, and the producer and primary consumer 2.

*(3 marks)*

**(e)** Nitrogen is passed on in a food web when organisms eat each other. Describe how nitrogen compounds in organisms are recycled back to atmospheric nitrogen. In your answer, you should describe the specific roles of named microorganisms.

*(4 marks)*

Module 6: Section 6 **Ecosystems**

# Module 6 — Section 7: Populations and Sustainability

## 1. Variation in Population Size

*The size of a population changes all the time for lots of different reasons. But to understand why a population grows and shrinks, first you need to know exactly what a population is...*

**Learning Objectives:**
- Know the factors that determine the size of a population.
- Understand the significance of limiting factors in determining the carrying capacity of a given environment and the impact of these factors on final population size.
- Understand how populations interact, including interspecific and intraspecific competition.
- Understand predator-prey relationships, including their effects on both prey and predator populations.

**Specification Reference 6.3.2**

### Populations
A **population** is all the organisms of one species in a habitat.

- Examples
  - All the foxes in a wood form a population.
  - All the people in a town form a population.

**Population size** is the total number of organisms of one species in a habitat. This number changes over time because of the effect of various factors.

### Abiotic factors and population size
The population size of any species varies because of abiotic factors, e.g. the amount of light, water or space available, the temperature of their surroundings or the chemical composition of their surroundings. When abiotic factors are ideal for a species, organisms can grow fast and reproduce successfully.

- Example
  When the temperature of a mammal's surroundings is the ideal temperature for metabolic reactions to take place, they don't have to use up as much energy maintaining their body temperature. This means more energy can be used for growth and reproduction, so their population size will increase.

When abiotic factors aren't ideal for a species, organisms can't grow as fast or reproduce as successfully.

- Example
  When the temperature of a mammal's surroundings is significantly lower or higher than their optimum body temperature, they have to use a lot of energy to maintain the right body temperature. This means less energy will be available for growth and reproduction, so their population size will decrease.

**Tip:** Remember — abiotic factors are the non-living features of the ecosystem.

### Biotic factors and population size
Population size can also vary because of biotic factors. These factors include interspecific competition, intraspecific competition and predation.

**Tip:** Remember — biotic factors are the living features of the ecosystem.

## 1. Interspecific competition

Interspecific competition is when organisms of different species compete with each other for the same resources. This can mean that the resources available to both populations are reduced, e.g. if they share the same source of food, there will be less available to both of them. This means both populations will be limited by a lower amount of food. They'll have less energy for growth and reproduction, so the population sizes will be lower for both species.

Interspecific competition can also affect the distribution of species. If two species are competing but one is better adapted to its surroundings than the other, the less well adapted species is likely to be out-competed — it won't be able to exist alongside the better adapted species.

**Tip:** Don't think it's only animals that compete with each other — plants compete with each other for things like minerals and light.

### Example

Grey squirrels were introduced to the UK. They now compete with the native red squirrels for the same food sources and habitats. As they share the same source of food, there is less available to both of them. So in areas where both red and grey squirrels live, both populations are smaller than they would be if there was only one species there.

Since the introduction of the grey squirrel to the UK, the native red squirrel has disappeared from large areas. The grey squirrel has a better chance of survival because it's larger and can store more fat over winter. It can also eat a wider range of food than the red squirrel.

## 2. Intraspecific competition

Intraspecific competition is when organisms of the same species compete with each other for the same resources. It can cause a cyclical change in population size, where the population grows, shrinks, grows again and so on (see Figure 1). This is because the population of a species increases when resources are plentiful. As the population increases, there'll be more organisms competing for the same amount of space and food. Eventually, resources such as food and space become limiting — there isn't enough for all the organisms. The population then begins to decline. A smaller population then means that there's less competition for space and food, which is better for growth and reproduction — so the population starts to grow again. The maximum stable population size of a species that an ecosystem can support is called the **carrying capacity**.

**Tip:** Don't get inter- and intra-specific competition mixed up. If you're struggling, just remember — in**ter** means diff**er**ent species, whereas intr**a** means the s**a**me species.

**Tip:** The stages of this graph are described on the next page.

### Example

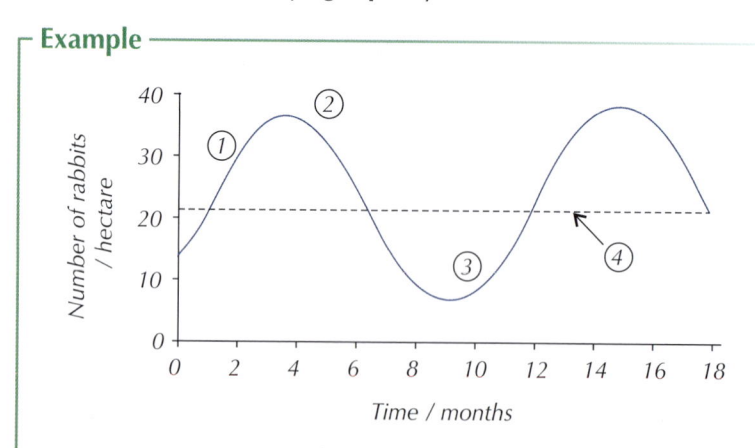

*Figure 1: Size of a rabbit population over time.*

1. There were lots of resources available so the population of rabbits grew.
2. The population grew so large that the resources became limiting. As there weren't enough resources, the rabbit population fell.
3. A smaller population of rabbits meant there was less competition, so the population of rabbits began to grow again.
4. The carrying capacity of the ecosystem was about 22 rabbits per hectare.

**Tip:** Although the population size rises above the carrying capacity, the ecosystem can't support a population this size over a long period of time — the population size isn't stable above the carrying capacity.

## 3. Predation

Predation is where an organism (the predator) kills and eats another organism (the prey), e.g. lions kill and eat (predate on) buffalo. The population sizes of predators and prey are interlinked — as the population of one changes, it causes the other population to change through **negative feedback** (see Figure 3). Negative feedback is when a system reacts to a change in a way that pushes it back towards a stable state.

In a predator-prey system, as the prey population increases, there's more food for predators, so the predator population grows. As the predator population increases, more prey is eaten so the prey population then begins to fall — this is a negative feedback effect that restores the prey population to a more stable size. This means there's less food for the predators, so their population decreases (another negative feedback effect), and so on.

**Figure 2:** Predation of snowshoe hares by lynxes causes the populations of both species to fluctuate over time.

— Example —

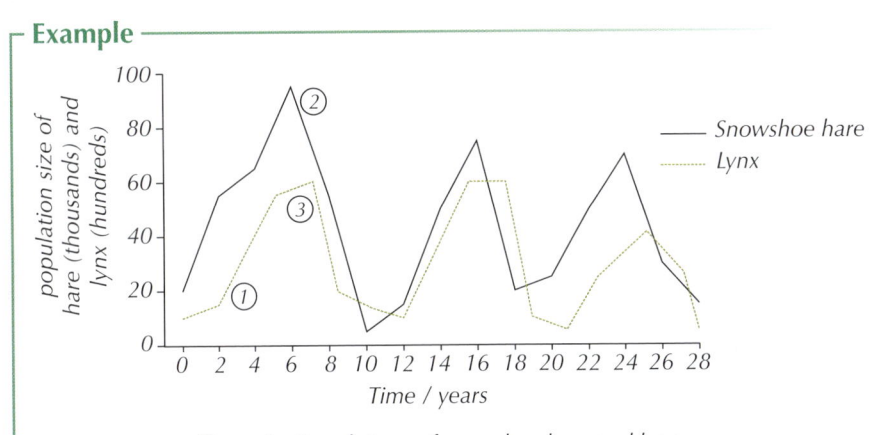

*Figure 3: Populations of snowshoe hare and lynx.*

1. In the graph above, the lynx population grew after the snowshoe hare population increased. This is because there was more food available for the lynx.
2. Greater numbers of lynx ate lots of snowshoe hares, so the population of hares fell. This is an example of negative feedback — the increase in the size of the lynx population pushed the snowshoe hare population back down.
3. Reduced snowshoe hare numbers meant there was less food for the lynx, so the population of lynx fell (again, a negative feedback effect).

Predator-prey relationships are usually more complicated than this though because there are other factors involved, like availability of food for the prey. E.g. it's thought that the population of snowshoe hare initially begins to decline because there's too many of them for the amount of food available. This is then accelerated by predation from the lynx.

## Limiting factors

Limiting factors stop the population size of a species increasing — they determine the carrying capacity of an ecosystem. Limiting factors can be abiotic or biotic.

**Tip:** Disease is another example of a biotic limiting factor of population growth — it could even make a population extinct.

### Example — an abiotic limiting factor
The amount of shelter in an ecosystem limits the population size of a species as there's only enough shelter for a certain number of individuals.

### Example — a biotic limiting factor
Interspecific competition limits the population size of a species because the amount of resources available to a species is reduced.

## Practice Questions — Application

A team investigated changes in the size of a population of owls and a population of mice over twenty years. They also monitored changes in temperature. Their results are shown on the graph below.

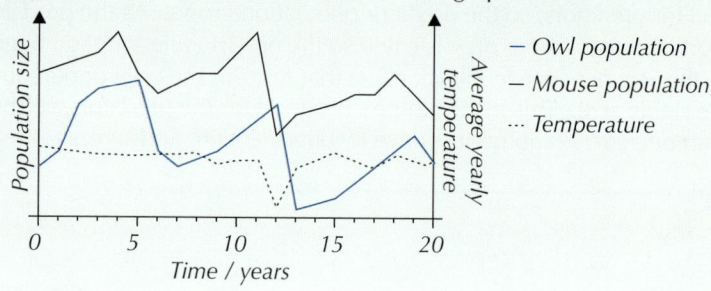

**Tip:** In the exam, if you're given a graph with two y-axes like the one on the left, make sure you read the key carefully so you know which line relates to which axis.

Q1 Give one factor affecting the population of owls which is biotic.

Q2 Describe how the fall in temperature between years 11 and 12 affected the mouse population size, and suggest a reason for the change in population size.

**Tip:** With 'suggest' questions, like in Q2 on the left, you probably won't have learned the exact answer — you need to use the information you're given and apply your own knowledge to answer the question.

Q3 Explain how variation in the mouse population size over the twenty year period could have caused changes in the owl population size.

## Practice Questions — Fact Recall

Q1 What is a population?

Q2 a) What is interspecific competition?
   b) Explain how interspecific competition may affect:
      i) the population sizes of two species competing.
      ii) the distribution of two species competing, if one species is better adapted to its surroundings.
   c) Describe an example of interspecific competition.

Q3 a) What is intraspecific competition?
   b) Explain why intraspecific competition causes a cyclical change in population size.

Q4 What is meant by the term 'carrying capacity'?

Q5 Explain how an increase in prey population will affect predator population.

Q6 What term is used to describe something that stops the population size of a species from growing?

Module 6: Section 7 Populations and Sustainability

# 2. Conservation of Ecosystems

*Ecosystems provide us with natural resources that we use in everyday life, such as food, fuel and drugs. It's important that we protect ecosystems so that species living in the ecosystems aren't destroyed and that these resources won't run out.*

## What is conservation?

Conservation is the protection and management of ecosystems so that the natural resources in them can be used without them running out. E.g. using rainforests for timber without any species becoming extinct and without any habitats being destroyed. This means the natural resources will still be available for future generations.

Conservation is a dynamic process — conservation methods need to be adapted to the constant changes (caused naturally and by humans) that occur within ecosystems. It involves the management of ecosystems — controlling how resources are used and replaced.

Conservation can also involve reclamation — restoring ecosystems that have been damaged or destroyed so they can be used again, e.g. restoring forests that have been cut down so they can be used again.

Conservation is important for many reasons:

### Economic reasons
Ecosystems provide resources for lots of things that humans need, e.g. rainforests contain species that provide things like drugs, clothes and food. These resources are economically important because they're traded on a local and global scale. If the ecosystems aren't conserved, the resources that we use now will be lost, so there will be less trade in the future.

### Social reasons
Many ecosystems bring joy to lots of people because they're attractive to look at and people use them for activities, e.g. birdwatching and walking. The species and habitats in the ecosystems may be lost if they aren't conserved, so future generations won't be able to use and enjoy them.

### Ethical reasons
Some people think we should conserve ecosystems simply because it's the 'right' thing to do — for example most people think organisms have a right to exist, so they shouldn't become extinct as a result of human activity. Some people think we have a moral responsibility to conserve ecosystems for future generations, so they can enjoy and use them.

### Ecological reasons
Conserving species and habitats can help to prevent climate change. E.g. when trees are burnt, $CO_2$ is released into the atmosphere, which contributes to global warming. If the trees are conserved, this doesn't happen. Conserving species and habitats also helps to prevent the disruption of food chains. Disruption of food chains can have knock-on effects on other organisms, e.g. some species of bear feed on salmon, which feed on herring — if the number of herring decreases it can affect both the salmon and the bear populations.

---

**Learning Objectives:**

- Understand the economic, social and ethical reasons for conservation of biological resources.
- Know the difference between conservation and preservation.
- Understand how the management of an ecosystem can provide resources in a sustainable way, including timber production and fishing.
- Understand how environmental resources can be managed and the effects of human activities on the environment.
- Understand how ecosystems can be managed to balance the conflict between conservation/preservation and human needs, for example in the Maasai Mara region of Kenya, the Terai region in Nepal, and with regards to peat bogs.

**Specification Reference 6.3.2**

**Tip:** Benefits people obtain from ecosystems are sometimes called 'ecosystem services'. These include things like the pollination of crop plants by wild insects as well as resources that can be harvested like wood and food. In recent years scientists and policy-makers have become more aware of ecosystem services, which has led to their increasing consideration in research and policy.

*Figure 1: Antarctica is a preserved ecosystem.*

**Tip:** Preservation has been the traditional way of protecting the natural environment. A greater understanding of the importance of balancing the needs of local populations with environmental considerations has made conservation more widely used.

**Tip:** Temperate woodland is found between the tropics and the polar circles (so the UK has temperate woodland).

*Figure 2: The plastic around this young tree was fitted to protect it while it grows.*

**Tip:** As the population of the Earth increases, it becomes more important to manage resources sustainably to ensure they're available for future generations.

# Preservation

Preservation is different from conservation — it's the protection of ecosystems so they're kept exactly as they are. Nothing is removed from a preserved ecosystem and they're only used for activities that don't damage them.

**Example**
Antarctica is a preserved ecosystem because it's protected from exploitation by humans — it's only used for limited tourism and scientific research, not mining or other industrial activities.

# Managing ecosystems in a sustainable way

Ecosystems can be managed to provide resources in a way that's sustainable — this means enough resources are taken to meet the needs of people today, but without reducing the ability of people in the future to meet their own needs.

## Temperate woodland

Temperate woodland can be managed in a sustainable way — for every tree that's cut down for timber, a new one is planted in its place. The woodland should never become depleted. Cutting down trees and planting new ones needs to be done carefully to be successful:

- Trees are cleared in strips or patches — woodland grows back more quickly in smaller areas between bits of existing woodland than it does in larger, open areas.
- The cleared strips or patches aren't too large or exposed — lots of soil erosion can occur on large areas of bare ground. If the soil is eroded, newly planted trees won't be able to grow.
- Timber is sometimes harvested by coppicing — cutting down trees in a way that lets them grow back. This means new trees don't need to be planted.
- Native tree species tend to be planted in preference to non-native species. This is better for biodiversity because native species have long-established interactions with other native species (e.g. plants, fungi, animals), so their presence should help species thrive in an area. Also some species might not adapt to the presence of non-native tree species.
- Planted trees are attached to posts to provide support, and are grown in plastic tubes to stop them being eaten by grazing animals — this makes it more likely the trees will survive to become mature adults.
- Trees aren't planted too close together — this means the trees aren't competing with each other for space or resources, so they're more likely to survive.

## Managing fishing

Overfishing has led to a decline in fish stocks in many parts of the world. This may lead to some species of fish disappearing altogether in some areas, and has the potential to severely disrupt ocean food chains.

Fish are an important part of many people's diets and fishing provides employment for many people, so we need to maintain fish stocks at a level where the fish continue to breed. This is sustainable food production — having enough food without using resources faster than they renew. There are a few different ways of managing fish stocks, including using fishing quotas and making regulations on mesh sizes (see next page).

Module 6: Section 7 Populations and Sustainability

## Fishing quotas

Fishing quotas are limits to the amount of certain fish species that fishermen are allowed to catch. Fishing quotas are supposed to help to conserve fish species by reducing the numbers that are caught and killed, so the populations aren't reduced too much and the species aren't at risk from becoming extinct.

To set fishing quotas, scientists study different species and decide how big their populations need to be for them to maintain their numbers. Then they decide how many it's safe for fishermen to take without reducing the population too much. International agreements are then made (e.g. the Common Fisheries Policy in the EU) that state the amount of fish each country can take, and where they're allowed to take them from.

There are problems with fishing quotas though — e.g. fish of the wrong species or size are still caught, but they end up being thrown back into the sea, often dead or dying, because the restrictions don't allow the fishermen to bring them ashore. However, new rules for the Common Fisheries Policy are banning the discarding of fish like this and the whole catch will have to be brought ashore to be counted against the quota.

## Mesh sizes

Governments can set limits for the mesh size of the fishing net, which vary depending on what's being fished. This reduces the number of 'unwanted' and discarded fish that are accidently caught, e.g. shrimp caught along with cod, as the 'unwanted' species can escape through the holes in larger meshes. It also means that younger fish will slip through the net, allowing them to reach breeding age.

However, it can be difficult to determine exactly how big the mesh size should be in areas where several different fish species are fished for at the same time. And two nets, each of which meets regulations, could be used one inside the other so that their meshes overlap — effectively reducing the reported mesh size.

**Figure 3:** *The fish in this picture are all 'unwanted' — they've been caught accidentally in a net intended to catch a different species.*

**Tip:** Managing conflicts between the environment and humans is difficult. For example, the best solution for fish stocks might be to completely ban fishing for a time, but this may not be acceptable to people who depend on fishing for their food and livelihoods. Policy-makers need to weigh up the ethical arguments relating to humans and the environment, as well as the scientific evidence, when making conservation decisions.

# Managing ecosystems and human needs

The goals of conservation and preservation are often in conflict with human needs. Ecosystems can be managed to reduce these conflicts.

### Example — the Terai Arc

The Terai Arc is an area of forest and grasslands on the border between Nepal and India. A variety of plants and animals are found there, including endangered species like the Bengal tiger and Asian elephant. Nearly 7 million people also live in this area and many of them depend on the forest's resources to survive.

Areas of the forest are also being destroyed to make way for more housing and other development — this destruction of habitat brings humans and animals into closer contact and increases conflict between the two. For example, elephants can eat and trample crop fields and tigers can kill livestock. This increases the likelihood of these animals being shot and killed.

Conservation charity the WWF has worked with local people to help balance their needs with conserving the forest and its wildlife. For example, the charity has provided people with things like solar cookers and biogas generators, so they don't need to use wood from the forest as fuel. Farmers are encouraged to plant mint hedges around their crops to keep animals (which don't like the taste of mint) away.

**Figure 4:** *The greater one-horned rhinoceros is found in the Terai Arc. Conservation efforts in the area have rescued it from the brink of extinction.*

Module 6: Section 7 Populations and Sustainability

**Tip:** Solutions like this, where alternative forms of income are developed, represent a sustainable long-term solution to conflicts between conservation and human needs, as they don't require indefinite funding from charities.

**Tip:** Ecotourism can be a useful way to make conservation economically viable, but it needs to be managed carefully to make sure that tourists don't damage the ecosystem they've come to visit.

**Tip:** Peat bogs are really useful to humans. By holding water in the landscape they can help to reduce flooding, and by storing $CO_2$ they may be useful in combatting climate change.

### Example — the Maasai Mara

The Maasai Mara is a national reserve in Kenya. It's a large area of grassland (savannah), which is home to huge populations of wildebeest and zebra, as well as lions and cheetahs. The Maasai Mara is named after the Maasai people who live in the area.

The Maasai people traditionally earn a living by raising livestock, such as cattle. This can bring them into conflict with conservationists — e.g. overgrazing by livestock can destroy grassland for wildlife.

Conservation trusts are working with the Maasai people to help them make money from their land through conservation and ecotourism projects rather than farming, and to farm in a sustainable way. So, the economic needs of the Maasai people are met, while still allowing the area to be conserved.

### Example — UK Peat Bogs

Lots of upland parts of the UK are home to peat bogs — areas of wet peat. These peat bogs store water and carbon dioxide, and are home to lots of different plants and animals, such as *Sphagnum* moss — these mosses actually help the peat bog form by retaining water.

Farmers use the peat bogs to graze sheep and deer. However, this can lead to conflict with conservationists because overgrazing causes loss of moss species, soil compaction (which increases water runoff down sheep paths, taking sediment with it) and general peat bog erosion.

Recent government-funded programmes, like the Environmental Stewardship Scheme, have given farmers money to use the peat bogs in a sustainable way, e.g. to carry out measures to reduce water runoff, to lower the number of livestock that use the peat bogs, and to remove livestock over winter.

### Practice Questions — Fact Recall

Q1 Outline an economic reason for conserving an ecosystem.

Q2 Give one reason why ecosystems might be conserved for social reasons.

Q3 Describe and explain two practices used when managing a woodland for sustainable timber production.

Q4 How can restrictions on fishing net mesh sizes help to make fishing sustainable?

Q5 Describe how human and environmental needs come into conflict in the Terai Arc.

Q6 Describe one way in which conflicts between human and environmental needs have been reduced in the Maasai Mara.

# 3. Human Impact on Ecosystems

*The animal and plant populations in important, but fragile, ecosystems have been affected by human activity in many places. We often need to conserve or preserve these ecosystems to try to reduce or counteract these effects.*

## The Galapagos Islands

Human activities have had a negative effect on the Galapagos Islands, a small group of islands in the Pacific Ocean about 1000 km off the coast of South America. Many species of animals and plants have evolved there that don't live anywhere else, e.g. the Galapagos giant tortoise and the Galapagos sea lion.

### Effects of human activities on the Galapagos Islands

- Explorers and sailors that visited the Galapagos Islands in the 19th century directly affected the populations of some animals by eating them.

  **Example**
  A type of giant tortoise found on Floreana Island was hunted to extinction for food.

- Non-native animals introduced to the islands eat some native species. This has caused a decrease in the populations of native species.

  **Examples**
  Non-native dogs, cats and black rats eat young giant tortoises and Galapagos land iguanas. Pigs also destroy the nests of the iguanas and eat their eggs. Goats have eaten much of the plant life on some of the islands.

- Non-native plants have also been introduced to the islands. These compete with native plant species, causing their populations to decrease.

  **Example**
  Quinine trees are taller than some native plants — they block out light to the native plants, which then struggle to survive.

- Fishing has caused a decrease in the populations of some of the sea life around the Galapagos Islands.

  **Examples**
  - The populations of sea cucumbers and hammerhead sharks have been reduced because of overfishing.
  - Galapagos green turtle numbers have also been reduced by overfishing and they're also killed accidentally when they're caught in fishing nets. They're now an endangered species.

- A recent increase in tourism (from 41 000 tourists in 1991 to over 210 000 in 2014) has led to an increase in development on the islands. The population on the islands has also increased due to the increased opportunities from tourism. This could lead to further development and so more damage to the ecosystems.

**Learning Objectives:**
- Understand how environmental resources can be managed and the effects of human activities on the environment.
- Understand the effects of human activities on animal and plant populations, and how these are controlled in environmentally sensitive ecosystems, e.g. the Galapagos Islands, Antarctica, Snowdonia National Park and the Lake District.

**Specification Reference 6.3.2**

**Tip:** Native plants and animals are those which naturally occur on the islands.

*Figure 1: The existence of the Galapagos land iguanas is under threat because of non-native animals introduced to the islands.*

*Figure 2: Satellite picture of the western Galapagos Islands.*

Module 6: Section 7 Populations and Sustainability  565

**Tip:** Balancing the interests of tourists and the needs of the environment is tricky. Although tourists can cause damage to sensitive ecosystems, they can provide money to fund conservation projects.

## Controlling the impact of humans on the Galapagos Islands

Eradication programmes have removed wild goats from some of the smaller islands and wild dogs from the largest island. Quinine trees are kept in check using chemical herbicides and by uprooting young trees. A marine protected area has been established around the islands, which sets limits and controls on fishing.

When people visit the Galapagos National Park they are expected to follow a list of rules, which includes not bringing any live plants or animals onto the islands, or moving them between the islands. People are also only allowed to visit the Galapagos National Park in the company of a licensed guide.

## Antarctica

Antarctica is the world's southernmost continent. It has a unique icy landscape with plants and animals that have adapted to its harsh conditions. For at least 200 years it has attracted visitors, e.g. research scientists and tourists. The waters around Antarctica support high levels of primary productivity during the Antarctic summer, and are home to penguins and numerous other seabirds, whales, seals and many species of fish.

**Tip:** Primary production is the conversion of the Sun's energy to chemical energy via photosynthesis. Photosynthetic algae grow well around Antarctica in the Antarctic summer, as days are long and the water is nutrient-rich.

### Effects of human activities on Antarctica

Historically, hunting of various animals around Antarctica was a large industry. During the twentieth century, whaling in the waters surrounding Antarctica was intense, leading to a huge decrease in whale numbers. As a result of this hunting, the Antarctic blue whale is critically endangered, and the populations of other species of whale have been severely depleted. Seal hunting in the nineteenth century drove the Antarctic fur seal to the brink of extinction. The seas around Antarctica are still exploited by fishing vessels.

Human activities can also lead to problems with pollution. In the past, visitors to Antarctica have dumped sewage into the sea and left behind rubbish. Shipping accidents have led to oil spills, which severely affect wildlife.

### Controlling the impact of humans on Antarctica

The continent of Antarctica is internationally protected by the Antarctic Treaty, and is now treated as a nature reserve. Commercial whaling was banned completely in the ocean surrounding Antarctica in 1994, and seal hunting has been banned for longer. Populations of the Antarctic fur seal have now recovered, but the populations of many species of whale are still considered to be dangerously low. Fishing still occurs, but within limits set with the help of scientists.

**Figure 3:** Antarctic fur seal

To reduce the impacts of pollution, all waste apart from food waste and sewage must be taken away by ship for disposal in other countries. Many research stations now treat their sewage before releasing it, to reduce its effects on the environment. Ships that use thick oil as a fuel are now banned from Antarctic waters, as heavy oil spills are likely to cause more damage and be harder to clean up than spills of lighter fuels. To prevent damage by tourists, tourist restrictions have been introduced — e.g. tourists are only allowed on land at certain locations for a few hours.

**Tip:** Antarctica is also threatened by global warming — changes in sea temperature could affect algae and fish populations, and the populations of animals that feed on them. Melting sea ice may negatively affect some of the species of penguin that breed in these areas.

# The Lake District and Snowdonia National Parks

The Lake District and Snowdonia are beautiful national parks — both are areas of hills and lakes, with the Lake District in North West England and Snowdonia in Wales. Both also attract millions of visitors per year.

## Effects of human activities on the Lake District and Snowdonia

Many of the visitors to the Lake District go walking on the region's footpaths. This leads to the erosion of the footpaths and the loss of soil from hillsides. Soil that ends up in waterways and lakes can disturb the pH of the water, causing knock-on effects for wildlife. As the paths become harder to walk on, people can start to trample and destroy the sensitive vegetation either side of the paths. It's a similar story in Snowdonia — a lot of rain falls in the Snowdonia hills, which leads to the erosion of the paths. Walkers often trample the surrounding vegetation as they try to walk around the floods.

The Lake District also has problems with water pollution in some areas. Phosphates in fertilisers used on farms, in detergents used for cleaning clothes and dishes and in water released by local sewage works have accumulated in some of the lakes. These act as fertilisers for algal growth, and can contribute to algal blooms, which deoxygenate the water and can kill fish.

## Controlling human impact on the Lake District and Snowdonia

To counteract footpath erosion in the Lake District, conservation charities and the Lake District National Park Authority attempt to carry out regular repair and maintenance work on the paths and encourage the regrowth of damaged vegetation. Walkers are also educated about the importance of sticking to the paths and not taking short cuts, as these increase erosion. In Snowdonia, volunteers have dug drains next to the paths to prevent them from flooding.

The pollution problem in the Lake District has been tackled by improving sewage treatment in the area, supplying grants to local farmers to improve farming practices and encouraging local businesses and residents to only use detergents that are phosphate-free.

*Figure 4: Windermere in the Lake District is very popular with tourists, including walkers and cyclists.*

### Practice Questions — Fact Recall

Q1 Describe two of the ways in which human activity has had a negative impact on the environment of the Galapagos Islands.

Q2 What actions have been taken to reduce the negative effects of human activity in Antarctica?

Q3 Outline one environmental effect of human activity in the Lake District.

## Section Summary

Make sure you know:

- That the size of a population varies because of the effect of abiotic factors (such as the temperature of the surroundings) and biotic factors (which include interspecific competition, intraspecific competition and predation).
- That interspecific competition is when individuals of different species compete with each other for the same resources.
- That intraspecific competition is when individuals of the same species compete with each other for the same resources.
- That the carrying capacity of an ecosystem is the maximum stable population size of a species that it can support.
- That population sizes of predators and prey are interlinked and have negative feedback effects on each other — as the prey population increases, there's more food for predators, so the predator population grows. As the predator population increases, more prey is eaten, so the prey population then begins to fall. This means there's less food available for predators, causing the predator population to decrease and allowing the prey population to increase once more.
- That limiting factors (e.g. amount of shelter) stop the population size of a species increasing.
- That conservation is the protection and management of ecosystems.
- How conservation is important for economic, social, ethical and ecological reasons.
- That preservation is the protection of ecosystems so that they're kept exactly as they are.
- That ecosystems (such as temperate woodland and oceans) can be managed in a sustainable way to make sure there are enough resources to meet the needs of people today and in the future.
- That human activities affect the environment, and that environmental resources can be managed to limit these effects.
- That ecosystems can be managed to balance the conflict between conservation and preservation and human needs, as in the Maasai Mara, the Terai Arc and peat bogs in the UK.
- That human activities have had an effect on environmentally sensitive ecosystems, such as the Galapagos Islands, Antarctica, Snowdonia National Park and the Lake District, and some of the ways that these effects can be controlled.

# Exam-style Questions

**1** Coral reefs are environmentally sensitive ecosystems that are popular with tourists. **Fig. 1.1** shows the annual number of tourists visiting a particular area of coral reef between 2009 and 2015.

What was the percentage increase in visitor numbers between 2009 and 2015?

**A** 21%   **B** 27%
**C** 33%   **D** 25%

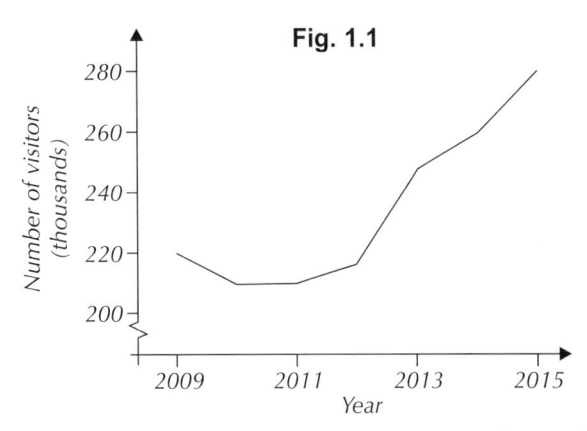

*(1 mark)*

**2** An investigation has been conducted on two species of grasshopper, species A and species B, in an area of grassy fields. **Fig. 2.1** shows changes in the population sizes of species A and B in the area under investigation.

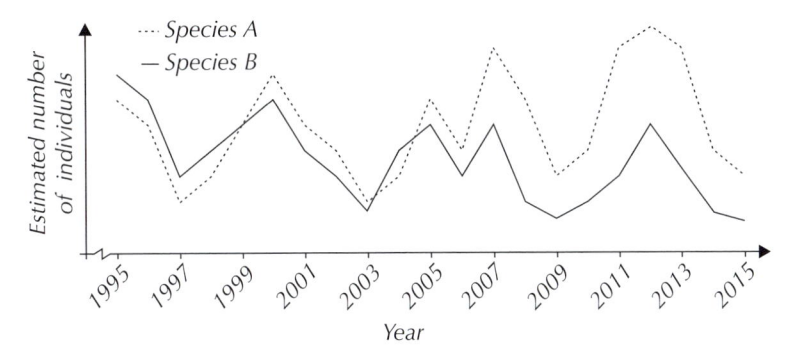

**Fig. 2.1**

(a) Describe **and** explain the trend shown by **Fig. 2.1**, with reference to the type of competition it shows.

*(3 marks)*

(b) The amount of food available prevents the population size of each grasshopper species from increasing further.
What term is used to describe the amount of food available in this case?

*(1 mark)*

(c) In a second area, species A is present but species B is not. The population of species A in this area remains roughly stable, with some smaller fluctuations.
State the name given to this stable population size.

*(1 mark)*

**3** Mangrove swamps are found in coastal areas in the tropics and sub-tropics. These swamps provide a unique habitat for many species of plant and fish. They also absorb wave energy, protecting the coastline behind them from storms.

Mangrove swamps have been cleared to make room for farming, settlements and tourist resorts. In some areas, wood is harvested from mangrove swamps at unsustainable levels. Mangrove swamps are globally threatened ecosystems.

(a) Suggest why the conservation of mangrove swamps is considered important by some people.

*(2 marks)*

A conservation charity is investigating methods for protecting a mangrove swamp in a Less Economically Developed Country in East Asia, where the swamp is threatened by overexploitation from the local population for charcoal making. Possible methods of protecting the swamp suggested by the charity include:

- Creating a nature reserve around the mangrove swamp and restricting access to the swamp to everyone except for conservation workers and scientists.
- Paying local people to only take wood from the mangrove swamp at sustainable levels.
- Promoting ecotourism in the area, based around the mangrove swamp.

(b)* Compare these options, giving the advantages and disadvantages of each.

*(9 marks)*

(c) Ecosystems can be protected through conservation or preservation.

  (i) Explain the difference between conservation and preservation.

*(1 mark)*

  (ii) State which of the methods outlined above represents a preservation method.

*(1 mark)*


**4** Many areas of woodland around the world are part of conservation projects.

(a) Outline **one** ethical reason for the conservation of woodland.

*(1 mark)*

(b) Ecosystems such as woodland can be managed in a sustainable way. Briefly describe what this means.

*(1 mark)*

(c) Complete the table below to give **two** different methods used to manage timber production in temperate woodland in a sustainable way **and** explain how each method works.

| Method | Explanation |
|--------|-------------|
|        |             |
|        |             |

*(4 marks)*

\* The quality of your response will be assessed in this question.

# Exam Help

# 1. The Exams

*You'll take three exams as part of OCR A A-level Biology. Everything you need to know about them is summarised below.*

It seems obvious, but if you know exactly what will be covered in each of the exams, how much time you'll have to do them and how they'll be structured, you can be better prepared. So let's take a look at the ins and outs of the exams you'll be facing for A-level Biology...

**Tip:** All this exam info is only relevant if you're taking the OCR A A-level in Biology. If you're taking the OCR A AS-level, you'll be sitting a completely different set of papers, which are structured in a different way. There are two AS-level papers that both test Modules 1 to 4.

## How are the exams structured?

OCR A A-Level Biology is examined in three papers. Papers 1 and 2 are each worth 37% of the total marks and Paper 3 is worth 26% of the total marks.

| | Paper | Total marks | Time | Modules assessed |
|---|---|---|---|---|
| 1 | Biological Processes | 100 | 2 hours 15 minutes | 1, 2, 3 & 5 |
| 2 | Biological Diversity | 100 | 2 hours 15 minutes | 1, 2, 4 & 6 |
| 3 | Unified Biology | 70 | 1 hour 30 minutes | 1 to 6 |

**Exam Tip**
All three A-level papers test you on practical skills.

- As you can see from the table, the modules assessed in each paper differs slightly — you'll need to make sure you plan your revision accordingly. The papers will contain some synoptic questions, which connect and test different areas of Biology from multiple modules.

**Exam Tip**
Synoptic means it tests you on different areas of Biology.

- The 'Biological Processes' and 'Biological Diversity' papers are both split into two sections — A and B. Section A of each paper contains 15 multiple choice questions and is worth 15 marks in total. Each multiple choice question will have four possible answers (A-D) but only one will be correct. Section B of these papers contains short answer questions and extended response questions. Section B is worth 85 marks in total.
- The 'Unified Biology' paper includes both short answer questions and extended response questions, but no multiple choice questions.
- Short answer questions may involve problem solving, calculations or a practical context (see next page). There's more about extended response questions below...

**Exam Tip**
Even though you're taking an A-level in Biology, you'll still need to do some maths in the exams — but it'll be set in a biological context.

## Extended response questions

In each of your three papers there will be one or more extended response questions. These questions are worth 6 or 9 marks and will require a long answer. They often want you to use a source (such as some text or a diagram, table or graph) to help you answer the question. Extended response questions are shown with an asterisk (*) next to their number.

Exam Help

You'll be awarded marks for the quality of your extended response as well as the content of your answer, so your answer needs to:
- Be legible (the same goes for all your written answers).
- Have a clear and logical structure.
- Show good reasoning — i.e. show that you have thought about and understood the question, and can justify your answer.
- Include information that's relevant to the question.

You can gain practice at extended response questions by doing the exam questions marked with an asterisk in this book.

**Tip:** To help you to structure your answer logically, you could briefly jot down the main points you want to include in your answer before you start writing.

## Solving problems in a practical context

In the exams, you'll get plenty of questions set in a 'practical context'. As well as answering questions about the methods used or the conclusions drawn, you'll need to be able to apply your scientific knowledge to solve problems set in these contexts.

**Exam Tip**
Make sure you read all the information you're given at the start of an exam question carefully, and pay attention to what's being shown in any figures that are included too.

— Example —

1   A scientist is investigating the effect on plant growth of adding additional $CO_2$ to the air in a greenhouse. The results are shown in **Fig. 1.1**.

Fig. 1.1

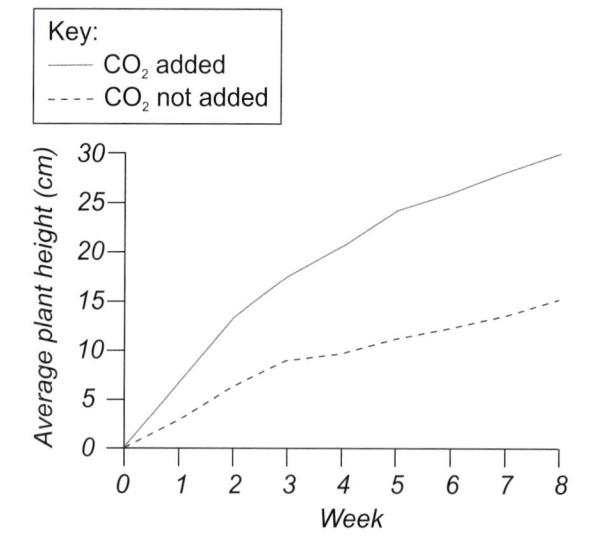

Key:
—— $CO_2$ added
---- $CO_2$ not added

[Graph: Average plant height (cm) vs Week, 0–8. "CO₂ added" curve rises to ~30 cm at week 8; "CO₂ not added" curve rises to ~15 cm at week 8.]

**Exam Tip**
Make sure you learn the language that goes with experiments too, e.g. precision, accuracy, validity — look back at Module 1 for more.

(a)   Explain the difference in the two curves shown on the graph.

*(3 marks)*

**Exam Tip**
Questions like this can look a bit scary, but you just have to apply what you already know about Biology to a real-life example. There are plenty of questions like this for you to have a go at in this book.

You should remember from Module 5 that plants use carbon dioxide to produce glucose by photosynthesis (see page 391). The more carbon dioxide plants have, the more glucose they can produce (until something other than $CO_2$ becomes a limiting factor) meaning they can also respire more. This gives them more ATP for DNA replication, cell division and protein synthesis, leading to increased plant growth.

572   Exam Help

## 2. Command Words

*Command words are just the bits of a question that tell you what to do.*

You'll find answering exam questions much easier if you understand exactly what they mean, so here's a brief summary table of the most common command words:

| Command word: | What to do: |
|---|---|
| Give / Name / State | Give a brief one or two word answer, or a short sentence. |
| Identify | Pick out information or say what something is. |
| Describe | Write about what something's like, e.g. describe the structure of fish gills. |
| Explain | Give reasons for something. |
| Suggest | Use your scientific knowledge to work out what the answer might be. |
| Compare | Give the similarities and differences between two things. |
| Outline | Write about the main points of a topic. |
| Calculate | Work out the solution to a mathematical problem. |
| Discuss | Write about a topic, considering different issues or ideas. |

Some questions will also ask you to answer 'using the information/data provided' (e.g. a graph, table or passage of text) or 'with reference to figure X' — if so, you must refer to the information, data or figure you've been given or you won't get the marks. Some questions may also ask you to answer 'using your calculation' — it's the same here, you need to use your answer to a particular calculation, otherwise you won't get the marks.

Not all of the questions will have command words, e.g. the multiple choice questions — instead they may just ask a which / what / how type of question.

**Exam Tip**
When you're reading exam questions, underline the command words. That way you'll know exactly what type of answer to give.

**Exam Tip**
If you're answering a longer 'compare' question make a mental list of the similarities and differences or pros and cons first, so you know what you want your answer to include before you start writing.

**Exam Tip**
Make sure you take a calculator and ruler into all your exams to help you with the calculation questions. A pencil and a spare pen may come in handy as well.

## 3. Time Management

*Time management is really important in your exams — it's no good writing a perfect answer to a 3 mark question if it takes you an hour.*

For each paper you get just over a minute per mark. This means if you get stuck on a short question it's sometimes worth moving onto another one and then coming back to it if you have time. However, bear in mind that you might want to spend a bit longer on the extended response questions, in which case you'll have to spend less time on the multiple choice and short answer questions.

If you've got any time left once you've finished the paper, hold off on celebrating and have a look back through the questions. You can use the time to go back to any questions you've skipped, check your answers to calculation questions and to make sure you haven't accidentally missed any questions out.

**Exam Tip**
If the question is only worth 1 mark, don't waste time writing more than you need to. Questions with more marks require longer answers.

Exam Help    573

# Answers

## Module 1

## Development of Practical Skills

### 1. Planning an Experiment

#### Page 8 — Application Questions
Q1 a) the light intensity / distance of light source from the shoot
b) E.g. temperature, shoot used
c) E.g. repeat the experiment three times at each distance and calculate a mean.
Q2 a) E.g. a gas syringe / an upturned measuring cylinder filled with water.
b) Hydrogen peroxide with no enzyme added.
*In reality, water should be added instead of the enzyme so that the overall volume of the reaction mixture is kept the same.*

#### Page 8 — Fact Recall Questions
Q1 That if you repeat the experiment (using the same equipment and method), you will get the same results.
Q2 Results that answer the original question.
Q3 The variable that's measured in an experiment.
Q4 It shows that only the independent variable (the variable being changed) is affecting the dependent variable.
Q5 It shows what a positive result should look like and that a positive result is possible for the experiment.
Q6 The dangers of the experiment. Who is at risk from any dangers. How the risk can be reduced.

### 2. Carrying Out an Experiment

#### Page 10 — Fact Recall Questions
Q1 $5.3 \text{ cm}^3$
Q2 To allow time for the water bath/solutions to heat up.
Q3 A table that shows you how many of each value there are.
Q4 A result that doesn't fit in with the rest of the results.

### 3. Processing Data

#### Page 12 — Application Questions
Q1 a) $4.2 - 3.1 = \textbf{1.1 dm}^3$
b) In numerical order, the results are:
3.1, 3.2, 3.4, 3.5, 3.5, 3.7, 3.9, 3.9, 3.9, 4.2
So the median is $(3.5 + 3.7) \div 2 = \textbf{3.6 dm}^3$
and the mode is $\textbf{3.9 dm}^3$.
Q2 Solution A: $(0.81 + 0.84 + 0.82) \div 3 = \textbf{0.82}$
Solution B: $(0.54 + 0.55) \div 2 = \textbf{0.55}$
Solution C: $(0.12 + 0.12 + 0.15) \div 3 = \textbf{0.13}$
*The third repeat for solution B is an anomalous result, so you should not include it when calculating the mean.*
Q3 Decrease in number of individuals: $292 - 105 = 187$
Difference in number of years: $2015 - 1995 = 20$
So the mean decrease per year was $187 \div 20 = \textbf{9.35}$.

#### Page 14 — Application Questions
Q1 $36 \div 65 = 0.55$
$0.55 \times 100 = \textbf{55\%}$
Q2 a) Hospital A:
percentage change $= \frac{(29 - 22)}{22} = \frac{7}{22} \times 100 = 32\%$
Hospital B:
percentage change $= \frac{(19 - 14)}{14} = \frac{5}{14} \times 100 = 36\%$
Hospital C:
percentage change $= \frac{(31 - 25)}{25} = \frac{6}{25} \times 100 = 24\%$
So the hospital with the largest percentage change is **B**.
b) 24 : 16
$24 \div 8 = 3$, $16 \div 8 = 2$
**3 : 2**

#### Page 16 — Application Questions
Q1 $4.5 \times 10^{-3}$
Q2 a) $4.53 \times 3.142 = 14.23326 = \textbf{14.2}$ (3.s.f.)
b) $0.315 \div 0.025 = 12.6 = \textbf{13}$ (2.s.f.)
Q3 There is a significant difference between the mean heights of the two groups of seedlings — the difference is not due to chance (at the 95% confidence limit).

### 4. Presenting Data

#### Page 22 — Application Questions
Q1 A histogram, because it is frequency data and the independent variable is continuous.
Q2 a) E.g. $3.8 \text{ cm}^3 \div 30 \text{ min} = \textbf{0.13 cm}^3\textbf{min}^{-1}$
b) For this answer you need to work out the equation of the graph in the form $y = mx + c$:
First, find the gradient, e.g. $2.2 \text{ cm}^3 \div 30 \text{ min} = 0.073 \text{ cm}^3 \text{min}^{-1}$ so $m = 0.073$
Then $c$ is where the line crosses the y-axis = 0.
So the equation of the line can be written as $y = 0.073x + 0$, or just $y = 0.073x$.
When $x = 50$ min, $y = 0.073 \times 50 = \textbf{3.7 cm}^3$
Q3

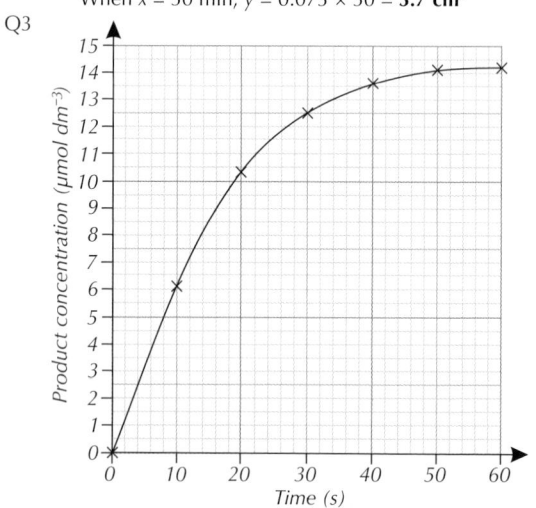

[Graph: Product concentration (μmol dm⁻³) vs Time (s), showing a curve rising from 0 and levelling off near 14 at 60s]

## 5. Drawing Conclusions and Evaluating

### Page 27 — Application Questions
Q1 a) ± 0.25 cm³
   b) (0.25 ÷ 6.0) × 100 = 4.2%
Q2 a) No — e.g. the highest rate of reaction shown on the graph is at 40 °C, but the investigation only measured the rate at 10 °C increases. The rate of reaction at in-between temperatures wasn't measured — it is possible that the enzyme could work best at a temperature between 30 °C and 40 °C or between 40 °C and 50 °C.
   b) E.g. the rate could be measured three times at each temperature and a mean rate of reaction could be calculated.
   c) No, because the results of the experiment are specific to enzyme X. It is not possible to tell if the results will be the same for any other enzyme.

### Exam-style Questions — page 29
1   D *(1 mark)*.
   Here are the answers for each option —
   A: (0.5 ÷ 50) × 100 = 1%, B: (0.05 ÷ 5) × 100 = 1%,
   C: (0.1 ÷ 10) × 100 = 1%, D: (0.25 ÷ 15) × 100 = 1.7%.
2   a) i) E.g. anomalous results (such as Repeat 1 at 10 °C) are easier to spot *(1 mark)*. A mean value can be calculated, which will reduce the effect of random error on the results/make the results more precise *(1 mark)*.
      ii) [graph: Mean time taken for cube to become colourless (s) vs Temperature (°C), showing negative linear trend from ~420 s at 10 °C to ~170 s at 40 °C]

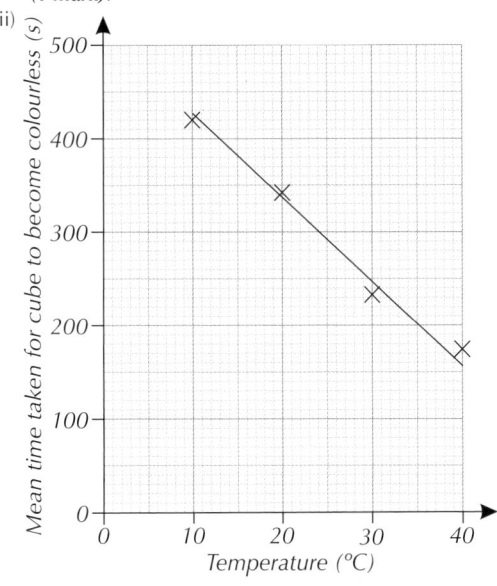

   *(3 marks — 1 mark for correctly labelled axes using appropriate scales, 1 mark for correctly plotted points, 1 mark for appropriate line of best fit.)*
   b) The graph shows negative correlation. *(1 mark)*
   Negative correlation is when one variable increases as the other decreases. Here, as the temperature increases, the mean time taken decreases.
   c) For temperatures between 10 °C and 40 °C, the time taken for the cube to turn colourless decreases as the temperature increases *(1 mark)*.
   d) E.g. by wearing gloves/lab coats/safety goggles for the duration of the experiment to protect the skin/eyes *(1 mark)*. By heating the acid in a water bath (rather than over a Bunsen burner) to prevent accidental boiling *(1 mark)*.
   e) Any two from: the method of preparing the agar / the size/surface area of the agar cubes / the concentration of hydrochloric acid / the volume of hydrochloric acid. *(1 mark for each)*
   You can read all about the method for this diffusion investigation on page 133.

# Module 2

## Section 1 — Cell Structure

### 1. Cells and Organelles

### Pages 42-43 — Application Questions
Q1 a) Mitochondria — these are the site of aerobic respiration in the cell / where ATP is produced.
   You should be able to tell that both organelles are mitochondria by the cristae (folded structures) inside them. Don't be thrown by their slightly odd shapes.
   b) Golgi apparatus — this processes and packages new lipids and proteins. It also makes lysosomes.
   c) Chloroplast — photosynthesis takes place here.
   You can clearly see the granum and lamellae in this organelle, which should tell you that it's a chloroplast.
   d) Cilia — used to move substances along the cell surface.
Q2 a) nucleolus
   b) cell wall
   c) Image B because there is a large vacuole and a cell wall present. Animal cells don't have either of these structures.

### Page 43 — Fact Recall Questions
Q1 A — cell wall, B — cytoplasm, C — mitochondrion, D — nucleus, E — chloroplast, F — vacuole, G — cell membrane, H — ribosome.
Q2 Any three from, e.g. cell wall / plasmodesmata / vacuole / chloroplasts.
Q3 The nucleus controls the cell's activities (by controlling the transcription of DNA). The nuclear pores allow substances to move between the nucleus and the cytoplasm. The nucleolus makes ribosomes.
Q4 Any one from: To digest invading cells. / To break down worn out components of the cell.
Q5 The rough endoplasmic reticulum is covered in ribosomes, whereas the smooth endoplasmic reticulum is not.
Q6 It synthesises and processes lipids.
Q7 Golgi apparatus
Q8 centriole
Q9 [diagram of cilium cross-section labelled "plasma membrane" and "microtubule pair"]

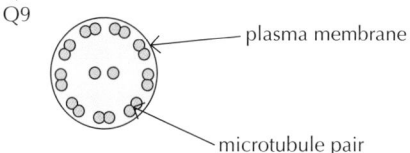

### 2. Organelles Working Together

### Page 45 — Application Questions
Q1 Normal Golgi apparatus would look like a group of flattened linear sacs, lined up next to each other, rather than appearing small, round and disconnected.
   Although normally you might expect to see some round vesicles adjacent to the Golgi apparatus.

Q2  E.g. proteins often undergo further processing (e.g. sugar chains are trimmed or more are added) in the Golgi apparatus. If the apparatus is deformed in some way, these modifications might not take place, and so the proteins produced may not function correctly or at all.

Q3  E.g. the cytoskeleton is involved in the transport of vesicles around the cell. Vesicles are used to transport proteins in protein synthesis. If the cytoskeleton is disrupted, proteins may not be transported between the RER and the Golgi apparatus, preventing them from being modified, or between the Golgi and the cell surface, preventing them from being secreted from the cell.

## Page 45 — Fact Recall Questions

Q1  The ribosomes on RER make proteins that are excreted or attached to the cell membrane. Proteins produced at the RER are folded and processed there.

Q2  The cytoskeleton supports the cell's organelles, keeping them in position. It also helps to strengthen the cell and maintain its shape. It transports organelles and materials within the cell. It can also cause the cell to move.

## 3. Prokaryotic Cells
## Page 46 — Fact Recall Questions

Q1  Any three from, e.g: prokaryotes are smaller than eukaryotes. / Prokaryotic DNA is circular, eukaryotic DNA is linear. / Prokaryotes don't have a nucleus, eukaryotes do. / In eukaryotes, if a cell wall is present, it is made of cellulose or chitin. The cell wall in prokaryotes is made of a polysaccharide that isn't cellulose or chitin. / Prokaryotes have fewer organelles than eukaryotes and no membrane-bound organelles, e.g. mitochondria. / Prokaryote flagella are made of the protein flagellin arranged in a helix, whereas in eukaryotes flagella are made of microtubules arranged in a '9 + 2' formation. / Prokaryotes have smaller ribosomes than eukaryotes.

Q2  Any one from, e.g: they both contain ribosomes/DNA/cytoplasm/a plasma (cell surface) membrane. / They may both contain flagella/a cell wall.

## 4. How Microscopes Work
## Page 48 — Application Questions

Q1  a) image size ÷ magnification = object size
8 mm ÷ 3150 = **0.0025 mm**
b) image size ÷ magnification = object size
18 mm ÷ 3150 = **0.0057 mm**
*Always make sure you show your working in questions like these — you could pick up some marks for using the correct calculation, even if you end up with the wrong final answer.*

Q2  object size × magnification = image size
0.00002 mm × 40 = **0.0008 mm**

Q3  First you need to convert 0.023 µm to millimetres by dividing by 1000.
0.023 µm ÷ 1000 = 0.000023 mm
magnification = image size ÷ object size
0.035 mm ÷ 0.000023 mm = **× 1522**

Q4  image size ÷ magnification = object size
13 mm ÷ 7000 = 0.0019 mm
Then times by 1000 to convert to µm
0.0019 mm × 1000 = **1.9 µm**

Q5  a) image size ÷ object size = magnification
16 mm ÷ 2 mm = **× 8**
b) object size × magnification = image size
3 mm × 50 = **150 mm**

Q6  First you need to convert 10 µm to millimetres by dividing by 1000.
10 µm ÷ 1000 = 0.01 mm
image size ÷ object size = magnification
10 mm ÷ 0.01 mm = **× 1000**

## Page 51 — Application Questions

Q1  *E. coli* bacterium — light microscope, TEM, SEM
nuclear pore — TEM, SEM
human egg cell — light microscope, TEM, SEM
DNA helix — TEM, SEM
mitochondrion — light microscope, TEM, SEM
influenza virus — TEM, SEM
*Answering this question is a lot easier if you know the maximum resolution for each type of microscope — it could come up in the exam, so make sure you learn it.*

Q2  E.g. Team One might use an SEM. HIV is 0.12 µm in diameter, so it needs to be viewed under an electron microscope as these have a higher maximum resolution than light microscopes. Also, the team is looking at surface proteins and SEM images can show the surface of a specimen and can be 3D. The second team might use a TEM as they want to view the virus's internal structures. A TEM would allow them to do this because it uses thin slices of the specimen material and has a higher maximum resolution than either light microscopes or SEMs.

Q3  The team could use a laser scanning confocal microscope. This type of microscope uses a laser beam which would cause the fluorescent dyes to give off fluorescent light and show where the different types of protein are located. This type of microscopy is also suitable for thick samples so can generate images at different depths within the tissue sample.

## Page 51 — Fact Recall Questions

Q1  magnification = image size ÷ object size

Q2  Magnification is how much bigger the image is than the specimen, whereas resolution is how detailed the image is and how well a microscope distinguishes between two points that are close together.

Q3  Fluorescent dyes

Q4  TEMs use electromagnets to focus a beam of electrons, which is then transmitted through the specimen.
Denser parts of the specimen absorb more electrons, which makes them look darker on the image you end up with.

Q5  SEMs scan a beam of electrons across the specimen. This knocks off electrons from the specimen, which are gathered in a cathode ray tube to form an image.

Q6  SEM

Q7  a) 0.2 µm
b) 0.0002 µm
c) 0.002 µm

Q8  TEM

Q9  TEM
*The maximum resolution of a light microscope is 0.2 µm and the maximum resolution of a SEM is 0.002 µm, so you wouldn't be able to see something that was 0.001 µm with either of these.*

## 5. Using Microscopes
### Page 55 — Application Question
Q1 a) Total length of 5 divisions on stage micrometer
= 2 µm × 5 = 10 µm
Length of each graticule division
= 10 µm ÷ 8 = **1.25 µm**

*For this question you first need to work out the total length of the 5 stage micrometer divisions. When you've got this you just need to divide this length by the number of eyepiece graticule divisions it's equal to, to give you the length represented by one eyepiece graticule division.*

b) 12 × 1.25 = **15 µm**

*The cell is the same width as 12 divisions on the eyepiece graticule scale, so you need to multiply the width of one division by 12.*

### Page 56 — Fact Recall Questions
Q1  To prevent the object being viewed from appearing white if it is completely transparent.
Q2  Particular stains can be used to make particular parts of cells show up.
Q3  Any two from: e.g. methylene blue, Giemsa stain, haematoxylin, eosin.
Q4  E.g. dry mounting and wet mounting.
Q5  cover slip
Q6  The eyepiece.
Q7  It is a microscope slide with an accurate scale that is used to work out the value of the divisions on the eyepiece graticule at a particular magnification.

### Exam-style Questions — pages 57-58
1  a) i)  Production of ATP *(1 mark)*.
      ii) Abnormal mitochondria might not produce as much ATP as normal mitochondria *(1 mark)*. This means the heart tissue may not have sufficient energy to work properly/for muscle contraction *(1 mark)*.
   b) i)  Any two from: abnormal mice have more mitochondria *(1 mark)* / smaller mitochondria *(1 mark)* / mitochondria with a smaller/lighter/less dense matrix *(1 mark)* / mitochondria with fewer cristae *(1 mark)*.
      ii) object size is 1.5 µm = 1.5 µm ÷ 1000 = 0.0015 mm
          magnification = image size ÷ object size
          = ~23 mm ÷ 0.0015 mm = **× 15333** (allow values between × 14667 to × 15333)
          *(2 marks for correct answer, 1 mark if only working is correct.)*
2  a) i)  No *(1 mark)*. The microscope has a resolution of 0.2 µm/200 nm so it can't be used to distinguish between objects that are smaller than 0.2 µm/200 nm — such as the ribosomes *(1 mark)*.

*If you convert the diameter of the ribosomes and the resolution of the microscope into the same units, (e.g. both nm or both µm) it's easier to see that the ribosomes are too small for the microscope to pick up.*

      ii) The ribosomes in the bacterial cells would be smaller than those in the stomach cells *(1 mark)*. This is because bacteria are prokaryotic cells which have smaller ribosomes than the eukaryotic stomach cells *(1 mark)*.
      iii) Any two from, e.g. the stomach cell would not have chloroplasts / a vacuole / a cell wall / plasmodesmata *(2 marks)*.
      iv) Using more than one stain would allow the scientist to see specific parts of the cell *(1 mark)*.
   b) object size = image size ÷ magnification
      = 4 ÷ 100 = **0.04 mm**
      *(2 marks for correct answer, 1 mark if only working is correct)*
   c) **5-6 marks:**
      The answer describes the full process of production and secretion of proteins (the digestive enzymes) that are to be released from the cell. There is a full explanation of the role of the ribosome(s), rough endoplasmic reticulum (RER), vesicle(s), Golgi apparatus and plasma membrane. The answer has a clear and logical structure. The information given is relevant and detailed.
      **3-4 marks:**
      The answer describes most of the process of production and secretion of proteins (the digestive enzymes) that are to be released from the cell. There is some explanation of the roles of the different organelles in the process. The answer has some structure. Most of the information given is relevant and there is some detail involved.
      **1-2 marks:**
      One or two steps involved in the process of production and secretion of proteins (the digestive enzymes) are referenced.
      The answer has no clear structure. The information given is basic and lacking in detail. It may not all be relevant.
      **0 marks:**
      No relevant information is given.
      **Here are some points your answer may include:**
      New proteins are made at the ribosomes on the rough endoplasmic reticulum. They're then folded and processed (e.g. sugar chains added) in the rough endoplasmic reticulum before being transported to the Golgi apparatus in vesicles. Here the proteins may undergo further processing (e.g. sugar chains trimmed). The proteins then enter vesicles to be transported to the plasma membrane where the proteins are secreted.
3  a) Bacteria are prokaryotic cells, so the penicillin inhibits the synthesis of their cell walls, eventually leading to cell lysis and death *(1 mark)*. Human cells are eukaryotic animal cells, and so have no cell wall, so penicillin antibiotics leave these cells unaffected *(1 mark)*.
   b) i) E.g. because electron microscopes have a higher resolution *(1 mark)* so they can be used to look at smaller objects (like bacteria) in more detail *(1 mark)*.
      ii) A transmission electron microscope/TEM *(1 mark)*. Transmission electron micrographs show a 2D cross section through a sample as seen in Fig 3.1 *(1 mark)*.
   c) Any two from, e.g. a prokaryotic cell is smaller than a eukaryotic cell *(1 mark)*. / There is no nucleus present in a prokaryotic cell *(1 mark)*. / There are fewer organelles present in a prokaryotic cell *(1 mark)*. / There are no mitochondria present in a prokaryotic cell *(1 mark)*. / Ribosomes are smaller in a prokaryotic cell than in a eukaryotic cell *(1 mark)*. / The DNA in a prokaryotic cell is circular, not linear *(1 mark)* / A prokaryotic cell may contain plasmids *(1 mark)*.

# Section 2 — Biological Molecules

## 1. Water
### Page 61 — Fact Recall Questions
Q1  Any three from: e.g. it is a reactant in lots of chemical reactions. / It transports substances. / It helps with temperature control. / It is a coolant. / It is a habitat. / It is a solvent.
Q2  Because it has a slight negative charge on one side and a slight positive charge on the other.
Q3  

[Diagram: water molecule showing O with δ−, two H atoms with δ+]

Q4  A weak bond between a slightly positively charged hydrogen atom in one molecule and a slightly negatively charged atom in another molecule.
Q5  E.g.

[Diagram: hydrogen bonds between water molecules]

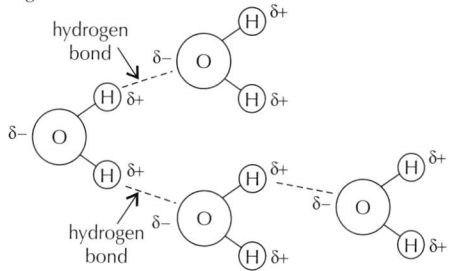

When drawing a hydrogen bond between two water molecules, make sure you draw it between one hydrogen atom and one oxygen atom.

Q6  Because when water is heated, a lot of the heat energy is absorbed by the hydrogen bonds between water molecules. So it takes a lot of energy to increase the temperature of the water.
Q7  Because it has a high latent heat of evaporation, which means it uses up a lot of (heat) energy when it evaporates from a surface. This cools the surface and helps to lower the temperature.
Q8  It makes water very cohesive and a good solvent.
Q9  a) B, e.g. because the water molecules are being held further apart in diagram B / the water molecules have formed a lattice shape.
    b) In cold temperatures ice forms an insulating layer on top of water. This means the organisms that live in the water below do not freeze and can still move around.
Q10 The slightly negatively charged ends of the water molecules will be attracted to the positive ion, meaning the positive ion will get surrounded by water molecules.

## 2. Macromolecules and Polymers
### Page 62 — Fact Recall Questions
Q1  A polymer is a large, complex molecule, composed of many monomers joined together.
Q2  A monomer is a small, basic molecular unit that makes up a polymer.
Q3  Any two from, e.g. monosaccharides / amino acids / nucleotides.
Q4  A chemical bond is formed between the monomers and a molecule of water is released.
Q5  A hydrolysis reaction.

## 3. Carbohydrates
### Page 65 — Application Question
Q1  a)

[Diagram: disaccharide structure]

This diagram looks a bit different from other disaccharide diagrams. It's because the OH group needed to form the glycosidic bond is at the top of the galactose molecule rather than the bottom.

b)

[Diagram: disaccharide with CH$_2$OH groups]

### Page 65 — Fact Recall Questions
Q1  Carbon, hydrogen and oxygen / C, H and O.
Q2  A hexose monosaccharide has six carbon atoms and a pentose monosaccharide has five carbon atoms.
Q3  a)

[Diagram: alpha glucose structure]

Be careful when drawing alpha glucose or beta glucose — it's only the groups on the right-hand side of the molecule that are different between the two types of glucose.

b)

[Diagram: beta glucose structure]

Q4 glycosidic
*There are lots of words similar to 'glycosidic' in biology so make sure you spell it right — you might not get the mark in the exam if you don't.*

Q5 α-glucose and fructose

Q6 Glycogen is made from long, branched chains of α-glucose. It has lots of side branches which means that stored glucose can be released quickly. It's a very compact molecule which makes it good for storage.

Q7 one cellulose molecule

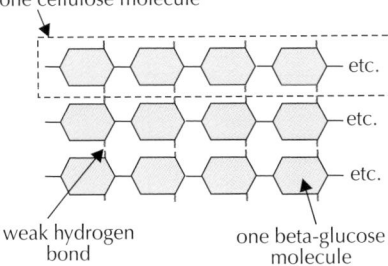

[Diagram showing chains of beta-glucose molecules with weak hydrogen bonds between them, labelled "one beta-glucose molecule"]

## 4. Lipids
### Page 68 — Fact Recall Questions
Q1 Carbon, hydrogen and oxygen / C, H and O.
Q2 A molecule of glycerol and three fatty acids.
Q3 ester bond
Q4 A saturated fatty acid doesn't have any double bonds between its carbon atoms, an unsaturated fatty acid does.
Q5 Because they contain lots of chemical energy and they're insoluble.
Q6 Phospholipid heads are hydrophilic and their tails are hydrophobic, so they form a double layer (the bilayer of cell membranes) with their heads facing out towards the water on either side. The centre of the bilayer is hydrophobic, so water-soluble substances can't easily pass through it.
Q7 They help to regulate the fluidity of the membrane by interacting with the phospholipid bilayer.

## 5. Proteins
### Page 70 — Application Questions
Q1 a) E.g. [structural diagram of dipeptide]
b) E.g. [structural diagram of dipeptide]
c) E.g. [structural diagram of tripeptide]

Q2 [structural diagrams of two amino acids]

### Page 73 — Fact Recall Questions
Q1 amino acids
Q2 A chain of more than two amino acids joined together.
Q3 [structural diagram of generic amino acid: $H_2N-C(R)(H)-COOH$]

You could have drawn your amino group like this; [alternative $NH_2$ structure] or your carboxyl group like this; $-C(=O)OH$
Both ways are fine and would get you marks in the exam.

Q4 Carbon, oxygen, hydrogen, nitrogen and sulfur.
Q5 peptide
Q6 a) condensation
b) hydrolysis
Q7 Hydrogen bonds form between the –NH and –CO groups of the amino acids in the chain. This makes it automatically coil into an alpha helix or beta pleated sheet.
*Don't get the secondary structure of a protein confused with the tertiary structure or quaternary structure. In the tertiary structure, hydrogen bonds form between some of the R groups on the polypeptide chain. In the quaternary structure, hydrogen bonds may form between different polypeptide chains.*

Q8 a) tertiary
b) A — hydrogen bond, B — ionic bond, C — disulfide bond
c) When two molecules of the amino acid cysteine come close together, the sulfur atom in one cysteine bonds to the sulfur in the other cysteine.

Q9 It is the way two or more polypeptide chains of a protein are assembled together.
Q10 The globular structure of haemoglobin means that the hydrophilic side chains are on the outside of the molecule and the hydrophobic side chains face inwards. This makes haemoglobin soluble in water, which makes it good for transporting oxygen in the blood.
Q11 A protein with a non-protein group attached.
Q12 E.g. they are soluble and reactive
Q13 a) It forms connective tissue in animals.
b) E.g. it's very strong so it can form rigid structures (such as bone).

## 6. Inorganic ions
### Page 75 — Application Question
Q1 C — Cl$^-$

### Page 75 — Fact Recall Questions
Q1 a) $H^+$
b) $NH_4^+$
c) $PO_4^{3-}$
d) $OH^-$
Q2 E.g. calcium ($Ca^+$) ion / phosphate ($PO_4^{3-}$) ion
Q3 E.g. sodium ($Na^+$) and potassium ($K^+$) ions
Q4 E.g. ammonium ($NH_4^+$) and nitrate ($NO_3^-$) ions
Q5 E.g. hydrogencarbonate ($HCO^{3-}$) ion
Q6 The pH would increase / the solution would become more alkaline.

Answers 579

## 7. Biochemical Tests for Molecules

### Page 76 — Application Questions
Q1 Orange juice and goat's milk.
Q2 As a (negative) control.

### Page 78 — Application Question
Q1 Solution A — no reducing sugars present, but non-reducing sugars might be present.
Solution B — reducing sugars are present.
*Here, think carefully about what sugars have been tested for and what the different colours of the results indicate. Remember that a negative result for a reducing sugar test doesn't rule out non-reducing sugars.*

### Page 81 — Application Question
Q1  8 mg cm$^{-3}$

### Page 81 — Fact Recall Questions
Q1 a) sodium hydroxide solution
   b) copper(II) sulfate solution
   c) It would be purple.
Q2 iodine test
Q3 Shake the sample with ethanol for about a minute then pour the solution into water. Any lipid will show up as a milky emulsion.
Q4 Add Benedict's reagent to a test sample and heat it in a water bath that's been brought to the boil. Look at the colour of the sample for the result. A positive result would be coloured green, yellow, orange or brick red and a negative result would be blue.
Q5 a) A device that measures the strength of a coloured solution by seeing how much light passes through it.
   b) Carry out the Benedict's test on the unknown solution. Remove the precipitate from the solution and use a colorimeter with a red filter to measure the absorbance of the Benedict's solution remaining in the tube. Finally using the calibration curve, read off an estimate for the glucose concentration of the sample.
*Make sure you're clear about what goes into the colorimeter — it's what's left in the tube after the precipitate has been removed, not the precipitate itself.*
Q6 A biosensor is a device that uses a biological molecule to detect a chemical. When it comes into contact with the chemical it detects, the biological molecule produces a signal which is then converted to an electrical signal by a transducer. The electrical signal is then processed.

## 8. Separating Molecules

### Page 84 — Application Question
Q1 a) $R_f$ value = $\dfrac{\text{distance moved by the solute}}{\text{distance moved by the solvent}}$

Solute A: $R_f$ value = 2.8 ÷ 7.2 = **0.39**
Solute B: $R_f$ value = 3.3 ÷ 7.2 = **0.46**
Solute C: $R_f$ value = 5.3 ÷ 7.2 = **0.74**

b) Solute A is alanine, solute B is tyrosine and solute C is leucine.

### Page 84 — Fact Recall Questions
Q1 Chromatography is used to separate out the components of a mixture.
Q2 A liquid solvent.
Q3 A thin layer of solid (e.g. silica gel) on a glass or plastic plate.
Q4 $R_f$ value = $\dfrac{\text{distance moved by the solute}}{\text{distance moved by the solvent}}$

### Exam-style Questions — pages 86-87

1. a)

| | Observation | Starch present |
|---|---|---|
| Plant A | dark, blue-black colour | Yes |
| Plant B | browny-orange colour | No |

   *(1 mark for each correct answer)*
   Make sure you emphasise that a positive result would be a dark colour — you won't get a mark in the exam if you just say it turns blue.
   b) i) amylopectin *(1 mark)*
      ii) Amylose is a long, unbranched chain of α-glucose *(1 mark)*. It has a coiled structure/cylindrical shape *(1 mark)*. These features make it compact meaning it's good for storage *(1 mark)*.
   c) i) Any three from: e.g. starch is used to store energy whereas cellulose is used to strengthen cell walls. / Starch is made from α-glucose whereas cellulose is made from β-glucose. / Starch has a compact shape whereas cellulose is a long, straight molecule. / The bonds between the glucose molecules in starch (amylose) are angled whereas the bonds between glucose molecules in cellulose are straight *(3 marks for 3 correct answers)*.
      ii) *(1 mark)*
      You have to flip the glucose molecule on the right-hand side, so that the –OH groups of both glucose molecules are close together — this is where the glycosidic bond forms and a molecule of water is lost.
      iii) During hydrolysis reactions *(1 mark)* molecules of water *(1 mark)* break apart the glycosidic bonds *(1 mark)*.

2. a) It is the sequence of amino acids in the polypeptide chain *(1 mark)* joined together with peptide bonds *(1 mark)*.
   b) ionic *(1 mark)*, disulfide *(1 mark)*, hydrogen *(1 mark)*, positively *(1 mark)*, negatively *(1 mark)*
   c) Add a few drops of sodium hydroxide solution to the test sample *(1 mark)*. Then add some copper(II) sulfate solution *(1 mark)*. If protein is present, the solution will turn purple *(1 mark)*. If there's no protein present, the solution will stay blue *(1 mark)*.

3. a) Different pigments will be spend different amounts of time in the mobile phase *(1 mark)*. The pigments that spend longer in the mobile phase will travel further, so the pigments separate out *(1 mark)*.
   b) $R_f$ value = 3.7 cm ÷ 9.0 cm = **0.41** *(1 mark)*
   c) Any two from: e.g. a different solvent was used / a different stationary phase was used / the experiment was carried out at a different temperature *(1 mark for each correct answer. Maximum of 2 marks available.)*.

# Section 3 — Nucleotides and Nucleic Acids

## 1. Nucleotides
### Page 90 — Fact Recall Questions
Q1 nucleotides
Q2 A = phosphate group, B = deoxyribose (sugar), C = (nitrogenous) base
Q3 Part B/the sugar would be ribose rather than deoxyribose.
Q4 adenine, guanine
Q5 cytosine, uracil
*Remember, uracil replaces thymine as a pyrimidine base in RNA.*
Q6 A purine base contains two carbon-nitrogen rings joined together, where as a pyrimidine base only has one carbon-nitrogen ring. (So a pyrimidine base is smaller than a purine base.)
Q7 One or more phosphate groups/inorganic phosphates ($P_i$).
Q8 A molecule of ADP is made from adenine, a ribose sugar and two phosphate groups.
*If you're asked to describe the structure of ADP in the exam, make sure you're specific and put that it's ribose. If you just put 'sugar' you won't get the mark.*

## 2. Polynucleotides and DNA
### Page 93 — Application Questions
Q1 a) TGACAGCATCAGCTACGAT
   b) ACGTGGTACACCATTTAGC
Q2 A white precipitate of DNA might not form, as the temperature in the water bath may not be high enough to stop the enzymes in the cells from working. This means the enzymes may break the DNA down and less DNA will be available to form a precipitate.
Q3 a) 22
   b) 12
   c) 12
*If there are 34 base pairs in total and 22 of them contain adenine, then the other 12 must contain both cytosine and guanine — it's all to do with complementary base pairing.*

### Page 93 — Fact Recall Questions
Q1 a) phosphodiester bonds
   b) The phosphate group of one nucleotide and the pentose sugar of another.
Q2 Two DNA polynucleotide strands join together by hydrogen bonding between complementary base pairs — A with T and G with C. The antiparallel strands then twist round each other to form the DNA double-helix.
Q3 E.g. break up the cells in your sample and mix with a solution of detergent, salt and distilled water. Incubate the mixture in a water bath at 60 °C for 15 minutes and then put it in an ice bath to cool down. When it's cooled, filter the mixture and transfer a sample of the mixture to a boiling tube. Add protease (and RNase) enzymes to the filtered mixture. Slowly dribble some cold ethanol down the side of the tube, so that it forms a layer on top of the DNA-detergent mixture. Leave the tube for a few minutes, and then remove any white precipitate of DNA that forms using a glass rod.

## 3. DNA Replication
### Page 95 — Application Question
Q1 a) In the bacteria that were grown in heavy nitrogen broth then light nitrogen broth, each DNA molecule contained 50% heavy nitrogen and 50% light nitrogen. This suggests that half of the new strands are from the original heavy nitrogen DNA, and therefore that the DNA has replicated semi-conservatively.
   b) It means that the original DNA strand can act as a template for the new strand — free-floating DNA nucleotides can join up with exposed bases on the original strand by complementary base pairing.
   c) E.g they could have controlled all the variables, e.g. the other nutrients in the broth. / They could have used a negative control, e.g. bacteria grown in broth without any nitrogen.
*If you get a question like this in the exam, try to give specific suggestions about how the results you're being asked about could be made valid — don't just talk about ways of improving validity in general.*

### Page 95 — Fact Recall Questions
Q1 hydrogen bonds
Q2 It joins nucleotides on the new DNA strand together.
Q3 To make sure genetic information is conserved (stays the same) each time the DNA in a cell is replicated.
Q4 A mutation is any change to the DNA base sequence.

## 4. Genes and Protein Synthesis
### Page 98 — Application Questions
Q1 a) 4
   b) 6
   c) 9
*To work out how many amino acids are coded for by a sequence you need to count the number of complete triplets that are in the sequence. Remember that the genetic code is non-overlapping.*
Q2 a) His-Tyr-Tyr-Arg-Gly-Cys-His-Arg-Gly
   b) Arg-Tyr-Asp-Asp-Cys-His-Gly-Tyr-His
*For questions like this, it's a good idea to split up the mRNA base sequence into groups of three letters (CAU/UAC/UAC, etc.). Then you'll be able to see what's going on more easily.*
Q3 E.g. GACUACUGCAGAAGAGGCUGCGGCUACCAU GGCGAC
*There are lots of possible combinations you could have given here, because each of the amino acids in the table is coded for by more than one codon.*

### Page 98 — Fact Recall Questions
Q1 It's the sequence of bases that codes for amino acids.
Q2 a) mRNA/messenger RNA
   b) tRNA/transfer RNA
*If you get a question like this in the exam you need to be specific. Always write down the type of RNA you mean (e.g. mRNA) rather than just 'RNA'.*
Q3 rRNA helps to catalyse the formation of peptide bonds between amino acids.

Q4 a) A sequence of three mRNA bases in a gene.
   b) Each mRNA codon codes for an amino acid or tells the cell when to start or stop production of a protein.
   c) triplet
Q5 a) Base triplets don't share their bases.
   b) The same specific base triplets code for the same amino acids in all living things.

## 5. Transcription and Translation
### Page 100 — Application Question
Q1 It will inhibit protein synthesis. By inhibiting RNA polymerase, α–amanitin will prevent the transcription of mRNA from DNA, preventing protein synthesis from taking place.

### Page 101 — Application Questions
Q1 E.g. it may affect the function of the ribosomes, preventing them from translating mRNA into amino acids. This could prevent/impair protein synthesis.
   *You don't need to have learnt about Diamond-Blackfan anaemia to answer this question — so long as you know the process of translation, you can work out the answer.*
Q2 It could be shorter and so could be a different protein. Translation of the mRNA sequence only continues until a stop codon is reached. Any codons after the stop codon would not be translated into amino acids.

### Pages 101-102 — Fact Recall Questions
Q1 An mRNA copy of a gene.
Q2 An enzyme. RNA polymerase attaches to the DNA double-helix, and it lines up free RNA nucleotides alongside the template strand. It then moves along the DNA strand, assembling a complementary mRNA sequence from free RNA nucleotides.
Q3 The hydrogen bonds between the strands re-form and the strands coil back into a double-helix.
Q4 a) A tRNA molecule with an anticodon that's complementary to the start codon on the mRNA attaches itself to the mRNA by complementary base pairing. A second tRNA molecule attaches itself to the next codon on the mRNA in the same way, and so on.
   b) translation
   *Don't get transcription and translation mixed up in the exam — it's easy to do and it means you'd miss out on a mark.*
   c) A stop codon on the mRNA molecule.

### Exam-style Questions — pages 103-104
1 D *(1 mark)*
2 A *(1 mark)*
3 a) AGCGGUUGUUGUGAG *(1 mark)*
     5 amino acids *(1 mark)*
   b) i) ribosome *(1 mark)*
      ii) **5-6 marks:**
          The answer describes the full process of translation with full and correct references to the roles that tRNA and rRNA play in the process.
          The answer has a clear and logical structure.
          The information given is relevant and detailed.
          **3-4 marks:**
          The answer describes most of the process of translation with some references to tRNA and rRNA. The answer has some structure. Most of the information given is relevant and there is some detail involved.
          **1-2 marks:**
          One or two steps involved in the process of translation are given, but with lack of reference to both tRNA and rRNA.
          The answer has no clear structure. The information given is basic and lacking in detail. It may not all be relevant.
          **0 marks:**
          No relevant information is given.
          **Here are some points your answer may include:**
          tRNA molecules carry amino acids to the ribosome. A tRNA molecule with an anticodon that's complementary to the start codon on the mRNA attaches itself to the mRNA by complementary base pairing. A second tRNA molecule attaches itself to the next codon on the mRNA in the same way and rRNA in the ribosome catalyses the formation of a peptide bond between the two amino acids. The first tRNA molecule moves away, leaving its amino acid behind. A third tRNA molecule binds to the next codon on the mRNA, its amino acid binds to the first two and the second tRNA molecule moves away. This process continues until there's a stop codon.
4 a) Deoxyribose sugar *(1 mark)*, a phosphate group *(1 mark)* and a nitrogenous base *(1 mark)*.
   b) i) The DNA will lose its double-helix structure/the two DNA strands will unravel *(1 mark)*. This is because the double helix/two DNA strands are held together by hydrogen bonding between the base pairs *(1 mark)*.
      ii) adenine *(1 mark)*, guanine *(1 mark)*
   *If you get a question in the exam that says, 'Name two...' don't hedge your bets and write down three or four possible answers — any wrong answers will cancel out the correct answers and you won't pick up any marks at all.*
   c) i) unzips *(1 mark)*, template *(1 mark)*, complementary *(1 mark)*, adenine *(1 mark)*, DNA polymerase *(1 mark)*
      ii) semi-conservative replication *(1 mark)*
5 a) The sugar in mRNA is ribose not deoxyribose *(1 mark)*. Uracil replaces thymine as a base in mRNA *(1 mark)*. mRNA is a single polynucleotide strand — a DNA molecule is made up of two polynucleotide strands *(1 mark)*.
   b) mRNA carries a complementary copy of a gene/section of DNA *(1 mark)* out of the nucleus to the ribosomes (in the cytoplasm) *(1 mark)*.

c) i) A sequence of DNA nucleotides that codes for a protein/polypeptide *(1 mark)*.
ii) E.g if there is a mutation in the sequence of DNA nucleotides, it could affect the amino acid sequence *(1 mark)*. This can cause an abnormal protein to be produced *(1 mark)*. The abnormal protein might function better than the normal protein — or it might not work at all *(1 mark)*.
d) The genetic code is described as degenerate because some amino acids are coded for by more than one base triplet *(1 mark)*.

# Section 4 — Enzymes
## 1. Action of Enzymes
### Page 108 — Application Question
Q1 No glucose was produced because, unlike with maltase, the shape of the active site of sucrase is not complementary to the shape of maltose. This means that maltose can't bind to sucrase to form an enzyme-substrate complex, so no reaction is catalysed.

### Page 108 — Fact Recall Questions
Q1 A substance that speeds up a chemical reaction without being used up in the reaction itself.
Q2 a) intracellular
   b) extracellular
   *Remember, intracellular enzymes are found inside cells, so extracellular enzymes are found outside cells.*
Q3 a) Because it breaks down the harmful hydrogen peroxide ($H_2O_2$) produced by some cellular reactions into oxygen ($O_2$) and water ($H_2O$), which are harmless.
   b) Intracellular
Q4 The hydrolysis of starch to maltose.
Q5 a) It catalyses the hydrolysis of peptide bonds — turning big polypeptides into smaller ones.
   b) Extracellular
Q6 The enzyme's tertiary structure.
Q7 An enzyme-substrate complex.
Q8 a) B
   b) The activation energy needed for the reaction with the presence of an enzyme.
Q9 Activation energy is needed to start a chemical reaction. The activation energy is often provided as heat. With the presence of an enzyme, the activation energy required to start a reaction is lowered. Therefore not as much heat is needed, so the reaction can take place at lower temperatures than it could do without an enzyme.
Q10 The substrate has a complementary shape to the active site. This means they fit together the same way that a key fits into a lock. They form an enzyme-substrate complex and catalyse the reaction.
Q11 In the 'lock and key' model the active site has a fixed shape that is complementary to the substrate, but in the 'induced fit' model the substrate has to make the active site change shape slightly to allow the substrate to bind tightly.

## 2. Factors Affecting Enzyme Activity
### Page 111 — Application Question
Q1 a) i) C — the enzyme is still active at 80 °C. This means the bacteria can live at very high temperatures and therefore is hyperthermophilic.
      ii) A — the enzyme is active at temperatures between 0 and 17 °C. This means the bacteria can live at very cold temperatures, so is psychrotrophic.
   b) A — There would be no enzyme activity at all as the enzyme would be denatured at temperatures over 17 °C.
      B — There would be some enzyme activity but the rate of reaction would gradually decrease until temperatures of around 70 °C were reached. At this point the enzyme would be denatured and there would be no further enzyme activity at higher temperatures.
      C — There would be an increasing amount of enzyme activity. The rate of reaction would gradually increase as the temperature increased.

### Page 111 — Fact Recall Questions
Q1 At higher temperatures there is more kinetic energy, so molecules move faster. This makes the substrate molecules more likely to collide with the enzymes' active sites. The energy of these collisions also increases, which means each collision is more likely to result in a reaction.
Q2 A very high temperature makes the enzyme's molecules vibrate more. This vibration breaks some of the bonds/hydrogen bonds and ionic bonds that hold the enzyme in shape. The active site changes shape and the enzyme and substrate no longer fit together. The enzyme is denatured.
Q3 That the rate of reaction quadruples when the temperature is raised by 10 °C.
Q4 e.g. pH
Q5 At first, increasing the enzyme concentration increases the rate of the reaction. This is because the more enzyme molecules there are in a solution, the more likely a substrate molecule is to collide with an active site and form an enzyme-substrate complex. The rate of reaction continues to increase until the substrate concentration becomes a limiting factor. At this point the rate of the reaction levels off.
Q6 The rate of reaction stays constant. All active sites are occupied so increasing the substrate concentration has no effect.
*Don't ever say that the enzymes are used up — say that all the active sites are occupied.*

## 3. Enzyme-Controlled Reactions
### Page 115 — Application Questions
Q1

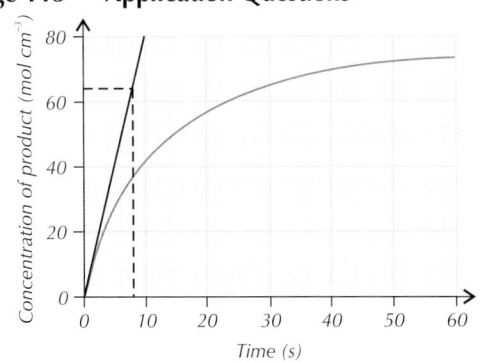

change in $y$ ÷ change in $x$ = 64 mol cm$^{-3}$ ÷ 8 s
= **8 mol cm$^{-3}$ s$^{-1}$**
(accept answers between 6.5 mol cm$^{-3}$ s$^{-1}$ and 10 mol cm$^{-3}$ s$^{-1}$)
*Tangents are tricky things to draw — there'll usually be a small range of acceptable answers that will get the mark.*
Q2 a) Any two from: e.g. temperature, pH, enzyme concentration.

b)

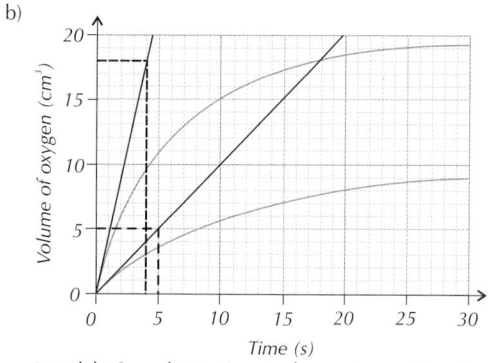

[Graph: Volume of oxygen (cm³) vs Time (s), showing curves for 2 mol dm⁻³ and 1 mol dm⁻³ with tangent lines drawn]

2 mol dm⁻³ — change in y ÷ change in x = 18 cm³ ÷ 4 s
= 4.5 cm³ s⁻¹
(accept answers between 3.3 cm³ s⁻¹ and 5 cm³ s⁻¹)
1 mol dm⁻³ — change in y ÷ change in x = 5 cm³ ÷ 5 s
= 1 cm³ s⁻¹
(accept answers between 0.8 cm³ s⁻¹ and 1.3 cm³ s⁻¹)
So 2 mol dm⁻³ : 1 mol dm⁻³ = **4.5 : 1**
Your answer depends on the values calculated for the tangents — it should fall between 6.25 : 1 and 2.5 : 1. See pages 13-14 for help on calculating ratios.

## Page 115 — Fact Recall Question
Q1 E.g. set up boiling tubes containing the same volume and concentration of hydrogen peroxide. To keep the pH constant, add equal volumes of a suitable buffer solution to each boiling tube. Fill a measuring cylinder with water, turn it upside down and place it in a trough of water. Feed a delivery tube attached to a bung into the measuring cylinder. Put each boiling tube in a water bath set to a different temperature (e.g. 10 °C, 20 °C, 30 °C and 40 °C) along with another tube containing catalase. Wait 5 minutes before moving onto the next step so the enzyme gets up to temperature. Use a pipette to add the same volume and concentration of catalase to each boiling tube. Then quickly attach the bung and delivery tube. Record how much oxygen is produced in the first minute (60 s) of the reaction. Use a stopwatch to measure the time. Repeat the experiment at each temperature three times, and use the results to find a mean volume of oxygen produced. Calculate the mean rate of reaction at each temperature by dividing the volume of oxygen produced by the time taken (i.e. 60 s).

## 4. Cofactors and Enzyme Inhibition
### Page 118 — Application Questions
Q1 a) Ethanol has a similar shape to methanol. This means it will act as a competitive inhibitor, binding to the active site of alcohol dehydrogenase and blocking methanol molecules. This means lower levels of methanol will be hydrolysed so the toxic product (formaldehyde) won't build up to fatal levels.

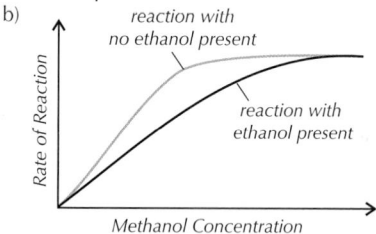

b) [Graph: Rate of Reaction vs Methanol Concentration, showing two curves — "reaction with no ethanol present" (upper) and "reaction with ethanol present" (lower)]

Your curve should be lower than the rate of reaction without any ethanol present. The reaction won't stop completely as some of the methanol molecules will still bind with the active sites. The plateau should be later as the reaction won't reach its maximum rate until the methanol concentration is much higher. The curve should start at zero.

Q2 a) A non-competitive inhibitor, because it binds to the enzyme away from the active site.
b) The rate of the reaction decreases because there are more inhibitor molecules present, which bind to glycogen phosphorylase molecules and alter the shape of their active sites. This means there are fewer active sites in the solution able to bind with glycogen, so the rate of the reaction slows down.
c) i) B. Increasing the concentration of the substrate won't make any difference to the rate of the reaction as enzyme activity will still be inhibited.
   ii) A. Increasing the concentration of the enzyme will mean there are more active sites available for the substrate so the rate of the reaction increases.

### Page 120 — Application Question
Q1 a) End-product inhibition.
b) The amount of substance two being produced would be reduced. This is because when enzyme five is inhibited, it increases the amount of substance four in pathway one, so that more substance five is made. Substance five inhibits enzyme one via end-product inhibition, so a higher concentration of substance five increases the amount of end-product inhibition on enzyme one. This reduces the amount of substance two being produced.
*This will continue until the amount of substance five decreases again, lifting the inhibition on enzyme one.*

### Page 120 — Fact Recall Questions
Q1 A non-protein substance that binds to an enzyme and activates it.
Q2 The coenzyme is used by an enzyme and is changed during the reaction. A second enzyme then uses the changed coenzyme. During this reaction the coenzyme is changed back to its original form.
Q3 A cofactor that is tightly bound to the enzyme.
Q4 a) Away from the active site.
   b) At the active site.
Q5 a) Weak, hydrogen or ionic bonds.
   b) Strong, covalent bonds.
Q6 E.g. cyanide is an irreversible, non-competitive inhibitor of cytochrome c oxidase. Cyanide molecules bind to cytochrome c oxidase away from the active site. This causes the active site to change shape so the substrate molecules can no longer bind to it. / Malonate is a competitive inhibitor of succinate dehydrogenase. Malonate molecules have a similar shape to the substrate, so they compete with the substrate molecules to bind to succinate dehydrogenase's active site. They block the active site, so no substrate molecules can fit in it. / Arsenic is a non-competitive inhibitor of pyruvate dehydrogenase. Arsenic molecules bind to pyruvate dehydrogenase away from the active site. This causes the active site to change shape so the substrate molecules can no longer bind to it.
*Don't fret if you've given a different example of a poison here. Just make sure when you mark it that it's spelt correctly and that you've clearly described how it works.*
Q7 Some enzymes are produced as inactive precursor enzymes, which are unable to catalyse reactions until they become activated.

### Exam-style Questions — pages 122-123

1. a) i) They lower it *(1 mark)*.
   ii) In synthesis reactions, attaching to the enzyme holds the substrate molecules close together, reducing any repulsion between them *(1 mark)*. In breakdown reactions, fitting into an enzyme's active site puts a strain on the bond in the substrate, causing it to break more easily *(1 mark)*.
   
   b) i) **5-6 marks:**
   The answer fully describes the induced fit model in reference to the context of the question.
   The answer has a clear and logical structure.
   The information given is relevant and detailed.
   **3-4 marks:**
   The answer describes most of the features of the induced fit model with some reference to the context of the question.
   The answer has some structure. Most of the information given is relevant and there is some detail involved.
   **1-2 marks:**
   Only one or two of the features of the induced fit model are referenced, and not in the context of the question.
   The answer has no clear structure. The information given is basic and lacking in detail. It may not all be relevant.
   **0 marks:**
   No relevant information is given.
   **Here are some points your answer may include:**
   Catechol and oxygen have a complementary shape to catecholase's active site. This lets them bind to the enzymes's active site. This forms an enzyme-substrate complex. Catechol and oxygen cause the active site to change shape slightly. This means that they bind more tightly to the enzyme. The enzyme-product complex is formed and then benzoquinone and water are released from catecholase.
   
   ii) The 'lock and key' model *(1 mark)*. In this model the active site does not change shape *(1 mark)*.
   
   c) In a fridge. At cooler temperatures the catechol, oxygen and catecholase molecules have less kinetic energy than they would at room temperature *(1 mark)*. This makes the substrate molecules/catechol and oxygen less likely to collide with the catecholase active sites *(1 mark)*. Also, the energy of the collisions is lower, meaning each collision is less likely to result in a reaction *(1 mark)*. Therefore, in a fridge the rate of the reaction would be lower/benzoquinone would be produced more slowly, so the apple would brown more slowly *(1 mark)*.
   *Accept reverse theory, i.e. more kinetic energy at higher temperatures.*
   
   d) i) Copper is an inorganic cofactor *(1 mark)* which binds to catecholase *(1 mark)* and helps it form an enzyme-substrate complex with catechol and oxygen more easily *(1 mark)*.
   *Even though the question doesn't tell you what type of cofactor copper is, you can work out that it must be inorganic because copper is a metal.*
   
   ii) E.g. inorganic cofactors don't directly participate in the reaction but organic cofactors do *(1 mark)*. Inorganic cofactors aren't used up or changed during the reaction but organic factors are changed/recycled *(1 mark)*.
   
   e) E.g. there would be less copper to bind to catecholase *(1 mark)* so fewer enzyme molecules would be able to form enzyme-substrate complexes *(1 mark)*. This would decrease the rate of the reaction, slowing the browning of the apple *(1 mark)*.

2. a) i) *(1 mark for a value between pH 4 and pH 5)*
   ii) pH 1 and pH 9 *(1 mark)*. There is no reaction at these pH levels *(1 mark)*.
   iii) The $H^+$ and $OH^-$ ions found in acids and alkalis can break the weak ionic bonds/hydrogen bonds that hold the enzyme's tertiary structure in place *(1 mark)*. This changes the shape of the active site *(1 mark)* so it is no longer complementary in shape to the substrate/will not bind to the substrate to catalyse the reaction *(1 mark)*.
   *Remember, it's the change in shape of the active site that means the reaction can't be catalysed.*
   iv) E.g. temperature *(1 mark)* and substrate concentration *(1 mark)*.
   
   b) i) A. The rate at which diglycerides and fatty acids are produced/the reaction rate is higher without the presence of orlistat *(1 mark)*.
   ii) Molecules of orlistat have a similar shape to triglycerides *(1 mark)*. They bind to the active sites of gastric lipase and block the entry of triglycerides *(1 mark)*. This means the reaction that produces diglycerides and fatty acids can't take place as quickly *(1 mark)*.

## Section 5 — Biological Membranes

### 1. Cell Membranes — The Basics
### Page 126 — Application Questions
Q1 a) E.g. to keep the enzymes needed for photosynthesis all in one place / to compartmentalise photosynthesis, making photosynthetic reactions more efficient.
   b) E.g. to control what substances enter and leave the cell. / To allow cell communication. / To allow cell recognition.
Q2 E.g. using carrier proteins/channel proteins in the membrane.
Q3 E.g. energy-releasing organelles require lots of substances (e.g. nutrients, enzymes, ATP) to travel across their membranes. Some of these substances will require help from proteins to get across the membrane, so these membranes will have a higher protein content.

### Page 129 — Application Questions
Q1 Freezing the raspberries will have caused ice crystals to form and pierce the cell-surface/plasma membranes, making the membranes highly permeable when they thawed. This will have caused the red pigment to leak out of the raspberry cells as they defrosted.
Q2 a) E.g. the size of the beetroot cubes. / The beetroot the cubes came from. / The volume of methanol solution the cubes were soaked in. / The temperature of the equipment and surroundings.
   b) Any two from: e.g. it should be turned on and left for five minutes to stabilise. / It should be set up so it's using the correct (blue) filter/a wavelength of about 470 nm. / It should be calibrated to zero (using a cuvette containing distilled water).

c) A. As the concentration of methanol increased, more of the lipids in the beetroot's cell membranes would dissolve. This would cause the cells to lose their structure and become more permeable. More pigment would be released from the beetroot cubes, so the absorbance of the surrounding liquid would increase.

## Page 129 — Fact Recall Questions
Q1 It allows some molecules through but not others.
Q2 Any three from: e.g. they act as a barrier between an organelle and the cytoplasm. / They can form vesicles to transport substances between different areas of the cell. / They control which substances enter and leave an organelle. / Membranes within organelles act as a barrier between the membrane contents and the rest of the organelle. / They can be the site of chemical reactions.
Q3 A = glycoprotein, B = glycolipid, C = cholesterol, D = protein channel, E = phospholipid (head)
Q4 'Hydrophilic' means 'attracts water'. Hydrophobic means 'repels water'.
Q5 The centre of the phospholipid bilayer is hydrophobic, so the membrane doesn't allow water-soluble substances through it.
Q6 Some proteins in the membrane allow the passage of large or charged particles that would otherwise find it difficult to cross the membrane.
Q7 a) Helps make the membrane more stable by regulating its fluidity. Creates a barrier to polar substances.
   b) Stabilise the membrane by forming hydrogen bonds with surrounding water molecules. Act as receptors in cell signalling. Are sites where drugs, hormones and antibodies bind. Act as antigens and allow self-recognition.
Q8 The phospholipid bilayer starts to melt and the membrane becomes more permeable. Water inside the cell expands, putting pressure on the membrane. Channel proteins and carrier proteins in the membrane denature so they can't control what enters or leaves the cell, further increasing the permeability of the membrane.

## 2. Cell Membranes and Signalling
## Page 131 — Application Questions
Q1 The drug is a complementary shape to the membrane-bound receptor — this means it will bind to the receptor, blocking the messenger molecule from doing so. This will prevent the messenger molecule from triggering a response in the cell.
Q2 The mutated receptor is not a complementary shape to the messenger molecule. This means the messenger molecule is unable to bind to it and trigger a response in the target cells.
Q3 The messenger molecule can only bind to receptors with a complementary shape. Different cells have different membrane-bound receptors. Only liver cells have the correct receptor, so only liver cells can respond to the messenger molecule.
*The key thing to remember here is that messenger molecules can only bind to membrane-bound receptors that have a <u>complementary shape</u> to their own.*

## 3. Diffusion and Osmosis
## Page 134 — Application Questions
Q1 The ink molecules are moving from an area of higher concentration (the original drop of ink) to an area of lower concentration (the surrounding water).
Q2 a) The distance the particles have to travel is further, so the rate of diffusion will decrease.
   b) The surface area of the cell will increase, so the rate of diffusion will increase.
   c) The concentration gradient will increase, so the rate of diffusion will increase.
Q3 a) E.g. she could cut equal-sized cubes of the agar jelly containing potassium permanganate. She could then prepare several boiling tubes containing the same concentration and volume of hydrochloric acid and place them in water baths set to different temperatures. She could then add one cube to each boiling tube and time how long it takes each cube to turn colourless.
   b) She should expect the cube in the highest temperature to go colourless fastest.

## Page 138 — Application Questions
Q1 a) Water molecules will move from the cheek cells into the salt solution.
   *A −300 kPa solution has a higher water potential (it's less negative) than a −325 kPa solution.*
   b) Water molecules will move into the apple slices from the beaker of water.
   c) There will be no net movement of water molecules as the water potential in both solutions is the same/the solutions are isotonic.
Q2 a) The potato cells have a lower water potential than the sucrose solution, so they gain water by osmosis. This causes the vacuoles to swell and the cell contents to push against the cell wall, making the cells turgid.
   b) E.g. The cells in both solutions will become flaccid (limp). This is because they have a higher water potential than the sucrose solutions, so will lose water by osmosis. The cells may lose so much water that they become plasmolysed.

## Page 138 — Fact Recall Questions
Q1 The net movement of particles from an area of higher concentration to an area of lower concentration.
Q2 It's a passive process.
Q3 Molecules that can pass freely through the membrane, e.g. small, non–polar molecules (and water).
Q4 E.g. The concentration gradient. The thickness of the exchange surface. The surface area of the exchange surface. The temperature.
Q5 osmosis
Q6 Water potential is the potential/likelihood of water molecules to diffuse out of or into a solution.
Q7 a) The cell will swell and could burst as water moves into it by osmosis.
   b) The cell will become turgid (swollen) as water moves into it by osmosis, causing the vacuole to swell and the contents of the vacuole and cytoplasm to push against the cell wall.
   c) The cell will become flaccid (limp) as water moves out of the cell by osmosis. The cell may eventually lose so much water that it becomes plasmolysed.

## 4. Facilitated Diffusion and Active Transport
### Pages 141-142 — Application Questions
Q1  a) vesicle
   b) Exocytosis. In step A, a vesicle containing the chemical messenger moves towards the membrane of neurone 1. In steps B and C, the vesicles fuse with the membrane and release their contents outside the cell.
   c) E.g. through a channel protein using facilitated diffusion.
Q2  a) As the rate of sodium ion active transport increases, so does the rate of oxygen consumption. This is because sodium ion active transport requires energy from ATP. As the rate of active transport increases, the rate of aerobic respiration must also increase in order to produce more ATP, which means the rate of oxygen consumption must increase too.
   *Remember, ATP is produced by the mitochondria during aerobic respiration — and aerobic respiration uses oxygen.*
   b) None. Facilitated diffusion doesn't require energy from ATP, so there would be no need for the rate of oxygen consumption to increase.

### Page 143 — Application Question
Q1

| Transport system | A plant cell taking in water | Calcium ions moving into a cell against a concentration gradient | A muscle cell taking in polar glucose molecules | White blood cell taking in anthrax bacteria |
|---|---|---|---|---|
| Osmosis | ✓ | ✗ | ✗ | ✗ |
| Facilitated diffusion using channel proteins | ✓ | ✗ | ✗ | ✗ |
| Facilitated diffusion using carrier proteins | ✗ | ✗ | ✓ | ✗ |
| Active transport using carrier proteins | ✗ | ✓ | ✓ | ✗ |
| Endocytosis | ✗ | ✗ | ✗ | ✓ |
| Exocytosis | ✗ | ✗ | ✗ | ✗ |

### Page 143 — Fact Recall Questions
Q1  In simple diffusion, small, non-polar molecules pass freely through the plasma membrane. Facilitated diffusion uses carrier proteins and channel proteins to aid the movement of large molecules and charged particles through the plasma membrane.
Q2  Similarity: both facilitated diffusion and active transport use carrier proteins to transport molecules across plasma membranes.
   Differences: in facilitated diffusion, molecules move down a concentration gradient. In active transport, molecules are moved against a concentration gradient.
   Facilitated diffusion is a passive process, it doesn't require energy. Active transport is an active process that does require energy.
Q3  a) A molecule attaches to a carrier protein in the membrane. The protein then changes shape and releases the molecule on the opposite side of the membrane.
   b) Channel proteins form pores in the membrane for charged particles to diffuse through.
Q4  A cell surrounds a substance or object with its plasma membrane. The membrane then pinches off to form a vesicle inside the cell, which contains the ingested substance or object.
Q5  E.g. a digestive enzyme / a hormone / a lipid

### Exam-style Questions — pages 145-146
1  a) i) The potential/likelihood of water molecules to diffuse out of or into a solution *(1 mark)*.
      ii) The cells in Fig. 1.2 have lost water by osmosis *(1 mark)*. This has caused the cytoplasm and plasma membranes to pull away from the cell walls *(1 mark)*. The cells are plasmolysed *(1 mark)*.
      iii) The net movement of water molecules will still be out of the cell by osmosis, causing the cell to shrink *(1 mark)*.
   b) i) Any four from: In the fluid mosaic model, phospholipid molecules form a continuous double layer/bilayer *(1 mark)*. Cholesterol molecules fit between and interact with the phospholipids, regulating membrane fluidity *(1 mark)*. Protein molecules are scattered throughout the bilayer, like tiles in a mosaic *(1 mark)*. Some protein molecules, called glycoproteins, have a polysaccharide/carbohydrate chain attached *(1 mark)*. / Some lipids, called glycolipids, also have a polysaccharide/carbohydrate chain attached *(1 mark)*.
      *(Maximum of 4 marks available.)*
      ii) E.g. any two from: Plasma membranes control which substances enter and leave the cell. / Plasma membranes allow recognition by other cells. / Plasma membranes allow cell communication.
      *(2 marks for 2 correct answers.)*
2  a) i) The centre of the phospholipid bilayer is hydrophobic *(1 mark)*. It forms a barrier to the diffusion of water-soluble substances including most polar molecules *(1 mark)*. Glucose is a polar molecule that can't diffuse directly across the membrane *(1 mark)*.
      ii) No. The glucose moves down its concentration gradient/facilitated diffusion is a passive process *(1 mark)*.
      iii) It is a carrier protein *(1 mark)* that changes shape when glucose binds to it, causing the glucose to be released on the opposite side of the membrane *(1 mark)*.
   b) The movement of molecules against their concentration gradient *(1 mark)* using energy (from ATP) *(1 mark)*.
3  a) E.g. in case the cubes did not all start out at exactly the same mass *(1 mark)*. / To enable a fair comparison between the cubes *(1 mark)*.
   b) 16% (accept 15-17%) *(1 mark)*
   *Don't forget that pure water is always 0 kPa.*
   c) i) The water potential in these three solutions must have been lower than the water potential of the potato cells *(1 mark)*, so water moved out of the cells by osmosis *(1 mark)*.
      ii) −425 kPa (accept any answer between −400 and −450 kPa) *(1 mark)*
   *The cells won't lose or gain any mass in an isotonic solution, so all you need to do is read the water potential off the graph where the change in mass equals zero.*

d) E.g. they could do repeats of the experiment for each concentration of sucrose solution and calculate a mean percentage change in mass *(1 mark)*.
There's more on precise results in Module 1 of this book.
e) Before 12 hours *(1 mark)* because the rate of osmosis will be faster due to the increase in surface area *(1 mark)*.

# Section 6 — Cell Division and Cellular Organisation

## 1. The Cell Cycle and Mitosis
### Page 150 — Application Question
Q1 a)

| Stage of Mitosis | Step Number |
|---|---|
| Anaphase | 3 |
| Telophase | 4 |
| Prophase | 1 |
| Metaphase | 2 |

b) i) B
   ii) C
To answer this you need to quickly go through each stage of mitosis in your head and think about the main thing that's happening, e.g. in metaphase all the chromosomes are in the middle of the cell. Then ask yourself if you can see that in the photo.
c) The centromeres are dividing, separating each pair of sister chromatids. The spindles are contracting, pulling chromatids to opposite ends of the cell, centromere first.

### Page 150 — Fact Recall Questions
Q1 The process that all body cells in multicellular organisms use to grow and divide.
Q2 interphase
Q3 It's checked for any damage that may have occurred.
Q4 For growth of multicellular organisms and for repairing damaged tissues.
Q5 During prophase the chromosomes condense, getting shorter and fatter. The centrioles start moving to opposite ends of the cell, forming the spindle. The nuclear envelope breaks down and chromosomes lie free in the cytoplasm.
Q6 metaphase
Q7 anaphase
Q8 A cleavage furrow forms to divide the cell membrane and the cytoplasm divides.
Q9 two
Q10 False
Mitosis produces two genetically identical daughter cells.

## 2. Sexual Reproduction and Meiosis
### Page 154 — Application Questions
Q1 a) metaphase 1
   b) anaphase 2
There are half the number of chromosomes in this cell (compared to the previous cell) and they're being pulled apart — that's how you know it must be in anaphase 2.
   c) prophase 1
   d) metaphase 2

Q2

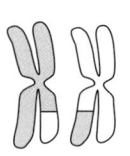

### Page 154 — Fact Recall Questions
Q1 a) diploid
   b) haploid
   c) diploid
Q2 a) The chromosomes condense, homologous chromosomes pair up and crossing-over occurs. The centrioles start moving to opposite ends of the cell, forming the spindle fibres, and the nuclear envelope breaks down.
   b) The homologous pairs line up across the centre of the cell and attach to the spindle fibres by their centromeres.
   c) The spindles contract, pulling the homologous pairs apart (one chromosome goes to each end of the cell).
   d) A nuclear envelope forms around each group of chromosomes and the cytoplasm divides so there are now two haploid daughter cells.
Q3 The two daughter cells from meiosis 1 undergo prophase 2, metaphase 2, anaphase 2 and telophase 2. Four haploid daughter cells are produced.
Q4 a) Crossing-over of chromatids and the independent assortment of chromosomes
   b) Crossing-over is when chromatids twist around each other and bits of chromatid swap over. The resulting chromosomes contain the same genes but now have a different combination of alleles. This means that when the chromatids separate at meiosis 2, each of the four daughter cells will contain chromatids with different alleles. The independent assortment of chromosomes is when different combinations of maternal and paternal chromosomes go into each daughter cell.

## 3. Stem Cells and Differentiation
### Pages 158-159 — Application Questions
Q1 a) If the cells on the outside of the cornea become damaged, the limbal stem cells will be able to differentiate into new cornea cells to replace them.
   b) Because the number of different types of cell that adult stem cells can differentiate into is limited, so they may not be able to differentiate into nerve cells, which are the type of cell required to treat Alzheimer's.
Q2 E.g. epithelial cells have microvilli, which increase the cell's surface area for absorption of nutrients.
The key thing here is to link what you know about epithelial cells to the information you're given in the question — in this case that they're found in the small intestine. Food is absorbed in the small intestine, so you should be able to work out the answer.

### Page 159 — Fact Recall Questions
Q1 An unspecialised cell that can develop into different types of cell.
Q2 The process by which a cell becomes specialised for its job.
Q3 a) i) red blood cells
      ii) white blood cells
You could remember that neutrophils are white blood cells by thinking of white as a neutral colour.
   b) In the bone marrow.

Q4  The stem cells that form xylem and phloem are found in the meristems. Stem cells of the vascular cambium divide and differentiate to become xylem vessels and phloem sieve tubes.

Q5  In heart disease, the heart tissue can become damaged. The body is unable to sufficiently replace damaged heart cells. Stem cells could be used to make replacement heart cells to repair the damaged tissue.

Q6  Parkinson's is caused by a loss of a type of nerve cell in the brain that produces a chemical called dopamine. Stem cells could be transplanted into patients to help regenerate the dopamine-producing cells.

Q7  a) Any one from: e.g. erythrocytes have a biconcave disc shape which provides a large surface area for gas exchange. / Erythrocytes don't have a nucleus so there's more room for haemoglobin, the protein that carries oxygen.
    b) Any one from: e.g. neutrophils have a flexible shape which allows them to engulf foreign particles or pathogens. / Neutrophils have a large number of lysosomes in their cytoplasm which contain digestive enzymes to break down engulfed foreign particles or pathogens.

*It's dead important that you know the functions and adaptations of erythrocytes, neutrophils, squamous and ciliated epithelial cells, sperm cells, palisade mesophyll cells, root hair cells and guard cells — you could be asked about any of them in the exam and they're easy marks if you learn them properly.*

Q8  a) To carry out photosynthesis.
    b) To absorb water and mineral ions from the soil.

Q9  In the light, guard cells take up water (into their vacuoles) and become turgid. Their thin outer walls and thickened inner walls force them to bend outwards, opening the stomata. This allows the leaf to exchange gases for photosynthesis.

## 4. Tissues, Organs and Systems
### Page 162 — Application Question
Q1  a) A = companion cell, B = ordinary plant cell, C = sieve cell
    b) Phloem tissue

### Pages 162-163 — Fact Recall Questions
Q1  A group of cells (plus any extracellular material secreted by them) that are specialised to work together to carry out a particular function.

Q2  false

Q3  a) Squamous epithelium is made up of a group of cells/a single layer of flat cells that are specialised to work together to provide a thin exchange surface for substances to diffuse across quickly.
    b) Ciliated epithelium is made up of a group of cells/a layer of cells covered in cilia, which are specialised to work together to move a substance along, e.g. mucus in the lungs.

*If you're asked why a particular tissue is classified as a tissue in the exam, make sure you include the function of that tissue in your answer.*

Q4  Muscle tissue is made up of bundles of elongated cells called muscle fibres.

Q5  Cartilage is a type of connective tissue that is found in the joints and also provides shape and support to the ears, nose and windpipe.

Q6  E.g. xylem, phloem.

Q7  A group of different tissues that work together to perform a particular function.

Q8  An organ system is where different organs work together to carry out a particular function.

Q9  E.g. the respiratory system. It is an organ system because it is made up of the lungs, trachea, larynx, nose, mouth and diaphragm which work together to carry out gas exchange.

### Exam-style Questions — pages 164-165
1  a) 12-16 hours and 36-40 hours *(1 mark)*, because the mass of DNA doubles *(1 mark)*.
   b) 24 hours and 48 hours *(1 mark)*, because the mass of DNA halves / the mass of the cell halves *(1 mark)*.
   c) E.g. the cell is growing *(1 mark)* and new organelles and proteins are made *(1 mark)*. The cell replicates it's DNA *(1 mark)* and checks the DNA for damage *(1 mark)*.
   d) i) Two (at 24 and 48 hours) *(1 mark)* because the mass of the cell and its DNA doubles and halves twice *(1 mark)*.
      ii) At 72 hours *(1 mark)*.

*In graphs with two scales, make sure you match the correct line (or bar) to the correct scale before you read off a value.*

   e) i) At opposite poles, chromatids uncoil and become long and thin again *(1 mark)*. A nuclear envelope forms around each group of chromosomes, so there are two nuclei *(1 mark)*.
      ii) Mitosis is important for growth *(1 mark)*, repair *(1 mark)*, and asexual reproduction *(1 mark)*.

*Don't forget that mitosis is not just used for growth and repair in multicellular organisms — some organisms use it for asexual reproduction too.*

2  a) Sperm cells use their tails to swim to the egg *(1 mark)*. If a large proportion of sperm cells can't do this successfully, there's less chance of a sperm cell successfully fertilising the egg *(1 mark)*.
   b) They have lots of mitochondria to provide the energy to swim *(1 mark)* and they have an acrosome, which contains digestive enzymes to enable the sperm to penetrate the surface of the egg *(1 mark)*.

3  a) Any two from: e.g. it has a large surface area for absorbing water and mineral ions from the soil *(1 mark)*. / It has a thin, permeable cell wall for absorbing water and mineral ions from the soil *(1 mark)*. / The cytoplasm contains extra mitochondria to provide the energy needed for active transport *(1 mark)*.
   b) i) In meristems / the vascular cambium *(1 mark)*.
      ii) Xylem is a group of cells, including xylem vessel cells and parenchyma cells *(1 mark)*, that are specialised to work together to transport water around the plant and support the plant *(1 mark)*.

4  a) i) The DNA is being replicated to produce two copies of each chromosome *(1 mark)*.
      ii) The chromosomes are condensing and are arranging themselves into homologous pairs *(1 mark)*.
      iii) Meiosis 1 occurs — the homologous pairs are separated, halving the chromosome number *(1 mark)*.
      iv) Meiosis 2 occurs — the pairs of sister chromatids are separated, generating haploid cells *(1 mark)*.

b) i) E.g. the daughter cells are genetically different *(1 mark)* and are haploid/contain half the number of chromosomes as the parent cell *(1 mark)*.
ii) When homologous chromosomes come together in meiosis 1, the chromatids are able to twist around each other and bits of the chromatids can swap over *(1 mark)*. Each of the chromatids now has a different combination of alleles *(1 mark)*, which means that each of the four daughter cells resulting from meiosis contain chromatids with different alleles *(1 mark)*.

# Module 3

## Section 1 — Exchange and Transport

### 1. Specialised Exchange Systems

**Page 167 — Application Question**

Q1 a) i) A — surface area = $6 \times 2 \times 2$ = **24 cm²**
B — surface area = $(4 \times 4 \times 2) + (2 \times 2 \times 2)$
    = $32 + 8$ = **40 cm²**
C — surface area = $4\pi r^2$
    = $4 \times \pi \times 2.5^2$
    = **79 cm²** (2 s.f.)

ii) A — volume = $2 \times 2 \times 2$ = **8 cm³**
B — volume = $2 \times 4 \times 2$ = **16 cm³**
C — volume = $\frac{4}{3}\pi r^3$
    = $\frac{4}{3}\pi \times 2.5^3$
    = **65 cm³** (2 s.f.)

iii) A — SA:V = 24:8 (or 3:1)
B — SA:V = 40:16 (or 5:2 or 2.5:1)
C — SA:V = 79:65 (or 1.2:1)

*You should have got the same answers for shape C whether you used π as 3.14 or the π button on your calculator. If an exam question specifies which value to use for π, make sure you do what it says.*

b) A
*Simplify all of the ratios to 1 in order to compare them, e.g. A = 3:1, B = 2.5:1 and C = 1.2:1 — it's then obvious that A is the largest ratio.*

**Page 170 — Application Questions**

Q1 The concentration gradient of oxygen between the alveoli and the capillaries will be lower than normal, so the rate of diffusion, and therefore gas exchange, will be slower.

Q2 Less air, and so less oxygen, would be inhaled in each breath. This means the concentration gradient of oxygen between the alveoli and the capillaries will be less steep, slowing the rate of diffusion.

Q3 a) The alveoli are enlarged/much larger in the diseased lungs than in the healthy lungs.
b) Having enlarged alveoli means there's a smaller surface area for gas exchange, slowing the rate of diffusion of oxygen into the blood. So a patient with emphysema would have a low level of oxygen in the blood.

*These questions are all asking you to think about factors that affect the efficiency of gas exchange surfaces. The key things to think about are the size of the surface area, how good the blood supply and/or ventilation is (to maintain steep concentration gradients) and the thickness of the exchange surface (or the length of the diffusion pathway).*

**Page 170 — Fact Recall Questions**

Q1 a) E.g. oxygen, glucose.
b) E.g. carbon dioxide, urea.

Q2 Some cells are deep within the body, so the distance between them and the outside environment is too great for diffusion to take place quickly. Larger animals have a low surface area : volume ratio. This means they don't have a large enough area exposed to the environment to be able to exchange all the substances they need quickly enough using diffusion. Multicellular organisms have a higher metabolic rate than single-celled organisms, so they use up oxygen and glucose faster than diffusion could provide them.

Q3 a) Plant roots are covered in root hair cells, which vastly increase the surface area of the root, so the rate of absorption of water and mineral ions from the soil is increased.
b) E.g. being thin and having a good blood supply and/or ventilation.

Q4 Fish gills contain a large network of capillaries, which keeps them well-supplied with blood. They're also well-ventilated by fresh water that constantly passes over them. These features help to maintain a concentration gradient of $O_2$, which increases the rate at which $O_2$ diffuses into the blood.

### 2. Gas Exchange in Mammals

**Page 173 — Application Question**

Q1 a) bronchus
b) A = cartilage, B = ciliated epithelium, C = elastic fibres

**Page 173 — Fact Recall Questions**

Q1 a) To secrete mucus.
b) To beat the mucus (plus trapped dust and microorganisms) away from the alveoli.

Q2 Elastic fibres help the process of breathing out. On breathing in, the lungs inflate and the elastic fibres are stretched. The fibres then recoil to help push air out of the lungs when exhaling. Elastic fibres are found in the trachea, bronchi, bronchioles and alveoli.

Q3 The trachea, bronchi and all but the smallest bronchioles.

Q4 Cartilage in the trachea is found in large C-shaped pieces/rings. Cartilage in the bronchi is found in smaller pieces and is interspersed with smooth muscle.

### 3. Ventilation in Mammals

**Page 176 — Application Questions**

Q1 Accept 0.5 dm³ or 0.55 dm³

Q2 11 breaths per minute

Q3 The air that's breathed out is a mixture of oxygen and carbon dioxide. The carbon dioxide is absorbed by the soda lime and the oxygen gets used up by respiration, so the total volume of gas in the spirometer decreases with time.

## 4. Gas Exchange in Fish and Insects

### Page 179 — Application Questions
**Q1** A concentration gradient would still be maintained between the water and the blood, but it would be less steep. This means the fish wouldn't be able to take in as much oxygen as it would in clean water.

**Q2** a) It increases steadily.
*To answer this question you need to look at the arrow head of the red line — it's pointing upwards so the oxygen concentration of the blood is increasing.*
b) It decreases steadily.
c) 80%
d) Because at point X the oxygen concentration of the water is higher than in the blood (about 92%) — so oxygen has diffused into the blood down its concentration gradient.

### Page 179 — Fact Recall Questions
**Q1** Each gill is made of lots of thin plates called gill filaments/primary lamellae. These are covered in lots of tiny structures called gill plates. Gill plates have a thin surface layer of cells and a good blood supply.

**Q2** The counter-current system works by maintaining a steep concentration gradient between the water and the blood. Blood flows through the gill plates in one direction and water flows over the gill plates in the opposite direction. This means that water with a relatively high oxygen concentration always flows next to blood with a lower oxygen concentration. Oxygen then diffuses into the blood from the water down the concentration gradient.

**Q3** The fish opens its mouth, which lowers the floor of the buccal cavity, causing its volume to increase. This causes the pressure inside the cavity to decrease, which causes water to be sucked into the cavity. When the fish closes its mouth, the floor of the buccal cavity is raised again. This causes the volume inside the cavity to decrease and the pressure inside to increase, forcing water out of the cavity and across the gill filaments.

**Q4** A bony flap that protects the gills of fish.

**Q5** The increase in pressure (caused by the decrease in volume of the buccal cavity) causes the operculum to open, to allow the water to leave the gills.

**Q6** Through the spiracles on the surface of the insect's body.

**Q7** Carbon dioxide from the cells moves down its concentration gradient towards the spiracles to be released into the atmosphere.

**Q8** Insects can use rhythmic movements to change the volume of their bodies and move air in and out of the spiracles. They can also use the movement of their wings whilst flying to pump their thoraxes.

## 5. Dissecting Gas Exchange Systems

### Page 181 — Application Question
**Q1** a) Because it can be easier to avoid damaging the tissue underneath where you're cutting when using scissors rather than a scalpel.
b) A network of very thin, silvery-grey tubes.
c) These are rings of chitin that act to support the tracheae.

### Page 181 — Fact Recall Questions
**Q1** To pin a specimen in place during the dissection.
**Q2** To hold and manipulate smaller parts of the specimen.
**Q3** Under the operculum.

### Exam-style Questions — pages 183-184
1. a) intercostal *(1 mark)*, contract *(1 mark)*, ribcage *(1 mark)*, volume *(1 mark)*, pressure *(1 mark)*
b) vital capacity *(1 mark)*
c) i) The person breathed out/expired *(1 mark)*.
*Watch out here — the spirometer trace shows the volume of gas in the lungs, not the volume of gas in the spirometer. The volume of gas in the lungs will decrease when the person breathes out.*
ii) 14 breaths / minute *(1 mark)*
*If the question doesn't tell you what units to give your answer in, just pick sensible ones.*
iii) The trace would slope downwards *(1 mark)*. This is because the volume of gas in the spirometer would decrease over time *(1 mark)*, as oxygen would be used up in respiration *(1 mark)* and carbon dioxide would be absorbed by the soda lime in the spirometer *(1 mark)*.
d) E.g. repeat the measurement several/at least three times and find the mean of the results *(1 mark)*.
*There are lots of possible answers here — just use your common sense. (See Module 1 for more on precise results.)*

2. a) surface area = $4\pi r^2$
$= 4 \times \pi \times 0.7^2$
$= 6$ μm² (1 s.f.)
volume $= \frac{4}{3}\pi r^3$
$= \frac{4}{3} \pi \times 0.7^3$
$= 1$ μm³ (1 s.f.)
surface area : volume = **6 : 1** *(1 mark)*
b) Because it is a single-celled organism with a short diffusion pathway *(1 mark)* and a large surface area to volume ratio *(1 mark)*. This means it can exchange substances quickly across its outer surface *(1 mark)*.
*To help you answer this question, think about why multicellular organisms do have a gaseous exchange system — it's because the diffusion pathway is too big, they have a small surface area : volume ratio and their rate of metabolism is higher, so they use up glucose and oxygen quicker. These characteristics mean that diffusion would be too slow.*

3. a) width of alveolus = width of image ÷ magnification
= 9 mm ÷ 60
= 0.15 mm × 1000 (to convert to micrometres)
= **150 μm**
*(1 mark for correct calculation, 2 marks for correct answer)*
*The question tells you to give your answer in μm, so you need to remember to convert your answer from mm to μm. If you're a bit rusty on this, check out p. 47.*
b) E.g. the walls of the alveoli have been destroyed in the diseased alveoli *(1 mark)*. Destruction of the alveolar walls reduces the surface area of the alveoli *(1 mark)*, so the rate of gaseous exchange would decrease *(1 mark)*.
c) There would be a steeper concentration gradient of oxygen between the alveoli and the capillaries *(1 mark)*. This would increase the rate of diffusion of oxygen into the blood *(1 mark)*.

4. a) To beat mucus (plus trapped dust and microorganisms) away from the alveoli *(1 mark)*.

b) i) Any one from, e.g. to support the trachea *(1 mark)*. / To stop the trachea from collapsing *(1 mark)*.
   ii) the bronchi *(1 mark)*
c) Any one from, e.g. goblet cells *(1 mark)* — to secrete mucus *(1 mark)*. / Smooth muscle *(1 mark)* — to control the trachea's diameter *(1 mark)*. / Elastic fibres *(1 mark)* — to recoil and push air out of the lungs whilst breathing out/expiring *(1 mark)*.

# Section 2 — Transport in Animals

## 1. Circulatory Systems
### Page 187 — Fact Recall Questions
Q1 Any two from: multicellular organisms are relatively big. / Multicellular organisms have a low surface area to volume ratio. / Many multicellular organisms have a high metabolic rate. / A lot of multicellular organisms are very active, so their cells need a constant, rapid supply of glucose and oxygen.
Q2 E.g. mammals.
Q3 a) Because blood only passes through the heart once for a complete circuit of the body.
   b) Because blood is enclosed inside blood vessels.
Q4 Because the blood isn't enclosed in blood vessels all the time. Instead it flows freely through the body cavity.

## 2. Blood Vessels
### Page 190 — Application Question
Q1 The water potential of the capillary is higher because there is less albumin in the blood so there is a lower oncotic pressure. This means less water is absorbed by osmosis back into the capillary at the venule end of the capillary bed, which leads to an increase in tissue fluid.

### Page 190 — Fact Recall Questions
Q1 a) Arteries need to carry blood away from the heart under high pressure so they have thick muscular walls with elastic tissue which stretch and recoil as the heart beats, helping to maintain the high pressure. They also have a folded endothelium which enables the artery to expand, again maintaining high pressure.
   b) Capillaries exchange substances like glucose and oxygen with body cells so the walls of capillaries are only one cell thick for efficient diffusion.
   c) Veins carry blood back to the heart under low pressure so they have a wide lumen, with little elastic or muscle tissue. They also contain valves to stop the blood flowing backwards.
Q2 Arterioles are much smaller than arteries and they have less elastic tissue.
Q3 venules
Q4 The fluid that surrounds cells in tissues.
Q5 At the arteriole end the hydrostatic pressure inside the capillaries is higher than the hydrostatic pressure in the tissue fluid. This means fluid is forced out of the capillaries and into the spaces around the cells, forming tissue fluid.
Q6 lymph vessels
Q7 a) E.g. any two from: blood contains red blood cells, tissue fluid does not. / Blood contains white blood cells, tissue fluid contains very few white blood cells. / Blood contains platelets, tissue fluid usually does not. / Blood contains proteins, tissue fluid contains very few proteins.
   b) E.g. tissue fluid contains very few white blood cells, most white blood cells are in the lymph.

## 3. Heart Basics
### Page 194 — Application Questions
Q1 The left atrium is contracting.
Q2 It is closed because the left ventricle is relaxing, so the pressure is higher in the aorta than in the ventricle, forcing the semi-lunar valve shut.
Q3 The left ventricle is relaxing.
Q4 The left atrium is filling up.
   At point D, the increase in atrial pressure can't be due to the left atrium contracting because the diagram shows that the left ventricle is relaxing — i.e. the left ventricle doesn't contract next. So you need to think about what happens in the left atrium as the left ventricle is relaxing — it's filling up with blood to prepare for the next atrial contraction.
Q5 It is open because the ventricle is relaxing, reducing the pressure in the chamber. The atrium has been filling, increasing the pressure in the chamber. So as the pressure in the atrium becomes higher than that in the ventricle, the atrioventricular valve will open.

### Page 194 — Fact Recall Questions
Q1 right side
Q2 A — inferior vena cava
   B — left atrium
   C — aorta
   D — right atrium
   E — coronary artery
   F — right ventricle
   G — left ventricle
   H — vena cava
Q3 a) semi-lunar valves
   b) They stop blood flowing back into the heart after the ventricles contract.
Q4 An ongoing sequence of contraction and relaxation of the atria and ventricles that keeps blood continuously circulating round the body.
Q5 The volume of the atria decreases and the pressure increases.
Q6 cardiac output = heart rate × stroke volume

## 4. Electrical Activity of The Heart
### Page 198 — Application Questions
Q1 a) From 1st R wave to 2nd R wave:
      1.24 − 0.42 = 0.82 s
      60 ÷ 0.82 = **73 bpm**
      *To work out heart rate (in bpm) you need to divide — not multiply — 60 by the length of one heartbeat (in s).*
   b) From 1st R wave to 2nd R wave:
      1.42 − 0.52 = 0.90 s
      60 ÷ 0.90 = **67 bpm**
Q2 ECG B shows a slower heart rate than that of ECG A (67 bpm compared to 73 bpm). ECG B shows a longer interval between contraction of the atria (the P wave) and contraction of the ventricles (QRS complex) than ECG A (about 0.3 s compared to 0.1 s).

## Page 198 — Fact Recall Questions

Q1  a) sino-atrial node
    b) It sets the rhythm of the heartbeat by sending regular waves of electrical activity over the atrial walls. This causes the right and left atria to contract at the same time.
Q2  non-conducting collagen tissue
Q3  It conducts waves of electrical activity from the atrioventricular node to the Purkyne tissue.
Q4  It carries the waves of electrical activity into the muscular walls of the right and left ventricles, causing them to contract simultaneously, from the bottom up.
Q5  a) electrocardiogram
    b) E.g. tachycardia / bradycardia / ectopic heartbeat / fibrillation

## 5. Haemoglobin
### Page 202 — Application Questions

Q1

[Graph: % saturation of haemoglobin with oxygen (y-axis, 0–100) vs partial pressure of $O_2$ / kPa (x-axis, 0–10). Two sigmoid curves shown: fetal haemoglobin (to the left) and adult haemoglobin (to the right).]

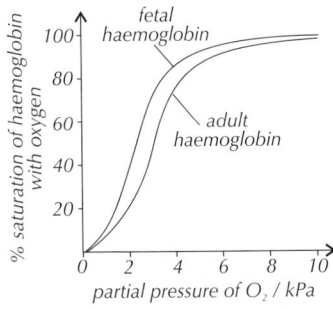

Q2  The dissociation curve for fetal haemoglobin is to the left of the dissociation curve for adult haemoglobin because it has a higher affinity for oxygen than adult haemoglobin. This means fetal haemoglobin takes up oxygen (becomes more saturated) in lower partial pressures of oxygen than adult haemoglobin.

*Don't get the dissociation curve for fetal haemoglobin mixed up with a curve showing the Bohr effect, which would be to the right of the normal adult haemoglobin dissociation curve.*

### Page 202 — Fact Recall Questions
Q1  oxyhaemoglobin
Q2  In the alveoli / lungs. This is the site where oxygen first enters the blood so it has the highest concentration of oxygen.
Q3  How saturated haemoglobin is with oxygen at any given partial pressure.
Q4  More oxygen is available to cells during activity.
Q5  It would shift the oxygen dissociation curve right.
Q6  carbonic anhydrase
Q7  a) It splits up to give hydrogen ions/$H^+$ and hydrogencarbonate ions/$HCO_3^-$.
    b) The increase in hydrogen ions/$H^+$ causes oxyhaemoglobin to unload its oxygen so that haemoglobin can take up the hydrogen ions/$H^+$.
Q8  The chloride shift is when chloride ions ($Cl^-$) diffuse into red blood cells to compensate for the loss of hydrogencarbonate ions ($HCO_3^-$) from them.

## Exam-style Questions — pages 204-205

1  B *(1 mark)*
The QRS complex is caused by contraction of the ventricles. The Purkyne tissue carries the electrical activity to the walls of both ventricles to make them contract simultaneously. The P wave is caused by contraction of the atria and a higher wave indicates more electrical charge is passing through the heart, which results in a stronger contraction. The T wave is due to relaxation (repolarisation) of the ventricles.

2  a) The semi-lunar valves are open *(1 mark)* so the pressure must be higher in the ventricles than the pulmonary artery/aorta *(1 mark)*. This means the blood is moving (from the ventricles) into the pulmonary artery/aorta *(1 mark)*.

*If you get a diagram of the heart in your exam that looks a bit different from this, just look to see where the valves are and whether they're open or closed — then you should be able to answer the question.*

   b) Atrioventricular valves / AV valves *(1 mark)*. They prevent the back-flow of blood into the atria when the ventricles contract *(1 mark)*.
   c) i) A double circulatory system means that blood passes through the heart twice for each complete circuit of the body *(1 mark)*.
      ii) One circuit sends deoxygenated blood from the heart to the lungs, then returns the blood to the heart after it has picked up oxygen *(1 mark)*. This oxygenated blood is then sent out from the heart round the rest of the body in the second circuit *(1 mark)*. The advantage of this system is that by returning to the heart to be pumped again, oxygenated blood travels to the rest of the body more quickly than if it was to travel directly from the lungs *(1 mark)*.

3  a) B. During the bike ride the man's respiration rate would have increased, raising the $pCO_2$ *(1 mark)*. This would have increased the rate of oxygen unloading, so the dissociation curve would have shifted to the right *(1 mark)*.
   b) The Bohr effect *(1 mark)*.
   c) The increased rate of respiration during the bike ride would have caused more carbon dioxide to be produced, most of which would have been converted in the red blood cells into carbonic acid *(1 mark)* by the enzyme carbonic anhydrase *(1 mark)*. The carbonic acid would then split to give hydrogen ions/$H^+$ and hydrogencarbonate ions/$HCO_3^-$, which would diffuse out of the red blood cells and into the plasma *(1 mark)*.

4  a) AVN — B *(1 mark)*, right ventricle — F *(1 mark)*, pulmonary vein — D *(1 mark)*
   b) It prevents the waves of electrical activity from being passed directly from the atria to the ventricles *(1 mark)*.
   c) There must be a delay so that the atria empty before the ventricles contract *(1 mark)*.
   d) The atrioventricular valve/AVN passes the waves of electrical activity onto the bundle of His *(1 mark)*. The bundle of His conducts the waves of electrical activity to the Purkyne tissue *(1 mark)*. The Purkyne tissue carries the waves of electrical activity into the muscular walls of the right and left ventricles *(1 mark)*.

5  a) i) X because it's an artery *(1 mark)*.
      As the blood travels round the circulatory system the pressure of the blood gradually decreases and it is returned to the heart at low pressure via the veins.
    ii) E.g. vessel Y contains valves, vessel X doesn't *(1 mark)*. Vessel X contains more elastic tissue than vessel Y *(1 mark)*. Vessel X contains a thicker muscle layer than vessel Y *(1 mark)*.
  b) At the start of the capillary bed the hydrostatic pressure inside the capillaries is higher than the pressure in the tissue fluid *(1 mark)*. The difference in pressure forces fluid out of the capillaries and into the spaces around the cells, forming tissue fluid *(1 mark)*.
  c) E.g. blood contains red blood cells, lymph doesn't *(1 mark)*. Blood contains platelets, lymph doesn't *(1 mark)*.

# Section 3 — Transport in Plants
## 1. Xylem and Phloem
### Page 209 — Application Questions
Q1  W, because it is situated underneath the xylem tissue.
Q2  a) sieve plate
    b) Pit — it allows water and mineral ions to move into and out of the xylem vessels.

### Page 210 — Fact Recall Questions
Q1  It would be too slow to meet their metabolic needs because plants are multicellular, so have a small surface area to volume ratio.
Q2 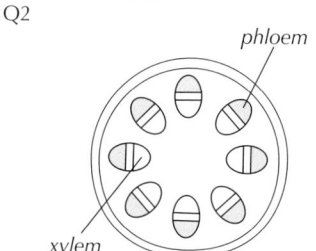  
    
    *phloem*
    
    *xylem*
    
    If you're drawing both the xylem and the phloem on a diagram remember to label them, so that the examiner knows which is which.
Q3  A — xylem
    B — phloem
Q4  water and mineral ions
    Remember, xylem vessels don't just transport water, they transport mineral ions too.
Q5  lignin
Q6  Sucrose/sugars.
Q7  a) living cells
    b) Any two from, e.g. they contain a very thin layer of cytoplasm. / They have no nucleus. / They have few organelles.
Q8  Companion cells carry out the living functions for sieve cells. (They provide energy for the active transport of solutes.)
Q9  E.g. use a scalpel to slice a thin cross-section of the stem (either longitudinal or transverse). Add a drop of water to a microscope slide and then place the section onto it. Add one or two drops of a stain, e.g. TBO, wait for about a minute and then carefully place the coverslip on the slide. View the specimen under a light microscope.

## 2. Water Transport
### Page 213 — Application Questions
Q1  root hair (cell)
Q2  C
Q3  Casparian strip
Q4  Structure E is the xylem, used to transport water (and mineral ions) to all parts of the plant. If the xylem is blocked some plant cells won't receive enough water and the plant may wilt.

### Page 213 — Fact Recall Questions
Q1  Water enters the root from the soil through the root hair cells. It then passes through the cortex, including the endodermis, before it reaches the xylem.
Q2  In the symplast pathway, water moves through the cytoplasm in the root cells to the xylem via osmosis. Plasmodesmata connect the cytoplasm of neighbouring cells. In the apoplast pathway water moves through the cell walls of the root. Water diffuses through the cell walls and passes through the spaces between them. However, the apoplast pathway is blocked at the endodermis cell layer by a waxy strip in the cell walls called the Casparian strip. The water then has to take the symplast pathway until it reaches the xylem.
    Be careful not to get the symplast and apoplast pathways mixed up — in the symplast pathway water moves through the cytoplasm.
Q3  The loss/evaporation of water from a plant's surface/leaves.
Q4  The movement of water from a plant's roots to its leaves.
Q5  Adhesion is where water molecules are attracted to the walls of the xylem vessels. It helps water rise up through the xylem vessels.

## 3. Transpiration
### Page 217 — Application Questions
Q1  B. E.g. there is a layer of hairs on the epidermis, which traps moist air around the stomata, reducing the water potential gradient between the leaf and the air, and slowing transpiration down. / The stomata are sunken in pits, which trap moist air, reducing transpiration by lowering the water potential gradient. / The leaf is curled, which traps moist air. This reduces the water potential gradient between the leaf and the air, slowing down transpiration. This also lowers the exposed surface area for losing water and protects the stomata from wind.
Q2  a) 10 °C — (15 + 12 + 14) ÷ 3 = **13.7 mm**
       20 °C — (19 + 16 + 19) ÷ 3 = **18.0 mm**
       30 °C — (25 + 22 + 23) ÷ 3 = **23.3 mm**
    b) See graph below. The bubble would move approximately 21 mm in 10 minutes at 25 °C.

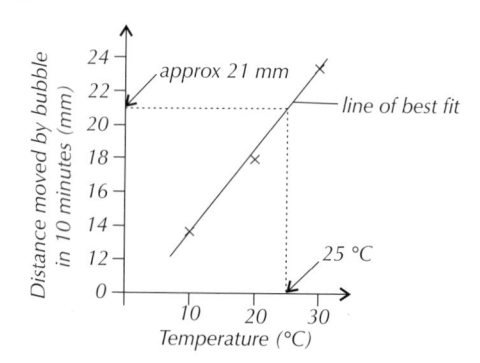

c) As the temperature increased, the distance moved by the bubble in 10 minutes increased too. This means the rate of transpiration increased with increasing temperatures. At higher temperatures water molecules have more energy so they evaporate from the cells inside the leaf faster. This increases the water potential between the inside and outside of the leaf, making water diffuse out of the leaf faster.

Q3 a) A hydrophyte because it lives in an aquatic habitat.
b) The stems may contain large air spaces to help the plant float. They may also be flexible because they are supported by the water around them, so they don't need rigid stems for support. Being flexible will also help to protect them from damage in strong water currents. The leaves may contain large air spaces to allow them to float, which increases the amount of light they receive. They may also have stomata on the upper surface of their leaves, which helps to maximise gas exchange, and be flexible (for the same reason as the stems).

## Page 217 — Fact Recall Questions
Q1 gas exchange/photosynthesis
Q2 An increase in wind increases transpiration rate. Lots of air movement blows away water molecules from around the stomata. This increases the water potential gradient, which increases the rate of transpiration.
Q3 E.g. light intensity, temperature and humidity.
Q4 That water uptake by a plant is directly related to water loss by the leaves.
Q5 Cacti have a thick, waxy layer on the epidermis — this reduces water loss by evaporation because the layer is waterproof (water can't move through it). They have spines instead of leaves — this reduces the surface area for water loss. Cacti also close their stomata at the hottest times of the day when transpiration rates are the highest.
Q6 e.g. water lilies

## 4. Translocation
## Page 220 — Application Questions
Q1 You would expect to see the sap flowing out more quickly near the leaves than at the bottom of the stem. This is because the pressure would be higher at the source (most likely the leaves), and lower towards the sink (most likely nearer the bottom of the plant).
Q2 The active loading of sucrose into the phloem requires ATP. ATP is needed to actively transport $H^+$ ions out of the companion cells into the surrounding tissue against their concentration gradient, which sets up a concentration gradient into the companion cells. $H^+$ ions then bind to a co-transport protein along with a molecule of sucrose. The movement of the $H^+$ ions down their concentration gradient is used to move sucrose into the companion cells against its concentration gradient. The same process occurs to move sucrose from the companion cells into the phloem tissue, where it is transported to the sink via translocation. A metabolic inhibitor would prevent this process from occurring so the process of active loading and translocation would stop.

## Page 220 — Fact Recall Questions
Q1 It's the movement of solutes/assimilates to where they're needed in a plant.
Q2 In a plant a source is where assimilates/solutes are made, whereas a sink is where assimilates/solutes are used up.

Q3 a) At the roots active transport is used to actively load solutes/assimilates into the sieve tubes. This lowers the water potential inside the sieve tubes, so water enters the tubes, from the xylem and companion cells, by osmosis.
*Remember, water always flows from a higher water potential to a lower water potential.*
b) At the sink solutes/assimilates are removed from the phloem to be used up. This increases the water potential inside the sieve tubes, so water leaves the tubes by osmosis.
Q4 The process used to move substances at the source into the companion cells from surrounding tissues, and from the companion cells into the sieve tubes, against a concentration gradient.

## Exam-style Questions — pages 222-223
1 C *(1 mark)*
The rate of water movement will decrease as it gets darker because the rate of transpiration will decrease (as the stomata close). Water is transported towards the xylem via osmosis, which is a passive process (so ATP is not needed). The water is moving by the apoplast pathway through the cell walls until it reaches the Casparian strip in the endodermis. Then it takes the symplast pathway through the cytoplasm. Water moves from an area of high water potential (in the roots) to an area of relatively lower water potential (in the leaves).

2 a) Y *(1 mark)*
b) The stem because, e.g. the xylem and phloem are distributed in a ring around the outside of the cross-section *(1 mark)*.
c) It helps support the walls of the xylem and stops them collapsing inwards *(1 mark)*. The spiral/ring pattern allows flexibility and prevents the stem from breaking *(1 mark)*.
d) Fig. 2.2 because there are lots of air spaces *(1 mark)*.
e) Any one from: e.g. stomata may only be present on the upper surface of floating leaves *(1 mark)*. / It may have flexible leaves/stems *(1 mark)*.

3 a) i) Reading off graph, distance moved by bubble in 5 minutes at 1.5 arbitrary units of light intensity
= 15 mm
15 ÷ 5 = **3 mm min$^{-1}$**
*(2 marks for the correct answer, otherwise 1 mark for showing a calculation of 'distance ÷ time')*
ii) The lighter it gets, the wider stomata open *(1 mark)*. This increases the rate at which water evaporates from the leaves, which creates more tension *(1 mark)*. The whole column of water moves up the xylem because water molecules are cohesive *(1 mark)*. The increased tension causes the water to move faster, meaning that the bubble moves further in a shorter amount of time *(1 mark)*.
b) E.g. the experiment should be repeated with a light intensity of zero *(1 mark)*.
c) E.g. when the stomata in a plant open to let carbon dioxide in / when stomata open for gas exchange *(1 mark)* this lets water move out down its water potential gradient *(1 mark)*.
d) The transpiration rate would not be as fast *(1 mark)* because with more water in the air, the water potential gradient between the air and the leaf would be lower *(1 mark)*.

4 a) i) Sieve plate *(1 mark)* — it allows sugars to pass from one sieve tube element to another / it connects cell cytoplasms *(1 mark)*.

ii) Cell B/the companion cell carries out the living functions for both itself and its sieve tube element *(1 mark)* because the sieve tube element can't survive on its own, e.g. it has no nucleus *(1 mark)*.
b) ATP is needed for the active loading of solutes/assimilates *(1 mark)*.
c) E.g. food storage organs *(1 mark)* / meristems/growth areas *(1 mark)*
d) **5-6 marks**
The answer identifies the pressure as being greater at the source end and explains the mechanism of translocation fully with correct reference to active loading, pressure gradients, water potential and osmosis.
The answer has a clear and logical structure. The information given is relevant and detailed.
**3-4 marks**
The answer identifies the pressure as being greater at the source end and partially explains the mechanism of translocation with some reference to active loading, pressure gradients, water potential and osmosis.
The answer has some structure. Most of the information given is relevant and there is some detail involved.
**1-2 marks**
The answer may identify the pressure as being greater at the source end and attempts to explain one aspect of the mechanism of translocation with partial reference to either active loading, pressure gradients, water potential or osmosis.
The answer has no clear structure. The information given is basic and lacking in detail. It may not all be relevant.
**0 marks**
No relevant information is given.
**Here are some points your answer may include:**
The pressure will be greatest at the source end. Active transport is used to actively load the solutes/assimilates into the sieve tubes of the phloem at the source end. Solutes/assimilates moving into the sieve tubes lowers the water potential inside the sieve tubes, so water enters the tubes from the xylem by osmosis. Water entering the sieve tubes creates a high pressure inside the sieve tubes at the source end of the phloem.
At the sink end, solutes/assimilates diffuse out of the phloem to be used up. The removal of solutes/assimilates increases the water potential inside the sieve tubes, so water leaves the tubes by osmosis. Water leaving the sieve tubes lowers the pressure inside the sieve tubes at the sink end. The result is a pressure gradient in the sieve tubes from the source to the sink end.

# Module 4

# Section 1 — Disease and the Immune System

## 1. Pathogens and Communicable Diseases

### Page 226 — Application Questions
Q1 a) E.g. an infected plant touching a healthy, but damaged plant / an infected plant growing from an infected seed.
b) E.g. by gardening tools / on a gardener's hands/gloves.
Q2 a) E.g. because they are closer together, so uninfected cattle are more likely to come into contact with an infected animal or spores.
b) indirect transmission
c) E.g. by washing hands and clothes after touching an infected cow or its environment / by wearing gloves while touching an infected cow or its environment.
Q3 Any two from: e.g. keep the person at home / increase ventilation in living spaces / person wears a mask (which will catch infected droplets) / monitor person's treatment (to make sure that the person is taking the antibiotics) / vaccinate people who are at increased risk of catching TB (as a longer term solution).
The spread of TB to the general public can also be controlled by isolating or quarantining people who are actively infected or suspected of being infected with the disease. It is usually enforced when the person is considered to be at high risk of spreading the disease and is only implemented in a minority of cases.

### Page 226 — Fact Recall Questions
Q1 An organism that causes disease.
Q2 A disease that can spread between organisms.
Q3 banana plant
Q4 fungus
Q5 potato/tomato late blight / malaria
Q6 E.g. droplet infection / sexual intercourse / touching an infected organism.
Q7 An intermediate organism that helps to transmit a disease from one organism to another.
Q8 People are less likely to be diagnosed and treated for HIV, and the most effective anti-HIV drugs are less likely to be available.
Q9 Those countries have the ideal climate for the malarial vectors (mosquitoes) to breed.

## 2. Defence Against Pathogens

### Page 229 — Application Questions
Q1 The mucous membranes in the lungs are coated in mucus, which traps the bacteria and contains antimicrobial enzymes that destroy the bacteria. These cells in the lung epithelium also have cilia that move the mucus up the trachea to the throat and mouth, so the bacteria are removed from the body.
Q2 The skin is a physical barrier against pathogens. When it is burnt, the barrier has been damaged, so bacteria that would not normally be able to enter the body are able to enter and cause disease.
Q3 To get to the sap, the aphids pierce the surface of the plant, which creates holes in its physical barriers against pathogens.

### Page 229 — Fact Recall Questions
Q1 It produces antimicrobial chemicals that can inhibit the growth of pathogens.
Q2 a mesh of protein/fibrin fibres
Q3 Increased tissue fluid isolates any pathogens that may be present and increased blood flow brings white blood cells to kill them.
Q4 E.g. a cough / sneeze
Q5 Any two from: e.g. waxy cuticle / cell wall / callose deposition
Q6 a) E.g. if the plant cell is stressed / infected.
b) Between the plasma membrane and cell wall, and at the plasmodesmata.
Q7 They inhibit the growth of pathogens.

## 3. The Immune System
### Page 233 — Application Questions
Q1  a) A = neutrophil
        B = monocyte
        C = red blood cell
    b) Neutrophils carry out phagocytosis.
Q2  With fewer T lymphocytes, fewer pathogens are killed directly. Also, with fewer T lymphocytes in the blood there are fewer cells to be activated by pathogen antigens presented by phagocytes. This means that fewer B lymphocytes are activated, so fewer antibodies are produced against the pathogens. With fewer antibodies, pathogens can survive longer in the body so opportunistic infections can cause problems.
Q3  Antibodies will be generated against antigens on the surface of *S. pyogenes*. These will then bind to antigens on the surface of heart cells because the antigens are so similar in shape. The immune system would then attack the heart cells and cause rheumatic fever.
*The command word in this question is 'suggest', so you're not expected to know the exact answer. You're expected to use what you know about the immune system to come up with a possible explanation.*

### Page 233 — Fact Recall Questions
Q1  The body's reaction to a foreign antigen.
Q2  Molecules found on the surface of cells.
Q3  Phagocytosis is the engulfment of pathogens.
Q4  A vesicle in the cytoplasm of a phagocyte (that contains engulfed pathogens).
Q5  It fuses with the phagosome and releases digestive enzymes that break down the (phagocytosed) pathogen.
Q6  cytokines
Q7  It presents the pathogen's antigens on its surface / becomes an antigen-presenting cell and the T lymphocytes that have complementary receptors to the presented antigens bind to them.
Q8  T helper cells release substances to activate B lymphocytes and T killer cells, T killer cells kill cells infected with a virus and T regulatory cells suppress the immune response from other white blood cells. Some activated T lymphocytes become memory cells. The function of plasma cells is to produce antibodies.
Q9  Phagocytosis → T-lymphocyte activation → B-lymphocyte activation and plasma cell production → Antibody production
Q10 E.g. T helper cells release interleukins that bind to receptors on B lymphocytes. This activates the B lymphocytes — the T helper cells are signalling to the B lymphocytes that there's a pathogen in the body.

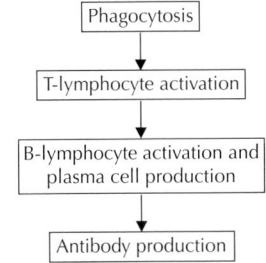

## 4. Antibodies
### Page 235 — Application Question
Q1  The anti-toxins bind to the toxins in the poison. This prevents the toxins from affecting human cells, so the toxins are neutralised (inactivated). The toxin-antibody complexes are then phagocytosed and destroyed.

### Page 235 — Fact Recall Questions
Q1  a) The variable region is complementary to a particular antigen and forms the antigen-binding site.
    b) The hinge region allows flexibility when an antibody binds to an antigen.
    c) The constant region allows the antibody to bind to receptors on immune system cells.
Q2  Antibodies have two antigen-binding sites. This is useful because it means that antibodies can bind to more than one pathogen at a time, so they can agglutinate the pathogens (clump them together).
Q3  Agglutinating groups of pathogens. Binding to and neutralising toxins produced by pathogens. Binding to receptors on pathogens and preventing them from entering host cells.

## 5. Primary and Secondary Immune Responses
### Page 237 — Application Questions
Q1  Mouse A had 10 units, Mouse B had 10 000 units.
Q2  Mouse B was already immune. You can tell this because the immune response was much quicker and stronger than the immune response of Mouse A.
Q3  a) Day 20
    b) The mouse's memory B lymphocytes rapidly divided and produced the antibody needed to bind to the antigen. The mouse's memory T lymphocytes rapidly divided into the correct type of T lymphocytes to kill the cell carrying the antigen.

### Page 237 — Fact Recall Questions
Q1  The primary response is slow because there aren't many T lymphocytes that can bind to the pathogen's antigens and there aren't many B lymphocytes that can make the right antibody to the antigens. The secondary response is faster because there are already memory T and B lymphocytes present that recognise the antigen and rapidly produce the right antibody to it.
Q2  Immunity doesn't always last forever because memory B and T lymphocytes have a limited lifespan. If the person is not exposed to the pathogen again, eventually all of the memory cells will die and the person will no longer be immune.
Q3  E.g. the primary response happens the first time a pathogen invades, the secondary response happens the second time a pathogen invades. / The primary response involves B and T lymphocytes, the secondary response involves memory cells. / There are symptoms with a primary response, but not with a secondary response.

## 6. Immunity and Vaccinations
### Page 241 — Application Questions
Q1  B
*A is an example of natural passive immunity, C is an example of natural active immunity and D is an example of artificial passive immunity.*
Q2  a) 75% (accept answers in the range of 74-76%)
    b) 1000 cases
    c) The number of cases decreased in a fluctuating pattern from a peak of around 6000 cases in the early 1960s to a peak of nearly 2000 cases around 1975. This is because more people were directly protected by the vaccine, and some people were protected by herd immunity.

Answers   597

## Page 241 — Fact Recall Questions

**Q1** Active immunity is the type of immunity you get when your immune system makes its own antibodies after being stimulated by an antigen.
Passive immunity is the type of immunity you get from being given antibodies made by a different organism — your immune system doesn't produce any antibodies of its own.

**Q2** a) A disease resulting from an abnormal immune response against the organism's own tissues.
b) The organism's immune system it isn't able to recognise certain self-antigens on the organism's cells / treats certain self-antigens on the cells as foreign antigens.

**Q3** The immune system attacking cells in the connective tissues.

**Q4** E.g. (rheumatoid) arthritis

**Q5** Vaccines contain substances that cause your body to produce memory cells against a particular pathogen. This makes you immune.

**Q6** Herd immunity is where unvaccinated people are protected because the occurrence of the disease is reduced by the number of people who are vaccinated.

**Q7** The influenza virus can change the antigens on its surface, so every year there are new strains of influenza circulating in the population.

## 7. Antibiotics and Other Medicines

## Page 244 — Application Questions

**Q1** D

**Q2** They are more likely to become infected with antibiotic-resistant bacteria and there are fewer antibiotics that are able to treat these infections.

**Q3** a) There was genetic variation in the *C. difficile* population that meant some of the bacteria had an allele that gave them resistance to fluoroquinolones. / A genetic mutation made some *C. difficile* more resistant to fluoroquinolones. This made them more likely to survive and reproduce in a host being treated with a fluoroquinolone. The bacteria passed the allele for fluoroquinolone resistance on to their offspring. Over time fluoroquinolone resistance became more common in the *C. difficile* population.
b) Patients who are already ill are more susceptible to infection because their immune systems are weakened. Hospitalised patients are also at risk because they are in an environment where lots of antibiotics are used, so *C. difficile* infections are more likely to be present.
Another factor here is that people who have recently been treated with antibiotics have lower amounts of harmless bacteria in their digestive systems, so there is more room for *C. difficile* to flourish.
c) Doctors should reduce their use of antibiotics / not prescribe them for minor infections or to prevent infections.
Patients should take all of the antibiotics they're prescribed to make sure the infection is fully cleared / all the bacteria have been killed.

## Page 244 — Fact Recall Questions

**Q1** Chemicals that kill or inhibit the growth of bacteria.
**Q2** penicillin
**Q3** e.g. MRSA (meticillin-resistant *Staphylococcus aureus*)
**Q4** a fungus

**Q5** Medicines that are tailored to an individual's DNA.
**Q6** The use of technology to design and make things such as artificial proteins, cells and even microorganisms.

## Exam-style Questions — pages 246-247

1  D *(1 mark)*
Malaria and tomato late blight are caused by a protoctist and ring rot is caused by a bacterium.

2  a) a bacterium *(1 mark)*
   b) i) The number of reported TB cases in the UK increased overall, from about 6750 cases in 2000 to about 9000 cases in 2009 *(1 mark)*.
      ii) 9000 − 7250 = 1750
          (1750 ÷ 7250) × 100 *(1 mark)* = **24.1%** *(1 mark)*
      iii) E.g. although the number of TB cases has risen by about 33% between 2000 and 2009, it doesn't necessarily mean this trend will continue *(1 mark)*. The graph shows the number of reported cases of TB, but the newspaper refers to the number of cases of TB — it may be that the reason for the increasing trend is just because more cases of TB are being reported (i.e. there's not an increase in overall number of cases) *(1 mark)*. The graph shows the number of reported cases of TB in the UK but the newspaper refers to the number of cases of TB in England, so this prediction doesn't fit the data shown in the graph *(1 mark)*.

Always read questions carefully — the introduction mentions that the graph shows the number of reported cases of TB in the UK. You'll miss this if you skim over the introduction and look at the graph first.

3  a) i) **5-6 marks:**
All of the stages of phagocytosis are described thoroughly and in the correct order.
The answer has a clear and logical structure.
The information given is relevant and detailed.
**3-4 marks:**
Some of the stages of phagocytosis are described and most of them are in order, but the answer is incomplete.
The answer has some structure. Most of the information given is relevant and there is some detail involved.
**1-2 marks:**
A few stages of phagocytosis are described briefly and not necessarily in the correct order.
The answer has no clear structure. The information given is basic and lacking in detail. It may not all be relevant.
**0 marks:**
No relevant information is given.
**Here are some points your answer may include:**
When a phagocyte recognises the antigens on a pathogen, the cytoplasm of the phagocyte moves around the pathogen, engulfing it. This may be made easier by the presence of opsonins — molecules in the blood that attach to foreign antigens to aid phagocytosis. The engulfed pathogen is contained in a phagosome inside the phagocyte. A lysosome fuses with the phagosome and the lysosomal enzymes from the lysosome break down the pathogen.
The phagocyte acts as an antigen-presenting cell by presenting the pathogen's antigens on its surface, in order to activate other immune system cells.

ii) They aid phagocytosis by attaching to foreign antigens *(1 mark)*.
iii) Receptors on the surface of T lymphocytes bind to the antigens presented by phagocytes, activating the T lymphocytes *(1 mark)*. When B lymphocytes, which are covered in antibodies, meet an antigen with a complementary shape they bind to it *(1 mark)*. This, along with substances released from T lymphocytes/ T helper cells, activates the B lymphocytes *(1 mark)*. The B lymphocytes then divide into plasma cells *(1 mark)*. The plasma cells then produce antibodies specific to the antigen *(1 mark)*.
b) After the first infection their B lymphocytes and T lymphocytes produced memory cells *(1 mark)*. When they were exposed for a second time these memory cells divided into plasma cells and the correct type of T lymphocytes to quickly destroy the virus *(1 mark)*.
c) The neuraminidase and haemagglutinin antigens on the Asian flu strain were different from the antigens on the Spanish flu strain *(1 mark)*, so any memory cells created against H1N1 would not detect H2N2 *(1 mark)*. So the immune system would have to start from scratch and carry out a primary immune response if exposed to Asian flu *(1 mark)*.

Make sure you use scientific terminology in your answer, e.g. 'antigens' and 'primary immune response'.

d) To make people immune to more than one strain of flu *(1 mark)*.

4   a) i) Vaccines contain substances (e.g. antigens or mRNA that codes for antigens) which activate T lymphocytes *(1 mark)*. The antigens and T lymphocytes activate B lymphocytes, some of which differentiate into memory B lymphocytes *(1 mark)*.
ii) They will benefit from herd immunity *(1 mark)*. If a large percentage of the population is vaccinated, then people who haven't been vaccinated are less likely to get the disease because there's no one to catch it from *(1 mark)*.
b) i) Variable region — forms the antigen-binding site *(1 mark)*.
Hinge region — allows flexibility when the antibody binds an antigen *(1 mark)*.
Constant region — allows binding to receptors on immune system cells *(1 mark)*.
ii)

| Agglutinating pathogens | ✓ |
| Killing pathogens directly | |
| Neutralising toxins | ✓ |
| Activating memory T lymphocytes | |
| Mutating pathogen DNA | |
| Stopping pathogens binding cells | ✓ |

*(1 mark for each correct answer, if more than three boxes are ticked remove 1 mark for each incorrect answer.)*

# Section 2 — Biodiversity
## 1. Investigating Biodiversity
### Page 253 — Application Questions
Q1 Any two from, e.g. she could sweep the net through the same depth of water. / She could make sure her net stays in the water for the same length of time for each sample. / She could take samples at the same time of day. / She could use the same net/type of net for each sample.

Standardise just means 'make the same' — so the question is asking for ways the environmental officer could collect each sample in the same way.

Q2 a) Pond A because the population sizes of the species are more similar than in pond B.
b) i) Pond A
$$D = 1 - \left(\left(\frac{3}{18}\right)^2 + \left(\frac{5}{18}\right)^2 + \left(\frac{2}{18}\right)^2 + \left(\frac{3}{18}\right)^2 + \left(\frac{1}{18}\right)^2 + \left(\frac{4}{18}\right)^2\right)$$
$$= \mathbf{0.802} \text{ (3 s.f.)}$$
ii) Pond B
$$D = 1 - \left(\left(\frac{13}{54}\right)^2 + \left(\frac{5}{54}\right)^2 + \left(\frac{7}{54}\right)^2 + \left(\frac{2}{54}\right)^2 + \left(\frac{18}{54}\right)^2 + \left(\frac{9}{54}\right)^2\right)$$
$$= \mathbf{0.776} \text{ (3 s.f.)}$$

If you have to calculate Simpson's Index of Diversity in the exam, always show your working out. You could pick up a mark for showing you understand the equation if nothing else.

c) Yes, because they both have a fairly high index of diversity. This means the populations are stable and capable of coping with change.

### Page 253 — Fact Recall Questions
Q1 a) The variety of living organisms in an area.
b) The area inhabited by a species.
c) A group of similar organisms able to reproduce to give fertile offspring.
Q2 Habitat diversity — the number of different habitats in an area. Species diversity — the number of different species (species richness) and the abundance of each species (species evenness) in an area. Genetic diversity — the variation of alleles within a species (or a population of a species).
Q3 a) It avoids bias in the results and makes it more likely that the sample is representative of the population as a whole.
b) E.g. If there's a lot of variety in the distribution of species in the habitat, you might want to make sure all the different areas in the habitat are sampled/all the different species in the habitat are sampled.
c) Systematic sampling, opportunistic sampling and stratified sampling.
Q4 a) The number of different species in an area.
b) It's a measure of the relative abundance of each species in an area.
Q5 The total number of organisms in one species.
The total number of all organisms.
Q6 That a habitat is highly diverse, making it stable and able to cope with change.

Answers    599

## 2. Genetic Diversity

### Page 255 — Application Questions

**Q1** a) proportion of polymorphic gene loci = number of polymorphic gene loci ÷ total number of loci
= 12 ÷ 80 = **0.15**
b) E.g. they could introduce gorillas from other zoos to breed with the existing population.
c) A population with a low genetic diversity might not be able to adapt to a change in the environment and the whole population could be wiped out by a single event (e.g. a disease).

**Q2** a) proportion of polymorphic gene loci = number of polymorphic gene loci ÷ total number of loci
= 66 ÷ 90 = 0.73...
percentage of genes with alleles = 0.73... × 100
= **73%** (2 s.f.)
b) proportion of polymorphic gene loci = 42 ÷ 90 = 0.46...
percentage of genes with alleles = 0.46... × 100
= **47%** (2 s.f.)
c) Species A, because it has a greater genetic diversity.

### Page 255 — Fact Recall Questions

**Q1** A locus that has two or more alleles.
**Q2** Take a sample of the genes in the population and work out what proportion or percentage of them are polymorphic.
**Q3** proportion of polymorphic gene loci = number of polymorphic gene loci ÷ total number of loci

## 3. Factors Affecting Biodiversity

### Page 258 — Application Question

**Q1** a) Sea surface temperature fluctuated around the average between 1950 and approximately 1978, then there was a steady increase between 1978 and 2000, up to just over 0.3 °C greater than the average. Subtropical plankton species were found in the sea south of the UK in 1958-1981. By 2000-2002 their distribution had moved further north along the west coast of the UK and Ireland to the Arctic Ocean.
b) The change in plankton distribution is correlated with the increase in sea surface temperature during the same period.
c) E.g. there could have been factors other than temperature involved, e.g. overfishing could have removed plankton predator species.
*Just because the difference in average temperature and the distribution of plankton have both changed over the same time period doesn't mean to say that one caused the other — there could be other factors involved. Remember, correlation and cause aren't the same thing (see page 23).*
d) E.g. biodiversity may have increased in the areas where the plankton moved to, as the plankton could have provided a new food source to support more marine organisms in those areas.

### Page 258 — Fact Recall Questions

**Q1** E.g. the need to develop more land for housing and to produce food leads to the destruction of habitats, which reduces biodiversity. / There is a greater demand for resources (such as food, water and energy). This means a lot of resources are being used up faster than they can be replenished, which can reduce both habitat and species diversity. / Sprawling cities and major road developments can isolate species, meaning populations are unable to interbreed and genetic diversity is decreased. / The increase in waste and pollution can kill species or destroy habitats, both of which decrease biodiversity.

**Q2** E.g. monoculture affects biodiversity because habitats are lost as land is cleared to make way for the large fields. There is also a loss of local and naturally occurring plants and animals as they are seen as weeds and pests, and so are destroyed with pesticides and herbicides, reducing species diversity. Heritage (traditional) varieties of crops are lost because they don't make enough money and so are not planted any more, which reduces species diversity.

## 4. Biodiversity and Conservation

### Page 261 — Application Question

**Q1** E.g. prairie dogs are a keystone species because they maintain the environment needed for the ecosystem. Their removal would disrupt food chains as several animals and birds of prey rely on them as a food source, and the numbers of these species may decline as a result.
The numbers of burrowing owls may also decline as they wouldn't have a supply of burrows in which to nest and lay eggs to produce more young. Plant growth would also be affected as the soil quality wouldn't be maintained and this may affect other species who rely on the plants for food.

### Page 264 — Application Question

**Q1** a) i) Any one from, e.g. both the Northern Quoll and its habitat are conserved which means that larger populations can be protected than with *ex situ* conservation. / *In situ* conservation is less disruptive than removing Northern Quoll from their habitats. / The chances of the Northern Quoll population recovering are greater than with *ex situ* methods.
ii) Any one from, e.g. it can be used to protect individual Northern Quolls in a controlled environment — things like predation and hunting can be managed more easily than in *in situ* conservation. / It's possible to reduce competition between Northern Quoll and other animals in *ex situ* conservation but not in *in situ* conservation. / It's easier to check on the health of Northern Quoll and treat them for diseases in *ex situ* than *in situ* conservation. / It's easier to manipulate breeding e.g. through the use of reproductive hormones and IVF, in *ex situ* than *in situ* conservation.
b) *In situ* conservation would involve eradicating the cane toads. Without the cane toads to eat the sugarcane pests, the yield of the sugarcane crops could fall, lowering farmers' income from the crop / forcing the farmers to spend more money on pesticides.

## Page 264 — Fact Recall Questions

**Q1** It's important to maintain biodiversity to protect species. Organisms in an ecosystem are interdependent — they depend on each other to survive. This means that the loss of just one species can have pretty drastic effects on an ecosystem, such as the disruption of food chains and the disruption of nutrient cycles. Protecting keystone species is particularly important as they often keep populations of prey in check and can also maintain the environment needed for the ecosystem. It is also important to maintain biodiversity to maintain genetic resources. We need to maintain genetic resources as they provide us with a variety of everyday products, such as food, drink, drugs and fuels. These products are important to the global economy as they are traded on a local and global scale. Genetic resources also allow us to adapt to changes in the environment.

**Q2**
a) E.g. to reduce soil depletion, so that crop yields don't decrease and spending on fertilisers doesn't need to increase.
b) E.g. to protect beautiful landscapes.

**Q3** The protection and management of species and habitats.

**Q4**
a) Conservation on site. / Protecting a species in its natural habitat.
b) Any two from: e.g. establishing protected areas such as national parks/wildlife reserves/marine conservation zones. / Controlling or preventing the introduction of species that threaten local biodiversity. / Protecting habitats. / Restoring damaged areas. / Promoting particular species. / Giving legal protection to endangered species.

**Q5**
a) Conservation off site. / Protecting a species by removing part of the population from a threatened habitat and placing it in a new location.
b) Any two from: e.g. relocating an organism to a safer area. / Breeding organisms in captivity/in animal sanctuaries/in zoos. / Growing plants in botanic gardens. / Storing plant seeds in seed banks.
c) Any one from e.g. usually only a small number of individuals can be cared for. / It can be difficult and expensive to create and sustain the right environment. / It is usually less successful than *in situ* methods as many species can't breed in captivity or don't adapt to their new environment when moved to a new location.

**Q6** An international agreement that aims to develop international strategies on the conservation of biodiversity and how to use animal and plant resources in a sustainable way.

**Q7** An agreement designed to increase international cooperation in regulating trade in wild animal and plant specimens.

**Q8** Any two from, e.g. regenerating hedgerows / leaving grassy margins around the edges of fields where wildflowers could grow / grazing upland areas to keep down bracken.

## Exam-style Questions — pages 266-267

1 B *(1 mark)*

2
a) The number of different species *(1 mark)* and the abundance of each species in an area *(1 mark)*.
b) Any two from, e.g. the sample was biased/not collected at random/the sample was only collected from one area *(1 mark)*. All the samples were collected on the same day/at the same time *(1 mark)*. / The student's method only collected insects that live on the ground *(1 mark)*.
c) Any one from, e.g. that one or two species dominate the habitat *(1 mark)*. / That insect diversity is low *(1 mark)*.
d) E.g. use the same sampling method/set up the pitfall traps in the same way *(1 mark)*.

3 *5-6 marks:*
The answer gives a detailed explanation of how climate change may affect the population of polar bears and makes several suggestions as to how, due to their role as a keystone species, this will affect the Arctic ecosystem.
The answer has a clear and logical structure.
The information given is relevant and detailed.
*3-4 marks:*
The answer describes how climate change may affect the population of polar bears and makes one or two suggestions as to how this might have a knock on effect on the Arctic ecosystem.
Most of the information given is relevant and there is some detail involved.
*1-2 marks:*
The answer suggests how climate change may affect the polar bears. An effect this may have on other Arctic organisms may be mentioned.
The answer has no clear structure. The information given is basic and lacking in detail. It may not all be relevant.
*0 marks:*
No relevant information is given.
**Here are some points your answer may include:**
Climate change includes global warming (the increasing global average temperature), which could cause the ice sheets to melt. This could reduce the overall area of the ice sheets/break up the ice sheets, leaving the polar bears a smaller area in which to hunt. This could make it harder for the bears to find food as a result. The lack of food could lead to a decrease in the number of polar bears/a change in their distribution. A decrease in the number of polar bears could mean fewer seals are eaten, causing the seal population to increase. This could have knock-on effects for the populations of organisms eaten by the seals. A decrease in the population of polar bears may also reduce the amount of food available for scavengers such as the Arctic fox and Arctic birds. These scavenger populations may also decrease as a result.

4
a) Wood
$$D = 1 - \left(\left(\frac{15}{101}\right)^2 + \left(\frac{18}{101}\right)^2 + \left(\frac{17}{101}\right)^2 + \left(\frac{19}{101}\right)^2 + \left(\frac{9}{101}\right)^2 + \left(\frac{8}{101}\right)^2 + \left(\frac{7}{101}\right)^2 + \left(\frac{8}{101}\right)^2 + \left(\frac{0}{101}\right)^2\right)$$
= **0.857** (3 s.f.)
*(2 marks for the correct answer, 1 mark for evidence of the correct calculation.)*
Town
$$D = 1 - \left(\left(\frac{1}{41}\right)^2 + \left(\frac{3}{41}\right)^2 + \left(\frac{2}{41}\right)^2 + \left(\frac{1}{41}\right)^2 + \left(\frac{1}{41}\right)^2 + \left(\frac{2}{41}\right)^2 + \left(\frac{20}{41}\right)^2 + \left(\frac{6}{41}\right)^2 + \left(\frac{5}{41}\right)^2\right)$$
= **0.714** (3 s.f.)
*(2 marks for the correct answer, 1 mark for evidence of the correct calculation.)*
b) Both areas have a relatively high index of diversity/an index of biodiversity close to 1 *(1 mark)*. This means that both areas have a relatively high biodiversity and so are likely to be fairly stable habitats that are able to withstand change *(1 mark)*.

c) Any two from: e.g. the red squirrels could be relocated to a safer area. / The red squirrels could be bred in captivity and reintroduced into the wild elsewhere. / The remaining woodland could be made a protected area.
*(1 mark for each correct answer up to a maximum of 2 marks.)*
*There are lots of possible right answers here — just apply your scientific knowledge to the situation and make two sensible suggestions.*

# Section 3 — Classification and Evolution

## 1. Classification Basics
### Pages 270-271 — Application Questions
Q1  a) sharks
    b) salamanders
    c) (i) crocodiles
       (ii) lizards
Q2

| Taxonomic Group | |
|---|---|
| Domain | Eukarya |
| Kingdom | Animalia |
| Phylum | Chordata |
| Class | Mammalia |
| Order | Perrisodactyla |
| Family | Equidae |
| Genus | Equus |
| Species | asinus |

### Page 271 — Fact Recall Questions
Q1  The act of arranging organisms into groups based on their similarities and differences.
Q2  Each species is given a two-part Latin name. The first part is the genus name and the second part is the species name.
Q3  Any three from, e.g. eukaryotic / multicellular / cell walls made of cellulose / can photosynthesise / contain chlorophyll / autotrophic.
Q4  The smallest group of organisms that shares a common ancestor.

## 2. The Evolution of Classification Systems
### Page 274 — Application Questions
Q1  Species A: TCGACGTGGGTAATCGAGC
    Species B: TCCACGTGTGTAATCGAGT
    Species C: ACGCCGAGTGTTATGGAGT
Q2  3
*Take your time with questions like this. Once you've got your answer, recount it to make sure it's right.*
Q3  7
Q4  Species B. There are fewer base differences in the DNA when comparing A and B than A and C.
Q5  Species B. There are only 6 base differences between species C and B. This is fewer than for species C and A, so species C and B are more likely to be closely related.

### Page 274 — Fact Recall Questions
Q1  You can compare the amino acid sequence of a particular protein that's shared between organisms. The more similar the amino acid sequence, the more closely related the species are likely to be.
Q2  In the three domain system, organisms with cells that contain a nucleus/eukaryotes are placed in the domain Eukarya. Organisms without a nucleus/prokaryotes are separated into two domains — Archaea and Bacteria.
Q3  Any one from, e.g. the RNA polymerase enzyme is different in Bacteria and Archaea. / Archaea have similar histones to Eukarya, but Bacteria don't. / The bonds of the lipids in the cell membranes of Bacteria and Archaea are different. / The development and composition of flagellae are different in Bacteria and Archaea.

## 3. Variation
### Page 277 — Application Question
Q1  a) continuous
    *Head circumference can take any value within a range, so it's continuous data. This indicates that head circumference is an example of continuous variation.*
    b) The mean difference in head circumference is approximately 0.5 cm for identical twins, 3 cm for non-identical twins and 8.5 cm for unrelated individuals. So the mean difference in head circumference is much larger for unrelated individuals than for either identical twins or non-identical twins.
    c) The data suggests that genetic factors have a larger effect on head circumference, because the mean difference in head circumference is much larger for unrelated individuals than for either identical twins or non-identical twins. However, the mean difference for identical twins wasn't zero, so environmental factors appear to play some role.
    d) The mean difference in the number of steps taken is between 800 and 900 for all three sample groups. Identical twins and non-identical twins show the lowest difference and unrelated individuals the highest but the margins are very small. This suggests that environmental factors play a more important role than genetic factors in determining activity level when measured by the number of steps taken per day.

### Page 277 — Fact Recall Questions
Q1  a) Variation within a species.
    b) Variation between different species.
Q2  Continuous variation is when the individuals in a population vary within a range — there are no distinct categories, e.g. height in humans. Discontinuous variation is when there are two or more distinct categories and each individual falls into only one of these categories — there are no intermediates, e.g. blood group in humans.
Q3  E.g. height in humans/plants / whether a microorganism grows a flagellum.

## 4. Investigating Variation

### Page 281 — Application Questions
Q1 a) i) The mean wing span is approximately 27 cm for species A and 31 cm for species B. Both curves follow a normal distribution. Species A has a higher standard deviation than species B.
ii) Species A, because it has a higher standard deviation.
iii) E.g. genetics, because species A and species B live in the same environment, so the difference in wing span is probably a result of genetic factors.
b) $(31 - 27) \div 27 \times 100 =$ **14.8%**

*Make sure you're confident at calculating percentages — they're a common mathsy-type question that examiners like to ask.*

Q2 Work out the mean length of snakes:
$\bar{x} = (177 + 182 + 190 + 187 + 191) \div 5 = 185.4$ cm
Work out $(x - \bar{x})^2$ for each snake length:
A = $(177 - 185.4)^2 = (-8.4)^2 = 70.56$,
B = $(182 - 185.4)^2 = (-3.4)^2 = 11.56$,
C = $(190 - 185.4)^2 = (4.6)^2 = 21.16$,
D = $(187 - 185.4)^2 = (1.6)^2 = 2.56$,
E = $(191 - 185.4)^2 = (5.6)^2 = 31.36$
Work out $\Sigma = (x - \bar{x})^2$:
$70.56 + 11.56 + 21.16 + 2.56 + 31.36 = 137.2$
Divide it by the number of values, n, minus 1:
$137.2 \div 4 = 34.3$
Square root it:
$\sqrt{34.3} =$ **5.86 to 3 s.f.**

### Page 283 — Application Question
Q1 a)

| Space per cow (km$^2$) | Rank | Average Daily Milk Yield (dm$^3$) | Rank | Difference between ranks (d) | d$^2$ |
|---|---|---|---|---|---|
| 0.004 | 8 | 32.1 | 8 | 0 | 0 |
| 0.005 | 7 | 36.2 | 5 | 2 | 4 |
| 0.006 | 6 | 37.4 | 3 | 3 | 9 |
| 0.007 | 5 | 34.3 | 6 | 1 | 1 |
| 0.008 | 4 | 36.7 | 4 | 0 | 0 |
| 0.009 | 3 | 38.9 | 1 | 2 | 4 |
| 0.010 | 2 | 37.6 | 2 | 0 | 0 |
| 0.011 | 1 | 33.4 | 7 | 6 | 36 |

$r_s = 1 - \dfrac{6\Sigma d^2}{n(n^2 - 1)}$

$r_s = 1 - \dfrac{6 \times (0 + 4 + 9 + 1 + 0 + 4 + 0 + 36)}{8 \times (8^2 - 1)}$

$r_s = 1 - \dfrac{6 \times 54}{8 \times 63}$

$r_s = 1 - \dfrac{324}{504}$

= **0.357** (3 s.f.)

b) Accepted, because the result is lower than the critical value of 0.738.

### Page 283 — Fact Recall Questions
Q1 Divide the total of all the values in your data by the number of values in your data.
Q2 Bell shaped
Q3 How much the values in a single sample vary / the spread of the values about the mean.

## 5. Adaptations

### Page 285 — Application Question
Q1 a) Light flexible wings = anatomical. Male bats make mating calls to attract females = behavioural. Bats lower their metabolism to hibernate over winter = physiological.
b) E.g. light, flexible wings — allow the bat to fly after insects, increasing its chances of catching prey and so surviving. Mating calls — increase the bat's chance of finding a mate and reproducing successfully. Hibernation — saves the bat's energy when food is scarce and so increases the bat's chances of surviving.

### Page 286 — Application Question
Q1 a) Anatomical
b) Both animals have evolved in similar environments to fill a similar ecological niche. Having opposable thumbs is beneficial for both types of animal because they both need to grip trees/branches. This means that individuals with opposable thumbs are more likely to survive and successfully reproduce, so the alleles responsible for the adaptation becomes widespread over generations.

### Page 286 — Fact Recall Questions
Q1 Because it increases the organism's chances of survival and successful reproduction
Q2 A process inside of an organism's body that increases its chance of survival.
Q3 Any five from: e.g. small or nonexistent eyes — because they don't need to be able to see underground. / No external ears — to keep the head streamlined for burrowing. / Scoop-shaped front paws — which are good for digging. / Powerful front paws — which are good for digging. / Specialised claws — which are specialised for digging. / Tube shaped body — which makes it easier to push through sand or soil. / Cone shaped head — which makes it easier to push through sand or soil.

## 6. The Theory of Evolution

### Page 289 — Application Questions
Q1 E.g. scientists could compare the amino acid sequence of cytochrome C in different organisms. Cytochrome C is present in almost all living organisms, so it suggests that we all evolved from a common ancestor. The more similar the amino acid sequence of cytochrome C in different organisms, the more recently the organisms are likely to have diverged away from one another.
Q2 Some individuals in the population had an allele for darker colouring that helped them to blend into their environment (wooded areas) better. This was beneficial because it helped them to avoid predators and sneak up on prey. So these individuals were more likely to survive, reproduce and pass on the allele for darker colouring. After some time most organisms in the population carried the allele for darker colouring.

*Whatever adaptation you're asked about in the exam, make sure you get the phrase, 'it helps the organism to survive, reproduce and pass on their alleles' into your answer.*

## Page 289 — Fact Recall Questions

**Q1** Any two from, e.g. organisms produce more offspring than survive. / There's variation in the characteristics of members of the same species. / Some characteristics can be passed on from one generation to the next. / Individuals that are best adapted to their environment are more likely to survive.

**Q2** Any environmental factor that creates a struggle for survival.

**Q3** (Alfred Russel) Wallace

**Q4** a) By arranging fossils in chronological (date) order, gradual changes in organisms can be observed that provide evidence of evolution.
b) Scientists can analyse DNA base sequences. The theory of evolution suggests that all living organisms evolved from a common ancestor, so organisms that diverged away from each other more recently should have more similar DNA than those that diverged less recently (as less time has passed for changes in the DNA sequence to occur).

## 7. More on Evolution
## Page 291 — Application Question

**Q1** a) There was variation in the *P. falciparum* population. Genetic mutations made some of the population naturally resistant to chloroquine. When the population was exposed to chloroquine, only the resistant *P. falciparum* survived to reproduce. The alleles for chloroquine resistance were then passed on to the next generation. Over many generations, the population evolved to become resistant to chloroquine.
b) i) E.g. it could take doctors longer to figure out which drugs will get rid of their malaria, during which time the patient could become very ill or die.
ii) E.g. it means that the drug companies have to keep developing more anti-malarial drugs, which takes time and costs money.

## Exam-style Questions — pages 293-294

**1** a)

| Domain | Archaea |
| --- | --- |
| Kingdom | Euryarchaeota |
| Phylum | Euryarchaeota |
| **Class** | Halobacteria |
| Order | Halobacteriales |
| **Family** | Halobacteriaceae |
| **Genus** | *Halobacterium* |
| Species | *salinarum* |

*(1 mark for each correct column)*

b) i) Any two from, e.g. no nucleus *(1 mark)* / unicellular *(1 mark)* / less than 5 µm *(1 mark)*
ii) Under the three domain system, organisms that would be in the Prokaryotae kingdom are split into two separate domains/Archaea and Bacteria *(1 mark)*. This is because of new evidence/molecular evidence that showed large differences between the two domains/Archaea and Bacteria *(1 mark)*.
iii) Any one from, e.g. the Protoctista/Plantae/Fungi/Animalia kingdom is present in both systems *(1 mark)*. / Four out of five kingdoms are present in both systems *(1 mark)*. / The hierarchy below domain (e.g. kingdom, phylum, class, order, family, genus, species) stays the same *(1 mark)*.

**2** a) E.g. he/she could analyse the DNA base sequences of the genes *(1 mark)*. The more similar the base sequences, the more closely related the plant species are likely to be *(1 mark)*.
b) It is present in all plants, so any two species of plant can be compared by looking at RuBisCO *(1 mark)*.
c) The amino acid sequences of the RuBisCO enzyme can be compared *(1 mark)*. The more similar the amino acid sequences are, the more closely related the plant species are likely to be *(1 mark)*.
d) E.g. scientists don't always agree on the relative importance of different features *(1 mark)*. Groups based solely on physical features may not show how closely related organisms are *(1 mark)*.

**3** a) i) At first, as the use of the pesticide increases, the number of aphids falls *(1 mark)*. After a period of time, the number of aphids plateaus and pesticide use increases less steeply *(1 mark)*. The number of aphids then begins to increase *(1 mark)*.
ii) E.g. the number of aphids fell as they were being killed by the pesticide *(1 mark)*. Random mutations may have occurred in the aphid DNA, resulting in pesticide resistance *(1 mark)*. Any aphids resistant to the pesticide were more likely to survive and pass on their alleles *(1 mark)*. Over many generations, the number of aphids increased as those carrying pesticide-resistant alleles became more common *(1 mark)*.
b) E.g. if the aphids are resistant to lots of other pesticides as well as this one, it might take the farmer a long time to find one that works *(1 mark)* — in that time the entire crop could be destroyed *(1 mark)*. / If the insects are resistant to specific pesticides, farmers might need to use broader pesticides *(1 mark)*, which might kill beneficial insects *(1 mark)*.

**4** a) i) A feature of an organism that increases its chances of survival and reproduction *(1 mark)* and also the chances of its offspring reproducing successfully *(1 mark)*.
ii) behavioural *(1 mark)*, physiological *(1 mark)*
b) Individuals within the *Anoura fistulata* population showed variation in their phenotypes due to differences in their alleles *(1 mark)*. The bats with longer tongues were more likely to survive, reproduce and pass on their alleles *(1 mark)*. Over time the number of individuals with a longer tongue increased *(1 mark)*. Over generations this led to evolution as the alleles that caused the longer tongue became more common in the population *(1 mark)*.

Always try to use the correct scientific language in your answers — here you should be talking about organisms passing on 'alleles', not 'features' or 'characteristics'.

c) *Anoura fistulata*'s DNA base sequence could be compared with the other species' DNA base sequence *(1 mark)*. Species that diverged away from each other more recently should have more similar DNA than those that diverged less recently *(1 mark)*. Also, *Anoura fistulata*'s other molecules, such as proteins/antibodies, could be compared with the other species' proteins/antibodies *(1 mark)*. Species that diverged away from each other more recently should also have more similar proteins/antibodies than those that diverged less recently *(1 mark)*.

# Module 5

## Section 1 — Communication and Homeostasis

### 1. Communication Basics

**Page 295 — Fact Recall Questions**
Q1  To increase their chances of survival.
Q2  E.g. to make sure that the activities of different organs are coordinated to keep the organism working effectively.
Q3  The way in which cells communicate with other cells.

### 2. The Nervous System

**Page 299 — Application Questions**
Q1  threshold level
Q2  a) B, because its generator potential reaches -60 mV/the threshold level.
    b) Approximately -87.5 mV (accept any value between -87 mV and -88 mV)
    *Make sure you always read the axes carefully — especially on graphs to do with potential differences across cell membranes, because they nearly always involve negative numbers.*

**Page 299 — Fact Recall Questions**
Q1  a) To transmit nerve impulses from receptors to the CNS.
    b) To transmit nerve impulses from the CNS to effectors.
    c) To transmit nerve impulses between sensory neurones and motor neurones.
Q2  A — dendrite, B — cell body, C — axon, D — axon terminal
Q3  E.g. any two from: the dendrites in a sensory neurone are further away from the cell body than they are in a motor neurone. / The axon in a sensory neurone is shorter than the axon in a motor neurone. / A sensory neurone has one long dendron whereas a motor neurone doesn't have a dendron. / Dendrites connect directly to the cell body in a motor neurone but not in a sensory neurone.
    *The questions asks for two structural differences, so you need to concentrate on the structure — not the function — of the different types of neurone.*
Q4  Receptor cells detect a stimulus. Sensory neurones transmit electrical impulses from the receptors to the CNS. The CNS processes the information, decides what to do with it and sends impulses along motor neurones to effectors, which respond.
Q5  Because they convert the energy of a stimulus into electrical energy. / Because they convert one form of energy into another.
Q6  When a stimulus is detected, the cell membrane is excited and becomes more permeable, allowing more ions to move in and out of the cell. This alters the potential difference across the cell membrane and therefore produces a generator potential.
Q7  A bigger stimulus excites the membrane more, causing a bigger movement of ions and a bigger change in potential difference, so a bigger generator potential is produced.
Q8  When a Pacinian corpuscle is stimulated, the lamellae are deformed and press on the sensory nerve ending. This causes deformation of stretch-mediated sodium channels in the sensory neurone's cell membrane. The sodium ion channels open and sodium ions diffuse into the cell, creating a generator potential. If the generator potential reaches the threshold, it triggers an action potential.

### 3. The Nervous Impulse

**Page 304 — Application Questions**
Q1  A — The neurone is stimulated.
    B — Depolarisation / Voltage-gated sodium ion channels are open and lots of sodium ions are diffusing into the neurone.
Q2  –40 mV
Q3  –60 mV
    *Remember to always include units in your answer when they're given on the graph.*
Q4  a) At a potential difference of +40 mV the sodium ion channels close and the potassium ion channels open. The membrane is more permeable to potassium so potassium ions diffuse out of the neurone down the potassium ion concentration gradient. This starts to get the membrane back to its resting potential. At the bottom of the curve the potassium ion channels are slow to close so there's a slight 'overshoot' where too many potassium ions diffuse out of the neurone. The potential difference (–70 mV) is more negative than the resting potential (–60 mV). The sodium-potassium pump then returns the membrane to its resting potential (–60 mV).
    b) refractory period
Q5  The action potential would have the same potential difference values as the graph shown because once the threshold is reached, an action potential will always fire with the same change in voltage, no matter how big the stimulus is. However, there may be another action potential shown on the graph because a bigger stimulus will cause action potentials to fire more frequently.

**Page 304 — Fact Recall Questions**
Q1  Sodium-potassium pumps and potassium ion channels.
    *Sodium ion channels are involved when a stimulus excites the neurone cells membrane but they're not involved in maintaining the resting membrane potential.*
Q2  Sodium ions diffuse into the neurone down the sodium ion electrochemical gradient. This makes the inside of the neurone less negative and so decreases the potential difference across the membrane.
Q3  a) More sodium ions diffuse into the neurone because sodium ion channels open.
    b) positive feedback
Q4  a) The ion channels are recovering and can't be made to open.
    b) It makes action potentials discrete/separate impulses. It makes action potentials unidirectional.

Q5  During an action potential, some of the sodium ions that enter the neurone diffuse sideways. This causes sodium ion channels in the next region of the neurone to open and sodium ions diffuse into that part. This causes a wave of depolarisation.

Q6  A myelinated neurone has a myelin sheath. The myelin sheath is made of a type of cell called a Schwann cell which is wrapped around the axon (and/or dendron). Between the Schwann cells are tiny patches of bare membrane called the nodes of Ranvier. Sodium ion channels are concentrated at the nodes of Ranvier.

Q7  In a myelinated neurone depolarisation/action potentials only happen at the nodes of Ranvier. However in a non-myelinated neurone, depolarisation/action potentials occur as a wave along the whole length of the axon membrane. Conduction along a myelinated neurone is faster than along a non-myelinated neurone.

Q8  Axon diameter and temperature.

## 4. Synapses

### Page 307 — Application Question
Q1  Carbachol mimics the action of ACh so the presence of carbachol will activate even more cholinergic receptors. This will make more action potentials fire in the postsynaptic neurone, so more saliva will be produced.

### Page 308 — Fact Recall Questions
Q1  a) The action potential stimulates voltage-gated calcium ion channels in the presynaptic neurone to open, so calcium ions diffuse into the synaptic knob.
    b) The influx of calcium ions into the synaptic knob causes the synaptic vesicles to fuse with the presynaptic membrane. The vesicles release ACh into the synaptic cleft. ACh diffuses across the synaptic cleft and binds to specific cholinergic receptors on the postsynaptic membrane. This causes sodium ion channels in the postsynaptic neurone to open. If the threshold is reached, the influx of sodium ions into the postsynaptic neurone causes an action potential on the postsynaptic membrane.

Q2  a) Information from one neurone can be dispersed to different areas of the body (as one neurone connects to many neurones).
    b) Information from many neurones can be amplified (as many neurones connect to one neurone).

Q3  a) Where two or more presynaptic neurones converge and release their neurotransmitters at the same time onto the same postsynaptic neurone, the small amount of neurotransmitter released from each of these neurones can be enough altogether to reach the threshold in the postsynaptic neurone. This makes an action potential more likely.
    b) Where two or more nerve impulses arrive in quick succession from the same presynaptic neurone, more neurotransmitter is released into the synaptic cleft. This makes an action potential more likely.

## Exam-style Questions — pages 309-310

1  a) i) Action potentials have a refractory period *(1 mark)*. During this period the ion channels are recovering and can't be made to open *(1 mark)*. This means that no more sodium ions can diffuse into the neurone to trigger another action potential *(1 mark)*.
      ii) There are 5 action potentials in 20 ms.
          500 ms ÷ 20 ms = 25. So 5 x 25 = **125 action potentials**.
          *(2 marks for correct answer, otherwise 1 mark for correct working.)*
   b) i) *5-6 marks:*
         The answer correctly identifies the stages of the action potential at each time and explains fully what is happening during those stages, including the movement of specific ions across the membrane. The answer has a clear and logical structure. The information given is relevant and detailed.
         *3-4 marks:*
         The answer correctly identifies the stages of the action potential at each time and explains briefly what is happening during those stages.
         The answer has some structure. Most of the information given is relevant and there is some detail involved.
         *1-2 marks:*
         The answer includes a basic explanation of at least one stage of an action potential. The answer has no clear structure. The information given is basic and lacking in detail. It may not all be relevant.
         *0 marks:*
         No relevant information is given.
         **Here are some points your answer may include:**
         Time 1 shows repolarisation because the sodium ion channels are closed and the potassium ion channels are open. The membrane is more permeable to potassium so potassium ions diffuse out of the neurone down their concentration gradient.
         Time 2 shows hyperpolarisation/the refractory period because both the sodium and potassium ion channels are closed. There is no movement of sodium or potassium through their ion channels (by facilitated diffusion).

   *If a question tells you to 'use evidence' from a source (like a diagram, graph, table, etc.) this means you need to include figures or descriptions from the source. So in this case, you need to say which ion channels are open and closed in the diagram.*

      ii) Sodium-potassium pumps use active transport *(1 mark)* to move three sodium ions out of the cell *(1 mark)* for every two potassium ions moved in *(1 mark)*.
      iii) The potassium ion channel is slow to close so too many potassium ions diffuse out of the neurone *(1 mark)*. The potential difference is more negative than the neurone cell membrane's resting potential, so the pump returns the membrane to its resting potential *(1 mark)*.

c) Sodium ions won't be able to diffuse into the neurone through voltage-gated sodium ion channels *(1 mark)*. This means that the neurone won't be depolarised so there will be no action potentials/no nervous impulses *(1 mark)*.

2  a) i) Schwann cell *(1 mark)*
   ii)

| | Structure | Function |
|---|---|---|
| B | axon | Carries nerve impulses from the cell body to effector cells / axon terminal. |
| C | dendrites | Carry nerve impulses from the central nervous system to the cell body. |

*(1 mark for each correct answer)*
The diagram shows a <u>motor neurone</u>, so dendrites carry information <u>from the CNS</u>.

b) i) To transmit nerve impulses from receptors to the central nervous system *(1 mark)*.
   ii) To transmit nerve impulses between sensory neurones and motor neurones *(1 mark)*.

c) Conduction of nervous impulses in non-myelinated neurones is slower than in myelinated neurones *(1 mark)*. If the myelin is damaged then the nerve impulse may be conducted much more slowly or not at all, resulting in muscle weakness or paralysis *(1 mark)*.

3  a) The action potential arrives in the synaptic knob of the motor neurone and stimulates voltage-gated calcium ion channels to open *(1 mark)*. Calcium ions diffuse into the synaptic knob *(1 mark)* and cause the synaptic vesicles to fuse with the presynaptic membrane *(1 mark)*. The vesicles release acetylcholine (ACh) into the synaptic cleft by exocytosis *(1 mark)*.

b) i) (temporal) summation *(1 mark)*
   ii) More neurotransmitter/ACh will be released into the synaptic cleft *(1 mark)*. This means more neurotransmitter/ACh will bind to receptors on the postsynaptic membrane/muscle cell *(1 mark)*. This causes more sodium ion channels to open *(1 mark)* and a greater influx of sodium ions *(1 mark)*, which makes the muscle cell more likely to reach threshold and fire an action potential *(1 mark)*.

c) Tubocurarine prevents ACh from binding to the cholinergic receptors *(1 mark)*. This means sodium ion channels on the muscle cell do not open *(1 mark)* so there's no influx of sodium ions into the muscle cell *(1 mark)*. No action potentials can be fired so the muscles cannot be stimulated to contract/move *(1 mark)*.

## 5. The Hormonal System and Glands

### Pages 313-314 — Application Questions
Q1

| Molecule / Structure | Name |
|---|---|
| Hormone | Oxytocin |
| Target cells | Myoepithelial cells |
| Target tissue | Epithelial tissue |
| Endocrine gland | Posterior pituitary gland |

Q2  E.g. because oxytocin has to travel in the blood to the target cells, which may take several minutes.

### Page 314 — Fact Recall Questions
Q1  A group of cells that is specialised to secrete hormones.
Q2  A change in concentration of a specific substance/another hormone, electrical impulses.
Q3  Each hormone will only bind to specific receptors for that hormone, found on the membranes of target cells.
Q4  a) cyclic AMP/cAMP
    b) It activates a cascade of enzyme reactions to make more glucose available to the cell by catalysing the breakdown of glycogen into glucose.
    c) adrenaline
Q5  a) The outer part is called the cortex and the inner part is called the medulla.
    b) The medulla secretes catecholamine hormones, such as adrenaline and noradrenaline. These act to make more energy available in the short-term by increasing heart and breathing rate, causing cells to break down glycogen into glucose and constricting some blood vessels so that blood is diverted to the brain and muscles.
Q6  a) islet of Langerhans
    b) i) glucagon
       ii) insulin

## 6. Homeostasis Basics

### Page 317 — Application Questions
Q1  A is an example of negative feedback because increasing respiration rate will increase the rate at which carbon dioxide is removed from the body. This will increase the pH of the blood back to the normal level. B is an example of positive feedback because more oestrogen being released will increase the levels of LH further and amplify the change.

Q2  a) i) At point A low concentrations of calcium in the blood are detected. This stimulates the secretion of PTH, which travels in the blood to effectors.
At point B effectors are responding by increasing the concentration of calcium in the blood.
   ii) At point C high concentrations of calcium in the blood are detected. This stimulates the secretion of calcitonin which travels in the blood to effectors.
At point D effectors are responding by decreasing the concentration of calcium in the blood.

b) The concentration of calcium in the blood may fall very low. This is because less PTH will be released to bring the levels back up to normal.

## Page 317 — Fact Recall Questions

**Q1** The maintenance of a constant internal environment.
**Q2** So that metabolic reactions can occur at an optimum rate. Low temperatures make metabolic reactions slower, but if the temperature gets too high the reaction essentially stops.
**Q3** A — receptors detect change, B — communication via hormonal or nervous system, C — effectors respond.
**Q4** A positive feedback mechanism amplifies a change from the normal level, whereas a negative feedback mechanism restores the level to normal.

# 7. Control of Body Temperature

## Pages 318-319 — Application Questions

**Q1** a) The external temperature was low/it was cold because the snake is an ectotherm and appears dark/is not radiating any heat/is cold.
b) The mouse because it's warmer than the snake, meaning it has more energy available (from metabolic reactions) for activity.
**Q2** a) The internal temperature of the chuckwalla increases as the external temperature increases. This suggests that the chuckwalla is an ectotherm as its internal temperature depends on the external temperature. The internal temperature of the hoatzin stays roughly the same as the external temperature increases. This suggests that the hoatzin is an endotherm as it can control its internal body temperature by homeostasis.
b) The chuckwalla because its internal temperature varied the most, meaning its metabolic reactions would have been most disrupted.

*Remember, metabolic reactions are controlled by enzymes and enzyme activity is greatest at an optimum temperature. Any variation from the optimum temperature will reduce enzyme activity and therefore slow down metabolic reactions.*

## Page 321 — Application Questions

**Q1** The hot water in the bath heats up the temperature of the skin. Thermoreceptors in the skin detect body temperature is too high and send impulses to the hypothalamus. The hypothalamus then sends impulses to the arterioles near the surface of the skin causing them to dilate. More blood then flows through the capillaries in the surface layers of the dermis so more heat is lost by radiation and the body temperature is lowered. The increased blood flow in the capillaries might make the skin appear pink.
**Q2** A cold external environment. When internal body temperature falls the body's responses include shivering and increased release of adrenaline and thyroxine. These mechanisms increase the rate of metabolism, which means more glucose is used. Blood glucose concentration will fall, so feelings of hunger will occur more quickly than they would do in a hot environment.
**Q3** In hot weather the internal body temperature rises. Normally one of the ways the body responds to this is by vasodilation to increase heat loss. However, cocaine causes the opposite effect — vasoconstriction. This will reduce heat loss so the internal temperature will remain high. Also, an increase in muscular activity will increase respiration, so more heat will be produced. This will increase the internal body temperature further and make the person at risk of hyperthermia.

## Page 321 — Fact Recall Questions

**Q1** a) By changing behaviour.
b) Internally by homeostasis as well as by changing behaviour.
**Q2** Ectotherms have a variable metabolic rate and endotherms have a constantly high metabolic rate.
**Q3** When the body's too hot sweat glands secrete more sweat. The water in sweat evaporates from the surface of the skin and takes heat from the body so the skin is cooled. When the body's too cold sweat glands secrete much less sweat, reducing the amount of heat lost.

*In this question you need to write about how sweat glands help the body lose heat and how they help it to conserve heat.*

**Q4** Muscles in the body contract in spasms when it's cold. This makes the body shiver and more heat is produced from increased respiration. The hormones adrenaline and thyroxine are released, which increases metabolism, so more heat is produced.
**Q5** They constrict.
**Q6** The hypothalamus.
**Q7** Thermoreceptors in the skin/peripheral temperature receptors detect external/skin temperature and send impulses via sensory neurones to the brain/hypothalamus.
**Q8** When thermoreceptors detect body temperature is too low, they send impulses to the hypothalamus, which sends impulses to effectors. Effectors respond to decrease heat loss from the body and increase heat production so body temperature returns to normal.

# 8. Control of Blood Glucose Concentration

## Page 323 — Application Questions

**Q1** It will increase blood glucose concentration.
*Remember, glycogenolysis is the process of breaking down glycogen into glucose. So when this process is activated, blood glucose concentration increases.*
**Q2** Carbohydrates are broken down into glucose, so their blood glucose concentration will increase. When the pancreas detects the blood glucose concentration is too high, the β cells will secrete insulin and the α cells will stop secreting glucagon. Insulin will then bind to receptors on liver and muscle cells (the effectors). These cells will respond by taking up more glucose, activating glycogenesis and by respiring more glucose. Blood glucose concentration will then return to normal.
**Q3** Glycogenolysis and gluconeogenesis both increase blood glucose concentration. If these processes don't work properly then when blood glucose concentration falls (i.e. if the person doesn't eat regularly) the body will be unable to raise the blood glucose concentration back to normal, so the person will suffer from hypoglycaemia.

## Page 326 — Application Questions

**Q1** The person with Type 2 diabetes doesn't produce as much insulin as the person without diabetes. / The body's cells don't respond properly to the insulin that's produced. Insulin lowers blood glucose concentration when it's too high, so if there's not enough insulin/the body can't respond to insulin properly, this process will be much slower.

**Q2** A person with Type 1 diabetes wouldn't produce any insulin. This means that blood glucose concentration would remain high for much longer than for the person with Type 2 diabetes.

**Q3** 22.5 minutes. This is because this is the time when the blood glucose concentration is at its upper limit / 110 mg per 100 cm$^3$.
*You're told the normal range for blood glucose concentration in the introduction to the question — make sure you always read questions thoroughly in the exam.*

**Q4** Insulin is a hormone, so it takes time to travel in the blood to receptor cells.

**Q5** When blood glucose concentration falls below 82 mg per 100 cm$^3$ the pancreas is stimulated to secrete glucagon and stop secreting insulin. Glucagon binds to specific receptors on liver cells. The liver cells respond to increase blood glucose concentration — glycogenolysis is activated, gluconeogenesis is activated and the cells respire less glucose.

## Page 327 — Fact Recall Questions

**Q1** It increases the permeability of liver and muscle cell membranes to glucose, activates enzymes that convert glucose into glycogen/activates glycogenesis and increases the rate of respiration of glucose in those cells.

**Q2** glycogenesis

**Q3** Gluconeogenesis — fatty acids or amino acids are converted to glucose. Glycogenolysis — glycogen is converted to glucose.

**Q4** a) The potassium ion channels are open and the calcium ion channels are closed.
b) The potassium ion channels close and the calcium ion channels open.

**Q5** a) It is an auto-immune disease, in which the body attacks and destroys the β cells in the islets of Langerhans.
b) For most people with Type 1 diabetes insulin therapy involves having regular insulin injections throughout the day. For some people it involves using an insulin pump — a machine that continuously delivers insulin into the body via a tube inserted beneath the skin.
c) Type 1 diabetes can be treated by having islet cell transplantation. This involves receiving healthy islet cells from a donor so the person's pancreas can produce some insulin (although they usually still need some additional insulin therapy).

**Q6** Type 2 diabetes is initially managed through lifestyle changes, such as eating a healthy, balanced diet, getting regular exercise and losing weight if needed. If blood glucose concentration can't be controlled through lifestyle changes alone, then medication may be prescribed. In some people with Type 2 diabetes, these types of medication are not enough to control blood glucose concentration so insulin therapy is used in addition or instead.

**Q7** Any three from: e.g. producing insulin using GM bacteria is cheaper than extracting it from animal pancreases. / Larger quantities of insulin can be produced using GM bacteria. / GM bacteria make human insulin, which is more effective than animal insulin and less likely to trigger an allergic response or be rejected by the immune system. / Some people prefer insulin from GM bacteria for ethical or religious reasons.

**Q8** Stem cells could be grown into β cells which would then be implanted into the pancreas of a person with Type I diabetes. This means the person would be able to make insulin as normal.

## Exam-style Questions — pages 330-331

1   B *(1 mark)*
Eating a healthy balanced diet will reduce the amount of insulin that a person with Type 1 diabetes needs to inject but, as they cannot produce insulin, it won't control the diabetes by itself.

2   a) adrenal medulla *(1 mark)*
b) Adrenaline binds to specific receptors in the cell membrane *(1 mark)*, which activates an enzyme/adenylyl cyclase in the cell membrane *(1 mark)*. The activated enzyme/adenylyl cyclase catalyses the production of cyclic AMP/cAMP from ATP *(1 mark)*, which triggers a cascade.
c) i) glycogenolysis *(1 mark)*
ii) glucagon *(1 mark)*

3   a) A mechanism that restores a level back to normal in a system *(1 mark)*.
b) i) β cell *(1 mark)*
ii) The person will have had a high blood glucose concentration, which caused more glucose to enter the β cell by facilitated diffusion *(1 mark)*, which increased the respiration rate and caused more ATP to be made *(1 mark)*. The rise in ATP triggered the potassium ion channels to close *(1 mark)*.
iii) The build up of potassium ions inside the cell depolarises the cell membrane *(1 mark)*. This triggers the calcium ion channels in the cell membrane to open *(1 mark)*. Calcium ions diffuse into the cell *(1 mark)*, which causes the vesicles to move to and fuse with the cell membrane and release insulin by exocytosis *(1 mark)*.
c) Glycogenesis is the process of forming glycogen from glucose *(1 mark)*.

4   a) As the temperature increases the activity level of Organism A increases, and as the temperature decreases the activity level of Organism A decreases / there is a positive correlation between the activity level of Organism A and temperature *(1 mark)*. The activity level of Organism B changes randomly as the temperature changes / there is no correlation between the activity level of Organism B and temperature *(1 mark)*.
b) i) Organism A because an ectotherm is more active in warmer external temperatures than it is in colder temperatures *(1 mark)*.
ii) Squirrels are endotherms so they can control their body temperature internally by homeostasis *(1 mark)*. This means their internal temperature is much less affected by external temperature compared to tortoises, so they can survive in a wider range of external temperatures *(1 mark)*.

c) i) Point X was relatively cold, so thermoreceptors/ peripheral temperature receptors in the squirrel's skin will have detected the low temperature *(1 mark)*. The thermoreceptors/peripheral temperature receptors will have sent impulses to the hypothalamus *(1 mark)* which will have sent impulses to erector pili muscles/ effectors to make the hairs stand up *(1 mark)* to trap more air and so prevent heat loss *(1 mark)*.

ii) Any two from: e.g. more sweat may be secreted from the squirrel's sweat glands *(1 mark)*. When the sweat evaporates it will take heat from the body so the skin is cooled *(1 mark)*. / The squirrel's erector pili muscles may relax so its hairs lie flat *(1 mark)*. This means less air is trapped, so the skin is less insulated and heat can be lost more easily *(1 mark)*. / Vasodilation may occur near the surface of the squirrel's skin *(1 mark)*. This means more heat is lost from the skin by radiation so the temperature of the skin is lowered *(1 mark)*. *(Maximum of 4 marks available.)*

# Section 2 — Excretion

## 1. The Liver and Excretion

### Page 336 — Application Questions

Q1 a) The level of argininosuccinate in the blood would be low. This is because argininosuccinate would still be used up in the cycle but there would be a lack of AS to convert citrulline to more argininosuccinate.
b) The level of citrulline would be high. This is because citrulline would still be made in the cycle but it would not be converted to argininosuccinate, so it would build up in the blood.

Q2 The proteins that we eat are made up of amino acids, which contain nitrogenous substances. Via deamination, these nitrogenous substances enter the ornithine cycle in the form of ammonia. If a person suffering from AS deficiency eats a low protein diet then fewer excess amino acids will be produced by digestion, so less ammonia will enter the ornithine cycle.

### Page 336 — Fact Recall Questions

Q1 The removal of the waste products of metabolism from the body.
Q2 e.g. carbon dioxide, nitrogenous waste
Q3 Excretion helps to keep the levels of certain substances in the blood roughly constant by removing the waste products of metabolism.
Q4 The duodenum and the ileum / the small intestine.
Q5 the hepatic vein
Q6 The capillaries that connect the hepatic artery and the hepatic portal vein to the central vein in the liver.
Q7 X — central vein, Y — sinusoids
Q8 First, the nitrogen-containing amino groups (–NH$_2$) are removed from any excess amino acids, forming ammonia (NH$_3$) and organic acids. This process is called deamination. Ammonia is then combined with CO$_2$ in the ornithine cycle to create urea (and water).
Q9 It is the process in which harmful substances, such as excess hormones/alcohol/drugs/excess insulin, are broken down by the liver into less harmful substances so they can be excreted.
Q10 The liver converts excess glucose to glycogen via glycogenesis and stores it as granules in its cells.

## 2. The Kidneys and Excretion

### Page 341 — Application Questions

Q1 A — Bowman's capsule
B — loop of Henle
C — distal convoluted tubule/DCT
D — ureter

Q2 a) X — basement membrane
Y — epithelium / podocyte
b) E.g. the structure of the barrier normally prevents larger molecules such as proteins from entering the tubules. If its structure is affected, large molecules such as proteins may be able to pass into the tubules and eventually end up in the urine, producing proteinuria.

### Page 341 — Fact Recall Questions

Q1 a) afferent arteriole
b) Bowman's capsule
c) Because vessel A/the afferent arteriole is larger in diameter than vessel B/the efferent arteriole, the blood in the glomerulus is under high pressure. The high pressure forces liquid and small molecules in the blood out of the capillary and into the Bowman's capsule (ultrafiltration).
*If you're struggling to remember the difference between the afferent and efferent arterioles, think afferent comes first, because it's first alphabetically.*

Q2 Any three from: e.g. glucose / amino acids / vitamins / salts / urea / water.
Q3 X — renal capsule, Y — renal pyramid / medulla, Z — renal calyx / renal pelvis
Q4 a) The wall of the artery will be thicker than the wall of the vein. The ureter is likely to have the most adipose (fatty) tissue round it.
b) You would expect to see the cone-shaped renal pyramids, which would probably appear stripy.

## 3. The Kidneys and Water Potential

### Page 344 — Application Questions

Q1 a) The runner is dehydrated because he has sweated a lot and not replaced any of the fluids he has lost. This has caused his blood water content/potential to drop.
b) The low water potential of the runner's blood is detected by osmoreceptors in his hypothalamus.
c) ADH molecules bind to receptors on the plasma membranes of cells of the runner's distal convoluted tubule/DCT and collecting duct. When this happens, protein channels called aquaporins are inserted into the plasma membrane. These channels allow water to pass through via osmosis, so make the walls of the DCT and collecting duct more permeable to water. This allows water to be reabsorbed from these tubules into the medulla and into the blood by osmosis, therefore conserving water in the runner's body.

d) The presence of sodium (Na⁺) and chloride (Cl⁻) ions in the sports drink increases the concentration of Na⁺ and Cl⁻ in the runner's filtrate. These ions are used to lower the water potential of the medulla in the loop of Henle in order to create a water potential gradient to drive the reabsorption of water back into the blood by osmosis.

*Make sure you understand water potential. If you don't, it makes understanding the regulation of water content by the kidneys pretty tricky. Remember, high water potential means a high concentration of water molecules and low water potential means a low concentration of water molecules. Water moves from a region of higher water potential to a region of lower water potential — from where there are more water molecules to where there are fewer.*

Q2 a) Normally if a person has consumed too much fluid, the osmoreceptors in the hypothalamus detect that the water content of the blood, and so its water potential, has risen. This causes the posterior pituitary gland to release less ADH into the blood. Less ADH means that the DCT and collecting duct are less permeable, so less water is reabsorbed into the blood by osmosis. This causes a large amount of dilute urine to be produced and so more water is lost.

b) If the body can't suppress ADH production, the DCT and collecting duct will continue to be made permeable, so water is reabsorbed into the blood by osmosis. This means that the excess water is not excreted and therefore accumulates, potentially affecting the balance of fluid in cells.

## Page 344 — Fact Recall Questions
Q1 the ascending limb
Q2 A longer ascending limb allows more ions to be actively pumped out into the medulla, which creates a really low water potential in the medulla. This means more water moves out of the nephron and collecting duct into the capillaries, giving very concentrated urine.

## 4. Kidney Failure

## Page 347 — Application Questions
Q1 a) In order to maintain a steep concentration gradient between the two fluids. This increases the rate of diffusion of waste products and excess water and ions across the membrane out of the blood and into the dialysis fluid.
b) E.g. the patient will have to undergo a major operation, which is risky. / The patient's immune system may reject the transplant.

Q2 a) If there is 0 mg of glucose in the urine, all the glucose filtered out of the blood must be reabsorbed. So:
5200 × 0.9 = 4680 mg hour⁻¹
4680 ÷ 60 = **78 mg min⁻¹**
b) e.g. kidney failure / kidney infection / high blood pressure

## Page 347 — Fact Recall Questions
Q1 It can be detected by measuring the glomerular filtration rate (GFR)/rate at which blood is filtered from the glomerulus into the Bowman's capsule.
Q2 Kidney infections can cause inflammation of the kidneys. This can damage the cells and create problems with reabsorption.
Q3 Any two from: e.g. waste products that the kidneys would normally remove begin to build up in the blood. / Fluid starts to accumulate in the tissues. / The balance of electrolytes (ions) in the body becomes unbalanced. / Long-term kidney failure can cause anaemia.
Q4 During haemodialysis, blood is passed through a dialysis machine. Blood flows on one side of a partially permeable membrane and dialysis fluid flows on the other side. The blood and dialysis fluid flow in opposite directions, which creates a concentration gradient. This means that waste products, excess water and electrolytes diffuse out of the blood into the dialysis fluid, restoring the balance of electrolytes in the blood.
Q5 Any two from: e.g. there's a risk of infection around the tube. / The patient has to have dialysis everyday, which can be inconvenient. / It can be an expensive treatment option.

## 5. Detecting Chemicals

## Page 349 — Application Questions
Q1 Test strips use antibodies which are specific to different molecules/drugs and so only bind to a particular type of molecule/drug.
Q2 a) Codeine may have a similar structure to opiates or the breakdown products of opiates and so would bind to the same antibodies.
b) The urine sample could be analysed using gas chromatography/mass spectrometry / GC/MS. This would determine whether the molecule producing the positive result was codeine or an illegal opiate.

## Page 349 — Fact Recall Questions
Q1 human chorionic gonadotropin (hCG)
Q2 white / it won't change colour
*Remember, the test strip will only change colour in a positive pregnancy test (when hCG is present).*
Q3 a) gas chromatography/mass spectrometry / GC/MS
b) In gas chromatography the urine sample is vaporised and passed through a column containing a polymer. Different substances move through the column at different speeds, so substances in the urine sample separate out. The mass spectrometer converts them into ions, then separates the ions depending on their mass and charge. The results are analysed by a computer and the substances are identified by comparing them to the results of known substances.

## Exam-style Questions — pages 351-352

1. **D** *(1 mark)*
The urine of pregnant women contains the hormone human chorionic gonadotropin (hCG). This binds to monoclonal antibodies on the application area of the test stick, which are attached to coloured beads. As the urine moves up the stick, the hCG binds to more monoclonal antibodies that are fixed in position on the test strip. This concentrates the coloured beads in this area, so the strip changes colour.

2. a) Microvilli *(1 mark)*. The epithelium of the wall of the PCT has microvilli to provide a large surface area *(1 mark)* for the selective reabsorption of useful materials from the filtrate into the blood *(1 mark)*.
   b) i) glomerulus *(1 mark)*
      ii) E and F *(1 mark)*
      iii) The longer the loop of Henle, the more water that can be reabsorbed from the filtrate *(1 mark)*. When there's a longer ascending limb, more ions are actively pumped out into the medulla *(1 mark)*, which creates a really low water potential in the medulla *(1 mark)*. This means more water moves out of the nephron and collecting duct into the capillaries, giving very concentrated urine *(1 mark)*.

3. a) i)

| Substance | TF/P ratio of 1.0 |
|---|---|
| glucose | ✓ |
| serum albumin (protein) | ✗ |
| sodium ions (Na$^+$) | ✓ |
| urea | ✓ |
| red blood cells | ✗ |

   **(2 marks for 3 correct answers, 1 mark for 2 correct)**
   Don't let the numbers throw you in this question. All you're really being asked is which substances can cross the filtration barrier and which can't.
   ii) The protein serum albumin is too large to pass through the filtration barrier into the tubular fluid, so it stays in the blood *(1 mark)*.
   iii) E.g. high blood pressure can damage the capillaries in the glomeruli *(1 mark)*. This means larger molecules like proteins may be able to get through the capillary walls and into the tubular fluid *(1 mark)*. This could cause the concentration of proteins like serum albumin to be the same in the plasma as in the tubular fluid, producing a TF/P ratio of 1.0 *(1 mark)*.
   b) i) 100 − 98.2 = 1.8% of the filtrate is not reabsorbed so must be urine *(1 mark)*
   1.8% of 1200 = $\frac{1.8}{100} \times 1200$
   = 21.6 cm$^3$ hour$^{-1}$ *(1 mark)*
   21.6 × 24 = **518.4 cm$^3$ day$^{-1}$** *(1 mark)*

   ii) The reabsorption of Na$^+$ from the kidney tubule back into the capillaries lowers the water potential of the medulla *(1 mark)*. This drives the reabsorption of water from the kidney tubule via osmosis *(1 mark)*. If the amount of sodium reabsorbed is decreased then the amount of water reabsorbed will also decrease *(1 mark)*. This means more water will be removed from the body in the urine, lowering the water content of the blood *(1 mark)*. This in turn will reduce blood volume, and therefore blood pressure *(1 mark)*.
   c) i) hepatic vein *(1 mark)*
   Remember, blood leaves the liver via the hepatic vein.
   ii) In the ornithine cycle, ammonia produced from the deamination of amino acids *(1 mark)* is combined with carbon dioxide, which produces urea (and water) *(1 mark)*.
   iii) E.g. weight loss *(1 mark)* / vomiting *(1 mark)*

# Section 3 — Animal Responses

## 1. The Nervous System

### Page 354-355 — Application Questions
Q1 a) cerebrum / (left) cerebral hemisphere
   b) cerebellum
   c) i) E.g. vision / hearing / learning / thinking
      ii) E.g. controls breathing rate / controls heart rate
      iii) E.g. maintains body temperature at a normal level / produces hormones that control the pituitary gland / involved in regulation of blood water potential
Q2 The cerebellum plays an important role in muscle coordination and coordination of balance. If the cerebellum is abnormally developed it could lead to problems with balance and coordination. This could make tasks such as throwing and catching difficult and make people more likely to fall over.

### Page 356 — Application Question
Q1 a) The response is automatic and happens quickly.
   b) Receptors in the hand/skin detect the heat stimulus and send a nerve impulse along a sensory neurone to a relay neurone in the CNS. The nerve impulse is then passed to a motor neurone, which carries the impulse to muscle cells (effectors) in the arm. The muscle cells contract to pull the hand away from the source of heat.

## Page 356 — Fact Recall Questions
Q1 The brain and the spinal cord.
Q2 To control unconscious activities of the body.
Q3 Pituitary gland. It releases hormones and stimulates other glands to release their hormones.
Q4 At the base of the brain / top of the spinal cord.
Q5 A reflex action is where the body responds to a stimulus without making a conscious decision to respond.
Q6 Sensory nerve endings in the cornea detect the touch stimulus. A nerve impulse is sent along the sensory neurone to a relay neurone in the CNS. The impulse is then passed from the relay neurone to motor neurones. The motor neurones send impulses to the effectors, the (orbicularis oculi) muscles that move your eyelids. These muscles contract causing your eyelids to close quickly.

## 2. 'Fight or Flight' Response and Heart Rate
## Page 359 — Application Questions
Q1 The chemoreceptors in a person with anaemia will detect low oxygen levels in the blood. The chemoreceptors will send impulses along sensory neurones to the cardiovascular centre, which will send impulses along sympathetic neurones. These neurones will secrete noradrenaline, which will bind to receptors on the sino-atrial node/SAN and cause the heart rate to increase.
Q2 a) The 'fight or flight' response. This response prepares the body for action in reaction to a threat.
b) The sympathetic nervous system.
c) 

| Response | Increased or decreased? |
|---|---|
| strength of contraction of heart muscle | increased |
| depth of breathing | increased |
| blood supply to the gut | decreased |
| blood supply to the skeletal muscles | increased |
| blood glucose level | increased |
| blood supply to the skin | decreased |

## Page 362 — Application Question
Q1 a) The chest strap of the heart rate monitor contains electrodes/sensors, which detect the electrical activity of the heart as it beats. The information picked up by the electrodes/sensors is transmitted wirelessly to a monitor worn on the wrist, which displays the data as a heart rate in beats per minute.
b) Null hypothesis: there is no significant difference between the mean heart rate of the people who were given caffeine and those who were not.
Find the mean for each data set:
Mean of data set 1 (caffeine) = (71 + 90 + 82 + 76 + 88 + 85 + 66) ÷ 7 = **79.7**
Mean of data set 2 (no caffeine) = (58 + 72 + 65 + 67 + 60 + 74 + 78) ÷ 7 = **67.7**
Find the standard deviation for each data set:

Data set 1

| $x$ | $(x - \bar{x})^2$ |
|---|---|
| 71 | 75.7 |
| 90 | 106.1 |
| 82 | 5.3 |
| 76 | 13.7 |
| 88 | 68.9 |
| 85 | 28.1 |
| 66 | 187.7 |
| Total | 485.5 |

Standard deviation for data set 1 = $\sqrt{(485.5 ÷ 6)} = \sqrt{80.9}$ = **9.0**

Data set 2

| $x$ | $(x - \bar{x})^2$ |
|---|---|
| 58 | 94.1 |
| 72 | 18.5 |
| 65 | 7.3 |
| 67 | 0.5 |
| 60 | 59.3 |
| 74 | 39.7 |
| 78 | 106.1 |
| Total | 325.5 |

Standard deviation for data set 2 = $\sqrt{(325.5 ÷ 6)} = \sqrt{54.3}$ = **7.4**
Use the formula for Student's t-test to calculate $t$.

$$t = \frac{79.7 - 67.7}{\sqrt{(9.0^2 / 7) + (7.4^2 / 7)}} = \frac{12}{4.4} = \mathbf{2.7}$$

*Remember you can ignore the sign for your t value — if you've used the data set after exposure to caffeine as data set 1 you won't get a negative value here anyway.*
Degrees of freedom = (7 + 7) − 2 = **12**
The critical value at P = 0.05 is 2.179. The $t$ value (2.7) is greater than 2.179. So the null hypothesis is rejected and the difference in heart rate between the people who were given caffeine and those who was not is concluded to be significant.
*You are asked to use a 95% confidence limit — this means using a P value of 0.05 (or 5%).*

## Page 362 — Fact Recall Questions
Q1 hypothalamus
Q2 a) baroreceptor/pressure receptor
   b) aorta and carotid arteries
Q3 They cause the heart rate to slow down/decrease.
Q4 E.g. you could record the heart rate of a group of people under normal controlled conditions using pulse measurements or an electronic heart rate monitor. You could then record their heart rate shortly after a loud noise using the same method. You could determine if any change in heart rate was significant by using a statistical test.

## 3. Muscle Contraction
## Page 365 — Application Questions
Q1 a) B
   b) C
   c) A and C
   d) B
Q2 Option 1. The A-band has stayed the same length, the I-band is shorter and the H-zone is shorter.
*Remember, the A-band is the length of the myosin filament and this doesn't get shorter during contraction. During contraction more of the actin filament slides over the myosin filament so the sections with only actin (the I-bands) get shorter and the sections with only myosin (the H-zones) get shorter too.*

## Page 367-368 — Application Questions
Q1 The influx of calcium ions triggers muscle contraction, so more calcium ions in the sarcoplasm would increase the strength of contraction of cardiac/heart muscle, which would help to pump more blood around the body of patients with heart failure.
Q2 a) i) X. The $Ca^{2+}$ concentration is low, suggesting that the muscle is at rest. Muscle fibres are longest when they are relaxed.
      ii) Y. There is an influx of $Ca^{2+}$ ions into the sarcoplasm following an action potential, and the $Ca^{2+}$ ions bind to troponin.
      iii) Y. The $Ca^{2+}$ ion concentration is high and $Ca^{2+}$ ions activate ATPase.
   b) The $Ca^{2+}$ ions are moved by active transport from the sarcoplasm back into sarcoplasmic reticulum, where they're stored.
   c) An action potential from a motor neurone stimulates a muscle cell and depolarises the sarcolemma. Depolarisation spreads down the T-tubules to the sarcoplasmic reticulum, causing the sarcoplasmic reticulum to release stored $Ca^{2+}$ ions into the sarcoplasm.

## Page 370 — Fact Recall Questions
Q1 a) They help to spread electrical impulses throughout the sarcoplasm so they reach all parts of the muscle fibre.
   b) It stores and releases calcium ions that are needed for muscle contraction.
   c) They provide the ATP that's needed for muscle contraction.
Q2 An A-band contains myosin filaments and some overlapping actin filaments. Under an electron microscope it appears as a dark band.
Q3 Myosin and actin filaments slide over one another to make the sarcomeres contract (the myofilaments themselves don't contract).
Q4 Troponin and tropomyosin.
Q5 Calcium ions in the sarcoplasm bind to troponin in the myofibrils, causing troponin to change shape. This pulls the attached tropomyosin out of the actin-myosin binding site on the actin filament. This exposes the binding site, which allows the myosin head to bind and form an actin-myosin cross bridge.
Q6 ATP is broken down by ATPase to provide the energy needed to move the myosin head from side to side, which pulls the actin filament along in a rowing action. ATP also provides the energy needed to break the myosin-actin cross bridge, so the myosin head detaches from the actin filament after it's moved.
Q7 a) Advantage: e.g. the ATP-CP system generates ATP very quickly / it can be used during short bursts of vigorous exercise / it's anaerobic/doesn't need oxygen / it's alactic/ doesn't form any lactate.
   Disadvantage: e.g. CP runs out after only a few seconds.
   b) Aerobic respiration and anaerobic respiration.
Q8

|  | Skeletal | Involuntary | Cardiac |
|---|---|---|---|
| Number of nuclei | many | one | one |
| Length | e.g. can be many centimetres | ~ 0.2 mm | ~ 0.1 mm |
| Shape of muscle fibres | e.g. long, straight shape | spindle-shaped (with pointed ends) | cylinder shaped / branched |
| Are cross-striations visible under a light microscope? | yes | no | yes (a few) |

Q9 To pump blood around the body.

## 4. Nerve Impulses and Muscle Contraction

### Page 373 — Application Questions
**Q1** They might have weaker muscle responses than normal. If receptors are destroyed at neuromuscular junctions then there will be fewer receptors for acetylcholine/ACh to bind to, so there will be less chance of depolarisation being triggered in the postsynaptic cell. This means fewer muscle cells will be stimulated.

**Q2** Galantamine would stop acetylcholinesterase/AChE breaking down acetylcholine/ACh, so there would be more ACh in the synaptic cleft and it would be there for longer. This means more nicotinic cholinergic receptors would be stimulated.

**Q3** a) The athlete is relaxing/resting the muscle in his forearm.
b) The maximum amplitude of the electrical activity recorded during time period A is lower than it is during time period B. This could be because, e.g. the person is picking up a heavier weight during time period B. The amplitude of the trace increases because more motor units are required to lift the heavier weight.
c) The trace would continue to increase in amplitude because the brain would be trying to activate more motor units to generate the force needed to hold the weight up.

### Page 373 — Fact Recall Questions
**Q1** A synapse between a motor neurone and a muscle cell.
**Q2** acetylcholine/ACh
**Q3** It is broken down by the enzyme acetylcholinesterase (AChE), which is released from clefts on the postsynaptic membrane.
**Q4** They may prevent the action potential from being passed on to the muscle, so the muscle won't contract. If they affect the muscles involved in breathing, e.g. the diaphragm and intercostal muscles, ventilation can't take place and the organism can't respire aerobically.
**Q5** Two electrodes (sensors) are placed on the skin near the muscle to be monitored and a third electrode is placed on an inactive point on the body to act as a control. The electrodes are connected to an amplifier and a computer. When the muscle contracts, the electrodes detect the electrical activity caused by nervous impulses arriving at neuromuscular junctions in the muscle. Information from the electrodes is transferred to the computer where it is displayed on a screen.

### Exam-style Questions — Pages 375-376
1  A *(1 mark)*
2  a) Medulla oblongata *(1 mark)*. Controls breathing and heart rate *(1 mark)*.
   b) i) Y *(1 mark)*
   Structure Y is the cerebellum.
   ii) The somatic nervous system because this is the part of the nervous system that is responsible for conscious activities *(1 mark)*.
   iii) In a reflex action the pathway of communication goes through the spinal cord/unconscious parts of the brain so doesn't involve the cerebellum *(1 mark)*.
   iv) Acetylcholine is released at neuromuscular junctions and binds to nicotinic cholinergic receptors on the motor end plate/postsynaptic membrane *(1 mark)*, which triggers depolarisation in the muscle cell *(1 mark)*. If nicotinic cholinergic receptors are being blocked by trihexyphenidyl, less depolarisation of the muscle cells will occur and the muscle won't be able to contract *(1 mark)*.

3  a) i) The adrenal glands / adrenal medulla *(1 mark)*.
   ii) E.g. it causes the cardiac muscle to contract more frequently *(1 mark)* and with more force *(1 mark)*.
   iii) E.g. muscles in the arterioles supplying the skin and gut constrict, and muscles in the arterioles supplying the heart, lungs and skeletal muscles dilate *(1 mark)*. This means that blood is diverted from the skin and gut to the heart, lungs and skeletal muscles *(1 mark)*. This increases blood flow to skeletal muscles (e.g. in the legs), making them ready for action *(1 mark)*.
   b) Cardiac muscle is composed of branched *(1 mark)*, cylinder-shaped muscle fibres *(1 mark)* that are connected by intercalated discs *(1 mark)*. The muscle fibres are uninucleate *(1 mark)*. **(Maximum of 2 marks available.)**

4  a) A — H-zone *(1 mark)*, B — I-band *(1 mark)*, C — A-band *(1 mark)*.
   b) A/the H-zone and B/the I-band will appear longer *(1 mark)* and C/the A-band will stay the same length *(1 mark)*.
   c) i) Myosin filaments have globular heads that are hinged *(1 mark)*. Each myosin head has a binding site for actin *(1 mark)* and a binding site for ATP *(1 mark)*.
   ii) **5-6 marks:**
   The answer explains fully how energy released from ATP enables the movement of the myosin filament and is required for the breaking of the actin-myosin cross bridge.
   The answer has a clear and logical structure.
   The information given is relevant and detailed.
   **3-4 marks:**
   The answer explains briefly how energy released from ATP enables the movement of the myosin filament and is required for the breaking of the actin-myosin cross bridge.
   The answer has some structure. Most of the information given is relevant and there is some detail involved.
   **1-2 marks:**
   The answer includes a basic explanation as to either how energy released from ATP enables the movement of the myosin filament or how it is required for the breaking of the actin-myosin cross bridge.
   The answer has no clear structure. The information given is basic and lacking in detail. It may not all be relevant.
   **0 marks:**
   No relevant information is given.
   **Here are some points your answer may include:**
   The myosin head binds to the actin filament and forms an actin-myosin cross bridge. Energy released from ATP moves the myosin head to the side, which pulls the actin filament along in a rowing action/power stroke. ATP also provides the energy to break the actin-myosin cross bridge so the myosin head detaches from the actin filament after it's moved. The myosin head then returns to it's starting position and reattaches to a different binding site further along the actin filament. As the cycle is repeated, the myosin head pulls the actin filament along, causing the muscle to contract.

d) i) ATP is made by phosphorylating ADP *(1 mark)* with a phosphate group taken from creatine phosphate *(1 mark)*.
Remember, the ATP-creatine phosphate (CP) system is used during short bursts of vigorous exercise.
   ii) ATP is generated very quickly *(1 mark)*. / No oxygen is needed / the process is anaerobic *(1 mark)*. / The process is alactic / no lactate is formed *(1 mark)*.
e) Any three from: e.g. a skeletal muscle fibre/muscle fibre in the biceps is multinucleate whereas an involuntary muscle fibre/muscle fibre in a blood vessel is uninucleate *(1 mark)*. / A skeletal muscle fibre/muscle fibre in the biceps is much longer than an involuntary muscle fibre/muscle fibre in a blood vessel *(1 mark)*. / A skeletal muscle fibre/muscle fibre in the biceps has a long, straight shape whereas an involuntary muscle fibre/muscle fibre in a blood vessel is spindle-shaped with pointed ends *(1 mark)*. / A skeletal muscle fibre/muscle fibre in the biceps has cross-striations visible under a microscope whereas an involuntary muscle/muscle in a blood vessel doesn't *(1 mark)*. **(Maximum of 3 marks available.)**
Always read exam questions carefully — this one asks for three structural differences, so you won't get marks for comparing the functions.

# Section 4 — Plant Responses and Hormones

## 1. Plant Responses

### Pages 381-382 — Application Questions
Q1 a) The auxin will have diffused straight down from the sponge into the left-hand side of the shoot. This will have stimulated the cells on this side to elongate, so the shoot grew towards the right.
b) Equal amounts of auxin will have diffused down both sides, making all the cells elongate at the same rate.
c) The shoots in experiment B were exposed to a light source. This will have caused the auxin to diffuse into the shoot and accumulate on the shaded side (left-hand side) regardless of where the sponge was placed. All the shoots grew towards the right because most auxin accumulated on the left, stimulating cell elongation there.
d) Sponge D was a negative control (a sponge soaked in water rather than auxin), included to show that it was the auxin having an effect and nothing else.
e) The sponges were soaked in glucose so that the shoots would have energy to grow in the dark, as no photosynthesis can take place.
Sponges from experiment B were also soaked in glucose, even though they were in the light, so were able to photosynthesise. This is done in order to keep the set-up of both experiments as similar as possible.

Q2 a) positive
The shoot is bending <u>towards</u> the stimulus.
b) Y because this is where cell elongation is taking place, causing the shoot to bend towards the opposite side.

### Page 382 — Fact Recall Questions
Q1 Anything harmful that's natural, but non-living.
Q2 E.g. producing toxic chemicals (e.g. tannins and alkaloids) to act as chemical defences / releasing pheromones to signal to other organisms / folding up in response to being touched.
Q3 Growth away from a (directional) stimulus.
Q4 phototropism
Q5 The growing regions of the plant / shoot and root tips.
Q6 inhibit growth
Q7 E.g. indoleacetic acid/IAA
Q8 a) by active transport and diffusion
b) via the phloem
Q9 a) Auxins move to the more shaded parts of the shoot. This means the cells on the shaded part of the shoot grow faster than the cells most exposed to light. This pattern of growth causes the shoot to bend towards the light.
b) Auxins move to the underside of roots. This means the growth of cells on the underside of the root is inhibited so they don't grow as quickly as the cells on the upper side. This pattern of growth causes the root to grow downwards in the same direction as gravity.

## 2. The Effects of Plant Hormones

### Page 387 — Application Questions
Q1 To minimise the differences between plants at the start of the experiment. The more variables the student controls, the more valid her results will be. Choosing plants of a similar age, height, mass, etc., makes it less likely that any differences observed between the three experimental conditions will result from differences between the plants.
Q2 The plants watered with a 100 mg dm$^{-3}$ gibberellin solution. Gibberellins are growth hormones that stimulate the stems of plants to grow by stem elongation, so the higher the concentration of gibberellin, the taller the plant will grow.
This is only true up to a point though — as the concentration of gibberellin gets higher, the effect it has on the plant changes and it doesn't stimulate the plant to grow any further.
Q3 a) Total growth = 26 cm − 8 cm = 18 cm
6 weeks = 6 × 7 days = 42 days
Average growth rate = 18 ÷ 42 = **0.43 cm day$^{-1}$**
b) Total growth = 18 cm
Percentage increase = (18 ÷ 8) × 100 = 2.25 × 100 = **225%**
To calculate percentage increase, divide the total growth by the initial plant height and then multiply your answer by 100.

616 Answers

## Page 387 — Fact Recall Questions

**Q1** It saves the plants' energy and prevents side shoots from the same plant competing with the shoot tip for light. This allows a plant in an area where there are many other plants to grow tall very fast, past smaller plants, to reach the sunlight (instead of wasting energy growing side shoots).

**Q2** Gibberellins stimulate seed germination by triggering the breakdown of starch into glucose in the seed. The plant embryo in the seed can then use the glucose to begin respiring and release the energy it needs to grow.

**Q3** a) Losing their leaves helps plants to conserve water, which is lost from the leaves.
*Remember, in winter it might be difficult for plants to absorb water from the soil because the soil water may be frozen.*
b) Auxins inhibit leaf loss.
c) Ethene stimulates the cells in the abscission layer to expand, breaking the cells walls and causing the leaf to fall off.

**Q4** a) guard cells
b) abscisic acid/ABA

**Q5** Ethene stimulates enzymes that break down cell walls, break down chlorophyll and convert starch into sugars. This makes the fruit ripen.

## Exam-style Questions — pages 389-390

**1** B *(1 mark)*

**2** a) phototropism *(1 mark)*
b) The seedling should have been from a Goosegrass plant and potted in soil from the same source *(1 mark)*. There should have been no lamp/light from any direction present *(1 mark)*.
c) E.g. to make sure that only the variable being tested (light intensity) was changing *(1 mark)*. / To keep all variables other than light intensity the same *(1 mark)*.
d) Seedling A will be bent to the right because it will have grown towards the light *(1 mark)*. Seedling B will have grown straight up because the rotation of the seedling means that the light is not continuously coming from one direction *(1 mark)*. Seedling C will be bent towards the right but may have a kink in, so that it is not a smooth bend because it will have grown to the right for five days, then to the left for five days and to the right again for the last five days, as the position of the light source was changed during the experiment *(1 mark)*.
e) IAA/auxins moved to the more shaded parts of the plant/shoots *(1 mark)*. This meant the shaded parts of the shoot grew faster/elongated more than the parts exposed to light *(1 mark)*. This uneven growth led to the shoots bending towards the light *(1 mark)*.

**3** a) lateral buds *(1 mark)*
b) i) Removing bud 1 from the plant means that the plant would no longer produce auxins *(1 mark)*. Auxins cause apical dominance, inhibiting the growth of side shoots from lateral buds, so removing bud 1 would allow side shoots to develop from lateral buds/buds 2-5 by cell division and cell elongation *(1 mark)*.
ii) Applying a source of auxin (the gel) to where the tip had been removed would result in the inhibition of side shoot development, so side shoots would not develop from lateral buds/buds 2-5 *(1 mark)*.
iii) E.g. as a source of rooting hormones / a substance for promoting root growth in a plant stem cutting *(1 mark)*.
c) E.g. ethene stimulates ripening, so exposing the plants to ethene gas would help to speed up the ripening of the fruits/tomatoes and help to ensure that they all ripen at roughly the same time/uniformly for harvesting *(1 mark)*.

**4** a) pheromones *(1 mark)*
b) E.g. tannins have a bitter taste *(1 mark)*. / In some herbivores, such as cattle, they can bind to proteins in the gut, making the plant hard to digest *(1 mark)*.
c) E.g. boosting the levels of defensive chemicals that crop plants produce might enable their defences against herbivory to be more effective, resulting in less tissue damage *(1 mark)*.

# Section 5 — Photosynthesis

## 1. Storing and Releasing Energy

### Page 393 — Application Question

**Q1** a) 07:30 and 16:30
*Anything between 07:20 and 07:40 would be acceptable for the first compensation point. Anything between 16:20 and 16:40 would be OK for the second one.*
b) The rate of photosynthesis depends partly on the intensity of light. 07:30 is shortly after the Sun has risen. The light intensity has increased to a level where the rate of photosynthesis has increased to match the rate of respiration. 16:30 is shortly before the Sun completely sets. The light intensity has decreased to a level where the rate of photosynthesis has decreased to match the rate of respiration.

### Page 393 — Fact Recall Questions

**Q1** Any three from, e.g. photosynthesis / active transport / DNA replication / cell division.

**Q2** Carbon dioxide and water are products of respiration and are also raw materials used in photosynthesis. Photosynthesis produces oxygen and glucose, which are raw materials used in respiration.

**Q3** ATP is the immediate source of energy in a cell.

**Q4** A molecule of ATP is made from adenine, a ribose sugar and three phosphate groups.
*If you're asked to describe the structure of ATP in the exam, make sure you're specific and put that it's a 'ribose sugar'. If you just put 'sugar' you won't get the mark.*

**Q5** a) ADP and $P_i$
b) hydrolysis

## 2. Photosynthesis and the Light-dependent Reaction

### Page 398 — Application Questions
Q1 a) proton/hydrogen ion/H⁺
b) Because this forms a proton gradient across the membrane. Protons move down their concentration gradient, into the stroma, via an enzyme called ATP synthase. The energy from this movement combines ADP and inorganic phosphate ($P_i$) to form ATP.
Q2 PSII / photosystem II
Q3 D
Q4 ATP
*Cyclic photophosphorylation doesn't produce any reduced NADP or $O_2$ — just ATP.*

### Page 398 — Fact Recall Questions
Q1 A – circular DNA
B – outer membrane of envelope
C – inner membrane of envelope
D – stroma
E – granum
F – thylakoid
G – thylakoid membrane
H – lamella
I – starch grain
Q2 a) Coloured substances that absorb the light energy needed for photosynthesis.
b) chlorophyll a
Q3 Accessory pigments that surround the reaction centres. They transfer light energy to the reaction centres to boost the energy available for electron excitement to take place.
Q4 Photosystem I and photosystem II / PSI and PSII
Q5 hydrogen
Q6 the thylakoid membranes
Q7 ATP and reduced NADP
*In the exam, always read the question very carefully. For example, this question didn't ask for all the products of the light-dependent reaction — it specifically asked for the products that are needed for the light-independent reaction. So if you put oxygen it would be wrong because it's not needed for the light-independent reaction.*
Q8 The process of adding phosphate to a molecule using light.
Q9 A chain of proteins through which excited electrons flow.
Q10 a) protons, electrons and oxygen
b) To replace excited electrons in PSII.
Q11 a) Photosystems: photosystem I/PSI and photosystem II/PSII
Products: ATP, reduced NADP and oxygen
b) Photosystem: photosystem I/PSI
Product: ATP

## 3. Light-independent Reaction

### Page 401 — Application Questions
Q1 X = ribulose bisphosphate (RuBP)
Y = glycerate 3-phosphate (GP)
Z = triose phosphate (TP)
Q2 A = ribulose bisphosphate carboxylase (RuBisCO)
B = reduced NADP
Q3

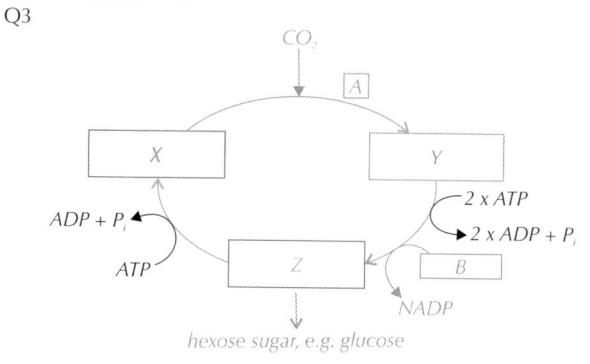

*[Calvin cycle diagram: $CO_2$ enters via A to combine with X, forming Y. Y is converted to Z using 2 × ATP → 2 × ADP + $P_i$ and B. Z regenerates X releasing ADP + $P_i$ ← ATP. Z also produces hexose sugar, e.g. glucose. NADP released.]*

### Page 401 — Fact Recall Questions
Q1 It is combined with ribulose bisphosphate to form glycerate 3-phosphate.
Q2 a)

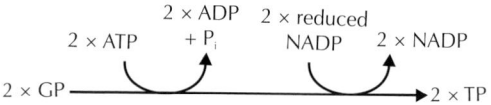

2 × GP → 2 × TP (using 2 × ATP → 2 × ADP + $P_i$ and 2 × reduced NADP → 2 × NADP)

(GP is glycerate 3-phosphate and TP is triose phosphate)
b) reduction
*Although the conversion of GP to TP is a reduction reaction, ATP and reduced NADP are both oxidised.*
Q3 In the Calvin cycle ATP is needed for the reduction of glycerate 3-phosphate (GP) to triose phosphate (TP). It's also needed for the regeneration of ribulose bisphosphate (RuBP) from triose phosphate.
Q4 five
Q5 a) six
*Six turns of the Calvin cycle produces 12 molecules of triose phosphate (TP). Ten of these molecules (5 out of every 6) are used to make ribulose bisphosphate (RuBP) and two are used to make one hexose sugar.*
b) 18
*Six turns of cycle × 3 ATP molecules per turn = 18 ATP*
c) 12
*Six turns of cycle × 2 reduced NADP molecules per turn = 12 reduced NADP*
Q6 a) Two triose phosphate molecules are joined together to produce a hexose sugar. Large carbohydrates are then made by joining the hexose sugars together.
b) Lipids are made from glycerol and fatty acids. Glycerol is synthesised from triose phosphate, while fatty acids are made from glycerate 3-phosphate.
c) Some amino acids are made from glycerate 3-phosphate.

## 4. Limiting Factors in Photosynthesis

### Page 406 — Application Questions

Q1  a) Outside plants week 2 height = 12 cm (accept 11-14 cm).
Outside plants week 5 height = 30 cm
Difference in plant height = 30 − 12 = 18 cm
% difference in plant height =
(difference ÷ original) × 100 = (18 ÷ 12) × 100 = **150%**
Greenhouse plants week 2 height = 28 cm (accept 26-29 cm).
Greenhouse plants week 5 height = 45 cm (accept 44-46 cm).
Difference in plant height = 45 − 28 = 17 cm
% difference in plant height = (17 ÷ 28) × 100 = **60.7%**

b) E.g. the farmer may have increased the carbon dioxide concentration in the greenhouse by burning a small amount of propane in a carbon dioxide generator. / The farmer may have used lamps to provide light at night. / The farmer may have made use of heaters and cooling systems in order to keep a constant optimum temperature.

Q2  a) When plants don't have enough water, their stomata close to preserve what water they do have. This can lead to a decrease in the rate of photosynthesis because less $CO_2$ is able to enter the leaves, so $CO_2$ becomes a limiting factor.

b) Unlike electric heaters, the paraffin heaters would produce $CO_2$, which would increase the atmospheric $CO_2$ concentration of the greenhouse. The loss of this source of $CO_2$ could result in the atmospheric $CO_2$ concentration decreasing to a level where it becomes a limiting factor to photosynthesis.

Q3  a) Plant B. This is because plant A has been under a green light, which is reflected by the plant, reducing the rate of photosynthesis. However, plant B has been under blue light, which is absorbed by photosynthetic pigments, increasing the rate of photosynthesis. This means plant B will have made more glucose and so had more energy for growth.

b) E.g. even though the plant is getting enough light and water, it is exposed to high temperatures of around 40 °C. At these temperatures its stomata may close to avoid losing too much water. This means less carbon dioxide can enter the leaf, so photosynthesis will slow right down. In turn, the plant will produce much less glucose, which means it'll have much less energy to carry out all its life processes and may die.

### Page 406 — Fact Recall Questions

Q1  A low light intensity will slow down the light-dependent reaction, so that less ATP and reduced NADP are produced. This means there will be less ATP and reduced NADP entering the Calvin cycle, which means the Calvin cycle will slow down.

Q2  a) The concentration of RuBP will decrease.
The level of RuBP decreases at low light intensities because the light-dependent reaction is slower, so less ATP and reduced NADP are produced and the conversion of GP to TP and RuBP is slower.

b) The concentration of RuBP will decrease.
The level of RuBP decreases at low temperatures because the enzymes in the Calvin cycle work more slowly.

c) The concentration of RuBP will increase.
The level of RuBP increases at low $CO_2$ concentrations because there is less $CO_2$ and so less RuBP will be combined with $CO_2$ to produce GP.

## 5. Photosynthesis Experiments

### Page 408 — Application Question

Q1  a) $R_f$ value = $\dfrac{\text{distance moved by the solute}}{\text{distance moved by the solvent}}$
= 7.90 cm ÷ 9.00 cm = **0.878** (3 s.f.)

b) Using paper chromatography means a different stationary phase and solvent would have been used, which would have affected the $R_f$ values. An $R_f$ value for a pigment is obtained under specific conditions.

### Page 409 — Fact Recall Question

Q1  A test tube containing the pondweed and water is connected to a capillary tube full of water, which is connected to a syringe. A source of white light is placed at a specific distance from the pondweed. The pondweed is left to photosynthesise for a set amount of time. At the end of the experiment, the syringe is used to draw the gas bubble in the tube up alongside a ruler and the length of the gas bubble (proportional to the volume of $O_2$) is measured. The experiment is repeated and the average length of gas bubble is calculated. The whole experiment is then repeated with the light source placed at different distances from the pondweed.

# Exam-style Questions — pages 411-412

1.  a) i) A – stroma *(1 mark)*
        B – thylakoid membrane / lamella *(1 mark)*
        C – outer membrane of envelope *(1 mark)*
    ii) A/stroma *(1 mark)*
    b) Primary pigments are reaction centres, where electrons are excited during the light-dependent reaction *(1 mark)*. Accessory pigments make up light-harvesting systems, which surround reaction centres and transfer light energy to them to boost the energy available for electron excitement to take place *(1 mark)*.
    c) i) **5-6 marks:**
        A full description of all the steps in the process is given in the correct order, including an explanation of the involvement of ATP, hydrogen ions, reduced NADP and ribulose bisphosphate carboxylase (RuBisCO) in the process.
        The answer has a clear and logical structure.
        The information given is relevant and detailed.
        **3-4 marks:**
        Some of the steps are described and they are in the correct order, but the answer is incomplete. The answer includes an explanation of the involvement of at least one from ATP, hydrogen ions, reduced NADP and ribulose bisphosphate carboxylase (RuBisCO).
        The answer has some structure. Most of the information given is relevant and there is some detail involved.
        **1-2 marks:**
        A few of the steps in the process are described briefly and not necessarily in the right order.
        The answer has no clear structure. The information given is basic and lacking in detail. It may not all be relevant.
        **0 marks:**
        No relevant information is given.
        **Here are some points your answer may include:**
        Carbon dioxide enters the leaf through the stomata and diffuses into the stroma of the chloroplast. Here, it's combined with ribulose bisphosphate (RuBP), a 5-carbon compound. This gives an unstable 6-carbon compound, which quickly breaks down into two molecules of glycerate 3-phosphate (GP). Ribulose bisphosphate carboxylase (RuBisCO) catalyses the reaction between carbon dioxide and RuBP. GP is then reduced to the 3-carbon compound called triose phosphate (TP), which glucose is synthesised from. ATP from the light-dependent reaction provides the energy to do this. This reaction also requires H$^+$ ions, which come from reduced NADP.
    ii) ATP is used *(1 mark)* to convert the five molecules of triose phosphate/TP/the 3-carbon compound back into ribulose bisphosphate/RuBP *(1 mark)*.
    d) respiration *(1 mark)*
2.  a) In tube B light energy was absorbed by photosystem I in the chloroplasts *(1 mark)* and electrons were excited to a very high energy level *(1 mark)*. Then these excited electrons were transferred to DNIP to produce reduced DNIP *(1 mark)*.
    *NADP is a coenzyme that can accept from or give hydrogen (and therefore electrons) to another molecule. The question says DNIP is an artificial hydrogen acceptor. This means it can accept hydrogen (and therefore electrons) from other molecules too — it works in the same way as NADP.*
    b) Tube A receives no light energy so the light-dependent reaction of photosynthesis can't take place *(1 mark)*. The chloroplasts in test tube C have been boiled, which will have denatured the enzymes in the chloroplast, therefore preventing photosynthesis from taking place *(1 mark)*.
    c) Glycerate 3-phosphate/GP is reduced to triose phosphate/TP *(1 mark)* using hydrogen ions from reduced NADP *(1 mark)*.
3.  a) No. The student hasn't taken into account the amount of oxygen that the plant has used for respiration *(1 mark)*.
    b) i) In experiment 1, the rate of photosynthesis increased with increasing light intensity *(1 mark)*. However, after about 100 µmoles m$^{-2}$ s$^{-1}$ the rate of photosynthesis levelled off *(1 mark)* because light intensity was no longer the limiting factor *(1 mark)*.
    ii) The limiting factor in experiment 2 must be temperature because the graph for experiment 3 levels off at a higher point *(1 mark)* but experiment 3 had the same light intensity and CO$_2$ concentration as experiment 2 *(1 mark)*.
    c) The level of RuBP will have increased because there would have been less CO$_2$ to combine with RuBP to form GP / because RuBP is still being made but isn't being used up *(1 mark)*. The level of TP will have decreased because it's being used up to make RuBP but isn't being remade *(1 mark)*.

*If you get a question like this in the exam, make sure you think of the substances before the reactant in the cycle as well as those that come after it.*

# Section 6 — Respiration

## 1. Aerobic Respiration

### Page 414 — Application Questions
Q1  a) ATP
    b) reduced NAD
    c) inorganic phosphate (P$_i$)
    d) hexose bisphosphate
    e) triose phosphate
    f) H$^+$ ions/hydrogen ions
Q2  a) phosphorylation
    b) oxidation
Q3  The formation of hexose phosphate in the first part of the reaction and the formation of 4ATP from 4ADP + 4P$_i$ in the second part of the reaction.

### Page 416 — Application Questions
Q1  a) oxaloacetate = 4C, citrate = 6C
    b) Decarboxylation and dehydrogenation occur, producing one molecule of reduced FAD and two of reduced NAD. ATP is produced by substrate-level phosphorylation.
Q2  24
    *Two molecules of carbon dioxide are produced per turn of the Krebs cycle and the Krebs cycle turns twice for each molecule of glucose. So for one molecule of glucose four molecules of carbon dioxide are produced. Therefore if six molecules of glucose were respired, 24 (6 x 4) molecules of carbon dioxide would be produced in the Krebs cycle.*
Q3  Acetyl coenzyme A can enter the Krebs cycle, leading to the formation of reduced coenzymes, which are then used in oxidative phosphorylation

## Page 417 — Application Questions

**Q1** Carrier 1 will be in a reduced state because it has received electrons from reduced NAD but can't pass them on. Carrier 3 will be in an oxidised state because it has passed its electrons onto oxygen, but hasn't received any more from carrier 2.
*If a substance gains electrons it is reduced. If a substance loses electrons it is oxidised.*

**Q2** Antimycin A inhibits carrier 2 and so stops electrons moving down the electron transport chain. This means no more energy will be lost from electrons moving down the chain, so H⁺ ions will not be transported across the inner mitochondrial membrane and the electrochemical gradient across the membrane won't be maintained. This means the synthesis of ATP by ATP synthase will stop. If a fish can't produce ATP it will die as energy from ATP is needed to fuel all biological processes.
*Don't write that H⁺ ions/protons are prevented from moving into or out of the inner mitochondrial membrane — they're prevented from moving across it.*

## Page 419 — Fact Recall Questions

**Q1** In the cytoplasm.
**Q2** ATP is used to phosphorylate glucose, making triose phosphate.
**Q3** By active transport.
**Q4** In the mitochondrial matrix.
**Q5** a) Pyruvate is decarboxylated — one carbon atom is removed from pyruvate in the form of carbon dioxide. Then NAD is reduced to NADH — it collects hydrogen from pyruvate, changing pyruvate into acetate.
b) It combines with acetate to form acetyl coenzyme A.
c) Acetyl coenzyme A enters the Krebs cycle. Reduced NAD is used in oxidative phosphorylation. Carbon dioxide is released as a waste product.
**Q6** substrate-level phosphorylation
**Q7** a) It is reused in the link reaction.
b) It is regenerated for use in the next Krebs cycle.
**Q8** They lose energy.
**Q9** It's the process of ATP production driven by the movement of H⁺ ions across a membrane (due to electrons moving down an electron transport chain).
**Q10** oxygen
**Q11** E.g. the conversion of pyruvate to acetate in the link reaction. / The conversion of citrate to the 5-carbon compound in the Krebs cycle. / The conversion of the 5-carbon compound to oxaloacetate in the Krebs cycle.
*Every time $CO_2$ is lost in a reaction, decarboxylation is happening.*
**Q12**

| Substance | Glycolysis | Link reaction | Krebs cycle | Oxidative phosphorylation |
|---|---|---|---|---|
| ATP | X | | X | X |
| reduced NAD | X | X | X | |
| reduced FAD | | | X | |
| $CO_2$ | | X | X | |

*Remember, oxidative phosphorylation also produces (oxidised) NAD and FAD, and water.*

## 2. Anaerobic Respiration

### Page 421 — Application Questions

**Q1** a) anaerobically
b) two
c)
$$glucose \xrightarrow{glycolysis} pyruvate \xrightarrow{\text{reduced NAD} \to \text{NAD}} lactate\ (lactic\ acid)$$

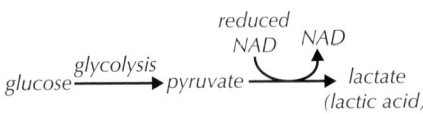

**Q2** a) i) lactate/lactic acid
  ii) pyruvate
  iii) ethanol
b) i) A
  ii) B
  iii) A
c) two

### Page 421 — Fact Recall Questions

**Q1** In the cytoplasm.
**Q2** E.g. both start with glycolysis. / Both produce ATP. / Both require NAD.
**Q3** a) E.g. mammals / some bacteria
b) E.g. yeast / plants
**Q4** Reduced NAD (from glycolysis) transfers hydrogen to pyruvate to form lactate and NAD.
**Q5** Reduced NAD (from glycolysis) transfers hydrogen to ethanal to form ethanol and NAD.
**Q6** a) 30 fewer ATP
*If aerobic respiration can produce 32 molecules of ATP per molecule of glucose and anaerobic respiration produces 2 molecules of ATP, then 32 − 2 = 30 fewer.*
b) Because anaerobic respiration only includes one energy-releasing stage (glycolysis), whereas aerobic respiration includes more energy-releasing stages (Krebs cycle, oxidative phosphorylation).

## 3. Respiratory Substrates

### Page 423 — Application Questions

**Q1** a) RQ = molecules of $CO_2$ released ÷ molecules of $O_2$ consumed = 57 ÷ 80 = **0.71**
b) A lipid because lipids have a respiratory quotient of 0.7. Carbohydrates have an RQ of 1 and proteins have an RQ of 0.9.
**Q2** a) RQ = volume of $CO_2$ released ÷ volume of $O_2$ consumed = 180 ÷ 250 = **0.72**
b) E.g. more carbohydrates are being respired. / Fewer fats are being respired.
*An increase or decrease in an organism's RQ doesn't mean that it is respiring more or less substrate overall — it just means that the type of substrate being respired has changed.*

### Page 423 — Fact Recall Questions

**Q1** Any biological molecule that can be broken down in respiration to release energy.
**Q2** Because lipids contain more hydrogen atoms per unit of mass than carbohydrates or proteins. Hydrogen atoms are required for the oxidative phosphorylation stage of aerobic respiration, in which most ATP is synthesised, so respiratory substrates that contain more hydrogen atoms per unit of mass will cause more ATP to be produced when respired.
**Q3** carbohydrates
**Q4** They can be used to determine what kind of respiratory substrates an organism is respiring and what type of respiration it's using.

## 4. Respiration Experiments

### Pages 425-426 — Application Question

Q1 a) E.g. the scientist could have set up a test tube containing a known volume and concentration of substrate (e.g. glucose) solution and a buffer solution at specific pH. She could then have added a known mass of dried yeast of species A to the tube and stirred until the yeast dissolved. Next, she could have sealed the test tube with a bung and attached it via a tube to a gas syringe in order to catch the $CO_2$ produced by the respiring yeast. At regular intervals (e.g. every minute) for a set amount of time (e.g. 10 minutes), the scientist could have recorded the volume of gas present in the gas syringe. By repeating the experiment (e.g. three times) at this pH, she could then have calculated the mean rate of $CO_2$ production at this pH. She could then have repeated the experiment at a range of pH levels by using buffer solutions of different pH levels. She could have done the same thing for species B.

b) Respiration is a series of reactions controlled by enzymes. The enzymes used in respiration by the different species of yeast may have different optimum pH levels, at which they are able to catalyse the reactions most effectively.

c) Mean rate of $CO_2$ production of species A at pH 5.5 = 1.75 $cm^3$ $min^{-1}$
*Anything between 1.7 and 1.8 $cm^3$ would be acceptable here.*
Mean rate of $CO_2$ production of species B at pH 5.5 = 3.75 $cm^3$ $min^{-1}$
*Anything between 3.7 and 3.8 $cm^3$ would be acceptable here.*
Percentage change in rate from species A to species B = $((1.75 - 3.75) \div 1.75) \times 100$ = **114% faster**
*Your final answer may differ a little depending on what you got for the mean rates of $CO_2$ production for the two species.*

d) Boiled yeast won't respire as the boiling will have killed it. Therefore, it acts as a negative control to show that the $CO_2$ production is a result of the respiring yeast and not any other reactions that may be happening in the tube.

### Page 427 — Fact Recall Questions

Q1 To stop oxygen getting into the yeast solution, forcing the yeast to respire anaerobically.

Q2 E.g. prepare and treat a test tube in the same way as the others in the investigation, but do not put any yeast in it.

Q3 It absorbs any $CO_2$ produced by the respiring organisms.

Q4 10 g
*You know the answer here is 10 g because the mass of the peas and the mass of the glass beads in the control tube have to be the same.*

### Exam-style Questions — pages 429-430

1 a) i) A – mitochondrial matrix *(1 mark)*
B – crista/inner mitochondrial membrane *(1 mark)*
C – outer mitochondrial membrane *(1 mark)*
ii) There is less folding of the inner membrane/fewer crista *(1 mark)*.

b) i) Because glycolysis takes place in the cytoplasm of the cell *(1 mark)*.
*Because glycolysis takes place in the cytoplasm and not the mitochondria, it doesn't matter whether you have functioning mitochondria or not — glycolysis can still happen.*

ii) Any three from: Glucose is phosphorylated by adding a phosphate from a molecule of ATP *(1 mark)*. / This creates one molecule of hexose phosphate *(1 mark)*. / Hexose phosphate is phosphorylated by ATP to form hexose bisphosphate *(1 mark)*. / Two molecules of ADP are produced overall *(1 mark)*.

iii) In the oxidation of triose phosphate to pyruvate, NAD collects the hydrogen ions from triose phosphate *(1 mark)*, forming reduced NAD *(1 mark)*.

c) RQ = molecules of $CO_2$ released ÷ molecules of $O_2$ consumed = 6 ÷ 7 = **0.86**
*(2 marks for correct answer, otherwise 1 mark for correct working).*

2 D *(1 mark)*
3 B *(1 mark)*
4 a) i) The oxidation of triose phosphate to pyruvate produces one molecule of reduced NAD *(1 mark)*. The conversion of pyruvate to acetate produces one molecule of reduced NAD *(1 mark)*. The conversion of citrate to a 5-carbon compound in the Krebs cycle produces one molecule of reduced NAD *(1 mark)*. The conversion of this 5-carbon compound to oxaloacetate produces another two molecules of reduced NAD *(1 mark)* and one molecule of reduced FAD *(1 mark)*.

ii) The electrons move along the electron transport chain *(1 mark)* losing energy at each electron carrier *(1 mark)*. Finally they are passed onto oxygen as it is the final electron acceptor *(1 mark)*.

b) There would be no electrochemical gradient produced across the inner mitochondrial membrane *(1 mark)*. This means there would be no movement of ions across the mitochondrial membrane to drive ATP synthase *(1 mark)* so no ATP would be made *(1 mark)*. The cells would only get ATP from anaerobic respiration *(1 mark)*.
*Even though $H^+$ ions will still be pumped across the inner mitochondrial membrane into the intermembrane space, the uncoupler will be moving them back into the matrix at the same time — so no gradient would be produced.*

# Module 6

## Section 1 — Cellular Control

### 1. Regulating Gene Expression

#### Page 434 — Application Questions
Q1 Any three from, e.g. temperature / the presence of other nutrients in the medium / the length of time the bacteria were left for / volume of culture / number of bacteria / amount of lactose/glucose added.
Q2 The normal *E. coli* have been included as a negative control. They show that any differences in the results were down to the mutations and nothing else.
Q3 a) E.g. Mutant 1 always produces mRNA and β-galactosidase, even in the absence of lactose. This may mean that Mutant 1 has a faulty lac repressor. If the repressor is faulty, it may not be able to bind to the operator and block transcription even in the absence of lactose (so mRNA and β-galactosidase are always produced).
   b) E.g. in Mutant 2, mRNA is produced in the presence of lactose, but active β-galactosidase isn't. This suggests that Mutant 2 is producing faulty β-galactosidase (e.g. because a mutation has affected its active site) / Mutant 2 isn't producing any β-galactosidase (e.g. because the mutation has affected a protein involved in translation).
Q4 They are reproducible.

#### Page 434 — Fact Recall Questions
Q1 a) A protein that binds to DNA and switches genes on or off by increasing or decreasing the rate of transcription.
   b) Activators — start/activate transcription.
      Repressors — stop/repress transcription.
   c) Specific DNA sites near the start of their target genes/the genes they control the expression of.
Q2 a) These code for useful proteins, e.g. enzymes.
   b) These include a promoter (a DNA sequence located before the structural genes that RNA polymerase binds to) and an operator (a DNA sequence that transcription factors bind to).
   c) This codes for a transcription factor.
Q3 The *lac* operon contains a regulatory gene (lacI), control elements and three structural genes (lacZ, lacY and lacA). When lactose is not present, lacI produces the lac repressor, which binds to the operator and blocks the transcription of lacZ, lacY and lacA. This means no mRNA is produced so no proteins are made.
Q4 Introns are removed / mature mRNA is produced.
Q5 Molecules like hormones can bind to cell membranes. This triggers the production of cyclic AMP (cAMP) within the cell. cAMP then activates proteins in the cell by changing their 3D structure.

### 2. Body Plans

#### Page 437 — Application Questions
Q1 a) Cells are broken down/killed.
   b) E.g. it may refine plant parts created by mitosis and differentiation by removing unwanted structures.
Q2 a) Hox genes code for proteins that control the development of the body plan. The ag-1 mutation alters the body plan (by causing petals to grow in place of stamens), so ag-1 must be a Hox gene.
   b) A homeobox sequence codes for a part of the protein called the homeodomain. The homeodomain binds to specific sites on DNA, enabling the protein to work as a transcription factor. The protein binds to DNA at the start of developmental genes, activating or repressing transcription and so altering the production of proteins involved in the development of the body plan.
   c) Because other organisms (e.g. animals and fungi) have similar Hox genes to plants, so the development of their body plans will be controlled in a similar way.

#### Page 437 — Fact Recall Questions
Q1 The general structure of an organism.
Q2 Hox genes.
Q3 Because it's controlled by similar Hox genes in each type of organism.
Q4 Enzymes inside the cell break down cell components, e.g. proteins and DNA. The cell shrinks and breaks up into fragments. The fragments are engulfed by phagocytes and digested.
Q5 Mitosis creates the bulk of the body parts.
Q6 Internal stimuli (e.g. DNA damage) and external stimuli (e.g. stress caused by a lack of nutrient availability).

### 3. Gene Mutations

#### Page 440 — Application Questions
Q1 a) Mutation A = a substitution mutation
      The third base along is now C, not T.
      Mutation B = a substitution mutation
      The seventh base along is now C, not G.
      Mutation C = a deletion mutation
      The fourth base, C, has been deleted.
      Mutation D = an insertion mutation
      The second triplet, TAT, has been inserted.
   b) Mutation A: Leu-His-Asp-Thr
      Mutation B: Leu-His-His-Thr
      Mutation C: Leu-Met-Ile
      Mutation D: Leu-Tyr-His-Asp-Thr
Q2 a) Mutation A is likely to have the least serious effect on the protein's structure. CTC still codes for Leu so the amino acid sequence/primary structure of the protein won't change from the original sequence.
   b) Mutation C is likely to have the most serious effect on the protein's structure as it is a frameshift mutation, and has caused all the amino acids coded for after the mutation to be different compared to the original sequence.

## Page 441 — Fact Recall Questions
Q1  A change in the DNA base (nucleotide) sequence.
Q2  E.g. if the mutation changes a base in a triplet, but the amino acid the triplet codes for doesn't change. If the mutation produces a triplet that codes for a different amino acid, but the amino acid is chemically similar to the original so it functions like the original amino acid. If the mutated triplet codes for an amino acid not involved with the protein's function.
Q3  It may alter the function of the protein produced so that it increases the organism's chance of survival.
Q4  E.g. a mutation at the start of a gene could result in RNA polymerase not being able to bind to the gene, which would mean that the protein coded for by the gene wouldn't be produced.

## Exam-style Questions — page 442
1   B *(1 mark)*
    Remember, similar Hox genes are found in plants, animals and fungi — they are not identical.
2   a) By the order of bases in the glucagon gene *(1 mark)*.
    b) E.g. glucagon could bind to cell membranes causing the production of cAMP inside the cell *(1 mark)*. cAMP would then activate the protein inside the cells by changing its three-dimensional structure *(1 mark)*.
    c) Once bound to the promoter, RNA polymerase begins the transcription of the structural genes in the *lac* operon *(1 mark)*. The structural genes produce proteins/enzymes that help the bacteria to digest lactose *(1 mark)*. This means the bacteria are able to respire lactose instead of glucose *(1 mark)*.
3   a) A single-base deletion will cause a frameshift *(1 mark)* and this could cause a change in the amino acid sequence/primary structure of the protein *(1 mark)*. This could change the tertiary structure of the protein and prevent it from functioning *(1 mark)*.
    b) A single-base substitution will only affect one amino acid *(1 mark)*, whereas a single-base deletion will probably alter all the amino acids after the mutation *(1 mark)*.
    c) Mutations that have a neutral effect on a protein's function won't affect an organism overall *(1 mark)*. This may happen because the mutation doesn't change the amino acid coded for by a triplet *(1 mark)* or because it changes the amino acid to one that is chemically similar to the original *(1 mark)*. Alternatively, the mutation may affect an amino acid that isn't involved in the protein's function *(1 mark)*.

# Section 2 — Patterns of Inheritance

## 1. Types and Causes of Variation
### Page 445 — Application Questions
Q1  a) monogenic
    b) Both. MAOA production is controlled by a gene, but it is also influenced by the environment (e.g. taking anti-depressants or smoking tobacco causes it to drop).
Q2  Environmental factors (temperature) affect mean percentage germination. All three genotypes showed variation in mean percentage germination at each temperature. For all genotypes, the highest percentage germination was at 30 °C and the lowest was at 35 °C. Genetic factors also affect mean percentage germination. The mean percentage germination was highest for genotype B at all three temperatures, and genotype C is higher than genotype A at all three temperatures.
*If you're asked to give evidence from a study, make sure you quote some figures to back up what you're saying.*

### Page 445 — Fact Recall Questions
Q1  polygenic
Q2  When a plant grows abnormally long and spindly because it's not getting enough light.
Q3  continuous

## 2. Genetic Terms
### Page 447 — Application Questions
Q1  A = tufted tail, B = tufted tail, C = non-tufted tail
Q2  a) yellow
    b) YY
    c) yy

## 3. Genetic Diagrams — Monogenic Crosses
### Pages 450-451 — Application Questions
Q1  The only possible genotype of offspring is heterozygous, e.g. Tt. Worked example:
    T — tall dominant allele
    t — dwarf recessive allele

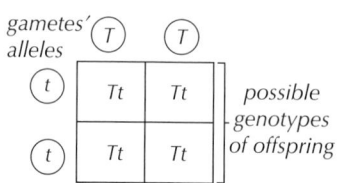

|  gametes'/alleles | T | T |  |
| --- | --- | --- | --- |
| t | Tt | Tt | possible genotypes of offspring |
| t | Tt | Tt |  |

*The question asked you to show your working. So even though you know that a monogenic cross with two homozygous parents always produces all heterozygous offspring, you must draw a genetic diagram of some kind to show how you would work that out.*

Q2  The phenotype ratio of curly hair : smooth hair for the offspring will be 3 : 1 / 75% of offspring will have curly hair and 25% will have smooth hair.
(8 ÷ 4) × 3 = **6 puppies**
Worked example:
H — curly hair allele
h — smooth hair allele

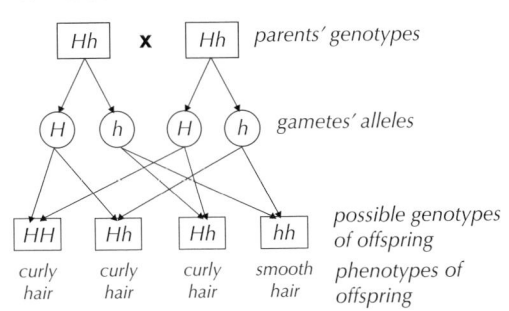

Parents' genotypes: Hh × Hh
Gametes' alleles: H, h, H, h
Possible genotypes of offspring: HH, Hh, Hh, hh
Phenotypes of offspring: curly hair, curly hair, curly hair, smooth hair

Q3 a) Worked example:
$H^N$ — normal allele
$H^S$ — sickle-cell allele

Parents' genotypes: $H^N H^N$ × $H^S H^S$
Gametes' alleles: $H^N$, $H^N$, $H^S$, $H^S$
Possible genotypes of offspring: $H^N H^S$, $H^N H^S$, $H^N H^S$, $H^N H^S$
Phenotypes of offspring: sickle-cell trait, sickle-cell trait, sickle-cell trait, sickle-cell trait

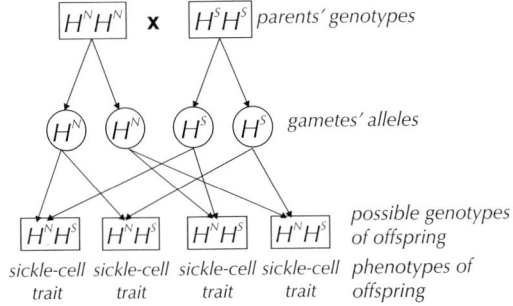

b) There is a 25% chance that any of these children will have sickle-cell anaemia. Worked example:
$H^N$ — normal allele
$H^S$ — sickle-cell allele

Parents' genotypes: $H^N H^S$ × $H^N H^S$
Gametes' alleles: $H^N$, $H^S$, $H^N$, $H^S$
Possible genotypes of offspring: $H^N H^N$, $H^N H^S$, $H^S H^N$, $H^S H^S$
Phenotypes of offspring: Normal, sickle-cell trait, sickle-cell trait, sickle-cell anaemia

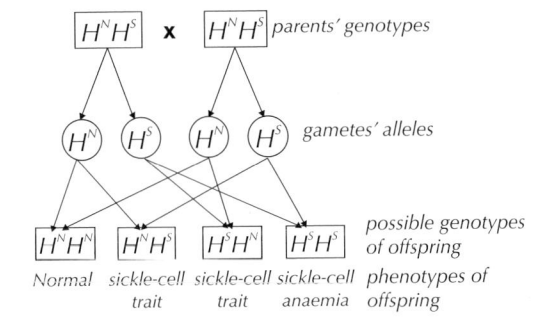

Q4  ½ / 0.5 / 50%. Worked example:
D — polydactyly dominant allele
d — normal recessive allele

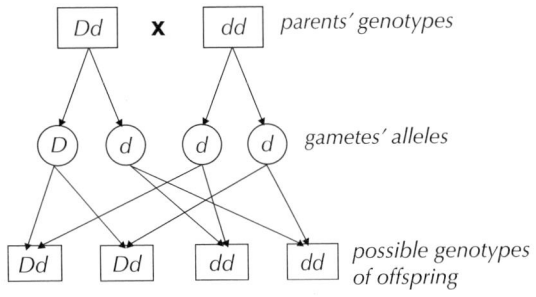

Parents' genotypes: Dd × dd
Gametes' alleles: D, d, d, d
Possible genotypes of offspring: Dd, Dd, dd, dd

Q5  1 : 0 : 1 ratio of blue : yellow : striped organisms / 1 : 1 ratio of blue : striped organisms. Worked example:
$C^Y$ — yellow allele
$C^B$ — blue allele

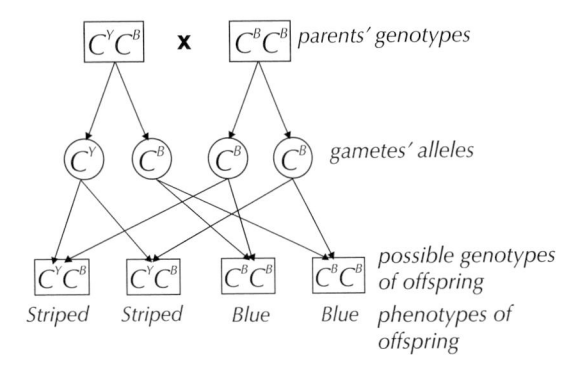

Parents' genotypes: $C^Y C^B$ × $C^B C^B$
Gametes' alleles: $C^Y$, $C^B$, $C^B$, $C^B$
Possible genotypes of offspring: $C^Y C^B$, $C^Y C^B$, $C^B C^B$, $C^B C^B$
Phenotypes of offspring: Striped, Striped, Blue, Blue

## Page 451 — Fact Recall Questions

Q1  Monogenic inheritance is the inheritance of a characteristic controlled by a single gene.
Q2  The ratio of different phenotypes in the offspring.
Q3  Codominant alleles are alleles that are both expressed in the phenotype, and neither one is recessive.
Q4  a) 3 : 1 ratio of dominant : recessive characteristics
    b) 1 : 2 : 1 ratio of homozygous for one allele : heterozygous : homozygous for the other allele

*The phenotypic ratios are always the same for these types of crosses, so it's well worth learning them.*

## 4. Genetic Diagrams — Multiple Allele and Dihybrid Crosses

### Page 454 — Application Questions

**Q1** The possible striping patterns are Abyssinian (50%) and Mackerel (50%). Worked example:

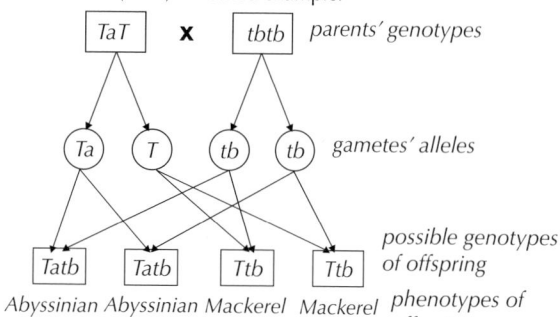

TaT × tbtb — parents' genotypes

Gametes' alleles: Ta, T, tb, tb

Possible genotypes of offspring: Tatb, Tatb, Ttb, Ttb

Phenotypes of offspring: Abyssinian, Abyssinian, Mackerel, Mackerel

**Q2** a) Melanic (M) is dominant to both of the other alleles, insularia is dominant to typical only and typical is recessive to all. / The dominance of the alleles is M > M' > m.

b) All heterozygous melanic (Mm). Worked example:

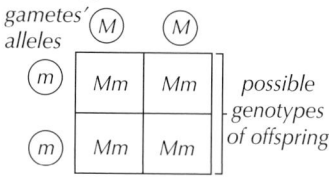

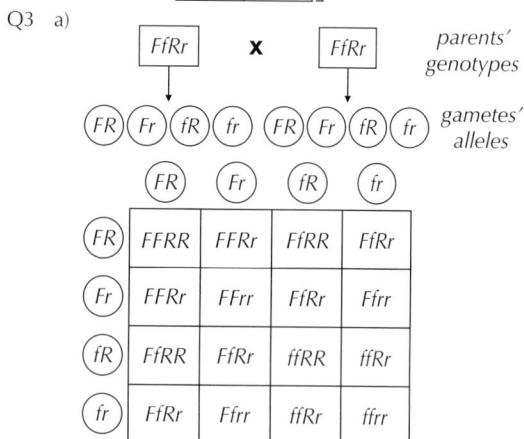

|  | M | M |
|---|---|---|
| m | Mm | Mm |
| m | Mm | Mm |

possible genotypes of offspring

**Q3** a)

FfRr × FfRr — parents' genotypes

Gametes' alleles: FR, Fr, fR, fr × FR, Fr, fR, fr

|  | FR | Fr | fR | fr |
|---|---|---|---|---|
| FR | FFRR | FFRr | FfRR | FfRr |
| Fr | FFRr | FFrr | FfRr | Ffrr |
| fR | FfRR | FfRr | ffRR | ffRr |
| fr | FfRr | Ffrr | ffRr | ffrr |

b) 9 : 1 ratio of round, red tomatoes to pear-shaped, yellow tomatoes.
Round, red tomatoes = FFRR, FFRr, FfRR, FfRr
Pear-shaped, yellow tomatoes = ffrr

**Q4** a) The offspring would all be heterozygous (BbPp).
The red cow with horns must have a homozygous recessive phenotype (bbpp). Dihybrid crosses between homozygous dominant and homozygous recessive parents will always produce heterozygous offspring in the $F_1$ generation.

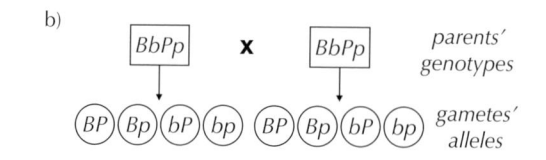

b)

BbPp × BbPp — parents' genotypes

Gametes' alleles: BP, Bp, bP, bp × BP, Bp, bP, bp

|  | BP | Bp | bP | bp |
|---|---|---|---|---|
| BP | BBPP | BBPp | BbPP | BbPp |
| Bp | BBPp | BBpp | BbPp | Bbpp |
| bP | BbPP | BbPp | bbPP | bbPp |
| bp | BbPp | Bbpp | bbPp | bbpp |

Black with no horns = BBPP, BBPp, BbPP, BbPp = 9
Black with horns = BBpp, Bbpp = 3
Red with no horns = bbPP, bbPp = 3
Red with horns = bbpp = 1

Phenotypic ratio: 9 : 3 : 3 : 1

### Page 454 — Fact Recall Questions

**Q1** one

**Q2** Dihybrid inheritance is the inheritance of two characteristics, which are controlled by different genes.

**Q3** 9 : 3 : 3 : 1 ratio of dominant both : dominant first, recessive second : recessive first, dominant second : recessive both.

## 5. Linkage

### Page 459 — Application Questions

**Q1** $X^FX^F$ (affected female), $X^FY$ (affected male), $X^FX^f$ (affected female), $X^fY$ (unaffected male). Worked example:

$X^FY$ — affected male
$X^FX^f$ — affected heterozygous female

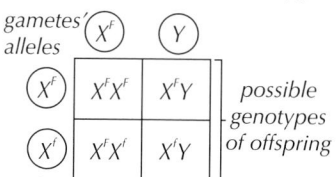

Gametes' alleles: $X^F$, Y

|  | $X^F$ | Y |
|---|---|---|
| $X^F$ | $X^FX^F$ | $X^FY$ |
| $X^f$ | $X^FX^f$ | $X^fY$ |

possible genotypes of offspring

This question doesn't ask you to show your working, but it's best to always do so. Then if you write an answer down wrong for any reason, you could still pick up marks in your exam for your working.

**Q2** Y-linked characteristics can only be passed on down the male (XY) line. So for a child to have a Y-linked disorder, its father must also have the disorder. So if a child has hairy ears but its dad doesn't, the dad might question if he was the father.
This is fairly tricky, but drawing a quick diagram would help you out:

$XY^N$ — unaffected male
XX — female

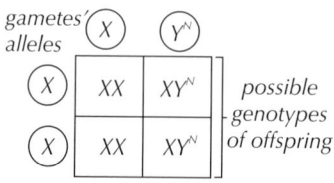

Gametes' alleles: X, $Y^N$

|  | X | $Y^N$ |
|---|---|---|
| X | XX | $XY^N$ |
| X | XX | $XY^N$ |

possible genotypes of offspring

An unaffected male can't have a child with the disorder.

Q3 ¼ / 0.25 / 25%. Worked example:
$X^N Y$ — unaffected male
$X^N X^n$ — female carrier

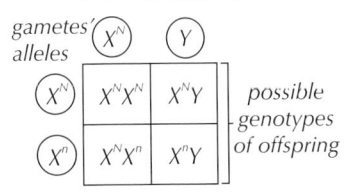

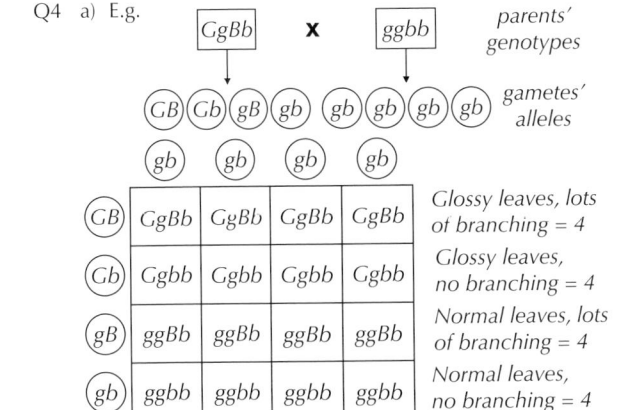

| gametes/alleles | $X^N$ | $Y$ |
|---|---|---|
| $X^N$ | $X^N X^N$ | $X^N Y$ |
| $X^n$ | $X^N X^n$ | $X^n Y$ |

possible genotypes of offspring

Q4 a) E.g.

GgBb × ggbb — parents' genotypes

Gametes' alleles: GB, Gb, gB, gb × gb, gb, gb, gb

|  | GB | Gb | gB | gb |
|---|---|---|---|---|
| gb | GgBb | Ggbb | ggBb | ggbb |
| gb | GgBb | Ggbb | ggBb | ggbb |
| gb | GgBb | Ggbb | ggBb | ggbb |
| gb | GgBb | Ggbb | ggBb | ggbb |

Glossy leaves, lots of branching = 4
Glossy leaves, no branching = 4
Normal leaves, lots of branching = 4
Normal leaves, no branching = 4

Expected phenotypic ratio = 1 : 1 : 1 : 1
b) Observed phenotypic ratio = 1.7 : 1.1 : 1 : 1.8
c) The GB alleles and the gb alleles in the GgBb parent may have been linked. This would mean that the GgBb parent produced mostly GB and gb gametes and would make the GgBb and ggbb genotypes more common in the offspring. As a result, a higher proportion of the offspring would have their parents' phenotypes, instead of the even split of phenotypes predicted.

## Page 459 — Fact Recall Questions
Q1 ½ / 0.5 / 50%
Q2 If a characteristic is sex-linked it means that the allele that codes for it is located on a sex chromosome (X or Y).
Q3 Males are more likely than females to have X-linked disorders because males only have one X chromosome. Because they only have one copy of any alleles on the X chromosome, they express the characteristic of those alleles even if they're recessive, whereas women would need to inherit two copies to express the same characteristics.
Q4 An autosome is any chromosome that isn't a sex chromosome.
Q5 Genes on the same autosome are said to be linked because being on the same autosome usually means they'll stay together during the independent assortment of chromosomes in meiosis I. This means their alleles will be passed on to the offspring together (unless crossing over splits them up first).

## 6. Epistasis

## Page 462 — Application Questions
Q1 a) i) EEBB, EeBB, EEBb, EeBb
For the dog to be black it must be able to express the dark pigment, so it much have at least one dominant E allele. Also, it must have at least one copy of the dominant B allele for the black pigment to be shown in the phenotype.
ii) Eebb, EEbb
For the dog to be chocolate it must be able to express the dark pigment, so it much have at least one dominant E allele. Also, it must have two copies of the recessive b allele for the chocolate pigment to be shown in the phenotype.
iii) eeBB, eeBb, eebb
For the dog to be yellow it must have two copies of the recessive e allele, so that it can't express the dark pigment. Gene 1 is epistatic over gene 2, so it doesn't matter what B or b alleles the dog has — it will still be yellow.
b) A cross between EEBB and eebb parents will give a 9 : 3 : 4 phenotypic ratio in the $F_2$ generation of black : chocolate : yellow. This is because gene 1 has a recessive epistatic allele (e) and two copies of the recessive epistatic allele (ee) will mask the expression of gene 2. Here's the cross to prove it:
B = black pigment, b = chocolate pigment, E = can express dark pigment, e = can't express dark pigment

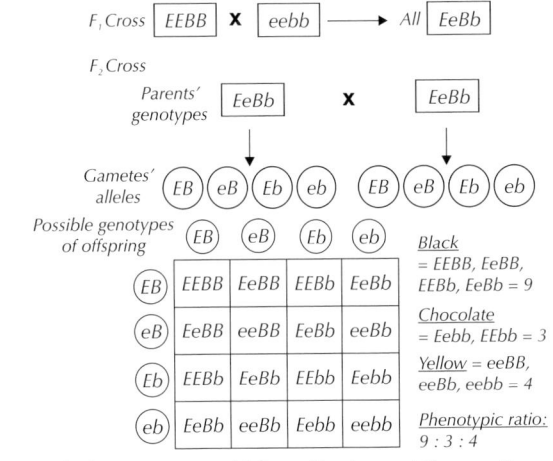

$F_1$ Cross: EEBB × eebb → All EeBb

$F_2$ Cross:
Parents' genotypes: EeBb × EeBb
Gametes' alleles: EB, eB, Eb, eb × EB, eB, Eb, eb

Possible genotypes of offspring:

|  | EB | eB | Eb | eb |
|---|---|---|---|---|
| EB | EEBB | EeBB | EEBb | EeBb |
| eB | EeBB | eeBB | EeBb | eeBb |
| Eb | EEBb | EeBb | EEbb | Eebb |
| eb | EeBb | eeBb | Eebb | eebb |

Black = EEBB, EeBB, EEBb, EeBb = 9
Chocolate = Eebb, EEbb = 3
Yellow = eeBB, eeBb, eebb = 4
Phenotypic ratio: 9 : 3 : 4

In the exam, you wouldn't need to draw out the genetic cross unless the question specifically asked you to. We've just included it here to help you out.

Q2 a) dominant epistasis
b) A cross between WWPP and wwpp produces a 48 : 12 : 4 or 12 : 3 : 1 phenotypic ratio in the $F_2$ generation of white : purple : red. This is because gene 1 has a dominant epistatic allele (W) and one or more copies of the dominant epistatic allele (Ww or WW) will mask the expression of gene 2.

c) W = white pigment, w = red pigment, P = purple pigment, p = no purple pigment

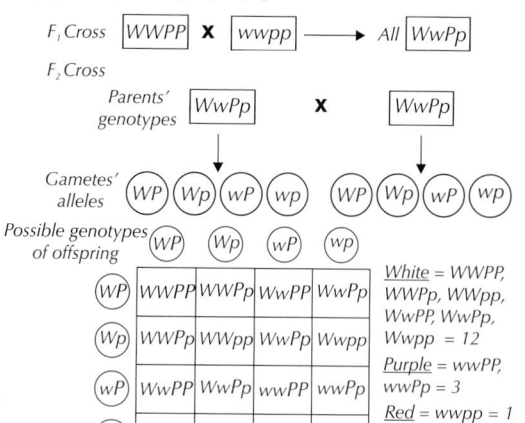

$F_1$ Cross: WWPP × wwpp → All WwPp

$F_2$ Cross:
Parents' genotypes: WwPp × WwPp

Gametes' alleles: (WP)(Wp)(wP)(wp)  (WP)(Wp)(wP)(wp)

Possible genotypes of offspring:

|  | (WP) | (Wp) | (wP) | (wp) |
|---|---|---|---|---|
| (WP) | WWPP | WWPp | WwPP | WwPp |
| (Wp) | WWPp | WWpp | WwPp | Wwpp |
| (wP) | WwPP | WwPp | wwPP | wwPp |
| (wp) | WwPp | Wwpp | wwPp | wwpp |

<u>White</u> = WWPP, WWPp, WWpp, WwPP, WwPp, Wwpp = 12
<u>Purple</u> = wwPP, wwPp = 3
<u>Red</u> = wwpp = 1
<u>Phenotypic ratio</u>: 12 : 3 : 1

## 7. The Chi-Squared Test

### Pages 466-467 — Application Questions

**Q1 a)** Yes, the difference would be significant because the chi-squared value is greater than the critical value (6.20 > 5.99).
*If the difference is significant it means the difference is unlikely to be due to chance and that the null hypothesis is rejected.*

**b)** No, the difference would not be significant because the chi-squared value is smaller than the critical value (4.85 < 5.99).
*If the difference is not significant it means the difference is likely to be due to chance — we're unable to reject the null hypothesis.*

**Q2**

| Phenotype | Ratio | Expected result (E) | Observed result (O) | O − E | (O − E)² | (O − E)²/E |
|---|---|---|---|---|---|---|
| Grey body | 3 | 48 | 45 | −3 | 9 | 0.19 |
| Ebony body | 1 | 16 | 19 | 3 | 9 | 0.56 |

$\chi^2 = \Sigma \frac{(O-E)^2}{E} = 0.75$

Therefore $\chi^2 = $ **0.75**

**Q3 a)**

| Phenotype | Ratio | Expected result (E) | Observed result (O) | O − E | (O − E)² | (O − E)²/E |
|---|---|---|---|---|---|---|
| Round, green | 9 | 72 | 74 | 2 | 4 | 0.06 |
| Round, yellow | 3 | 24 | 21 | −3 | 9 | 0.38 |
| Wrinkled, green | 3 | 24 | 26 | 2 | 4 | 0.17 |
| Wrinkled, yellow | 1 | 8 | 7 | −1 | 1 | 0.13 |

$\chi^2 = \Sigma \frac{(O-E)^2}{E} = 0.74$

Therefore $\chi^2 = $ **0.74**

**b)** There are 4 phenotypes which means there are 4 − 1 = 3 degrees of freedom. From the table, the critical value for a test with 3 degrees of freedom and a 0.05 probability level is 7.82. The chi-squared value is smaller than the critical value (0.74 < 7.82) so the difference between the observed and expected results is not significant. This means we're unable to reject the null hypothesis.

**Q4 a)** That there is no significant difference between the observed and expected results.

**b)**

| Phenotype | Ratio | Expected result (E) | Observed result (O) | O − E | (O − E)² | (O − E)²/E |
|---|---|---|---|---|---|---|
| Tall | 3 | 39 | 43 | 4 | 16 | 0.41 |
| Dwarf | 1 | 13 | 9 | −4 | 16 | 1.23 |

$\chi^2 = \Sigma \frac{(O-E)^2}{E} = 1.64$

Therefore $\chi^2 = $ **1.64**.
There are two phenotypes (tall and dwarf) which means there is 2 − 1 = 1 degree of freedom. From the table, the critical value for a test with 1 degree of freedom and a 0.05 probability level is 3.84. The chi-squared value is smaller than the critical value (1.64 < 3.84) so the difference between the observed and expected results is not significant. This means that the null hypothesis can't be rejected, so the results from this experiment support the scientist's theory.

**Q5 a)**

| Phenotype | Ratio | Expected result (E) | Observed result (O) | O − E | (O − E)² | (O − E)²/E |
|---|---|---|---|---|---|---|
| Red | 1 | 40 | 24 | −16 | 256 | 6.40 |
| Pink | 2 | 80 | 92 | 12 | 144 | 1.80 |
| White | 1 | 40 | 44 | 4 | 16 | 0.40 |

$\chi^2 = \Sigma \frac{(O-E)^2}{E} = 8.60$

Therefore $\chi^2 = $ **8.6**.
There are 3 phenotypes which means there are 3 − 1 = 2 degrees of freedom. From the table, the critical value for a test with 2 degrees of freedom and a 0.05 probability level is 5.99. The chi-squared value is greater than the critical value (8.6 > 5.99) so the difference between the observed and expected results is significant. This means that the null hypothesis is rejected, so this is unlikely to be an example of codominance.
*Be careful — the order that observed results are written in the question won't necessarily be the same as the order that things need to be written in the table.*

**b)**

| Phenotype | Ratio | Expected result (E) | Observed result (O) | O − E | (O − E)² | (O − E)²/E |
|---|---|---|---|---|---|---|
| Pink | 9 | 90 | 92 | 2 | 4 | 0.04 |
| Red | 3 | 30 | 24 | −6 | 36 | 1.20 |
| White | 4 | 40 | 44 | 4 | 16 | 0.40 |

$\chi^2 = \Sigma \frac{(O-E)^2}{E} = 1.64$

Therefore $\chi^2 = $ **1.64**.
The critical value is 5.99 (the same as for part a). This time the chi-squared value is smaller than the critical value (1.64 < 5.99) so the difference between the observed and expected results is not significant. This means that the null hypothesis can't be rejected and it is likely that recessive epistasis is involved.
*The critical value is the same here as in part a) because the number of degrees have freedom haven't changed (there are still 3 phenotypes involved).*

## Exam-style Questions — pages 469-470

1. a) Number of agouti offspring = (256 ÷ 4) × 3 = **192** *(1 mark)*
   A normal case of monogenic inheritance would give a phenotypic ratio of 3 : 1 of agouti : solid coloured. So three-quarters of the offspring would have agouti coat colour.
   b) ppAA, ppAa, ppaa *(1 mark)*
   The allele for pigmentation is <u>controlled</u> by the gene (P) — you need to have a gene for coat colour <u>as well as</u> the control gene to get the albino phenotype.
   c) A cross between PPAA and ppaa parents will give a 9 : 3 : 4 phenotypic ratio in the $F_2$ generation of agouti : solid coloured : albino *(1 mark)*. This is because the P gene has a recessive epistatic allele (p) and two copies of the recessive epistatic allele (pp) will mask the expression of the pigmentation gene *(1 mark)*. A dihybrid cross will only give a phenotypic ratio of 9 : 3 : 3 : 1 in the $F_2$ generation if the two genes do not interact and are not linked *(1 mark)*.

2. a)

   | Genotype | Growth on substance 1 |
   |---|---|
   | AaBb | ✓ |
   | aaBb | ✗ |
   | AAbb | ✗ |
   | AABb | ✓ |

   *(1 mark for all three correct)*
   b) They must have the genotype aaBb or aaBB *(1 mark)*. They can't produce enzyme A but can produce enzyme B *(1 mark)*, so if they're given substance 2 they can convert it to substance 3 *(1 mark)*.
   c) E.g.

   AaBb × aabb  parents' genotypes
   gametes' alleles: AB, Ab, aB, ab × ab, ab, ab, ab

   |  | ab | ab | ab | ab |
   |---|---|---|---|---|
   | AB | AaBb | AaBb | AaBb | AaBb |
   | Ab | Aabb | Aabb | Aabb | Aabb |
   | aB | aaBb | aaBb | aaBb | aaBb |
   | ab | aabb | aabb | aabb | aabb |

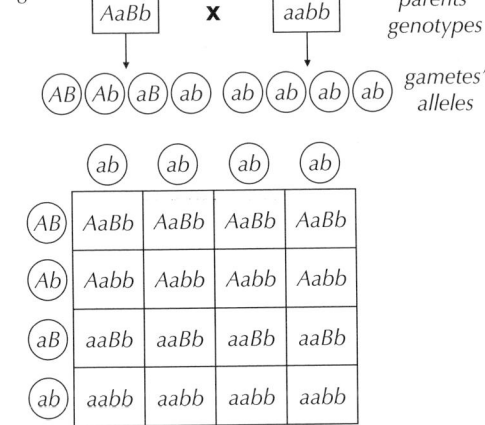

   *(1 mark for correct gametes, 1 mark for correct $F_1$ genotypes)*
   The ratio of genotypes AaBb : Aabb : aaBb : aabb is 1 : 1 : 1 : 1 *(1 mark)*.
   (12 ÷ 16) × 100 = **75%** *(1 mark)*
   Offspring with the genotype Aabb, aaBb and aabb would not be able to grow in medium containing substance 1.

3. a) $X^hY$ — haemophiliac male
   $X^HX^h$ — female carrier

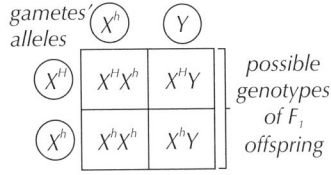

   gametes/alleles: $X^h$, Y across; $X^H$, $X^h$ down

   |  | $X^h$ | Y |
   |---|---|---|
   | $X^H$ | $X^HX^h$ | $X^HY$ |
   | $X^h$ | $X^hX^h$ | $X^hY$ |

   possible genotypes of $F_1$ offspring

   Possible phenotypes of $F_1$ offspring: carrier female ($X^HX^h$), unaffected male ($X^HY$), haemophiliac female ($X^hX^h$) and haemophiliac male ($X^hY$).
   *(1 mark for correct gametes, 1 mark for correct $F_1$ genotypes, 1 mark for $F_1$ phenotypes matched to correct $F_1$ genotypes.)*

   b) i)

   | Phenotype | Ratio | E | O | O − E | (O − E)² | $\frac{(O-E)^2}{E}$ |
   |---|---|---|---|---|---|---|
   | Carrier female | 1 | 68 | 72 | 4 | 16 | 0.24 |
   | Haemophilic female | 1 | 68 | 70 | 2 | 4 | 0.06 |
   | Unaffected male | 1 | 68 | 69 | 1 | 1 | 0.02 |
   | Haemophilic male | 1 | 68 | 61 | −7 | 49 | 0.72 |

   $\chi^2 = \Sigma \frac{(O-E)^2}{E} = 1.04$

   Therefore $\chi^2 =$ **1.04**.
   *(3 marks for correct answer, otherwise 1 mark for correct expected results, 1 mark for correct $(O-E)^2 \div E$ calculation.)*
   ii) The difference between the observed and expected results is not significant at the 0.05 probability level *(1 mark)*.
   This is because the critical value for this test is 7.82 and the chi-squared value (1.04) is less than this.

# Section 3 — Evolution

## 1. Evolution by Natural Selection and Genetic Drift

### Page 475 — Application Questions
Q1 a) The frequency of the three alleles in Population 1 is relatively even. However in Population 2 there is a very high frequency of the white allele and much lower frequencies of the purple and pink alleles.
   b) By chance, the white allele was passed onto offspring more than the other alleles. As a result, the number of individuals with the white allele increased and the number of individuals with purple and pink alleles fell.
   c) Population 2, because genetic drift has a much greater effect in smaller populations.
Q2 a) The peak in allele frequency in 2000 was most likely a result of the fire in 1999. The peak may be due to an increase in the number of mammals emigrating to the south from the north as a result of the fire. The northern population had a slightly higher frequency of the allele, so an influx from this population could have caused an increase in the allele frequency in the south.

b) From 1998 to 2002 there was a big increase in the dark fur allele in the northern population. In 1999, a fire destroyed a large area in the north of the forest. This would have left a large area of barren, darkened forest and blackened soil. Mammals with darker fur would have a selective advantage and so be more likely to survive, reproduce and pass on their alleles for darker fur, causing an increase in the frequency of the dark fur allele.

## Page 475 — Fact Recall Questions
Q1 a) The complete range of alleles in a population.
b) How often an allele appears in a population.
Q2 Evolution is the change in the frequency of an allele in a population over time.
Q3 Because individuals vary, it means that some organisms are better adapted to selection pressures than others. These individuals are more likely to survive, reproduce and pass on their beneficial alleles to their offspring than others so that, over many generations, these alleles become more common in a population.
Q4 It makes it more likely that individuals with alleles for characteristics towards the middle of the range will survive and reproduce. This reduces the range of possible phenotypes.
Q5 An event that causes a big reduction in the size of a population. Evolution by genetic drift has a greater effect on a population if there's a genetic bottleneck.
Q6 The founder effect describes the effect of starting a population from just a few individuals — when this happens, the number of alleles present in the new population will be much smaller than in the original population, so the frequency of these alleles will be much higher than in the original population. If, by chance, one of these alleles represents a genetic disorder, this could lead to an increased incidence of that disorder in the new population.

## 2. The Hardy-Weinberg Principle

## Page 478 — Application Questions
Q1 a) $p + q = 1$
$p = 1 - q$
$p = 1 - 0.10 =$ **0.90**
You're given one allele frequency in the table and are asked to find the other, so its the simple equation.
b) $p = 0.9$, $q = 0.1$, so $2pq = 2 \times 0.9 \times 0.1 =$ **0.18**
c) No, it does not apply. The frequency of the allele changes between the generations, and the Hardy-Weinberg principle is only true in cases where the allele frequency stays the same.
Q2 $q = 0.16$ and $p + q = 1$, so $p = 1 - q$
$p = 1 - 0.16 = 0.84$
homozygous dominant genotype frequency = $p^2$
$p^2 = 0.84^2 =$ **0.71**
Q3 recessive wrinkled allele = $q^2 = 31\% \div 100 = 0.31$
$q = \sqrt{0.31} = 0.557$
$p + q = 1$, so $p = 1 - q$
$p = 1 - 0.557 = 0.443$
Heterozygous genotype = $2pq$
$2pq = 2 \times 0.443 \times 0.557 = 0.49$
$0.49 \times 100 = 49$, so **49%** of the population have a heterozygous genotype.

## Page 478 — Fact Recall Questions
Q1 The Hardy-Weinberg principle is a mathematical model that predicts that the frequencies of alleles in a population won't change from one generation to the next as long as the population is large, there's no immigration, emigration, mutations or natural selection, and mating is totally random.
Q2 $p + q = 1$ and $p^2 + 2pq + q^2 = 1$, where $p$ = the frequency of the dominant allele, $q$ = the frequency of the recessive allele, $p^2$ = the frequency of the homozygous dominant genotype, $q^2$ = the frequency of the homozygous recessive genotype and $2pq$ = the frequency of the heterozygous genotype.

## 3. Artificial Selection

## Page 480 — Fact Recall Questions
Q1 Artificial selection is where humans select individuals in a population to breed together to get desirable traits.
Q2 a) E.g. females with large udders and males whose mothers had large udders were selected and bred together. The offspring with the largest udders were then selected and bred together. This process was continued over several generations until a cow with very large udders was produced.
b) E.g. high milk yield / high milk quality / a long lactation period / resistance to mastitis/disease / a calm temperament
Q3 E.g. bread wheat has been selectively bred to have a high wheat yield/large ears / a high tolerance to the cold / short stalks / uniform stalk height.
Q4 E.g. selective breeding can reduce the gene pool of a species, which could lead to problems in the future with resistance to new strains of diseases. Selective breeding can also cause unforeseen health problems for the organisms involved.

## 4. Speciation

## Pages 482-483 — Application Questions
Q1 E.g. the two elephant populations separated and became geographically isolated. The different habitats caused different selective pressures, so in each habitat elephants with different alleles were more likely to survive, reproduce and pass on their advantageous alleles. Over time this caused the frequencies of the advantageous alleles in each habitat to increase. Mutations also took place independently in each population, which also altered the allele frequencies in each habitat. Eventually the differences in allele frequencies resulted in the phenotypes of the two populations changing so much that they became reproductively isolated. Speciation had occurred.
Q2 a) Test whether they are able to breed with each other to produce fertile offspring.
b) Sympatric speciation. The two populations occur in the same area.

## Page 483 — Fact Recall Questions
Q1 a) When populations of the same species can no longer breed together to produce fertile offspring (as a result of changes in allele frequencies).
b) When a physical barrier divides two populations of a species.
c) The development of a new species.

Q2  In allopatric speciation the populations are geographically isolated before they become reproductively isolated. In sympatric speciation, reproductive isolation evolves between two populations without geographical isolation.

Q3  E.g. individuals could develop different flowering or mating seasons. Changes in genitalia may prevent individuals from mating successfully. A group of individuals may develop courtship rituals that aren't attractive to the main population.

## Exam-style Questions — pages 485-486

1  a) stabilising selection
   b) Birds could evolve to breed earlier in the year *(1 mark)*, as sufficient food will be available to allow them to breed earlier in the year, and offspring that hatch earlier in the year are more likely to survive *(1 mark)*.

2  a) i) artificial selection / selective breeding *(1 mark)*
      ii) E.g. males and females which grew quickly, converted food into body mass efficiently and produced a high proportion of breast meat were selected and bred together. Their offspring that showed these traits most strongly were then selected and bred together *(1 mark)*. This process continued over multiple generations, to give chickens that grew quickly and efficiently to produce a high proportion of breast meat *(1 mark)*.
   b) E.g. because broiler chickens grow quickly and can be slaughtered at a younger age, producing chicken is quicker, meaning a large volume of meat can be generated easily *(1 mark)*. The fact that broiler chickens are efficient at converting food to body mass also reduces costs, and means raising broiler chickens uses fewer resources than normal chickens (which is good for the environment) *(1 mark)*. However, selective breeding appears to have increased broiler chickens' vulnerability to some health problems, such as cardiovascular problems and walking issues, and many people don't think it's fair to artificially select traits that cause the organism to suffer *(1 mark)*.

3  a) The change may be due to genetic drift *(1 mark)* or it may be due to natural selection for smaller body size in the smaller forest fragment *(1 mark)*.
   b) Genetic drift is random, but natural selection increases the frequency of traits that increase an organism's chances of survival, so the scientists could distinguish between the two possibilities by looking at whether smaller beetles in the small forest fragment have a higher chance of survival *(1 mark)*. If they do, then the change is likely to be due to natural selection *(1 mark)*.

4  a) $q^2 = 5 \div 1000 = 0.005$
      $q = \sqrt{0.005} = 0.0707$
      $p = 1 - 0.0707 = 0.9293$
      $2pq = 0.1314$
      $0.1314 \times 100 = \mathbf{13.14\%}$
      *(2 marks for the correct answer, otherwise 1 mark for identifying 2pq as the frequency of heterozygotes in the population.)*
   b) Genetic drift *(1 mark)*. The syndrome does not increase a person's chance of surviving, so the allele must have become more common in the population by chance *(1 mark)*.

5  a) *7-9 marks:*
      The answer gives a detailed discussion of the selection pressures on both islands, and how the population sizes on the two islands will have affected their ability to respond to the selection pressures. Scientific terminology is used correctly, and the answer demonstrates a detailed understanding of the process of evolution, including the founder effect and genetic drift.
      The answer has a clear and logical structure.
      The information given is relevant and detailed.
      *4-6 marks:*
      The selection pressures on both islands are discussed, but no reference is made to the effect of population size. Scientific terminology is used correctly, and the answer is mostly well-structured.
      Most of the information given is relevant and there is some detail involved.
      *1-3 marks:*
      The selection pressures on Pod Mrcaru are discussed, but no comparisons are made to Pod Kopiste. Use of scientific terminology is poor.
      The answer has no clear structure. The information given is basic and lacking in detail. It may not all be relevant.
      *0 marks:*
      No relevant information is given
      **Here are some points your answer may include:**
      On Pod Mrcaru, more vegetation is available to eat than on Pod Kopiste. This has acted as a selection pressure on Pod Mrcaru, favouring individuals with alleles that make them better able to eat and digest vegetation. The individuals introduced to Pod Mrcaru included some individuals who were better able to eat vegetation, due to having stronger jaws, and individuals who were better able to digest vegetation due to the structure of their gut. These individuals were more likely to survive and reproduce, and pass on their alleles, leading to an increase in the frequency of these alleles over time and a change in jaw strength and gut structure across generations. The speed of this change may have been increased by the effect of genetic drift, and also by the founder effect, as the population of Pod Mrcaru was initially very small.
      On Pod Kopiste, on the other hand, as less vegetation is present, the selection pressure to be able to eat and process vegetation will have been lower. The population of lizards on Pod Kopiste will also have initially been larger, meaning that there was less of a chance of alleles for features that would make it easier to eat and digest vegetation increasing in frequency by chance via genetic drift. This weaker selection pressure and lack of drift will have meant that the ability to eat and digest vegetation efficiently has not evolved on Pod Kopiste within the same timescale as on Pod Mrcaru.
   b) i) allopatric speciation *(1 mark)*
      ii) The two populations would need to become reproductively isolated *(1 mark)*.

# Section 4 — Manipulating Genomes

## 1. Common Techniques

### Page 491 — Application Questions
Q1  a) top strand = CGTA, bottom strand = GGTA
    b) $2 \times 2 \times 2 \times 2 \times 2 \times 2 \times 2 = $ **128**
    *Remember, you start with two single stands of DNA. The amount of DNA then doubles with each PCR cycle.*

Q2  There is a *Bam*HI site on the left-hand side of the fragment and an *Eco*RI site towards the right-hand side. The DNA sample could be incubated with *Bam*HI and *Eco*RI, which would cut the DNA via a hydrolysis reaction at these sites. This is because the shape of each recognition sequence is complementary to each enzyme's active site.
    *Make sure you use the correct terms in the exam, e.g. the shape of the recognition sequence is* complementary *to the enzyme's active site,* not *the same as the enzyme's active site.*

Q3  a) It helps the samples to sink to the bottom of the wells and makes them easier to see.
    b) Make sure the tip of the micropipette is in the buffer solution and just above the opening of the well. Be careful not to pierce the bottom of the well by sticking the tip of the micropipette too far into the well. Also, use a clean micropipette tip for each different sample.
    c) Put the lid on the gel box and connect the leads from the gel box to the power supply. Then turn on the power supply and set it to the required voltage so an electrical current will pass through the gel. Let the gel run for about 30 minutes before turning off the power supply.

### Page 491 — Fact Recall Questions
Q1  polymerase chain reaction
Q2  A sequence of DNA that consists of antiparallel base pairs/base pairs that read the same in opposite directions.
Q3  Small tails of unpaired bases at the end of a DNA fragment. They can be used to bind/anneal the DNA fragment to another piece of DNA that has sticky ends with complementary sequences.
Q4  At the top / near the negative electrode.
Q5  You need to mix them with a chemical that denatures the proteins so they all have the same charge.
Q6  E.g. it could be used to identify the proteins present in urine or blood samples, which may help to diagnose disease.

## 2. DNA profiling

### Page 492 — Fact Recall Question
Q1  DNA profiling can be used to compare samples of DNA collected from crime scenes to samples of DNA from possible suspects. The DNA is isolated from all the collected samples (from the crime scene and from the suspects) and PCR is used to amplify multiple areas containing different sequence repeats. The PCR products are run on an electrophoresis gel and the DNA profiles produced are compared to see if any match. If the samples match, it links a person to the crime scene.

## 3. Genetic Engineering

### Page 494 — Application Question
Q1  a) Vector DNA was cut with the same restriction enzymes as the DNA fragment, so complementary sticky ends were produced. The DNA fragment and cut vector were mixed with DNA ligase, which joined together the sugar-phosphate backbones of the two pieces to form the recombinant DNA.
    b) electroporation

### Page 494 — Fact Recall Questions
Q1  The manipulation of an organism's DNA.
Q2  recombinant DNA
Q3  a) It transfers the fragment of DNA containing the desired gene into the host cell.
    b) E.g. plasmids and bacteriophages.
Q4  It means that the sticky ends of the vector DNA are complementary to the sticky ends of the DNA fragment containing the gene (allowing them to be joined).
Q5  DNA ligase is used to join the sticky ends of the DNA fragment containing the desired gene to the sticky ends of the vector DNA. They join together the sugar-phosphate backbones of the two bits of DNA.

## 4. Genetically Modified Organisms

### Pages 498 — Application Questions
Q1  a) E.g. the desired genes from the maize plant and soil bacterium could have been isolated using restriction enzymes and inserted into a plasmid from a bacterium, such as *A. tumefaciens*. The plasmid could then have been put back into *A. tumefaciens* and the rice plant cells infected with the transformed *A. tumefaciens* bacteria. The desired genes would then get inserted into the rice plant cells, creating the genetically modified rice.
    b) E.g. Golden Rice could be used to feed people in areas where people suffer from a vitamin A deficiency.
Q2  E.g. people with diabetes are now able to obtain human insulin instead of pig insulin, animals are not involved in the process, and the drugs can be made in large quantities, making them more available.
Q3  a) The DNA fragments that code for the production of alpha-1-antitrypsin could have been injected into a sheep embryo. The embryo could then have been implanted into a female sheep. When the offspring was born it could have been tested to see if it could make alpha-1-antitrypsin. If it could, selective breeding would have been used to produce more sheep that produce alpha-1-antitrypsin in their milk.
    b) The company may want legal protection for making the product so that they can control who uses the product and when. It also means that they will receive money for selling the product.

## Page 498 — Fact Recall Questions

**Q1** a) E.g. to prevent yields of soybean plants being greatly reduced by insect pests that feed on them.
b) *Bacillus thuringiensis* (Bt)
c) The gene codes for a protein that is toxic to some of the insects that feed on soybean plants.

**Q2** a) Pharming is where pharmaceuticals are produced using genetically modified organisms.
b) There are positive ethical issues with 'pharming' — e.g. drugs made this way can be made in large quantities compared to other methods of production. This can make them more available to more people. However, the creation of genetically modified animals raises negative ethical issues, e.g. there is concern that manipulating an animal's genes could cause harmful side-effects for the animal, and that using an animal in this way is enforcing the idea that animals are merely 'assets' that can be treated however we choose.

**Q3** E.g. it could lead to new treatments for disease.

**Q4** The sharing of knowledge, skills and technology between scientists at different institutions.

**Q5** E.g. they may not be able to afford patented genetically modified seeds. / They may not be allowed to plant and grow any of the seeds from one crop without paying again.

## 5. Gene Therapy

### Page 500 — Application Questions

**Q1** The virus is acting as a vector — it is being used to carry the normal FIX gene into the body cells of the sufferers of haemophilia.

**Q2** $(2 + 2 + 3 + 4 + 8 + 12) \div 6 = 5.16... = $ **5.2%** (2 s.f.)

**Q3** E.g. Yes. The maximum level after gene therapy was more than 1% for all the patients, which could improve their health.

**Q4** E.g. this therapy could prolong the lives of people with haemophilia B and could provide people with haemophilia B with a greater quality of life, as they may not have to receive injections for the protein multiple times a week in the future. It could save health authorities money, as the injections usually required by sufferers are expensive.

### Page 500 — Fact Recall Questions

**Q1** A possible treatment option for genetic disorders and some cancers that involves altering defective alleles inside cells.

**Q2** Somatic gene therapy involves altering the alleles in body cells (particularly those most affected by the disorder being treated). Germ line gene therapy involves altering the alleles in sex cells.

## 6. Sequencing Genes and Genomes

### Page 506 — Application Question

**Q1** a) A single-stranded template of the bone's DNA, DNA polymerase, lots of DNA primer, free nucleotides and a fluorescently-labelled modified nucleotide (a different one for each tube).
b) The tubes undergo PCR, which produces many strands of DNA all of different lengths. The DNA fragments in each tube are separated by electrophoresis and visualised under UV light. The complementary base sequence can then be read from the gel.
c) ATAAGCCATTCG
Remember — DNA sequencing gels are read from the bottom up. This will give you a DNA sequence that is complementary to the original sequence (TATTCGGTAAGC). To get the original sequence, remember that A always pairs with T and C pairs with G.
d) Species 2, because it has the same DNA sequence as the bone.

### Page 507 — Fact Recall Questions

**Q1** a) You need to chop up the genome into smaller pieces because the chain termination method can only be used for DNA fragments up to about 750 bp long.
b) bacterial artificial chromosomes (BACs)

**Q2** a) They are techniques that can sequence a lot faster than original methods (e.g. up to 1000 times more bases in a given time), at a fraction of the cost.
b) E.g. pyrosequencing

**Q3** You can use DNA sequencing to sequence a gene and work out the sequence of amino acids that a gene codes for. From this you can predict the primary structure of a polypeptide, which allows biological molecules to be created from scratch. This has led to the development synthetic biology.

**Q4** E.g. computational biology and bioinformatics.

**Q5** Computerised comparisons between the genomes of people that have a disease and those that don't can be used to detect particular mutations that could be responsible for an increased risk of the disease.

**Q6** Whole genomes of different species can be sequenced and then analysed using computer software to tell us how closely related different species are.

### Exam-style Questions — pages 509-510

1 B *(1 mark)*

2 a) PCR is used to amplify multiple areas containing different sequence repeats in each DNA sample *(1 mark)*. The PCR products from each sample are run on an electrophoresis gel *(1 mark)*. Shorter DNA fragments move faster and travel further through the gel, so the DNA fragments separate according to length, with longer pieces nearer the top *(1 mark)*. The fragments are stained before electrophoresis so that the bands produced for each sample can be seen — these are the DNA profiles *(1 mark)*.
b) DNA profiling technology involves comparing the number of times repetitive, non-coding base sequences *(1 mark)* are repeated at a number of different, specific places (loci) in a genome *(1 mark)*. The probability of two individuals having the same DNA profile is very low because the chance of two individuals having the same number of sequence repeats at each locus tested is very low *(1 mark)*.

c) Yes. The DNA profile of the stolen horse and DNA profile of horse 3 have exactly the same band pattern, so the DNA that produced both DNA profiles must have come from the same horse *(1 mark)*.
d) It can be used in medical diagnosis to analyse the risk of genetic disorders *(1 mark)*.

3  a) A reaction mixture is set up that contains the plant DNA sample, free nucleotides, primers and DNA polymerase *(1 mark)*. The DNA mixture is heated to 95 °C to break the hydrogen bonds between the two strands of DNA *(1 mark)*. The mixture is then cooled to 50-65 °C so that the primers can bind to the strands *(1 mark)*. The reaction mixture is heated to 72 °C, so that DNA polymerase can create new DNA strands *(1 mark)*. Two new copies of the DNA fragment are formed and then the cycle of heating and cooling is repeated many times *(1 mark)*.
b) It would show a band at the same point on the gel as that for the GM soybean plant *(1 mark)*.
c) The farmer's non-GM soybean plant *(1 mark)*.
d) E.g. there may be concerns that growing a genetically modified crop could encourage monoculture *(1 mark)*. Monoculture decreases biodiversity and could leave the whole crop vulnerable to disease, because all the plants are genetically identical *(1 mark)*.

4  a) E.g. plasmids / BACs/bacterial artificial chromosomes / liposomes *(1 mark)*
   *Bacteriophages are vectors too, but they are a type of virus that infects bacteria, so this doesn't answer the question. Make sure you read the question carefully before and, if you've time, after you answer it.*
b) i) Nine out of the ten patients had a functional immune system after gene therapy *(1 mark)*. However, two out of the ten patients developed leukaemia within 3 years of the treatment *(1 mark)*.
   ii) Any two from: e.g. a larger sample size could be used *(1 mark)*. / The patients could be followed for longer than three years after treatment *(1 mark)*. / Indicators other than developing leukaemia could be used to check the health status of the patients *(1 mark)*.
c) E.g. the technology could be used in ways other than for medical treatment, e.g. to reverse the cosmetic effects of aging *(1 mark)*. / There's the potential to do more harm than good by using the technology, e.g. by causing the overexpression of genes *(1 mark)*. / Gene therapy is expensive and the resources may be better spent on treatments that have already passed clinical trials *(1 mark)*.

# Section 5 — Cloning and Biotechnology

## 1. Plant Cloning

### Page 514 — Application Questions

Q1 a) Micropropagation. Clone the plant using tissue culture, then take cells from the developing clone. Subculture the cells in fresh medium to make even more clones, then repeat the process.
   b) E.g. the unusual pattern on the petals will always be passed on to the clones. / The plant could be reproduced in any season. / Less space is required by tissue culture/ micropropagation than would be needed to produce the same number of plants by conventional growing methods. / If the plant takes a long time to produce seeds it can be reproduced very quickly.
Q2 E.g. any undesirable characteristics the strawberry plant has will be passed on to all the clones. The cloned strawberry plant population will have no genetic variability and so a single disease could kill them all.

### Page 514 — Fact Recall Questions

Q1 Vegetative propagation is the natural production of plant clones from non-reproductive tissues, e.g. roots, leaves and stems.
Q2 E.g. cover the whole pot with a plastic bag. / Put the pot in a propagator.
Q3 Stem, leaf and root.
Q4 Any two from: e.g. to reproduce plants that don't readily reproduce naturally. / To reproduce plants that are rare or endangered. / To grow whole plants from genetically engineered plant cells.

## 2. Animal Cloning

### Page 518 — Application Questions

Q1 a) He could extract an egg cell from a female mouse and fertilise it in a Petri dish. He would then leave the fertilised egg to divide at least once, forming an embryo. Next, the individual cells from the embryo would be separated and each one put into a separate Petri dish. Each cell would divide and develop normally, so an embryo would form in each Petri dish. He would then implant the embryos into female mice. The embryos would continue to develop inside the surrogate mice, and eventually the offspring/cloned mice would be born.
   b) Cloned mice are all genetically identical, so the variables that come from genetic differences are removed. Controlling variables in this way will increase the validity of the results of the drug trial.
Q2 a) Somatic cell nuclear transfer/SCNT
   b) The embryo would be implanted into a surrogate mother and eventually a puppy would be born. The puppy would be a clone of the dog that the body/somatic cell nucleus came from.

## Page 518 — Fact Recall Questions

**Q1** During sexual reproduction, once an egg has been fertilised, it splits during the very early stages of development and develops into multiple embryos with the same genetic information. The embryos develop as normal to produce offspring that are all genetically identical — they are clones.

**Q2** To increase the number of animals with desirable characteristics to breed from.

**Q3** E.g. for research purposes (e.g. in medicine). / To help save endangered species from extinction. / To produce many animals that have been genetically modified to produce a useful substance.

**Q4** Arguments for — any three from: e.g. desirable genetic characteristics are always passed onto the clones. / Infertile animals can be reproduced. / Animals can be cloned at any time. / Increasing the population of endangered species helps to preserve biodiversity. / Cloning can help to develop new treatments for disease.
Arguments against — any three from: e.g. cloned animals have no genetic variability/undesirable genetic characteristics are always passed on to the clones. / Cloning is very difficult/expensive/time-consuming. / Clones may not live as long as natural offspring. / Using cloned human embryos as a source of stem cells in controversial.

## 3. Biotechnology — The Use of Microorganisms

### Page 522 — Application Questions

**Q1** Bioremediation could be used. This is the process of using organisms to remove pollutants from contaminated sites. Bioremediation could be used in this case by, e.g. providing extra nutrients and optimising growing conditions for microorganisms that occur naturally at the site and are capable of biodegrading/breaking down the pollutants. This would allow these microorganisms to thrive, so they would break down the pollutants into less harmful products more quickly, cleaning up the soil.

**Q2** a) E.g. the hot climate may make it difficult to grow crops or rear livestock on a large scale and the rapid population growth means that the demand for food will be constantly increasing. Single-cell protein would be advantageous in this environment because the microorganisms cultured to produce single-cell protein have simple growth requirements so they can be cultured anywhere if the right equipment is available. Also, single-cell protein can be produced using many different organic substrates (including waste materials) and only needs a relatively small area of land to produce food on a large scale. These factors mean that once the initial equipment has been bought and installed, single-cell protein is cheap, easy and quick to produce.
b) Any two from: e.g. the food could easily get contaminated with unwanted bacteria, which could be dangerous to humans / spoil the food. / The food may not be popular, as people may not like the idea of eating food that has been grown using waste products / single-cell protein doesn't have the same texture or flavour as real meat. / If single-cell protein is consumed in high quantities, health problems could be caused due to the high levels of uric acid released when the large amounts of amino acids are broken down.

## Page 522 — Fact Recall Questions

**Q1** The industrial use of living organisms to produce food, drugs and other products.

**Q2** Any three from: e.g. their ideal growth conditions can be easily created. / They have a short life-cycle, so they grow rapidly under the right conditions, meaning products can be made quickly. / They can grow on a range of inexpensive materials, so they're economical. / They can be grown at any time of the year.

**Q3** a) Brewing uses yeast to produce alcohol/ethanol by fermenting glucose from the grain.
b) Yeast is used in baking to produce $CO_2$ to make bread rise.
c) The enzyme chymosin, which is required to clot the milk, can be obtained from yeast cells that have been genetically modified to produce the enzyme. Cheese making also involves lactic acid bacteria, which convert the lactose in milk into lactic acid, making it turn sour and contribute to its solidifying. The production of blue cheeses also involves the addition of fungi to make the characteristic blue veins.
d) Yoghurt production uses lactic acid bacteria to clot the milk and cause it to thicken.
e) *Penicillium* fungi are grown under stress in industrial fermenters to produce penicillin on a massive scale.
f) Insulin is made by genetically modified bacteria, which have had the gene for human insulin production inserted into their DNA. These bacteria are grown in an industrial fermenter on a massive scale.

## 4. Biotechnology — Culturing Microorganisms

### Page 529 — Application Questions

**Q1** a) E.g. the turbidity of a sample of broth that doesn't have any bacteria added should be measured over time at room temperature. It should be used to make sure that the bacteria are responsible for the increasing turbidity rather than anything else in the broth.
b) Any two from: e.g. tie long hair back to prevent it from falling into anything. / Work near a Bunsen flame. / Regularly disinfect work surfaces to minimise contamination. / Sterilise the instrument used to transfer cultures. / Briefly flame the neck of the container of broth just after it's opened and just before it's closed. / Sterilise all glassware before and after use, e.g. in an autoclave.
c) Aseptic techniques are important because they prevent contamination of cultures by unwanted microorganisms, which may affect the growth of the microorganism being cultured. Contaminated cultures in laboratory experiments give imprecise results and may be hazardous to health.
d) E.g. turbidity increased more quickly for species 1 and species 1 spent more time in the exponential growth phase/took longer to reach the stationary phase. This is likely to be because the growing conditions were more favourable for species 1 than for species 2.

Q2 E.g. prepare separate samples of the bacteria in broth, each mixed in with a buffer solution at each of the pH levels under investigation. Next, apply the same volume of one of the bacterial broth samples to three separate agar plates and spread the broth across the entire surface of the agar using a sterile plastic spreader. Repeat this step for the other two bacterial broth samples. Put the lids on the plates and tape them shut. Put the plates upside down either in an incubator or leave them at room temperature, in a place where the temperature will remain constant. Also put another lidded agar plate, which has broth without any bacteria added to it, in the same place. This will act as a negative control. Leave all the plates for the same amount of time, then count the number of colonies that have formed on each plate and record the results in a table. Work out the mean number of colonies formed at each pH level.

## Page 529 — Fact Recall Questions

Q1 A population of one type of microorganism that's been grown under controlled conditions.
Q2 Any three from: e.g. pH / temperature / oxygen supply / contamination / nutrient concentration.
Q3 When growth of microorganisms takes place in a vessel that's isolated from the external environment.
Q4 a) Lag phase, exponential/log phase, stationary phase and decline phase.
b) Lag phase — the population size increases very slowly because the microorganisms have to make enzymes and other molecules before they can reproduce. This means the reproduction rate is low.
Exponential/log phase — the population size increases quickly because the culture conditions are at their most favourable for reproduction. The number of microorganisms doubles at regular intervals.
Stationary phase — the population size stays level because the death rate of the microorganisms equals their reproductive rate. Microorganisms die because there's not enough food and poisonous waste products build up.
Decline phase — the population size falls because the death rate is greater than the reproductive rate. This is because food is very scarce and waste products are at toxic levels.

## 5. Immobilised Enzymes

## Page 532 — Application Questions

Q1 By immobilising the enzyme (attaching the enzyme to an insoluble material so it can't become mixed with the products).
Q2 a) Columns of immobilised enzymes can be washed and reused, which reduces the cost of running the reaction on an industrial scale because the company doesn't have to keep buying new enzymes. Also, because the desired product won't be mixed in with the enzyme, no time and money has to be spent separating them.
b) Extra equipment is required, compared to using free enzymes, which can be expensive to buy. Immobilised enzymes are also more expensive to buy than free enzymes, so may not be economical if they aren't going to be used a lot.

## Page 532 — Fact Recall Questions

Q1 Encapsulation in jelly-like alginate beads, which act as a semi-permeable membrane. Trapping in a silica gel matrix. Covalent bonding to cellulose or collagen fibres.
Q2 The substrate solution is run through the column, where it binds to the active sites of the enzymes, which catalyse the reaction. The solution that flows out of the column contains the desired product.
Q3 Any three from: e.g. immobilised lactase — used in the breakdown of lactose in the production of lactose-free dairy products. / Immobilised penicillin acylase — used in the production of semi-synthetic penicillins. / Immobilised glucoamylase — used in the production of glucose and glucose syrup. / Immobilised glucose isomerase — used to convert glucose to fructose. / Immobilised aminoacylase — used to separate L and D amino acids. / Immobilised nitrilase — used to convert acrylonitrile to acrylamide.
*This isn't a comprehensive list of immobilised enzymes and their uses. There are loads more examples that aren't listed here, but would be acceptable.*

## Exam-style Questions — pages 534-535

1 a) i) Any three from: e.g. pH probe — monitors the pH and keeps it at an optimum level so enzymes work more efficiently *(1 mark)*. / Water jacket — keeps the temperature at an optimum level so enzymes work more efficiently *(1 mark)*. / Paddles — circulate the medium around the vessel so the bacteria can always access the nutrients needed for growth *(1 mark)*. / Sterile air-in pipe — pumps oxygen into the vessel when needed, so the microorganisms can always respire to provide energy for growth *(1 mark)*.
*The question asks you to identify three features of the fermentation vessel in Fig. 1.1., so make sure you only write about features shown on the vessel in the diagram or you won't get the marks.*
ii) It prevents unwanted microorganisms from entering the vessel and contaminating the culture *(1 mark)*. If the culture is contaminated, it may mean that product yield will be reduced as the bacteria will be competing for nutrients / the whole batch will have to be thrown away, which will be very costly *(1 mark)*.
b) i) 25 minutes *(1 mark)*. *(Accept answers in range 22 minutes – 28 minutes.)*
*To answer this question, the first thing you need to do is identify the exponential growth phase. Then you pick a number of cells during this phase and read the time at which there are this many cells (e.g. 500 cells). Next, read off the time at which this number of cells has doubled. The difference between these two times gives you the answer.*
ii) E.g. because the bacteria have to make enzymes and other molecules before they can reproduce *(1 mark)*.

iii) E.g.

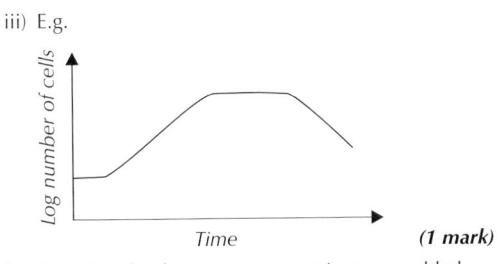

Graph: x-axis "Time", y-axis "Log number of cells"; curve shows lag, exponential rise, plateau, then decline. *(1 mark)*

iv) In a closed culture, no extra nutrients are added and waste products aren't removed, so after a time, there's not enough food and waste products start to build up *(1 mark)*. This causes the bacteria to reproduce more slowly and die faster *(1 mark)*. The graph levels off when death rate equals reproduction rate and decreases when death rate is higher than reproduction rate *(1 mark)*. In a culture like the one in Fig. 1.2, this doesn't happen because the constant addition of nutrients and removal of waste products keep conditions favourable for growth *(1 mark)*.

c) A somatic/body cell could be taken from a patient with diabetes and its nucleus removed *(1 mark)*. This nucleus could then be inserted into an enucleated egg cell/oocyte *(1 mark)*. These would then be fused together and stimulated to divide *(1 mark)*, which would produce an embryo from which embryonic stem cells could be harvested *(1 mark)*.

2  a) Any two from: e.g. rhizomes are stem structures that grow horizontally underground away from the parent plant. They have 'nodes' from which new shoots and roots can develop *(1 mark)*. / Stolons/runners are stem structures that grow above the ground, on the surface of the soil. New shoots and roots can either develop from nodes or form at the end of the stolon *(1 mark)*. / Suckers are shoots that grow from sucker buds/undeveloped shoots present on the shallow roots of a parent plant *(1 mark)*. / Tubers are large underground plant structures that act as a food store for the plant. They're covered in 'eyes', each of which is able to sprout and form a new plant *(1 mark)*. / Bulbs are underground food stores. New bulbs are able to develop from the original bulb and form new individual plants *(1 mark)*.

b) He should remove any leaves from the lower end of the cutting and dip it in rooting powder *(1 mark)*. He should then plant the cutting in a pot of suitable growth medium *(1 mark)* and place the pot in a propagator / cover it completely with a plastic bag *(1 mark)*. Once the cutting has developed its own roots, he should plant it in a suitable place to continue growing *(1 mark)*. **(Maximum of 3 marks available.)**

c) i) These cells are stem cells *(1 mark)*, so they can develop into any of the cell types needed to produce a new plant *(1 mark)*.

ii) Any two from: e.g. desirable characteristics will always be passed onto the clones *(1 mark)*. / Less space is required by tissue culture than would be needed to produce the same number of plants by conventional growing methods *(1 mark)*. / Plants that take a long time to produce seeds can be reproduced quickly *(1 mark)*.

d) i) The clones are all genetically identical, so they will all be susceptible to the bacterial infection *(1 mark)*.

ii) Any two from: e.g. their ideal growth conditions can be easily created *(1 mark)*. / Due to their short life-cycle they grow rapidly, so products can be made very quickly *(1 mark)*. / They can grow on a range of inexpensive materials, so are economical to use *(1 mark)*. / They can be grown at any time of year *(1 mark)*.

# Section 6 — Ecosystems

## 1. Ecosystems and Energy Flow

### Page 542 — Application Questions

Q1 a) net productivity = gross productivity – respiratory loss
net productivity = 22 861 – 17 000 = **5861 kJm$^{-2}$yr$^{-1}$**

b) % efficiency of energy transfer =
(net productivity of trophic level ÷ net productivity of previous trophic level) × 100
= (627 ÷ 5861) × 100 = **10.7%**

Q2 a) respiratory loss = gross productivity – net productivity
respiratory loss = 8072 – 2073 = **5999 kJm$^{-2}$yr$^{-1}$**

*The total amount of energy taken in is the gross productivity. Once you have identified this you can plug the numbers into the equation to work out the respiratory loss (you already know the net productivity from the diagram).*

b) gross productivity = net productivity + respiratory loss
gross productivity = 119 + 450 = **569 kJm$^{-2}$yr$^{-1}$**
converting m$^{-2}$ to km$^{-2}$ gives:
569 × 1 000 000 = **5.69 × 10$^8$ kJkm$^{-2}$yr$^{-1}$**

*There are 1000 m in 1 km so (1000 × 1000 =) 1 000 000 m$^2$ in 1 km$^2$.*

c) E.g. because some parts of the small fish aren't eaten so the energy isn't taken in. / Because some parts of the small fish are indigestible and will pass through the large fish and come out as waste.

*Some questions like this are tricky to work out — you need to think about what the key phrases, like gross productivity and net productivity, actually mean. Here the question is actually asking you 'Why is the energy absorbed by the large fish less than the energy available to them from the small fish?'*

d) % efficiency of energy transfer =
(net productivity of trophic level ÷ net productivity of previous trophic level) × 100
Between plant plankton and animal plankton =
(8105 ÷ 31 023) × 100 = **26.1%**
Between animal plankton and small fish =
(2073 ÷ 8105) × 100 = **25.6%**
Between small fish and large fish =
(119 ÷ 2073) × 100 = **5.7%**

*This example of a food chain is a bit different — the efficiency of energy transfer decreases as you go up it. But you don't need to worry about this when you're doing the calculations — just use the equation as normal.*

## Page 542 — Fact Recall Questions

**Q1** Biotic factors are the living features of an ecosystem (e.g. the presence of predators or food).

**Q2** a) E.g. tides (affecting pH, salinity, temperature).
b) E.g. rainfall making the soil waterlogged / sunlight affecting growth.
c) E.g. drought conditions.

**Q3** a) An organism that produces organic molecules using sunlight energy.
b) An organism that eats other organisms.

**Q4** photosynthesis

**Q5** gross productivity

**Q6** Carnivores, because more of the food they eat is digestible.
*Remember, herbivores only eat plants, which contain a lot of indigestible material. This means lots of the available energy is lost as waste, e.g. in faeces.*

**Q7** Measure the dry mass/biomass of the organisms.

**Q8** Any two from: e.g. herbicides — these kill weeds that compete with crops for energy. Reducing competition means crops receive more energy, so they grow faster and become larger. / Fungicides — these kill fungal infections, so the crops use more energy for growth and less for fighting infection. / Insecticides — these kill insect pests so less biomass is lost from crops. / Natural predators are introduced to the ecosystem. These eat the pest species so crops lose less energy and biomass. / Fertilisers — these replace minerals in the soil, so more energy from the ecosystem can be used to grow. / Intensive rearing of livestock — this controls the conditions animals live in and when they're slaughtered, so more of their energy is used for growth and less is used for other activities, so more energy is transferred to their biomass.

## 2. Recycling in Ecosystems

## Page 545 — Fact Recall Questions

**Q1** E.g. carbon is absorbed by plants when they carry out photosynthesis — it becomes carbon compounds in plant tissues. Carbon is passed on through the food chain by feeding. All living organisms die and are broken down by microorganisms called decomposers. Decomposers secrete enzymes onto dead organic material to digest the carbon compounds in them. They then absorb the products of digestion. Carbon is returned to the air (and water) as all living organisms (including the decomposers) carry out respiration, which produces $CO_2$.

**Q2** The carbon comes from fossil fuels, such as oil and coal. These are formed when dead organic matter ends up in places where there aren't any decomposers (e.g. deep oceans or bogs), and then is subject to heat and pressure over millions of years.

**Q3** Rock, such as limestone, can be weathered chemically by rainwater and physically, e.g. by plant roots, animals, etc. Chemical weathering causes mineral ions and bicarbonate ions to be released from the rock into solution and enter groundwater, from where they are transported into rivers and the oceans. There they combine to form carbon-containing compounds such as $CaCO_3$.

**Q4** $CO_2$ dissolves directly into the oceans from the atmosphere.

**Q5** To make proteins/nucleic acids. / For growth.

**Q6**

| Name of process | Bacteria responsible |
|---|---|
| Nitrogen fixation | *Rhizobium* and *Azotobacter* |
| Ammonification | Decomposers |
| Nitrification | *Nitrosomonas* and *Nitrobacter* |
| Denitrification | Denitrifying bacteria |

**Q7** Nitrogen compounds from dead organisms and animal waste are turned into ammonia by decomposers, which goes on to form ammonium ions.

**Q8** denitrification

## 3. Succession

## Page 548 — Application Questions

**Q1** Primary succession, because there is no soil present in 1800.
*Remember, the key difference between primary and secondary succession is soil — it's present in secondary succession, but not in primary succession. If you have a good look at the graph you'll see that there's no soil moisture in 1800. That's a pretty good sign that there's no soil, either.*

**Q2** The dominant plant species would have been adapted to survive without much water/in a soil with low moisture content and fluctuating ground temperatures. They would have had seeds that could remain viable for long periods of time. They would have been species of small plants / they would not have been tree species.
*There's a lot going on in the graph with all the different lines — and you could get something like this in the exam. Don't let the graph's complexity put you off though. Take your time and make sure you really understand what the graph is showing, and read the questions carefully so you pick out the right bits from the graph for your answers.*

**Q3** E.g. the average length of time dominant plant seeds remained viable for was relatively high between 1800 and 1860. This might have been because seeds that remained viable for a long time could lie dormant until conditions were favourable enough to germinate. Between about 1860 and 1880 the average length of time fell sharply, and then continued to fall more slowly until levelling off at around 1960. This may have been because the plants that were dominant between 1800 and 1860 were succeeded by other plant species which were more suited to the changed conditions, e.g. a higher soil moisture content, so they no longer needed to be viable for long periods of time.

**Q4** Between 1800 and 1920 because there were no tree species present during this time, so there would have been more light / less shade cast by the trees.

Q5 The soil moisture content is 0 between 1800 and 1820 because there is no soil. The soil moisture content increased gradually from 1820 until 1940 as the soil developed, then it increased more rapidly between 1940 and 2000 because the addition of decomposed organic material helped to increase soil moisture content and the deeper soil was able to retain more water.

### Page 549 — Fact Recall Questions
Q1 The process by which an ecosystem changes over time.
Q2 primary succession
Q3 pioneer species
Q4 The largest and most complex community of plants and animals that an ecosystem can support.
Q5 E.g. deforestation / volcanic eruption / fire
Q6 The climax community for a particular climate.
Q7 The climax community that exists when succession is stopped artificially by human activities.

## 4. Investigating Ecosystems

### Page 553 — Application Questions
Q1 a) She could place the quadrat on the ground at random locations across the field and count how much of the quadrat is covered by daisies. A square should be counted if it's more than half-covered.
   b) E.g. the student could divide the field into a grid and use a random number generator to select coordinates. The quadrat could then be placed at these coordinates and the number of daisies in each quadrat counted.
Q2 a) The kite diagram shows that species A is present between 20 and 45 m from the road with a low percentage cover. It's also present between 80-140 m, and is most abundant between 130-140 m. Species B is present between 55-130 m from the road, and is most abundant between 60-85 m. Species C is present between 0-50 m from the road and is most abundant between 0-20 m. The graph shows that soil salinity is high between 0-30 m from the road, falls sharply between 30-40 m, continues to fall until around 50 m and then remains low.
   b) Species C, as it is present between 0-50 m from the road and is the most abundant species between 0-30 m from the road, where soil salinity is highest.
   c) The data shows that at a high soil salinity there is an absence of species B, but this doesn't prove that salt spray from the road is the cause. Species B might be absent for other reasons, e.g. because it is out-competed by species C.

### Page 553 — Fact Recall Questions
Q1 a) The number of individuals of one species in a particular area.
   b) Where a particular species is in the area being investigated.
Q2 a) Because it would be too time-consuming to measure the abundance of the entire species in the area being investigated.
   b) To avoid biased results.
Q3 It would be put on the ground at random points within the field. Pins would be dropped through the holes in the frame and every plant that each pin touched would be recorded.
   *In the exam, if you're asked to describe a method you could use to investigate a population, don't forget to say that you would use random samples of the area you are investigating.*
Q4 For a line transect, a tape measure is placed along the transect and the species that touch the tape measure are recorded. For a belt transect, data is collected along the transect using frame quadrats placed next to each other.
Q5 To capture ground insects.

### Exam-style Questions — pages 555-556
1 B *(1 mark)*
2 D *(1 mark)*
3 a) i) E.g. they could set up a belt transect / place quadrats next to each other along a transect *(1 mark)* leading from the edge of the field that's next to the stream into the middle of the field *(1 mark)*.
     ii) E.g. they could count how many squares of each quadrat are covered by marsh marigolds by counting a square if it's more than half-covered *(1 mark)*. Measuring percentage cover is a quick way to investigate the abundance of marsh marigolds *(1 mark)* and they wouldn't have to count all the individual marsh marigolds *(1 mark)*.
  b) The non-living features of an ecosystem *(1 mark)*.
  c) Regular grazing would prevent the normal climax community from developing *(1 mark)*, so succession would be deflected from its natural course *(1 mark)*.
4 a) Light / the Sun *(1 mark)*
  b) gross productivity (secondary consumer 1)
     = net productivity (primary consumer 1) – energy lost
     = 2619 – 476 = 2143 kJm$^{-2}$yr$^{-1}$
     net productivity = gross productivity – respiratory loss
     net productivity = 2143 – 1571 = **572 kJm$^{-2}$yr$^{-1}$**
     *(1 mark for correct working only, 2 marks for correct answer)*
  c) E.g. because some parts of food, e.g. roots or bones, aren't eaten by organisms so the energy isn't taken in *(1 mark)*. Also, some parts of food are indigestible so pass through organisms and come out as waste, e.g. faeces *(1 mark)*.
  d) percentage efficiency of energy transfer =
     (net productivity of trophic level ÷ net productivity of previous trophic level) × 100
     between the producer and primary consumer 1 = (2619 ÷ 38750) × 100 = 6.76%
     between the producer and primary consumer 2 = (1265 ÷ 38750) × 100 = 3.26%
     6.76 – 3.26 = **3.5%**
     *(1 mark for each correct percentage efficiency of energy transfer or 3 marks for correct answer)*
  e) Nitrogen compounds from dead organisms and animal waste are turned into ammonia by decomposers (e.g. bacteria or fungi), which goes on to form ammonium ions (ammonification) *(1 mark)*. *Nitrosomonas* change ammonium ions into nitrites *(1 mark)*. *Nitrobacter* change nitrites into nitrates (nitrification) *(1 mark)*. Nitrates are converted into nitrogen gas by denitrifying bacteria (denitrification) *(1 mark)*.

# Section 7 — Populations and Sustainability

## 1. Variation in Population Size

### Page 560 — Application Questions
Q1  the number of mice
*Remember, biotic factors are the living things in an ecosystem.*
Q2  As the temperature fell, the size of the mouse population decreased. This could have been because the cold weather caused the temperature of the surroundings to fall below the body temperature of the mice. Mice are mammals, so if that had happened the mice would have used up more energy maintaining their body temperature. This would have meant less energy was available for growth and reproduction, causing their population size to fall.
Q3  As the mouse population size increased, there was more food for the owls and so the owl population grew. As the owl population increased, more mice were eaten and so the mice population began to fall. This meant there was less food for the owls, so their population decreased — and so this cycle continued.

### Page 560 — Fact Recall Questions
Q1  All organisms of one species in a habitat.
Q2  a)  Interspecific competition is when organisms of different species compete with each other for the same resources.
    b)  i)  The population size of both of the species competing will be lowered. This is because there are fewer resources available to both populations, so they will both be less likely to reproduce.
        ii) The less well adapted species will be outcompeted and won't be able to exist alongside the better adapted species.
    c)  E.g. grey squirrels and red squirrels in the UK compete for the same food sources and habitats. In areas where they both live, both populations are smaller than they would be if only one species lived there. The red squirrel has also disappeared from large areas as the grey squirrel is better adapted to the surroundings.
Q3  a)  Intraspecific competition is when organisms of the same species compete with each other for the same resources.
    b)  The population of a species increases when resources are plentiful. As the population increases, there'll be more organisms competing for the same amount of space and food. Eventually, resources such as food and space become limiting, so the population begins to decline. A smaller population then means that there's less competition for space and food, which is better for growth and reproduction, so the population starts to grow again.
Q4  It is the maximum stable population size of a species that an ecosystem can support.
Q5  It will cause the predator population to increase as well because there is more food available for the predators.
Q6  limiting factor

## 2. Conservation of Ecosystems

### Page 564 — Fact Recall Questions
Q1  Ecosystems provide resources for lots of things that humans need and these are traded on a local and global scale. If the ecosystems aren't conserved, the resources that we use now will be lost, so there will be less trade in the future.
Q2  E.g. because people use them for activities such as walking.
Q3  Any two from, e.g. trees are cleared in strips or patches rather than over large areas, as this allows trees to grow back more quickly and reduces soil erosion. / Trees can be coppiced rather than cut down, which allows the same tree to grow back, rather than requiring a new one to be planted. / Native trees are preferentially planted, which are considered better for biodiversity due to their long-established interactions with other native species. / Young trees are surrounded by protective tubes which prevents them from being damaged by grazing animals. / Young trees are attached to posts, which provide support and make them more likely to grow successfully. / Trees are spaced out when they are planted, reducing competition between them for light and other resources, and making it more likely that they'll survive and grow successfully.
Q4  Restricting mesh sizes can reduce the number of unwanted fish of the wrong species that are caught and can allow younger fish to escape the net, meaning they are more likely to reach breeding age and maintain the population.
Q5  Many plants and animals live in the forests in the Terai Arc, but the forest is being put at risk by local populations who need wood from the forests for fuel and from people who want to clear areas of the forest to make way for housing and other developments. Elephants and tigers can come into conflict with farmers as they can eat and trample crops and kill livestock.
Q6  Ecotourism projects have been developed in the Maasai Mara, which allow people to make money from the environment without damaging it. This alternative source of income reduces the reliance of the local population on farming, and therefore reduces damage to the grasslands caused by overgrazing.

## 3. Human Impact on Ecosystems

### Page 567 — Fact Recall Questions

**Q1** Any two from: e.g. explorers and sailors many years ago ate some of the animals which directly affected their populations. / Non-native animals have been introduced to the islands by humans. The non-native animals eat some native species, causing a decrease in the populations of native species. / Non-native plants have been introduced to the islands by humans. The non-native species compete with native plant species, causing a decrease in their populations. / Fishing has caused a decrease in the populations of some of the sea life. / An increase in tourism has caused damage to the ecosystems as more land is cleared and pollution is increased.

**Q2** E.g. commercial whaling has been banned from the ocean surrounding Antarctica, and seal hunting has also been banned. Fishing limits have been set. Many research stations treat their sewage before releasing it, to reduce its effect on the environment, and all waste other than food and sewage is removed by ship for disposal in other countries, in order to reduce pollution. There are tourists restrictions to prevent them from causing damage to the ecosystems of the area. Ships that use thick oil as a fuel have been banned from the area, as heavy oil spills are likely to cause more damage and be harder to clean up than spills of lighter fuels.

**Q3** E.g. erosion of footpaths can cause soil to be washed into lakes and rivers, altering the pH of the water and negatively affecting organisms living in aquatic environments. Erosion of footpaths can also cause people to walk on the vegetation on either side of the path, destroying vegetation. / Phosphates in fertilisers, in detergents and in the water released by local sewage works have accumulated in some of the lakes. These can contribute to algal blooms, which deoxygenate the water and can kill fish.

### Exam-style Questions — pages 569-570

1   B *(1 mark)*
    visitor numbers in 2015: 280 000
    visitor numbers in 2009: 220 000
    280 000 − 220 000 = 60 000
    (60 000 ÷ 220 000) × 100 = 27.27... = 27%

2   a) The population sizes of species A and B rise and fall cyclically over the 20 year period *(1 mark)*. The population sizes increase when resources are plentiful but decrease when resources become limited *(1 mark)*. This is because of intraspecific competition / organisms of species A are competing with each other for the same resources, and organisms of species B are competing with each other for the same resources *(1 mark)*.
    b) (biotic) limiting factor *(1 mark)*
    c) The carrying capacity of the ecosystem *(1 mark)*.

3   a) E.g. mangrove swamps are a unique ecosystem, and some people believe we have an ethical duty to protect them *(1 mark)*. People may also believe it is important to preserve mangrove swamps because of the protection they give the coastline, which could protect other ecosystems and people *(1 mark)*.
    *You don't actually need to know anything about mangrove swamps to answer this question — the command word 'suggest' means that you're expected to use your scientific knowledge of the benefits of conservation to come up with possible reasons. So your answer could include any sensible economic, social, ethical or ecological reasons that people may have for supporting conservation.*

   b) *7-9 marks:*
   The answer gives a detailed discussion of all three methods for protecting the mangrove habitat, giving well-explained disadvantages and advantages of each. Scientific terminology is used correctly, and the answer demonstrates a detailed understanding of the conservation of ecosystems. The answer has a clear and logical structure.
   The information given is relevant and detailed.
   *4-6 marks:*
   The answer includes a discussion of each of the three methods for protecting the habitat, but it may not include both advantages and disadvantages for all three, so the comparison of the methods is limited. Scientific terminology is used correctly, and the answer is mostly well-structured.
   Most of the information given is relevant and there is some detail involved.
   *1-3 marks:*
   The answer doesn't consider all of the habitat protection methods mentioned, and the discussion of the advantages and disadvantages of any of the methods is very limited. Use of scientific terminology is poor.
   The answer has no clear structure. The information given is basic and lacking in detail. It may not all be relevant.
   *0 marks:*
   No relevant information is given.
   **Here are some points your answer may include:**
   Creating a nature reserve and heavily restricting access would be an effective way of preserving the mangrove swamp, as it would prevent any further damage to the ecosystem by local populations. However, this suggestion doesn't take the needs of the local population into account, so doesn't represent an ethical solution to the problem. In addition, maintaining restrictions to access in the long term will require continued investment from the charity, so the solution isn't economically sustainable.
   On the other hand, paying local people to limit their use of the mangrove swamp to sustainable levels may represent an effective way of conserving the ecosystem whilst taking the needs of the local population into account. It allows them to continue using resources from the swamp, but at a reduced level, and offers them financial compensation. However, like the nature reserve suggestion, this solution requires a continued investment from the charity, so doesn't represent an economically sustainable solution. It may also be hard to enforce, as it requires constant monitoring of what is being taken from the swamp.
   The final suggestion, of developing ecotourism in the area, may be an effective way of protecting the mangrove swamp. By providing an alternative income for local populations it could reduce their need to take wood from the swamp to make charcoal, and gives the local population an incentive to conserve the swamp effectively. Unlike the other two suggestions, it may not require long-term investment from the conservation charity, so may be self-sustaining. It would, however, require careful management to make sure that tourists did not damage the ecosystem. Of these suggestions, ecotourism therefore seems like the best long-term solution for conserving the mangrove swamp, as it takes the needs of local people into account and doesn't require indefinite investment from the charity.
   c) i) Preservation keeps ecosystems exactly as they are, so nothing is removed, and human activity is limited. Conservation, on the other hand, does allow the removal of resources from ecosystems *(1 mark)*.
      ii) Creating a nature reserve and restricting access *(1 mark)*.

4  a) E.g. it's the right thing to do, especially if the ecosystem is at risk because of human activity. / There is a moral responsibility to conserve ecosystems for future generations, so they can enjoy and use them. *(1 mark)*

*If the question tells you to 'outline' a reason for something (like this one), you need to give a bit more than a one word answer — make sure you include a little bit of detail.*

b) It means taking enough resources from the woodland to meet the needs of people today without reducing the ability of people in the future to meet their own needs *(1 mark)*.

c) Any two from: e.g.

| Method | Explanation |
| --- | --- |
| Trees cleared in strips or patches. | Woodland grows back more quickly in smaller areas between bits of existing woodland than it does in larger, open areas. |
| Cleared strips or patches of woodland aren't too large or exposed. | Lots of soil erosion can occur on large areas of bare ground. If the soil is eroded, newly planted trees won't be able to grow. |
| Timber is harvested by coppicing/cut down in a way that lets them grow back. | New trees don't need to be planted. |
| Native species are preferentially planted. | Native species are better for biodiversity. |
| Planted trees are attached to posts / grown in plastic tubes. | This makes it more likely the trees will survive to become mature adults as they're supported/protected. |
| Trees aren't planted too close together. | The trees aren't competing with each other for space or resources, so they're more likely to survive. |

*(Maximum of 4 marks available — 1 mark for each correct method up to a maximum of 2 marks and 1 mark for each correctly matched explanation of how the method works).*

Answers

# Glossary

## A

**Abiotic factor**
A non-living feature of an ecosystem.

**Abiotic stress**
Something that's potentially harmful to a plant that's natural but non-living, e.g. a drought (water stress).

**Abscisic acid (ABA)**
A plant hormone that can trigger stomatal closure.

**Abscission layer**
A layer of cells at the bottom of a leaf stalk, which expand when stimulated by ethene, breaking the cell walls and causing the leaf to fall off.

**Abundance**
The number of individuals of one species in a particular area.

**Accurate result**
A result that is really close to the true answer.

**Acetylcholine (ACh)**
A type of neurotransmitter that binds to cholinergic receptors.

**Actin**
The thin myofilament protein in muscle fibres.

**Actin-myosin cross bridge**
The bond formed when a myosin head binds to an actin filament.

**Activation energy**
The energy that needs to be supplied before a chemical reaction will start.

**Activator**
A transcription factor that starts transcription.

**Active immunity**
The type of immunity you get when your immune system makes its own antibodies after being stimulated by an antigen.

**Active loading**
A process that happens at a source in a plant, in which assimilates are moved against their concentration gradient from surrounding tissues into the phloem. It requires energy.

**Active site**
The part of an enzyme where a substrate molecule binds.

**Active transport**
Movement of molecules and ions across plasma membranes, against a concentration gradient. Requires energy.

**Adaptation**
A feature of an organism that increases its chances of survival and reproduction, and also the chances of its offspring reproducing successfully.

**ADP (adenosine diphosphate)**
A molecule made up of adenine, a ribose sugar and two phosphate groups. ATP is synthesised from ADP and a phosphate group.

**Adrenal gland**
An endocrine gland that secretes hormones including cortisol, aldosterone, adrenaline and noradrenaline.

**Adrenaline**
A hormone secreted from the adrenal glands that has many effects, including increasing the blood glucose concentration.

**Aerobic respiration**
Process where energy is released from glucose using oxygen.

**Affinity for oxygen**
The tendency a molecule has to bind with oxygen.

**Agglutinin**
A substance (e.g. an antibody) that causes particles to clump together.

**Alcoholic fermentation**
A type of anaerobic respiration that occurs in yeast (and plants). Ethanol is the final product.

**Alkaloid**
A nitrogen-containing chemical produced by plants, which may have a bitter taste, noxious smell or poisonous characteristics to protect against herbivory.

**Allele**
One or more alternative versions of the same gene.

**Allele frequency**
How often an allele occurs in a population.

**Allopatric speciation**
When populations become reproductively isolated through a combination of geographical isolation and natural selection.

**Alpha ($\alpha$) cell**
A type of cell found in the islets of Langerhans, which secretes glucagon.

**Alveolus**
A microscopic air sac in the lungs where gas exchange occurs.

**Alzheimer's disease**
A disease where nerve cells in the brain die in increasing numbers, which results in symptoms such as severe memory loss.

**Amino acid**
A monomer of proteins.

**Ammonification**
The process in which nitrogen compounds from dead organisms or waste material are turned into ammonia by decomposers. This ammonia then goes on to form ammonium ions.

**Anaerobic respiration**
Process where energy is released from glucose without oxygen.

**Anomalous result**
A measurement that falls outside the range of values you'd expect or any pattern you already have.

**Anti-toxin**
An antibody that binds to a toxin produced by a pathogen and inactivates it.

**Antibiotic**
A chemical that kills or inhibits the growth of bacteria.

**Antibiotic resistance**
When bacteria are able to survive in the presence of antibiotics.

**Antibody**
A protein produced by B lymphocytes in response to the presence of a pathogen.

**Antidiuretic hormone (ADH)**
A hormone which regulates the water potential of the blood by controlling the permeability of the cells of the distal convoluted tubule and the collecting duct in the kidney.

**Antigen**
A molecule found on the surface of a cell. A foreign antigen triggers an immune response.

**Antigen-presenting cell**
An immune system cell that processes and presents antigens on its surface to activate other immune system cells.

**Apical dominance**
When the apical bud (tip of a plant shoot) grows more than the side shoots.

**Apoplast pathway**
A route that water takes through a plant root to the xylem, through cell walls.

**Apoptosis**
A highly controlled process by which cells are broken down.

**Artificial embryo twinning**
A technique for cloning animals. The technique involves manually separating embryos into individual cells, which each develop into further embryos that are implanted into surrogate animals.

**Artificial selection**
When humans select individuals in a population to breed together to get desirable traits.

**Aseptic technique**
A technique used to prevent the unwanted growth or transfer of microorganisms.

**Asexual reproduction**
A form of reproduction where the parent cell divides into two daughter cells (by mitosis). The daughter cells are genetically identical to the parent cell.

**Assimilate (in a plant)**
A substance that becomes incorporated into the plant tissue, e.g. sucrose.

**ATP (adenosine triphosphate)**
A molecule made up of adenine, a ribose sugar and three phosphate groups. It is the immediate source of energy in a cell.

**ATP-creatine phosphate (CP) system**
A system that generates ATP very quickly by phosphorylating ADP using a phosphate group from creatine phosphate.

**ATP synthase**
An enzyme which catalyses the synthesis of ATP from ADP and a phosphate group.

**ATPase**
An enzyme which catalyses the hydrolysis of ATP into ADP and a phosphate group.

**Atrioventricular node (AVN)**
A group of cells in the heart wall that are responsible for passing waves of electrical activity from the SAN on to the bundle of His.

**Atrioventricular (AV) valve**
A valve in the heart linking the atria to the ventricles.

**Autoimmune disease**
A disease resulting from the immune system launching an immune response against the organism's own tissues.

**Autonomic nervous system**
A division of the peripheral nervous system that controls unconscious activities, e.g. heart rate.

**Autosomal linkage**
When alleles on the same chromosome end up in the same daughter cell and so are inherited together.

**Autosome**
A chromosome that isn't a sex chromosome.

**Auxin**
A type of plant growth hormone produced in the tips of shoots, which stimulates cell elongation.

## B

**B lymphocyte**
A type of white blood cell involved in the immune response. It produces antibodies.

**BAC (Bacterial artificial chromosome)**
A man-made plasmid used in gene technology.

**Batch fermentation**
Where microorganisms are grown in individual batches in a fermentation vessel — when one culture ends it's removed and a different batch of microorganisms is grown.

**Benedict's test**
A biochemical test for the presence of sugars.

**Beta (β) cell**
A type of cell found in the islets of Langerhans, which secretes insulin.

**Binomial system**
The nomenclature (naming system) used for classification, in which each organism is given a two-part scientific (Latin) name.

**Biodiversity**
The variety of living organisms in an area.

**Bioinformatics**
Developing and using computer software that can analyse, organise and store biological data.

**Biomass**
The mass of living material in an organism.

**Bioremediation**
A process that uses organisms (usually microorganisms) to remove pollutants from contaminated sites.

**Biotechnology**
The industrial use of living organisms (or parts of living organisms) to produce food, drugs and other products.

**Biotic factor**
A living feature of an ecosystem.

**Biuret test**
A biochemical test for the presence of polypeptides and proteins.

**Body plan**
The general structure of an organism.

**Bohr effect**
An effect by which an increase of carbon dioxide in the blood results in a reduction of haemoglobin's affinity for oxygen.

**Bowman's capsule**
A hollow ball at the start of a nephron, which contains the glomerulus where ultrafiltration takes place.

**Breathing rate**
How many breaths are taken per unit time.

**Buccal cavity**
The space inside the mouth of a fish.

**Bundle of His**
A group of muscle fibres in the heart, responsible for conducting waves of electrical activity from the AVN to the Purkyne tissue.

# C

**Callose**
A plant polysaccharide.

**Calvin cycle**
Another name for the light-independent reaction of photosynthesis (see that entry).

**Carbon cycle**
The movement of carbon through living organisms and the non-living environment.

**Cardiac cycle**
An ongoing sequence of contraction and relaxation of the atria and ventricles that keeps blood continuously circulating around the body.

**Carrier (inheritance)**
A person carrying an allele which is not expressed in the phenotype but that can be passed on to offspring.

**Carrier protein**
A protein that carries molecules across a plasma membrane.

**Carrying capacity**
The maximum stable population size of a species that an ecosystem can support.

**Casparian strip**
A waxy strip in the cell wall of an endodermis cell.

**Catalyst**
A substance that speeds up a chemical reaction without being used up itself.

**Causal relationship**
Where a change in one variable causes a change in the other.

**Cell cycle**
The process that all body cells in multicellular organisms use to grow and divide.

**Cell signalling**
The process by which cells communicate with each other.

**Cell wall**
A rigid structure that surrounds the plasma membrane of some cells, e.g. plant cells. Supports the cell.

**Cellulose**
A polysaccharide made of long, unbranched chains of β-glucose.

**Central nervous system (CNS)**
Part of the nervous system made up of the brain and spinal cord.

**Centriole**
A small, hollow cylinder, containing a ring of microtubules. Involved with the separation of chromosomes during cell division.

**Centromere**
The point at which two strands of a chromosome are joined together.

**Cerebellum**
Part of the brain, which plays an important role in muscle coordination, posture and coordination of balance.

**Cerebrum**
The largest part of the brain, which plays an important role in vision, hearing, learning and thinking.

**Chain termination method**
A technique used to sequence DNA.

**Channel protein**
A membrane protein that forms a pore through which ions or small, polar molecules move.

**Chemiosmosis**
The movement of protons ($H^+$ ions) across a membrane which generates ATP.

**Chi-squared test**
A statistical test that that's used to see if the results of an experiment support a theory.

**Chloride shift**
The process in which chloride ions diffuse from the plasma into red blood cells to compensate for the loss of hydrogencarbonate ions from red blood cells. It helps to maintain the pH of the blood.

**Chlorophyll**
A photosynthetic pigment found in chloroplasts. There are different types of this pigment, e.g. chlorophyll a.

**Chloroplast**
A small, flattened organelle found in plant cells. It is the site of photosynthesis.

**Chlorosis**
Where a plant doesn't produce enough chlorophyll and turns yellow.

**Cholesterol**
A lipid (fat) containing a hydrocarbon tail attached to a hydrocarbon ring and a hydroxyl group.

**Cholinergic synapse**
A synapse that uses the neurotransmitter acetylcholine.

**Chromatid**
One 'arm' of a double stranded chromosome.

**Ciliated epithelium**
A layer of cells covered in cilia, found in animals (e.g. in the trachea or the bronchi).

**Cilium**
A small, hair-like structure found on the surface membrane of some animal cells. Used to move substances along the cell surface.

**Cladistics**
A method of classifying organisms based on their evolutionary relationships (phylogeny).

**Classification**
The act of arranging organisms into groups based on their similarities and differences.

**Climate change**
A significant long-term change in an area's climate.

**Climax community**
The largest and most complex community of plants and animals an ecosystem can support.

**Cloning**
The process of producing genetically identical cells or organisms from the cells of an existing organism.

**Closed circulatory system**
A circulatory system where the blood is enclosed inside blood vessels.

**Closed culture**
A culture which has been grown in a vessel that's isolated from the external environment.

**Codominant allele**
An allele whose characteristic appears together with another allele in the phenotype because neither allele is recessive.

**Coenzyme**
A molecule that aids the function of an enzyme. They work by transferring a chemical group from one molecule to another.

**Coenzyme A (CoA)**
A type of coenzyme involved in respiration. It transfers acetate from one molecule to another.

**Cofactor**
A non-protein substance that binds to an enzyme and activates it. It can be organic or inorganic.

**Collagen**
A fibrous protein that forms supportive tissue in animals.

**Communicable disease**
A disease that can be passed between individuals and is caused by infection with a pathogen.

**Companion cell**
A type of plant cell located next to a sieve tube element in phloem tissue, which carries out living functions for itself and the sieve cell.

**Compensation point (for light intensity)**
The level of light intensity at which the rate of photosynthesis exactly matches the rate of respiration.

**Competitive inhibitor**
A molecule with a similar shape to that of a substrate, so it competes with the substrate to bind to the enzyme's active site.

**Complementary base pairing**
Hydrogen bonds between specific pairs of bases on opposing polynucleotide strands, e.g. A always pairs with T and C always pairs with G.

**Computational biology**
Using computers to study biology, e.g. to create computer simulations and mathematical models.

**Concentration gradient**
The path from an area of higher concentration to an area of lower concentration.

**Condensation reaction**
A reaction that releases a water molecule when it links molecules together.

**Conjugated protein**
A protein with a non-protein group attached.

**Conservation (of ecosystems)**
A dynamic process that involves the protection, management and sometimes the reclamation of ecosystems.

**Consumer**
An organism that eats other organisms.

**Continuous fermentation**
Where microorganisms are continually grown in a fermentation vessel without stopping.

**Continuous variation**
When the individuals in a population vary within a range — there are no distinct categories.

**Control group**
A group in a study that is treated in exactly the same way as the experimental group, apart from the factor you're investigating.

**Control variable**
A variable you keep constant throughout an experiment.

**Convergence (at a synapse)**
When many neurones connect to one neurone.

**Convergent evolution**
When two species evolve similar characteristics independently of one another because they've adapted to live in similar environments.

**Correlation**
A relationship between two variables.

**Counter-current system**
The system in which blood flows in one direction and water flows in the opposite direction across the gills of a fish.

**Culture (microorganisms)**
A population of one type of microorganism that's been grown under controlled conditions.

**Cutting (plant)**
A section of a plant (e.g. from a stem, root or leaf) that can be used to produce new plants via vegetative propagation.

**Cyclic AMP (cAMP)**
A molecule that activates proteins inside cells by altering their 3D structures.

**Cytokine**
A protein that acts as a messenger molecule.

**Cytokinesis**
The process by which the cytoplasm divides in eukaryotic cells.

**Cytoplasm**
A gel-like substance where most of the chemical reactions in a cell happen.

**Cytoskeleton**
The network of protein threads contained in a cell.

# D

**Deamination**
The process by which nitrogen-containing amino groups are removed from amino acids, forming ammonia and organic acids.

**Decarboxylation**
The removal of carbon dioxide from a molecule.

**Deciduous plant**
A plant that loses its leaves in winter.

**Decomposer**
An organism that breaks down dead or undigested organic material.

**Dehydrogenation**
The removal of hydrogen from a molecule.

**Denatured**
The point at which an enzyme no longer functions as a catalyst.

**Denitrification**
The process in which nitrates in the soil are converted into nitrogen gas by denitrifying bacteria.

**Dependent variable**
The variable you measure in an experiment.

**Depolarisation**
A decrease in the potential difference across a cell's membrane, making it less negative (i.e. more positive) than the resting potential.

**Detoxification**
The process by which harmful substances are broken down by the liver into less harmful compounds, which can then be excreted from the body.

**Diabetes mellitus (Type I)**
A condition in which blood glucose concentration can't be controlled properly because the body doesn't produce any insulin.

**Diabetes mellitus (Type II)**
A condition in which blood glucose concentration can't be controlled properly because the body doesn't produce enough insulin or the body's cells don't respond properly to insulin.

**Differentiation**
The process by which a cell becomes specialised.

**Diffusion**
The net movement of particles from an area of higher concentration to an area of lower concentration.

**Dihybrid inheritance**
The inheritance of two characteristics which are controlled by different genes.

**Dipeptide**
A molecule formed from two amino acids.

**Diploid**
When a cell contains two copies of each chromosome.

**Direct transmission**
When a disease is transmitted directly from one organism to another.

**Directional selection**
Where individuals with alleles for characteristics of an extreme type are more likely to survive, reproduce and pass on their alleles.

**Disaccharide**
A molecule formed from two monosaccharides.

**Discontinuous variation**
When there are two or more distinct categories in a population — each individual falls into only one of these categories and there are no intermediates.

**Disease**
A condition that impairs the normal functioning of an organism.

**Distribution**
Where a particular species is within an area being investigated.

**Disulfide bond**
A bond formed between two sulfur atoms, which links together two cysteine amino acids in a polypeptide chain.

**Divergence (at a synapse)**
When one neurone connects to many neurones.

**DNA (deoxyribonucleic acid)**
A nucleic acid containing the pentose sugar deoxyribose. Stores genetic information in cells.

**DNA helicase**
An enzyme that breaks the hydrogen bonds between the two polynucleotide DNA strands during DNA replication.

**DNA ligase**
An enzyme that joins together the sticky ends of DNA fragments by joining up their sugar-phosphate backbones.

**DNA polymerase**
An enzyme that joins together the nucleotides on a new strand of DNA during DNA replication.

**DNA profile**
A DNA gel that shows the number of times repetitive, non-coding base sequences are repeated at different loci in an individual.

**DNA sequencing**
A technique used to determine the order of bases in a section of DNA.

**Dominant allele**
An allele whose characteristic appears in the phenotype even when there's only one copy.

**Double circulatory system**
A circulatory system where blood passes through the heart twice for each complete circuit of the body.

# E

**Ecosystem**
All the organisms living in a particular area and all the non-living (abiotic) conditions found there.

**Ectotherm**
An animal that can't control its body temperature internally.

**Effector**
A cell that brings about a response to a stimulus, to produce an effect.

**Electron carrier**
A protein that transfers electrons from one molecule to another.

**Electron transport chain**
A chain of proteins through which excited electrons flow.

**Electroporation**
A technique that uses an electric field to increase the permeability of cell membranes, which allows the cells to take up biological material, e.g. plasmids.

**Embryonic stem cell**
A stem cell harvested from an embryo, which can differentiate into any of the cell types in the body.

**Emulsion test**
A biochemical test for the presence of lipids.

**End-product inhibition**
When the final product in a metabolic pathway inhibits an enzyme that acts earlier on in the pathway.

**Endangered species**
A species whose population is so low that they could become extinct.

**Endocrine gland**
A group of cells specialised to secrete hormones directly into the blood.

**Endocytosis**
The process by which a cell surrounds substances with a section of its plasma membrane and takes them into the cell.

**Endotherm**
An animal that can control its body temperature internally by homeostasis.

**Enucleated cell**
A cell which has had the nucleus removed.

**Enzyme**
A globular protein that speeds up the rate of chemical reactions.

**Enzyme-product complex**
The intermediate formed when a substrate has been converted into its products, but they've not yet been released from the active site of an enzyme.

**Enzyme-substrate complex**
The intermediate formed when a substrate molecule binds to the active site of an enzyme.

**Epidemiology**
The study of health and disease within a population.

**Epistasis**
When an allele of one gene masks (blocks) the expression of the alleles of other genes.

**Erythrocyte**
A red blood cell.

**Esterification**
The process in which triglycerides are synthesised.

**Ethene (in plants)**
A plant hormone produced by ageing leaves, which stimulates leaf loss. It also stimulates enzymes which promote ripening.

**Etiolation**
Where a plant grows abnormally long and spindly because it's not getting enough light.

**Eukaryote**
Organism made up of a cell (or cells) containing a nucleus, e.g. animals and plants.

**Evolution**
The change in allele frequency in a population over time, characterised by the slow and continual change of organisms from one generation to the next.

***Ex situ* conservation**
Protecting a species by removing part of the population from a threatened habitat and placing it in a new location.

**Exchange organ**
An organ (e.g. the lungs) specialised to exchange substances.

**Excretion**
The removal of the waste products of metabolism from the body.

**Exocytosis**
The process by which a cell secretes substances using vesicles.

**Exon**
A section of DNA that codes for amino acids.

**Expulsive reflex**
An attempt to expel foreign objects, including pathogens, from the body automatically, e.g. a cough or sneeze.

**Extracellular**
Outside cells.

**Eyepiece graticule**
A transparent disc with a scale on it present inside the eyepiece of a microscope.

# F

**Facilitated diffusion**
The diffusion of particles through carrier proteins or channel proteins in the plasma membrane.

**FAD**
A type of coenzyme involved in respiration. It transfers hydrogen from one molecule to another.

**Fermentation vessel**
A large container in which microorganisms can be grown on an industrial scale.

**Fibrous protein**
An insoluble, rope-shaped protein.

**'Fight or flight' response**
A response involving the sympathetic nervous system and adrenaline, which prepares the body for action in reaction to a threat.

**Filtrate**
The liquid and small molecules present in the kidney tubules following ultrafiltration of the blood. Also called the tubular fluid.

**Final electron acceptor**
A molecule which accepts an electron at the end of an electron transport chain. E.g. oxygen in respiration.

**First messenger**
A chemical involved in cell signalling (e.g. a hormone) that binds to a receptor in a cell membrane and triggers activity inside the cell.

**Flaccid plant cell**
A plant cell which is limp due to lack of water.

**Flagellum**
Like a cilium, but longer, it sticks out from the cell surface and is surrounded by the plasma membrane. Used to move the cell.

**Fluid mosaic model**
Model describing the arrangement of molecules in a cell membrane.

**Founder effect**
The reduction in genetic diversity that occurs when just a few organisms from a population start a new colony.

**Frame quadrat**
A square frame, divided into a grid of 100 smaller squares, which can be used to investigate the abundance and distribution of organisms in an area.

# G

**Gamete**
A sex cell — e.g. the sperm cell in males or the egg cell in females.

**Gas exchange**
The process of taking in gases that are needed for life processes and getting rid of waste gases.

**Gas exchange surface**
A boundary between the outside environment and the internal environment of an organism, over which gas exchange occurs.

**Gel electrophoresis**
A technique that allows DNA fragments, RNA fragments or proteins to be separated on a gel according to size (length).

**Gene**
A sequence of DNA nucleotides that codes for a polypeptide, which results in a characteristic.

**Gene pool**
The complete range of alleles present in a population.

**Gene therapy**
Possible treatment option for genetic disorders and some cancers that involves altering defective alleles inside cells.

**Generator potential**
The change in potential difference across a cell membrane due to the presence of a stimulus.

**Genetic bottleneck**
An event that causes a big reduction in the size of a population.

**Genetic code**
The sequence of base triplets (codons) in mRNA which codes for specific amino acids.

**Genetic disorder**
An inherited disorder caused by an abnormal gene or chromosome.

**Genetic diversity**
The variation of alleles within a species (or a population of a species).

**Genetic drift**
The process whereby an allele becomes more common in a population due to chance.

**Genetic engineering**
The manipulation of an organism's DNA.

**Genetic resource**
Material from plants, animals or microorganisms, containing genes, that we find valuable.

**Genome**
All the genetic material in an organism.

**Genotype**
All the alleles an organism has.

**Geographical isolation**
When a physical barrier, e.g. a flood, divides a population of a species, causing some individuals to become separated from the main population.

**Geotropism**
The growth of a plant in response to gravity.

**Germ line gene therapy**
A possible cure for genetic disorders and some cancers that involves altering defective genes inside sex cells.

**Gibberellin**
A type of plant growth hormone that is produced in young leaves and in seeds. It stimulates seed germination, stem elongation, side shoot formation and flowering.

**Gill filament**
A thin plate, many of which make up a fish gill.

**Gill plate**
A tiny structure, which covers the gill filaments in a fish gill.

**Globular protein**
A soluble, round and compact protein.

**Glomerular filtration rate**
The rate at which blood is filtered from the glomerulus into the Bowman's capsule.

**Glomerulus**
A bundle of capillaries that loop inside the Bowman's capsule of a nephron. Where ultrafiltration takes place.

**Glucagon**
A hormone secreted by the pancreas that has an important role in raising blood glucose concentration.

**Gluconeogenesis**
The conversion of fatty acids or amino acids to glucose, activated by glucagon.

**Glycogen**
A polysaccharide made from a long, very branched chain of α-glucose.

**Glycogenesis**
The conversion of glucose to glycogen, activated by insulin.

**Glycogenolysis**
The conversion of glycogen to glucose, activated by glucagon.

**Glycolipid**
A lipid which has a carbohydrate chain attached.

**Glycolysis**
The first stage of aerobic respiration — here glucose is converted into pyruvate.

**Glycoprotein**
A protein which has a carbohydrate chain attached.

**Glycosidic bond**
A bond formed between monosaccharides.

**Golgi apparatus**
A group of fluid-filled flattened sacs. Involved with processing and packaging lipids and proteins, and making lysosomes.

**Gross productivity**
The energy available to organisms that is absorbed by them.

# H

**Habitat**
The area inhabited by a species.

**Habitat diversity**
The number of different habitats in an area.

**Haploid**
When a cell contains one copy of each chromosome.

**Hardy-Weinberg principle**
A mathematical model that predicts that the frequency of alleles in a population won't change from one generation to the next provided that certain conditions are met.

Glossary

**Herbivory**
When plants are eaten by animals (including insects).

**Herd immunity**
Where unvaccinated people are protected because the occurrence of the disease is reduced by the number of people who are vaccinated.

**Heterozygous**
When an organism carries two different alleles for the same characteristic.

**Hexose sugar**
A monosaccharide that has six carbon atoms, e.g. glucose.

**High-throughput sequencing**
DNA sequencing techniques that can sequence up to 1000 times more bases in a given time compared to original methods.

**Homeobox sequence**
A sequence in a homeotic gene that codes for the homeodomain (part of the protein that binds to DNA, allowing the protein to act as a transcription factor).

**Homeostasis**
The maintenance of a constant internal environment.

**Homologous chromosomes**
Pairs of matching chromosomes — each chromosome in the pair contains the same genes but different alleles.

**Homozygous**
When an organism carries two copies of the same allele.

**Hormone**
A chemical messenger secreted from an endocrine gland.

**Host cell**
A cell that is used to carry recombinant DNA.

**Hox genes**
Genes that encode proteins which control body plan development.

**Human chorionic gonadotropin (hCG)**
A hormone that is only found in the urine of pregnant women, which allows it to be used in pregnancy testing.

**Hydrogen bond**
A weak bond between a slightly positively charged hydrogen atom in one molecule and a slightly negatively charged atom in another molecule.

**Hydrolysis**
The splitting (lysis) of a molecule using water (hydro).

**Hydrophilic**
Attracts water.

**Hydrophobic**
Repels water.

**Hydrophytic plant**
A plant that is adapted to live in aquatic habitats.

**Hydrostatic pressure**
The pressure exerted by a liquid.

**Hyperpolarisation**
An increase in the potential difference across a cell's membrane, making it more negative than the resting potential.

**Hypothalamus**
A part of the brain that controls body temperature and monitors water potential of the blood.

**Hypothesis**
A specific testable statement, based on a theory, about what will happen in a test situation.

# I

**Immobilised enzyme**
An enzyme that is attached to an insoluble material so it can't become mixed with the products of a reaction.

**Immune response**
The body's reaction to a foreign antigen.

**Immunity**
The ability to respond quickly to an infection.

*In situ* **conservation**
Protecting species in their natural habitat.

**Inactive precursor**
An inactive form of an enzyme.

**Independent variable**
The variable you change in an experiment.

**Indirect transmission**
When a disease is transmitted from one organism to another via an intermediate.

**Indoleacetic acid (IAA)**
A type of auxin produced in the tips of shoots and roots in flowering plants.

**Inorganic ion**
An ion (charged particle) that doesn't contain carbon.

**Insulin**
A hormone secreted by the pancreas that has an important role in lowering blood glucose concentration.

**Interdependence (of organisms)**
The dependence of organisms in an ecosystem on each other for survival.

**Interphase**
A period of cell growth, consisting of $G_1$, S and $G_2$ phases, during which the cell's genetic material is copied and checked for DNA damage

**Interspecific competition**
Competition between organisms of different species for the same resources.

**Interspecific variation**
Variation between species.

**Intracellular**
Inside cells.

**Intraspecific competition**
Competition between organisms of the same species for the same resources.

**Intraspecific variation**
Variation within a species.

**Intron**
A section of DNA within a gene that doesn't code for amino acids.

**Iodine test**
A biochemical test for the presence of starch.

**Ionic bond (in a protein)**
An attraction between a negatively charged R group and a positively charged R group on different parts of the molecule.

**Islet of Langerhans**
An area of endocrine tissue in the pancreas, containing α and β cells.

**Isolated enzyme**
An enzyme not contained within the cells of organisms.

## K

**Keystone species**
A species that many of the other species in an ecosystem depend on and without which the ecosystem would change dramatically.

**Krebs cycle**
The third stage of aerobic respiration. It is a series of oxidation-reduction reactions that produces reduced coenzymes and ATP.

## L

***Lac* operon**
An operon containing the genes responsible for producing the enzymes needed to respire lactose in *E. coli*.

**Lactate fermentation**
A type of anaerobic respiration that occurs in mammals (and some bacteria). Lactate is the final product.

**Latent heat of evaporation**
The heat energy required to change a liquid to a gas.

**Light-dependent reaction**
The first stage of photosynthesis. Light energy is absorbed by photosynthetic pigments and converted to ATP and reduced NADP.

**Light-harvesting system**
A complex of proteins that surrounds a reaction centre and transfers light to it to boost the energy available for electron excitement to take place.

**Light-independent reaction**
The second stage of photosynthesis. Here ATP and reduced NADP (from the light-dependent reaction) are used to make glucose from carbon dioxide.

**Limiting factor of photosynthesis**
A variable that can slow down the rate of photosynthesis.

**Limiting factor of population size**
A biotic or abiotic factor that stops the population size of a species increasing.

**Link reaction**
The second stage of aerobic respiration where pyruvate is converted into acetyl coenzyme A.

**Locus**
The position on a chromosome where a particular allele is found.

**Loop of Henle**
Part of the kidney nephron responsible for establishing the water potential gradient, which allows water to be reabsorbed by the kidney.

**Lymph**
Excess tissue fluid that has drained into lymph vessels.

**Lysosome**
A round organelle that contains digestive enzymes.

## M

**Macromolecule**
A complex molecule with a relatively large molecular mass, e.g. a protein or lipid.

**Magnification**
How much bigger an image from a microscope is compared to the specimen.

**Margin of error**
The range in which the true value of a measurement lies.

**Mass flow hypothesis**
The best supported theory for how translocation works.

**Mature mRNA**
mRNA strands containing only exons — the introns have been removed.

**Mean**
The average of the values collected in a sample, obtained by adding all the values together and dividing by the total number of values in the sample.

**Medulla oblongata**
Part of the brain which automatically controls breathing rate and heart rate.

**Meiosis**
A type of cell division where a parent cell divides to create four genetically different haploid cells.

**Membrane-bound receptor**
A molecule (often a glycoprotein or glycolipid) that acts as a specific, complementary receptor for a messenger molecule in cell signalling.

**Memory cell**
A B or T lymphocyte which remains in the body for a long time and initiates a secondary immune response if a pathogen is re-encountered.

**Meristem**
Mitotically active tissue found in the growing parts of plants (e.g. the roots and shoots).

**Metabolism**
All the chemical reactions that occur within a living organism, which are essential for life.

**Microfilament**
A very thin protein strand in the cytoplasm of a cell.

**Micropropagation**
A technique where tissue culture is used to produce lots of cloned plants very quickly.

**Microtubule**
A tiny protein cylinder in the cytoplasm of a cell.

**Mitochondrion**
An oval-shaped organelle with a double membrane found in plant and animal cells. The site of aerobic respiration.

**Mitosis**
A type of cell division where a parent cell divides to produce two genetically identical daughter cells.

**Model (scientific)**
A simplified picture of what's physically going on.

**Monoculture**
The growing of a single variety of crop on a large area of land.

**Monogenic characteristic**
A characteristic influenced by one gene.

**Monogenic inheritance**
The inheritance of a single characteristic (gene) controlled by different alleles.

**Monomer**
A small, basic molecular unit, e.g. amino acids and monosaccharides.

**Monosaccharide**
A monomer of carbohydrates.

**mRNA (messenger RNA)**
A type of RNA that is the template for protein synthesis. It carries the genetic code from the DNA in the nucleus into the cytoplasm.

**Mucous membrane**
A membrane which protects body openings that are exposed to the environment (e.g. the mouth).

**Mucus**
A sticky substance that traps pathogens and contains antimicrobial enzymes.

**Mutation**
Any change in the DNA base (nucleotide) sequence.

**Myelin sheath (in the peripheral nervous system)**
A layer of Schwann cells around a neurone that acts as an electrical insulator and speeds up conduction of nervous impulses.

**Myofibril**
A long, cylindrical organelle within a muscle fibre that's highly specialised for contraction.

**Myogenic**
Produced by muscle cells without receiving a nerve's signal.

**Myosin**
The protein that makes up the thick myofilaments in myofibrils.

## N

**NAD**
A type of coenzyme involved in respiration. It transfers hydrogen from one molecule to another.

**NADP**
A coenzyme involved in photosynthesis. It transfers hydrogen from one molecule to another.

**Natural selection**
The process whereby an allele becomes more common in a population because it codes for an adaptation that makes an organism more likely to survive, reproduce and pass on its alleles to the next generation.

**Negative feedback mechanism**
When a system reacts to a change in a way that pushes it back towards a stable state.

**Nephron**
One of the filtering units of the kidney, responsible for removing waste substances such as urea from the blood.

**Net productivity**
The amount of energy that's available to the next trophic level in a food chain.

**Neuromuscular junction**
A specialised cholinergic synapse between a motor neurone and a muscle cell.

**Neurotransmitter**
A chemical that transmits a nerve impulse from one nerve cell to another nerve cell or to a muscle cell.

**Neutrophil**
A type of phagocyte.

**Nitrification**
The process in which ammonium ions in the soil are changed into nitrogen compounds by nitrifying bacteria called *Nitrosomonas* and *Nitrobacter*.

**Nitrogen cycle**
The conversion of nitrogen into a usable form and its movement through living organisms and the non-living environment.

**Nitrogen fixation**
The process in which nitrogen gas in the atmosphere is turned into ammonia by bacteria such as called *Rhizobium* and *Azotobacter*.

**Non-competitive inhibitor**
A molecule that binds to an enzyme away from its active site. This changes the shape of the active site so the substrate can no longer bind.

**Non-specific defence**
A defence that works the same against all pathogens.

**Nuclear envelope**
A double membrane found around the nucleus of a cell, which contains many pores.

**Nucleolus**
A structure inside the nucleus of a cell, which makes ribosomes.

**Nucleotide**
The monomer that makes up polynucleotides — consists of a pentose sugar, a phosphate group and a nitrogenous base.

**Nucleus**
A large organelle surrounded by a nuclear envelope. Contains DNA which controls the cell's activities.

## O

**Oncotic pressure**
The pressure which is generated by plasma proteins in a capillary.

**Oocyte**
An immature egg cell.

**Open circulatory system**
A circulatory system where the blood isn't enclosed in blood vessels all the time — it flows freely through the body cavity.

**Operator**
A DNA sequence that transcription factors bind to.

**Operculum**
A bony flap that covers and protects a fish gill.

**Operon**
A section of DNA that contains structural genes that are all transcribed together, control elements and sometimes a regulatory gene.

**Opsonin**
A molecule in the blood that attaches to foreign antigens to aid phagocytosis.

**Optimum pH**
The pH at which the rate of an enzyme-controlled reaction is at its fastest.

**Optimum temperature**
The temperature at which the rate of an enzyme-controlled reaction is at its fastest.

**Organ**
A group of different tissues that work together to perform a particular function.

**Organ system**
A group of organs that work together to perform a particular function.

**Organelle**
A part of a cell, e.g. the nucleus.

**Ornithine cycle**
A cycle of biochemical reactions in which ammonia is combined with carbon dioxide to create urea and water.

**Osmoreceptor**
A cell in the hypothalamus which monitors the water potential of the blood.

**Osmosis**
The diffusion of water molecules across a partially permeable membrane, from an area of higher water potential to an area of lower water potential.

**Oxidation**
A chemical reaction where a molecule loses electrons, and may have lost hydrogen or gained oxygen.

**Oxidative phosphorylation**
The final stage in aerobic respiration. Energy carried by electrons, from reduced coenzymes, is used to make ATP.

**Oxygen dissociation curve**
A curve on a graph that shows how saturated with oxygen haemoglobin is at any given partial pressure.

**Oxygen uptake (consumption)**
The rate at which a person uses up oxygen.

# P

**$pCO_2$**
Partial pressure of carbon dioxide — a measure of carbon dioxide concentration.

**$pO_2$**
Partial pressure of oxygen — a measure of oxygen concentration.

**Pacinian corpuscle**
A type of mechanoreceptor found in your skin.

**Palindromic sequence**
A sequence of DNA bases that consists of antiparallel base pairs (base pairs that read the same in opposite directions).

**Parasite**
An organism that lives on or in another organism (the host) and causes damage to that organism.

**Parasympathetic nervous system**
A division of the autonomic nervous system which calms the body down. It's the 'rest and digest' system.

**Parkinson's disease**
A disease which causes the loss of a particular type of nerve cell found in the brain, leading to uncontrollable tremors.

**Partially permeable membrane**
A membrane that lets some molecules through it, but not others.

**Passive immunity**
The type of immunity you get from being given antibodies made by a different organism.

**Pathogen**
An organism that can cause damage to the organism it infects (the host).

**PCR (polymerase chain reaction)**
A technique used to make millions of identical copies of a DNA fragment in a few hours.

**Peer review**
Where a scientific report is sent out to peers (other scientists) who examine the data and results, and if they think that the conclusion is reasonable it's published.

**Pentose sugar**
A sugar with five carbon atoms.

**Peptide bond**
A bond formed between the amino group of one amino acid and the carboxyl group of another amino acid.

**Peripheral nervous system**
Part of the nervous system that connects the CNS to the rest of the body. It consists of the somatic and autonomic nervous systems.

**Pesticide resistance**
When pests, e.g. insects, are able to survive in the presence of pesticides.

**Phagocyte**
A type of white blood cell that carries out phagocytosis, e.g. a neutrophil.

**Phagocytosis**
The engulfment of pathogens.

**Phagosome**
A type of vesicle in a cell that contains a phagocytosed pathogen.

**Pharming (genetics)**
Producing pharmaceuticals using genetically modified organisms, such as animals.

**Phenotype**
The characteristics an organism's alleles produce.

**Phenotypic ratio**
The ratio of different phenotypes in the offspring.

**Pheromone**
A signalling chemical, released by an organism, that produces a response in other organisms.

**Phloem**
A tissue in plants that transports sugars (e.g. sucrose) from their source to their sink.

**Phospholipid**
A lipid containing one molecule of glycerol attached to two fatty acids and a phosphate group. Main component of the cell membrane.

**Phosphorylation**
The process of adding phosphate to a molecule.

**Photolysis**
The splitting (lysis) of a molecule using light (photo) energy.

**Photomicrograph**
A photo of a microscopic object taken through a type of microscope.

**Photophosphorylation**
The process of adding phosphate to a molecule using light energy.

**Photosynthesis**
The process where energy from light is used to make glucose from carbon dioxide and water.

**Photosynthetic pigment**
A coloured substance (e.g. chlorophyll a) that absorbs the light energy needed for photosynthesis.

**Photosystem**
A protein and photosynthetic pigment structure found in the thylakoid membranes of chloroplasts in plants and algae.

**Phototropism**
The growth of a plant in response to light.

**Phylogeny**
The study of the evolutionary history of groups of organisms.

**Pioneer species**
The first species to colonise an area during succession.

**Pituitary gland**
A gland located beneath the hypothalamus in the brain, which releases hormones and stimulates other glands to release hormones.

**Placebo**
A dummy pill or injection that looks exactly like the real drug, but doesn't contain the drug.

**Plagioclimax**
The climax community produced when succession is artificially stopped by human activities.

**Plant growth hormone**
A chemical that speeds up or slows down plant growth.

**Plasma cell**
A type of B lymphocyte that produces antibodies.

**Plasma membrane**
The membrane found on the surface of animal cells and just inside the cell wall of plant cells and prokaryotic cells. Regulates the movement of substances into and out of the cell.

**Plasmodesmata**
Channels in plant cell walls for exchanging substances between neighbouring cells.

**Plasmolysis (plant cells)**
The pulling away of the cytoplasm and plasma membrane from the cell wall due to lack of water.

**Point quadrat**
A horizontal bar on two legs with a series of holes set at intervals along its length, through which pins are dropped. Can be used to investigate the abundance and distribution of organisms in an area.

**Polar molecule**
A molecule with a slight negative charge on one side and a slight positive charge on the other.

**Polygenic characteristic**
A characteristic influenced by many genes.

**Polymer**
A large, complex molecule composed of long chains of monomers, e.g. proteins and carbohydrates.

**Polymorphic gene locus**
A point on a chromosome that can have more than one allele.

**Polynucleotide**
A molecule made up of lots of nucleotides joined together in a long chain.

**Polypeptide**
A molecule formed from more than two amino acids.

**Polysaccharide**
A molecule formed from more than two monosaccharides.

**Population**
All the organisms of one species in a habitat.

**Positive feedback mechanism**
When a system reacts to a change in a way that amplifies it away from a stable state.

**Potential difference**
The voltage across a cell membrane.

**Precise result**
A result that is really close to the mean.

**Predation**
Where an organism (the predator) kills and eats another organism (the prey).

**Prediction**
See hypothesis.

**Preservation (of ecosystems)**
The protection of ecosystems so they're kept exactly as they are.

**Pressure filtration**
The process by which substances move out of capillaries into the tissue fluid, at the arteriole end of a capillary bed.

**Primary immune response**
The immune response triggered when a foreign antigen enters the body for the first time.

**Primary mRNA**
mRNA strand that contains both introns and exons.

**Primary succession**
Succession which happens on newly formed or exposed land with no soil.

**Primer**
A short piece of single stranded DNA that is complementary to the bases at the start of the DNA fragment you want.

**Probability**
How likely something is to happen.

**Producer**
An organism that produces organic molecules using sunlight energy.

**Product inhibition**
When an enzyme is inhibited by the product of the reaction it catalyses.

**Prokaryote**
Single-celled organism without a nucleus or membrane-bound organelles, e.g. bacteria.

**Promoter**
A DNA sequence (located before the structural genes in an operon) that RNA polymerase binds to.

**Prosthetic group**
A cofactor that is tightly bound to an enzyme.

**Purine**
A type of nucleotide base that contains two carbon-nitrogen rings joined together, e.g. adenine and guanine.

**Purkyne tissue**
Fine muscle fibres in the heart that carry waves of electrical activity into the muscular walls of the right and left ventricles.

**Pyrimidine**
A type of nucleotide base that contains one carbon-nitrogen ring joined together, e.g. cytosine, thymine and uracil.

## Q

**Qualitative result**
Non-numerical result.

**Quantitative result**
Numerical result.

## R

**Random error**
A difference in a measurement caused by an unpredictable factor, e.g. human error.

**Reaction centre**
A site where electrons are excited during the light-dependent reaction of photosynthesis.

**Receptor**
A cell, or protein on a cell surface membrane, that detects a specific stimulus.

**Recessive allele**
An allele whose characteristic only appears in the phenotype if there are two copies present.

**Recognition sequence**
A specific palindromic sequence in DNA recognised by a restriction enzyme.

**Recombinant DNA**
The name for DNA formed by joining together DNA from different sources.

**Redox reaction**
A chemical reaction that involves oxidation and reduction.

**Reduction**
A chemical reaction where a molecule gains electrons, and may have gained hydrogen or lost oxygen.

**Reflex action**
An automatic nervous response to a stimulus.

**Regulatory gene**
A gene that codes for a transcription factor (either an activator or repressor).

**Repeatable result**
A result that can be repeated by the same person using the same method and equipment.

**Repolarisation**
The return of a cell membrane to its resting potential.

**Repressor**
A transcription factor that stops transcription.

**Reproducible result**
A result that can be consistently reproduced in an independent experiment.

**Reproductive isolation**
When two populations of the same species are unable to breed together to produce fertile offspring.

**Resolution**
How well a microscope distinguishes between two points close together.

**Respiratory loss**
The amount of energy lost to the environment when organisms use energy produced from respiration for movement or body heat.

**Respiratory quotient**
The volume of carbon dioxide produced when a substrate is respired, divided by the volume of oxygen consumed, in a set period of time.

**Respiratory substrate**
Any biological molecule that can be broken down in respiration to release energy.

**Respirometer**
A device that can be used to measure the rate of oxygen being taken up by an organism.

**Resting potential**
The potential difference across a cell membrane when the cell is at rest.

**Restriction enzymes**
Enzymes that recognise specific recognition sequences and cut DNA at these places.

**Reverse transcriptase**
An enzyme that makes a DNA copy of RNA.

**$R_f$ value**
The distance a substance moves through the stationary phase during thin-layer chromatography, relative to the solvent.

**Ribosome**
A small organelle that makes proteins.

**Ribulose bisphosphate carboxylase (RuBisCo)**
An enzyme which catalyses the formation of glycerate 3-phosphate from carbon dioxide and ribulose bisphosphate (RuBP) in the light-independent reaction of photosynthesis.

**RNA (ribonucleic acid)**
A type of nucleic acid, similar to DNA but containing the pentose sugar ribose instead of deoxyribose and uracil instead of thymine.

**Rough endoplasmic reticulum (RER)**
A system of ribosome-covered membranes enclosing a fluid-filled space. Involved in protein synthesis.

**rRNA (ribosomal RNA)**
A type of RNA that forms the two subunits in a ribosome. It helps to catalyse the formation of peptide bonds between the amino acids.

## S

**Saltatory conduction**
The process in myelinated neurones by which a nervous impulse travels between nodes of Ranvier.

**Sample size**
The number of samples in the investigation, e.g. the number of people in a drug trial.

**Saprobiontic nutrition**
The process of feeding on dead organic matter used by decomposers.

**Sarcomere**
A short contractile unit that's part of a myofibril, made up of overlapping myosin and actin filaments.

**Saturation point (in photosynthesis)**
The point at which a particular factor no longer limits the rate of reaction. Here another factor has begun to limit the rate of reaction.

**Schwann cell**
The type of cell that makes up the myelin sheath around neurones in the peripheral nervous system.

**Second messenger**
A chemical that's produced inside a cell in response to a signal outside the cell. The chemical relays the signal to the inside of the cell.

**Secondary immune response**
The immune response triggered when a foreign antigen enters the body for the second time.

**Secondary succession**
Succession which happens on land cleared of all plants but where the soil remains, e.g. after a forest fire.

**Selection pressure**
Anything that affects an organism's chance of survival and reproduction.

**Selective breeding**
A process that involves humans selecting which strains of plants or animals to reproduce together in order to increase productivity.

**Selective reabsorption (kidneys)**
The reabsorption of useful substances along the kidney nephron back into the blood.

**Semi-conservative replication**
The process by which DNA molecules replicate. The two strands of a DNA double helix separate, each acting as a template for the formation of a new strand.

**Semi-lunar (SL) valve**
A valve in the heart linking the ventricles to the aorta and pulmonary artery.

**Sex-linked characteristic**
When the allele that codes for the characteristic is located on a sex chromosome (X or Y).

**Sexual reproduction**
A form of reproduction where two gametes join together at fertilisation to form a zygote, which divides and develops into a new organism.

**Sieve tube element**
Living plant cells that form the tube for transporting assimilates through a plant.

**Single circulatory system**
A circulatory system where blood only passes through the heart once for each complete circuit of the body.

**Sink (in a plant)**
Where assimilates (e.g. sucrose) are used up.

**Sino-atrial node (SAN)**
A group of cells in the wall of the right atrium that set the rhythm of the heartbeat by sending regular waves of electrical activity over the atrial walls.

**Sliding filament model**
The model that explains muscle contraction, in which myosin and actin filaments slide over one another to make sarcomeres contract.

**Smooth endoplasmic reticulum (SER)**
Similar to rough endoplasmic reticulum, but with no ribosomes. Involved in lipid synthesis.

**Somatic cell**
Any cell of a multicellular organism that isn't a reproductive cell.

**Somatic cell nuclear transfer (SCNT)**
A technique for cloning animals which involves taking a nucleus from a somatic cell and inserting it into an enucleated oocyte.

**Somatic gene therapy**
A possible treatment option for genetic disorders and some cancers that involves altering defective genes inside body cells.

**Somatic nervous system**
A division of the peripheral nervous system that controls conscious activities, e.g. running.

**Source (in a plant)**
Where assimilates (e.g. sucrose) are produced.

**Spatial summation**
Where two or more neurones release their neurotransmitters onto the same postsynaptic neurone at the same time, so the effect of their neurotransmitters is added together.

**Specialised cell**
A cell adapted to carry out specific functions.

**Speciation**
The development of a new species.

**Species**
A group of similar organisms that can reproduce to give fertile offspring.

**Species diversity**
The number of different species and the abundance of each species in an area.

**Species evenness**
A measure of the relative abundance of each species in an area.

**Species richness**
The number of different species in an area.

**Specific heat capacity**
The energy needed to raise the temperature of 1 gram of substance by 1 °C.

**Spiracle**
A pore on the surface of an insect.

**Squamous epithelium**
A single layer of flat cells lining a surface found in animals (e.g. in the alveoli).

**Stabilising selection**
Where individuals with alleles for characteristics towards the middle of the range are more likely to survive, reproduce and pass on their alleles.

**Stage micrometer**
A microscope slide with an accurate scale that's used to work out the value of the divisions on the eyepiece graticule at a particular magnification.

**Standard deviation**
A measure of the spread of values about the mean.

**Standard growth curve (for microorganisms)**
A curve with four phases that represents the growth of a population of microorganisms grown in a closed culture.

**Starch**
A carbohydrate molecule made up of two polysaccharides — amylose and amylopectin.

**Stem cell**
An unspecialised cell that can differentiate into different types of cell.

**Sticky end**
A small tail of unpaired DNA bases at each end of a DNA fragment.

**Stimulus**
A change in an organism's internal or external environment.

**Structural gene**
A gene that codes for a useful protein, e.g. an enzyme.

**Substrate**
A substance that interacts with an enzyme.

**Substrate-level phosphorylation**
When a phosphate group is directly transferred from one molecule to another.

**Succession**
The process by which an ecosystem changes over time.

**Surface area to volume ratio**
An organism's or structure's surface area in relation to its volume.

**Sympathetic nervous system**
A division of the autonomic nervous system which gets the body ready for action. It's the 'fight or flight' system.

**Sympatric speciation**
When a new species develops without geographical isolation.

**Symplast pathway**
A route that water takes through a plant root to the xylem, through the cytoplasm of cells.

**Synapse**
A junction between a neurone and another neurone, or between a neurone and an effector cell.

**Synthetic biology**
A large field of biology that includes building biological systems from artificially-made molecules, redesigning biological systems to perform better, and designing new biological systems and molecules that don't exist in the natural world.

## T

**T helper cell**
A differentiated form of a T lymphocyte which releases substances that activate B lymphocytes.

**T killer cell**
A differentiated form of a T lymphocyte which attaches to an antigen on a pathogen and kills the cell.

**T lymphocyte**
A type of white blood cell involved in the immune response. Some types activate B lymphocytes, some kill pathogens directly and some suppress the immune response.

**T regulatory cell**
A differentiated form of a T lymphocyte which suppresses the immune response from other white blood cells to stop immune system cells from mistakenly attacking the host's body cells.

**Tannin**
A bitter tasting chemical released by plants to protect against herbivory.

**Target cell (or target tissue)**
A cell (or tissue) that has specific receptors for a particular type of chemical, such as a hormone or a neurotransmitter.

**Taxonomy**
The study of classification.

**Technology transfer**
The sharing of knowledge, skills and technology.

**Temperature coefficient ($Q_{10}$)**
A value for a reaction that shows how much the rate of that reaction changes when the temperature is raised by 10 °C.

**Temporal summation**
Where one neurone is stimulated a lot in quick succession and the effects of all the neurotransmitters released onto the postsynaptic membrane are added together.

**Theory**
A possible explanation for something.

**Threshold level**
The level a generator potential needs to reach for an action potential to be generated.

**Tidal volume**
The volume of air in each breath.

**Tissue**
A group of cells (plus any extracellular material secreted by them) that are specialised to work together to carry out a particular function.

**Tissue culture (of plants)**
A technique for cloning plants which involves taking stem cells from the stem or root tips of a plant and growing them in culture.

**Tissue fluid**
The fluid that surrounds cells in tissues.

**Trachea (insects)**
A pipe that carries air between the external environment and the inside of an insect's body.

**Tracheole**
A small pipe that branches off the trachea in an insect and is used for gas exchange.

**Transcription**
The first stage of protein synthesis in which an mRNA copy of a gene is made from DNA in the nucleus.

**Transcription factor**
A protein that binds to DNA and switches a gene on or off by increasing or decreasing the rate of transcription.

**Transducer**
Something that converts one form of energy into another.

**Transect**
A line used to help measure how plants are distributed across an area, e.g. how species change from a hedge towards the middle of a field.

**Transformed cell**
A host cell that has taken up recombinant DNA.

**Transformed organism**
A organism that has had its genes altered by genetic engineering.

**Transgenic organism**
An organism that has been genetically engineered to include a gene from a different species.

**Translation**
The second stage of protein synthesis in which amino acids are joined together by ribosomes to make a polypeptide chain (protein).

**Translocation**
The movement of assimilates to where they're needed in a plant.

**Transpiration**
The evaporation of water from a plant's surface.

**Triglyceride**
A lipid containing one molecule of glycerol attached to three fatty acids.

**tRNA (transfer RNA)**
A type of RNA involved in translation. It carries the amino acids used to make proteins to the ribosomes.

Glossary

**Trophic level**
A stage in a food chain that's occupied by a particular group of organisms.

**Tropism**
The response of a plant to a directional stimulus.

**Turgid plant cell**
A cell which is swollen with water.

## U

**Ultrafiltration (kidneys)**
The filtering of the blood that takes place under high pressure, as blood passes from the glomerulus into the Bowman's capsule.

**Ultrastructure (of a cell)**
The details of a cell's internal structure and organelles that can be seen under an electron microscope.

**Uncertainty (of data)**
The amount of error measurements might have.

## V

**Vaccination**
The administering of a vaccine containing substances designed to stimulate the immune system and give immunity.

**Vacuole**
An organelle that contains cell sap (a weak solution of sugar and salts).

**Valid conclusion**
A conclusion that answers the original question.

**Variable**
A quantity that has the potential to change, e.g. weight, temperature, concentration.

**Variation**
The differences that exist between individuals.

**Vasoconstriction**
Constriction (narrowing) of a blood vessel.

**Vasodilation**
Dilation (widening) of a blood vessel.

**Vector (in disease)**
An organism that transmits a disease from one organism to another.

**Vector (in gene technology)**
Something used to transfer DNA into a cell, e.g. a plasmid or a bacteriophage.

**Vegetative propagation**
The natural production of plant clones from non-reproductive tissues, e.g. roots, leaves and stems.

**Vesicle**
A small fluid-filled sac in the cytoplasm. Transports substances in and out of the cell and between organelles.

**Vital capacity**
The maximum volume of air that can be breathed in or out.

## W

**Water potential**
The likelihood of water molecules to diffuse into or out of solution.

## X

**Xerophytic plant**
A plant that is adapted to live in dry climates.

**Xylem**
A tissue in plants that transports water and mineral ions.

# Acknowledgements

*OCR Specification reference points and practical activity requirements are adapted and reproduced by permission of OCR. OCR maintains the current version specification on the OCR website. You should always check for the latest version and any updates. https://www.ocr.org.uk/qualifications/as-and-a-level/biology-a-h020-h420-from-2015/*

**Data acknowledgements**

Data for graph showing glucose concentration vs absorbance on page 80 was obtained using a Mystrica colorimeter © Mystrica Ltd www.mystrica.com

Graph of whooping cough vaccine uptake on page 241 from Health in Scotland 2000, CMO Annual Report, September 2001. This information is licenced under the terms of the Open Government Licence http://www.nationalarchives.gov.uk/doc/open-government-licence/version/3/ (www.department.gov.uk/document, accessed November 2011).

With thanks to the HPA for permission to use the graph on page 246, adapted from Tuberculosis in the UK: Annual report on tuberculosis surveillance in the UK, 2010. London: Health Protection Agency Centre for Infections, October 2010

Data used to construct the graph of global sea temperature on page 258 © NASA/GISS.

Diagram showing the distribution of subtropical plankton on page 258 due to climate changes - North Sea. (February 2008). Hugo Ahlenius, UNEP/GRID-Arendal Maps and Graphics Library. http://maps.grida.no/go/graphic/plankton-distribution-changes-due-to-climate-changes-north-sea.

Critical values for the Spearman's rank test on page 283 abridged from Significance Testing of the Spearman Rank Correlation Coefficient by Jerrold H. Zar from the Journal of the American Statistical Association © 1972 Taylor & Francis, reprinted by the publisher Taylor & Francis Ltd, http://www.tandfonline.com

Data used to create graph on page 445 from Figure 1 of the following study Nascimento WM; Huber DJ; Cantliffe DJ. 2013. Carrot seed germination and ethylene production at high temperature in response to seed osmopriming. Horticultura Brasileira 31: 554-558

Information used in question 5 on page 486 from A. Herrel et al. 2008. Rapid large-scale evolutionary divergence in morphology and performance associated with exploitation of a different dietary resource. PNAS 105: 4792-4795. Copyright (2008) National Academy of Sciences, U.S.A.

Data used to produce the table on page 500 from A.C. Nathwani et al., Adenovirus-Associated Virus Vector–Mediated Gene Transfer in Hemophilia B: N Engl J Med 2011; 365:2357-2365

Data used to construct the graphs on page 510 from S. Hacein-Bey-Abina et al. SCIENCE 302: 415-419 (2003).

**Photograph acknowledgements**

Cover Photo iStock.com/**BlackJack3D**, p 1 **Dr Jeremy Burgess**/Science Photo Library, p 7 (top) **Andrew Lambert Photography**/Science Photo Library, p 7 (bottom) **Tek Image**/Science Photo Library, p 33 **Andrew Lambert Photography**/Science Photo Library, p 39 **Omikron**/Science Photo Library, p 40 (top) **Biophoto Associates**/Science Photo Library, p 40 (bottom) **Martin M Rother**/Science Photo Library, p 41 (top) **Science Photo Library**, p 41 (middle) **Don W Fawcett**/Science Photo Library, p 41 (bottom) **Biology Pics**/Science Photo Library, p 42 (top) **Don W Fawcett**/Science Photo Library, p 42 (bottom left) **Dr David Furness, Keele University**/Science Photo Library, p 42 (bottom right) **Science Photo Library**, p 43 (left) **Dr Kari Lounatmaa**/Science Photo Library, p 43 (right) **Prof. P. Motta/Dept. Of Anatomy/University La Sapienza**,

Rome/Science Photo Library, p 44 **Dr Torsten Wittmann**/Science Photo Library, p 45 **Juergen Berger**/Science Photo Library, p 46 **Ami Images**/Science Photo Library, p 48 (top) **Steve Gschmeissner**/Science Photo Library, p 48 (middle) **NIAID/CDC**/Science Photo Library, p 48 (bottom) **CNRI**/Science Photo Library, p 49 (Fig. 1 top) **Dr. Michael Gabridge, Visuals Unlimited**/Science Photo Library, p 49 (Fig. 1 bottom) **Heiti Paves**/Science Photo Library, p 49 (middle) **Andrew Brookes, National Physical Laboratory**/Science Photo Library, p 49 (Fig. 3 top) **Science Photo Library**, p 49 (Fig. 3 bottom) **Alfred Pasieka**/Science Photo Library, p 50 (right) **Professors P. Motta & T. Naguro**/Science Photo Library, p 50 (left) **K. R. Porter**/Science Photo Library, p 52 (Fig. 1) **Jack Bostrack, Visuals Unlimited**/Science Photo Library, p 52 (Fig. 2) **Eric Grave**/Science Photo Library, p 52 (bottom) **M. I. Walker**/Science Photo Library, p 54 **Martin Shields**/Science Photo Library, p 58 **CNRI**/Science Photo Library, p 61(left and right) **Clive Freeman/Biosym Technologies**/Science Photo Library, p 65 **Biophoto Associates**/Science Photo Library, p 72 (Fig. 8) **animante4.com**/Science Photo Library, p 72 (Fig. 10-12) **Laguna Design**/Science Photo Library, p 73 (top) **Susumu Nishinaga**/Science Photo Library, p 73 (bottom) **Biophoto Associates**/Science Photo Library, p 75 **Nigel Cattlin**/Science Photo Library, p 76 **Andrew Lambert Photography**/Science Photo Library, p 77 (top and bottom) **Andrew Lambert Photography**/Science Photo Library, p 78 (Fig. 8) **Andrew Lambert Photography**/Science Photo Library, p 78 (bottom) **Saturn Stills**/Science Photo Library, p 79 **Martyn F. Chillmaid**/Science Photo Library, p 81 **Jim Varney**/Science Photo Library, p 82 **Sinclair Stammers**/Science Photo Library, p 90 **ISM**/Science Photo Library, p 92 **Science Photo Library**, p 93 **Philippe Psaila**/Science Photo Library, p 100 **Ramon Andrade 3Dciencia**/Science Photo Library, p 106 **Clive Freeman, The Royal Institution**/Science Photo Library, p 116 **Jeff Daly, Visuals Unlimited**/Science Photo Library, p 125 **Russell Kightley**/Science Photo Library, p 134 **Andrew Lambert Photography**/Science Photo Library, p 135 (top and bottom) **J. C. Revy, ISM**/Science Photo Library, p 136 **Charles D. Winters**/Science Photo Library, p 140 **Science Picture Co**/Science Photo Library, p 141 **Don Fawcett**/Science Photo Library, p 145 (left and right) **J. C. Revy, ISM**/Science Photo Library, p 148 (all) **Pr. G Gimenez-Martin**/Science Photo Library, p 149 (top) **Pr. G Gimenez-Martin**/Science Photo Library, p 149 (bottom) **Herve Conge, ISM**/Science Photo Library, p 150 **Steve Gschmeissner**/Science Photo Library, p 151 **Eye Of Science**/Science Photo Library, p 152 **Science Pictures Ltd**/Science Photo Library, p 153 (top) **Pr. G Gimenez-Martin**/Science Photo Library, p 153 (bottom) **Adrian T Sumner**/Science Photo Library, p 155 (left) **Paul Gunning**/Science Photo Library, p 155 (right) **Dr. Tony Brain**/Science Photo Library, p 157 (top) **Steve Gschmeissner**/Science Photo Library, p 157 (middle) **Eye Of Science**/Science Photo Library, p 157 (bottom) **Steve Gschmeissner**/Science Photo Library, p 158 (top) **Dr Keith Wheeler**/Science Photo Library, p 158 (middle) **Microfield Scientific Ltd**/Science Photo Library, p 158 (bottom) **Dr Jeremy Burgess**/Science Photo Library, p 159 **Steve Gschmeissner**/Science Photo Library, p 160 **Martin Oeggerli**/Science Photo Library, p 161 (top) **Steve Gschmeissner**/Science Photo Library, p 161 (bottom) **Eye Of Science**/Science Photo Library, p 162 **Biophoto Associates**/Science Photo Library, p 165 **Power And Syred**/Science Photo Library, p 168 **Steve Gschmeissner**/Science Photo Library, p 169 **Science Vu, Visuals Unlimited**/Science Photo Library, p 170 (top) **Dr Keith Wheeler**/Science Photo Library, p 170 (bottom) **Manfred Kage**/Science Photo Library, p 171 **Dr. Richard Kessel & Dr. Gene Shih, Visuals Unlimited**/Science Photo Library, p 172 (top) **Science Photo Library**, p 172 (bottom) **Sinclair Stammers**/Science Photo Library, p 173 **Microscape**/Science Photo Library, p 175 **John Thys/Reporters**/Science Photo Library, p 177 **Power And Syred**/Science Photo Library, p 178 (bottom) **Microfield Scientific Ltd**/Science Photo Library, p 180 (top) **Science Photo Library**, p 180 (bottom) **Herve Conge, ISM**/Science Photo Library, p 181 **Dr Keith Wheeler**/Science Photo Library, p 184 (top left) **Eye Of Science**/Science Photo Library, p 184 (top right) **Dr. Fred Hossler, Visuals Unlimited**/Science Photo Library, p 184 (bottom) **Dr. Richard Kessel & Dr. Gene Shih, Visuals Unlimited**/Science Photo Library, p 188 (top) **Biophoto Associates**/Science Photo Library, p 188 (bottom) **Ralph Hutchings, Visuals Unlimited**/Science Photo Library, p 190 **Astrid & Hanns-Frieder Michler**/Science Photo Library, p 192 (top) **Science Picture Co**/Science Photo Library, p 195 **Simon Fraser/Coronary Care Unit/Hexham General Hospital**/Science Photo Library, p 196 **D. Varty, ISM**/Science Photo Library, p 198 **Dr P. Marazzi**/Science Photo Library, p 207 **Dr David Furness, Keele University**/Science Photo Library, p 208 (top) **Dr Keith Wheeler**/Science Photo Library, p 208 (bottom) **Herve Conge, ISM**/Science Photo Library, p 209 (Fig. 10) **Biophoto Associates**/Science Photo Library, p 209 (Fig. 11) **Dr Keith Wheeler**/Science Photo Library, p 209 (Q1 photo) **Dr Keith Wheeler**/Science Photo Library, p 209 (Figure A) **J. C. Revy, ISM**/Science Photo Library, p 209 (Figure B) **Power And Syred**/Science Photo Library, p 211 **Microfield Scientific Ltd**/Science Photo Library, p 216 **Dr Keith Wheeler**/Science Photo Library, p 217 (left) **Eye Of Science**/Science Photo Library, p 217 (right) **Power And Syred**/Science Photo Library, p 222 (both) **Dr Keith Wheeler**/Science Photo Library, p 225 (bottom) **A. Dowsett, Public Health England**/Science Photo Library, p 226 (top) **Dr Jeremy Burgess**/Science Photo Library, p 226 (bottom) **Norm Thomas**/Science Photo Library, p 227 (top) **Steve Gschmeissner**/Science Photo Library, p 227 (bottom) **Eye Of Science**/Science Photo Library, p 228 (top) **Dr P. Marazzi**/Science Photo Library, p 228 (bottom) **Nigel Cattlin**/Science Photo Library, p 229 **Scimat**/Science Photo Library, p 231 **Dr Olivier Schwartz, Institute Pasteur**/Science Photo Library, p 232 **Biophoto Associates**/Science Photo Library, p 233 **Biophoto Associates**/Science Photo Library, p 234 (top) **Phantatomix**/Science Photo Library, p 234 (bottom) **Science Photo Library**, p 235 **NIBSC**/Science Photo Library, p 239 (top) **Dr P. Marazzi**/Science Photo Library, p 239 (bottom) **Simon Fraser**/Science Photo Library, p 240 **CNRI**/Science Photo Library, p 243 (top) **D. Phillips**/Science Photo Library, p 243 (bottom) **Dr Jeremy Burgess**/Science Photo Library, p 250 **Nigel Cattlin**/Science Photo Library, p 256 **Dr Morley Read**/Science Photo Library, p 261 (top) **Simon Little**, p 262 (top) **Dr P. Marazzi**/Science Photo Library, p 262 (bottom) **Paul Shoesmith**/Science Photo Library, p 263 **John Reader**/Science Photo Library, p 264 **B. G Thomson**/Science Photo Library, p 269 (bacterium) **A. Dowsett, Public Health England**/Science Photo Library, p 269 (protoctista) **Michael Abbey**/Science Photo Library, p 273 (both) **Eye Of Science**/Science Photo Library, p 276 **Wally Eberhart, Visuals Unlimited**/Science Photo Library, p 284 (top) **David M Schleser**/**Nature's Images**/Science Photo Library, p 284 (bottom) **Duncan Shaw**/Science Photo Library, p 286 (top) © **Auscape International Pty Ltd**/Alamy Stock Photo, p 287 **Michael W. Tweedie**/Science Photo Library, p 289 **John Serrao**/Science Photo Library, p 296 **Steve Gschmeissner**/Science Photo Library, p 298 **Ray Simons**/Science Photo Library, p 303 **Dr David Furness, Keele University**/Science Photo Library, p 305 **Don Fawcett**/Science Photo Library, p 311 **Ramon Andrade 3Dciencia**/Science Photo Library, p 313 **CNRI**/Science Photo Library, p 314 **Steve Gschmeissner**/Science Photo Library, p 316 **CNRI**/Science Photo Library, p 318 **Adam Jones**/Science Photo Library, p 318 **Edward Kinsman**/Science Photo Library, p 325 **Dr P. Marazzi**/Science Photo Library, p 333 (top) **Prof. P. Motta/Dept. Of Anatomy/University La Sapienza, Rome**/Science Photo Library, p 333 (bottom) **Thomas Deerinck, NCMIR**/Science Photo Library, p 334 **CNRI**/Science Photo Library, p 335 **Science Photo Library**, p 336 **Biophoto Associates**/Science Photo Library, p 337 **Dr Keith Wheeler**/Science Photo Library, p 338 **Steve Gschmeissner**/Science Photo Library, p 339 (top) **ISM**/Science Photo Library, p 339 (bottom) **CNRI**/Science Photo Library, p 340 **Ralph Hutchings**/**Visuals Unlimited, Inc.**/Science Photo Library, p 341 **Science Photo Library**, p 343 (top) **Anthony Mercieca**/Science Photo Library, p 343 (middle) **Tom McHugh**/Science Photo Library, p 346 **Life In View**/Science Photo Library, p 347 **Life In View**/Science Photo Library, p 348 **Life In View**/Science Photo Library, p 349 **Mark Sykes**/Science Photo Library, p 351 **Steve Gschmeissner**/Science Photo Library, p 354 **Alfred Pasieka**/Science Photo Library, p 355 **Astrid & Hanns-Frieder Michler**/Science Photo Library, p 356 **PH. Gerbier**/Science Photo Library, p 363 **Steve Gschmeissner**/Science Photo Library, p 364 **Thomas Deerinck, NCMIR**/Science Photo Library, p 369 (top) **Eric Grave**/Science Photo Library, p 369 (bottom) **Science Photo Library**, p 370 **CNRI**/Science Photo Library, p 371 **Kent Wood**/Science Photo Library, p 375 **Dr Colin Chumbley**/Science Photo Library, p 378 (top, middle and bottom) **Martin Shields**/Science Photo Library, p 383 **David R. Frazier Photolibrary, Inc.**/Science Photo Library, p 384 **Scott Sinklier/AGStockUSA**/Science Photo Library, p 386 (top) **Dr Keith Wheeler**/Science Photo Library, p 387 **Andrew Lambert Photography**/Science Photo Library, p 395 **Dr Kari Lounatmaa**/Science Photo Library, p 401 **Biophoto Associates**/Science Photo Library, p 404 **iStock.com**/GAPS, p 407 **Sinclair Stammers**/Science Photo Library, p 411 **Dr. Jeremy Burgess**/Science Photo Library, p 413 **Dr David Furness, Keele University**/Science Photo Library, p 420 **Power And Syred**/Science Photo Library, p 423 **Philippe Psaila**/Science Photo Library, p 426 **Martin Shields**/Science Photo Library, p 432 **Mitchell Lewis, University Of Pennsylvania Medical Center**/Science Photo Library, p 435 **Eye**

Of Science/Science Photo Library, p 436 (top) **Dr Gopal Murti**/Science Photo Library, p 436 (middle) **Dr Keith Wheeler**/Science Photo Library, p 436 (bottom) **Claude Nuridsany & Marie Perennou**/Science Photo Library, p 437 **Dr Jeremy Burgess**/Science Photo Library, p 443 **Herve Conge, ISM**/Science Photo Library, p 444 **Geoff Kidd**/Science Photo Library, p 448 (top) **Wim Van Egmond, Visuals Unlimited**/Science Photo Library, p 448 (bottom) **J. C. Revy, ISM**/Science Photo Library, p 450 **Eye Of Science**/Science Photo Library, p 453 **Wally Eberhart, Visuals Unlimited**/Science Photo Library, p 461 **Ed Young/AGStockUSA**/Science Photo Library, p 463 **Science Photo Library**, p 479 **Dr. John Brackenbury**/Science Photo Library, p 481 **Dr Jeremy Burgess**/Science Photo Library, p 488 **Robert Longuehaye, NIBSC**/Science Photo Library, p 490 **Tek Image**/Science Photo Library, p 494 (top) **J. C. Revy, ISM**/Science Photo Library, p 494 (middle) **Biozentrum, University Of Basel**/Science Photo Library, p 496 **Philippe Psaila**/Science Photo Library, p 497 **Bill Barksdale/AGStockUSA**/Science Photo Library, p 498 Golden Rice image by International Rice Research Institute (IRRI) licenced under the Creative Commons Attribution 2.0 Generic license, p 502 **Geoff Tompkinson**/Science Photo Library, p 503 **James King-Holmes**/Science Photo Library, p 504 **Volker Steger**/Science Photo Library, p 506 **Martin Krzywinski**/Science Photo Library, p 511 **Michael P. Gadomski**/Science Photo Library, p 512 **Cordelia Molloy**/Science Photo Library, p 513 (top) **Tony Craddock**/Science Photo Library, p 513 (bottom) **Rosenfeld Images Ltd**/Science Photo Library, p 516 **James King-Holmes**/Science Photo Library, p 517 **Reinhard Dirscherl, Visuals Unlimited**/Science Photo Library, p 518 **Philippe Plailly**/Science Photo Library, p 520 (top) **Rosenfeld Images Ltd**/Science Photo Library, p 520 (bottom) **Andrew Mcclenaghan**/Science Photo Library, p 521 **Cordelia Molloy**/Science Photo Library, p 523 **Ed Young**/Science Photo Library, p 527 (top) **Trevor Clifford Photography**/Science Photo Library, p 527 (bottom) **Martyn F. Chillmaid**/Science Photo Library, p 543 **Cordelia Molloy**/Science Photo Library, p 544 **Simon Fraser**/Science Photo Library, p 545 (top) **Dr. Jeremy Burgess**/Science Photo Library, p 545 (bottom) **Alfred Pasieka**/Science Photo Library, p 546 **Annie Haycock**/Science Photo Library, p 547 **Simon Fraser**/Science Photo Library, p 548 (top) **Andrea Balogh**/Science Photo Library, p 548 (middle) **Simon Fraser**/Science Photo Library, p 548 (bottom) **Simon Fraser**/Science Photo Library, p 549 **Colin Varndell**/Science Photo Library, p 551 **Martyn F. Chillmaid**/Science Photo Library, p 559 **Jeff Lepore**/Science Photo Library, p 562 **Geoff Kidd**/Science Photo Library, p 563 (top) **Angel Fitor**/Science Photo Library, p 565 (top) **David Fleetham/Visuals Unlimited, Inc.**/Science Photo Library, p 565 (bottom) **PlanetObserver**/Science Photo Library, p 566 **Frans Lanting, Mint Images**/Science Photo Library, p 567 **Charlotte Sheridan**

Every effort has been made to locate copyright holders and obtain permission to reproduce sources. For those sources where it has been difficult to trace the originator of the work, we would be grateful for information. If any copyright holder would like us to make an amendment to the acknowledgements, please notify us and we will gladly update the book at the next reprint. Thank you.

# Index

## A

abiotic factors 536, 537, 557
abiotic stress 377
abscisic acid (ABA) 386
abundance 550
accuracy 5, 7
acetyl coenzyme A (acetyl CoA) 415
acetylcholine (ACh) 305, 358
acetylcholinesterase (AChE) 306, 371
actin filaments 363-367
actin-myosin cross bridges 366, 367
action potentials 298, 301, 302
  factors affecting speed of conduction 303
activation energy 106
active immunity 238
active loading 219, 220
active sites 105-111
active transport 140, 219
adaptations 284
adenylyl cyclase 312
adhesion (in plant water transport) 213
ADP (adenosine diphosphate) 89, 90, 392
adrenal glands 312, 313, 357
adrenaline 312, 357
aerobic respiration 413-418
  measuring the rate of 424, 426
affinity for oxygen 199
agar plates 527, 528
agglutinins 234
alcoholic fermentation 420
alkaloids 377
allele frequencies 471
  calculations of 476, 477
alleles 254, 276, 444, 446, 447
allopatric speciation 481
all-or-nothing principle (of action potentials) 302
alpha ($\alpha$) cells 313, 322
alveoli 169, 171, 172

Alzheimer's disease 156
amino acids 69, 96-98
  breakdown of 334, 335
ammonia 334, 335
ammonification 544, 545
ammonium ions 74
amylase 72, 105, 116
amylopectin 64
amylose 64
anabolic steroids 348
  testing for 349
anaerobic respiration 420, 421
  measuring the rate of 425
anaphase 148, 152
anatomical adaptations 284
animal cells 38
animal cloning 515-518
animal tissues 160
Animalia 269
anions 75
anomalous results 10
Antarctica 566
anti-toxins 235
antibiotic resistance 242, 243
antibiotics 242
antibodies 231-235
  structure of 234
anticodons 97, 100
antidiuretic hormone (ADH) 343, 344
antigen-presenting cells 230, 231
antigens 230-240
aorta 191-193
apical dominance 383, 384
apoplast pathway 212
apoptosis 436
aquaporins 343
arteries 188
arterioles 188
artificial embryo twinning 515
artificial immunity 238
artificial selection 479, 480
aseptic techniques 527
asexual reproduction 148, 149
assimilates 218
athlete's foot 224

ATP (adenosine triphosphate) 89, 90, 140, 220, 391, 392
  from aerobic respiration 418
  from anaerobic respiration 421
  in muscle contraction 368
ATP-creatine phosphate (ATP-CP) system 368
ATP synthase 392, 397, 417
ATPase 366, 392
atria 191-193
atrioventricular node (AVN) 195
atrioventricular valves 192, 193
autoimmune diseases 238
autonomic nervous system 353
autosomal linkage 457, 458
auxins 379, 383, 384, 386, 387
averages 11, 12
*Azotobacter* 545

## B

B lymphocytes 231
bacteria 46, 224, 327, 520, 521, 528, 529
bacterial artificial chromosomes (BACs) 502
bacterial meningitis 224
bacteriophages 493, 494
baking 520
baroreceptors 358
bases (nucleotides) 88, 89
batch fermentation 523
behavioural adaptations 284
Benedict's test 77-80
  quantitative testing 79
beta ($\beta$) cells 313, 322, 323
bias 27
bile ducts 332, 333
binomial system 268
biochemical tests for molecules 76-81
biodiversity 248-263
  collecting data on 248-250
  factors affecting 256-258
  maintenance of 259-263

bioinformatics 505
biomass 537, 538, 540, 541
bioremediation 520
biosensors 81
biotechnology 519-531
biotic factors 536, 557, 558
biuret test 76
black sigatoka 224
blinking reflex 355, 356
blood 190
   clotting 227
   smears 232
blood glucose concentration 322, 323
blood vessels 188
body plans 435, 436
body temperature 318-321
   control by hypothalamus 320, 321
   control mechanisms 319, 320
Bohr effect 201
bone marrow 155
Bowman's capsule 337, 338
bradycardia 197
brain 354
breathing rate 175
brewing 520
bronchi 171, 172
bronchioles 171, 172
buccal cavity 178
bundle of His 195

## C

cacti 215
calcium ion channels 324
calcium ions 74
calibration curves 80
callose deposition 228
Calvin cycle 395, 399-401
   limiting factors 404, 405
cAMP (cyclic AMP) 312, 433
capillaries 188, 189
capturing motile organisms 552
carbohydrates 63-65
carbon cycle 543, 544
carbonic acid 201, 202
carbonic anhydrase 116, 201, 202

cardiac cycle 193
cardiac muscle 369, 370
cardiac output 194
carrier proteins 139
carriers (inheritance) 447
carrying capacity 558, 560
cartilage 160, 172
Casparian strip 212
catalase 105, 112
cations 74
causal relationships 23
cell cycle 147-149
cell membranes 39, 124-131
   function of 124, 125
   investigating permeability of 128
   permeability of 127
   receptors 130, 131
   structure of 125, 126
cell signalling 130, 131, 232, 295
cell ultrastructure 38
cell walls 39
cells 38-42
cellulose 65
central nervous system (CNS) 354
centrioles 42
centromeres 148
cerebellum 354
cerebrum 354
channel proteins 139
cheese making 520
chemiosmotic theory 397, 417
chemoreceptors 358
chi-squared test 463-465
chloride ions 75, 116, 202
chloride shift 202
chloroplasts 41, 394
chlorosis 444
cholesterol 67, 68, 126
cholinergic synapses 306
chromatids 148, 153
chromatography 82-84, 407, 408
chromosomes 148
cilia 42, 171
ciliated epithelia 160, 171
circulatory systems 185-187
citations 35
CITES agreement 263
cladistics 270

classes 268
classification 268, 269
classification systems 272-274
   evidence for 272
   five kingdom system 269, 273
   three domain system 273
climate change 257
climax communities 547, 548
clonal expansion 231
clonal selection 231
cloning
   animals 515-518
   plants 511-514
closed circulatory systems 186
closed cultures 524
*Clostridium difficile* 243
co-transport proteins 219
codominant alleles 447
   inheritance of 450, 453
codons 96, 97
coenzyme A 413, 415
coenzymes 116
   in photosynthesis 395
   in respiration 413
cofactors 116
cohesion (of water molecules) 60
   in plant water transport 213
collagen 72
collecting ducts 338, 343, 344
colorimetry 79, 80, 128
command words 573
communicable diseases 224-226
communication systems 295
companion cells 208, 219, 220
compensation points 392, 393
competitive inhibitors 117
complementary base pairing 91
computational biology 505
conclusions 23, 26, 31
condensation reactions 62
conjugated proteins 72
conservation 259-263, 561-564
constant regions (of antibodies) 234
consumers 537
continuous data 18
continuous fermentation 523
continuous variation 275, 443
control elements 432
controls 6
convergent evolution 285
correlations 7, 23

counter-current systems  177
countercurrent multiplier mechanisms  342, 343
Countryside Stewardship Scheme (CSS)  263
creatine phosphate (CP)  368
critical values  361, 362, 465
crossing over (of chromatids)  153
cuttings (plant cloning)  304
cyclic AMP (cAMP)  312, 433
cyclic photophosphorylation  397
cytokines  230
cytokinesis  147, 149
cytoplasm  38, 39
cytoskeletons  44

# D

Darwin, Charles  287
data
  presenting  17-22
  processing  11-16
  recording  9, 10
  uncertainty in  24
data loggers  9, 175
deamination  334, 335
decarboxylation  415
deciduous plants  385, 386
decision making  4
decomposers  538, 543
deflecting succession  549
dehydrogenation  416
deletion mutations  438
denitrification  544, 545
dependent variables  5
depolarisation (of neurones)  301, 302
detoxification  335
diabetes mellitus  325-327
diaphragm  171, 174
differentiation (of cells)  155, 156
diffusion  132, 133
  investigating  133
dihybrid inheritance  452
dipeptides  69
diploid cells  151
direct transmission (of disease)  225
directional selection  472

disaccharides  64
discontinuous variation  276, 443
discrete data  17
dissection
  of gaseous exchange systems  180, 181
  of hearts  192
  of plant stems  209
distal convoluted tubule (DCT)  338, 343, 344
distribution  550
disulfide bonds  71
DNA (deoxyribonucleic acid)  88, 91-95
  analysis  487-492
  profiles  492
  purification of  92, 93
  replication  94, 95
  sequencing  501-504
DNA helicase  94
DNA ligase  493
DNA polymerase  94
Dolly the sheep  518
domains  268
dominant alleles  447
double circulatory systems  186
drug resistance  242, 243, 291

# E

ecosystems  536-552
  conservation of  561
  energy transfer through  537-541
  investigating  550-552
  management of  562, 563, 565-567
  preservation of  562
  recycling in  543-545
ectopic heartbeats  197
ectotherms  318
effectors  295, 315, 353
efficiency of energy transfer  539, 540
elastic fibres (in the airways)  172
elastin  73
electrocardiograms (ECGs)  195-198
electrochemical gradients  300, 417

electrolyte balance  345
electromyograms (EMGs)  372
electron carriers  396, 397, 417
electron micrographs  50
electron microscopes  49
electron transport chains  396, 397, 417
electrophoresis  489, 490
electroporation  494
embryonic stem cells  517
emulsion test  77
endocrine glands  311
endocrine systems  311-313
endocytosis  140
endotherms  318
energy transfer (through ecosystems)  537-541
  human control of  541
energy values (of respiratory substrates)  422
enucleation  516
environmental variation  276
enzyme-substrate complex  105, 106
enzymes  105-120
  action of  106
  denaturing  109
  factors affecting activity  109-111
  inhibition of  117-120
  investigating activity of  112, 113
  models of action  107
  structure of  105, 106
epidemics  239
epistasis  460, 461
epithelial cells  157
erythrocytes  155, 157
ester bonds  66
ethene (plant hormone)  386
ethical issues  7
  of animal cloning  517
  of artificial selection  480
  of gene therapy  499, 500
  of genetically modified organisms  495-497
  of using organisms in experiments  37
etiolation  444
eukaryotic cells  38, 46
evaluations  25, 26, 31
evidence  3

evolution 287-291, 471-474
  evidence for 288, 289
  of antibiotic resistance 242
  of drug resistance 291
  of pesticide resistance 290
exam structure 571
exchange surfaces 166-169
excretion 337
  role of kidneys in 337
  role of liver in 332
exercise (investigating effect on heart rate) 359, 360
exocytosis 141
exons 433
experimental design 5-7
expiration 174
expulsive reflexes 228
*ex situ* conservation 262
extended response questions 571
extracellular enzymes 105
eyepiece graticules 54

# F

facilitated diffusion 139, 140
FAD 413, 416-418
families (in classification) 268
fatty acids 66, 67
fermentation vessels 523, 524
fetal haemoglobin 200, 201
fibrillation 198
fibrous proteins 72, 73
'fight or flight' response 357
filtrate (kidneys) 338
first messengers 311
fishing quotas 563
five kingdom classification system 269
flaccid cells 135
flagella 42
fluid mosaic model 125
food chains 537
food webs 537
forensic science 492
fossil record 288
founder effect 474
frameshift mutations 438, 439
frequency tables 10
fungi 224, 520, 521
Fungi (kingdom) 269

# G

Galapagos Islands 565, 566
gametes 151
gas chromatography/mass spectrometry (GC/MS) 349
gaseous exchange (in plants) 214
gaseous exchange systems
  dissections of 180, 181
  in bony fish 177
  in insects 178
  in mammals 171, 172
gene
  expression 431-433
  mutations 438-440
  pools 471
  sequencing 501-504
  therapy 499, 500
genera 268
generator potentials 297
genes 96, 446
genetically modified (GM) organisms 495-497, 327, 520
genetic
  bottlenecks 473, 474
  code 96-98
  diagrams 448-462
  disorders 499, 500
  diversity 248, 254
  drift 473
  engineering 493-497
  resources 259, 260
  variation 153, 276, 444
genome sequencing 502-504
genotype frequencies 477, 478
genotypes 446
geographical isolation 481
geotropism 378, 379
  investigating 380, 381
germ line gene therapy 499
gibberellins 379, 384, 385
gill filaments 177
gill plates 177
gills 169, 177, 178, 180
  dissection of 180
glands 311
globular proteins 72
glomerular filtration rate (GFR) 345

glomeruli 337, 338
glucagon 322, 323
gluconeogenesis 322
glucose 63, 391, 414
  control of concentration in the blood 322, 323
  in photosynthesis and respiration 391
  test for 77, 78
glycerate 3-phosphate (GP) 399-401, 405
glycogen 65, 322, 323, 335
glycogen storage 335
glycogenesis 322, 323
glycogenolysis 322, 323
glycolipids 125, 126
glycolysis 414
glycoproteins 125, 126
glycosidic bonds 63, 64
goblet cells 171
Golgi apparatus 41, 44
graphs 17-22
  correlations 23
  finding the initial rate from 114
  finding the rate from 20-22
gross productivity 538
growth hormones in plants 379
guard cells 158

# H

habitat diversity 248
habitats 536
haemoglobin 199-202
  structure of 72
haemoglobinic acid 202
haploid cells 151
Hardy-Weinberg principle 476-478
hazards 32, 33
heart 191-198
  dissection of 192
  electrical activity of 195
  problems 197, 198
  structure of 191
  valves 192

heart rate
  calculating 196
  control of 357-359
  investigating 359, 360
  monitors 360
herbivory 377
herd immunity 239
heterozygotes 446
high-throughput sequencing 504
hinge regions (of antibodies) 234
histograms 18
histology
  kidney 339
  liver 334
  pancreas 313
HIV 224
homeobox sequences 435
homeostasis 315, 316
homologous chromosomes 151
homozygotes 446
hormonal systems 311-313
hormones 311-313
  as messenger molecules 130, 131
  in plants 379, 383-387
host cells 494
Hox genes 435
human chorionic gonadotropin (hCG) 348
human population growth 256
hydrogen bonding 60, 71, 91
hydrogen ions 74, 201, 202, 220
hydrogencarbonate ions 75, 201, 202
hydrolysis reactions 62
hydrophilic and hydrophobic interactions 71
hydrophytes 216
hydrostatic pressure 189
hydroxide ions 75
hypertonic solutions 135
hypothalamus 320, 343, 354, 357
hypotheses 1
hypotonic solutions 135

# I

immobilised enzymes 530
  uses of 531
immune response 230-232, 236, 237
immune system 230-232
immunity 236
*in situ* conservation 261
inactive precursors 120
independent assortment (of chromosomes) 154
independent variables 5
indirect transmission (of disease) 225
indoleacetic acid (IAA) 379
induced fit model 107
inflammation 228
influenza 224, 240
inheritance 448-462
initial rates of reaction 114
inorganic ions 74, 75
insect resistance 495
insertion mutations 438
inspiration 174
insulin 72, 322, 323
  from genetically modified bacteria 327, 520
  production 327, 520
  secretion 324
  therapy 325
intercostal muscles 171, 174
interdependent organisms 259
interleukins 232
interphase 147, 152
interspecific competition 558
interspecific variation 275
intracellular enzymes 105
intraspecific competition 558, 559
intraspecific variation 275
introns 433
involuntary muscle 369
iodine test 77
ionic bonds 71
islets of Langerhans 313, 322
isolated enzymes 519, 530
isotonic solutions 135

# K

keratin 73
keystone species 259
kidney failure 345-347
kidneys 337-340, 342-344
  dissection of 340
  histology 339
kidney transplants 347
kingdoms 268, 269
knee-jerk reflex 356
Krebs cycle 415, 416

# L

*lac* operon 432
lactate fermentation 420
lactose 64
Lake District 567
laser scanning confocal microscopes 49
latent heat of evaporation 60
leaf loss 385, 386
leaves 161, 212
ligation 493
light-dependent reaction 395-397
light-harvesting systems 394
light-independent reaction 395, 399-401
light microscopes 49, 54
lignin 207
limiting factors
  of photosynthesis 403-405
  of population sizes 560
line graphs 18
link reaction 415
linkage 455-458
lipids 66-68
  test for 77
liver 322, 323, 332-334
  histology 333, 334
loci 254, 446
lock and key model 107
logarithmic scales 526
logarithms 525
loop of Henle 338, 339, 342, 343
lungs 161, 171

lupus 238
lymph 189, 190
lymphocytes 231, 232
lymph vessels 189, 190
lysosomes 40, 230

# M

Maasai Mara 564
macromolecules 62
magnification 47, 50
malaria 224
maltose 64
manometers 426
margins of error 24
marram grass 216
marsupial moles 286
mass flow hypothesis 218, 219
mature mRNA 433
mean 11, 278
median 12
medicines
   personalised 244
   sources of 243
medulla oblongata 354, 358
meiosis 151-154
membrane-bound receptors 130, 131
memory cells 236, 239
meningitis C vaccine 239
meristems 156, 218
messenger molecules 130
metabolic pathways 119
metabolic poisons 119
metabolic rates 185
metabolic waste products 332
metaphase 148, 152
microfibrils 65
microfilaments 44
microorganisms
   culturing 523, 524, 527
   investigating factors affecting growth 528, 529
   standard growth curves 524-526
   use in biotechnology 519-521
micropropagation 513
microscope slides 53
microscopes 47
   how to use light microscopes 54
   types of 49, 50

microtubules 42, 44
migrations 258
*Mimosa pudica* 378
mitochondria 41, 413
mitosis 147-149, 436
   investigating 149
MMR 239
mode 12
models (scientific) 1
monoclonal antibodies (in pregnancy tests) 348
monocultures 257, 260, 495
monocytes 232
monogenic characteristics 444
monogenic inheritance 448-450
monomers 62
monosaccharides 63
motor neurones 296
mRNA (messenger RNA) 96, 99-101
   editing 433
MRSA 243
mucous membranes 227
multiple allele crosses 452
muscle contraction 363-368
   energy for 368
   investigating 372
   nervous control of 371
   sliding filament model of 364
muscle fibres (structure of) 363, 364
muscle tissue 160
muscle types 369, 370
mutations 95, 438-440
myelin sheaths 303
myelinated neurones 303
myofibrils 363, 364
myosin filaments 363-367

# N

NAD 413-418, 420
NADP 395, 397
natural immunity 238
natural selection 287, 471
negative controls 6
negative feedback 301, 315, 316
nephrons 337-339, 342, 343
nervous impulses 300-303
nervous system 296-298, 353-356
   control of heart rate 357, 358

net productivity 538, 539
neuromuscular junctions 371
neurones 296
neurotransmitters 305, 371
neutrophils 155, 157, 230, 232
nitrate ions 75
nitrification 544, 545
*Nitrobacter* 545
nitrogen cycle 544, 545
nitrogen fixation 544, 545
*Nitrosomonas* 545
nodes of Ranvier 303
non-competitive inhibitors 117
non-cyclic photophosphorylation 396
non-random sampling 249
non-reducing sugars 78
non-specific immune response 230
noradrenaline 358
normal distribution 278
nuclear envelope 40
nuclei 40
nucleic acids 88, 89
nucleotides 88-90
null hypotheses 16, 282, 360, 463

# O

oncotic pressure 189
open circulatory systems 187
operculum 178
operons 432
opportunistic sampling 249
opsonins 230
orders (in classification) 268
organelles 38-42
organ systems 162
organs 161
ornithine cycle 334, 335
osmoreceptors 343, 344
osmosis 134, 137
oxaloacetate 416
oxidative phosphorylation 417
oxygen dissociation curves 200, 201
oxygen uptake 175
oxyhaemoglobin 199

# P

Pacinian corpuscles 298
palindromic sequences 488
palisade mesophyll cells 158
pancreas 313
parasympathetic nervous system 353
Parkinson's disease 156
partial pressures
   of carbon dioxide ($pCO_2$) 201
   of oxygen ($pO_2$) 199
passive immunity 238
patents 497
pathogens 224
   in genetic engineering 496, 497
peat bogs 564
pedigree dogs 480
peer reviews 2
penicillin 242
   production of 520
pentose sugars (monosaccharides) 63, 88
peptide bonds 69
percentage error 24, 25
percentages 13
peripheral nervous system 353
peripheral temperature receptors 320
personalised medicines 244
pesticide resistance 290
phagocytosis 230, 234, 235
phagosomes 230
'pharming' 496
phenotypes 446
phenotypic ratios 449
   with epistasis 460, 461
   with linkage 458
phenotypic variation 443, 444
pheromones 377, 378
phloem 156, 161, 206-208
phosphate bonds 90
phosphate ions 75
phosphodiester bonds 91
phospholipids 67, 68, 125
phosphorylation 392
photolysis 396
photophosphorylation 396, 397

photosynthesis 391-409
   experiments 407-409
   factors affecting 402, 403
   in energy transfer 537
   in the carbon cycle 543
   light-dependent reaction 395-397
   light-independent reaction 395, 399-401
   limiting factors of 403-405
photosynthetic pigments 394, 402
   separation of 407, 408
photosystems 394
phototropism 378, 379
   investigating 380
phyla 268
phylogeny 270
physiological adaptations 284
phytoalexins 229
pioneer species 546
pituitary gland 343, 354
placebos 6
placental moles 286
plagioclimaxes 549
planning experiments 5-7
Plantae 269
plant cells 39
plant cloning 511-514
plant defences 228, 229
plant dissection 209
plant hormones 379, 383-387
   commercial uses of 386, 387
plant tissues 161
   examination of 208
plants 377-387
plasma cells 232
plasma membranes 39, 124
plasmids 493
plasmodesmata 39, 211, 228
plasmolysis 135
polar molecules 59
polygenic characteristics 444
polymerase chain reaction (PCR) 487, 488
polymers 62
polymorphism 254
polynucleotides 91-93
polypeptides 69
polysaccharides 63-65

populations (size of) 557
   investigating 550-552
positive controls 6
positive feedback 301
potassium ion channels 300, 324
potassium ions 74
potato/tomato late blight 224
potometers 215
practical activity groups (PAGs) 30, 36
Practical Endorsement 30
precision 5
predation 559
predator-prey relationships 559
predictions 1
pregnancy tests 348
presenting data 31
preservation 562, 564
pressure filtration 189
primary defences 227
primary immune response 236, 237
primary mRNA 433
primers 487
problem solving 30
processing data 31
producers 537
product inhibition 119
programmed cell death 436
Prokaryotae 269
prokaryotic cells 38, 46
prophase 148, 152
prosthetic groups 116
protein activation 433
protein synthesis 96-101
proteins 69-73
   structure of 70, 71
   test for 76
Protoctista 224, 269
proximal convoluted tubule (PCT) 338
pulmonary artery 191-193
pulmonary vein 191, 193
pulse rate measurements 359, 360
Punnett squares 449
purines 89
Purkyne tissue 195
pyrimidines 89
pyrosequencing 504
pyruvate 414, 415

Index

## Q

$Q_{10}$ (temperature coefficient) 109, 110
quadrats 550-552
qualitative data 17
quantitative data 17-19

## R

random sampling 249, 550
range 11
rates
  calculating from graphs 20-22
  of diffusion 132
ratios 13
rearing livestock 541
receptors 130, 131, 295, 315, 353
recessive alleles 447
recognition sequences 488
recombinant DNA 493, 494
recording data 9, 30
recording experiments 34
recreational drugs
  testing for 349
recycling (in ecosystems) 543-545
redox reactions 395
reduced NADP 395, 397
reducing sugars 77
references 35
reflex actions 355, 356
refractory periods 302
regulatory genes 432
relay neurones 296
renal dialysis 346
repeatable results 5, 6, 25
reproducible results 5, 25
reproductive isolation 481, 482
research skills 34, 35
resolution 48, 50
respiration 391, 413-427
  aerobic 413-418
  anaerobic 420, 421
  experiments 424-427
  in the carbon cycle 543
respiratory loss 538

respiratory quotients (RQs) 422
  uses of 423
respiratory substrates 422
respiratory system 162
respirometers 426, 427
resting potential
  of neurones 301
  of sensory receptors 297
restriction enzymes 488, 489, 493
$R_f$ values 83, 408
rheumatoid arthritis 239
*Rhizobium* 545
ribcage 171, 174
ribose 63, 89
ribosomes 40, 97, 100, 101
ribulose bisphosphate (RuBP) 399, 400, 405
ribulose bisphosphate carboxylase (RuBisCO) 399, 400
ring rot 224
ringworm 224
Rio Convention on Biological Diversity (CBD) 263
risk assessments 7, 32, 33
RNA (ribonucleic acid) 89, 96, 97
RNA polymerase 99
root hair cells 158, 168
rooting powders 387
rough endoplasmic reticulum (RER) 40, 44
routine vaccines 239
rRNA (ribosomal RNA) 97, 101

## S

saltatory conduction 303
sample sizes 6
sampling 249, 550
saponins 229
saprobiontic nutrition 543
sarcomeres 364
scanning electron microscopes (SEMs) 49
scattergrams 19
Schwann cells 303
scientific journals 2
second messengers 311

secondary immune response 236, 237
seed germination 384, 385
selection pressures 287
selective reabsorption (in the kidneys) 338, 339
self-antigens 238
semi-conservative replication 94
semi-lunar valves 192, 193
sensory neurones 296
sensory receptors 297, 298
sequencing 501-506
serial dilutions 79
sex-linkage 455, 456
sexual reproduction 151-154
sieve tube elements 207, 208, 219, 220
significant figures 14
Simpson's Index of Diversity 251, 252
single-cell proteins 521
single circulatory systems 185
sinks (in translocation) 218, 219
sino-atrial node (SAN) 195, 357
skeletal muscle 363, 369
  microscope examination of 369
skin 227
sliding filament model 364
smooth endoplasmic reticulum (SER) 40
smooth muscle (in the airways) 172
Snowdonia 567
sodium ions 74
sodium-potassium pumps 300
soil depletion 260
somatic cell nuclear transfer (SCNT) 516
somatic gene therapy 499
somatic nervous system 353
sources (in translocation) 218
sources of medicines 243
Spearman's rank correlation coefficient 281-283
specialised cells 157, 158
speciation 481, 482
species 268, 270
  diversity 248
  evenness 251
  richness 251

specific heat capacity 60
sperm cells 157
spindle fibres 148, 149, 152
spiracles 178
spirometers 175, 176
spores 225
squamous epithelia 160
stabilising selection 471, 472
stage micrometers 54
staining microscope samples 52
standard deviation 12, 279, 280, 361
standard form 15
standard growth curves 524-526
starch 64
   test for 77
statistical tests 16, 31
   chi-squared test 463-465
   Spearman's rank correlation coefficient 281-283
   Student's t-test 360-362
stem cells 155, 156
   as a potential cure for diabetes 327
   differentiation 155
   in animal cloning 517
   in plant cloning 513
   potential in medicine 156
stem elongation 384, 385
steroid hormones 312
steroids (anabolic) 348
   testing for 349
sticky ends 489
stimuli 301, 353, 377
stomata 212, 214
stomatal closure 386
stop codons 101
stratified sampling 249
structural genes 432
Student's t-test 360-362
studies 3
substitution mutations 438
substrate-level phosphorylation 416
succession 546-549
   deflected 549
   primary 546, 547
   secondary 548
sucrose 64
sugars 63
   test for 77, 78

superbugs 243
superkingdoms 273
surface area calculations 167
surface area: volume ratios 166
sustainability 562, 563
sympathetic nervous system 353, 357
sympatric speciation 482
symplast pathway 211
synapses 305-308
   disruption at 306
   summation at 307
synthetic biology 244, 505
systematic sampling 249

# T

T helper cells 231
T killer cells 231
T lymphocytes 231
T regulatory cells 231
tachycardia 197
tangents 21, 22, 114
tannins 377
target cells 130
taxonomic hierarchies 268
taxonomy 268
technology transfer 497
telophase 149, 152
temperate woodland 562
temperature coefficient ($Q_{10}$) 109
tension (in plant water transport) 213
Terai Arc 563
test strips (for glucose) 78
theories 1, 2
theory of evolution 287
thermoreceptors 320
thin-layer chromatography (TLC) 407, 408
three domains classification system 273
tidal volume (TV) 175
time management (in exams) 573
tissue culture 513
tissue fluid 189
tissues 160, 161
tobacco mosaic virus 224
trachea (windpipe) 171, 172

tracheae (in insects) 178, 181
tracheoles 178
transcription 96, 99
   control of 431, 432
transcription factors 431
transducers 297
transects 552
transformed organisms 495-497
transgenic organisms 493
translation 96, 100, 101
translocation 218-220
transmission (disease) 225, 226
transmission electron microscopes (TEMs) 49
transpiration 212, 214-216
   estimating rate of 215
   factors affecting 214
transpiration stream 213
transport systems
   in animals 185
   in plants 206
triglycerides 66-68
triose phosphate (TP) 399-401, 405
triplets (of bases) 96, 98
tRNA (transfer RNA) 97, 100, 101
trophic levels 537
tropisms 378
tropomyosin 365-367
troponin 365-367
trypsin 105
tuberculosis (TB) 224
turgid cells 135
Type 1 diabetes 325, 326
Type 2 diabetes 325, 326

# U

ultrafiltration (in the kidneys) 337, 338
uncertainty (of measurements) 24
unspecialised cells 155
urea 334, 335
urine 339, 342-344
   testing samples of 348, 349

## V

vaccination 239, 240
vaccination programmes 240
vacuoles 39
validity 5, 25
variable regions (antibodies) 234
variables 3, 5
variation 275-279, 281, 443-445
   causes 276
vascular system (in plants) 206
vasoconstriction 320
vasodilation 319
vectors
   in disease 225
   in genetic engineering 493
vegetative propagation 511
veins 188
vena cava 191, 193
ventilation
   in bony fish 178
   in insects 178
   in mammals 174
ventricles 191-193
venules 188
vesicles 41
viruses 224
vital capacity 175
volume calculations 167

## W

Wallace, Alfred Russel 288
water 59-61
   transport in plants 211-213
water lilies 216
water potential 134-137
   investigating effect on animal cells 137
   investigating effect on plant cells 136, 137
   of the blood 342-344
water stress 404
weathering 544
weedkillers 387
wound repair 228

## X

xerophytes 215, 216
xylem 156, 161, 206-209

## Y

yeast 420, 520
   in respiration experiments 424, 425
yoghurt production 520

## Z

zinc ions 116
zygotes 151